DIRECTORY OF POPULAR MUSIC

Third Edition

by
Leslie Lowe

D0308734

 **Waterlow**

Published by Waterlow Information Services Limited, London.

Third edition, April, 1992

First edition, 1975
Second edition, 1986

Third edition published by Music Master, Music House, 1 De Cham Avenue, Hastings, East Sussex. TN37 6HE.

Advertising enquiries: Telephone: 071-490-0049. Fax: 071-608-1163.

Editorial enquiries: Telephone: (0424) 715181. Fax: (0424) 422805.

Book trade enquiries: Music Sales, 8/9 Frith Street, London, W1V 5TZ. Telephone: 071-434-0066. Fax: 071-439-2848.

Private orders and record trade enquiries: Music Master Customer Services, Unit 4, Durham Road, Borehamwood, Hertfordshire, WD6 1LW. Telephone: 081-953-5433. Fax: 081-207-5814.

ISBN 0 904520 70 6

THE MUSIC MASTER TEAM: Production Manager: George Rankin. **Production Team:** Dave Kent, Jason Philpott, Clive Brown, Fiona Allman. **Editorial Manager:** Chris Spalding. **Editorial Team:** Pete Smith, Sylvia Davis, Karen Blackman, Jimmy Kent, Jenny Bellerose, Anita Ferrario. **Sales and Administration:** Marianne Hyne, Anna Sperni, Pam Brown.

Printed and bound in Great Britain by BPCC Wheatons Limited, Exeter, Devon.

Cover design by Jonathan Clegg, Design Communication.

MUSIC MASTER
DIRECTORY OF POPULAR MUSIC

CONTENTS

INTRODUCTION

The Directory of Popular Music is a comprehensive work of reference for popular music, listing around 9,000 songs and tunes originating in countries all over the world and which have proved their popularity over the years. The criteria for inclusion in this book is either by the amount of sheet music sold, the number of records sold or by consistent performances in films or on stage.

The various sections in the book are designed to enable quick reference by various routes, whether it be by year, composer, subject matter or simply alphabetically. The section headed *How to Use This Book* (page 7) gives more detail as to what each section contains and how to look up the various entries.

Entries in the book range from as early as 1813, culminating with up-to-date songs from 1990. This fascinating book is sure to provide answers to hundreds of questions and give the reader hours of pleasure simply browsing through it's many enthralling pages.

The author, Leslie Lowe, has been associated with music since he left school at the age of fourteen, when he was employed in the BBC Music Library until joining HM Forces. After serving with the Welsh Guards he returned to the BBC to work in the Gramophone Library and for ten years was concerned with commercial gramophone records for the Home and Light Programmes. He entered music publishing as the Professional Manager at Lorna Music Company and then moved to 20th Century Fox Music.

He has been awarded a Gold Badge of Merit by the British Academy of Songwriters, Composers and Authors for his services to the music business. His many years of experience in the music business have been brought to bear to produce this fascinating insight to the last 180 years or so of popular music.

HOW TO USE THIS BOOK

ALPHABETICAL SECTION

The key section of this book is the alphabetical section starting on page 11. Here, all the songs are listed in alphabetical order, with the relevant information pertaining to each song listed below the title.

Details listed in this section include the year the song first became popular, composers, publishers, country of origin and a list of the artists who have recorded the song, together with record label and catalogue number of the recordings.

If a song has featured in a film or show, the name of the film or show will be listed.

All the other sections and listings in this book refer back to the alphabetical section.

STAGE PRODUCTIONS

A comprehensive list of stage productions details the name of the show, the theatre at which it was first performed and the date. Where possible, dates for the first appearances in Britain and USA are shown separately.

FILMS

This section contains a list of all songs in this book that featured in films. The information is listed alphabetically by film title, with details of year, film company and details of songs from each film (where possible). The film company may be either the company that produced the film or the company that distributed the film.

CHRONOLOGICAL SECTION

For those wishing to find titles of songs relevant to a particular year or years, the chronological section is designed for quick and easy reference. All the song titles in the book are listed again here, but this time in chronological order beginning with the earliest year and finishing with the very latest year, 1990. Song titles are listed in alphabetical order within each year and only the song title is listed.

ACADEMY AWARD NOMINATIONS AND WINNING SONGS

This section is listed chronologically, with each song title in alphabetical order under each year. Winning songs are printed in italics. Those in plain text were nominated in that year, but did not win an award.

IVOR NOVELLO AWARDS AND NOMINATIONS

Again, this section is listed in chronological order. Songs are listed alphabetically under each year and song titles printed in italics are the winning songs in respect of each year. Those in plain text were nominated but did not win an award.

EUROVISION SONG CONTEST WINNERS AND ENTRANTS

This section is divided into two lists. The first is a list, by year, of all winning songs and shows the winning country. The second list details the UK entrants for each year, with an indication of the final placing in the competition.

THEME SONGS AND SIGNATURE TUNES

A short, but fascinating section, this is a list of signature tunes or theme tunes of some of the best known artists of all time. The listing is in alphabetical order by artist.

REVIVALS

This list makes interesting reading, as it details those songs which have been a hit more than once. The year the song first became popular is shown, followed by the year(s) it subsequently became a hit.

COMPOSERS' INDEX

This section contains an alphabetical list of composers. If you wish to see a list of all George Gershwin's songs which appear in this book, simply look under the heading *Gershwin, George.* All songs are then listed alphabetically under each composer's name.

SUBJECT CLASSIFICATION

This unusual index allows you to look up a particular song or songs by subject matter. The word, or classification, normally refers to a word or words in the title of a song, or may be of a more general nature.

FOREIGN LANGUAGE SONGS

A list of foreign language songs by country. Songs are listed alphabetically under each country. USA is excluded from this section. The country in each case is the country of origin of the song.

PROFESSIONAL AND TRADE ORGANISATIONS

A short list of some useful names, addresses and telephone numbers of organisations such as the Music Copyright Protection Society, etc.

PROFESSIONAL AND TRADE ORGANISATIONS

AMERICAN SOCIETY OF COMPOSERS, AUTHORS AND PUBLISHERS (A.S.C.A.P.)
Suite 10 & 11, 52 Haymarket, London, SW1Y 4RP
071 930 1121

BRITISH ACADEMY OF SONGWRITERS, COMPOSERS AND AUTHORS (B.A.S.C.A.)
34 Hanway Street, London, W1P 9DE
071 436 2261

BRITISH PHONOGRAPHIC INDUSTRY (B.P.I.)
Roxburghe House, 273-287 Regent Street, London, W1R 7PB
071 493 3667

BROADCAST MUSIC INCORPORATED (B.M.I.)
79 Marley House, Marylebone Road, London, NW1 5HN
071 935 8517

COUNTRY MUSIC ASSOCIATION (C.M.A.)
Suite 3, 52 Haymarket, London, SW1Y 4RP
071 930 2445

MECHANICAL COPYRIGHT PROTECTION SOCIETY (M.C.P.S.)
Elgar House, 41 Streatham High Road, London, SW16 1ER
081 769 4400

MUSIC PUBLISHERS ASSOCIATION (M.P.A.)
7th Floor, Kingsway House, 103 Kingsway, London, WC2B 6QX
071 831 7591

NATIONAL SOUND ARCHIVE
29 Exhibition Road, London, SW7 2AS
071 589 6603

PERFORMING RIGHT SOCIETY (P.R.S.)
29-33 Berners Street, London, W1P 4AA
071 580 5544

Songs listed alphabetically by title, giving the year the song first became popular and details of composer(s), publishers, films, shows and who has recorded the song.

007 (SHANTY TOWN) August 1967
Demond Decker
Island Music Ltd. . . . . UK
Desmond Dekker & The Aces Pyramid PYR 6004

10538 OVERTURE (see Ten Thousande Five Hundred And Thirty Eight Overture)

5-7-0-5 (See FIVE-SEVEN-ZERO-FIVE)

A.B.C. June 1970
"The Corporation"
Jobete Music (UK) Ltd. . . . . USA
The Jackson Five . . . . Tamla Motown TMG 738

'A' ROUND THE CORNER March 1952
Traditional, adapted by Joseph Marias
Campbell Connelly & Co. Ltd . . . . South Africa
Jo Stafford . . . . Philips BBL 7395
The Weavers . . . . Brunswick LAT 8357

A-TISKET A-TASKET 1938
Ella Fitzgerald / Al Feldman
Francis, Day & Hunter Ltd. . . . . USA
Film(s): . . . . Ride 'Em Cowboy / Two Girls and a Sailor
Chick Webb & his Orchestra,
vocal Ella Fitzgerald . . . . Brunswick LAT 8223
Glenn Miller & his Orchestra . . . . RCA RD 27145
Ella Fitzgerald . . . . HMV POP 380
Dodie Stevens . . . . London HLD 9174
Ella Fitzgerald appeared in *Ride 'Em Cowboy.*

'A' YOU'RE ADORABLE June 1949
Buddy Kaye / Fred Wise / Sidney Lippman
Campbell Connelly & Co. Ltd . . . . USA
Perry Como . . . . Camden CDN 110
Jo Stafford & Gordon MacRae . . . . Capitol CL 13089
The Adams Singers . . . . Pye NPL 28013
Tommy Sands . . . . Capitol T 848

ABA DABA HONEYMOON 1914
Arthur Fields / Walter Donovan
Ascherberg, Hopwood & Crew Ltd. . . . . USA
Film(s): . . . . Two Weeks With Love
The Two Bobs . . . . Edison Bell Winner 2876
Hoagy Carmichael & Cass Daley . . . . Brunswick 04698
Debbie Reynolds & Carleton Carpenter . . . . MGM 350
Freddy Martin & his Orchestra . . . . HMV B 10085
Debbie Reynolds & Carleton Carpenter appeared in *Two Weeks with Love.*

ABA NI BI June 1978
Ehud Manor / Nurit Hirsh
Heath Levy Music Ltd . . . . Israel
Izar Cohen & The Alphabeta . . . . Polydor 2001781
Israeli entry for the 1978 Eurovision Song Contest (Placed First).

ABACAB September 1981
Tony Banks / Phil Collins
Hit & Run Music . . . . UK
Genesis . . . . Charisma CB 388

ABDUL ABULBUL AMIR 1927
Percy French
Ascherberg, Hopwood & Crew Ltd. . . . . USA
Frank Crumit . . . . HMV 7EG 8181
George Melly . . . . Decca DFE 6557
Adapted by Frank Crumit.
Probably composed Circa 1877 first published 1886.

ABIE MY BOY 1920
L. Silberman / A. Grock / Herbert Rule & Tom McGhee
Campbell Connelly & Co. Ltd . . . . UK
Grock . . . . Columbia 2901
The Temperance Seven Plus One . . . . Argo RG 117

ABOUT A QUARTER TO NINE 1936
Al Dubin / Harry Warren
B. Feldman & Co. Ltd . . . . USA
Film(s): . . . . Casino de Paris / The Jolson Story
Curtis & Ames . . . . Panachord 25787

Wingy Manone & his Orchestra . . . . Brunswick 02064
Al Jolson . . . . Brunswick LA 8575
Al Jolson (soundtrack) . . . . RCA ZL 70136
Al Jolson appeared in *Casino de Paris.*

ABRACADABRA July 1982
Steve Miller
Heath Levy Music . . . . USA
The Steve Miller Band . . . . Mercury STEVE 3

ABRAHAM, MARTIN & JOHN June 1970
Dick Holler
Robert Melin Ltd. . . . . USA
Marvin Gaye . . . . Tamla Motown TMG 734

ABSOLUTE BEGINNERS October 1981
Paul Weller
Chappell & Co. Ltd . . . . UK
The Jam . . . . Polydor POSP 350

ABSOLUTE BEGINNERS April 1986
David Bowie
EMI Music . . . . UK
Film(s): . . . . Absolute Beginners
David Bowie . . . . Virgin VS 838
David Bowie appeared in *Absolute Beginners*

AC-CENT-TCHU-ATE THE POSITIVE 1945
Johnny Mercer / Harold Arlen
Edwin H. Morris & Co. Ltd. . . . . USA
Film(s): . . . . Here Come the Waves
Bing Crosby & The Andrews Sisters . . . . Brunswick Bing 9
Perry Como . . . . RCA RD 27078
Buddy Rich . . . . HMV CLP 1092
Sam Cooke . . . . HMV CLP 1273
Bing Crosby appeared in *Here Come the Waves.*
Nominated for an Academy Award 1945.

ACCORDION 1947
Marcel Paul / Fred Freed / Howard Barnes
Lawrence Wright Music Co. Ltd. . . . . France
Jean Caval . . . . HMV B 9542
Roy Fox & his Orchestra . . . . Decca F 8749

ACROSS THE ALLEY FROM THE ALAMO 1947
Joe Greene
Leeds Music Ltd. . . . . USA
The Mills Brothers . . . . Brunswick LAT 8369
Stan Kenton & his Orchestra,
vocal June Christy . . . . Capitol LC 6676
The Mills Brothers . . . . London HAD 2192
June Christy . . . . Capitol T 1202

ADDICTED TO LOVE June 1986
Robert Palmer
Island Music . . . . UK
Robert Palmer . . . . Island IS 270

ADELAIDE May 1955
Frank Loesser
Edwin H. Morris & Co. Ltd. . . . . USA
Film(s): . . . . Guys and Dolls
Sammy Davis Jnr . . . . Brunswick 05583
Jerry Vale . . . . Philips PB 614

ADELAIDE'S LAMENT September 1953
Frank Loesser
Edwin H. Morris & Co. Ltd. . . . . USA
Show(s): . . . . Guys and Dolls
Vivian Blaine . . . . Brunswick LAT 8022
Debbie Reynolds . . . . Reprise F 2016
Vivian Blaine appeared in both the American and British productions of *Guys and Dolls.*

ADELINE 1931
Joseph Gilbert / Horatio Nicholls
Lawrence Wright Music Co. Ltd . . . . UK
Jack Payne & The BBC Dance Orchestra . . . Columbia CB 143

ADIOS 1932
Enric Madriguera / Eddie Woods

Campbell Connelly & Co. Ltd. . . . . USA
Glenn Miller & his Orchestra . . . . **RCA RCX 1063**
Enric Madriguera & his Orchestra . . . . **Columbia FB 2818**
Jane Morgan . . . . **London HAR 2242**
Xavier Cugat & his Orchestra . . . . **RCA RD 27127**
Mel Tormé . . . . **HMV CLP 1315**

ADIOS MARIQUITA LINDA   1940
Marcos Jiminez / Ray Gilbert
Southern Music Publishing Co. Ltd . . . . Mexico
Film(s): . . . . Masquerade in Mexico
Artie Shaw & his Orchestra . . . . **HMV B 9079**
Gene Sutry appeared in *The Old Barn Dance.*
Dorothy Lamour . . . . **Brunswick 04488**
Los Valldemosa . . . . **Philips BBL 7480**
Dorothy Lamour appeared in *Masquerade In Mexico.*

ADIOS MUCHACHOS   1940
Julio Sanders / Caesar Vedani / Fred Stuart
Southern Music Publishing Co. Ltd. . . . . Argentina
Ella Logan . . . . **Parlophone R 2635**
Ramon Littee & his Orchestra . . . . **Parlophone MP 34**
Stanley Black & his Orchestra . . . . **Decca LK 4325**

ADORATION WALTZ, THE   June 1957
Larry Stock / Al Lewis
Sydney Bron Music Co. Ltd. . . . . USA
David Whitfield . . . . **Decca LK 4242**

AFFAIR TO REMEMBER, AN   October 1957
Harry Warren / Harold Adamson / Leo McCarey
Robbins Music Corporation Ltd . . . . USA
Film(s): . . . . An Affair to Remember
Joni James . . . . **MGM C 839**
Vic Damone . . . . **Philips BBR 8117**
Nominated for an Academy Award 1957.

AFRAID TO DREAM   1937
Mack Gordon / Harry Revel
Francis, Day & Hunter Ltd. . . . . USA
Film(s): . . . . You Can't Have Everything
Tony Martin & Alice Faye . . . . **Conifer CM SCD 004**
Connee Boswell . . . . **Brunswick 02480**
Les Allen . . . . **Columbia FB 1815**
Petula Clark . . . . **Nixa NPL 18007**
Tony Martin & Alice Faye appeared in *You Can't Have Everything.*

AFRICA   May 1983
David Paich / Jeffrey Porcard
April Music Ltd . . . . USA
Toto . . . . **CBS A 2510**

AFRICAN WALTZ   April 1961
Galt MacDermot
Key Music Ltd . . . . UK
Johnny Dankworth & his Orchestra . . . . **Columbia DB 4590**
Valerie Masters . . . . **Fontana H 367**
Ken Jones & his Orchestra . . . . **Columbia 33SX 1578**
Ivor Novello Award.

AFTER A WHILE   1945
Nick Kenny / Charles Kenny / Abner Silver
Noel Gay Music Co. Ltd. . . . . USA
Turner Layton . . . . **Columbia FB 3131**
Vera Lynn . . . . **Decca F 8556**

AFTER MY LAUGHTER CAME TEARS   1928
Charles Tobias / Roy Turk
B. Feldman & Co. Ltd . . . . USA
Layton & Johnstone . . . . **Saville SVL 180**
Bob Manning . . . . **Capitol CL 14234**
Johnnie Ray . . . . **Brunswick 05884**

AFTER THE BALL   1893
Charles K. Harris
W. Paxton & Co Ltd . . . . USA
Show(s): . . . . A Trip To Chinatown
Film(s): . . . . Lillian Russell, The Jolson Story
Florrie Forde . . . . **Rex 8528**
Vernon Dalhart . . . . **Columbia 15030 D**
Lester Lannin Orchestra . . . . **Philips BB 2008**
Bing Crosby . . . . **Capitol W 1363**
Anita Harris . . . . **Galaxy GY 156**
Cliff Adams Singers . . . . **Pickwick PWKS 656**

AFTER THE LOVE HAS GONE   August 1979
Donald Foster / Jay Graydon / Bill Champlin
Rondor Music (London) Ltd. USA
Earth Wind & Fire . . . . **CBS 7721**

AFTER THE STORM   1924
Jack Nelson
B. Feldman & Co. Ltd. . . . . USA
The Troubadours . . . . **HMV B 1848**
The Tuneful Twenties Dance Orchestra . . . **Parlophone R 3350**

AFTER YOU - WHO   1933
Cole Porter
Chappell & Co. Ltd. . . . . USA
Show(s): . . . . The Gay Divorce
Fred Astaire . . . . **Columbia DB 1215**
Jeri Southern . . . . **Capitol T 1173**
Lena Horne . . . . **RCA RD 27021**
Fred Astaire appeared in both the American and British productions of *The Gay Divorce.*

AFTER YOU GET WHAT YOU WANT, YOU DON'T WANT IT   1921
Irving Berlin
Irving Berlin Ltd . . . . USA
Film(s): . . . . There's No Business Like Show Business
Harry Roy & his Band . . . . **Decca F 9610**
Dolores Gray . . . . **Brunswick LAT 8059**
Anita Ellis . . . . **Philips PB 424**
Marilyn Monroe . . . . **HMV B 10847**
Marilyn Monroe appeared in *There's No Business Like Show Business.*

AFTER YOU'VE GONE   1918
Henry Creamer / Turner Layton
Francis, Day & Hunter Ltd . . . . USA
Film(s):For Me & My Gal / Jolson Sings Again / All That Jazz / The Five Pennies / Atlantic City
The Savoy Quartet . . . . **HMV B 1088**
Bessie Smith . . . . **Philips BBL 7042**
Sophie Tucker (1933) . . . . **Parlophone R 3353**
Judy Garland . . . . **Capitol LCT 6103**
Al Jolson . . . . **Brunswick LA 8502**
Eydie Gormé . . . . **HMV CLP 1170**
Danny Kaye & Louis Armstrong . . . . **Decca SAHU 6044**
Judy Garland appeared in *For Me & My Gal.*
Danny Kaye & Louis Armstrong appeared in *The Five Pennies.*

AFTERGLOW   1936
Al Stillman / Buck Ram / Phil Levant
Lawrence Wright Music Co. Ltd . . . . USA
Leo Reisman & his Orchestra . . . . **Vocalion 522**
Paul Whiteman & his Orchestra . . . . **HMV BD 5111**
Lelie Hutchinson (Hutch) . . . . **Parlophone F 644**

AGADOO   September 1984
Mya Simille / Michael Delancery / Giles Peram
Warner Chappell Music . . . . France
Black Lace . . . . **Flair FLA 107**

AGAIN   August 1949
Dorcas Cochrane / Lionel Newman
Robbins Music Corporation Ltd . . . . USA
Film(s): . . . . Road House
Mel Tormé . . . . **Capitol CL 13094**
Vic Damone . . . . **Mercury ZEP 10022**
Nat 'King' Cole . . . . **Capitol EAP 1-1211**
Dinah Washington . . . . **Mercury MMC 14055**

AGAIN AND AGAIN   September 1978
Richard Parfitt / Andy Bown / Paul Lynton
EMI Music Ltd . . . . UK
Status Quo . . . . **Vertigo QUO 1**

AGAINST ALL ODDS (Take a Look At Me Now)   May 1984
Phil Collins
Hit & Run Music . . . . UK
Film(s): . . . . Against All Odds
Phil Collins . . . . **Virgin VS 674**
Nominated for an Academy award 1984.
Ivor Novello Award.

AGGRAVATIN' PAPA   1923
Roy Turk / Russel Robinson
B. Feldman & Co. Ltd . . . . USA

Ladds Black Aces	HMV AL 3556
The Gin Bottle Seven	London LTZU 15115
Pearl Bailey	Columbia 33SX 1247

AH BUT IT HAPPENS — November 1948
Walter Kent / 'By' Dunham
Peter Maurice Music Co. Ltd . . . . USA
Tony Martin . . . . **HMV B 9708**
Sam Browne . . . . **Decca F 8998**

AH SWEET MYSTERY OF LIFE — 1910
Victor Herbert / Rida Johnson Young
B Feldman & Co Ltd . . . . USA
Show(s): . . . . Naughty Marietta
Film(s): . . . . Naughty Marietta / The Great Victor Herbert
Richard Crooks . . . . **Camden CDN 1019**
Jeanette MacDonald & Nelson Eddy . . . . **RCA RCX 1020**
Anne Ziegler & Webster Booth . . . . **HMV B 9051**
Richard Tauber . . . . **Parlophone RO 20482**
Paul Britten & his Orchestra . . . . **MGM C 779**
Jeanette MacDonald & Nelson Eddy appeared in the film *Naughty Marietta*.

AH-HA — 1925
Jimmy Monaco / Sidney Clare
Francis, Day & Hunter Ltd. . . . . USA
Paul Whiteman & his Orchestra . . . . **HMV B 2055**

AIN'T GONNA BUMP NO MORE — June 1977
B.L. McGinty / Buddy Killen
London Tree Music Ltd. . . . . USA
Joe Tex . . . . **Epic EPC 5035**

AIN'T GONNA KISS YA — September 1963
James Smith
Campbell Connelly & Co. Ltd . . . . USA
The Searchers . . . . **Pye NEP 24177**
Jean Martin . . . . **Decca F 11751**

AIN'T GONNA WASH FOR A WEEK — September 1961
Peter Udell / Gary Geld
Jewel Music Publishing Co. Ltd. . . . . USA
The Brook Brothers . . . . **Pye 7N 15369**
Eddie Hodges . . . . **London HLA 9369**

AIN'T GOT A DIME TO MY NAME — 1943
Johnny Burke / Jimmy Van Heusen
Victoria Music Co. Ltd . . . . USA
Film(s): . . . . Road to Morocco
Bing Crosby . . . . **Brunswick Bing 8**
Bing Crosby appeared in *Road to Morocco*.

AIN'T GOT NO — December 1968
Gerome Ragni / James Rado / Galt MacDermot
United Artists Music Co. Ltd. . . . . USA
Show(s): . . . . Hair
Film(s): . . . . Hair
Steve Curry, Lamont Washington & Melba Moore **RCA RD 7959**
Michael Feast, Peter Staker & Joanne White . . **Polydor 583043**
Nell Carter, Kurt Yahjian & Tony Watkins . . **RCA BL 03274**
Steve Curry, Lamont Washington & Melba Moore appeared in the American production of *Hair*.
Michael Feast, Peter Straker & Joanne White appeared in the British production of *Hair*.
Nell Carter, Kurt Yahjian & Tony Watkins appeared in the film of *Hair*.

AIN'T GOT NO - I GOT LIFE (Medley) — January 1969
Gerome Ragni / James Rado / Galt MacDermot
United Artists Music Co. Ltd. . . . . USA
Show(s): . . . . Hair
Film(s): . . . . Hair
Nina Simone . . . . **RCA 1743**
See also 'I Got Life'.

AIN'T IT A SHAME ABOUT MAME — 1941
Jimmy Monaco / Johnny Burke
Campbell Connelly & Co. Ltd . . . . USA
Film(s): . . . . Rhythm on the River
Mary Martin . . . . **Brunswick 03103**
Adelaide Hall . . . . **Decca F 7709**
Mary Martin appeared in *Rhythm on the River*.

AIN'T IT GRAND TO BE BLOOMIN' WELL DEAD — 1932
Leslie Sarony
Campbell Connelly & Co. Ltd. . . . . UK

| Leslie Sarony | Imperial 2688 |
| Primo Scala's Accordion Band | Decca F 9011 |

AIN'T LOVE A BITCH — March 1979
Rod Stewart / Gary Grainer
Riva Music . . . . UK
Rod Stewart . . . . **Riva 18**

AIN'T MISBEHAVIN' — 1929
Andy Razaf / Thomas Waller / Harry Brooks
Lawrence Wright Music Co. Ltd . . . . USA
Show(s): . . . . Hot Chocolates
Film(s):Stormy Weather / Follow the Band / Atlantic City / You Were Meant for Me / The Strip / Gentlemen Marry Brunettes
Louis Armstrong . . . . **Parlophone R 462**
'Fats' Waller & his Rhythm . . . . **Camden CDN 131**
Johnnie Ray (1956) . . . . **Philips PB 580**
Cleo Laine . . . . **Parlophone GEP 8613**
Tommy Bruce (1960) . . . . **Columbia DB 4453**
Fats' Waller & his Rhythm appeared in *Stormy Weather*.
The Louis Armstrong Orchestra appeared in *The Strip*.

AIN'T NO MOUNTAIN HIGH ENOUGH — October 1970
Nicholas Ashford / Valerie Simpson
Jobete Music (UK) Ltd. . . . . USA
Diana Ross . . . . **Tamla Motown TMG 751**
Vikki Carr . . . . **CBS SD 5161**

AIN'T NO PLEASING YOU — April 1982
Charles Hodges / David Peacock
Chas Dave Music . . . . UK
Chas & Dave . . . . **Rockney KOR 14**

AIN'T NO STOPPIN' US NOW — June 1979
Gene McFadden / John Whitehead / Jim Coen
Carlin Music Corporation . . . . USA
McFadden & Whitehead . . . . **Philadelphia PIR 7365**

AIN'T NO SUNSHINE — September 1972
Bill Withers
United Artists Music Co. Ltd. . . . . USA
Michael Jackson . . . . **Tamla Motown TMG 826**
Bill Withers . . . . **CBS 85049**

AIN'T NOBODY — April 1984
David Wolinski
Warner Chappell Music . . . . USA
Rufus & Chaka Khan . . . . **Warner Brothers RCK 1**
Rufus & Chaka Khan (1989) . . . . **Warner Brothers W 2800**

AIN'T NOBODY BETTER — May 1989
David Saunderson / Shanna Gray
Virgin Music . . . . UK
Inner City . . . . **Virgin TEN 252**

AIN'T NOBODY HEAR BUT US CHICKENS — 1947
Alex Kramer / Joan Whitney
Pickwick Music Ltd. . . . . USA
Louis Jordan & his Tympany Five . . . . **Brunswick 03778**
Pat Boone . . . . **London HAD 2049**
Louis Jordan . . . . **Mercury MPT 7521**

AIN'T NOTHIN' GOIN' ON BUT THE RENT — August 1986
Gwen Guthrie
Polygram Music . . . . USA
Gwen Guthrie . . . . **Polydor POSP 807**

AIN'T NOTHING BUT A HOUSEPARTY — April 1968
Del Sharn / Joe Thomas
Clairlyn Music . . . . USA
The Showstoppers . . . . **Beacon 3-100**

AIN'T SHE SWEET — 1927
Jack Yellen / Milton Ager
Lawrence Wright Music Co. Ltd. . . . . USA
Film(s): . . . . You Were Meant for Me / You're My Everything
The New York Syncopators . . . . **Parlophone E 5787**
Jack Hylton's Hyltonians . . . . **HMV B 5211**
Michael Holliday . . . . **Columbia 33SX 1170**
Sallie Blair . . . . **Parlophone PMC 1083**

AIN'T THAT A GRAND AND GLORIOUS FEELING — 1927
Jack Yellen / Milton Ager
Lawrence Wright Music Co. Ltd . . . . USA
Jack Hylton & his Orchestra . . . . **HMV B 5336**

Paul Ash & his Orchestra .... **Columbia 4563**
Max Bygraves with Ted Heath & his Music .... **Decca LK 4317**

AIN'T THAT A SHAME   November 1955
Antoine Domino / Dave Bartholomew
Francis, Day & Hunter Ltd. .... USA
Pat Boone .... **London HAD 2024**
Bobby Rydell .... **Columbia 33SX 1243**
Connie Francis .... **MGM C 804**
Fats Domino (1957) .... **London HAP 2041**

AIN'T THAT FUNNY   July 1962
Les Vandyke
Essex Music Ltd .... UK
Jimmy Justice .... **Pye 7N 15443**

AIN'T WE GOT FUN   1921
Gus Kahn / Ray Egan / Richard A. Whiting
B. Feldman & Co. Ltd .... USA
Film(s): .... By the Light of the Silvery Moon
The Benson Orchestra of Chicago .... **HMV B 1253**
Nat D. Ayer .... **Columbia 3080**
Bob Hope & Margaret Whiting .... **Capitol EAP 1-20071**
Doris Day & Danny Thomas .... **Philips BBL 7175**
Debbie Reynolds .... **London HAD 2326**
Doris Day & Gordon MacRae .... **Caliban 6019**
Doris Day & Gordon MacRae appeared in *By the Light of the Silvery Moon.*

AIR THAT I BREATHE, THE   March 1974
Albert Hammond / Mike Hazlewood
Rondor Music (London) Ltd. .... UK
The Hollies .... **Polydor 2058435**
Albert Hammond .... **CBS S 31643**
Ivor Novello Nomination.

AIRPORT   July 1978
Andy McMaster
Island Music Ltd .... UK
The Motors .... **Virgin VS 219**

ALABAMA JUBILEE   1915
George L. Cobb / Jack Yellen
Francis, Day & Hunter Ltd. .... USA
Red Foley .... **Brunswick 04852**
Ferlin Husky .... **Capitol EAP 2-1280**
Teresa Brewer .... **Coral LVA 9107**

ALABAMA MOON   1920
George Green
Francis, Day & Hunter Ltd .... USA
Olive Kline & Elsie Baker .... **HMV B 1207**

ALABAMY BOUND   1925
Bud Green / Buddy De Sylva / Ray Henderson
Keith Prowse Music Publishing Co. Ltd. .... USA
Show(s): .... Kid Boots
Film(s):The Great American Broadcast / Broadway / With a Song in
My Heart / Show Business
Fletcher Henderson & his Orchestra .... **Imperial 1420**
The Hannan Dance Band .... **Columbia 3634**
Bing Crosby .... **Brunswick LAT 8217**
Eddie Cantor .... **Brunswick 04284**
Al Jolson .... **Brunswick LAT 8322**
Dean Martin .... **Capitol EAP 1037**
Eddie Cantor appeared in *Kid Boots* and *Show Business.*

ALBATROSS   February 1969
Peter Green
Immediate Music Ltd. .... UK
Fleetwood Mac .... **Blue Horizon 573145**
Fleetwood Mac (1973) .... **CBS 8306**

ALEEZ VOUS-EN, GO AWAY   December 1954
Cole Porter
Chappell & Co. Ltd. .... USA
Show(s): .... Can-Can
Lilo .... **Capitol LCT 6010**
Irene Hilda .... **Parlophone PMD 1017**
Kay Starr .... **Capitol T 947**
Lilo appeared in the American production of *Can-Can.*
Irene Hilda appeared in the British production of *Can-Can.*

ALEXANDER'S RAGTIME BAND   1911
Irving Berlin

B. Feldman & Co. Ltd.
.... USA
Show(s): .... Hullo Ragtime
Film(s):Alexander's Ragtime Band / There's No Business Like Show
Business
Alice Faye .... **Reprise R 6029**
Herr Gottlieb's Orchestra .... **HMV B 161**
Al Jolson .... **Brunswick LAT 8267**
Harry Gold & his Band .... **Columbia SEG 8045**
Sarah Vaughan & Billy Eckstine .... **Mercury MPL 6530**
Ethel Merman, Donald O'Connor, Mitzi Gaynor, Dan Dailey &
Johnny Ray .... **Brunswick LAT 8059**
Alice Faye appeared in *Alexander's Ragtime Band*
Ethel Merman, Donald O'Connor, Mitzi Gaynor, Dan Dailey & Johnny
Ray appeared in *There's No Business Like Show Business.*

ALFIE   May 1966
Burt Bacharach / Hal David
Famous Chappell .... USA
Film(s): .... Alfie
Burt Bacharach Orchestra .... **A&M AMS 702**
Cilla Black .... **Parlophone R 5427**
Cher .... **Liberty LBL 83034**
Vikki Carr .... **Liberty LIB 83099**
Nominated for an Academy Award 1966.
The song was not in the film when first released in the UK.

ALGY THE PICCADILLY JOHNNY   1895
Harry Morris
Francis, Day & Hunter Ltd .... UK
Vesta Tilley .... **Edison 13603**
Ray Wallace .... **Parlophone R 1147**

ALI BABA'S CAMEL   1931
Noel Gay
Francis, Day & Hunter Ltd. .... UK
Cicely Courtneidge .... **HMV B 3985**
Jack Payne & his Orchestra,
vocal Jack Payne .... **Columbia CB 383**

ALICE BLUE GOWN   1920
Harry Tierney / Joseph McCarthy
Francis, Day & Hunter Ltd .... USA
Show(s): .... Irene
Film(s): .... Irene
Edith Day .... **HMV B 1115**
Edith Day .... **Columbia F 1044**
Bing Crosby .... **Warner Brothers WM 4021**
Edith Day appeared in both the British & American productions of
Irene.

ALICE WHERE ART THOU?   1861
Wellington Guernsey / Joseph Ascher
Unknown Publisher .... UK
The Francini Quartette .... **Zonophone T 1448**
Patricia Rossborough .... **Parlophone E 11188**
Neddle Nash .... **Columbia DB 792**
John Turner .... **HMV B 2760**

ALICE, I WANT YOU JUST FOR ME   January 1986
"Full Force"
Zomba Music .... UK
Full Force .... **CBS A 6640**

ALIVE AND KICKING   October 1985
"Simple Minds"
EMI Music .... UK
Simple Minds .... **Virgin VS 817**

ALL   April 1957
Alan Stranks / Reynell Wreford
Anglo-Continental Music Co. Ltd. .... UK
Robert Earl .... **Philips PB 684**
United Kingdom entry for the 1957 Eurovision Song Contest (Placed
Sixth).

ALL ABOARD FOR DIXIELAND   1914
George L. Cobb / Jack Yellen
Chappell & Co. Ltd. .... USA
Show(s): .... High Jinks
Ada Jones & The Peerless Quartet .... **Columbia 2443**

ALL ALONE   1911
Harry Von Tilzer / William Dillon
Francis, Day & Hunter Ltd. .... USA
Ada Jones & Herbert Scott .... **Columbia 1724**

Beth Tate . . . . Columbia 1793

ALL ALONE   **1925**
Irving Berlin
Francis, Day & Hunter Ltd. . . . . USA
Show(s): . . . . The Music Box Revue
Film(s): . . . . Alexander's Ragtime Band
The Savoy Orpheans . . . . **HMV B 1915**
Connee Boswell . . . . **Brunswick 02645**
Dinah Shore . . . . **Capitol T 1296**

ALL ALONE AM I   **February 1963**
Manos Hadjidakis / Arthur Altman
Leeds Music Ltd . . . . Greece
Brenda Lee . . . . **Brunswick 05882**
Johnny Tillotson . . . . **MGM C 972**

ALL ALONE MONDAY   **1930**
Bert Kalmar / Harry Ruby
Chappell & Co. Ltd . . . . USA
Show(s): . . . . The Ramblers
Film(s): . . . . The Cuckoos / Three Little Words
Van Philips & his Orchestra . . . . **Columbia DX 83**
The Melachrino Orchestra . . . . **HMV C 4045**

ALL ALONG THE WATCHTOWER   **November 1968**
Bob Dylan
B. Feldman & Co. Ltd. . . . . USA
Jimi Hendrix Experience . . . . **Track 604025**
Bob Dylan . . . . **CBS BPG 63252**

ALL AROUND MY HAT   **December 1975**
Traditional
Chrysalis Music Ltd . . . . UK
Steeleye Span . . . . **Chrysalis CHS 2078**

ALL AROUND THE WORLD   **August 1977**
Paul Weller
And Son Music . . . . UK
The Jam . . . . **Polydor 2058903**

ALL AROUND THE WORLD   **November 1989**
Lisa Stansfield / Ian Devaney / Andrew Morris
BMG Music . . . . UK
Lisa Stansfield . . . . **Arista 112693**
Ivor Novello Award 1989 & 1990.

ALL BECAUSE OF YOU   **May 1973**
Victor Malcolm
Red Bus Music . . . . UK
Geordie . . . . **EMI 2008**

ALL BY MYSELF   **1921**
Irving Berlin
Irving Berlin Ltd . . . . USA
Film(s): . . . . Blue Skies
Art Hickman & his New York-London Five . . . . . . **HMV B 1269**
Bing Crosby . . . . **Brunswick Bing 10**
Ella Fitzgerald . . . . **HMV CLP 1183**
Bing Crosby appeared in *Blue Skies*.

ALL BY MYSELF   **May 1976**
Eric Carmen
Campbell Connelly & Co. Ltd . . . . USA
Eric Carmen . . . . **Arista 42**
Based on Piano Concerto No.2 by Sergi Racmaninof (1873 - 1943).

ALL BY YOURSELF IN THE MOONLIGHT   **1929**
C. Jay Wallis
Campbell Connelly & Co. Ltd . . . . UK
The New Mayfair Orchestra . . . . **HMV B 5562**
Tommy Handley . . . . **Piccadilly 157**
Primo Scala's Accordion Band . . . . **Decca F 9010**

ALL CRIED OUT   **November 1984**
Alison Moyet / Steve Jolley / Tony Swain
Rondor Music . . . . UK
Alison Moyet . . . . **CBS A 4757**

ALL DAY AND ALL OF THE NIGHT   **November 1964**
Ray Davies
Edward Kassner Music Co. Ltd . . . . UK
The Kinks . . . . **Pye 7N 15714**
The Stranglers (1988) . . . . **Epic VICE 1**

ALL DRESSED UP WITH A BROKEN HEART October 1948
Fred Patrick / Claude Reese / Jack Val
Cinephonic Music Co. Ltd. . . . . USA
Buddy Clark . . . . **Columbia DB 2449**
Peggy Lee . . . . **Capitol CL 13001**
Chris Connor . . . . **London LZ 14036**

ALL FOR A SHILLING A DAY   **1935**
Noel Gay / Clifford Grey
Cinephonic Music Co. Ltd . . . . UK
Film(s): . . . . Me and Marlborough
Cicely Courtneidge & Jack Hulbert . . . . **HMV C 2668**
Ciceley Courtneidge & Jack Hulbert appeared in *Me and Marlborough*.

ALL FOR YOU   **1915**
Victor Herbert / Henry Blossom
B. Feldman & Co. Ltd. . . . . USA
Show(s): . . . . The Princess Pat
Film(s): . . . . The Great Victor Herbert
Peter Yorke & his Orchestra . . . . **Brunswick LAT 8035**
Allan Jones & Mary Martin . . . . **Caliban 6033**
Allan Jones & Mary Martin appeared in *The Great Victor Herbert*.

ALL GOD'S CHILLUN GOT RHYTHM   **1937**
Bronislaw Kaper / Walter Jurmann / Gus Kahn
Francis, Day & Hunter Ltd. . . . . USA
Film(s): . . . . A Day at the Races
Bunny Berigan & his Orchestra . . . . **HMV B 8638**
Judy Garland . . . . **Brunswick 02478**
June Christy . . . . **Capitol T 1076**

ALL I ASK OF YOU   **November 1986**
Andrew LLoyd Webber / Charles Hart / Richard Stilgoe
Really Useful Music . . . . UK
Show(s): . . . . Phantom of the Opera
Cliff Richard & Sarah Brightman . . . . **Polydor POSP 802**
Steve Barton & Sarah Brightman . . . . **Polydor PODV 9**
Steve Barton & Sarah Brightman appeared in *Phantom of the Opera*.
Ivor Novello Nomination.

ALL I DO IS DREAM OF YOU   **1934**
Arthur Freed / Nacio Herb Brown
Robbins Music Corporation Ltd . . . . USA
Film(s):Sadie McKee / Singin' in the Rain / The Boy Friend / Broadway Melody of 1936
Ray Noble & his Orchestra, vocal Al Bowlly . . . . . . **HMV B 6508**
Elsie Carlisle . . . . **Decca F 5122**
Debbie Reynolds . . . . **MGM 493**
Dean Martin . . . . **Capitol T 1150**
Pat Boone . . . . **London HAD 2030**
Twiggy . . . . **MGM 1SE 32**
Debbie Reynolds appeared in *Singin' in the Rain*.
Twiggy appeared in the film *The Boy Friend*.

ALL I EVER NEED IS YOU   **February 1972**
Jimmy Holiday / Eddie Reeves
United Artists Music Co. Ltd . . . . USA
Sonny & Cher . . . . **MCA MU 1145**
Ray Charles . . . . **Probe SPB 1039**

ALL I HAVE TO DO IS DREAM   **July 1958**
Boudleaux Bryant
Acuff-Rose Music Ltd. . . . . USA
The Everly Brothers . . . . **London HLA 8618**
Roy Orbison . . . . **London HAU 8108**
Bobby Gentry & Glenn Campbell . . . . **Capitol CL 15619**

ALL I REALLY WANT TO DO   **September 1965**
Bob Dylan
Blossom Music Ltd . . . . USA
The Byrds . . . . **CBS 201796**
Cher . . . . **Liberty LIB 66114**

ALL I SEE IS YOU   **November 1966**
Clive Westlake / Ben Weisman
Belinda (London) Ltd. . . . . UK
Dusty Springfield . . . . **Philips BF 1510**

ALL I WANNA DO IS MAKE LOVE TO YOU   **May 1990**
Robert John Lange
Zomba Music . . . . UK
Heart . . . . **Capitol CL 569**
Ivor Novello Nomination.

15

ALL I WANT IS YOU   November 1974
Bryan Ferry
E.G. Music . . . . UK
Roxy Music . . . . **Island WIP 6208**

ALL KINDS OF EVERYTHING   May 1970
Derry Linsay / Jackie Smith
Mews Music . . . . Ireland
Dana . . . . **Rex R 11054**
Irish entry for the 1970 Eurovision Song Contest (Placed First).

ALL MY LOVE   January 1951
Henri Contet / Paul Durand / Mitchell Parish
Peter Maurice Music . . . . USA
Allan Jones . . . . **HMV B 9989**
Xavier Cugat Orchestra . . . . **Columbia DB 2741**
Denny Dennis . . . . **Decca F 9220**
Guy Lombardo & his Royal Canadians . . . . . **Brunswick 04633**

ALL MY LOVE   January 1968
Monti Arduini / Peter Callander
Shapiro-Bernstein & Co. Ltd. Italy
Cliff Richard . . . . **Columbia DB 8293**

ALL MY LOVING   December 1963
John Lennon / Paul McCartney
Northern Songs Ltd . . . . UK
Film(s): . . . . A Hard Day's Night
The Beatles . . . . **Parlophone PMC 1206**
George Martin & his Orchestra . . . . **Parlophone R 5135**
Keely Smith . . . . **Reprise R 6142**
The Beatles appeared in *A Hard Day's Night.*
Ivor Novello Nomination.

ALL NIGHT LONG   March 1980
Ritchie Blackmore / Roger Glover
Panache . . . . UK
Rainbow . . . . **Polydor POSP 104**

ALL NIGHT LONG   November 1983
Lionel Richie
Warner Brothers Music . . . . USA
Lionel Richie . . . . **Motown TMG 1319**

ALL OF ME   1932
Seymour Simons / Gerald Marks
Francis, Day & Hunter Ltd. . . . . USA
Film(s): Careless Lady / Meet Danny Wilson / Lady Sings the Blues
Louis Armstrong & his Orchestra . . . . **Parlophone R 1894**
Willy Lewis & his Orchestra . . . . **Columbia DB 5017**
Connee Boswell . . . . **RCA RD 27116**
Frank Sinatra (1947) . . . . **Philips BBL 7168**
Helen O'Connell . . . . **Warner Brothers WM 4033**
Frank Sinatra appeared in *Meet Danny Wilson.*
Diana Ross appeared in *Lady Sings the Blues.*

ALL OF ME LOVES ALL OF YOU   November 1974
Bill Martin / Phil Coulter
Martin-Coulter Music Ltd. . . . . UK
The Bay City Rollers . . . . **Bell 1382**

ALL OF MY HEART   September 1982
Martin Fry / David Palmer / Stephen Singleton & Mark White
Virgin Music . . . . UK
ABC . . . . **Phonogram NT 104**

ALL OF MY LIFE   February 1974
Michael Randell
Jobete Music (UK) Ltd. . . . . USA
Diana Ross . . . . **Tamla Motown TMG 880**

ALL OF YOU   May 1957
Cole Porter
Chappell & Co. Ltd. . . . . USA
Show(s): . . . . Silk Stockings
Film(s): . . . . Silk Stockings
Fred Astaire . . . . **MGM C 760**
Trudie Richards . . . . **Capitol T 383**
Sammy Davis . . . . **Brunswick 05629**
Helen Merrill . . . . **Mercury MMB 12000**
Fred Astaire appeared in the film *Silk Stockings.*

ALL OR NOTHING   October 1966
Steve Marriott / Ronald Lane

Robbins Music Corporation Ltd. . . . . UK
The Small Faces . . . . **Decca F 12470**

ALL OR NOTHING AT ALL   1943
Arthur Altman / Jack Lawrence
Leeds Music Ltd . . . . USA
Film(s): . . . . Weekend Pass
Frank Sinatra . . . . **Columbia DB 2145**
Donna Hightower . . . . **Capitol T 1273**
Steve Lawrence . . . . **HMV CLP 1326**

ALL OUR TOMORROWS   1943
Jimmy Kennedy
Campbell Connelly & Co. Ltd . . . . UK
The R.A.F. Dance Orchestra . . . . **Decca F 8315**

ALL OUT OF LOVE   November 1980
Graham Russell / Clive Davis
Riva Music Ltd. . . . . Australia
Air Supply . . . . **Arista ARIST 362**

ALL OVER ITALY   1933
Ralph Butler / Ronnie Munro
Dash Music Ltd. . . . . UK
Anona Winn . . . . **Columbia DB 1138**
Ray Noble & his Orchestra . . . . **HMV B 6364**

ALL OVER THE PLACE   1941
Noel Gay / Frank Eyton
Noel Gay Music Co. Ltd . . . . UK
Film(s): . . . . Sailors Three
Tommy Trinder . . . . **Columbia FB 2531**
Leslie Hutchinson (Hutch) . . . . **HMV BD 882**
The New Mayfair Dance Orchestra . . . . **HMV BD 5642**
Tommy Trinder appeared in *Sailors Three.*

ALL OVER THE WORLD   August 1980
Jeff Lynne
Jet Music Ltd . . . . UK
The Electric Light Orchestra . . . . **Jet 195**

ALL OVER THE WORLD (Dans Le Monde Entier) May 1965
Franciose Hardy / Julian More
Rogers Music Co. Ltd . . . . France
Francois Hardy . . . . **Pye 7N 15802**

ALL PALS TOGETHER   1914
Reginald Sloan
B. Feldman & Co. Ltd. . . . . UK
London Piano-Accordian Band . . . **Regal Zonophone MR 3278**

ALL RIGHT NOW   August 1970
Andy Fraser / Paul Rodgers
Blue Mountain Music . . . . UK
Free . . . . **Island WIP 6082**
Free (1973) . . . . **Island WIP 6082**

ALL SHOOK UP   July 1957
Otis Blackwell / Elvis Presley
Belinda (London) Ltd. . . . . USA
Elvis Presley . . . . **RCA RB 16069**
Jim Dale . . . . **Parlophone R 4356**

ALL STOOD STILL   June 1981
William Currie / Christopher Cross / Warren Cann & Midge Ure
Island Music . . . . UK
Ultravox . . . . **Chrysalis CHS 2522**

ALL THE LOVE IN THE WORLD   January 1981
Barry Gibb / Robin Gibb / Maurice Gibb
Gibb Brothers Music . . . . UK
Dionne Warwick . . . . **Arista ARIST 507**

ALL THE THINGS SHE SAID   April 1986
"Simple Minds"
EMI Music . . . . UK
Simple Minds . . . . **Virgin VS 860**

ALL THE THINGS YOU ARE   1941
Jerome Kern / Oscar Hammerstein II
Chappell & Co. Ltd . . . . USA
Film(s):Till The Clouds Roll By / Because You're Mine / Broadway Rhythm
Tony Martin . . . . **Decca F 7645**
Joan Regan . . . . **Decca LK 4153**

Mario Lanza . . . . **RCA RB 16002**
Sammy Davis . . . . **Brunswick LAT 8274**
Tony Martin appeared in *Broadway Rhythm*.
Mario Lanza appeared in *Because You're Mine*.

ALL THE TIME AND EVERYWHERE   January 1953
Bob Merrill
Cinephonic Music Co. Ltd . . . . USA
Dickie Valentine . . . . **Decca LF 1163**
Mindy Carson . . . . **Columbia DB 3212**

ALL THE WAY   November 1957
Sammy Cahn / Jimmy Van Heusen
Barton Music Co. Ltd . . . . USA
Film(s): . . . . The Joker is Wild
Frank Sinatra . . . . **Capitol EAP 20062**
Jane Morgan . . . . **London HAD 2256**
The Five Dallas Boys . . . . **Columbia SEG 8035**
Frank Sinatra appeared in *The Joker is Wild*.
Academy Award winning song of 1957.

ALL THE WAY FROM MEMPHIS   October 1973
Ian Hunter
Island Music Ltd. . . . . UK
Mott the Hoople . . . . **CBS 1764**

ALL THE WORLD WILL BE JEALOUS OF ME   1917
Ernest Ball / Al Dubin
B. Feldman & Co. Ltd. . . . . USA
Violet Loraine . . . . **HMV 03647**
Herbert Payne . . . . **Zonophone Twin 1809**

ALL THE YOUNG DUDES   September 1972
David Bowie
Chrysalis Music Ltd. . . . . UK
Mott the Hoople . . . . **CBS 8271**
David Bowie . . . . **RCA APL 20771**

ALL THIS AND HEAVEN TOO   1941
Eddie De Lange / Jimmy Van Heusen
B. Feldman & Co. Ltd . . . . USA
Tommy Dorsey & his Orch, vocal Frank Sinatra . **HMV BD 5656**
Dick Todd . . . . **HMV BD 894**
Mel Tormé . . . . **London HAN 2016**
Chris Connor . . . . **Parlophone GEP 8778**

ALL THOSE YEARS AGO   May 1981
George Harrison
Ganja Music . . . . UK
George Harrison . . . . **Dark Horse K 17807**

ALL THROUGH THE DAY   1946
Jerome Kern / Leo Robin / Oscar Hammerstein II
Chappell & Co. Ltd. . . . . USA
Film(s): . . . . Centennial Summer
Frank Sinatra . . . . **Columbia DB 2227**
Perry Como . . . . **Camden CDN 142**
Joni James . . . . **MGM C 777**
Nominated for an Academy Award 1946.

ALL THROUGH THE NIGHT   1935
Cole Porter
Chappell & Co. Ltd . . . . USA
Show(s): . . . . Anything Goes
Film(s): . . . . Anything Goes
Jack Whiting . . . . **Columbia DX 698**
Bing Crosby . . . . **Brunswick Bing 15**
Ella Fitzgerald . . . . **HMV CLP 1083**
Johnny Ray . . . . **Philips BBL 7285**
Jack Whiting appeared in the British production of *Anything Goes*.
Bing Crosby appeared in both the 1936 and 1956 films of *Anything Goes*.

ALL TOGETHER NOW   December 1990
Peter Hooton / Stephen Grimes
Virgin Music . . . . UK
The Farm . . . . **Produce MILK 103**

ALL YOU NEED IS LOVE   August 1967
John Lennon / Paul McCartney
Northern Songs Ltd. . . . . UK
Film(s): . . . . Yellow Submarine
The Beatles . . . . **Parlophone R 5620**
The Beatles appeared in *Yellow Submarine*.

ALLAH'S HOLIDAY   1917
Rudolf Frimi / Otto Harbach
B. Feldman & Co. Ltd. . . . . USA
Show(s): . . . . Katinka
Herman Finck & his Orchestra . . . . **Columbia DX 943**
Red Nichols & his Five Pennies . . . . **Brunswick 01853**
Ray Noble & his Orchestra . . . . **HMV 7EG 8056**
Red Nichols & his Five Pennies . . . . **Capitol T 1228**

ALLEGHENY MOON   July 1956
Al Hoffman / Dick Manning
Cinephonic Music Co. Ltd. . . . . USA
Guy Mitchell . . . . **Philips BBL 7246**
Janie Marden . . . . **Decca F 10765**
Patti Page . . . . **Mercury MPT 7506**

ALLENTOWN JAIL   October 1951
Irving Gordon
Bourne Music Ltd . . . . USA
Lita Roza . . . . **Decca LF 1187**
Jo Stafford . . . . **Philips BBL 7395**
Lita Roza . . . . **Nixa N 15204**

ALLEY'S TARTAN ARMY   April 1978
Samuel Dennison
EMI Music Ltd . . . . UK
Andy Cameron . . . . **Klub 03**

ALLEY-OOP   July 1960
Dallas Frazier
Leeds Music Ltd . . . . USA
The Hollywood Argyles . . . . **London HLU 9146**

ALLIGATOR CRAWL   1938
Thomas Waller
Keith Prowse Music Publishing Co. Ltd . . . . USA
'Fats' Waller (piano solo) . . . . **HMV B 8784**
Ralph Sutton . . . . **Fontana TFR 6002**
'Fats' Waller & his Rhythm . . . . **HMV CLP 1042**

ALMAZ   February 1987
Randy Crawford
Warner Brothers Music . . . . USA
Randy Crawford . . . . **Warner Brothers W 8583**

ALMOST LIKE BEING IN LOVE   May 1949
Alan Jay Lerner / Frederick Loewe
Keith Prowse Music Publishing Co. Ltd . . . . USA
Show(s): . . . . Brigadoon
Film(s): . . . . Brigadoon
David Brooks & Marion Bell . . . . **HMV B 9748**
Gene Kelly . . . . **MGM D 133**
Jo Stafford . . . . **Captiol CL 13076**
Sallie Blair . . . . **Parlophone PMC 1083**
David Brookes & Marion Bell appeared in both the American and British productions of *Brigadoon*.
Gene Kelly appeared in the film of *Brigadoon*.

ALMOST THERE   October 1965
Jerry Keller / Gloria Shayne
Cinephonic Music Co. Ltd . . . . USA
Film(s): . . . . I'd Rather be Rich
Andy Williams . . . . **CBS 201813**
The Lettermen . . . . **Capitol T 2270**
Brenda Lee . . . . **Brunswick LAT 8614**
Andy Williams appeared in *I'd Rather Be Rich*.

ALONE   1936
Arthur Freed / Nacio Herb Brown
Francis, Day & Hunter Ltd . . . . USA
Film(s): . . . . A Night at the Opera / Born to Sing
Allan Jones . . . . **HMV B 9886**
Greta Keller . . . . **Decca F 5965**
Petula Clark . . . . **Nixa NPL 18007**
David Whitfield . . . . **Decca LK 4384**
Allan Jones appeared in *A Night At The Opera*.

ALONE   November 1957
Morton Craft / Selma Craft
Duchess Music Ltd . . . . USA
Petula Clark . . . . **Nixa NPT 19022**
The Kaye Sisters . . . . **Philips BBE 12166**

ALONE   **August 1987**
William Steinberg / Tom Kelly
Warner Brothers Music . . . . USA
Heart . . . . **Capitol CL 488**

ALONE AGAIN (Naturally)   **April 1972**
Gilbert O'Sullivan
M.A.M. (Music Publishing) Ltd . . . . UK
Gilbert O'Sullivan . . . . **MAM 66**
Ivor Novello Nomination.

ALONE AT A TABLE FOR TWO   **1937**
Billy Hill / Ted Fiorito / Dan Richman
Dash Music Co. Ltd. . . . . USA
Ted Fiorito & his Orchestra,
vocal Stanley Hickman . . . . **Decca F 5909**
Turner Layton . . . . **Columbia FB 1369**

ALONE TOGETHER   **1932**
Howard Dietz / Arthur Schwartz
Chappell & Co. Ltd. . . . . USA
Show(s): . . . . Flying Colours
Artie Shaw & his Orchestra . . . . **HMV B 9341**
Peggy Lee . . . . **Capitol T 1049**
Julie London . . . . **London HAU 2083**

ALONE WITHOUT YOU   **September 1985**
Paul King
CBS Songs . . . . UK
King . . . . **CBS A 6308**

ALONG CAME CAROLINE   **September 1960**
Paul Stephens / Michael Cox / Terence McGrath & M. Steel
Southern Music Publishing Co. Ltd . . . . UK
Michael Cox . . . . **HMV POP 789**

ALONG THE NAVAJO TRAIL   **1946**
Eddie De Lange / Dick Charles / Larry Marks
Peter Maurice Music Co. Ltd. . . . . USA
Film(s): . . . . Along the Navajo Trail / Don't Fence Me in
Roy Rogers . . . . **HMV 7EG 8145**
Bing Crosby & The Andrews Sisters . . . . **Brunswick 03634**
Sam Cooke . . . . **HMV CLP 1273**
Roy Rogers appeared in both *Along the Navajo Trail* and *Don't Fence Me In.*

ALONG THE SANTA FE TRAIL   **1941**
Al Dubin / Will Grosz / Edwina Coolidge
Bradbury Wood Ltd . . . . USA
Film(s): . . . . Santa Fe Trail
Bing Crosby . . . . **Brunswick 03142**
The Sons of The Pioneers . . . . **RCA RD 27016**

ALPHABET STREET   **June 1988**
"Prince"
Warner Chappell Music . . . . USA
Prince . . . . **Paisley Park W 7900**

ALRIGHT, ALRIGHT, ALRIGHT   **August 1973**
Jacques Dutronc / Jacques Lanzman / Joe Strange
United Artists Music Co. Ltd. . . . . France
Mungo Jerry . . . . **Dawn DNS 1037**

ALRIGHT, OKAY, YOU WIN   **December 1955**
Syd Wyche / Mamie Watts
Southern Music Publishing Co. Ltd. USA
Count Basie & his Orchestra,
vocal Joe Williams . . . . **Columbia 33CX 10026**
Peggy Lee . . . . **Capitol T 1049**
Ottie Patterson . . . . **Columbia SEG 7915**

ALSO SPRACH ZARATHUSTRA   **May 1973**
Richard Strauss / Arranged by Eumir Deodato
Unknown Publisher . . . . Germany
Film(s): . . . . 2001 A Space Odyssey
Deodato . . . . **Creed Taylor CTI 4000**
An arrangement of a tone poem by Richard Strauss (1864 - 1949).

ALTERNATE TITLE   **August 1967**
Mickey Dolenz
Screen Gems Music Ltd. . . . . USA
The Monkees . . . . **RCA 1604**

ALVIN'S HARMONICA   **April 1959**
Ross Bagdasarian

Chappell & Co. Ltd . . . . USA
David Seville & his Orchestra,
vocal The Chipmunks . . . . **London HAU 2205**
The Cool Men . . . . **Parlophone GEP 8739**

ALWAYS   **1925**
Irving Berlin
Francis, Day & Hunter Ltd. . . . . USA
Film(s): . . . . Christmas Holiday / Blue Skies
The Savoy Orpheans . . . . **HMV B 2171**
Deanna Durbin . . . . **Brunswick LAT 8285**
Kathryn Grayson . . . . **MGM EP 636**
Dinah Shore . . . . **Capitol T 1296**

ALWAYS   **1934**
Kenneth Leslie Smith / James Dyrenforth
Chappell & Co. Ltd. . . . . UK
Frank Titterton . . . . **Decca F 5008**
Webster Booth . . . . **HMV B 9534**
Ronnie Hilton . . . . **HMV 7EG 8121**

ALWAYS   **June 1987**
David Wayne / Jonathan Lewis
Jodaway Music . . . . USA
Atlantic Starr . . . . **Warner Brothers W 8455**

ALWAYS AND FOREVER   **December 1978**
Rodney Temperton
Rondor Music (London) Ltd . . . . UK
Heatwave . . . . **GTO GT 236**

ALWAYS IN MY HEART   **1942**
Kim Gannon / Ernesto Lecuona
Southern Music Publishing Co. Ltd . . . . USA
Film(s): . . . . Always in My Heart
Jimmy Dorsey & his Orchestra,
vocal Bob Eberly . . . . **Brunswick 03356**
Perez Prado & his Orchestra . . . . **RCA RD 27046**
Jodi Sands . . . . **HMV POP 533**
Valerie Carr . . . . **Columbia 33SX 1228**
Nominated for an Academy Award 1942.

ALWAYS ON MY MIND   **January 1973**
Wayne Thompson / Mark James / John Christopher
Screen Gems Music Ltd. . . . . USA
Elvis Presley . . . . **RCA 2304**
The Pet Shop Boys (1987) . . . . **Parlophone R 6171**

ALWAYS SOMETHING THERE TO REMIND ME   **Nov 1964**
Hal David / Burt Bacharach
December Music Ltd . . . . USA
Sandie Shaw . . . . **Pye 7N 15704**

ALWAYS THERE   **October 1986**
Simon May / Leslie Osborne / Don Black
Lawrence Wright Music . . . . UK
Marti Webb . . . . **BBC RESL 190**
The vocal version of the theme to the BBC Television series *Howards Way.*
See also "Howards Way Theme".

ALWAYS TRUE TO YOU IN MY FASHION   **March 1951**
Cole Porter
Chappell & Co. Ltd . . . . USA
Show(s): . . . . Kiss Me Kate
Film(s): . . . . Kiss Me Kate
Lisa Kirk . . . . **Philips BBL 7244**
Julie Wilson . . . . **Columbia SEG 7721**
Ann Miller & Tommy Rall . . . . **MGM C 753**
Lisa Kirk appeared in the American production of *Kiss Me Kate.*
Julie Wilson appeared in the British production of *Kiss Me Kate.*
Ann Miller & Tommy Rall appeared in the film of *Kiss Me Kate.*

ALWAYS YOURS   **July 1974**
Gary Glitter / Mike Leander
Leeds Music Ltd. . . . . UK
Gary Glitter . . . . **Bell 1359**

AM I BLUE   **1929**
Harry Akst / Grant Clarke
B. Feldman & Co. Ltd . . . . USA
Film(s):On With the Show / Is Everybody Happy / So Long Letty / The Eddy Duchin Story / Funny Girl
Ethel Waters . . . . **CBS BPG 62547**
Anona Winn . . . . **HMV B 3174**

The Dorsey Brothers Orchestra .... Parlophone R 2475
Mary Ann McCall .... Coral EEP 2041
Dorothy Provine .... Warner Brothers WM 4035
Barbra Streisand .... Arista ARTY 101
Barbra Streisand appeared in *Funny Girl*.

AM I THAT EASY TO FORGET   March 1968
Carl Belew / W.S. Stevenson
Palace Music Co. Ltd. .... USA
Engelbert Humperdinck .... Decca F 12722

AM I WASTING MY TIME ON YOU   1926
Irving Bibo / Howard Johnson
Lawrence Wright Music Co. Ltd. .... USA
The Denza Dance Band .... Columbia 4092
Frankie Vaughan (1958) .... Philips PB 865
Vera Lynn .... Decca LK 4305
Mike Preston .... Decca DFE 6679

AMADO MIO   1946
Allan Roberts / Doris Fisher
Chappell & Co. Ltd. .... USA
Film(s): .... Gilda
Leslie Hutchinson (Hutch) .... HMV BD 1133
Anne Shelton .... Decca F 8636
Dick Haymes .... Brunswick 03007

AMANDA   April 1973
Brian Hall
Peter Maurice Music Co. Ltd. .... UK
Stuart Gillies .... Philips 6006293

AMAPOLA   1941
Joseph M. Lacalle / Albert Gamse
Campbell Connelly & Co. Ltd .... Mexico
Film(s): .... First Love
Deanna Durbin .... Brunswick 03007
**Jimmy Dorsey & his Orchestra, vocal Bob Eberley & Helen
O'Connell** .... Brunswick 03170
**Jimmy Dorsey & his Orchestra, vocal Dottie Reid & Tommy
Mercer** .... HMV CLP 1132
Bob Eberly & Helen O'Connell .... Warner Brothers WM 4033
Deanna Durbin appeared in *First Love*.

AMATEUR HOUR   August 1974
Ron Mael
Island Music Ltd. .... UK
Sparks .... Island WIP 6203

AMAZING GRACE   February 1971
Traditional
.... USA
Judy Collins (1971) .... Elektra 2101020
The Band of the Royal Scots Dragoon Guards (1972) . RCA 2191

AMAZON (River Of Dreams)   1921
Rex Halm / Jay Eltinge
B. Feldman & Co. Ltd .... USA
Walter Jefferies .... HMV B 1260
Richard Silver .... Columbia 3034

AMERICAN PATROL   1943
F.W. Meacham
Keith Prowse Music Publishing Co. Ltd .... USA
Film(s): .... Orchestra Wives / The Glenn Miller Story
Glenn Miller & his Orchestra .... RCA RCX 1096
Joe Loss & his Orchestra .... HMV BD 5789
The Universal International Studio Orch .. Brunswick LA 8647
Ray Anthony & his Orchestra .... Capitol T 1200
Glenn Miller appeared in *Orchestra Waves*.
The Universal Int. Studio Orchestra appeared in *The Glenn Miller Story*.
Originally published in 1891.

AMERICAN PIE   March 1972
Don McLean
United Artists Music Co. Ltd .... USA
Don McLean .... United Artists UP 35325

AMERICANOS   April 1989
Holly Johnson
Warner Chappell Music .... UK
Holly Johnson .... MCA MCA 1323

AMIGO   October 1980
Elroy Baily / Anthony Brightly

Wise Owl Music .... UK
Black Slate .... Ensign ENY 42

AMITYVILLE (The House on the Hill)   June 1986
Steve Loeb / Curtis Blow / Mervin Rhymes
EMI Music .... USA
Lovebug Starski .... Epic A 7182

AMONG MY SOUVENIRS   1927
Edgar Leslie / Horatio Nicholls
Lawrence Wright Music Co. Ltd. .... UK
Film(s): .... Paris, The Best Years of Our Lives
The Kit Kat Band .... Columbia 4563
Aileen Stanley .... Brunswick 01722
Bing Crosby .... Brunswick OE 9363
Frank Sinatra (1947) .... Fontana TFL 5082
Connie Francis (1959) .... MGM EP 731

AMOR   1944
Gabriel Ruiz / Ricardo Mendez / Sunny Skylar
Southern Music Publishing Co. Ltd. .... Mexico
Film(s): .... Broadway Rhythm / Swing in the Saddle
Bing Crosby .... Brunswick LAT 8331
The Modernaires .... Vogue LVA 9080
Michael Holliday .... Columbia 33SX 1262

AMOROUS GOLDFISH, THE   1896
Sidney Jones / Harry Greenbank
Ascherberg, Hopwood & Crew Music .... UK
Show(s): .... The Geisha
Anne Welch .... Decca K 548
Gwen Catley .... Pye CEC 32001

AMOUR TOUJOURS L'AMOUR, L'   1922
Rudolf Frimi / Catherine Cushing
Chappell & Co. Ltd .... USA
Richard Crooks .... HMV DA 1142
Arthur Tracey (The Street Singer) ...... Decca LF 1077
101 Strings, conducted by Rudolph Friml ..... Pye GGL 0057

AMOUREUSE   December 1973
Veronique Sanson / Gary Osborne
Warner Brothers Music Ltd. .... France
Kiki Dee .... Rocket PIG 4

'AMPSTEAD WAY, THE   October 1946
Johnny Burk / Jimmy Van Heusen
Edwin H. Morris .... USA
Beryl Davis .... Decca F 8676
Tessie O'Shea .... Columbia DB 2232
The Skyrockets Dance Orchestra .... HMV BD 5941

AMY, WONDERFUL AMY   1930
Horatio Nicholls / Joe Gilbert
Lawrence Wright Music Co. Ltd .... UK
Jack Hylton & his Orchestra .... HMV B 5836
Debroy Somers & his Band .... Columbia CB 83

AN EVERLASTING LOVE   September 1978
Barry Gibb
Chappell & Co. Ltd .... UK
Andy Gibb .... RSO 015

AN INNOCENT MAN   March 1984
Billy Joel
CBS Songs .... USA
Billy Joel .... CBS A 4142

AN OCCASIONAL MAN (See OCCASIONAL MAN, AN)

ANCHORS AWEIGH   1907
Charles Zimmerman
Francis, Day & Hunter .... USA
Film(s): .... Anchors Aweigh
The U.S. Navy Band .... HMV B 2778
The Royal Marines School of Music Band ..... HMV CLP 1411

AND HE'D SAY "OO-LA-LA WEE-WEE"   1919
George Jessel / Harry Ruby
B. Feldman & Co. Ltd .... USA
Billy Murray .... Columbia 2957
Clinton Ford .... Oriole PS 40021

**AND HER GOLDEN HAIR WAS HANGING DOWN HER
BACK (See Her Golden Hair Was Hanging Down Her Back)**

AND HER MOTHER CAME TOO   1921
Ivor Novello / Dion Titheradge
Ascherberg, Hopwood & Crew .... UK
Show(s): .... A To Z / Jack and Jill
Jack Buchanan   **HMV 7EG 8307**
Reginald Purdell .... **Decca F 3408**

AND HER TEARS FLOWED LIKE WINE   1945
Joe Greene / Stanley Kenton / Charles Lawrence
Robbins Music Corporation Ltd. .... USA
Film(s): .... Two Guys From Milwaukee
Stan Kenton & his Orchestra,
vocal Anita O'Day .... **Capitol LC 6676**
Ella Fitzgerald .... **Brunswick 03566**

AND I LOVE YOU SO   June 1973
Don McLean
United Artists Music Co. Ltd. .... USA
Perry Como .... **RCA 2346**

AND MIMI   April 1948
Nat Simon / Jimmy Kennedy
Campbell Connelly & Co. Ltd. .... USA
Dick Haymes .... **Brunswick 03820**
Jean Caval .... **HMV B 9620**
Al Jolson .... **Brunswick LAT 8294**

AND SHE WAS   February 1986
David Byrne / Chris Frantz / Tina Weymouth & Jerry Harrison
Warner Brothers Music .... UK
Talking Heads .... **EMI 5543**

AND SO TO SLEEP AGAIN   November 1951
Sunny Skylar / Joe Marsala
Yale Music Corporation Ltd .... USA
Larry Cross .... **Parlophone R 3459**
April Stevens .... **HMV B 10152**
Dick Haymes .... **Brunswick 04815**
Vera Lynn .... **Decca LF 1102**

AND THE ANGELS SING   1939
Johnny Mercer / Ziggy Elman
Francis, Day & Hunter Ltd. .... USA
Film(s): .... And the Angels Sing / The Benny Goodman Story
Benny Goodman & his Orchestra,
vocal Martha Tilton .... **RCA RCX 1019**
Ziggy Elman & his Orchestra .... **MGM 101**
Benny Goodman & his Orchestra,
vocal Martha Tilton .... **Brunswick LAT 8103**
Eydie Gormé .... **HMV CLP 1404**

AND THE BANDS PLAYED ON   April 1981
"Saxon"
Carlin Music .... UK
Saxon .... **Carrere CAR 180**

AND THE BEAT GOES ON   March 1980
Leon Sylvers / Stephen Shockley / William Shelby
Chappell & Co. Ltd .... UK
The Whispers .... **Solar SO 1**

**AND THE BIRDS WERE SINGING (Et Les Oiseaux Chan-
taient)**   October 1980
Alain Morisod
Eaton Music Ltd. .... France
The Sweet People .... **Polydor POSP 179**

AND THE GREAT BIG SAW CAME NEARER   1936
R.P. Weston / E.H. Weston / Bert Lee
Francis Day & Hunter Ltd .... UK
Leslie Sarony .... **Regal Zonophone MR 2036**
Benny Lee .... **Columbia 33SX 1124**

AND THE HEAVENS CRIED   April 1961
Gwyan Elias / Irving Reid
Tin Pan Alley Music Co. Ltd .... USA
Anthony Newley .... **Decca F 11331**
Ronnie Savoy .... **MGM 1122**

AND THEN YOU KISSED ME   1944
Jule Styne / Sammy Cahn
Robbins Music Corporation Ltd .... USA
Film(s): .... Step Lively
Stanley Black & his Orchestra,
vocal Johnny Green .... **Decca F 8494**

AND THIS IS MY BELOVED   April 1955
Robert Wright / George Forrest
Frank Music Co. Ltd. .... USA
Show(s): .... Kismet
Film(s): .... Kismet
Alfred Drake, Dorretta Morrow, Richard Kiley
& Henry Calvin .... **Philips BBL 7023**
Howard Keel, Ann Blyth & Vic Damone .... **MGM C 758**
Adapted from the Nocturne of "String Quartet in D Major No.2" by
Alexander Borodin (1833 - 1887).
Alfred Drake & Doretta Morrow appeared in both the American and
British productions of *Kismet*.
Richard Kiley & Henry Calvin appeared in the American production of
Kismet.
Howard Keel, Ann Blyth & Vic Damone appeared in the film *Kismet*.

ANFIELD RAP, THE   May 1988
Craig Johnson
Virgin Music .... UK
The Liverpool Football Club .... **Virgin LFC 1**

ANGEL   December 1972
Jimi Hendrix
Schroeder Music Ltd. .... USA
Rod Stewart .... **Mercury 6052198**
Jimi Hendrix .... **Track 2408101**

ANGEL   October 1985
Madonna Ciccone / Steve Bray
Warner Brothers Music .... USA
Madonna .... **Sire W 8881**

ANGEL CHILD   1922
Benny Davis / George Price / Abner Silver
B. Feldman & Co. Ltd .... USA
The Benson Orchestra of Chicago .... **HMV B 1363**
Glenn Miller Orchestra .... **HMV CLPC 3**
Louis Armstrong & his Orchestra .... **Brunswick LAT 8210**

ANGEL EYES   August 1979
Benny Andersson / Bjorn Ulvaeus
Bocu Music Ltd. .... Sweden
Abba .... **Epic EPC 7499**

ANGEL EYES   September 1979
Bryan Ferry / Andrew McKay
E.G. Music .... UK
Roxy Music .... **Polydor POSP 67**

ANGEL EYES (Home and Away)   January 1988
Tom Cunningham / Neil Mitchell / Marti Pellow & Graham Clark
Chrysalis Music .... UK
Wet Wet Wet .... **Precious JEWEL 6**

ANGEL FACE   April 1974
John Rossall / Gerry Shephard
Rock Artistes Music .... UK
The Glitter Band .... **Bell 1348**

ANGEL FINGERS   September 1973
Roy Wood
Carlin Music Corporation .... UK
Wizzard .... **Harvest HAR 5076**

ANGEL OF HARLEM   January 1989
"U2"
Blue Mountain Music .... UK
U2 .... **Island IS 402**

ANGEL OF THE GREAT WHITE WAY   1937
Elton Box / Desmond Cox / Don Pelosi / Paddy Roberts
Peter Maurice Music Co. Ltd. .... UK
Sam Costa .... **Parlophone F 714**
Joe Petersen .... **Rex 8980**

ANGELA JONES   July 1960
John D. Loudermilk
Southern Music Publishing Co. Ltd .... USA
Michael Cox .... **Triumph RGM 1011**
Johnny Ferguson .... **MGM 1059**

ANGELA MIA   1928
Erno Rapee / Lew Pollack
Campbell Connelly & Co. Ltd. .... USA
Film(s): .... Street Angel
Donald Novis .... **Decca F 6722**

Paul Whiteman & his Orchestra . . . . HMV B 5510
Vic Damone . . . . Philips BBL 7234

ANGELA MIA   March 1960
Paul Conrad
Robbins Music Corporation Ltd . . . . USA
David Whitfield . . . . Decca F 11221

ANGELO   September 1977
Tony Hiller / Lee Sheridan / Martin Lee
A.T.V. Music Ltd. . . . . UK
Brotherhood of Man . . . . Pye 7N 45699
Ivor Novello Nomination.

ANGIE   September 1973
Keith Richard / Mick Jagger
Essex Music Ltd. . . . . UK
The Rolling Stones . . . . Rolling Stones RS19105
Ivor Novello Nomination.

ANGIE BABY   March 1975
Alan O'Day
Warner Brothers Music Ltd . . . . USA
Helen Reddy . . . . Capitol CL 15799

ANGRY   1926
Dudley Mecum / Henry & Merritt Brunies / Jules Cassard
Keith Prowse Music Publishing Co. Ltd. . . . . USA
Ted Lewis & his Band . . . . Columbia 3784
Bob Scobey's Frisco Band . . . . Vogue LVA 12145
Perry Como . . . . RCA RD 27035

ANIMAL   August 1987
Steven Clark / Phillip Collen / Robert Lange / Joseph Elliot & Richard Savage
Zomba Music . . . . UK
Def Leppard . . . . Bludgeon LEP 1

ANIMAL CRACKERS IN MY SOUP   1936
Ted Koehler / Irving Caeser / Ray Henderson
Keith Prowse Music Publishing Co. Ltd . . . . USA
Film(s): . . . . Curly Top
Shirley Temple . . . . Top Rank JKR 8003
Mae Questal . . . . Decca F 6117
Shirley Temple appeared in *Curly Top.*

ANNA   April 1953
Vatro Roman / F. Giordano / William Engvick
Southern Music Publishing Co. Ltd . . . . Italy
Film(s): . . . . Anna
Silvana Mangano . . . . MGM 624
Jane Morgan . . . . London HAR 2183
Silvana Mangano appeared in *Anna.*

ANNIE DOESN'T LIVE HERE ANYMORE   1934
Joe Young / Johnny Burke / Harold Spina
Francis, Day & Hunter Ltd. . . . . USA
Ramona . . . . HMV B 8115
Leslie Holmes . . . . Rex 8094
Marlene Dietrich . . . . Philips BBL 7322
Eartha Kitt . . . . HMV B 10584

ANNIE, I'M NOT YOUR DADDY   October 1982
August Darnell
Island Music . . . . USA
Kid Creole & The Coconuts . . . . Island WIP 6801

ANNIE'S SONG   October 1974
John Denver
A.T.V. Music Ltd. . . . . USA
John Denver . . . . RCA APBO 0295
Vince Hill . . . . CBS S 80742
James Galway (Flute) (1978) . . . . RCA RB 5085

ANNIVERSARY SONG, THE   1947
Al Jolson / Saul Chaplin
Campbell Connelly & Co. Ltd. . . . . USA
Film(s): . . . . The Jolson Story
Al Jolson . . . . Brunswick LA 8570
Bing Crosby . . . . Brunswick LA 8585
The McGuire Sisters . . . . Coral LVA 9140
Adapted from "Danube Waves" by J. Ivanovici.

ANNIVERSARY WALTZ, THE   1942
Al Dubin / Dave Franklin

Edwin H. Morris & Co. Ltd . . . . USA
Bing Crosby . . . . Brunswick 03289
Jack Payne & his Orchestra . . . . HMV 7EG 8441
Joe Loss & his Orchestra . . . . HMV 7EG 8512
Anita Harris (1968) . . . . CBS 3211

ANOTHER BRICK IN THE WALL   January 1980
Roger Waters
Pink Floyd Music . . . . UK
Film(s): . . . . The Wall
Pink Floyd . . . . Harvest HAR 5194
Ivor Novello Nomination 1979.
Ivor Novello Award 1980.
Ivor Novello Nomination 1982.

ANOTHER DAY   April 1971
Paul McCartney
Northern Songs Ltd . . . . UK
Paul McCartney . . . . Apple R 5889

ANOTHER DAY IN PARADISE   November 1989
Phil Collins
Hit & Run Music . . . . UK
Phil Collins . . . . Virgin VS 1234
Ivor Novello Nomination.

**ANOTHER LITTLE DRINK WOULDN'T DO US
ANY HARM**   1916
Nat. D. Ayer / Clifford Grey
B. Feldman & Co. Ltd. . . . . USA
Show(s): . . . . The Bing Boys are Here
Violet Loraine, George Robey & Alfred Lester . Columbia L 1034
Nat Ayer . . . . HMV B 642
The Regulars . . . . Columbia DB 3207
Violet Loraine, George Robey & Alfred Lester appeared in *The Bing Boys Are Here.*

ANOTHER NIGHT LIKE THIS   1947
Ernesto Lecuona / Harry Ruby
Campbell Connelly & Co. Ltd. . . . . Cuba
Film(s): . . . . Carnival in Costa Rica
Dick Haymes . . . . Brunswick 03777
Roberto Inglez & his Orchestra . . . . Parlophone F 2224
Dick Haymes appeared in *Carnival in Costa Rica.*

ANOTHER ONE BITES THE DUST   October 1980
John Deacon
EMI Music Ltd . . . . UK
Queen . . . . EMI 5102
Ivor Novello Nomination.

ANOTHER SATURDAY NIGHT   June 1963
Sam Cooke
Kags Music Ltd . . . . USA
Sam Cooke . . . . RCA 1341
Cat Stevens (1974) . . . . Island WIP 6206

ANOTHER STEP CLOSER TO YOU   May 1987
Kim Wilde / Steve Byrd
Rickim Music . . . . UK
Kim Wilde & Junior . . . . MCA KIM 5

ANOTHER SUITCASE IN ANOTHER HALL   April 1977
Tim Rice / Andrew Lloyd Webber
Leeds Music Ltd . . . . UK
Show(s): . . . . Evita
Barbara Dickson . . . . MCA 266
Elaine Paige . . . . WEA X 9670
Elaine Paige appeared in the British and American productions of *Evita.*

ANOTHER TIME ANOTHER PLACE   October 1971
Mike Leander / Edward Seago
Leeds Music Ltd . . . . UK
Engelbert Humperdinck . . . . Decca F 13212

ANSWER ME   December 1953
Carl Sigman / Gerhard Winkler / Fred Rouch
Bourne Music Ltd. . . . . Germany
David Whitfield . . . . Decca LF 1165
Frankie Laine . . . . Philips BBL 7263
Barbara Dickson (1976) . . . . RSO 2090174

ANT RAP   December 1981
Adam Ant

EMI Music .... UK
Adam & The Ants .... **CBS A 1738**

ANTMUSIC January 1981
Adam Ant / Marco Pirroni
EMI Music .... UK
Adam & The Ants .... **CBS 9352**

ANY OLD IRON 1911
Charles Collins / Fred Terry / E.A. Sheppard
Herman Darewski Music Publishing Co. Ltd .... UK
Harry Champion .... **Zonophone 729**
Harry Champion .... **Regal Zonophone 3347**
Billy Howard .... **Decca LK 4026**
Stanley Holloway .... **Pye NPL 18056**
Peter Sellers (1957) .... **Parlophone R 4337**

ANY TIME February 1952
Herbert Lawson
Victoria Music Co. Ltd .... USA
Eddie Fisher .... **HMV B 10190**
Dorothy Squires .... **Columbia DB 3042**
Dick Haymes .... **Brunswick 03996**
Connie Francis .... **MGM C 812**
First Published 1921.

ANY TIME'S KISSING TIME 1916
Frederick Norton / Oscar Asche
Keith Prowse Music Publishing Co. Ltd. .... UK
Show(s): .... Chu Chin Chow
Film(s): .... Chu Chin Chow
Violet Essex & Courtice Pounds .... **HMV D 417**
Aileen D'Orme .... **Columbia L 1114**
Julie Bryant & Inia Te Wiata .... **HMV CLP 1269**
Violet Essex, Courtice Pounds and Aileen D'Orme appeared in the
British production of *Chu Chin Chow.*

ANY WAY THE WIND BLOWS 1924
Henry Creamer / James Hanley
Keith Prowse Music Publishing Co. Ltd. .... USA
Fred Waring & his Pennsylvanians .... **HMV B 1904**

ANYONE CAN BE A MILLIONAIRE July 1955
Ed Franks
Lawrence Wright Music Co. Ltd. .... UK
Film(s): .... Fun at St. Fanny's
Max Bygraves .... **HMV 7EG 8123**

ANYONE CAN FALL IN LOVE August 1986
Simon May / Leslie Osborne / Don Black
Lawrence Wright Music .... UK
Anita Dobson .... **BBC RESL 191**
The vocal version of the theme to the television series *Eastenders.*

ANYONE WHO HAD A HEART March 1964
Hal David / Burt Bacharach
Hill & Range Songs (London) Ltd .... USA
Cilla Black .... **Parlophone R 5101**
Dionne Warwick .... **Pye NPL 28037**
Dusty Springfield .... **Philips BL 7594**

ANYTHING FOR YOU September 1988
Gloria Estefan
SBK Songs .... USA
Gloria Estefan & The Miami Sound Machine ...... **Epic 651673**

ANYTHING GOES 1935
Cole Porter
Chappell & Co. Ltd .... USA
Show(s): .... Anything Goes
Film(s): .... Anything Goes
Jeanne Aubert & The Four Admirals .... **Columbia DX 697**
Ethel Merman .... **Caliban 6043**
Cole Porter .... **HMV B 8332**
Frank Sinatra .... **Capitol LCT 6106**
Mitzi Gaynor .... **Brunswick LAT 8118**
Harper's Bizarre (1967) .... **Warner Brothers WB 7063**
Ethel Merman appeared in the American production and the 1936 film
of *Anything Goes.*
Jeanne Aubert & The Four Admirals appeared in the British production
of *Anything Goes.*
Mitzi Gaynor appeared in the 1956 film of *Anything Goes.*

ANYTHING I DREAM IS POSSIBLE December 1948
Billy Reid

Billy Reid Music Ltd. .... UK
Dorothy Squires .... **Columbia DB 2439**
Pearl Carr .... **Decca F 9043**

ANYTHING YOU CAN DO 1947
Irving Berlin
Irving Berlin Ltd. .... USA
Show(s): .... Annie Get Your Gun
Film(s): .... Annie Get Your Gun
Ethel Merman & Ray Middleton .... **Brunswick LAT 8002**
Dolores Gray & Bill Johnson .... **Columbia SEG 7711**
Betty Hutton & Howard Keel .... **MGM CD 1**
Ethel Merman & Ray Middleton appeared in the American production
of *Annie Get Your Gun.*
Dolores Gray & Bill Johnson appeared in the British production of
Annie Get Your Gun.
Betty Hutton & Howard Keel appeared in the film of *Annie Get Your Gun.*

ANYTIME, ANYDAY, ANYWHERE 1921
Louis Weslyn / Max Kortlander
Francis, Day & Hunter Ltd .... USA
Paul Whiteman & his Orchestra .... **HMV B 1178**
Glenn Miller & his Orchestra .... **Brunswick OE 9169**

ANYWAY THAT YOU WANT ME January 1967
Chip Taylor
Dick James Music Ltd. .... UK
The Troggs .... **Page One POF 010**

ANYWAY, ANYHOW, ANYWHERE July 1965
Peter Townshend / Roger Daltrey
Essex Music Ltd .... UK
The Who .... **Brunswick 05935**

ANYWHERE I WONDER December 1952
Frank Loesser
Edwin H. Morris & Co. Ltd .... USA
Show(s): .... Hans Andersen
Film(s): .... Hans Christian Andersen
Danny Kaye .... **Brunswick LA 8572**
Fred Waring & his Pennsylvanians .... **Capitol T 936**
Julius La Rosa .... **London HAA 2031**
Tommy Steele .... **Pye NSPL 18451**
Danny Kaye appeared in *Hans Christian Andersen.*
Tommy Steele appeared in *Hans Andersen.*

APACHE September 1960
Jerry Lordan
Francis, Day & Hunter Ltd .... UK
The Shadows .... **Columbia DB 4484**
Bert Weedon (guitar) .... **Top Rank JAR 415**
Ivor Novello Award.

APEMAN January 1971
Ray Davies
Carlin Music Corporation .... UK
The Kinks .... **Pye 7N 45016**

APOLLO 9 October 1984
Adam Ant / Marco Pirroni
EMI Music .... UK
Adam Ant .... **CBS A 4719**

APPLE BLOSSOM WEDDING, AN 1947
Nat Simon / Jimmy Kennedy
Campbell Connelly & Co. Ltd. .... USA
Russ Morgan & his Orchestra,
vocal Kenny Baker .... **Brunswick 03816**
Cyril Stapleton & his Orchestra .... **Decca F 8809**

APPLE FOR THE TEACHER, AN 1939
Johnny Burke / Jimmy Monaco
Campbell Connelly & Co. Ltd. .... USA
Film(s): .... The Star Maker
Bing Crosby & Connee Boswell .... **Brunswick Bing 5**
Bing Crosby appeared in *The Star Maker.*

APPLEJACK October 1963
Les Vandyke
Essex Music Ltd .... UK
Jet Harris & Tony Meehan .... **Decca F 11710**

APRIL IN PARIS 1934
E.Y. Harburg / Vernon Duke
Chappell & Co. Ltd. .... USA

Show(s): . . . . Walk a Little Faster
Film(s): . . . . April in Paris / Both Ends of the Candle / Paris Holiday
The BBC Dance Orchestra . . . . **Columbia CB 705**
Doris Day . . . . **Columbia SEG 7515**
Gogi Grant . . . . **RCA RD 27054**
Bob Hope . . . . **London HAT 2143**
Shirley Bassey . . . . **Columbia SEG 8027**
Ella Fitzgerald with the Count Basie Orch . . **Columbia LX 1621**
Doris Day appeared in *April in Paris*.
Bob Hope appeared in *Paris Holiday*.

APRIL IN PORTUGAL (Coimbra)   June 1953
Paul Ferrao / Jose Galhardo / Jimmy Kennedy
Chappell & Co. Ltd . . . . Portugal
Roberto Inglez & his Orchestra . . . . **Parlophone R 3376**
Amalia Rodrigues . . . . **Columbia 33CS 19**
Jane Morgan . . . . **Parlophone R 3699**
The Melachrino Strings . . . . **RCA RD 27124**
Eve Boswell . . . . **Parlophone PMD 1039**

APRIL LOVE   December 1957
Sammy Fain / Paul Francis Webster
Robbins Music Corporation . . . . USA
Film(s): . . . . April Love
Pat Boone . . . . **London HAD 2078**
Pat Boone appeared in *April Love*.
Nominated for an Academy Award 1957.

APRIL PLAYED THE FIDDLE   1940
Jimmy Monaco / Johnny Burke
Campbell Connelly & Co. Ltd . . . . USA
Film(s): . . . . If I Had My Way
Bing Crosby . . . . **Brunswick Bing 5**
Glenn Miller & his Orchestra, vocal Ray Eberle . **HMV 7EG 8043**
Bing Crosby appeared in *If I Had My Way*.

APRIL SHOWERS   1922
Louis Silvers / Buddy De Sylva
Chappell & Co. Ltd . . . . USA
Show(s): . . . . Bombo
Film(s):The Jolson Story / April Showers / Jolson Sings Again / The
Eddie Duchin Story
Paul Whiteman & his Orchestra . . . . **HMV B 1333**
Al Jolson (1947) . . . . **Brunswick OE 9336**
Eddy Duchin & his Orchestra . . . . **Philips BBL 7081**
Eydie Gormé . . . . **HMV CLP 1290**
Al Jolson appeared in *Bombo*.

AQUARIUS   November 1968
Gerome Ragni / James Rado / Galt MacDermot
United Artists Music Co. Ltd. . . . . USA
Show(s): . . . . Hair
Film(s): . . . . Hair
Ronald Dyson with Orchestra & Chorus . . . . . **RCA RD 7959**
Vince Edwards with Orchestra & Chorus . . . . . **Polydor 583043**
Ren Woods & Chorus . . . . **RCA BL 03274**
Ronald Dyson appeared in the American production of *Hair*.
Vince Edwards appeared in the British production of *Hair*.
Ren Woods appeared in the film *Hair*.

AQUARIUS - LET THE SUN SHINE IN (Medley)   May 1969
Gerome Ragni / James Rado / Galt MacDermot
United Artists Music Co. Ltd. . . . . USA
Show(s): . . . . Hair
Film(s): . . . . Hair
The Fifth Dimension . . . . **Liberty LBF 15198**

ARABY   1915
Irving Berlin
B. Feldman & Co. Ltd. . . . . USA
The Versatile Four . . . . **HMV C 645**

ARCADY IS EVER YOUNG   1909
Lionel Monckton / Arthur Wimperis / Howard Talbot
Chappell & Co. Ltd. . . . . UK
Show(s): . . . . The Arcadians
Florence Smithson . . . . **Columbia 542**
Gwen Catley . . . . **Pye CEC 32001**
June Bronhill . . . . **Columbia TWO 233**
Florence Smithson appeared in *The Arcadians*.

ARCHIBALD, CERTAINLY NOT   1909
Alfred Glover / John L. St. John
Francis, Day & Hunter . . . . UK

George Robey . . . . **Columbia 2985**

ARE WE DOWNHEARTED? NO!   1914
Lawrence Wright / Worton David
Lawrence Wright Music Co. Ltd. . . . . UK
Harrison Latimer . . . . **Regal G 6817**
Leon Cortez & his Costa Pals . . . . . **Regal Zonophone MR 2548**

ARE WE TO PART LIKE THIS   1912
Harry Castling / Charles Collins
B. Feldman & Co. Ltd . . . . UK
Kate Carney . . . . **Eclipse 200**
Kate Carney . . . . **Ace of Clubs ACL 1170**
Stella Moray . . . . **Decca LK 4628**

ARE YOU FROM DIXIE   1915
Jack Yellen / Will Cobb
B. Feldman & Co. Ltd. . . . . USA
The Two Rascals & Jacobson . . . . **Regal G 7400**
The Happy Harts . . . . **London HAR 2060**
Grandpa Jones . . . . **Parlophone GEP 8766**

ARE YOU HAVING ANY FUN   1939
Jack Yellen / Sammy Fain
Chappell & Co. Ltd. . . . . USA
Show(s):George White's Scandals of 1939 / The Little Dog Laughed
Jack Hylton & his Orchestra, vocal Dolly Elsie . . **HMV BD 5554**
Flanagan & Allen . . . . **Ace of Clubs ACL 1092**
Tony Bennett . . . . **Columbia 33SX 1174**
Flanagan & Allen appeared in *The Little Dog Laughed*.

ARE YOU LONESOME TONIGHT   1928
Roy Turk / Lou Handman
Francis, Day & Hunter Ltd. . . . . USA
Al Jolson . . . . **Brunswick LA 8705**
Elvis Presley (1961) . . . . **RCA 1216**
Helen Shapiro . . . . **Columbia 33SX 1397**

ARE YOU READY TO ROCK   January 1975
Roy Wood
Carlin Music Corporation . . . . UK
Wizzard . . . . **Warner Brothers K 16497**

ARE YOU SINCERE   April 1958
Wayne Walker
Southern Music Publishing Co. Ltd . . . . USA
Marty Wilde . . . . **Philips BBL 7342**
Andy Williams . . . . **London HLA 8587**

ARE YOU SURE   March 1961
Bob Allison / John Allison
Alice Music Ltd. . . . . UK
The Allisons . . . . **Fontana H 294**
United Kingdom entry for the 1961 Eurovision Song Contest (Placed
Second).
Ivor Novello Nomination.

ARE 'FRIENDS' ELECTRIC   July 1979
Gary Numan
Numan Music Ltd. . . . . UK
Tubeway Army . . . . **Beggars Banquet BEG 18**

AREN'T YOU GLAD YOU'RE YOU   1946
Johnny Burke / Jimmy Van Heusen
Edwin H. Morris & Co. Ltd. . . . . USA
Film(s): . . . . The Bells of St. Mary's
Bing Crosby . . . . **Brunswick Bing 9**
Joanie Sommers . . . . **Warner Brothers WM 4045**
June Christy . . . . **Capitol T 1398**
Bing Crosby appeared in *The Bells of St. Mary's*.
Nominated for an Academy Award 1945.

ARGENTINA   1935
Stanley Damerell / Tolchard Evans
Peter Maurice Music Co. Ltd . . . . UK
Troise & his Mandoliers . . . . **Rex 8354**

ARIA   October 1976
Sergio Bardotti / Dario Baldan Bembo
Fresh Air Music . . . . Italy
Acker Bilk (Clarinet) . . . . **Pye 7N 45607**
Dario Baldan . . . . **Fresh Air 6121125**

ARIZONA   1916
Melville Gideon / James Heard

Herman Darewski Music Publishing Co. Ltd. . . . . UK
Show(s): . . . . Flying Colours
Melville Gideon . . . . **Columbia D 1356**
The Unity Quartette . . . . **Columbia D 2750**
Melville Gideon appeared in *Flying Colours*.

ARMED AND EXTREMELY DANGEROUS   June 1973
Norman Harris / Alan Felder
Carlin Music Corporation . . . . USA
First Choice . . . . **Bell 1297**

ARMEN'S THEME   January 1957
Ross Bagdasarian
Bourne Music Ltd. . . . . USA
David Seville & his Orchestra . . . . **London HAU 2153**
Ted Heath & his Music . . . . **Decca LK 4210**

ARMS OF MARY, THE   May 1976
Iain Sutherland
Island Music Ltd . . . . UK
The Sutherland Brothers & Quiver . . . . **CBS 4001**

ARMY AIR CORPS SONG, THE   1943
Robert Crawford
Keith Prowse Music Publishing Co. Ltd . . . . USA
Show(s): . . . . Winged Victory
Film(s): . . .Follow The Band / Ice Capades Revue / Winged Victory
Fred Waring & his Pennsylvanians . . . . **Brunswick 03374**
The U.S. 3rd Air Force Band . . . . **HMV 7EG 8590**
Tony Bennett . . . . **Philips BBL 7219**

ARMY GAME, THE   June 1958
Sid Colin / Patrick Napper
Phoenix Music . . . . UK
Michael Medwin, Alfie Bass, Bernard Bresslaw
& Leslie Fyson . . . . **HMV POP 490**
Theme of the television series *The Army Game*.
Ivor Novello Nomination.

ARMY OF TODAY'S ALRIGHT, THE   1914
Fred W. Leigh / Kenneth Lyle
Francis, Day & Hunter Ltd. . . . . UK
Film(s): . . . . After the Ball
Vesta Tilley . . . . **Regal G 7079**
Ray Wallace . . . . **Parlophone R 1147**

ARMY, THE NAVY AND THE AIR FORCE, THE   1939
Herman Darewski
Keith Prowse Music Publishing Co. Ltd. . . . . UK
Herman Darewski & his Band,
vocal Cyril Norman . . . . **Parlophone F 1500**

AROUND THE CORNER AND UNDER THE TREE   1930
Gus Kahn / Art Kassell
Francis, Day & Hunter Ltd . . . . USA
Frank Crumit . . . . **HMV B 3528**
Gracie Fields . . . . **HMV B 3494**

AROUND THE WORLD   May 1957
Victor Young / Harold Adamson
Chappell & Co. Ltd. . . . . USA
Film(s): . . . . Around the World in Eighty Days
Victor Young & his Orchestra . . . . **Brunswick LAT 8185**
Bing Crosby . . . . **Brunswick 05674**
Gracie Fields . . . . **Columbia DB 3953**
Ronnie Hilton . . . . **HMV POP 338**

ARRIVEDERCI DARLING (Arrivederci Roma)   January 1956
Renato Rascel / S. Giovannini / P. Garinei, Carl Sigman & Jack Fishman
Berry Music Ltd. . . . . Italy
Film(s): . . . . The Seven Hills of Rome
Lys Assia . . . . **Decca DFE 6383**
Anne Shelton . . . . **HMV POP 146**
Nat 'King' Cole . . . . **Capitol EAP 2-1031**
Mario Lanza . . . . **RCA RA 13001**
Mario Lanza appeared in *The Seven Hills of Rome*.

ART FOR ART'S SAKE   January 1976
Eric Stewart / Graham Gouldman
St Annes Music Ltd . . . . UK
10 CC . . . . **Mercury 6008017**

ARTHUR MURRAY TAUGHT ME DANCING IN A HURRY   1942
Victor Schertzinger / Johnny Mercer

Victoria Music Co. Ltd . . . . USA
Film(s): . . . . The Fleet's In
Jimmy Dorsey & his Orchestra . . . . **Brunswick 03369**
Helen O'Connell . . . . **Warner Brothers WM 4033**
Jimmy Dorsey & Helen O'Connell appeared in *The Fleet's In*.

ARTHUR'S THEME   February 1982
Christopher Cross / Peter Allen / Burt Bacharach & Carol Bayer-Sager
Warner Brothers Music . . . . USA
Film(s): . . . . Arthur
Christopher Cross . . . . **Warner Brothers K 17847**
Academy Award winning song for 1981

AS I LOVE YOU   March 1959
Jay Livingston / Ray Evans
Macmelodies Ltd . . . . USA
Film(s): . . . . The Big Beat
Shirley Bassey . . . . **Philips BBL 7325**
Carmen McRae . . . . **Brunswick OE 9463**

AS IF I DIDN'T HAVE ENOUGH ON MY MIND   1946
Charles Henderson / Lionel Newman / Harry James
Edwin H. Morris & Co. Ltd. . . . . USA
Film(s): . . . . Do You Love Me
Dick Haymes . . . . **Brunswick 03726**
Paul Fenoulhet & the Skyrockets Dance Orchestra,
vocal Cyril Shane . . . . **HMV BD 5935**
Dick Haymes appeared in *Do You Love Me*.

AS LONG AS HE NEEDS ME   September 1960
Lionel Bart
Lakeview Music Publishing Co . . . . UK
Show(s): . . . . Oliver
Film(s): . . . . Oliver
Georgia Brown (UK) . . . . **Decca LK 4359**
Georgia Brown (USA) . . . . **RCA LOCD 2004**
Shirley Bassey . . . . **Columbia DB 4490**
Shani Wallis . . . . **RCA RB 6777**
Georgia Brown appeared in both the American and British productions
of *Oliver*.
Shani Wallis appeared in the film *Oliver*.
Ivor Novello Award.

AS LONG AS I LIVE   1934
Ted Koehler / Harold Arlen
Peter Maurice Music Co. Ltd . . . . USA
Lew Stone & his Band, vocal Al Bowlly . . . . **Decca F 5132**
Barbara Caroll . . . . **HMV 7EG 8138**
Ella Fitzgerald . . . . **HMV CLP 1267**

AS LONG AS I'M DREAMING   1947
Johnny Burke / Jimmy Van Heusen
Edwin H. Morris & Co. Ltd. . . . . USA
Film(s): . . . . Welcome Stranger
Bing Crosby . . . . **Brunswick Bing 11**
Bing Crosby appeared in *Welcome Stranger*.

AS TEARS GO BY   September 1964
Mick Jagger / Keith Richards / Andrew Loog Oldham
Forward Music Ltd . . . . UK
Marianne Faithfull . . . . **Decca F 11923**

AS TIME GOES BY   1932
Herman Hupfeld
Chappell & Co. Ltd. . . . . USA
Show(s): . . . . Everybody's Welcome
Film(s): . . . . Casablanca
Binnie Hale . . . . **Columbia DB 755**
Ambrose & his Orchestra, vocal Anne Shelton . . **Decca F 8307**
Perry Como . . . . **RCA RD 27070**
Petula Clark . . . . **Nixa NPL 18007**
Billy Eckstine . . . . **Columbia 33SX 1249**
Dooley Wilson . . . . **United Artists USD 311**
Dooley Wilson appeared in *Casabalanca*.

AS USUAL   February 1964
Alex Zanetis
Jewel Music Publishing Co. Ltd . . . . USA
Brenda Lee . . . . **Brunswick 05899**

AS WE ARE TODAY   January 1951
Ernesto Lecuona / Charles Tobias
B. Feldman & Co. Ltd . . . . USA

Film(s): . . . . The Daughter of Rosie O'Grady
Vic Shoen & his Orchestra, vocal Don Burke Brunswick 04664
Hugo Winterhalter & his Orchestra & Chorus . . . HMV B 10021

AS YOU DESIRE ME   1932
Allie Wrubel
Francis, Day & Hunter Ltd. . . . . USA
Russ Columbo & his Orchestra . . . . HMV B 6265
Peggy Lee . . . . **Capitol T 1401**

AS YOU LIKE IT   June 1962
Les Vandyke
Downbeat Publishing Co. Ltd. . . . . UK
Adam Faith . . . . **Parlophone R 4896**
Jess Conrad . . . . **Decca F 11620**

ASHBY DE LA ZOUCH (CASTLE ABBEY)   1946
Al Hoffman / Jerry Livingston / Milton Drake
Clover Music Co. Ltd. . . . . USA
Lou Preager & his Orchestra,
vocal Paul Rich . . . . **Columbia FB 3199**
Lew Stone & his Band, vocal Helen Mack
& Ronnie O'Dell . . . . **Decca F 8614**

ASHES OF ROSES   September 1950
Harry Tobias / Lew Porter / Sidney Mitchell
Campbell Connelly & Co. Ltd . . . . USA
The Deep River Boys . . . . **HMV 7EG 8133**
Steve Conway . . . . **Columbia SEG 7649**

ASHES TO ASHES   September 1980
David Bowie
Fleur Music . . . . UK
David Bowie . . . . **RCA BOW 6**

ASK A POLICEMAN   1889
A.E. Durandeau / E.W. Rogers
Francis, Day & Hunter Ltd. . . . . UK
The Columbia Light Opera Company . . . . **Columbia DX 640**
The Variety Singers . . . . **Columbia SEG 7712**

ASK ANYONE WHO KNOWS   June 1948
Eddie Seiler / Sol Marcus / Al Kaufman
B. Feldman & Co. Ltd. . . . . USA
Sammy Kaye & his Orchestra,
vocal Don Cornell . . . . **HMV BD 6009**
Kate Smith . . . . **MGM 128**
Leslie Hutchinson (Hutch) . . . . **HMV B 9650**

ASK ME NO QUESTIONS   May 1950
David Saxon / Robert Wells
B. Feldman & Co. Ltd . . . . USA
Bing Crosby & The Andrews Sisters . . . . **Brunswick 04489**
Dinah Shore & Dusty Walker . . . . **Columbia DB 2709**

ASLEEP IN THE DEEP   1897
Henry W. Petrie / Arthur Lamb
Herman Darewski Music Publishing Co. Ltd. . . . . USA
Norman Allin . . . . **Columbia DX 270**
Peter Dawson . . . . **HMV B 3542**
Warren Biggs . . . . **London HAF 2051**

AT A GEORGIA CAMP MEETING   1897
Kerry Mills
Herman Darewski Music . . . . USA
Film(s): . . . . Birth of the Blues
Sousa's Band . . . . **HMV B 246**
Lu Watters Yerba Buena Jazz Band . . . . **Melodisc 1123**
The Firehouse Five Plus Two . . . . **Vogue LDG 169**
Chris Barber Jazz Band . . . . **Columbia SX 1245**

AT DAWNING   1906
Nelle Richmond Eberhart / Charles Wakefield Cadman
Boosey & Hawkes Music Publishers Ltd. . . . . USA
John McCormack . . . . **HMV DA 303**
Paul Robeson . . . . **HMV 7EG 8631**
The Roger Wagner Chorale . . . . **Capitol P 8491**

AT LAST   1942
Mack Gordon / Harry Warren
Sun Music Publishing Co. Ltd . . . . USA
Film(s):Sun Valley Serenade / Orchestra Wives / The Glenn Miller
Story
Glenn Miller & his Orchestra . . . . **RCA RCX 1062**
The Four Freshmen . . . . **Capitol T 1378**

Glenn Miller appeared in *Sun Valley Serenade* and *Orchestra Wives*.

AT LAST, AT LAST   February 1952
Charles Trenet / Florence Miles
Pickwick Music Ltd . . . . France
Charles Trenet . . . . **Columbia 33CS 19**
Lee Lawrence . . . . **Decca F 9878**
Tony Martin . . . . **HMV B 10219**

AT LONG LAST LOVE   1941
Cole Porter
Chappell & Co. Ltd . . . . USA
Show(s): . . . . You Never Know
Film(s): . . . . At Long Last Love
Lena Horne . . . . **RCA RD 27098**
Vic Damone . . . . **Capitol T 1944**
Nancy Wilson . . . . **Capitol T 2351**
Lionel Newman Orchestra . . . . **RCA ABL 2-0976**

AT PEACE WITH THE WORLD   1926
Irving Berlin
Francis, Day & Hunter Ltd. . . . . USA
The Roger Wolfe Kahn Orchestra . . . . **HMV B 5088**

AT SANTA BARBARA   1912
Frederick E. Weatherly / Kennedy Russell
Chappell & Co. Ltd . . . . UK
Dennis Noble . . . . **Columbia DB 158**
Peter Dawson . . . . **HMV B 2661**

AT SUNDOWN   1927
Walter Donaldson
Francis, Day & Hunter Ltd . . . . USA
Film(s):Glorifying the American Girl / The Fabulous Dorseys / Love
Me or Leave Me / The Rat Race
Melville Gideon . . . . **HMV B 2533**
Muggsy Spanier's Ragtime Band . . . . **RCA RD 27132**
Doris Day . . . . **Philips BBL 7047**
Eddie Fisher . . . . **Camden CDN 123**
Gisele MacKenzie . . . . **RCA RD 27033**
Doris Day appeared in *Love Me or Leave Me*.

AT THE BALALAIKA   1936
George Posford / Eric Maschwitz
Keith Prowse Music Publishing Co. Ltd . . . . UK
Show(s): . . . . Balalaika
Film(s): . . . . Balalaika
Nelson Eddy . . . . **Columbia 33S 1012**
Greta Keller . . . . **Decca F 6263**
Richard Tauber . . . . **Parlophone PMD 1010**
Nelson Eddy appeared in the film *Balalaika*.

AT THE CAFE CONTINENTAL   1936
Will Grosz / Jimmy Kennedy
Peter Maurice Music Co. Ltd . . . . UK
Ambrose & his Orchestra . . . . **Decca F 6009**
Mantovani & his Tipica Orchestra . . . . . . **Columbia FB 1480**
Maurice Winnick & his Orchestra . . . . **Parlophone F 507**

AT THE CANDLELIGHT CAFE   October 1948
Mack David
Peter Maurice Music Co. Ltd. . . . . USA
Vera Lynn . . . . **Decca F 8845**
Dick Haymes . . . . **Brunswick 03850**
Al Jolson . . . . **Brunswick LAT 8387**

AT THE CLUB   June 1972
Gerry Goffin / Carole King
Screen Gems Music Ltd . . . . USA
The Drifters . . . . **Atlantic K 10148**

AT THE CROSSROADS   1943
Ernesto Leucona / Bob Russell
Francis, Day & Hunter Ltd . . . . Cuba
Vaughn Monroe . . . . **HMV BD 5804**
Mel Tormé . . . . **HMV CLP 1315**
Adapted from "Malaguena" by Ernesto Leucona.

AT THE END OF THE DAY   June 1951
Donald O'Keefe
Chappell & Co. Ltd . . . . UK
Gracie Fields . . . . **Decca DFE 6314**
Webster Booth . . . . **HMV B 10092**
Steve Conway & The Hastings Girls Choir . **Columbia DB 2913**

AT THE FOXTROT BALL 1915
Nat. D. Ayer
B. Feldman & Co. Ltd. .... USA
Show(s): .... 5064 Gerard
The Mayfair Orchestra .... **HMV B 287**
Clara Beck .... **HMV B 534**

AT THE HOP March 1958
Artie Singer / J. Medora / D. White
Yale Music Corporation Ltd .... USA
Film(s): .... Woodstock
Danny & The Juniors .... **HMV POP 436**
Nick Todd .... **London HLD 8537**
Sha Na Na .... **Atlantic K 6006**
Sha Na Na appeared in *Woodstock*.

AT THE JAZZ BAND BALL 1919
Dominic J. La Rocca / Larry Shields
Francis, Day & Hunter Ltd. .... USA
The Original Dixieland Jazz Band .... **HMV DLP 1065**
Bix Beiderbecke & his Orchestra .... **Philips BBE 12125**
Muggsy Spanier's Ragtime Band .... **RCA RD 27132**
Bing Crosby & Louis Armstrong .... **MGM C 844**

AT TRINITY CHURCH 1894
Fred Gilbert
Francis, Day & Hunter Ltd .... UK
Tom Costello .... **World Records SH 357**
Reg Grant .... **Parlophone E 6372**
Barrel Organ .... **HMV B 2514**
Warren Mitchell .... **Allegro ALL 850**

AT YOUR COMMAND 1932
Harry Barris / Bing Crosby / Harry Tobias
Keith Prowse Music Publishing Co. Ltd. .... USA
Bing Crosby .... **Brunswick LA 8741**
Gertrude Lawrence .... **Decca F 2577**

ATLANTIS July 1963
Jerry Lordan
Francis, Day & Hunter Ltd .... UK
The Shadows .... **Columbia DB 7047**

ATMOSPHERE February 1985
Eddie Tucker / Ben Findon / Stephen Rodway
Black Sheep Music .... UK
Russ Abbot .... **Spirit FIRE 4**

ATOMIC March 1980
Deborah Harry / James Destri
EMI Music Ltd .... UK
Blondie .... **Chrysalis CHS 2410**

ATTENTION TO ME May 1981
Ben Findon / Mike Myers / Robert Puzey
Black Sheep Music .... UK
The Nolans .... **Epic EPC 9571**

AU REVOIR BUT NOT GOODBYE 1936
Joseph Gilbert
Peter Maurice Music Co. Ltd .... UK
Al Bowlly .... **HMV BD 762**
Morton Downey .... **Rex 8854**

AUF WIEDERSEH'N 1916
Sigmund Romberg / Herbert Reynolds
Chappell & Co. Ltd. .... USA
Show(s): .... The Blue Paradise
Film(s): .... Deep in My Heart
Nelson Eddy .... **Camden CDN 157**
Helen Traubel .... **MGM C 755**
Helen Traubel appeared in *Deep in My Heart*.

AUF WIEDERSEH'N MY DEAR 1932
Milton Ager / Ed G. Nelson / Al Goodhart / Al Hoffman
Lawrence Wright Music Co. Ltd. .... USA
The Comedy Harmonists .... **HMV 7EG 8268**
Greta Keller .... **Decca LK 4126**
Les Howard .... **Columbia DB 4476**

AUF WIEDERSEH'N SWEETHEART July 1952
Eberhard Storch / John Sexton / John Turner
Peter Maurice Music Co. Ltd .... Germany
Vera Lynn .... **Decca LF 1102**

Vera Lynn .... **Decca LK 4120**

AUNT HAGAR'S BLUES 1923
William C. Handy / J. Tym Brym
Francis, Day & Hunter Ltd .... USA
Film(s): ....Hi Good Lookin' / St. Louis Blues
The Roseland Dance Orchestra .... **Imperial 1253**
Ladds Black Aces .... **London Al 3556**
The Dinning Sisters .... **Capitol CL 13294**
Jack Teagarden & his Music .... **Capitol T 721**
Pearl Bailey .... **Columbia 33SX 1094**
Jack Teagarden appeared in *Hi Good Lookin'*.

AURORA 1941
Mario Lago / Roberto Roberti / Harold Adamson
Sun Music Publishing Co. Ltd .... Brazil
Film(s): .... Hold That Ghost
The Andrews Sisters .... **Brunswick 03213**
Jimmy Dorsey & his Orchestra,
vocal Helen O'Connell .... **Brunswick 03209**
The Andrews Sisters .... **Capitol T 6132**
Ronnie Harris .... **Columbia SCM 5266**
The Andrews Sisters appeared in *Hold That Ghost*.

AUTOBAHN June 1975
Florian Elseben-Schneider / Ralf Hutter / Emil Schult
Famous-Chappell Music Ltd. .... Germany
Kraftwerk .... **Vertigo 6147012**

AUTOMATIC May 1984
Patrick Walsh / Mark Golenberg
MCA Music .... USA
The Pointer Sisters .... **Planet RPS 105**

AUTOMATIC LOVER May 1978
Gary Unwin / Patti Unwin
Martin-Coulter Music Ltd .... Germany
Dee D. Jackson .... **Mercury 6007171**

AUTOMATICALLY SUNSHINE August 1972
William Robinson
Jobete Music (UK) Ltd. .... USA
The Supremes .... **Tamla Motown TMG 821**

AUTUMN ALMANAC November 1967
Ray Davies
Carlin Music Corporation .... UK
The Kinks .... **Pye 7N 17400**

AUTUMN CONCERTO September 1956
Camillo Bargoni / Paul Siegel / Geoffrey Parsons & John Turner
Macmelodies Ltd. .... Italy
Joan Small .... **Parlophone R 4211**
Ted Heath & his Music .... **Decca F 10777**
Norrie Paramor & his Orchestra .... **Columbia DB 3815**
The Melachrino Strings .... **HMV 7EG 8601**

AUTUMN IN NEW YORK November 1954
Vernon Duke
Chappell & Co. Ltd. .... USA
Show(s): .... Thumbs Up
Frank Sinatra .... **Philips BBL 7180**
The Hi Lo's .... **Philips BBL 7411**
Sarah Vaughan .... **Mercury MMC 14024**

AUTUMN LEAVES September 1950
Joseph Kosma / Jacques Prevert / Johnny Mercer
Peter Maurice Music Co. Ltd .... France
Film(s): .... Hey Boy! Hey Girl!
Bing Crosby .... **Brunswick 04602**
Eve Boswell .... **Parlophone PMD 1039**
Gordon MacRae .... **Capitol T 1146**
Keely Smith .... **Capitol T 1160**
Roger Williams & his Orchestra .... **London HAR 2058**
Keely Smith appeared in *Hey Boy, Hey Girl*.

AVALON 1920
Al Jolson / Vincent Rose / Buddy De Sylva
B. Feldman & Co. Ltd .... USA
Show(s): .... Sinbad
Film(s):The Jolson Story / The Benny Goodman Story / Both Ends of
the Candle
Paul Whiteman & his Orchestra .... **HMV C 1002**
Al Jolson .... **Brunswick LA 8570**

The Benny Goodman Quartet .... **HMV 7EG 8003**
Bing Crosby .... **Brunswick LAT 8217**
The Benny Goodman Quartet (Sound Track) . **Brunswick LAT 8103**
Gogi Grant .... **RCA RD 27054**
Gogi Grant dubbed the singing voice of Ann Blyth who appeared in the film *Both Ends of the Candle*.

AXEL F July 1985
Harold Faltermeyer
Famous Music .... Germany
Harold Faltermeyer .... **MCA MCA 949**

AY, AY, AY 1927
Osman Perez-Freire / Max Gartman
G. Ricordi & Co. (London) Ltd. .... Spain
Tito Schipa .... **HMV DB 1051**
Michele Fleta .... **HMV DB 1483**
Webster Booth .... **HMV B 9009**
Mario Lanza .... **HMV ALP 1405**

AY AY AY AY MOOSEY December 1981
Geoffrey Deane / David Jaymes
April Music Ltd .... UK
Modern Romance .... **WEA K 18883**

BABALU 1942
Marguerita Leucona / Bob Russell
Southern Music Publishing Co. Ltd .... Cuba
Film(s): .... Two Girls and a Sailor / Pan-Americana
Xavier Cugat & his Orchestra,
vocal Miguelito Valdez .... **Parlophone R 2811**
Yma Sumac .... **Capitol CL 13766**
Hermanas Manguez .... **HMV CLP 1241**
Xavier Cugat Orchestra appeared in *Two Girls and a Sailor*.

BABE February 1980
Dennis De Yong
Rondor Music (London) Ltd .... UK
Styx .... **A&M AMS 7489**

BABETTE 1925
Horatio Nicholls / Ray Morelle
Lawrence Wright Music Co. Ltd. .... UK
Jack Hylton & his Orchestra .... **HMV B 2088**
Cyril Newton .... **HMV B 2151**
Joe Loss & his Orchestra .... **HMV DLP 1113**

BABOOSHKA August 1980
Kate Bush
EMI Music Ltd .... UK
Kate Bush .... **EMI 5085**
Ivor Novello Nomination.

BABY BABY May 1957
Milton Subotsky / Glen Moore
Chappell & Co. Ltd .... USA
Film(s): .... Rock Rock Rock
Frankie Lyman .... **Columbia DB 3878**

BABY COME BACK July 1968
Edmund Grant
Edward Kassner Music Co. Ltd. .... UK
The Equals .... **President PT 135**

BABY COME TO ME March 1983
Rodney Temperton
Rondor Music .... UK
Patti Austin & James Ingram .... **Quest K 15005**

BABY DOLL March 1952
Johnny Mercer / Harry Warren
Francis, Day & Hunter Ltd .... USA
Film(s): .... The Belle of New York
Fred Astaire .... **MGM EP 628**
Ella Fitzgerald .... **Brunswick 05008**
Fred Astaire appeared in *The Belle of New York*.

BABY DON'T CHANGE YOUR MIND July 1977
Van McCoy
Warner Brothers Music Ltd .... USA
Gladys Knight & The Pips .... **Buddah DBS 458**

BABY DON'T GO October 1965
Sonny Bono
Edward Kassner Music Co. Ltd .... USA

Sonny & Cher .... **Reprise R 20309**

BABY FACE 1926
Harry Akst / Benny Davis
Francis, Day & Hunter Ltd. .... USA
Film(s):Jolson Sings Again / Glorifying the American Girl / Thoroughly Modern Millie
Jack Smith .... **HMV B 2383**
The Savoy Orpheans .... **HMV B 5147**
Al Jolson (1949) .... **Brunswick LAT 8322**
Art Mooney & his Orchestra .... **MGM D 136**
Little Richard (1959) .... **London HAU 2126**
Dorothy Provine .... **Warner Brothers WM 4053**
Wing And A Prayer Fife & Drum Band ...... **Atlantic K 10705**
Julie Andrews .... **Brunswick LAT 8685**
Julie Andrews appeared in *Thoroughly Modern Millie*.

BABY I DON'T CARE August 1961
Jerry Leiber / Mike Stoller
Belinda (London) Ltd. .... USA
Film(s): .... Jailhouse Rock
Elvis Presley .... **RCA RCX 106**
Buddy Holly .... **Coral Q 72432**
Cliff Richard .... **Columbia 33SX 1147**
Elvis Presley appeared in *Jailhouse Rock*.

BABY I DON'T CARE May 1989
Nick Sayer
Cinepop Music .... UK
Transvision Vamp .... **MCA TVV 6**

BABY I KNOW March 1977
John Richardson / Alan Williams
State Music .... UK
The Rubettes .... **State STAT 37**

BABY I LOVE YOU February 1964
Phil Spector / Ellie Greenwich / Jeff Barry
Belinda (London) Ltd .... USA
The Ronettes .... **London HL 9826**
Bob B. Sox & The Blue Jeans .... **London HAU 8121**
Dave Edmunds (1973) .... **Rockfield ROC 1**
The Ramones (1980) .... **Sire SIR 4031**

BABY I LOVE YOU, O.K. July 1975
Bill Martin / Phil Coulter
Martin-Coulter Music Ltd .... UK
Kenny .... **Rak 207**

BABY I LOVE YOUR WAY / FREEBIRD January 1989
Peter Frampton
Rondor Music .... UK
Will To Power .... **Epic 653094**

BABY I'M... A WANT YOU February 1972
David Gates
Screen Gems Music Ltd .... UK
Bread .... **Elektra K 12033**

BABY IT'S COLD OUTSIDE October 1949
Frank Loesser
Edwin H. Morris Ltd .... USA
Film(s): .... Neptune's Daughter
Esther Williams & Ricardo Montalban .... **MGM C 789**
Dinah Shore & Buddy Clark .... **Columbia DB 2582**
Carmen McRae & Sammy Davis .... **Brunswick 05830**
Esther Williams & Ricardo Montalban appeared in *Neptune's Daughter*. Academy Award winning song of 1949.

BABY JANE July 1983
Rod Stewart / Jay Davis
Carlin Music .... USA
Rod Stewart .... **Warner Brothers W 9608**

BABY JUMP March 1971
Ray Dorset
Our Music .... UK
Mungo Jerry .... **Dawn DNX 2505**

BABY LOVE November 1964
Brian Holland / Eddie Holland / Lamont Dozier
Belinda (London) Ltd .... USA
The Supremes .... **Stateside SS 350**
The Supremes (1974) .... **Tamla Motown TMG 915**

BABY LOVER   May 1958
Wandra Merrell
Cromwell Music Ltd. . . . . USA
Film(s): . . . . .Six Five Special
Petula Clark   **Nixa N 15126**

BABY MAKE IT SOON   July 1969
Tony Macaulay
Welbeck Music Co. Ltd. . . . . UK
Marmalade . . . . **CBS 4287**

BABY MINE   1942
Ned Washington / Frank Churchill / Oliver Wallace
Chappell & Co. Ltd . . . . USA
Film(s): . . . . Dumbo (cartoon)
Sound Track   **HMV BD 1285**
Joe Loss & his Orch, vocal Chick Henderson . . **HMV BD 6734**
Nominated for an Academy Award 1941.

BABY NOW THAT I'VE FOUND YOU   December 1967
John MacLeod / Tony Macauley
Schroeder Music Ltd. . . . . UK
The Foundations . . . . **Pye 7N 17366**

BABY PLEASE DON'T GO   February 1965
Joe Williams
Leeds Music Ltd . . . . USA
Them . . . . **Decca F 12018**

BABY SITTIN' BOOGIE   April 1961
Johnny Parker
Edwin H. Morris & Co. Ltd . . . . USA
Buzz Clifford . . . . **Fontana H 297**

BABY STOP CRYING   September 1978
Bob Dylan
Big Ben Music . . . . USA
Bob Dylan . . . . **CBS 6499**

**BABY WE BETTER TRY TO GET IT
TOGETHER**   September 1976
Barry White
Schroeder Music Ltd . . . . USA
Barry White . . . . **20th Century BTC 2298**

BABY WON'T YOU PLEASE COME HOME   1919
Clarence Williams / Charles Warfield
Pickwick Music Ltd. . . . . USA
Film(s): . . . . That's the Spirit
Frankie Trumbauer & his Orchestra . . . . . . **Parlophone R 1978**
The Mills Brothers . . . . **Brunswick 01255**
Kay Starr . . . . **London HAU 2039**
Della Reese . . . . **RCA RD 27167**

BABYLON'S BURNING   July 1979
Malcolm Owen / John Jennings / Paul Fox & Glen Ruffy
Virgin Music (Publishers) Ltd. UK
The Ruts . . . . **Virgin VS 271**

BACH GOES TO TOWN   1939
Alec Templeton
Francis, Day & Hunter Ltd. . . . . USA
Arthur Young (Novachord) . . . . **Decca F 7201**
Benny Goodman & his Orchestra . . . . **Camden CDN 148**
The Neal Hefti Orchestra . . . . **RCA RD 27058**

BACHELOR BOY   January 1963
Bruce Welch / Cliff Richard
Elstree Music Ltd . . . . UK
Film(s): . . . . Summer Holiday
Cliff Richard . . . . **Columbia DB 4950**
The Bachelors . . . . **Decca LK 4519**
Cliff Richard appeared in *Summer Holiday*.
Ivor Novello Nomination.

BACHELOR GAY, A   1917
James W. Tate / Clifford Harris / Arthur Valentine
Francis, Day & Hunter Ltd. . . . . UK
Show(s): . . . . The Maid of the Mountains
Thorpe Bates . . . . **Columbia L 1159**
Peter Dawson . . . . **HMV DLP 1180**
Stanley Holloway . . . . **Pye NPL 18056**
Barry Kent . . . . **HMV 7EG 8413**
Thorpe Bates appeared in the British production of *The Maid of the Mountains*.

BACK AGAIN TO HAPPY-GO-LUCKY-DAYS   1932
Raymond Wallace
Campbell Connelly & Co. Ltd. . . . . UK
Ray Noble & The New Mayfair Dance Orchestra . . **HMV B 6169**

BACK AND FORTH   May 1987
Kevin Kendrick / Tom Jenkins / Nathan Leftenant & Lonnie Blackman
Polygram Music . . . . UK
Cameo . . . . **Club JAB 49**

BACK HOME   June 1970
Bill Martin / Phil Coulter
Mews Music . . . . UK
The England World Cup Squad . . . . **Pye 7N 17920**

BACK HOME IN TENNESSEE   1915
Walter Donaldson / William Jerome
B. Feldman & Co. Ltd. . . . . USA
De Groot & his Picadilly Orchestra . . . . . . **HMV B 691**
G.H. Elliott . . . . **Regal G 7294**
The George Mitchell Singers . . . . **HMV CLP 1399**

BACK IN YOUR OWN BACK YARD   1928
Dave Dreyer / Al Jolson / Billy Rose
Francis, Day & Hunter . . . . USA
Film(s): . . . . .Jolson Sings Again / Say it With Songs
Fletcher Henderson & his Orchestra . . . . **Vocalion S 86**
Al Jolson . . . . **Brunswick LA 8509**
The Andrews Sisters . . . . **Capitol T 973**
Brenda Lee . . . . **Brunswick LAT 8319**
Al Jolson appeared in *Say it With Songs*.

BACK OFF BOOGALOO   May 1972
Richard Starkey
Essex Music Ltd . . . . UK
Ringo Starr . . . . **Apple R 5944**

BACK STAGE   March 1966
Fred Anisfield / Willie Denson
Bron Music Co. Ltd. . . . . USA
Gene Pitney . . . . **Stateside SS 490**

BACK STREET LUV   September 1971
Darryl Way / Sonja Linwood / Ian Eyre
Island Nusic Ltd . . . . UK
Curved Air . . . . **Warner Brothers K 36015**

BACK TO LIFE   July 1989
Beresford Romeo / Caron Wheeler / Simon Law & Nellee Hooper
Virgin Music . . . . UK
Soul II Soul . . . . **10 TEN 265**
Ivor Novello Nomination.

BACK TO THOSE HAPPY DAYS   1935
Horatio Nicholls
Lawrence Wright Music Co. Ltd . . . . UK
Geraldo's Accordion Band . . . . **Columbia FB 1026**
Max Bygraves . . . . **Decca LK 4360**
Theme song of Herman Darewski.

BACK TOGETHER AGAIN   July 1980
James Mtume / Reggie Lucas
Famous-Chappell . . . . USA
Roberta Flack & Donny Hathaway . . . . **Atlantic K 11481**

BAD   October 1987
Michael Jackson
Warner Brothers Music . . . . USA
Michael Jackson . . . . **Epic 651155**

BAD BAD BOY   August 1973
"Nazareth"
Carlin Music Corporation . . . . UK
Nazareth . . . . **Mooncrest MOON 9**

BAD BOY   January 1960
Marty Wilde
Youngstar Music . . . . UK
Marty Wilde . . . . **Philips BBL 7380**

BAD BOY   June 1986
Lawrence Derner / Joe Galdo / Rafael Vigil
CBS Songs . . . . USA
Miami Sound Machine . . . . **Epic A 6537**

BAD BOYS June 1983
George Michael
Morrison Leahy Music . . . . UK
Wham . . . . **Inner Vision A 3143**

BAD MOON RISING October 1969
John Fogerty
Burlington Music Co. Ltd. . . . . USA
Creedence Clearwater Revival . . . . **Liberty LBF 15230**

BAD OLD DAYS, THE May 1978
Stephanie De Sykes / Stuart Slater
A.T.V. Music Ltd . . . . UK
Co-Co . . . . **Ariola AHA 513**
United Kingdom entry for the 1978 Eurovision Song Contest (Placed
Eleventh).

BAD PENNY BLUES June 1956
Humphrey Lyttelton
Essex Music Ltd. . . . . UK
Humphrey Lyttelton & his Band . . . . . . **Parlophone GEP 8645**

BAD TO ME September 1963
John Lennon / Paul McCartney
Northern Songs Ltd . . . . UK
Billy J. Kramer . . . . **Parlophone R 5049**

BADGE FROM YOUR COAT, THE 1941
Horatio Nicholls / Annette Mills
Lawrence Wright Music Co. Ltd . . . . UK
Alice Delysia . . . . **Decca F 7822**
Jay Wilbur & his Orchestra, vocal Sam Browne . . . . . **Rex 9908**

BAGGY TROUSERS October 1980
Graham McPherson / Chris Foreman / Mike Barson
Warner Brothers Music Ltd . . . . UK
Madness . . . . **Stiff BUY 84**

BAIA 1945
Ary Barroso / Ray Gilbert
Lawrence Wright Music Co. Ltd. . . . . Brazil
Film(s): . . . . The Three Caballeros (Cartoon)
Bing Crosby . . . . **Brunswick LAT 8331**
Jane Morgan . . . . **London HAR 2244**
Xavier Cugat & his Orchestra . . . . **RCA RD 27127**

BAKER STREET April 1978
Gerry Rafferty
Island Music Ltd . . . . UK
Gerry Rafferty . . . . **United Artists UP 36346**
Ivor Novello Award.

BALI HA'I November 1951
Richard Rodgers / Oscar Hammerstein II
Williamson Music Ltd . . . . USA
Show(s): . . . . South Pacific
Film(s): . . . . South Pacific
Juanita Hall . . . . **Philips BBL 7157**
Muriel Smith . . . . **Columbia SEG 7668**
Juanita Hall . . . . **RCA RB 16065**
Juanita Hall appeared in the American production of *South Pacific* and
also the film *South Pacific*.
Muriel Smith appeared in the British production of *South Pacific*.

BALL OF CONFUSION October 1970
Norman Whitfield / Barrett Strong
Jobete Music (UK) Ltd. . . . . USA
The Temptations . . . . **Tamla Motown TMG 749**

BALL PARK INCIDENT January 1973
Roy Wood
Carlin Music Corporation . . . . UK
Wizzard . . . . **Harvest HAR 5062**

BALLAD OF BETHNAL GREEN, THE July 1959
Paddy Roberts
Essex Music Ltd . . . . UK
Paddy Roberts . . . . **Decca LF 1322**
Beatrice Lillie . . . . **Decca DFE 6697**
Ivor Novello Award.

BALLAD OF BONNIE AND CLYDE, THE February 1968
Mitch Murray / Peter Callander
Clan Music . . . . UK
Georgie Fame . . . . **CBS 3124**

Ivor Novello Nomination.

BALLAD OF DAVY CROCKETT, THE February 1956
George Bruns / Tom Blackburn
Walt Disney Music co. Ltd. . . . . USA
Film(s): . . . . Davy Crockett, King of the Wild Frontier
Gary Miller . . . . **Nixa NPT 19015**
Fess Parker . . . . **Philips PB 534**
Eddy Arnold . . . . **RCA RD 27155**
Tennessee Ernie Ford . . . . **Capitol CL 14506**
Bill Hayes . . . . **London HLA 8220**
Fess Parker appeared in *Davy Crockett, King of the Wild Frontier.*

BALLAD OF JOHN AND YOKO, THE July 1969
John Lennon / Paul McCartney
Northern Songs Ltd. . . . . UK
The Beatles . . . . **Apple R 5786**

BALLAD OF THE PALADIN, THE September 1962
Richard Boone / Sam Rolfe / Johnny Western
Greenwich Music Ltd . . . . USA
Duane Eddy (guitar) . . . . **RCA 1300**
Lawrence Welk & his Orchestra . . . . **Coral LVA 9117**
Theme of the T.V. series *Have Gun, Will Travel.*

BALLERINA July 1948
Carl Sigman / Bob Russell
Peter Maurice Music Co. Ltd. . . . . USA
Bing Crosby . . . . **Brunswick 03889**
Vaughn Monroe . . . . **RCA RCX 1043**
Vaughn Monroe . . . . **London HLT 9123**

BALLIN' THE JACK 1913
Chris Smith / James Burris
Francis, Day & Hunter Ltd. . . . . USA
Show(s): . . . . The Passing Show of 1915
Film(s): . . . . For Me & My Gal / On the Riviera / Jazz Dance
Elsie Janis & Basil Hallam . . . . **HMV B 485**
Jerry Roll Morton's Jazzmen . . . . **HMV B 9218**
Danny Kaye (1948) . . . . **Brunswick LA 8660**
Brenda Lee . . . . **Brunswick LAT 8319**
Danny Kaye appeared in *On The Riviera.*
Elsie Janis & Basil Hallam appeared in *The Passing Show of 1915.*

BALLOONS (Who'll Buy My Nice Balloons) 1933
Frank Magine / Nelson Shawn
Keith Prowse Music Publishing Co. Ltd. . . . . USA
Lew Stone & his Orchestra, vocal Al Bowlly . . . . **Decca F 3314**
Gracie Fields . . . . **HMV B 4362**

BALLROOM BLITZ October 1973
Mike Chapman / Nicky Chinn
Chinnichap Music . . . . UK
The Sweet . . . . **RCA 2403**

'BAM 'BAM 'BAMMY SHORE 1926
Ray Henderson / Mort Dixon
Francis, Day & Hunter Ltd. . . . . USA
The Savoy Havana Band . . . . **HMV B 2186**
The Revellers . . . . **HMV B 2276**

BAMBI 1942
Larry Morey / Frank Churchill
Campbell Connelly & Co. Ltd . . . . USA
Film(s): . . . . Bambi (cartoon)
Sound Track . . . . **Top Rank JKP 2032**

BANANA ROCK July 1974
Mike Batt
Batt Songs . . . . UK
The Wombles . . . . **CBS 2465**

BANANA SPLITS May 1979
Richie Adams / Mark Barkan
Aaron Schroeder Music . . . . USA
The Dickies . . . . **A&M AMS 7431**

BANC, UN ARBRE, UNE RUE, UN June 1971
Jean-Pierre Bourtayre / Yves Dessca
. . . . Monaco
Severine (in French) . . . . **Philips 6009135**
Monaco entry for the 1971 Eurovision Song Contest (Placed First).

BAND OF GOLD October 1970
Ronald Dunbar / Edith Wayne

29

Gold Fever Music .... USA
Freda Payne .... **Invictus INV 502**

BAND OF GOLD, THE   March 1956
Bob Musel / Jack Taylor
Essex Music Ltd.. USA
Petula Clark .... **Nixa NPT 19015**
Don Cherry .... **Philips BBR 8084**

BAND ON THE RUN   August 1974
Paul McCartney
McCartney Music .... UK
Paul McCartney & Wings .... **Apple R 5997**

BAND PLAYED ON, THE   1895
Charles Ward / John Palmer
B. Feldman & Co. Ltd...................................... USA
Film(s): .... Lillian Russell / The Strawberry Blonde
Ambrose & his Orchestra, vocal Sam Browne . **Decca F 7966**
Vaughn Monroe .... **RCA RD 27049**
Frank D'Rone .... **Mercury AMT 1123**
Alice Faye .... **Reprise R 6029**
Alice Faye appeared in *Lillian Russell.*

BANDANA DAYS   1922
Noble Sissle / Eubie Blake
B. Feldman & Co. Ltd .... USA
Show(s): .... Shuffle Along
Eubie Blake & his Shuffle Along Orchestra ...... **HMV B 1297**

BANDANNA BABIES   1928
Dorothy Fields / Jimmy McHugh
Lawrence Wright Music Co. Ltd. .... USA
Show(s): .... Blackbirds of 1928
Duke Ellington & his Cotton Club Orchestra ..... **HMV B 8652**

BANDIT, THE (O'Cangaceiro)   April 1954
Alfredo Nascimento / John Turner
Peter Maurice Music Co. Ltd. .... Brazil
The Johnston Brothers .... **Decca DFE 6249**
Frank Weir & his Orchestra .... **Decca DFE 6226**
Tex Ritter .... **Capitol CL 14177**
Manuel & his Music of The Mountains ... **Columbia 33SX 1359**

BANG BANG   September 1979
B.A. Robertson / Terry Britten
United Artists Music Co. Ltd. .... UK
B.A. Robertson .... **Asylum K 13152**

BANG BANG (My Baby Shot Me Down)   June 1966
Sonny Bono
Edward Kassner Music Co. Ltd. .... USA
Cher .... **Liberty LIB 66160**

BANG ZOOM (Let's Go Go)   July 1986
Howie Tee
Zomba Music .... USA
The Real Roxanne & Hitman Howie Tee   **Cooltempo COOL 124**

BANGIN' MAN   July 1974
Noddy Holder / Jimmy Lea
Barn Publishing Ltd. .... UK
Slade .... **Polydor 2058492**

BANGLA DESH   August 1971
George Harrison
Harrisongs Ltd .... UK
George Harrison .... **Apple R 5912**

BANJO'S BACK IN TOWN, THE   October 1955
Alden Shuman / Earle Shuman / Marshall Brown
Leeds Music .... USA
Alma Cogan .... **HMV B 10917**
Suzi Miller .... **Decca F 10593**
Teresa Brewer .... **Coral Q 72098**

BANK ROBBER   September 1980
Joe Strummer / Mick Jones
Nineden Music .... UK
Clash .... **CBS 8323**

BANKS OF THE OHIO, THE   December 1971
Traditional
Carlin Music Corporation .... USA
Olivia Newton-John .... **Pye 7N 25568**

BANNER MAN, THE   July 1971
Roger Greenaway / Roger Cook / Herbie Flowers
Cookaway Music .... UK
Blue Mink .... **Regal Zonophone RZ 3034**

BARBADOS   August 1975
Jeff Calvert / Max West
Gull Songs Ltd .... UK
Typically Tropical .... **Gull GULS 14**

BARBARA   1927
Abner Silver / Billy Rose
Chappell & Co. Ltd. .... USA
Jack Hylton & his Orchestra,
vocal Jack Jackson & chorus .... **HMV B 5388**

BARBARA ANN   April 1966
Fred Fassert
Planetary Nom (London) Ltd. .... USA
The Beach Boys .... **Capitol CL 15432**

BARCELONA   1926
Tolchard Evans / Huntley Trevor
Peter Maurice Music Co. Ltd. .... UK
The Savoy Orpheans .... **HMV B 5045**
The Tuneful Twenties Dance Orchestra ... **Parlophone R 3497**
David Rose & his Orchestra .... **MGM C 788**

BARCELONA   November 1987
Freddie Mercury / Mike Moran
Queen Music .... UK
Freddie Mercury & Montserrat Caballe ..... **Polydor POSP 887**

BARNACLE BILL THE SAILOR   1931
Carson Robison / Frank Luther
Francis, Day & Hunter Ltd .... USA
Frank Luther .... **Decca F 5346**
Hoagy Carmichael & his Orchestra,
vocal Carson Robison .... **Camden CDN 112**

BARNEY GOOGLE   1923
Con Conrad / Billy Rose
Francis, Day & Hunter Ltd .... USA
The Great White Way Orchestra,
vocal Billy Murray .... **HMV B 1715**
The Andrews Sisters .... **Capitol T 973**

BASIN STREET BLUES   1930
Spencer Williams
Lawrence Wright Music Co. Ltd .... USA
Film(s): .... The Glenn Miller Story / The Strip
Louis Armstrong & his Orchestra .... **Philips BBL 7202**
Bing Crosby & Connee Boswell .... **Brunswick LA 88558**
Paul Whiteman & his Orchestra,
vocal Jack Teagarden .... **London HAZ 2365**
The Mills Brothers .... **Brunswick LA 8702**
Louis Armstrong appeared in *The Strip.*

BATDANCE   July 1989
"Prince"
Warner Chappell Music .... USA
Prince .... **Warner Brothers W 2924**

BATHING IN THE SUNSHINE   1931
Horatio Nicholls / Joe Gilbert
Lawrence Wright Music Co. Ltd. .... UK
Layton & Johnstone .... **Columbia DB 429**
Ambrose & his Orchestra, vocal Sam Browne ... **HMV B 5980**

BATTLE OF NEW ORLEANS, THE   August 1959
Traditional arranged by Jimmy Driftwood
Acuff-Rose Publishing Co. Ltd .... USA
Lonnie Donegan .... **Pye NEP 24114**
Johnny Horton .... **Philips BBL 7464**
Glen Mason .... **Parlophone R 4562**
Jimmy Driftwood .... **RCA RCX 159**

BAUBLES, BANGLES AND BEADS   April 1955
Robert Wright / George Forrest
Frank Music Co. Ltd. .... USA
Show(s): .... Kismet
Film(s): .... Kismet
Doretta Morrow .... **Philips BBL 7023**
Ann Blyth .... **MGM C 758**
Doretta Morrow appeared in both the American and British productions

of *Kismet*.
Ann Blyth appeared in the film *Kismet*.
Adapted from "String Quartet in D Major" by Alexander Borodin (1833 - 1887).

BE A CLOWN   October 1948
Cole Porter
Chappell & Co. Ltd. . . . . USA
Show(s): . . . . Singin' in the Rain
Film(s): . . . . The Pirate
Judy Garland & Gene Kelly   **MGM C 763**
Roy Castle . . . . **Safari RAIN 1**
Judy Garland & Gene Kelly appeared in *The Pirate*.
Roy Castle appeared in *Singin' in the Rain*.

BE ANYTHING - BUT BE MINE   June 1952
Irving Gordon
Cinephonic Music Co. Ltd . . . . USA
Jimmy Young . . . . **Polygon P 1042**
Peggy Lee . . . . **Brunswick 04939**
Sarah Vaughan . . . . **Mercury MPL 6542**

BE-BOP-A-LULA   August 1956
Gene Vincent / Tex Davis
Carlin Music Ltd. . . . . USA
Film(s): . . . . The Girl Can't Help it
Gene Vincent . . . . **Capitol CL 14599**
Gene Vincent appeared in *The Girl Can't Help it*.

BE CAREFUL IT'S MY HEART   1942
Irving Berlin
Irving Berlin Ltd . . . . USA
Film(s): . . . . Holiday Inn
Bing Crosby . . . . **Brunswick Bing 7**
Pat Boone . . . . **London HAD 2082**
The Four Freshmen . . . . **Capitol T 1378**
Bing Crosby appeared in *Holiday Inn*.

BE HONEST WITH ME   1943
Gene Autry / Fred Rose
Peter Maurice Music Co. Ltd . . . . USA
Film(s): . . . . Strictly in the Groove / Ridin' on a Rainbow
Gene Autry . . . . **Regal Zonophone MR 3477**
Bing Crosby . . . . **Brunswick LAT 8253**
Gene Autry appeared in *Ridin' on a Rainbow*.
Nominated for an Academy Award 1941.

BE MINE   March 1960
J. Menke / M. Panas / T. Luth & Marcel Stellman
Southern Music Publishing Co. Ltd . . . . Germany
Lance Fortune . . . . **Pye 7N 15240**

BE MY BABY   November 1963
Phil Spector / Ellie Greenwich / Jeff Barry
Belinda (London) Ltd . . . . USA
The Ronettes . . . . **London HL 9793**
Grazina . . . . **HMV POP 1212**

BE MY COMRADE TRUE   1912
Leo Fall
Chappell & Co. Ltd . . . . Germany
Show(s): . . . . Princess Caprice
Clara Evelyn . . . . **HMV 03297**
Clara Evelyn appeared in *Princess Caprice*.

BE MY GIRL   November 1957
Artie Singer
Chappell & Co. Ltd . . . . USA
Jim Dale . . . . **Parlophone R 4343**
Frankie Brent . . . . **Nixa N 15103**

BE MY LIFE'S COMPANION   April 1952
Bob Hilliard / Milton De Lugg
Edwin H. Morris & Co. Ltd . . . . USA
The Johnston Brothers . . . . **Decca LF 1145**
The Mills Brothers . . . . **Brunswick LA 8664**
Rosemary Clooney . . . . **Philips BBL 7301**
The Mills Brothers . . . . **London HAD 2192**

BE MY LITTLE BABY BUMBLE BEE   1919
Stanley Murphy / Henry Marshall
B. Feldman & Co. Ltd . . . . USA
Show(s): . . . . The Ziegfeld Follies of 1911
Film(s): Hoppity Goes to Town / By the Light of the Silvery Moon / When Irish Eyes are Smiling

Ada Jones & Billy Murray . . . . **Zonophone Twin 1115**
Gordon MacRae & June Hutton . . . . **Capitol LC 6599**
Doris Day . . . . **Philips BBL 7175**
Julie London . . . . **London HAW 2225**
Doris Day & Gordon McRae appeared in *By the Light of the Silvery Moon*.

BE MY LOVE   March 1951
Nicholas Brodszky / Sammy Cahn
Robbins Music Corporation Ltd . . . . USA
Film(s): . . . . The Toast of New Orleans / Looking For Love
Mario Lanza . . . . **RCA RCXZ 1025**
Mario Lanza & Kathryn Grayson . . . . **MCA 2368075**
Dorothy Squires . . . . **Columbia DB 2855**
Connie Francis . . . . **MGM C 983**
Mario Lanza & Kathryn Grayson appeared in *The Toast of New Orleans*.
Connie Francis appeared in *Looking For Love*.
Theme song of Mario Lanza.
Nominated for an Academy Award 1950.

BE STILL MY HEART   1935
Jack Egan / Allan Flynn
Francis, Day & Hunter Ltd . . . . USA
Al Bowlly . . . . **Decca F 5326**
Jane Froman . . . . **Capitol LC 6605**
The Four Coins . . . . **Fontana H 168**

BEACH BABY   July 1974
John Carter / Gillian Shakespeare
John Carter Music . . . . UK
First Class . . . . **UK UK 66**

BEALE STREET BLUES   1917
William C. Handy
Francis, Day & Hunter Ltd. . . . . USA
Film(s): . . . . St. Louis Blues / It's Trad Dad
Ted Lewis & his Band . . . . **Columbia 4609**
Jack Teagarden & his Orchestra,
vocal Jack Teagarden . . . . **Parlophone R 2735**
Ella Fitzgerald . . . . **HMV 7EG 8392**
Nat 'King' Cole . . . . **Capitol LCT 6156**
Jack Teagarden . . . . **Capitol T 721**
Ella Fitzgerald & Nat 'King' Cole appeared in *St. Louis Blues*.

BEAT DIS   March 1988
Emilio Pasquez / Tim Simeon
MCA Music . . . . UK
Bomb the Bass . . . . **Rhythm King DOOD 1**

BEAT IT   March 1983
Michael Jackson
Carlin Music . . . . USA
Michael Jackson . . . . **Epic EPC 3258**

BEAT ME DADDY, EIGHT TO THE BAR   1941
Don Raye / Hughie Prince / Eleanor Sheehy
Leeds Music Ltd . . . . USA
The Andrews Sisters . . . . **Brunswick 03082**
The Andrews Sisters . . . . **Capitol LCT 6132**
Ella Fitzgerald . . . . **HMV CLP 1455**

BEAT OUT DAT RHYTHM ON A DRUM   March 1955
Georges Bizet / Oscar Hammerstein II
Williamson Music Ltd. . . . . USA
Show(s): . . . . Carmen Jones
Film(s): . . . . Carmen Jones
June Hawkins, Cozy Cole & Chorus . . . . **Brunswick LAT 8057**
Pearl Bailey & Chorus . . . . **HMV CLP 1034**
June Hawkins & Cozy Cole appeared in the American production of *Carmen Jones*.
Pearl Bailey appeared in the film of *Carmen Jones*.
Based on 'The Gypsy Song' from the opera 'Carmen' by Georges Bizet (1838 - 1875).

BEAT SURRENDER   December 1982
Paul Weller
Morrison Leahy Music . . . . UK
The Jam . . . . **Polydor POSP 540**

BEAT THE CLOCK   August 1979
Ron Mael / Russell Mael
Island Music Ltd. . . . . UK
Sparks . . . . **Virgin VS 270**

BEATNIK FLY, THE   April 1960
Tom King / Ira Mack
Duchess Music Ltd . . . . USA
Johnny & The Hurricanes . . . . London HL 9072
Based on *The Bluetail Fly.*

BEAUTIFUL BROWN EYES   May 1951
Arthur Smith / Alton Delmore
Campbell Connelly & Co. Ltd . . . . USA
Jimmy Wakely . . . . Capitol CL 13484
Evelyn Knight . . . . Brunswick 04697
The Brothers Four . . . . Philips PB 1072

BEAUTIFUL DREAMER   1940
Stephen Foster
Out of copyright . . . . USA
Film(s): . . . . Swanee River
Richard Crooks . . . . HMV DA 1599
Al Jolson . . . . Brunswick LA 8554
Bing Crosby . . . . Brunswick LA 8571
Al Jolson appeared in *Swanee River.*

BEAUTIFUL EYES   April 1949
Frankie Adams / Leonard Rosen / Nell Madagalia
Leeds Music Ltd . . . . USA
Joe Loss & his Orchestra . . . . HMV BD 6041
Dickie Valentine . . . . Decca DFE 6427

BEAUTIFUL GARDEN OF ROSES, A   1909
Johann Schmidt / J.E. Dempsey
B. Feldman & Co. Ltd. . . . . USA
Philip Maxwell . . . . Zonophone 364
Charles Kullman . . . . Columbia DB 1439

BEAUTIFUL ISLE OF SOMEWHERE, THE   1897
Jessie Pounds / John Fearis
Unknown Publisher . . . . USA
John McCormack . . . . HMV DA 497
Richard Crooks . . . . HMV DA 1265
Moira Anderson . . . . Decca SKL 5073
Jo Stafford . . . . Philips PB 175

BEAUTIFUL LADY WALTZ (See My Beautiful Lady)

BEAUTIFUL LOVE   1932
Haven Gillespie / Victor Young / Wayne King / Egbert Van Alstyne
Keith Prowse Music Publishing Co. Ltd. . . . . USA
Film(s): . . . . Sing a Jingle
George Seversky . . . . Parlophone R 1269
Bing Crosby . . . . Brunswick 03633
Mario Lanza . . . . RCA RB 16085

BEAUTIFUL NOISE   November 1976
Neil Diamond
April Music Ltd . . . . USA
Neil Diamond . . . . CBS 4601

BEAUTIFUL OHIO   1918
Mary Earl / Ballard MacDonald
B. Feldman & Co. Ltd. . . . . USA
The Mayfair Dance Orchestra . . . . HMV C 917
Tony Martin . . . . Decca F 8901
Ted Heath & his Music . . . . Decca LK 4167
Joe Reisman & his Orchestra . . . . Columbia SEG 8020
Glenn Miller & his Orchestra . . . . HMV BD 5644

BECAUSE   1902
Guy D'Hardelot / Edward Teschemacher
Chappell & Co. Ltd. . . . . UK
Film(s): . . . . Three Smart Girls Grow Up / The Great Caruso
Maggie Teyte . . . . HMV 3629
Enrico Caruso (in French) . . . . HMV DA 107
Deanna Durbin (1940) . . . . Brunswick LAT 8285
Helen Traubel . . . . London HAR 2117
Mario Lanza . . . . RCA RD 86218
Deanna Durbin appeared in *Three Smart Girls Grow Up.*
Mario Lanza appeared in *The Great Caruso.*

BECAUSE I LOVE YOU   1927
Irving Berlin
Francis, Day & Hunter Ltd. . . . . USA
Melville Gideon . . . . HMV B 2421
Jack Hylton & his Orchestra . . . . HMV B 5161
Gracie Fields . . . . Regal Zonophone MR 1938

BECAUSE I LOVE YOU (SLADE) (see Coz I Love You)

BECAUSE MY BABY DON'T MEAN MAYBE NOW   1929
Walter Donaldson
Keith Prowse Music Publishing Co. Ltd . . . . USA
Paul Whiteman & his Orchestra,
vocal Bing Crosby . . . . Fontana TFE 17061
George Olsen & his Music . . . . HMV B 5518
The Betty Smith Quintet . . . . Decca DFE 6446

BECAUSE OF LOVE   November 1962
Ruth Batchelor / Bob Roberts
Hill & Range Songs (London) Ltd . . . . USA
Film(s): . . . . Girls, Girls, Girls
Billy Fury . . . . Decca F 11508
Elvis Presley . . . . RCA RD 7534
Elvis Presley appeared in *Girls, Girls, Girls.*

BECAUSE OF RAIN   January 1952
Ruth Poll / Bill Harrington / Nat Cole
Magna Music Co. Ltd . . . . USA
Nat 'King' Cole . . . . Capitol CL 13637
Ella Fitzgerald . . . . Brunswick 04866

BECAUSE OF YOU   July 1951
Dudley Wilkinson / Arthur Hammerstein
Dash Music Ltd . . . . USA
Tony Bennett . . . . Columbia DB 2924
Teddy Johnson . . . . Columbia DB 2944
Donna Hightower . . . . Capitol CL 15048
Sammy Davis . . . . Brunswick LAT 8296
Theme song of Tony Bennett.

BECAUSE THE NIGHT   June 1978
Patti Smith / Bruce Springsteen
Intersong Music . . . . USA
Film(s): . . . . That Summer
Patti Smith Group . . . . Arista 181

BECAUSE THEY'RE YOUNG   August 1960
Aaron Schroeder / Wally Gold / Don Costa
Chappell & Co. Ltd . . . . USA
Film(s): . . . . Because They're Young
Duane Eddy (guitar) . . . . London HLW 9162
James Darren . . . . Pye NEP 4404
Duane Eddy appeared in *Because They're Young.*

BECAUSE YOU'RE MINE   November 1952
Nicholas Brodszky / Sammy Cahn
Robbins Music Corporation Ltd . . . . USA
Film(s): . . . . Because You're Mine
Mario Lanza . . . . RCA 1166
Vera Lynn . . . . MGM C 843
Nat 'King' Cole (1953) . . . . Capitol CL 13811
Mario Lanza appeared in *Because You're Mine.*
Nominated for an Academy Award 1952.

BED SITTER   December 1981
David Ball / Marc Almond
Warner Brothers Music . . . . UK
Soft Cell . . . . Some Bizarre BZS 6

BEDS ARE BURNING   May 1989
"Midnight Oil"
Warner Chappell Music . . . . UK
Midnight Oil . . . . Spirit OIL 3

BEDTIME STORY, A   1932
Leo Towers / Harry Leon / Horatio Nicholls
Lawrence Wright Music Co. Ltd. UK
Jack Hylton & his Orchestra . . . . Decca F 3223
Layton & Johnstone . . . . Columbia DB 986

BEEP BEEP   December 1958
Donald Claps / Carl Cicchetti
Planetary Nom (London) Ltd . . . . USA
The Playmates . . . . Columbia DB 4224

BEER BARREL POLKA, THE   1939
Jaromir Vejvoda / Wladimir Timm / Lew Brown
Keith Prowse Music Publishing Co. Ltd. . . . . Czechoslovkia
Show(s): . . . . Yokel Boy
Film(s): . . . . A Night in Casablanca
The Andrews Sisters . . . . Brunswick 02769

Wille Glahe & his Orchestra . . . . **HMV 7EG 8283**
The Andrews Sisters & his Orchestra . . . . **Capitol LCT 6132**
Cyril Stapleton & his Orchestra . . . . **Decca LK 4258**

BEER, BEER, GLORIOUS BEER   1896
Harry Anderson / Steve Leggett / Will Godwin
Francis, Day & Hunter Ltd. . . . . UK
The Kerbstone Serenaders . . . . **Rex 8317**
Leon Cortez & his Costa Pals . . . . **Regal Zonophone MR 3214**
The Tony Osborne Orch & Chorus . . . . . **Parlophone PMC 1127**

BEG STEAL OR BORROW   April 1972
Tony Cole / Graham Hall / Steve Wolfe
Valley Music . . . . UK
The New Seekers . . . . **Polydor 2058201**
United Kingom entry for the 1972 Eurovision Song Contest (Placed 2nd).
Ivor Novello Award.

BEGGAR IN LOVE, A   June 1951
Bob Merrill
Cinephonic Music Co. Ltd. . . . . USA
Guy Mitchell . . . . **Columbia DB 2871**
David Hughes . . . . **HMV B 10104**

BEGIN THE BEGUINE   1939
Cole Porter
Chappell & Co. Ltd. . . . . USA
Show(s): . . . . Jubilee
Film(s): . . . . Broadway Melody of 1940 / Night and Day
Leslie Hutchinson (Hutch) . . . . **Parlophone GEP 8505**
Ambrose Orchestra, vocal Anne Shelton . . . . . . **Decca F 7521**
Artie Shaw & his Orchestra . . . . **RCA RCX 1061**
The Andrews Sisters . . . . **Brunswick 02752**
Bing Crosby . . . . **Brunswick LAT 8053**
The Andrews Sisters . . . . **Capitol LCT 6132**
Julio Inglesias (1981) . . . . **CBS A 1612**
Theme song of Leslie Hutchinson (Hutch).

BEGINNER'S LUCK   1937
George Gershwin / Ira Gershwin
Chappell & Co. Ltd. . . . . USA
Film(s): . . . . Shall We Dance
Fred Astaire . . . . **Brunswick 02424**
Ella Fitzgerald . . . . **HMV CLP 1338**
Fred Astaire appeared in *Shall We Dance*.

BEHIND A PAINTED SMILE   May 1969
George Hunter / Beatrice Verdi
Jobete Music (UK) Ltd. . . . . USA
The Isley Brothers . . . . **Tamla Motown TMG 693**

BEHIND THE GROOVE   July 1980
Teena Marie / Richard Rudolph
Jobete Music (UK) Ltd. . . . . USA
Teena Marie . . . . **Motown TMG 1185**

DEI MIR BIST DU SCHON   1938
Shalom Secunda / Jacob Jacobs / Saul Chaplin / Sammy Cahn
Chappell & Co. Ltd. . . . . USA
Film(s): . . . . Love, Honour and Behave
The Andrews Sisters . . . . **Brunswick LA 8728**
June Christy . . . . **Capitol T 1006**
The Andrews Sisters . . . . **Capitol LCT 6132**
Nina & Frederik . . . . **Columbia SEG 7997**
Louis Prima & Keely Smith . . . . **London HAD 2243**
Theme song of The Andrews Sisters.

BEING BOILED   January 1982
Philip Oakey / Martyn Wave / Ian Marsh
Virgin Music . . . . UK
Human League . . . . **EMI FAST 4**

BEING WITH YOU   June 1981
W.S. Robinson
Jobete Music . . . . USA
Smokey Robinson . . . . **Motown TMG 1223**

BELFAST   December 1977
Drafi Deutscher / Joe Meke / Jimmy Billsbury
A.T.V. Music Ltd. . . . . Germany
Boney M . . . . **Atlantic K 11020**

BELFAST CHILD   March 1989
Traditional, arranged by the group "Simple Minds"

Virgin Music . . . . UK
Simple Minds . . . . **Virgin SMXT 3**
Originally an Irish song called 'She Moved Through the Fair'.

BELIEVE IN ME (Sur Ma Vie)   September 1956
Charles Aznavour / Geoffrey Parsons / John Turner
Macmelodies Ltd. . . . . France
Robert Earl . . . . **Philips PB 593**
Charles Aznavour . . . . **London DEP 95014**

BELIEVE IT BELOVED   1935
George Whiting / Nat Schwartz / J.C. Johnson
Sun Music Publishing Co. Ltd . . . . USA
'Fats' Waller & his Rhythm . . . . **HMV DLP 1056**
Phil Green & his Band . . . . **Decca MW 368**
Al Hibbler . . . . **HMV 7EG 8326**

BELL BOTTOM BLUES   March 1954
Hal David / Leon Carr
Michael Reine Music Co. Ltd. . . . . USA
Alma Cogan . . . . **HMV B 10653**
Billie Anthony . . . . **Columbia DB 3446**

BELL BOTTOM TROUSERS   1945
Moe Jaffe
Campbell Connelly & Co. Ltd. . . . . USA
Jack Payne & his Orchestra . . . . **HMV BD 5897**
Mitch Miller & the Gang . . . . **Philips BBL 7258**

BELLA MUSICA   September 1952
Marc Fontenoy / George Koger / Geoffrey Parsons
Peter Maurice Music Co. Ltd . . . . France
Anne Shelton . . . . **Decca F 9962**
Dinah Shore . . . . **HMV 7M 119**

BELLE OF THE BALL   February 1952
Leroy Anderson
Mills Music Ltd . . . . USA
Leroy Anderson & his Orchestra . . . . **Brunswick OE 9021**
The Boston Promenade Orchestra . . . . **HMV DLP 1142**
David Hughes . . . . **Philips PB 101**

BELLE, BELLE, MY LIBERTY BELLE   September 1951
Bob Merrill
Dash Music Ltd . . . . USA
Guy Mitchell . . . . **Philips BBL 7265**

BELLS ACROSS THE MEADOW   1924
Albert Ketelbey
Keith Prowse Music Publishing Co. Ltd. . . . . UK
Albert Ketelbey & his Concert Orchestra . . . . . **Columbia 9410**
The New Symphony Orchestra,
conductor Stanford Robinson . . . . **Decca LK 4080**

BELLS OF ST. MARY'S, THE   1917
A. Emmett Adams / Douglas Furber
Ascherberg, Hopwood & Crew Ltd. . . . . UK
Film(s): . . . . The Bells of St. Mary's
Ruby Heyl . . . . **HMV C 785**
The Unity Quartette . . . . **Columbia 2885**
Bing Crosby . . . . **Brunswick Bing 9**
Gordon MacRae . . . . **Capitol T 1251**
Bing Crosby appeared in *The Bells of St. Mary's*.

BELOVED BE FAITHFUL   December 1950
Ervin Drake / Jimmy Shirl
Pickwick Music Ltd . . . . USA
Teddy Johnson . . . . **Columbia DB 2759**
Russ Morgan & his Orchestra . . . . **Brunswick 04540**

BEN   December 1972
Don Black / Walter Sharp
Jobete Music (UK) Ltd. . . . . USA
Film(s): . . . . Ben
Michael Jackson . . . . **Tamla Motown TMG 834**
Marti Webb . . . . **Starblend STAR 6**
Nominated for an Academy Award 1972.

BENCH IN A PARK, A   1931
Jack Yellen / Milton Ager
Lawrence Wright Music Co. Ltd . . . . USA
Film(s): . . . . The King of Jazz
Paul Whiteman & his Orchestra,
vocal The Rhythm Boys . . . . **Columbia CB 86**
Harry Hudson's Melody Men . . . . **Edison 1360**

Ambrose & his Orchestra . . . . HMV B 5842
Paul Whiteman Orchestra & The Rhythm Boys appeared in *The King of Jazz*.

BEND IT   October 1966
Ken Howard / Alan Blaikley
Lynn Music Ltd. . . . . UK
Dave Dee, Dozy, Beaky, Mick & Tich . . . . Fontana TF 711

BEND ME SHAPE ME   March 1968
Scott English / Laurence Weiss
Carlin Music Corporation . . . . USA
Amen Corner . . . . Deram DM 172

BENEATH THE LIGHTS OF HOME   1941
Bernie Grossman / Walter Jurmann
B. Feldman & Co. Ltd . . . . USA
Film(s): . . . . Nice Girl
Deanna Durbin . . . . Brunswick 03201
Geraldo & his Orchestra,
vocal Dorothy Carless . . . . Parlophone F 1847
The Beverley Sisters . . . . Columbia 33SX 1285
Deanna Durbin appeared in *Nice Girl*.

BERNADETTE   April 1967
Brian Holland / Eddie Holland / Lamont Dozier
Carlin Music Corporation . . . . USA
The Four Tops . . . . Tamla Motown TMG 601

BERNADINE   September 1957
Johnny Mercer
Essex Music Ltd. . . . . USA
Film(s): . . . . Bernadine
Pat Boone . . . . London HAD 2098
Pat Boone appeared in *Bernadine*.

BESAME MUCHO (Kiss Me)   1944
Consuelo Velasquez / Sunny Skylar
Southern Music Publishing Co. Ltd. . . . . Mexico
Film(s): . . . . Follow the Boys
Jimmy Dorsey & his Orchestra,
vocal Bob Eberly & Kitty Kallen . . . . Brunswick 03495
Eydie Gormé & Steve Lawrence . . . . Vogue LVA 9086
Connie Francis . . . . MGM C 836

BESIDE A BABBLING BROOK   1923
Walter Donaldson / Gus Kahn
Francis, Day & Hunter Ltd . . . . USA
The Great White Way Orchestra . . . . HMV B 1676

BESIDE MY CARAVAN   1934
Karel Vacek / Jimmy Kennedy
B. Feldman & Co. Ltd. . . . . UK
Roy Fox & his Orchestra, vocal Denny Dennis . . . Decca F 3964

BESS YOU IS MY WOMAN NOW   1935
George Gershwin / Ira Gershwin
Chappell & Co. Ltd . . . . USA
Show(s): . . . . Porgy and Bess
Film(s): . . . . Porgy and Bess
Todd Duncan & Anne Brown . . . . Brunswick LAT 8021
Lawrence Tibbett & Helen Jepson . . . . HMV DB 3392
Sound Track recording of *Porgy and Bess* . . . Philips ABL 3282
Todd Duncan & Anne Brown appeared in the American production of *Porgy and Bess*.

BEST, THE   October 1989
Holly Knight / Mike Chapman
Zomba Music . . . . UK
Tina Turner . . . . Capitol CL 543

BEST OF ALL   December 1949
Ray Sonin / Wally Dewar
Campbell Connelly & Co. Ltd . . . . UK
Steve Connelly . . . . Columbia DB 2616

BEST OF ME, THE   June 1989
Jeremy Lubbox / Richard Marx / David Foster
Warner Chappell Music . . . . USA
Cliff Richard . . . . EMI EM 92

BEST OF MY LOVE, THE   October 1977
Maurice White / Al McKay
Carlin Music Corporation . . . . USA
The Emotions . . . . CBS 5555

BEST THING THAT EVER HAPPENED TO ME, THE   August 1975
Jim Weatherly
Ardmore & Beechwood Ltd . . . . USA
Gladys Knight & the Pips . . . . Buddah BDS 432

BEST THINGS IN LIFE ARE FREE, THE   1928
Buddy De Sylva / Lew Brown / Ray Henderson
Chappell & Co. Ltd. . . . . USA
Show(s): . . . . Good News
Film(s): . . . . Good News / The Best Things in Life are Free
Jack Smith . . . . HMV B 2766
Ambrose & his Orchestra . . . . Brunswick LAT 8267
Al Jolson . . . . Brunswick LAT 8267
June Allyson & Peter Lawford . . . . MGM 167
June Allyson & Peter Lawford appeared in the 1947 film of *Good News*.

BEST YEARS OF OUR LIVES   January 1983
David Jaymes / Geoffrey Rozelaar
April Music Ltd . . . . UK
Modern Romance . . . . WEA ROM 1

BETCHA BY GOLLY WOW   August 1972
Thomas Bell / Linda Creed
Carlin Music Corporation . . . . USA
The Stylistics . . . . Avco 6105011

BETTE DAVIS EYES   May 1981
Donna Weiss / Jackie De Shannon
Plain & Simple Music . . . . USA
Kim Carnes . . . . EMI EA 121

BETTER LOVE NEXT TIME   February 1980
Steve Pippen / Larry Keith / Johnny Slate
Sunbury Music Ltd . . . . USA
Dr Hook . . . . Capitol CL 16112

BETTER NOT ROLL THOSE BLUE BLUE EYES   1943
Al Goodhart / Kay Twomey
Sterling Music Publishing Co. Ltd . . . . USA
Film(s): . . . . Johnny Doughboy
Carroll Gibbons & his Orchestra,
vocal Carroll Gibbons . . . . Columbia FB 2945

BETTER THE DEVIL YOU KNOW   June 1990
Mike Stock / Matt Aitken / Peter Waterman
All Boys Music . . . . UK
Kylie Minogue . . . . PWL PWL 56

BETTY CO-ED   1931
Rudy Vallee / Ed Lockton / J. Paul Fogarty
Keith Prowse Music Publishing Co. Ltd . . . . USA
Rudy Vallee . . . . Capitol LC 6698
Jack Hylton & his Orchestra . . . . HMV B 5987

BETWEEN 18TH AND 19TH ON CHESTNUT STREET   1940
Dick Rogers / Will Osborne
Leeds Music Ltd . . . . USA
Bing Crosby & Connee Boswell . . . . Brunswick LA 8558

BETWEEN THE DEVIL AND THE DEEP BLUE SEA   1936
Ted Koehler / Harold Arlen
Lawrence Wright Music Co. Ltd . . . . USA
Frankie Trumbauer & his Orchestra . . . . . . Columbia DB 5007
Frances Langford . . . . Brunswick 02964
Perry Como . . . . RCA RD 27078
Carmen McRae . . . . Brunswick LAT 8257

BEWITCHED, BOTHERED AND BEWILDERED   1941
Richard Rodgers / Lorenz Hart
Chappell & Co. Ltd . . . . USA
Show(s): . . . . Pal Joey
Film(s): . . . . Pal Joey
Carol Bruce . . . . Philips PB 279
Bill Snyder (piano) (1950) . . . . Parlophone MSP 6005
Doris Day . . . . Philips BBL 7120
Frank Sinatra . . . . Capitol LCT 6148
Ella Fitzgerald . . . . HMV CLP 1117
Carol Bruce appeared in the British production of *Pal Joey*.
Frank Sinatra appeared in the film of *Pal Joey*.
Theme tune of Bill Snyder.

BEYOND THE BLUE HORIZON   1930
Richard A. Whiting / Leo Robin / Franke Harling
Chappell & Co. Ltd . . . . USA

Film(s): . . . . Monte Carlo / Follow the Boys
Jeanette MacDonald . . . . **RCA RCX 1044**
Artie Shaw & his Orchestra . . . . **HMV B 9320**
Jane Morgan . . . . **London HAR 2133**
Jeanette MacDonald appeared in both Monte Carlo *and* Follow The Boys.

BEYOND THE SEA   February 1960
Charles Trenet / Jack Lawrence
Chappell & Co. Ltd . . . . France
Bobby Darin . . . . **London HAE 2172**
See also *La Mer.*

BEYOND THE STARS   March 1955
Annunzio Mantovani / Bunny Lewis
Robbins Music Ltd. . . . . UK
David Whitfield . . . . **Decca F 10458**

BIBBIDI-BOBBIDI-BOO   October 1950
Al Hoffman / Jerry Livingston / Mack David
Walt Disney Music Ltd . . . . USA
Film(s): . . . . Cinderella
Dinah Shore . . . . **Columbia DB 2735**
Sound Track of Cinderella . . . . **Top Rank JKP 2030**
Bing Crosby . . . . **Brunswick 04580**
Betty Woolfe . . . . **HMV 7EG 116**
Nominated for an Academy Award 1950.

BICYCLE RACE   November 1978
Freddie Mercury
EMI Music Ltd . . . . UK
Queen . . . . **EMI 2870**

BICYCLETTES DE BELSIZE   November 1968
Les Reed / Barry Mason
Donna Music Ltd. . . . . UK
Film(s): . . . . Bicyclettes De Belsize
Engelbert Humperdinck . . . . **Decca F 12834**
Les Reed Orchestra . . . . **Polydor 583728**
Joe Loss & his Orchestra . . . . **Columbia SX 6301**
Mantovani Orchestra . . . . **Decca LK 4989**

BIDIN' MY TIME   1932
George Gershwin / Ira Gershwin
Chappell & Co. Ltd. . . . . USA
Show(s): . . . . Girl Crazy
Film(s): . . . . . Girl Crazy / Rhapsody in Blue / The Glenn Miller Story
The Blue Jeans Orchestra . . . . **HMV B 6209**
Dickie Valentine . . . . **Decca DFE 6549**
Ella Fitzgerald . . . . **HMV CLP 1347**

BIG APPLE   October 1983
"Kajagoogoo"
Tritec Music . . . . UK
Kajagoogoo . . . . **EMI 5423**

BIG BAD JOHN   November 1961
Jimmy Dean
Acuff-Rose Publishing Co. Ltd. . . . . USA
Jimmy Dean . . . . **Philips PB 1187**

BIG CITY BLUES   1929
Con Conrad / Sidney Mitchell / Archie Gottler
Campbell Connelly & Co. Ltd . . . . USA
Film(s): . . . . Fox Movietone Follies of 1929
Annette Hanshaw . . . . **Columbia 5425**

BIG EIGHT   May 1973
Ted Lemmon / Alex Hughes
Warner Brothers Music Ltd. . . . . UK
Judge Dread . . . . **Big Shot BI 619**

BIG FUN   January 1988
Lonnie Simmons / Rudy Taylor
Miner Music . . . . UK
The Gap Band . . . . **RCA FB 49779**

BIG FUN   October 1988
James Pennington / Art Forest / Shanna Jackson & Kevin Saunderson
Virgin Music . . . . USA
Inner City . . . . **10 TEN 240**

BIG GIRLS DON'T CRY   February 1963
Bob Crewe / Bob Gaudio
Ardmore & Beechwood Ltd . . . . USA

The Four Seasons . . . . **Brunswick 05882**
The Orlons . . . . **MGM C 972**

BIG HEAD   August 1953
Jack Meadows
Lawrence Wright Music Co. Ltd . . . . UK
Max Bygraves . . . . **HMV B 10546**

BIG HUNK OF LOVE, A   August 1959
Aaron Schroeder / Sid Wyche
Hill & Range Songs (London) Ltd . . . . USA
Elvis Presley . . . . **RCA RD 27159**

BIG IN JAPAN   September 1984
Marian Gold / Frank Mertens / Bernard Lloyd
Warner Brothers Music . . . . Germany
Alphaville . . . . **WEA X 9505**

BIG LOVE   May 1987
Lindsey Buckingham
EMI Music . . . . UK
Fleetwood Mac . . . . **Warner Brothers W 8398**

BIG MAMOU   June 1953
Link Davis
Southern Music Publishing Co. Ltd . . . . USA
Dolores Gray . . . . **Brunswick 05111**
Frank Chacksfield & his Orchestra . . . . **Parlophone R 3702**

BIG MAN   July 1958
Bruce Bellan / Glen Larson
Grosvenor Music Ltd . . . . USA
The Four Preps . . . . **Capitol T 1291**

BIG NOISE FROM WINNETKA   1944
Gil Rodin / Bob Crosby / Ray Bauduc & Bob Haggart
Lafleur & Co. Ltd . . . . USA
Film(s): . . . . Reveille With Beverly / Let's Make Music
Bob Crosby & his Orchestra . . . . **Decca F 7835**
Bob Haggart & Ray Bauduc . . . . **Decca F 7005**
The Gene Krupa Quartet . . . . **Columbia LB 10108**
Kenny Ball & his Jazzmen . . . . **Pye NJL 28**
Bob Haggart, Ray Bauduc & Bob Crosby & his Orchestra appeared in *Reveille with Beverly.*
Bob Crosby & his Orchestra appeared in *Let's Make Music.*

BIG ROCK CANDY MOUNTAIN, THE   November 1949
Traditional
Francis, Day & Hunter Ltd . . . . USA
Burl Ives . . . . **Brunswick LAT 8048**

BIG SEVEN   January 1973
Ted Lemmon / Alex Hughes
Warner Brothers Music Ltd. . . . . UK
Judge Dread . . . . **Big Shot BI 613**

BIG SHIP   June 1969
Raymond Froggatt
Edwin H. Morris & Co. Ltd. . . . . USA
Cliff Richard . . . . **Columbia DB 8581**

BIG SIX   October 1972
Alex Hughes / Alvin Ranglin
Warner Brothers Music Ltd. . . . . UK
Judge Dread . . . . **Big Shot BI 608**

BIG SPENDER   December 1967
Dorothy Fields / Cy Coleman
Campbell, Connelly & Co. Ltd. . . . . USA
Show(s): . . . . Sweet Charity
Film(s): . . . . Sweet Charity
Helen Gallagher & Thelma Oliver . . . . **Columbia KOL 6500**
Josephine Blake & Paula Kelly . . . . **CBS BRG 70035**
Chorus & Orchestra (Soundtrack) . . . . **MCA MUCS 133**
Peggy Lee . . . . **Capitol CL 15512**
Shirley Bassey . . . . **United Artists ULP 1160**
Helen Gallagher & Thelma Oliver appeared in the American production of *Sweet Charity.*
Josephine Baker & Paula Kelly appeared in the British production of *Sweet Charity.*

BIG TEN   October 1975
Ted Lemmon / Alex Hughes
Warner Brothers Music Ltd . . . . UK
Judge Dread . . . . **Cactus CT 77**

BIG YELLOW TAXI   August 1970
Joni Mitchell
Warner Brothers Music Ltd. . . . . USA
Joni Mitchell . . . . **Reprise RS 20906**

BIGGEST ASPIDISTRA IN THE WORLD, THE   1938
Jimmy Harper / Will Haines / Tommie Connor
Cameo Music Publishing Co. . . . . UK
Gracie Fields . . . . **Regal Zonophone MR 2889**
Gracie Fields . . . . **Ace of Clubs ACL 1042**

BILL   1928
Jerome Kern / Oscar Hammerstein II / P.G. Wodehouse
Chappell & Co. Ltd. . . . . USA
Show(s): . . . . Show Boat
Film(s): . . . Show Boat / The Man I Love / Both Ends of the Candle
Helen Morgan . . . . **HMV BD 343**
Marie Burke . . . . **Columbia 9427**
Ava Gardner . . . . **MGM D 104**
Gogi Grant . . . . **RCA RD 27054**
Helen Morgan appeared in the American production of *Show Boat*
and the 1929 and 1936 films of *Show Boat*.
Marie Burke appeared in the British production of *Show Boat*.
Ava Gardner appeared in the 1951 film of *Show Boat*.
Gogi Grant dubbed the singing voice of Ann Blyth who appeared in
the film *Both Ends of the Candle*.
Theme song of Helen Morgan.

BILLIE JEAN   March 1983
Michael Jackson
Carlin Music . . . . USA
Michael Jackson . . . . **Epic EPC 3083**

BILLY DON'T BE A HERO   April 1974
Mitch Murray / Peter Callander
Intune Ltd. . . . . UK
Paper Lace . . . . **Bus Stop BUS 1014**
Ivor Novello Nomination.

BILLY MUGGINS   1906
Charles Ridgewell
Francis, Day & Hunter Ltd. . . . . UK
Harry Dainton Orchestra . . . . **Columbia DX 8399**

BIMBO   May 1954
Rodney Morris
Macmelodies Ltd . . . . USA
Jim Reeves . . . . **London HL 8014**
Ruby Wright . . . . **Parlophone R 3816**
Suzi Miller & The Stargazers . . . . **Decca F 10264**

BIMBO, EL   August 1975
Claude Morgan
Burlington Music Co. Ltd . . . . France
Bimbo Jet . . . . **EMI 2317**

BIMINI BAY   1922
Richard A. Whiting / Gus Kahn / Raymond Egan
B. Feldman & Co. Ltd . . . . USA
The Benson Orchestra of Chicago . . . . **HMV B 1309**

BIRD DOG   December 1959
Boudleaux Bryant
Acuff-Rose Publishing Co. Ltd . . . . USA
The Everly Brothers . . . . **London HAA 2266**

BIRD IN A GILDED CAGE, A   1899
Harry Von Tilzer / Arthur Lamb
B. Feldman & Co. Ltd. . . . . USA
Film(s): . . . . Ringside Maisie
Maurice J. Gunsky . . . . **Zonophone Twin 5336**
Marie Kendall . . . . **Decca F 5169**
Virginia O'Brien . . . . **Brunswick 04234**
Dennis Bowen . . . . **Piccadilly NPL 38002**

BIRD OF PARADISE   January 1984
Terry White
White Flames Music . . . . UK
Snowy White . . . . **Towerbell TOW 42**

BIRD ON THE WING   1936
Jimmy Kennedy / Will Grosz
Peter Maurice Music Co. Ltd . . . . UK
Greta Keller . . . . **Decca F 5863**

BIRD SONGS AT EVENTIDE   1926
Eric Coates / Royden Barry
Chappell & Co. Ltd. . . . . UK
John McCormack . . . . **HMV DA 973**
The Golden Guinea Concert Orchestra . . . . . . **Pye GGL 0063**

BIRDHOUSE IN YOUR SOUL   April 1990
John Flansburgh / John Linnell
Intersong Music . . . . USA
They Might Be Giants . . . . **Elektra EKR 104**

BIRDIE SONG, THE   October 1981
Werne Thomas / Terrence Rendell
Valentine Music . . . . Belgium
The Tweets . . . . **PRT 7P 219**

BIRDS AND THE BEES, THE   July 1956
Mack David / Harry Warren
Chappell & Co. Ltd. . . . . USA
Film(s): . . . . The Birds and the Bees
Alma Cogan . . . . **HMV POP 223**
Ruth Adams & Loulie Jean Normon . . . . **MGM 908**
Dave King . . . . **Decca F 10741**

BIRTH OF THE BLUES, THE   1927
Buddy De Sylva / Lew Brown / Ray Henderson
Chappell & Co. Ltd. . . . . USA
Show(s): George White's Scandals / One Damn Thing After Another
Film(s):Birth of the Blues / Painting the Clouds with Sunshine / The
Best Things in Life are Free
Edith Baker (piano) . . . . **Columbia 9217**
Leo Reisman & his Orchestra . . . . **Columbia 4392**
Harry Richman . . . . **Brunswick 03944**
Bing Crosby (1942) with Jack
Teagarden & his Orchestra . . . . **Brunswick BING 6**
Shirley Bassey . . . . **Philips BBR 8130**
Perry Como . . . . **RCA RD 27078**
Gordon MacRae . . . . **Capitol LCT 6119**
Edith Baker appeared in *One Damn Thing After Another*.
Harry Richman appeared in *George White's Scandals*.
Bing Crosby & Jack Teagarden appeared in *Birth of the Blues*.
Gordon MacRae appeared in *The Best Things in Life are Free*

BITS AND PIECES   March 1964
Dave Clark / Mike Smith
Ardmore & Beechwood Ltd . . . . UK
The Dave Clark Five . . . . **Columbia DB 7210**

BITTEREST PILL, THE   September 1982
Paul Weller
Morrison Leahy Music . . . . UK
The Jam . . . . **Polydor POSP 505**

BLACK AND WHITE   August 1971
Dave Arkin / Earl Robinson
Durham Music . . . . USA
Greyhound . . . . **Trojan TR 7820**

BLACK AND WHITE RAG   1911
George Botsford
Francis, Day & Hunter Ltd. . . . . USA
Piano Roll Recording (1908) . . . . **Riverside RLP 12-110**
Lawrence Coates (Xylophone) . . . . **Columbia 2025**
Winifred Atwell (1951) . . . . **Ace of Clubs ACL 1005**
Joe 'Fingers' Carr . . . . **Capitol T 760**

BLACK BETTY   October 1977
Traditional, arranged by Huddie Leadbetter
Kensington Music Ltd . . . . USA
Ram Jam . . . . **Epic EPC 5492**
Leadbelly (Huddie Leadbetter) . . . . . . **Melodisc MLP 515**

BLACK BOTTOM, THE   1926
Buddy De Sylva / Lew Brown / Ray Henderson
Chappell & Co. Ltd. . . . . USA
Show(s): . . . . George White's Scandals
Film(s): . . . . A Star is Born
The Denza Dance Band . . . . **Columbia 4153**
Johnny Hamp's Kentucky Serenaders . . . . **HMV B 5173**
Eddie Condon & his Orchestra . . . . **Brunswick 04571**
Judy Garland . . . . **Philips BBL 7007**
Judy Garland appeared in *A Star is Born*.

BLACK HILLS OF DAKOTA, THE   June 1954
Sammy Fain / Paul Francis Webster

Campbell Connelly & Co. Ltd. . . . . USA
Film(s): . . . . Calamity Jane
Doris Day . . . . **Philips BBL 7297**
Doris Day appeared in *Calamity Jane.*

BLACK IS BLACK   August 1966
Steve Wadey / Tony Hayes / Michael Grainger
Robert Mellin Ltd. . . . . UK
Los Bravos . . . . **Decca F 22419**
La Belle Epoque (1977) . . . . **Harvest HAR 5133**

BLACK MOONLIGHT   1933
Sam Coslow / Arthur Johnston
Victoria Music Co. Ltd. . . . . USA
Film(s): . . . . Too Much Harmony
Bing Crosby . . . . **Fontana TFR 6006**
Perry Como . . . . **RCA RCX 136**
Bing Crosby appeared in *Too Much Harmony.*

BLACK NIGHT   October 1970
"Deep Purple"
Hec Music . . . . UK
Deep Purple . . . . **Harvest HAR 5020**

BLACK PEARL   October 1970
Phil Spector / Toni Wine / Irwin Levine
Rondor Music (London) Ltd . . . . USA
Horace Faith . . . . **Trojan TR 7790**

BLACK SKIN BLUE EYED BOY   January 1971
Edmond Grant
Edward Kassner Music Co. Ltd . . . . UK
The Equals . . . . **President PT 325**

BLACK SUPERMAN (Muhammed Ali)   February 1975
John Wakelin
Francis, Day & Hunter Ltd . . . . UK
Johnny Wakelin & The Kinshasa Band . . . . **Pye 7N 45420**

BLACK VELVET   May 1990
Christopher Ward / David Tyson
Zomba Music . . . . Canada
Alannah Myles . . . . **Atlantic A 8742**

BLACK VELVET BAND, THE   October 1967
Traditional
This edition by Solomon Music . . . . UK
The Dubliners . . . . **Major Minor MM 530**

BLACK-EYED BOYS, THE   September 1974
Mitch Murray / Peter Callander
Intune Music . . . . UK
Paper Lace . . . . **Bus Stop BUS 1019**

BLACKBERRY WAY   February 1969
Roy Wood
Essex Music Ltd. . . . . UK
The Move . . . . **Regal Zonophone RZ 3015**

BLACKSMITH BLUES, THE   May 1952
Jack Holmes
Chappell & Co. Ltd . . . . USA
Ella Mae Morse . . . . **Capitol CL 13727**
Ted Heath & his Music, vocal Lita Roza . . . . **Decca LF 1187**
Sy Oliver & his Orchestra,
vocal Trudy Richards . . . . **Brunswick 04906**
The Ira Ironstrings Dance Band . . . . **Warner Brothers WM 4011**

BLAME IT ON THE BOOGIE   November 1978
Mick Jackson / Dave Jackson / Elmar Krohn
Carlin Music Corporation . . . . USA
Michael Jackson . . . . **Atlantic K 11102**
The Jacksons . . . . **Epic EPC 6683**
Big Fun (1989) . . . . **Jive JIVE 217**

BLAME IT ON THE PONY EXPRESS   January 1971
Tony Macaulay / Roger Greenaway / Roger Cook
Mustard Music . . . . UK
Johnny Johnson & The Bandwagon . . . . **Bell BLL 1128**

BLANKET ON THE GROUND   September 1975
Roger Bowling
Campbell Connelly & Co. Ltd . . . . USA
Film(s): . . . . Convoy
Billie Jo Spears . . . . **United Artists UP 35805**

Billie Jo Spears . . . . **Capitol EST 24590**
Billie Jo Spears appeared in *Convoy*

BLAZE AWAY   1901
Abe Holzmann
B. Feldman & Co. Ltd. . . . . USA
St. Hilda's Colliery Prize Band . . . . **Regal G 7485**
The Royal Marines Band,
conducted by Lt. Col. F. Vivian Dunn . . . . **HMV 7EG 8686**

BLESS 'EM ALL   1941
Jimmy Hughes / Frank Lake
Keith Prowse Music Publishing Co. Ltd . . . . UK
The R.A.F. Band & chorus . . . . **HMV RAF 9**
Bertha Wilmot . . . . **Decca F 7692**
The Henry Hall Dance Orchestra,
vocal The Coronets . . . . **Columbia 33SX 1067**

BLESS THIS HOUSE   1927
Helen Taylor / May Brahe
Boosey & Hawkes Music Publishers Ltd. . . . . UK
Essie Ackland . . . . **HMV B 4439**
John McCormack . . . . **HMV DA 1285**
The Kentucky Minstrels . . . . **HMV BD 761**
Gracie Fields . . . . **Decca LF 1080**

BLESS YORE BEAUTIFUL HIDE   March 1955
Johnny Mercer / Gene De Paul
Robbins Music Corporation Ltd. . . . . USA
Film(s): . . . . Seven Brides for Seven Brothers
Howard Keel . . . . **MGM D 146**
Howard Keel appeared in *Seven Brides for Seven Brothers.*

BLESS YOU   1946
Eddie Lane / Don Baker
Noel Gay Music Co. Ltd. . . . . USA
The Ink Spots . . . . **Brunswick 03040**
Glenn Miller & his Orchestra, vocal Ray Eberle . **HMV DLP 1145**
Jan Holland . . . . **Parlophone R 4810**

BLESS YOU   October 1961
Barry Mann / Cynthia Weil
Nevins-Kirshner Ltd. . . . . USA
Gary Mills . . . . **Decca F 11383**
Tony Orlando . . . . **Fontana H 330**

BLIND PLOUGHMAN, THE   1913
Marguerite Radclyffe-Hall / R. Coningsby-Clarke
Chappell & Co. Ltd . . . . UK
Benjamin Luxon . . . . **Argo ZFB 96**
Ester Ackland . . . . **Regal T 5717**
Nelson Eddy . . . . **Columbia DB 2114**
Roy Henderson . . . . **Decca F 1987**

BLIND VISION   May 1983
Neil Arthur / Steven Luscombe
Cherry Red Music . . . . UK
Blancmange . . . . **London BLANC 5**

BLINDED BY THE LIGHT   October 1976
Bruce Springsteen
Intersong Music . . . . USA
Manfred Mann's Earthband . . . . **Bronze BRO 29**

BLOCKBUSTER   February 1973
Mike Chapman / Nicky Chinn
Chinnichap Music . . . . UK
The Sweet . . . . **RCA 2305**
Ivor Novello Nomination.

BLOODNOKS ROCK 'N' ROLL   October 1956
Spike Milligan / Pat Dixon
Unknown Publisher . . . . UK
The Goons . . . . **Decca F 10780**

BLOOP BLEEP   1947
Frank Loesser
Chappell & Co. Ltd. . . . . USA
Danny Kaye . . . . **Brunswick 03812**

BLOSSOM FELL, A   February 1955
Howard Barnes / Harold Cornelius / Dominic John
John Fields Music Co. Ltd. . . . . UK
Dickie Valentine . . . . **Decca LF 1211**
Nat 'King' Cole . . . . **Capitol T 954**

| Vera Lynn | Decca LK 4120 |
| Patti Page | Mercury MMC 14013 |

Ivor Novello Nomination.

BLOW THE HOUSE DOWN — March 1989
Albert Hammond / Marcus Vere

| Empire Music | UK |
| **Living In A Box** | **Chrysalis LIB 5** |

BLOW, GABRIEL, BLOW — 1935
Cole Porter / Ira Gershwin

Chappell & Co. Ltd	USA
Show(s):	Anything Goes
Film(s):	Anything Goes
Ethel Merman	**Brunswick LA 8636**
Jeanne Aubert & The Four Admirals	**Columbia DX 698**
Bing Crosby, Mitzi Gaynor, Donald O'Connor & Jeanmaire	**Brunswick Bing 15**
Chris Connor	**London LTZK 15151**
Ethel Merman	**Reprise R 6032**

Ethel Merman appeared in both the American production and the 1936 film of *Anything Goes*. Jeanne Aubert & The Four Admirals appeared in the British production of *Anything Goes*.

BLOWING IN THE WIND — November 1963
Bob Dylan

Blossom Music Ltd	USA
Peter, Paul & Mary	**Warner Brothers WB 104**
Nina & Frederik	**Columbia 33SX 1683**
Jackie De Shannon	**Liberty LBY 1182**

BLOWING WILD — February 1954
Paul Francis Webster / Dimitri Tiomkin

Campbell Connelly & Co. Ltd	USA
Film(s):	Blowing Wild
Frankie Laine	**Philips PB 207**

BLUE — 1922
Grant Clarke / Edgar Leslie / Lou Handman

Francis, Day & Hunter Ltd	USA
The Virginians	**HMV B 1408**
Lionel Hampton & his Orchestra, vocal Nat 'King' Cole	**HMV B 9137**
The Jonah Jones Quartet	**Capitol T 1405**

BLUE AGAIN — 1931
Dorothy Fields / Jimmy McHugh

Keith Prowse Music Publishing Co. Ltd	USA
Show(s):	The Vanderbilt Revue
Leslie Hutchinson (Hutch)	**Parlophone R 897**
Louis Armstrong & his Orchestra	**Parlophone R 2365**
Alma Cogan	**HMV B 10929**
Molly Bee	**Capitol T 1097**

BLUE ANGEL — January 1961
Roy Orbison / Joe Melson

| Acuff-Rose Publishing Co. Ltd | USA |
| **Roy Orbison** | **London HL 9207** |

BLUE BAYOU — October 1963
Roy Orbison / Joe Melson

| Acuff-Rose Publishing Co. Ltd | USA |
| **Roy Orbison** | **London HL 9777** |

BLUE BELL POLKA — July 1952
F. Stanley

Essex Music Ltd.	UK
Jimmy Shand & his Band	**Parlophone PMC 1144**
Alma Cogan	**HMV 7EG 8169**

BLUE BELLS OF BROADWAY, THE — June 1954
Sammy Fain / Paul Francis Webster

Campbell Connelly & Co. Ltd.	USA
Film(s):	Lucky Me
Doris Day	**Philips PB 295**
Jean Campbell	**Columbia 33SX 1271**

Doris Day appeared in *Lucky Me*.

BLUE EYES — 1916
Horatio Nicholls / Fred Godfrey

Lawrence Wright Music Co. Ltd.	UK
Dorothy Ward	**Regal G 7170**
The Debroy Somers Band, conducted by Horatio Nicholls	**Columbia DX 673**
Harry Davidson & his Orchestra	**Columbia SCD 2033**

BLUE EYES — July 1968
Richard Kerr / Joan Maitland

| Essex Music Ltd. | UK |
| **Don Partridge** | **Columbia DB 8416** |

BLUE EYES — April 1982
Elton John / Gary Osborne

| Big Pig Music | UK |
| **Elton John** | **Rocket XPRES 71** |

BLUE GUITAR — November 1975
Justin Hayward

| Justunes Ltd | UK |
| **Justin Hayward & John Lodge** | **Threshold TH 21** |

BLUE HAWAII — 1937
Leo Robin / Ralph Rainger

Victoria Music Co. Ltd.	USA
Film(s):	Waikiki Wedding / Blue Hawaii
Bing Crosby	**Brunswick Bing 3**
Andy Williams	**London HAA 2203**
Elvis Presley	**RCA RD 27238**

Bing Crosby appeared in *Waikiki Wedding*.
Elvis Presley appeared in *Blue Hawaii*.

BLUE IS THE COLOUR — March 1972
Daniel Boone / Rod McQueen

| Sterling Music Publishing Co. Ltd | UK |
| **The Chelsea Football Team** | **Penny Farthing PEN 782** |

BLUE JEAN — October 1984
David Bowie

| EMI Music | UK |
| **David Bowie** | **EMI EA 181** |

BLUE MOMENTS (Without You Dear) — 1933
Morey Davidson / Art Berman / Buddy Fields

Dash Music Ltd.	USA
Roy Fox & his Orchestra	**Decca F 3768**
Layton & Johnstone	**Columbia DB 1253**

BLUE MONDAY — May 1983
Stephen Morris / Peter Hook / Bernard Dicken & Gillian Gilbert

Warner Chappell Music	UK
New Order	**Factory FAC 73**
New Order (1988)	**Factory FAC 73R**

BLUE MOON — 1935
Richard Rodgers / Lorenz Hart

| Robbins Music Corporation Ltd | USA |

Film(s):Words and Music / With a Song in My Heart / Torch Song / This Could be the Night / Kiss Them for Me / Grease

Layton & Johnstone	**Columbia DB 1530**
Frances Langford	**Brunswick 02961**
Mel Tormé	**Capitol CL 13123**
Jane Froman	**Capitol CL 13719**
Elvis Presley	**RCA RD 27128**
Rosemary Clooney	**Vogue LVA 9112**
Ray Anthony & his Orchestra	**MGM C 761**
The Marcels (1961)	**Pye 7N 25073**
Sha Na Na	**RSO 2479-210**

Mel Tormé appeared in *Words and Music*.
Ray Anthony Orchestra appeared in *This Could be the Night*.
Sha Na Na appeared in *Grease*.
Jane Froman dubbed the singing voice of Susan Hayward who appeared in the film *With a Song in My Heart*.

BLUE PACIFIC MOONLIGHT — 1930
Jack Payne / Wallace Herbert

Campbell Connelly & Co. Ltd.	UK
George Metaxa	**HMV B 3549**
Jack Payne & The BBC Dance Orchestra	**Columbia CB 76**
Jack Payne & his Orchestra	**HMV CLP 1160**

BLUE PRELUDE — 1933
Gordon Jenkins / Joe Bishop

Chappell & Co. Ltd.	USA
Bing Crosby	**Fontana TFR 6000**
Isham Jones & his Orchestra	**HMV B 4980**
Woody Herman & his Orchestra	**Brunswick 03048**
Judy Garland	**Capitol LCT 6136**

Theme song of Woody Herman.

BLUE RIBBON GAL — July 1949
Irwin Dash / Ross Parker

Dash Music Ltd . . . . UK
The Radio Revellers . . . . **Columbia FB 3504**
Peter Lind Hayes . . . . **Brunswick 04421**

BLUE ROOM, THE   1927
Richard Rodgers / Lorenz Hart
Chappell & Co. Ltd. . . . . USA
Show(s): . . . . The Girl Friend
Film(s): . . . . Words and Music / The Eddy Duchin Story
Melville Gideon . . . . **HMV B 2538**
The Revellers . . . . **HMV B 2541**
Hildegarde . . . . **Decca F 7754**
Layton & Johnstone . . . . **Columbia 4565**
Ella Fitzgerald . . . . **HMV CLP 1117**
Eydie Gormé & Steve Lawrence . . . . **HMV CLP 1463**

BLUE SAVANNAH   March 1990
Vincent Clarke / Andrew Bell
Sonet Music . . . . UK
Erasure . . . . **Mute MUTE 109**
Ivor Novello Award.

BLUE SHADOWS AND WHITE GARDENIAS   1942
Harry Owens / Mack Gordon
Bregman, Vocco & Conn Ltd . . . . USA
Film(s): . . . . Song of the Islands
Bing Crosby . . . . **Brunswick 03355**

BLUE SKIES   1927
Irving Berlin
Francis, Day & Hunter Ltd. . . . . USA
Show(s): . . . . .Betsy / Blue Skies
Film(s):The Jazz Singer / Glorifying the American Girl / Alexander's
Ragtime Band / Blue Skies / White Christmas
Jack Smith . . . . **HMV B 2494**
The Savoy Havana Band . . . . **HMV B 5220**
Bing Crosby . . . . **Brunswick Bing 10**
Benny Goodman & his Orchestra,
vocal Art Lund . . . . **Parlophone R 3018**
Bing Crosby & Danny Kaye . . . . **Brunswick LAT 8044**
Brook Benton . . . . **Mercury MMC 14022**
Jack Smith appeared in the show *Blue Skies*.
Bing Crosby appeared in the film *Blue Skies* and also in *White Christmas*.
Danny Kaye appeared in *White Christmas*.

BLUE SKIES ARE ROUND THE CORNER   1939
Hugh Charles / Ross Parker
Dash Music Ltd. . . . . UK
Ambrose & his Orchestra, vocal Denny Dennis . **Decca F 6914**
Jack Hylton & his Orchestra . . . . **HMV BD 5446**
Ross Parker & Hugh Charles . . . . **Decca F 7356**

BLUE STAR (The Medic Theme)   August 1955
Victor Young / Edward Hoyman
Chappell & Co. Ltd. . . . . USA
Cyril Stapleton & his Orch, vocal Julie Dawn . . **Decca LF 1265**
Eve Boswell . . . . **Parlophone R 4082**
Victor Young & his Singing Strings . . . . . **Brunswick LAT 8283**

BLUE SUEDE SHOES   May 1956
Carl Perkins
Aberbach (London) Ltd. . . . . USA
Film(s): . . . . G.I. Blues
Elvis Presley . . . . **RCA RD 27192**
Carl Perkins . . . . **London HAS 2202**
Elvis Presley appeared in *G.I. Blues*.

BLUE TANGO   February 1952
Leroy Anderson
Mills Music Ltd . . . . USA
Leroy Anderson & his Orchestra . . . . **Brunswick LAT 8337**
Johnny Gregory & his Orchestra . . . . **Fontana TFL 5090**
Ray Martin Orchestra . . . . **Columbia DB 3051**

BLUE TURNING GREY OVER YOU   1937
Andy Razaf / Thomas Waller
Lawrence Wright Music Co. Ltd. . . . . USA
'Fats' Waller & his Rhythm . . . . **HMV DLP 1017**
Frankie Laine . . . . **Philips BBL 7155**

BLUE TURNS TO GREY   April 1966
Mick Jagger / Keith Richard
Kags Music Ltd. . . . . UK

Cliff Richard . . . . **Columbia DB 7866**

BLUE VELVET   October 1990
Bernie Wayne / Lee Morris
Chappell & Co. . . . . USA
Bobby Vinton . . . . **Epic 6505240**
Originaly published 1951.

BLUEBELL   1904
Edward Madden / Theodore Morse
Francis, Day & Hunter Ltd. . . . . USA
Film(s): . . . . The Jolson Story
Alf Gordon . . . . **Nicole 4332**
The Empire Military Band . . . . **Parlophone R 1648**
Noel Coward . . . . **HMV C 2431**
Merle Travis (Guitar) . . . . **Capitol EAP 2-650**

BLUEBERRY HILL   1941
Al Lewis / Larry Stock / Vincent Rose
Victoria Music Co. Ltd . . . . USA
Film(s): . . . . The Singing Hill
Gene Autry . . . . **Regal Zonophone MR 3404**
Ambrose & his Orchestra, vocal Anne Shelton . . **Decca F 7671**
'Fats' Domino (1956) . . . . **London HAP 2073**
Louis Armstrong . . . . **London HAR 8190**
Gene Autry appeared in *The Singing Hill*.

BLUES IN THE NIGHT   1942
Harold Arlen / Johnny Mercer
Chappell & Co. Ltd . . . . USA
Film(s): . . . . Birth of the Blues
Bing Crosby . . . . **Brunswick LAT 8138**
Dinah Shore . . . . **Regal Zonophone MR 3642**
Jo Stafford & Johnny Mercer . . . . **Capitol LC 6633**
Bing Crosby appeared in *Blues in the Night*.
Nominated for an Academy Award in 1941.

BLUES MY NAUGHTY SWEETIE GAVE TO ME, THE   1919
Charles McCarron / Carey Morgan / A. Swanstone
Campbell Connelly & Co. Ltd. . . . . USA
Ted Lewis & his Band . . . . **Columbia 4239**
Jimmy Noone's Apex Club Band . . . . **Vogue LRA 10026**
Dinah Shore . . . . **HMV 7EG 8161**
The Clyde Valley Stompers, vocal Fiona Duncan . . **Pye NJL 26**

BO DIDDLEY   July 1963
Elias McDaniel
Good Music Ltd . . . . USA
Bo Diddley . . . . **Pye 7N 25210**
Buddy Holly & The Fireballs . . . . **Coral Q 72463**
Bobby Vee & The Crickets . . . . **Liberty LBY 1086**

BOA NOITE   1941
Harry Warren / Mack Gordon
Francis, Day & Hunter Ltd . . . . USA
Film(s): . . . . That Night In Rio
Tony Martin . . . . **Decca F 7913**
The New Mayfair Dance Orchestra . . . . **HMV BD 5690**

BOAT THAT I ROW, THE   May 1967
Neil Diamond
Ardmore & Beechwood Ltd. . . . . USA
Lulu . . . . **Columbia DB 8169**

BOB WHITE   1937
Johnny Mercer / Bernie Hanighan
B. Feldman & Co. Ltd. . . . . USA
Bing Crosby & Connee Boswell . . . . **Brunswick LA 8558**
Bobby Darin & Johnny Mercer . . . . **London HAK 2363**

BOBBY'S GIRL   November 1962
Henry Hoffman / Gary Klein
Edward Kassner Music Co. Ltd . . . . USA
Susan Maughan . . . . **Philips 326544 BF**
Marcie Blane . . . . **London HLU 9599**

BODY AND SOUL   1930
Johnny Green / Edward Heyman / Robert Sour / Frank Eyton
Chappell & Co. Ltd . . . . USA
Show(s): . . . . .Three's a Crowd
Film(s):The Man I Love / The Eddy Duchin Story / Both Ends of the Candle
Ambrose & his Orchestra, vocal Sam Browne . . **Decca M 118**
Frances Langford . . . . **Brunswick 02963**
Perry Como . . . . **HMV DLP 1026**

Julie London . . . . **London HAU 2083**
Gogi Grant . . . . **RCA RD 27054**
Gogi Grant dubbed the singing voice of Ann Blyth who appeared in the film *Both Ends of the Candle*.

BODY AND SOUL   September 1985
Eric Van Tijn / Jochem Fluitsma
Fader Songs . . . . Holland
Mai Tai . . . . **Virgin VS 801**

BODY ROCK   October 1985
Sylvester La Vay / John Bettis
Warner Brothers Music . . . . USA
Film(s): . . . . Body Rock
Maria Vidal . . . . **EMI EA 189**

BODY TALK   July 1981
Tony Swain / Steve Jolly / Leee John & Ashley Ingram
Red Bus Music . . . . UK
Imagination . . . . **R&B RBS 201**

BOHEMIA   1916
Paul Rubens / Adrian Ross
Chappell & Co. Ltd. . . . . UK
Show(s): . . . . Happy Days
Jose Collins & chorus . . . . **Columbia L 1048**
The Pro Arte Orchestra,
conducted by Stanford Robinson . . . . **Pye CML 33003**
Jose Collins appeared in *Happy Day*.

BOHEMIAN RHAPSODY   January 1976
Freddie Mercury
B. Feldman & Co Ltd . . . . UK
Queen . . . . **EMI 2375**
Ivor Novello Award.

BOILED BEEF AND CARROTS   1909
Charles Collins / Fred Murray
B. Feldman & Co. Ltd. . . . . UK
Harry Champion . . . . **John Bull 40751**
The Two Bills from Bermondsey . . . . **Parlophone R 3953**
Billy Cotton & his Band . . . . **Columbia DB 4555**

BONAPARTE'S RETREAT   August 1950
Pee Wee King
Anglo-Pic Music Co. Ltd . . . . USA
Kay Starr . . . . **Capitol T 950**
Kitty Wells . . . . **Brunswick LAT 8361**

BONNIE CAME BACK   February 1960
Lee Hazlewood / Duane Eddy
Burlington Music Co. Ltd . . . . USA
Duane Eddy (guitar) . . . . **London HAW 2325**
Based on *My Bonnie Lies Over The Ocean*.

BOO HOO   1937
Edward Heyman / Carmen Lombardo / John J. Loeb
Francis, Day & Hunter Ltd. . . . . USA
Wingy Manone & his Orchestra . . . **Regal Zonophone MR 2414**
The Bell Sisters . . . . **HMV B 10294**
Guy Lombardo & his Royal Canadians . . . . . **Capitol LCT 6117**

BOOGIE NIGHTS   March 1977
Rodney Temperton
Rondor Music (London) Ltd . . . . UK
Heatwave . . . . **GTO GT 77**
Ivor Novello Nomination.

BOOGIE ON REGGAE WOMAN   February 1975
Stevie Wonder
Jobete Music (UK) Ltd. . . . . USA
Stevie Wonder . . . . **Tamla Motown TMG 928**

BOOGIE OOGIE OOGIE   August 1978
Janice Johnson / Perry kibble
Carlin Music Corporation . . . . USA
Taste of Honey . . . . **Capitol CL 15988**

BOOGIE WONDERLAND   June 1979
Maurice White / Al McKay
Rondor Music (London) Ltd. . . . . USA
Earth Wind & Fire . . . . **CBS 7292**

BOOGIE WOOGIE   1939
Clarence 'Pinetop' Smith

Herman Darewski Music Publishing Co. Ltd. . . . . USA
Count Basie's Blue Five,
vocal Jimmy Rushing . . . . **Fontana TFL 5064**
'Pinetop' Smith (Piano) . . . . **Vogue LVA 9069**
Tommy Dorsey & his Orchestra . . . . **RCA RCX 1002**
The Clark Sisters . . . . **London HAD 2128**

BOOGIE WOOGIE BUGLE BOY   1941
Don Raye / Hughie Prince
Leeds Music Ltd . . . . USA
Film(s): . . . . Buck Privates / Swingtime Johnny
The Andrews Sisters . . . . **Brunswick 03147**
The Andrews Sisters . . . . **Capitol LCT 6132**
The Andrews Sisters appeared in both *Buck Privates* and *Swingtime Johnny*.
Nominated for an Academy Award 1941.

BOOK OF LOVE   June 1958
Warren Davies / George Melone / Charles Patrick
Francis, Day & Hunter Ltd . . . . USA
The Mudlarks . . . . **Columbia SEG 7854**

BOOK, THE   February 1954
Hans Gottwald / Paddy Roberts
Edward Kassner Music Co. Ltd. . . . . UK
David Whitfield . . . . **Decca LF 1165**
Anne Shelton . . . . **HMV B 10641**

BOOM   1939
Charles Trenet / Roma Campbell-Hunter
Keith Prowse Music Publishing Co. Ltd. . . . . France
Charles Trenet . . . . **Columbia SEG 7819**
Jack Hylton & his Orchestra, vocal Dolly Elsie . . **HMV BD 5553**
Charles Trenet . . . . **Columbia 33SX 1376**

BOOM BANG-A-BANG   April 1969
Peter Warne / Alan Moorhouse
Chappell & Co. Ltd. . . . . UK
Lulu . . . . **Columbia DB 8550**
United Kingdom entry for the 1969 Eurovision Song Contest (Placed First).
Four Contries tied for first place: France, Holland, Spain & United Kingdom.
Ivor Novello Nomination.

BOOMERANG   May 1955
Mark Lotz / Alan Gold / Tom Harrison
Lawrence Wright Music Co. Ltd. . . . . UK
The Radio Revellers . . . . **Polygon P 1165**

BOOMPS-A-DAISY   1939
Annette Mills
Lawrence Wright Music Co. Ltd. . . . . UK
Show(s): . . . . Hellzapoppin
Joe Loss & his Band,
vocal Annette Mills . . . . **Regal Zonophone MR 3027**
Billy Cotton & his Band . . . . **Decca DFE 6224**

BOOTS AND SADDLE   1935
Walter G. Samuels / Leonard Whitcup / Teddy Powell
Southern Music Publishing Co. Ltd . . . . USA
Film(s): . . . . Call of the Canyon
Chick Bullock . . . . **Rex 8565**
Bing Crosby . . . . **Brunswick LAT 8152**
Jimmy Wakely . . . . **Brunswick LAT 8179**

BORDERLINE   February 1986
Reggie Lucas
Brampton Music . . . . USA
Madonna . . . . **Sire W 9260**

BORN FREE   May 1966
Don Black / John Barry
Screens Gems - Columbia Music Ltd. . . . . UK
Film(s): . . . . Born Free
John Barry & his Orchestra (Sound Track) . . . . **MGM C 8010**
Matt Monro . . . . **Capitol CL 15436**
Connie Francis . . . . **MGM 1336**
Ivor Novello Award.

BORN IN THE USA   July 1985
Bruce Springsteen
Zomba Music . . . . USA
Bruce Springsteen . . . . **CBS A 6342**

BORN TO BE ALIVE August 1979
Patrick Hernandez
Leosong Copyright Service Ltd. France
Patrick Hernandez . . . . **Gem GEM 4**

BORN TO BE WITH YOU September 1956
Don Robertson
Edwin H. Morris & Co. Ltd. . . . . USA
The Chordettes . . . . **London HAA 2000**
The Echoes . . . . **Top Rank JAR 399**
The Beverley Sisters . . . . **Decca DFE 6401**
Dave Edmunds (1973) . . . . **Rockfield ROC 2**

BORN TOO LATE October 1958
Fred Tobias / Charles Strouse
Anglo-Pic Music Co. Ltd . . . . USA
The Poni-Tails . . . . **HMV POP 516**

BORN WITH A SMILE ON MY FACE August 1974
Roger Holman / Simon May
A.T.V. Music Ltd. . . . . UK
Stephanie De Sykes & Rain . . . . **Bradleys BRAD 7406**

BORSALINO December 1972
Claude Bolling
Chappell & Co. Ltd. . . . . France
Film(s): . . . . .Borsalino
Claude Bolling (piano) & Orchestra
(sound track recording) . . . . **ABC ABCL 5076**

BOSSA NOVA BABY November 1963
Jerry Leiber / Mike Stoller
Trio Music Ltd . . . . USA
Elvis Presley . . . . **RCA 1374**

BOSTON TEA PARTY, THE July 1976
Harvey McKenna
Panache Music Ltd. . . . . UK
The Sensational Alex Harvey Band . . . . **Mountain TOP 12**

BOSTON TWO STEP 1908
Thomas Walton / Luke Everett
Francis, Day & Hunter . . . . UK
London Novelty Orchestra . . . . **Regal MR 256**
Sydney Baynes Orchestra . . . . **HMV B 6428**
Harry Davidson Orchestra . . . . **Columbia DX 1191**

BOTCH-A-ME (Baciami) August 1952
H. Morbelli / L. Astore / Eddie Stanley
Edward Kassner Music Co. Ltd . . . . USA
Rosemary Clooney . . . . **Philips BBL 7301**
Ted Heath & his Music, vocal Lita Roza . . . . **Decca F 9980**

BOTH SIDES NOW March 1970
Joni Mitchell
Essex Music Ltd. . . . . USA
Judy Collins . . . . **Elektra EKSN 45043**
Frank Sinatra . . . . **Reprise RLP 1027**
Joni Mitchell . . . . **Reprise RS 23402**

BOULEVARD OF BROKEN DREAMS 1934
Al Dubin / Harry Warren
B. Feldman & Co. Ltd. . . . . USA
Film(s): . . . . Moulin Rouge
Ambrose & his Orchestra, vocal Sam Browne Brunswick 01721
Frances Langford . . . . **Brunswick 02962**
Billy Eckstine . . . . **Mercury ZEP 10110**

BOUQUET (I Shall Always Think Of You) 1925
Horatio Nicholls / Ray Morelle
Lawrence Wright Music Co. Ltd. . . . . UK
Percival Mackey & his Orchestra . . . . **Columbia 3687**

BOUQUET OF ROSES, A March 1949
Steve Nelson / Bob Hilliard
Chappell & Co. Ltd . . . . USA
Eddy Arnold . . . . **HMV BD 1234**
Lou Preager & his Orchestra,
vocal Paul Rich . . . . **Columbia FB 3460**
Dickson Hall . . . . **London RER 1158**

BOWERY, THE 1892
Percy Gaunt / Charles Hoyt
Francis, Day & Hunter . . . . USA
Show(s): . . . . .A Trip To Chinatown

Bing Crosby . . . . **Warner Brothers WM 4021**
Mitch Miller . . . . **Philips BBL 7419**

BOXER, THE June 1969
Paul Simon
Pattern Music Ltd. . . . . USA
Simon & Garfunkel . . . . **CBS 10029**

BOXERBEAT April 1983
Dig Wayne / Robert March / David Collard
Zomba Music . . . . UK
Jo Boxers . . . . **RCA BOX 1**

BOY FROM NEW YORK CITY June 1978
John Taylor
West One Music Ltd . . . . USA
Darts . . . . **Magnet MAG 116**

BOY FROM NOWHERE May 1987
Mike Leander / Edward Seago
Matador Music . . . . UK
Film(s): . . . . Matador
Tom Jones & John Springate . . . . **Epic OLE 1**

BOY NAMED SUE, A October 1969
Shel Silverstein
Essex Music Ltd. . . . . USA
Johnny Cash . . . . **CBS 63629**

BOY NEXT DOOR, THE 1944
Hugh Martin / Ralph Blane
Robbins Music Corporation & Co. Ltd. . . . . USA
Film(s): . . . . .Meet Me In St.Louis
Judy Garland . . . . **Brunswick 03558**
Judy Garland . . . . **Capitol LCT 6103**
Joni James . . . . **MGM C 839**
Judy Garland appeared in *Meet Me in St. Louis.*
See also *The Girl Next Door.*

BOYS (Summertime Love) July 1988
Claudio Ceccnetto / Matteo Bosanto / Roberto Rossi / Malcolm Charlton
London Music . . . . Italy
Sabrina . . . . **London IBIZ 1**

BOYS ARE BACK IN TOWN, THE July 1976
Phil Lynnot
Pippin The Friendly Ranger Music . . . . UK
Thin Lizzy . . . . **Vertigo 6059139**

BOYS CRY March 1964
Buddy Kaye / Tommy Scott
One Four Two Music Ltd . . . . UK
Eden Kane . . . . **Fontana TF 438**

BOYS IN THE BACK ROOM, THE 1940
Frederick Hollander / Frank Loesser
Robbins Music Corporation Ltd . . . . USA
Film(s): . . . . Destry Rides Again
Marlene Dietrich . . . . **Brunswick LAT 8339**
Marlene Dietrich . . . . **Philips BBL 7386**
Marlene Dietrich appeared in *Destry Rides Again.*

BRAND NEW KEY, A February 1972
Melanie Safka
Keith Prowse Music Publishing Co. Ltd . . . . USA
Melanie . . . . **Buddah 2011105**

BRANDY November 1971
Scott English / Richard Kerr
Grahple Music Ltd . . . . UK
Scott English . . . . **Horse HOSS 7**
This song has the same melody as *Mandy.*

BRASS IN POCKET January 1980
Chrissie Hynde / James Honeyman-Scott
A.T.V. Music Ltd. . . . . UK
The Pretenders . . . . **Real ARE 11**

BRAZIL 1943
Ary Barroso / Bob Russell
Southern Music Publishing Co. Ltd . . . . Brazil
Film(s):Saludos Amigos / The Eddy Duchin Story / The Girl He Left Behind
Jimmy Dorsey & his Orchestra,
vocal Bob Eberly & Helen O'Connell . . . . **Brunswick 03403**
Xavier Cugat & his Orchestra . . . . **Fontana TFR 5020**

Bing Crosby & Rosemary Clooney .... **RCA RD 21705**
Frank Sinatra .... **Capitol LCT 6154**

BREAD AND BUTTER WOMAN, A   January 1948
Allan Roberts / Lester Lee
Campbell Connelly & Co. Ltd. .... USA
Danny Kaye & The Andrews Sisters .... **Brunswick 03836**

BREAK AWAY   July 1969
Brian Wilson / Reggie Dunbar
Immediate Music Ltd. .... USA
The Beach Boys .... **Capitol CL 15598**

BREAK MY STRIDE   February 1984
Matthew Wilder / Gregory Prestopino
Warner Chappell Music .... USA
Matthew Wilder .... **Epic A 3908**

BREAK OF DAY   1943
Hans May / Alan Stranks
Keith Prowse Music Publishing Co. Ltd .... UK
Show(s): .... Old Chelsea
The Melachrino Orchestra,
conducted by Richard Tauber .... **Columbia DX 1256**
Webster Booth .... **HMV B 9633**
The Luton Girls Choir .... **Parlophone R 3118**
Richard Tauber .... **Parlophone RO 20539**
Richard Tauber appeared in *Old Chelsea*.

BREAK THE NEWS TO MOTHER   1897
Charles K. Harris
Herman Darewski Music Publishing Co. Ltd. .... USA
Film(s): .... Wait Till the Sun Shines Nellie
Gerald Adams .... **Regal Zonophone MR 143**
The Mills Brothers .... **Brunswick 03659**

BREAK THE RULES   June 1974
Francis Rossi / Robert Young / Ritchie Parfitt, Alan Lancaster &
John Coghlan
Valley Music .... UK
Status Quo .... **Vertigo 6059101**

BREAKAWAY   April 1983
Jackie De Shannon / Sharon Sheeley
United Artists Music .... USA
Tracy Ullman .... **Stiff BUY 168**
Irma Thomas .... **Liberty LIB 66013**
Beryl Marsden .... **Columbia DB 7797**

BREAKAWAY, THE   1929
Con Conrad / Sidney Mitchell / Archie Gottler
Campbell Connelly & Co. Ltd .... USA
Film(s): .... Fox Movietone Follies of 1929
The Dorsey Brothers Orchestra .... **Parlophone E 6197**
Jack Hylton & his Orchestra .... **HMV B 5658**
The Big Ben Banjo Band .... **Columbia 33SX 1188**

BREAKDANCE PARTY   June 1984
Jaques Morali / Fred Zarr / Henry Belola / Ken Rodgers
Leosong .... USA
Break Machine .... **Record Shack SOHO 20**

BREAKFAST IN AMERICA   August 1979
Richard Davies / Roger Hodgson
Rondor Music (London) Ltd. .... USA
Supertramp .... **A&M AMS 7451**

BREAKFAST IN BED   July 1988
Donnie Fritts / Eddie Hinton
EMI Music .... UK
UB40 & Chrissie Hynde .... **DEP International DEP 29**

BREAKIN'... THERE'S NO STOPPING US   July 1984
Ollie Brown / Jerry Knight
Rondor Music .... USA
Ollie & Jerry .... **Polydor POSP 690**

BREAKING DOWN THE WALLS
OF HEARTACHE   December 1968
Sandy Linzer / Denny Randell
Screen Gems Music Ltd. .... USA
Johnny Johnson & The Bandwagon .... **Direction 583670**

BREAKING IN A BRAND NEW BROKEN HEART   August 1961
Howard Greenfield / Jack Keller

Nevins-Kirshner Ltd. .... USA
Connie Francis .... **MGM 1136**
The Wilburn Brothers .... **Brunswick LAT 8501**

BREAKING UP IS HARD TO DO   September 1962
Howard Greenfield / Neil Sedaka
Aldon Music Ltd. .... USA
Neil Sedaka .... **RCA 1298**
Shelley Fabares .... **Pye 7N 25166**
The Partridge Family (1972) .... **Bell Mabel 1**

BREAKOUT   November 1986
Martin Jackson / Corinne Drewery / Andrew Connell
Phonogram Music .... UK
Swing Out Sister .... **Mercury SWING 2**

BREATHLESS   May 1958
Otis Blackwell
Carlin Music .... USA
Jerry Lee Lewis .... **London HLS 8592**

BREEZE (Blow My Baby Back To Me)   1922
Ballard MacDonald / Joe Goodwin / James Hanley
B. Feldman & Co. Ltd .... USA
Will Strong & Chorus .... **HMV B 1292**
Papa Bue's Viking Jazz Band .... **Parlophone PMC 1141**

BREEZE AND I, THE   1940
Ernesto Leucona / Al Stillman
Francis, Day & Hunter Ltd .... Cuba
Film(s): .... Cuban Pete
Ethel Smith (organ) .... **Brunswick 03787**
Jimmy Dorsey & his Orchestra,
vocal Bob Eberly .... **Brunswick 03027**
Bob Eberly .... **Warner Brothers WM 4033**
Caterina Valente (1955) .... **Polydor LPHM 46065**
The Troubadours .... **London HAR 2095**
Ethel Smith appeared in *Cuban Pete*.
Adapted from "Andalucia" by Ernesto Leucona.

BREEZE, THE (That's Bringing My Honey Back To Me)   1934
Tony Sacco / Dick Smith / Al Lewis
Campbell Connelly & Co. Ltd .... USA
Brian Lawrence .... **Decca F 5111**
Kay Starr .... **Capitol T 1358**
Patti Page .... **Mercury ZEP 10073**

BREEZIN' ALONG WITH THE BREEZE   1927
Richard A. Whiting / Seymour Simons / Haven Gillespie
Francis, Day & Hunter Ltd. .... USA
Film(s): .... Both Ends of the Candle
Jack Hylton's Kit Kat Band .... **HMV B 5119**
The Merry Macs .... **Decca F 7589**
Gogi Grant .... **RCA RD 27054**
Perry Como .... **RCA RD 27070**
Gogi Grant dubbed the singing voice of Ann Blyth who appeared in
the film *Both Ends of the Candle*.

BRIDGE OF SIGHS, THE   July 1953
Billy Reid
Peter Maurice Music Co. Ltd .... UK
David Whitfield .... **Decca LF 1165**
Anne Shelton .... **HMV B 10596**

BRIDGE OVER TROUBLED WATER   April 1970
Paul Simon
Pattern Music Ltd. .... USA
Simon & Garfunkel .... **CBS S 4790**

BRIDGE TO YOUR HEART   September 1987
Andrew Gold / Graham Gouldman
Island Music .... UK
Wax .... **RCA PB 41405**

BRIDGET THE MIDGET   April 1971
Ray Stevens
Peter Maurice Music Co. Ltd .... USA
Ray Stevens .... **CBS S 7070**

BRIGHT EYES   1921
Harry B. Smith / Otto Motzan / M.K. Jerome
B. Feldman & Co. Ltd .... USA
Paul Whiteman & his Orchestra .... **HMV B 1226**
Al Jolson .... **Brunswick LAT 8322**
Ben Light (piano) .... **Oriole LB 1079**

BRIGHT EYES   **May 1979**
Mike Batt
April Music Ltd. .... UK
Film(s): .... Watership Down
Art Garfunkel .... **CBS 6947**
Ivor Novello Award 1978 & 1979.

BRING A LITTLE WATER SYLVIE   **October 1956**
Traditional, arranged by Lonnie Donegan
Kensington Music .... UK
Lonnie Donegan .... **Pye Nixa N 15071**

BRING IT ON HOME TO ME   **May 1965**
Sam Cooke
Kags Music Ltd .... USA
The Animals .... **Columbia DB 7539**
Rod Stewart (1974) .... **Mercury 6167033**

BRING YOUR SMILE ALONG   **October 1955**
Benny Davis / Carl Fischer
Dash Music Ltd. .... USA
Film(s): .... Bring Your Smile Along
Frankie Laine .... **Philips PB 510**
Billy Cotton & his Band, vocal Alan Breeze .. **Decca F 10630**
Frankie Laine appeared in *Bring Your Smile Along.*

BRINGING ON BACK THE GOOD TIMES   **August 1969**
Philip Goodhand-Tait / John Cokell
Josid Music Ltd. .... UK
The Love Affair .... **CBS 4300**

BRITISH HUSTLE, THE   **September 1978**
Ken Joseph / Dave Joseph / Paul Philips / Jeffrey Guishard
Screen Gems Music .... Canada
Hi Tension .... **Island WIP 6446**

BRITTANIA RAG   **December 1952**
Winifred Atwell
Francis, Day & Hunter Ltd .... UK
Winifred Atwell (piano) .... **Decca F 10015**

BROADWAY MELODY, THE   **1929**
Nacio Herb Brown / Arthur Freed
Francis, Day & Hunter Ltd .... USA
Film(s): .... Broadway Melody / Broadway Melody of 1936
Charles King .... **HMV B 3087**
Layton & Johnstone .... **Columbia 5292**
Nat Shilkret & his Orchestra .... **HMV B 5635**
Frank Chacksfield & his Orchestra ..... **Decca LK 4151**
The King Brothers .... **Parlophone GEP 8665**
Charles King appeared in *Broadway Melody.*

BROADWAY RHYTHM   **1936**
Arthur Freed / Nacio Herb Brown
Robbins Music Corporation Ltd .... USA
Film(s): .... Broadway Melody of 1936 / Babes in Arms
Richard Himber & his Ritz-Carlton Orchestra ... **HMV BD 5020**
Ambrose & his Orchestra .... **Decca F 5740**
Charles Young .... **Columbia 33SX 1180**
Judy Garland .... **Caliban 6038**
Judy Garland appeared in *Babes in Arms.*

BROADWAY ROSE   **1921**
Martin Fried / Otis Spencer / Eugene West
Francis, Day & Hunter Ltd .... USA
The Original Dixieland Jazz Band .... **HMV B 1216**

BROKEN DOLL   **1915**
James W. Tate
Francis, Day & Hunter Ltd .... UK
Show(s): .... Samples
Film(s): ....The Courtneys of Curzon Street
Clarice Mayne & "That" .... **Columbia L 1041**
Brian Lawrence .... **Decca F 5981**
The Coronets .... **Columbia SEG 7617**

BROKEN DOWN ANGEL   **June 1973**
"Nazareth"
Carlin Music Corporation .... UK
Nazareth .... **Mooncrest MOON 1**

BROKEN HEARTED   **1928**
Buddy De Sylva / Lew Brown / Ray Henderson
Campbell Connelly & Co. Ltd. .... USA

Show(s): .... Artists and Models
Film(s): .... The Best Things in Life are Free
Aileen Stanley .... **HMV B 2590**
Johnny Ray (1952) .... **Columbia DB 3006**
Jim Lowe .... **London HAD 2108**

BROKEN HEARTED (Cuore Cuore)   **January 1971**
Edilio Capostosti / Antonello Da Simone / Bill Owen
Leeds Music Ltd .... Italy
Ken Dodd .... **Columbia DB 8725**

BROKEN HEARTED CLOWN   **1937**
Don Pelosi / Art Noel
Southern Music Publishing Co. Ltd. .... UK
Harry Richman .... **Columbia DB 1711**
Kevin Scott .... **Parlophone R 4540**

BROKEN HEARTED MELODY   **October 1959**
Sherman Edwards / Hal David
Peter Maurice Music Co. Ltd .... USA
Sarah Vaughan .... **Mercury ZEP 10041**
Maureen Evans .... **Embassy WB 356**
Tony Raymond .... **Fontana H 213**

BROKEN RECORD, THE   **1936**
Charles Tobias / Cliff Friend / Boyd Bunch
Chappell & Co. Ltd .... USA
Mae Questal .... **Decca F 5899**
Henry Hall & the B.B.C. Dance Orchestra ... **Columbia FB 1288**
The Radio Revellers .... **Columbia FB 3485**

BROKEN WINGS   **March 1953**
John Jerome / Bernard Grun
John Fields Music Co. Ltd .... UK
Dickie Valentine .... **Decca F 9954**
Art & Dotti Todd .... **HMV B 10399**
The Stargazers .... **Decca LF 1186**

BROKEN WINGS   **January 1986**
Richard Page / Steve George / John Lang
Warner Brothers Music .... USA
Mr Mister .... **RCA PB 49945**

BRONTOSAURUS   **May 1970**
Roy Wood
Essex Music Ltd. .... UK
The Move .... **Regal Zonophone RZ 3026**

BROTHER CAN YOU SPARE A DIME   **1933**
E.Y. Harburg / Jay Gorney
Chappell & Co. Ltd. .... USA
Show(s): .... Americana
Bing Crosby .... **Columbia DB 1829**
Steve Conway .... **Columbia FB 3416**
Rudy Vallee & his Connecticut Yankees .... **Columbia CB 552**

BROTHER LOUIE   **May 1973**
Errol Brown / Tony Wilson
Rak Music Ltd. .... UK
Hot Chocolate .... **Rak 149**

BROTHER LOUIS   **September 1986**
Dieter Bohlem
Intersong Music .... Germany
Modern Talking .... **RCA PB 40875**

BROWN BIRD SINGING, A   **1922**
J.M. Barrie / Haydn Wood
Chappell & Co. Ltd .... UK
John McCormack .... **HMV DA 780**
Sydney Coltham .... **HMV B 1646**
Peggy Lee .... **Brunswick LAT 8266**
Roy Castle .... **Philips BBL 7457**

BROWN EYED HANDSOME MAN   **April 1963**
Chuck Berry
Jewel Music Publishing Co. Ltd .... USA
Buddy Holly .... **Coral Q 72459**
Wanda Jackson .... **Capitol T 1596**
Chuck Berry .... **Pye NPL 28027**

BROWN EYES WHY ARE YOU BLUE   **1926**
George Meyer / Alfred Bryan
B.Feldman & Co. Ltd. .... USA

Nick Lucas . . . . Brunswick 02961
The Savoy Orpheans . . . . HMV B 2552
Mickey Rooney . . . . RCA RD 27038

BROWN GIRL IN THE RING   **June 1978**
Traditional, arranged by Frank Farian
Hansa Music Ltd . . . . Germany
Boney M . . . . **Atlantic K 11120**

BROWN SUGAR   **June 1971**
Mick Jagger / Keith Richards
Mirage Music Ltd . . . . UK
The Rolling Stones . . . . **Rolling Stones COC 59100**

BRUSH THOSE TEARS FROM YOUR EYES   **February 1949**
Oakley Haldeman / Al Trace / Jimmy Lee
Leeds Music Ltd . . . . USA
Film(s): . . . . The Blazing Sun
Buddy Clark . . . . **Columbia DB 2525**
Evelyn Knight . . . . **Brunswick 04015**

BUCKLE DOWN WINSOCKI   **1942**
Hugh Martin / Ralph Blane
Chappell & Co. Ltd . . . . USA
Show(s): . . . . Best Foot Forward
Film(s): . . . . Best Foot Forward
Lester Lanin & his Orchestra . . . . **Fontana TFR 6020**
Fred Waring & his Pennsylvanians . . . . **Capitol LCT 6174**

BUFFALO BILLY   **April 1951**
John Redmond / Frank Weldon / James Cavanaugh
Campbell Connelly & Co. Ltd . . . . USA
Roy Rogers . . . . **HMV 7EG 8182**

BUFFALO GALS   **January 1983**
Traditional
CBS Songs . . . . UK
Malcolm McLaren . . . . **Charisma MALC 1**
Based on "Lubly Fan" by John Hodges (Circa 1844).

BUFFALO SOLDIER   **June 1983**
Bob Marley / Noel Williams
Rondor Music . . . . USA
Bob Marley & The Wailers . . . . **Island IS 108**

BUFFALO STANCE   **January 1989**
Neneh Cherry / Cameron McVey / Phil Ramacon & Jamie Morgan
Warner Chappell Music . . . . UK
Neneh Cherry . . . . **Circa VR 21**
Ivor Novello Nomination

BUGLE CALL RAG   **1924**
Elmer Schoebel / Billy Meyers / Jack Pettis
Lawrence Wright Music Co. Ltd. . . . . USA
Film(s): . . . . Orchestra Wives / The Benny Goodman Story
The Friars Society Orchestra . . . . **London AL 3536**
The Chocolate Dandies . . . . **Parlophone R 1645**
Harry Roy & his Orchestra . . . . **Parlophone R 1734**
Glenn Miller & his Orchestra . . . . **RCA RD 27057**
Benny Goodman & his Orchestra . . . . **RCA RCX 1026**
Humphrey Lyttleton & his Band . . . . **Columbia 33SX 1329**
Benny Goodman & his Orchestra . . . . **Brunswick LAT 8102**
Glenn Miller appeared in *Orchestra Wives.*

BUILD ME UP BUTTERCUP   **January 1969**
Tony Macaulay / Mike D'Abo
Immediate Music Ltd. . . . . UK
The Foundations . . . . **Pye 7M 17636**
Ivor Novello Award.

BULLFROG PATROL, THE   **1922**
Jerome Kern / Anne Caldwell
Chappell & Co Ltd . . . . USA
Show(s): . . . . She's a Good Fellow
The Duncan Sisters . . . . **Columbia 5182**
Shirley Abicair . . . . **Fontana TFE 17159**
Dan Dailey, Carol Burnet & Steve Lawrence . . . **RCA RD 27062**
The Duncan Sisters appeared in *She's a Good Fellow.*

BUMBLE BOOGIE   **March 1948**
Arranged by Jack Fina
Chappell & Co. Ltd. . . . . USA
Film(s): . . . . Melody Time
Freddy Martin Orchestra with Jack Fina (piano) . . **HMV B 9621**

Adapted from 'The Flight of the Bumble Bee' by Nikolai Rimsky-Korsakov (1844 - 1908).

BUMP, THE   **February 1975**
Bill Martin / Phil Coulter
Martin-Coulter Music Ltd . . . . UK
Kenny . . . . **Rak 186**

BUNGALOW, A PICCOLO AND YOU, A   **1933**
Al Lewis / Al Sherman / Lee David
Campbell Connelly & Co. Ltd. . . . . USA
Henry Hall & The B.B.C. Dance Orchestra . . . **Columbia CB 481**

BUONA SERA   **February 1961**
Carl Sigman / Peter De Rose
Mills Music Ltd . . . . USA
Louis Prima . . . . **Capitol T 1531**
Acker Bilk & his Jazz Band . . . . **Columbia DB 4544**

BURLESQUE   **November 1972**
John Whitney / Roger Chapman
United Artists Music Co. Ltd. . . . . UK
Family . . . . **Reprise K 14196**

BURLINGTON BERTIE FROM BOW   **1915**
William Hargreaves
Lawrence Wright Music Co. Ltd. . . . . UK
Film(s): . . . . Star / Mother Wore Tights
Ella Shields . . . . **Columbia 629**
Ella Shields . . . . **Ace of Clubs ACL 1077**
Elsa Lanchester . . . . **HMV CLP 1417**
Julie Andrews . . . . **Stateside SL 10233**
Julie Andrews appeared in *Star.*

BURN IT UP   **October 1988**
"Beatmasters"
Zomba Music . . . . UK
The Beatmasters & P.P. Arnold . . . . **Rhythm King LEFT 27**

BURNING BRIDGES   **January 1989**
Francis Rossi / Andy Brown
Birchwood Music . . . . UK
Status Quo . . . . **Vertigo QUO 25**

BURNING HEARTS   **March 1986**
Jim Peterick / Frank Sullivan
Warner Brothers Music . . . . USA
Survivor . . . . **Scotti Brothers A 6708**

BURNING LOVE   **November 1972**
Dennis Linde
Keith Prowse Music Publishing Co. Ltd. . . . . USA
Elvis Presley . . . . **RCA 2267**

BUS STOP   **July 1966**
Graham Gouldman
Hournew Music Ltd. . . . . UK
The Hollies . . . . **Parlophone R 5469**

BUSHEL AND A PECK, A   **August 1953**
Frank Loesser
Edwin H. Morris & Co. Ltd . . . . USA
Show(s): . . . . Guys and Dolls
Vivian Blaine & Robert Alda . . . . **Brunswick LAT 8022**
Julie Wilson & chorus . . . . **Philips PB 142**
Margaret Whiting & Jimmy Wakely . . . . **Capitol CL 13923**
Vivian Blaine appeared in both the American and British productions of *Guys and Dolls.*
Robert Alda appeared in the American production of *Guys and Dolls.*

BUSY DOING NOTHING   **June 1949**
Johnny Burke / Jimmy Van Heusen
Edwin H. Morris & Co. Ltd . . . . USA
Film(s): . . . . A Yankee in King Arthur's Court
Bing Crosby, William Bendix &
Sir Cedric Hardwicke . . . . **Brunswick Bing 12**
Bing Crosby, William Bendix & Sir Cedric Hardwicke appeared in *A Yankee In King Arthur's Court.*

BUSY LINE   **April 1950**
Murray Semos / Frank Stanton
Southern Music Publishing Co. Ltd . . . . USA
Rose Murphy . . . . **HMV B 9901**
Peter Skellern . . . . **Mercury MER 137**

BUT BEAUTIFUL   February 1948
Johnny Burke / Jimmy Van Heusen
Edwin H. Morris & Co. Ltd. . . . . USA
Film(s): . . . . Road to Rio
Bing Crosby . . . . **Brunswick Bing 11**
Lena Horne . . . . **RCA RD 27141**
Brook Benton . . . . **Mercury ZEP 10091**
Bing Crosby appeared in *Road to Rio*.

BUT I DO   July 1961
Paul Gayton / Robert Guidry
Jewel Music Publishing Co. Ltd. . . . . USA
Clarence 'Frogman' Henry . . . . **Pye 7N 25078**
Tab Hunter . . . . **London HAD 2401**

BUT NOT FOR ME   1932
George Gershwin / Ira Gershwin
Chappell & Co. Ltd. . . . . USA
Show(s): . . . . Girl Crazy
Film(s): . . . . Girl Crazy
Teddy Wilson & his Orchestra,
vocal Helen Ward . . . . **Parlophone R 2815**
Kate Smith . . . . **Capitol T 854**
Anne Shelton . . . . **Philips BBL 7291**
Dennis Lotis . . . . **Pye NPL 18002**
Ethel Merman . . . . **Reprise R 6032**

BUT YOU LOVE ME DADDY   January 1970
Pat Twitty
Burlington Music Co. Ltd. . . . . USA
Jim Reeves . . . . **RCA 1899**
The Krankies . . . . **Rubber ADUB 5**

BUTTERFINGERS   June 1957
Tommy Steele / Lionel Bart
Peter Maurice Music . . . . UK
Tommy Steele . . . . **Decca F 10877**

BUTTERFLIES IN THE RAIN   1933
Stanley Damerell / Robert Hargreaves / Sherman Myers
Cecil Lennox Music Co. Ltd. . . . . UK
Ray Noble & his Orchestra, vocal Al Bowlly . . . . . **HMV B 6316**

BUTTERFLY   July 1957
Anthony September
Aberbach (London) Ltd. . . . . USA
Andy Williams . . . . **London HLA 8399**
Tommy Steele . . . . **Decca F 10915**
Billy Williams . . . . **Vogue LVA 9092**

BUTTERFLY   October 1971
Danyel Gerard / Ralph Bernet / Howard Barnes
April Music Ltd . . . . France
Danyel Gerard . . . . **CBS S 7454**

BUTTON UP YOUR OVERCOAT   1929
Buddy De Sylva / Low Brown / Ray Henderson
Chappell & Co. Ltd . . . . USA
Show(s): . . . . Follow Through
Film(s): . . . . Follow Through / The Best Things in Life Are Free
Ruth Etting . . . . **Columbia 5600**
The Ray Charles Singers . . . . **MGM 630**
Eydie Gormé . . . . **HMV CLP 1201**

BUTTONS AND BOWS   September 1948
Jay Livingston / Ray Evans
Victoria Music Co. Ltd. . . . . USA
Film(s): . . . . The Paleface / Son of Paleface
Dinah Shore . . . . **Philips BBL 7331**
Bob Hope . . . . **Capitol CL 19001**
The King Brothers . . . . **Parlophone PMC 1060**
Bob Hope appeared in *The Paleface* and *Son of Paleface*.
Academy Award winning song for 1948.

BY A WATERFALL   1934
Irving Kahal / Sammy Fain
B. Feldman & Co. Ltd. . . . . USA
Film(s): . . . . Footlight Parade
Dick Powell & Ruby Keeler . . . . **United Artists UAG 29421**
Val Rosing . . . . **Rex 8090**
Henry Hall & The B.B.C. Dance Orchestra . . . **Columbia CB 700**
Harry Roy & his Orchestra . . . . **Parlophone R 1725**
Dick Powell & Ruby Keeler appeared in *Footlight Parade*.

BY CANDLELIGHT   1942
Sonny Miller / Hugh Charles
Dash Music Ltd . . . . UK
Ambrose & his Orchestra, vocal Denny Dennis . . **Decca F 8102**
Robert Farnon & his Orchestra . . . . **Decca LK 4086**

BY HECK   1914
L. Wolfe Gilbert / S.R. Henry
Francis, Day & Hunter Ltd. . . . . USA
Show(s): . . . . Push and Go
John Henning . . . . **Columbia 2584**
The Metropolitan Dance Orchestra . . . . **HMV C 602**
David Carroll & his Orchestra . . . . **Mercury MMC 14061**
John Henning appeared in *Push and Go*.

BY MYSELF   1937
Howard Dietz / Arthur Schwartz
Chappell & Co. Ltd . . . . USA
Show(s): . . . . Between The Devil
Film(s): . . . . Band Wagon / I Could Go On Dancing
Fred Astaire . . . . **MGM C 752**
Judy Garland . . . . **Capitol W 1861**
Fred Astaire appeared in *Band Wagon*
Judy Garland appeared in *I Could Go On Dancing*.

BY STRAUSS   1951
George Gershwin / Ira Gershwin
Chappell & Co. Ltd . . . . USA
Show(s): . . . . The Show Is On
Film(s): . . . . An American In Paris
Ella Fitzgerald . . . . **HMV CLP 1339**
Cleo Laine . . . . **RCA PL 12407**
Gene Kelly, Oscar Levant & George Guetary . . **CBS AK 545391**
Kiri Te Kanawa . . . . **EMI EL 270274**
Gene Kelly, Oscar Levant & George Guetary appeared in *An American In Paris*

BY THE BEAUTIFUL SEA   1914
Harry Carroll / Harold Atteridge
Francis, Day & Hunter Ltd. . . . . USA
Film(s):The Story of Vernon & Irene Castle / Some Like it Hot / For
Me and My Gal / Atlantic City
Jackie Gleeson & his Orchestra . . . . **Capitol LCT 6153**
The Society Syncopaters . . . . **London HAT 2176**
Julie London . . . . **London HAW 2225**

BY THE CAMPFIRE   1919
Percy Wenrich / Mabel Girling
Francis, Day & Hunter Ltd. . . . . USA
Show(s): . . . . Bran Pie
Beatrice Lillie & Jose De Moraes . . . . **Columbia F 1009**
Beatrice Lillie & Jose de Moraes appeared in *Bran Pie*.

BY THE FIRESIDE   1932
Ray Noble / James Campbell / Reginald Connelly
Campbell Connelly & Co. Ltd. . . . . UK
Ray Noble & his Orchestra, vocal Al Bowlly . . . . **HMV B 8186**
Jack Hylton & his Orchestra . . . . **Decca LF 1143**
The Johnston Brothers . . . . **Decca LK 4266**
Jo Stafford . . . . **Philips BBL 7187**

BY THE FOUNTAINS OF ROME   August 1956
Matyas Seiber / Norman Newell
Chappell & Co. Ltd. . . . . UK
David Hughes . . . . **Philips BBE 12088**
Ivor Novello Award.

BY THE LIGHT OF THE SILVERY MOON   1909
Gus Edwards / Edward Madden
B. Feldman & Co. Ltd. . . . . USA
Show(s): . . . . The Ziegfeld Follies of 1909
Film(s):Birth of the Blues / Sunbonnet Sue / The Jolson Story / Two
Weeks With Love / By the Light of the Silvery Moon
Bing Crosby . . . . **Brunswick 05000**
Al Jolson . . . . **Brunswick LA 8570**
Jane Powell . . . . **MGM EP 633**
Teresa Brewer . . . . **Coral LVA 9138**
The George Mitchell Singers . . . . **HMV CLP 1399**
Bing Crosby appeared in *Birth of the Blues*.
Jane Powell appeared in *Two Weeks With Love*.

BY THE RIVER OF THE ROSES   1944
Joe Burke / Marty Symes
Francis, Day & Hunter Ltd. . . . . USA

45

Ambrose & his Orchestra,
  vocal George Melachrino . . . . Decca F 8403
Donald Peers . . . . Decca F 8418

BY THE RIVER SAINT MARIE   1931
Edgar Leslie / Harry Warren
Keith Prowse Music Publishing Co. Ltd . . . . USA
Jimmy Lunceford & his Orchestra . . . . Brunswick 02615
The Deauville Dance Band, vocal Al Bowlly . . Edison Bell 1558
Tony Martin . . . . Decca F 8921
The Platters . . . . Mercury MMC 14045

BY THE SHALIMAR   1923
Ted Koehler / Frank Magine / Del Delbridge
Herman Darewski Music Publishing Co. Ltd . . . . USA
Paul Specht & his Orchestra . . . . Columbia 3298

BY THE SIDE OF THE ZUYDER ZEE   1906
Bennett Scott / A.J. Mills
B. Feldman & Co. Ltd. . . . . UK
Florrie Forde . . . . Zonophone X 43117
Ronnie Ronalde . . . . Columbia SEG 8087

BY THE SLEEPY LAGOON   1931
Eric Coates
Chappell & Co. Ltd . . . . UK
Film(s): . . . . Sleepy Lagoon
Albert Sandler & his Orchestra . . . . Columbia DB 1061
The Eric Coates Symphony Orchestra . . . . Columbia DB 1945
Reg Owen & his Orchestra . . . . RCA RD 27040

BY THE WATERS OF MINNETONKA   1919
Thurlow Lieurance / J.M. Cavanass
Chappell & Co. Ltd. . . . . USA
Dame Nellie Melba . . . . HMV DA 334
The Lancers . . . . London HAP 2307

BY YOU, BY YOU, BY YOU   March 1957
Bob Davie / Marvin Moore
Cinephonic Music Co. Ltd. . . . . USA
Pauline Shepherd . . . . Nixa NPT 19019

BYE BYE BABY   October 1953
Leo Robin / Jule Styne
Edward Kassner Music Co. Ltd. USA
Show(s): . . . . Gentlemen Prefer Blondes
Film(s): . . . . Gentlemen Prefer Blondes
Carol Channing & Jack McCauley . . . . Philips BBL 7232
Marilyn Monroe . . . . MGM D 116
Billy Daniels . . . . HMV CLP 1200
Dora Bryan & Donald Stewart . . . . HMV CLP 1602
Carol Channing & Jack McCauley appeared in the American produc-
tion of *Gentlemen Prefer Blondes.*
Marilyn Monroe appeared in the film *Gentlemen Prefer Blondes.*
Dora Bryan & Donald Stewart appeared in the British production of
Gentlemen Prefer Blondes.

BYE BYE BABY (Baby Goodbye)   April 1975
Bob Crewe / Bob Gaudio
Keith Prowse Music Publishing Co. Ltd . . . . USA
The Bay City Rollers . . . . Bell 1409
The Symbols . . . . President PT 144

BYE BYE BABY, GOODBYE   November 1959
Frank McNulty
Southern Music Publishing Co. Ltd . . . . USA
Teresa Brewer . . . . Coral Q 72375

BYE BYE BLACKBIRD   1926
Ray Henderson / Mort Dixon
Francis, Day & Hunter Ltd. . . . . USA
Film(s): Rainbow Round My Shoulder / The Eddie Cantor Story / Pete
Kelly's Blues
George Olson & his Music . . . . HMV B 5114
Turner Layton . . . . Columbia RB 2578
Eddie Cantor . . . . Capitol LC 6652
Peggy Lee . . . . Brunswick LAT 8078
Helen Merrill . . . . Mercury MMB 12000

BYE BYE BLUES   1930
Fred Hamm / Dave Bennett / Bert Lown / Chauncey Gray
Francis, Day & Hunter Ltd . . . . USA
Bert Lown & his Orchestra . . . . Columbia CB 139
George Metaxa . . . . HMV B 3648
Eydie Gormé . . . . HMV CLP 1392

Bing Crosby & Louis Armstrong . . . . MGM C 844
Theme song of Bert Lown Orchestra.

BYE BYE LOVE   August 1957
Felice Bryant / Boudleaux Bryant
Acuff-Rose Publishing Co. Ltd. USA
The Everly Brothers . . . . London HAA 2081
Connie Francis . . . . MGM C 812

C'EST LA VIE   January 1987
Robbie Nevil / Duncan Pain / Mark Holding
Screen Gems Music . . . . USA
Robbie Nevil . . . . Manahattan MT 14

C'EST MAGNIFIQUE   November 1954
Cole Porter
Chappell & Co. Ltd. . . . . USA
Show(s): . . . . Can-Can
Film(s): . . . . Can-Can
Lilo & Peter Cookson . . . . Capitol LCT 6010
Irene Hilda & Edmund Hockridge . . . . . Parlophone PMD 1017
Frank Sinatra . . . . Capitol W 1301
Kay Starr . . . . Capitol T 1374
Teddy Johnson . . . . Columbia DB 3521
Lilo & Peter Cookson appeared in the American production of *Can-
Can.*
Irene Hilda & Edmund Hockridge appeared in the British production
of *Can-Can.*
Frank Sinatra appeared in the film *Can-Can.*

C'EST SI BON   May 1950
Henri Betti / Jerry Seelen / Andre Hornez
Peter Maurice Music Co. Ltd . . . . France
Show(s): . . . . Latin Quarter
Film(s): . . . . New Faces
Danny Kaye . . . . Brunswick LA 8668
Eartha Kitt (1954) . . . . RCA RD 27067
Louis Armstrong . . . . Brunswick LAT 8085
Eartha Kitt . . . . London HAR 2296
Eartha Kitt appeared in *New Faces.*

C'EST VOUS (It's You)   1927
Abner Greenberg / Abner Silver / Harry Richman
Campbell Connelly & Co. Ltd. . . . . USA
The Jacques Renard Orchestra . . . . HMV B 5349

C'MON AND GET MY LOVE   November 1989
Danny Poku
EMI Music . . . . UK
D Mob & Cathy Dennis . . . . London F 117

C'MON EVERYBODY   April 1959
Eddie Cochran / Jerry Capeheart
Burlington Music Co. Ltd . . . . USA
Eddie Cochran . . . . London HAG 2267
Adam Faith . . . . Parlophone PMC 1101
The Sex Pistols (1979) . . . . Virgin VS 272

CA C'EST L'AMOUR   December 1957
Cole Porter
Chappell & Co. Ltd . . . . USA
Film(s): . . . . Les Girls
Tania Elg . . . . MGM C 763
Tony Bennett . . . . Philips BBE 12159
Tina Robin . . . . Vogue Q 72294
Tania Elg appeared in *Les Girls.*

CA C'EST PARIS   1927
Jose Padilla / Jacques Charles / Hake P. Jordan
Ascherberg, Hopwood & Crew Ltd. . . . . France
The Rio Grande Tango Band . . . . HMV B 5251
Anona Winn . . . . Decca F 3408
Patachou . . . . Audio Fidelity AFLP 1814
Mistinguett . . . . Parlophone GEP 8659

CA PLANE POUR MOI   June 1978
Yves Lacomblez / Lou Depryck
Hansa Music Ltd . . . . Belgium
Plastic Bertrand . . . . Sire 6078616

CABARET   April 1968
John Kander / Fred Ebb
Valando Music Co. Ltd. . . . . USA
Show(s): . . . . Cabaret
Film(s): . . . . Cabaret

Jill Haworth .... Columbia KOL 6640
Judi Dench .... CBS 70039
Liza Minelli .... ABC ABCL 5019
Louis Armstrong .... HMV POP 1615
Frankie Vaughan .... Philips BF 1536
Jill Haworth appeared in the American production of *Cabaret*.
Judi Dench appeared in the British production of *Cabaret*.
Liza Minelli appeared in the film *Cabaret*.

CABIN IN THE SKY   1942
John Latouche / Vernon Duke
Robbins Music Corporation Ltd .... USA
Show(s): .... Cabin in the Sky
Film(s): .... Cabin in the Sky
Ethel Waters .... World Record ST 949
Ella Fitzgerald .... Brunswick LA 8581
Gordon MacRae .... Capitol T 875
Rosemary Clooney .... RCA RD 27218
Ethel Waters appeared in the show and the film *Cabin in the Sky*.

CAFE IN VIENNA   1934
Karel Vacek / Jimmy Kennedy
B. Feldman & Co. Ltd. .... UK
John Hendrick .... Parlophone R 1819
Gordon Little .... Decca F 3991

CAGE IN THE WINDOW, A   1934
Clark Gibson / Ray Morton
Dash Music Ltd. .... UK
Harry Roy & his Band .... Parlophone R 1677
Roy Fox & his Band .... Decca F 3760

CAISSONS GO ROLLING ALONG, THE   1942
Edmund Gruber
Shapiro-Bernstein & Co. Ltd .... USA
Film(s): .... Ice Capades Revue
Fred Waring & his Pennsylvanians .... Brunswick 03374
Buddy Williams & his Orchestra ..... Columbia 33SX 1182

CAKE WALKING BABIES FROM HOME   1925
Chris Smith / Henry Troy / Clarence Williams
B. Feldman & Co. Ltd. .... USA
Bessie Smith .... Philips BBL 7042
The Clarence Williams Blue Five .... Fontana TFL 5087
Mick Mulligans Jazz Band, vocal George Melly Tempo TAP 11

CALDONIA   1946
Fleecie Moore
Edwin H. Morris & Co. Ltd. .... USA
Film(s): .... Swing Parade of 1946
Woody Herman & his Orchestra,
vocal Woody Herman ...... Parlophone R 2990
Louis Jordan & his Tympany Five .... Brunswick 04041
Woody Herman & the First Herd .... Fontana TFR 6015
Louis Jordan & his Tympany Five .... Mercury MPT 7521
Louis Jordan appeared in *Swing Parade of 1946*.

CALENDAR GIRL   March 1961
Howard Greenfield / Neil Sedaka
Nevins-Kirshner Ltd .... USA
Neil Sedaka .... RCA 1220

CALIFORNIA DREAMIN'   May 1966
John Phillips / Michelle Phillips
.... USA
The Mama's & The Papa's (1966) .... RCA 1503
River City People .... EMI EM 145

CALIFORNIA HERE I COME   1924
Buddy De Sylva / Al Jolson / Joseph Meyer
B. Feldman & Co. Ltd. .... USA
Show(s): .... Bombo / Big Boy
Film(s):Lucky Boy / Rose of Washington Square / The Jolson Story /
You're My Everything / Jolson Sings Again / With a Song in My Heart
The California Ramblers .... Columbia 3419
Al Jolson .... Brunswick LA 8512
Freddie Mills .... Parlophone R 4376
Ray Charles .... HMV CLP 1387
Dorothy Provine .... Warner Brothers WM 4053
Al Jolson appeared in *Bombo*, *Big Boy* and *Rose of Washington Square*.
Song added to *Dombo* in 1924.

CALIFORNIA MAN   June 1972
Roy Wood

Carlin Music Corporation .... UK
The Move .... Harvest HAR 5050

CALL HER YOUR SWEETHEART   January 1967
Leon Payne
Acuff-Rose Publishing Co. Ltd. .... USA
Frank Ifield .... Columbia DB 8078

CALL ME   May 1980
Deborah Harry / Giorgio Moroder
Famous-Chappell .... UK
Film(s): .... American Gigolo
Blondie .... Chrysalis CHS 2414

CALL ME   June 1985
Peter Cox / Richard Drummie
ATV Music .... UK
Go West .... Chrysalis GOW 1

CALL ME   August 1987
Ivana Spagna / Giorgio Spagna / Alfredo Pignagnoli
Labelle Music .... Italy
Spagna .... CBS 650279

CALL ME DARLING   1931
Bert Reisfeld / Rolf Marbot / Mart Fryberg / Dorothy Dick
Keith Prowse Music Publishing Co. Ltd. .... Germany
Arthur Tracey (The Street Singer) .... Decca F 5608
Ernestine Anderson .... Mercury ZEP 10057
Donna Douglas .... Fontana H 256

CALL ME IRRESPONSIBLE   May 1962
Sammy Cahn / Jimmy Van Heusen
Chappell & Co. Ltd. .... USA
Film(s): .... Papa's Delicate Condition
Frank Sinatra .... Reprise R 20151
Nancy Wilson .... Capitol T 2082
Andy Williams .... CBS BPG 62372
Brook Benton .... RCA RD 7797
Academy Award winning song for 1963.

(CALL ME) NUMBER ONE   December 1969
Alan Blaikley / Len Hawkes
Gale Music Ltd .... UK
The Tremeloes .... CBS 4582

CALL OF THE CANYON, THE   1941
Billy Hill
Francis, Day & Hunter Ltd .... USA
Film(s): .... Call of the Canyon
Big Bill Campbell & his Rocky Mountaineers .... Rex 9921
Tony Martin .... Decca F 7799
Tommy Dorsey Orchestra,vocal Frank Sinatra   Camden CDN 153

CALL OF THE FARAWAY HILLS, THE   July 1953
Mack David / Victor Young
Chappell & Co. Ltd .... USA
Film(s): .... Shane
Jack Hilliard .... Columbia DB 3326
Victor Young & his Orchestra .... Brunswick LAT 8029
Bill Lowe .... Philips PB 180

CALL ROUND ANY OLD TIME   1908
Charles Moore / E.W. Rogers
B. Feldman & Co. Ltd. .... UK
Victoria Monks .... Ariel 1829

CALLING ALL THE HEROES   August 1986
Francis Dunnery / Richard Nolan
Virgin Music .... UK
It Bites .... Virgin VS 872

CALLING OCCUPANTS OF
INTERPLANETARY CRAFT   November 1977
L.M. Carpenter / Helen Benson
A.T.V. Music Ltd. .... USA
The Carpenters .... A&M AMS 7318

CALLING YOUR NAME   December 1983
"Marilyn" / Paul Caplin
Intersong Music .... UK
Marilyn .... Mercury MAZ 1

CAMBODIA   December 1981
Marty Wilde / Ricky Wilde

47

Rak Music . . . . UK
Kim Wilde . . . . **Rak 336**

CAMOUFLAGE   August 1986
Stan Ridgeway
Illegal Music . . . . USA
Stan Ridgeway . . . . **IRS RMT 114**

CAN ANYONE EXPLAIN   November 1950
Bennie Benjamin / George Weiss
Dash Music Ltd . . . . USA
Al Morgan . . . . **London LK 766**
Dinah Shore . . . . **Columbia DB 2751**
Dick Haymes . . . . **Brunswick 04589**

CAN CAN   July 1981
Jacques Offenbach, arranged by "Bad Manners"
. . . . UK
Bad Manners . . . . **Magnet MAG 190**
Adapted from "Orpheus In The Underworld" by Jacques Offenbach
(1819-1880)
(See also 'French Can-Can Polka')

CAN I CANOE YOU UP THE RIVER   April 1951
Marjorie Goetschius / Edna Osser
Leeds Music . . . . USA
Billy Cotton & his Band . . . . **Decca F 9619**
Joe Loss Orchestra . . . . **HMV BD 6089**
Arthur Godfrey . . . . **Columbia 2767**

CAN I FORGET YOU   1937
Jerome Kern / Oscar Hammerstein II
Chappell & Co. Ltd. . . . . USA
Film(s): . . . . High Wide and Handsome
Phyllis Robins . . . . **Rex 9165**
Bing Crosby . . . . **Brunswick 02484**
David Whitfield . . . . **Decca LK 4384**
Gwen Catley . . . . **Pye CEC 32006**

CAN I PLAY WITH MADNESS   March 1988
Adrian Smith / Paul Dickinson / Steve Harris
Zomba Music . . . . UK
Iron Maiden . . . . **EMI EM 49**

CAN I TAKE YOU HOME LITTLE GIRL   January 1976
Roger Greenaway / Barry Mason
Cookaway Music . . . . UK
The Drifters . . . . **Bell 1462**

CAN IT BE LOVE   1915
Paul Rubens / Adrian Ross
Chappell & Co. Ltd. . . . . UK
Show(s): . . . . Betty
Aimee Maxwell . . . . **HMV C 656**
The New Mayfair Orchestra . . . . **HMV BD 489**
Henry Hall & The B.B.C. Dance Orchestra . . . . **Capitol FB 1157**

CAN THE CAN   June 1973
Mike Chapman / Nicky Chinn
Chinnichap Music . . . . UK
Suzi Quatro . . . . **Rak 150**

CAN THIS BE LOVE   November 1954
Irene Roper / Terence Roper / Robert Raglan
B. Feldman & Co. Ltd. . . . . UK
Joan Regan . . . . **Decca F 10397**

CAN YOU DO IT   July 1973
Victor Malcolm
Red Bus Music . . . . UK
Geordie . . . . **EMI 2031**

CAN YOU FEEL IT   May 1981
Michael Jackson / Jackie Jackson
Carlin Music . . . . USA
The Jacksons . . . . **Epic EPC 9554**

CAN YOU FEEL THE FORCE   March 1979
Chris Amoo / Eddie Amoo
Open Choice Music . . . . UK
The Real Thing . . . . **Pye 7N 46147**

CAN YOU PARTY   November 1988
Terry Todd
Champion Music . . . . USA

Royal House . . . . **Champion CHAMP 79**

CAN'T BE WITH YOU TONIGHT   May 1987
Felix Da Silva
Reward Music . . . . UK
Judy Boucher . . . . **Orbiton OR 721**

CAN'T BUY ME LOVE   April 1964
John Lennon / Paul McCartney
Northern Songs Ltd . . . . UK
Film(s): . . . . A Hard Day's Night
The Beatles . . . . **Parlophone R 5114**
Ella Fitzgerald . . . . **Verve VS 519**
Keely Smith . . . . **Reprise R 6142**
The Beatles appeared in *A Hard Day's Night*.
Ivor Novello Nomination.

CAN'T GET ENOUGH OF YOUR LOVE BABE   September 1974
Barry White
Schroeder Music Ltd. . . . . USA
Barry White . . . . **Pye 7N 25661**

CAN'T GET INDIANA OFF MY MIND   1940
Hoagy Carmichael / Robert De Leon
Campbell Connelly & Co. Ltd . . . . USA
Bing Crosby . . . . **Brunswick 03073**
Nat Gonella & his Georgians . . . . **Parlophone MP 47**

CAN'T GET OUT OF THIS MOOD   1943
Jimmy McHugh / Frank Loesser
Southern Music publishing Co. Ltd . . . . USA
Film(s): . . . . Seven Days Leave
Anne Shelton . . . . **Decca F 8291**
Lita Roza . . . . **Decca LK 4171**
Johnny Mathis . . . . **Fontana TFL 5039**

CAN'T GET USED TO LOSING YOU   May 1963
Doc Pomus / Mort Shuman
Manor Music Co. Ltd . . . . USA
Andy Williams . . . . **CBS AAG 138**
Jimmy Justice . . . . **Pye NPL 18085**
Skeeter Davis . . . . **RCA RD 7604**
The Beat(1983) . . . . **Go Feet FEET 17**

CAN'T GIVE YOU ANYTHING (But My Love)   August 1975
Hugo Peretti / Luigi Creatore / George Weiss
Cyril Shane Music . . . . USA
The Stylistics . . . . **Avco 6105039**

CAN'T HELP FALLING IN LOVE   April 1962
Hugo Peretti / Luigi Creatore / George Weiss
Manor Music Co. Ltd. . . . . USA
Film(s): . . . . Blue Hawaii
Elvis Presley . . . . **RCA 1270**
George Maharis . . . . **Columbia 33SX 1444**
Alma Cogan . . . . **Columbia 33SX 1469**
Andy Williams (1970) . . . . **CBS 4818**
The Stylistics (1976) . . . . **Avco 6105050**
Elvis Presley appeared in *Blue Hawaii*.
Based on 'Plaisir D'Amour' by Giovanni Martini (1741 - 1816).

CAN'T HELP LOVIN' DAT MAN   1928
Jerome Kern / Oscar Hammerstein II
Chappell & Co. Ltd. . . . . USA
Show(s): . . . . Show Boat
Film(s):Show Boat / Till the Clouds Roll By / Both Ends of the Candle
Marie Burke . . . . **Columbia 9427**
Ava Gardner . . . . **MGM D 104**
Lena Horne . . . . **MGM D 143**
Gogi Grant . . . . **RCA RD 27054**
Marie Burke appeared in the British production of *Show Boat*.
Ava Gardner appeared in the 1951 film of *Show Boat*.
Lena Horne appeared in *Till the Clouds Roll By*.
Gogi Grant dubbed the singing voice of Ann Blyth who appeared in
the film *Both Ends of the Candle*.

CAN'T HELP SINGING   1945
Jerome Kern / E.Y. Harburg
Chappell & Co. Ltd. . . . . USA
Film(s): . . . . Can't Help Singing
Deanna Durbin & Robert Paige . . . . **Brunswick 0171**
Deanna Durbin & Robert Paige appeared in *Can't Help Singing*.

CAN'T I   September 1953
Leroy Lovett

Southern Music Publishing Co.Ltd . . . . USA
Nat 'King' Cole . . . . **Capitol CL 13937**

CAN'T KEEP IT IN   February 1973
Cat Stevens
Freshwater Music . . . . UK
Cat Stevens . . . . **Island WIP 6152**

CAN'T SHAKE THE FEELING   December 1989
Mike Stock / Matt Aitken / Peter Waterman
All Boys Music . . . . UK
Big Fun . . . . **Jive JIVE 234**

CAN'T STAND LOSING YOU   August 1979
"Sting"
Virgin Music (Publishers) Ltd. . . . . UK
Police . . . . **A&M AMS 7381**

CAN'T STAY AWAY FROM YOU   March 1989
Gloria Estefan
SBK Songs . . . . USA
Gloria Estefan & The Miami Sound Machine . . . . . **Epic 651444**

CAN'T STOP THE MUSIC
(La Musique N'a Pas De Fin)   September 1980
Jacques Morali / Henri Belolo / Philip Hurt / P. Whitehead
Zomba Music Publishers . . . . France
Film(s): . . . . Can't Stop the Music
The Village People . . . . **Mercury MER 16**

CAN'T TAKE MY EYES OFF YOU   May 1968
Bob Crewe / Bob Gaudio
Ardmore & Beechwood Ltd. . . . . USA
Andy Williams . . . . **CBS 3928**
Boystown Gang (1982) . . . . **ERC 101**

CAN'T WAIT ANOTHER MINUTE   May 1986
Susan Sheridan / Paul Chiten
Famous Music . . . . USA
Five Star . . . . **RCA PB 40697**

CAN'T WE BE FRIENDS   1931
Kay Swift / Paul James
Chappell & Co. Ltd . . . . USA
Show(s): . . . . The Little Show
Bing Crosby . . . . **Columbia DB 2035**
Ella Fitzgerald . . . . **HMV CLP 1322**
Frank Sinatra . . . . **Capitol LC 6702**

CAN'T WE TALK IT OVER   1932
Ned Washington / Victor Young
B. Feldman & Co. Ltd. . . . . USA
Film(s): . . . . Illegal
Bing Crosby . . . . **Brunswick 02695**
Toni Arden . . . . **Columbia DB 2880**
Claire Austin . . . . **Vogue LAC 12139**
Jane Russell . . . . **MGM EP 702**

CAN'T YOU HEAR ME CALLING CAROLINE   1914
William Gardner / Caro Roma
B. Feldman & Co. Ltd. . . . . USA
The Mills Brothers . . . . **Brunswick 04449**
Jerry Colonna . . . . **Brunswick LA 8711**

CAN'T YOU HEAR ME SAY I LOVE YOU   1928
Charles Derickson / Burton Brown
Lawrence Wright Music Co. Ltd. . . . . USA
The Troubadours . . . . **HMV B 5468**

CAN'T YOU READ BETWEEN THE LINES   1945
Jule Styne / Sammy Cahn
Francis, Day & Hunter Ltd. . . . . USA
Geraldo & his Orchestra, vocal Carol Carr . . **Parlophone F 2086**
Ambrose & his Orchestra, vocal Jack Powers . . **Decca F 8563**

CAN'T YOU SEE THAT SHE'S MINE   June 1964
Dave Clark / Mike Smith
Ardmore & Beechwood Ltd. . . . . UK
The Dave Clark Five . . . . **Columbia DB 7291**

CANADIAN CAPERS   1915
Gus Chandler / Henry Cohen / Bert White
B. Feldman & Co. Ltd. . . . . USA
Film(s): . . . . My Dream is Yours
Paul Whiteman & his Orchestra . . . . **HMV B 1310**

The Milt Herth Trio . . . . **Brunswick 03302**
Doris Day . . . . **Philips BBE 12167**
Doris Day appeared in *My Dream is Yours*.

CANDIDA   February 1971
Tony Wine / Irwin Levine
Carlin Music Corporation . . . . USA
Dawn . . . . **Bell BLL 1118**

CANDLE IN THE WIND, A   April 1974
Elton John / Bernie Taupin
Dick James Music Ltd. . . . . UK
Elton John . . . . **DJM DJS 297**
Elton John (1988) . . . . **Rocket EJS 15**

CANDY   1945
Joan Whitney / Alex Kramer
Robbins Music Corporation Ltd. . . . . USA
Joe Loss & his Orchestra, vocal Harry Kaye . . . . **HMV BD 5890**
Jo Stafford . . . . **Philips PB 1034**
Something Smith & The Redheads . . . . **Fontana TFE 17107**
Ray Charles . . . . **HMV CLP 1449**

CANDY AND CAKE   July 1950
Bob Merrill
Dash Music Ltd . . . . USA
Evelyn Knight . . . . **Brunswick 04542**
Mindy Carson . . . . **HMV B 9919**

CANDY GIRL   June 1983
Maurice Starr / Michael Jonzun
Chrysalis Music . . . . USA
New Edition . . . . **London LON 21**

CANDY KISSES   June 1949
George Morgan
Chappell & Co. Ltd . . . . USA
Film(s): . . . . Down Dakota Way
Danny Kaye . . . . **Brunswick 04087**
Slim Whitman . . . . **London HAP 2139**
Molly Bee . . . . **Capitol T 1097**

CANDY MAN   March 1964
Beverly Ross / Fred Neil
Aaron Schroeder Ltd. . . . . USA
Brian Poole & The Tremeloes . . . . **Decca F 11823**
The Hollies . . . . **Parlophone PMC 1220**

CANOE SONG, THE   1935
Mischa Spoliansky / Arthur Wimperis
Campbell Connelly & Co. Ltd . . . . UK
Film(s): . . . . Sanders of the River
Paul Robeson . . . . **HMV 7EG 8185**
Paul Robeson appeared in *Sanders of the River*.

CANTEEN BOUNCE, THE   1944
Jimmy Fortis / Max Spickol
Campbell Connelly & Co. Ltd. . . . . USA
The R.A.F. Dance Orchestra . . . . **Decca F 8442**
Joe Loss & his Orchestra . . . . **HMV BD 5861**

CAPRICE VIENNOIS   1910
Fritz Kreisler
Schott & Co Ltd. . . . . Austria
Fritz Kreisler (Violin) . . . . **HMV DB 1091**
Yehudi Menuhin (Violin) . . . . **HMV DA 1832**
Mischa Elman (Violin) . . . . **Philips AL 3423**

CAPSTICK COMES HOME   April 1981
Tony Capstick
Tyke Music . . . . UK
Carlton Main Frickley Colliery Band . . . . **Dingles SID 27**
Based on the second movement ("Largo") of Symphony No.9 in E
minor by Antonin Dvorak (1841-1904)

CAPTAIN BEAKY   February 1980
Jeremy Lloyd / Jim Parker
Chappell & Co. Ltd . . . . UK
Keith Michell . . . . **Polydor POSP 106**

CAPTAIN GINGAH   1910
George Bastow / Fred W. Leigh
Francis, Day & Hunter Ltd. . . . . UK
George Bastow . . . . **Columbia 1824**
Harry Fay . . . . **HMV B 4011**

Archie Harradine . . . . Columbia DB 2917

CAPTAIN OF HER HEART   February 1986
Malou Haug
E.G. Music . . . . UK
Double . . . . Polydor POSP 779

CAPTAIN OF YOUR SHIP   April 1968
Kenny Young / B. Yardley
Carlin Music Corporation . . . . USA
Reparata & The Delrons . . . . Bell 1002

CAR 67   February 1979
Paul Phillips / Peter Zorn
Logo Music Ltd. . . . . UK
Driver 67 . . . . Logo GO 336

CAR WASH   February 1977
Norman Whitfield
Leeds Music Ltd . . . . USA
Rose Royce . . . . MCA 267

CARA MIA   July 1954
Tulio Trapani / Lee Lange
Robbins Music Corporation Ltd. . . . . UK
David Whitfield . . . . Decca LF 1244
Gordon MacRae . . . . Capitol T 1050

CARAVAN   1937
Duke Ellington / Juan Tizol / Irving Mills
Lafleur & Co. Ltd. . . . . USA
Duke Ellington & his Orchestra . . . . . . Philips BBE 12404
The Mills Brothers . . . . Brunswick OE 9060
Ralph Marterie & his Orchestra . . . . . . Oriole CB 1175
Ella Fitzgerald . . . . HMV CLP 1213
David Carroll & his Orchestra . . . . Mercury MMC 14066

CARAVAN OF LOVE   January 1987
Marvin Isley / Chris Jasper
Warner Brothers Music . . . . UK
The Housemartins . . . . Go Discs GOD 16

CARELESS   1940
Lew Quadling / Eddie Howard / Dick Jurgens
Bradbury Wood Ltd . . . . USA
Al Bowlly . . . . HMV BD 828
Dick Jurgens & his Orchestra . . . . . Regal Zonophone MR 3246
Sarah Vaughan . . . . Mercury AMT 1044

CARELESS HANDS   June 1949
Bob Hilliard / Carl Sigman
Edwin H. Morris & Co. Ltd . . . . USA
Mel Tormé . . . . Capitol CL 13094
Michael Holliday . . . . Columbia DB 4216
Bing Crosby . . . . Brunswick 04098
Bryan Johnson . . . . Decca LK 4362
Des O'Connor (1968) . . . . Columbia DB 8275

CARELESS LOVE   1922
William C. Handy / Spencer Williams / Martha Koenig
Francis, Day & Hunter Ltd . . . . USA
Film(s): . . . . St. Louis Blues
Bessie Smith . . . . Philips BBL 7019
Louis Armstrong's All Stars . . . . Philips BBL 7445
The Chris Barber Jazz Band, vocal Ottile Patterson . . Nixa NJL 500
Nat 'King' Cole . . . . Capitol LCT 6156
Nat 'King' Cole appeared in *St. Louis Blues*.

CARELESS WHISPER   September 1984
George Michael / Andrew Ridgeley
Morrison Leahy Music . . . . UK
George Michael . . . . Epic A 4603
Ivor Novello Award

CARELESSLY   1937
Nick & Charles Kenny / Norman Ellis
Avenue Music Publishing Co. Ltd. . . . . USA
Turner Layton . . . . Columbia FB 1710
Greta Keller . . . . Decca F 6439
Bunny Berigan & his Orchestra,
  vocal Gail Reese . . . . Camden CDN 159

CARIOCA, THE   1934
Gus Kahn / Edward Eliscu / Vincent Youmans
Chappell & Co. Ltd. . . . . USA

Film(s): . . . . Flying Down to Rio
Connee Boswell . . . . Brunswick 01783
The Andrews Sisters . . . . Brunswick 04834
Artie Shaw & his Orchestra . . . . RCA RCX 1011
Mel Tormé . . . . London LTZN 15009
Nominated for an Academy Award 1934.

CARNAVALITO   January 1954
Edmundo Zaldiver
Southern Music Publishing Co. Ltd. . . . . Argentina
Cyril Stapleton & his Orchestra . . . . Decca LF 1159
Edmundo Ros & his Orchestra . . . . Decca LK 4111
Michel Legrand & his Orchestra . . . . Philips BBL 7262

CARNIVAL IS OVER, THE   December 1965
Tom Springfield
Springfield Music Ltd . . . . UK
The Seekers . . . . Columbia DB 7711

CAROLINA   1945
Max Nesbitt / Harry Nesbitt / Jack Stodel
Dash Music Ltd. . . . . UK
Lou Preager & his Orchestra,
  vocal Paul Rich . . . . Columbia FB 3178
Billy Cotton & his Band, vocal Alan Breeze . . . . Rex 10230

CAROLINA IN THE MORNING   1923
Gus Kahn / Walter Donaldson
Francis, Day & Hunter Ltd . . . . USA
Show(s): . . . . The Passing Show of 1922
Film(s):The Dolly Sisters / April Showers / Jolson Sings Again / I'll See You in My Dreams
Paul Whiteman & his Orchestra . . . . HMV B 1516
Al Jolson . . . . Brunswick LA 8509
The King Brothers . . . . Parlophone GEP 8651
Debbie Reynolds . . . . MGM EP 670

CAROLINA MOON   1929
Joe Burke / Benny Davis
Lawrence Wright Music Co. Ltd . . . . USA
Jesse Crawford . . . . HMV B 3069
Perry Como . . . . HMV BD 1202
Bonnie Guitar . . . . London HAD 2122
Connie Francis (1958) . . . . MGM 985
Dean Martin . . . . Capitol EAP 1007

CAROLINE   October 1973
Francis Rossi / Robert Young
Valley Music . . . . UK
Status Quo . . . . Vertigo 6059085

CAROUSEL WALTZ, THE   June 1950
Richard Rodgers
Williamson Music Ltd . . . . USA
Show(s): . . . . Carousel
Film(s): . . . . Carousel
The Carousel Orchestra . . . . Brunswick LAT 8006
Alfred Newman & his Orchestra
  (from the Sound Track of the film) . . . . . . Capitol LCT 6105

CARRIBEAN QUEEN   November 1984
Keith Diamond / Billy Ocean
Zomba Music . . . . UK
Billy Ocean . . . . Jive JIVE 77
Ivor Novello Nomination

CARRIE   March 1980
Terry Britten / B.A. Robertson
United Artists Music Co. Ltd . . . . UK
Cliff Richard . . . . EMI 5006

CARRIE ANNE   July 1967
Allan Clarke / Graham Nash / Tony Hicks
Gralto Music Ltd. . . . . UK
The Hollies . . . . Parlophone R 5602

CARRY ME BACK TO GREEN PASTURES   1933
Harry S. Pepper
B. Feldman & Co. Ltd. . . . . UK
Melville Gideon . . . . Imperial 2911
Paul Robeson . . . . HMV 7P 226
The Kentucky Minstrels . . . . HMV C 3085

CARRY ME BACK TO THE LONE PRAIRIE   1935
Carson Robison

Campbell Connelly & Co. Ltd .... USA
Film(s): .... Stars Over Broadway
Nick Lucas .... **Rex 8306**
Jimmy Wakely .... **Brunswick LAT 8179**
The Sons of The Pioneers .... **RCA RD 27016**

CARRY ON   **1932**
Jack O'Hagen / Girvan Dundas
Peter Maurice Music Co. Ltd. .... Australia
The Masqueraders .... **Columbia CB 401**

CARS   **September 1979**
Gary Numan
Andrew Heath Music Ltd. .... UK
Gary Numan .... **Beggars Banquet BEG 23**

CASANOVA   **October 1980**
Joseph Armstead / Milton Middlebrook
Planetary-Nom (London) Ltd .... USA
Coffee .... **De Lite MER 38**

CASANOVA   **September 1987**
Reggie Calloway
Chappell & Co. Ltd .... UK
Levert .... **Atlantic A 9217**

CASEY JONES   **1912**
Lawrence Selbert / Eddie Newton
Francis, Day & Hunter Ltd. .... USA
The Two Bobs .... **Columbia 1932**
Carson Robinson's Pioneers .... **Columbia DX 365**
Russ Morgan & his Orchestra .... **Columbia DB 5039**

CAST YOUR FATE TO THE WIND   **February 1965**
Vincent Gauraldi
Robert Mellin Ltd .... USA
Sounds Orchestral .... **Piccadilly 7N 35206**

CASTLE ROCK   **October 1951**
Ervin Drake / Jimmy Shirl / Al Sears
Southern Music Publishing Co. Ltd .... USA
Frank Sinatra with Harry James
& his Orchestra .... **Fontana TFL 5030**

CASTLES IN THE SAND   **1933**
Dick Sandford / George McConnel / Bud Green
Dash Music Ltd. .... USA
Sam Browne .... **Panachord 25464**
Derickson & Brown .... **HMV B 4436**

CASTLES IN THE SAND   **May 1951**
Bob Hilliard / Dave Mann
Leeds Music Ltd .... USA
The Smith Brothers .... **London L 959**
Larry Cross .... **Parlophone R 3400**
The Ink Spots .... **Brunswick 04719**

CAT AMONG THE PIGEONS   **December 1988**
Matthew Goss / Luke Goss
Warner Chappell Music .... UK
Bros .... **CBS ATOM 6**

CAT CREPT IN, THE   **May 1974**
Nicky Chinn / Mike Chapman
Chinnichap Music .... UK
Mud .... **Rak 170**

CAT'S WHISKERS, THE   **1923**
Felix Austed / Edward Gladstone
Chappell & Co. Ltd .... USA
The Benson Orchestra of Chicago .... **HMV 1717**

CATCH A FALLING STAR   **February 1958**
Lee Pockriss / Paul Vance
B. Feldman & Co. Ltd .... USA
Perry Como .... **RCA RD 27100**
Jane Morgan .... **London HAR 2133**
Mark Murphy .... **Capitol T 1299**

CATCH THE WIND   **April 1965**
"Donovan"
Southern Music Publishing Co. Ltd .... UK
Donovan .... **Pye 7N 15801**
Ivor Novello Award.

CATCH US IF YOU CAN   **August 1965**
Dave Clark / Leonard Davidson
Ivy Music Ltd .... UK
Film(s): .... Catch Us if You Can
The Dave Clark Five .... **Columbia DB 7625**
The Dave Clark Five appeared in *Catch Us If You Can*.

CATHY'S CLOWN   **May 1960**
Don Everly / Phil Everly
Acuff-Rose Publishing Co. Ltd .... USA
The Everly Brothers .... **Warner Brothers WM 4028**
Pat Boone .... **London HAD 2354**

CAUSING A COMMOTION   **October 1987**
Madonna Ciccone / Steven Bray
Warner Brothers Music .... USA
Madonna .... **Sire W 8224**

CECILIA   **1926**
Herman Ruby / Dave Dreyer
Francis, Day & Hunter Ltd. .... USA
Jack Smith .... **HMV B 2226**
Johnny Mercer .... **Capitol LC 6648**
Max Bygraves with Ted Heath & his Music ..... **Decca LK 4317**
Tony Brent .... **Columbia 33SX 1200**

CELEBRATIN'   **1936**
Harry Woods
Cinephonic Music Co. Ltd .... UK
Jack Hulbert .... **HMV BD 335**
Tennessee Ernie Ford .... **Capitol CL 13909**

CELEBRATION   **December 1980**
Ronald Bell / Robert 'Kool' Bell / George Brown / Larry Gittins
Planetary-Nom (London) Ltd .... USA
Kool & The Gang .... **De Lite KOOL 10**

CELEBRATION RAG   **May 1953**
Rodd Arden / Jimmy Harper
Bradbury Wood Ltd .... UK
Donald Peers .... **HMV B 10487**
Bob & Alf Pearson .... **Parlophone F 2515**
The Stargazers .... **Decca F 10133**

CEMENT MIXER   **1946**
Lee Ricks / Slim Gaillard
World Wide Music Co. Ltd. .... USA
Film(s): .... The Sweetheart of Sigma Chi
The Squadronaires Dance Orchestra .... **Decca F 8644**
Mel Tormé .... **Vogue LVA 9032**
The Radio Revellers .... **Columbia FB 3311**
Slim Gaillard Trio .... **HEP HEP 28**
Slim Gaillard appeared in *The Sweetheart of Sigma Chi*.

CENTERFOLD   **February 1982**
Seth Justman
Rondor Music .... USA
J. Geils Band .... **EMI EA 135**

CERTAIN SMILE, A   **August 1958**
Sammy Fain / Paul Francis Webster
Robbins Music CorporationLtd .... USA
Film(s): .... A Certain Smile
Johnny Mathis .... **Fontana TFL 5083**
Andy Russell .... **RCA 1076**
The Kaye Sisters .... **Philips BBE 12256**
The Four Preps .... **Capitol T 1216**
Nominated for an Academy Award 1958.

CHAIN GANG   **March 1956**
Sol Quasha / Hank Yakus
Bluebird Music Co. Ltd. .... USA
Jimmy Young .... **Decca F 10694**
Bobby Scott .... **London HL 8254**

CHAIN GANG   **October 1960**
Sam Cooke / Charles Cooke
Kags Music Ltd .... USA
Sam Cooke .... **RCA 1202**
Ronnie Carroll .... **Philips PB 1060**

CHAIN REACTION   **March 1986**
Barry Gibb / Robin Gibb / Maurice Gibb
Chappell & Co. Ltd .... UK

Diana Ross . . . . Capitol CL 386
Ivor Novello Award

CHAINS OF LOVE   June 1988
Vincent Clarke / Andrew Bell
Sonet Music . . . . UK
Erasure . . . . Mute MUTE 83

CHANCE   September 1983
Stuart Adamson / Mark Brezicki / Bruce Watson / Tony Butler
Virgin Music . . . . UK
Big Country . . . . Mercury COUNT 4

CHANCES ARE   November 1957
Robert Allen / Al Stillman
Dominion Music Co. Ltd . . . . USA
Michael Desmond . . . . Columbia DB 4018
Johnny Mathis . . . . Fontana TFL 5058
The McGuire Sisters . . . . Vogue LVA 9146

CHANGE   February 1983
Roland Orzabal
Dick James Music . . . . UK
Tears For Fears . . . . Mercury IDEA 4

CHANGE PARTNERS   1938
Irving Berlin
Irving Berlin Ltd. . . . . USA
Film(s): . . . . .Carefree
Fred Astaire . . . . Philips BBL 7052
Elsie Randolph . . . . HMV BD 621
Fred Astaire . . . . London HAR 2219
Roy Hamilton . . . . Fontana TFE 17163
Fred Astaire appeared in *Carefree*.
Nominated for and Academy Award 1938.

CHANGING OF THE GUARD, THE   1932
Flotsam & Jetsam / (B.C. Hilliam / Malcolm McEachern)
Peter Maurice Music Co. Ltd. . . . . UK
Malcolm McEachern . . . . Columbia DB 630
Frank Barber & his Orchestra . . . . Columbia 33SX 1193
John Hanson . . . . Oriole MC 20015
The Grenadier Guards Band . . . . Decca DFE 6390

CHANGING PARTNERS   January 1954
Larry Coleman / Joe Darion
Robert Mellin Ltd. . . . . USA
Patti Page . . . . Oriole CB 1254
Kay Starr . . . . Capitol CL 14050
Bing Crosby . . . . Brunswick LAT 8281
Miki & Griff . . . . Pye NPL 18058

CHANSON D'AMOUR   March 1977
Wayne Shanklin
Carlin Music Corporation . . . . USA
Manhattan Transfer . . . . Atlantic K 10886
Steve Martin . . . . Philips PB 820
Ray Conniff Orchestra . . . . CBS BPG 62132

CHANT NUMBER ONE   August 1981
Gary Kemp
Reformation Music . . . . UK
Spandau Ballet . . . . Chrysalis CHS 2528

CHANTEZ CHANTEZ   June 1957
Albert Gamse / Irving Fields
Essex Music Ltd. . . . . USA
Marion Ryan . . . . Nixa NEP 24041
Eve Boswell . . . . Parlophone R 4299

CHANTILLY LACE   February 1959
J.P. Richardson
Southern Music Publishing Co. Ltd . . . . USA
Big Bopper . . . . Mercury MMC 14008

CHAPEL OF THE ROSES, THE   April 1957
Abel Baer / Remus Harris
Bregman, Vocco & Conn Ltd. . . . . USA
Malcolm Vaughan . . . . HMV 7EG 8272
Dickie Valentine . . . . Decca F 10874

CHARIOTS OF FIRE   June 1981
"Vangelis"
Warner Brothers Music . . . . USA
Film(s): . . . . Chariots of Fire

Vangelis . . . . Polydor POSP 246

CHARLESTON   1925
James P. Johnson / Cecil Mack
Chappell & Co. Ltd. . . . . USA
Show(s): . . . . Running' Wild
Film(s): . . . . You're My Everything
The Hannan Dance Band . . . . Columbia 3716
The California Ramblers . . . . Riverside RLP 12-801
James P. Johnson (Piano) . . . . London AL 3553
Eddie Condon & his Orchestra . . . . Brunswick LAT 8271
Pee Wee Hunt & his Band . . . . Capitol CL 13188

CHARLEY MY BOY   1924
Gus Kahn / Ted Fiorito
Francis, Day & Hunter Ltd. . . . . USA
The California Ramblers . . . . Columbia 3542
The Andrews Sisters . . . . Brunswick 04428
Teddy Philips & his Orchestra . . . . London L 524
Peggy Lee . . . . Capitol T 1131

CHARLIE BROWN   April 1959
Jerry Leiber / Mike Stoller
Progressive Music Ltd . . . . USA
The Coasters . . . . London HAK 2237
Ray Ellington . . . . Nixa N 15189
The Chordettes . . . . London HAA 2388

CHARM OF YOU, THE   1946
Jule Styne / Sammy Cahn
Robbins Music Corporation Ltd. . . . . USA
Film(s): . . . . Anchors Aweigh
Frank Sinatra . . . . Fontana TFE 17043
Beverly Kenny . . . . Vogue VA 160141
Frank Sinatra appeared in *Anchors Aweigh*.

CHARMAINE   1927
Erno Rapee / Lew Pollack
Keith Prowse Music Publishing Co. Ltd. . . . . USA
Film(s): . . . . Sunset Boulevard
Florence Oldham . . . . Columbia 4675
The Savoy Orpheans . . . . HMV B 5330
The Mantovani (1951) . . . . Decca LK 4105
The Four Freshmen . . . . Capitol CL 14731
Johnny Gregory & his Orchestra . . . Fontana TFL 5090
The Bachelors (1963) . . . . Decca F 11559

CHATTANOOGA CHOO CHOO   1942
Mack Gordon / Harry Warren
Robbins Music Corporation Ltd . . . . USA
Film(s):Sun Valley Serenade / Springtime in the Rockies / The Glenn Miller Story
Glenn Miller & his Orchestra . . . . RCA RCX 1035
The Andrews Sisters . . . . Brunswick 03290
Tex Beneke & The Modernaires . . . . . Vogue LVA 9103
Carmen Miranda . . . . MCA MCL 1703
Nominated for an Academy Award 1941.
Carmen Miranda appeared in *Springtime in the Rockies*.
Glenn Miller appeared in *Sun Valley Serenade*

CHATTANOOGIE SHOESHINE BOY   March 1950
Harry Stone / Jack Stapp
Anglo-Pic Music Co. Ltd . . . . USA
Film(s): . . . . Indian Territory
Donald Peers . . . . HMV B 9899
Bing Crosby . . . . Brunswick 04442
Red Foley . . . . Brunswick 04467
Phil Harris . . . . HMV B 9895
Pat Boone . . . . London HAD 2030

CHEATIN' ON ME   1925
Jack Yellen / Lew Pollack
Lawrence Wright Music Co. Ltd. . . . . USA
The California Ramblers . . . . Riverside RLP 12-801
Jimmy Lunceford & his Orchestra . . . . Philips BBL 7037
Julie London . . . . London HAG 2353

CHECK OUT THE GROOVE   April 1980
Rodney Brown / Willie Lester
Peterman Music Co. . . . . USA
Bobby Thurston . . . . Epic EPC 8348

CHECK THIS OUT   June 1988
Lee Adams

Polygram Music . . . . USA
L.A. Mix . . . . **A&M USA 629**

CHEE CHEE-OO-CHEE   **May 1955**
Saverio Serachini / John Turner / Geoffrey Parsons
Peter Maurice Music Co. Ltd. . . . . Italy
Alma Cogan . . . . **HMV 7M 293**
The Johnston Brothers . . . . **Decca F 10513**
Dean Martin . . . . **Capitol CL 14311**

CHEEK TO CHEEK   **1935**
Irving Berlin
Irving Berlin Ltd . . . . USA
Film(s): . . . . Top Hat
Fred Astaire . . . . **HMV 7EG 8463**
Ginger Rogers . . . . **Decca F 5747**
Fred Astaire . . . . **Philips BBL 7052**
Eydie Gormé & Steve Lawrence . . . . **HMV CLP 1372**
Fred Astaire & Ginger Rogers appeared in *Top Hat*.
Nominated for an Academy Award in 1935.

CHEERFUL LITTLE EARFUL   **1931**
Harry Warren / Billy Rose / Ira Gershwin
Francis, Day & Hunter Ltd . . . . USA
Show(s): . . . . Sweet and Low
Ben Selvin & his Orchestra . . . . **Columbia CB 225**
Jack Hylton & his Orchestra . . . . **HMV B 5972**
Jerry Fielding & his Orchestra . . . . **London HAPB 1027**

CHEERIE BEERIE BE   **1928**
Mabel Wayne / Sam M. Lewis / Joe Young
Francis, Day & Hunter Ltd. . . . . USA
Paul Whiteman & his Orchestra . . . . **HMV B 5376**

CHEQUERED LOVE   **May 1981**
Marty Wilde / Ricky Wilde
Rak Music . . . . UK
Kim Wilde . . . . **Rak RAK 330**

CHERIE   **1921**
Leo Wood / Irving Bibo
Francis, Day & Hunter Ltd . . . . USA
Paul Whiteman & his Orchestra . . . . **HMV B 1253**

CHERISH   **July 1985**
Ronald Bell / James Taylor
Warner Chappell Music . . . . USA
Kool & The Gang . . . . **De Lite DE 20**

CHERISH   **September 1989**
Madonna Ciccone / Patrick Leonard
Warner Chappell Music . . . . USA
Madonna . . . . **Sire W 2883**

CHEROKEE   **1939**
Ray Noble
Peter Maurice Music Co. Ltd. . . . . UK
Film(s): . . . . Jam Session / Drum Crazy
Ray Noble & his Orchestra . . . . **Columbia FB 2102**
Charlie Barnet & his Orchestra . . . . **RCA RCX 1008**
The Clark Sisters . . . . **London HAD 2128**
Sarah Vaughan . . . . **Emarcy EJL 100**
Joannie Sommers . . . . **Warner Brothers WM 4045**
Charlie Barnet appeared in *Jam Session*.

CHERRY PINK AND APPLE BLOSSOM WHITE **April 1955**
'Louiguy' / Jacques Larue / Mack David
Chappell & Co. Ltd. . . . . France
Film(s): . . . . Under Water
Perez Prado & his Orchestra . . . . **RCA RCX 1001**
Eddie Calvert & his Orchestra . . . . **Columbia SCM 5168**
Ted Heath & his Music . . . . **Decca LK 4386**
Modern Romance (1982) . . . . **WEA K 19245**
Perez Prado appeared in *Under Water*.

CHERRY STONES   **May 1950**
John Jerome
John Fields Music . . . . UK
Joy Nichols . . . . **Decca F 9333**
The Radio Revellers . . . . **Columbia DB 2666**
The Tanner Sisters . . . . **HMV B 9900**
Vera Lynn & Lee Lawrence . . . . **Decca F 9448**

CHESTNUT TREE, THE   **1938**
Jimmy Kennedy / Tommie Connor / Hamilton Kennedy
Peter Maurice Music Co. Ltd. . . . . UK
Jack Hylton & his Orchestra . . . . **HMV BD 5439**
Joe Loss & his Orchestra . . . . **Regal Zonophone MR 2966**
Dick James . . . . **Parlophone GEP 8708**

CHEWING A PIECE OF STRAW   **1945**
Howard Barnes / Hedley Grey
Bradbury Wood Ltd. . . . . UK
Jack Payne & his Orchestra,
vocal The Crackerjacks . . . . **HMV BD 5894**
Geraldo & his Orchestra,
vocal Carol Carr & Len Camber . . . . **Parlophone F 2081**

CHEWING GUM   **1933**
Art Kassel
Campbell Connelly & Co. Ltd. . . . . USA
Ray Noble & his Orchestra . . . . **HMV B 6369**
Roy Fox & his Band . . . . **Decca F 3570**

CHI MAI   **April 1981**
Ennio Morricone
EMI Music . . . . Italy
Ennio Morricone Orchestra . . . . **BBC RESL 92**
Theme of the television series *The Life and Times of David Lloyd George*.

CHI-BABA CHI-BABA   **1947**
Mack David / Al Hoffman / Jerry Livingston
Sun Music Publishing Co. Ltd. . . . . USA
Perry Como . . . . **HMV BD 1180**
Denny Dennis . . . . **Decca F 8810**

CHICA CHICA BOOM CHIC   **1941**
Harry Warren / Mack Gordon
Robbins Music Corporation Ltd . . . . USA
Film(s): . . . . That Night In Rio
Carmen Miranda . . . . **Brunswick 03207**
Xavier Cugat & his Orchestra,
vocal Lena Romay . . . . **Parlophone R 2801**
Carmen Miranda appeared in *That Night in Rio*.

CHICAGO (That Toddlin' Town)   **1922**
Fred Fisher
B. Feldman & Co. Ltd . . . . USA
Film(s): . . . . Oh! You Beautiful Doll / With a Song in My Heart
Paul Whiteman & his Orchestra . . . . **HMV B 1526**
Tommy Dorsey & his Orchestra . . . . **RCA RCX 1012**
The Clark Sisters . . . . **London HAD 2128**
Frank Sinatra (1957) . . . . **Capitol EAP 20062**
Eddie Condon's Chicagoans . . . . . . **Warner Brothers WM 4009**

CHICK   **April 1959**
Joe Henderson
Henderson Music Ltd . . . . UK
Joe 'Mr. Piano' Henderson . . . . **Nixa N 15187**

CHICK A BOOM   **November 1953**
Bob Merrill
Dash Music Ltd. . . . . USA
Film(s): . . . . Those Redheads from Seattle
Guy Mitchell . . . . **Philips BBR 8031**
The Keynotes . . . . **Decca F 10185**
Guy Mitchell appeared in *Those Redheads from Seattle*.

CHICK CHICK CHICKEN   **1925**
Thomas McGhee / Fred Holt / Irving King
Campbell Connelly & Co. Ltd. . . . . UK
Cyril Newton . . . . **HMV B 2156**
Jack Hylton & his Orchestra . . . . **HMV B 2121**

CHICKEN REEL, THE   **1912**
Joseph.M. Daly
Francis, Day & Hunter Ltd . . . . USA
The Flanagan Brothers . . . . **Regal MR 682**
Jimmy Dorsey & his Orchestra . . . . **Brunswick 02364**
Ronnie Munro Orchestra . . . . **HMV BD 5298**
The Robin Hood Band . . . . **Columbia 33SX 1344**
Les Paul (guitar) . . . . **Capitol CL 13466**

CHICKEN SONG, THE   **May 1986**
Phil Pope / Rob Grant / Douglas Naylor
Island Music . . . . UK
Spitting Image . . . . **Virgin SPIT 1**

CHICKERY CHICK 1946
Sidney Lippman / Sylvia Dee
Campbell Connelly & Co. Ltd. . . . . USA
Evelyn Knight . . . . **Brunswick 03629**
Carroll Gibbons & The Savoy Orpheans,
vocal Rita Williams . . . . **Columbia FB 3191**
Ambrose & his Orchestra, vocal Alan Dean . . . . . **Decca F 8620**

CHILD'S PRAYER, A September 1975
Errol Brown
Rak Music Ltd . . . . UK
Hot Chocolate . . . . **Rak 212**

CHILDREN OF THE REVOLOUTION, THE October 1972
Marc Bolan
Wizard Music . . . . UK
T. Rex . . . . **T. Rex MARC 2**

CHILI BEAN 1921
Albert Von Tilzer / Lew Brown
Francis, Day & Hunter Ltd . . . . USA
Show(s): . . . . Pot Luck
Frank Crumit . . . . **Columbia 3003**
The Mayfair Orchestra . . . . **HMV C 1062**
The Benson Orchestra of Chicago . . . . **HMV B 1180**

CHILI BOM BOM 1924
Cliff Friend / Walter Donaldson
Francis, Day & Hunter Ltd. . . . . USA
The Savoy Orpheans . . . . **Columbia 3435**
Jack Jackson & his Orchestra . . . . **HMV B 6550**
The Tuneful Twenties Dance Orchestra . . . **Parlophone R 3326**

CHIM CHIM CHEREE February 1965
Richard M. Sherman / Robert B. Sherman
Walt Disney Music Co. Ltd . . . . USA
Film(s): . . . . Mary Poppins
Julie Andrews & Dick Van Dyke . . . . **HMV CLP 1794**
Julie Andrews & Dick Van Dyke appeared in *Mary Poppins*.
Academy Award winning song of 1964.

CHIN CHIN CHINAMAN 1896
Sidney Jones / Percy Greenbank
Ascherberg, Hopwood & Crew Ltd . . . . UK
Show(s): . . . . The Geisha
S.H. Dudley . . . . **Berliner 2-2165**
Victor Conway . . . . **Decca K 548**
John Gower . . . . **Discourses ABK 12**

CHINA BOY 1923
Dick Winfree / Phil Boutelje
Francis, Day & Hunter Ltd . . . . USA
Film(s): . . . . The Benny Goodman Story
Ambrose & his Embassy Club Orchestra . . . . . **Columbia 3285**
Gene Austin . . . . **Panachord 26027**
The Benny Goodman Trio . . . . **Brunswick LAT 8103**
Benny Goodman & his Orchestra . . . . **Fontana TFE 17184**

CHINA GIRL June 1983
David Bowie / Iggy Pop
Fleur Music . . . . USA
David Bowie . . . . **EMI EA 157**

CHINA IN YOUR HAND November 1987
Carol Decker / Ronald Rogers
Virgin Music . . . . UK
T'Pau . . . . **Siren SRN 64**
Ivor Novello Nomination

CHINA TEA September 1959
Trevor Stanford
Mills Music Ltd . . . . UK
Russ Conway (piano) . . . . **Columbia DB 4337**

CHINAMAN'S SONG, THE 1921
Percy Fletcher / Oscar Asche
Ascherberg, Hopwood & Crew Ltd. UK
Show(s): . . . . Cairo
Frank Cochrane . . . . **Columbia 3109**
Frank Cochrane appeared in *Cairo*.

CHINATOWN MY CHINATOWN 1910
William Jerome / Jean Schwartz
Francis, Day & Hunter Ltd. . . . . USA
Show(s): . . . . Up and Down Broadway / Push and Go

Film(s):Bright Lights / Is Everybody Happy / Jolson Sings Again /
Eddie Foy and the Seven Little Foys
Shirley Kellog . . . . **Columbia 557**
The Mills Brothers . . . . **Brunswick 01331**
Bing Crosby . . . . **Brunswick LAT 8217**
Al Jolson . . . . **Brunswick LAT 8294**
The Alex Welsh Band . . . . **Columbia 33SX 1322**
Bob Hope . . . . **HMV DLP 1088**
Louis Armstrong & his Orchestra . . . . **Parlophone R 1159**
Bob Hope appeared in *Eddie Foy and the Seven Little Foys*.
Shirley Kellog appeared in *Push and Go*.

CHINESE LAUNDRY BLUES 1932
Jack Cottrell / George Formby
B. Feldman & Co. Ltd. . . . . UK
George Formby . . . . **Decca DFE 6144**

CHIP OFF THE OLD BLOCK 1908
Harold Simpson / W.H. Squire
Chappell & Co. Ltd . . . . UK
Robert Radford . . . . **HMV E 73**
Peter Dawson . . . . **HMV B 3378**

CHIQUITA 1928
Mabel Wayne / L. Wolfe Gilbert
Francis, Day & Hunter Ltd. . . . . USA
Paul Whiteman & his Orchestra . . . . **Columbia 4981**

CHIQUITA BANANA 1946
Lew MacKenzie / Garth Montgomery / William Wirges
Dash Music Ltd. . . . . USA
Roberto Inglez & his Orchestra . . . . **Parlophone F 2183**
Edmundo Ros & his Orchestra . . . . **Decca F 8725**
Xavier Cugat & his Orchestra,
vocal Buddy Clark . . . . **Columbia DB 2682**

CHIQUITITA February 1979
Benny Andersson / Bjorn Ulvaeus
U.N.I.C.E.F. . . . . Sweden
Abba . . . . **Epic EPC 7030**

CHIRPY CHIRPY CHEEP CHEEP August 1971
Claudio Fabi / Harold Stott
Flamingo Music Ltd . . . . Italy
Middle of the Road . . . . **RCA 2047**

CHITTY CHITTY BANG BANG February 1969
Richard M. Sherman / Robert B. Sherman
United Artists Music Co. Ltd. . . . . USA
Film(s): . . . . Chitty Chitty Bang Bang
Dick Van Dyke, Sally Ann Howes,
Adrian Hall & Heather Ripley . . . . **United Artists ULP 1200**
Dick Van Dyke, Sally Ann Howes, Adrian Hall & Heather Ripley
appeared in *Chitty Chitty Bang Bang*.
Nominated for an Academy Award 1968.

CHLOE 1928
Gus Kahn / Neil Moret
Francis, Day & Hunter Ltd. . . . . USA
Film(s): . . . . Bring on the Girls
Adelaide Hall . . . . **Decca F 7460**
The New Mayfair Orchestra . . . . **HMV B 5563**
Duke Ellington & his Orchestra . . . . **RCA RD 27133**
Dinah Shore . . . . **HMV BD 1026**
Spike Jones & his City Slickers (1946) . . . . **HMV BD 1107**
Ted Heath & his Music . . . . **Decca LK 4224**
Spike Jones & the City Slickers appeared in *Bring on the Girls*.

CHON KINA 1896
Sidney Jones / Percy Greenbank
Ascherberg, Hopwood & Crew Ltd . . . . UK
Show(s): . . . . The Geisha
Denise Orme . . . . **HMV GC 3665**
Ann Welch . . . . **Decca K 548**

CHONG (He Come From Hong Kong) 1920
Harold Weeks
Francis, Day & Hunter Ltd . . . . USA
Show(s): . . . . Bran Pie
Odette Myrtil . . . . **Columbia F 1012**
The London Dance Orchestra . . . . **Columbia 800**
The Mayfair Dance Orchestra . . . . **HMV C 941**

CHOO CHOO 1931
Matty Malneck / Frankie Trumbauer

54

Lafleur & Co. Ltd .... USA
Frankie Trumbauer & his Orchestra .... Parlophone R 821
Jack Payne & The BBC Dance Orchestra .... Columbia CB 228
Jack Hylton & his Orchestra .... HMV B 5973

CHOO CHOO CH'BOOGIE   1947
Vaughan Horton / Denver Darling / Milton Gabler
Victoria Music Co. Ltd. .... USA
Louis Jordan & his Tympany Five .... Brunswick 03696
Bill Haley & his Comets .... Brunswick LAT 8139
Quincy Jones & his Orchestra .... Mercury ZEP 10047

CHOO'N' GUM   June 1950
Vic Mizzy / Mann Curtis
Chappell & Co. Ltd .... USA
Teresa Brewer .... London L 678
Dean Martin .... Capitol CL 13290
The Tanner Sisters .... HMV B 9923

CHOSEN FEW, THE   October 1979
Ben Findon
Black Sheep Music .... UK
The Dooleys .... GTO GT 258

CHRISTMAS ALPHABET   December 1955
Buddy Kaye / Jules Loman
Pickwick Music Ltd. .... USA
Dickie Valentine .... Decca DFE 6408
The McGuire Sisters .... Coral Q 72108

CHRISTMAS AND YOU   December 1956
Russell Faith / Clarence Kehner
Leeds Music Ltd. .... USA
Joni James .... MGM 696
Dave King .... Decca DFE 6408

CHRISTMAS DREAMING   1947
Irving Gordon / Lester Lee
Leeds Music Ltd. .... USA
Lou Preager & his Orchestra .... Columbia FB 3352
Dick Haymes .... Brunswick 03927
Frank Sinatra .... Philips BBR 8114

CHRISTMAS ISLAND   January 1957
Lyle Moraine
Macmelodies Ltd .... USA
The Andrews Sisters (1948) .... Brunswick 03947
Dickie Valentine .... Decca F 10798

CHRISTOPHER COLUMBUS   April 1951
Dob Merrill / Terry Gilkyson
Campbell Connelly & Co. Ltd .... USA
Guy Mitchell .... Columbia DB 2831
Cyril Stapleton & his Orchestra,
vocal the Strangers .... Decca F 9777

CHRISTOPHER ROBIN AT BUCKINGHAM PALACE   1924
A.A. Milne / Harold Fraser-Simson
Ascherberg, Hopwood & Crew Ltd. .... UK
Petula Clark .... Nixa NEP 24006
Max Bygraves .... Decca LK 4333

CHRISTOPHER ROBIN IS SAYING HIS PRAYERS   1935
A.A. Milne / Harold Fraser-Simson
Ascherberg, Hopwood & Crew Ltd .... UK
John Morel .... Parlophone R 1541
Gracie Fields .... Regal Zonophone MR 2893
Ann Stephens .... HMV 7EG 8187
The Hull Orpheus Choir .... Pye CMT 34000

CHURCH OF THE POISON MIND   April 1983
George O'Dowd / Jonathan Moss / Michael Craig / Roy Hay
Virgin Music .... UK
Culture Club .... Virgin VS 571

CIAO CIAO BAMBINA (Piove)   April 1959
Domenico Modungo / 'Verde' / Mitchell Parish
Robbins Music Corporation Ltd .... Italy
Domenico Modungo .... Oriole MG 10023
The Marino Marini Quartet .... Durium TLU 97020
Connie Francis .... MGM C 821
The Four Aces .... Brunswick OE 9458

CIELITO LINDO   1923
Sebastian Yradier / Carlo Fernandez / Neil Wilson

Herman Darewski Music Publishing Co. Ltd .... Mexico
Film(s): .... Casino de Paree
The Lecuona Cuban Boys .... Columbia 33S 1075
Deanna Durbin .... Brunswick 03375
The Trio Los Panchos .... Philips BBL 7469
Percy Faith & his Orchestra .... Philips BBL 7487
Al Jolson .... Sandy Hook SH 2030
Al Jolson appeared in *Casino de Paree.*

CIGAREETS, WHUSKY AND WILD WILD WOMEN   March 1949
Tim Spencer
Chappell & Co. Ltd .... USA
Red Ingle & The Natural Seven .... Capitol EAP 20052

CIGARETTE   1904
Herbert Haines / Evelyn Baker / Charles Taylor
Francis, Day & Hunter Ltd. .... UK
Show(s): .... The Catch of the Season
Stanley Kirby .... HMV GC 3-2176

CINDERELLA ROCKAFELLA   April 1968
Mason Williams / Nancy Ames
Rondor Music (London) Ltd. .... USA
Esther & Abi Ofarim .... Philips BF 1640

CINDERELLA STAY IN MY ARMS   1938
Jimmy Kennedy / Michael Carr
Peter Maurice Music Co. Ltd. .... UK
Joe Loss & his Band .... Regal Zonophone MR 2873
Ambrose & his Orchestra, vocal Vera Lynn ..... Decca F 6869
Dick Lee .... Columbia SCM 5094

CINDERELLA SWEETHEART   1938
Art Strauss / Bob Dale
Lawrence Wright Music Co. Ltd. .... UK
Leslie Hutchinson (Hutch) .... Parlophone F 1268
Ambrose & his Orchestra, vocal Vera Lynn ..... Decca F 6869
Jack Hylton & his Orchestra .... HMV BD 5426

CINDY INCIDENTALLY   March 1973
Rod Stewart / Ron Wood / Ian McLagan
Warner Brothers Music Ltd. .... UK
Faces .... Warner Brothers K 16247

CINDY, OH CINDY   November 1956
Bob Barron / Burt Long
Dash Music Ltd. .... USA
Eddie Fisher .... HMV POP 273
Tony Brent .... Columbia DB 3844

CIRCLES   July 1972
Harry Chapin
Ampar Music .... USA
The New Seekers .... Polydor 2058242

CIRCLES IN THE SAND   June 1988
Richard Nowells / Ellen Shipley
Virgin Music .... USA
Belinda Carlisle .... Virgin VS 1074

CIRCUS   October 1949
Louis Alter / Bob Russell
Anglo-Pic Music Co. Ltd .... USA
Tony Martin .... HMV B 9854
Dick Haymes .... Brunswick 04280
The Four Freshmen .... Capitol T 1008

CIRCUS   October 1987
Vincent Clarke / Andrew Bell
Sonet Music .... UK
Erasure .... Mute MUTE 66

CIRIBIRIBIN   1910
Alberto Pestalozza / Rudolf Thaler
Out of Copyright .... Italy
Film(s): .... One Night of Love / Hit the Deck
Lucrezia Bori .... HMV DA 900
Grace Moore (1935) .... Brunswick 01922
Bing Crosby & The Andrews Sisters .... Brunswick 02881
Harry James & his Orchestra (1944) ...... Parlophone R 2908
Frank Sinatra .... Columbia DB 2145
Harry James & his Orchestra .... Capitol LC 6800
Jane Powell, Debbie Reynolds, Tony Martin, Vic Damone &
Russ Tamblyn .... MGM EP 525

Grace Moore appeared in *One Night of Love*.
Jane Powell, Debbie Reynolds, Tony Martin, Vic Damone & Russ Tamblyn appeared in *Hit The Deck*.
First published in Italy in 1898.
Theme song of Harry James.
New Lyric added by Jack Lawrence in 1944.

CIVILIZATION   **January 1948**
Bob Hilliard / Carl Sigman
Edwin H. Morris & Co. Ltd. .... USA
Show(s): .... Angel in the Wings
Danny Kaye & The Andrews Sisters .... **Brunswick 03836**
The King Brothers .... **Parlophone GEP 8760**

CLAIR   **November 1972**
Gilbert O'Sullivan
M.A.M. (Music Publishing) Ltd. .... UK
Gilbert O'Sullivan .... **MAM 84**
Ivor Novello Nomination.

CLAIRVOYANT, THE   **December 1988**
Steve Harris
Zomba Music .... UK
Iron Maiden .... **EMI EM 79**

CLANCY LOWERED THE BOOM   **July 1949**
Hy Heath / Johnny Lange
Leeds Music Ltd .... USA
Dan Daley & The Andrews Sisters .... **Brunswick 04088**
Dennis Day .... **Capitol T 741**

CLAP HANDS, HERE COMES CHARLEY   **1926**
Billy Rose / Ballard MacDonald / Joseph Meyer
Lawrence Wright Music Co. Ltd. .... USA
Film(s): .... Funny Lady
The California Ramblers .... **Riverside RLP 12-801**
Charlie Kunz (Piano) .... **Decca F 9862**
The Jazzpickers .... **Emarcy EJL 1265**
Big' Tiny Little .... **Vogue LVA 9136**
Barbra Streisand .... **Arista ARTY 101**
Signature tune of Charlie Kunz.
Barbra Streisand appeared in *Funny Lady*.

CLAP YO' HANDS   **1927**
George Gershwin / Ira Gershwin
Chappell & Co. Ltd. .... USA
Show(s): .... Oh Kay
Film(s): .... Rhapsody in Blue / Funny Face
Claude Hulbert .... **Columbia 4617**
George Gershwin (piano) .... **Columbia 4538**
Fred Astaire & Kay Thompson .... **HMV CLP 1119**
Doris Day .... **Philips BBL 7471**
Claude Hulbert appeared in the British production of *Oh Kay*.
Fred Astaire & Kay Thompson appeared in *Funny Face*.

CLAPPING SONG, THE   **June 1965**
Lincoln Chase
Gallico Music Ltd .... USA
Shirley Ellis .... **London HL 9961**
The Belle Stars (1982) .... **Stiff BUY 155**

CLASSIC   **March 1982**
Adrian Gurvitz
Rak Music .... UK
Adrian Gurvitz .... **Rak RAK 339**

CLASSICAL GAS   **October 1968**
Mason Williams
Rondor Music (London) Ltd. .... USA
Mason Williams .... **Warner Brothers WB 7190**

CLEMENTINE   **April 1960**
Traditional, new lyric by Woody Harris
Southern Music Publishing Co. Ltd .... USA
Bobby Darin .... **London HAK 2235**

CLIMB EV'RY MOUNTAIN   **September 1961**
Richard Rodgers / Oscar Hammerstein II
Williamson Music Ltd. .... USA
Show(s): .... Sound of Music
Film(s): .... Sound of Music
Patricia Neway .... **Philips ABL 3370**
Constance Shacklock .... **HMV CLP 1453**
Peggy Wood .... **RCA RB 6616**
Shirley Bassey .... **Columbia DB 4685**

Patricia Neway appeared in the American production of *Sound of Music*.
Constance Shacklock appeared in the British production of *Sound of Music*.
Peggy Wood appeared in the film of *Sound of Music*.

CLIMBING UP   **1937**
Eric Maschwitz / Mischa Spoliansky
Cinephonic Music Co. Ltd. .... UK
Film(s): .... King Solomon's Mines
Paul Robeson .... **HMV 7EG 8687**
Paul Robeson .... **HMV CLP 1415**
Paul Robeson appeared in *King Soloman's Mines*.

CLOPIN CLOPANT   **March 1949**
Bruno Coquatrix / Pierre Dudan / Kermit Goell
Imperia Music Co. Ltd .... France
Show(s): .... Latin Quarter
George Guetary .... **Columbia DB 2513**
Jean Caval .... **HMV B 0744**
Josephine Baker .... **RCA RD 27177**
Paul Anka .... **Columbia 33SX 1196**
George Guetary appeared in *Latin Quarter*.

CLOSE (To The Edit)   **February 1985**
Anne Dudley / Trevor Horn / Gary Langan / Jonathan Jeczlik & Paul Morley
Perfect Songs .... UK
The Art of Noise .... **ZTT ZTPS 1**

CLOSE AS PAGES IN A BOOK   **1946**
Sigmund Romberg / Dorothy Fields
Chappell & Co. Ltd. .... USA
Show(s): .... Up in Central Park
Film(s): .... Up in Central Park
Bing Crosby .... **Brunswick LA 8675**
Vic Damone .... **Philips BBL 7259**

CLOSE THE DOOR
(They're Coming in the Window)   **September 1955**
Fred Ebb / Paul Klein
Duchess Music Ltd. .... USA
The Stargazers .... **Decca LF 1297**
Benny Lee .... **Parlophone GEP 8561**
Jim Lowe .... **London HAD 2108**

CLOSE TO YOU   **1943**
Jerry Livingston / Al Hoffman / Carl Lampl
Dash Music Ltd .... USA
Ambrose & his Orchestra, vocal Rex Eaton ..... **Decca F 8359**
Frank Sinatra .... **Capitol T 6130**
Sarah Vaughan .... **Mercury MMC 14059**

CLOSE TO YOU   **October 1970**
Burt Bacharach / Hal David
Carlin Music Corporation .... USA
The Carpenters .... **A&M AMS 800**
Matt Monro .... **Capitol ST 22546**
Richard Chamberlain .... **MGM 1211**

CLOSE TO YOU   **July 1990**
Gary Benson / Winston Sela
Warner Chappell Music .... UK
Maxi Priest .... **Ten TEN 294**

CLOSE YOUR EYES   **1934**
Bernice Petkere
Keith Prowse Music Publishing Co. Ltd. .... USA
Ruth Etting .... **Brunswick 01614**
Ray Noble & his Orchestra, vocal Al Bowlly ... **HMV 7EG 8186**
Doris Day .... **Philips BBL 7211**

CLOSEST THING TO HEAVEN   **August 1984**
Martin Brammer / Dave Brewis
ATV Music .... UK
The Kane Gang .... **London SK 15**

CLOUD LUCKY SEVEN   **December 1953**
Charles Tobias / Peter De Rose
Robbins Music Corporation Ltd. .... USA
Guy Mitchell .... **Philips BBL 7265**
Frankie Vaughan .... **HMV 7M 167**

CLOUD NINE   **September 1969**
Barrett Strong / Norman Whitfield
Jobete Music (UK) Ltd. .... USA
The Temptations .... **Tamla Motown TMG 707**

CLOUDS ACROSS THE MOON　　　　April 1985
Richard Hewson
Chappell & Co. Ltd . . . . UK
The Rah Band . . . . RCA PB 40025

CLOUDS WILL SOON ROLL BY, THE　　　　1932
Harry Woods / George Brown
Lawrence Wright Music Co. Ltd. . . . . USA
Layton & Johnstone . . . . Columbia DB 920
Tony Brent . . . . Columbia DB 4066

CLUB TROPICANA　　　　August 1983
George Michael / Andrew Ridgely
Morrison Leahy Music . . . . UK
Wham . . . . Inner Vision A 3613

CO-CO　　　　July 1971
Mike Chapman / Nicky Chinn
Chinnichap Music . . . . UK
The Sweet . . . . RCA 2087

COAL BLACK MAMMY　　　　1921
Ivy St. Helier / Laddie Cliff
Francis, Day & Hunter Ltd . . . . UK
Show(s): . . . . The Co-Optimists
Walter Jefferies . . . . HMV B 1289
The 'Queens' Dance Orchestra . . . . HMV B 1275
The George Mitchell Singers . . . . HMV CLP 1399
Al Jolson . . . . Murray Hill P 15531

COAX ME A LITTLE BIT　　　　1946
Charles Tobias / Nat Simon
Victoria Music Co. Ltd. . . . . USA
Dinah Shore . . . . Columbia DB 2271
Edmundo Ros & his Orchestra . . . . Decca F 8649
The Andrews Sisters . . . . Brunswick 03729

COBBLER'S SONG, THE　　　　1916
Frederick Norton / Oscar Asche
Keith Prowse Music Publishing Co. Ltd. . . . . UK
Show(s): . . . . Chu Chin Chow
Film(s): . . . . Chu Chin Chow
Bryn Gwyn . . . . Homophone H 530
Frank Cochrane . . . . Columbia D 1379
Peter Dawson . . . . HMV DLP 1180
Inia Te Wiata . . . . HMV CLP 1311
Bryn Gwyn & Frank Cochrane appeared in the British production of
Chu Chin Chow.

COCK-EYED OPTIMIST, A　　　　December 1951
Richard Rodgers / Oscar Hammerstein II
Williamson Music Ltd . . . . USA
Show(s): . . . . South Pacific
Film(s): . . . . South Pacific
Mary Martin . . . . Philips BBL 7157
Mitzi Gaynor . . . . RCA RB 16065
Mary Martin appeared in both the American and British productions
of *South Pacific.*
Mitzi Gaynor appeared in the film *South Pacific.*

COCKTAILS FOR TWO　　　　1934
Sam Coslow / Arthur Johnston
Victoria Music Co. Ltd. . . . . USA
Film(s): . . . Murder at the Vanities / She Loves Me Not / Ladies Man
Carl Brisson . . . . Decca F 5014
Carroll Gibbons & his Orchestra . . . . Columbia CB 775
Spike Jones & his City Slickers (1945) . . . . RCA RCX 1030
Keely Smith . . . . Capitol T 1073
Carl Brisson appeared in *Murder at the Vanities.*
Spike Jones & The City Slickers appeared in *Ladies Man*
Bing Crosby appeared in *She Loves Me Not*
Theme song of Carl Brisson.

COFFEE SONG, THE　　　　1947
Bob Hilliard / Dick Miles
Southern Music Publishing Co. Ltd. . . . . USA
Show(s): . . . . Piccadilly Hayride
The Andrews Sisters . . . . Brunswick 03789
Frank Sinatra . . . . Columbia DB 2376
The King Brothers . . . . Parlophone GEP 8760

COKEY COKEY, THE　　　　1945
Traditional, English lyric by Jimmy Kennedy
Campbell Connelly & Co. Ltd . . . . USA
Lou Preager & his Orchestra, vocal Paul Rich . . Columbia FB 3123

Billy Cotton & his Band, vocal Alan Breeze . . Decca DFE 6224
Russ Morgan & his Orchestra . . . . Brunswick LA 8707
Also known as 'The Hokey Cokey'.

COLD COLD HEART　　　　November 1951
Hank Williams
Acuff-Rose Publishing Co. Ltd . . . . USA
Tony Bennett . . . . Columbia DB 2924
Ellenn Wilson . . . . Brunswick 04809
Petula Clark . . . . Polygon P 1021
Hank Williams . . . . MGM D 137

COLD TURKEY　　　　November 1969
John Lennon
Northern Songs Ltd. . . . . UK
The Plastic Ono Band . . . . Apple 1001

COLETTE　　　　March 1960
Billy Fury
Peter Maurice Music Co. Ltd . . . . UK
Billy Fury . . . . Decca F 11200

COLLEGIATE　　　　1925
Moe Jaffe / Nat Bonx / Lew Brown
Keith Prowse Music Publishing Co. Ltd. . . . . USA
Show(s): . . . . Gay Paree
Film(s): . . . . . The Time, The Place and The Girl / Animal Crackers
The Denza Dance Band . . . . Columbia 3743
The California Ramblers . . . . Riverside RLP 12-801
The Swinging Sophomores . . . . Columbia 3957
The Andrews Sisters . . . . Capitol T 973

COLOURS　　　　July 1965
"Donovan"
Southern Music Publishing Co. Ltd . . . . UK
Donovan . . . . Pye 7N 15866

COMANCHEROS, THE　　　　February 1962
Tillman Franks
Robbins Music Corporation Ltd. . . . . USA
Lonnie Donegan . . . . Pye 7N 15410
Claude King . . . . Philips PB 1199

COMBINE HARVESTER　　　　June 1976
Melanie Safka
Keith Prowse Music Publishing Co. Ltd . . . . UK
The Wurzels . . . . EMI 2450
Parody of "Brand New Key".

COME AND GET IT　　　　February 1970
Paul McCartney
Northern Songs Ltd. . . . . UK
Film(s): . . . . The Magic Christian
Badfinger . . . . Apple 20

COME AND STAY WITH ME　　　　March 1965
Jackie De Shannon
Metric Music Ltd . . . . USA
Marianne Faithfull . . . . Decca F 10275

COME BACK AND FINISH WHAT YOU STARTED　　　August 1978
Van McCoy / Joe Cobb
United Artists Music Co. Ltd . . . . USA
Gladys Knight & The Pips . . . . Buddah BDS 473

COME BACK AND SHAKE ME　　　　May 1969
Kenny Young
April Music Ltd. . . . . UK
Clodagh Rodgers . . . . RCA 1792

COME BACK AND STAY　　　　October 1983
Jack Lee
Chrysalis Music . . . . UK
Paul Young . . . . CBS A 3636

COME BACK MY LOVE　　　　March 1978
Bobby Mansfield
Carlin Music Corporation . . . . USA
Darts . . . . Magnet MAG 110

COME BACK TO ERIN　　　　1868
Charlotte Barnard
. . . . UK
Nellie Melba . . . . HMV 3616
Frank Titterton . . . . Decca F 6101

Bing Crosby .... Warner Brothers WM 4046
The Bill Sheperd Singers .... Ace of Hearts AH 124

COME BACK TO SORRENTO (Tourna a Surriento)   1936
Ernesto De Curtis / Claude Aveling
G. Ricordi & Co. (London) Ltd .... Italy
Film(s): .... Paramount on Parade
Benjamino Gigli .... HMV DLP 1100
Richard Tucker .... Philips ABE 10067
Bing Crosby (1947) .... Brunswick 04134
Gracie Fields .... Decca LF 1140

COME CLOSER TO ME (Acercate Mas)   1946
Osvaldo Farres / Al Stewart
Southern Music Publishing Co. Ltd. .... Mexico
Film(s): .... Easy to Wed
Edmundo Ros & his Orchestra .... Decca F 8681
Nat 'King' Cole .... Capitol EAP 2-1031
Julie Dawn .... Columbia 33SX 1124

COME DOWN MA EVENING STAR   1912
John Stromberg / Robert B. Smith
B. Feldman & Co. Ltd. .... USA
Show(s): .... Twirly-Whirly
Film(s): .... Broadway to Hollywood / Lillian Russell
Alice Faye .... Caliban 6016
Alice Faye appeared in *Lillian Russell.*

COME HOME TO MY ARMS   December 1956
Leslie Baguley / Emily Jane
Chappell & Co. Ltd. .... UK
Dorothy Squires .... Nixa NPT 19019
The Beverley Sisters .... Decca F 10813
The Chordettes .... London HAA 2088

COME INTO MY LIFE   February 1987
Joyce Sims
Chrysalis Music .... USA
Joyce Sims .... London LON 161

COME JOSEPHINE IN MY FLYING MACHINE   1910
Alfred Bryan / Fred Fisher
B. Feldman & Co. Ltd. .... USA
Film(s): The Story of Vernon & Irene Castle / Oh You Beautiful Doll
Ada Jones .... Zonophone 1193

COME LIVE WITH ME   July 1983
Glen Gregory / Ian Marsh / Martyn Ware
Virgin Music .... UK
Heaven 17 .... Virgin VS 607

COME NEXT SPRING   April 1956
Max Steiner / Lenny Adelson
Frank Music Co. Ltd. .... USA
Film(s): .... Come Next Spring
Tony Bennett .... Philips BBR 8084
Joan Small .... Parlophone MSP 6219

COME ON AND GET MY LOVE (See C'mon And Get My Love)

COME ON A MY HOUSE   August 1951
Ross Bagdasarian / William Saroyan
Leeds Music Ltd .... USA
Film(s): .... Stars are Singing
Rosemary Clooney .... Philips BBL 7301
Kay Starr .... Capitol CL 13576
Della Reese .... RCA RD 27208
Rosemary Clooney appeared in *Stars are Singing.*

COME ON EILEEN   August 1982
Kevin Rowland / James Patterson / Kevin Adams
EMI Music .... UK
Dexy's Midnight Runners
& The Emerald Express .... Mercury DEXYS 9
Ivor Novello Award

COME ON FEEL THE NOISE (See Cum On Feel The Noise)

COME ON LETS GO   December 1958
Ritchie Valens
Essex Music Ltd .... USA
Tommy Steele .... Decca DFE 6551
Ritchie Valens .... Pye N 25000

COME ON OVER TO MY PLACE   October 1972
Barry Mann / Cynthia Weill
Screen Gems Music Ltd. .... USA
The Drifters .... Atlantic K 10216

COME OUT, COME OUT, WHEREVER YOU ARE   1945
Jule Styne / Sammy Cahn
Chappell & Co. Ltd. .... USA
Film(s): .... Step Lively
Geraldo & his Orchestra, vocal Len Camber . Parlophone F 2052
Johnny Green .... Decca F 8494

COME OUTSIDE   June 1962
Charles Blackwell
Southern Music Publishing Co. Ltd. .... UK
Mike Sarne .... Parlophone R 4902

COME PRETTY ONE (See Coom Pretty One)

COME PRIMA (More Than Ever)   December 1958
Mario Panzeri / S. Paola-Tacani / Mary Bond
Chappell & Co. Ltd .... Italy
Marino Marini .... Durium DLU 96034
Malcolm Vaughan .... HMV POP 538
Eve Boswell .... Parlophone R 4479

COME RAIN OR COME SHINE   1946
Johnny Mercer / Harold Arlen
Chappell & Co. Ltd. .... USA
Show(s): .... St. Louis Woman
Billie Holiday .... Columbia 33CX 10019
Dinah Shore .... Columbia SEG 7543
Steve Lawrence .... Coral FEP 2012
June Christy .... Capitol T 1202

(COME ROUND HERE) I'M THE ONE YOU NEED   March 1971
Eddie Holland / Brian Holland / Lamont Dozier
Carlin Music Corporation .... USA
Smokey Robinson & The Miracles ... Tamla Motown TMG 584

COME SOFTLY TO ME   May 1959
Garry Troxel / Barbara Ellis / Gretchen Christopher
Edwin H. Morris & Co. Ltd .... USA
The Fleetwoods .... London HAG 2339
Frankie Vaughan & The Kaye Sisters .... Philips PB 913
The New Seekers (1973) .... Polydor 2058315

COME TO BABY DO   1946
Inez James / Sidney Miller
Leeds Music Ltd. .... USA
Jimmy Dorsey & his Orchestra,
vocal Inez James .... Brunswick 03724
Duke Ellington & his Orchestra,
vocal Joya Sherrill .... HMV B 9492
Geraldo & his Orchestra, vocal Carol Carr .. Parlophone F 2161

COME TO ME   June 1978
Gene Price
Acoustic Music .... USA
Ruby Winters .... Creole CR 153

COME TO THE BALL   1910
Lionel Monckton / Adrian Ross / Percy Greenbank
Chappell & Co. Ltd .... UK
Show(s): .... The Quaker Girl
George Carvey .... HMV 02298
Gracie Leigh .... HMV 03298
The Columbia Light Opera Orchestra .... Columbia DX 413
Eric Robinson & his Orchestra .... Argo RG 40
George Carvey & Gracie Leigh appeared in the British production of
The Quaker Girl.

COME TO THE FAIR   1917
Helen Taylor / Easthope Martin
Edwin Ashdown Ltd. .... UK
Herbert Thorpe & Foster Richardson . Regal Zonophone G 5678
Ted & Julie Andrews (vocal)
and Barbara Andrews (piano) .... Columbia DB 2470
Frederick Harvey .... HMV CLP 1680

COME TOGETHER   November 1969
John Lennon / Paul McCartney
Northern Songs .... UK
The Beatles .... Apple R 5814

COME TOMORROW February 1965
Bob Elgin / Dolores Philips / Frank Augustus
Aberbach (London) Ltd. . . . . USA
Manfred Mann . . . . **HMV POP 1381**
Marie Knight . . . . **Fontana H 354**
Tommy Kinsman & his Orchestra . . . . **Fontana TL 5249**

COME WHAT MAY (Apres Toi) May 1972
Mario Panas / Yves Dessca / Klaus Munro & Norman Newell
Louvigny-Marquee Music Co. . . . . Luxembourg
Vicky Leandros . . . . **Philips 6000049**
Luxembourg entry for the 1972 Eurovision Song Contest (Placed First).

COME WITH ME MY HONEY 1945
Mack David / Joan Whitney / Alex Kramer
Campbell Connelly & Co. Ltd. . . . . USA
Film(s): . . . . Meet Miss Bobby Socks
Guy Lombardo & his Royal Canadians . . . . . **Brunswick 04163**
Edmundo Ros & his Orchestra . . . . **Decca F 8508**

COMES A-LONG A-LOVE January 1953
Al Sherman
Kassner Music . . . . USA
Kay Starr . . . . **Capitol CL 13808**
The Tanner Sisters . . . . **HMV B 10390**

COMES LOVE 1939
Lew Brown / Sammy Stept / Charles Tobias
Chappell & Co. Ltd. . . . . USA
Show(s): . . . . Yokel Boy / Funny Side Up
Film(s): . . . . Yokel Boy
Carroll Gibbons & his Orchestra,
  vocal Anne Lenner . . . . **Columbia FB 2339**
Billy Daniels . . . . **HMV DLP 1174**
Helen Merrill . . . . **Emarcy EJL 7501**
Sarah Vaughan . . . . **Mercury MMC 14024**

COMIN' HOME BABY January 1963
Ben Tucker / Bob Dorough
Belinda (London) Ltd . . . . USA
Mel Tormé . . . . **London HL 9643**

COMING AROUND AGAIN March 1987
Carly Simon
Warner Chappell Music . . . . USA
Carly Simon . . . . **Arista ARIST 687**

COMING HOME 1945
Billy Reid
Macmelodies Ltd. . . . . UK
Dorothy Squires . . . . **Parlophone F 2076**
Dorothy Squires . . . . **Nixa NPL 18015**

COMING IN ON A WING AND A PRAYER 1943
Harold Adamson / Jimmy McHugh
Francis, Day & Hunter Ltd . . . . USA
The Song Spinners . . . . **Brunswick 03469**
Ambrose & his Orchestra, vocal Anne Shelton . . **Decca F 8328**

COMING UP May 1980
Paul McCartney
McCartney Music . . . . UK
Paul McCartney . . . . **Parlophone T 6035**

COMMUNICATION March 1983
Gary Kemp
Reformation Music . . . . UK
Spandau Ballet . . . . **Chrysalis CHS 2668**

COMPLEX December 1979
Gary Numan
Andrew Heath Music Ltd. . . . . UK
Gary Numan . . . . **Beggars Banquet BEG 29**

COMPUTER LOVE January 1982
Ralf Hutter / Florian Schneider
EMI Music . . . . Holland
Kraftwerk . . . . **EMI 5207**

COMRADES 1890
Felix McGlennon / Tom Costello
Francis, Day & Hunter Ltd. . . . . UK
Film(s): . . . . Variety Jubilee
The Pavement Artists . . . . **Regal Zonophone MR 563**
Raymond Newell . . . . **Decca LK 4026**

CONCERTO FOR CLARINET 1941
Artie Shaw
Campbell Connelly & Co. Ltd . . . . USA
Film(s): . . . . Second Chorus
Artie Shaw & his Orchestra . . . . **RCA RD 27065**
Carl Barriteau & his Orchestra . . . . **Decca F 8409**
The Melachrino Orchestra . . . . **HMV CLP 1197**
Artie Shaw and his Orchestra appeared in *Second Chorus.*

CONCHITA, MARQUITA, LOLITA, PEPITA, ROSITA, JUANITA LOPEZ 1942
Herb Magidson / Jule Styne
Victoria Music Co. Ltd . . . . USA
Film(s): . . . . Priorities on Parade
The R.A.F. Dance Orchestra, vocal Jimmy Miller . . **Decca F 8194**
Bing Crosby . . . . **Brunswick 03390**

CONCRETE AND CLAY April 1965
Tommy Moeller / Brian Parker
Apollo Music Ltd . . . . UK
Unit Four Plus Two . . . . **Decca F 12071**
Randy Edelman (1976) . . . . **20th Century BTC 2261**

CONFIDENTIALLY October 1949
Reg Dixon
Chappell & Co. Ltd . . . . UK
Reg Dixon . . . . **Decca F 9192**
Danny Kaye . . . . **Brunswick 04490**

CONFUSION December 1979
Jeff Lynne
United Artists Music Co. Ltd. . . . . UK
The Electric Light Orchestra . . . . **Jet 166**

CONGRATULATIONS December 1952
Paul Weston / Sid Robin
Bourne Music Ltd . . . . USA
Jo Stafford . . . . **Capitol EAP 1-20154**
Gary Miller . . . . **Philips PB 102**
Ruby Murray . . . . **Columbia 33SX 1244**

CONGRATULATIONS May 1968
Bill Martin / Phil Coulter
Keith Prowse Music Publishing Co. Ltd. . . . . UK
Cliff Richard . . . . **Columbia DB 8376**
United Kingdom entry for the 1968 Eurovision Song Contest (Placed Second). Ivor Novello Award.

CONSEQUENCES (See Life's Full Of Consequences)

CONSIDER YOURSELF June 1960
Lionel Bart
Lakeview Music Publishing Co. Ltd . . . . UK
Show(s): . . . . Oliver
Film(s): . . . . Oliver
Keith Hamshere & Martin Horsey . . . . **Decca LK 4359**
Michael Goodman & Bruce Prochnik . . . . . . **RCA LOCD 2004**
Max Bygraves . . . . **Decca F 11251**
David Kossoff . . . . **Oriole EP 7039**
Jack Wild, Mark Lester & chorus . . . . **RCA RB 6777**
Michael Goodman & Bruce Prochnik appeared in the American production of *Oliver.*
Keith Hamshere & Martin Horsey appeared in the British production of *Oliver.*
Jack Wild & Mark Lester appeared in the film *Oliver.*

CONSTANTINOPLE 1928
Harry Carleton
Lawrence Wright Music Co. Ltd. . . . . UK
Clarkson Rose . . . . **Zonophone 5091**
Paul Whiteman & his Orchestra . . . . **Columbia 4951**
Jack Hylton & his Orchestra . . . . **HMV B 5501**
The Big Ben Banjo Band . . . . **Columbia 33SX 1188**

CONSTANTLY 1943
Johnny Burke / Jimmy Van Heusen
Victoria Music Co. Ltd . . . . USA
Film(s): . . . . Road to Morocco
Bing Crosby . . . . **Brunswick Bing 8**
Anne Shelton . . . . **Decca F 8247**
Bing Crosby appeared in *Road to Morocco.*

CONSTANTLY (L'Edera) June 1964
Saverio Seracini / Michael Julien
World Wide Music Co. Ltd . . . . Italy

Cliff Richard .... Columbia DB 7272

CONTACT February 1979
Edwin Starr / A.E. Pullan
A.T.V. Music Ltd. .... USA
Edwin Starr .... 20th Century BTC 2396

CONTINENTAL, THE 1934
Herb Magidson / Con Conrad
Sterling Music Publishing Co. Ltd .... USA
Film(s): .... The Gay Divorcee
Ambrose & his Orchestra .... Decca F 5317
Frank Sinatra .... Philips BBR 8003
Eddie Fisher .... HMV CLP 1095
Maureen McGovern .... 20th Century BTC 2222
Academy Award winning song for 1934.

CONVERSATIONS August 1969
Roger Cook / Roger Greenaway / Jerry Lordan
Cookaway Music .... UK
Cilla Black .... Parlophone R 5785

CONVOY March 1976
C.W. McCall / Bill Fries / Chip Davis
Chappell & Co. Ltd .... USA
Film(s): ....Convoy
C.W. McCall .... MGM 2006560

CONVOY G.B. May 1976
C.W. McCall / Bill Fries / Chip Davis / Louis Davis
Chappell & Co. Ltd .... USA
Laurie Lingo & The Dipsticks .... State STAT 23
See also 'Convoy'.

COOL FOR CATS April 1979
Glen Tilbrook / Chris Difford
Rondor Music (London) Ltd. .... UK
Squeeze .... A&M AMS 7436

COOL MEDITATION February 1979
Michael Cooper
Blue Mountain Music .... Jamaica
Third World .... Island WIP 6469

COOL WATER November 1948
Bob Nolan
B. Feldman & Co. Ltd .... USA
Film(s): .... Hands Across the Border
The Sons of The Pioneers .... Brunswick 04001
Cliffie Stone .... Capitol CL 14996
The Sons of The Pioneers .... RCA RD 27016
Bing Crosby .... Brunswick LAT 8152
Frankie Laine (1955) .... Philips PB 465
The Sons of the Pioneers appeared in *Across the Border*.

COOM PRETTY ONE 1934
Leslie Sarony
Lawrence Wright Music Co. Ltd. .... UK
Film(s): .... Rolling in Money
Leslie Sarony .... Rex 8183
Tommy Handley .... Decca F 3982
Leslie Sarony appeared in *Rolling in Money*.

COPENHAGEN 1925
Walter Melrose / Charles Davis
Herman Darewski Music Publishing Co. Ltd. .... USA
The Wolverines .... Brunswick 02205
Sid Philips & his Band .... HMV DLP 1164
Teresa Brewer .... London HAPB 1006
Eddie Condon & his Band .... London LTZD 15158

COPPER CANYON March 1950
Jay Livingston / Ray Evans
Victoria Music Co. Ltd .... USA
Film(s): .... Copper Canyon
Teresa Brewer & Bobby Wayne .... London L 562
Johnny Dennis & his Ranchers .... Decca F 9397

COQUETTE 1928
Gus Kahn / Carmen Lombardo / John Green
Francis, Day & Hunter Ltd. .... USA
Film(s): .... Cockeyed Cavaliers / Easy to Love
Guy Lombardo & his Royal Canadians,
vocal Kenny Gardner .... Capitol LCT 6117

The Ink Spots .... Brunswick LA 8590
Billy Eckstine .... MGM D 138
Johnny Ray .... Philips BBL 7254
Theme song of Guy Lombardo.

CORN SILK 1941
Wayne King / Hal Bellis / Irving Kahal
Cavendish Music Co. Ltd .... USA
The Milt Herth trio .... Brunswick 03196
The King Brothers .... Parlophone PMC 1060

CORNISH RHAPSODY 1944
Hubert Bath
Keith Prowse Music Publishing Co. Ltd. .... UK
Film(s): .... Love Story / Sincerly Yours
Harriet Cohen (Piano) with The London Symphony
Orchestra, conductor Hubert Bath .... Columbia DX 1171
Rawicz & Landauer .... Columbia DB 2164
Liberace with Paul Weston& his Orchestra .. Philips BBL 7030

CORONATION RAG June 1953
Winifred Atwell
Magna Music .... UK
Winifred Atwell (piano) .... Decca F 10110

CORONATION WALTZ, THE 1937
Jimmy Kennedy
Peter Maurice Music Co. Ltd. .... UK
Ambrose & his Orchestra .... Decca F 6369
Gracie Fields .... Decca F 6403

COTTAGE FOR SALE 1930
Larry Conley / Willard Robison
Victoria Music Co. Ltd .... USA
Jack Hylton & his Orchestra .... HMV B 58411
The Beverley Sisters .... Columbia 33SX 1285
Billy Eckstine .... Columbia 33SX 1249
Matt Monro .... Ace of Clubs ACL 1069

COTTON FIELDS July 1970
Traditional
.... USA
The Beach Boys .... Capitol CL 156409

COULD BE 1939
Walter Donaldson / Johnny Mercer
Campbell Connelly & Co. Ltd. .... USA
Wally Bishop .... Regal Zonophone MR 3014
Mitchell Ayers & his Orchestra,
vocal Mary Ann Mercer .... Columbia FB 2192
Geraldo & his Orchestra .... HMV BD 5468

COULD HAVE TOLD YOU SO February 1990
Raymond St. John
MCA Music .... UK
Halo James .... Epic HALO 2

COULD IT BE FOREVER June 1972
Wes Farrell / Danny Janssen
Carlin Music Corporation .... USA
David Cassidy .... Bell 1224

COULD IT BE I'M FALLING IN LOVE June 1973
Melvin Steals
Carlin Music Corporation .... USA
The Detroit Spinners .... Atlantic K 10283
David Grant & Jaki Graham (1985) .... Chrysalis GRAN 6

COULD YOU BE LOVED August 1980
Bob Marley
Rondor Music (London) Ltd .... UK
Bob Marley & The Wailers .... Island WIP 6610

COULD'VE BEEN April 1988
Lois Blaisch
Eaton Music .... USA
Tiffany .... MCA TIFF 2

COULDN'T GET IT RIGHT November 1976
"The Climax Blues Band"
A.I.R. Music .... UK
The Climax Blues Band .... BTM SBT 105

COUNT EVERY STAR August 1950
Bruno Coquatrix / Sammy Gallop

Imperia Music Co. Ltd .... USA
Dick Hayes .... **Brunswick 04557**
Ray Anthony & his Orchestra,
vocal Dick Noel .... **Capitol CL 13342**
Al Hibbler .... **Brunswick LAT 8140**

COUNT YOUR BLESSING   May 1948
Edith Temple / Reginald Morgan
Ascherberg, Hopwood & Crew Ltd. .... UK
Joseph Locke .... **Columbia DB 2409**
The Luton Girls Choir .... **Parlophone GEP 8619**
Harry Secombe .... **Philips BBL 7501**

COUNT YOUR BLESSINGS
INSTEAD OF SHEEP   November 1954
Irving Berlin
Chappell & Co. Ltd. .... USA
Film(s): .... White Christmas
Bing Crosby .... **Brunswick LAT 8044**
Rosemary Clooney .... **Philips BBR 8047**
Gordon MacRae .... **Capitol T 1050**
Bing Crosby appeared in *White Christmas*.
Nominated for an Academy Award 1954.

COUNTING TEARDROPS   January 1961
Howard Greenfield / Barry Mann
Nevins-Kirshner Ltd .... USA
Emile Ford .... **Pye 7N 15314**
Barry Mann .... **HMV CLP 1559**

COUNTRY GARDENS   1919
Percy Grainger
Schott & Co. Ltd. .... UK
Percy Grainger (Piano) .... **Columbia D 1664**
Mark Hambourg (Piano) .... **HMV B 4437**
Capitol Symphony Orchestra,
conducted by Carmen Dragon .... **Capitol P 8466**

COUNTRY STYLE   1947
Johnny Burke / Jimmy Van Heusen
Edwin H. Morris & Co. Ltd. .... USA
Film(s): .... Welcome Stranger
Bing Crosby .... **Brunswick Bing 11**
Bing Crosby appeared in *Welcome Stranger*.

COUPLE OF SWELLS, A   September 1949
Irving Berlin
Irving Berlin Ltd .... USA
Film(s): .... Easter Parade
Judy Garland & Fred Astaire .... **MGM D 140**
Judy Garland & Fred Astaire appeared in *Easter Parade*.

COUSIN NORMAN   October 1971
Hugh Nicholson
Catrine Music .... UK
Marmalade .... **Decca F 13214**

COVER GIRL   May 1990
Maurice Starr
EMI Music .... USA
New Kids On The Block .... **CBS BLOCK 5**

COW COW BOOGIE   1944
Benny Carter / Don Raye / Gene De Paul
Leeds Music Ltd. .... USA
Film(s): .... Reveille with Beverly
Freddie Slack Orchestra,
vocal Ella Mae Morse .... **Capitol CL 13007**
Ella Fitzgerald .... **Brunswick 03503**
Valerie Masters .... **Fontana H 253**
Freddie Slack Orchestra & Ella Mae Morse appeared in *Reveille with Beverly*.

COWARD OF THE COUNTY   March 1980
Roger Bolling / B.E. Wheeler
EMI Music Ltd .... USA
Kenny Rogers .... **United Artists UP 614**

COWBOY   1937
Michael Carr
Peter Maurice Music Co. Ltd. .... UK
Bob Mallin .... **Rex 9018**
Roy Fox & his Orchestra, vocal Denny Dennis .. **HMV BD 5161**

COZ I LUV YOU   December 1971
Noddy Holder / Jim Lea

Barn Publishing Ltd .... UK
Slade .... **Polydor 2058155**

CRACKLIN' ROSIE   January 1971
Neil Diamond
Ardmore & Beechwood Ltd .... USA
Neil Diamond .... **Uni UN 529**

CRADLE OF LOVE   June 1960
Jack Fautheree / Wayne Gray
Good Music Ltd .... USA
Johnny Preston .... **Mercury AMT 1092**

CRASH   March 1988
Paul Court / Steven Dullagham / Tracy Spencer
Complete Music Co. .... UK
The Primitives .... **RCA PB 41761**

CRAZY   April 1973
Mike Chapman / Nicky Chinn
Rak Music Ltd. .... UK
Mud .... **Rak 146**

CRAZY CRAZY NIGHTS   October 1987
Paul Stanley / Adam Mitchell
MCA Music .... UK
Kiss .... **Vertigo KISS 7**

CRAZY FOR YOU
John Bettis / John Lind
Warner Brothers Music Ltd. .... USA
Madonna .... **Geffen A 6323**

CRAZY HORSES   December 1972
Alan Osmond / Wayne Osmond / Merrill Osmond
Intersong Music .... USA
The Osmonds .... **MGM 2006142**

CRAZY LITTLE THING CALLED LOVE   November 1979
Freddie Mercury
EMI Music Ltd. .... UK
Queen .... **EMI 5001**

CRAZY OTTO RAG   July 1955
Mack Wolfson / Emile Trent / Eddie White & Fred Lawrence
Edward Kassner Music Co. Ltd. .... USA
Crazy Otto (Piano) .... **Polydor LPHM 46014**
The Stargazers .... **Decca F 10523**

CRAZY PEOPLE   1932
Edgar Leslie / Jimmy Monaco
Francis, Day & Hunter Ltd. .... USA
Film(s): .... The Big Broadcast
The Boswell Sisters .... **Brunswick 1416**
Jean Campbell & Benny Lee .... **Columbia 33SX 1124**
Something Smith & The Redheads .... **Fontana TFE 17107**
The Boswell Sisters appeared in *The Big Broadcast*.

CRAZY RHYTHM   1928
Irving Caesar / Joseph Meyer / Roger Wolfe Kahn
Chappell & Co. Ltd. .... USA
Show(s): .... Here's Howe / Lucky Girl
Film(s): .... You Were Meant for Me / Tea for Two
The Roger Wolfe Kahn Orchestra .... **HMV B 5535**
Ray Noble & his Orchestra .... **Columbia FB 2002**
The Coleman Hawkins' All Star Jam Band .. **HMV DLP 1055**
Doris Day .... **Columbia SEG 7507**
Tony Bennett .... **Philips BBL 7219**
Shirley Bassey .... **Philips BBL 7325**
Doris Day appeared in *Tea for Two*.

CRAZY WORDS, CRAZY TUNE   1927
Jack Yellen / Milton Ager
Lawrence Wright Music Co. Ltd. .... USA
The California Ramblers .... **Riverside RLP 12-801**
Jerry Lewis .... **Capitol LC 6591**
Dorothy Provine .... **Warner Brothers WM 4035**

CREEP, THE   February 1954
Andy Burton / Carl Sigman
Robbins Music Corporation .... USA
Ken Mackintosh .... **HMV BD 1295**
Ted Heath & his Music .... **Decca F 10222**
Jack Parnell Orchestra .... **Parlophone R 3802**
The Johnson Brothers .... **Decca F 10234**

CREEQUE ALLEY August 1967
John Phillips / Michelle Gillian
Ampar Music . . . . USA
The Mamas & The Papas . . . . **RCA 1613**

CREOLE LOVE CALL 1932
Duke Ellington
Lawrence Wright Music Co. Ltd. . . . . USA
Duke Ellington & his Orchestra . . . . **Brunswick 116**
The Monty Sunshine Band . . . . **Columbia DB 4681**
Duke Ellington & his Orchestra . . . . **RCA RD 27133**

CREST OF A WAVE, THE 1934
Ralph Reader
Cinephonic Music Co. Ltd . . . . UK
Ralph Reader . . . . **Decca F 5186**
The Original Gang Show Boys . . . . **Decca F 10815**
The Ken Jones Orchestra & chorus . . . . . **Fontana TFL 5104**
Theme song of the Boy Scouts Gang Shows.

CRITICIZE December 1987
Garry Johnson / Alexander O'Neal
EMI Music . . . . USA
Alexander O'Neal . . . . **Tabu 6512117**

CROCKETT'S THEME October 1987
Jan Hammer
MCA Music . . . . USA
Jan Hammer . . . . **MCA MCA 1193**

CROCODILE ROCK December 1972
Elton John / Bernie Taupin
Dick James Music Ltd. . . . . UK
Elton John . . . . **DJM DJS 271**
Ivor Novello Nomination.

CROONING 1921
William Caeser / Al Dubin / Herbert Weise
B. Feldman & Co. Ltd . . . . USA
The Benson Orchestra of Chicago . . . . **HMV B 1251**
The Ballyhooligans . . . . **HMV BD 5198**

CROSS MY BROKEN HEART April 1988
Mike Stock / Matt Aitken / Peter Waterman
All Boys Music . . . . UK
Sinitta . . . . **Fanfare FAN 15**

CROSS OVER THE BRIDGE April 1954
Bennie Benjamin / George Weiss
Chappell & Co. Ltd. . . . . USA
Patti Page . . . . **Oriole CB 1269**
The Beverley Sisters . . . . **Philips PB 257**
Anne Shelton . . . . **HMV 7M 197**

CROWN, THE August 1983
Stevie Wonder / Gary Byrd
Jobete Music . . . . USA
Gary Byrd & The G.B. Experience . . . . . . **Motown TMGT 1312**

CRUEL SEA, THE August 1963
Mike Maxfield
Jaep Music Ltd . . . . UK
The Dakotas . . . . **Parlophone R 5044**
The Ventures . . . . **Liberty LIB 96**

CRUEL SUMMER August 1983
Tony Swain / Steve Jolly / "Bananarama"
Red Bus Music . . . . UK
Bananarama . . . . **London NANA 5**

CRUEL TO BE KIND October 1979
Nick Lowe / Robert Gomm
Albion Music . . . . UK
Nick Lowe . . . . **Radar ADA 43**

CRUISING DOWN THE RIVER 1946
Eily Beadell / Nellie Tollerton
Cinephonic Music Co. Ltd. . . . . UK
Film(s): . . . . Cruising Down the River
Lou Preager & his Orchestra,
 vocal Paul Rich . . . . **Columbia FB 3180**
Russ Morgan & his Orchestra . . . . **Brunswick OE 9417**
Vera Lynn . . . . **MGM C 840**
Winner of the 'Write a Song Contest' 1945.

CRUNCH, THE August 1977
Richard Hewson
Rah Music . . . . UK
The Rah Band . . . . **Goodearth GD 7**

CRUSH ON YOU March 1987
Jerry Knight / Aaron Zigman
Rondor Music . . . . USA
The Jets . . . . **MCA MCA 1048**

CRY January 1952
Churchill Kohlman
Francis, Day & Hunter Ltd . . . . USA
Johnnie Ray . . . . **Philips BBL 7264**
Jimmy Young . . . . **Polygon P 1033**
Brenda Lee . . . . **Brunswick LAT 8376**
Theme song of Johnnie Ray.

CRY JUST A LITTLE BIT November 1983
Bob Heatlie
EMI Music . . . . UK
Shakin' Stevens . . . . **Epic A 3774**

CRY ME A RIVER March 1956
Arthur Hamilton
Frank Music Co. Ltd. . . . . USA
Film(s): . . . . The Girl Can't Help it
Julie London . . . . **London HAU 2005**
Shirley Bassey . . . . **Columbia 33SX 1178**
Julie London appeared in *The Girl Can't Help it*.

CRY OF THE WILD GOOSE, THE May 1950
Terry Gilkyson
Campbell Connelly & Co. Ltd . . . . USA
'Tennessee' Ernie Ford . . . . **Capitol T 1380**
Stan Wilson . . . . **Columbia SEB 10041**
Terry Gilkyson & The Easy Riders . . . . . **London HAR 2301**
Frankie Laine . . . . **Philips BBL 7568**

CRY WOLF January 1987
Pal Waaktaar / Magne Furholmen
ATV Music . . . . UK
A-Ha . . . . **Warner Brothers W 8500**

CRY, BABY, CRY 1938
Jimmy Eaton / Terry Shand
B. Feldman & Co. Ltd. . . . . USA
Judy Garland . . . . **Brunswick 02611**
Turner Layton . . . . **Columbia FB 2050**

CRYING October 1961
Roy Orbison / Joe Melson
Acuff-Rose Music Ltd. . . . . USA
Roy Orbison . . . . **London HLU 9405**
Don McLean (1980) . . . . **EMI 5051**

CRYING FOR THE CAROLINES 1930
Sam M. Lewis / Joe Young / Harry Warren
Francis, Day & Hunter Ltd . . . . USA
Film(s): . . . . Spring is Here
Arthur Schutt & his Orchestra . . . . **Parlophone R 619**
Ruth Etting . . . . **Columbia DB 83**
Ruth Adams . . . . **Parlophone R 3815**

CRYING GAME, THE September 1964
Geoff Stevens
Southern Music Publishing Co. Ltd . . . . UK
Dave Berry . . . . **Decca F 11937**

CRYING IN THE CHAPEL January 1954
Artie Glenn
Edwin H. Morris & Co. . . . . USA
Lee Lawrence . . . . **Decca F 10177**
June Valli . . . . **HMV B 10568**
The Orioles . . . . **London L 1201**
Elvis Presley (1965) . . . . **RCA 1455**

CRYING IN THE RAIN February 1962
Howard Greenfield / Carole King
Screen Gems Music . . . . USA
The Everly Brothers (1962) . . . . **Warner Brothers WB 56**
A-Ha (1990) . . . . **Warner Brothers W 9547**

CRYING LAUGHING LOVING LYING　　　April 1972
Labi Siffre
M.A.M. (Music Publishing) Ltd . . . . UK
Labi Siffre . . . . **Pye 7N 25576**

CRYING OVER YOU　　　January 1975
Lloyd Charmer
B&C Music . . . . UK
Ken Boothe . . . . **Trojan TR 7944**

CRYSTAL GAZER, THE　　　March 1949
Frank Petch
Dash Music Ltd . . . . UK
Reggie Goff . . . . **Decca F 9072**
Eric Winstone & his Orchestra, vocal Julie Dawn . . . . **MGM 178**

CUANTO LE GUSTA　　　August 1948
Gabriel Ruiz / Ray Gilbert
Southern Music Publishing Co. Ltd. . . . . Mexico
Film(s): . . . . A Date With Judy
Carmen Miranda & The Andrews Sisters . . . . **Brunswick 03917**
Edmundo Ros Rumba Band . . . . **Decca F 9046**
Percy Faith & his Orchestra . . . . **Philips BBL 7245**
Carmen Miranda appeared in *A Date With Judy*.

CUBA　　　March 1980
Daniel Vangarde / Jean Kluger
Blue Mountain Music . . . . France
Film(s): . . . . The Bitch
The Gibson Brothers . . . . **Island WIP 6561**

CUBAN LOVE SONG　　　1931
Herbert Stothart / Dorothy Fields / Jimmy McHugh
Keith Prowse Music Publishing Co. Ltd. . . . . USA
Film(s): . . . . Cuban Love Song
Lawrence Tibbett . . . . **HMV DA 1251**
Tony Martin . . . . **Decca F 8900**
Edmundo Ros Orchestra . . . . **Decca LK 4353**
Eva Boswell . . . . **Parlophone PMC 1105**
Lawrence Tibbett appeared in *Cuban Love Song*.
Theme song of Edmundo Ros.

CUBAN PETE　　　1936
Jose Norman
J. Norris Music Publishing Co. Ltd . . . . UK
Film(s): . . . . Cuban Pete
Mantovani & his Tipica Orchestra . . . . **Columbia FB 1420**
Ambrose & his Orchestra . . . . **Decca F 5994**

CUCARACHA, LA　　　1935
Traditional
Chappell & Co. Ltd . . . . Mexico
The Pan American Marimba Band . . . . **HMV D 0557**
Ambrose & his Orchestra . . . . **Decca F 72025**
Percy Faith & his Orchestra . . . . **Philips BBL 7245**
The Capitol Symphony Orchestra . . . . **Capitol P 8412**

CUCKOO WALTZ, THE　　　1929
J.E. Johansen
Keith Prowse Music Publishing Co. Ltd . . . . Sweden
The International Novelty Quartet . . . . . . **Regal T 5002**
Joe Loss & his Orchestra . . . . **HMV BD 6027**
Ken Griffin (organ) (1948) . . . . **Philips BBL 7115**

CUDDLE UP A LITTLE CLOSER　　　1909
Otto Harbach / Karl Hoschna
B. Feldman & Co. Ltd. . . . . USA
Show(s): . . . . The Three Twins
Film(s):The Story of Vernon and Irene Castle / Birth of the Blues / Is Everybody Happy / On Moonlight Bay / Coney Island
Josephine Bradley & her Orchestra . . . . **Decca F 8394**
The McGuire Sisters . . . . **Vogue LVA 9024**
Vic Damone . . . . **Philips BBL 7259**
Julie London . . . . **London HAW 2225**
Doris Day . . . . **Philips BBL 7175**
Doris Day appeared in *On Moonlight Bay*.

CUDDLY TOY　　　February 1989
Andrew Roachford
Polygram Music . . . . UK
Roachford . . . . **CBS ROAT 4**

CUFF OF MY SHIRT, THE　　　March 1954
Bob Merrill

Campbell Connelly & Co. Ltd . . . . USA
Guy Mitchell . . . . **Philips PB 225**

CUM ON FEEL THE NOIZE　　　April 1973
Noddy Holder / Jimmy Lea
Barn Publishing Ltd. . . . . UK
Slade . . . . **Polydor 2058339**

CUMBANCHERO, EL　　　August 1952
Rafael Hernandez
Southern Music Publishing Co. Ltd . . . . Mexico
Film(s): . . . . Cuban Pete
Winifred Atwell (piano) . . . . **Ace of Clubs ACL 1005**
Pepe Jaramillo & his Orchestra . . . . . . **Parlophone PMC 1080**
Dolores Ventura (piano) . . . . **Pye GGL 0087**

CUMBERLAND GAP, THE　　　March 1957
Traditional, additional Lyrics Lonnie Donnegan
An edition by Essex Music Ltd. . . . . USA
Lonnie Donegan . . . . **Nixa NEP 24040**
The Vipers Skiffle Group . . . . **Parlophone GEP 8615**

CUMPARSITA, LA　　　1916
G. Matos Rodriguez
G. Ricordi & Co. (London) Ltd. . . . . Argentina
Xavier Cugat & his Waldorf Astoria Orchestra . . . **HMV B 9072**
The Mantovani Orchestra . . . . **Decca LK 4061**
Billy Vaughan & his Orchestra . . . . **London HAD 2151**
Stanley Black & his Orchestra . . . . **Decca LK 4325**

CUP OF COFFEE, A SANDWICH AND YOU, A　　　1926
Joseph Meyer / Billy Rose / Al Dubin
Chappell & Co. Ltd. . . . . USA
Show(s): . . . . . . Charlot Revue of 1926 / The Charlot Show of 1926
Gertrude Lawrence . . . . **HMV C 2835**
Nick Lucas . . . . **Brunswick 3052**
Vocal Trio . . . . **Warner Brothers WM 4035**
Gertrude Lawrence appeared in the *Charlot Revue of 1926*.

CUPBOARD LOVE　　　March 1963
Les Vandyke
Essex Music Ltd . . . . UK
John Leyton . . . . **HMV POP 1122**

CUPID　　　September 1961
Sam Cooke
Kags Music Ltd. . . . . USA
Sam Cooke . . . . **RCA 1242**
Johnny Nash (1969) . . . . **Major Minor MM 603**
The Detroit Spinners (1980) . . . . **Atlantic K 11498**

CURLY　　　August 1969
Roy Wood
Essex Music Ltd. . . . . UK
The Move . . . . **Regal Zonophone RZ 3021**

CURSE OF AN ACHING HEART　　　1914
Al Piantadosi / Henry Fink
Ascherberg, Hopwood & Crew Ltd. . . . . USA
Film(s): . . . . Show Business
Will Oakland . . . . **Zonophone 1225**
Frank Sinatra . . . . **Reprise R 20010**

CUT YOURSELF A PIECE OF CAKE (And Make Yourself At Home)　　　1923
Billy James
Francis, Day & Hunter Ltd . . . . USA
Paul Whiteman & his Orchestra . . . . **HMV B 1729**

CUTTER, THE　　　February 1983
"Echo & The Bunnymen"
Warner Brothers Music . . . . UK
Echo & The Bunnymen . . . . **Korova KOW 26**

CYNTHIA'S IN LOVE　　　1946
Jack Owen / Billy Gish / Earl White
Chappell & Co. Ltd. . . . . USA
**Carroll Gibbons & his Orchestra,
vocal Denny Vaughan** . . . . **Columbia FB 3227**
Chris Dane . . . . **London HLA 8165**

CZARDAS　　　1904
Vittorio Monti
Yvonn Curtis (violin) . . . . **Columbia 19041**
Mario De Pietro (mandolin) . . . . **Decca F 1952**

Freddy Martin Orchestra . . . . **HMV B 9716**
The Hollywood Bowl Symphony Orchestra . . . **Capitol P 834-2**
The London Symphony Orchestra . . . . **EMI TWOD 2005**

D-DAYS   April 1981
Hazel O'Connor
Albion Music . . . . UK
Hazel O'Connor . . . . **Albion ION 1009**

DA DA DA   July 1982
Stephen Remmler"Kralle"
EMI Music . . . . Germany
Trio . . . . **Phonogram CORP 5**

DA DOO RON RON   August 1963
Phil Spector / Ellie Greenwich / Jeff Barry
Belinda (London) Ltd . . . . USA
The Crystals . . . . **London HL 9732**
The Searchers . . . . **Pye NPL 18086**
The Crystals (1974) . . . . **Warner Brothers K 19010**

DA' YA THINK I'M SEXY   December 1978
Rod Stewart / Carmine Appice
Warner Brothers Music Ltd . . . . UK
Rod Stewart . . . . **Riva 17**

DA-DAR DA-DAR   1933
Stanley Damerell / Robert Hargreaves / Tolchard Evans
Box & Cox (Publications) Ltd. . . . . UK
Bertha Wilmot . . . . **Decca F 7446**
Barbara Lyon & Ronnie Harris . . . . **Columbia DB 3749**
Clinton Ford . . . . **Columbia 33SX 1560**

DADDY   1941
Bobby Troup
Chappell & Co. Ltd . . . . USA
Film(s): . Two Latins From Manhattan / Gentlemen Marry Brunettes
Ambrose & his Orchestra, vocal Anne Shelton . . **Decca F 7953**
The Andrews Sisters . . . . **Brunswick 04834**
Sallie Blair . . . . **MGM 1000**
Pat Suzuki . . . . **RCA 1069**
Jane Russell & Anita Ellis . . . . **Vogue LVA 9003**
Jane Russell & Anita Ellis appeared in *Gentlemen Marry Brunettes.*

DADDY COOL   February 1977
Frank Farian / George Reyam
A.T.V. Music Ltd. . . . . Germany
Boney M . . . . **Atlantic 10827**

DADDY COOL - THE GIRL CAN'T HELP IT   December 1977
Frank Slay / Bob Crewe
Jewel Music Publishing Co. Ltd . . . . USA
The Darts . . . . **Magnet MAG 100**

DADDY DON'T YOU WALK SO FAST   October 1971
Peter Callander / Geoff Stevens
Intune Ltd . . . . UK
Daniel Boone . . . . **Penny Farthing PEN 764**

DADDY WOULDN'T BUY ME A BOW-WOW   1892
Joseph Tabrar
Francis, Day & Hunter Ltd . . . . UK
Film(s): . . . . Evergreen
Vesta Victoria . . . . **Columbia DX 290**
Bertha Wilmott . . . . **Parlophone E 6341**
Barbara Windsor . . . . **Parlophone PMC 1127**

DADDY'S HOME   December 1981
James Shepherd / William Miller
Planetary-Nom Music Ltd . . . . USA
Cliff Richard . . . . **EMI 5251**

DADDY'S LITTLE GIRL   June 1950
Horace Gerlach / Bobbie Burke
Yale Music Corporation Ltd . . . . USA
Steve Conway . . . . **Columbia SEG 7573**
Dick James . . . . **Parlophone R 4498**
The Mills Brothers . . . . **Brunswick 04487**
The Mills Brothers . . . . **London HAD 2319**

DAISY BELL   1893
Harry Dacre
Francis, Day & Hunter Ltd. . . . . UK
Film(s): . . . . I'll Be Your Sweetheart

Reg Grant . . . . **Parlophone E 6293**
Florrie Forde . . . . **Rex 8528**
John Rorke . . . . **Decca LK 4026**

DAM BUSTERS MARCH, THE   October 1955
Eric Coates
Chappell & Co. Ltd. . . . . UK
Film(s): . . . . The Dam Busters
The R.A.F. Central Band . . . . **HMV 7EG 8265**
Eric Coates & his Orchestra . . . . **Nixa NPT 19015**
Ivor Novello Award.

DANCE AWAY   June 1979
Bryan Ferry
E.G. Music . . . . UK
Roxy Music . . . . **Polydor POSP 44**

DANCE IN THE OLD FASHIONED WAY (See Old Fashioned Way)

DANCE LITTLE LADY   1928
Noel Coward
Chappell & Co. Ltd. . . . . UK
Show(s): . . . . This Year of Grace
Noel Coward . . . . **HMV B 2720**
Hildegarde . . . . **Decca F 7310**
Beatrice Lillie . . . . **Decca LK 4129**
Peter Knight & his Orchestra . . . . **Pye NPL 18051**
Noel Coward appeared in the American production of *This Year of Grace.*

DANCE LITTLE LADY, DANCE   October 1976
Biddu' / Gerry Shury / Ron Roker
Rondor Music (London) Ltd . . . . UK
Tina Charles . . . . **CBS 4480**

DANCE ME LOOSE   April 1952
Mel Howard / Lee Erwin
Magna Music Ltd . . . . USA
Russ Morgan & his Orchestra . . . . **Brunswick 04886**
The Stargazers . . . . **Decca F 9905**
Eve Boswell . . . . **Parlophone R 3549**

DANCE ON   January 1963
Valerie Murtagh / Elaine Murtagh / Ray Adams
Sydney Bron Music Co. Ltd . . . . UK
The Shadows (January) . . . . **Columbia DB 4948**
Kathry Kirby (September) . . . . **Decca F 11682**
Ivor Novello Nomination.

DANCE TO THE MUSIC   August 1968
Sylvester Stewart
Cralin Music Corporation . . . . USA
Film(s): . . . . Woodstock
Sly & the Family Stone . . . . **Direction 583568**
Sly & The Family Stone appeared in *Woodstock.*

DANCE WITH A DOLLY   1944
Terry Shand / Jimmy Easton / Mickey Leader
Campbell Connelly & Co. Ltd . . . . USA
Film(s): . . . . On Stage Everybody / Her Lucky Night
Geraldo & his Orchestra,
vocal Johnny Green . . . . **Parlophone F 2048**
Evelyn Knight . . . . **Brunswick LA 8538**

DANCE WITH ME HENRY (Wallflower)   May 1955
Etta James / Johnny Otis / Hank Ballard
Sheridan Music Co. . . . . USA
Georgia Gibbs . . . . **Mercury MB 3223**
Suzi Miller . . . . **Decca F 10512**

DANCE WITH THE DEVIL   February 1974
Phil Dennys / Michael Hayes
Rak Music Ltd. . . . . UK
Cozy Powell . . . . **Rak 164**

DANCE WITH THE GUITAR MAN (See Guitar Man)

DANCE YOURSELF DIZZY   April 1980
Adrian Baker / Eddie Seago
A.T.V. Music Ltd. . . . . UK
Liquid Gold . . . . **Polo 1**

DANCE, DANCE, DANCE   January 1978
Kenny Lehman / Bernard Edwards / Nile Rodgers
Warner Brothers Music Ltd . . . . USA

Chic . . . . Atlantic K 11038

DANCE, EVERYONE, DANCE   October 1958
Sid Danoff
Bourne Music Ltd . . . . USA
Sallie Terri . . . . **Capitol CL 14919**
Connie Francis . . . . **MGM 861**
Based on *Hava Noguila.*

DANCIN' IN THE MOONLIGHT   September 1977
Phil Lynott
Pippin The Friendly Ranger Music . . . . UK
Thin Lizzy . . . . **Vertigo 6059177**

DANCIN' PARTY   September 1962
Kal Mann / Dave Appell
Carlin Music Corporation . . . . USA
Chubby Checker . . . . **Columbia DB 3876**
Showaddywaddy (1977) . . . . **Arista 149**

DANCIN' WITH SOMEONE   May 1953
Bennie Benjamin / George Weiss / Alex Alstone
Valando Music Co. Ltd . . . . USA
Jimmy Young . . . . **Decca F 10108**
Molly Bee . . . . **Capitol CL 13911**
Carol Carr . . . . **HMV B 10486**
Teresa Brewer . . . . **Vogue LVA 9095**

DANCING GIRLS   May 1984
Nik Kershaw
Rondor Music . . . . UK
Nik Kershaw . . . . **MCA NIK 3**

DANCING IN THE CITY   August 1978
Julian Marshall / Kit Hain
Intersong Music . . . . USA
Marshall Hain . . . . **Harvest HAR 5157**

DANCING IN THE DARK   1932
Howard Dietz / Arthur Schwartz
Chappell & Co. Ltd. . . . . USA
Show(s): . . . . The Band Wagon
Film(s): . . . . Dancing in the Dark / The Band Wagon
Bing Crosby . . . . **Brunswick LA 8741**
Frank Sinatra . . . . **Capitol LCT 6179**
The MGM Studio Orchestra . . . . **MGM C 752**
Artie Shaw & his Orchestra . . . . **HMV B 9476**

DANCING IN THE DARK   February 1985
Bruce Springsteen
Zomba Music . . . . USA
Bruce Springsteen . . . . **CBS A 4436**

DANCING IN THE STREET   February 1969
William Stevenson / Marvin Gaye
Jobete Music (UK) Ltd. . . . . USA
Film(s): . . . . Cooley High
Martha Reeves & The Vandellas . . . . . **Tamla Motown TMG 684**
David Bowie & Mick Jagger (1985) . . . . **EMI EA 204**

DANCING ON A SATURDAY NIGHT   September 1973
Barry Blue / Lynsey De Paul
A.T.V. Music Ltd. . . . . UK
Barry Blue . . . . **Bell BELL 1295**

DANCING ON THE CEILING   1931
Richard Rodgers / Lorenz Hart
Chappell & Co. Ltd . . . . USA
Show(s): . . . . Ever Green
Film(s): . . . . Evergreen
Peggy Lee . . . . **HMV LAT 8171**
Jessie Matthews . . . . **Columbia DB 1403**
Jeri Southern . . . . **London T 1278**
Jessie Matthews appeared in both the show and the film of *Evergreen.*

DANCING ON THE CEILING   August 1986
Lionel Richie / Carlos Rios
Rondor Music . . . . USA
Lionel Richie . . . . **Motown L 10**

DANCING ON THE FLOOR   July 1981
Bunny Clarke
Blue Mountain Music . . . . USA
Third World . . . . **CBS A 1214**

DANCING QUEEN   October 1976
Benny Andersson / Bjorn Ulvaeus / Stig Anderson
Bocu Music Ltd . . . . Sweden
Abba . . . . **Epic EPC 4499**

DANCING TAMBOURINE   1927
W.C. Polla / Phil Ponce
Chappell & Co. Ltd. . . . . USA
The Piccadilly Revels Band . . . . **Columbia 4604**
The Robin Hood Dell Orchestra . . . . **Columbia DX 1581**
Bob Keene & his Band . . . . **Vogue VA 160158**

DANCING TIGHT   May 1981
Philip Fearon
Handle Music . . . . UK
Galaxy . . . . **Ensign ENY 501**

DANCING TIME   1921
Jerome Kern / George Grossmith
Chappell & Co. Ltd . . . . USA
Show(s): . . . . The Cabaret Girl
The 'Queens' Dance Orchestra . . . . **HMV B 1643**
Dorothy Dickson . . . . **HMV C 2946**
Tommy Kinsman & his Orchestra . . . . **Fontana TFL 5049**
Oscar Rabin Band . . . . **Decca F 7737**
Dorothy Dickson appeared in *The Cabaret Girl.*
Theme tune of Oscar Rabin Band.

DANCING WITH MY SHADOW   1935
Harry Woods
Cinephonic Music Co. Ltd . . . . UK
Elsie Carlisle . . . . **Decca F 5436**
The Kaye Sisters . . . . **Philips PB 925**
The Eric Jupp Orchestra . . . . **Columbia 33S 1097**

DANCING WITH TEARS IN MY EYES   1930
Al Dubin / Joe Burke
B. Feldman & Co. Ltd . . . . USA
Ruth Etting . . . . **Columbia DB 218**
Kate Smith . . . . **MGM D 145**
Dennis Hale . . . . **Parlophone R 3539**

DANCING WITH TEARS IN MY EYES   June 1984
Christopher Cross / Warren Cann / James Ure / William Currie
BMG Music . . . . UK
Ultravox . . . . **Chrysalis UV 1**

DANCING WITH THE CAPTAIN   November 1976
Dominic Bugatti / Frank Musker
April Music Ltd . . . . USA
Paul Nicholas . . . . **RSO 20902026**

DANGER AHEAD   November 1947
Billy Reid
Yale Music . . . . UK
Leslie Hutchinson (Hutch) . . . . **HMV BD 1173**
Dorothy Squires . . . . **Parlophone F 2244**
Denny Dennis . . . . **Decca F 8810**

DANGER, HEARTBREAK AHEAD   May 1955
Carl Stutz / Carl Barefoot
B. Feldman & Co. Ltd. . . . . USA
Patti Lewis . . . . **Philips PB 434**
Jay P. Morgan . . . . **HMV B 10868**

DANIEL   February 1973
Elton John / Bernie Taupin
Dick James Music Ltd. . . . . UK
Elton John . . . . **DJM DJS 275**
Ivor Novello Award.

DANNY BOY   1912
Traditional, lyric by Frederick Weatherly
Boosey & Hawkes Ltd . . . . UK
John McHugh . . . . **Columbia FB 2904**
Cavan O'Connor . . . . **Ace of Clubs ACL 1097**
Val Doonican . . . . **Philips 6326008**
Stuart Burrows . . . . **Decca 430 090-2**
Based on "The Londonderry Air".

DAPPER DAN   1921
Albert Von Tilzer / Lew Brown
Francis, Day & Hunter Ltd . . . . USA
Show(s): . . . . A To Z

Jack Buchanan & The Trix Sisters . . . . HMV B 1302
Ray Burns . . . . Columbia DB 3998
Jack Buchanan & The Trix Sisters appeared in *A to Z*.

DARDANELLA   1919
Fred Fisher / Felix Bernard / Johnny Black
Francis, Day & Hunter Ltd . . . . USA
Show(s): . . . . Afgar
Alice Delysia . . . . Columbia F 1043
The Adrian Rollini Trio . . . . Mercury MPT 7538
Bing Crosby & Louis Armstrong . . . . MGM C 844
Phil Napoleon & His Memphis Five . . . . Capitol T 1428
Alice Delysia appeared in *Afgar*.

DARK MOON   July 1957
Ned Miller
Francis, Day & Hunter Ltd. . . . . USA
The Kaye Sisters . . . . Philips BBE 12166
Teresa Brewer . . . . Vogue LVA 9023
Jim Reeves . . . . RCA RD 27193

DARKNESS ON THE DELTA   1933
Marty Symes / Al Neiburg / Jerry Livingston
Keith Prowse Music Publishing Co. Ltd. . . . . USA
Film(s): . . . . South of Dixie
The Southern Sisters . . . . Brunswick 01530
Ted Fiorito & his Orchestra . . . . Decca F 3511
Teresa Brewer . . . . Vogue LVA 9020

DARKTOWN POKER CLUB, THE   1947
Jean Havez / Will Vodery / Bert Williams
Francis, Day & Hunter Ltd. . . . . USA
Show(s): . . . . Ziegfeld Follies of 1914
Phil Harris . . . . Camden CDN 124

DARKTOWN STRUTTERS BALL, THE   1917
Shelton Brooks
Francis, Day & Hunter Ltd. . . . . USA
Film(s):The Story of Vernon & Irene Castle / Broadway / The Dolly
Sisters / Incendiary Blonde
The Jungle Kings . . . . London AL 3503
Elsie Janis . . . . HMV E 167
Gene Mayl's Dixieland Band . . . . London LTZU 15069
Lizzie Miles . . . . Capitol T 792

DARLIN'   February 1968
Brian Wilson / Mike Love
Rondor Music (London) Ltd. . . . . USA
The Beach Boys . . . . Capitol CL 15527
David Cassidy (1975) . . . . RCA 2622

DARLIN'   November 1978
Oscar Blandamer
Robert Kingston (Music) Ltd . . . . UK
Frankie Miller . . . . Chrysalis CHS 2255
Poacher . . . . RK RK 1009

DARLING NELLIE GRAY   1856
J. Bodewalt Lampe / Benjamin Hanby
B. Feldman & Co. Ltd . . . . USA
Carson Robinson . . . . Broadcast 3318
The Mills Brothers . . . . Brunswick 03659
The Chris Barber Jazz Band,
vocal Ottile Patterson . . . . Columbia 33SX 1158

DARLING, JE VOUS AIME BEAUCOUP   1936
Anna Sosenko
Francis, Day & Hunter Ltd . . . . USA
Hildegarde . . . . Columbia DB 1556
Bing Crosby . . . . Brunswick 04121
Greta Keller . . . . Decca LK 4126
Theme song of Hildegarde.

DARN THAT DREAM   1939
Eddie De Lange / Jimmy Van Heusen
Francis, Day & Hunter Ltd. . . . . USA
Show(s): . . . . Swingin' the Dream
Tony Bennett . . . . Philips BBR 8089
Doris Day . . . . Philips BBL 7120
Sarah Vaughan . . . . Mercury MMC 14021

DAT   March 1976
Leighton Shervington
Nems Publishing Ltd . . . . UK

Pluto Shervington . . . . Opal PAL 5

DAT'S LOVE   March 1955
Georges Bizet / Oscar Hammerstein II
Williamson Music Ltd. . . . . USA
Show(s): . . . . Carmen Jones
Film(s): . . . . Carmen Jones
Muriel Smith & Chorus . . . . Brunswick LAT 8057
Marilyn Horne & Chorus . . . . HMV CLP 1034
Marilyn Horne appeared in the film *Carmen Jones*.
Muriel Smith appeared in the American production of *Carmen Jones*.
Based on 'The Habanera' from the opera 'Carmen' by Georges Bizet
(1838 - 1875).

DAUGHTER OF DARKNESS   May 1970
Les Reed / Geoff Stevens
Carlin Music Corporation . . . . UK
Tom Jones . . . . Decca F 13013

DAVY'S ON THE ROAD AGAIN   July 1978
John Simon / Robbie Robertson
Island Music Ltd . . . . UK
Manfred Mann's Earth Band . . . . Bronze BRO 52

DAY AFTER DAY   March 1972
Peter Ham
Apple Publishing . . . . UK
Badfinger . . . . Apple 40

DAY AFTER FOREVER, THE   1944
Johnny Burke / Jimmy Van Heusen
Victoria Music Co. Ltd. . . . . USA
Film(s): . . . . Going My Way
Bing Crosby . . . . Brunswick BING 8
Bing Crosby appeared in *Going My Way*.

DAY BY DAY   1946
Axel Stordahl / Sammy Cahn / Paul Weston
New World Publishers Ltd. . . . . USA
Frank Sinatra . . . . Fontana TFL 5082
Eydie Gormé . . . . HMV CLP 1156
Bing Crosby . . . . Brunswick 03731
The Four Freshmen . . . . Capitol T 1008

DAY BY DAY   March 1972
Stephen Schwartz
Carlin Music Corporation . . . . USA
Show(s): . . . . Godspell
Film(s): . . . . Godspell
Julie Covington . . . . Bell BELLS 203
Robin Lamont . . . . Bell BELLS 223
Holly Sherwood . . . . Bell 1182
Julie Covington appeared in the British production of *Godspell*.
Robin Lamont appeared in the film *Godspell*.

DAY DREAMING   1938
Johnny Mercer / Harry Warren
B. Feldman & Co. Ltd. . . . . USA
Film(s): . . . . .The Gay Imposter
Pat O'Regan . . . . Rex 9490
Rudy Vallee & his Connecticut Yankees . . . . HMV BD 5423

DAY DREAMING   1942
Gus Kahn / Jerome Kern
Chappell & Co. Ltd . . . . USA
Oscar Rabin & his Band, vocal Beryl Davis . . . . . Decca F 8108
Bing Crosby . . . . Brunswick 03300
Tony Osborne & his Orchestra . . . . HMV CLP 1270

DAY I MET MARIE, THE   October 1967
Hank B. Marvin
Shadows Music Ltd. . . . . UK
Cliff Richard . . . . Columbia DB 8245

DAY IN, DAY OUT   1939
Johnny Mercer / Rube Bloom
Sun Music Publishing Co. Ltd. . . . . USA
Adelaide Hall . . . . Decca F 7304
Lena Horne . . . . RCA RD 27021
Frank Sinatra . . . . Capitol LCT 6179

DAY OF JUBILO, THE   August 1952
Terry Gilkyson
Campbell Connelly & Co. Ltd . . . . USA
Guy Mitchell . . . . Columbia SEG 7598

The Stargazers . . . . Decca F 9960 | Academy Award winning song for 1962

DAY THE CIRCUS LEFT TOWN, THE   November 1955
Carolyn Leigh / E.D. Thomas
Edwin H. Morris & Co. Ltd. . . . . USA
Eartha Kitt . . . . **HMV B 10922**

DAY THE RAINS CAME, THE   January 1959
Gilbert Becaud / Pierre Delanoe / Carl Sigman
John Fields Music Co. Ltd . . . . France
Jane Morgan . . . . **London HAR 2158**
Gilbert Becaud . . . . **HMV POP 574**
Ronnie Hilton . . . . **HMV POP 556**
Vera Lynn . . . . **Decca F 11106**

DAY TRIP TO BANGOR   January 1980
Debbie Cook
Coley Music . . . . UK
Fiddlers Dram . . . . **Dingles SID 211**

DAY TRIPPER   December 1965
John Lennon / Paul McCartney
Northern Songs Ltd . . . . UK
The Beatles . . . . **Parlophone R 5389**

DAY WITHOUT LOVE, A   October 1968
Philip Goodhand-Tait
Dick James music Ltd. . . . . UK
The Love Affair . . . . **CBS 3674**

DAY YOU CAME ALONG, THE   1933
Sam Coslow / Arthur Johnston
Victoria Music Co. Ltd. . . . . USA
Film(s): . . . . Too Much Harmony
Bing Crosby . . . . **Columbia DB 2009**
Bing Crosby . . . . **Brunswick LAT 8251**
Jimmy Young . . . . **Decca LK 4219**
Bing Crosby appeared in *Too Much Harmony.*

DAY-O (Banana Boat Song)   February 1957
Out of copyright.This arrangement by "Lord" Burgess, Harry Bela-
fonte & William Attaway
Belafonte Music Ltd. . . . . USA
Harry Belafonte . . . . **RCA RD 27107**
Shirley Bassey . . . . **Philips PB 668**

DAYBREAK   1943
Ferde Grofé / Harold Adamson
Robbins Music Corporation Ltd . . . . USA
Film(s): . . . . Thousands Cheer
Cavan O'Connor . . . . **Rex 10175**
Jimmy Dorsey & his Orchestra . . . . **Brunswick 03435**
Al Hibbler . . . . **Brunswick 05420**
Dinah Washington . . . . **Mercury MMC 14063**
Adapted from "The Mississippi Suite" by Ferde Grofe

DAYDREAM   June 1966
John Sebastian
Robbins Music Corporation Ltd. USA
The Lovin' Spoonful . . . . **Pye 7N 25361**

DAYDREAM BELIEVER   February 1968
John Stewart
Screen Gems Music Ltd. . . . . USA
The Monkees . . . . **RCA 1645**

DAYDREAMER   November 1973
Terry Dempsey
Palace Music Co. Ltd. . . . . UK
David Cassidy . . . . **Bell BELL 1334**

DAYS   August 1968
Raymond Davies
Davray Music . . . . UK
The Kinks . . . . **Pye 7N 17573**
Kirsty MacColl . . . . **Virgin KMA 2**

DAYS OF WINE AND ROSES   September 1963
Johnny Mercer / Henry Mancini
Chappell & Co. Ltd . . . . USA
Film(s): . . . . Days of Wine and Roses
Henry Mancini & his Orchestra . . . . **RCA RD 7549**
Andy Williams . . . . **CBS BPG 62146**
Eydie Gormé . . . . **CBS BPG 62151**
Perry Como . . . . **RCA RD 7582**

DAYTONA DEMON   December 1973
Mike Chapman / Nicky Chinn
Rak Music Ltd. . . . . UK
Suzi Quatro . . . . **Rak 161**

DE DO DO DO, DE DA DA DA   January 1981
"Sting"
Virgin Music . . . . UK
Police . . . . **A&M AMS 7578**

DEAD END STREET   December 1966
Raymond Davies
Carlin Music Corporation . . . . UK
The Kinks . . . . **Pye 7N 17222**

DEAD GIVEAWAY   July 1983
Joey Gallo / Marcus Dare / Leon Sylvers
Chappell & Co. Ltd . . . . USA
Shalamar . . . . **Solar E 9819**

DEAD RINGER FOR LOVE   December 1981
Jim Steinman
Dick James Music . . . . USA
Meatloaf . . . . **Epic EPCA 1697**

DEADWOOD STAGE, THE   March 1954
Sammy Fain / Paul Francis Webster
Campbell Connelly & Co. Ltd. USA
Film(s): . . . . Calamity Jane
Doris Day . . . . **Philips BBL 7297**
Doris Day appeared in *Calamity Jane.*

DEAN AND I, THE   September 1973
Kevin Godley / Lol Creme
St. Annes Music Ltd. . . . . UK
10 CC . . . . **UK 48**

DEAR HEARTS AND GENTLE PEOPLE   January 1950
Sammy Fain / Bob Hilliard
Edwin H. Morris & Co. Ltd . . . . USA
Dinah Shore . . . . **Columbia DB 2634**
Bing Crosby . . . . **Brunswick LAT 8052**
Fred Waring & his Pennsylvanians . . . . **Capitol T 936**
Perry Como . . . . **RCA RD 27154**

DEAR JESSIE   January 1990
Madonna Ciccone / Patrick Leonard
Warner Chappell Music . . . . USA
Madonna . . . . **Sire W 2668**

DEAR JOHN   April 1982
John Gustafson / Jackie Macaulay
Shawbury Music . . . . Australia
Status Quo . . . . **Vertigo QUO 7**

DEAR LITTLE CAFE   1929
Noel Coward
Chappell & Co. Ltd . . . . UK
Show(s): . . . . Bitter Sweet
Film(s): . . . . Bitter Sweet
Peggy Wood & George Metaxa . . . . **HMV C 1746**
Nelson Eddy . . . . **Columbia DB 2023**
Vanessa Lee & Roberto Cardinali . . . . . **HMV CLP 1242**
Peggy Wood & George Metaxa appeared in the British production of
Bitter Sweet.
Nelson Eddy appeared in the 1940 film of *Bitter Sweet.*

DEAR LOVE MY LOVE   1921
Brian Hooker / Rudolf Friml
Chappell & Co. Ltd . . . . UK
Show(s): . . . . June Love
The Regal Dance Orchestra . . . . **Regal G 7899**
Lillian Davies . . . . **HMV B 3192**
John Hanson . . . . **Philips 6308147**

DEAR OLD DONEGAL   1946
Steve Graham
Leeds Music Ltd. . . . . USA
Bing Crosby . . . . **Brunswick LAT 8106**
Joseph Locke . . . . **Columbia DB 2429**
Dennis Martin . . . . **Decca LK 4366**

DEAR OLD PAL OF MINE — 1918
Gitz Rice / Harold Robe
G. Ricordi & Co. (London) Ltd. . . . . USA
John McCormack . . . . **HMV DA 965**

DEAR OLD SOUTHLAND — 1922
Henry Creamer / Turner Leyton
Francis, Day & Hunter Ltd . . . . USA
Leyton & Johnstone . . . . **Columbia 3512**
Louis Armstrong's All Stars . . . . **Brunswick LAT 8213**
Duke Ellington & his Orchestra . . . . **HMV BD 5766**
Theme song of Leyton & Johnston.

DEAR ONE — 1925
Mark Fisher / Cyril Richardson / Joe Burke
Francis, Day & Hunter Ltd. . . . . USA
The Gleneagles Hotel Orchestra . . . . **Columbia 3586**

DEAR PRUDENCE — October 1983
John Lennon / Paul McCartney
Northern Songs . . . . UK
The Beatles . . . . **Apple PMC 7067**
Siouxsie & The Banshees (1983) . . . . **Polydor SHE 4**

DEAREST LOVE — 1938
Noel Coward
Chappell & Co. Ltd. . . . . UK
Show(s): . . . . Operette
Peggy Wood . . . . **HMV B 8739**
Noel Coward . . . . **HMV B 8721**
Peggy Wood appeared in *Operette*.

DEARIE — April 1950
Bob Hilliard / Dave Mann
Campbell Connelly & Co. Ltd . . . . USA
Lisa Kirk & Fran Warren . . . . **HMV B 9919**
Ethel Merman & Ray Bolger . . . . **Brunswick 04456**
Donald Peers . . . . **HMV B 9933**
Billy Cotton & Kathy Kay . . . . **Columbia 33SX 1278**

DEARLY BELOVED — 1943
Jerome Kern / Johnny Mercer
Victoria Music Co. Ltd . . . . USA
Film(s): . . . . You Were Never Lovelier
Fred Astaire . . . . **Brunswick 03429**
Bing Crosby . . . . **Brunswick LA 8505**
Fred Astaire . . . . **Pye NPL 28002**
Helen Merrill . . . . **Mercury MMB 12000**
Fred Astaire appeared in *You Were Never Lovelier*.
Nominated for an Academy Award 1942.

DEATH OF A CLOWN, THE — September 1967
Raymond Davies / Dave Davies
Carlin Music Corporation . . . . UK
The Kinks . . . . **Pye 7N 17356**

DEBORA — May 1972
Marc Bolan
Cromwell Music Ltd . . . . UK
Tyrannosaurus Rex . . . . **Magic Fly ECHO 102**

DECEMBER — December 1949
Al Rinker / Floyd Huddlestone
Bregman, Vocco & Conn Ltd . . . . USA
Clive Wayne . . . . **HMV B 9840**
The Squadronaires Dance Orchestra,
vocal Roy Edwards . . . . **Decca F 9304**

DECEMBER '63 — March 1976
Bob Gaudio / Judy Parker
Jobete Music (UK) Ltd. . . . . USA
The Four Seasons . . . . **Warner Brothers K 16688**

DECK OF CARDS — January 1960
T. Texas Tyler
Campbell Connelly & Co. Ltd . . . . USA
Phil Harris . . . . **Camden CDN 124**
Wink Martindale (1960, 1963 & 1973) . . . . **London HL 8962**
T. Texas Tyler . . . . **London HAB 8156**
Max Bygraves (1973) . . . . **Pye 7N 45276**

DEDICATED FOLLOWER OF FASHION, A — April 1966
Ray Davies
Belinda (London) Ltd. . . . . UK
The Kinks . . . . **Pye 7N 17064**

Ivor Novello Nomination.

DEDICATED TO THE ONE I LOVE — June 1967
Lowman Pauling / Ralph Bass
Lois Music Ltd. . . . . USA
The Mamas & The Papas . . . . **RCA 1576**

'DEED I DO — 1927
Walter Hirsch / Fred Rose
Keith Prowse Music Publishing Co. Ltd. . . . . USA
Ben Pollack's Californians . . . . **HMV B 5281**
Lena Horne . . . . **MGM 111**
Perry Como . . . . **RCA RD 27035**
Billy Eckstine . . . . **Columbia 33SX 1327**

DEEP HENDERSON — 1926
Fred Rose
Keith Prowse Music Publishing Co. Ltd. . . . . USA
Ambrose & his Orchestra . . . . **Decca LF 1105**
The Coon-Sanders Orchestra . . . . **HMV B 5121**
Bob Scobey Band . . . . **Columbia LB 10078**

DEEP IN A DREAM — 1939
Eddie De Lange / Jimmy Van Heusen
Chappell & Co. Ltd. . . . . USA
Elsie Carlisle . . . . **HMV BD 663**
Artie Shaw & his Orchestra . . . . . . **Regal Zonophone MR 2979**
Monica Zetterlund . . . . **Columbia 33CSX 20**
Patti Page . . . . **Mercury MPL 6521**

DEEP IN MY HEART — 1926
Sigmund Romberg / Dorothy Donnelly
Chappell & Co. Ltd. . . . . USA
Show(s): . . . . The Student Prince
Film(s): . . . . The Student Prince Deep in My Heart
Harry Welchman & Rose Hignell . . . . **Columbia 9057**
Nelson Eddy & Rise Stevens . . . . **Philips SBF 117**
Ann Blyth . . . . **MGM MGM 766**
Mario Lanza . . . . **RCA RB 16113**
Harry Welchman & Rose Hignell appeared in the British production of *The Student Prince*.
Ann Blyth appeared in the 1954 film of *The Student Prince*.
Mario Lanza dubbed the singing voice of Edmund Purdom who appeared in the 1954 film of *The Student Prince*.

DEEP IN THE HEART OF TEXAS — 1942
June Hershey / Don Swander
Southern Music Publishing Co. Ltd . . . . USA
Film(s): . . . . Hi Neighbour / With a Song in My Heart
Bing Crosby with Woody Herman
& his Woodchoppers . . . . **Brunswick LAT 8253**
Joe 'Fingers' Carr (piano) . . . . **Capitol CL 14359**
Vera Lynn . . . . **MGM C 840**

DEEP NIGHT — 1929
Rudy Vallee / Charlie Henderson
Lawrence Wright Music Co. Ltd . . . . USA
Film(s): . . . . Both Ends of the Candle
Rudy Vallee & his Connecticut Yankees . . . . **Camden CDN 170**
Frank Sinatra . . . . **Columbia DB 3016**
Gogi Grant . . . . **RCA RD 27054**
Ann Richards . . . . **Capitol T 1078**

DEEP PURPLE — 1939
Peter De Rose / Mitchell Parish
Robbins Music Corporation Ltd. . . . . USA
Dick Todd . . . . **HMV BD 699**
Larry Clinton & his Orchestra . . . . **RCA RC 24003**
Bing Crosby . . . . **Brunswick LA 8514**
Duke Ellington & his Orchestra . . . . **Parlophone PMC 1136**
Billy Ward (1957) . . . . **London HLU 8500**
Pat Boone . . . . **London HAD 2127**
Nino Tempo & April Stevens (1964) . . . . . . **London HLK 9785**
Donnie & Marie Osmond (1976) . . . . **MGM 2006561**

DEER HUNTER THEME, THE (Cavatina) (He Was Beautiful) — June 1979
Stanley Myers / Cleo Laine
Robbins Music Ltd. . . . . UK
Film(s): . . . . Deer Hunter
The Shadows (June) . . . . **EMI 2939**
John Williams (Guitar) (June)
(Sound Track Recording) . . . . **Cube BUG 80**
Iris Williams (November) . . . . **Columbia DB 9070**

Lyric added to original composition.
Ivor Novello Award 1977.
Ivor Novello Nomination 1979.
Ivor Novello Nomination 1979 (for lyric).

DELAWARE   March 1960
Irving Gordon
Leeds Music Ltd . . . . USA
Perry Como . . . . **RCA 1170**

DELICADO   July 1952
Walter Azevedo
Lafleur & Co. Ltd . . . . Brazil
Frank Cordell & his Orchestra . . . . **HMV B 10305**
Stanley Black & his Orchestra . . . . **Decca LK 4306**

DELILAH   1917
Horatio Nicholls
Lawrence Wright Music Co. Ltd. . . . . UK
The Debroy Somers Band,
conducted by Horatio Nicholls . . . . **Columbia DX 673**
Harry Davidson & his Orchestra . . . . **Columbia 33S 1142**

DELILAH   May 1968
Les Reed / Barry Mason
Donna Music Ltd. . . . . UK
Tom Jones . . . . **Decca F 12747**
The Sensational Alex Harvey Band (1975) . . . **Vertigo ALEX 001**
Ivor Novello Award.

DELTA LADY   November 1969
Leon Russell
Louvigny-Marquee Music Co. . . . . USA
Film(s): . . . . Mad Dogs & Englishmen
Joe Cocker . . . . **Regal Zonophone RZ 3024**
Leon Russell . . . . **A&M AMLS 982**
Joe Cocker . . . . **A&M AMLS 6002**
Joe Cocker & Leon Russell appeared in *Mad Dogs & Englishmen.*

DELYSE   1937
Horatio Nicholls / Joseph Gilbert
Lawrence Wright Music Co. Ltd. . . . . UK
Jack Hylton & his Orchestra . . . . **HMV BD 5165**
Arthur Tracey (The Street Singer) . . . . **Decca F 6402**
Harry Davidson & his Orchestra . . . . **Columbia SCD 2033**

DENIS (Denise)   April 1978
Neil Levenson
Bright Music Ltd . . . . UK
Blondie . . . . **Chrysalis CHS 2204**

DESAFINADO   December 1962
Antonio Carlos Jobim / Jessie Cavanaugh / John Hendricks
Essex Music Ltd . . . . Brazil
Charlie Byrd (guitar) & Stan Getz
(tenor saxophone) . . . . **HMV POP 1061**
Ella Fitzgerald . . . . **Verve VS 502**
Laurindo Almeida (guitar) . . . . **Capitol T 1759**

DESERT SONG, THE   1927
Sigmund Romberg / Otto Harbach / Oscar Hammerstein II
Chappell & Co. Ltd. . . . . USA
Show(s): . . . . The Desert Song
Film(s): . . . . The Desert Song / Deep in My Heart
Harry Welchman & Edith Day . . . . **Columbia 9211**
Kathryn Grayson & Tony Martin . . . . **HMV DLP 1029**
Edmund Hockridge & June Bronhill . . . . . . **HMV CLP 1274**
Mario Lanza & Judith Raskin . . . . **RCA RB 16226**
Gordon MacRae . . . . **Capitol LCT 6114**
Harry Welchman & Edith Day appeared in the British production of *The
Desert Song.*
Kathryn Grayson & Gordon McRae appeared in the 1953 film of
The Desert Song.

DESIDERATA (You Are A Child Of The Universe)   April 1972
Fred Werner / Max Ehrmann
Screen Gems Music Ltd . . . . USA
Les Crane . . . . **Warner Brothers K 16119**

DESIRE   October 1988
Paul Hewson / David Evans / Larry Mullen Jnr. & Adam Clayton
Blue Mountain Music . . . . UK
U2 . . . . **Island IS 400**

DESPERATE DAN   January 1973
Robert Woodward / Nigel Fletcher
Makepeace Music Ltd. . . . . UK
Lieutenant Pigeon . . . . **Decca F 13365**

DESTINY WALTZ   1913
Sidney Baynes
Swan & Co. (Publishers) Ltd. . . . . UK
The Mayfair Orchestra . . . . **HMV C 333**
The Mantovani Orchestra . . . . **Decca LF 1015**
Michael Collins & his Orchestra . . . . . **Columbia 33SX 1194**

DETOUR AHEAD   April 1956
Herb Ellis / John Frigo / Lou Carter
Edwin H. Morris & Co. Ltd. . . . . USA
Jackie Paris . . . . **Vogue LRA 10038**
Joe Williams . . . . **London HBC 1065**
Jeri Southern . . . . **Columbia 33SX 1134**

DETROIT CITY   April 1967
Mel Tillis / Danny Hill
Meridian Music Publishing Co. Ltd. . . . . USA
Tom Jones . . . . **Decca F 22555**

DEVIL GATE DRIVE   March 1974
Mike Chapman / Nicky Chinn
Chinnichap Music . . . . UK
Suzi Quatro . . . . **Rak 167**

DEVIL WENT DOWN TO GEORGIA, THE   October 1979
*Charles Daniels / Fred Edwards / Tom Crain / James Marshall /
Charlie Hayward / Joel Digregorio*
April Music Ltd . . . . USA
The Charlie Daniels Band . . . . **Epic EPC 7737**

DEVIL WOMAN   November 1962
Marty Robbins
Acuff-Rose Publishing Co. Ltd . . . . USA
Marty Robbins . . . . **CBS AAG 114**
Brian Poole & The Tremeloes . . . . **Ace of Clubs ACL 1146**

DEVIL WOMAN   June 1976
Kristine Authors / Terry Britten
Chappell & Co. Ltd . . . . UK
Cliff Richard . . . . **EMI 2458**
Kristine . . . . **Power Exchange PX 229**

DEVILS' ANSWER, THE   August 1971
John Cann
G.H. Music . . . . UK
Atomic Rooster . . . . **B&C CB 157**

DEVOTION   August 1958
Otto Cesana
Cecil Lennox Music . . . . USA
Petula Clark . . . . **Nixa N 15152**

DIAMONDS   February 1963
Jerry Lordan
Francis, Day & Hunter Ltd . . . . UK
Jet Harris & Tony Meehan . . . . **Decca F 11563**
The Ventures . . . . **Liberty LBY 1150**

DIAMONDS ARE A GIRL'S BEST FRIEND   October 1953
Leo Robin / Jule Styne
Edward Kassner Music Co. Ltd. . . . . USA
Show(s): . . . . Gentlemen Prefer Blondes
Film(s): . . . . Gentlemen Prefer Blondes
Carol Channing . . . . **Philips BBL 7232**
Marilyn Monroe . . . . **MGM D 116**
Dora Bryan . . . . **HMV CLP 1602**
Carol Channing appeared in the American production of *Gentlemen
Prefer Blondes.*
Marilyn Monroe appeared in the film *Gentlemen Prefer Blondes.*
Dora Bryan appeared in the British production of *Gentlemen Prefer Blondes.*

DIAMONDS ARE FOREVER   February 1972
Don Black / John Barry
United Artists Music Co. Ltd . . . . UK
Film(s): . . . . Diamonds Are Forever
Shirley Bassey . . . . **United Artists UP 35293**
Ivor Novello Award.

DIANA   August 1957
Paul Anka

Robert Mellin Ltd. . . . . USA
Paul Anka . . . . **Columbia 33SX 1092**
Bobby Vee . . . . **London HAG 2374**

DIANE   1927
Erno Rapee / Lew Pollack
Keith Prowse Music Publishing Co. Ltd. . . . . USA
Layton & Johnstone . . . . **Columbia 4693**
Jack Hylton & his Orchestra . . . . **HMV B 5393**
The Mantovani Orchestra . . . . **Decca LK 4105**
Tony Williams . . . . **Mercury MMC 14027**
The Bachelors (1964) . . . . **Decca F 11799**

DIARY OF HORACE WIMP, THE   August 1979
Jeff Lynne
United Artists Music Co. Ltd. . . . . UK
The Electric Light Orchestra . . . . **Jet 150**

DICK-A-DUM DUM (KINGS ROAD)   June 1969
Jim Dale
Edwin H. Morris & Co. Ltd. . . . . UK
Des O'Connor . . . . **Columbia DB 8566**

DICKY BIRD HOP, THE   1926
Ronald Gourlay / Leslie Sarony
Keith Prowse Music Publishing Co. Ltd. . . . . UK
Ronald Gourlay . . . . **Edison 0222**
Ann Stevens & Ronald Gourlay . . . . **HMV 7EG 8187**
The Keynotes . . . . **Decca F 9502**
Theme song of Ronald Gourlay.

DID I REMEMBER   1936
Harold Adamson / Walter Donaldson
Francis, Day & Hunter Ltd . . . . USA
Film(s): . . . . Suzy
Dick Powell . . . . **Decca F 6044**
Guy Lombardo & his Royal Canadians . . . . . **Capitol LCT 6127**
Jay P. Morgan . . . . **MGM C 793**

**DID TOSTI RAISE HIS BOWLER HAT WHEN HE SAID
SORRY**   1925
Bill Mayerl / Gene Paul
Keith Prowse Music Publishing Co. Ltd. . . . . UK
Norah Blaney . . . . **Columbia 3790**

DID YOU EVER   October 1971
Bobby Braddock
London Tree Music Ltd. . . . . USA
Nancy Sinatra & Lee Hazlewood . . . . **Reprise K 14093**

**DID YOU EVER GET THAT FEELING
IN THE MOONLIGHT**   1946
James Cavanaugh / Larry Stock / Ira Schuster
Francis, Day & Hunter Ltd. . . . . USA
Perry Como . . . . **HMV BD 1120**
Geraldo & his Orchestra, vocal Carol Carr . . **Parlophone F 2114**
Guy Mitchell . . . . **Philips BBL 7465**

DID YOU EVER SEE A DREAM WALKING   1934
Mack Gordon / Harry Revel
Bradbury Wood Ltd. . . . . USA
Film(s): . . . . Sitting Pretty
Bing Crosby . . . . **Fontana TFR 6012**
Frances Day . . . . **HMV B 8096**
Lita Roza . . . . **Decca F 9992**
Michael Holliday . . . . **Columbia 33SX 1170**
Frankie Avalon . . . . **HMV CLP 1423**

DID YOUR MOTHER COME FROM IRELAND   1936
Jimmy Kennedy / Michael Carr
Peter Maurice Music Co. Ltd . . . . UK
Peggy Dell . . . . **Regal Zonophone MR 2246**

DIDJA EVER   August 1952
Vic Mizzy / Mann Curtis
Edward Cox Music . . . . USA
Debbie Reynolds & Carleton Carpenter . . . . **MGM 538**
Mary Small . . . . **Vogue V 9039**

DIED IN YOUR ARMS   September 1986
Nick Eede
Virgin Music . . . . UK
The Cutting Crew . . . . **Siren SIREN 21**

DIFFERENT CORNER   April 1986
George Michael
Morrison Leahy Music . . . . UK
George Michael . . . . **Epic A 7033**

DIGA DIGA DOO   1929
Dorothy Fields / Jimmy McHugh
Lawrence Wright Music Co. Ltd . . . . USA
Show(s): . . . . Blackbirds of 1928
Film(s): . . . . Stormy Weather
Duke Ellington & his Orchestra . . . . **HMV B 4959**
Adelaide Hall . . . . **Columbia SCX 6422**
The Mills Brothers . . . . **Brunswick 01520**
The Dick Charlesworth Band . . . . **Top Rank 35-104**
**Duke Ellington & his Orchestra,
vocal Irving Mills** . . . . **CBS BPG 62545**
Adelaide Hall appeared in *Blackbirds of 1928.*

DIGGING YOUR SCENE   March 1986
Robert Howard
BMG Music . . . . UK
The Blow Monkeys . . . . **RCA MONK 1**

DIME AND A DOLLAR, A   June 1954
Jay Livingston / Ray Evans
Maddox Music . . . . USA
Guy Mitchell . . . . **Philips PB 248**
Joe Loss Orchestra . . . . **HMV BD 6169**
The Keynotes . . . . **Decca F 10302**

DINAH   1926
Joe Young / Harry Akst / Sam M. Lewis
B. Feldman & Co. Ltd. . . . . USA
Show(s): . . . . Kid Boots
Film(s): . . . . Broadway / Show Business / The Big Broadcast
The Revellers . . . . **HMV B 2182**
Eddie Cantor . . . . **Brunswick 03974**
Bing Crosby & The Mills Brothers . . . . **Brunswick 03080**
Muggsy Spanier's Ragtime Band . . . . **RCA RD 27132**
Bing Crosby . . . . **Brunswick LA 8673**
Eddie Cantor appeared in *Kid Boots* and *Show Business.*
Bing Crosby appeared in *The Big Broadcast*
Theme song of Dinah Shore.

DING DONG THE WITCH IS DEAD   1940
Harold Arlen / E.Y. Harburg
Robbins Music Corporation . . . . USA
Film(s): . . . . The Wizard of Oz
The MGM Studio Orchestra & chorus . . . . **MGM C 757**
Ann Stephens . . . . **HMV BD 928**
June Christy . . . . **Capitol T 1398**

DING-A-DONG (Ding Dinge Dong)   May 1975
Wil Lukinga / Dick Baker / Eddy Owens
A.T.V. Music Ltd. . . . . Holland
Teach-In . . . . **Polydor 2058570**
Dutch entry for the 1975 Eurovision Song Contest (Placed First).

DINNER AT EIGHT   1933
Dorothy Fields / Jimmy McHugh
Campbell Connelly & Co. Ltd. . . . . USA
Film(s): . . . . Dinner at Eight
Carl Brisson . . . . **Decca F 3701**
Ray Noble & his Orchestra, vocal Al Bowlly . . . . . **HMV B 6409**
Frank Chacksfield & his Orchestra . . . . **Decca DFE 6442**

DINNER FOR ONE PLEASE JAMES   1935
Michael Carr
Peter Maurice Music Co. Ltd . . . . UK
Leslie Hutchinson (Hutch) . . . . **Parlophone F 311**
Hal Yates . . . . **HMV BD 307**
Nat 'King' Cole . . . . **Capitol LC 6627**

DIPPETY DAY   November 1978
Pierre Kartner / 'Linlee'
Burlington Music Co.Ltd . . . . Holland
Father Abraham & The Smurfs . . . . **Decca F 13798**

DIPSY DOODLE, THE   1938
Larry Clinton
Francis, Day & Hunter Ltd. . . . . USA
Film(s): . . . . Since You Went Away
Tommy Dorsey & his Orchestra . . . . **HMV B 8692**
Glenn Miller & his Orchestra . . . . **RCA RD 27090**

Larry Clinton & his Orchestra	RCA RC 24003
The Modernaires	Vogue LVA 10012

DIRTY CASH　　　　　　　　　　　　　　　May 1990
Steve Vincent / Mick Walsh
Warner Chappell Music .... UK
Adventures of Stevie V .... Mercury MER 311

DIRTY DIANA　　　　　　　　　　　　　　　July 1988
Michael Jackson
Warner Chappell Music .... USA
Michael Jackson .... Epic 651546

DIRTY HANDS, DIRTY FACE　　　　　　　　　　1923
Jimmy Monaco / Edgar Leslie / Grant Clarke / Al Jolson
Chappell & Co. Ltd .... USA
Show(s): .... Bombo
Film(s): .... The Jazz Singer
Al Jolson .... Brunswick 3790
Joe Raymond & his Orchestra .... HMV B 1717
Elsie Carlisle .... HMV BD 476
Judy Garland .... Capitol LCT 6121
Al Jolson appeared in both *Bombo* and *The Jazz Singer*.

DIS DONC, DIS DONC　　　　　　　　　　October 1958
*Marguerite Monnot / Alexandre Breffort / Julian More / David
Heneker & Monty Norman*
Trafalgar Music Ltd .... France
Show(s): .... Irma La Douce
Elizabeth Seal .... Philips BBL 7274
Line Renaud .... Columbia DB 2193
Elizabeth Seal appeared in both the American and British productions
of *Irma La Douce*.

D.I.S.C.O.　　　　　　　　　　　　　　October 1980
Daniel Vangarde / Jean Kluger
Heath Levy Music Ltd .... France
Ottowan .... Carrere CAR 161

DISCO CONNECTION, THE　　　　　　　　　May 1976
Isaac Hayes
Anchor Music Ltd .... USA
The Isaac Hayes Movement .... ABC 4100

DISCO DUCK　　　　　　　　　　　　　October 1976
Rick Dees
Chappell & Co. Ltd .... USA
Rick Dees & His Cast of Idiots .... RSO 2090204

DISCO QUEEN　　　　　　　　　　　　　　June 1975
Errol Brown / Tony Wilson
Rak Music Ltd .... UK
Hot Chocolate .... Rak 202

DISCO STOMP　　　　　　　　　　　　　　July 1975
Hamilton Bohannon
Burlington Music Co. Ltd .... USA
Hamilton Bohannon .... Brunswick BR 19

DISTANT DRUMS　　　　　　　　　　　December 1966
Cindy Walker
Acuff-Rose Music Ltd. .... USA
Jim Reeves .... RCA 1537

DIVINE EMOTIONS　　　　　　　　　　　　May 1988
Narada Michael Walden / Jeffrey Cohen
MCA Music .... USA
Narada .... Reprise W 7967

D.I.V.O.R.C.E.　　　　　　　　　　　　　July 1975
Bobby Braddock / Curly Putman
London Tree Music Co. .... USA
Film(s): .... Five Easy Pieces
Tammy Wynette .... Epic 3361
Tammy Wynette (Sound Track) .... Epic SEPC 70091
Billy Connolly (November) (Parody version) . Polydor 2058652
Tammy Wynette appeared in *Five Easy Pieces*.

DIZZY　　　　　　　　　　　　　　　　　June 1969
Tommy Roe / Freddy Weller
Lowery Music Co. .... USA
Tommy Roe .... Stateside SS 2143

DIZZY FINGERS　　　　　　　　　　　　　1928
Zez Confrey

Lawrence Wright Music Co. Ltd. .... USA
Film(s): .... The Eddy Duchin Story
Zez Confrey & his Orchestra .... HMV B 5354
Patricia Rossborough (Piano) .... Parlophone F 1128
Steve Race (Piano) .... Columbia SEG 7584
Frank Barron .... MGM CC 1
Carmen Cavallaro (piano) .... Brunswick LAT 8119

DO ANYTHING YOU WANNA DO　　　　September 1977
Ed Hollis / Graeme Douglas
Island Music Ltd .... UK
Film(s): .... That Summer
Eddie & The Hot Rods .... Island WIP 6401
Eddie & The Hot Rods appeared in *That Summer*.

DO DO DO　　　　　　　　　　　　　　　　1927
George Gershwin / Ira Gershwin
Chappell & Co. Ltd. .... USA
Show(s): .... Oh Kay
Film(s): .... Tea for Two / Both Ends of the Candle / Star
Gertrude Lawrence & Harold French .... Columbia 4617
Doris Day .... Columbia DB 2862
Gogi Grant .... RCA RD 27054
Julie Andrews .... Stateside SL 10233
Gertrude Lawrence appeared in both the British and American pro-
ductions of *Oh Kay*.
Harold French appeared in the British production of *Oh Kay*.
Doris Day appeared in *Tea for Two*.
Julie Andrews appeared in *Star*.
Gogi Grant dubbed the singing voice of Ann Blyth who appeared in
the film *Both Ends of the Candle*.

DO I DO　　　　　　　　　　　　　　　　July 1982
Stevie Wonder
Jobete Music .... USA
Stevie Wonder .... Motown TMG 1254

**DO I LOVE YOU BECAUSE
YOU'RE BEAUTIFUL**　　　　　　　　　December 1958
Richard Rodgers / Oscar Hammerstein II
Williamson Music Ltd .... USA
Show(s): .... Cinderella
Yana & Bruce Trent .... Decca LK 4303
Vic Damone .... Philips BBE 12245
Edmund Hockridge .... Nixa N 15167
Yana & Bruce Trent appeared in *Cinderella*.

DO I LOVE YOU, DO I　　　　　　　　　　　1941
Cole Porter
Chappell & Co. Ltd .... USA
Show(s): .... Dubarry Was a Lady / Black Vanities
Film(s): .... Du Barry Was a Lady / Night and Day
Frances Day .... Decca F 7867
Jimmy Young .... Columbia 33SX 1102
Judy Garland .... Capitol T 1036
Ethel Merman .... Reprise R 6032
Frances Day appeared in the British production of *Dubarry Was A
Lady* and also *Black Vanities*.
Ethel Merman appeared in the American production of *Dubarry Was
A Lady*.

DO I WORRY　　　　　　　　　　　　　　　1941
Stanley Cowan / Bobby North
Southern Music Publishing Co. Ltd .... USA
Film(s): .... Pardon My Sarong
The Ink Spots .... Brunswick LA 8728
Dorothy Squires .... Columbia DB 2659
Helen Carr .... London HAN 2065
The Ink Spots appeared in *Pardon My Sarong*.

DO IT AGAIN　　　　　　　　　　　September 1968
Brian Wilson / Mike Love
Immediate Music Ltd. .... USA
The Beach Boys .... Capitol CL 15554

**DO IT, DO IT AGAIN
(A Far L'Amore Comincia Tu)**　　　　　　May 1978
Daniele Pace / Franco Bracardi / A. Collins
Sugar Music Ltd .... Italy
Raffaella Carra .... Epic ENY 13

DO NOTHING　　　　　　　　　　　　　January 1981
Lynval Golding / Jerry Dammers
Plangent Visions Music .... UK
The Specials .... 2 Tone CHSTT 16

DO NOTHING TILL YOU HEAR FROM ME　　　　1944
Duke Ellington / Bob Russell
Robbins Music Corporation Ltd. . . . . USA
Duke Ellington & his Orchestra . . . . **RCA RD 27133**
Ed Townsend . . . . **Capitol T 1140**
Rosemary Clooney . . . . **Coral LVA 9112**
Dinah Shore . . . . **Capitol T 1354**
Adapted from "Concerto for Cootie" by Duke Ellington.

DO SOMETHING　　　　1929
Bud Green / Sammy Stept
Campbell Connelly & Co. Ltd . . . . USA
Film(s): . . . . Nothing But the Truth / Syncopation
Zelma O'Neal . . . . **Brunswick 3999**
Helen Kane . . . . **MGM EP 549**
Helen Kane appeared in *Nothing But The Truth*.

DO THAT TO ME ONE MORE TIME　　　March 1980
Toni Tennille
A.T.V. Music Ltd. . . . . USA
Captain & Tennille . . . . **Casablanca CAN 175**

DO THE CONGA　　　　December 1984
Peter Morris / Mick Flynn
Sonet Music . . . . UK
Black Lace . . . . **Flair FLA 108**

DO THE HUCKLEBUCK (See Hucklebuck, The)

(DO THE) SPANISH HUSTLE　　　　March 1976
Gerry Thomas
Intersong Music . . . . USA
The Fatback Band . . . . **Polydor 2066656**

DO THEY KNOW IT'S CHRISTMAS　　December 1984
Bob Geldof / Midge Ure
Warner Chappell Music . . . . UK
Band Aid . . . . **Mercury FEED 1**
Ivor Novello Award 1984.

DO WAH DIDDY DIDDY　　　　August 1964
Ellie Greenwich / Jeff Barry
West One Music Ltd . . . . USA
Manfred Mann . . . . **HMV POP 1320**
The Exciters . . . . **United Artists UP 1041**

DO WHAT YOU DO　　　　March 1985
Ralph Dino / Larry Ditomaso
MCA Music . . . . USA
Jermaine Jackson . . . . **Arista ARIST 609**

DO WHAT YOU GOTTA DO　　　　January 1969
Jim Webb
Carlin Music Corporation . . . . USA
Nina Simone . . . . **RCA 1743**
The Four Tops (October) . . . . . . **Tamla Motown TMG 710**

DO YA DO YA (Wanna Please Me)　　　July 1986
Michael Bissell / Graham Richardson
Zomba Music . . . . UK
Samatha Fox . . . . **Jive FOXY 2**

DO YOU CARE　　　　1942
Lew Quadling / Jack Elliott
Bradbury Wood Ltd . . . . USA
Bing Crosby . . . . **Brunswick 03278**
Alan Dean . . . . **MGM 523**
Dinah Shore . . . . **Regal Zonophone MR 3605**

DO YOU EVER THINK OF ME　　　　1921
Harry Kerr / John Cooper / Earl Burtnett
Herman Darewski Music Publishing Co. Ltd . . . . USA
Paul Whiteman & his Orchestra . . . . **HMV B 1225**
Bing Crosby & The Merry Macs . . . . **Brunswick 04104**
Matt Monro . . . . **Philips LF 1276**
Gisele MacKenzie . . . . **RCA RD 27033**

DO YOU FEEL MY LOVE　　　　December 1980
Eddy Grant
Intersong Music . . . . UK
Eddy Grant . . . . **Ensign ENY 45**

DO YOU KNOW THE WAY TO SAN JOSE　June 1968
Burt Bacharach / Hal David
Blue Seas Music . . . . USA

Dionne Warwick . . . . **Pye 7N 25457**

DO YOU KNOW WHERE YOU'RE GOING TO　May 1976
Michael Masser / Gerry Goffin
Screen Gems Music Ltd . . . . USA
Film(s): . . . . Mahogany
Diana Ross . . . . **Tamla Motown TMG 1010**
Diana Ross appeared in *Mahogany*.

DO YOU LOVE ME　　　　1946
Harry Ruby
Chappell & Co. Ltd. . . . . USA
Film(s): . . . . Do You Love Me
Dick Haymes . . . . **Brunswick 03726**
Paula Green . . . . **Columbia FB 3236**
Harry James & his Orchestra,
　vocal Ginnie Powell . . . . **Parlophone R 3015**
Dick Haymes appeared in *Do You Love Me*.

DO YOU LOVE ME　　　　October 1963
Berry Gordy Jnr
Dominion Music Co. Ltd . . . . USA
Brian Poole & The Tremeloes . . . . **Decca F 11739**
Dave Clark Five . . . . **Columbia SEG 8289**

DO YOU MIND　　　　April 1960
Lionel Bart
Macmelodies Ltd . . . . UK
Film(s): . . . . Let's Get Married
Anthony Newley . . . . **Decca F 11220**
Anthony Newley appeared in *Let's Get Married*.

DO YOU REALLY LOVE ME TOO (Fools Errand)　January 1964
Mark Barkan / Ben Raleigh
Shapiro-Bernstein & Co. Ltd . . . . USA
Billy Fury . . . . **Decca F 11792**
Barbara Chandler . . . . **London HLR 9823**

DO YOU REALLY WANT TO HURT ME　October 1982
George O'Dowd / Jonathan Moss / Michael Craig / Roy Hay
Virgin Music . . . . UK
Culture Club . . . . **Virgin VS 518**
Ivor Novello Nomination 1982 & 1983

DO YOU REMEMBER THE LAST WALTZ　　1911
Bennett Scott / A.J. Mills
B. Feldman & Co Ltd . . . . UK
Ernest Pike . . . . **Regal T 613**
Harry Davidson & his Orchestra . . . . . **Columbia DX 1856**

DO YOU WANNA DANCE　　　　November 1973
Barry Blue / Ron Roker / Gerry Shury
A.T.V. Music Ltd. . . . . UK
Barry Blue . . . . **Bell 1336**

DO YOU WANNA TOUCH ME　　　February 1973
Gary Glitter / Mike Leander
Leeds Music Ltd. . . . . UK
Gary Glitter . . . . **Bell BELL 1280**

DO YOU WANT TO KNOW A SECRET　　June 1963
John Lennon / Paul McCartney
Northern Songs Ltd . . . . UK
Billy J. Kramer & The Dakotas . . . . **Parlophone R 5023**
The Beatles . . . . **Parlophone PMC 1202**
Keely Smith . . . . **Reprise R 6142**

DO-RE-MI　　　　July 1961
Richard Rodgers / Oscar Hammerstein II
Williamson Music Ltd. . . . . USA
Show(s): . . . . Sound of Music
Film(s): . . . . Sound of Music
Mary Martin . . . . **Philips ABL 3370**
Jean Bayless . . . . **HMV CLP 1453**
Julie Andrews . . . . **RCA RB 6616**
Gracie Fields . . . . **Columbia DB 4622**
Mary Martin appeared in the American production of *Sound of Music*.
Jean Bayless appeared in the British production of *Sound of Music*.
Julie Andrews appeared in the film of *Sound of Music*.

DOCK OF THE BAY, THE　　　　April 1968
Steve Cropper / Otis Redding
Tee Pee Music . . . . USA
Otis Redding . . . . **Stax 601031**

DOCTOR BEAT September 1984
Enrique Garcia
EMI Music . . . . USA
The Miami Sound Machine . . . . **Epic A 4614**

DOCTOR! DOCTOR! March 1984
Tom Bailey / Alannah Currie / Joe Leeway
Point Music . . . . UK
The Thompson Twins . . . . **Arista TWINS 3**

DOCTOR KILDARE THEME April 1962
Jerry Goldsmith
Robbins Music Corporation Ltd. . . . . USA
Johnnie Spence & his Orchestra (April) . . . **Parlophone R 4872**
Nelson Riddle & his Orchestra . . . . **Capitol T 1771**
Theme of the TV series 'Doctor Kildare'.

DOCTOR KISS KISS August 1976
Tony Eyers
Intersong Music . . . . UK
5000 Volts . . . . **Philips 6006533**

DOCTOR LOVE January 1977
Biddu'
Dick James Music Ltd . . . . UK
Tina Charles . . . . **CBS 4779**

DOCTOR MY EYES March 1973
Jackson Brown
Lorna Music Co. Ltd. . . . . USA
The Jackson Five . . . . **Tamla Motown TMG 842**

DOCTOR'S ORDERS April 1974
Roger Cook / Roger Greenaway / Geoff Stevens
Cookaway Music . . . . UK
Sunny . . . . **CBS 2068**
Ivor Novello Nomination.

DOCTORIN' THE HOUSE March 1988
Jonathan Moore / Matthew Black / Winston Riley & Yasmin Evans
Big Life Music . . . . UK
Cold Cut featuring Yazz
& The Plastic Population **Ahead of Our Time CCUT 27**

DOCTORIN' THE TARDIS June 1988
Ron Grainer / Gary Glitter / Michael Chapman & Nicky Chinn
Warner Chappell Music . . . . UK
The Timelords . . . . **KLF KLF 003**

DOES SANTA CLAUS SLEEP WITH HIS WHISKERS 1934
Billy Bray / Fred Gibson
Victoria Music Co. Ltd. . . . . UK
Bobbie Comber . . . . **Broadcast 3359**
The BBC Dance Orchestra,
conducted by Henry Hall . . . . **Columbia CB 693**

DOES YOUR CHEWING GUM
LOSE IT'S FLAVOUR February 1959
Billy Rose / Marty Bloom / Ernest Brever
B. Feldman & Co. Ltd . . . . USA
Lonnie Donegan . . . . **Nixa NPL 18034**
Original title *Does the Spearmint Lose Its Flavour*.
First published in 1924.

DOES YOUR MOTHER COME FROM IRELAND (See Did
Your Mother Come From Ireland)

DOES YOUR MOTHER KNOW May 1979
Benny Andersson / Bjorn Ulvaeus
Bocu Music Ltd. . . . . Sweden
Abba . . . . **Epic EPC 7316**

DOG EAT DOG November 1980
Marco Pirroni / Adam Ant
EMI Music Ltd . . . . UK
Adam & The Ants . . . . **CBS 9039**

DOIN' THE DO June 1990
Alison Clarkson / Kenny Young
Rhythm King Music . . . . UK
Betty Boo . . . . **Rhythm King LEFT 39**

DOIN' THE NEW LOWDOWN 1929
Dorothy Fields / Jimmy McHugh
Lawrence Wright Music Co. Ltd . . . . USA
Show(s): . . . . Blackbirds of 1928

Duke Ellington & his Orchestra . . . . **Parlophone R 379**
The Mills Brothers . . . . **Brunswick 01518**
Pearl Bailey . . . . **Columbia 33SX 1269**

DOIN' THE RACCOON 1929
J. Fred Coots / Ray Klages
Francis, Day & Hunter Ltd . . . . USA
Film(s): . . . . The Time, the Place and the Girl
George Olsen & his Music . . . . **HMV B 5576**
Dorothy Provine . . . . **Warner Brothers WM 4053**
Laurie Johnson & His Orchestra . . . . **Pye 7N 15406**

DOIN' WHAT COMES NATURALLY 1947
Irving Berlin
Irving Berlin Ltd. . . . . USA
Show(s): . . . . .Annie Get Your Gun
Film(s): . . . . .Annie Get Your Gun
Ethel Merman . . . . **Brunswick LAT 8002**
Dolores Gray . . . . **Columbia SEG 7711**
Betty Hutton . . . . **MGM CD 1**
Ethel Merman appeared in the American production of *Annie Get Your Gun*.
Dolores Gray appeared in the British production of *Annie Get Your Gun*.
Betty Hutton appeared in the film of *Annie Get Your Gun*.

DOINA DE JALE September 1976
Traditional, arranged by Zamfir
Chappell & Co. Ltd . . . . Rumania
Georghe Zamfir . . . . **Epic EPC 4310**
Theme of the TV series *The Light of Experience*.

DOING ALRIGHT WITH THE BOYS July 1975
Gary Glitter / Mike Leander
Leeds Music Ltd . . . . UK
Gary Glitter . . . . **Bell 1429**

DOLCE VITA October 1983
Pierluigi Giombini / Paul Mazzolni
Warner Chappell Music . . . . Italy
Ryan Paris . . . . **Carrere CAR 289**

DOLL DANCE, THE 1927
Nacio Herb Brown
Keith Prowse Music Publishing Co. Ltd. . . . . USA
Nat Shilkret & his Orchestra . . . . **HMV B 2505**
Lou Busch & his Orchestra . . . . **Capitol T 1072**
Russ Morgan & his Orchestra . . . . **Brunswick 04795**

DOLL HOUSE January 1961
Lou Duhig / Ruby Berry
Newman Music . . . . USA
The King Brothers . . . . **Parlophone R 4715**
Donnie Brooks . . . . **London HLN 9253**

DOLLAR PRINCESSES 1909
Adrian Ross / Leo Fall
Ascherberg, Hopwood & Crew Ltd. USA
Show(s): . . . . .The Dollar Princess
The Dollar Princess Operatic Party . . . . **HMV GC 4622**

DOLLY MY LOVE August 1975
Tommy Keith
Sunbury Music Ltd . . . . USA
The Moments . . . . **All Platinum 6146306**

DOLORES 1941
Louis Alter / Frank Loesser
Victoria Music Co. Ltd . . . . USA
Film(s): . . . . The Gay City
Bing Crosby & The Merry Macs . . . . **Brunswick 03190**
Tommy Dorsey & his Orchestra . . . . **HMV BD 5688**
Tony Osborne & his Orchestra . . . . **HMV 7EG 8443**
Tommy Dorsey appeared in *The Gay City*.
Nominated for an Academy Award 1941.

DOMANI June 1955
Tony Velona / Ulpio Minucci
Larry Spier Ltd. . . . . USA
The Gaylords . . . . **Mercury ZEP 10086**
Julius La Rosa . . . . **London HAR 2031**
Dennis Lotis . . . . **Nixa NEP 24017**

DOMINIQUE December 1963
'Souer Sourire'
Flamingo Music Ltd . . . . Belgium
Film(s): . . . . The Singing Nun

Sister Sourire . . . . **Philips BF 1293**
Debbie Reynolds . . . . **MGM C 8011**
Debbie Reynolds appeared in *The Singing Nun.*

DOMINO December 1951
Jacques Plante / Louis Ferrari / Don Raye
Leeds Music Ltd . . . . France
Teddy Johnson . . . . **Columbia DB 2996**
Bing Crosby . . . . **Brunswick 04841**

DOMINO DANCING October 1988
Neil Tennant / Chris Lowe
Cage Music . . . . UK
The Pet Shop Boys . . . . **Parlophone R 6190**

DON QUIXOTE September 1985
Nik Kershaw
Rondor Music . . . . UK
Nik Kershaw . . . . **MCA NIK 8**

DON'T March 1958
Jerry Lieber / Mike Stoller
Belinda Music . . . . USA
Elvis Presley . . . . **RCA 1043**

DON'T ANSWER ME (Ti Vedo Uscuiri) July 1966
B. Zambrini / L. Enriques / Peter Callander
Shapiro-Bernstein & Co. Ltd. . . . . Italy
Cilla Black . . . . **Parlophone R 5463**

DON'T ASK ME WHY 1943
Robert Stolz / Joe Young
Campbell Connelly & Co. Ltd . . . . Germany
Richard Tauber . . . . **Parlophone RO 20526**
Tony Martin . . . . **Decca F 8286**
The Robert Stoltz Orchestra . . . . **MGM C 815**
Greta Keller . . . . **Decca LK 4126**

DON'T BE CRUEL October 1956
Otis Blackwell / Elvis Presley
Aberbach (London) Ltd. . . . . USA
Elvis Presley . . . . **HMV POP 249**
Connie Francis . . . . **MGM C 804**

DON'T BE THAT WAY 1938
Edgar Sampson / Benny Goodman / Mitchell Parish
Francis, Day & Hunter Ltd. . . . . USA
Benny Goodman Orchestra . . . . **RCA RCX 1036**
Harry Parry & his Radio Rhythm Club Sextet . **Parlophone R 2808**
The Andrews Sisters . . . . **Brunswick LA 8599**
Soundtrack of The Benny Goodman Story . **Brunswick LAT 8102**
Ella Fitzgerald . . . . **HMV CLP 1146**

DON'T BELIEVE A WORD February 1977
Phil Lynott
Pippin The Friendly Ranger Music . . . . UK
Thin Lizzy . . . . **Vertigo 001**

DON'T BLAME ME 1933
Dorothy Fields / Jimmy McHugh
Campbell Connelly & Co. Ltd. USA
Film(s): . . . . Dinner at Eight / Big City / The Strip
Val Rosing . . . . **Rex 8023**
Annette Hanshaw . . . . **Edison Bell Winner W 20**
Betty Garrett (1948) . . . . **MGM 148**
Sarah Vaughan (1948) . . . . **Parlophone R 3130**
Sammy Davis . . . . **Brunswick LAT 8248**
Frank Ifield (1964) . . . . **Columbia DB 7184**
Betty Garrett appeared in *Big City.*

DON'T BREAK MY HEART December 1985
"UB40"
ATV Music . . . . UK
UB40 . . . . **DEP International DEP 22**

DON'T BRING LULU 1925
Billy Rose / Lew Brown / Ray Henderson
Francis, Day & Hunter Ltd. . . . . USA
Jan Garber & his Orchestra . . . . **HMV B 2048**
The Andrews Sisters . . . . **Capitol T 973**
Max Bygraves with Ted Heath & his Music . . . . **Decca LK 4317**
Dorothy Provine (1961) . . . . **Warner Brothers WM 4035**

DON'T BRING ME DOWN November 1964
Johnnie Dee
Southern Music Publishing Co. Ltd . . . . UK
The Pretty Things . . . . **Fontana TF 503**

DON'T BRING ME DOWN July 1966
Gerry Goffin / Carole King
Screen Gems - Columbia Music Ltd. . . . . USA
The Animals . . . . **Decca F 12407**

DON'T BRING ME DOWN September 1979
Jeff Lynne
United Artists Music Co. Ltd. . . . . UK
The Electric Light Orchestra . . . . **Jet 153**

DON'T BRING ME POSIES (WHEN IT'S SHOESIES THAT I NEED) 1924
Fred Rose / Billy McCabe / Clarence Jennings
Ascherberg, Hopwood & Crew Ltd. . . . . USA
The Benson Orchestra of Chicago . . . . . **HMV B 1865**
Georgia Brown . . . . **Decca F 9665**

DON'T BRING ME YOUR HEARTACHES November 1965
Robin Conrad / Les Reed
Skidmore Music Ltd . . . . UK
Paul & Barry Ryan . . . . **Decca F 12260**

DON'T CRY DADDY April 1970
Scott Davis
Carlin Music Corporation . . . . USA
Elvis Presley . . . . **RCA 1916**

DON'T CRY FOR ME ARGENTINA February 1977
Tim Rice / Andrew Lloyd Webber
Leeds Music Ltd . . . . UK
Show(s): . . . . Evita
Julie Covington . . . . **MCA 260**
Elaine Paige . . . . **MCA 3527**
Patti Lupone . . . . **MCA MCA2 11007**
The Shadows (1979) . . . . **EMI 2890**
Elaine Paige appeared in the British production of *Evita.*
Patti Lupone appeared in the American production of *Evita.*
Ivor Novello Nomination 1976
Ivor Novello Award 1977.

DON'T CRY JOE
(Let Her Go, Let Her Go, Let Her Go) November 1949
Joe Marsala
B. Feldman & Co. Ltd . . . . USA
Gordon Jenkins & his Orchestra . . . . **Brunswick 8370**
The Kirby Stone Four . . . . **Philips BBE 12263**

DON'T CRY OUT LOUD December 1978
Peter Allen / Carole Bayer Sager
Chappell & Co. Ltd . . . . USA
Elkie Brooks . . . . **A&M AMS 7395**
Peter Allen . . . . **A&M AMLN 64739**

DON'T DILLY DALLY ON THE WAY 1919
Fred W. Leigh / Charles Collins
B. Feldman & Co. Ltd. . . . . UK
Marie Lloyd Jr. . . . . **Edison Bell 5623**
Leslie Douglas & his Band,
  vocal Pearl Carr . . . . **Regal Zonophone MR 3797**
Rita Williams . . . . **Parlophone PMC 1127**

DON'T DO IT BABY May 1975
Wayne Bickerton / Tony Waddington
A.T.V. Music Ltd. . . . . UK
Mac & Katie Kissoon . . . . **State STAT 4**

DON'T DO THAT TO THE POOR PUSS CAT 1928
Leslie Sarony / Frank Eyton
Keith Prowse Music Publishing Co. Ltd. . . . . UK
Leslie Sarony . . . . **HMV B 2714**

DON'T EVER CHANGE 1938
Louis Hirsch / Lou Handman
Campbell Connelly & Co. Ltd. . . . . USA
Film(s): . . . . Rhythm in the Clouds
Roy Fox & his Orchestra, vocal Mary Lee . . **HMV BD 5331**
Jay Wilbur & his Band, vocal Jack Cooper . . **Rex 9261**

DON'T EVER CHANGE August 1962
Gerry Goffin / Carole King

Aldon Music Ltd. .... USA
The Crickets .... Liberty LIB 55441
Gerry Reno .... Decca F 11477
Brian Poole & The Tremeloes .... Ace of Clubs ACL 1146

DON'T EVER LEAVE ME   1935
Jerome Kern / Oscar Hammerstein II
Chappell & Co. Ltd .... USA
Film(s): .... Sweet Adeline / Both Ends of the Candle
The Roy Fox Band .... Decca F 5601
Donald Stewart .... Decca F 5619
Gogi Grant .... RCA RD 27054
Gogi Grant dubbed the singing voice of Ann Blyth who appeared in
the film *Both Ends of the Candle*.

DON'T FALL IN LOVE   April 1947
Eddie Lisbona / Joe Lubin
Bradbury Wood Ltd .... USA
Geraldo & his Orchestra .... Parlophone F 2213
Joe Loss & his Orchestra .... HMV BD 5972

DON'T FEAR THE REAPER   July 1978
Donald Rosser
Carlin Music Corporation .... USA
Blue Oyster Cult .... CBS 6333

DON'T FENCE ME IN   1945
Cole Porter
Chappell & Co. Ltd. .... USA
Film(s): .... Hollywood Canteen / Don't Fence Me In
Bing Crosby & The Andrews Sisters ... Brunswick LAT 8369
Mitch Miller & The Gang .... Philips BBL 7258
Bryan Johnson .... Decca LK 4362
Roy Rogers .... Readers Digest RDS 6509
Roy Rogers and The Andrew Sisters appeared in *Hollywood Canteen*.

DON'T FORBID ME   February 1957
Charles Singleton
Campbell Connelly & Co. Ltd. .... USA
Pat Boone .... London HAD 2098
Glen Mason .... Parlophone R 4271

DON'T FORGET TO REMEMBER   October 1969
Barry Gibb / Maurice Gibb
Abigail Music .... UK
The Bee Gees .... Polydor 56343

DON'T GET AROUND MUCH ANYMORE   1943
Duke Ellington / Bob Russell
Robbins Music Corporation Ltd .... USA
Duke Ellington & his Orchestra .... RCA RCX 1055
The Ink Spots .... Brunswick LA 8710
Eydie Gormé .... HMV CLP 1170
The King Sisters .... Capitol T 1333
Based on "Never No Lament" by Duke Ellington.

DON'T GET ME WRONG   November 1986
Chrissie Hynde
Hynde House Music .... UK
The Pretenders .... Real YZ 85

DON'T GIVE UP   November 1986
Peter Gabriel
Cliofine Music Ltd .... UK
Peter Gabriel & Kate Bush .... Virgin PGS 2
Ivor Novello Award

DON'T GIVE UP ON US   February 1977
Tony Macaulay
Macaulay Music .... UK
David Soul .... Private Stock PVT 84
Ivor Novello Nomination.

DON'T GO   August 1982
Vincent Clarke
Sonet Music .... UK
Yazoo .... Mute YAZ 001

DON'T GO BREAKING MY HEART   August 1976
Ann Orson / Cart Blanche
Big Pig Music .... UK
Elton John & Kiki Dee .... Rocket ROKN 512
Ivor Novello Award.

DON'T GO DOWN THE MINE DAD   1910
William Geddes / Robert McDonnelly
Lawrence Wright Music Co. Ltd. .... UK
Stanley Kirby .... Zonophone Twin 342
Kenneth Walters .... Regal Zonophone G 6460

DON'T GO IN THE LIONS' CAGE TONIGHT   1906
John Gilroy / E. Ray Goetz
Francis, Day & Hunter Ltd .... USA
The Greenwood Singers .... London HAR 8308
Julie Andrews .... CBS BPG 62405

DON'T HAVE ANY MORE MISSUS MOORE   1926
Harry Castling / James Walsh
B. Feldman & Co. Ltd. .... UK
Lily Morris .... Columbia 9597
David Kossoff .... Oriole MG 20043

DON'T IT MAKE MY BROWN EYES BLUE   January 1978
Richard Leigh
United Artists Music Co. Ltd .... USA
Film(s): ....Convoy
Crystal Gayle .... United Artists UP 36307

DON'T KNOCK THE ROCK   March 1957
Robert Kent / Fred Karger
Chappell & Co. Ltd .... USA
Film(s): ....Don't Knock The Rock
Bill Haley & his Comets .... Brunswick 05640
Bill Haley & his Comets appeared in *Don't Knock The Rock*.

DON'T KNOW MUCH   December 1989
Barry Mann / Cynthia Weil / Tom Snow
ATV Music .... USA
Linda Ronstadt & Aaron Neville .... Elektra EKR 10

DON'T LAUGH AT ME   October 1952
Norman Wisdom / June Tremayne
David Toff Music Publishing Co. Ltd .... UK
Film(s): .... Trouble in Store
Norman Wisdom .... Columbia SEG 7612
Judy Wayne .... Capitol CL 14127
Norman Wisdom appeared in *Trouble in Store*.

DON'T LEAVE ME NOW   March 1954
Eddie Lisbona
Victoria Music .... USA
Don Cherry .... Brunswick 04926
Vera Lynn .... Decca F 10230
Dickie Valentine .... Decca F 10134

DON'T LEAVE ME THIS WAY   February 1977
Kenny Gamble / Leon Huff
Carlin Music Corporation .... USA
Harold Melvin & The Blue Notes .... CBS 4909
Thelma Houston .... Motown TMG 1060
The Communards (1986) .... London LON 103

DON'T LET IT DIE   July 1971
Eileen Smith
Rak Music Ltd .... UK
Hurricane Smith .... Columbia DB 8765
Ivor Novello Award.

DON'T LET ME BE MISUNDERSTOOD   March 1965
Bennie Benjamin / Sol Marcus / Gloria Caldwell
West One Music Ltd .... USA
The Animals .... Columbia DB 7445

DON'T LET THE STARS GET IN YOUR EYES   January 1953
Slim Willett
Edwin H. Morris & Co. Ltd .... USA
Red Foley .... Brunswick LA 8729
Gisele MacKenzie .... Capitol CL 13855
Perry Como .... RCA RD 27100

DON'T LET THE SUN CATCH YOU CRYING   May 1964
Gerry Marsden / Fred Marsden / Les Chadwick / Les Maguire
Pacermusic Ltd .... UK
Gerry & The Pacemakers .... Columbia DB 7268
Louise Cordet .... Decca F 11824

DON'T LET THE SUN GO DOWN ON ME   June 1974
Elton John / Bernie Taupin

Big Pig Music . . . . UK
Elton John . . . . **DMJ DJS 302**

DON'T LET YOUR LOVE GO WRONG   **1934**
George Whiting / F.C. Johnson / Nat Schwartz
Francis, Day & Hunter Ltd . . . . USA
The Boswell Sisters . . . . **Brunswick 01832**
Kay Starr . . . . **Capitol CL 13071**

DON'T LOOK DOWN   **December 1985**
Peter Cox
ATV Music . . . . UK
Go West . . . . **Chrysalis GOW 3**

DON'T MAKE ME WAIT   **September 1988**
Tim Simemon / Pascal Gabriel
Rhythm King Music . . . . UK
Bomb the Bass . . . . **Rhythm King DOOD 2**

DON'T MAKE MY BABY BLUE   **September 1965**
Cynthia Weill / Barry Mann
Screen Gems - Columbia Music Ltd . . . . USA
The Shadows . . . . **Columbia DB 7650**

DON'T MAKE WAVES   **May 1980**
Ben Findon / Mike Myers / Robert Puzey
Black Sheep Music . . . . UK
The Nolans . . . . **Epic EPC 8349**

DON'T MIND THE RAIN   **1924**
Ned Miller / Chester Cohn
Francis, Day & Hunter Ltd. USA
Paul Whiteman & his Orchestra . . . . **HMV B 1847**

DON'T PLAY THAT SONG (You Lied)   **September 1970**
Ahmet Ertgun / Betty Nelson
Progressive Music Ltd. . . . . USA
Aretha Franklin . . . . **Atlantic 2091027**
Benn E. King . . . . **London HLK 9544**

DON'T PLAY YOUR ROCK AND ROLL TO ME   **Nov. 1975**
Mike Chapman / Nicky Chinn
Chinnichap Music . . . . UK
Smokey . . . . **Rak 217**

DON'T PUSH IT - DON'T FORCE IT   **April 1980**
Leon Hayward
Sunbury Music Ltd . . . . USA
Leon Haywood . . . . **20th Century TC 2443**

**DON'T PUT YOUR DAUGHTER ON THE STAGE MRS
WORTHINGTON (See Mrs. Worthington)**

DON'T RAIN ON MY PARADE   **January 1965**
Bob Merrill / Jule Styne
Chappell & Co. Ltd . . . . USA
Show(s): . . . . Funny Girl
Film(s): . . . . Funny Girl
Barbra Streisand . . . . **Capitol W 2059**
Lisa Shane . . . . **Pye NEP 24257**
Barbra Streisand . . . . **CBS 70044**
Barbra Streisand appeared in both the American & British production
and the film of *Funny Girl*
Lisa Shane appeared in the British production of *Funny Girl*

DON'T RING-A DA BELL   **April 1956**
Johnny Reine / Sonny Miller
Michael Reine Music Co. Ltd. . . . . UK
Alma Cogan . . . . **HMV 7EG 8169**
Shani Wallis . . . . **Nixa N 15049**

DON'T SAY GOODBYE   **1932**
Robert Stolz
Chappell & Co. Ltd. . . . . Germany
Show(s): . . . . Wild Violets
Olive Groves . . . . **Decca F 3212**
Barbara Leigh . . . . **HMV 7EG 8467**

DON'T SIT UNDER THE APPLE TREE   **1942**
Sammy Stept / Charles Tobias / Lew Brown
Robbins Music Corporation Ltd . . . . USA
Film(s):Private Buckaroo / With a Song in My Heart / Kiss Them for Me
The Andrews Sisters . . . . **Brunswick 03337**
Glenn Miller & his Orchestra . . . . **RCA RCX 1024**
The Andrews Sisters . . . . **Capitol LCT 6132**

Marion Hutton, Tex Beneke & Modernaires . . **Vogue LVA 9103**
The Andrews Sisters appeared in *Private Buckaroo*.

DON'T SLEEP IN THE SUBWAY   **July 1967**
Tony Hatch / Jackie Trent
Welbeck Music Co. Ltd. . . . . UK
Petula Clark . . . . **Pye 7N 17325**
Ivor Novello Nomination.

DON'T STAND SO CLOSE TO ME   **October 1980**
"Sting"
Virgin Music (Publishers) Ltd . . . . UK
Police . . . . **A&M AMS 7564**
Ivor Novello Nomination.
Also re-released 1988, remix.

**DON'T STAY AWAY TOO LONG (Herzen Haben Keine
Fenster)**   **June 1974**
Henry Mayer / Bryan Blackburn
Pedro Music . . . . Germany
Peters & Lee . . . . **Philips 6006388**

DON'T STOP - TWIST   **February 1962**
Frankie Vaughan
Davon Music Ltd . . . . UK
Frankie Vaughan . . . . **Philips PB 1219**

DON'T STOP IT NOW   **April 1976**
Errol Brown
Rak Music Ltd . . . . UK
Hot Chocolate . . . . **Rak 230**

DON'T STOP ME NOW   **April 1979**
Freddie Mercury
EMI Music Ltd. . . . . UK
Queen . . . . **EMI 2910**

DON'T STOP THE CARNIVAL   **March 1968**
Sonny Rollins
Carlin Music Corporation . . . . USA
Alan Price . . . . **Decca F 12731**
Sonny Rollins (Tenor Saxophone) . . . . **RCA RD 7524**

DON'T STOP THE MUSIC   **January 1981**
Lonnie Simmons / Alisa Peoples / Jonah Ellis
Rachel Music . . . . USA
Yarborough & Peoples . . . . **Mercury MER 53**

DON'T STOP THE PARTYLINE   **April 1990**
Peter Neefs / Jean-Paul De Coster
MCA Music . . . . Belgium
Bizz Nizz . . . . **Cool Tempo COOL 203**

DON'T STOP TILL YOU GET ENOUGH   **October 1979**
Michael Jackson
Carlin Music Corporation . . . . USA
Michael Jackson . . . . **Epic EPC 7763**

DON'T SWEETHEART ME   **1944**
Charles Tobias / Clifford Friend
Chappell & Co. Ltd. . . . . USA
Film(s): . . . . Hi Beautiful
Donald Peers . . . . **Decca DFE 6387**
Geraldo & his Orch. vocal Sally Douglas . . . **Parlophone F 2040**

DON'T TAKE AWAY THE MUSIC   **November 1976**
Kenny St. Lewis / Freddie Perren / Chris Yarian
A.T.V. Music Ltd. . . . . USA
Tavares . . . . **Capitol CL 15886**

DON'T TAKE YOUR LOVE FROM ME   **1941**
Harry Nemo
B. Feldman & Co. Ltd . . . . USA
Artie Shaw & his Orchestra, vocal Lena Horne . . . **HMV B 9322**
The McGuire Sisters . . . . **Vogue LVA 9082**
Eydie Gormé . . . . **HMV POP 616**
Kay Starr . . . . **Capitol T 1303**

DON'T TALK TO HIM   **December 1963**
Cliff Richard / Bruce Welch
Shadows Music Ltd . . . . UK
Cliff Richard . . . . **Columbia DB 7150**

DON'T TALK TO ME ABOUT LOVE   **April 1983**
"Altered Images"

Warner Brothers Music . . . . UK
Altered Images . . . . Epic EPC A 3083

DON'T TELL ME   May 1984
Neil Arthur / Stephen Luscombe
Cherry Red Music . . . . UK
Blancmange . . . . **London BLANC 7**

DON'T THAT BEAT ALL   September 1962
Les Vandyke
Downbeat Publishing Co. Ltd . . . . UK
Adam Faith . . . . **Parlophone R 4930**
Johnny Keating & his Orchestra . . . . . . **Ace of Clubs ACL 1160**

DON'T THROW YOUR LOVE AWAY   May 1964
Billy Jackson / Jimmy Wisner
Welbeck Music Co. Ltd . . . . USA
The Searchers . . . . **Pye 7N 15630**
The Orlons . . . . **Cameo-Parkway C 287**

DON'T TREAT ME LIKE A CHILD   May 1961
Mike Hawker / John Schroeder
Lorna Music Co. Ltd . . . . UK
Helen Shapiro . . . . **Columbia DB 4589**

DON'T TURN AROUND   May 1964
Peter Lee Sterling / Barry Mason
Robbins Music Corporation Ltd . . . . UK
The Merseybeats . . . . **Fontana TF 459**

DON'T TURN AROUND   April 1988
Diane Warren / Albert Hammond
EMI Music . . . . UK
Aswad . . . . **Mango IS 341**

DON'T WANNA LOSE YOU   August 1989
Gloria Estefan
EMI Music . . . . USA
Gloria Estefan . . . . **Epic 6550540**

DON'T WASTE MY TIME   March 1986
Paul Hardcastle
Oval Music . . . . UK
Paul Hardcastle . . . . **Chrysalis PAUL 1**

DON'T WORRY   June 1955
Ed Franks
Vocable Music Co. Ltd. . . . . UK
Johnny Brandon . . . . **Nixa NEP 24003**

DON'T WORRY   November 1990
Kim Appleby / Craig Logan / George Deangelis
Perfect Music . . . . UK
Kim Appleby . . . . **Parlophone R 9272**
Ivor Novello Nomination.

DON'T WORRY 'BOUT ME   1940
Ted Koehler / Rube Bloom
Cinephonic Music Co. Ltd. . . . . USA
Kate Smith . . . . **HMV BD 718**
Pearl Bailey . . . . **Columbia SX 1269**
Gisele MacKenzie . . . . **RCA RD 27033**
Chris Connor . . . . **London LTZK 15195**

DON'T WORRY - BE HAPPY   October 1988
Bobby McFerrin
Noblem Music . . . . USA
Bobby McFerrin . . . . **Manhattan MT 56**

DON'T YOU FORGET ABOUT ME   May 1985
Keith Forsey / Steve Schiff
MCA Music . . . . UK
Simple Minds . . . . **Virgin VS 749**

DON'T YOU JUST KNOW IT   December 1985
Huey Smith / John Vincent
EMI Music . . . . UK
Amazulu . . . . **Island S 233**

DON'T YOU KNOW   June 1970
Chris Arnold / David Martin / Geoff Morrow
Sunbury Music Ltd. . . . . UK
Butterscotch . . . . **RCA 1937**

DON'T YOU KNOW IT   August 1961
Les Vandyke
Downbeat Publishing Co. Ltd. UK
Adam Faith . . . . **Parlophone R 4807**

DON'T YOU ROCK ME DADDY-O   January 1957
Wally Whyton / Bill Varley
Essex Music Ltd. . . . . UK
Bob Cort Skiffle Group . . . . **Decca DFE 6409**
Lonnie Donegan & his Skiffle Group . . . . **Nixa NPT 19022**
The Vipers Skiffle Group . . . . **Parlophone GEP 8615**

DON'T YOU THINK IT'S TIME   February 1963
Geoffrey Goddard / Joe Meek
Meridian Music Publishing Co. Ltd . . . . UK
Mike Berry . . . . **HMV POP 1105**

DON'T YOU WANT ME   December 1981
Philip Oakey / Jo Callis / Adrain Wright
Virgin Music . . . . UK
Human League . . . . **Virgin VS 466**
Ivor Novello Nomination 1981 & 1982

DONKEY SERENADE, THE   1938
Rudolf Frimi / Herbert Stothart / Robert Wright / Chet Forrest
Chappell & Co. Ltd. . . . . USA
Film(s): . . . . The Firefly
Allan Jones . . . . **HMV 7EG 8231**
Monte Ray . . . . **Parlophone F 1685**
Mario Lanza . . . . **RCA RB 16002**
Paul Britten & his Orchestra . . . . **MGM C 779**
Allan Jones appeared in *The Firefly*.
Theme song of Monte Rey.

DONKEY SONG, THE   November 1953
Nino Oliviero / Roberto Murolo / Ben Raleigh & Guy Wood
Aberbach (London) Ltd. . . . . Italy
Jane Morgan . . . . **Parlophone R 3762**
Robert Murolo . . . . **Durium DLU 96011**
David Carey . . . . **Columbia DB 3385**

DONNA   May 1959
Ritchie Valens
Aberbach (London) Ltd. . . . . USA
Marty Wilde . . . . **Philips BBE 12288**
Ritchie Valens . . . . **London HL 8803**
Cliff Richard . . . . **Columbia 33SX 1147**

DOO WACKA DOO   1925
Clarence Gaskill / Will Donaldson / George Horther
Francis, Day & Hunter Ltd. . . . . USA
Paul Whiteman & his Orchestra . . . . **HMV B 1937**
Pete Daily's Dixieland Band . . . . **Capitol CL 13380**

DOOR WILL OPEN, A   1946
Don George / John Benson Brooks
Southern Music Publishing Co. Ltd. . . . . USA
**Paul Fenoulhet & the Skyrockets Dance Orchestra, vocal Cyril
Shane** . . . . **HMV BD 5921**
Geraldo & his Orchestra, vocal Dick James **Parlophone F 2143**

DORMI, DORMI, DORMI   September 1958
Harry Warren / Sammy Cahn
Chappell & Co. Ltd . . . . USA
Film(s): . . . . Rock-A-Bye Baby
Jerry Lewis . . . . **Brunswick OE 9480**
Eydie Gormé . . . . **HMV 7EG 8409**
Jerry Lewis appeared in *Rock-A-Bye Baby*.

DOUBLE BARREL   May 1971
Winston Riley
B&C Music . . . . Jamaica
Dave & Ansil Collins . . . . **Technique TBL 162**

DOUBLE DUTCH   August 1983
Malcolm McLaren / Trevor Horn
CBS Songs . . . . UK
Malcolm McLaren . . . . **Charisma MALC 3**

DOWN AMONG THE SHELTERING PALMS   1915
James Brockman / Abe Olman
Sun Music Publishing Co. Ltd. USA
Film(s); . . . . That Midnight Kiss / Some Like it Hot
The Boswell Sisters . . . . **Brunswick 1347**
Al Jolson & The Mills Brothers . . . . **Brunswick LA 8705**

Bing Crosby .... RCA RD 27032

DOWN ARGENTINE WAY   1941
Harry Warren / Mack Gordon
Sun Music Publishing Co. Ltd .... USA
Film(s): ....Down Argentine Way
Bob Crosby & his Orchestra, vocal Bonnie King . Decca F 7701
Oscar Rabin & his Orchestra. Ken Beaumont ...... Rex 9913
Nominated for an Academy Award 1940.

DOWN AT THE OLD BULL AND BUSH (Under The An-
heuser Bush)   1903
Harry Von Tilzer / Andrew Sterling / Percy Krone / Russell Hunting
B. Feldman & Co. Ltd. .... USA
Florrie Forde .... **HMV GC 3563**
Anne Shelton .... **Decca F 8842**
Stanley Holloway .... **Pye NPL 18056**

DOWN BY THE O-HI-O   1940
Abe Olman / Jack Yellen
Francis Day & Hunter Ltd .... USA
Show(s): ....Zeigfled Follies of 1920
Ben Bernie & his Orch. vocal Bailey Sisters   Columbia FB 2548
The Andrews Sisters .... **Brunswick 03011**
Frankie Vaughan .... **Philips BBL 7482**

DOWN BY THE OLD MILL STREAM   1910
Tell Taylor
Herman Darewski Publishing Co. Ltd .... USA
Bing Crosby .... **Brunswick 02807**
Fred Waring & his Pennsylvanians **Brunswick LA 8704**
Mitch Miller & The Gang .... **Philips BBL 7528**
Bruce Hayes & Mary Mayo .... **Top Rank TR 5016**

DOWN BY THE STATION   June 1949
Lee Ricks / Slim Gaillard
Lawrence Wright Music Co. Ltd .... USA
Tommy Dorsey & his Orchestra, vocal Denny Dennis, Lucy
Anne Polk & The Sentimentalists .... **HMV BD 1243**
Guy Lombardo & his Royal Canadians ... **Brunswick 04078**
The Squadronaires Dance Orchestra .... **Decca F 9128**

DOWN DEEP INSIDE   September 1977
Donna Summer / John Barry
Screen Gems Music Ltd .... USA
Film(s): ....The Deep
Donna Summer .... **Casablanca CAN 111**

DOWN DOWN   January 1975
Francis Rossi / Robert Young
Valley Music .... UK
Status Quo .... **Vertigo 6059114**

DOWN FORGET-ME-NOT LANE   1941
Horatio Nicholls / Charlie Chester / Reg Morgan
Lawrence Wright Music Publishing Co. Ltd .... UK
The R.A.F. Dance Orchestra, vocal Jimmy Miller . Decca F 7926
Joe Petersen .... **Rex 10052**
Flanagan & Allen .... **Decca F 8009**

DOWN HOME RAG   1911
Wilbur Sweatman
Peter Maurice Music .... USA
Jim Europe's Society Orchestra .... **RCA PM 42402**
Ralph Sutton (piano solo) .... **Columbia 33CX 10061**
Humphrey Lyttelton & his Band .... **Parlophone PMD 1006**

DOWN IN JUNGLE TOWN   1908
Edward Madden / Theodore Morse
Francis, Day & Hunter Ltd. .... USA
De Groot & his Picadilly Orchestra .... **HMV 0649**
The Kid Ory Band .... **Columbia 33SX 10116**
The Georg Brunies All Stars .... **Tempo EXA 96**

DOWN IN THE GLEN   March 1949
Harry Gordon / Tommie Connor
Lawrence Wright Music Co. Ltd .... UK
Robert Wilson .... **HMV DLP 1086**
Joseph Locke .... **Columbia DB 2661**

DOWN IN THE VALLEY   1944
Frank Luther
Leeds Music Ltd. .... USA
Film(s): .... Moonlight and Cactus

The Andrews Sisters .... Brunswick 03502
Lou Preager & his Orchestra,
vocal Rita Williams .... Columbia FB 3260
The Andrews Sisters appeared in *Moonlight and Cactus*.

DOWN ON THE BEACH TONIGHT   November 1974
Tony Macaulay / Roger Greenaway
Cookaway Music .... UK
The Drifters .... **Bell 1381**

DOWN ON THE FARM   1924
Billy Dale / Charles Parrott / Jimmie Adams / Harry Harrison
Keith Prowse Music Publishing Co. Ltd .... USA
The Manhattan Merrymakers .... **HMV B 1761**
Stan Bradbury .... **Panachord 25903**

DOWN ON THE STREET   August 1984
Bill Sharpe / Roger O'Dell
Skratch Music .... UK
Shakatak .... **Polydor POSP 688**

DOWN SWEETHEART AVENUE   February 1948
Frank Chacksfield / Cedric Rushworth
Francis, Day & Hunter Ltd. .... UK
The Jack Simpson Sextet .... **Parlophone F 2262**

DOWN THE DUSTPIPE   July 1970
Carl Groszmann
Valley Music .... UK
Status Quo .... **Pye 7N 17907**

DOWN THE OLD OX ROAD   1933
Sam Coslow / Arthur Johnston
Victoria Music Co. Ltd. .... USA
Film(s): .... College Humour
Bing Crosby .... **Brunswick LAT 8251**
Bing Crosby .... **Columbia 33S 1036**
Bing Crosby appeared in *College Humour*.

DOWN THE OLD SPANISH TRAIL   August 1947
Jimmy Kennedy / Kenneth Leslie Smith
Peter Maurice Music .... UK
Monte Rey .... **Columbia FB 3321**
Issy Bonn .... **Decca F 8787**
Roy Rogers .... **Regal Zonophone MR 3810**

DOWN THE OREGON TRAIL   1935
Billy Hill / Peter De Rose
B. Feldman & Co. Ltd .... USA
Al & Bob Harvey .... **Decca F 5604**
Tex Ritter .... **Panachord 25802**

DOWN THE ROAD (Away Went Polly)   1893
Fred Gilbert
Francis, Day & Hunter Ltd .... UK
Gus Elen .... **Berliner 2362**
Leon Cortez & his Coster Pals .... **Regal MR 2257**
Warren Mitchell .... **Allegro ALL 850**
Mike Reid .... **Pye NSPL 18417**

DOWN THE TRAIL OF ACHING HEARTS   March 1952
Jimmy Kennedy / Nat Simon
Yale Music Corporation Ltd .... USA
Patti Page .... **Mercury MEP 9502**
Pearl Carr .... **Decca F 9825**

DOWN TO EARTH   February 1987
"Curiosity Killed The Cat"
Warner Brothers Music .... UK
Curiosity Killed The Cat .... **Mercury CAT 2**

DOWN TOWN   December 1964
Tony Hatch
Welbeck Music Co. Ltd .... UK
Petula Clark .... **Pye 7N 15722**
Sandie Shaw .... **Pye NPL 18110**
Petula Clark (1989) .... **PRT PYS 19**
Ivor Novello Award.

DOWN UNDER   February 1983
Colin Hay / Ronald Stryker
April Music Ltd .... UK
Men At Work .... **Epic EPC A 1980**

DOWN WHERE THE TRADE WINDS BLOW 1938
Harry Owens
Campbell Connelly & Co. Ltd. . . . . USA
Film(s): . . . . Hawaii Calls
Bobby Breen . . . . **HMV BD 573**
Harry Owens & his Royal Hawaiian Hotel Orchestra   Decca F 6724
Marty Robbins . . . . **Fontana TFE 17167**
Bobby Breen appeared in *Hawaii Calls*.

DOWN YONDER 1921
L. Wolfe Gilbert
B. Feldman & Co. Ltd . . . . USA
Nat D. Ayer & his Orchestra (1921) . . . . **Columbia 3080**
Del Wood (piano) (1952) . . . . **London L 1127**
Johnny & The Hurricanes (1960) . . . . **London HLX 9134**

DOWNHEARTED May 1953
Bob Hilliard / Dave Mann
New World Publishers Ltd . . . . USA
The Johnston Brothers . . . . **Decca F 10071**
Eddie Fisher . . . . **Camden CDN 123**
Guy Lombardo & his Royal Canadians . . . . . **Brunswick 05094**

DOWNTOWN TRAIN March 1990
Tom Waits
Warner Chappell Music . . . . UK
Rod Stewart . . . . **Warner Brothers W 2647**

DRAGNET December 1953
Walter Schuman
Aberbach (London) Ltd . . . . USA
Ray Anthony & his Orchestra . . . . **Capitol CL 13983**
Ted Heath & his Music . . . . **Decca LK 4344**
Theme of the Dragnet TV programme.

DRAMA October 1989
Vincent Clarke / Andrew Bell
Sonet Music . . . . UK
Erasure . . . . **Mute MUTE 89**

DREADLOCK HOLIDAY September 1978
Eric Stewart / Graham Gouldman
St. Annes Music Ltd . . . . UK
10 CC . . . . **Mercury 6008035**
Ivor Novello Nomination.

DREAM 1945
Johnny Mercer
Sterling Music Publishing Co. Ltd. USA
Film(s): . . . . Her Highness and the Bellboy / Daddy Long Legs
Geraldo & his Orchestra . . . . **Parlophone F 2082**
The Pied Pipers . . . . **Capitol T 9103**
Frank Sinatra . . . . **Capitol W 1417**
Etta James . . . . **Pye 7N 25113**
Theme song of The Pied Pipers.

DREAM A LITTLE DREAM OF ME 1931
Gus Kahn / Wilbur Schwandt / Fabian Andre
Francis, Day & Hunter Ltd . . . . USA
Nat 'King' Cole . . . . **Capitol LCT 6003**
June Hutton . . . . **Capitol LC 6808**
Bing Crosby . . . . **RCA RD 27032**
Frankie Laine . . . . **Philips BBL 7294**
Mama Cass (1968) . . . . **RCA 1726**

DREAM BABY May 1962
Cindy Walker
Acuff-Rose Publishing Co. Ltd. . . . . USA
Roy Orbison . . . . **London HL 9511**
Bruce Channel . . . . **Mercury MMC 14104**
Del Shannon . . . . **London REX 1387**

DREAM BOAT May 1955
Jack Hoffman
Leeds Music Ltd. . . . . USA
Alma Cogan . . . . **HMV 7EG 8122**
The Paulette Sisters . . . . **Capitol CL 14294**

DREAM IS A WISH YOUR HEART MAKES, A   October 1950
Al Hoffman / Jerry Livingston / Mack David
Walt Disney Music Ltd . . . . USA
Film(s): . . . . Cinderella
Ileen Woods . . . . **HMV B 9970**
Steve Conway . . . . **Columbia SEG 7649**

Barbara Leigh . . . . **HMV 7EG 116**

DREAM LOVER 1930
Victor Schertzinger / Clifford Grey
Campbell Connelly & Co. Ltd . . . . USA
Film(s): . . . . The Love Parade
Olive Groves . . . . **Decca F 1675**

DREAM LOVER 1930
Victor Schertzinger / Clifford Grey
Campbell Connelly & Co. Ltd . . . . USA
Film(s): . . . . The Love Parade
Jeanette MacDonald . . . . **HMV B 3289**
Robert Farnon & Orcheatra,
vocal Johnston Bros. . . . . **Decca LK 4055**
Jeanette MacDonald appeared in *The Love Parade*.

DREAM LOVER July 1959
Bobby Darin
Aldon Music Ltd. . . . . USA
Bobby Darin . . . . **London REE 1225**
Duffy Power . . . . **Fontana H 194**

DREAM MOTHER 1930
Al Lewis / Al Sherman / Joe Burke
Campbell Connelly & Co. Ltd . . . . USA
The New Mayfair Dance Orchestra . . . . **HMV B 5675**
The Andy Sanella Trio . . . . **Columbia 5558**

DREAM OF OLWEN, THE February 1948
Charles Williams
Lawrence Wright Music Co. Ltd. . . . . UK
Film(s): . . . . While I Live
Charles Williams & his Orchestra . . . . **Columbia SEG 7600**
Victor Young & his Singing Strings . . . . **Brunswick 04687**
Mantovani Orch. Rawicz & Landauer (pianos) . **Decca LK 4145**

DREAM TIME 1936
J. Fred Coots / Benny Davis
Campbell Connelly & Co. Ltd . . . . USA
Guy Lombardo & his Royal Canadians . . . . . . **HMV BD 5081**
Lew Stone & his Orchestra . . . . **Decca F 5971**

DREAM'S A DREAM, A May 1990
Simon Law / Beresford Romeo
Virgin Music . . . . UK
Soul II Soul . . . . **Ten TEN 300**

DREAM, DREAM, DREAM 1947
John Redman / Lou Ricca
Pickwick Music Ltd . . . . USA
The Mills Brothers . . . . **Brunswick 03804**

DREAMER March 1975
Roger Hodgson / Richard Davies
Rondor Music (London) Ltd . . . . UK
Supertramp . . . . **A&M AMS 7132**

DREAMER WITH A PENNY July 1949
Lester Lee / Allan Roberts
Magna Music Co. Ltd . . . . USA
Show(s): . . . . All For Love
Charles La Vere . . . . **Brunswick 04278**
Margaret Whiting . . . . **Capitol CL 13109**

DREAMER'S HOLIDAY, A October 1949
Kim Gannon / Mabel Wayne
Francis, Day & Hunter Ltd . . . . USA
Perry Como & The Fontane Sisters . . . . **Camden CDN 142**
Joy Nichols . . . . **Decca F 9234**

DREAMER, THE 1944
Arthur Schwartz / Frank Loesser
Sterling Music Publishing Co. Ltd. USA
Film(s): . . . . Thank Your Lucky Stars
Kay Armen & his Balladiers . . . . **Brunswick 03496**

DREAMIN' November 1960
Barry De Vorzon / Ted Ellis
Edwin H. Morris & Co. Ltd . . . . USA
Johnny Burnette . . . . **London HAG 2306**

DREAMIN' September 1980
Alan Tarney / Leo Sayer
Chrysalis Music Ltd . . . . UK

Cliff Richard .... **EMI 5095**

DREAMING 1932
Reginald Connelly / Bud Flanagan
Campbell Connelly & Co. Ltd. .... UK
Flanagan & Allen .... **Columbia FB 1289**
Layton & Johnstone .... **Columbia DB 1026**
Norrie Paramor & his Orchestra .... **Columbia 33SX 1258**
Arthur Tracey (The Street Singer) .... **Decca LK 4897**

DREAMING 1940
Miguel Prado / Anthony Stephan
Soutern Music Publishing Co. Ltd .... USA
Al Bowlly .... **HMV BD 834**
Beryl Davis .... **Decca F 7472**
The Michael Sammes Singers .... **Fontana TFL 5182**
This song has the same melody as *Time Was*.

DREAMING October 1979
Deborah Harry / Chris Stein
EMI Music Ltd. .... UK
Blondie .... **Chrysalis CHS 2350**

DREAMS CAN TELL A LIE February 1956
Howard Barnes / Harold Cornelius / Dominic John
John Fields Music .... UK
Nat 'King' Cole .... **Capitol CL 14513**
Dickie Valentine & The Keynotes ...... **Decca F 10667**

DRESS YOU UP December 1985
Margaret Staniale / Andre Larusso
Warner Brothers Music .... USA
Madonna .... **Sire W 8848**

DRIFTING AND DREAMING 1926
Haven Gillespie / Egbert Van Alstyne / Loyal Curtis / Erwin Schmidt
Campbell Connelly & Co. Ltd. .... USA
George Olsen & his Music .... **HMV B 5069**
Bing Crosby .... **Brunswick LAT 8334**
Nelson Riddle & his Orchestra .... **Capitol T 915**
Vera Lynn .... **Decca LK 4305**

DRIFTWOOD 1924
Benny Davis / Abe Lyman / Dohl Davis
Francis, Day & Hunter Ltd. .... USA
Leo Reisman & his Orchestra .... **Columbia 3537**
The Ink Spots .... **Brunswick 04188**

**DRINK, DRINK BROTHERS DRINK (Trink, Trink Bruder-
lein Trink)** 1931
Wilhelm Linderman / Harry S. Pepper
Chappell & Co. Ltd. .... Germany
The Columbia Vocal Gems Company ..... **Columbia DX 708**
BBC Dance Orch. conducted by Jack Payne **Columbia CB 251**
Stuart Robertson .... **HMV B 3842**

DRINKING SONG, THE 1926
Sigmund Romberg / Dorothy Donnelly
Chappell & Co. Ltd. .... USA
Raymond Marlowe, Paul Clemon & Olaf Olson **Columbia 9083**
Lauritz Melchoir .... **Brunswick LA 8626**
Mario Lanza .... **RCA RB 16113**
Raymond Marlowe, Paul Clemon & Olaf Olson appeared in the British
production of *The Student Prince*.
Mario Lanza dubbed the singing voice of Edmund Purdom who
appeared in the 1954 film of *The Student Prince*.

DRIVE November 1984
Richard Ocasek
Lido Music .... USA
The Cars .... **Elektra E 9706**

DRIVE-IN SATURDAY May 1973
David Bowie
Mainman Music .... UK
David Bowie .... **RCA 2352**

DRIVING IN MY CAR August 1982
Michael Barson
Warner Brothers Music .... UK
Madness .... **Stiff BUY 153**

DROP THE BOY April 1988
Matt & Luke Goss
Virgin Music .... UK

Bros .... **CBS ATOM 3**

DROWNING IN BERLIN February 1982
Russell Madge / David Blundell / Christopher Downton
Leosong .... UK
The Mobiles .... **Rialto RIA 3**

DRY BONES October 1949
Traditional
Leeds Music Ltd .... USA
Fred Waring & his Pennsylvanians .... **Brunswick 04257**
'Fats' Waller & his Rhythm .... **HMV B 9885**
Fred Waring & his Pennsylvanians .... **Capitol LCT 6143**

DUB BE GOOD TO ME March 1990
Norman Cook / James Harris / Terry Lewis
EMI Music .... UK
Beats International .... **Go Beat GOD 39**

DUKE OF EARL August 1979
Eugene Dixon / Berniece Williams / Earl Edwards
Carlin Music Corporation .... USA
The Darts .... **Magnet MAG 147**
Gene Chandler (1962) .... **Lightning OG 9030**

DUMMY SONG, THE March 1953
Billy Rose / Lew Brown / Ray Henderson
Keith Prowse Music .... USA
Anne Shelton .... **Decca F 10013**
Max Bygraves & Archie Andrews (Peter Brough) **HMV B 10444**
The Hoosier Hot Shots .... **Brunswick 04963**
First published in 1925

DURHAM TOWN (THE LEAVING) January 1970
Roger Whittaker
Tembo Music .... UK
Roger Whittaker .... **Columbia DB 8613**

DYNAMITE November 1973
Mike Chapman / Nicky Chinn
Rak Music Ltd. .... UK
Mud .... **Rak 159**

EACH TIME YOU BREAK MY HEART December 1986
Madonna Ciccone / Stephen Bray
Warner Brothers Music .... USA
Nick Kamen .... **WEA YZ 90**

EADIE WAS A LADY 1932
Richard A. Whiting / Nacio Herb Brown / Buddy De Sylva
Chappell & Co. Ltd. .... USA
Show(s): .... Take a Chance
Film(s): .... Take a Chance
Ethel Merman .... **Brunswick LA 8638**
The Cavendish Three .... **Columbia FB 2400**
Ethel Merman appeared in the show *Take a Chance*.

EARFUL OF MUSIC, AN 1935
Walter Donaldson / Gus Kahn
Francis, Day & Hunter Ltd .... USA
Film(s): .... Kid Millions
Eddie Cantor .... **Rex 8390**
Ethel Merman .... **Brunswick 01945**
Ethel Merman & Eddie Cantor appeared in *Kid Millions*.

EARLY IN THE MORNING August 1969
Mike Leander / Eddie Seago
Leeds Music Ltd. .... UK
Vanity Fair .... **Page One POF 142**

EARTH ANGEL June 1955
Curtis Williams
Chappell & Co. Ltd. .... USA
The Crew Cuts .... **Mercury MPT 7501**
Robb Storme .... **Decca F 11388**

EARTH DIES SCREAMING, THE November 1980
"UB40"
A.T.V. Music Ltd. .... UK
UB 40 .... **Graduate GRAD 10**

EAST OF THE SUN 1935
Brooks Bowman
Campbell Connelly & Co. Ltd .... USA
Arthur Tracey (The Street Singer) .... **Decca F 5697**

Tommy Dorsey & his Orch. vocal Frank Sinatra HMV 7EG 8070
The Modernaires . . . . Vogue LVA 9080
Dinah Shore . . . . Capitol T 1296

EAST SIDE OF HEAVEN   1939
Johnny Burke / Jimmy Monaco
Campbell Connelly & Co. Ltd. . . . . USA
Film(s): . . . . East Side of Heaven
Bing Crosby . . . . **Brunswick Bing 4**
Guy Mitchell . . . . **Philips BBL 7246**
Bing Crosby appeared in *East Side of Heaven.*

EASTER PARADE   1935
Irving Berlin
Irving Berlin Ltd . . . . USA
Show(s): . . . . As Thousands Cheer / Stop Press
Film(s): . . . Alexander's Ragtime Band / Holiday Inn / Easter Parade
Leo Reisman & his Orchestra, vocal Clifton Webb HMV BD 122
Dorothy Dickson . . . . HMV C 2946
Joan Edwards & Clarke Dennnis . . . . Brunswick 02856
Judy Garland & Fred Astaire . . . . MGM D 140
Bing Crosby . . . . Brunswick Bing 7
Al Jolson . . . . Brunswick LAT 8267
Sarah Vaughan & Billy Eckstine . . . . . Mercury MMC 14035
Clifton Webb appeared in *As Thousands Cheer.*
Dorothy Dickson appeared in *Stop Press.*
Bing Crosby appeared in *Holiday Inn.*
Judy Garland & Fred Astaire appeared in *Easter Parade.*

EASY   August 1977
Lionel Richie
Jobete Music (UK) Ltd. . . . . USA
The Commodores . . . . Motown TMG 1073
The Commodores (1988) . . . . Motown ZB 41793

EASY GOING ME   May 1961
Lionel Bart
Apollo Music Ltd . . . . UK
Adam Faith . . . . Parlophone R 4766

EASY LOVER   April 1985
Philip Bailey / Phil Collins / Nathan East
Warner Brothers Music . . . . UK
Phil Bailey & Phil Collins . . . . CBS A 4915
Ivor Novello Award.

EASY STREET   1943
Alan Rankin Jones
Robert Mellin Ltd . . . . USA
Martha Tilton . . . . Brunswick 03405
Julie London . . . . London HAU 2005
Pearl Bailey . . . . Mercury ZEP 10067

EASY TO LOVE   1936
Cole Porter
Victoria Music Co. Ltd . . . . USA
Film(s): . . . . Born to Dance / Night and Day / Easy to Love
Virginia Bruce . . . . Vocalion 523
The King Sisters . . . . Capitol CL 14777
Bing Crosby . . . . Brunswick LA 8513
Doris Day . . . . Philips BBL 7248
Virginia Bruce appeared in *Born To Dance.*

EBB TIDE   June 1953
Robert Maxwell / Carl Sigman
Robbins Music Corporation Ltd . . . . USA
Frank Chacksfield & his Orchestra . . . . Ace of Clubs ACL 1034
Stanley Black & his Orchestra . . . . Decca LK 4306
Bobby Maxwell (harp) . . . . MGM C 848
The Arthur Lyman Group . . . . Vogue VA 160174
The Righteous Brothers . . . . London HL 10011
Gisele MacKenzie . . . . RCA NL 89462
Jerry Colona (comedy version) . . . . Brunswick 05243

EBBTIDE   1938
Leo Robin / Ralph Rainger
Victoria Music Co. Ltd. . . . . USA
Film(s): . . . . Ebbtide
Connee Boswell . . . . Brunswick 02544

EBONY AND IVORY   May 1982
Paul McCartney
M.P.L. Music . . . . UK
Paul McCartney & Stevie Wonder . . . . Parlophone R 6054

Ivor Novello Award 1982

EBONY EYES   March 1961
John D. Loudermilk
Auff-Rose Publishing Co. Ltd . . . . USA
The Everly Brothers . . . . Warner Brothers WB 33

ECHO BEACH   April 1980
Mark Gane
Virgin Music (Publishers) Ltd . . . . Canada
Martha & The Muffins . . . . Dindisc DIN 9

ECHO OF A SERENADE, THE (Te Quieo Dijiste)   1941
Maria Grever / David Palmer
Southern Music Publishing Co. Ltd . . . . Mexico
Monte Ray . . . . Columbia FB 3043
Anne Shelton . . . . Decca F 8479
See also *Magic is the Moonlight.*

ECHO TOLD ME A LIE, THE   June 1949
Howard Barnes / Harold Fields / Dominic John
Chappell & Co. Ltd . . . . UK
Paul Adam & his Music . . . . Regal Zonophone MR 3820
Frank Chacksfield & his Orchestra . . . . Decca LK 4095
Based on the Italian folk song "Bella Ragazza Dalle Trecce Bionde".

ECSTASY   December 1952
Jose Belmonte
Sidney Bron Music . . . . UK
Ray Martin & his Orchestra . . . . Columbia DB 3199
Edmundo Ros & his Orchestra . . . . Decca F 9996
Geraldo & his Orchestra . . . . Philips PB 105
Sidney Torch & his Orchestra . . . . Parlophone R 3578

EDELWEISS   July 1961
Richard Rodgers / Oscar Hammerstein II
Williamson Music Ltd. . . . . USA
Show(s): . . . . Sound of Music
Film(s): . . . . Sound of Music
Mary Martin & Theadore Bikel . . . . Philips ABL 3370
Jean Bayless & Roger Dann . . . . HMV CLP 1453
Julie Andrews & Christopher Plummer . . . . RCA RB 6616
Vince Hill (1967) . . . . Columbia DB 8127
Jean Bayless & Roger Dann appeared in the British production of
Sound of Music. Julie Andrews & Christopher Plummer appeared in
the film *Sound of Music.*
Bill Lee Dubbed the Singing voice of Christopher Plummer.
Mary Martin & Theadore Bikel appeared in the American production
of *Sound of Music.*

EDGE OF HEAVEN   July 1986
George Michael
Morrison Leahy Music . . . . UK
Wham . . . . Epic FINE 1
Ivor Novello Nomination

EGYPTIAN REGGAE   December 1977
Jonathan Richman
Warner Brothers Music Ltd . . . . USA
Jonathan Richman & The Modern Lovers . . . Beserkley BZZ 2

EH CUMPARI   January 1954
Julius La Rosa / Archie Bleyer
Francis, Day & Hunter Ltd. . . . . USA
The Stargazers . . . . Decca F 10213
Julius La Rosa . . . . London L 1218
The Gaylords . . . . Mercury MMC 14032

EIGHTEEN WITH A BULLET   July 1975
Peter Wingfield
Island Music Ltd . . . . UK
Pete Wingfield . . . . Island WIP 6231

EIGHTH DAY   September 1980
Hazel O'Connor
Albion Music . . . . UK
Hazel O'Connor . . . . A&M AMS 7553

EILEEN ALANNA   1873
John Roger Thomas / Edward Marble
Unknown Publisher . . . . USA
John McCormack . . . . HMV DA 292
Ernest Pike . . . . Regal G 494
Danny Malone . . . . HMV B 8214
John O'Neill . . . . Embasy WLP 6020

EINSTEIN A GO-GO · April 1981
John Walters / Richard Burgess / Christopher Heaton / Andrew Pask / Peter Thomas
Sunbury Music . . . . UK
Landscape . . . . **RCA 22**

EL CAPITAN MARCH · 1896
John Philip Sousa
Unknown Publisher . . . . USA
Sousa's Band, conducted by J.P. Sousa . . . . . . **Pye GGL 0431**
The Band of the Coldstream Guards . . . . **HMV B 2941**
20th Century-Fox Studio Orchestra, conducted by Alfred Newman . . . . **MGM E 3508**

EL PASO · March 1960
Marty Robbins
Acuff-Rose Music Ltd. . . . . USA
Marty Robbins . . . . **Fontana H 233**

EL RELICARIO · 1920
Jose Padilla
Ascherberg, Hopwood & Crew Ltd. . . . . Spain
Raquel Meller . . . . **Parlophone R 1334**
Ramon Navarro . . . . **HMV B 8426**
Emanuel Vardi Orchestra . . . . **Brunswick LAT 8112**
Roland Shaw Orchestra . . . . **Decca PFS 4027**

ELEANOR RIGBY · September 1966
John Lennon / Paul McCartney
Northern Songs Ltd. . . . . UK
Film(s): . . . . Yellow Submarine
The Beatles . . . . **Parlophone R 5493**
The Beatles appeared in *Yellow Submarine.*

ELECTED · November 1972
Alice Cooper / Michael Bruce / Glen Buxton / Dennis Dunaway
Carlin Music Corporation . . . . USA
Alice Cooper . . . . **Warner Brothers K 16214**

ELECTION DAY · November 1985
Roger Taylor / Nick Rhodes / Simon Le Bon
Tritec Music . . . . UK
Arcadia . . . . **Parlophone NSR 1**

ELECTRIC AVENUE · February 1983
Eddy Grant
Intersong Music . . . . UK
Eddy Grant . . . . **Ice ICE 57**

ELENORE · November 1968
Howard Kaylan / Mark Volman / Al Nichol, John Barbata & Jim Pons
Carlin Music Corporation . . . . USA
The Turtles . . . . **London HL 10223**

ELEVEN MORE MONTHS AND TEN MORE DAYS · 1932
Fred Hall / Arthur Fields
Campbell Connelly & Co. Ltd. . . . . USA
Film(s): . . . . Ride Tenderfoot Ride
The Colt Brothers . . . . **Panachord 25029**
Ambrose & his Orchestra . . . . **HMV B 6119**
Clinton Ford . . . . **Oriole CB 1425**

ELEVEN THIRTY SATURDAY NIGHT (see 'leven Thirty Saturday Night)

ELIZABETH · 1930
Robert Katscher / Roland Leigh
Ascherberg, Hopwood & Crew Ltd . . . . Germany
Show(s): . . . . Wonder Bar
Elsie Randolph . . . . **Columbia DB 394**
Carl Brisson . . . . **Decca F 2397**
Joe Loss & his Orchestra . . . . **HMV DLP 1175**

ELIZABETHAN SERENADE · February 1957
Ronald Binge
Ascherberg, Hopwood & Crew Ltd. . . . . UK
Ron Goodwin & his Orchestra . . . . **Parlophone GEP 8699**
Ivor Novello Award.

ELMER'S TUNE · 1942
Elmer Albrecht / Dick Jurgens / Sammy Gallop
Francis, Day & Hunter Ltd . . . . USA
Film(s): . . . . Strictly in the Groove
The Andrews Sisters . . . . **Brunswick 03275**

Glenn Miller & his Orchestra . . . . **RCA RCX 1040**
Ray Eberle & The Modernaires . . . . **Vogue LVA 9103**

ELOISE · November 1968
Paul Ryan
Carlin Music Corporation . . . . UK
Barry Ryan . . . . **MGM 1442**
The Damned (1986) . . . . **MCA GRIM 4**

ELUSIVE BUTTERFLY, THE · May 1966
Bob Lind
Metric Music Ltd. . . . . USA
Bob Lind . . . . **Fontana TF 670**
Val Doonican . . . . **Decca F 12358**

EMBARRASSMENT · December 1980
Michael Barson / Lee Thompson
Warner Brothers Music Ltd . . . . UK
Madness . . . . **Stiff BUY 102**

EMBRACEABLE YOU · 1932
George Gershwin / Ira Gershwin
Chappell & Co. Ltd. . . . . USA
Show(s): . . . . Girl Crazy
Film(s):Girl Crazy / Nancy Goes to Rio / Rhapsody in Blue / An American in Paris / With a Song in my Heart / Sincerely Yours
Turner Layton . . . . **Columbia 2983**
Bing Crosby . . . . **Brunswick LA 8666**
Judy Garland . . . . **Brunswick 02993**
Frank Sinatra (1945) . . . . **Fontana TFL 5138**
Frank Sinatra . . . . **Capitol T 1417**
Judy Garland appeared in the 1943 film of *Girl Crazy.*

EMMA · April 1974
Errol Brown / Tony Wilson
Rak Music Ltd. . . . . UK
Hot Chocolate . . . . **Rak 168**

EMOTIONAL RESCUE · August 1980
Mick Jagger / Keith Richard
EMI Music Ltd . . . . UK
The Rolling Stones . . . . **Rolling Stones PSR 105**

EMOTIONS · April 1978
Barry Gibb / Robin Gibb
Chappell & Co. Ltd . . . . UK
Film(s): . . . . The Stud
Samantha Sang . . . . **Private Stock PVT 128**

EMPTY SADDLES · 1936
Billy Hill
B. Feldman & Co. Ltd . . . . USA
Film(s): . . . . Rhythm on the Range
Bing Crosby . . . . **Brunswick Bing 2**
The Diamonds . . . . **Mercury MMC 14039**
Bing Crosby appeared in *Rhythm on the Range.*

END OF MY OLD CIGAR, THE · 1914
R.P. Weston / Norton David
Francis, Day & Hunter Ltd . . . . UK
Harry Champion . . . . **Columbia DX 289**
Roy Hudd . . . . **Pye 7N 45666**

END OF THE ROAD, THE · 1926
Harry Lauder / William Dillon
Francis, Day & Hunter Ltd. . . . . UK
Harry Lauder . . . . **Camden CDN 130**
George Elrick . . . . **Ace of Clubs ACL 1024**
Kenneth McKellar . . . . **Decca LK 4295**

END OF THE WORLD, THE · April 1963
Sylvia Dee / Arthur Kent
Compass Music Ltd . . . . USA
Skeeter Davis . . . . **RCA 13428**
Valerie Masters . . . . **HMV POP 1125**
Ruby & The Romantics . . . . **London HAR 8078**
Vic Dana . . . . **Liberty LBY 1193**

ENDLESS LOVE · September 1981
Lionel Richie
Warner Brothers Music . . . . USA
Film(s): . . . . Endless Love
Diana Ross & Lionel Richie . . . . **Motown TMG 1240**
Nominated for an Academy Award 1981.

ENDLESS SLEEP   **August 1958**
Jody Reynolds / Dolores Nance
Hill & Range Music .... USA
Jody Reynolds .... **London HL 8651**
Marty Wilde .... **Philips PB 835**

ENERGY (see N.R.G.)

ENGLAND SWINGS   **February 1966**
Roger Miller
Burlington Music Co. Ltd .... USA
Roger Miller .... **Philips BF 1456**

ENGLISH COUNTRY GARDEN   **July 1962**
Traditional, new lyric by Robert Jordan
Tin Pan Alley Music Co. Ltd .... UK
Jimmy Rodgers .... **Columbia DB 4847**

ENGLISH ROSE   **1902**
Edward German / Basil Hood
Chappell & Co. Ltd. .... UK
Show(s): .... Merrie England
Robert Evett .... **Odeon 44189**
John Harrison Orch. conducted by Edward German   **HMV D 27**
Frank Titterton .... **Decca F 5530**
Robert Evett appeared in *Merrie England.*

ENJOY THE SILENCE   **March 1990**
Martin Gore
Sonet Music .... UK
Depeche Mode .... **Mute BONG 18**

ENJOY YOURSELF   **May 1950**
Herb Magidson / Carl Sigman
Edwin H Morris & Co. Ltd .... USA
Guy Lombardo & his Orchestra .... **Brunswick 04484**
Donald Peers .... **HMV B 9924**
Jimmy Silver & his Music, vocal Verdi .... **Decca LK 4290**

ENLLORO (Voodoo Moon)   **1946**
Obdulio Morales / Julio Blanco / Marion Sunshine
Leeds Music Ltd. .... USA
Film(s): .... Hollywood Canteen
Carmen Cavallaro & his Orchestra ... **Brunswick LAT 8320**
Carmen Cavallaro appeared in *Hollywood Canteen.*

ENOLA GAY   **November 1980**
George McClusky
Dinsong Ltd .... UK
Orchestral Manouvres in the Dark .... **DIndisc DIN 22**

ERNIE (The Fastest Milkman In The West)   **December 1971**
Benny Hill
.... UK
Benny Hill .... **Columbia DB 8833**
Ivor Novello Award.

ESO BESO (That Kiss)   **December 1962**
Joe Sherman / Noel Sherman
Spanka Music Ltd .... USA
Paul Anka .... **RCA 1318**
Georgie Fame .... **Columbia 33SX 1599**
Cliff Richard .... **Columbia 33SX 6039**

ESPECIALLY FOR YOU   **January 1989**
Mike Stock / Matt Aitken / Peter Waterman
All Boys Music .... UK
Kylie Minogue & Jason Donovan .... **PWL PWL 24**
Ivor Novello Nomination

ESTRELLITA   **1923**
Manuel Ponce / Frank La Forge
Boosey & Hawkes Music Publishers Ltd .... Mexico
Film(s): .... Two Girls and a Sailor
Jascha Heifetz (violin) .... **HMV DA 934**
Deanna Durbin .... **Brunswick LAT 8285**
Harry James & his Orchestra (1945) ...... **Parlophone R 2958**
Bob Sharples & his Orchestra .... **Decca LK 4287**
Trio Los Panchos .... **Philips BBL 7269**
The Harry James recording titled 'Little Star'.
Harry James Orchestra appeared in *Two Girls and a Sailor.*

ETERNAL FLAME   **April 1989**
Susanna Hoffs / Billy Steinberg / Tom Kelly
Warner Chappell Music .... USA

Bangles .... **CBS BANG 5**

ETERNALLY (Terry's Theme)   **June 1953**
Charles Chaplin / Geoffrey Parsons / John Turner
Bourne Music ltd .... USA
Film(s): .... Limelight
Jimmy Young .... **Decca DFE 6277**
See also *Limelight.*

ETON RIFLES   **November 1979**
Paul Weller
And Son Music .... UK
The Jam .... **Polydor POSP 83**

EUROPEAN FEMALE   **February 1983**
"The Stranglers"
EMI Music .... UK
The Stranglers .... **Epic EPCA 2893**

EV'RY HOUR, EV'RY DAY OF MY LIFE   **July 1958**
Clint Ballard
George Weiner Music Ltd .... USA
Malcolm Vaughan .... **HMV 7EG 8377**

EV'RY STREET'S A BOULEVARD   **August 1954**
Jule Styne / Bob Hilliard
Chappell & Co. Ltd. .... USA
Show(s): .... Hazel Flagg
Film(s): .... Living it Up
Dean Martin & Jerry Lewis ..... **Capitol EAP 1-533**
Norrie Paramor & his Orchestra .... **Columbia 33SX 1251**
Dean Martin & Jerry Lewis appeared in *Living It Up.*

EV'RY TIME WE SAY GOODBYE   **1945**
Cole Porter
Chappell & Co. Ltd. .... USA
Show(s): .... Seven Lively Arts
Ella Fitzgerald .... **HMV CLP 1083**
Gisele MacKenzie .... **RCA RD 27033**
Jeri Southern .... **Brunswick LA 8699**
Simply Red (1987) .... **WEA YZ 161**

EVE OF DESTRUCTION, THE   **October 1965**
P.F. Sloane
Dick James Music Ltd .... USA
Barry McGuire .... **RCA 1469**

EVE OF THE WAR   **December 1989**
Jeff Wayne
Jeff Wayne Music .... UK
Jeff Wayne .... **CBS 655126**

EVEN THE BAD TIMES ARE GOOD   **September 1967**
Peter Callander / Mitch Murray
Skidmore Music Ltd. .... UK
The Tremeloes .... **CBS 2930**

**EVER FALLEN IN LOVE (With Someone You
Shouldn't've)**   **November 1978**
Peter Shelley
Virgin Music (Publishers) Ltd .... UK
Buzzcocks .... **United Artists UP 36455**
Fine Young Cannibals (1987) .... **London LON 121**

EVER SO GOOSEY   **1929**
Ralph Butler / Raymond Wallace / Julian Wright
Campbell Connelly & Co. Ltd .... UK
Jack Hylton & his Orchestra .... **HMV B 5649**

EVERGREEN   **July 1977**
Barbra Streisand / Paul Williams
Warner Brothers Music Ltd .... USA
Film(s): .... A Star is Born
Barbra Streisand .... **CBS 4855**
Barbra Streisand appeared in *A Star Is Born*
Academy Award winning song for 1976.

EVERLASTING LOVE   **March 1968**
James Cason / Mac Gayden
Peter Maurice Music Co. Ltd. .... USA
The Love Affair .... **CBS 3125**
Robert Knight .... **Monument MNT 2106**

EVERMORE   **June 1955**
Gerry Levine / Paddy Roberts

Rogers Music Co. Ltd. . . . . UK
Ruby Murray . . . . **Encore ENC 104**

EVERY BEAT OF MY HEART   July 1986
Rod Stewart / Kevin Savigar
Island Music . . . . UK
Rod Stewart . . . . **Warner Brothers W 8625**

EVERY BREATH YOU TAKE   June 1983
"Sting"
Virgin Music . . . . UK
Police . . . . **A&M AMS 117**
Ivor Novello Award

EVERY DAY HURTS   November 1979
Paul Young / John Stimpson
St. Annes Music Ltd. . . . . UK
Sad Cafe . . . . **RCA PB 5180**

EVERY DAY I LOVE YOU MORE   September 1989
Mike Stock / Matt Aitken / Peter Waterman
All Boys Music . . . . UK
Jason Donovan . . . . **PWL PWL 43**

EVERY DAY OF MY LIFE   January 1955
Jimmy Crane / Al Jacobs
Robbins Music Corporation Ltd. . . . . USA
Malcolm Vaughan . . . . **HMV 7EG 8272**

EVERY LITTLE MOVEMENT   1910
Otto Harbach / Karl Hoschna
B. Feldman & Co. Ltd. . . . . USA
Show(s): . . . . Madame Sherry
Film(s): . . . . On Moonlight Bay / Presenting Lily Mars
The International Novelty Quartet . . **Regal Zonophone MR 846**
Ted Heath & his Music . . . . **Decca LK 4299**
Judy Garland & Connie Gilchrist . . . . **Caliban 6038**
Julie Andrews & Carol Burnett . . . . **CBS BPG 62139**
Judt Garland & Connie Gilchrist appeared in *Presenting Lily Mars.*

EVERY LITTLE STEP   June 1989
L.A. Reid"Babyface"
Warner Chappell Music . . . . UK
Bobby Brown . . . . **MCA MCA 1338**

EVERY LITTLE THING SHE DOES IS MAGIC   Nov 1981
"Sting"
Virgin Music . . . . UK
Police . . . . **A&M AMS 8174**

EVERY LITTLE WHILE   1916
James W. Tate
Francis, Day & Hunter Ltd. . . . . UK
Show(s): . . . . Some
Lee White . . . . **Columbia L 1058**
Sidney Thompson's Old Time
Dance Orchestra . . . . **Parlophone GEP 8512**

EVERY LOSER WINS   October 1986
Simon May / Stewart James / Bradley James
Simon May Music . . . . UK
Nick Berry . . . . **BBC RESL 204**
Ivor Novello Award.

EVERY NIGHT ABOUT THIS TIME   1943
Jimmy Monaco / Ted Koehler
Chappell & Co. Ltd . . . . USA
The Ink Spots . . . . **Brunswick 03433**
The Diamonds . . . . **Mercury MT 121**

EVERY ROSE HAS IT'S THORN   March 1989
Bruce Johannesson / Harry Kuykendall / Bret Michaels & Richard Ream
Zomba Music . . . . USA
Poison . . . . **Capitol CL 520**

EVERY SINGLE LITTLE TINGLE OF MY HEART   1935
Nat Simon / Jules Loman / Allan Roberts
Dash Music Ltd . . . . UK
Russ Morgan & his Orchestra . . . . **Columbia FB 1105**

EVERY TIME YOU GO AWAY   May 1985
Daryl Hall
Chappell & Co. Ltd . . . . USA
Paul Young . . . . **CBS A 6300**

EVERYBODY   October 1963
Tommy Roe
Chappell & Co. Ltd . . . . USA
Tommy Roe . . . . **HMV POP 1207**

EVERYBODY DANCE   May 1978
Bernard Edwards / Nile Rodgers
Warner Brothers Music Ltd . . . . USA
Chic . . . . **Atlantic K 11097**

EVERYBODY KNEW BUT ME   1946
Irving Berlin
Irving Berlin Ltd. . . . . USA
Geraldo & his Orchestra, vocal Dick James . . **Parlophone F 2119**

EVERYBODY KNOWS (I STILL LOVE YOU)   December 1967
Dave Clark / Lenny Davidson
Donna Music Ltd. . . . . UK
The Dave Clark Five . . . . **Columbia DB 8286**

EVERYBODY LOVES A LOVER   September 1958
Richard Adler / Robert Allen
Larry Spier . . . . USA
Doris Day . . . . **Philips PB 843**
Joe Loss & his Orchestra . . . . **HMV POP 524**

EVERYBODY LOVES MY BABY   1925
Jack Palmer / Spencer Williams
B. Feldman & Co. Ltd. . . . . USA
Film(s): . . . . It's Trad Dad / Love Me or Leave Me
Clarence Williams Blue Five,
vocal Eva Taylor . . . . **Fontana TFL 5087**
The Andrews Sisters . . . . **Capitol T 933**
Teresa Brewer . . . . **Vogue LVA 9107**
The Temperance Seven . . . . **Columbia 33SX 1412**
Doris Day . . . . **Philips BBL 7047**
The Temperance Seven appeared in *It's Trad Dad.*
Doris Day appeared in *Love Me or Leave Me.*

EVERYBODY LOVES SOMEBODY   October 1964
Ken Lane / Irving Taylor
Edwin H. Morris & Co. Ltd . . . . USA
Dean Martin . . . . **Reprise R 20281**

EVERYBODY STEP   1922
Irving Berlin
Irving Berlin Ltd . . . . USA
Show(s): . . . . The Music Box Revue
Film(s): . . . . Alexander's Ragtime Band / Blue Skies
Paul Whiteman & his Orchestra . . . . **HMV B 1318**
Sid Philips & his Band . . . . **HMV 7 EG 8461**
Bing Crosby . . . . **Brunswick Bing 10**
Bing Crosby appeared in *Blue Skies.*

EVERYBODY WANTS TO RULE THE WORLD   April 1985
Roland Orzabal / Ian Stanley / Chris Hughes
Virgin Music . . . . UK
Tears For Fears . . . . **Phonogram IDEA 9**
Tears For Fears (1986) . . . . **Mercury RACE 1**
Ivor Novello Nomination 1985.
1986 version titled 'Everybody Wants To Run The World' for Sports Aid.

EVERYBODY'S CRAZY ON THE FOXTROT   1915
Bennett Scott / A.J. Mills
B. Feldman & Co. Ltd. . . . . UK
The Two Bobs . . . . **Edison Bell Winner 2914**
Walter Jefferies . . . . **HMV B 567**

EVERYBODY'S DOING IT   1911
Irving Berlin
B.Feldman & Co. Ltd . . . . USA
Show(s): . . . . Everybody's Doing it
Film(s):Alexander's Ragtime Band / The Fabulous Dorseys / Easter Parade
Robert Hale & Ida Crispi . . . . **HMV 04093**
Jack Payne & his Band . . . . **Rex 8455**
Clinton Ford . . . . **Oriole CB 1623**
Robert Hale & Ida Crispi appeared in *Everbody's Doing It.*

EVERYBODY'S GOT TO LEARN SOMETIME   July 1980
James Warren
Heath Levy Music Ltd . . . . UK
The Korgis . . . . **Rialto TREB 115**

EVERYBODY'S LAUGHING   August 1984
Phil Fearon
Handle Music . . . . UK
Phil Fearon & Galaxy . . . . **Ensign ENY 514**

EVERYBODY'S SOMEBODY'S FOOL   September 1960
Howard Greenfield / Jack Keller
Nevins-Kirshner Ltd . . . . USA
Connie Francis . . . . **MGM EP 742**

EVERYBODY'S TWISTING   April 1962
Ted Koehler / Rube Bloom
Peter Maurice Music Co. Ltd. . . . . USA
Frank Sinatra . . . . **Reprise R 20063**
Adapted from "Truckin'".

EVERYDAY   April 1974
Noddy Holder / Jimmy Lea
Barn Publishing Ltd. . . . . UK
Slade . . . . **Polydor 2058453**

EVERYDAY IS LIKE SUNDAY   July 1989
Stephen Street / Steve Morrisey
Warner Brothers Music . . . . UK
Morrissey . . . . **HMV POP 1619**

EVERYONE'S A WINNER   April 1978
Errol Brown
Rak Music Ltd . . . . UK
Film(s): . . . . The Stud
Hot Chocolate . . . . **Rak 270**

EVERYONE'S GONE TO THE MOON   August 1965
Kenneth King
Marquis Music Ltd . . . . UK
Jonathan King . . . . **Decca F 12187**

EVERYTHING COUNTS   August 1983
Martin Gore
Sonet Music . . . . UK
Depeche Mode . . . . **Mute 7 BONG 3**

EVERYTHING I AM   February 1968
Dan Penn / Spooner Oldham
Essex Music Ltd. . . . . USA
Plastic Penny . . . . **Page One POF 051**

EVERYTHING I HAVE IS YOURS   1933
Harold Adamson / Burton Lane
Robbins Music Corporation Ltd. . . . . USA
Film(s): . . . . Strictly Dishonourable / Everything I Have is Yours
Al Bowlly . . . . **Decca F 3853**
Reg Owen & his Orchestra . . . . **RCA RD 27040**
Faron Young . . . . **Capitol T 1004**
Eddie Fisher (1953) . . . . **HMV B 10398**
Monica Lewis . . . . **MGM D 109**
Monica Lewis appeared in *Everything I Have is Yours*.

EVERYTHING I OWN   November 1974
David Gates
Screen Gems Music Ltd. . . . . USA
Ken Boothe . . . . **Trojan TR 7920**
Bread . . . . **Elektra K 12041**
Boy George (1987) . . . . **Virgin BOY 100**

EVERYTHING I'VE GOT   1943
Richard Rodgers / Lorenz Hart
Chappell & Co. Ltd . . . . USA
Show(s): . . . . By Jupiter
Ella Fitzgerald . . . . **HMV CLP 1117**
Annie Ross . . . . **Vogue LAE 12233**

EVERYTHING IS BEAUTIFUL   June 1970
Ray Stevens
Peter Maurice Music Co. Ltd. . . . . USA
Ray Stevens . . . . **CBS 4953**

EVERYTHING IS HOTSY TOTSY NOW   1925
Irving Mills / Jimmy McHugh
Lawrence Wright Music Co. Ltd. . . . . USA
The California Ramblers . . . . **Riverside RLP 12-801**
Georgie's Varsity Five . . . . **Vogue VA 160128**

EVERYTHING IS PEACHES DOWN IN GEORGIA   1919
Grant Clarke / Milton Ager / George W. Meyer

Francis, Day & Hunter Ltd. . . . . USA
Show(s): . . . . U.S.
Fred Douglas . . . . **Regal G 7461**
The Savoy Quartet . . . . **HMV B 1008**
Bob Scobey's Frisco Band . . . . **Vogue LDG 155**

EVERYTHING MUST CHANGE   January 1985
Paul Young / Ian Kewley
Bright Music . . . . UK
Paul Young . . . . **CBS A 4972**

EVERYTHING SHE WANTS   January 1985
George Michael
Morrison Leahy Music . . . . UK
Wham . . . . **Epic A 4949**

EVERYTHING STOPS FOR TEA   1935
Maurice Sigler / Al Hoffman / Al Goodhart
Cinephonic Music Co. Ltd . . . . UK
Film(s): . . . . Come Out of the Pantry
Jack Buchanan . . . . **Brunswick 02125**
The Syncopaters, vocal Babsie Kaye . . . . **Decca F 11359**
Jack Buchanan appeared in *Come Out of the Pantry*.

EVERYTHING'S ALRIGHT   May 1964
Nicholas Crouch / John Conrad / Simon Stavely / Stuart James & Keith Karlson
West One Music Ltd . . . . UK
The Mojos . . . . **Decca F 11853**

EVERYTHING'S COMING UP ROSES   March 1963
Stephen Sondheim / Jule Styne
Chappell Music Ltd . . . . USA
Show(s): . . . . Gypsy
Film(s): . . . . Gypsy
Ethel Merman . . . . **CBS APG 60003**
Angela Lansbury . . . . **RCA SER 5686**
Rosalind Russell . . . . **Warner Brothers WM 8120**
Ethel Merman appeared in the American production of *Gypsy*.
Angela Landsbury appeared in the British production of *Gypsy*.
Rosalind Russell appeared in the film of *Gypsy* Singing voice dubbed by Lisa Kirk.

EVERYTHING'S TUESDAY   March 1971
Daphne Dumas / Ronald Dunbar / Edith Wayne
Ardmore & Beechwood Ltd . . . . USA
Chairmen of the Board . . . . **Invictus INV 507**

EVERYTHING'S IN RHYTHM WITH MY HEART   1935
Maurice Sigler / Al Goodhart / Al Hoffman
Cinephonicx Music Co. Ltd . . . . UK
Film(s): . . . . First a Girl
Jessie Matthews . . . . **Decca F 5729**
Jessie Matthews appeared in *First a Girl*.

EVERYWHERE   July 1955
Larry Kahn / Tolchard Evans
Sydney Bron Music Co. Ltd. . . . . UK
David Whitfield . . . . **Decca LF 1265**
Ivor Novello Award.

EVERYWHERE   April 1988
Christine McVie
Bright Music . . . . USA
Fleetwood Mac . . . . **Warner Brothers W 8143**

EVERYWHERE YOU GO   1928
Larry Shay / Joe Goodwin / Mark Fisher
Chappell & Co. Ltd. . . . . USA
Will Perry & his Orchestra . . . . **Parlophone E 6016**
Doris Day (1949) . . . . **Columbia DB 2561**
Bing Crosby & Evelyn Knight (1949) . . . . **Brunswick 04139**

EVIL HEARTED YOU   November 1965
Graham Gouldman
Campbell Connelly & Co. Ltd . . . . UK
The Yardbirds . . . . **Columbia DB 7706**

EVIL THAT MEN DO   September 1988
Adrian Smith / Bruce Dickinson / Steve Harris
Zomba Music . . . . UK
Iron Maiden . . . . **EMI EM 64**

EVIL WOMAN   February 1976
Jeff Lynne

Jet Music Ltd . . . . UK
Electric Light Orchestra **Jet 764**

EXACTLY LIKE YOU **1930**
Dorothy Fields / Johnny McHugh
Lawrence Wright Music Co. Ltd . . . . USA
Show(s): . . . . The International Revue
Film(s): . . . . The Eddy Duchin Story
Gertrude Lawrence . . . . **MCA MUP 336**
Louis Armstrong & his Orchestra . . . . **Parlophone R 2042**
Carmen McRae . . . . **Brunswick LAT 8257**
Bing Crosby . . . . **RCA RD 27032**
Gertrude Lawrence appeared in *The International Revue*.

EXCERPT FROM A TEENAGE OPERA
(GROCER JACK) **October 1967**
Keith West / Mark Wirtz
Robbins Music Ltd. . . . . UK
Keith West . . . . **Parlophone R 5623**
Ivor Novello Award.

EXODUS **August 1977**
Bob Marley
Rondor Music (London) Ltd . . . . UK
Bob Marley & The Wailers . . . . **Island WIP 6390**

EXODUS THEME, THE **April 1961**
Ernest Gold
Chappell & Co. Ltd . . . . USA
Film(s): . . . . .Exodus
Ferrante & Teicher (piano duet) . . . . **London HL 9298**
The Sinfonia of London, cond. by Ernest Gold **RCA RD 27210**

EXPERIMENT **1933**
Cole Porter
Chappell & Co. Ltd. . . . . USA
Show(s): . . . . Nymph Errant
Gertrude Lawrence . . . . **HMV DLP 1099**
Virginia Somers . . . . **Decca LF 1213**
Gertrude Lawrence appeared in *Nymph Errant*.

EXPRESS YOURSELF **June 1989**
Madonna Ciccone / Steve Bray
Warner Chappell Music . . . . USA
Madonna . . . . **Sire W 2948**

EYE LEVEL **November 1973**
Jack Trombey
De Wolf Ltd. . . . . UK
Simon Park Orchestra . . . . **Columbia DB 8946**
Theme of the T.V. series "Van Der Valk".

EYE OF THE TIGER, THE **September 1982**
Jim Peterick / Frank Sullivan
Warner Brothers Music . . . . USA
Film(s): . . . . .Rocky III
Survivor . . . . **Scotti Brothers SCTA 2411**
Nominated for an Academy Award 1982.

FABULOUS **July 1957**
John Sheldon / Harry Land
Carlin Music . . . . USA
Charlie Grace . . . . **Parlophone R 4313**

FADE TO GREY **February 1981**
William Currie / Christopher Payne / Midge Ure
Island Music . . . . UK
Visage . . . . **Polydor POSP 194**

FADED SUMMER LOVE, A **1932**
Phil Baxter
Francis, Day & Hunter Ltd. . . . . USA
Ruth Etting . . . . **Regal Zonophone MR 458**
Bing Crosby . . . . **Brunswick LA 8741**
Kay Starr . . . . **Capitol T 1303**
Teresa Brewer . . . . **Vogue LVA 9100**

FAIR AND WARMER **1934**
Al Dubin / Harry Warren
B. Feldman & Co. Ltd . . . . USA
Film(s): . . . . Twenty Million Sweethearts
Ray Noble & his Orchestra . . . . **HMV B 6503**

FAIRY ON THE CHRISTMAS TREE, THE **1937**
Roma Campbell-Hunter / Harry Parr Davies

Keith Prowse Music Publishing Co. Ltd. . . . . UK
Gracie Fields . . . . **Regal Zonophone MR 3180**
The BBC Dance Orchestra . . . . **Columbia FB 1575**

FAIRY TALES **January 1977**
Paul Creddus
Heath Levy Music Ltd . . . . UK
Dana . . . . **GTO GT 66**

FAIRYTALE OF NEW YORK **December 1987**
Shane MacGowan / Jerri Finer
Stiff Music . . . . UK
The Pogues featuring Kirsty MacColl . . . . **Stiff NY 12**

FAITH **November 1987**
George Michael
Morrison Leahy Music . . . . UK
George Michael . . . . **Epic EMU 3**
Ivor Novello Award 1988.

FAITH CAN MOVE MOUNTAINS **November 1952**
Guy Wood / Ben Raleigh
Dash Music Ltd . . . . USA
Harry Secombe . . . . **HMV 7EG 8603**
Jimmy Young . . . . **Decca F 9986**
Johnnie Ray . . . . **Columbia DB 3154**
Nat 'King' Cole . . . . **Capitol CL 13811**

FAITHFUL FOREVER **1939**
Leo Robin / Ralph Rainger
Victoria Music Co. Ltd. . . . . USA
Film(s): . . . . Gulliver's Travels
Jay Wilbur & his Band, vocal Sam Browne . . . . **Rex 9703**
Dolly Elsie . . . . **HMV BD 804**
Glenn Miller & his Orchestra, vocal Ray Eberle . **HMV 7EG 8135**
Nominated for an Academy Award 1939.

FALL IN AND FOLLOW ME **1910**
A.J. Mills / Bennett Scott
B. Feldman & Co. Ltd . . . . UK
Lew Stone & his Band, vocal Sam Browne . . . . **Decca F 7278**
Sidney Thompson & his Orchestra . . . . . **Parlophone PMD 1013**
Billy Cotton Band . . . . **Columbia DB 4555**

FALL IN LOVE WITH YOU **April 1960**
Ian Samwell
Kalith Music Ltd . . . . UK
Cliff Richard . . . . **Columbia SEG 8050**

FALLING **June 1963**
Roy Orbison
Acuff-Rose Publishing Co. Ltd . . . . USA
Roy Orbison . . . . **London HL 9727**

FALLING **December 1990**
Angelo Badalamenti / David Lynch
MCA Music . . . . USA
Julee Cruise . . . . **Warner Brothers W 9544**

FALLING APART AT THE SEAMS **April 1976**
Tony Macaulay
Macaulay Music . . . . UK
Marmalade . . . . **Target TGT 105**

FALLING IN LOVE AGAIN **1930**
Frederick Hollander / Reginald Connelly
Campbell Connelly & Co. Ltd . . . . Germany
Film(s): . . . . The Blue Angel
Marlene Dietrich . . . . **HMV 7EG 8257**
May Britt . . . . **Top Rank JAR 230**
Marlene Dietrich appeared in the 1930 film of *The Blue Angel*.
May Britt appeared in the 1959 film of *The Blue Angel*.

FALLING IN LOVE WITH LOVE **1940**
Richard Rodgers / Lorenz Hart
Sterling Music Publishing Co. Ltd . . . . USA
Show(s): . . . . The Boys From Syracuse / Up and Doing
Film(s): .The Boys From Syracuse
Allan Jones . . . . **HMV B 9106**
Patrice Musnel & Vaughan Monroe . . . . **HMV B 10200**
Frank Sinatra . . . . **Reprise R 1002**
Anita O'Day . . . . **HMV CLP 1436**
Lynn Kennington . . . . **Decca LK 4564**
Allan Jones appeared in the film *The Boys From Syracuse*.

Lynn Kennington appeared in the British production of *The Boys From Syracuse*.

FALLING LEAVES   **1941**
Mack David / Frankie Carle
Dash Music Ltd .... USA
Glenn Miller & his Orchestra .... HMV BD 5651
Ambrose & his Orchestra, vocal Sam Browne .. Decca F 1841
Glenn Miller & his Orch. vocal Ray McKinley .. RCA RD 27079

FAME   **July 1982**
Michael Gore / Dean Pitchford
CBS Songs .... USA
Film(s): .... Fame
Irene Cara .... RSO RSO 9
Irene Cara appeared in *Fame*
Academy Award winning song for 1980.

FANCY OUR MEETING   **1929**
Joseph Meyer / Phil Charig / Douglas Furber
Chappell & Co. Ltd .... USA
Show(s): .... That's a Good Girl / Wake Up and Dream
Film(s): .... That's a Good Girl
Jack Buchanan & Elsie Randolph .... Columbia 9462
Al Bowlly .... Decca F 3472
Jack Buchanan appeared in both the show and the film of *That's A Good Girl* and also the show *Wake Up And Dream*.
Elsie Randolph appeared in both the show and the film of *That's A Good Girl*.

FANCY PANTS   **April 1975**
Bill Martin / Phil Coulter
Martin-Coulter Music Ltd .... UK
Kenny .... Rak 196

FANFARE FOR THE COMMON MAN   **July 1977**
Aaron Copland
Boosey & Hawkes Music Publishers Ltd .... USA
Emerson, Lake & Palmer .... Atlantic K 10946

FANLIGHT FANNY   **1935**
Harry Gifford / Fred Cliffe / George Formby
Cinephonic Music .... UK
George Formby .... Decca F 5569
Clinton Ford (1962) .... Oriole CB 1706

FANTASTIC DAY   **May 1982**
Nick Heyward
Bryan Morrison Music .... UK
Haircut 100 .... Arista CLIP 3

FANTASY   **March 1978**
Maurice White / Verdine White / Eddie Delbarrio
Chappell & Co. Ltd .... USA
Earth Wind & Fire .... CBS 6056
Black Box (1990) .... RCA PB 43895

FANTASY ISLAND   **May 1982**
Peter Souer / Martinus Duiser
Zomba Music .... Holland
Tightfit .... Jive JIVE 13

FAR AWAY PLACES   **February 1949**
Joan Whitney / Alex Kramer
Leeds Music Ltd .... USA
Dinah Shore .... Columbia DB 2494
Bing Crosby .... Brunswick LAT 8052
Steve Lawrence .... RCA RD 27062

FAR FAR AWAY   **November 1974**
Noddy Holder / Jimmy Lea
Barn Publishing Ltd. .... UK
Slade .... Polydor 2058522

FARE-THEE-WELL ANNABELLE   **1935**
Mort Dixon / Allie Wrubel
B. Feldman & Co. Ltd .... USA
Film(s): .... Sweet Music
Rudy Vallee .... HMV BD 185
The Boswell Sisters .... Brunswick 02043
Rudy Vallee appeared in *Sweet Music*.

FAREWELL   **October 1974**
Rod Stewart / Martin Quittenton
Warner Brothers Music Ltd. .... UK

Rod Stewart .... Mercury 6167033

FAREWELL BLUES   **1923**
Elmer Schoebel / Paul Mares / Leon Rappolo
Lawrence Wright Music Co. Ltd .... USA
The Friars Society Orchestra .... London Al 3536
The New Orleans Rhythm Kings ..... London Al 3536
Wilbur De Paris & his Band ...... London LTZK 15086
Glenn Miller & his Orchestra ...... RCA RD 27068
Red Nichols & The Charlestown Chasers .. Philips BBE 12350

FAREWELL IS A LONELY SOUND   **April 1970**
James Dean / Jack Goga / William Witherspoon
Jobete Music (UK) Ltd. .... USA
Jimmy Ruffin .... Tamla Motown TMG 726

FAREWELL MY SUMMER LOVE   **July 1984**
Kenneth Lewis
Jobete Music .... USA
Michael Jackson .... Motown TMG 1342

FASCINATING RHYTHM   **1926**
George Gershwin / Ira Gershwin
Chappell & Co. Ltd. .... USA
Show(s): .... Lady Be Good / Singin' in the Rain
Film(s): .... Lady Be Good / Girl Crazy / Rhapsody in Blue
Fred & Adele Astaire .... Columbia 3969
Jack Hylton & his Orchestra .... HMV C 1261
Tony Bennett .... Philips BBL 7308
Petula Clark .... Nixa NPT 19002
Tommy Steele .... Safari RAIN 1
Fred & Adele Astaire appeared in both the American and British productions of *Lady Be Good*.
Tommy Steele appeared in the show *Singin' in the Rain*.

FASCINATING RHYTHM   **October 1990**
William Orbit / Sharon Musgrave / Laurie Mayer / Stephen Roberts
Virgin Music .... USA
Bass-O-Matic .... Guerilla VS 1274

FASCINATION   **1932**
F.D. Marchetti / Maurice De Feraudy / Dick Manning
Southern Music Publishing Co. Ltd. .... France
Film(s): .... Love in the Afternoon
Orchestre Mascotte .... Parlophone R 1428
Jane Morgan .... London HAR 2086
Nat 'King' Cole .... Capitol EAP 1-813
The Mantovani Orchestra .... Decca LK 4316
Adapted from 'Valse Tzigane' by Marchetti.

FASHION   **November 1980**
David Bowie
Fleur Music .... UK
David Bowie .... RCA BOW 7

FAST CAR   **July 1988**
Tracy Chapman
SBK Songs .... USA
Tracy Chapman .... Elektra EKR 73

FAT LI'L' FELLER WID HIS MAMMY'S EYES   **1913**
Sheridan Gordon / F.L. Stanton
Chappell & Co. Ltd. .... UK
Paul Robeson .... HMV 7EG 8449

FATE   **1923**
Byron Gay
B. Feldman & Co. Ltd .... USA
Paul Whiteman & Co. Ltd .... HMV B 1637
Ted Lewis & his Band .... Columbia 3235
Harry Roy & his Tiger Ragamuffins .... Parlophone R 837

FATTIE BUM BUM   **October 1975**
Carl Malcolm
Campbell Connelly & Co. Ltd .... UK
Carl Malcolm .... UK 108

FAVOURITE SHIRT   **November 1981**
Nick Heyward
Bryan Morrison Music .... UK
Haircut 100 .... Arista CLIP 1

F.B.I.   **April 1961**
Peter Gormley
Shadows Music Ltd .... UK

The Shadows . . . . Columbia DB 4580

F.D.R. JONES (see FRANKLIN D. ROOSEVELT JONES)

FEATHER IN HER TYROLEAN HAT, THE   1937
Annette Mills
Campbell Connelly & Co. Ltd . . . . UK
Gracie Fields . . . . **Rex 8936**
Ambrose & his Orchestra . . . . **Decca F 6200**

FEATHER YOUR NEST   1921
James Kendis / Howard Johnson / James Brockman
Herman Darewski Music Publishing Co. Ltd . . . . USA
Show(s): . . . . .Tip Top
Art Hickman & his Orchestra . . . . **Columbia 3020**
The Happy Six . . . . **Columbia 3025**

FEEL SO REAL   November 1985
Steve Arrington / India Arrington
Screen Gems Music . . . . USA
Steve Arrington . . . . **Atlantic A 9576**

FEEL THE NEED IN ME   March 1973
Abrim Tilmon
Carlin Music Corporation . . . . USA
The Detroit Emeralds . . . . **Janus 6146020**
The Detroit Emeralds (1977) . . . . **Atlantic K 10945**

FEELINGS   November 1975
Morris Albert
Keith Prowse Music Publishing Co. Ltd . . . . Brazil
Morris Albert . . . . **Decca F 13591**

(FEELS LIKE) HEAVEN   February 1984
Kevin Patterson / Edward Jordan
Carlin Music . . . . UK
The Fiction Factory . . . . **CBS A 3996**

FEELS LIKE I'M IN LOVE   September 1980
Ray Dorset
Red Bus Music . . . . UK
Kelly Marie . . . . **Calibre 1**

FEET UP   September 1952
Bob Merrill
Cinephonic Music Co. Ltd . . . . USA
Guy Mitchell . . . . **Columbia SEG 7513**
Ray Ellington & The Stargazers . . . . **Decca F 10023**

FELIX KEPT ON WALKING   1924
Edward E. Bryant / Hubert W. David
Lawrence Wright Music Co. Ltd . . . . UK
The Two Gilberts . . . . **Regal G 8092**
Jack Hylton & his Orchestra . . . . **HMV B 1758**
Joe Loss & his Band . . . . **Regal Zonophone MR 2635**

FELLA WITH AN UMBRELLA, A   October 1948
Irving Berlin
Irving Berlin Ltd. . . . . USA
Film(s): . . . . Easter Parade
Bing Crosby . . . . **Brunswick 03965**
Judy Garland & Peter Lawford . . . . **MGM D 140**
Garry Miller . . . . **Nixa NPL 18008**
Judy Garland & Peter Lawford appeared in *Easter Parade*.

FELLOW NEEDS A GIRL, A   1947
Richard Rodgers / Oscar Hammerstein II
Williamson Music Ltd. . . . . USA
Show(s): . . . . Allegro
Doris Day . . . . **Philips BBL 7377**
Frank Sinatra . . . . **Philips BBL 7180**
Al Jolson . . . . **Brunswick LAT 8294**

FERDINAND THE BULL   1939
Larry Morey / Albert Hay Malotte
Chappell & Co. Ltd. . . . . USA
Film(s): . . . . Ferdinand the Bull (cartoon)
Dick Robertson & his Orchestra . . . . **Decca F 6922**
The Merry Macs . . . . **Decca F 6973**
Joe Loss & his Band . . . . **Regal Zonophone MR 2958**
Bill Hayes . . . . **HMV 7EG 8355**

FERNANDO   May 1976
Benny Andersson / Stig Anderson
Bocu Music Ltd . . . . Sweden

Abba . . . . Epic EPC 4036

FERRY 'CROSS THE MERSEY   January 1965
Gerry Marsden
Pacemusic Ltd . . . . UK
Film(s): . . . . Ferry Across The Mersey
Gerry & The Pacemakers . . . . **Columbia DB 7437**
The Christians (1989) . . . . **PWL 41**
Gerry & The Pacemakers appeared in *Ferry Across the Mersey*
1989 recording by various artists for charity.

FERRY BOAT INN, THE   November 1950
Don Pelosi / Jimmy Campbell
Campbell Connelly & Co. Ltd . . . . UK
Benny Lee . . . . **Decca F 9577**
The Beverley Sisters . . . . **Columbia DB 2786**

FERRY BOAT SERENADE (La Piccinina)   1941
Eldo Di Lazzaro / Harold Adamson
Francis, Day & Hunter Ltd . . . . Italy
The Andrews Sisters . . . . **Brunswick 03082**
Al Bowlly . . . . **HMV BD 892**
The Andrews Sisters . . . . **Capitol LCT 6132**
The Adams Singers . . . . **Pye NPL 28013**

FEUDIN' AND FIGHTIN'   1947
Al Dubin / Burton Lane
Chappell & Co. Ltd. . . . . USA
Show(s): . . . . Laffing Room Only
Film(s): . . . . Feudin', Fussin' and a-Fightin'
Bing Crosby & The Jesters . . . . **Brunswick LA 8579**
The Three Suns . . . . **RCA RD 27066**

FEVER   September 1958
John Davenport / Eddie Cooley
Redwood Music Ltd . . . . USA
Film(s): . . . . Hey Boy! Hey Girl!
Peggy Lee . . . . **Capitol T 1366**
Earl Grant . . . . **Brunswick LAT 8297**
Louis Prima & Keely Smith . . . . **Capitol T 1160**
Helen Shapiro . . . . **Columbia DB 7190**
Louis Prima & Keely Smith appeared in *Hey Boy! Hey Girl!*.

FIACRE, LE (The Cab)   1939
Leon Xanrof / Barry Gray
Peter Maurice Music Co. Ltd. . . . . France
Jean Sablon . . . . **HMV DLP 1041**
Gisele MacKenzie . . . . **Capitol CL 13686**

FIBBIN'   November 1958
Michael Merlo / Patrick Welch
Francis, Day & Hunter Ltd . . . . USA
Petula Clark . . . . **Nixa N 15168**
Patti Page . . . . **Mercury ZEP 10006**

FIDDLE FADDLE   August 1948
Leroy Anderson
Mills Music Ltd. . . . . USA
Leroy Anderson & his Orchestra . . . . **Brunswick LA 8613**
The Boston Promenade Orchestra . . . . **HMV DLP 1142**
The Eastman-Rochester 'Pops' Orchestra . **Mercury ZEP 10090**

FIELDS OF FIRE   April 1983
"Big Country"
Virgin Music . . . . UK
Big Country . . . . **Mercury COUNT 2**

FIESTA   1931
Walter G. Samuels / Leonard Whitcup
Campbell Connelly & Co. Ltd. . . . . USA
The Big Four . . . . **Columbia DB 535**
Billy Mayerl (piano) . . . . **Columbia DB 534**
The Carlo Sovino Orchestra . . . . **Durium TLU 97003**

FIFTY MILLION FRENCHMEN CAN'T BE WRONG   1927
Fred Fisher / Billy Rose / Will Raskin
Lawrence Wright Music Co. Ltd. . . . . USA
Nat Shilkret & his Orchestra . . . . **HMV B 5318**
Sophie Tucker . . . . **Columbia SEG 7766**

FIGARO   February 1978
Lee Sheridan / Tony Hiller
A.T.V. Music Ltd. . . . . UK
Brotherhood of Man . . . . **Pye 7N 46037**

FINAL COUNTDOWN   November 1986
Joey Tempest
EMI Music . . . . Holland
Europe . . . . **Epic A 7127**

FINCHLEY CENTRAL   July 1967
Geoff Stevens / Alan Klein
Meteor Music Ltd. . . . . UK
The New Vaudeville Band . . . . **Fontana TF 824**

FIND MY LOVE   August 1988
Mark Nevin
MCA Music . . . . UK
Fairground Attraction . . . . **RCA PB 42079**

FIND THE TIME   August 1986
Paul Gurvitz / Nick Trevisik
Island Music . . . . UK
Five Star . . . . **Tent PB 40799**

FINE AND DANDY   1931
Kay Swift / Paul James
Chappell & Co. Ltd . . . . USA
Show(s): . . . . Fine and Dandy
The Dorsey Brothers Orchestra . . . . **Parlophone R 993**
Doris Day . . . . **Columbia 33S 1038**
Anita O'Day . . . . **HMV CLP 1085**

FINE BROWN FRAME   December 1948
Guadalupe Cartiero / J. Mayo Williams
Unknown . . . . USA
Nellie Lutcher . . . . **Capitol EAP 20066**

FINE ROMANCE, A   1936
Jerome Kern / Dorothy Fields
Chappell & Co. Ltd . . . . USA
Film(s): . . . . Swing Time / Till the Clouds Roll By
Fred Astaire . . . . **Philips BBL 7052**
Bing Crosby & Dixie Lee . . . . **Brunswick LA 8505**
Eydie Gormé & Steve Lawrence . . . . **HMV CLP 1463**
Ella Fitzgerald & Louis Armstrong . . . . **HMV CLP 1147**
Fred Astaire appeared in *Swing Time.*

FINE TIME   February 1989
Andrew Caine / Jake Le Mesurier / Martin Glover
E.G. Music . . . . UK
Yazz . . . . **Big Life BLR 6**

FINE TIME   January 1989
"New Order"
Warner Chappell Music . . . . UK
New Order . . . . **Factory FAC 2237**

FINEST, THE   April 1986
Terry Lewis / James Harris
CBS Songs . . . . USA
The S.O.S. Band . . . . **Tabu A 6997**

FINGER OF SUSPICION, THE   January 1955
Paul Mann / Al Lewis
Pickwick Music Ltd. . . . . USA
Dickie Valentine . . . . **Decca LF 1244**
The Coronets . . . . **Columbia DB 3533**
Dickie Valentine & The Skyrockets
 Dance Orchestra . . . . **Ace of Clubs ACL 1082**

FINGS AIN'T WOT THEY USED T'BE   April 1960
Lionel Bart
World Wide Music Co. Ltd . . . . UK
Show(s): . . . . Fing's Ain't Wot They Used T'Be
Glyn Edwards & Miriam Karlin . . . . **Decca LK 4346**
Max Bygraves . . . . **Decca F 11214**
Billy Cotton . . . . **Columbia SEG 8024**
Glyn Edwards & Miriam Karlin appeared in *Fings Ain't Wot They Used T'Be.*

FIRE   August 1968
Arthur Brown / Vincent Crane / Peter Ker / 'Finesilver'
Essex Music Ltd. . . . . UK
The Crazy World of Arthur Brown . . . . **Track 604 022**

FIRE BRIGADE   March 1968
Roy Wood
Essex Music Ltd. . . . . UK
The Move . . . . **Regal Zonophone RZ 3005**

FIRE DOWN BELOW   September 1957
Ned Washington / Lester Lee
Dash Music Ltd. . . . . USA
Film(s): . . . . An Affair in Trinidad / Fire Down Below
Jeri Southern . . . . **Brunswick OE 9340**
Edric Connor . . . . **Oriole CB 1377**
Barbara Lyon . . . . **Columbia DB 3931**
Shirley Bassey . . . . **Philips PB 723**

FIREBALL   December 1971
Ritchie Blackmore / Ian Gillan / Ian Pace / Roger Glover & Jon Lord
Hec Music . . . . UK
Deep Purple . . . . **Harvest SHVL 793**

FIRST CUT IS THE DEEPEST   June 1967
Cat Stevens
Screen Gems Music Ltd. . . . . UK
P.P. Arnold . . . . **Immediate IM 047**
Cat Stevens . . . . **Deram FML 1018**
Rod Stewart . . . . **Riva 7**

FIRST LOVE, LAST LOVE, BEST LOVE   1918
Nat. D. Ayer / Clifford Grey
B. Feldman & Co. Ltd. . . . . UK
Show(s): . . . . The Bing Boys on Broadway
George Robey & Clara Evelyn . . . . **Columbia L 1236**
Violet Loraine . . . . **HMV C 2357**
George Robey & Clara Evelyn appeared in *The Bing Boys On Broadway.*

FIRST LULLABY, THE   1941
Michael Carr / Jack Popplewell
Peter Maurice Music Co. Ltd . . . . UK
Les Allen . . . . **Rex 9944**
Ambrose & his Orchestra, vocal Anne Shelton . . **Decca F 7730**
Doreen Stephens . . . . **RCA BD 923**

FIRST OF MAY, THE   March 1969
Barry Gibb / Robin Gibb / Maurice Gibb
Abigail Music . . . . UK
The Bee Gees . . . . **Polydor 56304**

FIRST ROW BALCONY   October 1956
Ben Raleigh / Sherman Edwards
Lawrence Wright Music Co. Ltd. . . . . USA
The Kaye Sisters . . . . **HMV POP 251**

FIRST TIME, THE   October 1963
Chris Andrews
Glissando Music Ltd . . . . UK
Adam Faith . . . . **Parlophone R 5061**

FIRST TIME, THE   December 1988
Gavin Spencer / Tom Anthony / Terry Boyle
EMI Music . . . . USA
Robin Beck . . . . **Mercury MER 270**

FIRST TIME EVER I SAW YOUR FACE, THE   July 1972
Ewan MacColl
Harmony Music Ltd. . . . . UK
Roberta Flack . . . . **Atlantic K 10161**
Ivor Novello Award.

FIRST TIME I SAW YOU, THE   1937
Nat Shilkret / Allie Wrubel
Campbell Connelly & Co. Ltd. . . . . USA
Film(s): . . . . The Toast of New York
Jimmy Lunceford & his Orchestra . . . . **Brunswick 02491**
Gracie Fields . . . . **Rex 9166**
Lew Stone & his Band, vocal Sam Costa . . . . . . **Decca F 6507**

FISHERMEN OF ENGLAND, THE   1921
Montague F. Philips / Gerald Dodson
Chappell & Co. Ltd . . . . UK
Show(s): . . . . The Rebel Maid
Thorpe Bates . . . . **Columbia F 1073**
Sidney Burchall . . . . **Decca F 7515**
Peter Dawson . . . . **HMV 7EG 8093**
Thorpe Bates appeared in *The Rebel Maid.*

FIT AS A FIDDLE   1933
Arthur Freed / Al Hoffman / Al Goodhart
Francis, Day & Hunter Ltd. . . . . USA
Show(s): . . . . Singin' in the Rain
Film(s): . . . . Singin' in the Rain

Annette Hanshaw	Panachord 25413
Elsie Carlisle	Decca F 3411
Gene Kelly & Donald O'Connor	MGM D 140
Doris Day	Philips BBL 7296
Tommy Steele & Roy Castle	Safari RAIN 1

Gene Kelly & Donald O'Connor appeared in the film *Singin' in the Rain*.

Tommy Steele & Roy Castle appeared in the show *Singin' in the Rain*.

FIVE FIFTEEN   October 1973
Peter Townshend

Fabulous Music Ltd.	UK
Film(s):	Quadrophenia
The Who	Track 2094115

The Who appeared in *Quadrophenia*.

FIVE FOOT TWO, EYES OF BLUE   1926
Sam M. Lewis / Joe Young / Ray Henderson

Francis, Day & Hunter Ltd.	USA
Film(s):	Has Anybody Seen My Gal
The California Ramblers	Riverside RLP 12-801
The Savoy Orpheans	HMV B 5005
The King Brothers	Parlophone PMC 1130

FIVE MINUTES MORE   1947
Jule Styne / Sammy Cahn

Chappell & Co. Ltd.	USA
Show(s):	Piccadilly Hayride
Film(s):	Sweetheart of Sigma Chi
Frank Sinatra	Fontana TFL 5074
The Four Winds	London HLU 8556
Robb Storme	Decca F 11313

FIVE O'CLOCK WHISTLE, THE   1941
Joseph Myrow / Kim Gannon / Gene Irwin

Chappell & Co. Ltd	USA
Jay Wilbur & his Band, vocal Dorothy Carless	Rex 9915
Duke Ellington & his Orch. vocal Ivie Anderson	HMV 7EG 8239
Ella Fitzgerald	Brunswick 03107

FIVE-FOUR-THREE-TWO-ONE   February 1964
Paul Jones / Mike Hugg / Manfred Mann

| Keith Prowse Music Publishing Co. Ltd | UK |
| Manfred Mann | HMV POP 1252 |

FIVE-SEVEN-ZERO-FIVE   August 1978
Lol Mason / Steve Broughton

| Chappell & Co. Ltd | UK |
| City Boy | Vertigo 6059207 |

FLAMINGO   1941
Ted Grouya / Edmund Anderson

Chappell & Co. Ltd	USA
Show(s):	Big Top
Leslie Hutchinson (Hutch)	HMV BD 1003
Earl Bostic & his Orchestra (1953)	Vogue V 2145
Teddi King	Coral FEP 2052
Peter Elliot	Parlophone R 4514
Caterina Valente	Polydor BM 6081

FLANAGAN   1910
C.W. Murphy / William Letters

Francis, Day & Hunter Ltd.	UK
Florrie Forde	Columbia 9780
Jack Hylton Orchestra	Decca K 624
The Big Ben Banjo Band	Columbia 33SX 1188

FLAPPERETTE   1927
Jesse Greer

Lawrence Wright Music Co. Ltd.	USA
Nat Shilkret & his Orchestra	HMV B 2505
Jack Hylton's Kit Kat Band	HMV B 5184
The Harry Breuer Quintet	Audio Fidelity AFLP 1825

FLASH   January 1981
Brian May

| EMI Music | UK |
| Queen | EMI 5126 |

FLASH BANG WALLOP   May 1963
David Heneker

Brittania Music	UK
Show(s):	Half a Sixpence
Tommy Steele	Decca SKL 5421

Tommy Steele appeared in *Half A Sixpence*
Ivor Novello Award.

FLASHBACK   December 1981
Tony Swain / Steve Jolly

| Red Bus Music | UK |
| Imagination | R&B RBS 206 |

FLASHDANCE - WHAT A FEELING   July 1983
Keith Forsey / Irene Cara / Giorgio Moroder

Famous Music	USA
Film(s):	Flashdance
Irene Cara	Casablanca CAN 1016

Academy Award winning song for 1983.

FLAT FOOT FLOOGIE, THE   1938
Slim Gaillard / Slam Stewart / Bud Green

World Wide Music Co. Ltd.	USA
Slim & Slam	Vocalion S 158
'Fats' Waller & his Rhythm	HMV 7EG 8341
Ray Ellington	Nixa NPL 18032

FLEET'S IN PORT AGAIN, THE   1936
Noel Gay

Cinephonic Music Co. Ltd	UK
Show(s):	Okay for a Sound
Jack Hylton & his Orchestra	HMV BD 5102
Billy Cotton & his Band	Decca LF 1124
The Singing Sailors	Decca F 11045

FLEET'S IN, THE   1942
Victor Schertzinger / Johnny Mercer

Victoria Music Co. Ltd	USA
Film(s):	The Fleet's In
The Johnston Brothers	Decca LK 4055
The "Sing It Again" Ensemble	Columbia 33SX 1124

FLIES CRAWLED UP THE WINDOW, THE   1932
Vivian Ellis / Douglas Furber

Chappell & Co. Ltd.	UK
Film(s):	Jack's the Boy
Jack Hulbert	HMV B 4263
Cicely Courtneidge & Jack Hulbert	HMV C 2868

Jack Hulbert appeared in *Jack's The Boy*.

FLIRTATION WALK   1935
Mort Dixon / Allie Wrubel

B. Feldman & Co. Ltd	USA
Film(s):	Flirtation Walk
Dick Powell	Decca F 5650
Gordon MacRae	Capitol T 875

Dick Powell appeared in *Flirtation Walk*.

FLIRTATION WALTZ, THE   January 1952
R. Haywood / Leslie Sarony

Bourne Music Ltd	UK
Frank Chacksfield & his Orchestra	Polydor P 1027
Joe 'Mr. Piano' Henderson	Nixa N 15224
Robert Farnon & his Orchestra	Decca LK 4083

F.L.M.   July 1987
Mike Stock / Matt Aitken / Peter Waterman

| All Boys Music | UK |
| Mel & Kim | Supreme SUPE 113 |

FLOAT ON   September 1977
W. Willis / A. Ingram / J. Mitchell

| Anchor Music Ltd | USA |
| The Floaters | ABC 4187 |

FLORAL DANCE, THE   1911
Katie Moss

Chappell & Co. Ltd	UK
Peter Dawson	Regal T 1005
Peter Dawson	HMV DLP 1180
Stanley Holloway	Riverside RLP 12-824
Brighouse & Rastrick Brass Band (1977)	Transatlantic BIG 548
Terry Wogan	Philips 6006 592

Ivor Novello Nomination 1978.

FLOWERS IN THE RAIN   October 1967
Roy Wood

| Essex Music Ltd. | UK |
| The Move | Regal Zonophone RZ 3001 |

Nancy Sinatra	Reprise K 14138
The Move	PRT Flashback FLB 1001

FLOY JOY   April 1972
William Robinson
Jobete Music (UK) Ltd. .... USA
The Supremes .... **Tamla Motown TMG 804**

FLY ME TO THE MOON (see In Other Words)

FLYING DOWN TO RIO   1934
Gus Kahn / Edward Eliscu / Vincent Youmans
Chappell & Co. Ltd. .... USA
Film(s): .... Flying Down to Rio
Fred Astaire .... **Columbia DB 1329**
Rudy Vallee & his Connecticut Yankees .... **HMV B 6466**
Roger Williams & his Orchestra .... **London HAR 2105**
Fred Astaire appeared in *Flying Down to Rio*.

FLYING DUTCHMAN, THE   1907
Paul Rubens
Chappell & Co. Ltd. .... UK
Show(s): .... Miss Hook of Holland
The Light Opera Company .... **HMV C 1989**
The Zonophone Light Opera Company ..... **Zonophone 5662**

FOG ON THE TYNE   November 1990
Alan Hull
Charisma Music .... UK
Gazza & Lindisfarne .... **Best ZB 44083**

FOGGY DAY, A   1937
George Gershwin / Ira Gershwin
Chappell & Co. Ltd. .... USA
Film(s): .... A Damsel in Distress
Fred Astaire with Ray Noble & his Orchestra   **Philips BBL 7052**
Les Allen .... **Columbia FB 1866**
Fred Astaire .... **London HAR 2219**
Shirley Bassey .... **Columbia SEG 8027**
Frank Sinatra .... **Reprise R 20035**
Fred Astaire appeared in *A Damsel in Distress*.

FOLD YOUR WINGS   1935
Ivor Novello / Christopher Hassell
Chappell & Co. Ltd .... UK
Show(s): .... Glamorous Night
Film(s): .... Glamorous Night
Mary Ellis & Trefor Jones .... **HMV DLP 1095**
Julie Bryan & Ivor Emanuel .... **HMV CLP 1258**
Mary Ellis & Trefor Jones appeared in both the show and the film of *Glamorous Night*.

FOLK SINGER, THE   April 1963
Mark Kilgore
Shapiro-Bermstein & Co. Ltd .... USA
Tommy Roe .... **HMV POP 1138**
Jimmy Justice .... **Pye NPL 18085**

FOLKS WHO LIVE ON THE HILL, THE   1000
Jerome Kern / Oscar Hammerstein II
Chappell & Co. Ltd. .... USA
Film(s): .... High Wide and Handsome
Bing Crosby .... **Brunswick 02484**
Roy Fox & his Orchestra, vocal Denny Dennis .. **HMV BD 5270**
Peggy Lee .... **Capitol T 864**
Michael Holliday .... **Columbia 33SX 1170**

FOLLOW THAT DREAM   June 1962
Ben Wiseman / Fred Wise
Seventeen Saville Row Ltd. .... USA
Film(s): .... Follow That Dream
Elvis Presley .... **RCA RCX 211**
Elvis Presley appeared in *Follow That Dream*.

FOLLOW THE SWALLOW   1925
Ray Henderson / Billy Rose / Mort Dixon
Francis, Day & Hunter Ltd. .... USA
Jack Hylton & his Orchestra .... **HMV B 1940**

FOLLOW YOU FOLLOW ME   April 1978
Michael Rutherford / Phil Collins / Tony Banks
Hit & Run Music .... UK
Genesis .... **Charisma CB 309**

FOLLOWING IN FATHER'S FOOTSTEPS   1902
E.W. Rogers
Francis, Day & Hunter Ltd. .... UK
Film(s): .... After the Ball
Alf Gordon .... **Zonophone 42258**
Jack Hylton & his Orchestra .... **HMV C 1783**
Ray Wallace .... **Parlophone R 1147**

FOLLOWING THE SUN AROUND   1929
Joseph McCarthy / Harry Tierney
Francis, Day & Hunter Ltd .... USA
Show(s): .... Rio Rita
Film(s): .... Rio Rita
Geoffrey Gwyther .... **Columbia DB 115**
Eve Boswell .... **Parlophone PMC 1105**
Geoffrey Gwyther appeared in the British production of *Rio Rita*.

FOOL   September 1973
James Last / Carl Sigman
Intersong Music .... Germany
Elvis Presley .... **RCA 2393**

FOOL (If You Think It's Over)   November 1978
Chris Rea
Magnet Music .... UK
Chris Rea .... **Magnet MAG 111**
Elkie Brooks (1982) .... **A&M AMS 8187**

FOOL AM I, A (Dimmelo Parlami)   November 1966
F. Carravesi / Peter Callander
Shapiro-Bernstein & Co. Ltd. .... Italy
Cilla Black .... **Parlophone R 5515**

FOOL FOR YOUR LOVIN'   May 1980
David Coverdale / Bernie Marsden / Mike Moody
Seabreeze Music .... UK
Whitesnake .... **United Artists BP 352**

FOOL SUCH AS I, A   May 1959
Bill Trader
Leeds Music Ltd .... USA
Elvis Presley .... **RCA RD 27159**
Tommy Edwards .... **MGM C 774**
Slim Whitman .... **Lodon HAP 2343**

FOOL TO CRY, A   June 1976
Keith Richard / Mick Jagger
Essex Music Ltd .... UK
The Rolling Stones .... **Rolling Stones RS 19121**

FOOLISH BEAT   July 1988
Debbie Gibson
EMI Music .... USA
Debbie Gibson .... **Atlantic A 9059**

FOOLS RUSH IN   1940
Johnny Mercer / Rube Bloom
Cavendish Music Co. Ltd .... USA
Tony Martin .... **Decca F 7557**
Vera Lynn .... **MGM C 843**
Tommy Dorsey & his Orchestra,
vocal Frank Sinatra .... **RCA RD 27104**
Brook Benton .... **Mercury MMC 14060**
Rick Nelson (1963) .... **Brunswick 05895**

FOOT TAPPER   April 1963
Hank B. Marvin / Bruce Welch
Elstree Music Ltd .... UK
Film(s): .... Summer Holiday
The Shadows .... **Columbia DB 4984**
The Shadows appeared in *Summer Holiday*.

FOOTLOOSE   May 1984
Dean Pitchford / Kenny Loggins
MCA Music Ltd. .... USA
Film(s): .... Footloose
Kenny Loggins .... **CBS A 4101**
Nominated for an Academy Award 1984.

FOOTSEE   February 1975
Nick Bohonos / John Peters
Planetary-Nom (London) Ltd .... USA
Wigan's Chosen Few .... **Pye DDS 111**

FOOTSTEPS   May 1960
Barry Mann / Hank Hunter
Nevins-Kirshner Ltd . . . . USA
Steve Lawrence . . . . **HMV POP 726**
Ronnie Carroll . . . . **Philips PB 1004**

FOR ALL WE KNOW   1934
Sam M. Lewis / J. Fred Coots
Francis, Day & Hunter Ltd . . . . USA
Greta Keller . . . . **Decca F 5216**
The Andrews Sisters . . . . **Brunswick 03290**
Joan Regan . . . . **Decca LK 4153**
Joannie Sommers . . . . **Warner Brothers WM 4045**

FOR ALL WE KNOW   October 1971
Fred Karlin / Arthur James / Robb Wilson
Leeds Music Ltd . . . . USA
Film(s): . . . . Lovers and Other Strangers
Shirley Bassey . . . . **United Artists UP 35267**
The Carpenters . . . . **A&M AMS 864**
Nominated for an Academy Award 1970.

FOR AMERICA   November 1986
Clark Toulson
Warner Brothers Music . . . . UK
Red Box . . . . **Sire YZ 84**

FOR EVERY MAN THERE'S A WOMAN   November 1948
Harold Arlen / Leo Robin
Edwin H. Morris & Co. Ltd. . . . . USA
Film(s): . . . . Casbah
Tony Martin . . . . **HMV B 9685**
Sammy Davis . . . . **Brunswick LAT 8330**
Tony Martin . . . . **RCA RD 27003**
Tony Bennett . . . . **Philips BBL 7455**
Tony Martin appeared in *Casbah*.
Nominated for an Academy Award 1948.

FOR ME AND MY GAL   1917
Edgar Leslie / Ray Goetz / George W. Meyer
B. Feldman & Co. Ltd. . . . . USA
Show(s): . . . . Here and There
Film(s): . . . . For Me & My Gal / Jolson Sings Again
The Savoy Quartette . . . . **HMV B 896**
Judy Garland & Gene Kelly . . . . **Brunswick LA 8725**
Al Jolson . . . . **Brunswick LAT 8267**
Kathie Kay & Billy Cotton . . . . . . **Columbia 33SX 1278**
Judy Garland . . . . **Capitol T 1118**
Judy Garland & Gene Kelly appeared in *For Me and My Gal*.

FOR OLD TIMES' SAKE   1898
Charles Osborne
Francis, Day & Hunter Ltd. . . . . UK
Florrie Forde . . . . **Rex 8258**
David Kossoff . . . . **Oriole MG 20043**

FOR OLD TIMES' SAKE   1929
Buddy De Sylva / Lew Brown / Ray Henderson
Campbell Connelly & Co. Ltd . . . . UK
Layton & Johnstone . . . . **Columbia 5198**

FOR ONCE IN MY LIFE   February 1969
Ron Miller / Orlando Murden
Jobete Music (UK) Ltd. . . . . USA
Stevie Wonder . . . . **Tamla Motown TMG 679**
Tony Bennett . . . . **CBS 3064**
Dorothy Squires . . . . **President PT 267**

FOR SENTIMENTAL REASONS   1947
Deke Watson / William Best
Peter Maurice Music Co. Ltd. . . . . USA
Ella Fitzgerald & The Delta Rhythm Boys . . **Brunswick 04312**
Eve Boswell . . . . **Parlophone R 4401**
Dinah Shore . . . . **Columbia DB 2247**
Vera Lynn . . . . **MGM C 843**
Frankie Avalon . . . . **HMV CLP 1423**

FOR THE FIRST TIME I'VE FALLEN IN LOVE   1944
Dave Kapp / Charles Tobias
Keith Prowse Music Publishing Co. Ltd. . . . . USA
Carroll Gibbons & The Savoy Hotel
Orpheans, vocal Edna Kaye . . . . **Columbia FB 2985**
Dich Haymes . . . . **Brunswick 03497**
Roger Williams & his Orchestra . . . . **London HLR 8422**

FOR THE GOOD TIMES   October 1973
Kris Kristofferson
Valentine Music Group . . . . USA
Perry Como . . . . **RCA 2402**
Kris Kristofferson . . . . **Monument 64631**

FOR YOU   1931
Al Dubin / Joe Burke
B. Feldman & Co. Ltd. . . . . USA
Film(s): . . . . Holy Terror
Debroy Somers & his Orchestra . . . . **Columbia CB 373**
Perry Como (1949) . . . . **HMV BD 6033**
Steve Conway (1949) . . . . **Columbia FB 3463**
Julie London . . . . **London HAU 2112**

FOR YOU ALONE   1909
Henry Geehl / P.J. O'Reilly
Leonard A. Gould Publishing . . . . UK
Enrico Caruso . . . . **HMV DA 108**
Richard Crooks . . . . **HMV DA 1163**
Lauritz Melchior . . . . **MGM 112**
Kenneth McKellar . . . . **Decca SKL 5269**

FOR YOU, FOR ME, FOR EVERYONE   1947
George Gershwin / Ira Gershwin
Victoria Music Co. Ltd. . . . . USA
Film(s): . . . . The Shocking Miss Pilgrim
Dick Haymes . . . . **Brunswick 03776**
Ella Fitzgerald . . . . **HMV CLP 1347**
Dick Haymes appeared in *The Shocking Miss Pilgrim*.

FOR YOUR EYES ONLY   August 1981
Bill Conti / Michael Leeson
United Artists Music . . . . USA
Film(s): . . . . For Your Eyes Only
Sheena Easton . . . . **EMI 5195**
Nominated for an Academy Award 1981.
Ivor Novello Nomination.

FOREVER   February 1974
Roy Wood
Carlin Music Corporation . . . . UK
Roy Wood . . . . **Harvest HAR 5078**

FOREVER AND EVER   June 1949
Franz Winkler / Malia Rosa
Francis, Day & Hunter Ltd . . . . Germany
Russ Morgan & his Orchestra . . . **Brunswick LAT 8370**
Dinah Shore . . . . **Columbia DB 2529**
Perry Como . . . . **Camden CDN 110**
The Franz Winkler Quartet . . . . **Decca C 16006**

FOREVER AND EVER   February 1976
Bill Martin / Phil Coulter
Martin-Coulter Music Ltd . . . . UK
Slik . . . . **Bell 1464**

FOREVER AUTUMN   August 1978
Paul Vigrass / Gary Osborne / Jeff Wayne
Leeds Music Ltd . . . . UK
Justin Hayward . . . . **CBS 6368**
Vigrass & Osborne . . . . **UNI UNS 5044**

FOREVER KIND OF LOVE, A   December 1962
Gerry Goffin / Jack Keller
Aldon Music Ltd. . . . . USA
Bobby Vee . . . . **Liberty LIB 10046**
Cliff Richard . . . . **Columbia SEG 8347**

FOREVER LIVE AND DIE   October 1986
"Orchestral Manoeuvres in the Dark"
Virgin Music . . . . UK
Orchestral Manoeuvres in the Dark . . . . **Virgin VS 888**

FORGET ABOUT YOU   September 1978
Andy McMaster
Island Music Ltd . . . . UK
The Motors . . . . **Virgin VS 222**

FORGET HIM   June 1963
Mack Anthony
Welbeck Music Co. Ltd . . . . UK
Bobby Rydell . . . . **Cameo-Parkway C 108**
Adam Faith . . . . **Parlophone PMC 1213**

FORGET ME NOT   December 1952
Johnny Reine / Johnny May / William Sinclair
Michael Reine Music . . . . UK
Vera Lynn . . . . **Decca F 9985**

FORGET ME NOT   February 1962
Les Vandyke
Essex Music Ltd. . . . . UK
Eden Kane . . . . **Decca F 11418**
Bobby Vee . . . . **Liberty LBY 1084**

FORGET ME NOTS   May 1982
Patrice Rushen / Fred Washington / Terry McFadden
Rachel Music . . . . USA
Patrice Rushen . . . . **Elektra K 13173**

FORGIVE ME   1927
Jack Yellen / Milton Ager
Lawrence Wright Music Co. Ltd. . . . . USA
Nat Shilkret & his Orchestra . . . . **HMV B 5284**
Pat Boone . . . . **London HAD 2030**
Peggy Lee . . . . **Brunswick 04939**

FORGOTTEN DREAMS   June 1957
Leroy Anderson
Mills Music Ltd. . . . . USA
Leroy Anderson & his Orchestra . . . . **Brunswick LAT 8049**
Joe 'Mr. Piano' Henderson . . . . **Pye NPT 19022**
The Mantovani Orchestra . . . . **Decca LK 4377**

FORT WORTH JAIL   May 1959
Dick Reinhart
Peter Maurice Music Co. Ltd . . . . USA
Woody Herman & his Woodchoppers . . . . . . **Brunswick 03459**
Lonnie Donegan . . . . **Nixa NEP 24114**
Skeets McDonald . . . . **Capitol EAP 1-1040**

FORTY MILES OF BAD ROAD   September 1959
Duane Eddy / Al Casey
Burlington Music Co. Ltd . . . . USA
Duane Eddy (guitar) . . . . **London HAW 2325**

FORTY-SECOND STREET   1933
Al Dubin / Harry Warren
B. Feldman & Co. Ltd. . . . . USA
Film(s): . . . . Forty-Second Street
Norrie Paramor & his Orchestra . . . **Columbia 33S 1098**
Dick Powell & Ruby Keeler . . . . **United Artists UAG 29421**
The Boswell Sisters . . . . **Brunswick 01376**
Dick Powell & Ruby Keeler appeared in *Forty-Second Street*.

FORTY-SEVEN GINGER HEADED SAILORS   1928
Leslie Sarony
Montgomery Successors Ltd. . . . . UK
Show(s): . . . . Clowns in Clover
Cicely Courtneidge . . . . **Columbia 5176**
Jack Hylton & his Orchestra . . . . **HMV B 5542**
Cicely Courtneidge appeared in *Clowns in Clover*.

FORTYEIGHT CRASH   August 1973
Mike Chapman / Nicky Chinn
Rak Music Ltd. . . . . UK
Suzi Quatro . . . . **Rak 158**

FOUR IN THE MORNING (see It's Four In The Morning)

FOUR LETTER WORD, A   January 1989
Marty Wilde / Ricky Wilde
Rickim Music . . . . UK
Kim Wilde . . . . **MCA KIM 10**

FOUR LITTLE HEELS   November 1960
Lee Pockriss / Paul Vance
Tin Pan Alley Music Co. Ltd . . . . USA
Brian Hyland . . . . **London HLR 9203**
The Avons . . . . **Columbia DB 4522**

FOUR WINDS AND THE SEVEN SEAS   September 1949
Don Rodney / Hal David
Bregman, Vocco & Conn Ltd . . . . USA
Mel Tormé . . . . **Capitol CL 13148**
Bing Crosby . . . . **Brunswick 04260**

FOX ON THE RUN   April 1975
Brian Connelly / Steve Priest / Mick Turner & Andy Scott

Essex Music Ltd . . . . UK
The Sweet . . . . **RCA 2524**

FOX ON THE RUN   February 1969
Tony Hazzard
Mann Music Publishers Ltd. . . . . UK
Manfred Mann . . . . **Fontana TF 985**
Hazzard & Barnes . . . . **Warner Brothers K 16724**

FRANKIE   July 1985
Denise Rich
I.D.G. Music . . . . USA
Sister Sledge . . . . **Atlantic A 9547**

FRANKLIN D. ROOSEVELT JONES   1939
Harold Rome
Chappell & Co. Ltd. . . . . USA
Show(s): . . . . Sing Out the News / The Little Dog Laughed
Film(s): . . . . Babes on Broadway
Flanagan & Allen . . . . **Decca LF 1125**
Judy Garland . . . . **Brunswick 03305**
Glenn Miller & his Orchestra . . . . **RCA RD 27057**
Flanagan & Allen appeared in *The Little Dog Laughed*.
Judy Garland appeared in *Babes on Broadway*.

FRASQUITA SERENADE (see Serenade Frasquita)

FREAK, LE   January 1979
Nile Rodgers / Bernard Edwards
Warner Brothers Music Ltd. . . . . USA
Chic . . . . **Atlantic K 11209**

FREE   May 1977
Deniece Williams / Susaye Green / Hank Redd & Nathan Watts
Island Music Ltd . . . . UK
Deniece Williams . . . . **CBS 4978**

FREEDOM   November 1984
George Michael
Morrison Leahy Music . . . . UK
Wham . . . . **Epic A 4743**

FREEDOM COME FREEDOM GO   October 1971
*Roger Greenaway / Roger Cook / Albert Hammond & Mike Hazle-
wood*
Cookaway Music . . . . UK
The Fortunes . . . . **Capitol CL 15693**
Ivor Novello Nomination.

FREIGHT TRAIN   May 1957
Paul James / Fred Williams
Pan-Musik Ltd. . . . . USA
The Charles McDevitt Skiffle Group,
   vocal Nancy Whiskey . . . . **Oriole EP 7002**
Rusty Draper . . . . **Mercury MPT 7523**

FRENCH CAN CAN POLKA   March 1950
Jacques Offenbach / Jimmy Kennedy
Campbell Connelly & Co. Ltd . . . . France
Michel Legrand & his Orchestra . . . . **Felsted ESD 3009**
Billy Cotton & his Band . . . . **Decca DFE 6224**
Ethel Smith (organ), vocal The Smith Singers . **Brunswick 04479**
Adapted from "Orpheus in the Underworld" by Jacques Offenbach
(1819 - 1880).
See also Can-Can

FRENCH KISS   August 1989
Lil Louis
Polygram Music . . . . UK
Lil Louis . . . . **London F 115**

FRENCH KISSIN' IN THE USA   December 1986
Chuck Lorre
EMI Music . . . . USA
Debbie Harry . . . . **Chrysalis CHS 3066**

FRENCH MILITARY MARCHING SONG   1927
Sigmund Romberg / Otto Harbach / Oscar Hammerstein II
Chappell & Co. Ltd . . . . USA
Show(s): . . . . The Desert Song
Film(s): . . . . The Desert Song
Dorett Morrow . . . . **Philips BBL 7212**
Edith Day . . . . **Columbia 9211**
Lucille Norman . . . . **Capitol LC 6606**
Edith Day appeared in the British production of *The Desert Song*

FRENESI 1941
Alberto Dominguez / Bob Russell / Ray Charles
Southern Music Publishing Co. Ltd .... Mexico
Artie Shaw & his Orchestra .... **RCA RCX 1011**
Xavier Cugat & his Orchestra .... **Philips BBL 7284**
Perez Prado & his Orchestra .... **RCA RD 27046**
Mel Tormé .... **HMV CLP 1315**

FRESH December 1984
James Taylor
Warner Chappell Music .... UK
Kool & The Gang .... **Phonogram DE 18**

FRIDAY NIGHT May 1983
Billy Falcon
April Music Ltd .... USA
Billy Falcon's Burning Rose .... **Philips 9103450**
The Kids From Fame .... **RCA 320**

FRIDAY ON MY MIND December 1966
George Young / Harry Vanda
United Artists Music Co. Ltd. .... USA
The Easybeats .... **United Artists UP 1157**

FRIEND O' MINE 1913
Frederick E. Weatherly / Wilfred Sanderson
Boosey & Hawkes Music Publishers Ltd. .... UK
Peter Dawson .... **HMV B 3839**
Kenneth Walters .... **Regal Zonophone G 8319**
Dennis Noble .... **HMV B 9125**
Owen Brannigan .... **HMV CLP 3639**

FRIEND OF YOURS, A 1945
Johnny Burke / Jimmy Van Heusen
Chappell & Co. Ltd. .... USA
Film(s): .... A Man Called Sullivan
Bing Crosby .... **Brunswick 03589**
Joe Loss & his Orchestra .... **HMV BD 5895**
Lena Horne .... **RCA RD 27141**

FRIEND OR FOE October 1982
Adam Ant / Marco Pirroni
EMI Music .... UK
Adam & The Ants .... **CBS A 2736**

FRIENDLY PERSUASION January 1957
Dimitri Tiomkin / Paul Francis Webster
Robbins Music Corporation Ltd. .... USA
Film(s): .... Friendly Persuasion
Pat Boone .... **London HAD 2098**
The Four Aces .... **Brunswick LAT 8249**
Nominated for an Academy Award 1956.

FRIENDS 1935
Stanley Damerell / Tolchard Evans
Sydney Bron Music Co Ltd .... UK
The Masqueraders .... **Columbia FB 1063**
Ambrose & his Orchestra .... **Decca F 5599**

FRIENDS January 1970
Terry Reid
Carlin Music Corporation .... UK
Arrival .... **Decca F 12986**

FRIENDS December 1982
William Shelby / Glen Barbee / Nidra Beard
Chappell & Co. Ltd .... USA
Shalamar .... **Solar CHUM 1**

FRIENDS January 1985
Mike Francis
Screen Gems Music .... UK
Amii Stewart .... **RCA 471**

FRIENDS AND NEIGHBOURS May 1954
Malcolm Lockyer / Marvin Scott
Michael Reine Music Co. Ltd. .... UK
Billy Cotton & his Band .... **Decca LF 1244**
Max Bygraves .... **HMV 7EG 8271**

FRIENDS WILL BE FRIENDS July 1986
Freddie Mercury / John Deacon
EMI Music .... UK
Queen .... **EMI QUEEN 8**

FRIENDSHIP 1942
Cole Porter
Chappell & Co. Ltd .... USA
Show(s): .... Dubarry Was a Lady
Film(s): .... Dubarry Was a Lady
Ethel Merman .... **Reprise R 6032**
Judy Garland & Johnny Mercer ...... **Brunswick 03393**
Ethel Merman was in the American production of *Dubarry Was A Lady*.

FRIGHTENED CITY, THE June 1961
Norrie Paramor
Filmusic Publishing Co. Ltd .... UK
Film(s): .... The Frightened City
The Shadows .... **Columbia DB 4637**

FROM A DISTANCE October 1990
Julie Gold
Rondor Music .... USA
Cliff Richard .... **EMI EM 155**
Bette Midler .... **Atlantic A 7820**

FROM A JACK TO A KING April 1963
Ned Miller
Burlington Music Co. Ltd .... USA
Ned Miller .... **London HL 9658**
Bobby Darin .... **Capitol T 1942**

FROM A WINDOW August 1964
John Lennon / Paul McCartney
Northern Songs .... UK
Billy J. Kramer .... **Parlophone R 5156**

FROM HERE TO ETERNITY December 1953
Fred Karger / Robert Wells
Dash Music Ltd. .... USA
Frank Sinatra .... **Capitol LCT 6123**
The Columbia Pictures Orchestra ...... **Brunswick LAT 8170**

FROM HERE TO ETERNITY November 1977
Giorgio Moroder / Pete Bellotte
Heath Levy Music Ltd .... USA
Giorgio .... **Oasis 1**

FROM ME TO YOU June 1963
John Lennon / Paul McCartney
Northern Songs Ltd .... UK
The Beatles .... **Parlophone R 5015**

FROM NEW YORK TO L.A. October 1977
Gilles Vignault / Gene Williams
Dick James Music Ltd .... France
Patsy Gallant .... **EMI 2620**

FROM RUSSIA WITH LOVE November 1963
Lionel Bart
United Artists Music Co. Ltd .... UK
Film(s): .... From Russia With Love
Sound Track Orchestra,
conducted by John Barry .... **United Artists ULP 1052**
Matt Monro .... **Parlophone R 5068**
Kenny Ball & his Jazzmen .... **Pye 7NJ 2070**

FROM THE TIME YOU SAY GOODBYE July 1952
Leslie Sturdy
Pickwick Music Ltd .... UK
Vera Lynn .... **Ace of Clubs ACL 1045**
Dinah Shore .... **HMV B 10299**
Gary Miller .... **Columbia DB 3111**

**FROM THE TOP OF YOUR HEAD (To The Tip Of Your
Toes)** 1935
Mack Gordon / Harry Revel
Victoria Music Co. Ltd .... USA
Film(s): .... Two for Tonight
Bing Crosby & The Dorsey Brothers Orch. .. **Brunswick Bing 1**
Ambrose & his Orchestra .... **Decca F 5751**
Bing Crosby appeared in *Two for Tonight*.

FROM THE UNDERWORLD October 1967
Howard Blaikley
Lynn Music .... UK
The Herd .... **Fontana TF 856**

FROM THE VINE CAME THE GRAPE March 1954
Leonard Whitcup / Paul Cunningham

Victoria Music Co. Ltd. . . . . USA
Frankie Vaughan . . . . **HMV B 10655**
The Hilltoppers . . . . **London HAD 2071**
Suzi Miller . . . . **Decca F 10275**

FROM THIS MOMENT ON   **July 1951**
Cole Porter
Chappell & Co. Ltd . . . . USA
Film(s): . . . . Kiss Me Kate
Frank Sinatra . . . . **Capitol LCT 6135**
Lena Horne . . . . **RCA RD 27021**
Mel Tormé . . . . **Vogue LVA 9004**
Tommy Rall, Ann Miller & Bobby Van . . . . **MGM C 753**
Tommy Rall, Ann Miller & Bobby Van appeared in *Kiss Me Kate*.

FROSTY THE SNOWMAN   **February 1951**
Steve Nelson / Jack Rollins
Aberbach (London) Ltd. . . . . USA
Gene Autry . . . . **Columbia FB 3584**
Vaughn Monroe . . . . **HMV B 9985**
Perry Como . . . . **RCA RCX 120**

FROZEN ORANGE JUICE   **July 1969**
Peter Sarstedt
Mortimer Music Co. . . . . UK
Peter Sarstedt . . . . **United Artists UP 35021**

FUHRER'S FACE, DER   **1943**
Oliver Wallace
Southern Music Publishing Co. Ltd . . . . USA
Film(s): . . . . Der Fuhrer's Face
Spike Jones & his City Slickers . . . . **HMV BD 5787**
Tommy Trinder . . . . **Columbia FB 2885**
Geraldo & his Orchestra . . . . **Parlophone F 1960**

FULL METAL JACKET   **October 1987**
Abigail Mead / Nigel Goulding
Warner Brothers Music . . . . USA
Film(s): . . . . Full Metal Jacket
Abigail Mead & Nigel Goulding . . . . . **Warner Brothers W 8187**

FULL MOON AND EMPTY ARMS   **1946**
Buddy Kaye / Ted Mossman
Boosey & Hawkes Music Publishers Ltd. . . . . USA
Frank Sinatra . . . . **Philips BBL 7180**
The Norman Luboff Choir . . . . **Philips BBL 7337**
Based on piano concerto No.2 in C minor opus 18 by Sergi Rachmaninov (1873 - 1943).

FUNERAL PYRE   **July 1981**
"The Jam"
Chappell & Co. Ltd . . . . UK
The Jam . . . . **Polydor POSP 257**

FUNKIN' FOR JAMAICA   **August 1980**
Tom Brown / Toni Smith
Intersong Music . . . . USA
Tom Brown (trumpet) . . . . **Arista ARIST 357**

FUNKY GIBBON, THE   **April 1975**
Bill Oddie
A.T.V. Music Ltd. . . . . UK
The Goodies . . . . **Bradleys BRAD 7504**

FUNKY MOPED, THE   **October 1975**
Chris Rohmann / Jasper Carrott
B. Feldman & Co. Ltd . . . . UK
Jasper Carrott . . . . **DJM DJS 388**
Chris Rohmann . . . . **Old Fangled OLDF 1**

FUNKY TOWN   **June 1980**
Steven Greenberg
Intersong Music . . . . USA
Lipps Inc . . . . **Casablanca CAN 194**
Pseudo Echo (1987) . . . . **RCA PB 49705**

FUNKY WEEKEND   **March 1976**
Hugo Peretti / Luigi Creatore
Cyril Shane Music . . . . USA
The Stylistics . . . . **Avco 6105044**

FUNNY FACE   **1928**
George Gershwin / Ira Gershwin
Chappell & Co. Ltd . . . . USA
Show(s): . . . . Funny Face

Film(s): . . . . Funny Face
George Gershwin (piano) . . . . **Columbia 5109**
Fred & Adele Astaire . . . . **Columbia 5174**
Fred Astaire . . . . **HMV CLP 1119**
Barbara Windsor . . . . **HMV POP 833**
Adele Astaire appeared in both the American and British productions of *Funny Face*.
Fred Astaire appeared in both the American and British productions and also the film of *Funny Face.*

FUNNY FAMILIAR FORGOTTEN FEELINGS   **June 1967**
Mickey Newbury
Acuff-Rose Publishing Co. Ltd. USA
Tom Jones . . . . **Decca F 12599**
Don Gibson . . . . **RCA SF 8005**

FUNNY FUNNY   **April 1971**
Mike Chapman / Nicky Chinn
April Music Ltd . . . . UK
The Sweet . . . . **RCA 2051**

FUNNY HOW LOVE CAN BE   **March 1965**
John Carter / Ken Lewis
Southern Music Publishing Co. Ltd . . . . UK
The Ivy League . . . . **Piccadilly 7N 35222**

FUNNY OLD HILLS, THE   **1939**
Leo Robin / Ralph Rainger
Victoria Music Co. Ltd. . . . . USA
Film(s): . . . . Paris Honeymoon
Bing Crosby . . . . **Brunswick Bing 4**
Oscar Rabin & his Band . . . . **Rex 9550**
Freddy Martin & his Orchestra . . . . **Regal Zonophone MR 2995**
Bing Crosby appeared in *Paris Honeymoon.*

FUTURE MRS 'AWKINS, THE   **1892**
Albert Chevalier
Reynolds & Co. Ltd . . . . UK
Albert Chevalier . . . . **HMV D 374**
Reg Grant . . . . **Parlophone E 6186**
Bill Owen . . . . **Decca LK 4628**

G'BYE NOW   **1943**
Ole Olsen / Chic Johnson / Ray Evans & Jay Levison
Campbell Connelly & Co. Ltd . . . . USA
Film(s): . . . . Hellzapoppin
Martha Tilton . . . . **Brunswick 03465**

G.I. JIVE, THE   **1944**
Johnny Mercer
Sterling Music Publishing Co. Ltd. . . . . USA
Glenn Miller & The U.S. Army Air Force Band . . **RCA RD 27135**

G.T.O.   **January 1988**
Mike Stock / Matt Aitken / Peter Waterman
All Boys Music . . . . UK
Sinitta . . . . **Fanfare FAN 14**

GABY GLIDE, THE   **1911**
Louis Hirsch / Harry Pilcer
B.Feldman & Co. Ltd . . . . USA
Show(s): . . . . Vera Violetta / Hullo Ragtime
The Bohemian Band . . . . **HMV B 161**
The Jolly Old Fellows . . . . **Regal Zonophone MR 113**
Jack Manning . . . . **Columbia 2100**

GAL IN CALICO, A   **1947**
Arthur Schwartz / Leo Robin
B. Feldman & Co. Ltd. . . . . USA
Film(s): . . . . The Time, the Place and the Girl
Bing Crosby . . . . **Brunswick 03775**
Tony Martin . . . . **Mercury MMC 14025**
Nominated for an Academy Award 1946.

GAL WITH THE YALLER SHOES, THE   **August 1959**
Sammy Cahn / Nicholas Brodsky
Robbins Music Corporation Ltd . . . . USA
Film(s): . . . . Meet Me in Las Vegas
Michael Holliday . . . . **Columbia SEG 7683**

GALLOPING MAJOR, THE   **1906**
George Bastow / Fred W. Leigh
Francis, Day & Hunter . . . . UK
Film(s): . . . . The Galloping Major
Harry Fay . . . . **HMV B 4011**

Stanley Holloway . . . . Pye NPL 18056

GALVESTON   June 1969
Jim Webb
Carlin Music Corporation . . . . USA
Glen Campbell . . . . Ember S 263

GALWAY BAY   June 1948
Arthur Colahan
Box & Cox (Publications) Ltd. . . . . UK
Bing Crosby . . . . Brunswick LAT 8278
Eileen Donaghy . . . . Fontana TFL 5036

GAMBLER   October 1985
Madonna Ciccone
Warner Brothers Music . . . . USA
Madonna . . . . Geffen A 6585

GAME OF LOVE, THE   March 1965
Clint Ballard
Shapiro-Bernstein & Co. Ltd . . . . USA
Wayne Fontana & The Mindbenders . . . . Fontana TF 535

GAMES PEOPLE PLAY   April 1969
Joe South
Lowery Music Co. . . . . USA
Joe South . . . . Capitol CL 15579

GAMES WITHOUT FRONTIERS   March 1980
Peter Gabriel
Hit and Run Music . . . . UK
Peter Gabriel . . . . Charisma CB 354

GANDY DANCERS BALL, THE   May 1952
Paul Weston / Paul Mason Howard
Walt Disney Music Co. Ltd . . . . USA
Film(s): . . . . Bring Your Smile Along
Frankie Laine . . . . Columbia SEG 7505
The Weavers . . . . Brunswick 04920
Frankie Laine appeared in *Bring Your Smile Along.*

GANG THAT SANG "HEART OF MY HEART", THE   1954
Ben Ryan
Francis, Day & Hunter Ltd. . . . . USA
Frankie Laine . . . . Oriole MG 10001
Max Bygraves . . . . HMV B 10654
The Coronets . . . . Columbia DB 3442
Vera Lynn . . . . Decca LK 4120
Mitch Miller & the Gang . . . . Philips BBL 7404

GANGSTERS   September 1979
Jerry Dammers
Plangent Visions Music . . . . UK
The Specials . . . . 2-Tone TT 1

GANGWAY   1937
Sol Lerner / Al Goodhard / Al Hoffman
Cinephonic Music Co. Ltd. . . . . UK
Film(s): . . . . Gangway
Jessie Matthews . . . . Decca F 6571
Jessie Matthews appeared in *Gangway.*

GARDEN IN THE RAIN, A   1928
Jimmy Dyrenforth / Carroll Gibbons
Campbell Connelly & Co. Ltd. . . . . UK
George Metaxa . . . . HMV B 2801
The Four Aces . . . . Brunswick 04883
Perry Como (1947) . . . . HMV BD 1156
Connie Francis . . . . MGM C 782

GARDEN OF EDEN, THE   January 1957
Dennise Norwood
Duchess Music Ltd. . . . . USA
Frankie Vaughan . . . . Philips BBL 7233
Matt Monro . . . . Ace of Clubs ACL 1069

GARDEN OF LOVE, THE   1904
Andre Messager / Lilian Eldee / Percy Greenbank
Chappell & Co. Ltd. . . . . France
Show(s): . . . . Veronique
Olive Groves . . . . Decca F 2361

GASOLINE ALLEY BRED   October 1970
Roger Cook / Roger Greenaway / Tony Macaulay
Cookaway Music . . . . UK

The Hollies . . . . Parlophone R 5862

GAUCHO SERENADE, THE   1940
James Cavanaugh / John Redmond / Nat Simon
B. Feldman & Co. Ltd. . . . . USA
Joe Loss & his Orchestra,
   vocal Chick Henderson . . . . Regal Zonophone MR 3232
David Rose & his Orchestra . . . . MGM EP 506

GAY CABALLERO, A   1929
Frank Crumit / Lou Klein
Campbell Connelly & Co. Ltd . . . . USA
Film(s): . . . . Dance Fools Dance
Frank Crumit . . . . HMV 7EG 8181

GAYE   August 1973
Clifford T. Ward
Island Music Ltd. . . . . UK
Clifford T. Ward . . . . Charisma CB 205

GEE BABY   October 1974
Peter Shelley
Magnet Music . . . . UK
Peter Shelley . . . . Magnet MAG 12

GEE WHIZ, IT'S YOU   May 1961
Hank B. Marvin / Ian Samwell
Belinda (London) Ltd . . . . UK
Cliff Richard . . . . Columbia SEG 8078

GENDARMES DUET, THE   1933
Jacques Offenbach
Unknown Publisher . . . . France
Show(s): . . . . Genevieve De Brabant
Malcolm MacEachern & Harold Williams . . . . Columbia DX 585
Robert Tear & Benjamin Luxon . . . . EMI 2095

GENERAL'S FAST ASLEEP, THE   1935
Jimmy Kennedy / Michael Carr
Peter Maurice Music Co. Ltd . . . . UK
Elsie Carlisle . . . . Decca F 5761
Lew Stone Orchestra . . . . World Records SH 178

GENIE WITH THE LIGHT BROWN LAMP   January 1965
Hank B. Marvin / Bruce Welch / John Rostill & Brian Bennett
Shadows Music Ltd . . . . UK
Show(s): . . . . Aladin and his Wonderful Lamp
The Shadows . . . . Columbia DB 7416
The Shadows appeared in *Aladin and his Wonderful Lamp.*

GENO   May 1980
Kevin Rowland / Kevin Archer
EMI Music Ltd . . . . UK
Dexy's Midnight Runners . . . . Parlophone R 6033

GENTLE ON MY MIND   April 1969
John Hartford
Acuff-Rose Publishing Co. Ltd. . . . . USA
Dean Martin . . . . Reprise RS 23343
Glen Campbell . . . . Ember S 249

GENTLEMAN IS A DOPE, THE   May 1948
Richard Rodgers / Oscar Hammerstein II
Chappell & Co. Ltd. . . . . USA
Show(s): . . . . Allegro
Eydie Gormé . . . . HMV CLP 1156
Diana Dors . . . . Pye NPL 18044

GENTLEMEN, THE KING   1935
Cyril Ray / Ivor McLaren
Lawrence Wright Music Co. Ltd . . . . UK
Cicely Courtneidge . . . . HMV BD 239

GEORGETTE   1922
Lew Brown / Ray Henderson
Cavendish Music Co. Ltd . . . . USA
Show(s): . . . . Greenwich Village Follies of 1922
The Club Royal Orchestra . . . . HMV B 1397

GEORGIA ON MY MIND   1932
Hoagy Carmichael / Stuart Gorrell
Campbell Connelly & Co. Ltd. . . . . USA
Hoagy Carmichael & his Orchestra,
   vocal Hoagy Carmichael . . . . HMV DLP 1106
Bing Crosby . . . . Brunswick LAT 8217

The Mills Brothers . . . . Brunswick OE 9060
Ray Charles . . . . HMV POP 792

GEORGIAN RUMBA   April 1956
Ivor Slaney
Bradbury Wood Ltd. . . . . UK
Dolores Ventura (Piano) with Orchestra, conducted by Ivor Sla-
ney . . . . Parlophone R 4160

GEORGY GIRL   April 1967
Jim Dale / Tom Springfield
Springfield Music Ltd. . . . . UK
Film(s): . . . . Georgy Girl
The Seekers . . . . Columbia DB 8134
Nominated for an Academy Award 1966.

GERONIMO   December 1963
Hank B. Marvin
Shadows Music Ltd . . . . UK
The Shadows . . . . Columbia DB 7163

GERTIE THE GIRL WITH THE GONG   1935
Ray Sonin / Ronnie Munro
Francis, Day & Hunter Ltd . . . . UK
Ambrose & his Orchestra,
vocal Elsie Carlisle & Sam Browne . . . . Decca F 6486

GET A LIFE   January 1990
Beresford Romeo / Hayden Brown
Virgin Music . . . . UK
Soul II Soul . . . . Ten TEN 284

GET AWAY   July 1966
Clive Powell
Carlin Music Corporation . . . . UK
Georgie Fame . . . . Columbia DB 7946

GET BACK   June 1969
John Lennon / Paul McCartney
Northern Songs Ltd . . . . UK
The Beatles . . . . Apple R 5777
Rod Stewart (1976) . . . . Riva 6
Ivor Novello Award.

GET DANCING   December 1974
Bob Crewe / Kenny Nolan
Intersong Music . . . . USA
Discotex & The Sex-O-Lettes . . . . Chelsea 2005013

GET DOWN   April 1973
Gilbert O'Sullivan
M.A.M. (Music Publishing) Ltd. . . . . UK
Gilbert O'Sullivan . . . . MAM MAM 96
Ivor Novello Award.

GET DOWN   March 1979
James Thompson
Leosong Copyright Service . . . . USA
Gene Chandler . . . . 20th Century BTC 1040

GET DOWN ON IT   January 1982
Ronald Bell / James Taylor
Planetary-Nom Music . . . . USA
Kool & The Gang . . . . De Lite DE 5

GET HAPPY   1930
Harold Arlen / Ted Koehler
Francis, Day & Hunter Ltd . . . . USA
Show(s): . . . . Nine-Fifteen Revue
Film(s): . . . . If You Feel Like Singing / With a Song in My Heart
Frankie Trumbauer & his Orchestra,
vocal Frankie Trumbauer, ... Parlophone R 2625
Frank Sinatra . . . . Capitol W 587
Judy Garland . . . . MGM 346
June Christy . . . . Capitol T 1006
Judy Garland appeared in *If You Feel Like Singing.*

GET IT   March 1979
Nigel Trubridge
Magnet Music . . . . UK
The Darts . . . . Magnet MAG 140

GET IT ON   August 1971
Marc Bolan
Essex Music Ltd . . . . UK

T. Rex . . . . Fly BUG 10

GET LOST   October 1961
Les Vandyke
Essex Music Ltd. . . . . UK
Eden Kane . . . . Decca F 11381

GET ME TO THE CHURCH ON TIME   May 1958
Alan Jay Lerner / Frederick Loewe
Chappell & Co. Ltd . . . . USA
Show(s): . . . . My Fair Lady
Film(s): . . . . My Fair Lady
Stanley Holloway (USA) . . . . Philips RBL 1000
Stanley Holloway & chorus (UK) . . . . CBS 70005
Rosemary Clooney . . . . RCA RD 27218
Stanley Holloway & chorus (film) . . . . CBS BRG 72237
Stanley Holloway appeared in the American and British productions
and the film *My Fair Lady.*

GET OFF OF MY CLOUD   November 1965
Mick Jagger / Keith Richards
Mirage Music Ltd . . . . UK
The Rolling Stones . . . . Decca F 12263

GET OUT AND GET UNDER   1913
Maurice Abrahams / Grant Clarke / Edgar Leslie
Francis, Day & Hunter Ltd. . . . . USA
Show(s): . . . . The Pleasure Seekers / Hullo Tango
Gerald Kirby . . . . HMV B 461
Jack Hylton & his Orchestra . . . . HMV C 1653
Harry Roy & his Orchestra, vocal Johnny Green . Decca F 9485
Clinton Ford . . . . Oriole EP 7027
Gerald Kirby appeared in *Hullo Tango.*

GET OUT AND GET UNDER THE MOON   1928
Larry Shay / William Jerome / Charles Tobias
Francis, Day & Hunter Ltd . . . . USA
Paul Whiteman & His Orch. vocal Bing Crosby . Columbia 4951
Bonnie Guitar . . . . London HAD 2112

GET OUT OF MY DREAMS, GET INTO MY CAR   March 1988
Robert Lange / Billy Ocean
Zomba Music . . . . UK
Billy Ocean . . . . Jive BOS 1
Ivor Novello Nomination

GET OUT OF TOWN   1939
Cole Porter
Chappell & Co. Ltd. . . . . USA
Show(s): . . . . Leave it to Me
Frances Langford . . . . Brunswick 02872
Chris Connor . . . . London HAK 2020
Lena Horne . . . . RCA RD 27098

GET OUT THOSE OLD RECORDS   March 1951
Carmen Lombardo / John Jacob Loeb
Chappell & Co. Ltd . . . . USA
Mary Martin & Larry Martin . . . . Columbia DB 2813

GET READY   April 1969
Smokey Robinson
Jobete Music (UK) Ltd. . . . . USA
The Temptations . . . . Tamla Motown TMG 688
Tom Jones . . . . Decca LK 4909
Ella Fitzgerald . . . . Reprise RS 20850

GET UP (BEFORE THE NIGHT IS OVER)   February 1990
Manuela Kamosi / Jo Bogaert
Brothers Organisation . . . . Belgium
Technotronic . . . . Swanyard SYR 8

GET UP AND BOOGIE   May 1976
Sylvester Levay / Stephen Praeger
Meridian Music Publishing Co. Ltd . . . . Germany
The Silver Convention . . . . Magnet MAG 55

GETTING AROUND AND ABOUT   1935
Lewis Ilda / Michael Carr
Dash Music Ltd . . . . UK
Carroll Gibbons & The Savoy Orpheans . . . . Columbia FB 1042

GETTING NOWHERE   1946
Irving Berlin
Irving Berlin Ltd. . . . . USA
Film(s): . . . . Blue Skies

Bing Crosby . . . . **Brunswick Bing 10**
Bing Crosby appeared in *Blue Skies*.

GETTING TO KNOW YOU   October 1953
Richard Rodgers / Oscar Hammerstein II
Williamson Music Ltd. . . . . USA
Show(s): . . . . The King and I
Film(s): . . . . The King and I
Gertrude Lawrence . . . . **Brunswick LAT 8026**
Valerie Hobson . . . . **Philips BBL 7002**
Deborah Kerr & Chorus . . . . **Capitol LCT 6108**
Gertrude Lawrence appeared in the American production of *The King & I*.
Valerie Hobson appeared in the British production of *The King and I*.
Deborah Kerr appeared in *The King and I*.
The Singing voice of Deborah Kerr was Dubbed by Marni Nixon.

GHETTO CHILD   November 1973
Linda Creed / Thomas Bell
Carlin Music Corporation . . . . USA
The Detroit Spinners . . . . **Atlantic K 10359**

GHETTO HEAVEN   May 1990
Peter Lord / Sandra St. Victor / Vernon Smith
EMI Music . . . . USA
The Family Stand . . . . **Atlantic A 7997**

GHOST OF A CHANCE, A   1932
Victor Young / Ned Washington / Bing Crosby
Peter Maurice Music Co. Ltd. . . . . USA
Film(s): . . . . The Man From the Folies Bergere
Bing Crosby . . . . **Fontana TFR 6012**
Frank Sinatra . . . . **Capitol LCT 6185**

GHOST RIDERS IN THE SKY   June 1949
Stan Jones
Edwin H. Morris & Co. Ltd . . . . USA
Film(s): . . . . Riders in the Sky
Vaughn Monroe . . . . **RCA RCX 1043**
Bing Crosby . . . . **Brunswick LAT 8370**
The Norman Luboff Choir . . . . **Philips DB 2529**
The Ramrods (1961) . . . . **London CDN 110**
The Shadows (1980) . . . . **EMI C 16006**

GHOST TOWN   July 1981
Jerry Dammers
Plangent Visions Music . . . . UK
The Specials . . . . **2 Tone CHSTT 17**

GHOSTBUSTERS   October 1984
Ray Parker Jnr
CBS Songs Ltd. . . . . USA
Film(s): . . . . Ghostbusters
Ray Parker Jnr . . . . **Arista ARIST 580**
Nominated for an Acadmey Award 1984.

GHOSTS   April 1982
David Sylvian
Virgin Music . . . . UK
Japan . . . . **Virgin VS 472**

GIANNINA MIA   1912
Rudolf Frimi / Otto Harbach
Chappell & Co. Ltd . . . . USA
Show(s): . . . . The Firefly
Film(s): . . . . The Firefly
Allan Jones . . . . **HMV 7EG 8231**
Mario Lanza . . . . **RCA RB 16002**
Harry Secombe . . . . **Philips BBE 12257**
Paul Britten & his Orchestra . . . . **MGM C 779**
Alan Jones appeared in the film *The Firefly*.

GIDDY-UP-A-DING-DONG   October 1956
Freddie Bell / Pep Lattanzi
Myers Music . . . . UK
Freddie Bell & The Bellboys . . . . **Mercury MT 122**

GIGI   January 1959
Alan Jay Lerner / Frederick Loewe
Chappell & Co. Ltd . . . . USA
Film(s): . . . . Gigi
Billy Eckstine . . . . **Mercury AMT 1018**
Louis Jordan . . . . **MGM C 770**
Vic Damone . . . . **Philips BBE 12245**
Louis Jordan appeared in *Gigi*.
Academy Award winning song for 1958.

GIGOLETTE   1924
Franz Lehar / William Cary
Chappell & Co. Ltd . . . . Austria
Show(s): . . . . The Three Graces
The Original Orchestra . . . . **Zonophone 2436**
Lucienne Boyer . . . . **Columbia DF 388**

GILBERT THE FILBERT   1914
Arthur Wimperis / Herman Finck
Francis, Day & Hunter Ltd. . . . . UK
Show(s): . . . . The Passing Show
Basil Hallam . . . . **HMV B 481**
Basil Hallam appeared in *The Passing Show*.

GILLY-GILLY OSSENFEFFER KATZEN ELLEN BOGEN
BY THE SEA   August 1954
Al Hoffman / Dick Manning
Larry Spier Ltd. . . . . USA
Max Bygraves . . . . **HMV 7M 237**
Max Bygraves . . . . **Decca LK 4333**

GIMME A LITTLE KISS, WILL YA, HUH   1926
Roy Turk / Jack Smith / Maceo Pinkard
Francis, Day & Hunter Ltd. . . . . USA
Film(s): . . . . Lady on a Train / Has Anybody Seen My Gal
Jean Goldkette & his Orchestra . . . . **HMV B 5080**
April Stevens . . . . **HMV JO 302**
Debbie Reynolds . . . . **London HAD 2326**

GIMME ALL YOUR LOVIN'   November 1984
Bill Gibbons / Dusty Hill / Frank Beard
Warner Brothers Music . . . . UK
ZZ Top . . . . **Warner Brothers W 9693**

GIMME DAT DING   May 1970
Mike Hazlewood / Albert Hammond
Shair Music . . . . UK
The Pipkins . . . . **Columbia DB 8662**
Ivor Novello Nomination.

GIMME GIMME GIMME   November 1979
Benny Andersson / Bjorn Ulvaeus
Bocu Music Ltd. . . . . Sweden
Abba . . . . **Epic EPC 7914**

GIMME GOOD LOVIN'   July 1969
Joey Levine / Richi Cordell
Dick James Music Ltd. . . . . USA
Crazy Elephant . . . . **Major Minor MM 609**

GIMME HOPE JO'ANNA   March 1988
Eddy Grant
Intersong Music . . . . UK
Eddy Grant . . . . **Ice 78701**

GIMME LITTLE SIGN   March 1968
Joe Hooven / Alfred Smith / Jerry Winn
Metric Music Ltd. . . . . USA
Brenton Wood . . . . **Liberty LBF 15021**

GIMME SOME   April 1977
H.W. Casey / Richard Finch
Sunbury Music Ltd . . . . USA
Brendon . . . . **Magnet MAG 80**

GIMME SOME LOVING   December 1966
Steve Winwood / Muff Winwood / Spencer Davis
Island Music Ltd. . . . . UK
The Spencer Davis Group . . . . **Fontana TF 762**

GINGER YOU'RE BARMY   1910
Fred Murray
B. Feldman & Co. Ltd. . . . . UK
Harry Champion . . . . **Columbia 1490**

GINNY COME LATELY   June 1962
Peter Udell / Gary Geld
Spanka Music Ltd. . . . . USA
Brian Hyland . . . . **HMV POP 1013**
Steve Perry . . . . **Decca F 11462**
Adam Faith . . . . **Parlophone PMC 1213**

GIPSY IN ME, THE   1935
Cole Porter
Chappell & Co. Ltd . . . . USA

Show(s): . . . . Anything Goes
The Anything Goes Foursome . . . . HMV B 8333

GIPSY IN MY SOUL 1938
Clay Boland / Moe Jaffe
World Wide Music Co. Ltd. . . . . USA
Nat Gonella & his Georgians,
vocal Nat Gonella . . . . Parlophone F 1085
Margaret Whiting . . . . London HAD 2109
Ella Fitzgerald . . . . HMV CLP 1455

GIPSY LOVE SONG, THE 1898
Victor Herbert / Harry B. Smith
B. Feldman & Co. Ltd. . . . . USA
Show(s): . . . . The Fortune Teller
Film(s): . . . . .Love Happy
W.F. Hooley . . . . HMV GC 2-2698
Charles Kullman . . . . Columbia DB 1812
Bing Crosby & Frances Langford . . . . Brunswick LA 8600
Mario Lanza . . . . RCA RB 16002

GIPSY MAIDEN 1911
Franz Lehar / Adrian Ross
Chappell & Co. Ltd . . . . Austria
Show(s): . . . . Gipsy Love
Anne Ziegler . . . . HMV C 4125

GIPSY MELODY 1930
Horatio Nicholls
Lawrence Wright Music Co. Ltd . . . . UK
Layton & Johnstone . . . . Columbia DB 347

GIPSY MOON 1932
Igor Borganoff / Frank Eyton
Chappell & Co. Ltd. . . . . Hungary
Foster Richardson . . . . Imperial 2740
Eve Boswell . . . . Parlophone PMD 1039

GIPSY, THE 1945
Billy Reid
Peter Maurice Music Co. Ltd. . . . . UK
Dorothy Squires&Orch. cond. by Billy Reid   Parlophone F 2085
The Ink Spots . . . . Brunswick LAT 8369

GIRL March 1966
John Lennon / Paul McCartney
Northern Songs Ltd. . . . . UK
St. Louis Union . . . . Decca F 12318
Truth . . . . Pye 7N 17035
The Beatles . . . . Parlophone PCS 3075

GIRL CAN'T HELP IT, THE April 1957
Bobby Troup
Robbins Music Ltd . . . . USA
Film(s): . . . . The Girl Can't Help It
Little Richard . . . . London HLO 8382

GIRL CRAZY April 1982
Eroll Brown
Rak Music . . . . UK
Hot Chocolate . . . . Rak 341

GIRL DON'T COME January 1965
Chris Andrews
Glissando Music Ltd . . . . UK
Sandie Shaw . . . . Pye 7N 15714

GIRLFRIEND, THE 1927
Richard Rodgers / Lorenz Hart
Chappell & Co. Ltd. . . . . USA
Show(s): . . . . The Girlfriend
The California Ramblers . . . . Columbia 4461
Frank Crumit . . . . HMV B 2526
Bing Crosby . . . . Brunswick 04914

GIRL FROM IPANEMA, THE July 1964
Antonio Carlos Jobim / Vinicius De Moraes / Norman Gimble
Leeds Music Ltd . . . . Brazil
Astrud Gilberto . . . . Verve V 8545
The Morgan-James Duo . . . . Philips BF 1350
Peggy Lee . . . . Capitol T 2096
Joe Loss & his Orchestra . . . . HMV CLP 1819

GIRL I'M GONNA MISS YOU November 1989
Frank Faran / Dieter Kawan / Peter Bischof-Fallenstein

E.G. Music . . . . Germany
Milli Vanilli . . . . Cooltempo COOL 191

GIRL IN THE ALICE BLUE GOWN, THE 1938
Ross Parker
Dash Music Ltd. . . . . UK
Lew Stone & his Band, vocal Al Bowlly . . . . . . Decca F 6607
Arthur Tracey (The Street Singer) . . . . Decca F 6636

GIRL IN THE CRINOLINE GOWN, THE 1924
Melville Gideon / Clifford Seyler
Francis, Day & Hunter Ltd. . . . . UK
Show(s): . . . . The Co-Optimists
Melville Gideon . . . . Columbia 3509
Eric Rogers & his Orchestra . . . . Decca LK 4225
Melville Gideon appeares in *The Co-Optimists*.

GIRL IN THE LITTLE GREEN HAT, THE 1933
Jack Scholl / Bradford Browne / Max Rich
Dash Music Ltd. . . . . USA
Roy Fox & his Orchestra . . . . Decca F 3537

GIRL IS MINE, THE December 1982
Michael Jackson
Warner Chappell Music . . . . USA
Michael Jackson & Paul McCartney . . . . Epic EPC 2729

GIRL LIKE YOU, A July 1961
Jerry Lordan
Francis, Day & Hunter Ltd. UK
Cliff Richard . . . . Columbia DB 4667

GIRL NEXT DOOR, THE
Hugh Martin / Ralph Blane
Robbins Music Ltd . . . . USA
Film(s): . . . . Athena
Vic Damone . . . . Mercury MB 3208
Vic Damone appeared in *Athena*
See also *The Boy Next Door*

GIRL OF MY BEST FRIEND, THE July 1960
Beverly Ross / Sam Bobrick
Hill & Range Songs (London) Ltd . . . . USA
Elvis Presley . . . . RCA RD 27171
Elvis Presley (1976) . . . . RCA 2729

GIRL OF MY DREAMS 1928
Sonny Clapp
Lawrence Wright Music Co. Ltd . . . . USA
Blue Steele & his Orchestra, vocal Kenny Sargent and featur-
ing Sonny Clapp (trombone) . . . . HMV B 5585
Bing Crosby . . . . Brunswick LA 8687
Perry Como (1958) . . . . RCA 108
The Four Aces . . . . Brunswick LAT 8221
Vic Damone . . . . Philips BBL 7476

GIRL ON THE MAGAZINE COVER, THE 1916
Irving Berlin
Irving Berlin Ltd. . . . . USA
Show(s): . . . . Stop, Look, Listen / Follow the Crowd
Film(s): . . . . Easter Parade
Joseph Coyne & Chorus . . . . HMV 02648
Fred Astaire . . . . London HAR 2219
Dick Haymes . . . . Brunswick LA 8516
Joseph Coyne appeared in *Follow the Crowd.*
Fred Astaire appeared in *Easter Parade.*

GIRL ON THE POLICE GAZETTE, THE 1937
Irving Berlin
Irving Berlin Ltd. . . . . USA
Show(s): . . . . Star and Garter
Film(s): . . . . On the Avenue
Dick Powell . . . . Decca F 6454
Sidney Lipton & his Orchestra . . . . Decca LK 4308
Dick Powell appeared in *On the Avenue.*

GIRL TALK 1966
Neil Hefti / Bobby Troup
Chappell Music Co. Ltd . . . . USA
Film(s): . . . . Harlow
Tony Bennett . . . . CBS BPG 62677
Stuart Gilles . . . . Philips 6308118

GIRL THAT I MARRY 1947
Irving Berlin

Irving Berlin Ltd. . . . . USA
Show(s): . . . . Annie Get Your Gun
Film(s): . . . . Annie Get Your Gun
Ray Middleton . . . . **Brunswick LAT 8002**
Bill Johnson . . . . **Columbia SEG 7711**
Howard Keel . . . . **MGM CD 1**
Ray Middleton appeared in the American production of *Annie Get Your Gun.*
Bill Johnson appeared in the British production of *Annie Get Your Gun.*
Howard Keel appeared in the film of *Annie Get Your Gun.*

GIRL WITH THE DREAMY EYES   1935
Michael Carr / Eddie Pola
Dash Music Ltd . . . . UK
Phyllis Robins . . . . **Rex 8469**
Jack Hylton & his Orchestra . . . . **HMV BD 164**

GIRL YOU KNOW IT'S TRUE   November 1988
Bill Pettaway / Sean Spencer / Kevin Lyles / Rodney Hollaman & Kayode Adeymo
I.Q. Music . . . . USA
Milli Vanilli . . . . **Cooltempo COOL 170**

GIRLFRIEND   April 1988
L.A. Reid / Kenny Edmonds
Warner Chappell Music . . . . USA
Pebbles . . . . **MCA MCA 1233**

GIRLIE GIRLIE   January 1986
Sangie Davis
Sangie Davis Music . . . . USA
Sophia George . . . . **Winner WIN W01**

GIRLS   April 1975
Al Goodman / Harry Ray / Venus Dodson
Sunbury Music Ltd . . . . USA
Moments & Whatnauts . . . . **All Platinum 6146302**

GIRLS JUST WANT TO HAVE FUN   February 1984
Robert Hazard
Warner Brothers Music . . . . USA
Cyndi Lauper . . . . **Epic A 3943**

GIRLS ON FILM   April 1981
"Duran Duran"
Carlin Music . . . . UK
Duran Duran . . . . **EMI 5206**

GIRLS TALK   August 1979
Elvis Costello
Plangent Visions Music . . . . UK
Dave Edmunds . . . . **Swansong SSK 19418**

GIRLS WERE MADE TO LOVE AND KISS   1937
Franz Lehar / A.P. Herbert
Francis, Day & Hunter Ltd. . . . . Austria
Show(s): . . . . Paganini
Richard Tauber . . . . **Parlophone PMB 1006**
Harry Secombe . . . . **Philips BBE 12131**
Richard Tauber appeared in *Paganini.*

GIRLS WERE MADE TO TAKE CARE OF BOYS   April 1950
Ralph Blane
B. Feldman & Co. Ltd . . . . USA
Film(s): . . . . One Sunday Afternoon
Rose Murphy . . . . **HMV B 9919**
Billie Holiday . . . . **Brunswick 04456**
Jo Stafford & Gordon MacRae . . . . **Capitol B 9933**
The King Sisters . . . . **Capitol 33SX 1278**

GIRLS, GIRLS, GIRLS   April 1976
Georg Kajanus
Edwin H. Morris & Co. Ltd . . . . Germany
Sailor . . . . **Epic EPC 3858**

GIVE A LITTLE LOVE   August 1975
Phil Wainman / John Goodison
Utopia Music . . . . UK
The Bay City Rollers . . . . **Bell 1425**

GIVE A LITTLE WHISTLE   1940
Ned Washington / Leigh Harline
Chappell & Co. Ltd . . . . USA
Film(s): . . . . Pinocchio (Cartoon)
Sound Track . . . . **Top Rank JKP 2033**

June Christy . . . . **Capitol T 1398**

GIVE HER MY LOVE   December 1956
Leslie Baguley / Tommy Connor / Michael Reine
Michael Reine Music Co. Ltd. . . . . UK
Anne Shelton . . . . **Philips BBE 12114**

GIVE IT UP   August 1983
Harry Casey / Deborah Carter
CBS Songs . . . . USA
K.C. & The Sunshine Band . . . . **Epic A 3017**

GIVE ME A LITTLE COSY CORNER   1918
James W. Tate / Clifford Harris
Francis, Day & Hunter Ltd. . . . . UK
Louis Leigh, Walter Jefferies & Eric Courtland . . . . **HMV B 984**
Clarice Mayne & "That" . . . . **Columbia L 1326**
Harry Davidson & his Orchestra . . . . **Columbia DX 1222**

GIVE ME A NIGHT IN JUNE   1927
Cliff Friend
Francis, Day & Hunter Ltd. . . . . USA
Noble Sissie & his Orchestra . . . . **Parlophone R 3449**

GIVE ME BACK MY HEART   April 1982
Simon Darlow / Trevor Horn
Island Music . . . . UK
Dollar . . . . **WEA BUCK 3**

GIVE ME HOPE JO'ANNA (see Gimme Hope Jo'anna)

GIVE ME JUST A LITTLE MORE TIME   September 1970
Ronald Dunbar / Edith Wayne
Gold Fever Music . . . . USA
Chairmen of the Board . . . . **Invictus INV 501**

GIVE ME LITTLE SIGN (see Gimme Little Sign)

GIVE ME LOVE (Give Me Peace On Earth)   June 1973
George Harrison
Unknown Publisher . . . . UK
George Harrison . . . . **Apple R 5988**

GIVE ME SOMETHING TO REMEMBER YOU BY (see Something To Remember You By)

GIVE ME THE MOONLIGHT   1917
Albert Von Tilzer / Lew Brown
Francis, Day & Hunter Ltd. . . . . USA
Show(s): . . . . Hullo America
Film(s): . . . . The Dolly Sisters
Elsie Janis . . . . **HMV D 435**
Frankie Vaughan (1955) . . . . **Philips BBL 7233**
Theme song of Frankie Vaughan.

GIVE ME THE NIGHT   August 1980
Rodney Temperton
Rodsongs . . . . USA
George Benson . . . . **Warner Brothers LV 40**

GIVE ME THE RIGHT   March 1955
Marty Gold / Tom Glazer
Keith Prowse Music Publishing Co. Ltd. . . . . USA
David Hughes . . . . **Philips PB 396**
Johnnie Francis . . . . **Decca F 10440**

GIVE ME THE SIMPLE LIFE   August 1951
Harry Ruby / Rube Bloom
Victoria Music Co. Ltd . . . . USA
Film(s): . . . . Wake Up and Dream
Bing Crosby . . . . **Brunswick 04746**
Buddy Greco . . . . **Vogue LVA 9021**
Rosemary Clooney . . . . **RCA RD 27189**

GIVE ME YOUR WORD   July 1954
Irving Taylor / George Wyle
Campbell Connelly & Co. Ltd. . . . . USA
Tennessee Ernie Ford . . . . **Capitol T 841**

GIVE MY REGARDS TO BROADWAY   1904
George M. Cohan
B. Feldman & Co. Ltd. . . . . USA
Show(s): . . . . Little Johnny Jones
Film(s):Little Johnny Jones / Broadway Melody / The Great America Broadcast / Yankee Doodle Dandy / Jolson Sings Again / With a Song

in My Heart
Al Jolson .... **Brunswick LA 8502**
Gerry Dorsey .... **Columbia 33SX 1180**
Mitch Miller & The Gang .... **Philips BBL 7404**
Theme song of George M. Cohan.

GIVE PEACE A CHANCE   **August 1969**
John Lennon / Paul McCartney
Northern Songs Ltd. .... UK
The Plastic Ono Band .... **Apple 13**
Ivor Novello Nomination.

GIVE YOURSELF A PAT ON THE BACK   **1930**
Ralph Butler / Raymond Wallace
Campbell Connelly & Co. Ltd .... UK
Bobbie Comber .... **Broadcast 489**

GIVIN' UP GIVIN' IN   **November 1978**
Giorgio Moroder / Pete Bellotte
Heath Levy Music Ltd .... USA
The Three Degrees .... **Ariola ARO 130**

GIVING IT ALL AWAY   **May 1973**
David Courtney / Leo Sayer
Blandell Music .... UK
Roger Daltrey .... **Track 2094110**

GLAD ALL OVER   **January 1964**
Dave Clark / Mike Smith
Ivy Music Ltd .... UK
Dave Clark Five .... **Columbia DB 7154**

GLAD IT'S ALL OVER   **April 1984**
Ray Burns / Tony Mansfield
Rondor Music .... UK
Captain Sensible .... **A&M CAP 6**

GLAD RAG DOLL   **1929**
Jack Yellen / Milton Ager / Dan Dougherty
Lawrence Wright Music Co. Ltd .... USA
Film(s): .... Glad Rag Doll
Ted Lewis & his Orchestra .... **Columbia 5268**
Sid Philips & his Band .... **HMV 7EG 8461**

GLAMOROUS NIGHT   **1935**
Ivor Novello / Christopher Hassell
Chappell & Co. Ltd .... UK
Show(s): .... Glamorous Night
Film(s): .... Glamorous Night
Mary Ellis .... **HMV DLP 1095**
Vanessa Lee .... **HMV 7EG 8513**
Mary Ellis appeared in both the show and the film of *Glamorous Night*.

GLASS OF CHAMPAGNE, A   **January 1976**
George Kajanus
Edwin H. Morris & Co. Ltd .... Germany
Sailor .... **Epic 3770**

GLENDORA   **September 1956**
Ray Stanley
Campbell Connelly & Co. Ltd. .... USA
Glen Mason .... **Parlophone R 4203**
Perry Como .... **HMV POP 240**

GLOBETROTTER   **February 1963**
Joe Meek
Ivy Music Ltd .... UK
The Tornados .... **Decca F 11562**

GLOOMY SUNDAY   **1936**
Laszio Javor / Rezso Seress / Sam Lewis
Chappell & Co. Ltd .... Hungary
Sari Barabas .... **Philips NBL 5011**
Paul Robeson .... **HMV B 8423**
Artie Shaw & his Orchestra .... **HMV B 9116**
Mel Tormé .... **HMV CLP 1238**

GLORIA   **February 1983**
Umberto Tozzi / Giancar Bigazzi
MCA Music .... USA
Laura Branigan .... **Atlantic K 11759**

GLORIOUS DEVON   **1905**
Edward German
Boosey & Hawkes Ltd .... UK

Robert Radford .... **HMV E 75**
Peter Dawson .... **HMV B 3280**
Forbes Robinson .... **Decca SPA R465**

GLORY OF LOVE, THE   **1936**
Billy Hill
Peter Maurice Music Co. Ltd .... USA
Hildegarde .... **Columbia FB 1401**
The Andrews Sisters .... **Brunswick 04599**
Roberta Sherwood .... **Brunswick LAT 8159**
The Platters .... **Mercury MMC 14010**
Peggy Lee .... **Capitol T 979**

GLORY OF LOVE, THE   **September 1986**
Peter Cetera / David Foster / Diana Nini
Warner Brothers Music .... USA
Film(s): .... Karate Kid Part II
Peter Cetera .... **Full Moon W 8662**
Nominated for an Academy Award 1986.

GLOW WORM, THE   **1907**
Paul Lincke / Lilla Cayley Robinson
Boosey & Hawkes Music publishers Ltd. .... Germany
Show(s): .... The Girl Behind the Counter
The New Light Symphony Orchestra .... **HMV C 1562**
The Mills Brothers (1952) .... **Brunswick LA 8664**
Johnny Mercer .... **Capitol CL 13520**
The Mills Brothers .... **London HAD 2192**
Henry Jerome & his Orchestra .... **Brunswick LAT 8354**
New lyric added by Johnny Mercer in 1952.

GO (Before You Break My Heart)   **June 1974**
Daniele Pace / Mario Panzeri / Lorenzo Pilat & Norman Newell
April Music Ltd. .... Italy
Gigiola Cinquetti .... **CBS 2294**
Italian entry for the 1974 Eurovision Song Contest (Placed Second).

GO AWAY LITTLE GIRL   **January 1963**
Gerry Goffin / Carole King
Aldon Music Ltd. .... USA
Mark Wynter .... **Pye 7N 15492**
Steve Lawrence .... **CBS AAG 127**
Ray Bennett .... **Decca F 11550**

GO HOME AND TELL YOUR MOTHER   **1930**
Dorothy Fields / Jimmy McHugh
Keith Prowse Music Publishing Co. Ltd .... USA
Film(s): .... Love in the Rough
Jack Hylton & his Orchestra .... **HMV B 5939**

GO NOW   **January 1965**
Larry Banks / Milton Bennett
Sparta Music Ltd .... USA
The Moody Blues .... **Decca F 12022**
Bessie Banks .... **Red Bird BC 106**

GO ON BY   **October 1955**
Stuart Hamblen
Bluebird Music Co. Ltd. .... USA
Suzi Miller .... **Decca F 10593**
Alma Cogan .... **HMV 7EG 8151**

GO WEST   **July 1979**
Jacques Morali / Henri Belolo / John Willis
Zomba Music Publishers .... France
The Village People .... **Mercury 6007221**

GO WILD IN THE COUNTRY   **May 1982**
Malcolm McLaren / Matthew Ashman / Leigh Gorman & Dave Barbarossa
CBS Songs .... UK
Bow Wow Wow .... **RCA 175**

GOD ONLY KNOWS   **September 1966**
Tony Asher / Brian Wilson
Immediate Music Ltd. .... USA
The Beach Boys .... **Capitol CL 15459**

GOGGLE EYE   **November 1964**
John D. Loudermilk
Acuff-Rose Publishing Co. Ltd .... USA
Sheb Wooley .... **MGM C 903**
The Nashville Teens .... **Decca F 12000**
John D. Loudermilk .... **RCA RD 7515**

GOIN' BACK   **August 1966**
Gerry Goffin / Carole King
Screen Gems - Columbia Music Ltd. . . . . USA
Dusty Springfield . . . . **Philips BF 1502**

GOIN' CO'TIN'   **January 1955**
Johnny Mercer / Gene De Paul
Robbins Music Corporation Ltd. . . . . USA
Film(s): . . . . Seven Brides for Seven Brothers
Jane Powell & The Brothers . . . . **MGM C 853**
Jane Powell & The Brothers appeared in *Seven Brides for Seven Brothers*.

GOING BACK TO MY ROOTS   **June 1981**
Lamont Dozier
April Music Ltd. . . . . USA
Odyssey (1981) . . . . **RCA RCA 85**
F.P.I. Project . . . . **Rumour RUMA 9**

GOING HOME   **August 1973**
Alan Osmond / Wayne Osmond / Merrill Osmond
Intersong Music . . . . USA
The Osmonds . . . . **MGM 2006288**

GOING IN WITH MY EYES OPEN   **April 1977**
Tony Macaulay
Macaulay Music . . . . UK
David Soul . . . . **Private Stock PVT 99**

GOING MY WAY   **1944**
Johnny Burke / Jimmy Van Heusen
Victoria Music Co. Ltd. . . . . USA
Film(s): . . . . Going My Way
Bing Crosby . . . . **Brunswick BING 8**
Ed Townsend . . . . **Capitol T 1140**
Bing Crosby appeared in *Going My Way*.

GOING UNDERGROUND   **April 1980**
Paul Weller
Chappell & Co. Ltd . . . . UK
The Jam . . . . **Polydor POSP 113**

GOING UP   **1918**
Otto Harbach / Louis Hirsch
B. Feldman & Co. Ltd. . . . . USA
Show(s): . . . . Going Up
The Cast of 'Going Up' . . . . **HMV C 860**
Joseph Coyne, Majorie Gordon, Evelyn Laye, Henry de Bray, Austin Melford & Clifton Alderson appeared in the British production of *Going Up*.

GOLD   **September 1983**
Gary Kemp
Reformation Music . . . . UK
Spandau Ballet . . . . **Chrysalis SPAN 2**

GOLD AND SILVER WALTZ, THE   **1904**
Franz Lehar
Boosey & Hawkes Music Publishers Ltd. . . . . Austria
Marek Weber & his Orchestra . . . . **HMV B 3726**
Andre Kostelanetz & his Orchestra . . . . **Columbia DX 1553**
Mantovani & his Orchestra . . . . **Decca LK 4150**

GOLD DIGGERS SONG (See We're In The Money)

GOLDEN BROWN   **January 1982**
Jean Burnell / Hugh Cornwell / Jet Black & David Greenfield
EMI Music . . . . UK
The Stranglers . . . . **Liberty BP 407**
Ivor Novello Award

GOLDEN DAYS   **1926**
Sigmund Romberg / Dorothy Donnelly
Chappell & Co. Ltd. . . . . USA
Show(s): . . . . The Student Prince
Film(s): . . . . The Student Prince
Allan Prior & Herbert Waterous . . . . **Columbia 3903**
Mario Lanza . . . . **RCA RB 16113**
Allan Prior & Herbert Waterous appeared in the British production of the *Student Prince*.
Mario Lanza dubbed the singing voice of Edmund Purdom who appeared in the 1954 film of *The Student Prince*.

GOLDEN EARRINGS   **1947**
Jay Livingston / Ray Evans / Victor Young

Chappell & Co. Ltd. . . . . USA
Film(s): . . . . Golden Earrings
Bing Crosby . . . . **Brunswick 03838**
Victor Young & his Singing Strings . . . . . **Brunswick LAT 8283**
The Troubadours . . . . **London HAR 2106**

GOLDEN HAIR WAS HANGING DOWN HER BACK, THE
(See And Her Golden Hair Was Hanging Down Her Back)

GOLDEN SONG, THE   **1923**
Franz Schubert / Adrian Ross
Chappell & Co. Ltd . . . . Austria
Show(s): . . . . Lilac Time
Clara Butterworth & Courtice Pounds . . . . . . **Vocalion K 05065**
Clara Butterworth & Courtice Pounds appeared in *Lilac Time*.

GOLDEN TANGO, THE   **February 1953**
Victor Silvester / Ernest Wilson
Lawrence Wright Music Co. Ltd . . . . UK
Victor Sylvester's Silver Strings . . . . **Columbia 33S 1013**
Frank Chacksfield & his Orchestra . . . . **Decca DFE 6185**

GOLDEN WEST, THE   **1925**
Horatio Nicholls
Lawrence Wright Music Co. Ltd. . . . . UK
Jack Hylton & his Orchestra . . . . **HMV B 1939**

GOLDEN YEARS   **January 1976**
David Bowie
Chrysalis Music Ltd . . . . UK
David Bowie . . . . **RCA 2640**

GOLDFINGER   **November 1964**
Leslie Bricusse / Anthony Newley / John Barry
United Artists Music Co. Ltd . . . . UK
Film(s): . . . . Goldfinger
Sound Track Orch, conducted by John Barry . . . . . **MGM C 903**
Shirley Bassey . . . . **Decca F 12000**
Ferrante & Teicher (piano duet) . . . . **RCA RD 7515**

GOLLIWOG'S CAKE WALK   **1907**
Claude Debussy
Unknown Publisher . . . . France
Claude Debussy (recorded from a piano roll) . **Columbia ML 4291**
Alfred Cortot (piano) . . . . **HMV DB 679**
Sergei Rachmaninov . . . . **Camden CAL 486**
Moura Lympany . . . . **EMI CDZ 762523**
Part of "The Childrens Corner Suite" by Claude Debussy (1862-1918)

GONE FISHIN'   **October 1950**
Nick Kenny / Charles Kenny
Francis, Day & Hunter Ltd . . . . USA
Bing Crosby & Louis Armstrong . . . . . **Brunswick LAT 8306**
Pat Boone . . . . **London HAD 2144**
Michael Holliday . . . . **Columbia 33SX 1354**

GONE WITH THE WIND   **1937**
Herb Magidson / Allie Wrubel
Chappell & Co. Ltd . . . . USA
Roy Fox & his Orchestra, vocal Denny Dennis . . **HMV BD 5279**
Matt Munro . . . . **Ace of Clubs ACL 1069**
Julie London . . . . **London HAU 2005**

GONNA BUILD A BIG FENCE AROUND TEXAS   **1945**
George Olsen / Clifford Friend / Katharine Philips
Robbins Music Corporation Ltd. . . . . USA
Eric Winstone & his Orchestra, vocal Alan Kane   **HMV BD 5878**

GONNA BUILD A MOUNTAIN   **October 1961**
Leslie Bricusse / Anthony Newley
Essex Music Ltd. . . . . UK
Show(s): . . . . Stop the World - I Want to Get Off
Film(s): . . . . Stop the World - I Want to Get Off
Anthony Newley . . . . **Decca LK 4408**
Matt Monro . . . . **Parlophone R 4819**
Eydie Gormé . . . . **CBS BPG 62181**
Tony Tanner . . . . **Warner Brothers B 1643**
Anthony Newley appeared in the British and American production of *Stop the World - I Want to Get Off.*
Tony Tanner appeared in the film *Stop the World - I Want to Get Off.*

GONNA FIND ME A BLUEBIRD   **August 1957**
Marvin Rainwater
Frank Music Co. Ltd . . . . USA
Marvin Rainwater . . . . **MGM 961**

Petula Clark . . . . **Nixa N 15096**
Russ Hamilton . . . . **MGM 1096**

GONNA GET A GIRL   1928
Paul Ash / Howard Simons / Al Lewis
Francis, Day & Hunter Ltd. . . . . USA
The Gilt-Edged Four . . . . **Columbia 4611**
Kay Starr . . . . **Capitol T 1303**

GONNA GET ALONG WITHOUT YOU NOW   January 1957
Milton Kellem
Francis, Day & Hunter Ltd. . . . . USA
Patience & Prudence . . . . **London REU 1087**
The Ken Colyer Jazz Band . . . . **Columbia 33SX 1297**
Viola Wills (1979) . . . . **Ariola AHA 546**

GONNA MAKE YOU A STAR   December 1974
David Essex
April Music Ltd. . . . . UK
David Essex . . . . **CBS 2492**

GONNA MAKE YOU AN OFFER YOU
CAN'T REFUSE   March 1973
Johnny Worth
Essex Music Ltd. . . . . UK
Jimmy Helms . . . . **Cube BUG 27**

GOO GOO BABARABAJAGAL (Love Is Hot)   August 1969
Donovan Leitch
Donovan Music Ltd. . . . . UK
Donovan & The Jeff Beck Group . . . . **Pye 7N 17778**

GOOD BYE-EE   1917
R.P. Weston / Bert Lee
Francis, Day & Hunter Ltd. . . . . UK
Fred Douglas . . . . **Regal G 7440**
Florrie Forde . . . . **Rex 8222**

GOOD COMPANIONS, THE   April 1957
C.A. Rossi / Paddy Roberts / Geoffrey Parsons
Peter Maurice Music Co. Ltd. . . . . UK
Film(s): . . . . The Good Companions
Janette Scott & John Fraser . . . . **Nixa NPT 19019**
Billy Cotton & his Band . . . . **Decca F 10857**
Janette Scott & John Fraser appeared in *The Good Companions.*

GOOD GOLLY MISS MOLLY   April 1964
John Marascalco / Robert Blackwell
Southern Music Publishing Co. Ltd . . . . USA
Little Richard . . . . **London HLU 8560**
The Swinging Blue Jeans . . . . **HMV POP 1273**

GOOD GRIEF CHRISTINA   May 1973
Giorgio Moroder / Pete Bellotti
A.T.V. Music Ltd. . . . . USA
Chicory Tip . . . . **CBS 1258**

GOOD HEART   December 1985
Maria McKee
E.G. Music . . . . UK
Feargal Sharkey . . . . **Virgin VS 808**

GOOD LIFE   January 1989
Kevin Saunderson / Paris Gray / Ray Holman
Virgin Music . . . . USA
Inner City . . . . **10 TEN 249**

GOOD LOVE CAN NEVER DIE   March 1975
Peter Shelley / Barry Mason
BumperSongs . . . . UK
Alvin Stardust . . . . **Magnet MAG 21**

GOOD LUCK CHARM   July 1962
Aaron Schroeder / Wally Gold
Belinda (London) Ltd . . . . USA
Elvis Presley . . . . **RCA 1280**

GOOD LUCK, GOOD HEALTH, GOD BLESS YOU   Feb 1951
Charles Adams / A. Le Royal
Carolin Music . . . . UK
Steve Conway & The Hastings Girls Choir . **Columbia SEG 7573**
Michael Holliday, Ruby Murray &
Eddie Calvert (trumpet) . . . . **Columbia SEG 7669**

GOOD MAN IS HARD TO FIND, A   1918
Eddie Green
Francis, Day & Hunter Ltd. . . . . USA
Show(s): . . . . Back Again
Lee White . . . . **Columbia F 1022**
Lizzie Miles . . . . **Capitol T 792**
Brenda Lee . . . . **Brunswick LAT 8319**
Lee White appeared in *Back Again.*

GOOD MORNING   1940
Nacio Herb Brown / Arthur Freed
Chappell & Co. Ltd . . . . USA
Show(s): . . . . Singin' in the Rain
Film(s): . . . . Babes in Arms / Singin' in the Rain
Gene Kelly, Debbie Reynolds & Donald O'Connor . **MGM D 140**
Joe Loss & his Orch. vocal chorus Regal Zonophone MR 3216
Judy Garland & Micky Rooney . . . . **JJA 19802**
Danielle Carson, Tommy Steele & Roy Castle . . . **Safari RAIN 1**
Gene Kelly, Debbie Reynolds & Donald O'Connor appeared in the
film *Singin' in the Rain.*
Judy Garland & Mickey Rooney appeared in *Babes in Arms.*
Danielle Carson, Tommy Steele & Roy Castle appeared in the show
Singin' in the Rain.

GOOD MORNING BROTHER SUNSHINE   1916
J.W. Foley / Liza Lehmann
Chappell & Co. Ltd . . . . UK
Hinge & Bracket . . . . **BBC REH 450**
Hull Orpheus Choir . . . . **Pye CMT 34000**
Olga Haley . . . . **HMV 03614**

GOOD MORNING FREEDOM   May 1970
Mike Hazlewood / Albert Hammond
Cookaway Music . . . . UK
Blue Mink . . . . **Philips BF 1838**

GOOD MORNING JUDGE   June 1977
Eric Stewart / Graham Gouldman
St. Annes Music Ltd . . . . UK
10 CC . . . . **Mercury 6008025**

GOOD MORNING MR ECHO   September 1951
Bill Putnam / Belinda Putnam
Pickwick Music Ltd . . . . USA
Buddy Morrow & his Orch., vocal The Quartette . **HMV B 10132**

GOOD MORNING STARSHINE   December 1968
Gerome Ragni / James Rado / Galt MacDermot
United Artists Music Co. Ltd. . . . . USA
Show(s): . . . . Hair
Film(s): . . . . Hair
Lynn Kellogg, Melba Moore, James Rado
& Gerome Ragni . . . . **RCA RD 7959**
Annabel Leventon, Linda Kendrick & Co. . . . . . **Polydor 583043**
Beverly D'Angelo, Annie Golden, Cheryl Barnes,
Don Dacus, Treat Williams & Dorsey Wright . **RCA BL 03274**
Oliver (1969) . . . . **CBS 4435**
Lynn Kellogg, Melba Moore, James Rado & Gerome Ragni appeared
in the American production of *Hair.*
Annabel Leventon, Linda Kendrick & Company appeared in the British
production of *Hair.*
Beverly D'Angelo, Annie Golden, Cheryl Barnes, Don Dacus, Treat
Williams & Dorsey Wright appeared in the film *Hair.*

GOOD NEWS   1928
Buddy De Sylva / Lew Brown / Ray Henderson
Chappell & Co. Ltd. . . . . USA
Show(s): . . . . Good News
Film(s): . . . . Good News / The Best Things in Life are Free
George Olsen & his Music . . . . **HMV B 5496**
Bill Savill & his Orchestra . . . . **Decca LK 4232**
George Olsen & his Music appeared in the American production of
Good News.

GOOD OLD ROCK 'N' ROLL   January 1970
M. Equine / Roy Michaels / Robert Smith / Bernie Packer / "Chinn"
Interworld Music . . . . USA
The Dave Clark Five . . . . **Columbia DB 8638**

GOOD THING   April 1989
David Steele / Roland Gift
Campbell Connelly & Co. Ltd . . . . UK
Fine Young Cannibals . . . . **London LON 218**

GOOD THING GOING, A　　　April 1981
"The Corporation"
Jobete Music . . . . USA
Sugar Minott . . . . **RCA 58**

GOOD TIMES　　　July 1979
Bernard Edwards / Nile Rodgers
Warner Brothers Music Ltd. USA
Chic . . . . **Atlantic K 11310**

GOOD TIMES (Better Times)　　　April 1969
Roger Cook / Roger Greenaway / Jerry Lordan
Francis, Day & Hunter Ltd . . . . UK
Cliff Richard . . . . **Columbia DB 8548**

GOOD TIMIN'　　　July 1960
Fred Tobias / Clint Ballard Jnr
Sheldon Music Ltd . . . . USA
Jimmy Jones . . . . **MGM C 832**

GOOD TRADITION　　　September 1988
Tanita Tickaram
Brogue Music . . . . UK
Tanita Tikaram . . . . **WEA YZ 196**

GOOD VIBRATIONS　　　December 1966
Mike Love / Brian Wilson
Immediate Music Ltd. . . . . USA
The Beach Boys . . . . **Capitol CL 15475**

GOOD YEAR FOR THE ROSES　　　November 1981
Jerry Chesnut
Valentine Music . . . . USA
Elvis Costello . . . . **F. Beat XX 17**

GOOD, GOOD, GOOD　　　1946
Allan Roberts / Doris Fisher
Campbell Connelly & Co. Ltd. . . . . USA
Film(s): . . . . Memory for Two
Lou Preager & his Orchestra,
vocal Rita Williams & Paul Rich . . . . **Columbia FB 3199**
Bing Crosby & The Andrews Sisters . . . . . . **Brunswick 03634**

GOOD, THE BAD AND THE UGLY, THE　　　December 1968
Ennio Morricone
United Artists Music Co. Ltd. . . . . USA
Film(s): . . . . The Good, the Bad and the Ugly
Hugo Montenegro Orchestra . . . . **RCA 1727**
Ray Conniff Orchestra . . . . **CBS 63423**

GOODBYE　　　1931
Robert Stolz / Ralph Benatzky / Harry Graham
Chappell & Co. Ltd . . . . Germany
Show(s): . . . . White Horse Inn
Richard Tauber . . . . **Parlophone Columbia PMB 1012**
Joseph Locke . . . . **Columbia SEG 7626**
Robert Stoltz & his Orchestra . . . . **MGM C 815**
Andy Cole . . . . **HMV CLP 1205**

GOODBYE　　　1937
Gordon Jenkins
Southern Music Publishing Co. Ltd . . . . USA
Gordon Jenkins & his Orchestra . . . . **Brunswick LA 8521**
Benny Goodman & his Orchestra . . . . **RCA RCX 1033**
Frank Sinatra . . . . **Capitol LCT 6168**
Julie London . . . . **London HAG 2280**
Closing theme of The Benny Goodman Orchestra.

GOODBYE　　　May 1969
John Lennon / Paul McCartney
Northern Songs Ltd. . . . . UK
Mary Hopkin . . . . **Apple 10**

GOODBYE BLUES　　　1932
Arnold Johnson / Dorothy Fields / Jimmy McHugh
Keith Prowse Music Publishing Co. Ltd. . . . . USA
Film(s): . . . . The Big Broadcast
Fletcher Henderson's Connie's Inn Orchestra . **Brunswick 01319**
The Mills Brothers . . . . **Brunswick 01296**
Burlington Bertie's Banjo Band . . . . **Philips BBL 7415**
The Mills Brothers appeared in *The Big Broadcast*.

GOODBYE CRUEL WORLD　　　January 1962
Gloria Shayne

Aldon Music Ltd. . . . . USA
James Darren . . . . **Pye 7N 25116**
Bill Forbes . . . . **Columbia DB 4747**

GOODBYE DOLLY GRAY　　　1900
Paul Barnes / Will Cobb
B. Feldman & Co. Ltd. . . . . USA
Film(s): . . . . Wait Till the Sun Shines Nellie
Florrie Forde . . . . **Imperial 2853**
Noel Coward . . . . **HMV C 2431**
Clinton Ford . . . . **Oriole MG 20046**
The Pavement Artists . . . . **Regal Zonophone MR 530**
Edward Woodward . . . . **DJM DJLPS 459**

GOODBYE HAWAII　　　1935
Harry Leon / Vic Robbins / Leo Towers / Dave Appolion
B. Feldman & Co. Ltd . . . . UK
Martin Duke (Hawaiian guitar) & Charles Smart (organ) . **Rex 8376**
A.P. Sharpe's Honolulu Hawaiians . . . . . . **Columbia SEG 7724**

GOODBYE JIMMY GOODBYE　　　June 1959
Jack Vaughn
Sydney Bron Music Ltd . . . . USA
Ruby Murray . . . . **Columbia DB 4305**
Kathy Linden . . . . **Felsted GEP 1002**
Kathy Kay . . . . **HMV POP 625**

GOODBYE MY LOVE　　　April 1965
R. Mosley / L. Swearingen / L. Simington
Aaron Schroeder Ltd. . . . . USA
The Searchers . . . . **Pye 7N 15794**

GOODBYE MY LOVE　　　February 1975
Gerry Shephard
Rock Artistes Music . . . . UK
The Glitter Band . . . . **Bell 1395**

GOODBYE SALLY　　　1940
Arthur Risco / J. Borelli
Francis, Day & Hunter Ltd. . . . . UK
Show(s): . . . . Shephard's Pie
Arthur Risco . . . . **Columbia FB 2323**
Arthur Risco appeared in *Shepherd's Pie*.

GOODBYE SAM, HELLO SAMANTHA　　　July 1970
Mitch Murray / Peter Callander / Geoff Stevens
Shadows Music Ltd. . . . . UK
Cliff Richard . . . . **Columbia DB 8685**

GOODBYE STRANGER　　　June 1987
Tambi Fernando / Iris Fernando / Wayne Brown
BMG Music . . . . UK
Pepsi & Shirlie . . . . **Polydor POSP 865**

GOODBYE SUMMER, SO LONG FALL, HELLO WINTER-
TIME　　　1913
Percy Wenrich / Edward Madden
B. Feldman & Co. Ltd. . . . . USA
The Peerless Quartet . . . . **Zonophone 1228**

GOODBYE TO JANE (See Gudbuy T'Jane)

GOODBYE TO LOVE　　　November 1972
Richard Carpenter / John Bettis
Rondor Music (London) Ltd. . . . . USA
The Carpenters . . . . **A&M AMS 7023**

GOODBYE VIRGINIA　　　1915
Grant Clarke / Jean Schwartz
B. Feldman & Co. Ltd. . . . . USA
Walter Jefferies . . . . **HMV B 566**

GOODBYE YELLOW BRICK ROAD　　　November 1973
Elton John / Bernie Taupin
Dick James Music Ltd. . . . . UK
Elton John . . . . **DJM DJS 285**

GOODNESS GRACIOUS ME　　　December 1960
Herbert Kretzmer / Dave Lee
Essex Music Ltd . . . . UK
Peter Sellers & Sophia Loren . . . . **Parlophone PMC 1131**
Dave Lee (piano) . . . . **Top Rank 35-112**
Ivor Novello Award.

GOODNIGHT   1929
Harry Woods / Irving Bibo / Con Conrad
Francis, Day & Hunter Ltd .... USA
Ted Lewis & his Band .... Columbia 5485
Ted Lewis & his Band .... Columbia FB 2814
Joe Loss & his Orchestra .... HMV DLP 1068

GOODNIGHT   March 1965
Roy Orbison / Bill Dees
Acuff-Rose Publishing Co. Ltd .... USA
Roy Orbison .... London HL 9951

GOODNIGHT (I'm Only A Strolling Vagabond)   1921
Edward Kunneke / Adrian Ross
B. Feldman & Co. Ltd .... Germany
Show(s): .... The Cousin From Nowhere
Russell Scott .... Columbia 3272
Cavan O'Connor .... Decca F 9039
Theme song Of Cavan O'Connor.

GOODNIGHT AND BLESS YOU   1941
Morton Fraser
B. Feldman & Co. Ltd .... UK
Joe Loss & his Orchestra,
vocal Sam Browne .... HMV BD 5667

GOODNIGHT ANGEL   1938
Herb Magidson / Allie Wrubel
Chappell & Co. Ltd. .... USA
Film(s): .... Radio City Revels
Al Bowlly .... HMV BD 565
Dick Robertson & his Orchestra,
vocal Dick Robertson .... Panachord 25977
Louis Armstrong .... Brunswick LAT 8210

GOODNIGHT CHILDREN, EVERYWHERE   1940
Gabby Rogers / Harry Philips
J. Norris Music Publishing Co. Ltd. .... UK
Vera Lynn .... Decca F 7339

GOODNIGHT IRENE   October 1950
Huddie Ledbetter / John Lomax
Leeds Music Ltd .... USA
The Weavers .... Brunswick OE 9429
Huddie Leadbetter .... Melodisc EPM 7-63
Billy Williams .... Vogue Q 72369

GOODNIGHT MIDNIGHT   August 1969
Kenny Young
April Music Ltd .... UK
Clodagh Rodgers .... RCA 1852

GOODNIGHT MY LOVE   1937
Mack Gordon / Harry Revel
Francis, Day & Hunter Ltd. .... USA
Film(s): .... Stowaway
Alice Faye .... Brunswick 02406
Leslie Hutchinson (Hutch) .... Decca LF 1207
Dean Martin .... Capitol T 1150
Alice Faye appeared in *Stowaway*.

GOODNIGHT SWEETHEART   1931
Ray Noble / James Campbell / Reginald Connelly
Campbell Connelly & Co. Ltd .... UK
Show(s): .... Earl Carroll's Vanities of 1931
Film(s): ...... The Big Broadcast of 1936 / You Were Meant for Me
Ray Noble & The New Mayfair Dance Orchestra, vocal Al
Bowlly .... HMV 7EG 8056
Rudy Vallee & his Connecticut Yankees .... HMV C 2802
Bing Crosby .... Brunswick LA 8740

GOODNIGHT TONIGHT   May 1979
Paul McCartney
A.T.V. Music Ltd. .... UK
Wings .... Parlophone R 6023

GOODNIGHT VIENNA   1932
Eric Maschwitz / George Posford
Keith Prowse Music Publishing Co. Ltd. .... UK
Film(s): .... Goodnight Vienna
Jack Buchanan .... HMV 7EG 8307
Frank Barber & his Orchestra .... Columbia 33SX 1233
Jack Buchanan appeared in *Goodnight Vienna*.

GOODNIGHT WHEREVER YOU ARE   1944
Dick Robertson / Al Hoffman / Frank Weldon
Campbell Connelly & Co. Ltd. .... USA
Mary Martin .... Brunswick 03563
Glenn Miller & his Orchestra, vocal Johnny Desmond & the
Crew Chiefs .... RCA RD 27090

GOODY GOODY   1936
Matty Malneck / Johnny Mercer
Victoria Music Co. Ltd .... USA
Film(s): .... The Benny Goodman Story
Benny Goodman & his Orchestra .... HMV B 8427
Benny Goodman & his Orchestra .... Brunswick LAT 8102
Ella Fitzgerald .... HMV CLP 1455
Rosemary Clooney .... Vogue LVA 9112

GOODY TWO SHOES   June 1982
Adam Ant / Marco Pirroni
EMI Music .... UK
Adam Ant .... CBS A 2367

GOOFUS   1932
Gus Kahn / Wayne King
Francis, Day & Hunter Ltd. .... USA
Wayne King & his Orchestra .... HMV B 6217
Tommy Dorsey & his Orchestra .... Brunswick 04654
David Seville & his Orchestra .... Camden CDN 124
Phil Harris .... Camden CDN 124

GORDON FOR ME, A   January 1950
Robert Wilson
Lawrence Wright Music Co. Ltd .... UK
Robert Wilson .... HMV DLP 1086
The Stargazers .... Decca DFE 6449

GOT A DATE WITH AN ANGEL   1931
Jack Waller / Joseph Tunbridge / Clifford Grey / Sonny Miller
Chappell & Co. Ltd. .... UK
Show(s): .... For the Love of Mike
Bobby Howes .... Columbia DB 697
Duke Ellington & his Orchestra .... Philips BBL 7315
Helen Carr .... London HAN 2065
Bobby Howes appeared in *For the Love of Mike*.

GOT A MATCH?   July 1958
Billy Mure / Dick Wolf
Cromwell Music ltd .... USA
Frank Gallop .... HMV POP 509

GOT MY MIND SET ON YOU   November 1987
Rudy Clark
Carlin Music .... USA
George Harrison .... Dark Horse W 8170

GOT TO BE CERTAIN   July 1988
Mike Stock / Matt Aitken / Peter Waterman
All Boys Music .... UK
Kylie Minogue .... PWL PWL 12

GOT TO BE THERE   March 1972
Elliot Willensky
Jobete Music (UK) Ltd. .... USA
Michael Jackson .... Tamla Motown TMG 797

GOT TO GET   January 1990
Robert Watz / Rasmus Lindwall
BMG Music .... Sweden
Rob & Raz featuring Leila K .... Arista 112696

GOT TO GET YOU INTO MY LIFE   September 1966
John Lennon / Paul McCartney
Northern Songs Ltd. .... UK
Cliff Bennett & The Rebel Rousers .... Parlophone R 5489
The Beatles .... Parlophone PCS 7009

GOT TO GIVE IT UP   June 1977
Marvin Gaye
Jobete Music (UK) Ltd. .... USA
Marvin Gaye .... Motown TMG 1069

GOT TO HAVE YOUR LOVE   February 1990
Curtis Khaleel / Bryce Wilson / E.D. Jon
Screen Gems .... USA
Mantronix featuring Wondress .... Capitol CL 559

GOT YOU ON MY MIND   November 1952
Howard Biggs / Joe Thomas
B. Feldman & Co. Ltd . . . . USA
Buddy Morrow & his Orch. vocal Frankie Lester . **HMV B 10371**

GOTTA BE THIS OR THAT   1946
Sunny Skylar
Victoria Music Co. Ltd. . . . . USA
Geraldo & his Orchestra, vocal Carol Carr . **Parlophone F 2106**
Ella Fitzgerald . . . . **HMV CLP 1267**

GOTTA GO HOME   September 1979
Frank Farian / Heinz Huth / Fred Jay
A.T.V. Music ltd. . . . . Germany
Boney M . . . . **Atlantic K 11351**

GOTTA HAVE SOMETHING IN THE BANK, FRANK   1957
Bob Hilliard / Mort Garson
Campbell Connelly & Co. Ltd . . . . USA
Frankie Vaughan & The Kaye Sisters . . . . . . **Philips BBL 7233**

GOTTA PULL MYSELF TOGETHER   November 1980
Ben Findon / Mike Myers / Robert Puzey
Black Sheep Music . . . . UK
The Nolans . . . . **Epic EPC 8878**

GRANADA   1932
Augustin Lara / Dorothy Dodd
Latin-American Music Publishing Co. Ltd. . . . . Mexico
Film(s):The Gay Ranchero / Because You're Mine / I'll Be Yours / Two
Girls and a Sailor
Bing Crosby . . . . **Brunswick LAT 8331**
Mario Lanza . . . . **RCA RCX 1039**
Frank Sinatra (1961) . . . . **Reprise R 20010**
Deanna Durbin . . . . **MCA MCG 6007**
Frankie Laine (1954) . . . . **Philips PB 242**
Mario Lanza appeared in *Because You're Mine.*
Deanna Durbin appeared in *I'll be Yours.*

GRAND COOLIE DAM   May 1958
Woody Guthrie
Essex Music . . . . USA
Lonnie Donegan . . . . **Pye NIXA N 15129**

GRANDAD   February 1971
Herbie Flowers / Kenneth Pickett
In-Music Ltd . . . . UK
Clive Dunn . . . . **Columbia DB 8726**
Ivor Novello Award.

GRANDFATHER'S CLOCK   1876
Henry Work
Unknown Publisher . . . . USA
George Baker . . . . **HMV B 4308**
Frank Crumit . . . . **HMV 7EG 8222**
The Radio Revellers . . . . **Columbia FB 3394**
Alasdair Gillies . . . . **Decca LK 5060**

GRANDMA'S PARTY   January 1977
Dominic Buggati / Frank Musker
April Music Ltd . . . . USA
Paul Nicholas . . . . **RSO 2090216**

GRANNY'S OLD ARM-CHAIR   1932
John Read
B. Feldman & Co. Ltd. . . . . UK
Frank Crumit . . . . **HMV B 10327**
George Melly . . . . **Decca DFE 6557**

GREASE   October 1978
Barry Gibb
Chappell & Co. Ltd . . . . UK
Film(s): . . . . Grease
Frankie Valli . . . . **RSO 12**
Ivor Novello Nomination.

GREASED LIGHTNING   December 1978
Warren Casey / Jim Jacobs
Chappell & Co. Ltd . . . . USA
Show(s): . . . . Grease
Film(s): . . . . Grease
Timothy Meyers . . . . **MGM 1SE 34 OC**
John Travolta . . . . **RSO 2479210**
Timothy Meyers appeared in the show *Grease.*
John Travolta appeared in the film *Grease.*

GREAT BALLS OF FIRE   January 1958
Jack Hammer / Otis Blackwell
Aberbach (London) Ltd. . . . . USA
Film(s): . . . . Jamboree
Jerry Lee Lewis . . . . **London HLS 8529**
Don Lang . . . . **Ace of Clubs ACL 1111**
Jerry Lee Lewis appeared in *Jamboree.*

GREAT DAY   1930
Vincent Youmans / Edward Eliscu / Billy Rose
Campbell Connelly & Co. Ltd . . . . USA
Show(s): . . . . Great Day
Film(s): . . . . Funny Girl
Paul Whiteman & his Orchestra,
  vocal Bing Crosby . . . . **Columbia CB 116**
Edmund Hockridge . . . . **Nixa NPL 18021**
The Robin Hood Band . . . . **Columbia 33SX 1344**
Barbra Streisand . . . . **Arista ARTY 101**
Barbra Streisand appeared in *Funny Girl.*

GREAT PRETENDER, THE   October 1956
Buck Ram
Southern Music Publishing Co. Ltd. . . . . USA
Film(s): . . . . Rock Around the Clock / The Girl Can't Help it
The Platters . . . . **Mercury MT 117**
Pat Boone . . . . **London HLD 2382**
Jimmy Parkinson . . . . **Columbia DB 3729**
Anne Shelton . . . . **Philips PB 567**
Stan Freiberg (comedy version) . . . . . **Capitol CL 14571**
Freddie Mercury (1987) . . . . **Parlophone R 6151**
The Platters appeared in *The Girl Can't Help it.*

GREATEST LOVE OF ALL   May 1986
Michael Masser / Linda Creed
CBS Songs . . . . USA
Film(s): . . . . The Greatest
George Benson . . . . **Arista 133**
Whitney Houston . . . . **Arista ARIST 658**

GREATEST MISTAKE OF MY LIFE, THE   1937
James Netson
Dash Music Ltd. . . . . UK
Chick Henderson . . . . **Regal Zonophone MR 2516**
Arthur Tracey (The Street Singer) . . . . . **Decca F 6452**
The Monograms . . . . **Parlophone R 4515**

GREEN COCKATOO, THE   1946
Don Rellegro
Cinephonic Music Co. Ltd. . . . . UK
Roberto Inglez & his Orchestra . . . . . . **Parlophone F 2183**
Ethel Smith (organ) . . . . **Brunswick LA 8566**
Mickey Ashman's Ragtime Band . . . . . **Pye NJL 29**

GREEN DOOR, THE   November 1956
Marvin Moore / Bob Davie
Francis, Day & Hunter Ltd. . . . . USA
Frankie Vaughan . . . . **Philips BBL 7233**
Jim Lowe . . . . **London HAD 2108**
Shakin' Stevens (1981) . . . . **Epic EPC A 1354**

GREEN EYES (Aquellos Ojos Verdes)   1941
Milo Menendez / Adolfo Utrera / L. Wolfe Gilbert
Campbell Connelly & Co. Ltd . . . . Cuba
Film(s): . . . . The Fabulous Dorseys
Jimmy Dorsey & his Orchestra, vocal Bob Eberly & Helen
O'Connell . . . . **Brunswick LAT 8369**
Bob Eberly & Helen O'Connell . . . . . **Warner Brothers WM 4033**

GREEN FIELDS   April 1960
Terry Gilkyson / Richard Dehr / Frank Miller
Montclare Music Co. Ltd . . . . USA
The Brothers Four . . . . **Philips PB 1009**

GREEN GREEN GRASS OF HOME, THE   February 1967
Curly Putman
Burlington Music Co. Ltd. . . . . USA
Porter Wagoner . . . . **RCA RCX 7178**
Tom Jones . . . . **Decca F 22511**
Dean Martin . . . . **Reprise RLP 6250**
Diana Trask . . . . **Ember NR 5086**

GREEN LEAVES OF SUMMER, THE   June 1962
Dimitri Tiomkin / Paul Francis Webster
Robbins Music Corporation Ltd. . . . . USA

Film(s): . . . . The Alamo
Kenny Ball's Jazzmen . . . . **Pye 7NJ 2054**
The Brothers Four . . . . **Philips BBL 7429**
The Mantovani Orchestra . . . . **Decca LK 4377**
Nominated for an Academy Award 1960.

GREEN MANALISHI, THE   **July 1970**
Peter Green
Fleetwood Music . . . . UK
Fleetwood Mac . . . . **Reprise RS 27007**

GREEN ONIONS   **February 1980**
Booker T. Jones / Steve Cropper / Al Jackson / Lewis Steinberg
Carlin Music Corporation . . . . USA
Booker T & The MG's . . . . **Atlantic K 40432**

GREEN TAMBOURINE   **March 1968**
Shelley Pinz / Paul Leka
Kama Sutra Music Ltd. . . . . USA
The Lemon Pipers . . . . **Pye 7N 25444**

GREY DAY   **May 1981**
Michael Barson
Warner Brothers Music . . . . UK
Madness . . . . **Stiff BUY 112**

GRINZING (Ich Muss Wieder Einmal In Grinzing Sein) **1934**
Ralph Benatzky
Peter Maurice Music Co. Ltd . . . . Germany
Franz Hoffman . . . . **Parlophone R 1279**
Ray Noble & his Orchestra, vocal Al Bowlly . . . . **HMV B 6519**
Jack Hylton & his Orchestra . . . . **HMV C 2856**
Cyril Stapleton & his Orchestra . . . . **Decca LK 4321**

GROCER JACK (See Excerpt From A Teenage Opera)

GROOVE IS IN THE HEART   **September 1990**
Kieren Kirby / Towa Tei / Herbie Hancock
Virgin Music . . . . USA
Deee-Lite . . . . **Elektra EKR 114**

GROOVE, THE   **May 1980**
Rodney Franklin
Leosong Copyright Service Ltd . . . . USA
Rodney Franklin . . . . **CBS 8529**

GROOVE LINE, THE   **February 1978**
Rodney Temperton
Rondor Music (London) Ltd . . . . UK
Heatwave . . . . **GTO GT 115**

GROOVER   **July 1973**
Marc Bolan
Wizard Music . . . . UK
T. Rex . . . . **EMI MARC 5**

GROOVIN'   **July 1967**
Felix Cavaliere / Eddie Brigati
Sparta Music Ltd. . . . . USA
The Young Rascals . . . . **Atlantic 584 111**

GROOVIN'   **June 1984**
Paul Weller / Michael Talbot
EMI Music . . . . UK
The Style Council . . . . **Polydor TSC 6**

GROOVIN' WITH MR. BLOE   **July 1970**
*Bobbie Gentry / Paul De Naumann / Kenneth Laguna / Bernard
Cochrane*
Dick James Music Co. Ltd. . . . . USA
Mr. Bloe . . . . **DJM DJS 216**

GROOVY KIND OF LOVE, A   **April 1966**
Tony Wine / Carole Bayer Sager
Screens Gems - Columbia Music Ltd. USA
The Mindbenders . . . . **Fontana TF 644**
Phil Collins (1988) . . . . **Virgin VS 1117**

GROOVY TRAIN   **September 1990**
Peter Hooton / Stephen Grimes
Virgin Music . . . . UK
The Farm . . . . **Produce MILK 102**

GUAGLIONE(The Man Who Plays the Mandolin) **Nov 1956**
Giovanni Fanciulli'Nisa' / Marilyn Keith & Alan Bergman

Mills Music Ltd. . . . . Italy
Film(s): . . . . Ten Thousand Bedrooms
Ourilio Fierro . . . . **Durium TLU 97007**
Dean Martin . . . . **Capitol CL 14690**
Dean Martin appeared in *Ten Thousand Bedrooms*.

GUANTANAMERA   **November 1966**
Jose Marti / Hector Angulo / Pete Seeger
Harmony Music Ltd. . . . . USA
The Sandpipers . . . . **Pye 7N 25380**

GUDBUY T'JANE   **December 1972**
James Lea / Neville Holder
Barn Publishing Ltd. . . . . UK
Slade . . . . **Polydor 2058312**

GUESS WHO I SAW TODAY   **1955**
Murray Grand / Elisse Boyd / June Carroll
Campbell Connelly & Co. Ltd . . . . USA
Film(s): . . . . New Faces
June Carroll . . . . **RCA LOC 1008**
Chris Conor . . . . **Columbia 33SX 1377**
Eydie Gormé . . . . **HMV CLP 1156**
Julie London . . . . **Liberty LBX 1113**
June Carroll appeared in *New Faces*

GUILTY   **1932**
Harry Akst / Gus Kahn / Richard A. Whiting
Francis, Day & Hunter Ltd. . . . . USA
The New Mayfair Dance Orchestra,
vocal Al Bowlly . . . . **HMV B 6097**
Ruth Etting . . . . **Regal Zonophone MR 458**
Steve Conway (1947) . . . . **Columbia FB 3308**
Jack Payne & his Orchestra . . . . **HMV CLP 1160**
Ella Fitzgerald . . . . **Brunswick OE 9062**
Ronnie Hilton . . . . **HMV POP 865**

GUILTY   **July 1974**
Ron Parker / Gerry Shurdy
A.T.V. Music Ltd. . . . . UK
The Pearls . . . . **Bell 1352**

GUITAR BOOGIE SHUFFLE   **May 1959**
Arthur Smith
Francis, Day & Hunter Ltd . . . . USA
Bert Weedon . . . . **Top Rank JAR 117**
The Virtues . . . . **HMV POP 621**

GUITAR MAN   **December 1962**
Duane Eddy / Lee Hazlewood
Shapiro-Bernstein & Co. Ltd . . . . USA
Dunae Eddy (guitar) & The Rebeletts . . . . **RCA 1316**

GUITAR MAN   **October 1972**
David Gates
Screen Gems Music Ltd. . . . . USA
Bread . . . . **Elektra K 12066**

GUITAR TANGO   **September 1962**
G. Lieferman / Norman Maine
Mills Music Ltd . . . . France
The Shadows . . . . **Columbia DB 4870**
Joe Loss & his Orchestra . . . . **HMV CLP 1697**

GURNEY SLADE THEME, THE   **December 1960**
Max Harris
Robbins Music Corporation Ltd . . . . UK
Max Harris & his Group . . . . **Fontana H 282**
Alyn Ainsworth & his Orchestra . . . . **Parlophone R 4719**
Theme of the television production *The Strange World of Gurney
Slade*.

GUY IS A GUY, A   **May 1952**
Oscar Brand
Leeds Music Ltd . . . . USA
Doris Day . . . . **Columbia DB 3058**
Diana Coupland . . . . **Decca F 9918**

GYPSYS TRAMPS AND THIEVES   **December 1971**
Bob Stone
Campbell Connelly & Co. Ltd . . . . USA
Cher . . . . **MCA MU 1142**

H.A.P.P.Y. RADIO   June 1979
Edwin Starr
A.T.V. Music Ltd. .... USA
Edwin Starr .... **RCA TC 2408**

HA HA SAID THE CLOWN   May 1967
Anthony Hazzard
Sydney Bron Music Co. Ltd. .... UK
Manfred Mann .... **Fontana TF 812**

HAIL CALEDONIA   1912
Hugh Ogilvie / Arthur Stroud
Francis, Day & Hunter Ltd .... UK
Tom Moss .... **Beltona 1750**
Reginald Talbot .... **Parlophone F 3164**
Stuart Gillies .... **EMI NTS 140**

HAIR OF GOLD, EYES OF BLUE   September 1948
Sunny Skylar
Chappell & Co. Ltd. .... USA
Film(s): .... Riders of the Whistling Pines
Bob Eberly .... **Brunswick 03976**
Benny Lee .... **Decca F 8970**
Gordon MacRae .... **Capitol CL 13031**

HAJJI BABA   December 1954
Dimitri Tiomkin / Ned Washington
Campbell Connelly & Co. Ltd. .... USA
Film(s): .... The Adventures of Hajji Baba
Nat 'King' Cole .... **Capitol CL 14155**
Dimitri Tiomkin & his Orchestra .... **Vogue LVA 9006**

HALF AS MUCH   August 1952
Curley Williams
Robbins Music Corporation Ltd .... USA
Rosemary Clooney .... **Philips BBL 7301**
Alma Cogan .... **HMV B 10338**
Connie Francis .... **MGM C 812**

HALF AS NICE   March 1969
Lucio Battisti / Jack Fishman
Cyril Shane Music .... Italy
Amen Corner .... **Immediate IM 073**

HALFWAY DOWN THE STAIRS   June 1977
A.A. Milne / H. Frazer Simpson
Ascherberg, Hopwood & Crew Ltd .... UK
The Muppets .... **Pye 7N 35698**

HALFWAY TO PARADISE   July 1961
Gerry Goffin / Carole King
Nevins-Kirshner Ltd. .... USA
Tony Orlando .... **Columbia SEG 8238**
Billy Fury .... **Decca F 11349**

HALLELUJAH   1927
Vincent Youmans / Leo Robin / Clifford Grey
Chappell & Co. Ltd. .... USA
Show(s): .... Hit the Deck
Film(s): .... Hit the Deck
Layton & Johnstone .... **Columbia SEG 7778**
Tony Martin, Vic Damone & Russ Tamblyn ...... **MGM EP 526**
Dennis Lotis .... **Columbia SEG 7955**
The Rita Williams Singers .... **HMV CLP 1311**
Tony Martin, Vic Damone & Russ Tamblyn appeared in the 1955 film of *Hit the Deck*.

HALLELUJAH   May 1979
Shimrit Orr / Kobi Oshrat
Intersong Music Ltd. .... Israel
Milk & Honey .... **Polydor 2001870**
Israeli entry for the 1979 Eurovision Song Contest (Placed first).

HALLELUJAH FREEDOM   November 1972
Junior Campbell
Camel Music .... UK
Junior Campbell .... **Deram DM 364**

HAMSTEAD WAY, THE (See 'Amstead Way, The)

HAND ON YOUR HEART   May 1989
Mike Stock / Matt Aitken / Peter Waterman
All Boys Music .... UK
Kylie Minogue .... **PWL PWL 35**

HANDFUL OF SONGS, A   September 1957
Tommy Steele / Lionel Bart / Michael Pratt
Peter Maurice Music Co. Ltd .... UK
Film(s): .... The Tommy Steele Story
Tommy Steele .... **Decca LF 1288**
Tommy Steele appeared in *The Tommy Steele Story*.
Ivor Novello award.

HANDS ACROSS THE SEA   1899
John Philip Sousa
Boosey & Hawkes Ltd .... USA
The American Legion Band .... **Decca F 7011**
The Band of the Royal Marines ...... **HMV CLP 3637**
American Military Band .... **Elite Special SOLP 351**

HANDS ACROSS THE TABLE   1934
Jean Delettre / Mitchell Parish
Campbell Connelly & Co. Ltd. .... USA
Show(s): .... Continental Varieties
Lucienne Boyer .... **Columbia DC 231**
Lee Wiley .... **Brunswick 01945**
Sarah Vaughan .... **Columbia 33SX 1252**
Pat Boone .... **London HAD 2265**

HANDS OFF - SHE'S MINE   March 1980
Roger Charlery / Andy Cox / Everett Morton / David Steele / Dave Wakeling
Zomba Music Publishers .... UK
The Beat .... **Go-Feet FEET 1**

HANDS TO HEAVEN   September 1988
David Glasper / Marcus Lillington
Virgin Music .... UK
Breathe .... **Siren SRN 68**

HANDS UP (Give Me Your Heart)   September 1981
Jean Kluger / Daniel Vangarde
Heath Levy Music .... France
Ottawan .... **Carrere CAR 183**

HANDSOME TERRITORIAL, A   1939
Jimmy Kennedy / Michael Carr
Peter Maurice Music Co. Ltd. .... UK
Jack Hylton & his Orchestra .... **HMV BD 5489**
Henry Hall & his Orchestra .... **Columbia FB 2234**
Billy Cotton & his Band .... **Rex 9577**

HANDY MAN   May 1960
Otis Blackwell / Jimmy Jones
Sheldon Music Ltd .... USA
Jimmy Jones .... **MGM C 832**

HANG ON IN THERE BABY   October 1974
Johnny Bristol
Heath Levy Music Ltd. .... USA
Johnny Bristol .... **MGM 2006443**

HANG ON SLOOPY   October 1965
Bert Russell / Wes Farrell
Robert Mellin Ltd .... USA
The McCoys .... **Immediate IM 001**
The Vibrations .... **London HLK 9875**

HANG ON THE BELL NELLIE   August 1949
Clive Erard / Ross Parker / Tommie Connor
Magna Music Co. Ltd .... UK
Lou Preager & his Orchestra .... **Columbia FB 3486**
Billy Cotton & his Band .... **Decca F 9149**

HANG ON TO YOUR LOVE   April 1990
Mike Stock / Matt Aitken / Peter Waterman
All Boys Music .... UK
Jason Donovan .... **PWL PWL 51**

HANG OUT THE STARS IN INDIANA   1931
Harry Woods / Billy Moll
Peter Maurice Music Co. Ltd. .... USA
The New Mayfair Dance Orchestra, vocal Al Bowlly   **HMV B 6058**
Florence Oldham .... **Columbia DB 724**

HANG YOUR HEART ON A HICKORY LIMB   1940
Johnny Burke / Jimmy Monaco
Campbell Connelly & Co. Ltd .... USA
Film(s): .... East Side of Heaven
Bing Crosby .... **Brunswick Bing 4**
Bing Crosby appeared in *East Side of Heaven*.

HANGIN' TOUGH — January 1990
Maurice Starr
EMI Music . . . . USA
New Kids On The Block . . . . CBS BLOCK 3

HANGING ON — June 1974
Mize Allen
Pedro Music . . . . USA
Cliff Richard . . . . EMI 2150
Cher . . . . Atco 228026
Conway Twitty & Loretta Lynn . . . . MCA MUPS 429

HANGING ON A STRING (Contemplating) — April 1985
Carl McIntosh / Jane Eugene / Steve Nichol
Virgin Music . . . . UK
Loose Ends . . . . Virgin VS 748

HANGING ON THE TELEPHONE — December 1978
Jack Lee
Chrysalis Music Ltd . . . . USA
Blondie . . . . Chrysalis CHS 2266

HANKY PANKY — August 1990
Madonna Ciccone / Patrick Leonard
Warner Chappell Music . . . . USA
Madonna . . . . Sire W 9789

HAPPENIN' ALL OVER AGAIN — February 1990
Mike Stock / Matt Aitken / Peter Waterman
All Boys Music . . . . UK
Lonnie Gordon . . . . Supreme SUPE 159

HAPPENING, THE — June 1967
Brian Holland / Eddie Holland / Lamont Dozier & Frank Devol
Carlin Music Corporation . . . . USA
The Supremes . . . . Tamla Motown TMG 607

HAPPINESS IS A THING CALLED JOE — 1942
Harold Arlen / E. Y. Harburg
Robbins Music Corporation Ltd . . . . USA
Film(s): . . . . Cabin in the Sky / I'll Cry Tomorrow
Lillian Roth . . . . Philips BBL 7079
Carroll Gibbons & The Savoy Hotel
Orpheans, vocal Edna Kay . . . . Columbia FB 2933
Ethel Waters . . . . World Records ST 949
Frances Wayne . . . . Vogue LVA 9096
Susan Hayward . . . . MGM EP 555
Ethel Waters appeared in *Cabin In The Sky*.
Susan Hayward appeared in *I'll Cry Tomorrow*.
Nominated for an Academy Award 1943.

HAPPINESS STREET — December 1956
Mack Wolfson / Edward White
Sydney Bron Music Co. Ltd. . . . . UK
Patti Lewis . . . . Columbia DB 3825
Tony Bennett . . . . Philips PB 628
Jill Day . . . . HMV POP 254

HAPPY ANNIVERSARY — November 1959
Al Stillman / Robert Allan
Dominion Music Co. Ltd . . . . USA
Film(s): . . . . Happy Anniversary
Mitzi Gaynor . . . . Top Rank JAR 2053
Joan Regan . . . . Nixa N 15238
Mitzi Gaynor appeared in *Happy Anniversary*.

HAPPY ANNIVERSARY — October 1974
Garry Paxton
Francis, Day & Hunter Ltd. . . . . USA
Slim Whitman . . . . United Artists UP 35728

HAPPY BIRTHDAY (Altered Images) — November 1981
"Altered Images"
Warner Brothers Music . . . . UK
Altered Images . . . . Epic EPC A 1522

HAPPY BIRTHDAY SWEET SIXTEEN — January 1962
Howard Greenfield / Neil Sedaka
Aldon Music Ltd. . . . . USA
Neil Sedaka . . . . RCA 1266

HAPPY CHRISTMAS (War is Over) — December 1972
John Lennon / Yoko Ono

Northern Songs . . . . UK
John & Yoko . . . . Apple R 5970

HAPPY DAYS AND LONELY NIGHTS — 1929
Fred Fisher / Billy Rose
Lawrenec Wright Music Co. Ltd . . . . USA
Ruth Etting . . . . Columbia 5110
June Pursell . . . . Brunswick 39828
Ruby Murray (1955) . . . . Columbia SEG 7588
Kay Starr . . . . Capitol T 1438

HAPPY DAYS ARE HERE AGAIN — 1930
Jack Yellen / Milton Ager
Lawrence Wright Music Co. Ltd . . . . USA
Film(s): . . . . Chasing Rainbows / Rain or Shine
Jack Payne & the BBC Dance Orchestra . . . . . Columbia CB 9
Sid Philips & his Band . . . . HMV POP 525
The 'Sing It Again' Ensemble . . . . Columbia 33SX 1271

HAPPY ENDING — 1933
Harry Parr-Davies
Francis, Day & Hunter Ltd. . . . . UK
Film(s): . . . . This Week of Grace
Gracie Fields . . . . Regal Zonophone MR 2040
Gracie Fields appeared in *This Week of Grace*.

HAPPY FEET — 1930
Jack Yellen / Milton Ager
Lawrence Wright Music Co. Ltd . . . . USA
Film(s): . . . . The King of Jazz
Paul Whiteman & his Orchestra . . . . Columbia CB 86
Horace Henderson & his Orchestra . . . . Parlophone GEP 8614
Lorrie Mann . . . . Pye 7N 25069
Paul Whiteman appeared in *The King Of Jazz*.

HAPPY GO LUCKY YOU, & BROKEN HEARTED ME — 1932
Al Hoffman / John Murray / Al Goodhart
Dash Music Ltd. . . . . USA
Bing Crosby . . . . Columbia SEG 7522
Steve Conway . . . . Columbia FB 3363

HAPPY HEART — July 1969
James Last / Jackie Rae
Donna Music Ltd. . . . . Germany
Andy Williams . . . . CBS 4062
James Last Orchestra . . . . Polydor 2371054

HAPPY HOLIDAY — 1942
Irving Berlin
Irving Berlin Ltd . . . . USA
Film(s): . . . . Holiday Inn
Bing Crosby . . . . Brunswick Bing 7
Jo Stafford . . . . Philips BBL 7100
Bing Crosby appeared in *Holiday Inn*.

HAPPY HOUR — July 1986
Stan Cullimore / Paul Heaton
Go Disc Music . . . . UK
The Housemartins . . . . Go Discs GOD 11

HAPPY JACK — January 1967
Peter Townshend
Fabulous Music Ltd. . . . . UK
The Who . . . . Reaction 591010

HAPPY TALK — November 1951
Richard Rodgers / Oscar Hammerstein II
Williamson Music Ltd . . . . USA
Show(s): . . . . South Pacific
Film(s): . . . . South Pacific
Juanita Hall . . . . Philips BBL 7157
Muriel Smith . . . . Columbia SEG 7688
Juanita Hall . . . . RCA RB 16065
Captain Sensible (1982) . . . . A&M CAP 1
Juanita Hall appeared in the American production of *South Pacific* and also the film *South Pacific*.
Muriel Smith appeared in the British production of *South Pacific*.

HAPPY TIMES — August 1950
Sylvia Fine
B. Feldman & Co. Ltd . . . . USA
Danny Kaye . . . . Brunswick 04505

Dinah Shore . . . . Columbia DB 2684
Benny Lee . . . . Decca F 9423

HAPPY TO BE ON AN ISLAND IN THE SUN   January 1976
David Lewis
EMI Music Ltd . . . . UK
Demis Roussos . . . . **Philips 6042033**

HAPPY WANDERER, THE   January 1954
Friedrich Wilhelm Moller / Antonia Ridge
Bosworth & Co. Ltd. . . . . Germany
The Obenkirchen Children's Choir . . . . . **Parlophone GEP 8529**
Frank Weir & his Orchestra . . . . **Decca LF 1297**
The Obenkirchen Children's Choir . . . . . **Parlophone PMC 1121**
Max Bygraves . . . . **Decca LK 4333**

HAPPY WHISTLER, THE   June 1956
Don Robertson
Sydney Bron Music . . . . USA
Don Robertson . . . . **Capitol CL 14575**
Ronnie Ronalde . . . . **Columbia DB 3785**

HARBOUR LIGHTS   1937
Jimmy Kennedy / Hugh Williams
Peter Maurice Music Co. Ltd. . . . . UK
Roy Fox & his Orchestra . . . . **HMV BD 5172**
Bing Crosby . . . . **Brunswick 04602**
The Platters (1960) . . . . **Mercury MMC 14045**
Pat Boone . . . . **London HAD 2030**

HARD DAY'S NIGHT, A   September 1964
John Lennon / Paul McCartney
Northern Songs Ltd . . . . UK
Film(s): . . . . A Hard Day's Night
The Beatles . . . . **Parlophone R 5160**
Keely Smith . . . . **Reprise R 6142**
Peter Sellers (1966) . . . . **Parlophone R 5393**
The Beatles appeared in *A Hard Day's Night.*
Ivor Novello Nomination.

HARD HABIT TO BREAK   November 1984
Steve Kipner / John Parker
SBK Songs . . . . USA
Chicago . . . . **Full Moon W 9214**

HARD HEADED WOMAN   August 1958
Claude De Metruis
Belinda (London) Ltd . . . . USA
Film(s): . . . . King Creole
Elvis Presley . . . . **RCA RD 27088**
Elvis Presley appeared in *King Creole.*

HARD HEARTED HANNAH   1924
Jack Yellen / Charles Bates / Bob Bigelow
Lawrence Wright Music Co. Ltd. USA
Film(s): . . . . Pete Kelly's Blues
Brooke Johns . . . . **HMV 1886**
Ella Fitzgerald . . . . **Brunswick 8078**
The Temperance Seven . . . . **Argo RG 117**
Kay Starr . . . . **Capitol T 1438**
Dorothy Provine . . . . **Warner Brothers WM 4053**
The Temperance Seven (1961) . . . . **Parlophone R 4823**
Ella Fitzgerald appeared in *Pete Kelly's Blues.*

HARD RAIN'S GONNA FALL, A   October 1973
Bob Dylan
Blossom Music Ltd. . . . . USA
Bryan Ferry . . . . **Island WIP 6170**
Bob Dylan . . . . **CBS 67239**

HARD TO HANDLE   September 1968
Alan Jones / Isbell Alvertis / Otis Redding
Carlin Music Corporation . . . . USA
Otis Redding . . . . **Atlantic 584199**

HARD TO SAY I'M SORRY   October 1982
Peter Cetera / David Foster
Chappell & Co. Ltd . . . . USA
Chicago . . . . **Full Moon K 79301**

HARDCORE UPROAR   August 1990
Jonathan Donaghy / Suddi Raval / Mark Hall
Virgin Music . . . . UK
Together . . . . **London F 143**

HARDER I TRY, THE   September 1988
Mike Stock / Matt Aitken / Peter Waterman
All Boys Music . . . . UK
Brother Beyond . . . . **Parlophone R 6184**

HARLEM NOCTURNE   1944
Earle Hagen / Dick Rogers
Peter Maurice Music Co. Ltd . . . . USA
Ray Noble & his Orchestra . . . . **Columbia FB 2568**
David Rose & his Orchestra . . . . **MGM SP 1009**
Les Brown & his Band of Renown . . . . **Capitol T 746**
Ernestine Anderson . . . . **Mercury MMC 14037**

HARLEM SHUFFLE   April 1969
Bob Relf / Ernest Nelson
Campbell Connelly & Co. Ltd. . . . . USA
Bob & Earl . . . . **Island WIP 6599**

HARPER VALLEY P.T.A.   December 1968
Tom T. Hall
Keith Prowse music Publishing Co. Ltd. . . . . USA
Jeannie C. Riley . . . . **Polydor 56748**

HARRIGAN   1907
George M. Cohan
B. Feldman & Co. Ltd. . . . . USA
Show(s): . . . . Fifty Miles from Boston
Film(s): . . . . Yankee Doodle Dandy
Mickey Rooney . . . . **RCA RD 27038**
Bing Crosby . . . . **Warner Brothers WM 4034**

HARRY LIME THEME, THE   November 1949
Anton Karas
Chappell & Co. Ltd . . . . UK
Film(s): . . . . The Third Man
Anton Karas (Zither) . . . . **Decca LF 1053**
Stanley Black & his Orchestra . . . . **Decca LK 4306**
Ethel Smith (organ) . . . . **Brunswick 04480**
Johnny Gregory & his Orchestra . . . . **Fontana TFL 5090**

HARRY'S GAME   November 1982
Paul Brennan
Television Music . . . . UK
Clannad . . . . **RCA 292**
Theme of the television series *Harry's Game.*

HARVEST FOR THE WORLD   August 1976
Marvin Isley / Ernest Isley / Rudolph Isley / O' Kelly Isley / Ronald Isley / Christopher Jasper
Carlin Music Corporation . . . . USA
The Isley Brothers (1976) . . . . **Epic EPC 4369**
The Christians (1988) . . . . **Island IS 395**

HARVEST OF LOVE   July 1963
Benny Hill
Welbeck Music Co. Ltd . . . . UK
Benny Hill . . . . **Pye 7N 15520**
Ivor Novello Award.

HAS ANYBODY HERE SEEN KELLY   1909
C.W. Murphy / William Letters
Francis, Day & Hunter Ltd . . . . UK
Show(s): . . . . The Jolly Bachelors
Film(s): . . . . Variety Jubilee
Florrie Forde . . . . **Rex 8189**
Jack Hylton & his Orchestra . . . . **HMV C 1681**
Dennis Martin . . . . **Decca LK 4366**

HAS ANYBODY SEEN OUR SHIP   1936
Noel Coward
Chappell & Co. Ltd . . . . UK
Show(s): . . . . Tonight at Eight-Thirty
Film(s): . . . . Star
Noel Coward & Gertrude Lawrence . . . . **HMV CLP 1050**
Julie Andrews & Daniel Massey . . . . **Stateside SL 10233**
Noel Coward & Gertrude appeared in the British production of *Tonight At Eight-Thirty.*
Julie Andrews & Daniel Massey appeared in *Star.*

HATS OFF TO LARRY   October 1961
Del Shannon
Vicki Music Ltd. . . . . USA
Del Shannon . . . . **London HL 9402**

HAVA NAGILA   March 1963
Traditional, arranged by Bo Winberg
Leeds Music Ltd ....
The Spotniks .... Oriole CB 1790

HAVE A DRINK ON ME   June 1961
Traditional, additional lyric by Lonnie Donegan & Peter Buchanan
Essex Music Ltd .... USA
Lonnie Donegan .... Pye 7N 15354

HAVE A LITTLE FAITH IN ME   1930
Harry Warren / Sam M. Lewis / Joe Young
Francis, Day & Hunter Ltd .... USA
Film(s):..Spring is Here
Arthur Schutt & his Orchestra .... Parlophone R 619
Guy Lombardo & his Royal Canadians ...... Columbia CB 38
Bert & Bob .... Decca F 1846

HAVE I THE RIGHT   May 1964
Howard Blaikley
Ivy Music Ltd .... UK
The Honeycombs .... Pye 7N 15664
The Dead End Kids (1977) .... CBS 4972

HAVE I TOLD YOU LATELY THAT I LOVE YOU   Sept 1950
Scott Wiseman
Leeds Music Ltd .... USA
Bing Crosby & The Andrews Sisters ...... Brunswick 044553
Vera Lynn .... Decca F 11129
Tex Ritter .... Capitol CL 13355

HAVE YOU EVER BEEN IN LOVE   April 1982
Andy Hill / Peter Sinfield / John Dantier
Paper Music .... UK
Leo Sayer .... Chrysalis CHS 2596
Ivor Novello Award

HAVE YOU EVER BEEN LONELY   1933
George Brown / Peter De Rose
Lawrence Wright Music Co. Ltd. .... USA
Val Rosing .... Imperial 2841
Ray Noble & his Orchestra, vocal Al Bowlly ..... HMV B 6319
Ronnie Hilton (1955) .... HMV B 10924
Joan Regan .... HMV POP 593

HAVE YOU GOT A LIGHT BOY (See Hev Yew Gotta Loight Boy)

HAVE YOU GOT ANY CASTLES BABY   1938
Richard A. Whiting / Johnny Mercer
Sterling Music Publishing Co. Ltd. .... USA
Film(s):....................................... The Varsity Show
Dick Powell .... Decca F 6637
Bobby Darin .... London HAK 2235
Dick Powell appeared in *The Varsity Show.*

HAVE YOU HEARD   May 1953
Roy Rodde / Frank Lavere / Lew Douglas
Francis, Day & Hunter Ltd .... USA
Dick James .... Parlophone R 3670
Lita Roza .... Decca F 10109
Joni James .... MGM SP 1025

HAVE YOU MET MISS JONES   1940
Richard Rodgers / Lorenz Hart
Chappell & Co. Ltd. .... USA
Show(s):...........................I'd Rather be Right / All Clear
Film(s):........................... Gentlemen Marry Brunettes
Adelaide Hall .... Decca F 7305
Bing Crosby .... HMV CLP 1088
Rudy Vallee, Jane Russell, Anita Ellis,
Scott Brady & Alan Young .... Vogue LVA 9003
Rudy Vallee, Jane Russell, Anita Ellis, Scott Brady & Alan Young
appeared in *Gentlemen Marry Brunettes.*

HAVE YOU SEEN HER   February 1972
Eugene Record / Barbara Acklin
Burlington Music Co. Ltd .... UK
The Chi-Lites (1972) .... MCA MU 1146
The Chi-Lites (1975) .... Brunswick BR 20
M.C. Hammer (1990) .... Capitol CL 590

HAVE YOU SEEN YOUR MOTHER, BABY, STANDING IN THE SHADOW   November 1966
Mick Jagger / Keith Richard
Mirage Music Ltd. .... UK

The Rolling Stones .... Decca F 12497

HAVE YOURSELF A MERRY LITTLE CHRISTMAS   1944
Hugh Martin / Ralph Blane
Sun Music Publishing Co. Ltd .... USA
Film(s):...........................Meet Me In St.Louis
Judy Garland .... Brunswick 03572
Frank Sinatra .... Capitol LCT 6144
Ella Fitzgerald .... HMV CLP 1397
Judy Garland appeared in *Meet Me In St. Louis*

HAVING MY BABY   November 1974
Paul Anka
M.A.M. (Music Publishing) Ltd. .... USA
Paul Anka .... United Artists UP 35713

HAWAIIAN BUTTERFLY   1917
Joseph Santly / George Little / Billy Baskette
Herman Darewski Music Publishing Co. Ltd. .... USA
Show(s):... Bubbly
Teddie Gerrard .... Columbia L 1188
Herbert Payne .... Regal 1808
Terrie Gerrard appeared in *Bubbly.*

HAWAIIAN WAR CHANT, THE   1941
"Leleichaku" / Johnny Noble / Ralph Freed
Keith Prowse Music Publishing Co. Ltd .... USA
Film(s):................It's a Date / Song of the Islands
Roland Peachy & his Royal Hawaiians .... Decca F 7855
Tommy Dorsey & his Orchestra .... HMV 7EG 8011
The Tommy Dorsey Orchestra, conducted by
Warren Covington .... Brunswick LAT 8282
The King Sisters .... Capitol T 808
Chuck "Kaipo" Miller's Royal Hawaiian Serenaders Capitol T 1229

HAWAIIAN WEDDING SONG   January 1959
Charles E. King / Al Hoffman / Dick Manning
Pickwick Music Ltd .... Hawaii
Film(s):... Blue Hawaii
Andy Williams .... London HLA 8784
Billy Vaughan & his Orchestra .... London HAD 2201
Julie Rogers (1965) .... Mercury MF 849
Elvis Presley .... RCA RD 27238
Elvis Presley appeared in *Blue Hawaii.*

HAWKEYE   December 1955
Boudleaux Bryant
Good Music .... USA
Frankie Laine .... Philips PB 519

HE AIN'T HEAVY, HE'S MY BROTHER   November 1969
Bobby Russell / Bobby Scott
Cyril Shane Music .... USA
The Hollies .... Parlophone R 5806
Matt Monro .... Capitol ST 22546
The Hollies (1988) .... EMI EM 74

HE AIN'T NO COMPETITION   November 1988
Mike Stock / Matt Aitken / Peter Waterman
All Boys Music .... UK
Brother Beyond .... Parlophone R 6193

HE PLAYED HIS UKULELE AS THE SHIP WENT DOWN   1932
Arthur Le Clerq
Campbell Connelly & Co. Ltd. .... UK
Ambrose & his Orchestra .... HMV B 6137

HE WAS REALLY SAYING SOMETHING   May 1982
Norman Whitfield / Eddie Holland / William Stevenson
Jobete Music .... USA
Bananarama & Fun Boy Three .... Deram NANA 1

HE'LL HAVE TO GO   July 1960
Joe Allison / Audrey Allison
Campbell Connelly & Co. Ltd .... USA
Jim Reeves .... RCA RD 27176

HE'S A COUSIN OF MINE   1906
Cecil Mack / Christopher Smith / Silvio Hein
Campbell Connelly & Co. Ltd. .... USA
Show(s):... Marrying Mary
Mac Perrin .... Fontana TFL 5019

HE'S A RAG PICKER   1914
Irving Berlin

B. Feldman & Co. Ltd. . . . . USA
Show(s): . . . . 5064 Gerard
Jack Morrison . . . . **Columbia 2553**
The Two Bobs . . . . **Edison Bell Winner 2876**
Harry Roy & his Orchestra . . . . **Parlophone F 338**
Jack Morrison appeared in *5064 Gerard.*

HE'S A REAL GONE GUY   April 1949
Nellie Lutcher
Campbell Connelly & Co. Ltd . . . . USA
Nellie Lutcher . . . . **Capitol EAP 20066**

HE'S A REBEL   January 1963
Gene Pitney
Aaron Schroeder Ltd. . . . . USA
The Crystals . . . . **London HL 9611**
The Breakaways . . . . **Pye 7N 15471**

HE'S DEAD BUT HE WON'T LIE DOWN   1932
Will Haines / Maurice Beresford / James Harper
Campbell Connelly & Co. Ltd. . . . . UK
Gracie Fields . . . . **HMV B 4258**
Leonard Henry . . . . **Regal T 6227**

HE'S GONNA STEP ON YOU AGAIN   July 1971
John Kongos / Chris Demetriou
Westminster Music . . . . UK
John Kongos . . . . **Fly BUG 8**
See also under Step On.

HE'S GOT NO LOVE   August 1965
Chris Curtis / Mike Pender
Toby Music Ltd . . . . UK
The Searchers . . . . **Pye 7N 15878**

HE'S GOT THE WHOLE WORLD IN HIS HANDS   Dec 1957
Traditional
An edition by Mills Music Ltd . . . . USA
Laurie London . . . . **Parlophone GEP 8664**

HE'S HIS OWN GRANDPA (See I'm My Own Grandpa)

HE'S IN TOWN   November 1964
Gerry Goffin / Carole King
Aldon Music Ltd. . . . . USA
The Rocking Berries . . . . **Piccadilly 7N 35203**
The Tokens . . . . **Fontana TF 500**

HE'S MISSTRA KNOW IT ALL   May 1974
Stevie Wonder
Jobete Music (UK) Ltd. . . . . USA
Stevie Wonder . . . . **Tamla Motown TMG 892**

HE'S MY GUY   1943
Don Raye / Gene De Paul
Leeds Music Ltd. . . . . USA
Film(s): . . . . Who Done it / Follow the Band
Dinah Shore . . . . **HMV BD 1031**
Ella Fitzgerald . . . . **Brunswick 03441**
Peggy Lee . . . . **Capitol T 864**

HE'S SO FINE   May 1963
Ronald Mack
Peter Maurice Music Co. Ltd . . . . USA
The Chiffons . . . . **Stateside SS 172**

HE'S TALL AND DARK AND HANDSOME   1928
Charles Tobias / Al Sherman
Lawrence Wright Music Co. Ltd. . . . . USA
Sophie Tucker . . . . **Columbia 4942**

HE'S THE GREATEST DANCER   April 1979
Nile Rodgers / Bernard Edwards
Warner Brothers Music Ltd. . . . . USA
Sister Sledge . . . . **Atlantic K 11257**

HEAD OVER HEELS   July 1985
Roland Orzabal / Curt Smith
Virgin Music . . . . UK
Tears For Fears . . . . **Phonogram IDEA 10**

HEAD OVER HEELS IN LOVE   1937
Mack Gordon / Harry Revel
Cinephonic Music Co. Ltd. USA

Film(s): . . . . Head Over Heels
Jessie Matthews . . . . **Decca F 6286**
Lilli Palmer . . . . **HMV B 8544**
Jessie Matthews appeared in *Head Over Heels.*

HEAR MY SONG VIOLETTA (Hor Mein Lied Violetta) 1938
Rudolph Luckesch / Othmar Klose / Harry S. Pepper
Dix Music Ltd. . . . . Austria
Arthur Tracey (The Street Singer) . . . . **Decca LF 1077**
Jimmy Dorsey & his Orchestra,
vocal Bob Eberly . . . . **Brunswick 03133**
Joseph Locke . . . . **Columbia SCD 2153**
David Whitfield . . . . **Decca F 11289**

HEAR THE DRUMMER GET WICKED   June 1990
Chad Jackson
Marylebone Music . . . . UK
Chad Jackson . . . . **Big Wave BWR 36**

HEART   March 1957
Richard Adler / Jerry Ross
Frank Music Co. Ltd. . . . . USA
Show(s): . . . . Damn Yankees
Film(s): . . . . What Lola Wants
American Cast of Damn Yankees . . . . **HMV CLP 1108**
The McGuire Sisters . . . . **Coral Q 72238**
Sound Track of What Lola Wants . . . . **RCA RD 27103**

HEART   April 1988
Neil Tennant / Chris Lowe
Cage Music . . . . UK
The Pet Shop Boys . . . . **Parlophone R 6177**

HEART AND SOUL   1939
Hoagy Carmichael
Bradbury Wood Ltd. . . . . USA
Film(s): . . . . A Song is Born / Some Like it Hot
Paul Whiteman & his Orchestra . . . . **Brunswick 02675**
Jay Wilbur & his Band . . . . **Rex 9475**
Hoagy Carmichael Orchestra . . . . **MCA 1819**
Carole Carr . . . . **HMV B 10420**
Sue Raney . . . . **Capitol T 964**

HEART AND SOUL   September 1988
Carol Decker / Ronald Rogers
Virgin Music . . . . UK
T'Pau . . . . **Siren SRN 41**

HEART BREAKER   April 1948
Frank Capano / Max Freedman / Morty Berk
Leeds Music Ltd. . . . . USA
The Andrews Sisters . . . . **Brunswick 03916**
Sam Browne & the Keynotes . . . . **Decca F 8872**
Art Mooney & his Orchestra & Chorus . . . . **MGM D 136**

HEART FULL OF SOUL   August 1965
Graham Gouldman
B. Feldman & Co. Ltd . . . . UK
The Yardbirds . . . . **Columbia DB 7594**

HEART OF A MAN   August 1959
Peggy Cochrane / Paddy Roberts
David Toff Music Publishing Co. Ltd . . . . UK
Film(s): . . . . Heart of a Man
Frankie Vaughan . . . . **Philips BBE 12317**
Frankie Vaughan appeared in *Heart of a Man.*

HEART OF A ROSE   1918
Horatio Nicholls / Worton David
Lawrence Wright Music Co. Ltd. . . . . UK
Freda Fairchild . . . . **Zonophone 1852**
Anne Ziegler & Webster Booth . . . . **HMV B 9760**
Reggie Goff . . . . **Decca F 9336**

HEART OF A TEENAGE GIRL   May 1960
Bill Crompton / Morgan Jones
Park Gate Music Ltd . . . . UK
Craig Douglas . . . . **Top Rank JAR 340**

HEART OF GLASS, A   February 1979
Deborah Harry / Christopher Stein
EMI Music Ltd. . . . . UK
Blondie . . . . **Chrysalis CHS 2275**

HEART OF GOLD April 1972
Neil Young
Warner Brothers Music Ltd .... USA
Neil Young .... **Reprise K 14140**

HEART OF MY HEART (See Gang That Sang Heart Of My Heart, The)

HEART OF STONE April 1973
Phil Coulter / Bill Martin
Mews Music .... UK
Kenny .... **Rak 144**

HEART ON MY SLEEVE July 1976
Benny Gallagher / Graham Lyle
Rondor Music (London) Ltd .... UK
Gallagher & Lyle .... **A&M AMS 7227**
Ivor Novello Nomination.

HEARTACHE February 1987
Tambi Fernando / Iris Fernando / Wayne Brown
Handle Music .... UK
Pepsi & Shirlie .... **Polydor POSP 837**

HEARTACHE AVENUE January 1983
Mark Tibenham / Lawrence Mason
ATV Music .... UK
The Maisonettes .... **RSG RSG 1**

HEARTACHES 1931
John Klenner / Al Hoffman
Campbell Connelly & Co. Ltd .... USA
Bert Lown & his Hotel Biltmore Orchestra .... **HMV B 6051**
Ted Weems & his Orchestra (1947) .... **Brunswick OE 9420**
The Four Aces .... **Brunswick LAT 8221**
Pat Boone .... **London HAD 2127**
Vince Hill (1966) .... **Columbia DB 7852**

HEARTACHES BY THE NUMBER February 1960
Harlan Howard
Joy Music Ltd .... USA
Guy Mitchell .... **Philips BBE 12336**

HEARTBEAT September 1975
Bob Montgomery / Norman Petty
Southern Music Publishing Co. Ltd .... USA
Showaddywaddy .... **Bell 1450**
Buddy Holly .... **Coral Q 72346**
The England Sisters .... **HMV POP 710**

HEARTBEAT January 1955
Jerry Stevens
Edward Kassner Music Co. Ltd. .... USA
Ruby Murray .... **Columbia SEG 7631**
Lita Roza .... **Decca F 10427**
Karen Chandler .... **Vogue Q 2030**

HEARTBREAK HOTEL April 1956
Mae Boren Axton / Elvis Presley / Tommy Durden
Mills Music Ltd. .... USA
Elvis Presley .... **HMV POP 182**
Connie Francis .... **MGM C 804**

HEARTBREAKER November 1982
Barry Gibb / Robin Gibb / Maurice Gibb
Gibb Brothers Music .... UK
Dionne Warwick .... **Arista ARIST 496**
Ivor Novello Nomination.

HEARTLESS March 1954
Ken Morris
Bluebird Music Co. Ltd. .... UK
Frankie Vaughan .... **HMV B 10635**
Johnny Brandon .... **Polygon P 1103**

HEARTS AND FLOWERS 1899
Theodore Tobani
W. Paxton & Co. Ltd. .... USA
The New Light Symphony Orchestra .... **HMV C 1562**
Paul Whiteman & his Orchestra .... **HMV B 2185**
Peter Yorke & his Orchestra .... **Columbia DB 2340**
Adapted from *Winter Story* by Alphonse Czibulka.

HEAT IS ON, THE April 1985
Keith Forsey / Harold Faltermeyer

Famous Music .... USA
Film(s): .... Beverly Hills Cop
Glen Frey .... **MCA MCA 941**

HEAT WAVE 1934
Irving Berlin
Irving Berlin Ltd. .... USA
Show(s): .... As Thousands Cheer
Film(s):Alexander's Ragtime Band / Thousands Cheer / Blue Skies /
There's No Business Like Show Business
Ethel Waters .... **Columbia DB 1436**
Delores Gray .... **Brunswick LAT 8059**
Eve Boswell .... **Parlophone PMC 1105**
Bing Crosby .... **HMV CLP 1088**
Ethel Waters appeared in *As Thousands Cheer.*
Bing Crosby appeared in *Blue Skies.*

HEATHER ON THE HILL, THE April 1949
Alan Jay Lerner / Frederick Loewe
Keith Prowse Music Publishing Co. Ltd .... USA
Show(s): .... Brigadoon
Film(s): .... Brigadoon
David Brooks & Marion Bell .... **HMV B 9748**
Jack Cassidy & Shirley Jones .... **Philips BBL 7257**
Gene Kelly .... **MGM D 133**
David Brooks & Marion Bell appeared in the American production of
Brigadoon.
Gene Kelly appeared in the film of *Brigadoon.*

HEATSEEKER January 1988
Angus Young / Malcolm Young / Brian Johnson
Chappell & Co. Ltd .... Australia
AC/DC .... **Atlantic A 9136**

HEAVEN (See (Feels Like) Heaven)

HEAVEN CAN WAIT 1939
Eddie De Lange / Jimmy Van Heusen
B. Feldman & Co. Ltd. .... USA
The Casa Loma Orchestra .... **Decca F 7057**
Nelson Riddle & his Orchestra ...... **Capitol T 1018**
The Four Aces .... **Brunswick LA 8614**
Dean Martin .... **Capitol T 1442**

HEAVEN IS A PLACE ON EARTH January 1988
Richard Nowells / Ellen Shipley
Virgin Music .... USA
Belinda Carlisle .... **Virgin VS 1036**

HEAVEN KNOWS I'M MISERABLE NOW June 1984
Steven Morrisey / John Marr
Warner Brothers Music .... UK
The Smiths .... **Rough Trade RT 156**

HEAVEN MUST BE MISSING AN ANGEL August 1976
Kenny St. Lewis / Freddie Perren
Heath Levy Music Ltd .... USA
Film(s): .... The World Is Full of Married Men
Tavares .... **Capitol CL 15876**
Tavares appeared in *The World is Full of Married Men.*

HEAVEN MUST HAVE SENT YOU June 1971
Eddie Holland / Brian Holland / Lamont Dozier
Jobete Music (UK) Ltd. .... USA
The Elgins .... **Tamla Motown TMG 583**

HEIGH-HO 1938
Larry Morey / Frank Churchill
Walt Disney Music Co. Ltd. .... USA
Film(s): .... Snow White and the Seven Dwarfs
Sound Track .... **HMV BD 514**
Sound Track .... **Disneyland DLP 39003**
Freddie Rich & his Orchestra .... **Decca F 6629**

HELEN WHEELS December 1973
Paul McCartney
McCartney Music .... UK
Paul McCartney & Wings .... **Apple R 5993**

HELENE March 1949
D. Katrivanou / John Howells
Peter Maurice Music Co. Ltd .... Greece
Lee Lawrence .... **Decca F 9090**

HELL RAISER   May 1973
Mike Chapman / Nicky Chinn
Chinnichap Music . . . . UK
The Sweet . . . . **RCA 2316**

HELLO   April 1984
Lionel Richie
Warner Brothers Music . . . . USA
Lionel Richie . . . . **Motown TMG 1330**

HELLO BLUEBIRD   1927
Cliff Friend
Francis, Day & Hunter Ltd. . . . . USA
The Cliquot Club Eskimos . . . . **Columbia 4271**
Jack Hylton & his Orchestra . . . . **HMV B 5189**

HELLO DOLLY   July 1964
Jerry Herman
Edwin H. Morris & Co. Ltd . . . . USA
Show(s): . . . . Hello Dolly
Film(s): . . . . Hello Dolly
Mary Martin . . . . **RCA RD 7768**
The Kenny Ball Jazzmen . . . . **Pye 7NJ 2071**
Louis Armstrong . . . . **London HL 9878**
Frankie Vaughan . . . . **Philips BF 1339**
Barbra Streisand . . . . **Stateside SSL 10292**
Louis Armstrong . . . . **Stateside SSL 10292**
The Bachelors (1966) . . . . **Decca F 12309**
Mary Martin appeared in both the American and British productions
of *Hello Dolly*
Barbra Streisand & Louis Armstrong appeared in the film *Hello Dolly.*

HELLO FRISCO HELLO   1915
Louis Hirsch / Gene Buck
Francis, Day & Hunter Ltd. . . . . USA
Show(s): . . . . The Ziegfeld Follies of 1915
Film(s): . . . . Wharf Angel
Red Nichols & his Orchestra,
   vocal The Boswell Sisters . . . . **Brunswick 108**
The Merry Macs . . . . **Decca F 7179**
Vivian Blaine . . . . **Mercury MPL 6518**

HELLO GOODBYE   January 1968
John Lennon / Paul McCartney
Northern Songs Ltd. . . . . UK
The Beatles . . . . **Parlophone R 5655**
Ivor Novello Nomination.

HELLO HAPPINESS   April 1976
Les Reed / Roger Greenaway
Cookaway Music . . . . UK
The Drifters . . . . **Bell 1469**

HELLO HAWAII, HOW ARE YOU   1915
Jean Schwartz / Bert Kalmar / Edgar Leslie
B. Feldman & Co. Ltd. . . . . USA
Stanley Kirkby . . . . **Regal G 7362**
The Royal Cremona Orchestra . . . . **Zonophone Twin 1687**

HELLO HELLO I'M BACK AGAIN   May 1973
Gary Glitter / Mike Leander
Leeds Music Ltd. . . . . UK
Gary Glitter . . . . **Bell BELL 1299**

HELLO HURRAY   March 1973
Rolf Kempf
Warner Brothers Music Ltd. . . . . USA
Alice Cooper . . . . **Warner Brothers K 16248**

HELLO I LOVE YOU   October 1968
Robert Krieger / James Morrison / Ray Manzarak & John Densmore
Campbell, Connelly & Co. Ltd. . . . . USA
The Doors . . . . **Elektra EKSN 45037**

HELLO LITTLE GIRL   October 1963
John Lennon / Paul McCartney
Northern Songs Ltd . . . . UK
The Fourmost . . . . **Parlophone R 5056**

HELLO MA BABY   1899
Joseph Howard / Ida Emerson
Francis, Day & Hunter Ltd . . . . USA
Film(s): . . . . I Wonder Who's Kissing Her Now
Sophie Tucker . . . . **Mercury MPL 6503**
Bing Crosby . . . . **Warner Brothers WM 4034**

HELLO MARY LOU, GOODBYE HEART   July 1961
Gene Pitney
Aaron Schroeder Ltd. . . . . USA
Ricky Nelson . . . . **London HL 9347**
Gene Pitney . . . . **HMV CLP 1566**

HELLO MOM   1944
Arthur Jones / Frank Loesser / Eddie Dunstedter
B. Feldman & Co. Ltd. . . . . USA
Bing Crosby . . . . **Brunswick 03510**
Turner Layton . . . . **Columbia FB 3091**

HELLO MUDDAH, HELLO FADDUH   October 1963
Amicare Ponchielli
Peter Maurice Music Co. Ltd . . . . USA
Alan Sherman . . . . **Warner Brothers WB 106**
Adapted from *Dance of the Hours* from Act3 of *La Gioconda* by
Amilcare Ponchielli (1834 - 1886).
See also 'Like I Do'.

HELLO MY DEARIE   1917
Gene Buck / Dave Stamper
Francis, Day & Hunter Ltd. . . . . USA
Show(s): . . . . Zig-Zag
Cicely Debenham & Bertram Wallis . . . . **Columbia L 1138**
Cicely Debenham & Bertram Wallis appeared in *Zig-Zag.*

HELLO SUMMERTIME   September 1974
Bill Backer / Billy Davis / Roger Greenaway & Roger Cook
Cookaway Music . . . . UK
Bobby Goldsboro . . . . **United Artists UP 35705**

HELLO SUSIE   July 1969
Roy Wood
Essex Music Ltd. . . . . UK
Amen Corner . . . . **Immediate IM 081**

HELLO THIS IS JOANNIE   January 1979
Paul Evans / Fred Tobias
Singatune Publishing . . . . USA
Paul Evans . . . . **Spring 2066932**

HELLO YOUNG LOVERS   October 1953
Richard Rodgers / Oscar Hammerstein II
Williamson Music Ltd. . . . . USA
Show(s): . . . . The King and I
Film(s): . . . . The King and I
Gertrude Lawrence . . . . **Brunswick LAT 8026**
Valerie Hobson . . . . **Philips BBL 7002**
Marni Nixon . . . . **Capitol LCT 6108**
Gertrude Lawrence appeared in the American production of *The King
and I.*
Valerie Hobson appeared in the British production of *The King and I.*
Deborah Kerr appeared in the film *The King and I.*
The Singing voice of Deborah Kerr was Dubbed by Marni Nixon.

HELLO, HELLO, WHO'S YOUR LADY FRIEND   1914
Worton David / Bert Lee / Harry Fragson
B. Feldman & Co. Ltd. . . . . UK
Film(s): . . . . The Story Of Vernon & Irene Castle
Florrie Forde . . . . **Imperial 2853**
Leslie Sarony . . . . **Decca LK 4026**
Stanley Holloway . . . . **Philips BBI 7237**

HELP   August 1965
John Lennon / Paul McCartney
Northern Songs Ltd . . . . UK
Show(s): . . . . John, Paul, George, Ringo and Bert
Film(s): . . . . Help
The Beatles . . . . **Parlophone R 5305**
Alma Cogan . . . . **Columbia DB 7786**
Barbara Dickson . . . . **RSO 239141**
Bananarama (1989) . . . . **London LON 222**
The Beatles appeared in *Help.*
Barbara Dickson appeared in *John, Paul, George, Ringo and Bert.*
Ivor Novello Nomination.

HELP ME GIRL   November 1966
Scott English / Laurence Weiss
Schroeder Music Ltd. . . . . USA
Eric Burdon & The Animals . . . . **Decca F 12502**

HELP ME MAKE IT THROUGH THE NIGHT   January 1973
Kris Kristofferson
Keith Prowse Music Publishing Co. Ltd. . . . . USA

Gladys Knight & the Pips .... Tamla Motown TMG 830
John Holt (1975) .... Trojan TR 7944

HELP YOURSELF (Gli Occhi Miei)　　　September 1968
C. Donida / Jack Fishman
Valley Music .... Italy
Tom Jones .... Decca F 12812

HER BATHING SUIT NEVER GOT WET　　　1946
Charles Tobias / Nat Simon
Leeds Music Co. Ltd. .... USA
The Andrews Sisters .... Brunswick 03742
Edmundo Ros & his Orchestra .... Decca F 8708

HER GOLDEN HAIR WAS HANGING DOWN HER BACK 1884
Monroe H. Rosenfield / Felix McGlennon
Francis, Day & Hunter Ltd .... USA
Show(s): .... The Shop Girl
George Gaskin .... Berliner 938
Seymour Hicks .... HMV C 2432
Seymour Hicks appeared in *The Shop Girl*

HER NAME IS MARY　　　　　　　　　　1933
Bruce Sievier / Harold Ramsey
Chappell & Co. Ltd. .... UK
Charles Kullman .... Columbia DB 1006
Debroy Somers & his Band .... Columbia CB 536
Jack Hylton & his Orchestra .... Decca F 3515

HERE COMES COOKIE　　　　　　　　　　1935
Mack Gordon / Harry Revel
Victoria Musioc Co. Ltd .... USA
Film(s): .... Love in Bloom
Cleo Brown .... Brunswick 02013
Jay Wilbur & his Band .... Rex 8486

HERE COMES HEAVEN AGAIN　　　　　　　1946
Harold Adamson / Jimmy McHugh
Robbins Music Corporation Ltd. .... USA
Film(s): .... Come Back to Me
Carroll Gibbons & The Savoy Orpheans ... Columbia FB 3209

HERE COMES MY BABY　　　　　　　March 1967
Cat Stevens
Angussa Music .... UK
The Tremeloes .... CBS 202519

HERE COMES SUMMER　　　　　September 1959
Jerry Keller
Mills Music Ltd .... USA
Jerry Keller .... London HAR 2261
Cliff Richard .... Columbia 33SX 1192

HERE COMES THAT FEELING　　　　　July 1962
Dorsey Burnette / Joe Osborne
Peter Maurice Music Co. Ltd .... USA
Brenda Lee .... Brunswick 05871

HERE COMES THE JUDGE　　　　　August 1968
Bob Astor / Dick Allen / Sarah Harvey / Dewey Markham
Jewel Music Publishing Co. Ltd. .... USA
Pigmeat Markham .... Chess CRS 8077

HERE COMES THE NIGHT　　　　　　April 1965
Bert Berns
Robert Mellin Ltd .... USA
Them .... Decca F 12094

HERE COMES THE RAIN AGAIN　　　February 1984
Annie Lennox / Dave Stewart
RCA Music .... UK
Eurythmics .... RCA DA 5

HERE COMES THE SUN　　　　　　August 1976
George Harrison
Northern Songs Ltd .... UK
Show(s): .... John, Paul, Georgo Ringo & Bert
Steve Harley .... EMI 2505
Barbara Dickson .... RSO 2394141
The Beatles .... Parlophone PCS 7088
Barbara Dickson appeared in *John, Paul, George, Ringo & Bert.*

HERE I AM IN LOVE AGAIN　　　　　April 1957
Moose Charlap / Chuck Sweeney
Chappell & Co. Ltd. .... USA

The Modernaires .... Vogue LVA 9080
Debbie Reynolds .... London HAD 2200
Buddy Greco .... Vogue LVA 9021

HERE I GO AGAIN　　　　　　　　　June 1964
Mort Shuman / Clive Westlake
Belinda (London) Ltd .... UK
The Hollies .... Parlophone R 5137

HERE I GO AGAIN　　　　　　September 1976
Joe McDonald
Sonet Publishing .... USA
Twiggy .... Mercury 6007100
'Country' Joe McDonald .... Vanguard SVRL 19048

HERE I GO AGAIN　　　　　　November 1987
David Coverdale / Bernard Marsden
Warner Brothers Music .... UK
Whitesnake .... EMI EM 35

HERE IN MY ARMS　　　　　　　　　　1927
Richard Rodgers / Lorenz Hart
Chappell & Co. Ltd. .... USA
Show(s): .... Dearest Enemy / Lido Lady
Film(s): .... Tea for Two
Phyllis Dare & Jack Hulbert .... Columbia 4426
Don Cherry .... Brunswick 04607
Ella Fitzgerald .... HMV CLP 1117
Phyllis Dare & Jack Hulbert appeared in *Lido Lady.*

HERE IN MY HEART　　　　　　November 1952
Bill Borrelli / Pat Genaro / Lou Levinson
Robert Mellin Ltd .... USA
Al Martino .... Capitol EAP 1-20153
Lee Lawrence .... Decca F 9970
Keely Smith .... London HLD 9240

HERE IT COMES AGAIN　　　　　November 1965
Barry Mason / Les Reed
Donna Music Ltd .... UK
The Fortunes .... Decca F 12243

HERE LIES LOVE　　　　　　　　　　　1933
Leo Robin / Ralph Rainger
Chappell & Co. Ltd. .... USA
Film(s): .... The Big Broadcast
Bing Crosby .... Columbia DB 1990
Frankie Laine .... Philips BBL 7260
Chris Connor .... London LTZK 15151
Bing Crosby appeared in *The Big Broadcast.*

HERE WE ARE, HERE WE ARE, HERE WE ARE AGAIN 1914
Charles Knight / Kenneth Lyle
Francis, Day & Hunter Ltd. .... UK
Mark Sheridan .... HMV 02550
Debroy Somers & his Band ...... Columbia DX 199
Tommy Handley & chorus .... HMV C 3039

HERE WE GO ROUND THE MULBERRY BUSH　Jan 1968
Chris Wood / Dave Mason / Stevie Winwood & Jim Capaldi
United Artists Music Co. Ltd. .... UK
Film(s): .... Here We Go Round the Mulberry Bush
Traffic .... Island WIP 6025
Traffic .... United Artists ULP 1186
Traffic appeared in *Here We Go Round the Mulberry Bush.*

HERE'S THAT RAINY DAY　　　　　　　1954
Johnny Burke / Jimmy Van Heusen
Chappell & Co. Ltd. .... USA
Show(s): .... Carnival in Flanders
Frank Sinatra .... Capitol LCT 6185
Peggy Lee .... Capitol T 1630
Perry Como .... RCA RD 27232
Tony Bennett .... CBS S 64849
Nancy Wilson .... Capitol T 2433

HERE'S TO LOVE　　　　　　　　　　1912
Paul Rubens / Arthur Wimperis
Chappell & Co. Ltd .... UK
Show(s): .... The Sunshine Girl
The Columbia Light Opera Orchestra .... Columbia 9896

HERE'S TO ROMANCE　　　　　　　　1936
Herb Magidson / Con Conrad

Sam Fox Publishing Co. (London) Ltd . . . . USA
Film(s): . . . . Here's to Romance
Nino Martini . . . . **HMV B 8401**
Bob Crosby & his Orchestra . . . . **Decca F 5870**
Nino Martini appeared in *Here's to Romance.*

HERNANDO'S HIDEAWAY   September 1955
Richard Adler / Jerry Ross
Frank Music Co. Ltd. . . . . USA
Show(s): . . . . The Pajama Game
Film(s): . . . . The Pajama Game
Carol Haney . . . . **Philips BBL 7050**
Elizabeth Seal & Edmund Hockridge . . . . **HMV CLP 1062**
Carol Haney . . . . **Philips BBL 7197**
The Johnston Brothers . . . . **Decca F 10608**
Carol Haney appeared in both the American production and the film
of *The Pajama Game.*
Elizabeth Seal & Edmund Hockridge appeared in the British produc-
tion of *The Pajama Game.*

HEROES AND VILLAINS   September 1967
Brian Wilson / Van Dyke Parks
Rondor Music . . . . USA
The Beach Boys . . . . **Capitol CL 15510**

HERSHAM BOYS   August 1979
Jimmy Pursey / David Parsons
Singatune Publishing . . . . USA
Sham 69 . . . . **Polydor POSP 64**

HEV YEW GOTTA LOIGHT BOY   December 1966
Alan Smetherst
Dick James Music Ltd. . . . . UK
The Singing Postman (Alan Smetherst) . . **Parlophone GEP 8956**
Rolf Harris . . . . **Columbia DB 8014**

HEY BABY   May 1962
Margaret Cobb / Bruce Channel
Peter Maurice Music Co. Ltd. . . . . USA
Bruce Channel . . . . **Mercury AMT 1171**
Paul & Paula . . . . **Philips 652026 BL**

HEY GIPSY (Play Gipsy)   1926
Emmerich Kalman / Clifford Grey / N. Foley
B. Feldman & Co. Ltd. . . . . Austria
Show(s): . . . . Countess Maritza
John Garrick . . . . **HMV B 8787**
Al Bowlly (1939) . . . . **HMV BD 709**
The Mantovani Orchestra . . . . **Decca LK 4347**
Harry Secombe . . . . **Philips BBL 7387**
Also known as *Play Gipsy Play* and *Come Gipsy Come.*
John Garrick appeared in the British production of *Countess Maritza.*

HEY GIRL   June 1966
Steve Marriott / Ronald Lane
Robbins Music Corporation Ltd. . . . . UK
The Small Faces . . . . **Decca F 12393**

HEY GIRL DON'T BOTHER ME   October 1971
Ray Whitley
Chappell & Co. Ltd . . . . USA
The Tams . . . . **Probe PRO 532**

HEY GOOD LOOKING   December 1951
Hank Williams
Chappell & Co. Ltd . . . . USA
Jo Stafford & Frankie Laine . . . . **Columbia DB 2948**
Hank Williams . . . . **MGM D 137**
Bobby Rydell . . . . **Columbia 33SX 1308**

HEY JOE   November 1953
Boudleaux Bryant
Robbins Music Ltd . . . . USA
Frankie Laine . . . . **Philips PB 172**

HEY JOE   February 1967
Will Roberts
. . . . USA
The Leaves . . . . **Fontana TF 713**
The Byrds . . . . **CBS BPG 62783**
Deep Purple . . . . **Parlophone PMC 7005**
The Jimi Hendrix Experience . . . . **Polydor 56139**

HEY JUDE   October 1968
John Lennon / Paul McCartney

Northern Songs Ltd. . . . . UK
The Beatles . . . . **Apple R 5722**
Wilson Pickett (1969) . . . . **Atlantic 584-236**
The Beatles (1976) . . . . **Apple R 5722**
Ivor Novello Award.

HEY LITTLE GIRL   April 1962
Del Shannon
Vicki Music Ltd. . . . . USA
Del Shannon . . . . **London HL 9515**

HEY LITTLE HEN   1941
Ralph Butler / Noel Gay
Noel Gay Music Co. Ltd . . . . UK
Donald Peers . . . . **Decca F 7941**
Bunny Doyle . . . . **HMV BD 939**

HEY LOOK ME OVER   March 1961
Carolyn Leigh / Cy Coleman
Edwin H. Morris & Co. Ltd . . . . USA
Show(s): . . . . Wildcat
Lucille Ball & Paula Stewart . . . . **RCA LOC 1060**
Cy Coleman (vocal) with Orchestra . . . . . . **CBS BPG 63075**
Lucille Ball Paula Stewart appeared in *Wildcat.*

HEY MATTHEW   October 1987
Karel Fialka
Illegal Music . . . . UK
Karel Fialka . . . . **I.R.S. IRM 140**

HEY MISTER BANJO   July 1955
Freddy Morgan / Norman Malkin
Bradbury Wood Ltd. . . . . USA
The Coronets with the Big Ben Banjo Band **Columbia SEG 7593**
The Stargazers . . . . **Decca F 10523**

HEY MUSIC LOVER   March 1989
Sylvester Stewart
Warner Brothers Music . . . . USA
S'Xpress featuring Eric & Billy . . . . **Rhythm King LEFT 30**

HEY NEIGHBOUR   August 1950
Ross Parker
Lawrence Wright Music Co. Ltd . . . . UK
Show(s): . . . . Knights of Madness
Flanagan & Allen . . . . **Columbia 33S 1010**
Flanagan & Allen appeared in *Knights of Madness.*

HEY PAULA   March 1963
Ray Hildebrand
Tin Pan Alley Music Co. Ltd . . . . USA
Paul & Paula . . . . **Philips 304012 BF**
Elaine & Derek . . . . **Piccadilly 7N 35105**
The Avons . . . . **Decca F 11588**

HEY ROCK AND ROLL   July 1974
"Showaddywaddy"
Bailey Music Publishing . . . . UK
Showaddywaddy . . . . **Bell 1357**

HEY THERE   October 1955
Richard Adler / Jerry Ross
Frank Music Co. Ltd. . . . . USA
Show(s): . . . . The Pajama Game
Film(s): . . . . The Pajama Game
John Raitt . . . . **Philips BBL 7050**
Edmund Hockridge . . . . **HMV CLP 1062**
John Raitt . . . . **Philips BBL 7197**
Johnnie Ray . . . . **Philips PB 495**
Rosemary Clooney . . . . **Philips BBL 7301**
John Raitt appeared in both the American production and film of *The
Pajama Game.*
Edmund Hockridge appeared in the British production of *The Pajama
Game.*

HEY YOU THE ROCKSTEADY CREW   November 1983
Steven Hague / R. Blue / Buddy Soldier
Charisma Music . . . . USA
The Rocksteady Crew . . . . **Virgin RSC 1**

HEY-BA-BA-RE-BOP   1946
Lionel Hampton / Curley Hamner
Leeds Music Ltd. . . . . USA
Lionel Hampton & his Orchestra . . . . **Brunswick LA 8527**

HEYKENS SERENADE (See Serenade)

HI DIDDLE DIDDLE 1926
Carlton A. Coon / Hal Keidel
Francis, Day & Hunter Ltd. .... USA
Ted Lewis & his Band .... **Decca 4033**
Phil Harris & his Orchestra .... **HMV B 10392**
Bob Scobey Band .... **Columbia B 5121**

HI HI HI February 1973
Paul McCartney / Linda McCartney
McCartney Music .... UK
Wings .... **Apple R 5973**

HI HO SILVER March 1986
Jim Diamond / Chris Parren
Rondor Music .... UK
Jim Diamond .... **A&M AM 296**
From the television series *Boon*

HI HO SILVER LINING May 1967
Scott English / Lawrence Weiss
EMI Music Ltd. .... USA
Jeff Beck (1967) .... **Columbia DB 8151**
Jeff Beck (1972) .... **RAK RR3**

HI TIDDLEY HI TI ISLAND 1937
Ralph Stanley / Leslie Alleyn
B. Feldman & Co. Ltd. .... UK
George Formby .... **Columbia SEG 7550**

HI-DIDDLE-DEE-DEE (An Actors Life For Me) 1940
Ned Washington / Leigh Harline
Chappell & Co. Ltd .... USA
Film(s): .... Pinocchio (Cartoon)
Sound Track .... **HMV BD 822**
Jay Wilbur & his Band .... **Rex 9757**
Walter Catlett .... **Disneyland DLP 39002**

HI-FIDELITY September 1982
Enid Levine
April Music Ltd .... USA
The Kids From Fame .... **RCA RCA 254**
From the television series *Fame*.

HI-JIG-A-JIG (Follow The Band) May 1947
Sim Simmons
Box & Cox Music Co. .... UK
Lou Preager Orchestra .... **Columbia FB 3293**

HI-LILLI HI-LO January 1953
Helen Deutch / Bronislaw Kaper
Robbins Music Corporation Ltd .... USA
Film(s): Lilli
Leslie Caron & Mel Ferrer .... **MGM D 109**
The Four Aces .... **Brunswick LAT 8249**
Doretta Morrow .... **RCA RD 27062**
Alan Price (1966) .... **Decca F 12442**
Leslie Caron & Mel Ferrer appeared in *Lilli*.

HIAWATHA'S LULLABY 1933
Walter Donaldson / Joe Young
Francis, Day & Hunter Ltd. .... USA
Layton & Johnstone .... **Columbia DB 1149**
Derickson & Brown .... **HMV B 4462**

HIAWATHA'S MELODY OF LOVE 1922
Alfred Bryan / Artie Mehlinger / George W. Meyer
B. Feldman & Co. Ltd .... USA
Show(s): .... Midnight Rounders of 1920
De Groot & his Picadilly Orchestra .... **HMV C 1102**
Louis James .... **Regal G 7745**

HIDE AND SEEK March 1984
Howard Jones
Warner Brothers Music .... UK
Howard Jones .... **WEA HOW 3**

HIDEAWAY July 1966
Ken Howard / Alan Blaikley
Lynn Music Ltd. .... UK
Dave Dee, Dozy, Beaky, Mick & Tich .... **Fontana TF 711**

HIGH AND THE MIGHTY, THE November 1954
Dimitri Tiomkin / Ned Washington
Campbell Connelly & Co. Ltd. .... USA
Film(s): .... The High and the Mighty
Victor Young & his Orchestra .... **Brunswick LAT 8203**
Dimitri Tiomkin & his Orchestra .... **Vogue LVA 9006**

HIGH CLASS BABY December 1958
Ian Samwell
Kalith Music Ltd .... UK
Cliff Richard .... **Columbia DB 4203**

HIGH ENERGY June 1984
Ian Levine / Fiachra Trench
Leosong .... UK
Evelyn Thomas .... **Record Shack SOHO 18**

HIGH HOPES October 1959
Sammy Cahn / Jimmy Van Heusen
Barton Music Co. Ltd .... USA
Film(s): .... Hole in the Head
Frank Sinatra .... **Capitol EAP 1-1224**
Dave King .... **Pye 7N 25032**
Frank Sinatra appeared in *A Hole in the Head*.
Academy Award winning song for 1959.

HIGH IN THE SKY September 1968
Arthur King
Carlin Music Corporation .... UK
Amen Corner .... **Deram DM 197**

HIGH LIFE March 1983
David Jaymes / John Du Prez
April Music Ltd .... UK
Modern Romance .... **WEA ROM 2**

HIGH NOON September 1952
Ned Washington / Dimitri Tiomkin
Robbins Music Corporation Ltd .... USA
Film(s): .... High Noon
Frankie Laine .... **Philips BBL 7263**
Tex Ritter .... **Capitol CL 13668**
Jimmy Rodgers .... **Columbia 33SX 1217**
Dimitri Tiomkin & his Orchestra .... **Vogue LVA 9006**
Academy Award winning song for 1952.

HIGH SCHOOL CONFIDENTIAL February 1959
Jerry Lee Lewis / Ron Hargrave
Aberbach (London) Ltd. .... USA
Film(s): .... High School Confidential
Jerry Lee Lewis .... **London HAS 2138**
Adam Faith .... **HMV POP 557**
Jerry Lee Lewis appeared in *High School Confidential*.

HIGH SOCIETY 1907
Porter Steele / Walter Melrose
Herman Darewski Music Publishing Co. Ltd. .... USA
King Oliver's Creole Jazz Band .... **Philips BBL 7181**
Bunk Johnson & his New Orleans Band .... **HMV B 9820**
The Chris Barber Jazz Band .... **Columbia 33SX 1274**

HIGH TIME December 1966
Mike Leander / Charles Mills
Mirage Music Ltd. .... UK
Paul Jones .... **HMV POP 1544**

HIGH UP ON A HILL TOP 1929
Abel Baer / George Whiting / Ian Campbell
Francis, Day & Hunter Ltd .... USA
Frankie Trumbauer & his Orchestra ...... **Parlophone R 2644**
June Pursell .... **Brunswick 03928**

HIGHER & HIGHER June 1969
Gary Jackson / Carl Miller / Raynard Milner
United Artists Music Co. Ltd. .... USA
Jackie Wilson .... **MCA MU 1131**

HINDUSTAN 1918
Oliver Wallace / Harold Weeks
Francis, Day & Hunter Ltd. .... USA
Show(s): .... Joy Bells
The Mayfair Dance Orchestra .... **HMV C 921**
Bob Crosby's Bob Cats .... **Decca F 7155**
Bing Crosby & Rosemary Clooney .... **RCA RD 27105**

HIPPY HIPPY SHAKE, THE February 1964
Chan Romero

Ardmore & Beechwood Ltd . . . . USA
Chan Romero . . . . **Columbia DB 4341**
The Swinging Blue Jeans . . . . **HMV POP 1242**

HIS LATEST FLAME   November 1961
Doc Pomus / Mort Shuman
Aberbach (London) Ltd. . . . . USA
Elvis Presley . . . . **RCA 1258**
Del Shannon . . . . **London HAX 2402**

HIS MAJESTY THE BABY   1935
Mabel Wayne / Neville Fleeson / Arthur Terker
Chappell & Co. Ltd . . . . USA
Elsie Carlisle . . . . **Decca F 5380**
Mabel Wayne . . . . **Columbia DX 672**
Harry Roy & his Orchestra . . . . **Parlophone F 109**

HIS ROCKING HORSE RAN AWAY   1944
Johnny Burke / Jimmy Van Heusen
Victoria Music Co. Ltd. . . . . USA
Film(s): . . . . And the Angels Sing
Betty Hutton . . . . **Capitol CL 13019**
Betty Hutton appeared in *And the Angels Sing.*

HISTORY   July 1985
Eric Von Tijn / Jochem Fluitsma
Intersong Music . . . . Holland
Mai Tai . . . . **Virgin VS 733**

HIT AND MISS   April 1960
John Barry
Mills Music Ltd . . . . UK
The John Barry Seven . . . . **Columbia DB 4414**
Theme of T.V. production *Juke Box Jury.*
Ivor Novello Nomination.

HIT ME WITH YOUR RHYTHM STICK   January 1979
Ian Dury / Charles Jankel
Blackhill Music . . . . UK
Ian Dury & The Blockheads . . . . **Stiff BUY 38**

HIT THAT PERFECT BEAT   January 1986
Steve Bronski / John Foster / Larry Steinbachek
Bronski Music . . . . UK
Bronski Beat . . . . **London BITE 6**
Ivor Novello Nomination 1985

HIT THE ROAD JACK   November 1961
Percy Mayfield
Tangerine Music Ltd. . . . . USA
Ray Charles . . . . **HMV POP 935**
Don Lang . . . . **Ace of Clubs ACL 1111**

HIT THE ROAD TO DREAMLAND   1943
Harold Arlen / Johnny Mercer
Victoria Music Co. Ltd. . . . . USA
Film(s): . . . . Star Spangled Rhythm / That Certain Feeling
Mel Tormé . . . . **HMV CLP 1382**
Margaret Whiting . . . . **London HAD 2109**
Dean Martin . . . . **Capitol T 1150**

HITCHIN' A RIDE   February 1970
Mitch Murray / Peter Callander
Intune Ltd. . . . . UK
Vanity Fare . . . . **Page One POF 158**

HITCHY-KOO   1912
Lewis Muir / Maurice Abrahams / L. Wolfe Gilbert
Francis, Day & Hunter Ltd. . . . . USA
Show(s): . . . . Hullo Ragtime
Lew Hearn & Bonita . . . . **HMV C 557**
The Jolly Old Fellows . . . . . . **Regal Zonophone MR 144**
Jack Hylton & his Orchestra . . . . **HMV C 1653**

HO HUM   1931
Edward Heyman / Dana Suesse
Chappell & Co. Ltd. USA
Show(s): . . . . Monkey Business
Annette Hanshaw . . . . **Parlophone R 967**
Bing Crosby & Loyce Whitman . . . . . . **RCA RD 27075**

HOBNAILED BOOTS THAT FARVER WORE, THE   1907
R.P. Weston / Fred Barnes
Francis, Day & Hunter Ltd . . . . UK
Billy Williams . . . . **Zonophone TWIN 557**

David Kossoff . . . . **Oriole MG 20043**

HOKEY COKEY, THE (See Cokey Cokey, The)

HOLD BACK THE DAWN   1944
Hedley Grey
Lawrence Wright Music Co. Ltd. . . . . UK
Anne Shelton . . . . **Decca F 8402**

HOLD BACK THE NIGHT   November 1975
Ronald Baker / Norman Harris / Earl Young
Carlin Music Corporation . . . . USA
The Trammps . . . . **Buddah BDS 437**

HOLD BACK TOMORROW   September 1959
Eddie Pierce / James Watson / Wynn Stewart
Chappell & Co. Ltd . . . . USA
Miki & Griff . . . . **Nixa NEP 24129**

HOLD ME   1933
Jack Little / Dave Oppenheim / Ira Schuster
Campbell Connelly & Co. Ltd. . . . . USA
Eddy Duchin & his Orchestra . . . . **HMV B 6363**
Jackie Gleason & his Orchestra . . . . . **Capitol LCT 6131**
Peggy Lee . . . . **Capitol LC 6817**
Brook Benton . . . . **Mercury MMC 14015**
P.J. Proby (1964) . . . . **Decca F 11904**

HOLD ME   November 1981
B.A. Robertson
Campbell Connelly & Co. Ltd . . . . UK
B.A. Robertson & Maggie Bell . . . . . . **Swansong BAM 1**

HOLD ME CLOSE   October 1975
David Essex
April Music Ltd . . . . UK
David Essex . . . . **CBS 3572**

HOLD ME IN YOUR ARMS   March 1989
Rick Astley
All Boys Music . . . . UK
Rick Astley . . . . **RCA PB 42615**

HOLD ME NOW   December 1983
Tom Bailey / Alannah Currie / Joe Leeway
Point Music . . . . UK
The Thompson Twins . . . . **Artista TWINS 2**

HOLD ME NOW   June 1987
Johnny Logan
MCA Music . . . . UK
Johnny Logan . . . . **Epic LOG 1**
Irish entry for the 1987 Eurovision Song Contest (Placed First).

HOLD ME TIGHT   September 1968
Johnny Nash
Writers Workshop Ltd. . . . . USA
Johnny Nash . . . . **Regal Zonophone RZ 3010**

HOLD ME, THRILL ME, KISS ME   April 1953
Harry Noble
Mills Music Ltd . . . . USA
Muriel Smith . . . . **Philips PB 122**
Noble & King . . . . **Parlophone R 3432**
Roberta Lee . . . . **Brunswick 05059**
Alma Cogan . . . . **HMV B 10460**
Karen Chandler . . . . **Vogue LVA 9096**

HOLD MY HAND   1934
Jack Yellen / Irving Caeser / Ray Henderson
Sam Fox Publishing Co. (London) Ltd . . . . USA
Film(s): . . . . George White's Scandals
Frances Langford . . . . **Rex 8231**
Ray Noble & his Orchestra, vocal Al Bowlly . . . . **HMV B 6499**

HOLD MY HAND   October 1954
Jack Lawrence / Richard Meyers
Bradbury Wood Ltd. USA
Film(s): . . . . Susan Slept Here
Don Cornell . . . . **Vogue LVA 9098**
Lorrae Desmond . . . . **Decca F 10375**
Ronnie Harris . . . . **Columbia SCM 5138**
Nominated for an Academy Award 1954.

HOLD ON June 1990
Thomas McElroy / Denzil Foster
Rondor Music . . . . USA
En Vogue . . . . **Atlantic A 7908**

HOLD ON July 1990
Chynna Philips / Glen Ballard / Carrie Wilson
EMI Music . . . . USA
Wilson Philips . . . . **SBK SBK 6**

HOLD ON TIGHT September 1981
Jeff Lynne
April Music Ltd . . . . UK
The Electric Light Orchestra . . . . **JET 7011**

HOLD ON TO LOVE May 1975
Peter Skellern
Warner Brothers Music Ltd . . . . UK
Peter Skellern . . . . **Decca F 13568**

HOLD ON TO MY LOVE May 1980
Blue Weaver / Robin Gibb
Chappell & Co. Ltd . . . . UK
Jimmy Ruffin . . . . **RSO 57**

HOLD THE LINE March 1979
David Paich
April Music Ltd. . . . . USA
Film(s): . . . . Yesterdays Heroes
Toto . . . . **CBS 6784**

HOLD TIGHT May 1966
Ken Howard / Alan Blaikley
Lynn Music Ltd. . . . . UK
Dave Dee, Dozy, Beaky, Mick & Tich . . . . **Fontana TF 671**

HOLD TIGHT, HOLD TIGHT 1939
Leonard Kent / Jerry Brandow / Leonard Ware & William Spotswood
Lafleur & Co. Ltd. . . . . USA
'Fats' Waller & his Rhythm . . . . **HMV BD 5469**
The Andrews Sisters . . . . **Brunswick 02717**
The Andrews Sisters . . . . **Capitol LCT 6132**
Mel Tormé . . . . **Vogue LVA 9032**

HOLD YOUR HAND OUT NAUGHTY BOY 1913
C.W. Murphy / Worton David
Francis, Day & Hunter Ltd. UK
Florrie Forde . . . . **Columbia 9780**
Ella Retford . . . . **Jumbo 1088**
Jack Hylton & his Orchestra . . . . **HMV C 2082**
Florrie Forde . . . . **Rex 8189**
Paddie O'Neil . . . . **Decca LK 4026**

HOLD YOUR HEAD UP April 1972
Rod Argent / Chris White
Verulam Music . . . . UK
Argent . . . . **Epic EPC 7786**

HOLDING BACK THE YEARS June 1986
Mick Hucknall / Neil Moss
CBS Songs . . . . UK
Simply Red . . . . **WEA YZ 70**

HOLDING OUT FOR A HERO October 1985
Jim Steinman / Dean Pitchford
Famous Music . . . . USA
Film(s): . . . . Footloose
Bonnie Tyler . . . . **CBS A 4251**

HOLE IN MY SHOE October 1967
Dave Mason
Island Music . . . . UK
Traffic . . . . **Island WIP 6017**
Neil (1984) . . . . **WEA YZ 10**

HOLE IN THE GROUND March 1962
Ted Dicks / Myles Rudge
Noel Gay Music Co. Ltd. . . . . UK
Bernard Cribbins . . . . **Parlophone R 4869**

HOLIDAY February 1984
Curtis Hudson / Lisa Stevens
Warner Chappell Music . . . . USA
Madonna . . . . **Sire W 9405**

HOLIDAY FOR STRINGS 1944
David Rose
Chappell & Co. Ltd. . . . . USA
Film(s): . . . . Ladies Man
David Rose & his Orchestra . . . . **HMV 7EG 8081**
Spike Jones & his City Slickers . . . . **HMV BD 1115**
Stanley Black & his Orchestra . . . . **Decca LK 4306**
David Rose & his Orchestra . . . . **MGM D 103**
Spike Jones appeared in *Ladies Man*.

HOLIDAYS IN THE SUN November 1977
Steve Jones / Paul Cook / Sid Vicious & Johnny Hotten
Warner Brothers Music Ltd . . . . UK
The Sex Pistols . . . . **Virigin VS 191**

HOLY CITY, THE 1892
Stephen Adams / Frederick E. Weatherly
Boosey & Hawkes Ltd . . . . UK
William Paul . . . . **HMV 2-2174**
Dame Clara Butt . . . . **Columbia 7375**
Gracie Fields . . . . **Regal Zonophone MR 2892**
The Morriston Orpheus Choir . . . **Columbia 33SX 6211**
Moira Anderson . . . . **Decca F 12989**
Benjamin Luxon . . . . **Argo ZFB 96**

HOLY COW December 1966
Allen Toussaint
Ardmore & Beechwood Ltd. . . . . USA
Lee Dorsey . . . . **Stateside SS 552**

HOMBURG October 1967
Keith Reid / Gary Brooker
Essex Music Ltd. . . . . UK
Procol Harum . . . . **Regal Zonophone RZ 3003**

HOME 1932
Harry Clarkson / Jeff Clarkson / Peter Van Steeden
Peter Maurice Music Co. Ltd. . . . . USA
Mildred Bailey . . . . **HMV B 4084**
Dick Haymes . . . . **Brunswick 04172**
Dave King . . . . **Decca F 11061**
Margaret Whiting . . . . **London HAD 2109**

HOME AGAIN 1935
Mabel Wayne
Chappell & Co. Ltd . . . . USA
Henry Hall & the B.B.C. Dance Orchestra . . **Columbia FB 1040**
Colli Knox . . . . **Decca F 5481**

HOME COOKING September 1950
Jay Livingston / Ray Evans
Victoria Music Co. Ltd . . . . USA
Film(s): . . . . Fancy Pants
Bing Crosby . . . . **Brunswick LA 8724**
Bob Hope & Margaret Whiting . . . **Capitol EAP 1-20071**
Bob Hope appeared in *Fancy Pants*.

(HOME IN) PASADENA 1924
Harry Warren / Grant Clarke / Edgar Leslie
Lawrence Wright Music Co. Ltd. . . . . USA
Fred Douglas . . . . **Regal G 8179**
The Savoy Havana Band . . . . **Columbia 3435**
The Tuneful Twenties Dance Orchestra . . **Parlophone R 3330**
The Temperance Seven (1961) . . . . **Parlophone R 4781**

HOME JAMES AND DON'T SPARE THE HORSES 1935
Fred Hillebrand
Southern Music Publishing Co. Ltd . . . . USA
Elsie Carlisle & Sam Browne . . . . **Decca F 6926**
Fred Hillebrand . . . . **Decca F 5323**
Jack Jackson & his Orchestra . . . . **HMV BD 115**

HOME LOVIN' MAN December 1970
Roger Cook / Roger Greenaway / Tony Macaulay
Schroeder Music Ltd . . . . UK
Andy Williams . . . . **CBS S 65151**
Ivor Novello Award.

HOME ON THE RANGE 1933
Traditional, arranged by Ted Ezra
An edition by Lawrence Wright Music Co. Ltd. . . . . . . USA
Bing Crosby . . . . **Columbia DB 1829**
Bing Crosby . . . . **Brunswick LAT 8152**
The Sons of The Pioneers . . . . **RCA RD 27016**

HOME TOWN   **1937**
Jimmy Kennedy / Michael Carr
Peter Maurice Music Co. Ltd. . . . . UK
Show(s): . . . . London Rhapsody
Flanagan & Allen . . . . **Columbia SEG 7709**
The Adams Singers . . . . **Pye NPL 28013**
Flanagan & Allen appeared in *London Rhapsody*.

HOMECOMING WALTZ, THE   **1943**
Bob Musel / Ray Sonin / Reginald Connelly
Campbell Connelly & Co. Ltd . . . . UK
Ivy Benson & her Girls Band . . . . **HMV BD 1061**
Donald Peers . . . . **Decca F 8391**
Ray Burns . . . . **Columbia SCM 5115**

HOMELY GIRL   **May 1974**
Eugene Record / Stan McKenny
Intersong Music . . . . USA
The Chi-Lites . . . . **Brunswick BR 9**
UB40 (1989) . . . . **DEP DEP 33**

HOMESICK   **1923**
Irving Berlin
Irving Berlin Ltd . . . . USA
Paul Whiteman & his Orchestra . . . . **HMV B 1637**

HOMESICK, THAT'S ALL   **1946**
Gordon Jenkins
Sterling Music Publishing Co. Ltd. USA
Frank Sinatra . . . . **Columbia DB 2216**
Ambrose & his Orchestra, vocal Rita Marlowe . . . **Decca F 8620**

HOMEWARD BOUND   **May 1966**
Paul Simon
Lorna Music Co. Ltd. . . . . USA
Simon & Garfunkel . . . . **CBS 202045**

HOMING   **1917**
Arthur Salmon / Teresa Del Riego
Chappell & Co. Ltd . . . . UK
Muriel Brunskill . . . . **Columbia 3328**
Eva Turner . . . . **Columbia LB 11**
Walter Midgley . . . . **Columbia DB 1922**
Webster Booth . . . . **HMV B 9264**
Maryetta & Vernon Midgley . . . . **MVM 1124**

HOMING WALTZ, THE   **September 1952**
Tommie Connor / Michael Reine
Michael Reine Music Co. Ltd . . . . UK
Alma Cogan & Larry Day . . . . **HMV B 10307**
Dickie Valentine . . . . **Decca F 9954**
Vera Lynn . . . . **Decca F 9959**

HONALOOCHIE BOOGIE   **July 1973**
Ian Hunter
Island Music Ltd. . . . . UK
Mott the Hoople . . . . **CBS 1530**

HONEY   **1929**
Richard A. Whiting / Howard Simons / Haven Gillespie
Francis, Day & Hunter Ltd . . . . USA
Film(s): . . . . .Her Highness and the Bellboy
Mildred Hunt . . . . **HMV B 3140**
Arthur Godfrey . . . . **Columbia DB 3415**
The Andrews Sisters . . . . **Brunswick 03275**
Kay Starr . . . . **Top Rank JKP 2042**

HONEY   **June 1968**
Bobby Russell
Peter Maurice Music Co. Ltd. . . . . USA
Bobby Goldsboro . . . . **United Artists UP 2215**

HONEY   **May 1975**
Bobby Goldoro / Bob Montgomery
Keith Prowse Music Publishing Co Ltd . . . . USA
Bobby Goldsboro . . . . **United Artists UP 356633**

HONEY BUN   **November 1951**
Richard Rodgers / Oscar Hammerstein II
Williamson Music Ltd . . . . USA
Show(s): . . . . South Pacific
Film(s): . . . . South Pacific
Mary Martin . . . . **Philips BBL 7157**

Mitzi Gaynor . . . . **RCA RB 16065**
Mary Martin appeared in both the American and British productions
of *South Pacific*.
Mitzi Gaynor appeared in the film *South Pacific*.

HONEY COME BACK   **July 1970**
Jim Webb
Jobete Music (UK) Ltd. . . . . USA
Glen Campbell . . . . **Capitol CL 15638**

HONEY HONEY   **September 1974**
Benny Andersson / Bjorn Ulvaeus / Stig Anderson
A.T.V. Music Ltd. . . . . Sweden
Sweet Dreams . . . . **Bradleys BRAD 7408**
Abba . . . . **Epic EPC 80179**

HONEY I'M IN LOVE WITH YOU   **1925**
Con Conrad / William Friedlander
Francis, Day & Hunter Ltd. . . . . USA
Show(s): . . . . Mercenary Mary
Sonny Hale & June . . . . **Columbia 3807**
Kathlyn Hilliard & George Baker . . . . **HMV B 2195**
Sonny Hale & June appeared in the British production of *Mercenary
Mary*.

HONEYSUCKLE AND THE BEE, THE   **1901**
Albert Fitz / William Penn
Francis, Day & Hunter Ltd. . . . . USA
Film(s): . . . . I'll Be Your Sweetheart / Broadway to Hollywood
Belle Davies & her Pickaninnies . . . . **HMV GC 3244**
Ellaline Terris & Seymour Hicks . . . . **HMV C 2432**
George Adams . . . . **Regal Zonophone MR 345**
Stanley Holloway . . . . **Pye NPL 18056**

HONEYSUCKLE ROSE   **1930**
Andy Razaf / Thomas Waller
Campbell Connelly & Co. Ltd . . . . USA
Film(s): . . . . Tin Pan Alley / Thousands Cheer
'Fats' Waller & his Rhythm . . . . **RCA RCX 1010**
Coleman Hawkins & his All Star Jam Band . . . . . . **HMV B 8754**
Dinah Shore . . . . **Regal Zonophone MR 3569**
The Mills Brothers . . . . **Brunswick LAT 8235**
Lena Horne . . . . **RCA RD 27021**
Lena Horne appeared in *Thousands Cheer*.

HONG KONG BLUES   **1939**
Hoagy Carmichael
Chappell & Co. Ltd. . . . . USA
Film(s): . . . . To Have and Have Not
Hoagy Carmichael (1939) . . . . **Columbia DB 5053**
Hoagy Carmichael . . . . **Brunswick LA 8663**
Hoagy Carmichael . . . . **Warner Brothers WM 4050**
Hoagy Carmichael appeared in *To Have and Have Not*.

HONG KONG GARDEN   **September 1978**
John McKay / Kenneth Morris / Susan Ballion & Steven Bailey
Signatue Publishing . . . . UK
Siouxsie & The Banshees . . . . **Polydor 2059052**

HONKY TONK WOMEN   **August 1969**
Mick Jagger / Keith Richard
Mirage Music Ltd. . . . . UK
Film(s): . . . . Mad Dogs & Englishmen
The Rolling Stones . . . . **Decca F 12952**
Joe Cocker . . . . **A&M AMLS 6002/1**
Joe Cocker appeared in *Mad Dogs & Englishmen*.
Ivor Novello Nomination.

HOOP DEE-DOO   **July 1950**
Frank Loesser / Milton De Lugg
Edwin H. Morris & Co. Ltd . . . . USA
Perry Como . . . . **HMV B 9925**
Kay Starr . . . . **Capitol CL 13309**
Doris Day . . . . **Philips BBL 7137**

HOORAY FOR HOLLYWOOD   **1939**
Richard A. Whiting / Johnny Mercer
Sterling Music . . . . USA
Film(s): . . . . Hollywood Hotel, Pepe
Benny Goodman Orchestra . . . . **United Artists UAG 29644**
Louis Levy & his Orchestra . . . . **HMV BD 542**
Doris Day . . . . **Philips BBL 7247**

Frances Langford, Dick Powell,
Johnny 'Scat' Davis & The Sammy Davis Jnr .. **Pye NPL 28015**
Frances Langford, Dick Powell, Johnny 'Scat' Davis & The Benny
Goodman Orchestra appeared in *Hollywood Hotel*
Sammy Davis Jnr appeared in *Pepe*

HOORAY FOR LOVE December 1948
Harold Arlen / Leo Robin
Edwin H. Morris & Co. Ltd . . . . USA
Film(s): . . . . Casbah
Tony Martin . . . . **HMV B 9686**
Gordon MacRae . . . . **Capitol T 875**
Debbie Reynolds . . . . **London HAD 2200**
Rosemary Clooney . . . . **RCA RD 27189**
Tony Martin appeared in *Casbah*.

HOORAY, HOORAY, IT'S A HOLI HOLIDAY May 1979
Frank Farian / Fred Jay
A.T.V. Music Ltd. . . . . Germany
Boney M . . . . **Atlantic K 11279**

HOOTS MON January 1959
Harry Robinson
Southern Music Publishing Co. Ltd . . . . UK
Lord Rockingham's Eleven . . . . **Decca F 11059**

HOP SCOTCH POLKA October 1949
William 'Billy' Whitlock / Gene Rayburn / Carl Sigman
Leeds Music Ltd . . . . UK
Billy Whitlock . . . . **Decca F 9233**
The Tanner Sisters . . . . **HMV B 9846**
Guy Lombardo & his Royal Canadians . . . . . **Brunswick 04281**

HOPELESSLY DEVOTED TO YOU November 1978
John Farrar
Chappel & Co. Ltd . . . . UK
Film(s): . . . . Grease
Olivia Newton-John . . . . **RSO 2479-210**
Olivia Newton-John appeared in *Grease*.
Nominated for an Academy Award 1978.

HORA STACCATO 1930
Grigoras Dinicu / Jascha Heifetz
Boosey & Hawkes Music Publishing Ltd . . . . Romania
Dinicu & his Orchestra . . . . **Columbia 5684**
Jascha Heifetz (violin) . . . . **RCA RB 16243**
Freddie Martin & his Orchestra . . . . **HMV B 9621**
Victor Young & his Orchestra . . . . **Brunswick LAT 8033**
The Eastman-Rochester 'Pops' Orchestra . **Mercury MMA 11092**

HORS D'OEUVRES 1915
David Comer
B. Feldman & Co. Ltd. . . . . UK
Show(s). . . . . 5064 Gerard
Murray's Ragtime Trio . . . . **HMV C 399**
Donald Peers . . . . **HMV B 10002**
Sid Philips & his Band (1949) . . . . **HMV DLP 1102**
Bob Crosby & his Orchestra . . . . **Capitol CL 13663**
Murray's Ragtime Trio appeared in *5064 Gerard*.

HORSE WITH NO NAME, A February 1972
Dewey Burnell
Warner Brothers Music Ltd . . . . USA
America . . . . **Warner Brothers K 16128**

HORSES 1926
Richard A. Whiting / Byron Gay
Francis, Day & Hunter Ltd. . . . . USA
Paul Specht's Original Georgians . . . . **Columbia 4016**

HORSEY KEEP YOUR TAIL UP 1924
Walter Hirsch / Bert Kaplan
B. Feldman & Co. Ltd. . . . . USA
The Romaine Orchestra . . . . **HMV B 1802**
Freddie 'Schnichelfritz' Fisher & his Band . . . . . **Decca F 7195**
Joe Loss & his Orchestra . . . . **HMV 7EG 8195**

HORSEY, HORSEY 1938
Elton Box / Desmond Cox / Paddy Roberts / Ralph Butler
Sun Music Publishing Co. Ltd. . . . . UK
Jack Jackson & his Band . . . . **Decca F 6552**
Billy Cotton & his Band . . . . **Rex 9149**
Henry Hall & his Orchestra,
vocal The Coronets . . . . **Columbia 33SX 1067**

HOT CANARY, THE November 1948
Paul Nero / Ray Gilbert
Leeds Music Ltd. . . . . Austria
Paul Nero (Violin) with Orchestra . . . . **Capitol LC 6547**
Florian Zabach (Violin) with Orchestra . . . **Brunswick LAT 8371**
Percy Faith & his Orchestra & chorus . . . . . **Columbia DB 2881**
Paul Weston & his Orch.with Paul Nero (Violin) . **Capitol LC 6821**
Adapted from "Le Caneri" by F. Poliakin.

HOT DIGGITY May 1956
Al Hoffman / Dick Manning
Peter Maurice Music Co. Ltd. . . . . USA
Perry Como . . . . **RCA RD 27100**
Michael Holliday . . . . **Columbia DB 3783**
The Stargazers . . . . **Decca DFE 6362**
Adapted from 'Espana' (Spanish Rhapsody) by Emmanuel Chabrier
(1841 - 1894).

HOT IN THE CITY February 1988
Billy Idol
Chrysalis Music . . . . UK
Billy Idol . . . . **Chrysalis IDOL 12**

HOT LEGS February 1978
Rod Stewart / Gary Grainger
Riva Music . . . . UK
Rod Stewart . . . . **Riva 10**

HOT LIPS 1922
Henry Busse / Jack Lange / Lou Davis
Francis, Day & Hunter Ltd . . . . USA
Film(s): . . . . Rat Race
Paul Whiteman & His Orchestra
(featuring Henry Busse (trumpet)) . . . . **HMV B 1396**
Mistinguett . . . . **Pathé 6603**
Harry Roy & his Tiger Ragamuffins . . . . **Parlophone R 624**
The Wilbur De Paris Band . . . . **London LTZK 15024**

HOT LOVE May 1971
Marc Bolan
Essex Music Ltd . . . . UK
T. Rex . . . . **Fly BUG 6**
Ivor Novello Nomination.

HOT STUFF June 1979
Peter Bellotte / Harry Faltermeir
Heath Levy Music Ltd. . . . . USA
Donna Summer . . . . **Casablanca CAN 151**

HOT TODDY May 1953
Ralph Flanagan / Herb Hendler
Aberbach (London) Ltd. . . . . USA
Ted Heath & his Music . . . . **Decca LK 4064**
Ralph Flanagan & his Orchestra . . . . **RCA RCX 1021**
The Clark Sisters . . . . **London HAD 2177**

HOTEL CALIFORNIA May 1977
Don Felder / Don Henley / Glen Frey
Warner Brothers Music Ltd . . . . USA
The Eagles . . . . **Asylum K 13079**

HOUND DOG September 1956
Jerry Leiber / Mike Stoller
Edwin H. Morris & Co. Ltd. . . . . USA
Film(s): . . . . Grease
Elvis Presley . . . . **RCA RB 16069**
George Melly . . . . **Decca LK 4226**
Sha Na Na . . . . **RSO 2479-211**
Sha Na Na appeared in the film *Grease*.

HOUR NEVER PASSES, AN 1944
Jimmy Kennedy
Campbell Connelly & Co. Ltd. . . . . UK
Leslie Hutchinson (Hutch) . . . . **HMV BD 1080**
Ambrose & his Orchestra,
vocal George Melachrino . . . . **Decca F 8421**
Joe Loss & his Orchestra . . . . **HMV BD 5849**

HOUR OF PARTING, THE 1931
Gus Kahn / Mischa Spoilansky
Chappell & Co. Ltd . . . . USA
De Groot & his Orchestra . . . . **HMV B 3207**
Benny Goodman & his Orchestra . . . . **Columbia 33SX 1038**
Stanley Black & his Orchestra . . . . **Decca LK 4114**

HOUSE ARREST — January 1988
Cassius Campbell / Mark Gamble / Ruth Joy
MCA Music . . . . UK
Krush . . . . **Club JAB 63**

HOUSE IS HAUNTED, THE — 1934
Basil G. Adlam / Billy Rose
Francis, Day & Hunter Ltd. . . . . USA
Val Rosing . . . . **Rex 8220**
Gracie Fields . . . . **Regal Zonophone MR 1949**
Kay Starr . . . . **RCA RD 27056**
Don Neilson . . . . **Philips PB 1058**

HOUSE NATION — September 1987
Kevin Jones
Leosong . . . . UK
The Housemaster Boyz
& The Rude Boys of House . . . . **Magnetic Dance MAGDT 1**

HOUSE OF BAMBOO, THE — July 1958
Norman Murrells / Bill Crompton
Sydney Bron Music Co. Ltd . . . . UK
Neville Taylor . . . . **Parlophone R 4447**
Andy Williams . . . . **London HAA 2388**
Earl Grant . . . . **Brunswick 05824**

HOUSE OF BLUE LIGHTS, THE — 1947
Freddie Slack / Don Raye
Francis, Day & Hunter Ltd. . . . . USA
The Andrews Sisters . . . . **Brunswick 03701**
Freddie Slack & his Orchestra,
vocal Ella Mae Morse . . . . **Capitol CL 13007**

HOUSE OF DAVID BLUES, THE — 1923
Elmer Schoebel / Billy Meyers / Irving Mills
Lawrence Wright Music Co. Ltd . . . . USA
The Original Capitol Orchestra . . . . **Zonophone 2411**
Jack Hylton & his Orchestra . . . . **HMV B 1702**
The Connie's Inn Orchestra . . . . **Brunswick 1205**

HOUSE OF FUN — January 1982
Michael Barson / Lee Thompson
Warner Brothers Music . . . . UK
Madness . . . . **Stiff BUY 146**

HOUSE OF SINGING BAMBOO, THE — March 1951
Harry Warren / Arthur Freed
Francis, Day & Hunter Ltd . . . . USA
Film(s): . . . . Pagan Love Song
Howard Keel . . . . **MGM EP 667**
Guy Mitchell & Rosemary Clooney . . . . **Columbia DB 331**
Howard Keel appeared in *Pagan Love Song*.

HOUSE OF THE RISING SUN, THE — February 1964
Traditional, arranged by Alan Price
Keith Prowse Music Publishing Co. Ltd . . . . USA
The Animals . . . . **Columbia DB 7301**
Frijid Pink (1970) . . . . **Deram DM 228**
The Animals (1982) . . . . **RAK RR 1**

HOUSE THAT JACK BUILT — April 1983
Paul Barry
EMI Music . . . . UK
Tracie . . . . **Respond KOB 701**

HOUSE THAT JACK BUILT, THE — September 1967
Alan Price
Alan Price Music . . . . UK
The Alan Price Set . . . . **Decca F 12641**

HOUSE WITH LOVE IN IT, A — November 1956
Sidney Lippman / Sylvia Dee
Lawrence Wright Music Co. Ltd. . . . . USA
Vera Lynn . . . . **Decca F 10799**
Ronnie Harris . . . . **Columbia DB 3836**
Gordon MacRae . . . . **Capitol T 1251**

HOW 'BOUT US — June 1981
Dana Walden
April Music Ltd . . . . USA
Champaign . . . . **CBS A 1046**

HOW ABOUT ME — 1929
Irving Berlin
Francis, Day & Hunter Ltd . . . . USA

Morton Downey . . . . **HMV B 2998**
Julius La Rosa . . . . **Columbia 33SX 1164**
Julie London . . . . **London HAG 2299**

HOW ABOUT THAT — October 1960
Les Vandyke
Mills Music Ltd . . . . UK
Adam Faith . . . . **Parlophone GEP 8841**

HOW ABOUT YOU — 1942
Ralph Freed / Burton Lane
Sun Music Publishing Co. Ltd . . . . USA
Film(s): . . . . Babes on Broadway / Kiss Them For Me
Judy Garland . . . . **Brunswick 03305**
Bing Crosby & Rosemary Clooney . . . . **RCA RD 27105**
Frank Sinatra . . . . **Capitol LCT 6106**
Joni James . . . . **MGM C 825**
Judy Garland appeared in *Babes On Broadway*.
Nominated for an Academy Award 1942.

HOW AM I SUPPOSED TO LIVE WITHOUT YOU — Mar 1990
Michael Bolton / Douglas James
EMI Music . . . . USA
Michael Bolton . . . . **CBS 6553977**

HOW AM I TO KNOW — 1930
Dorothy Parker / Jack King
Robbins Music Corporation Ltd . . . . USA
Film(s): . . . . Dynamite / Pandora and the Flying Dutchman
Frankie Trumbauer & his Orchestra . . . . **Parlophone R 618**
Tommy Dorsey & his Orchestra,
vocal Jack Leonard . . . . **HMV BD 5851**
Ava Gardner . . . . **MGM EP 703**
Rosemary Clooney . . . . **RCA RD 27218**
Ava Gardner appeared in *Pandora and The Flying Dutchman*.

HOW ARE THINGS IN GLOCCA MORRA — 1947
E.Y. Harburg / Burton Lane
Chappell & Co. Ltd. . . . . USA
Show(s): . . . . Finian's Rainbow
Film(s): . . . . Finian's Rainbow
Ella Logan . . . . **Philips BBE 12255**
Dick Haymes . . . . **Brunswick 03810**
Gracie Fields . . . . **Decca F 8808**
Jeannie Carson . . . . **RCA RCX 199**
Petula Clark . . . . **Warner Brothers WF 2550**
Ella Logan appeared in the American production of *Finian's Rainbow*.
Petula Clark appeared in the film of *Finian's Rainbow*.

HOW BLUE THE NIGHT — 1944
Harold Arlen / Jimmy McHugh
Francis, Day & Hunter Ltd. . . . . USA
Film(s): . . . . Four Jills in a Jeep
Dick Haymes . . . . **Brunswick 03535**
Denny Dennis . . . . **Decca F 8481**
Dick Haymes appeared in *Four Jills in a Jeep*.

HOW CAN I BE SURE — October 1972
Felix Cavaliere / Eddie Brigati
Sparta Music Ltd. . . . . USA
David Cassidy . . . . **Bell 1258**

HOW CAN I MEET HER — June 1962
Gerry Goffin / Jack Keller
Aldon Music Ltd. . . . . USA
The Everly Brothers . . . . **Warner Brothers WB 67**

HOW CAN WE BE LOVERS — June 1990
Michael Bolton / Diane Warren / Desmond Child
EMI Music . . . . USA
Michael Bolton . . . . **CBS 6559187**

HOW CAN YOU BUY KILLARNEY — April 1949
Hamilton Kennedy / Ted Steels / Freddie Grant / Gerard Morrison
Peter Maurice Music Co. Ltd . . . . UK
Lee Lawrence . . . . **Decca F 9090**
Bing Crosby . . . . **Brunswick LAT 8278**
Ruby Murray . . . . **Columbia 33S 1079**

HOW CAN YOU TELL — December 1965
Chris Andrews
Glissando Music Ltd . . . . UK
Sandie Shaw . . . . **Pye 7N 15987**

HOW COME February 1974
Ronnie Lane / Clive Westlake
Warner Brothers Music Ltd. .... UK
Ronnie Lane .... **G.M. GMS 011**

HOW COME YOU DO ME LIKE YOU DO 1925
Gene Austin / Roy Bergere
B. Feldman & Co. Ltd. .... USA
Show(s): ....That's the Spirit / Three for the Show
The Original Memphis Five .... **Brunswick 3713**
Spike Hughes & his Orchestra,
vocal Henry Allen .... **Decca LK 4173**
Jane Powell .... **HMV CLP 1131**
Jimmy Rushing .... **Philips BBL 7484**
Julie London .... **London HAW 2225**

HOW COULD YOU BELIEVE ME, WHEN I SAID I
LOVE YOU, WHEN YOU KNOW I'VE BEEN A LIAR ALL
MY LIFE March 1951
Alan Jay Lerner / Burton Labe
Chappell & Co. Ltd .... USA
Film(s): ....Wedding Bells
Fred Astaire & Jane Powell .... **MGM EP 635**
Edmund Hockridge & Joan Regan ..... **Pye NPL 18048**
Danny Kaye & Carole Richards .... **Brunswick 04683**
Fred Astaire & Jane Powell appeared in *Wedding Bells*.

HOW DEEP IS THE OCEAN 1933
Irving Berlin
Francis, Day & Hunter Ltd. .... USA
Film(s): .... Blue Skies / Meet Danny Wilson
Bing Crosby .... **Fontana TFE 17179**
Gracie Fields .... **HMV B 4343**
Pat Boone .... **London HAD 2082**
Lita Roza .... **Pye NPL 18047**
Bing Crosby appeared in *Blue Skies*.

HOW DEEP IS YOUR LOVE December 1977
Robin Gibb / Maurice Gibb / Barry Gibb
Abigail Music .... UK
Film(s): .... Saturday Night Fever
The Bee Gees .... **RSO 2090259**
Ivor Novello Award.

HOW DO YOU DO IT April 1963
Mitch Murray
Dick James Music Ltd .... UK
Gerry & The Pacemakers .... **Columbia DB 4987**

HOW GREEN WAS MY VALLEY 1942
Benny Davis / Abner Silver
Peter Maurice Music Publishing Co. Ltd .... USA
Ambrose & his Orchestra, vocal Anne Shelton .. **Decca F 8122**
Joe Loss & his Orchestra, vocal Pat McCormack **HMV BD 5746**
Vera Lynn .... **Decca F 8137**
Vera Lynn .... **MGM C 855**

HOW HIGH THE MOON December 1949
Nancy Hamilton / Morgan Lewis
Chappell & Co. Ltd .... USA
Film(s): .... Two For the Show
Nat 'King' Cole .... **Capitol CL 13204**
Les Paul & Mary Ford (1951) .... **Capitol T 1438**
Ella Fitzgerald .... **HMV CLP 1391**
Sarah Vaughan .... **Mercury MPL 6542**
Theme song of Les Paul & Mary Ford.

HOW IMPORTANT CAN IT BE April 1955
Bennie Benjamin / George Weiss
Valando Music Co. Ltd. .... USA
Joni James .... **MGM 811**
Teresa Brewer .... **Vogue Q 72065**
Connee Boswell .... **Brunswick 05397**

HOW IT LIES, HOW IT LIES, HOW IT LIES July 1949
Paul Francis Webster / Sonny Burke
Edwin H. Morris & Co. Ltd .... USA
Bing Crosby & Evelyn Knight .... **Brunswick 04139**
Doris Day .... **Columbia DB 3123**

HOW LITTLE WE KNOW 1945
Hoagy Carmichael / Johnny Mercer
B. Feldman & Co. Ltd. .... USA
Film(s): .... To Have and Have Not

Eric Winstone & his Orchestra, vocal Julie Dawn .. **HMV BD 5898**
Dennis Lotis .... **Columbia 33SX 1089**

HOW LONG HAS THIS BEEN GOING ON 1929
George Gershwin / Ira Gerswin
Chappell & Co. Ltd .... USA
Show(s): .... Rosalie
Film(s): .... Funny Face
June Christy .... **Capitol LC 6802**
Audrey Hepburn .... **HMV CLP 1119**
Tony Bennett .... **Philips BBL 7452**
Audrey Hepburn appeared in *Funny Face*.

HOW LUCKY YOU ARE 1947
Eddie Cassen / Desmond O'Connor
Edward Kassner Music Co. Ltd. .... UK
The Andrews Sisters .... **Brunswick 03823**
Lou Preager & his Orchestra .... **Columbia FB 3293**
Joni James .... **MGM 918**

HOW MANY HEARTS HAVE YOU BROKEN 1944
Marty Symes / Al Kaufman
B. Feldman & Co. Ltd .... USA
Geraldo & his Orch. vocal Johnny Green .. **Parlophone F 2048**
The Ambassadors Dance Orchestra,
vocal Leslie Douglas .... **Rex 10212**

HOW MANY TEARS September 1961
Gerry Goffin / Carole King
Nevins-Kirchner Ltd. .... USA
Bobby Vee .... **London HL 9389**

HOW MUCH LOVE May 1977
Leo Sayer / Barry Mann
Screen Gems Music Ltd .... USA
Leo Sayer .... **Chrysalis CHS 2140**

HOW SOON September 1964
Al Stillman / Henry Mancini
Compass Music Ltd .... USA
Henry Mancini & his Orchestra .... **RCA 1414**
Ken Thorne & his Orchestra
with The Michael Sammes Singers .... **HMV POP 1278**
Theme from the *Richard Boone Show* T.V. series.

HOW SWEET YOU ARE 1944
Arthur Schwartz / Frank Loesser
B. Feldman & Co. Ltd .... USA
Film(s): .... Thank Your Lucky Stars
Kay Armen & his Balladiers .... **Brunswick 03496**
Ivy Benson's Girls Band, vocal Rita Williams .... **HMV BD 1069**
Jimmy Young .... **Columbia 33SX 1102**

HOW TO HANDLE A WOMAN October 1964
Alan Jay Lerner / Frederick Loewe
Chappell & Co. Ltd .... USA
Show(s): .... Camelot
Film(s): .... Camelot
Richard Burton .... **CBS APG 60004**
Laurence Harvey .... **HMV CLP 1756**
Richard Harris .... **Warner Brothers W 1712**
Richard Burton appeared in the American production of *Camelot*.
Laurence Harvey appeared in the British production of *Camelot*.
Richard Harris appeared in the film *Camelot*.

HOW WILL I KNOW February 1986
George Merrill / Sharron Rubicam / Narada Michael Walden
Carlin Music .... USA
Whitney Houston .... **Arista ARIST 656**

HOW WONDERFUL TO KNOW (Aneme e Core) July 1961
Salve D'Esposito / Tito Manlio / Kermit Goell
Macmelodies Ltd. .... Italy
Joan Regan .... **Pye 7N 15334**
Teddy Johnson & Pearl Carr .... **Columbia DB 4603**
Andy Williams .... **CBS BPG 62658**

HOW YA GONNA KEEP 'EM DOWN ON THE FARM 1919
Sam M. Lewis / Joe Young / Walter Donaldson
B. Feldman & Co. Ltd .... USA
Film(s): .... For Me & My Gal / The Eddie Cantor Story
The Savoy Quartet .... **HMV B 1060**
Jacob's Trocaderians .... **Columbia 2867**
Eddie Cantor .... **Brunswick LA 8658**
Verdi .... **Decca LK 4290**

Eddie Cantor . . . . Capitol LC 6652

HOW'D YA LIKE TO LOVE ME 1938
Frank Loesser / Burton Lane
Victoria Music Co. Ltd. . . . . USA
Film(s): . . . . Swing Teacher Swing
Abe Lyman & his Orchestra . . . . . . Regal Zonophone MR 2779
Roy Fox & his Orchestra, vocal Mary Lee . . . . . . HMV BD 5371
Jimmy Dorsey & his Orchestra . . . . Decca F 6740

HOW'S CHANCES 1935
Irving Berlin
Chappell & Co. Ltd . . . . USA
Show(s): . . . . As Thousands Cheer / Stop Press
Film(s): . . . . Thousands Cheer
Henry Hall & the B.B.C. Dance Orchestra . . Columbia FB 1024
Ella Fitzgerald . . . . HMV CLP 1184

HOWARD'S WAY THEME November 1985
Simon May / Leslie Osborne
Lawrence Wright Music . . . . UK
Simon May Orchestra . . . . BBC RESL 174
Theme of the television series *Howards Way*
See also "Always There"

HOWZAT November 1976
Garth Porter / Tony Mitchell
Heath Levy Music Ltd . . . . Australia
Sherbert . . . . Epic EPC 4574

HUCKLEBUCK, THE March 1981
Roy Alfred / Andy Gibson
Leeds Music . . . . USA
Coast To Coast . . . . Polydor POSP 214

HUGGIN' AND CHALKIN' 1947
Kermit Goell / Clancy Hayes
Peter Maurice Music co. Ltd. . . . . USA
Hoagy Carmichael . . . . Brunswick 03709
The Leslie Douglas Band . . . . Regal Zonophone MR 3792
Bob Scobey's Band, vocal Clancy Hayes . . . . . Vogue LDG 155

HULA HOOP SONG, THE November 1958
Carl Maduri / Donna Kohler
Leeds Music Ltd . . . . USA
Georgia Gibbs . . . . Columbia DB 4201
Teresa Brewer . . . . Coral FEP 2013

HUMAN September 1986
James Harris / Terry Lewis
CBS Songs . . . . UK
Human League . . . . Virgin VS 880

HUMMING 1921
Ray Henderson / Louis Breau
Chappell & Co. Ltd . . . . USA
Show(s): . . . . Faust on Toast
Nellie Walker & Chorus . . . . HMV B 1224
Paul Whiteman & his Orchestra . . . . HMV B 1234

HUMPTY DUMPTY HEART 1942
Johnny Burke / Jimmy Van Heusen
Southern Music Publishing Co. Ltd . . . . USA
Film(s): . . . . Playmates
Ambrose & his Orchestra, vocal Anne Shelton . . Decca F 8155
Glenn Miller & his Orchestra, vocal Ray Eberle . HMV BD 5749

HUNDRED POUNDS OF CLAY May 1961
Bob Elgin / Luther Dixon / Kay Rogers
Tin Pan Alley Music Co. Ltd . . . . USA
Craig Douglas . . . . Top Rank JAR 556
Gene McDaniels . . . . London HAG 2384

HUNDRED YEARS FROM TODAY, A 1934
Victor Young / Ned Washington
Francis, Day & Hunter Ltd. . . . . USA
Show(s): . . . . Blackbirds of 1933 / Blackbirds of 1934
Film(s): . . . . The Girl from Missouri
Jack Teagarden & his Orchestra . . . . Brunswick 03365
June Christy . . . . Capitol T 1202
Jack Teagarden & his Orchestra . . . . Columbia SX 1303
Don Cornell . . . . Vogue LVA 9037

HUNGRY LIKE THE WOLF June 1982
"Duran Duran"

Carlin Music . . . . UK
Duran Duran . . . . EMI 5295

HUNTING HIGH AND LOW June 1986
Pal Waaktaar
ATV Music . . . . UK
A-Ha . . . . Warner Brothers W 6663

HURDY GURDY MAN, THE 1937
Sammy Cahn / Saul Chaplin
Sun Music Publishing Co. Ltd . . . . USA
Film(s): . . . . Wake Up and Live
Jimmy Dorsey & his Orchestra,
vocal Louis Armstrong . . . . Decca F 6145
Nat Gonella & his Georgians . . . . Parlophone F 783

HURDY GURDY MAN, THE July 1968
Donovan Leitch
Donovan Music Ltd. . . . . UK
Donovan . . . . Pye 7N 17537

HURRY ON DOWN January 1949
Nellie Lutcher
Campbell Connelly & Co. Ltd . . . . USA
Nellie Lutcher . . . . Capitol LC 6506
Theme song of Nellie Lutcher.

HURRY UP HARRY November 1978
Jimmy Pursey / David Parsons
Singatune Publishing . . . . UK
Sham 69 . . . . Polydor POSP 7

HURT November 1976
Al Jacobs / Jimmy Crane
Big 3 Music . . . . USA
The Manhattans . . . . CBS 4562
Timi Yuro . . . . London HLG 9403
Elvis Presley . . . . RCA 2674
First published 1953.

HURT SO GOOD May 1975
Phillip Mitchell
Warner Brothers Music Ltd . . . . USA
Susan Cadogan . . . . Magnet MAG 23

HUSH NOT A WORD TO MARY July 1968
Mitch Murray / Peter Callander
Intune Ltd. . . . . UK
John Rowles . . . . MCA MU 1023

HUSTLE TO THE MUSIC August 1988
Mark Brydon / Carl Munson / Richard Parrot / Gerry Thomas & June Stewart
MCA Music . . . . UK
The Funky Worm . . . . WEA FUN 15

HUSTLE, THE July 1975
Van McCoy
Warner Brothers Music Ltd . . . . USA
Van McCoy . . . . Avco 6105037

HUT SUT SONG 1941
Jack Owens / Ted McMichael / Leo Killion
Chappell & Co. Ltd . . . . USA
Film(s): . . . . San Antonio Rose
Lew Stone & his Orchestra, vocal Carl Barriteau Decca F 7919
The Merry Macs . . . . Decca F 7960
Elsie Carlisle . . . . Rex 10021
Mel Tormé . . . . Vogue LVA 9032
The Merry Macs appeared in *San Antonio Rose*.

HYMN December 1982
William Currie / Warren Cann / Christopher Allen / James Ure
Mood Music . . . . UK
Ultravox . . . . Chrysalis CHS 2657

HYMN TO HER January 1987
Meg Keene
Hynde House Music . . . . UK
The Pretenders . . . . Real YZ 93

I (WHO HAVE NOTHING) (Uno Dei Tanti) November 1963
C. Donida / Jerry Leiber / Mike Stoller
Shapiro-Bernstein & Co. Ltd . . . . Italy
Ben E. King . . . . London HL 9778

Shirley Bassey . . . . Columbia DN 7113
Ken Kirkham . . . . HMV POP 1208

**I AIN'T GONNA GIVE NOBODY NONE O'THIS JELLY
ROLL** 1919
Clarence Williams / Spencer Williams
B. Feldman & Co. Ltd . . . . USA
Emmett Miller . . . . Parlophone R 2163
Sharkey & His Kings Of Dixieland . . . . Capitol LC 6600
The Dutch Swing College Band . . . . Philips BBL 7390
Bobby Darin & Johnny Mercer . . . . London HAK 2363

I AIN'T GONNA STAND FOR IT January 1981
Stevie Wonder
Jobete Music . . . . USA
Stevie Wonder . . . . Motown TMG 1215

I AIN'T GOT NOBODY 1928
Spencer Williams / Roger Graham
Campbell Connelly & Co. Ltd. . . . . USA
Film(s): . . . . Paris Honeymoon / Atlantic City
Sophie Tucker . . . . Parlophone R 3353
Bing Crosby, Woody Herman &
his Woodchoppers . . . . Brunswick Bing 4
Rosemary Clooney . . . . RCA RD 27218
Bing Crosby appeared in *Paris Honeymoon*.

I AIN'T NOBODY'S DARLING 1923
Robert King / Elmer Hughes
Keith Prowse Music Publishing Co. Ltd . . . . USA
Norah Blaney & Gwen Farrar . . . . HMV B 1513
Jack Hylton & his Orchestra . . . . HMV B 1524

I AM A CIDER DRINKER October 1976
Tony Baylis / Tommy Banner / Pete Budd
Noon Music . . . . UK
The Wurzels . . . . EMI 2520
Parody version of "Una Paloma Blanca".

I AM A CLOWN April 1973
Tony Romeo
Carlin Music Corporation . . . . USA
David Cassidy . . . . Bell MABEL 4

I AM THE BEAT January 1981
Jonathan Whetsone / Michael Bass
Big Brother Music . . . . UK
The Look . . . . MCA MCA 647

I AM THE STARLIGHT May 1984
Andrew Lloyd Webber / Richard Stilgoe
Really Usefull Music . . . . UK
Show(s): . . . . Starlight Express
Lon Statton . . . . Starlight Express LNER 1
Lon Statton appeared in *Starlight Express*.

I AM...I SAID June 1971
Neil Diamond
A&B Music . . . . USA
Neil Diamond . . . . Uni UN 532

I APOLOGISE 1932
Ed Nelson / Al Goodhart / Al Hoffman
Victoria Music Co. Ltd. . . . . USA
Kate Smith . . . . Columbia DB 734
Bing Crosby . . . . Brunswick LA 8741
Billy Eckstine (1951) . . . . MGM EP 749
Billy Eckstine . . . . Columbia 33SX 1249
P.J. Proby (1965) . . . . Liberty LIB 10188

I BEG YOUR PARDON April 1989
Barry Harris / Joe South
Warner Chappell Music . . . . USA
Kon Kan . . . . Atlantic A 8969

I BEGGED HER 1945
Jule Styne / Sammy Cahn
Robbins Music Corporation Ltd. . . . . USA
Film(s): . . . . Anchors Aweigh
Frank Sinatra . . . . Fontana SET 303A
Geraldo & his Orchestra,
vocal Len Camber . . . . Parlophone F 2087
The Bill Shepherd Orchestra & chorus . . . . Nixa NPL 18018
Frank Sinatra appeared in *Anchors Aweigh*.

I BELIEVE May 1953
Ervin Drake / Jimmy Shirl / Irvin Graham & Al Stillman
Cinephonic Music Co. Ltd . . . . USA
David Whitfield . . . . Decca LF 1165
Frankie Laine . . . . Philips BBL 7263
Perry Como . . . . RCA RCX 161
The Bachelors (1964) . . . . Decca F 11857

I BELIEVE (In Love) October 1971
Tony Wilson / Errol Brown
Rak Music Ltd . . . . UK
Hot Chocolate . . . . Rak 118

I BELIEVE IN FATHER CHRISTMAS December 1975
Greg Lake / Peter Sinfield
Manticore Group . . . . UK
Greg Lake . . . . Manticor K 13511
Adapted from the "Lieutenant Kije Suite, Opus 60" by Sergei Prokofiev
(1891 - 1953).

I BELIEVE IN MIRACLES 1935
Pete Wendling / George Meyer / Sam M. Lewis
Francis, Day & Hunter Ltd . . . . USA
Val Rosing . . . . Regal Zonophone MR 1649
Hildegarde . . . . Columbia DB 1552
Dick Powell . . . . Decca F 5503
'Fats' Waller & his Rhythm . . . . Camden CDN 131

I BELONG TO GLASGOW 1920
Will Fyffe
Francis, Day & Hunter Ltd . . . . UK
Will Fyffe . . . . Regal G 7693
Max Bygraves . . . . HMV 7 EG 8271
Gracie Fields . . . . Columbia 33SX 1198

I BOUGHT MYSELF A BOTTLE OF INK 1934
Arthur Le Clerq / Stanley Damerell / Tolchard Evans
Sidney Bron Music Co. Ltd . . . . UK
Henry Hall & the B.B.C. Dance Orchestra . . . Columbia CB 790
Jack Jackson & his Orchestra . . . . HMV B 6526
Leslie Holmes . . . . Rex 8293

I BRING A LOVE SONG 1931
Sigmund Romberg / Oscar Hammerstein II
B. Feldman & Co. Ltd . . . . USA
Film(s): . . . . Viennese Nights
Richard Crooks . . . . HMV DA 1174
The Mantovani Orchestra . . . . Decca LK 4082

I CAIN'T SAY NO 1947
Richard Rodgers / Oscar Hammerstein II
Williamson Music Ltd. . . . . USA
Show(s): . . . . Oklahoma
Film(s): . . . . Oklahoma
Celeste Holm . . . . Brunswick LAT 8001
Dorothy MacFarland . . . . HMV 7EP 7023
Gloria Graham . . . . Capitol LCT 6100
Celeste Holm appeared in the American production of *Oklahoma*.
Dorothy MacFarland appeared in the British production of *Oklahoma*.
Gloria Graham appeared in the film of *Oklahoma*.

I CAME HERE TO TALK FOR JOE 1943
Lew Brown / Charles Tobias / Sammy Stept
Francis, Day & Hunter Ltd . . . . USA
Glen Gray & The Casa Loma Orchestra,
vocal Kenny Sargent . . . . Brunswick 03417

I CAME, I SAW, I CONGA'D 1941
James Cavanaugh / John Redmond / Frank Weldon
Campbell Connelly & Co. Ltd . . . . USA
Celia Lipton . . . . Columbia FB 2646
Phil Tate & his Band . . . . Oriole EP 7052

I CAN DO IT April 1975
Wayne Bickerton / Tony Waddington
A.T.V. Music Ltd. . . . . UK
The Rubettes . . . . State STAT 1

I CAN DREAM ABOUT YOU September 1985
Dan Hartman
CBS Songs . . . . USA
Dan Hartman . . . . MCA MCA 988

I CAN DREAM CAN'T I 1938
Irving Kahal / Sammy Fain

Francis, Day & Hunter Ltd. . . . . USA
Show(s): . . . . Right this Way
Al Bowlly & his Orchestra . . . . **HMV BD 5363**
The Andrews Sisters (1949) . . . . **Brunswick OE 9429**
Millicent Martin . . . . **Columbia DB 4466**

I CAN GIVE YOU THE STARLIGHT   1939
Ivor Novello / Christopher Hassall
Chappell & Co. Ltd. . . . . UK
Show(s): . . . . The Dancing Years
Film(s): . . . . The Dancing Years
Mary Ellis . . . . **HMV DLP 1028**
Sound Track . . . . **HMV B 9966**
Vanessa Lee . . . . **HMV CLP 1258**
Hilde Gueden . . . . **Decca LK 4196**
Mary Ellis appeared in the show *The Dancing Years*.

I CAN HEAR MUSIC   April 1969
Phil Spector / Jeff Barry / Ellie Greenwich
Carlin Music Corporation . . . . USA
The Beach Boys . . . . **Capitol CL 15584**

I CAN HEAR THE GRASS GROW   May 1967
Roy Wood
Essex Music Ltd. . . . . UK
The Move . . . . **Deram DM 117**

I CAN HELP   January 1975
Billy Swan
Keith Prowse Music Publishing Co. Ltd. . . . . USA
Billy Swan . . . . **Monument MNT 2752**
Elvis Presley . . . . **RCA RS 1011**

I CAN MAKE YOU FEEL GOOD   May 1982
Howard Hewett / Renwick Jackson / William Shelby
Chappell Music Co. . . . . USA
Shalamar . . . . **Solar K 12599**

I CAN PROVE IT   August 1986
Tony Etoria
Chrysalis Music . . . . UK
Phil Fearon . . . . **Ensign PF 1**
Tony Etoria . . . . **GTO GT 89**

I CAN SEE CLEARLY NOW   August 1972
Johnny Nash
Rondor Music (London) Ltd. . . . . USA
Johnny Nash . . . . **CBS 8113**

I CAN SEE FOR MILES   November 1967
Peter Townshend
Fabulous Music . . . . UK
The Who . . . . **Track 604011**

I CAN SING A RAINBOW   August 1969
Arthur Hamilton
Edwin H. Morris & Co. Ltd. . . . . USA
Film(s): . . . . Pete Kelly's Blues
The Dells . . . . **Philips 9299331**
Peggy Lee . . . . **Brunswick 05472**
Peggy Lee appeared in *Pete Kelly's Blues*.

I CAN TAKE OR LEAVE YOUR LOVING   February 1968
Rick Jones
Active Music . . . . UK
Herman's Hermits . . . . **Columbia DB 8327**

I CAN'T ASK FOR ANYTHING MORE THAN YOU   Oct 1976
Ken Gold / Micky Denne
Screen Gems Music Ltd . . . . USA
Cliff Richard . . . . **EMI 2499**

I CAN'T BEGIN TO TELL YOU   1946
Mack Gordon / Jimmy Monaco
Bregman, Vocca & Conn Ltd. . . . . USA
Film(s): . . . . The Dolly Sisters / You're My Everything
Harry James Orchestra, vocal Ruth Haag . . **Columbia DB 2642**
Steve Conway . . . . **Columbia FB 3186**
Bing Crosby . . . . **Brunswick OE 9424**
Jane Morgan . . . . **London HLR 8925**
Brook Benton . . . . **Mercury MMC 14015**
Ruth Haag is pseudonym for Betty Grable.
Betty Grable appeared in *The Dolly Sisters*.
Nominated for an Academy Award 1946.

I CAN'T BELIEVE THAT YOU'RE IN LOVE WITH ME   1927
Jimmy McHugh / Clarence Gaskill
Lawrence Wright Music Co. Ltd. . . . . USA
Show(s): . . . . On With the Show
Film(s): . . . . The Caine Mutiny / Looking for Love
Walter Williams & Winnie Collins . . . . **Regal G 8876**
Bing Crosby (1954) . . . . **Brunswick 05273**
Dinah Shore . . . . **Capitol T 1354**
Dean Martin . . . . **Capitol T 1442**
Connie Francis . . . . **MGM C983**
Connie Francis appeared in *Looking for Love*.

I CAN'T CONTROL MYSELF   November 1966
Reginald Presley
Dick James Music Ltd. . . . . UK
The Troggs . . . . **Page One POF 001**

I CAN'T DANCE, I GOT ANTS IN MY PANTS   1936
Clarence Williams / Charles Gaines
Pickwick Music Ltd . . . . USA
The Dorsey Brothers Orchestra . . . . **Brunswick 01867**
Harry Parry & his Radio Rhythm Sextet . . . **Parlophone R 2851**

I CAN'T DO MY BALLY BOTTOM BUTTON UP   1916
John P. Long
B. Feldman & Co. Ltd. . . . . UK
Ernie Mayne . . . . **Edison Bell Winner 2985**
Ian Wallace . . . . **Parlophone R 4726**

I CAN'T DO WITHOUT YOU   1928
Irving Berlin
Francis, Day & Hunter Ltd . . . . USA
Gus Arnheim & His Orchestra . . . . **Parlophone F 638**

I CAN'T ESCAPE FROM YOU   1936
Leo Robin / Richard A. Whiting
Sterling Music Publishing Co. Ltd . . . . USA
Film(s): . . . . Rhythm on the Range
Bing Crosby . . . . **Brunswick Bing 2**
Carmen McRae . . . . **Brunswick LAT 8257**
Johnnie Ray . . . . **Philips BBL 7285**
Bing Crosby appeared in *Rhythm on the Range*.

I CAN'T EXPLAIN   April 1965
Peter Townshend
Essex Music Ltd . . . . UK
The Who . . . . **Brunswick 05926**

I CAN'T GET BY WITHOUT YOU   October 1976
Chris Gold / Micky Denne
Screen Gems Music Ltd . . . . USA
The Real Thing . . . . **Pye 7N 45618**
The Real Thing (1986) . . . . **PRT 7P 352**

I CAN'T GET NEXT TO YOU   February 1970
Norman Whitfield / Barrett Strong
Jobete Music (UK) Ltd. . . . . USA
The Temptations . . . . **Tamla Motown TMG 722**

I CAN'T GET NO SATISFACTION (See Satisfaction)

I CAN'T GET STARTED   1936
Vernon Duke / Ira Gershwin
Chappell & Co. Ltd . . . . USA
Show(s): . . . . The Ziegfeld Follies of 1936
Bunny Berigan & his Orchestra,
vocal Bunny Berigan . . . . **RCA RCX 1005**
The Clark Sisters . . . . **London HAD 2177**
Frank Sinatra . . . . **Capitol LCT 6185**

I CAN'T GET YOU OUTA MY MIND   October 1977
Beatrice Verdi / Christian yarian
A.T.V. Music Ltd. . . . . USA
Yvonne Elliman . . . . **RSO 2090251**

I CAN'T GIVE YOU ANYTHING BUT LOVE   1928
Dorothy Fields / Jimmy McHugh
Lawrence Wright Music Co. Ltd. . . . . USA
Show(s): . . . . Blackbirds of 1928 / Singin' in the Rain
Film(s):I Can't Give You Anything But Love / Stormy Weather / Jam
Session / Born Yesterday / Both Ends of the Candle
The Goofus Five . . . . **Parlophone R 218**
Ethel Waters . . . . **Brunswick 01518**
Adelaide Hall . . . . **HMV B 8849**

Gogi Grant . . . . **RCA RD 27054**
Ella Fitzgerald . . . . **HMV CLP 1396**
Danielle Carson . . . . **Safari RAIN 1**
Ethel Waters appeared in *Stormy Weather*.
Adelaide Hall appeared in *Blackbirds of 1928*.
Gogi Grant dubbed the singing voice of Ann Blyth who appeared in the film *Both Ends of the Candle*.
Danielle Carson appeared in the show of *Singin' in the Rain*.

I CAN'T GO FOR THAT (No Can Do)   February 1982
Daryl Hall / John Oates / Sara Allen
Interwood Music . . . . USA
Daryl Hall & John Oates . . . . **RCA RCA 172**

I CAN'T HELP MYSELF   August 1965
Brian Holland / Eddie Holland / Lamont Dozier
Jobete Music (UK) Ltd. . . . . USA
The Four Tops . . . . **Tamla Motown TMG 515**
The Four Tops (1970) . . . . **Tamla Motown TMG 732**
Donnie Elbert (1972) . . . . **Avco 6105009**

I CAN'T LEAVE YOU ALONE   November 1974
H.W. Casey / Richard Finch
Southern Music Publishing Co. Ltd. . . . . USA
George McRae . . . . **Jayboy BOY 90**

I CAN'T LET GO   April 1966
Chip Taylor / Al Gorgoni
April Music Co. Ltd. . . . . USA
The Hollies . . . . **Parlophone R 5409**

I CAN'T LET MAGGIE GO   May 1968
Pete Dello
Ambassador Music Ltd. . . . . UK
Honeybus . . . . **Deram DM 182**

I CAN'T LOVE YOU ANYMORE   1940
Herb Magidson / Allie Wrubel
Francis, Day & Hunter Ltd . . . . USA
Bebe Daniels . . . . **Decca F 7574**
Trudy Richards . . . . **London L 1192**
Debbie Reynolds . . . . **London HAD 2294**

I CAN'T STAND IT   October 1990
Ruud Van Rijen / Henning Reith
Carlin Music . . . . Holland
Twenty 4 Seven . . . . **BCM BCMR 395**

I CAN'T STAND THE RAIN   March 1978
Donald Bryant / Ann Peebles / Bernard Miller
Burlington Music Co. Ltd . . . . USA
Eruption . . . . **Hansa K 11060**
Ann Peebles . . . . **London HLU 10428**

I CAN'T STAND UP FOR FALLING DOWN   March 1980
Homer Banks / Alan Jones
Warner Brothers Music Ltd . . . . UK
Elvis Costello . . . . **F-Beat XX 1**

I CAN'T STOP   June 1974
Wes Farrell / Jerry Goldstein
Carlin Music Corporation . . . . USA
The Osmonds . . . . **MCA 129**

I CAN'T STOP LOVIN' YOU   October 1978
Billy Nicholls
G.H. Music . . . . UK
Leo Sayer . . . . **Chrysalis CHS 2240**

I CAN'T STOP LOVING YOU   August 1962
Don Gibson
Acuff-Rose Music Ltd. . . . . USA
Don Gibson . . . . **RCA 1056**
Ray Charles . . . . **HMV POP 1034**
Connie Francis . . . . **MGM C 916**

I CAN'T TELL A WALTZ FROM A TANGO   November 1954
Al Hoffman / Dick Manning
Michael Reine Music Co. Ltd. . . . . USA
Alma Cogan . . . . **HMV 7M 271**
Patti Page . . . . **Mercury MB 3161**

I CAN'T TELL THE BOTTOM FROM THE TOP   May 1970
Guy Fletcher / Doug Flett
Abacus Music . . . . UK

The Hollies . . . . **Parlophone R 5837**

I CAN'T WAIT   June 1986
Johnny Smith
Warner Brothers Music . . . . USA
Nu Shooz . . . . **Atlantic A 9446**

I CLOSE MY EYES AND COUNT TO TEN   August 1968
Clive Westlake
Carlin Music Corporation . . . . UK
Dusty Springfield . . . . **Philips BF 1682**
Ivor Novello Award.

I CONCENTRATE ON YOU   1941
Cole Porter
Chappell & Co. Ltd . . . . USA
Film(s): . . . . **Broadway Melody of 1940**
Fred Astaire . . . . **HMV CLP 1304**
Julie Dawn . . . . **Columbia 33SX 1180**
The Modernaires . . . . **Vogue LVA 9080**
Joanie Sommers . . . . **Warner Brothers WM 4045**
Fred Astaire appeared in *Broadway Melody of 1940*.

I COULD BE HAPPY   January 1982
"Altered Images"
Warner Brothers Music . . . . UK
Altered Images . . . . **Epic EPCA 1834**

I COULD BE HAPPY WITH YOU   February 1954
Sandy Wilson
Chappell & Co. Ltd. . . . . UK
Show(s): . . . . **The Boy Friend**
Film(s): . . . . **The Boy Friend**
Anne Rogers & Anthony Hayes . . . . **HMV DLP 1078**
Julie Andrews . . . . **RCA LOC 1018**
Twiggy & Christopher Gable . . . . **MGM 1 SE 32 ST**
Anne Rogers & Anthony Hayes appeared in the British production of *The Boy Friend*.
Julie Andrews appeared in the American production of *The Boy Friend*.
Twiggy & Christopher Gable appeared in the film of *The Boy Friend*.

I COULD BE SO GOOD FOR YOU   December 1980
Pat Waterman / Gerard Kenny
Chappell & Co. Ltd . . . . UK
Dennis Waterman . . . . **EMI 5009**
Theme of the TV series *Minder*.
Dennis Waterman appeared in *Minder*.
Ivor Novello Award.

I COULD EASILY FALL   January 1965
Hank B. Marvin / Bruce Welch / John Rostill & Brian Bennett
Shadows Music Ltd . . . . UK
Show(s): . . . . **Aladdin and his Wonderful Lamp**
Cliff Richard . . . . **Columbia DB 7420**
Cliff Richard appeared in *Aladdin and his Wonderful Lamp*.

I COULD HAVE DANCED ALL NIGHT   April 1958
Alan Jay Lerner / Frederick Loewe
Chappell & Co. Ltd . . . . USA
Show(s): . . . . **My Fair Lady**
Film(s): . . . . **My Fair Lady**
Julie Andrews . . . . **Philips RBL 1000**
Julie Andrews & Betty Wolfe . . . . **CBS 70005**
Diane Todd . . . . **Decca DFE 6474**
Lita Roza . . . . **Pye NEP 24076**
Audrey Hepburn & chorus . . . . **CBS BRG 72237**
Julie Andrews appeared in both the American and British productions of *My Fair Lady*.
Diane Todd appeared in the American production of *My Fair Lady*.
Betty Wolfe appeared in the British production of *My Fair Lady*.
Audrey Hepburn appeared in the film *My Fair Lady*.
Marni Nixon dubbed the singing voice of Audrey Hepburn in the film of *My Fair Lady*.

I COULD WRITE A BOOK   1942
Richard Rodgers / Lorenz Hart
Chappell & Co. Ltd . . . . USA
Show(s). . . . . **Pal Joey**
Film(s): . . . . **Pal Joey**
Harold Lang & Vivienne Segal . . . . **Columbia 33SX 1027**
Frank Sinatra . . . . **Capitol LCT 6148**
Ella Fitzgerald . . . . **HMV CLP 1117**
Harold Lang appeared in both the American and British productions of *Pal Joey*.

Vivienne Segal appeared in the American production of *Pal Joey*.
Frank Sinatra appeared in the film of *Pal Joey*.

I COULDN'T LIVE WITHOUT YOUR LOVE   August 1966
Tony Hatch / Jackie Trent
Welbeck Music Co. Ltd. . . . . UK
Petula Clark . . . . **Pye 7N 17133**

I COULDN'T SLEEP A WINK LAST NIGHT   1944
Harold Adamson / Jimmy McHugh
Chappell & Co. Ltd. . . . . USA
Film(s):   Higher and Higher / Radio Stars on Parade / The Blue Veil
Frank Sinatra . . . . **Fontana TFL 5138**
Frank Sinatra . . . . **Capitol LCT 6130**
Frank Sinatra appeared in *Higher and Higher*.
Nominated for an Academy Award 1944.

I COVER THE WATERFRONT   1933
Edward Heyman / Johnny Green
Victoria Music Co. Ltd. . . . . USA
Annette Hanshaw . . . . **Panachord 25551**
The Ink Spots . . . . **Brunswick LA 8710**
Ray Conniff & his Orchestra & chorus . . . . . **Philips BBL 7281**
Kay Starr . . . . **Capitol T 1254**

I CRIED FOR YOU   1923
Gus Arnheim / Abe Lyman / Arthur Freed
Herman Darewski Music Publishing Co. Ltd . . . . USA
Film(s):Babes in Arms / Bathing Beauty / Somebody Loves Me / Love
Me or Leave Me / Lady Sings the Blues
Cliff Edwards . . . . **Disneyland WDL 3003**
Connee Boswell . . . . **Brunswick 01298**
Judy Garland (1939) . . . . **MGM C 887**
Harry James Orchestra (1944) . . . . **Parlophone R 2869**
Kay Starr . . . . **London HAU 2039**
Connie Francis (1958) . . . . **MGM D 153**
Vic Damone . . . . **Philips BBL 7476**
Doris Day . . . . **Silva Screen ACS 8773**
Ricky Stevens (1961) . . . . **Columbia DB 4739**
Diana Ross . . . . **Tamla Motown STML 11311-2**
Judy Garland appeared in *Babes in Arms*.
Harry James Orchestra appeared in *Bathing Beauty*.
Doris Day appeared in *Love Me or Leave Me*.
Diana Ross appeared in *Lady Sings the Blues*.

I DID WHAT I DID FOR MARIA   July 1971
Peter Callander / Mitch Murray
Intune Ltd . . . . UK
Tony Christie . . . . **MCA MK 5064**

I DIDN'T KNOW ABOUT YOU   1944
Duke Ellington / Bob Russell
Sun Music Publishing Co. Ltd. . . . . USA
Yvonne Blanc & her Trio . . . . **HMV DA 4975**
Frank Weir & his Astor Club Seven . . . . **Decca F 8522**
The King Sisters . . . . **Capitol T 1333**
Duke Ellington & his Orchestra . . . . **RCA RD 27258**
Jo Stafford . . . . **Philips BBL 7488**
Adapted from "Sentimental Lady" by Duke Ellington.

I DIDN'T KNOW I LOVED YOU (Till I Saw You Rock 'N' Roll)   October 1972
Gary Glitter / Mike Leander
Leeds Music Ltd. . . . . UK
Gary Glitter . . . . **Bell 1259**

I DIDN'T KNOW WHAT TIME IS WAS   1941
Richard Rodgers / Lorenz Hart
Chappell & Co. Ltd . . . . USA
Show(s): . . . . Too Many Girls
Film(s): . . . . Too Many Girls / Pal Joey
Artie Shaw & his Orch. vocal Helen Forrest . **Camden CDN 137**
Frank Sinatra . . . . **Capitol LCT 6148**
Ella Fitzgerald . . . . **HMV CLP 1117**
Frank Sinatra appeared in *Pal Joey*.

I DIDN'T MEAN TO TURN YOU ON   August 1986
James Harris / Terry Lewis
CBS Songs . . . . UK
Robert Palmer . . . . **Island IS 283**

I DIE, YOU DIE   September 1980
Gary Numan
Numan Music Ltd . . . . UK
Gary Numan . . . . **Beggars Banquet BEG 46**

I DO LIKE TO BE BESIDE THE SEASIDE   1909
John A. Glover-Kind
Chappell & Co. Ltd. . . . . UK
Film(s): . . . . The Adventures of Sherlock Holmes
Florrie Forde . . . . **Imperial 2827**
Reg Grant . . . . **Parlophone R 1332**
Dick James . . . . **Parlophone GEP 8708**
Reginald Dixon (Organ) . . . . **Columbia SEG 7845**
Theme song of Reginald Dixon.

I DON'T BELIEVE IN IF ANY MORE   June 1970
Roger Whittaker
Tembo Music . . . . UK
Roger Whittaker . . . . **Columbia DB 8664**

I DON'T BLAME YOU AT ALL   July 1971
William Robinson
Jobete Music (UK) Ltd. . . . . USA
Smokey Robinson & The Miracles . . . **Tamla Motown TMG 774**

I DON'T CARE   1905
Jean Lenox / Harry Sutton
Francis, Day & Hunter . . . . USA
Film(s): . . . . In the Good Old Summertime
Judy Garland . . . . **MGM D 134**
Eydie Gormé . . . . **HMV CLP1257**
Judy Garland appeared in *In The Good Old Summertime*.
Theme song of Eva Tanguay.

I DON'T CARE IF THE SUN DON'T SHINE   August 1950
Mack David
Chappell & Co. Ltd . . . . USA
Dean Martin . . . . **Capitol CL 13331**
Jimmy Young . . . . **Decca LK 4219**
Patti Page . . . . **Mercury MMC 14013**

I DON'T KNOW ANYBODY ELSE   March 1990
Daniela Davoli / Mirko Limoni / Valerie Semplici
Warner Chappell Music . . . . Italy
Black Box . . . . **Deconstruction PB 43479**

I DON'T KNOW ENOUGH ABOUT YOU   1946
Peggy Lee / Dave Barbour
Bradbury Wood Ltd. . . . . USA
Joe Loss & his Orchestra,
vocal Elizabeth Batey & Howard Jones . . . . **HMV BD 5950**
Peggy Lee . . . . **Brunswick LAT 8287**
Brook Benton . . . . **Mercury MMC 14060**

I DON'T KNOW HOW TO LOVE HIM   March 1972
Tim Rice / Andrew Lloyd Webber
Leeds Music Ltd . . . . UK
Show(s): . . . . Jesus Christ - Superstar
Film(s): . . . . Jesus Christ - Superstar
Yvonne Elliman . . . . **MCA MMKS 5077**
Yvonne Elliman . . . . **MCA MDKS 8012**
Yvonne Elliman appeared in both the American production and the
film *Jesus Christ - Superstar*.
Ivor Novello Award.

I DON'T KNOW WHY   May 1969
Don Hunter / Lulu Hardaway / Paul Riser & Stevie Wonder
Jobete Music (UK) Ltd. . . . . USA
Stevie Wonder . . . . **Tamla Motown TMG 690**

I DON'T KNOW WHY - I JUST DO   1931
Fred Ahlert / Roy Turk
Francis, Day & Hunter Ltd. . . . . USA
Film(s): . . . . Faithfull in My Fashion
Kate Smith . . . . **Columbia DB 709**
Frank Sinatra (1946) . . . . **Philips BBL 7137**
Louis Prima & Keely Smith . . . . **London HAD 2243**
Linda Scott . . . . **Columbia DB 4748**
Eden Kane (1962) . . . . **Decca F 11460**

I DON'T LIKE MONDAYS   August 1979
Bob Geldof
Sewer Fire Hits . . . . UK
The Boomtown Rats . . . . **Ensign ENY 30**
Ivor Novello Award.

I DON'T SEE ME IN YOUR EYES ANYMORE   June 1949
Bennie Benjamin / George Weiss
Campbell Connelly & Co. Ltd . . . . USA
Buddy Clark . . . . **Columbia DB 2534**

The Star Dusters . . . . Brunswick 04082
Ernestine Anderson . . . . Mercury MMC 14016
Carl Perkins . . . . Philips PB 983

I DON'T WANNA DANCE November 1982
Eddy Grant
Intersong Music . . . . UK
Eddy Frant . . . . Ice ICE 56
Ivor Novello Award.

I DON'T WANNA GET HURT June 1989
Mike Stock / Matt Aitken / Peter Waterman
All Boys Music . . . . UK
Donna Summer . . . . Warner Brothers U 7567

I DON'T WANNA LOSE YOU May 1979
Dave Most / Steven Glen / Michael Burns
Rak Music Ltd. . . . . UK
Kandidate . . . . Rak 289

I DON'T WANNA LOSE YOU December 1989
Albert Hammond / Graham Lyle
Rondor Music . . . . UK
Tina Turner . . . . Capitol CL 553

I DON'T WANT A LOVER
John McElhone / Sharleen Spiteri
10 Music . . . . UK
Texas . . . . Mercury TEX 1

I DON'T WANT OUR LOVING TO DIE May 1968
Howard / Blaikley
Lynn Music Ltd. . . . . UK
The Herd . . . . Fontana TF 925

I DON'T WANT TO BE A HERO September 1987
Clark Datchler
Virgin Music . . . . Holland
Johnny Hates Jazz . . . . Virgin VS 1000

I DON'T WANT TO GET WELL 1918
Harry Jentes / Howard Johnson / Harry Pease
Francis, Day & Hunter Ltd. . . . . USA
Film(s): . . . . Show Business
The Savoy Quartet . . . . HMV B 962
Eddie Cantor . . . . Caliban 6034
Eddie Cantor appeared in Show Business.

I DON'T WANT TO PLAY IN YOUR YARD 1894
Philip Wingate / H.W. Petrie
Herman Darewski Music Publishing Co. Ltd. . . . . USA
Frank Luther . . . . Decca F 6792
Evelyn Griffiths &
Charles Hawtrey . . . . Regal Zonophone MR 142
Peggy Lee . . . . Brunswick LAT 8266
Rita Williams &
Barbara Windsor . . . . Parlophone PMC 1127

I DON'T WANT TO PUT A HOLD ON YOU April 1977
Mike Flint / Berni Flint
Sparta Music Ltd . . . . UK
Berni Flint . . . . EMI 2599
Ivor Novello Nomination.

I DON'T WANT TO SET THE WORLD ON FIRE 1941
Eddie Dunham / Eddie Seiler / Sol Marcus & Bennie Benjamin
Bradbury Wood Ltd . . . . USA
The Ink Spots . . . . Brunswick LA 8710
Geraldo & his Orchestra,
vocal Dorothy Carless . . . . Parlophone F 1873
Neville Taylor . . . . Parlophone R 4476

I DON'T WANT TO TALK ABOUT IT June 1977
Danny Whitten / Cat Stevens
Rondor Music (London) Ltd . . . . UK
Rod Stewart . . . . Riva 7

I DON'T WANT TO TALK ABOUT IT August 1988
Danny Whitten
Rondor Music . . . . USA
Everything But The Girl . . . . Blanco Y Negro NEG 34

I DON'T WANT TO WALK WITHOUT YOU 1942
Jule Styne / Frank Loesser
Chappell & Co. Ltd . . . . USA

Film(s): . . . . Sweater Girl
Betty Jane Rhodes . . . . Brunswick 03315
Helen Forrest . . . . Warner Brothers WM 4050
Jo Stafford . . . . Philips BBL 7290
Gogi Grant . . . . London HAB 2032
Betty Jane Rhodes appeared in Sweater Girl.

I DOUBLE DARE YOU 1938
Jimmy Eaton / Terry Shand
Sun Music Publishing Co. Ltd. . . . . USA
Woody Herman & his Orchestra,
vocal Woody Herman . . . . Panachord 25971
Carroll Gibbons . . . . Columbia FB 1893
Jimmy Lloyd . . . . Philips PB 1055

I DREAM OF YOU 1946
Marjorie Goetschius / Edna Osser
Macmelodies Ltd. . . . . USA
Frank Sinatra . . . . Fontana TFL 5048
Johnny Nash . . . . HMV CLP 1251
Alma Cogan . . . . Columbia 33SX 1345

I DREAM TOO MUCH 1936
Jerome Kern / Dorothy Fields
Chappell & Co. Ltd . . . . USA
Film(s): . . . . I Dream Too Much
Lily Pons . . . . HMV DA 1456
Doreen Hulme . . . . Fontana TFE 17344
Lily Pons appeared in I Dream Too Much.

I DREAMED January 1957
Charles Grean / Marvin Moore
Duchess Music Ltd. . . . . USA
The Beverley Sisters . . . . Decca DFE 6401
Betty Johnson . . . . London HLU 8365

I DROVE ALL NIGHT July 1989
William Steinberg / Tom Kelly
Warner Chappell Music . . . . UK
Cyndi Lauper . . . . Epic CYN 4

I EAT CANNIBALS September 1982
Barry Blue / Paul Greedus / Roy Nicolson
Heath Levy Music . . . . UK
Toto Coelo . . . . Radialchoice TIC 10

I ENJOY BEING A GIRL August 1958
Richard Rodgers / Oscar Hammerstein II
Williamson Music Ltd . . . . USA
Show(s): . . . . Flower Drum Song
Film(s): . . . . Flower Drum Song
Pat Suzuki . . . . Philips ABL 3302
Yama Saki . . . . HMV CLP 1359
Nancy Kwan . . . . Brunswick LAT 8302
Pat Suzuki appeared in the American production of Flower Drum Song
Yama Saki appeared in the British production of Flower Drum Song.
Nancy Kwan appeared in the film of Flower Drum Song.

I FALL IN LOVE TOO EASILY 1946
Jule Styne / Sammy Cahn
Robbins Music Corporation Ltd. . . . . USA
Film(s): . . . . Anchors Aweigh
Frank Sinatra . . . . Fontana TFE 17043
Jo Stafford . . . . Philips BBL 7290
Frank Sinatra appeared in Anchors Aweigh.
Nominated for an Academy Award 1945.

I FALL IN LOVE WITH YOU EVERY DAY 1946
Sammy Stept
Clover Music Co. Ltd. . . . . USA
Frank Sinatra . . . . Columbia DB 2238
Ruby Wright . . . . Parlophone MSP 6209
Johnny Desmond . . . . MGM 419

I FAW DOWN AN' GO BOOM 1929
James Brockman / Leonard Stevens
Keith Prowse Music Publishing Co. Ltd . . . . USA
Jack Smith . . . . HMV B 2968

I FEEL A SONG COMING ON 1936
Dorothy Fields / Jimmy McHugh
Robbins Music Corporation Ltd . . . . USA

Film(s): . . . . . . Every Night at Eight / Follow the Boys / The Stooge
Frances Langford . . . . **Brunswick 02084**
Eve Boswell . . . . **Parlophone DP 518**
Dean Martin . . . . **Capitol LC 6590**
Edmund Hockridge . . . . **Pye NPL 18021**
Connee Boswell . . . . **Brunswick 02127**
Frances Langford appeared in *Every Night at Eight.*
Dean Martin appeared in *The Stooge.*

I FEEL FINE — December 1964
John Lennon / Paul McCartney
Northern Songs Ltd . . . . UK
The Beatles . . . . **Parlophone R 5200**
Frank Chacksfield & his Orchestra . . . . . . **Decca LK 4666**
Ivor Novello Nomination.

I FEEL FOR YOU — November 1984
"Prince"
Island Music . . . . USA
Chaka Khan . . . . **Warner Brothers W 9209**

I FEEL LIKE A FEATHER IN THE BREEZE — 1936
Mack Gordon / Harry Revel
Victoria Music Co. Ltd . . . . USA
Film(s): . . . . The Charm School / The Stooge
The Rhythm Maniacs . . . . **Decca F 5927**
Dean Martin . . . . **Capitol LC 6590**
Doris Day . . . . **Philips BBL 7296**
Dean Martin appeared in *The Stooge.*

I FEEL LIKE BUDDY HOLLY — June 1984
Mike Batt
Chappell Music Co. . . . . UK
Alvin Stardust . . . . **Chrysalis CHS 2784**

I FEEL LOVE — August 1977
Donna Summer / Giorgio Moroder / Pete Bellotte
Heath Levy Music Ltd . . . . USA
Donna Summer . . . . **GTO GT 100**

I FEEL PRETTY — January 1959
Leonard Bernstein / Stephen Sondheim
Chappell & Co. Ltd . . . . USA
Show(s): . . . . West Side Story
Film(s): . . . . West Side Story
Carol Lawrence, Marilyn Cooper,
Carmen Guilterrez & Elizabeth Taylor . . . . **CBS BPG 62060**
Marlys Watters . . . . **HMV 7EG 8429**
Marni Nixon . . . . **CBS BPG 62058**
Carol Lawrence, Marilyn Cooper, Carmen Guilterrez & Elizabeth Taylor appeared in the American production of *West Side Story.*
Marlys Watters appeared in the British production of *West Side Story.*
Natalie Wood appeared in the film *West Side Story* (singing voice dubbed by Marni Nixon).

I FEEL THE EARTH MOVE — November 1989
Carole King
Screen Gems Music . . . . UK
Martika . . . . **CBS 655294**

I FOUND A MILLION DOLLAR BABY — 1932
Mort Dixon / Harry Warren / Billy Rose
Francis, Day & Hunter Ltd. . . . . USA
Show(s): . . . . Crazy Quilt
Film(s): . . . . Million Dollar Baby / Funny Lady
Bing Crosby . . . . **Brunswick LA 8740**
The Mills Brothers . . . . **London HAE 2140**
Bobby Darin . . . . **London HLD 8553**
Barbra Streisand . . . . **Arista ARTY 101**
Barbra Streisand appeared in *Funny Lady.*

I FOUND A NEW BABY — 1926
Spencer Williams / Jack Palmer
B. Feldman & Co. Ltd. . . . . USA
Film(s): . . . . Sweet and Lowdown
The Mills Brothers . . . . **Brunswick 01761**
Isham Jones & his Orchestra . . . . **Brunswick 01894**
Bing Crosby . . . . **Brunswick 04117**
Benny Goodman & his Orchestra . . . . **HMV B 8481**
Mindy Carson . . . . **Philips BBL 7249**
Benny Goodman Orchestra appeared in *Sweet and Lowdown.*

I FOUND LOVIN' — October 1987
Michael Walker / John Flippen

Minder Music . . . . USA
Steve Walsh . . . . **A1 A 2199**
The Fatback Band . . . . **Master Mix CHE 8401**

I FOUND SOMEONE — January 1988
Michael Bolton / Mark Mangold
SBK Songs . . . . USA
Cher . . . . **Geffen GEF 31**

I FOUND YOU — 1931
Ray Noble / James Campbell / Reginald Connelly
Campbell Connelly & Co. Ltd. . . . . UK
Jack Gordon . . . . **Imperial 2533**
Ambrose & his Orchestra . . . . **HMV B 6039**
Jack Payne & The BBC Dance Orchestra . . . . **Columbia CB 320**

I GET A KICK OUT OF YOU — 1935
Cole Porter
Chappell & Co. Ltd . . . . USA
Show(s): . . . . Anything Goes
Film(s): . . Anything Goes / Night and Day / Sunny Side of the Street
Ethel Merman . . . . **Brunswick LA 8636**
Jeanne Aubert & The Four Admirals . . . . . . **Columbia DX 697**
Tony Travis . . . . **HMV CLP 1195**
Ella Fitzgerald . . . . **HMV CLP 1083**
Patti Page . . . . **Mercury MMC 14036**
Ethel Merman . . . . **Reprise R 6032**
Gary Shearston (1974) . . . . **Charisma CB 234**
Ethel Merman appeared in the American production and the 1936 film of *Anything Goes.*
Jeanne Aubert & The Four Admirals appeared in the British production of *Anything Goes.*

I GET A LITTLE SENTIMENTAL OVER YOU — April 1974
Tony Macaulay / Geoff Stevens
Mustard Music . . . . UK
The New Seekers . . . . **Polydor 2058439**

I GET ALONG WITHOUT YOU VERY WELL — 1939
Hoagy Carmichael
Chappell & Co. Ltd. . . . . USA
Film(s): . . . . Las Vegas Story
Leslie Hutchinson (Hutch) . . . . **Parlophone F 1485**
Dick Todd . . . . **HMV BD 719**
Jimmy Dorsey & his Orchestra,
vocal Bob Eberly . . . . **Brunswick 02778**
Jimmy Young . . . . **Columbia 33SX 1102**
Rosemary Clooney . . . . **RCA RD 27218**
Hoagy Carmichael . . . . **MCA 1819**

I GET AROUND — August 1964
Brian Wilson
Burlington Music Co. Ltd . . . . USA
The Beach Boys . . . . **Capitol CL 15350**

I GET SO LONELY — April 1954
Pat Ballard
Edwin H. Morris & Co. Ltd. . . . . USA
Bing Crosby . . . . **Brunswick OE 9003**
Anne Shelton . . . . **HMV B 10680**
Geraldo & his Orchestra, vocal Jill Day . . . . **Philips OB 262**
The Four Knights . . . . **Capitol CL 14076**

I GET THE NECK OF THE CHICKEN — 1943
Frank Loesser / Jimmy McHugh
Southern Music Publishing Co. Ltd. . . . . USA
Film(s): . . . . Seven Days Leave
Carroll Gibbons & The Savoy Hotel Orpheans **Columbia FB 2897**

I GET THE SWEETEST FEELING — September 1972
Van McCoy / Alicia Evelyn
Carlin Music Corporation . . . . USA
Jackie Wilson . . . . **MCA MU 1160**
Jackie Wilson (1987) . . . . **SMP SKM 1**

I GET UP EVERY MORNING (What Do I Do, What Do I Do, What Do I Do) — 1947
Joe Lubin / Eddie Lisbona
Bradbury Wood Ltd. . . . . USA
The Skyrockets Dance Orchestra . . . . **HMV BD 5979**
Gordon MacRae . . . . **Capitol LC 6592**
The Barry Sisters . . . . **Columbia DB 4215**

I GET WEAK — March 1988
Diane Warren

EMI Music .... USA
Belinda Carlisle .... **Virgin VS 1046**

I GIVE MY HEART   1932
Karl Millocker / Rowland Leigh
Chappell & Co. Ltd. .... Austria
Show(s): .... The Dubarry
Anny Ahlers .... **Parlophone GEP 8623**
Grace Moore .... **HMV DA 1309**
Maria Perilli .... **Philips BBE 12436**
Anny Ahlers appeared in the British production of *The Dubarry*.
Grace Moore appeared in the American production of *The Dubarry*.

I GO APE   May 1959
Neil Sedaka / Howard Greenfield
Aldon Music Ltd. .... USA
Neil Sedaka .... **RCA RCX 116**
Roy Young .... **Parlophone PMC 1101**

I GO TO SLEEP   December 1981
Ray Davies
Kassner Music .... UK
The Pretenders .... **Real ARE 18**

I GOT IT BAD, AND THAT AIN'T GOOD   1942
Duke Ellington / Paul Francis Webster
Francis, Day & Hunter Ltd .... USA
Film(s): ..... The Benny Goodman Story / This Could be the Night
**Duke Ellington & his Orchestra,
vocal Ivie Anderson** .... **RCA RD 27134**
Mel Tormé .... **London HAN 2016**
Cleo Laine .... **Parlophone MSP 6147**
Dinah Washington .... **Mercury MMC 14063**
Julie Wilson .... **MGM C 761**
Julie Wilson appeared in *This Could be the Night*.

I GOT LIFE   November 1968
Gerome Ragni / James Rado / Galt MacDermot
United Artists Music Co. Ltd. .... USA
Show(s): .... Hair
Film(s): .... Hair
James Rado .... **RCA RD 7959**
Paul Nicholas .... **Polydor 583043**
Treat Williams .... **RCA BL 03274**
James Rado appeared in the American production of *Hair*.
Paul Nicholas appeared in the British production of *Hair*.
Treat Williams appeared in the film *Hair*.
See also 'Ain't Got No - I Got Life' and 'Ain't Got No'.

I GOT LOST IN HIS ARMS   1947
Irving Berlin
Irving Berlin Ltd. .... USA
Show(s): .... Annie Get Your Gun
Film(s): .... Annie Get Your Gun
Ethel Merman .... **Brunswick LAT 8002**
Dolores Gray .... **Columbia DX 1379**
Betty Hutton .... **MGM CD 1**
Ethel Merman appeared in the American production of *Annie Get Your Gun*.
Dolores Gray appeared in the British production of *Annie Got Your Gun*.
Betty Hutton appeared in the film of *Annie Get Your Gun*.

I GOT PLENTY OF NUTTIN'   1935
George Gershwin / Ira Gershwin
Chappell & Co. Ltd .... USA
Show(s): .... Porgy and Bess
Film(s): .... Porgy and Bess
Todd Duncan .... **Brunswick LAT 8021**
Frank Sinatra .... **Capitol LCT 6135**
Sound Track recording of *Porgy and Bess* ... **Philips ABL 3282**
Todd Duncan appeared in the American production of *Porgy and Bess*.

I GOT RHYTHM   1932
George Gershwin / Ira Gershwin
Chappell & Co. Ltd. .... USA
Show(s): .... Girl Crazy
Film(s): ...... Girl Crazy / Rhapsody in Blue / An American in Paris
Ethel Merman .... **Brunswick LA 8638**
Gene Kelly .... **MGM D 133**
Ella Fitzgerald .... **HMV CLP 1353**
Ethel Merman .... **Reprise R 6032**
Ethel Merman appeared in the show *Girl Crazy*.
Gene Kelly appeared in *An American in Paris*.
Theme song of Ethel Merman

I GOT STUNG   February 1959
Aaron Schroeder / David Hill
Hill & Range (London) Ltd .... USA
Elvis Presley .... **RCA RD 27159**

I GOT THE SUN IN THE MORNING   1947
Irving Berlin
Irving Berlin Ltd. .... USA
Show(s): .... Annie Get Your Gun
Film(s): .... Annie Get Your Gun
Ethel Merman .... **Brunswick LAT 8002**
Vocal Company of British Production .... **Columbia SEG 7711**
Betty Hutton .... **MGM CD 1**
Dolores Gray .... **Columbia SEG 7711**
Ethel Merman appeared in the American production of *Annie Get Your Gun*.
Dolores Gray appeared in the British production of *Annie Get Your Gun*.
Betty Hutton appeared in the film of *Annie Get Your Gun*.

I GOT YOU BABE   August 1965
Sonny Bono
Aberbach (London) Ltd. .... USA
Film(s): .... Good Times
Sonny & Cher .... **Atlantic AT 4035**
UB40 with Chrissie Hynde (1985) .... **Virgin DEP 20**
Sonny & Cher appeared in *Good Times*.

I GOTTA GET A MESSAGE TO YOU   October 1968
Barry Gibb / Robin Gibb / Maurice Gibb
Abigail Music .... UK
The Bee Gees .... **Polydor 56273**

I GOTTA RIGHT TO SING THE BLUES   1933
Ted Koehler / Harold Arlen
Chappell & Co. Ltd. .... USA
Show(s): .... Earl Carroll's Vanities of 1932
Film(s): .... Hats Off to Rhythm
Ethel Merman .... **HMV B 4348**
Perry Como .... **RCA RD 27070**
Billie Holiday .... **Columbia 33CX 10064**
Julie London .... **London HAU 2091**
Billy Eckstine .... **Mercury MMB 12002**

I GUESS I'LL ALWAYS LOVE YOU   February 1969
Brian Holland / Eddie Holland / Lamont Dozier
Jobete Music (UK) Ltd. .... USA
The Isley Brothers .... **Tamla Motown TMG 683**

I GUESS I'LL GET THE PAPERS AND GO HOME   1947
Hughie Prince / Dick Rogers / Hal Kanner
New World Publishers Ltd. .... USA
The Mills Brothers .... **Brunswick 04638**
Geraldo & his Orchestra, vocal Dick James .. **Parlophone F 2193**
The Mills Brothers .... **London HAD 2319**

I GUESS I'LL HAVE TO CHANGE MY PLAN   1932
Howard Dietz / Arthur Schwartz
Chappell & Co. Ltd. .... USA
Show(s): .... The Little Show
Film(s): .... The Band Wagon
Ambrose & his Orchestra .... **HMV B 6261**
Fred Astaire & Jack Buchanan .... **MGM C 752**
Julie London .... **London HAU 2186**
Bobby Darin .... **London HAK 2394**
Fred Astaire & Jack Buchanan appeared in *The Band Wagon*.

I GUESS I'LL HAVE TO DREAM THE REST   1941
Mickey Stoner / Martin Block / Harold Green
Bradbury Wood Ltd .... USA
Leslie Hutchinson (Hutch) .... **HMV BD 972**
**Tommy Dorsey & his Orchestra,
vocal Frank Sinatra** .... **RCA RD 27069**
Les Brown & his Band of Renown .... **Vogue LVA 9084**

I GUESS THAT'S WHY THEY
CALL IT THE BLUES   July 1983
Elton John / Bernie Taupin / Davey Johnstone
Big Pig Music .... UK
Elton John .... **Rocket XPRES 91**

I HAD THE CRAZIEST DREAM   1943
Mack Gordon / Harry Warren
Bregman, Vocco & Conn Ltd .... USA
Film(s): .... Springtime in the Rockies
Geraldo & his Orchestra, vocal Len Camber .. **Parlophone F 1971**

Harry James & his Orchestra . . . . **Philips BBE 12211**
Tony Martin . . . . **Decca F 8286**
Doris Day . . . . **Philips BBL 7248**
Perry Como . . . . **RCA RD 27035**
Harry James appeared in *Springtime in the Rockies*.

I HADN'T ANYONE TILL YOU   1938
Ray Noble
Chappell & Co. Ltd. . . . . USA
Film(s): . . . . Sunny Side of the Street
Ray Noble & his Orchestra,
vocal Tony Martin . . . . **Columbia FB 2024**
Benny Goodman & his Orchestra,
vocal Martha Tilton . . . . **Philips BBL 7010**
Roberta Sherwood . . . . **Brunswick LAT 8159**
Judy Garland . . . . **Capitol T 1036**

I HATE MEN   April 1951
Cole Porter
Chappell & Co. Ltd . . . . USA
Show(s): . . . . Kiss Me Kate
Film(s): . . . . Kiss Me Kate
Patricia Morison . . . . **Philips BBL 7224**
Patricia Morison . . . . **Columbia SEG 7721**
Kathryn Grayson . . . . **MGM C 753**
Patricia Morison appeared in both the American and British productions of *Kiss Me Kate*.
Kathryn Grayson appeared in the film *Kiss Me Kate*.

I HAVE A DREAM   January 1980
Benny Andersson / Bjorn Ulvaeus
Bocu Music Ltd . . . . Sweden
Abba . . . . **Epic EPC 8088**

I HAVE EYES   1939
Leo Robin / Ralph Rainger
Victoria Music Co. Ltd. . . . . USA
Film(s): . . . . Paris Honeymoon
Bing Crosby . . . . **Brunswick Bing 4**
Ambrose & his Orchestra, vocal Denny Dennis . . **Decca F 7029**
Adelaide Hall . . . . **Decca F 7049**
Bing Crosby appeared in *Paris Honeymoon*.

I HAVEN'T TIME TO BE A MILLIONAIRE   1940
Jimmy Monaco / Johnny Burke
Campbell Connelly & Co. Ltd . . . . USA
Film(s): . . . . If I Had My Way
Bing Crosby . . . . **Brunswick Bing 5**
Al Bowlly . . . . **HMV BD 865**
Harry Roy & his Band,
vocal Harry Roy . . . . **Regal Zonophone MR 3338**
Bing Crosby appeared in *If I Had My Way*.

I HEAR A RHAPSODY   1941
George Frajos / Dick Gasparre / Jack Baker
Campbell Connelly & Co. Ltd . . . . USA
Film(s): . . . . Casa Manana / Clash By Night
Lew Stone & his Band, vocal Benny Lee . . . . **Decca F 7919**
Connee Boswell . . . . **Brunswick 03194**
Fran Warren . . . . **MGM 502**
Billy Eckstine . . . . **Columbia 33SX 1249**

I HEAR MUSIC   August 1956
Burton Lane / Frank Loesser
Chappell & Co. Ltd. . . . . USA
Film(s): . . . . Dancing on a Dime
Nat 'King' Cole . . . . **Capitol LC 6830**
Chris Connor . . . . **London HBN 1074**
Peggy Lee . . . . **Capitol T 979**

I HEAR YOU CALLING ME   1908
Harold Herford / Charles Marshall
Boosey & Hawkes Music Publishers Ltd. . . . . UK
Film(s): . . . . Song of My Heart
John McCormack . . . . **Camden CDN 1002**
Webster Booth . . . . **HMV B 9173**
Dennis Noble . . . . **Argo RG 53**
John McCormack appeared in *Song of My Heart*.

I HEAR YOU KNOCKING   February 1956
Dave Bartholomew / Pearl King
Francis, Day & Hunter Ltd. . . . . USA
Gale Storm . . . . **London HLD 8222**
Jill Day . . . . **HMV POP 158**

Connie Francis . . . . **MGM C 804**
Dave Edmunds (1971) . . . . **MAM MAM 1**

I HEAR YOU NOW   February 1980
Jon AndersonVangelis
Warner Brothers Music Ltd . . . . UK
Jon & Vangelis . . . . **Polydor POSP 96**

I HEARD A RUMOUR   August 1987
Sarah Dillon / Siobhan Fahey / Karen Woodward / Mike Stock / Matt Aitken & Peter Waterman
All Boys Music . . . . UK
Bananarama . . . . **London NANA 13**

I HEARD IT THROUGH THE GRAPEVINE   April 1969
Norman Whitfield / Barrett Strong
Jobete Music (UK) Ltd. . . . . USA
Marvin Gaye . . . . **Tamla Motown TMG 686**
Gladys Knight & the Pips . . . . **Tamla Motown TMG 629**
Creedence Clearwater Revival . . . . **Liberty LBS 83388**
Marvin Gaye (1986) . . . . **Tamla Motown ZB 40701**

I HEARD YOU CRIED LAST NIGHT   1944
Jerry Kruger / Ted Grouya
Campbell Connelly & Co. Ltd. . . . . USA
Film(s): . . . . Cinderella Swings it
Dick Haymes . . . . **Brunswick 03478**
Adelaide Hall . . . . **Decca F 8485**
Joe Loss & his Orchestra, vocal Harry Kaye . . **HMV BD 5846**
The Four Freshman . . . . **Capitol T 1074**

I HOPE TO DIE IF I TOLD A LIE   1945
Jack Little
Campbell Connelly & Co. Ltd. . . . . USA
Vera Lynn . . . . **Decca F 8556**
The Ink Spots . . . . **Brunswick 03606**

I JUST CALLED TO SAY I LOVE YOU   October 1984
Stevie Wonder
Jobete Music . . . . USA
Film(s): . . . . Woman In Red
Stevie Wonder . . . . **Motown TMG 1349**
Academy Award winning song for 1984

I JUST CAN'T HELP BELIEVING   February 1972
Barry Mann / Cynthia Weill
Screen Gems Music Ltd . . . . USA
Elvis Presley . . . . **RCA 2158**

I JUST CAN'T MAKE MY EYES BEHAVE   1906
Will Cobb / Gus Edwards
Francis, Day & Hunter Ltd . . . . USA
Show(s): . . . . Parisian Model
Film(s): . . . . Strike Up The Music
Joan Morris & William Bolcom . . . . . . **Nonesuch H 71330**

I JUST CAN'T STOP LOVING YOU   August 1987
Michael Jackson
Warner Brothers Music . . . . USA
Michael Jackson . . . . **Epic 650202**

I JUST DIED IN YOUR ARMS (See Died In Your Arms)

I JUST DON'T HAVE THE HEART   September 1989
Mike Stock / Matt Aitken / Peter Waterman
All Boys Music . . . . UK
Cliff Richard . . . . **EMI EM 101**

I JUST DON'T KNOW WHAT
TO DO WITH MYSELF   August 1964
Burt Bacharach / Hal David
December Music Ltd . . . . USA
Dusty Springfield . . . . **Philips BF 1348**
The Andrew Oldham Orchestra . . . . . . **Ace of Clubs ACL 1180**

I KEEP FORGETTING TO REMEMBER   1947
Joe Lubin / Eddie Lisbona
Bradbury Wood Ltd. . . . . USA
Anne Shelton . . . . **Decca F 8751**
Lou Preager & his Orchestra,
vocal Paul Rich . . . . **Parlophone F 3288**

I KISS YOUR HAND MADAME
(Ich Kusse Ihr Hand Madame)   1929
Fritz Rotter / Ralph Erwin / Sam M. Lewis / Joe Young

Chappell & Co. Ltd .... Germany
Film(s): ....The Emporer Waltz
George Metaxa .... **HMV B 2944**
Bing Crosby .... **Brunswick Bing 11**
David Whitfield .... **Decca LK 4321**
Vic Damone .... **Philips BBL 7529**
Bing Crosby appeared in *The Emporer Waltz*.

I KNEW YOU WERE WAITING (FOR ME)   **February 1987**
Simon Climie / Dennis Morgan
Chrysalis Music .... UK
Aretha Franklin & George Michael .... **Epic DUET 2**
Ivor Novello Nomination

I KNOW A LOVELY GARDEN   **1903**
Guy D'Hardelot / Edward Teschemacher
Chappell & Co. Ltd. .... UK
Derek Oldham .... **HMV B 3068**
Hon. W. Brownlow .... **Columbia DB 1650**

I KNOW A PLACE   **April 1965**
Tony Hatch
Welbeck Music Ltd .... UK
Petula Clark .... **Pye 7N 15772**

I KNOW HIM SO WELL   **February 1985**
Tim Rice / Bkorn Ulvaeuss / Benny Andersson
Bocu Music .... UK
Show(s): .... Chess
Elaine Paige & Barbara Dickson .... **RCA CHESS 1**
Ivor Novello Award.

I KNOW OF TWO BRIGHT EYES   **1901**
George H. Clutsam
Edwin Ashdown Ltd .... UK
John McCormack .... **Odeon 0513**
Frank Mullings .... **Columbia 3947**
Derek Oldham .... **IIMV D 2070**
Webster Booth .... **HMV B 3735**
Stuart Burrows .... **Oiseau Lyre DSLO 44**

I KNOW THAT YOU KNOW   **1926**
Vincent Youmans / Anne Caldwell
Chappell & Co. Ltd. .... USA
Show(s): .... Oh Please
Film(s): .... Tea for Two / Hit the Deck
Jimmy Noone & his Orchestra .... **Vocalion S 216**
Nat 'King' Cole .... **Capitol LCT 6133**
Kevin Scott .... **HMV 7EG 8458**
Jane Powell & Vic Damone .... **MGM EP 526**
Jane Powell & Vic Damone appeared in *Hit the Deck*.

I KNOW WHERE THE FLIES GO IN WINTERTIME   **1920**
Sam Mayo / J.P. Harrington
Herman Darewski Music Publishing Co. Ltd .... UK
Show(s): .... Just Fancy
Walter Williams .... **Columbia F 3**
Walter Williams appeared in *Just Fancy*.

I KNOW WHY   **1942**
Mack Gordon / Harry Warren
Sun Music Publishing Co. Ltd .... USA
Film(s): .... Sun Valley Serenade / The Glenn Miller Story
Glenn Miller & his Orchestra .... **HMV DLP 1024**
The Modernaires .... **Vogue LVA 9103**
Mel Tormé .... **Parlophone GEP 8773**
Glenn Miller appeared in *Sun Valley Serenade*.

**I LEAVE MY HEART IN AN
ENGLISH GARDEN**   **December 1950**
Harry Parr-Davies / Christopher Hassell
Sun Music Publishing Co. Ltd .... UK
Show(s): .... Dear Miss Phoebe
Lee Lawrence .... **Decca F 9575**
The Luton Girls Choir .... **Parlophone R 3373**
Edmund Hockridge .... **HMV B 10001**

I LEFT MY HEART AT THE STAGE DOOR CANTEEN   **1943**
Irving Berlin
Irving Berlin Ltd .... USA
Show(s): .... This is the Army
Film(s): .... This is the Army
Corporal Earl Oxford .... **Brunswick 03489**
Jo Stafford .... **Philips BBL 7290**

Corporal Earl Oxford appeared in both the American and British productions of *This is the Army*.

I LEFT MY HEART IN SAN FRANCISCO (See In San Francisco)

I LEFT MY SUGAR STANDING IN THE RAIN   **1927**
Irving Kahal / Sammy Fain
B. Feldman & Co. Ltd. .... USA
**Paul Whiteman & his Orchestra,
vocal The Rhythm Boys** .... **HMV B 2562**
Harry Roy & his Tiger Ragamuffins .... **Parlophone F 589**

I LET A SONG GO OUT OF MY HEART   **1938**
Duke Ellington / Irving Mills / Henry Nemo
Lawrence Wright Music Co. Ltd. .... USA
Duke Ellington & his Orchestra ...... **Philips BBE 12404**
Mildred Bailey .... **Parlophone R 2568**
Gogi Grant .... **London HAB 2032**
Billy Eckstine .... **MGM EP 583**

I LIFT UP MY FINGER AND I SAY TWEET TWEET   **1929**
Leslie Sarony
Francis, Day & Hunter Ltd .... UK
Show(s): .... Love Lies
Jack Hylton & his Orchestra,vocal Leslie Sarony . **Columbia 5354**
Stanley Lupino .... **Columbia 5354**
Gracie Fields .... **HMV B 2999**
Stanley Lupino appeared in *Love Lies*.

I LIKE BANANAS BECAUSE THEY HAVE NO BONES   **1936**
Chris Yacich
Sterling Music Publishing Co. Ltd .... USA
The BBC Dance Orchestra .... **Columbia FB 1425**
George Formby .... **Regal Zonophone MR 2162**

I LIKE IT   **July 1963**
Mitch Murray
Jaep Music Ltd .... UK
Gerry & The Pacemakers .... **Columbia DB 7041**

I LIKE MOUNTAIN MUSIC   **1933**
James Cavanaugh / Frank Weldon
B. Feldman & Co. Ltd. .... USA
Big Bill Campbell & his Hill Billy Band ..... **Columbia FB 1784**
**The BBC Dance Orchestra,
conducted by Henry Hall** .... **Columbia CB 622**
Roy Acuff .... **Brunswick 05635**

I LIKE THE LIKES OF YOU   **1934**
E.Y. Harburg / Vernon Duke
Chappell & Co. Ltd. .... USA
Show(s): .... The Ziegfeld Follies of 1934
Debbie Reynolds .... **London HAD 2200**
Vic Damone .... **Philips BBL 7347**
Eydie Gormé & Steve Lawrence .... **HMV CLP 1463**

I LIKE TO RECOGNIZE THE TUNE   **1944**
Richard Rodgers / Lorenz Hart
Chappell & Co. Ltd. .... USA
Show(s): ....Too Many Girls
Film(s): ....Meet the People
Mel Tormé .... **London LTZN 15009**

I LIVE IN TRAFALGAR SQUARE   **1902**
C.W. Murphy
Francis, Day & Hunter Ltd. .... UK
Stanley Holloway .... **Philips BBL 7237**
Georgia Brown with Ted Heath & his Music .... **Decca LK 4411**
Warren Mitchell .... **Allegro ALL 850**

I LOST MY HEART IN HEIDELBERG   **1932**
Ernest Neubach / Freddy Raymond / Harry S. Pepper
B. Feldman & Co. Ltd. .... Germany
Layton & Johnstone .... **Columbia DB 826**
**The BBC Dance Orchestra,
conducted by Henry Hall** .... **Columbia CB 445**

**I LOST MY HEART TO A
STARSHIP TROOPER**   **December 1978**
Jeffrey Calvert / Geraint Hughes
Heath Levy Music Ltd .... UK
Sarah Brightman & Hot Gossip .... **Ariola AHA 527**

I LOST MY SUGAR IN SALT LAKE CITY   **1943**
Johnny Lange / Leon Rene

Campbell Connelly & Co. Ltd .... USA
Film(s): .... Stormy Weather / Jam Session
Jan Garber & his Orchestra ... **Hollwood Soundstage HS 5014**
Peggy Lee .... **Capitol T 1219**
Rosemary Squires .... **HMV 7EG 8588**
Jan Garber & his Orchestra appeared in *Jam Session*.

I LOVE A LASSIE 1905
Harry Lauder / Gerald Grafton
Francis, Day & Hunter Ltd. .... UK
Harry Lauder .... **Regal GO 81**
George Elrick .... **Beltona ABL 509**
Robert Wilson .... **HMV CLP 1378**
Theme song of Harry Lauder.

I LOVE A PIANO 1916
Irving Berlin
Chappell & Co. Ltd. .... USA
Show(s): .... Stop, Look, Listen / Follow the Crowd
Film(s): .... Easter Parade
Ethel Levey .... **HMV 03476**
Judy Garland & Fred Astaire .... **MGM D 140**
Ethel Levey appeared in *Follow the Crowd*. Judy Garland & Fred Astaire appeared in *Easter Parade*.

I LOVE HOW YOU LOVE ME January 1962
Barry Mann / Larry Kolber
Screen Gems-Columbia Music Ltd. .... USA
The Paris Sisters .... **Top Rank JAR 588**
Jimmy Crawford .... **Columbia DB 4717**
Maureen Evans .... **Oriole CB 1906**
Paul & Barry Ryan (1966) .... **Decca F 12445**
Barry Mann .... **HMV CLP 1559**

I LOVE ME 1923
Edwin J. Weber / Jack Hoins / Will Mahoney
Lawrence Wright Music Co. Ltd .... USA
Alfred Lester .... **HMV C 1114**
The Savoy Havana Band .... **Columbia 3351**
Mel Blanc .... **Capitol CL 13951**

I LOVE MUSIC March 1976
Kenny Gamble / Leon Huff
Carlin Music Corporation .... USA
The O'Jays .... **Philadelphia PIR 3879**

I LOVE MY BABY, MY BABY LOVES ME 1926
Harry Warren / Bud Green
Keith Prowse Music Publishing Co. Ltd. .... USA
Film(s): .... Drum Crazy
Isham Jones & his Band .... **Brunswick 3015**
Sheila Buxton .... **Columbia DB 3887**
Suzi Miller .... **Decca F 10848**
Ruby Lane .... **HMV CLP 1352**
Ruby Lane appeared in *Drum Crazy*.

I LOVE MY RADIO February 1987
Graziano Pegorado / Claudio Cecchetto / Pier Bozzetti
EMI Music .... Italy
Taffy .... **Transglobal TYPE 1**

I LOVE PARIS September 1954
Cole Porter
Chappell & Co. Ltd. .... USA
Show(s): .... Can-Can
Film(s): .... Can-Can
Lilo .... **Capitol LCT 6010**
Irene Hilda .... **Parlophone PMD 1017**
Frank Sinatra & Maurice Chevalier .... **Capitol W 1301**
Ronnie Harris .... **Columbia SCM 5139**
Lilo appeared in the American production of *Can-Can*.
Irene Hilda appeared in the British production of *Can-Can*.
Frank Sinatra & Maurice Chevalier appeared in the film *Can-Can*.

I LOVE ROCK 'N' ROLL May 1982
Jake Hooker / Alan Merrill
Rak Music .... USA
Joan Jett & The Blackhearts .... **Epic EPCA 2152**

I LOVE THE MOON 1912
Paul Rubens
Chappell & Co. Ltd .... UK
Show(s): .... Naughty Cinderella
The Savoy Havana Band .... **HMV B 1936**

Hubert Eisdell .... **Columbia 4811**
Doris Vane .... **Columbia 3798**

I LOVE THE NAME OF MARY 1913
Richard Oldham / Helen Taylor
Enoch & Sons Ltd. .... UK
Ernest Payne .... **Zonophone Twin 976**

I LOVE THE SOUND OF BREAKING GLASS April 1978
Nick Lowe / Andrew Bodnar / Stephen Golding
Rock Artistes Music .... UK
Nick Lowe .... **Radar ADA 1**

I LOVE THE SUNSHINE OF YOUR SMILE October 1951
Jimmy MacDonald / Jack Hoffman
New World Publishers Ltd .... USA
The Four Knights .... **Capitol CL 13587**
Donald Peers .... **HMV B 10377**

I LOVE THE WAY YOU SAY 'GOODNIGHT' December 1951
Eddie Pola / George Wyle
Campbell Connelly & Co. Ltd .... USA
Film(s): .... Lullaby of Broadway
Maurice Winnick & his Orchestra .... **HMV BD 6115**
Doris Day .... **Philips BBL 7137**
Doris Day appeared in *Lullaby of Broadway*.

I LOVE TO BOOGIE July 1976
Marc Bolan
Wizard Music .... UK
T. Rex .... **EMI MARC 14**

I LOVE TO LOVE (But My Baby Just Loves To Dance) March 1976
Jack Robinson / James Bolden
Mautoglade .... France
Tina Charles .... **CBS 3937**

I LOVE TO SING 1943
Paul Misraki / Tommie Connor / Michael Carr
Peter Maurice Music Co. Ltd .... France
Film(s): .... Rhythm Serenade
The New Mayfair Dance Orchestra .... **HMV BD 5820**
Josephine Bradley & her Ballroom Orchestra ... **Decca F 8367**
Alma Cogan .... **HMV CLP 1152**

I LOVE TO WHISTLE 1938
Harold Adamson / Jimmy McHugh
Francis, Day & Hunter Ltd. .... USA
Film(s): .... Mad About Music
Deanna Durbin .... **MCA MCG 6007**
'Fats' Waller & his Rhythm .... **HMV BD 5360**
Betty Driver .... **HMV BD 545**
Gracie Fields .... **Rex 9328**
Deanna Durbin appeared in *Mad About Music*.

I LOVE YOU 1924
Harry Archer / Harlan Thompson
Francis, Day & Hunter Ltd .... USA
Show(s): .... Little Jesse James
Film(s): .... The Sun Also Rises
Paul Whiteman & his Orchestra .... **HMV B 1740**
Jackie Gleason & his Orchestra .... **Capitol EAP 2-509**
Billy Eckstine .... **Columbia 33SX 1249**
Jane Powell .... **MGM EP 701**

I LOVE YOU 1945
Cole Porter
Chappell & Co. Ltd. .... USA
Show(s): .... Mexican Hayride
Film(s): .... Mexican Hayride
Bing Crosby .... **Brunswick LA 8513**
Perry Como .... **Camden CDN 110**
Julie London .... **London HAU 2005**

I LOVE YOU December 1960
Bruce Welch
Belinda (London) Ltd .... UK
Cliff Richard .... **Columbia DB 4547**

I LOVE YOU BABY December 1957
Paul Anka
Sherwin Music Co. .... USA
Paul Anka .... **Columbia 33SX 1282**

I LOVE YOU BECAUSE   **May 1964**
Leon Payne
Bourne Music Ltd . . . . USA
Leon Payne . . . . **Capitol CL 13474**
Jim Reeves . . . . **RCA 1385**
Brenda Lee . . . . **Brunswick LAT 8576**

I LOVE YOU LOVE ME LOVE   **January 1974**
Gary Glitter / Mike Leander
Leeds Music Ltd. . . . . UK
Gary Glitter . . . . **Bell 1337**
Ivor Novello Award.

I LOVE YOU SAMANTHA   **April 1961**
Cole Porter
Chappell & Co. Ltd . . . . USA
Film(s): . . . . High Society
Kenny Ball's Jazzmen . . . . **Pye 7NJ 2040**
Bing Crosby . . . . **Capitol LCT 6166**
Bing Crosby appeared *High Society*.

I LOVE YOU SO (The Merry Widow Waltz)   **1907**
Franz Lehar / Adrian Ross
Chappell & Co. Ltd. . . . . Austria
Show(s): . . . . The Merry Widow
Film(s): . . . . The Merry Widow
Richard Tauber . . . . **Parlophone R 20493**
Jeanette MacDonald . . . . **HMV B 8247**
Lucille Norman & Gordon MacRae . . . . **Capitol LC 6564**
Trudy Erwin & Fernando Lamas . . . . **MGM D 107**
Jeanette MacDonald appeared in the 1934 film of *The Merry Widow*.
Trudy Erwin & Fernando Lamas appeared in the 1952 film of *The Merry Widow*.

I LOVE YOU TRULY   **1906**
Carrie Jacobs-Bond
. . . . USA
Arthur Tracey (The Street Singer) . . . . **Decca F 7318**
Bing Crosby . . . . **Brunswick LAT 8053**
Jo Stafford & Nelson Eddy . . . . **Columbia SEG 7516**
The McGuire Sisters . . . . **Vogue LVA 9140**

I LOVES YOU PORGY   **1935**
George Gershwin / Ira Gershwin
Chappell & Co. Ltd . . . . USA
Show(s): . . . . Porgy and Bess
Film(s): . . . . Porgy and Bess
Todd Duncan & Anne Brown . . . . **Brunswick LAT 8021**
Sound Track recording of *Porgy and Bess* . . . **Philips ABL 3282**
Todd Duncan & Anne Brown appeared in the American production of *Porgy and Bess*.

I MAY BE CRAZY   **1902**
Leslie Stuart
Francis, Day & Hunter Ltd. . . . . UK
Eugene Stratton . . . . **HMV C 556**
The George Mitchell Minstrels . . . . **HMV CLP 1399**

I MAY BE WRONG BUT I THINK YOU'RE WONDERFUL   **1930**
Harry Ruskin / Henry Sullivan
Lawrence Wright Music Co. Ltd . . . . USA
Show(s): . . . . John Murray Anderson's Almanac
Film(s):Wallflower / You're My Everything / Young Man of Music / Sunny Side of the Street / Starlift
Jack Hylton & his Orchestra . . . . **HMV B 5760**
Dinah Shore . . . . **Columbia DB 2331**
Perry Como . . . . **RCA RD 27078**
Doris Day . . . . **Philips BBL 7175**
Doris Day appeared in *Young Man of Music* and *Starlift*.

I MAY NEVER PASS THIS WAY AGAIN   **April 1958**
Murray Wizell / Irving Melcher
Chappell & Co. Ltd . . . . USA
Robert Earl . . . . **Philips PB 805**
Ronnie Hilton . . . . **HMV POP 468**
Joan Regan . . . . **Decca F 11009**
Perry Como . . . . **RCA 1062**

I MEAN TO MARRY A MAN   **1906**
Howard Talbot / Arthur Anderson
Chappell & Co. Ltd . . . . UK
Show(s): . . . . The Girl Behind the Counter
Isobel Jay . . . . **Favourite 1-66015**
Isobel Jay appeared in *The Girl Behind the Counter*.

I MET HER ON MONDAY   **1942**
Allie Wrubel / Lionel Newman
Bradbury Wood Ltd . . . . USA
Geraldo & his Orchestra, vocal Derek Roy . **Parlophone F 1964**
Donald Peers . . . . **Decca F 8280**
The Mills Brothers . . . . **Brunswick 03436**

I MIGHT BE YOUR ONCE IN A WHILE   **1921**
Victor Herbert / Robert B. Smith
Chappell & Co. Ltd . . . . USA
Show(s): . . . . Angel Face
Film(s): . . . . The Great Victor Herbert
Joseph C. Smith's Orchestra . . . . **HMV B 1198**
Bing Crosby . . . . **Brunswick LA 8600**

I MISS MY SWISS - MY SWISS MISS MISSES ME   **1925**
L. Wolfe Gilbert / Abel Baer
Francis, Day & Hunter Ltd. . . . . USA
Show(s): . . . . Chauve Souris
Paul Whiteman & his Orchestra . . . . **HMV B 2117**
Ronnie Ronalde . . . . **Columbia DB 3002**
The Tuneful Twenties Dance Orchestra . . . **Parlophone R 3326**

I MUST BE SEEING THINGS   **March 1965**
Al Kooper / Bob Brass / Irwin Levine
Aaron Schroeder Ltd. . . . . USA
Gene Pitney . . . . **Stateside SS 390**

I NEED LOVE   **October 1987**
Todd Smith / Bob Erving / Darryl Pierce & Duane Simon
Island Music . . . . USA
L.L. Cool J . . . . **Def Jam 6511016**

I NEED YOU   **August 1988**
Nathan Rodgers / S. Hill / Frederick Byrd
EMI Music . . . . USA
B.V.S.M.P. . . . . **Debut DEPT 3044**

I NEED YOU NOW   **October 1954**
Jimmy Crane / Al Jacobs
B. Feldman & Co. Ltd. . . . . USA
Eddie Fisher . . . . **HMV B 10755**
The Stargazers . . . . **Decca F 10379**
Joni James . . . . **MGM 1064**

I NEED YOUR LOVIN'   **September 1989**
Fred Gordon / Vincent Bell
Island Music . . . . UK
Alyson Williams . . . . **Def Jam 6551436**

I NEVER KNEW (I Could Love Anybody)   **1921**
Tom Pitts / Ray Egan / Roy Marsh
Francis, Day & Hunter Ltd . . . . USA
Film(s): . . . . Strictly in the Groove
Paul Whiteman & his Orchestra . . . . **HMV B 1225**
The Darktown Strutters . . . . **HMV BD 5050**
Josephine Bradley & her Orchestra . . . . **Decca F 8887**
Sid Philips & his Band . . . . **HMV BD 6198**
The King Sisters . . . . **Capitol T 1333**

I NEVER KNEW (That Roses Grew)   **1926**
Gus Kahn / Ted Fiorito
Francis, Day & Hunter Ltd. . . . . USA
Film(s): . . . . Pete Kelly's Blues
The Savoy Orpheans . . . . **HMV B 5028**
Tommy Dorsey & his Orchestra . . . . **HMV BD 5864**
Bing Crosby . . . . **Brunswick LA 8673**
Peggy Lee . . . . **Brunswick LAT 8078**
Peggy Lee appeared in *Pete Kelly's Blues*.

I NEVER KNEW HOW WONDERFUL YOU WERE   **1926**
Joe Burke / Dorothy Terriss
Francis, Day & Hunter Ltd. . . . . USA
Paul Whiteman & his Orchestra . . . . **HMV B 5039**

I NEVER MENTION YOUR NAME, OH NO   **1944**
Walter Kent / Don George / Mack Davis
Bradbury Wood Ltd . . . . USA
Carroll Gibbons & The Savoy Hotel
Orpheans, vocal Valerie Davis . . . . **Decca F 8392**
Dick Haymes . . . . **MGM C 777**

I NEVER SEE MAGGIE ALONE   **1926**
Harry Tilsley / Everett Lynton

Cecil Lennox Music Co. Ltd. .... UK
Bert Ralton .... **Columbia 4092**
Bob Hannon & Johnny Ryan .... **Brunswick 04352**
Max Miller .... **HMV B 9878**
Slim Whitman (1949) .... **London HLP 8835**

I ONCE HAD A HEART MARGARITA   1937
J. Schmitz / Eddie Lisbona / Tommie Connor
Francis, Day & Hunter Ltd. .... Germany
Turner Layton .... **Columbia FB 1629**
Alfredo & his Orchestra .... **HMV B 8514**

I ONLY HAVE EYES FOR YOU   1935
Al Dubin / Harry Warren
B. Feldman & Co. Ltd .... USA
Film(s): ....Dames / Tea for Two / Jolson Sings Again
Leslie Hutchinson (Hutch) .... **Parlophone R 2002**
Phil Regan .... **Regal Zonophone MR 1491**
Frank Sinatra (1946) .... **Philips BBL 7168**
Al Jolson .... **Brunswick LA 8655**
Doris Day .... **Columbia DB 2769**
Art Garfunkel (1975) .... **CBS 3575**
Dick Powell & Ruby Keeler .... **United Artists UAG 29421**
Phil Regan, Dick Powell & Ruby Keeler appeared in *Dames*.
Doris Day appeared in *Tea for Two*.

I ONLY WANNA BE WITH YOU   January 1964
Mike Hawker / Ivor Raymonde
Springfield Music Ltd .... UK
Dusty Springfield .... **Philips BF 1292**
The Bay City Rollers (1976) .... **Bell 1493**
The Tourists (1979) .... **Logo GO 370**
Samantha Fox (1989) .... **Jive FOXY 11**

I OWE YOU NOTHING   July 1988
Matt Goss / Luke Goss
Warner Chappell Music .... UK
Bros .... **CBS ATOM 4**

I PAID FOR THAT LIE I TOLD YOU   1939
Enoch Light / Al Sherman / Al Hoffman
Campbell Connelly & Co. Ltd. .... USA
Arthur Tracey (The Street Singer) .... **Decca F 7082**
Dick Todd .... **HMV BD 730**
Ambrose & his Orchestra, vocal Vera Lynn ..... **Decca F 7115**

I PITCH MY LONELY CARAVAN AT NIGHT   1921
Eric Coates / Annette Horey
Chappell & Co. Ltd .... UK
Hubert Eisdell .... **Columbia D 1451**
Walter Glynne .... **HMV B 3412**

I POURED MY HEART INTO A SONG   1939
Irving Berlin
Irving Berlin Ltd. .... USA
Film(s): .... Second Fiddle
Rudy Vallee .... **Decca F 7211**
Steve Conway .... **Columbia FB 3377**
Tony Brent .... **Columbia SEG 8019**
Rudy Vallee appeared in *Second Fiddle*.
Nominated for an Academy Award 1939.

I PRETEND   August 1968
Les Reed / Barry Mason
Patricia Music .... UK
Des O'Connor .... **Columbia DB 8397**

I PROMISE YOU   1945
Johnny Mercer / Harold Arlen
Victoria Music Co. Ltd. .... USA
Film(s): .... Here Come the Waves
Bing Crosby .... **Brunswick Bing 9**
Michael Holliday .... **Columbia 33SX 1262**
Bing Crosby appeared in *Here Come the Waves*.

I PUT A SPELL ON YOU   May 1966
Jay Hawkins
Sheldon Music Ltd. .... USA
The Alan Price Set .... **Decca F 12367**
Nina Simone .... **Philips BF 1736**

I QUIT   October 1988
Matt Goss / Luke Goss
Virgin Music .... UK

Bros .... **CBS ATOM 5**

I REMEMBER ELVIS PRESLEY   October 1977
Eddie Ouwens / Dick Bakker / R. Dunhills
Island Music .... Holland
Danny Mirror .... **Sonet SON 2121**

I REMEMBER THE CORNFIELDS   July 1950
Martyn Mayne / Harry Ralton
Arcadia Music Publishing Co. Ltd .... UK
Evelyn Knight .... **Brunswick 04459**
Anne Shelton .... **Decca F 9477**
Dorothy Squires .... **Columbia DB 2722**

I REMEMBER YESTERDAY   October 1977
Donna Summer / Pete Bellotte / Giorgio Moroder
Heath Levy Music Ltd .... USA
Donna Summer .... **GTO GT 107**

I REMEMBER YOU   1942
Victor Schertzinger / Johnny Mercer
Chappell & Co. Ltd .... USA
Film(s): .... The Fleet's In
Jimmy Dorsey & his Orchestra,
vocal Bob Eberly .... **Brunswick 03328**
Doris Day .... **Philips BBL 7142**
Sue Raney .... **Capitol T 964**
Frank Ifield (1962) .... **Columbia DB 4856**
Jimmy Dorsey & Bob Eberly appeared in *The Fleet's In*.

I SAID MY PYJAMAS (And Put On My Prayers)   April 1950
Eddie Pola / George Wyle
Leeds Music Ltd .... USA
Fran Warren & Tony Martin .... **HMV B 9888**
Ethel Merman & Ray Bolger .... **Brunswick 04456**

I SAW HER AGAIN LAST NIGHT   September 1966
John Phillips / Dennis Doherty
Leeds Music Ltd .... USA
The Mamas & The Papas .... **RCA 1533**

I SAW HIM STANDING THERE   July 1988
John Lennon / Paul McCartney
Northern Songs .... UK
Tiffany .... **MCA TIFF 3**
Original title "I Saw Her Standing There"

I SAW MOMMY KISSING SANTA CLAUS   October 1953
Tommie Connor
Edwin H. Morris & Co. Ltd. .... USA
Jimmy Boyd .... **Columbia SCM 5072**
Billy Cotton & his Band .... **Decca F 10206**
The Beverley Sisters .... **Decca DFE 6611**

I SAW STARS   1934
Al Hoffman / Maurice Sigler / Al Goodhart
Robbins Music Corporation Ltd. .... USA
Paul Whiteman & his Orchestra .... **HMV B 6532**
Morton Downey .... **Rex 8339**
Carroll Gibbons & The Savoy Orpheans .... **Columbia CB 803**
Teddi King .... **Vogue LDE 142**

I SAY A LITTLE PRAYER   September 1968
Burt Bacharach / Hal David
Shapiro-Bernstein & Co. Ltd. .... USA
Aretha Franklin .... **Atlantic 584206**

I SECOND THAT EMOTION   January 1968
Smokey Robinson / Al Cleveland
Jobete Music (UK) Ltd. .... USA
Smokey Robinson & the Miracles (1968) . **Tamla Motown TMG 631**
Diana Ross, The Supremes
& The Temptations (1969) .... **Tamla Motown TMG 709**
Japan (1982) .... **Hansa HANSA 12**

I SEE A STAR   June 1974
H. Van Hemert
A.T.V. Music Ltd. .... Holland
Mouth & McNeal .... **Decca F 13504**

I SEE THE MOON   April 1954
Meredith Wilson
B. Feldman & Co. Ltd. .... USA
Dick Todd .... **Brunswick 05259**
The Stargazers .... **Decca LF 1186**

I SEE YOUR FACE BEFORE ME　　　　　**April 1955**
Howard Dietz / Arthur Schwartz
Chappell & Co. Ltd. . . . . USA
Show(s): . . . . .Between the Devil
Frank Sinatra　　　　　　　　　**Capitol LC 6702**
Doris Day　　　　　　　　　　　**Philips BBL 7211**

I SHALL ALWAYS REMEMBER YOU SMILING　　**1939**
Ross Parker / Hugh Charles
Dash Music Ltd. . . . . UK
Les Allen　　　　　　　　　　**Columbia FB 2152**
Ambrose & his Orchestra, vocal Vera Lynn . . . . . **Decca F 6966**
Ross Parker & Hugh Charles　　　　**Decca F 7356**
Jack Hylton & his Orchestra . . . . **HMV BD 5456**

I SHALL BE WAITING　　　　　　　　**1940**
Ross Parker / Hugh Charles / Joe Irwin
Dash Music Ltd. . . . . UK
Vera Lynn　　　　　　　　　　　**Decca F 7330**
Ross Parker & Hugh Charles　　　　**Decca F 7356**
Issy Bonn . . . . **HMV BD 797**

I SHOT THE SHERIFF　　　　　　**August 1974**
Bob Marley
Tuff Gong Music . . . . UK
Eric Clapton　　　　　　　　　　**RSO 2090132**
Bob Marley & The Wailers　　　　**Island ILPS 9376**

I SHOULD BE SO LUCKY　　　　　　**May 1988**
Mike Stock / Matt Aitken / Peter Waterman
All Boys Music . . . . UK
Kylie Minogue . . . . **PWL PWL 8**
Ivor Novello Award

I SHOULD CARE　　　　　　　　　　**1945**
Axel Stordahl / Paul Weston / Sammy Cahn
Southern Music Publishing Co. Ltd. . . . . USA
Film(s): . . . . Thrill of a Romance
Jimmy Dorsey & his Orchestra,
vocal Teddy Walters　　　　　　**Brunswick 03591**
The R.A.F. Dance Orchestra . . . . **Decca F 8548**
Julie London　　　　　　　　　**London HAU 2005**
Matt Monro　　　　　　　　　**Parlophone PMC 1134**

I SHOULD HAVE KNOWN BETTER　　**December 1984**
Jim Diamond / Graham Lyle
Rondor Music . . . . UK
Jim Diamond . . . . **A&M AM 220**
Ivor Novello Nomination

I SHOULDA LOVED YA　　　　　　**May 1980**
Narada Michael Walden / T.M. Stevens / Allee Willis
Rondor Music (London) Ltd . . . . USA
Narada Michael Walden　　　　　**Atlantic K 11413**

I STILL BELIEVE　　　　　　　**December 1954**
Billy Reid
Macmelodies Ltd. . . . . UK
Ronnie Harris　　　　　　　**Columbia SCM 5139**
Al Martino　　　　　　　　　　**Capitol CL 14192**
Dorothy Squires . . . . **Nixa NPL 18015**

I STILL GET A THRILL (Thinking Of You)　　**1931**
J. Fred Coots / Benny Davis
Francis, Day & Hunter Ltd . . . . USA
Ambrose & his Orchestra　　　　　**HMV B 5916**
Dick Haymes　　　　　　　　**Brunswick 04547**
Patti Page　　　　　　　　　**Mercury MMC 14036**

I STILL HAVEN'T FOUND WHAT I'M LOOKING FOR　**June 1987**
"U2"
Blue Mountain Music . . . . UK
U2 . . . . **Island IS 328**
The Chimes (1990) . . . . **CBS CHIM 1**

I STILL LOVE YOU ALL　　　　　　**May 1961**
Norbert Glanzberg / Don Raye
Leeds Music Ltd . . . . France
Kenny Ball's Jazzmen . . . . **Pye 7NJ 2042**
See also 'Padam Padam'.

I SURRENDER　　　　　　　　**February 1981**
Russ Ballard
Island Music . . . . UK

Rainbow . . . . **Polydor POSP 221**

I SURRENDER DEAR　　　　　　　　**1931**
Gordon Clifford / Harry Barris
Lawrence Wright Music Co. Ltd. . . . . USA
Bing Crosby . . . . **HMV 7EG 8139**
Jack Payne & his Orchestra . . . . **HMV CLP 1160**
Bing Crosby　　　　　　　　　**Brunswick LAT 8251**
Tony Brent　　　　　　　　　　**Columbia DB 4238**

I TAKE TO YOU　　　　　　　　　　**1942**
Mack Gordon / Harry Warren
Robbins Music Corporation Ltd . . . . USA
Film(s): . . . . The Great American Broadcast
The Johnny Long Orchestra　　　　**Brunswick 03244**
Adelaide Hall　　　　　　　　　　**Decca F 8030**

I TALK TO THE TREES　　　　　　**July 1953**
Alan Jay Lerner / Frederick Loewe
Chappell & Co. Ltd . . . . USA
Show(s): . . . . Paint Your Wagon
Film(s): . . . . Paint Your Wagon
Tony Bavaar . . . . **HMV CLP 1005**
Ken Cantrill　　　　　　　　　**Columbia DB 3289**
Edmundo Ros & his Orchestra . . . . **Decca LK 4264**
Clint Eastwood　　　　　　　**Paramount PMS 1001**
Tony Bavaar appeared in the American production of *Paint Your
Wagon*
Ken Cantrill appeared in the British production of *Paint Your Wagon*.
Clint Eastwood appeared in the film *Paint Your Wagon*.

I TAUT I TAW A PUDDY TAT　　　　**January 1951**
Alan Livingston / Billy May / Warren Foster
Harms-Connelly Ltd . . . . USA
Mel Blanc . . . . **Capitol CL 14950**
Benny Lee & Mary　　　　　　　**Decca F 9577**
Danny Kaye . . . . **Brunswick LAT 8350**

I THINK OF YOU　　　　　　　　**March 1964**
Peter Lee Sterling
Robbins Music Corporation Ltd . . . . UK
The Merseybeats . . . . **Fontana TF 431**

I THINK OF YOU
(Il Faut Trouver Le Temp D'Aimer)　　**June 1971**
Rod McKuen / Francis Lai
Melanie Music . . . . France
Perry Como　　　　　　　　　　**RCA 2075**
Rod McKuen　　　　**Warner Brothers WS 3015**

I THINK WE'RE ALONE NOW　　　**March 1987**
Ritchie Cordell
Chappell Music Co. . . . . USA
Tommy James . . . . **Major Minor MM 511**
Lena Lovich . . . . **Stiff BUY 32**
Tiffany (1987) . . . . **MCA MCA 1211**

I THOUGHT OF YOU LAST NIGHT　　**April 1952**
Ralph Freed
Bregman, Vocco & Conn Ltd . . . . USA
Jeri Southern . . . . **Brunswick 04910**
The Beverley Sisters . . . . **Columbia DB 4523**
Jeri Southern . . . . **Capitol T 1278**

I THREW A KISS IN THE OCEAN　　　　**1942**
Irving Berlin
Bradbury Wodd Ltd . . . . USA
Jimmy Dorsey & his Orchestra,
vocal Helen O'Connell . . . . **Brunswick 03349**
Eric Winstone & his Orchestra,
vocal Julie Dawn . . . . **Regal Zonophone MR 3647**

I TOOK MY HARP TO A PARTY　　　　**1934**
Noel Gay / Desmond Carter
Chappell & Co. Ltd. . . . . UK
Gracie Fields . . . . **HMV B 8065**
Leslie Sarony . . . . **Rex 8063**
Gracie Fields . . . . **Decca LK 4182**

I TRAVEL THE ROAD　　　　　　　　**1932**
Donovan Parsons / Pat Thayer
Keith Prowse Music Publishing Co. Ltd. . . . . UK
Peter Dawson . . . . **HMV B 3812**
Raymond Newell . . . . **Columbia DB 228**
Dennis Noble . . . . **HMV B 9212**

I UNDERSTAND 1941
Mabel Wayne / Kim Gannon
Sun Music Publishing Co. Ltd .... USA
Jimmy Dorsey & his Orchestra,
vocal Bob Eberly .... **Brunswick 03189**
Bob Eberly .... **Warner Brothers WM 4033**
Nat 'King' Cole .... **Capitol LCT 6149**

I UNDERSTAND December 1964
Pat Best
Maddox Music Co. Ltd .... USA
Freddie & The Dreamers .... **Columbia DB 7381**
Herman's Hermits .... **Columbia SEG 8380**

I UPS TO HER, AND SHE UPS TO ME 1939
Al Hoffman / Al Goodheart / Manny Kurtz
Sun Music Publishing Co. Ltd. .... USA
Lew Stone & his Band .... **Decca F 6929**
Guy Lombardo & his Royal Canadians ..... **Brunswick 02699**
Henry Hall & his Orchestra .... **Columbia FB 2154**

I USED TO BE COLOUR BLIND 1938
Irving Berlin
Irving Berlin Ltd. .... USA
Film(s): .... Carefree
Fred Astaire .... **Columbia DB 1809**
Ginger Rogers .... **HMV B 8822**
Mildred Bailey .... **Parlophone R 2610**
Anita O'Day .... **HMV DLP 1169**
Fred Astaire .... **HMV CLP 1304**
Fred Astaire & Ginger Rogers appeared in *Carefree*.

I USED TO LOVE YOU (But It's All Over Now) 1921
Lew Brown / Albert Von Tilzer
Francis, Day & Hunter Ltd .... USA
Louis Armstrong & his Orchestra .... **Decca F 8163**
'Fats' Waller & his Rhythm .... **RCA RD 27185**
Rosemary June .... **Pye N 25015**

I USED TO SIGH FOR THE SILVERY MOON 1909
Herman Darewski / Lester Barrett
Francis, Day & Hunter .... UK
G.H. Elliott (The Chocolate
Coloured Coon) .... **Columbia SEG 7614**
Herman Darewski Orchestra ...... **Columbia FB 1567**
G.H. Elliott .... **Fontana TFL 5043**

I WANNA BE LOVED BY YOU 1932
Herbert Stothart / Harry Ruby / Bert Kalmar
Victoria Music Co. Ltd. .... USA
Show(s): .... Good Boy
Film(s):Three Little Words / Gentleman Marry Brunettes / Some Like
it Hot
Helen Kane (1925) .... **HMV B 4042**
Rose Murphy .... **Brunswick 04585**
Jane Russell, Anita Ellis & Rudy Vallee ...... **Vogue LVA 9003**
Helen Kane (1950) .... **MGM D 139**
Marilyn Monroe .... **London HAT 2176**
Dorothy Provine .... **Warner Brothers WM 4035**
Helen Kane appeared in *Good Boy*.
Jane Russell, Anita Ellis & Rudy Vallee appeareed in *Gentleman
Marry Brunettes.*.
Marilyn Monroe appeared in *Some Like it Hot.*

I WANNA BE YOUR DRILL INSTRUCTOR (See Full Metal Jacket)

I WANNA BE YOUR MAN January 1964
John Lennon / Paul McCartney
Northern Songs Ltd .... UK
The Rolling Stones .... **Decca F 11770**
The Beatles .... **Parlophone PMC 1206**

I WANNA DANCE WIT CHOO (Do Dat Dance) May 1975
Bob Crewe / Denny Randell
Carlin Music Corporation .... USA
Disco Tex & The Sex-O-Lettes ..... **Chelsea 2005024**

I WANNA DANCE WITH SOMEBODY
(Who Loves Me) June 1987
George Merrill / Sharron Rubicam
Rondor Music .... USA
Whitney Houston .... **Arista RIST 1**

I WANNA DO IT WITH YOU November 1982
Laying Martine

138

Chappell Music Co. .... USA
Barry Manilow .... **Arista ARIST 495**

I WANNA GET MARRIED 1945
Dan Shapiro / Milton Pascal / Phil Charig
Robbins Music Ltd. .... USA
Show(s): .... Follow the Girls
Gertrude Niesen .... **Brunswick 03602**
Gertrude Niesien appeared in the American production of *Follow the Girls*.

I WANNA GO HOME June 1960
Traditional
Essex Music Ltd .... USA
Lonnie Donegan .... **Pye 7N 15267**
Jimmy Rodgers .... **Columbia 33SX 1292**

I WANNA SAY HELLO January 1952
Jimmy MacDonald / Jack Hoffman
Chappell & Co. Ltd .... USA
'Sir' Hubert Pimm & Orchestra ...... **London REU 1032**
Billy Cotton & his Band .... **Decca F 9827**
Sophie Tucker .... **Mercury MPL 6503**

I WANNA STAY WITH YOU April 1976
Benny Gallagher / Graham Lyle
Rondor Music (London) Ltd .... UK
Gallagher & Lyle .... **A&M AMS 7211**

I WANT A GIRL JUST LIKE THE GIRL THAT MARRIED
DEAR OLD DAD 1918
Harry Von Tilzer / William Dillon
Francis, Day & Hunter Ltd. .... USA
Film(s): .... Show Business / The Jolson Story
Dorothy Ward .... **Columbia 2062**
Al Jolson .... **Brunswick LA 8575**
The Saints Jazz Band .... **Parlophone R 3427**
Red Foley .... **Brunswick LAT 8343**

I WANT CANDY September 1965
Jerry Goldstein / Bob Feldman / Richard Gottener & Bert Berns
Dominion Music .... USA
Brian Poole & The Tremeloes .... **Decca F 12197**
Bow Wow Wow (1982) .... **RCA RCA 238**

I WANT IT ALL May 1989
"Queen"
EMI Music .... UK
Queen .... **Parlophone QUEEN 10**

I WANT SOME MONEY 1922
Herbert Rule / Fred Holt / L. Silberman / Tom McGhee
Campbell Connelly & Co. Ltd .... UK
The Two Gilberts .... **Regal G 7829**
The New Mayfair Dance Orchestra ...... **HMV B 4318**
The Serenaders .... **Columbia FB 3429**

I WANT THAT MAN November 1989
Allanah Currie / Tom Bailey
Point Music .... UK
Deborah Harry .... **Chrysalis CHS 3369**

I WANT TO BE A MILITARY MAN 1900
Leslie Stuart / Owen Hall
Francis, Day & Hunter Ltd. .... UK
Show(s): .... Florodora
Light Opera Company .... **Columbia DX 126**

I WANT TO BE FREE June 1981
Toyah Willcox / Joel Bogen
Sweet & Sour Songs .... UK
Toyah .... **Safari SAFE 34**

I WANT TO BE HAPPY 1925
Vincent Youmans / Irving Caesar / Otto Harbach
Chappell & Co. Ltd. .... USA
Show(s): .... No No Nanette
Film(s): .... No No Nanette / Tea for Two
Binnie Hale & Joseph Coyne .... **Columbia 3630**
Bruce Trent .... **Fontana TFE 5016**
Doris Day .... **Philips BBL 7471**
June Christy .... **Capitol T 1-1327**
Binnie Hale & Joseph Coyne appeared in the British production of *No
No Nanette*.
Doris Day appeared in *Tea for Two*.

I WANT TO BE IN DIXIE 1912
Irving Berlin / Ted Snyder
B. Feldman & Co. Ltd . . . . USA
The American Ragtime Octet . . . . **HMV 2-4039**
Willie Solar . . . . **HMV B 471**
Geraldo & his Orchestra . . . . **Parlophone F 1998**
The George Mitchell Singers . . . . **HMV CLP 1399**

I WANT TO BREAK FREE May 1984
John Deacon
EMI Music . . . . UK
Queen . . . . **EMI QUEEN 2**

I WANT TO GO BACK TO MICHIGAN 1914
Irving Berlin
B. Feldman & Co. Ltd. . . . . USA
Show(s): . . . . 5064 Gerard
Film(s): . . . . Easter Parade
The Mayfair Orchestra . . . . **HMV B 287**
The Harry Davidson Orchestra . . . . **Columbia DX 1789**
Beatrice Lillie . . . . **Decca LK 4293**

I WANT TO HOLD YOUR HAND January 1964
John Lennon / Paul McCartney
Northern Songs Ltd . . . . UK
The Beatles . . . . **Parlophone R 5084**
The Boston 'Pops' Orch.conducted by Arthur Fiedler . **RCA 1408**
Dollar (1980) . . . . **Carrere CAR 131**
Ivor Novello Nomination.

I WANT TO KNOW WHAT LOVE IS January 1985
Mick Jones
Warner Brothers Music . . . . UK
Foreigner . . . . **Atlantic A 9596**
Ivor Novello Nomination.

I WANT TO SING IN OPERA 1910
Worton David / Georgie Arthurs
Francis, Day & Hunter Ltd . . . . UK
Wilkie Bard (1910) . . . . **Jumbo 563**
Reg Grant . . . . **Parlophone R 1332**

I WANT TO STAY HERE September 1963
Gerry Goffin / Carole King
Aldon Music Ltd. . . . . USA
Steve Lawrence & Eydie Gormé . . . . **CBS AAG 163**
Miki & Griff . . . . **Pye 7N 15555**

I WANT TO WAKE UP WITH YOU September 1986
Benjamin Peters
Lawrence Welk Music . . . . USA
Boris Gardiner . . . . **Revue REV 733**

I WANT WHAT I WANT WHEN I WANT IT 1906
Henry Blossom / Victor Herbert
Chappell & Co. Ltd . . . . USA
Show(s): . . . . Mlle. Modiste
George Alexander . . . . **Columbia A 293**
Kenneth Smith . . . . **Readers Digest RDM 50**
Lauritz Melchior . . . . **RCA CAL 424**

I WANT YOU August 1966
Bob Dylan
Warner Brothers Music Ltd. . . . . USA
Bob Dylan . . . . **CBS 202258**

I WANT YOU BACK March 1970
"The Corporation"
Jobete Music (UK) Ltd. . . . . USA
The Jackson Five . . . . **Tamla Motown TMG 724**
The Jackson Five (1988) . . . . **Motown ZB 41913**

I WANT YOU BACK May 1988
Sarah Dallin / Siobhan Fahey / Karen Woodward / Mike Stock / Matt Aitken & Peter Waterman
All Boys Music . . . . UK
Bananarama . . . . **London NANA 16**

I WANT YOU TO WANT ME TO WANT YOU January 1950
Bob Shafer / Fred Fisher / Alfred Bryan
B. Feldman & Co. Ltd . . . . USA
Film(s): . . . . Oh You Beautiful Doll
The Mills Brothers . . . . **Brunswick 04418**
Gordon MacRae . . . . **Capitol CL 13307**

Tony Martin . . . . **HMV JO 215**

I WANT YOU, I NEED YOU, I LOVE YOU July 1956
Maurice Mysels / Ira Kosloff
Aberbach (London) Ltd. . . . . USA
Elvis Presley . . . . **RCA RB 16069**

I WANT YOUR LOVE March 1979
Bernard Edwards / Nile Rodgers
Warner Brothers Music Ltd. . . . . USA
Chic . . . . **Atlantic LV 16**

I WANT YOUR LOVE August 1988
Nick Sayer
Cinepop Music . . . . UK
Transvision Vamp . . . . **MCA TVV 3**

I WANT YOUR SEX June 1987
George Michael
Morrison Leahy Music . . . . UK
George Michael . . . . **Epic LUST 1**

I WAS A GOOD LITTLE GIRL TILL I MET YOU 1914
Clifford Harris / James W. Tate
Francis, Day & Hunter Ltd. . . . . UK
Ella Retford . . . . **Favourite 854**
Clarice Mayne & "That" . . . . **Columbia L 1041**
Georgia Brown . . . . **Decca LK 4411**

I WAS BORN TO LOVE YOU May 1985
Freddie Mercury
EMI Music . . . . UK
Freddie Mercury . . . . **CBS A 6019**

I WAS KAISER BILL'S BATMAN May 1967
Roger Greenaway / Roger Cook
Mills Music Ltd. . . . . UK
Whistling Jack Smith . . . . **Deram DM 112**

I WAS MADE FOR DANCIN' February 1979
Michael Lloyd
Carlin Music Corporation . . . . USA
Leif Garrett . . . . **Atlantic K 11202**

I WAS MADE TO LOVE HER August 1967
Stevie Wonder / Sylvia Moy / Henry Cosby & Lula Hardaway
Jobete Music (UK) Ltd. . . . . USA
Stevie Wonder . . . . **Tamla Motown TMG 613**

I WAS NEVER KISSED BEFORE 1947
Vivian Ellis
Chappell & Co. Ltd. . . . . UK
Show(s): . . . . Bless the Bride
George Guetary & Lizbeth Webb . . . . **Columbia SEG 7551**
Anthony Newley . . . . **Decca LK 4406**
George Guetary & Lizbeth Webb appeared in *Bless the Bride*.

I WENT TO YOUR WEDDING November 1952
Jessie Mae Robinson
Victoria Music Co. Ltd . . . . USA
Patti Page . . . . **Oriole CB 1129**
Joyce Frazer . . . . **Columbia DB 3191**
Dick James . . . . **Parlophone R 3606**
Spike Jones & his City Slickers (Comedy version) . **HMV B 10482**

I WHISTLE A HAPPY TUNE September 1953
Richard Rodgers / Oscar Hammerstein II
Williamson Music Ltd. . . . . USA
Show(s): . . . . The King and I
Film(s): . . . . The King and I
Gertrude Lawrence . . . . **Brunswick LAT 8026**
Valerie Hobson . . . . **Philips BBL 7002**
Deborah Kerr & Rex Thompson . . . . **Capitol LCT 6108**
Gertrude Lawrence appeared in the American production of *The King and I*.
Valerie Hobson appeared in the British production of *The King and I*.
Deborah Kerr & Rex Thompson appeared in the film of *The King and I*.
The Singing voice of Deborah Kerr was dubbed by Marni Nixon.

I WILL May 1964
Dick Glasser
Bens Music Ltd . . . . USA
Vic Dana . . . . **Liberty LIB 51**
Billy Fury . . . . **Decca F 11888**
Skeeter Davis . . . . **RCA RD 7604**
Ruby Winter (1977) . . . . **Creole CR 141**

I WILL DRINK THE WINE   March 1971
Paul Ryan
Ryan Music Ltd . . . . UK
Frank Sinatra . . . . **Reprise RS 23487**

I WILL RETURN   November 1971
Philip Cordell
Jigsaw Music . . . . UK
Springwater . . . . **Polydor 2058141**

I WILL SURVIVE   July 1970
Frank Collins
Westminster Music . . . . UK
Arrival . . . . **Decca F 13026**

I WILL SURVIVE   March 1979
Dino Fekaris / Freddie Perren
A.T.V. Music Ltd. . . . . USA
Gloria Gaynor . . . . **Polydor 2095097**

I WISH   February 1977
Stevie Wonder
Jobete Music (UK) Ltd. . . . . USA
Stevie Wonder . . . . **Motown TMG 1054**

I WISH I COULD SHIMMY LIKE MY SISTER KATE   1923
Armand Piron / Peter Bocage
Lawrence Wright Music Co. Ltd . . . . USA
The Virginians . . . . **HMV B 1459**
Muggsy Spanier's Ragtime Band . . . . **RCA RD 27132**
Bunk Johnson & his New Orleans Band . . . . **HMV B 9517**
Kid Ory's Creole Jazz Band . . . . **HMV CLP 1329**

I WISH I DIDN'T LOVE YOU SO   1947
Frank Loesser
Victoria Music Co. Ltd. . . . . USA
Film(s): . . . . The Perils of Pauline
Helen Forrest . . . . **MGM 110**
Steve Conway . . . . **Columbia FB 3344**
The Four Freshmen . . . . **Capitol T 1189**
Nominated for an Academy Award 1947.

I WISH I HAD A GIRL   1908
Gus Kahn / Grace Le Boy
Herman Darewski Music . . . . USA
Film(s): . . . . I'll See You in My Dreams
Al Jolson . . . . **Brunswick 04145**
Doris Day . . . . **Columbia DB 3093**
Doris Day appeared in *I'll See You in My Dreams*.

I WISH I KNEW   1945
Mack Gordon / Harry Warren
Chappell & Co. Ltd. . . . . USA
Film(s): . . . . The Diamond Horseshoe
Dick Haymes . . . . **Brunswick 03582**
Petula Clark . . . . **Nixa NPL 18007**
The Four Freshmen . . . . **Capitol T 1189**
Dick Haymes appeared in *The Diamond Horseshoe*.

I WISH I WERE IN LOVE AGAIN   1938
Richard Rodgers / Lorenz Hart
Chappell & Co. Ltd. . . . . USA
Show(s): . . . . Babes in Arms
Film(s): . . . . Words and Music
Judy Garland . . . . **Brunswick 04887**
Judy Garland & Mickey Rooney . . . . **MGM C 853**
Frank Sinatra . . . . **Capitol LCT 6135**
Rosemary Clooney . . . . **Vogue LVA 9112**
Judy Garland and Mickey Rooney appeared in *Words and Music*.

I WISH I WERE TWINS   1934
Edgar Leslie / Frank Loesser / Joseph Meyer
Francis, Day & Hunter Ltd . . . . USA
The American Ramblers, vocal Ella Logan . . **Brunswick 01775**
'Fats' Waller & his Rhythm . . . . **HMV DLP 1118**

I WISH I WUZ   November 1951
Sid Kuller / Lyn Murray
Peter Maurice Music Co. Ltd. USA
Film(s): . . . . Slaughter Trail
Gloria De Haven . . . . **Brunswick 04389**
Teresa Brewer . . . . **London L 1085**
Donald Peers . . . . **HMV B 10158**

**I WISH IT COULD BE CHRISTMAS
EVERYDAY**   December 1973
Roy Wood
Carlin Music Corporation . . . . UK
Wizzard . . . . **Harvest HAR 5079**

I WISH IT WOULD RAIN DOWN   February 1990
Phil Collins
Hit & Run Music . . . . UK
Phil Collins . . . . **Virgin VS 1240**

I WISHED ON THE MOON   1936
Ralph Rainger / Dorothy Parker
Victoria Music Co. Ltd . . . . USA
Film(s): . . . . The Big Broadcast of 1936
Little Jack Little & his Orchestra . . . . **Columbia FB 1104**
**Bing Crosby with The Dorsey
Brothers Orchestra** . . . . **Brunswick Bing 1**
June Christy . . . . **Capitol T 1114**
Mel Tormé . . . . **HMV CLP 1445**
Bing Crosby appeared in *The Big Broadcast of 1936*.

I WON'T COME IN WHILE HE'S THERE   March 1967
Gene Davis
Metric Music Ltd. . . . . USA
Jim Reeves . . . . **RCA 1563**

I WON'T DANCE   1935
*Jerome Kern / Otto Harbach / Dorothy Fields / Jimmy McHugh /
Oscar Hammerstein II*
Chappell & Co. Ltd . . . . USA
Film(s): . . . . . . Roberta / Till the Clouds Roll By / Lovely to Look at
Jack Hylton & his Orchestra . . . . **HMV BD 200**
Fred Astaire . . . . **HMV CLP 1100**
Mitzi Gaynor . . . . **HMV 7EG 8460**
Marge & Gower Champion . . . . **MGM D 141**
Margaret Whiting . . . . **HMV CLP 1418**
Fred Astaire appeared in *Roberta*.
Marge & Gower Champion appeared in *Lovely to Look At*.

I WON'T FORGET YOU   July 1964
Harlan Howard
One Four Two Music Ltd . . . . USA
Jim Reeves . . . . **RCA 1400**
Joe Henderson (piano) . . . . **Pye GGL 0292**

I WON'T LAST A DAY WITHOUT YOU   October 1972
Paul Williams / Roger Nichols
Rondor Music . . . . USA
The Carpenters . . . . **A&M AMS 7023**
Paul Williams . . . . **A&M AMLS 64367**
Maureen McGovern . . . . **Pye 7N 25627**

I WON'T LET THE SUN GO DOWN ON ME   July 1984
Nik Kershaw
Rondor Music . . . . UK
Nik Kershaw . . . . **MCA NIK 4**
Ivor Novello Nomination

I WON'T LET YOU DOWN   May 1982
Anthony Hymas / James Diamond
Rondor Music . . . . UK
PH.D . . . . **WEA K 79209**

I WON'T RUN AWAY   December 1984
John David
Warner Brothers Music . . . . UK
Alvin Stardust . . . . **Chrysalis CHS 2829**

I WON'T TELL A SOUL (That I Love You)   1938
Ross Parker / Hugh Charles
Dash Music Ltd. . . . . UK
Leslie Hutchinson (Hutch) . . . . **Parlophone F 1164**
Vera Lynn . . . . **Decca F 6731**
Frances Langford . . . . **Brunswick 02872**
Ross Parker & Hugh Charles . . . . **Decca F 7356**

I WONDER   June 1955
Sam M. Lewis / Pete Wendling / Joseph Meyer
Macmelodies Ltd. . . . . USA
Dickie Valentine . . . . **Decca LF 1265**
Jane Froman . . . . **Capitol EAP 1-600**
Vera Lynn . . . . **Decca DFE 6312**

I WONDER **August 1963**
Cecil Grant / Raymond Leveen
Leeds Music Ltd .... USA
Brenda Lee .... **Brunswick 05891**
Ray Charles .... **HMV CLP 1626**
Woody Herman & his Orchestra,
vocal Woody Herman .... **CBS BPG 62158**

I WONDER HOW I LOOK WHEN I'M ASLEEP **1927**
Buddy De Sylva / Lew Brown / Ray Henderson
Campbell Connelly & Co. Ltd. .... USA
Vaughan De Leath .... **Columbia 4443**

I WONDER IF I TAKE YOU HOME **August 1985**
"Full Force"
Chrysalis Music .... USA
Lisa Lisa & Cult Jam .... **CBS A 6057**

I WONDER IF LOVE IS A DREAM **1914**
Dorothy Foster / Edward Teschemacher
Chappell & Co. Ltd. .... UK
Ruth Vincent .... **HMV E 25**

I WONDER WHAT'S BECOME OF SALLY **1924**
Jack Yellen / Milton Ager
Lawrence Wright Music Co. Ltd. .... USA
Jack Hylton & his Orchestra .... **HMV B 1925**
Bing Crosby .... **Brunswick LA 8620**
Al Jolson .... **Brunswick LA 8294**

I WONDER WHERE MY BABY IS TONIGHT **1926**
Gus Kahn / Walter Donaldson
Francis, Day & Hunter Ltd. .... USA
Show(s): .... The Co-Optimists
Melville Gideon .... **HMV B 2287**
Harry Roy & his Tiger Ragamuffins ...... **Parlophone R 1912**
The Ira Ironstrings Orchestra .... **Warner Brothers WEP 6026**
Melville Gideon appeared in *The Co-Optimists*.

I WONDER WHO'S KISSING HER NOW **1909**
Joseph Howard / Frank Adams / William Hough
B. Feldman & Co. Ltd .... USA
Show(s): .... Prince for Tonight
Film(s):The Time, the Place and the Girl / I Wonder Who's Kissing
Her Now / Moonlight in Havana
Arthur George .... **Pathé 78811**
Harry Fay .... **Zonophone 388**
Michael Holliday .... **Columbia DB 4663**
Danny Kaye (1947) .... **Brunswick 03812**

I WONDER WHY **April 1978**
Ricardo Weeks / Melvin Anderson
United Artists Music Co. Ltd .... UK
Showaddywaddy .... **Arista 174**
Dion & The Belmonts .... **London HLU 8646**

I WOULDN'T LEAVE MY LITTLE
WOODEN HUT FOR YOU **1905**
Tom Mellor / Charles Collins
Francis, Day & Hunter .... UK
Film(s): .... Evergreen
Burt Shepard .... **HMV GC 3-2342**
Tessa Deane & John Rorke ...... **Regal Zonophone MR 1435**
Roma Creswell .... **Piccadilly NPL 38002**

I WOULDN'T TRADE YOU FOR THE WORLD **September 1964**
Bill Taylor / Bill Smith / Curtis Kirk
Le Bill Music Ltd .... USA
The Bachelors .... **Decca F 11949**

I WRITE THE SONGS **August 1975**
Bruce Johnstone
Sunbury Music Ltd .... USA
David Cassidy .... **RCA 2571**
Barry Manilow .... **Arista ARTV 2**

I YI YI YI YI I LIKE YOU VERY MUCH **1941**
Harry Warren / Mack Gordon
Francis, Day & hunter Ltd .... USA
Film(s): .... That Night In Rio
Carmen Miranda .... **Brunswick 03207**
The Andrews Sisters .... **Brunswick 03195**
Petula Clark .... **Nixa NPL 18007**
Carmen Miranda appeared in *That Night In Rio*.

I'D CLIMB THE HIGHEST MOUNTAIN
(If I Knew I'd Find You) **1926**
Lew Brown / Sidney Clare
Francis, Day & Hunter Ltd. .... USA
Jack Smith .... **HMV B 2319**
Lillian Roth .... **Philips BBL 7079**
The Ink Spots .... **Brunswick LA 8590**
The Platters .... **Mercury MMC 14010**
Based on Humoresque opus 101 no.7 by Antonin Dvorak (1841 - 1904).

I'D DO ANYTHING **September 1960**
Lionel Bart
Lakeview Music Publishing Co .... UK
Show(s): .... Oliver
Film(s): .... Oliver
Martin Horsey, Georgia Brown,
Keith Hamshere, Diane Gray & Ron Moody .... **Decca LK 4359**
Michael Goodman, Georgia Brown,
Bruce Prochnik, Alice Playten & Clive Revill . **RCA LOCD 2004**
Shani Wallis, Jack Wild, Mark Lester,
Shelia White, Ron Moody & chorus .... **RCA RB 6777**
Martin Horsey, Keith Hamshere & Diane Grey appeared in the British
production of *Oliver*.
Michael Goodman, Bruce Prochnik, Alice Pleyten & Clive Revill
appeared in the American production of *Oliver*.
Georgia Brown appeared in both the British and American productions of *Oliver*.
Shani Wallis, Jack Wild, Shelia White & Mark Lester appeared in the film *Oliver*.
Ron Moody appeared in both the British production and the film of *Oliver*.

I'D GIVE THE WORLD (Liebeslied) **May 1957**
Heino Gaze / Harold Spina
Macmelodies Ltd. .... Germany
David Whitfield .... **Decca LK 4242**
Ronnie Harris .... **HMV 7EG 8270**

I'D LIKE TO TEACH THE WORLD TO SING **February 1972**
Roger Greenaway / Roger Cook
Cookaway Music .... UK
The New Seekers .... **Polydor 2058184**

I'D LOVE TO FALL ASLEEP **March 1953**
Louis Gaste / Sonny Miller
B. Feldman & Co Ltd .... USA
Line Renaud .... **Columbia DB 3247**
Penny Nicholls .... **HMV B 10447**
Muriel Smith .... **Philips PB 122**

I'D LOVE TO FALL ASLEEP AND WAKE UP IN MY
MAMMY'S ARMS **1921**
Sam M. Lewis / Joe Young / Fred Ahlert
B. Feldman & Co. Ltd .... USA
Fred Douglas .... **Regal G 7631**
The Benson Orchestra of Chicago .... **HMV B 1179**

I'D LOVE TO LIVE IN LOVELAND
WITH A GIRL LIKE YOU **1910**
W.R. Williams
Sun Music Publishing Co. Ltd .... USA
Bing Crosby (1938) .... **Brunswick LA 8624**
Lou Preager & his Orchestra, vocal Paul Rich . **Columbia FB 3452**
Stanley Klines .... **Fontana TFL 5019**

I'D LOVE YOU TO WANT ME **July 1974**
Kent Lavoie
Carlin Music Corporation .... USA
Lobo .... **UK UK 68**
Ray Conniff Orchestra .... **CBS S 65430**

I'D NEVER FIND ANOTHER YOU **January 1962**
Gerry Goffin / Carole King
Nevins-Kirshner Ltd. .... USA
Billy Fury .... **Decca F 11409**
Tony Orlando .... **Fontana TFL 5167**
Paul Anka .... **Columbia 33SX 1432**

I'D RATHER BE ME **1945**
Felix Bernard / Eddie Cherkose / Sam Coslow
Edwin H. Morris Co. Ltd. .... USA
Film(s): .... Out of This World
Bing Crosby .... **Brunswick Bing 10**

I'D RATHER GO BLIND **June 1969**
Ellington Jordan / Bill Foster
Jewel Music Publishing Co. Ltd. ,,,,,,,,, USA
Chicken Snack .... **CBS 1832**

Etta James . . . . **Chess CRS 8063**

I'D RATHER JACK   **March 1989**
Mike Stock / Matt Aitken / Peter Waterman
All Boys Music . . . . UK
The Reynolds Girls . . . . **PWL PWL 25**

I'D'VE BAKED A CAKE   **May 1950**
Al Hoffman / Bob Merrill / Clem Watts
Chappell & Co. Ltd . . . . USA
Eve Young . . . . **London L 658**
Eileen Barton . . . . **Vogue Q 72075**
Ethel Merman & Ray Bolger . . . . **Brunswick 04491**
Donald Peers . . . . **HMV B 9903**

I'LL ALWAYS BE IN LOVE WITH YOU   **1929**
Sammy Stept / Bud Green / Harry Ruby
Campbell Connelly & Co. Ltd . . . . USA
Film(s): . . . . Stepping High / Syncopation
Fred Waring & his Pennsylvanians . . . . **HMV B 5648**
Michael Holliday . . . . **Columbia DB 4155**
Vera Lynn . . . . **Decca LK 4305**
Fred Waring & his Pennsylvanians appeared in *Syncopation*.

I'LL ALWAYS BE WITH YOU   **1945**
Marjorie Goetschius / Edna Osser
Keith Prowse Music Publishing Co. Ltd. . . . . USA
Perry Como . . . . **HMV BD 1118**
Denny Dennis . . . . **Decca F 8573**
Malcolm Dodds . . . . **Brunswick 05774**

I'LL ALWAYS LOVE YOU   **April 1951**
Jay Livingston / Ray Evans
Victoria Music Co. . . . . USA
Eileen Wilson & Don Cherry . . . . **Brunswick 04624**
Teddy Johnson . . . . **Columbia DB 2799**
Roberto Inglez & his Orchestra . . . . . . **Parlophone R 3367**

I'LL BE AROUND   **1943**
Alec Wilder
Cavendish Music Co. Ltd . . . . USA
Film(s): . . . . The Joe Louis Story
The Mills Brothers . . . . **Brunswick 03464**
Eve Boswell . . . . **Parlophone R 3455**
The Mills Brothers . . . . **London HAD 2192**
Frank Sinatra . . . . **Capitol EAP 2-581**
Brook Benton . . . . **Mercury MMC 14060**

I'LL BE GOOD BECAUSE OF YOU   **1931**
Ray Noble / Alan Murray
Chappell & Co. Ltd . . . . UK
The New Mayfair Dance Orchestra . . . . **HMV B 5956**
Gracie Fields . . . . **HMV B 3600**

I'LL BE HOME   **May 1956**
Ferdinand Washington / Stan Lewis
Box & Cox (Publications) Ltd. . . . . USA
Pat Boone . . . . **London HAD 2024**

I'LL BE LOVING YOU (FOREVER)   **March 1990**
Maurice Starr
EMI Music . . . . USA
New Kids On The Block . . . . **CBS BLOCK 4**

I'LL BE SATISFIED   **November 1982**
Berry Gordy Jnr / Tyran Carlo
Planetary-Nom Music . . . . USA
Shakin' Stevens . . . . **Epic A 2846**
Jackie Wilson (1959) . . . . **Coral Q 72372**

I'LL BE SEEING YOU   **1944**
Irving Kahal / Sammy Fain
Francis, Day & Hunter Ltd. . . . . USA
Show(s): . . . . Right this Way
Film(s): . . . . I'll be Seeing You
Ambrose & his Orchestra, vocal Rita Marlowe . . . **Decca F 8440**
Bing Crosby . . . . **Brunswick LAT 8055**
Jo Stafford . . . . **Philips BBL 7290**
The Poni-Tails . . . . **HMV POP 663**
Dinah Shore . . . . **Capitol T 1422**

I'LL BE THERE   **June 1955**
Jerry Wayne
Lawrence Wright Music Co. Ltd. . . . . UK

Kathie Kay . . . . **Polygon P 1168**
Edna Savage . . . . **Parlophone R 4017**
Les Howard . . . . **Columbia DB 4391**

I'LL BE THERE   **April 1965**
Bobby Darin
Seventeen Savile Row Ltd . . . . USA
Gerry & The Pacemakers . . . . **Columbia DB 7504**

I'LL BE THERE   **January 1971**
Berry Gordy Jnr / Willie Hutch / Bob West / Hal Davis
Jobete Music (UK) Ltd. . . . . USA
The Jackson Five . . . . **Tamla Motown TMG 758**

I'LL BE TRUE TO YOU, YES I WILL   **March 1965**
Gerry Goffin / Russ Titleman
Screen Gems - Columbia Music . . . . USA
The Hollies . . . . **Parlophone R 5225**

I'LL BE WITH YOU IN APPLE BLOSSOM TIME   **1920**
Neville Fleeson / Albert Von Tilzer
Francis, Day & Hunter Ltd . . . . USA
Film(s): . . . . Buck Privates
The Andrews Sisters . . . . **Brunswick LA 8728**
Rosemary June . . . . **Pye N 25005**
The Andrews Sisters . . . . **Capitol LCT 6132**
Eydie Gormé . . . . **HMV CLP 1404**
The Andrews Sisters appeared in *Buck Privates*.

I'LL BE YOUR BABY TONIGHT   **November 1990**
Bob Dylan
B. Feldman & Co. Music . . . . USA
Robert Palmer & UB40 . . . . **EMI EM 167**

I'LL BE YOUR SWEETHEART   **1899**
Harry Dacre
B. Feldman & Co. Ltd. . . . . UK
Film(s): . . . . I'll Be Your Sweetheart
Marie Kendall . . . . **Decca F 5169**
Billy Cotton & his Band, vocal Allan Breeze
& Edna Kaye . . . . **Rex 10226**
June Marlow & Franklin Boyde . . . . **Columbia 33SX 1271**

I'LL BUILD A STAIRWAY TO PARADISE   **1923**
George Gershwin / Buddy De Sylva / Arthur Francis (Ira Gershwin)
Chappell & Co. Ltd . . . . USA
Show(s): . . . . George White's Scandals of 1922 / Stop Flirting
Film(s): . . . . Rhapsody in Blue / An American in Paris
Paul Whiteman & his Orchestra . . . . **HMV B 1518**
Billie Holiday . . . . **Columbia 33C 9023**
George Guetary . . . . **MGM EP 580**
Pat Boone . . . . **London HAD 2144**
Paul Whiteman appeared in *George White's Scandals Of 1922*.
George Guetary appeared in *An American In Paris*.

I'LL BUY THAT DREAM   **1946**
Herb Magidson / Allie Wrubel
Edwin H. Morris & Co. Ltd. . . . . USA
Film(s): . . . . Sing Your Way Home
Dick Haymes & Helen Forrest . . . . **Brunswick 03637**
Eve Boswell . . . . **Parlophone PMC 1038**
Nominated for an Academy Award 1945.

I'LL BUY YOU A STAR   **March 1958**
Arthur Schwartz / Dorothy Fields
Chappell & Co. Ltd . . . . USA
Show(s): . . . . A Tree Grows in Brooklyn
Ronnie Hilton . . . . **HMV 7EG 8375**
Dave King . . . . **Decca F 10973**

I'LL CAPTURE YOUR HEART   **1942**
Irving Berlin
Irving Berlin Ltd . . . . USA
Film(s): . . . . Holiday Inn
Bing Crosby & Fred Astaire . . . . **Brunswick Bing 7**
Bing Crosby & Fred Astaire appeared in *Holiday Inn*.

I'LL CLOSE MY EYES   **1946**
Billy Reid
World Wide Music Co. Ltd. . . . . UK
Film(s): . . . . Six Five Special
Dorothy Squires . . . . **Parlophone F 2102**
Sarah Vaughan . . . . **Mercury MMC 14011**
Dorothy Squires . . . . **Pye NPL 18015**

I'LL COME TO YOU

J.B. Boldi / Sonny Miller
No Publisher .... No Origin
Jan Zalski .... **Regal Zonophone MR 3678**
Mantovani & his Orchestra .... **Decca F 8265**
Adapted from 'Chanson Bohemienné' by J.B. Boldi.

I'LL COME WHEN YOU CALL   September 1955

Josephine Caryll / David Caryll
Michael Reine Music Co. Ltd. .... UK
Ruby Murray .... **Columbia SEG 7620**
Janie Marden .... **Decca F 10605**

I'LL DANCE AT YOUR WEDDING   March 1948

Herb Magidson / Ben Oakland
Edwin H. Morris & Co. Ltd. .... USA
Jeanie Leitt .... **Brunswick 03854**
Tony Martin .... **HMV B 9635**

I'LL FIND MY WAY HOME   January 1982

Jon Anderson / Vangelis
Warner Brothers Music .... UK
Jon & Vangelis .... **Polydor JV 1**

I'LL FIND YOU   April 1957

Tolchard Evans / Richard Mullan
Robbins Music Corporation Ltd. .... UK
Film(s): .... Sea Wife
David Whitfield .... **Decca LK 4242**
Ivor Novello Nomination.

I'LL FLY FOR YOU   September 1984

Gary Kemp
Reformation Music .... UK
Spandau Ballet .... **Chrysalis SPAN 4**

I'LL FOLLOW MY SECRET HEART   1934

Noel Coward
Chappell & Co. Ltd. .... UK
Show(s): .... Conversation Piece
Yvonne Printemps & Noel Coward ..... **HMV DLP 1050**
Anne Ziegler .... **HMV C 3636**
Hilde Gueden .... **Decca LK 4196**
Noel Coward .... **Philips BBL 7108**
Yvonne Printemps & Noel Coward appeared in the British production
of *Conversation Piece.*

I'LL FOLLOW YOU   1932

Fred Ahlert / Roy Turk
Campbell Connelly & Co. Ltd. .... USA
Ethel Merman .... **HMV B 4348**
Paul Whiteman & his Orchestra ..... **HMV B 6275**
Bing Crosby .... **Columbia DB 2019**
Al Bowlly .... **Decca F 3304**

I'LL GET BY   1929

Roy Turk / Fred Ahlert
Francis, Day & Hunter Ltd .... USA
Film(s):A Guy Named Joe / Follow the Boys / Puttin' on the Ritz / You
Were Meant for Me / I'll Get By' a Star is Born / Both Ends of the
Candle
The Ipana Troubadours, vocal Bing Crosby ... **Columbia 5391**
Ruth Etting .... **Columbia DB 5446**
The Ink Spots (1944) .... **Brunswick LA 8590**
Judy Garland .... **Philips BBL 7007**
Jack Payne & his Orchestra ..... **HMV CLP 1160**
Gogi Grant .... **RCA RD 27054**
Shirley Bassey (1961) .... **Columbia DB 4737**
Judy Garland appeared in *A Star Is Born.*
Gogi Grant dubbed the singing voice of Ann Blyth who appeared in
the film *Both Ends of the Candle.*

I'LL KEEP THE LOVELIGHT BURNING   April 1949

Bennie Benjamin / George Weiss
Campbell Connelly & Co. Ltd .... USA
Vera Lynn .... **Decca F 9127**
Patti Page .... **Oriole CB 1251**
Dick Haymes .... **Brunswick 04275**
Dick Haymes .... **Brunswick 04275**

I'LL KEEP YOU SATISFIED   December 1963

John Lennon / Paul McCartney
Northern Songs Ltd .... UK
Billy J. Kramer .... **Parlophone R 5073**

I'LL MAKE A MAN OF YOU   1914

Herman Finck / Arthur Wimperis
Francis, Day & Hunter Ltd. .... UK
Show(s): .... The Passing Show
Gwendoline Brogden .... **HMV B 481**

I'LL MAKE UP FOR EVERYTHING   1947

Ross Parker
Macmelodies Ltd. .... UK
Steve Conway .... **Columbia FB 3344**
The Ink Spots .... **Brunswick 03840**

I'LL MEET YOU AT MIDNIGHT   October 1976

Mike Chapman / Nicky Chinn
Rak Music Ltd .... UK
Smokie .... **Rak 241**

I'LL NEVER BE THE SAME   1932

Gus Kahn / Matt Maineck / Frank Signoelli
Keith Prowse Music Publishing Co. Ltd. .... USA
Greta Keller .... **Decca F 3184**
Nat 'King' Cole .... **Capitol LC 6593**
Teddi King .... **Vogue LVA 9096**
Jeri Southern .... **Columbia 33SX 1134**

I'LL NEVER FALL IN LOVE AGAIN   September 1967

Jimmy Currie / Lonnie Donegan
Tyler Music Ltd. .... UK
Tom Jones .... **Decca F 12639**

I'LL NEVER FALL IN LOVE AGAIN   October 1969

Burt Bacharach / Hal David
Edwin H. Morris & Co. Ltd. .... USA
Show(s): .... Promises Promises
Jill O'Hara & Jerry Orbach .. **United Artists UAS 9902**
Betty Buckley & Anthony Roberts .. **United Artists UAS 29075**
Bobbie Gentry .... **Capitol CL 15606**
Jill O'Hara & Jerry Orbach appeared in the American production of
Promises Promises.
Betty Buckley & Anthony Roberts appeared in the British production
of *Promises Promises.*

I'LL NEVER FIND ANOTHER YOU   February 1965

Tom Springfield
Springfield Music Ltd .... UK
The Seekers .... **Columbia DB 7431**
Ivor Novello Award.

I'LL NEVER GET OVER YOU   September 1963

Gordon Mills
Leeds Music Ltd .... UK
Johnny Kidd .... **HMV POP 1173**
The Viscounts .... **Pye 7N 15536**

I'LL NEVER LET A DAY PASS BY   1941

Victor Schertzinger / Frank Loesser
Victoria Music Co. Ltd .... USA
Film(s): .... Kiss The Boys Goodbye
Tommy Dorsey & his Orchestra,
vocal Frank Sinatra .... **HMV BD 5712**
The R.A.F. Dance Orchestra .... **Decca F 7967**

I'LL NEVER SAY "NEVER AGAIN" AGAIN   1935

Harry Woods
Francis, Day & Hunter Ltd .... USA
The Dorsey Brothers Orchestra .. **Brunswick RL 256**
Ambrose & his Orchestra,
vocal Connee Boswell .... **Brunswick 02046**
Lita Roza .... **Nixa NPL 18020**
The Four Aces .... **Brunswick LAT 8299**
Dinah Shore .... **RCA 1054**

I'LL NEVER SMILE AGAIN   1940

Ruth Lowe
Campbell Connelly & Co. Ltd .... USA
Film(s): .... Gay City
Tony Martin .... **Decca F 7610**
Tommy Dorsey & his Orchestra,
vocal Frank Sinatra .... **RCA RCX 1060**
Frank Sinatra .... **Capitol EAP 1-1221**
Patti Page .... **Mercury MPL 6521**
The Platters .... **Mercury MMC 14014**
Tommy Dorsey & his Orchestra appeared in *Gay City.*

I'LL NEVER STOP LOVING YOU   October 1955
Sammy Cahn / Nicholas Brodszky
Robbins Music Corporation Ltd. . . . . USA
Film(s): . . . . Love Me or Leave Me
Doris Day . . . . **Philips BBL 7047**
Doris Day appeared in *Love Me or Leave Me*.
Nominated for an Academy Award 1955.

I'LL PICK A ROSE FOR MY ROSE   February 1969
Jimmy Dean / William Witherspoon / Marv Johnson
Jobete Music (UK) Ltd. . . . . USA
Marv Johnson . . . . **Tamla Motown TMG 680**

I'LL PRAY FOR YOU   1940
Roy King / Stanley Hill
Noel Gay Music Co. Ltd . . . . UK
Vera Lynn . . . . **Decca F 7330**

I'LL PUT YOU TOGETHER AGAIN   January 1979
Don Black / Geoff Stevens
Dick James Music Ltd. . . . . UK
Hot Chocolate . . . . **Rak 286**

I'LL REMEMBER APRIL   1944
Don Raye / Gene De Paul / Patricia Johnston
Leeds Music Ltd. . . . . USA
Film(s):Ride 'Em Cowboy / I'll Remember April / Strictly in the Groove
Kitty Carlisle . . . . **Brunswick 03537**
Carmen McRae . . . . **Brunswick LAT 8104**
June Christy . . . . **Capitol T 1006**
Shirley Bassey . . . . **Columbia 33SX 1178**

I'LL SAY FOREVER MY LOVE   August 1970
James Dean / William Witherspoon / Stephen Bowden
Jobete Music (UK) Ltd. . . . . USA
Jimmy Ruffin . . . . **Tamla Motown TMG 740**

I'LL SAY SHE DOES   1919
Gus Kahn / Al Jolson / Buddy De Sylva
B. Feldman & Co. Ltd. . . . . USA
Show(s): . . . . Sinbad
Maurice Chevalier . . . . **MGM C 813**

I'LL SEE YOU AGAIN   1929
Noel Coward
Chappell & Co. Ltd . . . . UK
Show(s): . . . . Bitter Sweet
Film(s): . . . . Bitter Sweet
Peggy Wood & George Metaxa . . . . **HMV C 1746**
Evelyn Laye . . . . **HMV DB 1870**
Noel Coward . . . . **HMV CLP 1050**
Nelson Eddy . . . . **Columbia 33S 1012**
Anne Ziegler & Webster Booth . . . . **HMV B 9120**
Vanessa Lee & Roberto Cardinali . . . . **HMV CLP 1242**
Peggy Wood & George Metaxa appeared in the British production of
Bitter Sweet.
Noel Coward & Evelyn Laye appeared in the American production of
Bitter Sweet.
Nelson Eddy appeared in the 1940 film of *Bitter Sweet*.
Theme song of Noel Coward.

I'LL SEE YOU IN C-U-B-A   1921
Irving Berlin
Chappell & Co. Ltd . . . . USA
Show(s): . . . . Greenwich Village Follies
Film(s): . . . . Blue Skies
The Palace Trio . . . . **HMV B 1161**
Bing Crosby & Trudy Irwin . . . . **Brunswick Bing 10**
Bing Crosby appeared in *Blue Skies*.

I'LL SEE YOU IN MY DREAMS   1925
Gus Kahn / Isham Jones
Francis, Day & Hunter Ltd. . . . . USA
Film(s):Follow the Boys / I'll See You in My Dreams / Pardon My
Rhythm.
The Corona Dance Orchestra . . . . **Regal G 8441**
Paul Whiteman & his Orchestra . . . . **HMV B 1982**
Jeanette MacDonald . . . . **Hollywood Soundstage HS 5012**
Doris Day . . . . **Philips BBL 7302**
The Pied Pipers . . . . **Capitol CL 13105**
Tony Martin . . . . **Mercury MPT 7005**
Pat Boone (1962) . . . . **London HL 9504**
Jeanette MacDonald appeared in *Follow the Boys*.
Doris Day appeared in *I'll See You in My Dreams*.

Theme song of Tony Martin.

I'LL SING YOU A THOUSAND LOVE SONGS   1937
Al Dubin / Harry Warren
B. Feldman & Co. Ltd . . . . USA
Film(s): . . . . Cain and Mabel
Russ Morgan & his Orchestra . . . . **Vocalion 516**
Les Allen . . . . **Columbia FB 1584**
Arthur Tracey (The Street Singer) . . . . **Decca F 6235**

I'LL STOP AT NOTHING   March 1965
Chris Andrews
Glissando Music Ltd . . . . UK
Sandie Shaw . . . . **Pye 7N 16783**

I'LL STRING ALONG WITH YOU   1934
Al Dubin / Harry Warren
B. Feldman & Co. Ltd . . . . USA
Film(s): . . . . Twenty Million Sweethearts / My Dream is Yours
Dick Powell . . . . **Decca F 5106**
The Four Aces . . . . **Brunswick LAT 8299**
Brook Benton . . . . **Mercury MMC 14015**
Doris Day & Buddy Clark (1949) . . . . **Capitol DB 2584**
Jo Stafford & Gordon MacRae (1950) . . . . **Capitol CL 13258**
Dick Powell . . . . **RCA ZL 70136**
Dick Powell appeared in *Twenty Million Sweethearts*.
Doris Day appeared in *My Dream is Yours*.

I'LL TAKE ROMANCE   1938
Ben Oakland / Oscar Hammerstein II
Chappell & Co. Ltd. . . . . USA
Film(s): . . . . I'll Take Romance / The Eddy Duchin Story
Betty Driver . . . . **HMV BD 545**
Jeri Southern . . . . **Brunswick LAT 8100**
Marion Ryan . . . . **Pye NPL 18030**

I'LL TAKE YOU HOME AGAIN KATHLEEN   1914
Thomas Westendorf
 . . . . USA
William Thomas . . . . **Regal G 6614**
Bing Crosby (1946) . . . . **Brunswick LA 8278**
John McHugh . . . . **Columbia DX 1864**
Brendan O'Dowda . . . . **Columbia 33SX 1283**
Slim Whitman (1957) . . . . **London HLP 8403**

I'LL WALK ALONE   1944
Sammy Cahn / Jule Styne
Edwin H.Morris & Co. Ltd. . . . . USA
Film(s): . . . . Follow the Boys / With a Song in My Heart
Ambrose & his Orchestra, vocal Anne Shelton . . **Decca F 8430**
Mary Martin . . . . **Brunswick LA 8638**
Jo Stafford . . . . **Philips BBL 7290**
Jane Froman . . . . **Capitol LC 6554**
Pat Boone . . . . **London GAD 2127**
Nominated for an Academy Award 1944.
Jane Froman dubbed the singing voice of Susan Hayward who
appeared in the film *With a Song in My Heart*.

I'LL WALK BESIDE YOU   1939
Alan Murray / Edward Lockton
Chappell & Co. Ltd. . . . . UK
John McCormack . . . . **HMV BLP 1084**
Joseph Locke . . . . **Columbia DB 2980**
Harry Secombe . . . . **Philips BBL 7349**

I'M A BELIEVER   February 1967
Neil Diamond
Screen Gems Music Ltd. . . . . USA
The Monkees . . . . **RCA 1560**
Robert Wyatt . . . . **Virgin VS 114**

I'M A BOY   October 1966
Peter Townshend
Fabulous Music Ltd. . . . . UK
The Who . . . . **Reaction 591004**

I'M A DING DONG DADDY (From Dumas)   1929
Phil Baxter
Francis, Day & Hunter Ltd . . . . USA
Film(s): . . . . Hollywood Hotel
Louis Armstrong & his Orchestra . . . . **Philips BBL 7218**
Phil Harris . . . . **HMV B 9918**
George Melly . . . . **Decca F 10763**
Benny Goodman Quartet . . . . **HMV B 8734**

Benny Goodman appeared in *Hollywood Hotel*.

I'M A DREAMER, AREN'T WE ALL 1930
Buddy De Sylva / Lew Brown / Ray Henderson
Campbell Connelly & Co. Ltd .... USA
Film(s):Sunny Side Up / Holy Terror / The Best Things in Life are Free
The High Hatters .... **HMV B 5745**
Gracie Fields .... **HMV B 3259**
Lucille Mapp .... **Columbia DB 4168**
Carmen McRae .... **Brunswick LAT 8133**

I'M A LITTLE BLACKBIRD LOOKING FOR
A BLUEBIRD 1925
George Meyer / Arthur Johnston / Roy Turk / Grant Clarke
Francis, Day & Hunter Ltd. .... USA
Show(s):.............................Dixie to Broadway
Clarence Williams Blue Five, vocal Eva Taylor Fontana TFL 5087
Gwen Farrar .... **Vocalion X 9888**
Lucille Mapp .... **Columbia SEG 7726**

I'M A MAN March 1967
Steve Winwood / Jimmy Miller
Island Music Ltd. .... UK
The Spencer Davis Group .... **Fontana TF 785**
Chicago (1970) .... **CBS 4715**

I'M A ONE MAN GIRL 1929
Leo Robin / Clifford Grey / Richard Myers
Chappell & Co. Ltd .... USA
Show(s):.................................Mister Cinders
Binnie Hale & Bobby Howes .... **Columbia 5334**
Binnie Hale & Bobby Howes appeared in *Mister Cinders*.

(I'M A) ROAD RUNNER May 1969
Eddie Holland / Brian Holland / Lamont Dozier
Jobete Music (UK) Ltd. .... USA
Film(s): .... Cooley High
Junior Walker & The All Stars .... **Tamla Motown TMG 691**
Junior Walker & The All Stars appeared in *Cooley High*.

I'M A TIGER December 1968
Marty Wilde / Ronnie Scott
Valley Music .... UK
Lulu .... **Columbia DB 8500**

I'M A WONDERFUL THING (Baby) June 1982
August Darnell / Peter Schott
Island Music .... USA
Kid Creole & The Coconuts .... **Island WIP 6756**

I'M AFRAID TO COME HOME IN THE DARK 1907
Egbert Van Alstyne / Harry Williams
Francis, Day & Hunter .... USA
Ella Retford .... **Jumbo 151**
Jack Hylton & his Orchestra .... **HMV C 2307**
Primo Scala's Accordion Band, vocal Sam Browne .. **Rex 9707**

I'M AFRAID TO LOVE YOU 1947
Harry Stride / Pat McCarthy / Bert Douglas
Leeds Music Ltd. .... USA
The Mills Brothers .... **Brunswick 03704**
The Radio Revellers .... **Columbia FB 3346**
The Mills Brothers .... **London HAD 2319**

I'M ALIVE July 1965
Clint Ballard
Shapiro-Bernstein & Co. Ltd .... USA
The Hollies .... **Parlophone R 5287**

I'M ALONE BECAUSE I LOVE YOU 1931
Joe Young
B. Feldman & Co. Ltd .... USA
Bud & Joe Billings .... **Zonophone 5834**
Glen Mason .... **Parlophone R 4390**
Tab Hunter .... **London RED 1134**

I'M ALWAYS CHASING RAINBOWS 1919
Harry Carroll / Joseph McCarthy
Francis, Day & Hunter Ltd. .... USA
Show(s):...................................... Oh Look
Film(s): .... The Ziegfeld Girl / The Dolly Sisters
Al Jolson .... **Brunswick LAT 8220**
Judy Garland .... **Brunswick 03128**
Perry Como (1946) .... **HMV BD 1130**

Judy Garland appeared in *The Ziegfeld Girl*.
Adapted from 'Fantaisie Impromptu' in C sharp minor opus 66 by Frederic Chopin (1810 - 1849).

(I'M ALWAYS TOUCHED BY YOUR) PRESENCE
DEAR May 1978
Gary Valentine
EMI Music Ltd .... USA
Blondie .... **Chrysalis CHS 2217**

I'M AN OLD COW-HAND 1936
Johnny Mercer
Sun Music Publishing Co. Ltd .... USA
Film(s): .... Rhythm on the Range / King of the Cowboys
Bing Crosby .... **Brunswick Bing 2**
The Sons of The Pioneers .... **Panachord 25873**
Ray Conniff & his Orchestra & chorus .... **Philips BBE 12226**
Bing Crosby appeared in *Rhythm on the Range*.
The Sons of the Pioneers appeared in *King of the Cowboys*.

I'M BEGINNING TO SEE THE LIGHT 1945
Duke Ellington / Harry James / Johnny Hodges & Don George
Campbell Connelly & Co. Ltd. .... USA
Film(s): .... The Man From Oklahoma
Duke Ellington & his Orchestra,
vocal Joya Sherrill .... **RCA RCX 1055**
Ella Fitzgerald & The Ink Spots ...... **Brunswick 03584**
Peggy Lee .... **Capitol T 1049**

I'M COMING HOME January 1968
Les Reed / Barry Mason
Donna Music Ltd. .... UK
Tom Jones .... **Decca F 12693**

I'M COMING OUT December 1980
Bernard Edwards / Nile Rodgers
Warner Brothers Music Ltd .... USA
Diana Ross .... **Motown TMG 1210**

I'M COMING VIRGINIA 1927
Donald Heywood / Will Marion Cook
Francis, Day & Hunter Ltd. .... USA
Show(s):.. Africana
Film(s): .... The Benny Goodman Show
Frankie Trumbauer & his Orchestra with Bix Beiderbecke
(Trumpet) .... **Philips BBL 7014**
Maxine Sullivan .... **Columbia DB 5045**
Bing Crosby .... **RCA RD 27075**
Tony Bennett .... **Philips BBL 7495**

I'M CONFESSIN' 1931
Doc Dougherty / Al Neiburg / Ellis Reynolds
Francis, Day & Hunter Ltd .... USA
Louis Armstrong .... **Parlophone R 909**
Ella Fitzgerald & The Song Spinners ... **Brunswick 03566**
Perry Como (1946) .... **Camden CDN 110**
Tommy Sands .... **Capitol T 1123**
Frank Ifield (1963) .... **Columbia DB 7062**

I'M CRAZY 'BOUT MY BABY 1932
Thomas Waller / Alexander Hill
Lawrence Wright Music Co. Ltd. .... USA
'Fats' Waller (Piano Solo) .... **Parlophone R 1197**
'Fats' Waller & his Rhythm .... **HMV BD 5120**
Louis Armstrong & his Orchestra .... **Philips BBL 7064**
Ottie Patterson .... **Columbia DB 4760**

I'M CRAZY OVER YOU 1929
Al Sherman / Al Lewis
Campbell Connelly & Co. Ltd .... USA
Jack Smith .... **HMV B 2962**
The Trix Sisters .... **Columbia 5236**

I'M CRYING October 1964
Alan Price / Eric Burdon
Ivy Music Ltd .... UK
The Animals .... **Columbia DB 7354**

I'M DOING FINE NOW September 1973
Thom Bell / Sherman Marshall
Gamble-Huff Music .... USA
New York City .... **RCA 2351**

I'M EVERY WOMAN January 1979
Nicholas Ashford / Valerie Simpson

Warner Brothers Music Ltd. . . . . USA
Chaka Khan . . . . **Warner Brothers K 17269**
Chaka Khan (1989) . . . . **Warner Brothers W 2963**

I'M FALLING   May 1984
Robert Hodgems / Ken McClusky
ATV Music . . . . UK
The Bluebells . . . . **London LON 45**

I'M FALLING IN LOVE WITH SOMEONE   1910
Victor Herbert / Rida Johnson Young
B. Feldman & Co. Ltd. . . . . USA
Show(s): . . . . Naughty Marietta
Film(s): . . . . Naughty Marietta / The Great Victor Herbert
Nelson Eddy . . . . **HMV DA 1418**
Nelson Eddy . . . . **Philips NBE 11116**
Paul Britten & his Orchestra . . . . **MGM C 779**
Nelson Eddy appeared in the film *Naughty Marietta*.

I'M FEELING LIKE A MILLION   1937
Arthur Freed / Nacio Herb Brown
Robbins Music Corporation Ltd. . . . . USA
Film(s): . . . . Broadway Melody of 1938
Hildegarde . . . . **Columbia FB 1768**
Nat Gonella & his Georgians,
vocal Nat Gonella . . . . **Parlophone F 904**
The Casa Loma Orchestra, vocal Pee Wee Hunt **Brunswick 02462**

I'M FOREVER BLOWING BUBBLES   1919
John Kellette / Jaan Kenbrovin
Francis, Day & Hunter Ltd . . . . USA
Show(s): . . . . The Passing Show of 1918
Film(s): . . . . On Moonlight Bay
The Original Dixieland Jazz Band . . . . **Columbia 33S 1133**
William Thomas . . . . **Regal G 7481**
Doris Day & Jack Smith . . . . **Columbia DB 3487**
The Merry Macs . . . . **Capitol T 850**
Doris Day appeared in *Moonlight Bay*.

I'M FREE   September 1973
Peter Townshend
Track Music Ltd. . . . . UK
Film(s): . . . . Tommy
Roger Daltrey & The London Symphony Orchestra . . . **Ode 66302**
Roger Daltrey appeared in *Tommy*.

I'M FREE   August 1990
Mick Jagger / Keith Richards
Westminster Music . . . . UK
Soup Dragons . . . . **Big Life RTV 9**

I'M GETTING SENTIMENTAL OVER YOU   1933
George Bassman / Ned Washington
Campbell Connelly & Co. Ltd. USA
Film(s): . . . . Du Barry Was a Lady
Jack Jackson & his Orchestra,
vocal Denny Dennis . . . . **HMV B 6392**
Frances Langford . . . . **Brunswick 02537**
Tommy Dorsey & his Orchestra (1938) . . . . . . **RCA RCX 1023**
Patti Page . . . . **Mercury MPT 7531**
The Ink Spots . . . . **Brunswick LA 8590**
The Four Freshmen . . . . **Capitol T 1485**
Tommy Dorsey & his Orchestra appeared in *Du Barry Was a Lady*.
Theme song of Tommy Dorsey.

I'M GETTING TIRED SO I CAN SLEEP   1943
Irving Berlin
Irving Berlin Ltd . . . . USA
Show(s): . . . . This is the Army
Film(s): . . . . This is the Army
Private Stuart Churchill . . . . **Brunswick 03490**
Kenny Baker . . . . **Brunswick 03472**
Private Stuart Churchill appeared in both the American and British
productions of *This is the Army*.

I'M GLAD THERE IS YOU   November 1952
Paul Madeira / Jimmy Dorsey
Edwin H. Morris & Co. Ltd . . . . USA
Peggy Lee . . . . **Brunswick LAT 8356**
Frank Sinatra . . . . **Philips BBR 8040**
June Christy . . . . **Capitol T 1076**

I'M GOIN' SHOPPIN' WITH YOU   1936
Al Dubin / Harry Warren

B. Feldman Co. Ltd . . . . USA
Film(s): . . . . Gold Diggers of 1935
Dick Powell . . . . **Decca F 5548**
The Dorsey Brothers Orchestra,
vocal Bob Crosby . . . . **Brunswick RL 246**
Dick Powell appeared in *Gold Diggers of 1935*.

I'M GOING BACK TO HIMAZAS   1927
Fred Austin
Lawrence Wright Music Co. Ltd. . . . . UK
Harry Gordon . . . . **Beltona 1295**
John Butler with The George Mitchell Minstrels . . **HMV CLP 3579**

I'M GOING BACK TO OLD NEBRASKA   1928
Harry Revel / Noble Sissle
Campbell Connelly & Co. Ltd. USA
Noble Sissle with Orchestra,
conducted by Harry Revel . . . . **Parlophone R 3522**
Melville Gideon . . . . **Parlophone B 2815**
Jack Hylton & his Orchestra . . . . **Parlophone B 5444**
The George Mitchell Minstrels . . . . **Parlophone CLP 1599**

I'M GOING SOUTH   1924
Abner Silver / Harry Woods
B. Feldman & Co. Ltd . . . . USA
Show(s): . . . . Bombo
Paul Specht & his Orchestra . . . . **Columbia 3419**

I'M GOING TO SEE YOU TODAY   1942
Joyce Grenfell / Richard Addinsell
Keith Prowse Music Publishing Co. Ltd . . . . UK
Joyce Grenfell accompanied by
Richard Addinsell (piano) . . . . **HMV B 9295**
Hildegarde . . . . **Brunswick 04251**
Joyce Grenfell . . . . **HMV CLP 1810**

I'M GONNA BE   September 1988
Charles Reid / Craig Reid
Warner Chappell Music . . . . UK
The Proclaimers . . . . **Chrysalis CLAIM 2**

I'M GONNA BE STRONG   December 1964
Barry Mann / Cynthia Weill
Screen Gems - Columbia Music . . . . USA
Frankie Laine . . . . **CBS AAG 167**
Gene Pitney . . . . **Stateside SS 358**

I'M GONNA CHARLESTON BACK TO CHARLESTON 1925
Roy Turk / Lou Handman
Francis, Day & Hunter Ltd. . . . . USA
The Coon-Sanders Original Night Hawk Orchestra . . **HMV B 2122**
The Firehouse Five Plus Two . . . . **Vogue LAG 12087**
Dorothy Provine . . . . **Warner Brothers WM 4053**

I'M GONNA GET LIT UP   1943
Hubert Gregg
Peter Maurice Music Co. Ltd . . . . UK
Joe Loss & his Orchestra . . . . **HMV BD 5800**
Vanessa Lee . . . . **Oriole MG 20015**

I'M GONNA GET ME A GUN   May 1967
Cat Stevens
Cat Music . . . . UK
Cat Stevens . . . . **Deram DM 118**

I'M GONNA KNOCK ON YOUR DOOR   April 1974
Aaron Schroeder / Sid Wayne
Aberbach (London) Ltd. . . . . USA
Jimmy Osmond . . . . **MGM 2006389**
The Isley Brothers . . . . **RCA 1172**

I'M GONNA LIVE TILL I DIE   May 1952
Al Hoffman / Mann Curtis / Walter Kent
Campbell Connelly & Co. Ltd . . . . USA
Film(s): . . . . Sunny Side of the Street / This Could be the Night
Frankie Laine . . . . **Oriole CB 1086**
Sammy Davis . . . . **Reprise R 2003**
Julie Wilson . . . . **MGM C 761**
Frankie Laine appeared in *Sunny Side of The Street*.
Julie Wilson appeared in *This Could Be The Night*.

I'M GONNA LOCK MY HEART AND THROW AWAY THE
KEY   1938
Jimmy Eaton / Terry Shand
Keith Prowse Music Publishing Co. Ltd. . . . . USA

Jay Wilbur & his Orchestra, vocal Sam Costa .... **Rex 9385**
Greta Keller .... **Decca F 6821**

I'M GONNA LOVE THAT GUY 1945
Frances Ash
Lawrence Wright Music Co. Ltd. .... UK
Adelaide Hall .... **Decca F 8517**
Paula Green .... **Columbia FB 3099**

I'M GONNA MAKE YOU LOVE ME March 1969
Kenny Gamble / Jerry Ross
Jobete Music (UK) Ltd. .... USA
**Diana Ross, The Supremes &
The Temptations** .... **Tamla Motown TMG 685**

I'M GONNA MAKE YOU MINE November 1969
Tony Romeo
Carlin Music Corporation .... USA
Lou Christie .... **Buddah BDS 431**

I'M GONNA MOVE TO THE OUTSKIRTS OF TOWN 1944
William Weldon / Roy Jacobs / Andy Razaf
Leeds Music Ltd. .... USA
Jimmy Lunceford & his Orchestra ...... **Brunswick 03361**
Johnnie Ray .... **Philips BBL 7148**
Margaret Whiting .... **London HAD 2109**

I'M GONNA RING THE BELL TONIGHT July 1953
Vernon Duke / Sammy Cahn
Harms-Connelly Ltd .... USA
Film(s): .... April in Paris
Doris Day .... **Columbia SCM 5045**
Doris Day appeared in *April in Paris.*

I'M GONNA RUN AWAY FROM YOU July 1971
Bert Berns
Shapiro-Bernstein & Co. Ltd .... USA
Tammi Lynn .... **Mojo 2092001**

I'M GONNA SIT RIGHT DOWN AND WRITE MYSELF A LETTER 1935
Joe Young / Fred Ahlert
Sterling Music Publishing Co. Ltd .... USA
'Fats' Waller & his Rhythm .... **RCA RCX 1053**
Bing Crosby .... **RCA RD 27032**
Billy Williams (1957) .... **Coral Q 72266**
Gary Miller .... **Pye NPL 18059**

I'M GONNA TEAR YOUR PLAYHOUSE DOWN October 1984
Earl Randle
Burlington Music .... USA
Paul Young .... **CBS A 4786**

I'M GONNA WASH MY HANDS OF YOU 1935
Franz Vienna / Eddio Pola
Peter Maurice Music Co. Ltd .... UK
Ambrose & his Orchestra .... **Decca F 5318**
Nat Gonella & his Georgians .... **Parlophone F 116**

I'M GONNNA WASH THAT MAN RIGHT OUT OF MY HAIR November 1951
Richard Rodgers / Oscar Hammerstein II
Williamson Music Ltd .... USA
Show(s): .... South Pacific
Film(s): .... South Pacific
Mary Martin .... **Philips BBL 7157**
Mitzi Gaynor .... **RCA RB 16065**
Mary Martin appeared in both the American and British productions
of *South Pacific.*
Mitzi Gaynor appeared in the film *South Pacific.*

I'M HAPPY WHEN I'M HIKING 1931
*Ralph Butler / Raymond Wallace / Reginald Connelly / James
Campbell*
Campbell Connelly & Co. Ltd. .... UK
The Pearly Kings .... **Parlophone R 951**
**The BBC Dance Orchestra,
conducted by Jack Payne** .... **Columbia CB 299**
The Bowman-Hyde Singers .... **Parlophone PMC 1155**

I'M HENERY THE EIGHTH 1910
R.P. Weston / Fred Murray
Francis, Day & Hunter Ltd. .... UK
Harry Champion .... **Columbia 1621**
Stanley Holloway .... **Philips BBL 7237**

I'M HUMMING, I'M WHISTLING, I'M SINGING 1934
Mack Gordon / Harry Revel
Victoria Music Co. Ltd .... USA
Film(s): .... She Loves Me Not
Bing Crosby .... **Columbia DB 2068**
Harry Roy & his Orchestra .... **Parlophone R 1918**
Bing Crosby appeared in *She Loves Me Not.*

I'M IN A DANCING MOOD 1936
Maurice Sigler / Al Goodhart / Al Hoffman
Cinephonic Music Co. Ltd .... UK
Show(s): .... This'll Make You Whistle
Show(s): .... This'll Make You Whistle
Jack Buchanan & Elsie Randolph .... **Brunswick 02348**
Anne Shelton .... **Philips BBL 7291**
Jack Buchanan & Elsie Randolph appeared in both the show and the
film of *This'll Make You Whistle.*

I'M IN FAVOUR OF FRIENDSHIP May 1955
Bob Hilliard / Dave Mann
Campbell Connelly & Co. Ltd. .... USA
Diana Decker .... **Columbia SEG 7593**
The Five Smith Brothers .... **Decca F 10527**

I'M IN LOVE AGAIN 1927
Cole Porter
Chappell & Co. Ltd. .... USA
Show(s): . The Greenwich Village Follies of 1924 / Up With the Lark
Sam Lanin's Troubadours .... **Imperial 1803**
The Revellers .... **HMV B 2518**
April Stevens .... **HMV B 10091**
Petula Clark .... **Pye NPL 18039**

I'M IN LOVE WITH A WONDERFUL GUY December 1951
Richard Rodgers / Oscar Hammerstein II
Williamson Music Ltd .... USA
Show(s): .... South Pacific
Film(s): .... South Pacific
Mary Martin .... **Philips BBL 7157**

I'M IN LOVE WITH TWO SWEETHEARTS 1945
Elton Box / Desmond Cox / Lewis Ilda
Dash Music Ltd. .... UK
Issy Bonn .... **Decca F 8577**
Russ Hamilton .... **Oriole MG 20031**

I'M IN LOVE WITH VIENNA 1939
Johann Strauss / Oscar Hammerstein II
Chappell & Co. Ltd. .... USA
Film(s): .... The Great Waltz
Alfred Piccaver .... **Brunswick 02750**
Richard Tauber .... **Parlophone PMB 1007**
Harry Secombe .... **Philips BBR 8099**

I'M IN THE MARKET FOR YOU 1930
Joseph McCarthy / James Hanley
Keith Prowse Music Publishing Co. Ltd .... USA
Film(s): .... High Society Blues
Frankie Trumbauer & his Orchestra .... **Parlophone R 778**
Ambrose & his Orchestra, vocal Sam Browne .... **HMV B 5824**
Jim Dale .... **Parlophone PMD 1055**
Anne Richards .... **Capitol T 1087**

I'M IN THE MOOD FOR DANCING February 1980
Ben Findon / Mike Myers / Robert Puzey
Black Sheep Music .... UK
The Nolan Sisters .... **Epic EPC 8068**

I'M IN THE MOOD FOR LOVE 1935
Dorothy Fields / Jimmy McHugh
Robbins Music Corporation Ltd .... USA
Film(s): .... Every Night at Eight / Between Two Women
Frances Langford .... **Brunswick 02085**
Julie London .... **London HAU 2005**
Dennis Lotis .... **Parlophone PMC 1101**
Frances Langford appeared in *Every Night At Eight.*

I'M INTO SOMETHING GOOD October 1964
Gerry Goffin / Carole King
Aldon Music Ltd. .... USA
Herman's Hermits .... **Columbia DB 7338**
Earl Jean .... **Colpix PX 729**
Joy Marshall .... **Decca LK 4678**

I'M JUST A BABY   August 1962
Jerry Lordan
Francis, Day & Hunter Ltd . . . . UK
Louise Cordet . . . . **Decca F 11476**

I'M JUST A VAGABOND LOVER   1929
Rudy Vallee / Leon Zimmerman
Francis, Day & Hunter Ltd . . . . USA
Film(s): . . . . . . The Vagabond Lover / Glorifying the American Girl
Rudy Vallee . . . . **HMV C 2802**
Eddie Fisher . . . . **HMV CLP 1040**
Rudy Vallee . . . . **Capitol LC 6698**
Rudy Vallee appeared in both *The Vagabond Lover* and *Glorifying The American Girl*.

I'M JUST WILD ABOUT HARRY   1922
Eubie Blake / Noble Sissle
B. Feldman & Co. Ltd . . . . USA
Film(s):Babes in Arms / Rose of Washington Square / Broadway / Is Everybody Happy / Jolson Sings Again / Greenwich Village
Paul Whiteman & his Orchestra . . . . **HMV B 1407**
Eubie Blake & his Shuffle Along Orchestra . . **HMV B 1297**
Judy Garland . . . . **Brunswick 02969**
Al Jolson . . . . **Brunswick LA 8502**
Noble Sissle Orchestra, (piano: Eubie Blake) **Top Rank JKP 2008**
Dorothy Provine . . . . **Warner Brothers WM 4053**
Judy Garland appeared in *Babes in Arms*.

I'M KNEE DEEP IN DAISIES   1925
Joe Goodwin / Larry Shay / Paul Ash
Francis, Day & Hunter Ltd. . . . . USA
Jack Smith . . . . **HMV B 2192**
The Savoy Havana Band . . . . **HMV B 2054**

I'M LEAVING IT UP TO YOU   September 1974
Dewey Terry / Don Harris
A.T.V. Music Ltd. . . . . USA
Donny & Marie Osmond . . . . **MGM 2006446**
Dale & Grace . . . . **London HL 9807**
Sonny & Cher . . . . **Atlantic 587006**

I'M LOOKING FOR A GIRL NAMED MARY   1927
Sammy Stept
Lawrence Wright Music Co. Ltd. . . . . USA
The Savoy Orpheans . . . . **HMV B 5261**

I'M LOOKING OUT OF THE WINDOW   June 1962
John Jacob Niles
Chappell & Co. Ltd . . . . USA
Cliff Richard . . . . **Columbia DB 4828**

I'M LOOKING OVER A FOUR-LEAF CLOVER 1927
Mort Dixon / Harry Woods
Francis, Day & Hunter Ltd. . . . . USA
Film(s): . . . . Jazz Singer / Jolson Sings Again
Jack Hylton & his Orchestra . . . . **HMV B 5267**
Art Mooney & his Orchestra . . . . **MGM D 136**
The Merry Melody Makers (1948) . . . . . . **HMV BD 1203**
Russ Morgan & his Orchestra (1948) . . . . **Brunswick 03877**
Al Jolson . . . . **Brunswick LA 8502**
The Johnston Brothers . . . . **Decca F 10962**

I'M MAKING BELIEVE   1944
Mack Gordon / Jimmy Monaco
Bradbury Wood Ltd. . . . . USA
Film(s): . . . . Sweet and Lowdown
Ella Fitzgerald & the Ink Spots . . . . **Brunswick 03573**
Connee Boswell . . . . **Capitol CL 14236**
Nominated for an Academy Award 1944.

I'M MANDY, FLY ME   April 1976
Eric Stewart / Graham Gouldman / Lol Creme
St. Annes Music Ltd . . . . UK
Film(s): . . . . Sunburn
10 CC . . . . **Mercury 6008019**

I'M MY OWN GRANDPA   May 1948
Dwight Latam / Moe Jaffe
Leeds Music . . . . USA
Guy Lombardo & his Royal Canadians . . . . . **Brunswick 03878**
Phil Harris . . . . **HMV BD 1222**

I'M NOBODY'S BABY   1921
Lester Santley / Milton Ager / Benny Davis

Francis, Day & Hunter Ltd . . . . USA
Film(s): . . . . Andy Hardy Meets the Debutante
Judy Garland . . . . **Brunswick 03038**
Betty Hutton . . . . **Capitol CL 14131**
Connie Francis . . . . **MGM D 153**
Judy Garland appeared in *Andy Hardy Meets the Debutante*.

I'M NOT IN LOVE   July 1975
Graham Gouldman / Eric Stewart
St. Annes Music Ltd . . . . UK
10 CC . . . . **Mercury 6008014**
Ivor Novello Award.

I'M NOT SCARED   April 1988
Neil Tennant / Chris Lowe
Cage Music . . . . UK
Eighth Wonder . . . . **CBS SCARE 1**

I'M OLD FASHIONED   1943
Jerome Kern / Johnny Mercer
Chappell & Co. Ltd . . . . USA
Film(s): . . . . You Were Never Lovelier
Fred Astaire . . . . **Brunswick 03428**
Michael Holliday . . . . **Columbia 33S 1114**
Steve Lawrence . . . . **HMV CLP 1326**
Fred Astaire appeared in *You Were Never Lovelier*.

I'M ON A SEE-SAW   1934
Vivian Ellis / Desmond Carter
Chappell & Co. Ltd . . . . UK
Show(s): . . . . Jill Darling
Louise Brown & John Mills . . . . **HMV B 8279**
Jack Jackson & his Orchestra . . . . **HMV B 6565**
Cleo Laine . . . . **Esquire 15-007**
Louise Brown & John Mills appeared in *Jill Darling*.

I'M ON FIRE   September 1975
Tony Eyers
Intersong Music . . . . UK
5000 Volts . . . . **Philips 6006464**

I'M ON FIRE   July 1985
Bruce Springsteen
Zomba Music . . . . USA
Bruce Springsteen . . . . **CBS A 6342**

I'M POPEYE THE SAILOR MAN   1935
Sammy Lerner
Famous Music . . . . USA
Billy Costello . . . . **Regal Zonophone MR 2897**
Frank Luther . . . . **Decca F 5259**

I'M PRAYING TO SAINT CHRISTOPHER   March 1953
Albert Von Tilzer / Larry McPherson
Dash Music Ltd . . . . USA
Joyce Frazer . . . . **Columbia DB 3230**
Anne Shelton . . . . **Decca F 10061**
Toni Arden . . . . **Philips PB 148**

I'M PUTTING ALL MY EGGS IN ONE BASKET 1936
Irving Berlin
Irving Berlin Ltd . . . . USA
Film(s): . . . . Follow the Fleet
Fred Astaire . . . . **Columbia DB 1634**
Ginger Rogers . . . . **Decca F 5963**
Gordon MacRae . . . . **Brunswick LAT 8147**
Ella Fitzgerald & Louis Armstrong . . . . **HMV CLP 1147**
Fred Astaire & Ginger Rogers appeared in *Follow The Fleet*.

I'M RIDING FOR A FALL   1944
Arthur Schwartz / Frank Loesser
Sterling Music Publishing Co. Ltd . . . . USA
Film(s): . . . . Thank Your Lucky Stars
Phil Green & his Orchestra . . . . **Decca MW 204**

I'M SENDING A LETTER TO SANTA CLAUS   1939
Spencer Williams / Lanny Rogers
B. Feldman & Co. Ltd. . . . . USA
Phyllis Robins . . . . **Parlophone F 1602**
Vera Lynn . . . . **Decca F 8992**

I'M SHOOTING HIGH   1936
Ted Koehler / Jimmy McHugh
Francis, Day & Hunter Ltd . . . . USA

Film(s): . . . . King of Burlesque
Alice Faye . . . . **Rex 8778**
Carolyn Marsh . . . . **Columbia FB 1367**
Chris Connor . . . . **London LTZK 15142**
Alice Faye appeared in *King of Burlesque.*

I'M SHY, MARY ELLEN I'M SHY   1910
Charles Ridgewell / George Stevens
Francis, Day & Hunter Ltd . . . . UK
Jack Pleasants . . . . **Edison Bell Winner 2089**
David Kossoff . . . . **Oriole MG 20043**

I'M SITTING HIGH ON A HILLTOP   1935
Gus Kahn / Arthur Johnston
Robbins Music Corporation Ltd . . . . USA
Film(s): . . . . Thanks a Million
Dick Powell . . . . **Decca F 5823**
Edmund Hockridge . . . . **Pye NPL 18021**
Dick Powell appeared in *Thanks A Million.*

I'M SITTING ON TOP OF THE WORLD   1926
Sam M. Lewis / Joe Young / Ray Henderson
Francis, Day & Hunter Ltd . . . . USA
Film(s):The Singing Fool / The Jolson Story / I'll Cry Tomorrow / Love
Me or Leave Me
Al Jolson . . . . **Brunswick 3014**
Al Jolson . . . . **Brunswick LA 8509**
Les Paul & Mary Ford (1953) . . . . **Capitol T 1438**
Susan Hayward . . . . **MGM EP 555**
The King Brothers . . . . **Parlophone GEP 8651**
Al Jolson appeared in *The Singing Fool.*
Susan Hayward appeared in *I'll Cry Tomorrow.*

I'M SO ALL ALONE   1946
Paul Durand / Jean Casanova / Rose Noel / Joseph Gilbert
Peter Maurice Music Co. Ltd. . . . . France
Steve Conway . . . . **Columbia FB 3179**
Leslie Hutchinson (Hutch) . . . . **HMV BD 1122**

I'M SO EXCITED   November 1984
Anita Pointer / June Pointer / Ruth Pointer & Trevor Lawrence
Rondor Music . . . . USA
The Pointer Sisters . . . . **Planet RPS 108**

I'M SO RIGHT TONIGHT   March 1948
'By' Dunham / Terry Shand
Pickwick Music Ltd. . . . . USA
Phil Harris . . . . **HMV BD 1194**
Beth Douglas . . . . **Polydor P 1155**

I'M SORRY   August 1960
Ronnie Self / Dud Albritton
Peter Maurice Music Ltd . . . . USA
Brenda Lee . . . . **Brunswick LAT 8347**
Bobby Vee . . . . **London HAG 2320**

I'M SORRY I MADE YOU CRY   1918
N.J. Clesi / Theodore Morse
B. Feldman & Co. Ltd. . . . . USA
Film(s): . . . . . . Rose of Washington Square / Somebody Loves Me
Violet Loraine . . . . **HMV 03646**
Eddie Condon & his Orchestra . . . . **Odeon PO 66**
Frank Sinatra . . . . **Columbia DB 2330**
Connie Francis . . . . **MGM C 831**

I'M STEPPING OUT WITH A MEMORY TONIGHT   1940
Herb Magidson / Allie Wrubel
Sun Music Puiblishing Co. Ltd . . . . USA
Film(s): . . . . Footlight Parade
Al Bowlly with Jimmy Messene (guitar) . . . . **HMV BD 865**
Tony Martin . . . . **Decca F 7602**
Jeff Southern . . . . **Columbia 33SX 1134**

I'M STILL STANDING   September 1983
Elton John / Bernie Taupin
Big Pig Music . . . . UK
Elton John . . . . **Rocket EJS 1**

I'M STILL WAITING   September 1971
Deke Richards
Jobete Music (UK) Ltd. . . . . USA
Diana Ross . . . . **Tamla Motown TMG 781**

I'M STONE IN LOVE WITH YOU   November 1972
Anthony Bell / Linda Creed / Thomas Bell
Carlin Music Corporation . . . . USA
The Stylistics . . . . **Avco 6105015**
Johnny Mathis (1975) . . . . **CBS 2653**

I'M SURE OF EVERYTHING BUT YOU   1933
Pete Wendling / George Meyer / Charles O'Flynn
Francis, Day & Hunter Ltd. . . . . USA
Greta Keller . . . . **Decca F 3470**
Annette Hanshaw . . . . **Panachord 25413**
Layton & Johnstone . . . . **Columbia DB 1079**

I'M TELLING THE BIRDS, TELLING THE BEES, HOW I
LOVE YOU   1927
Cliff Friend / Lew Brown
Francis, Day & Hunter Ltd. . . . . USA
Jack Smith . . . . **HMV B 2414**
The Savoy Orpheans . . . . **HMV B 5214**

I'M TELLING YOU NOW   September 1963
Freddie Garrity / Mitch Murray
B. Feldman & Co. Ltd . . . . UJ
Freddie & The Dreamers . . . . **Columbia DB 7086**

I'M THE BELLE OF NEW YORK (See She Is The Belle
Of New York)

I'M THE LEADER OF THE GANG (I Am)   August 1973
Gary Glitter / Mike Leander
Leeds Music Ltd. . . . . UK
Gary Glitter . . . . **Bell BELL 1321**

I'M THE LONELY ONE   February 1964
Gordon Mills
Eugene Music Ltd . . . . UK
Cliff Richard . . . . **Columbia DB 7203**

I'M THE LONESOMEST GAL IN TOWN   1912
Lew Brown / Albert Von Tilzer
Francis, Day & Hunter Ltd. . . . . USA
Film(s): . . . . Make Believe Ballroom
Ella Fitzgerald . . . . **Brunswick 03188**
Kay Starr . . . . **Capitol T 1358**

I'M THE ONE   February 1964
Gerry Marsden
Pacermusic Ltd . . . . UK
Gerry & The Pacemakers . . . . **Columbia DB 7189**

I'M THE URBAN SPACEMAN   January 1969
Neil Innes
Sydney Bron Music Co. Ltd. . . . . UK
The Bonzo Dog Doo Dah Band . . . . **Liberty LBF 15144**
Ivor Novello Award.

I'M THINKING TONIGHT OF MY BLUE EYES   1943
A.P. Carter / Don Marcotte
Southern Music Publishing Co. Ltd . . . . USA
Film(s): . . . . The Man From Music Mountain
Bing Crosby . . . . **Brunswick 03456**
Burl Ives . . . . **Brunswick LA 8552**

I'M THROUGH WITH LOVE   1932
Gus Kahn / Matt Malneck / Fud Livingston
Keith Prowse Music Publishing Co. Ltd. . . . . USA
Film(s): . . . . Some Like it Hot
Bing Crosby . . . . **Ace of Hearts AH 40**
Sarah Vaughan . . . . **MGM EP 572**
Joni James . . . . **MGM EP 530**
Marilyn Monroe . . . . **London HLT 8862**
Marilyn Monroe appeared in *Some Like it Hot.*

I'M TICKLED TO DEATH I'M SINGLE   1923
Melville Gideon / Clifford Seyler
Francis, Day & Hunter Ltd . . . . UK
Melville Gideon . . . . **HMV B 1551**
**Olive Groves, Effie Atherton, Webster Booth & Stewart Robert-
son** . . . . **HMV C 2800**

I'M TWENTY-ONE TODAY   1911
Alec Kendall
B. Feldman & Co. Ltd . . . . UK
Stanley Kirkby . . . . **Beka 500**
Albert Whelan . . . . **Jumbo 813**

John Rorke . . . . **Parlophone GEP 8590**

I'M WALKING BEHIND YOU   May 1953
Billy Reid
Peter Maurice Music Co. Ltd . . . . UK
Dorothy Squires . . . . **Polygon P 1068**
Frank Sinatra . . . . **Capitol CL 13294**
Dorothy Squires . . . . **Pye NPL 18015**
Eddie Fisher . . . . **Camden CDN 167**
Jerry Keller . . . . **London HAR 2261**

I'M WISHING   1938
Larry Morey / Frank Churchill
Walt Disney Music Co. Ltd. . . . . USA
Film(s): . . . . Snow White and the Seven Dwarfs
Sound Track . . . . **HMV BD 515**
Sound Track . . . . **Disneyland DLP 39003**

I'M YOUR BABY TONIGHT   November 1990
L.A. Reid / "Babyface"
Warner Chappell Music . . . . USA
Whitney Houston . . . . **Arista 113594**

I'M YOUR MAN   November 1985
George Michael
Morrison Leahy Music . . . . UK
George Michael . . . . **Epic A 6716**

I'M YOUR PUPPET   June 1976
Lindon Oldham / Dan Penn
Lowery Music Co. . . . . USA
James & Bobby Purify . . . . **Mercury 6167324**

I'M YOURS   1931
E.Y. Harburg / Johnny Green
Chappell & Co. Ltd . . . . USA
Film(s): . . . . The Stooge
Ruth Etting . . . . **Columbia DB 409**
Dinah Shore . . . . **Columbia DB 2438**
Don Cherry . . . . **Philips BBL 7128**
Tommy Sands . . . . **Capitol T 1123**

I'M YOURS   July 1952
Robert Mellin
Robert Mellin Music . . . . USA
David Hughes . . . . **Columbia DB 3112**
Eddie Fisher . . . . **HMV B 10278**
Eve Boswell . . . . **Parlophone R 3561**

I'VE BEEN A BAD BAD BOY   February 1967
Mike Leander
Leeds Music Ltd. . . . . UK
Film(s): . . . . Privilege
Paul Jones . . . . **HMV POP 1576**

I'VE BEEN HURT   October 1973
Ray Whitley
Chappell & Co. Ltd. . . . . UK
Guy Darrell . . . . **Santo Ponsa PNS 4**

I'VE BEEN LOSING YOU   October 1984
Pal Waaktaar
ATV Music . . . . UK
A-Ha . . . . **Warner Brothers W 8594**

I'VE BEEN THINKING ABOUT YOU   October 1990
William Henshall / Jimmy Helms / George Chandler / James Chambers
Warner Chappell Music . . . . UK
London Beat . . . . **Anxious ANX 14**

I'VE GOT A CRUSH ON YOU   1930
George Gershwin / Ira Gershwin
Chappell & Co. Ltd . . . . USA
Show(s): . . . . Strike Up the Band
Film(s):Meet Danny Wilson / Three for the Show / Both Ends of the Candle
Ella Fitzgerald . . . . **Brunswick LA 8648**
Frank Sinatra . . . . **Fontana TFL 5030**
Gogi Grant . . . . **RCA RD 27054**
Gogi Grant dubbed the singing voice of Ann Blyth who appeared in the film *Both Ends of the Candle*.

I'VE GOT A FEELIN' YOU'RE FOOLIN'   1936
Arthur Freed / Nacio Herb Brown
Robbins Music Corporation Ltd . . . . USA

Film(s):Broadway Melody of 1936 / Singin' in the Rain / With a Song in My Heart
Eleanor Powell . . . . **HMV B 8396**
Joan Regan . . . . **Decca LK 4151**
Helen Carr . . . . **London HAN 2065**
Eleanor Powell appeared in *Broadway Melody of 1936*.

I'VE GOT A FEELING I'M FALLING   1929
Billy Rose / Harry Link / Thomas Waller
Campbell Connelly & Co. Ltd . . . . USA
Film(s): . . . . Applause
Thomas 'Fats' Waller . . . . **HMV B 3243**
Miff Mole's Molers . . . . **Philips BBL 7432**
Ada Moore . . . . **Philips BBL 7105**
Louis Armstrong's All Stars . . . . **Philips BBL 7064**

I'VE GOT A GAL IN KALAMAZOO   1942
Mack Gordon / Harry Warren
Bregman, Vocco & Conn Ltd . . . . USA
Film(s): . . . . Orchestra Wives / Kiss Them for Me
Glenn Miller & his Orchestra . . . . **HMV DLP 1059**
Marion Hutton, Ray Eberle & Modernaires . . **Vogue LVA 9103**
Glenn Miller appeared in *Orchestra Wives*.
Nominated for an Academy Award 1942.

I'VE GOT A LOVELY BUNCH OF COCONUTS   July 1949
Fred Heatherton
Box & Cox (Publications) Ltd . . . . UK
Billy Cotton & his Band . . . . **Decca LF 1185**
Danny Kaye . . . . **Brunswick LA 8660**
Dick James . . . . **Parlophone GEP 8554**

I'VE GOT A POCKETFUL OF DREAMS   1939
Jimmy Monaco / Johnny Burke
Campbell Connelly & Co. Ltd. . . . . USA
Film(s): . . . . Sing You Sinners
Bing Crosby . . . . **Brunswick Bing 3**
Henry Hall & his Orchestra . . . . **Columbia FB 2114**
Guy Mitchell . . . . **Philips BBR 7465**
Bing Crosby appeared in *Sing You Sinners*.

I'VE GOT A RIGHT TO SING THE BLUES (See I Gotta Right To Sing The Blues)

I'VE GOT FIVE DOLLARS   1931
Richard Rodgers / Lorenz Hart
Chappell & Co. Ltd. . . . . USA
Show(s): . . . . America's Sweetheart / The Show is on
Film(s): . . . . Gentlemen Marry Brunettes
The Rhythm Maniacs . . . . **Decca F 2999**
Ella Fitzgerald . . . . **HMV CLP 1117**
Bing Crosby . . . . **HMV CLP 1088**
Jane Russell & Scott Brady . . . . **Vogue LVA 9003**
Jane Russell & Scott Brady appeared in *Gentlemen Marry Brunettes*.

I'VE GOT MY CAPTAIN WORKING FOR ME NOW   1920
Irving Berlin
Irving Berlin Ltd . . . . USA
Film(s): . . . . Blue Skies
The Original Dixieland Jazz Band . . . . . . **Columbia 33S 1133**
Bing Crosby . . . . **Brunswick Bing 10**
Bing Crosby appeared in *Blue Skies*.

I'VE GOT MY EYES ON YOU   1940
Cole Porter
Chappell & Co. Ltd . . . . USA
Film(s): . . . . Broadway Melody of 1940
Dinah Shore . . . . **Regal Zonophone MR 3317**
Turner Layton . . . . **Columbia FB 2455**
Lita Roza . . . . **Nixa NPL 18020**
Fred Astaire . . . . **Verve 2317082**
Fred Astaire appeared in *Broadway Melody of 1940*.

I'VE GOT MY FINGERS CROSSED   1936
Ted Koehler / Jimmy McHugh
Francis, Day & Hunter Ltd . . . . USA
Film(s): . . . . King of Burlesque
'Fats' Waller . . . . **HMV BD 5052**
Louis Armstrong & his Orchestra . . . . **Decca F 5869**
Alice Faye . . . . **Rex 8779**
Fats' Waller appeared in *King of Burlesque*.

I'VE GOT MY LOVE TO KEEP ME WARM   1937
Irving Berlin

Irving Berlin Ltd. . . . . USA
Film(s): . . . . On the Avenue
Dick Powell . . . . **Decca F 6453**
Sarah Vaughan & Billy Eckstine . . . . **Mercury MMC 14035**
Frank Sinatra . . . . **Reprise R 1001**
Les Brown Band . . . . **Columbia DB 2533**
Dick Powell appeared in *On the Avenue*

I'VE GOT NO STRINGS   1940
Ned Washington / Leigh Harline
Chappell & Co. Ltd . . . . USA
Film(s): . . . . Pinocchio (Cartoon)
Sound Track . . . . **HMV BD 822**
Sound Track . . . . **Top Rank JKP 2033**

I'VE GOT RINGS ON MY FINGERS   1911
R.P. Weston / F.J. Barnes / Maurice Scott
Francis, Day & Hunter . . . . UK
Show(s): . . . . The Midnight Sons
Harry Carlton . . . . **HMV 4-2082**
The Merry Macs . . . . **Capitol T 850**
Teresa Brewer . . . . **Coral LVA 9138**

I'VE GOT SIXPENCE (As I Go Rolling Home)   1941
Elton Box / Desmond Cox / Desmond Hall
Bradbury Wood Ltd . . . . UK
The R.A.F. Dance Orchestra & Chorus . . . . **HMV RAF 9**
Glenn Miller & his Orchestra . . . . **HMV CLP 1081**
Mitch Miller & The Gang . . . . **Philips BBL 7258**

I'VE GOT THE SWEETEST GIRL IN MARYLAND   1919
Walter Donaldson
B. Feldman & Co. Ltd. . . . . USA
Lee White . . . . **Edison Bell 3232**
The Billy Jones Dixieland Band . . . . **Parlophone F 478**

I'VE GOT THE WORLD ON A STRING   1932
Harold Arlen / Ted Koehler
Peter Maurice Music Co. Ltd. . . . . USA
Film(s): . . . . I'll Get By
**Duke Ellington & his Orchestra,
vocal Ivie Anderson** . . . . **Columbia SEG 7677**
**Woody Herman & his Orchestra,
vocal Woody Herman** . . . . **Parlophone R 3017**
Bing Crosby . . . . **Fontana TFR 6012**
Perry Como . . . . **RCA RD 27070**
Ella Fitzgerald . . . . **HMV CLP 1479**

I'VE GOT TO SING A TORCH SONG   1933
Al Dubin / Harry Warren
B. Feldman & Co. Ltd. . . . . USA
Film(s): . . . . Gold Diggers of 1933
Rudy Vallee & his Connecticut Yankees . . . . **Columbia CB 638**
Bing Crosby . . . . **Brunswick 01615**
**Chorus from Soundtrack of
'Gold Diggers of 1933'** . . . . **United Artists UAG 29421**

I'VE GOT YOU ON MY MIND   1933
Cole Porter
Chappell & Co. Ltd. . . . . USA
Show(s): . . . . The Gay Divorce
Fred Astaire . . . . **HMV B 6398**
Ambrose & his Orchestra . . . . **Brunswick 01623**
Fred Astaire appeared in both the American and British productions
of *The Gay Divorce*.

I'VE GOT YOU UNDER MY SKIN   1937
Cole Porter
Chappell & Co. Ltd. . . . . USA
Film(s): . . . Born to Dance / Night and Day / This Could be the Night
Virginia Bruce . . . . **Vocalion 523**
Frances Day . . . . **HMV B 8526**
Steve Lawrence . . . . **Coral FEP 2010**
Ray Anthony & his Orchestra . . . . **MGM C 761**
Anita O'Day . . . . **HMV CLP 1332**
Frank Sinatra . . . . **Reprise R 1010**
The Four Seasons (1966) . . . . **Philips BF 1511**
Virginia Bruce appeared in *Born to Dance*. Ray Anthony appeared in
This Could Be the Night.
Nominated for an Academy Award 1936.

I'VE GROWN ACCUSTOMED TO HER FACE   May 1958
Alan Jay Lerner / Frederick Loewe
Chappell & Co. Ltd . . . . USA

Show(s): . . . . My Fair Lady
Film(s): . . . . My Fair Lady
Rex Harrison (USA) . . . . **Philips RBL 1000**
Rex Harrison (UK) . . . . **CBS 70005**
Rex Harrison (Soundtrack) . . . . **CBS BRG 72237**
Rex Harrison appeared in the American and British productions and
the film *My Fair Lady*.

I'VE HAD MY MOMENTS   1935
Walter Donaldson / Gus Kahn
Robbins Music Corporation Ltd . . . . USA
Film(s): . . . . The Girl from Missouri / Hollywood Party
Eddy Duchin & his Orchestra . . . . **HMV B 6495**
Frank Sinatra . . . . **Capitol LCT 6130**

I'VE HAD THE TIME OF MY LIFE (See Time Of My Life, The)

I'VE HEARD THAT SONG BEFORE   1942
Jule Styne / Sammy Cahn
Edwin H. Morris & Co. Ltd . . . . USA
Film(s): . . . . Youth on Parade
Carroll Gibbons & Orch,vocal Edna Kaye . . . **Columbia FB 2926**
**Harry James & his Orchestra,
vocal Helen Forrest** . . . . **Capitol T 952**
Patti Page . . . . **Mercury MMC 14007**
Pat Boone . . . . **London HAD 2144**
Nominated for an Academy Award 1942.

I'VE LOST YOU   December 1970
Kenneth Howard / Alan Blaikley
Carlin Music Corporation . . . . UK
Elvis Presley . . . . **RCA 1999**

I'VE NEVER BEEN IN LOVE BEFORE   July 1953
Frank Loesser
Edwin H.Morris & Co. Ltd . . . . USA
Show(s): . . . . Guys and Dolls
Robert Alda & Isabel Bigley . . . . **Brunswick LAT 8022**
Jerry Wayne . . . . **Philips PB 146**
Edmund Hockridge . . . . **Parlophone R 3697**
Robert Alda & Isabel Bigley appeared in the American production of
Guys and Dolls.
Jerry Wayne & Edmund Hockridge appeared in the British production
of *Guys and Dolls*.

I'VE NEVER BEEN TO ME   June 1982
Ron Miller / Ken Hirsch
Jobete Music . . . . USA
Charlene . . . . **Motown TMG 1260**

I'VE NEVER SEEN A STRAIGHT BANANA   1926
Ted Waite
Lawrence Wright Music Co. Ltd. . . . . UK
Jack Hylton & his Orchestra . . . . **HMV B 5197**
Jimmy Edwards . . . . **Fontana H 260**
**Tony Mercer & Dai Francis with
The George Mitchell Minstrels** . . . . **HMV CLP 3579**

I'VE TOLD EVERY LITTLE STAR   1932
Jerome Kern / Oscar Hammerstein II
Chappell & Co. Ltd. . . . . USA
Show(s): . . . . Music in the Air
Film(s): . . . . Music in the Air
Irene Dunne . . . . **Brunswick 03340**
Mary Ellis & chorus . . . . **Columbia DB 1139**
David Allen . . . . **Vogue VA 160127**
Linda Scott (1961) . . . . **Columbia DB 4638**
Irene Dunn appeared in the American production of *Music in the Air.*
Mary Ellis appeared in the British production of *Music in the Air.*

I'VE WAITED SO LONG   May 1959
Jerry Lordan
Pan-Musik Ltd . . . . UK
Film(s): . . . . Idle on Parade
Anthony Newley . . . . **Decca DFE 6566**
Jerry Lordan . . . . **Parlophone PMC 1133**
Anthony Newley appeared in *Idle On Parade*.

I.O.U.   August 1983
Arthur Baker
Intersong Music . . . . USA
Freeez . . . . **Beggars Banquet BEG 96**

ICE CREAM   1928
Howard Johnson / Billy Moll / Robert King

Lawrence Wright Music Co. Ltd. . . . . USA
Fred Waring & his Pennsylvanians . . . . **HMV B 5436**
The Chris Barber Jazz Band . . . . **Decca LK 4246**
The Humphrey Lyttleton Band . . . . **Parlophone R 3292**

ICE CREAM MAN   June 1963
Joe Meek
Filmusic Publishing Co. Ltd . . . . UK
Film(s): . . . . Farewell Performance
The Tornados . . . . **Decca F 11662**
The Tornados appeared in *Farewell Performance*.

ICE ICE BABY   December 1990
"Vanilla Ice"
Ice Baby Music . . . . UK
Vanilla Ice . . . . **SBK SBK 18**

ICE IN THE SUN   October 1968
Marty Wilde / Ronnie Scott
Valley Music . . . . UK
Status Quo . . . . **Pye 7N 17581**
Marty Wilde . . . . **Philips SBL 7877**

ICH LIEBE DICH, MY DEAR   1932
Jack Hart / Tom Bright
Chappell & Co. Ltd . . . . UK
Gloria Swanson . . . . **HMV B 4357**
Robert Naylor . . . . **Parlophone R 1401**
Lew Stone & his Orchestra, vocal Al Bowlly . . . . . **Decca F 3372**

IDA, SWEET AS APPLE CIDER   1937
Eddie Leonard / Eddie Munson
Peter Maurice Music Co. Ltd. . . . . USA
Show(s): . . . . Roly Boly Eyes
Film(s):Babes in Arms / Incendiary Blonde / The Eddie Cantor Story
Eddie Cantor . . . . **Brunswick LA 8658**
Bing Crosby . . . . **Brunswick LAT 8228**
The Mills Brothers . . . . **Brunswick 01863**
Tony Williams . . . . **Mercury MMC 14027**
Eddie Leonard appeared in *Roly Boly Eyes*.
Theme song of Eddie Cantor.
First Published in 1903.

IDAHO   1942
Jesse Stone
Chappell & Co. Ltd . . . . USA
Film(s): . . . . Idaho
Guy Lombardo & his Royal Canadians . . . . . **Brunswick 03407**
Geraldo & his Orchestra . . . . **Parlophone F 1949**
Johnny Dankworth & his Orchestra . . . . **Parlophone PMC 1079**
Dakota Staton . . . . **Capitol T 1170**

IDEAL WORLD   January 1988
Henry Priestman / Mark Herman
10 Music . . . . UK
The Christians . . . . **Island IS 347**

IDLE GOSSIP   April 1954
Joseph Meyer / Floyd Huddleston
Sydney Bron Music Co. Ltd. . . . . USA
Perry Como . . . . **HMV 7M 200**
Lita Roza . . . . **Decca F 10335**
Sarah Vaughan . . . . **Mercury MPL 6532**

IF   1934
Tolchard Evans / Robert Hargreaves / Stanley Damerell
Sydney Bron Music Co. Ltd. . . . . UK
Frank Titterton . . . . **Rex 8149**
Tolchard Evans (piano) . . . . **Decca F 11173**
Allan Jones . . . . **HMV B 9973**
Billy Eckstine (1950) . . . . **MGM 380**
Perry Como . . . . **RCA RCX 136**

IF   March 1975
David Gates
Screen Gems Music Ltd . . . . USA
Telly Savalas . . . . **MCA 174**
Bread . . . . **Elektra K 52062**

IF ANYONE FINDS THIS, I LOVE YOU   March 1955
Sidney Lippman / Sylvia Dee
Michael Reine Music Co. Ltd. USA
Kay Starr . . . . **HMV 7M 300**
Ruby Murray . . . . **Columbia SCM 5169**

Jimmy Young . . . . **Decca F 10483**

IF DREAMS CAME TRUE   September 1958
Robert Allen / Al Stillman
Grosvenor Music . . . . USA
Pat Boone . . . . **London HLD 8675**
Rickki Henderson . . . . **Embassy WB 302**

IF EVER I WOULD LEAVE YOU   November 1964
Alan Jay Lerner / Frederick Loewe
Chappell & Co. Ltd . . . . USA
Show(s): . . . . Camelot
Film(s): . . . . Camelot
Robert Goulet . . . . **CBS APG 60004**
Barry Kent . . . . **HMV CLP 1756**
Franco Nero . . . . **Warner Brothers W 1712**
Robert Goulet appeared in the American production of *Camelot*.
Barry Kent appeared in the British production of *Camelot*.
Franco Nero appeared in the film *Camelot*.

IF EVERYDAY WAS LIKE CHRISTMAS   December 1966
Red West
Lorna Music Co. Ltd. . . . . USA
Elvis Presley . . . . **RCA 1557**

IF I CAN DREAM   March 1969
W. Earl Brown
Carlin Music Corporation . . . . USA
Elvis Presley . . . . **RCA 1795**

IF I CAN HELP SOMEBODY   February 1951
Alma Bazel Androzzo
Boosey & Hawkes Music Publishers Ltd . . . . USA
Joseph Locke . . . . **Columbia DB 2784**
Gracie Fields . . . . **Decca LF 1140**
Michael Holliday . . . . **Columbia 33S 1114**
Harry Secombe . . . . **Philips BBL 7501**

IF I CAN'T HAVE YOU   June 1978
Robin Gibb / Maurice Gibb / Barry Gibb
Chappell & Co. Ltd . . . . UK
Film(s): . . . . Saturday Night Fever
Yvonne Elliman . . . . **RSO 2090266**

IF I COULD BE WITH YOU (ONE HOUR TONIGHT)   1932
Henry Creamer / James P. Johnson
Francis, Day & Hunter Ltd . . . . USA
Film(s): . . . . The Man I Love / Flamingo Road
Maurice Chevalier . . . . **MGM C 778**
Ruth Etting . . . . **Columbia DB 341**
The Mound City Blue Blowers . . . . **Camden CDN 139**
Bing Crosby . . . . **Brunswick LAT 8217**
Della Reese . . . . **RCA RD 27167**

IF I COULD TURN BACK TIME   October 1989
Diane Warren
EMI Music . . . . USA
Cher . . . . **Geffen GEF 59**

IF I DIDN'T CARE   1939
Jack Lawrence
Sterling Music Publishing Co. Ltd. . . . . USA
Film(s): . . . . The Great American Broadcast
The Ink Spots . . . . **Brunswick LA 8728**
Connie Francis . . . . **MGM 1012**
The Platters . . . . **Mercury 14014**
David Cassidy (1974) . . . . **Bell 1350**
The Ink Spots appeared in *The Great American Broadcast*.
Theme song of The Ink Spots.

IF I GAVE MY HEART TO YOU   October 1954
Jimmy Brewster / Jimmy Crane / Al Jacobs
Robbins Music Corporation Ltd. . . . . USA
Dinah Shore . . . . **HMV B 10756**
Nat 'King' Cole . . . . **Capitol CL 14203**
Doris Day . . . . **Philips BBL 7297**
Joan Regan . . . . **Decca LF 1244**

IF I HAD A GOLDEN UMBRELLA   August 1953
Bob Merrill
Cinephonic Music Co. Ltd . . . . USA
Diana Decker . . . . **Columbia DB 3325**
Alma Cogan . . . . **HMV B 10530**
The Cloverleafs . . . . **MGM 656**

IF I HAD A HAMMER   October 1963
Les Hayes / Pete Seeger
Essex Music Ltd .... USA
Trini Lopez   **Reprise R 20198**

IF I HAD A MILLION DOLLARS   1935
Johnny Mercer / Matt Malneck
Chappell & Co. Ltd .... USA
Film(s): ....Transatlantic Merry-Go-Round
The Boswell Sisters   **Brunswick 01957**
The Boswell Sisters appeared in *Transatlantic Merry-Go-Round*

IF I HAD A TALKING PICTURE OF YOU   1930
Buddy De Sylva / Lew Brown / Ray Henderson
Campbell Connelly & Co. Ltd .... USA
Film(s): ...... Sunny Side Up / The Best Things in Life are Free
Layton & Johnston   **Columbia 5668**
Jack Hylton & his Orchestra   **HMV B 5741**
Eve Boswell   **Parlophone R 4517**
The Syncopators   **Decca F 11359**

IF I HAD MY LIFE TO LIVE OVER   February 1950
Larry Vincent / Henry Tobias / Moe Jaffe
Bradbury Wood Ltd .... USA
Lee Lawrence   **Decca F 9315**
Kate Smith   **MGM D 145**
The Raindrops   **Oriole CB 1544**
First Published 1939.

IF I HAD MY WAY   1913
James Kendis / Lew Klein
Campbell Connelly & Co. Ltd. .... USA
Film(s): .... If I Had My Way / Sunbonnet Sue
Bing Crosby   **Brunswick Bing 5**
The Mills Brothers   **Brunswick 04452**
Vera Lynn   **MGM C 840**
Bing Crosby appeared in *If I Had My Way*.

IF I HAD WORDS   February 1978
Jonathan Hodge
Rak Music Ltd .... UK
Scott Fitzgerald & Yvonne Keeley .... **Pepper UP 36333**
Adapted from a theme from the 3rd Movement of "Symphony No.3, opus 78" by Charles Camille Saint-Saens (1835 - 1921).

IF I HAD YOU   1929
Ted Shapiro / James Campbell / Reginald Connelly
Campbell Connelly & Co. Ltd .... UK
Film(s): .... Under the Clock / You Were Meant for Me
Ambrose & his Orchestra .... **HMV B 5605**
Jeri Southern   **Brunswick LAT 8209**
Dinah Shore .... **Capitol T 1422**

IF I KNEW THEN (What I Know Now)   November 1968
Charles Tobias / Harry Tobias / Henry Tobias
Cinephonic Music Co. Ltd. .... USA
Val Doonican .... **Pye 7N 17616**

IF I LOST YOU   March 1957
Tolchard Evans / Richard Mullan
Robbins Music Corporation Ltd. .... UK
David Whitfield .... **Decca LK 4242**

IF I LOVED YOU   June 1950
Richard Rodgers / Oscar Hammerstein II
Williamson Music Ltd .... USA
Show(s): .... Carousel
Film(s): .... Carousel
Jan Clayton & John Raitt .... **Brunswick LAT 8006**
Iva Withers & Stephen Douglas .... **Columbia SED 5536**
Gordon MacRae .... **Capitol LCT 6105**
Jan Clayton & John Raitt appeared in the American production of *Carousel*.
Iva Withers & Stephen Douglas appeared in the British production of *Carousel*.
Gordon MacRae appeared in the film of *Carousel*.

IF I ONLY HAD A HEART   1940
Harold Arlen / E.Y. Harburg
Robbins Music Corporation Ltd .... USA
Film(s): .... The Wizard of Oz
Jack Haley .... **MGM C 757**
Victor Young & his Orchestra .... **Brunswick 02888**
Jack Haley appeared in *The Wizard of Oz*.

IF I ONLY HAD TIME (Je N'aurai Pas Le Temps)   May 1968
Michael Fugain / Jack Fishman
Valley Music .... France
John Rowles .... **MCA MU 1000**
Michael Fugain .... **Festival FX 1532**

IF I ONLY HAD WINGS   1940
Sid Colin / Ronnie Aldrich
Peter Maurice Music Co. Ltd .... UK
Nat Gonella & his New Georgians .... **Columbia FB 2502**
Bebe Daniels .... **Decca F 7651**
Vera Lynn .... **HMV CLP 3590**

IF I RULED THE WORLD   September 1963
Leslie Bricusse / Cyril Ornadel
Chappell & Co. Ltd .... UK
Show(s): .... Pickwick
Harry Secombe .... **Philips AL 3431**
Tony Bennett .... **CBS BPG 62544**
Nancy Wilson .... **Capitol T 2321**
Harry Secombe appeared in both the British and American productions of *Pickwick*
Ivor Novello Award.

IF I SAID YOU HAVE A BEAUTIFUL BODY   October 1979
David Bellamy
Famous-Chappell .... USA
The Bellamy Brothers .... **Warner Brothers K 17405**

IF I SHOULD FALL IN LOVE AGAIN   1940
Jack Popplewell
Peter Maurice Music Co. Ltd .... UK
Denny Dennis .... **Rex 9803**
Ronnie Hilton .... **HMV DLP 1109**
Carmita .... **Fontana TFE 17121**

IF I SHOULD PLANT A TINY SEED OF LOVE   1909
James W. Tate / Ballard MacDonald
B. Feldman & Co. Ltd. .... UK
Norman Blair .... **Panachord 25331**
Frank Williams .... **Regal T 90**
Helen Clare .... **Decca LK 4026**
Stanley Holloway .... **Pye NPL 18056**

IF I WAS   October 1985
Midge Ure / Daniel Mitchell
BMG Music .... UK
Midge Ure .... **Chrysalis URE 1**

IF I WERE A BELL   July 1953
Frank Loesser
Edwin H. Morris & Co. Ltd .... USA
Show(s): ....Guys and Dolls
Film(s): ....Guys and Dolls
Isabel Bigley .... **Brunswick LAT 8022**
Jean Simmons .... **Brunswick OE 9241**
Isabel Bigley appeared in the American production of *Guys and Dolls*.
Jean Simmons appeared in the film of *Guys and Dolls*.

IF I WERE A BLACKBIRD   August 1950
Traditional
Box & Cox (Publications) Ltd .... UK
Delia Murphy .... **Regal Zonophone MR 3379**
Ronnie Ronalde .... **Columbia DB 2654**
Joseph Locke .... **Columbia DB 2763**

IF I WERE A CARPENTER   December 1966
Tim Hardin
Robbins Music Corporation Ltd. .... USA
Bobby Darin .... **Atlantic 584051**
The Four Tops (1968) .... **Tamla Motown TMG 647**

IF I WERE A RICH MAN   August 1967
Sheldon Harnick / Jerry Bock
Chappell & Co. Ltd. .... USA
Show(s): .... Fiddler on the Roof
Film(s): .... Fiddler on the Roof
Zero Mostel .... **RCA RD 7843**
Topol .... **CBS BRG 70030**
Topol .... **United Artists UP 35307**
Zero Mostel appeared in the American production of *Fiddler on the Roof*.
Topol appeared in both the British production and the film of *Fiddler on the Roof*.

IF I'M LUCKY   1947
Eddie De Lange / Joseph Myrow
Chappell & Co. Ltd. . . . . USA
Film(s): . . . . If I'm Lucky
Perry Como . . . . **HMV BD 1154**
Julie London . . . . **London HAU 2186**
Perry Como appeared in *If I'm Lucky*.

IF IT HAPPENS AGAIN   October 1984
"UB40"
ATV Music . . . . UK
UB40 . . . . **DEP DEP 11**

IF IT WASN'T FOR THE 'OUSES IN BETWEEN   1894
Edgar Bateman / George Le Brunn
Francis, Day & Hunter Ltd. . . . . UK
Gus Elen . . . . **Sterno 789**
Gus Elen . . . . **Regal Zonophone MR 2630**
David Kossoff . . . . **Oriole MG 20043**
Jimmy Hanley . . . . **Piccadilly NPL 38002**

IF MY FRIENDS COULD SEE ME NOW   November 1967
Dorothy Fields / Cy Coleman
Campbell, Connelly & Co. Ltd. . . . . USA
Show(s): . . . . Sweet Charity
Film(s): . . . . Sweet Charity
Gwen Verdon . . . . **Columbia KOL 6500**
Juliet Prowse . . . . **CBS BPG 70035**
Shirley MacLaine . . . . **MCA MUCS 133**
Gwen Verdon appeared in the American production of *Sweet Charity*.
Juliet Prowse appeared in the British production of *Sweet Charity*.
Shirley MacLaine appeared in the film *Sweet Charity*.

IF NOT FOR YOU   April 1971
Bob Dylan
B. Feldman & Co. Ltd . . . . USA
Olivia Newton-John . . . . **Pye 7N 25543**
Bob Dylan . . . . **CBS S 69001**

IF NOT YOU   November 1976
Dennis Locorriere
Sunbury Music Ltd . . . . USA
Dr. Hook . . . . **Capitol CL 15885**

IF ONLY I COULD   October 1989
Sydney Youngblood / Markus Staab / Ralf Hamm & Claus Zundel
Virgin Music . . . . Germany
Sydney Youngblood . . . . **Circa YR 34**

IF ONLY I COULD LIVE MY LIFE AGAIN   March 1959
Gilbert Becaud / Pierre Delanoe / L. Amade & Elly Leighton
Peter Maurice Music Co. Ltd . . . . France
Jane Morgan . . . . **London HAR 2371**
Gilbert Becaud . . . . **HMV CLP 1262**
Teddy Johnson & Pearl Carr . . . . **Columbia DB 4275**

IF SHE SHOULD COME TO YOU (La Montana)   August 1960
Augusto Alguero / Georges Moreu / Alec Wilder
Essex Music Ltd . . . . Spain
Anthony Newley . . . . **Decca DFE 6555**

IF THE KIDS ARE UNITED   August 1978
Jimmy Pursey / David Parsons
Signatune Publishing . . . . UK
Sham 69 . . . . **Polydor 2059050**

IF THE WHOLE WORLD STOPPED LOVING   February 1968
Benjamin Peters / Shelby Singleton
Immediate Music Ltd. . . . . USA
Val Doonican . . . . **Pye 7N 17396**

IF THIS ISN'T LOVE   1947
E.Y. Harburg / Burton Lane
Chappell & Co. Ltd. . . . . USA
Show(s): . . . . Finian's Rainbow
Film(s): . . . . Finian's Rainbow
Ella Logan & Donald Richards . . . . **Philips BBL 7466**
Gracie Fields . . . . **Decca F 8808**
Sarah Vaughan . . . . **Mercury MPL 6522**
Petula Clark & Fred Astaire . . . . **Warner Brothers WF 2550**
Ella Logan & Donald Richards appeared in the American production of *Finian's Rainbow*.
Petula Clark & Fred Astaire appeared in the film *Finian's Rainbow*.

IF THOSE LIPS COULD ONLY SPEAK   1905
Charles Ridgewell / Will Godwin
Francis, Day & Hunter . . . . UK
George Baker . . . . **HMV B 4308**
Charles Young . . . . **Parlophone PMC 1127**

IF WINTER COMES   1922
Melville Gideon / Clifford Grey
Francis, Day & Hunter Ltd . . . . UK
Melville Gideon . . . . **Zonophone 2246**
Eric Randolph . . . . **Regal G 7831**
The 'Queens' Dance Orch, conductor Jack Hylton HMV B 1386

IF YOU ARE BUT A DREAM   1946
Moe Jaffe / Jack Fulton / Nat Bonx
Campbell Connelly & Co. Ltd. . . . . USA
Jimmy Dorsey & his Orchestra,
vocal Bob Eberly . . . . **Brunswick 03591**
Frank Sinatra . . . . **Fontana TFL 5030**
Frank Sinatra . . . . **Capitol LCT 6155**
Brook Benton . . . . **Mercury MMC 14060**
Adapted from "Romance in E flat" by Anton Rubinstein (1829-1894).

IF YOU BELIEVE   May 1955
Irving Berlin
Francis, Day & Hunter Ltd . . . . USA
Film(s): . . . . There's No Business Like Show Business
Johnnie Ray . . . . **Philips PB 379**
Johnnie Ray appeared in *There's No Business Like Show Business*

IF YOU CAN'T GIVE ME LOVE   April 1978
Mike Chapman / Nicky Chinn
Rak Music Ltd . . . . UK
Suzi Quatro . . . . **Rak 271**

IF YOU CAN'T STAND THE HEAT   January 1983
Andy Hill / Ian Bairson
Paper Music . . . . UK
Bucks Fizz . . . . **RCA 300**

IF YOU COULD CARE FOR ME   1918
Herman Darewski / Arthur Wimperis
Herman Darewski Music Publishing Co. Ltd. . . . . UK
Show(s): . . . . As You Were
Film(s): . . . . The Time, The Place and the Girl / Task Force
Alice Delysia & John Humphries . . . . **Columbia L 1268**
Richard Tauber . . . . **Parlophone R 20528**
Bruce Forsythe . . . . **Parlophone PMC 1132**
Alice Delysia & J. Humphries was in the British production of *Going Up*.

IF YOU DON'T KNOW ME BY NOW   February 1973
Kenny Gamble / Leon Huff
Carlin Music Corporation . . . . USA
Harold Melvin & The Bluenotes . . . . **CBS 8496**
Simply Red (1989) . . . . **Elektra YZ 377**

IF YOU EVER GO TO IRELAND   1944
Art Noel
Cinephone Music Co. Ltd. . . . . UK
Joe Loss & his Orchestra, vocal Pat McCormack . HMV BD 5855
Dennis Martin . . . . **Parlophone R 3145**

IF YOU GO (Si Tu Partais)   February 1952
Michael Ember / Geoffrey Parsons
Peter Maurice Music Co. Ltd . . . . France
Film(s): . . . . Night Without Stars
Edith Piaf . . . . **Decca C 16096**
Vera Lynn . . . . **Decca LF 1102**
Frankie Laine . . . . **Philips BBL 7238**

IF YOU GO AWAY (Ne Me Quitte Pas)   August 1974
Jacques Brel / Rod McKuen
Flamingo Music Ltd. . . . . France
Terry Jacks . . . . **Bell 1362**
Shirley Bassey . . . . **United Artists UP 1176**
Jacques Brel (in French) . . . . **Philips B 76487**

IF YOU GOTTA GO, GO NOW   October 1965
Bob Dylan
Blossom Music Ltd . . . . USA
Manfred Mann . . . . **HMV POP 1466**

IF YOU GOTTA MAKE A FOOL OF SOMEBODY   April 1963
Rudy Clark

B. Feldman & Co. Ltd .... USA
Freddie & The Dreamers .... Columbia DB 7032
Timi Yuro .... Liberty LBY 1154

IF YOU HADN'T GONE AWAY   1925
Lew Brown / Ray Henderson / Billy Rose
Keith Prowse Music Publishing Co. Ltd. .... USA
Norah Blaney .... Columbia 4273
The Kit Kat Band .... HMV B 2197
The Sid Philips Quintet .... Decca F 7888

IF YOU KNEW SUSIE   1925
Buddy De Sylva / Joseph Meyer
Keith Prowse Publishing Co. Ltd. .... USA
Show(s): .... Big Boy
Film(s):The Great Ziegfeld / The Eddie Cantor Story / The Benny
Goodman Story
Ramon Newton .... HMV B 2241
The Corona Dance Orchestra .... Regal G 8441
Eddie Cantor .... Brunswick LA 8658
Mitch Miller & The Gang .... Philips BBL 7494

IF YOU LEAVE ME NOW   November 1976
Peter Cetera
Island Music Ltd .... USA
Chicago .... CBS 4603

IF YOU LET ME STAY   April 1987
Terence Trent D'Arby
Virgin Music .... UK
Terence Trent D'Arby .... CBS TRENT 1

IF YOU LOVE ME (Hyme A L'Amour)   November 1953
Marguerite Monnot / Edith Piaf / Geoffrey Parsons
World Wide Music Co. Ltd. .... France
Edith Piaf .... Columbia 33CSX 5
Bing Crosby .... Brunswick 05313
Kay Starr .... Capitol LC 6835
Vera Lynn .... Decca LK 4120

IF YOU LOOK IN HER EYES   1918
Otto Harbach / Louis Hirsch
B. Feldman & Co. Ltd. ....USA
Show(s): ....Going Up
Majorie Gordon & Evelyn Laye .... HMV 04233
Majorie Gordon & Evelyn Laye appeared in the British production of
Going Up

IF YOU PLEASE   1943
Johnny Burke / Jimmy Van Heusen
Victoria Music Co. Ltd .... USA
Film(s): .... Dixie
Bing Crosby .... Brunswick Bing 8
Carroll Gibbons & The Savoy Hotel
Orpheans, vocal Edna Kaye .... Columbia FB 2958
Billy Ward .... London HAU 2116
Bing Crosby appeared in *Dixie*.

IF YOU STUB YOUR TOE ON THE MOON   May 1949
Johnny Burke / Jimmy Van Heusen
Edwin H. Morris & Co. Ltd .... USA
Film(s): ....A Yankee in King Arthur's Court
Bing Crosby .... Brunswick Bing 12
Frank Sinatra .... Columbia DB 2522
Bing Crosby appeared in *A Yankee In King Arthurs' Court*.

IF YOU THINK YOU KNOW HOW TO LOVE ME   August 1975
Mike Chapman / Nicky Chinn
Rak Music Ltd .... UK
Smokey .... Rak 206

IF YOU WANT THE RAINBOW   1929
Billy Rose / Mort Dixon / Oscar Levant
Francis, Day & Hunter Ltd .... USA
Film(s): .... My Man
Ben Selvin & his Orchestra .... Columbia 5306
Fanny Brice .... HMV B 3004
Fanny Brice appeared in *My Man*.

IF YOU WERE THE ONLY GIRL IN THE WORLD   1916
Nat. D. Ayer / Clifford Grey
B. Feldman & Co. Ltd. .... UK
Show(s): ....The Bing Boys are Here
Film(s): .... The Vagabond Lover / Both Ends of the Candle
Violet Loraine & George Robey .... Columbia L 1035

Rudy Vallee .... HMV C 2802
Dick Haymes .... Brunswick LA 8530
Gogi Grant .... RCA RD 27054
Stanley Holloway .... Pye NPL 18056
Violet Loraine & George Robey appeared in *The Bing Boys are Here*.
Rudy Vallee appeared in *The Vagabond Lover*.
Gogi Grant dubbed the singing voice of Ann Blyth who appeared in
the film *Both Ends of the Candle*.

IF YOU'RE IN LOVE YOU'LL WALTZ   1930
Joseph McCarthy / Harry Tierney
Francis, Day & Hunter Ltd .... USA
Show(s): .... Rio Rita
Film(s): .... Rio Rita
Bebe Daniels .... HMV B 3211
Edith Day & Geoffrey Gwyther .... Columbia DX 55
Edith Day & Geoffrey Gwyther appeared in the British production of
Rio Rita.
Bebe Daniels appeared in the film of *Rio Rita*.

IF YOU'RE IRISH COME INTO THE PARLOUR   1920
Shaun Glenville / Frank Miller
B. Feldman & Co. Ltd .... UK
James Mullan .... Regal Zonophone MR 695
Ruby Murray .... Columbia 33S 1079
Eileen Donaghy .... Fontana TFE 17342

IF YOU'RE LOOKIN' FOR A WAY OUT   November 1980
Sandy Linzer / Ralph Kotov
Chappell & Co. Ltd .... USA
Odyssey .... RCA 5

IKO IKO   July 1982
Marylin Jones / Sharon Jones / Joe Jones / Jessie Thomas
Carlin Music .... USA
The Dixie Cups .... Red Bird RB 10024
The Belle Stars .... Stiff BUY 150
Natasha (1982) .... Towerbell TOW 22

ILO - A VOICE FROM MUMMY LAND   1921
James Black
Francis, Day & Hunter Ltd .... USA
The 'Queens' Dance Orchestra .... HMV B 1258

IMAGE OF A GIRL   September 1960
Richard Clasky / Lee Rosenberg
Duchess Music Ltd .... USA
Mark Wynter .... Decca F 11263
Nelson Keen .... HMV POP 771

IMAGINATION   1940
Johnny Burke / Jimmy Van Heusen
Chappell & Co. Ltd .... USA
Ella Fitzgerald .... Brunswick LAT 8056
June Christy .... Capitol T 833
Pat Boone .... London HAD 2265
The King Sisters .... Capitol CL 14729

IMAGINE   November 1975
John Lennon
Northern Songs Ltd .... UK
John Lennon (1975) .... Apple R 6009
John Lennon (1981) .... Apple R 6009

IMPORTANCE OF YOUR LOVE, THE (Importance C'est La
Rose)   July 1968
Gilbert Becaud / Norman Newell
Metric Music Ltd. .... France
Vince Hill .... Columbia DB 8414
Gilbert Becaud .... Columbia DB 8392

IMPOSSIBLE DREAM, THE   May 1968
Joe Darion / Mitch Leigh
Sam Fox (London) Ltd. .... USA
Show(s): .... Man of La Mancha
Film(s): .... Man of La Mancha
Richard Kiley .... London HAR 8362
Keith Michell .... MCA MUP 334
Peter O'Toole .... United Artists VAS 9906
Jack Jones .... London HLR 10088
Matt Monro .... Capitol CL 15573
Richard Kiley appeared in the American production of *Man of La Mancha*.
Keith Michell appeared in the British production of *Man of La Mancha*.
Peter O'Toole appeared in the film *Man of La Mancha*.
Simon Gilbert dubbed the singing voice of Peter O'Toole.

IN A BROKEN DREAM   November 1972
David Bentley
Young Blood Music . . . . UK
Python Lee Jackson . . . . **Young Blood YB 1002**

IN A GOLDEN COACH   March 1953
Ronald Jamieson / Harry Leon
Box & Cox (Publications) Ltd . . . . UK
Donald Peers . . . . **HMV B 10487**
Billy Cotton & his Band . . . . **Decca F 10058**
Dickie Valentine . . . . **Decca F 10098**

IN A LITTLE GIPSY TEAROOM   1935
Joe Burke / Edgar Leslie
Campbell Connelly . . . . USA
Greta Keller . . . . **Decca F 5595**
Harry Roy & his Orchestra . . . . **Parlophone F 190**
Bob Crosby & his Orchestra . . . . **Brunswick 02041**

IN A LITTLE SECONDHAND STORE   1933
Harry Pease / Ed Nelson / Dave Dreyer
Francis, Day & Hunter Ltd. . . . . USA
Layton & Johnstone . . . . **Columbia DB 1161**
Connee Boswell . . . . **Brunswick 01528**

IN A LITTLE SPANISH TOWN   1927
Mabel Wayne / Sam M. Lewis / Joe Young
Francis, Day & Hunter Ltd. . . . . USA
Film(s): . . . . Thousands Cheer
Melville Gideon . . . . **HMV B 2421**
Mabel Wayne . . . . **Columbia DX 672**
Bing Crosby . . . . **Brunswick LAT 8331**
Virginia O'Brien . . . . **Brunswick 04234**
Virginia O'Brien appeared in *Thousands Cheer.*

IN A MOMENT OF MADNESS   1945
Ralph Freed / Jimmy McHugh
Sun Music Publishing Co. Ltd. . . . . USA
Film(s): . . . . Two Girls and a Sailor
Helen Forrest . . . . **Brunswick 03559**
Helen Forrest appeared in *Two Girls and a Sailor.*

IN A MONASTERY GARDEN   1918
Albert Ketelbey
Boosey & Hawkes Music Publishers Ltd. . . . . UK
The Mayfair Orchestra . . . . **HMV B 872**
Albert Ketelbey & his Concert Orchestra . . . **Columbia 9403**
**The New Symphony Orchestra of London,
conductor Bob Sharples** . . . . **Decca LK 4329**
Peter Dawson . . . . **HMV DLP 1180**

IN A PERSIAN MARKET   1921
Albert Ketelbey
Bosworth & Co. Ltd . . . . UK
**The Court Symphony Orchestra,
conducted by Albert Ketelbey** . . . . **Columbia 896**
Albert Ketelbey & his Concert Orchestra . . . **Columbia 9404**
**The New Symphony Orchestra of London,
conductor Bob Sharples** . . . . **Decca LK 4329**

IN A SENTIMENTAL MOOD   1936
Duke Ellington / Irving Mills / Mann Kurtz
Lafleur & Co. Ltd . . . . USA
Duke Ellington & his Orchestra . . . . **Brunswick 02038**
Duke Ellington & his Famous Orchestra . . . **HMV DLP 1007**
Ella Fitzgerald . . . . **HMV CLP 1227**

IN A SHADY NOOK BY A BABBLING BROOK 1927
E.G. Nelson / Harry Pease
Keith Prowse Music Publishing Co. Ltd. . . . . USA
Johnny Marvin . . . . **HMV B 2541**
Donald Peers (1944) . . . . **Decca DFE 6387**

IN A SHANTY IN OLD SHANTY TOWN   1932
Joe Young / John Siras / Jack Little
B. Feldman & Co. Ltd. USA
Film(s): . . . . Lullaby of Broadway / The Crooner
Layton & Johnstone . . . . **Columbia DB 946**
Bud Flanagan & the Radio Revellers . . . . . **Columbia DB 2594**
Doris Day . . . . **Columbia 33S 1038**
Max Bygraves . . . . **Decca DFE 6505**
Johnny Long & his Orchestra . . . . **Brunswick LA 8650**
Vera Lynn . . . . **MGM C 840**
Doris Day appeared in *Lullaby of Broadway.*

IN AN EIGHTEENTH CENTURY DRAWING ROOM 1939
Raymond Scott / Jack Lawrence
Cinephone Music Co. Ltd. . . . . USA
Hal Kemp & his Orchestra . . . . **HMV BD 5534**
The Milt Herth Trio . . . . **Brunswick 02827**
Tommy Kinsman & his Orchestra . . . . **Fontana TFL 5049**
The Bowman-Hyde Singers & Players . . **Parlophone PMC 1155**
Adapted from 'Piano Sonata No. 3 in C' by Wolfgang Amadeus Mozart
(1756 - 1791).

IN AN OLD DUTCH GARDEN   1940
Mack Gordon / Will Grosz
Chappell & Co. Ltd . . . . USA
Ambrose & his Orchestra, vocal Jack Cooper . . **Decca F 7451**
Bebe Daniels . . . . **Decca F 7474**
Glenn Miller & his Orchestra, vocal Ray Eberle . **HMV DLP 1145**

IN AN OLD FASHIONED TOWN   1914
Ada Leonora Harris / W.H. Squire
Boosey & Hawkes Music . . . . UK
Joan Foster & Peter Macready . . . . **Regal MR 292**
Derek Oldham . . . . **HMV B 3725**
Peter Dawson . . . . **HMV OXLP 7662**
Felicity Palmer . . . . **Argo ZK 97**

IN AND OUT OF LOVE   January 1968
Brian Holland / Eddie Holland / Lamont Dozier
Carlin Music Corporation . . . . USA
Diana Ross & The Supremes . . . . **Tamla Motown TMG 632**

IN BETWEEN   1939
Roger Edens
Francis, Day & Hunter Ltd. . . . . USA
Film(s): . . . . Love Finds Andy Hardy
Judy Garland . . . . **Brunswick LA 8727**
Judy Garland appeared in *Love Finds Andy Hardy.*

IN BETWEEN DAYS   August 1985
Robert Smith
APB Music . . . . UK
The Cure . . . . **Fiction FICS 22**

IN BETWEENIES, THE   January 1974
Bill Oddie
A.T.V. Music Ltd. . . . . UK
The Goodies . . . . **Bradleys BRAD 7421**

IN CALIENTE   1936
Allie Wrubel / Mort Dixon
B. Feldman & Co. Ltd . . . . USA
Film(s): . . . . In Caliente
The Masqueraders . . . . **Columbia FB 1219**

IN CHI-CHI CASTENANGO   1945
Jay Gorney / Henry Myers
Campbell Connelly & Co. Ltd. . . . . USA
Show(s): . . . . Meet the People
George Guetary . . . . **Columbia DB 2398**

IN CROWD, THE   June 1974
Billy Page
Cross Music Ltd. . . . . USA
Bryan Ferry . . . . **Island WIP 6196**
Dobie Gray . . . . **London HL 9953**
Petula Clark . . . . **Pye NPL 18118**

IN DREAMS   May 1963
Roy Orbison
Acuff-Rose Publishing Co. Ltd . . . . USA
Roy Orbison . . . . **London HL 9676**

IN DULCE JUBILO   January 1976
Traditional, arranged by Mike Oldfield
Mike Oldfield . . . . **Virgin VS 131**

IN FOR A PENNY   November 1975
Neville Holder / James Lea
Barn Publishing Ltd . . . . UK
Slade . . . . **Polydor 2058663**

IN LOVE FOR THE VERY FIRST TIME December 1955
Jack Woodman / Paddy Roberts
Essex Music Ltd. . . . . UK
Film(s): . . . . An Alligator Named Daisy
Jean Carson . . . . **HMV POP 124**

Diana Dors . . . . **Pye NPL 18044**
Diana Dors appeared in *An Alligator Named Daisy*.
Ivor Novello Award.

IN MY ARMS 1943
Ted Grouya / Frank Loesser
B. Feldman & Co. Ltd . . . . USA
Film(s): . . . . See Here Private Hargrove
Dick Haymes . . . . **Brunswick 03468**
Geraldo & his Orchestra, vocal Derek Roy . . . **Parlophone F 1909**
Mitch Miller & his Orchestra & chorus . . . . . **Columbia DB 2781**

IN MY DREAMS February 1949
Jimmy Shearer
Dash Music Ltd . . . . USA
Vaughn Monroe . . . . **HMV BD 6035**
Ella Fitzgerald . . . . **Brunswick 04031**
Reggie Goff . . . . **Decca F 9040**

IN MY LITTLE BOTTOM DRAWER 1934
Will Haines / Jimmy Harper / Maurice Beresford
Campbell Connelly & Co. Ltd . . . . UK
Film(s): . . . . Sing as We Go
Gracie Fields . . . . **HMV B 8209**
Gracie Fields . . . . **Conquest CL 1001**
Gracie Fields appeared in *Sing as We Go*.

IN MY LITTLE RED BOOK 1938
Al Stillman / Ray Bloch / Nat Simon
Peter Maurice Music Co. Ltd. . . . . USA
Ted Weems & his Orch,vocal Perry Como . . **Panachord 25974**
Dick Powell . . . . **Decca F 6694**
Al Morgan . . . . **London L 884**
Vera Lynn . . . . **HMV CLP 1791**

IN MY LITTLE SNAPSHOT ALBUM 1938
Harry Parr-Davies / Jimmy Harper / Will E. Haines
Lawrence Wright Music Co. Ltd. . . . . UK
Film(s): . . . . I See Ice
George Formby . . . . **Regal Zonophone MR 2753**
George Formby appeared in *I See Ice*.

IN MY MERRY OLDSMOBILE 1905
Vincent Bryan / Gus Edwards
B. Feldman & Co. Ltd . . . . USA
Bing Crosby . . . . **Brunswick 02841**
Jean Goldkette & his Orchestra . . . . **Sunbeam BIX 4**

IN MY OWN TIME September 1971
John Whitney / Roger Chapman
United Artists Music Co. Ltd . . . . UK
Family . . . . **Reprise K 14090**

IN OLD LISBON (Lisboa Antigua) August 1948
Raul Portela / Jose Galhardo / Amadou Do Valé & Harry Dupree
Latin-American Music Publishing Co. Ltd. . . . . Portugal
Film(s): . . . . Lisbon
Amalia Rodrigues . . . . **Columbia SEG 7922**
Los Clippers Orchestra . . . . **Decca C 16023**
Frank Chacksfield & his Orchestra . . . . **Ace of Clubs ACL 1080**
Nelson Riddle & his Orchestra . . . . **Capitol CL 15110**

IN OTHER WORDS (Fly Me To The Moon) November 1964
Bart Howard
Essex Music Ltd . . . . USA
Johnny Mathis . . . . **Fontana TFL 5011**
Nat 'King' Cole . . . . **Capitol W 1675**
Peggy Lee . . . . **Capitol T 1401**
Frank Sinatra . . . . **Reprise R 1012**

IN PRIVATE December 1989
Neil Tennant / Chris Lowe
Cage Music . . . . UK
Dusty Springfield . . . . **Parlophone R 6234**

IN SAN FRANCISCO December 1962
George Cory / Douglas Cross
Dash Music Ltd . . . . USA
Tony Bennett . . . . **CBS BPG 62201**
Brenda Lee . . . . **Brunswick LAT 8530**

IN SHADOWLAND 1925
Fred Ahlert / Ruth Brooks / Sam M. Lewis / Joe Young
B. Feldman & Co. Ltd . . . . USA

The Savoy Havana Band . . . . **HMV B 1935**

IN SUMMER August 1963
Elaine Murtagh / Valerie Murtagh / Ray Adams
Skidmore Music Ltd . . . . UK
Billy Fury . . . . **Decca F 11701**
Mark Wynter . . . . **Pye NEP 24176**

IN SUMMERTIME ON BREDON 1911
Graham Peel / A.E. Housman
Chappell & Co Ltd . . . . UK
Gervase Elwes . . . . **Columbia L 1101**
Robert Irwin . . . . **HMV B 9673**

IN THE AIR TONIGHT February 1981
Phil Collins
Hit & Run Music . . . . UK
Phil Collins . . . . **Virgin VSK 102**
Phil Collins (1988) . . . . **Virgin VS 102**
Ivor Novello Award 1981

IN THE ARMS OF LOVE October 1966
Jay Livingston / Ray Evans / Henry Mancini
Compass Music Ltd. . . . . USA
Film(s): . . . . What Did You Do in the War Daddy
Andy Williams . . . . **CBS 202300**

IN THE BAD BAD OLD DAYS April 1969
John McLeod / Tony Macaulay
Welbeck Music Co. Ltd. . . . . UK
The Foundations . . . . **Pye 7N 17702**

IN THE BLUE OF EVENING 1943
Alphonso D'Artega / Tom Adair
Campbell Connelly & Co. Ltd . . . . USA
Anne Shelton . . . . **Decca F 8330**
Jane Froman . . . . **Capitol EAP 1-889**
Jackie Wilson . . . . **Vogue LVA 9108**

IN THE BUSH December 1978
Patrick Adams / Sandra Cooper
Leeds Music Ltd . . . . USA
Musique . . . . **CBS 6791**

IN THE CHAPEL IN THE MOONLIGHT 1937
Billy Hill
Dash Music Ltd . . . . USA
Ruth Etting . . . . **Decca F 6257**
Gracie Fields . . . . **Rex 8968**
The Mariners . . . . **Philips BBR 8035**
The Bachelors (1965) . . . . **Decca DE 12256**

IN THE COOL, COOL, COOL OF THE EVENING October 1951
Hoagy Carmichael / Johnny Mercer
Victoria Music Co. Ltd . . . . USA
Film(s): . . . . Here Comes the Groom
Bing Crosby & Jane Wyman . . . . **Brunswick Bing 13**
Jo Stafford & Frankie Laine . . . . **Columbia DB 2900**
Bing Crosby & Jane Wyman appeared in *Here Comes the Groom*.
Academy Award winning song of 1951.

IN THE COUNTRY January 1967
Hank B. Marvin / Bruce Welch / Brian Bennett & John Rostill
Shadamm Music . . . . UK
Show(s): . . . . Cinderella
Cliff Richard . . . . **Columbia DB 8094**
Cliff Richard appeared in *Cinderella*.

IN THE DIM DIM DAWNING 1933
Al Hoffman / Al Goodhart / Stanley Adams
Peter Maurice Music Co. Ltd. . . . . USA
Paul Whiteman & his Orchestra . . . . **HMV B 6311**

IN THE GARDEN OF MY HEART 1908
Ernest Ball / Caro Roma
B. Feldman & Co. Ltd. . . . . USA
Herbert Payne . . . . **Zonophone Twin 1004**

IN THE GHETTO August 1969
Mac Davis
Carlin Music Corporation . . . . USA
Elvis Presley . . . . **RCA 1831**

IN THE GLOAMING 1877
Meta Orred / Annie Fortesue Harrison

```
.....................................................................UK
Film(s): ............................When You're In Love
Will Oakland .......................Zonophone TWIN 1180
Grace Moore .........................................Caliban 6044
Jeannie Carson ..............................HMV POP 515
Stuart Burrows ..................Oiseay Lyre DSLO 43
Felicity Palmer ......................................Argo ZK 97
```

IN THE GOOD OLD SUMMERTIME   1902
Ren Shields / George Evans
Herman Darewski Music Publishing Co. Ltd. ....USA
Show(s): ....The Defender
Film(s): ....In the Good Old Summertime
The Big Four ....Columbia DX 288
The Andrews Sisters ....Brunswick 04085
Les Paul & Mary Ford ....Capitol EAP 20048
Bing Crosby ....Warner Brothers WM 4034

IN THE HEART   May 1984
Robert Bell / Ronald Bell / James Taylor / Kool & The Gang
Planetary-Nom Music ....UK
Kool & The Gang ....De Lite DE 17

IN THE JAILHOUSE NOW   1931
Jimmy Rodgers
Southern Music Publishing Co. Ltd ....USA
Jimmy Rodgers ....Zonophone 5808
Webb Pierce ....Brunswick OE 9253
Jimmy Rodgers ....RCA RD 27203

IN THE LAND OF BEGINNING AGAIN   1919
Grant Clarke / George Meyer
B. Feldman & Co. Ltd. ....USA
Film(s): ....The Bells of St. Mary's
Bing Crosby ....Brunswick Bing 9
Ambrose & his Orchestra, vocal Rita Marlowe ... Decca F 8633
Archie Lewis (1946) ....Parlophone F 2140
Bing Crosby appeared in *The Bells of St. Mary's.*

IN THE MIDDLE OF A DARK DARK NIGHT   September 1957
Bob Merrill
Joy Music Ltd ....USA
Guy Mitchell ....Philips BBE 12145

IN THE MIDDLE OF A KISS   1935
Sam Coslow
Victoria Music Co. Ltd ....USA
Film(s): ....College Scandal / The Clock Strikes Eight
Connee Boswell ....Brunswick 02050
Morton Downey ....Rex 8620
Julie London ....London HAU 2171

IN THE MIDDLE OF AN ISLAND   August 1957
Ted Varnick / Nick Acquaviva
Edwin H. Morris & Co. Ltd. ....USA
Tony Bennett ....Philips BBE 12159
Marion Keene ....HMV POP 375

IN THE MIDDLE OF NOWHERE   July 1965
Beatrice Verdi / Buddy Kaye
Raintree Music Ltd ....USA
Dusty Springfield ....Philips PB 1418

IN THE MIDDLE OF THE HOUSE   October 1956
Bob Hilliard
John Fields Music Co. Ltd. ....USA
Jimmy Parkinson ....Columbia DB 3833
Alma Cogan ....HMV POP 261
Milton Berle ....Vogue Q 72197

IN THE MIDNIGHT HOUR   October 1965
Steve Cropper / Wilson Pickett
West One Music Ltd ....USA
Wilson Pickett ....Atlantic AT 4036

IN THE MOOD   1940
Andy Razaf / Joe Garland
Peter Maurice Music Co. Ltd ....USA
Film(s): ....Sun Valley Serenade / The Glenn Miller Story
Glenn Miller & his Orchestra ....RCA RD 27057
Joe Loss & his Orchestra ....Regal Zonophone MR 3243
The Andrews Sisters ....Brunswick 05109
The Clark Sisters ....London HAD 2177
The Universal International

Studio Orchestra ....Brunswick LA 8647
Ralph Marterie & his Orchestra ....Mercury AMT 1074
Glenn Miller Orchestra (1976) ....RCA 2644
Glenn Miller appeared in *Sun Valley Serenade.*
The Universal International Orchestra appeared in *The Glenn Miller Story.*
Theme song of Joe Loss.

IN THE NAVY   April 1979
Richard Jobson / Stuart Adamson
Zomba Music Publishers ....USA
The Village People ....Mercury 6007209

IN THE QUARTERMASTER'S STORES   1940
Elton Box / Desmond Cox / Bert Reed
Cavendish Music Co. Ltd ....UK
Murgatroyd & Winterbottom
(Ronald Frankau & Tommy Handley) ....Parlophone F 1669
Billy Cotton & his Band ....Rex 9737
Eric Delaney & his Band ....Nixa NEP 24006

IN THE RAIN   June 1973
Phil Spector / Barry Mann / Cynthia Weill
Screen Gems Music Ltd. ....USA
The Partridge Family ....Bell 1293
The Walker Brothers ....Philips BF 1576
The Ronettes ....London HLU 9931

IN THE SHADE OF THE OLD APPLE TREE   1905
Egbert Van Alstyne / Harry Williams
Francis, Day & Hunter Ltd ....USA
Charles Holland ....Zonophone X 42358
Norman Blair ....Panachord 25624
The Mills Brothers ....Brunswick LA 8681

IN THE SHADOWS   1910
Herman Finck / Ray Goetz
Boosey & Hawkes Music Publishers Ltd ....USA
The Bohemia Orchestra ....HMV 0650
The London Novelty Orchestra .....Regal Zonophone MR 95
Mantovani & his Orchestra ....Columbia FB 2405

IN THE SPIRIT OF THE MOMENT   1944
Walter Jurmann / Bernie Grossman
Southern Music Publishers ....USA
Film(s): ....His Butler's Sister
Deanna Durbin ....MCA MCL 1668
Deanna Durbin appeared in *His Butler's Sister*

IN THE STILL OF THE NIGHT   1938
Cole Porter
Chappell & Co. Ltd. ....USA
Film(s): ....Rosalie / Night and Day
Maurice Winnick & his Orchestra,
vocal Al Bowlly ....Decca F 6605
Allan Jones ....HMV 7EG 8179
Johnny Mathis ....Fontana TFL 5050

IN THE SUMMERTIME   August 1970
Ray Dorset
Our Music ....UK
Mungo Jerry ....Dawn DNX 2502
Ivor Novello Award.

IN THE TWI-TWI-TWILIGHT   1908
Herman Darewski / Charles Wilmot
Francis, Day & Hunter Ltd ....UK
Show(s): ....The Dairymaids
Film(s): ....Variety Jubilee
Reg Grant ....Parlophone R 1518
Leslie Sarony ....Decca LK 4026

IN THE VALLEY OF THE MOON   1933
Joe Burke / Charles Tobias
Campbell Connelly & Co. Ltd. ....USA
Derickson & Brown ....HMV B 4462
Hank Thompson ....Capitol EAP 1-1111

IN THE WOODSHED SHE SAID SHE WOULD   1928
Howard Johnson / Tommy Tucker / Monty Siegel
Campbell Connelly & Co. Ltd. ....USA
Gracie Fields ....HMV B 2782

IN THE YEAR 2525   October 1969
Rick Evans

Essex Music Ltd. . . . . USA
Zager & Evans . . . . **RCA 1860**

IN THOUGHTS OF YOU   **August 1965**
Geoff Morrow / Chris Arnold
Coda Music Ltd . . . . UK
Billy Fury . . . . **Decca F 12178**

IN TOO DEEP   **July 1986**
Anthony Banks / Phil Collins / Mike Rutherford
Hit & Run Music . . . . UK
Genesis Virgin   **GENS 1**
Ivor Novello Nomination.

IN YOUR CAR   **July 1985**
Steven McIntosh
Zomba Music . . . . UK
The Cool Notes . . . . **Abstract AD 4**

IN YOUR EYES   **October 1983**
Michael Masser / Daniel Hill
Rondor Music . . . . USA
George Benson . . . . **Warner Brothers W 9487**

IN ZAIRE   **August 1976**
John Wakelin
Francis, Day & Hunter Ltd . . . . UK
Johnny Wakelin . . . . **Pye 7N 45595**

INCOMMUNICADO   **June 1987**
"Marillion"
Charisma Music . . . . UK
Marillion . . . . **EMI MARIL 6**

INDIAN LOVE CALL   **1925**
Rudolf Frimi / Otto Harbach / Oscar Hammerstein II
Chappell & Co. Ltd. . . . . USA
Show(s): . . . . Rose Marie
Film(s): . . . . Rose Marie / One Night of Love
Edith Day & Derek Oldham . . . . **Columbia 9038**
Jeanette MacDonald & Nelson Eddy . . . . **RCA RCX 1020**
Slim Whitman (1952) . . . . **London L 1149**
Ann Blyth & Fernado Lamas . . . . **MGM D 128**
Edith Day & Derek Oldham appeared in the British production of *Rose Marie*.
Jeanette MacDonald & Nelson Eddy appeared in the 1936 film of *Rose Marie*.
Ann Blyth & Fernando Lamas appeared in the 1954 film of *Rose Marie*.

INDIAN RESERVATION   **November 1970**
John D. Loudermilk
Acuff Rose Publishing Co. Ltd . . . . USA
Don Fardon . . . . **Young Blood YB 1015**

INDIAN SUMMER   **1920**
Victor Herbert / Al Dubin
Chappell & Co. Ltd . . . . USA
Bing Crosby . . . . **Brunswick LA 8600**
Gordon MacRae . . . . **Capitol T 1146**
Tony Martin . . . . **Decca F 7449**
The Four Freshmen . . . . **Capitol T 1008**

INDIANA   **1917**
James Hanley / Ballard MacDonald
B. Feldman & Co. Ltd. . . . . USA
Film(s):With a Song in My Heart / Satchmo the Great / Drum Crazy /
Five Pennies
The Original Dixieland Jazz Band . . . . **Columbia 2903**
Red Nichols & his Five Pennies . . . . **Brunswick 01590**
Dick Haymes . . . . **Brunswick 04315**
Louis Armstrong's All Stars . . . . **Philips BBL 7216**
Sound Track of Drum Crazy . . . . **HMV CLP 1352**
Danny Kaye . . . . **London HAU 2189**
Red Nichols & his Five Pennies . . . . **Brunswick LAT 8307**
Bobby Darin & Johnny Mercer . . . . **London HAK 2363**
The Louis Armstrong All Stars appeared in *Satchmo the Great*.
Danny Kaye appeared in *The Five Pennies*.

INDIANA WANTS ME   **June 1971**
R. Dean Taylor
Jobete Music (UK) Ltd. . . . . USA
R. Dean Taylor . . . . **Tamla Motown TMG 763**

INDIANOLA   **1919**
Domenico Savino
Herman Darewski Music Publishing Co. Ltd. . . . . USA
The Mayfair Dance Orchestra . . . . **HMV C 906**

The Six Swingers . . . . **Columbia FB 1988**

INFINITY   **March 1990**
Paul Walden
Virgin Music . . . . UK
Guru Josh . . . . **Deconstruction PB 43475**

INKA DINKA DOO   **1934**
Ben Ryan / Dave Dreyer / Harry Donnelly / Jimmy Durante
Francis, Day & Hunter Ltd. . . . . USA
Film(s):The Great Schnozzle / This Time for Keeps / Two Girls and a Sailor
Jimmy Durante . . . . **Columbia DB 1806**
Jimmy Durante . . . . **Brunswick LAT 8312**
Jimmy Durante appeared in *The Great Schnozzle*, *Two Girls and a
Sailor* and *This Time For Keeps*.
Theme song of Jimmy Durante.

INNOCENT MAN (See An Innocent Man)

INSIDE OUT   **July 1982**
Jessie Rae
MCA Music . . . . USA
Odyssey . . . . **RCA RCA 226**

INSTANT KARMA   **March 1970**
John Lennon
Northern Songs Ltd. . . . . UK
**John Lennon & Yoko Ono with
The Plastic Ono Band** . . . . **Apple 1003**

INSTANT REPLAY   **December 1978**
Dan Hartman
EMI Music Ltd . . . . USA
Dan Hartman . . . . **Blue Sky 6706**
Yell (1990) . . . . **Fanfare FAN 22**

INSTINCTION   **May 1982**
Gary Kemp
Reformation Music . . . . UK
Spandau Ballet . . . . **Chrysalis CHS 2602**

INTERMEZZO (Souvenir de Vienne)   **1941**
Heinz Provost / Robert Henning
Southern Music Publishing Co. Ltd . . . . Sweden
Film(s): . . . . Escape to Happiness
Allan Jones . . . . **HMV B 9234**
Sidney Torch & his Orchestra . . . . **Parlophone R 3084**
Percy Faith & his Orchestra . . . . **Philips BBL 7336**

INTERNATIONAL RAG   **1913**
Irving Berlin
B. Feldman & Co. Ltd. . . . . USA
Film(s): . . . . Alexander's Ragtime Band / Call Me Madam
Collins & Harlan . . . . **Zonophone 1231**
Ethel Merman . . . . **Brunswick LA 8603**
Ethel Merman appeared in *Call Me Madam*.

INTERNATIONAL RESCUE   **April 1989**
*Joanne Dunne / Margaret Dunne / Tina O'Neil / Victoria Perks &
Liam Sternberg*
Warner Chappell Music . . . . UK
Fuzzbox . . . . **WEA YZ 347**

INTO EACH LIFE SOME RAIN MUST FALL   **1945**
Doris Fisher / Allan Roberts
Pickwick Music Ltd. . . . . USA
Ella Fitzgerald & The Ink Spots . . . . . **Brunswick 9429**
The Hilltoppers . . . . **London HAD 2029**
Kay Starr . . . . **Capitol T 1303**

INTO THE GROOVE   **July 1985**
Madonna Ciccone / Steve Bray
Warner Brothers Music . . . . USA
Madonna . . . . **Sire W 8934**

INTO THE VALLEY   **March 1979**
Richard Jobson / Stuart Adamson
Virgin Music (Publishers) Ltd. . . . . USA
The Skids . . . . **Virgin VS 241**

INTUITION   **April 1981**
David Grant / Peter Martin
Solid Music . . . . UK
Linx . . . . **Chrysalis CHS 2500**

INVISIBLE SUN October 1981
"Sting"
Virgin Music . . . . UK
The Police . . . . **A&M AMS 8164**

INVISIBLE TOUCH June 1986
Anthony Banks / Phil Collins / Mike Rutherford
Hit & Run Music . . . . UK
Genesis . . . . **Virign GENS 1**

IRE FEELINGS (SKANGA) December 1974
Rupie Edwards
Creole Music . . . . UK
Rupie Edwards . . . . **Cactus CT 38**

**IRELAND MUST BE HEAVEN FOR MY MOTHER CAME
FROM THERE** 1916
Joseph McCarthy / Howard Johnson / Fred Fisher
Herman Darewski Music Publishing Co. Ltd. . . . . USA
Film(s): . . . . Oh You Beautiful Doll
Jack Daly . . . . **Regal Zonophone MR 3087**
Joseph Locke . . . . **Columbia DB 2688**

IRENE 1920
Harry Tierney / Joseph McCarthy
Francis, Day & Hunter Ltd . . . . USA
Show(s): . . . . .Irene
Film(s): . . . . .Irene
Edith Day . . . . **HMV B 1115**
Edith Day . . . . **Columbia F 1044**
Edith Day appeared in both the American & British productions of *Irene*.

IRISH ROVER, THE April 1987
Traditional
The Pogues & The Dubliners . . . . **Stiff BUY 258**

IRRESISTIBLE YOU 1945
Don Raye / Gene De Paul
Chappell & Co. Ltd. . . . . USA
Film(s): . . . . Broadway Rhythm
**Woody Herman & his Orchestra,
vocal Frances Wayne** . . . . **Brunswick LAT 8092**
Mark Murphy . . . . **Brunswick LAT 8172**
June Christy . . . . **Capitol T 833**

IS IT A SIN 1947
Emma Carus / Vincent Bryan / J. Walter Leopold
Lawrence Wright Music Co. Ltd. . . . . USA
The Ink Spots . . . . **Brunswick 03653**

IS IT ANY WONDER August 1953
Bob Hayes / Roy Rodde
Leeds Music Ltd. . . . . USA
Joni Jones . . . . **MGM 642**
Jimmy Young . . . . **Decca F 10130**
Donald Peers . . . . **HMV B 10506**
Joan Dowling . . . . **Columbia DB 3307**

IS IT LOVE YOUR AFTER January 1980
Miles Gregory
Warner Brothers Music Ltd . . . . USA
Rose Royce . . . . **Whitfield K 17456**

IS IT TIME TO GET FUNKY
Dany Poku / Courtney Coulson / Basil Reynolds / Chris Scarlett
EMI Music . . . . UK
D Mob Featuring L.R.S. . . . . **London F 107**

IS IT TRUE WHAT THEY SAY ABOUT DIXIE 1936
Irving Caesar / Sammy Lerner / Gerald Marks
Bradbury Wood Ltd . . . . USA
Film(s): . . . . Jolson Sings Again
Frances Langford . . . . **Brunswick 02216**
Al Jolson . . . . **Brunswick LA 8502**
Dean Martin . . . . **Encore 103**
Phil Harris (1950) . . . . **Camden CDN 124**
Sid Philips Band (1950) . . . . **HMV BD 6064**

IS MY BABY BLUE TONIGHT 1944
William Tracey / Lou Handman
Dash Music Ltd. . . . . USA
**Geraldo & his Orchestra,
vocal Johnny Green** . . . . **Parlophone F 2019**
The R.A.F. Dance Orchestra, vocal Jimmy Miller . . . **Decca F 8424**

IS SHE MY GIRL FRIEND 1928
Jack Yellen / Milton Ager
Lawrence Wright Music Co. Ltd. . . . . USA
**Jack Hylton & his Orchestra,
vocal Jack Jackson & chorus** . . . . **HMV B 5422**

IS SHE REALLY GOING OUT WITH HIM September 1979
Joe Jackson
Albion Music . . . . UK
Joe Jackson . . . . **A&M AMS 7459**

IS THERE SOMETHING I SHOULD KNOW April 1983
"Duran Duran"
Carlin Music . . . . UK
Duran Duran . . . . **EMI 5371**

IS THIS LOVE March 1978
Bob Marley
Rondor Music (London) Ltd . . . . UK
Bob Marley & The Wailers . . . . **Island WIP 6420**

IS THIS LOVE January 1987
Alison Moyet / Dave Stewart
RCA Music . . . . UK
Alison Moyet . . . . **CBS MOYET 1**

IS THIS LOVE July 1987
David Coverdale / John Sykes
Warner Brothers Music . . . . UK
Whitesnake . . . . **EMI EM 3**

IS THIS THE WAY TO AMARILLO December 1971
Neil Sedaka / Howard Greenfield
ATV Music Ltd . . . . USA
Tony Christie . . . . **MCA MKS 5073**

IS YOU IS, OR IS YOU AIN'T MY BABY 1944
Louis Jordan / Billy Austin
Leeds Music Ltd . . . . USA
Film(s): . . . . Follow the Boys / On Stage Everybody
Louis Jordan & his Tympany Five . . . . **Brunswick 03545**
Bing Crosby & The Andrews Sisters . . . **Brunswick LAT 8306**
Marilyn Moore . . . . **Parlophone GEP 8755**
Louis Jordan appeared in *Follow The Boys*.
The Andrew Sisters appeared in *On Stage Everybody*.

ISLAND GIRL November 1975
Elton John / Bernie Taupin
Big Pig Music . . . . UK
Elton John . . . . **DJM DJS 610**
Ivor Novello Nomination.

ISLAND IN THE SUN July 1957
Harry Belafonte / Irving Burgess
B. Feldman & Co. Ltd. . . . . USA
Film(s): . . . . Island in the Sun
Harry Belafonte . . . . **RCA 1007**
Harry Belafonte appeared in *Island in the Sun*.

ISLAND OF DREAMS March 1963
Tom Springfield
Chappell & Co. Ltd . . . . UK
The Springfields . . . . **Philips 326557 BF**
The Kestrels . . . . **Piccadilly NPL 38009**

ISLANDS IN THE STREAM December 1983
Barry Gibb / Robin Gibb / Maurice Gibb
Gibb Brothers Music . . . . UK
Kenny Rogers & Dolly Parton . . . . **RCA RCA 378**

ISLE OF CAPRI 1934
Jimmy Kennedy / Will Grosz
Peter Maurice Music Co. Ltd . . . . UK
Ray Noble & his Orchestra, vocal Al Bowlly . . . . . **HMV B 6519**
Gracie Fields . . . . **HMV B 8232**
Bing Crosby & Rosemary Clooney . . . . **RCA RD 27105**

ISLE OF INNISFREE August 1952
Richard Farrelly
Peter Maurice Music Co. Ltd . . . . UK
Bing Crosby . . . . **Brunswick LAT 8278**
Vera Lynn . . . . **Decca F 10029**
Eileen Donaghy . . . . **Fontana TFL 5150**

ISN'T IT KINDA FUN   1946
Richard Rodgers / Oscar Hammerstein II
Williamson Music .... USA
Film(s): .... State Fair
Ann-Margret .... **London HAD 2453**
Dick Haymes .... **MCA MCFM 2720**
Dick Haymes appeared in the 1945 film *State Fair*
Ann-Margret appeared in the 1962 film *State Fair*

ISN'T IT ROMANTIC   1933
Richard Rodgers / Lorenz Hart
Victoria Music Co. Ltd. .... USA
Film(s): ....Love Me Tonight
Jeanette MacDonald .... **HMV B 4288**
Hildegarde .... **Decca F 7853**
Carmen McRae .... **London HAR 2185**
Ella Fitzgerald .... **HMV CLP 1117**
Jeanette MacDonald appeared in *Love Me Tonight*.

ISN'T LIFE STRANGE   June 1972
John Lodge
Threshold Music .... UK
The Moody Blues .... **Threshold TH 9**

ISN'T SHE LOVELY   February 1977
Stevie Wonder
Jobete Music (UK) Ltd. .... USA
David Parton .... **Pye 7N 45663**
Stevie Wonder .... **Motown TMSP 6002**

ISN'T THIS A LOVELY DAY   1935
Irving Berlin
Irving Berlin Ltd .... USA
Film(s): .... Top Hat
Fred Astaire .... **Brunswick RL 297**
Ginger Rogers .... **Decca F 5746**
Fred Astaire .... **HMV 7EG 8463**
Marion Ryan .... **Pye NPL 18030**
Fred Astaire & Ginger Rogers appeared in *Top Hat*.

ISRAELITES, THE   May 1969
Desmond Dacres / Leslie Kong
Sparta Music Ltd. .... Jamaica
Desmond Dekker & The Aces .... **Pyramid PYR 6058**
Desmond Dekker (1975) .... **Cactus CT 57**

ISTANBUL (Not Constantinople)   December 1953
Jimmy Kennedy / Nat Simon
Aberbach (London) Ltd. .... USA
The Malcolm Mitchell Trio .... **Parlophone R 3783**
Edmundo Ros & his Orchestra .... **Decca DFE 6147**
The Four Lads .... **Philips BBL 7331**

IT AIN'T GONNA RAIN NO MO'   1924
Wendell Hall
Francis, Day & Hunter Ltd. .... USA
Show(s): .... The Punch Bowl
Film(s): .... Has Anybody Seen My Gal
Will Hall (Wendell Hall) .... **Edison Bell Winner 4027**
The Two Gilberts .... **Regal G 8184**
Norah Blaney & Gwen Farrar .... **HMV BD 254**
Jack Hylton & his Orchestra .... **HMV B 1878**
The 'Sing Along' Minstrels .... **Ace of Clubs ACL 1090**
Norah Blaney & Gwen Farrar appeared in *The Punch Bowl*.

IT AIN'T NECESSARILY SO   1935
George Gershwin / Ira Gershwin
Chappell & Co. Ltd .... USA
Show(s): .... Porgy and Bess
Film(s): ....Rhapsody in Blue / Porgy and Bess
Todd Duncan & Choir .... **Brunswick LAT 8021**
Sound Track recording of *Porgy and Bess* ... **Philips ABL 3282**
Todd Duncan appeared in the American production of *Porgy and Bess*.

IT AIN'T NOBODY'S BUSINESS IF I DO (See T'aint No-body's Business If I Do)

IT AIN'T WHAT YOU DO, IT'S THE WAY THAT YOU DO IT (See T'aint What You Do)

IT ALL COMES BACK TO ME NOW   February 1949
Hy Zaret / Joan Whitney / Alex Kramer
Cinephonic Music Co. Ltd .... USA
Oscar Rabin & his Band, vocal 'Diane' ..... **Parlophone F 2337**

Perry Como .... **Brunswick 04018**
Ferlin Husky .... **Capitol T 880**

IT ALL DEPENDS ON YOU   1927
Buddy De Sylva / Lew Brown / Ray Henderson
Chappell & Co. Ltd. .... USA
Show(s): .... Big Boy / Lido Lady
Film(s):The Singing Fool / The Best Things in Life are Free / Love Me or Leave Me
Al Jolson .... **Brunswick 04996**
Phyllis Dare .... **Columbia 4227**
Fred Rich & his Orchestra .... **Columbia 4392**
Frank Sinatra .... **Philips BBL 7168**
Doris Day .... **Philips BBL 7047**
Al Jolson appeared in *Big Boy* and *The Singing Fool*.
Phyllis Dare appeared in *Lido Lady*.
Song added to *Big Boy* in 1926.
Doris Day appeared in *Love Me or Leave Me*.

IT CAN'T BE WRONG   1943
Max Steiner / Kim Gannon
Victoria Music Co. Ltd .... USA
Film(s): .... Now Voyager
Vera Lynn .... **Decca F 8388**
Dick Haymes .... **Brunswick 03488**
Anne Shelton .... **Philips BBL 7291**
Dennis Lotis .... **Columbia 33SX 1089**
Vera Lynn .... **MGM C 843**
Melody only used in *Now Voyager*.

IT COSTS SO LITTLE   1942
Horatio Nicholls / Alf Ritter / J. Lester Smith
Lawrence Wright Music Co. Ltd .... UK
Anne Shelton .... **Decca F 8243**
Joe Loss & his Orchestra .... **HMV BD 5781**

IT COULD HAPPEN TO YOU   1944
Johnny Burke / Jimmy Van Heusen
Victoria Music Co. Ltd. .... USA
Film(s): .... And the Angels Sing
Bing Crosby .... **Brunswick LA 8595**
Kate Smith .... **Capitol LC 6672**
Lena Horne .... **RCA RD 27141**
Dakota Staton .... **Capitol T 1054**

IT DIDN'T MATTER   February 1987
Paul Weller / Mick Talbot
FMI Music .... UK
The Style Council .... **Polydor TSC 12**

IT DOESN'T HAVE TO BE   March 1987
Vincent Clarke / Andrew Bell
Sonet Music .... UK
Erasure .... **Mute MUTE 66**

IT DOESN'T HAVE TO BE THIS WAY   February 1987
Robert Howard
RCA Music .... UK
The Blow Monkeys .... **RCA MONK 4**

IT DOESN'T MATTER ANYMORE   April 1959
Paul Anka
Monarch Music Ltd .... USA
Buddy Holly .... **Coral LVA 9105**
Vince Eager .... **Parlophone PMC 1101**

IT DON'T COME EASY   May 1971
Richard Starkey
Essex Music Ltd .... UK
Ringo Starr .... **Apple R 5898**

IT DON'T MEAN A THING (If It Ain't Got That Swing)   1932
Duke Ellington / Irving Mills
Lawrence Wright Music Co. Ltd. .... USA
Duke Ellington & his Orchestra .... **Philips BBE 12404**
The Mills Brothers .... **Brunswick OE 9060**
The Boswell Sisters with
The Dorsey Brothers Orchestra .... **Columbia DB 1994**
Duke Ellington & his Orchestra .... **HMV DLB 1007**
June Christy .... **Capitol T 1076**

IT GOES LIKE THIS (That Funny Melody)   1929
Irving Caesar / Cliff Friend
Francis, Day & Hunter Ltd. .... USA
Cliff Edwards (Ukulele Ike) .... **Columbia 5113**

161

Sid Philips & his Band . . . .   HMV POP 269

IT HAD TO BE YOU   **1924**
Gus Kahn / Isham Jones
Francis, Day & Hunter Ltd. . . . . USA
Film(s):Show Business / Incendiary Blonde / Her Kind of Man / I'll See
You in My Dreams
Layton & Johnstone . . . .   **Columbia 3511**
Bing Crosby . . . .   **Brunswick OE 9359**
Dick Haymes & Helen Forrest (1945) . . . .   **Brunswick 03552**
Doris Day . . . .   **Philips BBL 7137**
Patti Page . . . .   **Mercury MMC 14007**
Doris Day appeared in *I'll See You in My Dreams*.

IT HAPPENED IN ADANO   **May 1949**
Don Pelosi / Harold Fields
Peter Maurice Music Co. Ltd . . . . UK
Donald Peers . . . .   **HMV B 9773**
Anne Shelton . . . .   **Decca F 9153**

IT HAPPENED IN MONTEREY   **1930**
Mabel Wayne / Billy Rose
Francis, Day & Hunter Ltd . . . . USA
Film(s): . . . . The King of Jazz
John Boles . . . .   **HMV B 3456**
Paul Whiteman & his Orchestra . . . .   **Columbia CB 87**
Mabel Wayne . . . .   **Columbia DX 672**
Frank Sinatra . . . .   **Capitol LCT 6106**
Bing Crosby & Rosemary Clooney . . . . . .   **RCA RD 27105**
John Boles & Paul Whiteman appeared in *The King of Jazz*.

IT HAPPENED IN SUN VALLEY   **1942**
Mack Gordon / Harry Warren
Sun Music Publishing Co. Ltd . . . . USA
Film(s): . . . . .Sun Valley Serenade
Glenn Miller & his Orchestra . . . .   **RCA RCX 1034**
Jo Stafford . . . .   **Philips BBL 7187**
Glenn Miller appeared in *Sun Valley Serenade*.

IT HURTS SO MUCH TO SEE YOU GO   **February 1965**
Billy Guitar / Jim Reevs
Hyde Park Music Ltd . . . . USA
Jim Reeves . . . .   **RCA 1437**

IT IS ONLY A TINY GARDEN   **1916**
Hadyn Wood / Lillian Glanville
Chappell & Co. Ltd. . . . . UK
Carmen Hill . . . .   **HMV E 8**
Sydney Coltham . . . .   **HMV B 2576**

IT IS TIME TO GET FUNKY   **June 1989**
Danny Poku / Courtney Coulson / Basil Reynolds & Chris Scarlett
EMI Music . . . . UK
D Mob featuring LRS . . . .   **London F 107**

IT LOOKS LIKE RAIN IN CHERRY BLOSSOM LANE   **1937**
Joe Burke / Edgar Leslie
Campbell Connelly & Co. Ltd. . . . . USA
Dick Robertson . . . .   **Panachord 25929**
Art Lund . . . .   **Vogue LVA 9056**
Patti Page . . . .   **Mercury MMC 14013**
Sue Raney . . . .   **Capitol T 964**

IT MAKES NO DIFFERENCE NOW   **1940**
Jimmy Davis / Floyd Tillman
Southern Music Publishing Co. Ltd. USA
Film(s): . . . . Down the Wyoming Trail / Strictly in the Groove
Jimmy Davis . . . .   **Panachord 26041**
Bing Crosby . . . .   **Brunswick 03456**
Ernest Tubb . . . .   **Brunswick LAT 8292**

IT MAY BE WINTER OUTSIDE
(But In My Heart It's Spring)   **March 1975**
P. Politi / Barry White
Edward Kassner Music Co. Ltd . . . . USA
Love Unlimited . . . .   **20th Century BTC 2149**
Felice Taylor . . . .   **President PT 120**

IT MEK   **July 1969**
Desmond Dacres / Leslie Kong
Blue Mountain Music . . . . UK
Desmond Dekker . . . .   **Pyramid PYR 6068**

IT MIGHT AS WELL BE SPRING   **1946**
Richard Rodgers / Oscar Hammerstein II
Chappell & Co. Ltd. . . . . USA
Film(s): . . . . State Fair
Dick Haymes . . . .   **Brunswick 03620**
Gordon MacRae . . . .   **Capitol T 1146**
Billy Eckstine . . . .   **Columbia 33SX 1327**
Anita Gordon . . . .   **London HAD 2453**
Dick Haymes appeared in the 1945 film of *State Fair*.
Anita Gordon appeared in the 1962 film of *State Fair*.
Academy Award winning song for 1945.

IT MIGHT AS WELL RAIN UNTIL SEPTEMBER   **October 1962**
Gerry Goffin / Carole King
Aldon Music Ltd. . . . . USA
Carole King . . . .   **London HL 9591**
The De Laine Sisters . . . .   **Piccadilly 7N 35070**
Helen Shapiro . . . .   **Columbia 33SX 1661**

IT MUST BE HIM (Seul Sur Son Etoile)   **August 1967**
Gilbert Becaud / Mack David
Metric Music Ltd. . . . . France
Vicki Carr . . . .   **Liberty LIB 55917**

**IT MUST BE JELLY, 'CAUSE JAM DON'T SHAKE LIKE
THAT**   **1944**
George Williams / J.C. McGregor / Sunny Skylar
Chappell & Co. Ltd. . . . . USA
Woody Herman & his Orchestra,
vocal Woody Herman & Frances Wayne . . . .   **Brunswick 03541**
Glenn Miller & his Orchestra . . . .   **HMV CLPC 2**

IT MUST BE LOVE   **January 1972**
Labi Siffre
M.A.M. (Music Publishing) Ltd . . . . USA
Labi Siffre . . . .   **Pye 7N 25572**
Madness (1982) . . . .   **Stiff BUY 134**

IT MUST BE TRUE   **1930**
Harry Barris / Gus Arnheim / Gordon Clifford
Lawrence Wright Music Co. Ltd . . . . USA
Film(s): . . . . .The Eddy Duchin Story
Bing Crosby . . . .   **Brunswick LA 8684**
Jeri Southern . . . .   **Brunswick LAT 8209**
Bing Crosby . . . .   **RCA RD 27075**

IT MUST HAVE BEEN LOVE   **July 1990**
Per Gessle
EMI Music . . . . Sweden
Roxette . . . .   **EMI EM 141**

IT NEVER ENTERED MY MIND   **1941**
Richard Rodgers / Lorenz Hart
Chappell & Co. Ltd . . . . USA
Show(s): . . . . Higher and Higher
Patty Andrews . . . .   **Brunswick 04923**
Ella Fitzgerald . . . .   **HMV CLP 1116**
Frank Sinatra . . . .   **Fontana TFL 5048**

IT ONLY HAPPENS WHEN I DANCE WITH YOU   **July 1948**
Irving Berlin
Irving Berlin Ltd. . . . . USA
Film(s): . . . . .Easter Parade
Fred Astaire . . . .   **MGM 174**
Chris Connor . . . .   **London LTZK 15142**
Art Lund . . . .   **MGM 144**
Fred Astaire appeared in *Easter Parade*.

IT ONLY TAKES A MINUTE   **July 1976**
Dennis Lambert / Brian Potter
Anchor Music Ltd . . . . USA
One Hundred Ton & A Feather . . . .   **UK 135**

IT ONLY TOOK A MINUTE   **January 1963**
Mort Garson / Hal David
Shapiro-Bernstein & Co. Ltd . . . . USA
Joe Brown & The Bruvvers . . . .   **Piccadilly 7N 35082**

IT SHOULD HAVE BEEN ME   **March 1976**
Norman Whitfield / William Stevenson
Jobete Music (UK) Ltd. . . . . USA
Yvonne Fair . . . .   **Tamla Motown TMG 1013**

IT STARTED ALL OVER AGAIN   **October 1962**
Gerry Goffin / Jack Keller

Aldon Music Ltd. . . . . USA
Brenda Lee . . . . **Brunswick 05876**

IT STARTED WITH A KISS   August 1982
Eroll Brown
Rak Music . . . . UK
Hot Chocolate . . . . **Rak 344**

IT SURE BRINGS OUT THE LOVE IN YOUR EYES   June 1978
Tony Macaulay / Geoff Stevens
Cookaway Music . . . . UK
David Soul . . . . **Private Stock PVT 137**

IT TAKES TWO   March 1967
Sylvia Moy / William Stevenson
Carlin Music Corporation . . . . USA
Marvin Gaye & Kim Weston . . . . **Tamla Motown TMG 590**
Rod Stewart & Tina Turner (1990) . . . . **Warner Brothers ROD 1**

IT'LL BE ME   October 1962
Jack Clement
Aberbach (London) Ltd. . . . . USA
Jerry Lee Lewis . . . . **London HLS 8457**
Cliff Richard . . . . **Columbia DB 4886**

IT'S A BIT OF A RUIN THAT CROMWELL KNOCKED
ABOUT A BIT   1912
Harry Bedford / Terry Sullivan
B.Feldman & Co. Ltd . . . . UK
Marie Lloyd Jr. . . . . **Broadcast 518**
Marie Lloyd Jr. . . . . **Fontana TFL 5043**

IT'S A BLUE WORLD   1940
Robert Wright / Chet Forrest
Bradbury Wood Ltd . . . . USA
Film(s): . . . . Music in My Heart
Woody Herman & his Orchestra,
vocal Woody Herman . . . . **Brunswick 02952**
Tony Martin . . . . **Decca F 7494**
The Four Freshmen . . . . **Capitol T 1008**
Julie London . . . . **London HAW 2229**
Tony Martin appeared in *Music In My Heart*.
Nominated for an Academy Award 1940.

IT'S A BOY   September 1958
Paddy Roberts
Francis, Day & Hunter Ltd . . . . UK
Lita Roza . . . . **Nixa N 15155**
Lisa Noble . . . . **Decca F 11051**

IT'S A CRUEL CRUEL WORLD   June 1949
Abner Silver / Bennie Davis
Campbell Connelly & Co. Ltd . . . . USA
Cass Daley . . . . **Brunswick 04258**
The Beverley Sisters . . . . **Columbia DB 2843**

IT'S A GOOD DAY   1947
Dave Barbour / Peggy Lee
Victoria Music Co. Ltd. . . . . USA
Film(s): . . . . .With a Song in my Heart
Jane Froman . . . . **Capitol LC 6554**
Peggy Lee . . . . **Capitol LC 6817**
Perry Como . . . . **RCA RD 27070**
Jane Froman dubbed the singing voice of Susan Hayward who
appeared in the film *With a Song in My Heart*.

IT'S A GRAND NIGHT FOR SINGING   1946
Richard Rodgers / Oscar Hammerstein II
Chappell & Co. Ltd. . . . . USA
Film(s): . . . . State Fair
Dick Haymes . . . . **Brunswick 03628**
Bobby Darin, Anita Gordon & Bob Smart . . **London HAD 2453**
Dick Haymes appeared in the 1945 film of *State Fair*.
Bobby Darin, Anita Gordon & Bob Smart appeared in 1962 film of
State Fair.

IT'S A GREAT BIG SHAME   1895
Edgar Bateman / George Le Brunn
Francis, Day & Hunter Ltd. . . . . UK
Gus Elen . . . . **Ace of Clubs ACL 1077**
John Hewer . . . . **Parlophone PMC 1127**
David Kossoff . . . . **Oriole MG 20043**

IT'S A GREAT DAY FOR THE IRISH   1941
Roger Edens

Robbins Music Corporation Ltd . . . . USA
Film(s): . . . . .Little Nellie Kelly
Judy Garland . . . . **Brunswick 03211**
Ruby Murray . . . . **Columbia S 1079**
Dennis Martin . . . . **Decca LK 4366**
Judy Garland appeared in *Little Nellie Kelly*.

IT'S A HAP-HAP-HAPPY DAY   1940
Sammy Timberg / Winston Sharples / Al Neiburg
Victoria Music Co. Ltd. . . . . USA
Film(s): . . . . Gulliver's Travels
Phyllis Robins . . . . **Parlophone F 1643**
Gracie Fields . . . . **Regal Zonophone MR 3226**
Dick Todd . . . . **HMV BD 811**

IT'S A HARD LIFE   August 1984
Freddie Mercury
EMI Music . . . . UK
Queen . . . . **EMI QUEEN 3**

IT'S A HEARTACHE   January 1978
Ronnie Scott / Stevie Wolfe
Rak Music Ltd . . . . UK
Bonnie Tyler . . . . **RCA PB 5057**
Ivor Novello Nomination.

IT'S A HUNDRED TO ONE I'M IN LOVE   1940
Dick Jurgens / Ronnie Kemper
Robbins Music Corporation Ltd. USA
Dick Todd . . . . **HMV BD 779**
Jan Savitt & his Tophatters, vocal "Bon-Bon" . . **Brunswick 03101**

IT'S A LONG WAY TO TIPPERARY   1912
Jack Judge / Harry Williams
B. Feldman & Co. Ltd. . . . . UK
Show(s): . . . . Chin Chin / Dancing Around
Film(s): . . . . Wait Till the Sun Shines Nellie
John McCormack . . . . **HMV DA 475**
Harry Fay . . . . **Zonophone 1070**
Florrie Forde . . . . **Columbia 9780**
Kenneth McKellar . . . . **Decca F 11022**

IT'S A LOVE THING   April 1981
William Shelby / Dana Meyers
Chappell & Co. Ltd . . . . USA
The Whispers . . . . **Solar SO 16**

IT'S A LOVELY DAY TODAY   March 1952
Irving Berlin
Irving Berlin Ltd . . . . USA
Show(s): . . . . Call Me Madam
Film(s): . . . . Call Me Madam
Eileen Wilson & Dick Haymes . . . . **Brunswick LAT 8016**
Shani Wallis & Jeff Warren . . . . **Columbia 33SX 1002**
Carole Richards & Donald O'Connor . . . . . . **Brunswick LA 8603**
Shani Wallis & Jeff Warren appeared in the British production of *Call
Me Madam*.
Donald O'Connor appeared in the film *Call Me Madam*.
Carole Richards dubbed the singing voice for Vera-Ellen who ap-
peared in the film *Call Me Madam*.

IT'S A LOVELY DAY TOMORROW   1940
Irving Berlin
Victoria Music Co. ltd . . . . USA
Show(s): . . . . Louisiana Purchase
Film(s): . . . . Louisiana Purchase
Binnie Hale . . . . **Columbia FB 2386**
Al Bowlly . . . . **HMV BD 828**
Ron Goodwin & his Orchestra . . . . **Parlophone PMD 1038**

IT'S A MIRACLE   April 1984
George O'Dowd / Roy Hay / Michael Craig / John Moss / Phil Pickett
Warner Brothers Music . . . . UK
Culture Club . . . . **Virgin VS 662**

IT'S A MOST UNUSUAL DAY   May 1948
Harold Adamson / Jimmy McHugh
Robbins Music Corporation Ltd. USA
Film(s): . . . . A Date With Judy
Vera Lynn . . . . **Decca F 9078**
Chris Connor . . . . **London LTZK 15142**

IT'S A PITY TO SAY GOODNIGHT   1946
Billy Reid

Peter Maurice Music Co. Ltd.	UK
Dorothy Squires	Parlophone F 2146
Ella Fitzgerald	Brunswick 04312
Dorothy Squires	Pye NPL 18015
Pat Boone	London HAD 2144

IT'S A SHAME (MY SISTER) October 1990
Monie Love / David Steele
Virgin Music .... USA
Monie Love featuring True Image ..... **Cool Tempo COOL 219**

IT'S A SIN July 1987
Neil Tennant / Chris Lowe
10 Music .... UK
The Pet Shop Boys .... **Parlophone R 6158**
Ivor Novello Nomination

IT'S A SIN TO TELL A LIE 1936
Billy Mayhew
Francis, Day & Hunter Ltd .... USA
Ruth Etting .... **Rex 8853**
Henry Hall & the B.B.C. Dance Orchestra .. **Columbia FB 1506**
The Ink Spots .... **Brunswick 03653**
'Fats' Waller & his Rhythm .... **RCA RCX 1053**
Max Bygraves .... **Decca LK 4360**
Gerry Monroe (1971) .... **Chapter One CH 144**

IT'S A WONDERFUL WORLD March 1959
Harold Adamson / Jan Savitt / Johnny Watson
Robbins Music Ltd .... USA
Ralph Marterie & his Orchestra .... **Mercury MPT 7508**
Peggy Lee .... **Capitol T 1049**
Jan Savitt Orchestra .... **Brunswick LAT 8368**
Frank Sinatra .... **Reprise R 1002**

IT'S ALL IN THE GAME February 1952
Charles Dawes / Carl Sigman
Blossom Music Ltd .... USA
Jimmy Young .... **Polygon P 1032**
Nat 'King' Cole .... **Capitol LCT 6129**
Tommy Edwards (1958) .... **MGM C 774**
Louis Armstrong with
Gordon Jenkins Orchestra .... **Brunswick 04858**
Cliff Richard (1958) .... **Columbia DB 7089**
The Four Tops (1970) ...... **Tamla Motown TMG 736**
Adapted from *Melodie* by Charles Dawes.

IT'S ALL OVER May 1967
Don Everly
Acuff-Rose Publishing Co. Ltd. .... USA
Cliff Richard .... **Columbia DB 8150**

IT'S ALL OVER BABY BLUE September 1965
Bob Dylan
Blossom Music Ltd .... USA
Joan Baez .... **Fontana TF 604**

IT'S ALL OVER NOW January 1947
Sunny Skylar / Don Marcotte
Campbell Connelly & Co. Ltd .... USA
Joe Loss & his Orchestra .... **HMV BD 5953**
Rita Williams .... **Columbia FB 3269**
Russ Morgan & his Orchestra .... **Brunswick 04011**

IT'S ALL OVER NOW August 1964
Shirley Womack / Bob Womack
Kags Music Ltd .... USA
The Rolling Stones .... **Decca F 11934**

IT'S ALL RIGHT IN THE SUMMERTIME 1904
Fred Murray / George Everard
Francis, Day & Hunter Ltd. .... UK
Vesta Victoria .... **Columbia DX 290**
Gemma Jones .... **BBC RESL 45**

IT'S ALL RIGHT WITH ME September 1954
Cole Porter
Chappell & Co. Ltd. .... USA
Show(s): .... Can-Can
Film(s): .... Can-Can
Peter Cookson .... **Capitol LCT 6010**
Edmund Hockridge .... **Parlophone PMD 1017**
Eileen Barton .... **Vogue LVA 9096**
Lena Horne .... **RCA RD 27021**

Frank Sinatra .... **Capitol W 1310**
Peter Cookson appeared in the American production of *Can-Can*.
Edmund Hockridge appeared in the British production of *Can-Can*.
Frank Sinatra appeared in the film *Can-Can*.

IT'S ALMOST TOMORROW February 1956
Gene Adkinson / Wade Buff
Macmelodies Ltd. .... USA
Jo Stafford .... **Philips BBR 8084**
The Dream Weavers .... **Brunswick 05515**
Mark Wynter (1963) .... **Pye 7N 15577**

IT'S ALRIGHT July 1989
Sterling Void
EMI Music .... UK
The Pet Shop Boys .... **Parlophone R 6220**

IT'S ALRIGHT (Baby's Coming Back) January 1986
Annie Lennox / Dave Stewart
RCA Music .... UK
Eurythmics .... **RCA PB 40375**
Ivor Novello Award

IT'S ALWAYS YOU 1941
Johnny Burke / Jimmy Van Heusen
Victoria Music Co. Ltd .... USA
Film(s): .... Road to Zanzibar
Bing Crosby .... **Brunswick Bing 6**
Jimmy Young .... **Columbia 33SX 1102**
Vera Lynn .... **Decca LK 4152**
June Christy .... **Capitol T 833**
Bing Crosby appeared in *Road to Zanzibar*.

IT'S AN OPEN SECRET March 1964
Joy Webb
B. Feldman & Co. Ltd .... UK
The Joy Strings .... **Regal RZ 501**

IT'S BEEN A LONG LONG TIME 1945
Jule Styne / Sammy Cahn
Edwin H. Morris & Co. Ltd. .... USA
Film(s): ....I'll Get By
Bing Crosby .... **Brunswick LAT 8334**
Peggy Lee .... **Capitol T 1049**
Brook Benton .... **Mercury MMC 14060**

IT'S BEEN SO LONG 1936
Walter Donaldson / Harold Adamson
Sun Music Publishing Co. Ltd .... USA
Film(s): .... The Great Ziegfeld / The Benny Goodman Story
Ruth Etting .... **Brunswick 02218**
Bunny Berigan & his Orchestra .... **Philips BBL 7086**
Patti Page .... **Mercury MPL 6524**
Benny Goodman & his Orchestra .... **Brunswick LAT 8102**

IT'S BEEN SO LONG September 1975
Richard Finch / H.W. Casey
April Music Ltd .... USA
George McCrae .... **Jayboy BOY 100**

IT'S D'LOVELY 1938
Cole Porter
Chappell & Co. Ltd. .... USA
Show(s): .... Red Hot and Blue / The Fleet's Lit Up
Film(s): .... Anything Goes
Frances Day .... **HMV B 8790**
The Peters Sisters .... **Decca F 6893**
Ethel Merman .... **Brunswick LA 8634**
Mitzi Gaynor & Donald O'Connor ..... **Brunswick LAT 8118**
Ethel Merman appeared in *Red Hot and Blue*. Frances Day appeared in *The Fleet's Lit Up*.
Mitzi Gaynor & Donald O'Connor appeared in the 1956 film of *Anything Goes*.

IT'S DIFFERENT FOR GIRLS February 1980
Joe Jackson
Albion Music .... UK
Joe Jackson .... **A&M AMS 7493**

IT'S DREAMTIME 1947
Jack Brooks / Walter Schumann
Sun Music Publishing Co. Ltd. .... USA
Film(s): ....I'll Be Yours
The Skyrockets Dance Orchestra, conducted
by Paul Fenhoulet vocal Doreen Lundy .... **HMV BD 5967**

Mel Tormé . . . . **Parlophone R 3094**

IT'S EASY TO REMEMBER 1935
Richard Rodgers / Lorenz Hart
Victoria Music Co. Ltd . . . . USA
Film(s): . . . . Mississippi
Bing Crosby . . . . **Brunswick Bing 1**
Dinah Shore . . . . **Capitol T 1296**
Perry Como . . . . **RCA RD 27035**
Bing Crosby appeared in *Mississippi*.

IT'S FOOLISH BUT IT'S FUN 1941
Gus Kahn / Robert Stoltz
B. Feldman & Co. Ltd . . . . USA
Film(s): . . . . Spring Parade
Deanna Durbin . . . . **Brunswick 03163**
Petula Clark . . . . **Nixa NPL 18007**
Deanna Durbin appeared in *Spring Parade*.

IT'S FOR YOU August 1964
John Lennon / Paul McCartney
Northern Songs Ltd . . . . UK
Cilla Black . . . . **Parlophone R 5162**

IT'S FOUR IN THE MORNING September 1972
Jerry Chesnut
Burlington Music Co. Ltd. . . . . USA
Faron Young . . . . **Mercury 6052140**

IT'S FUNNY TO EVERYONE BUT ME 1940
Jack Lawrence
B. Feldman & Co. Ltd . . . . USA
The Ink Spots . . . . **Brunswick 02812**
Kay Starr . . . . **RCA RD 27056**
Dinah Shore . . . . **Capitol T 1354**

IT'S GETTING BETTER October 1969
Barry Mann / Cynthia Weil
Screen Gems Music Ltd. . . . . USA
Mama Cass . . . . **Stateside SS 8021**

IT'S GONNA BE A COLD COLD CHRISTMAS November 1975
Roger Greenaway / Geoff Stevens
Cookaway Music . . . . UK
Dana . . . . **GTO GT 45**

IT'S GOOD NEWS WEEK November 1965
Kenneth King
Jonjo Music Co. . . . . UK
Hedghoppers Anonymous . . . . **Decca F 12241**

IT'S IMPOSSIBLE (Somos Novios) April 1971
Ganch Manzanero / Sid Wayne
Sunbury Music Ltd . . . . Mexico
Perry Como . . . . **RCA 2043**

IT'S IN HIS KISS August 1975
Rudy Clark
T.M. Music Ltd . . . . USA
Linda Lewis . . . . **Arista 17**
Betty Everett . . . . **President PT 215**
Ramona King . . . . **Warner Brothers WB 125**

IT'S IN THE AIR 1939
Harry Parr-Davies
Keith Prowse Music Publishing Co. Ltd. . . . . UK
Film(s): . . . . It's in the Air
George Formby . . . . **Regal Zonophone MR 2891**
The R.A.F. Orchestra, conducted by R.P. O'Donnell . . **HMV RAF 5**
George Formby appeared in *It's in the Air*

IT'S JUST A MATTER OF TIME January 1959
Brook Benton / Clyde Otis / Belford Hendricks
Francis, Day & Hunter Ltd . . . . USA
Brook Benton . . . . **Mercury AMT 1014**

IT'S LATE May 1959
Dorsey Burnette
Commodore-Imperial Music Ltd . . . . USA
Ricky Nelson . . . . **London HAP 2159**
Vince Eager . . . . **Parlophone PMC 1101**
Shakin' Stevens (1983) . . . . **Epic A 3565**

IT'S LOVE AGAIN 1936
Sam Coslow

Cinephonic Music Co. Ltd . . . . UK
Film(s): . . . . It's Love Again
Jessie Matthews . . . . **Decca F 5982**
Ruth Etting . . . . **Rex 8852**
Lew Stone & his Band . . . . **Decca F 5984**
Jessie Matthews appeared in *It's Love Again*.

IT'S LOVE, LOVE, LOVE 1944
Mack David / Joan Whitney / Alex Kramer
Campbell Connelly & Co. Ltd. . . . . USA
Film(s): . . . . Stars on Parade / That Wonderful Urge
Dorothy Morrow's Aristocrats . . . . **Columbia FB 3037**
Donald Peers . . . . **Decca DFE 6387**
Lou Preager & his Orchestra,
vocal Edna Kaye . . . . **Regal Zonophone MR 3737**

IT'S MAGIC January 1949
Jule Styne
Campbell Connelly & Co. Ltd . . . . USA
Film(s): . . . . It's Magic / Starlift
Doris Day . . . . **Columbia DB 2493**
Sarah Vaughan . . . . **Mercury ZEP 10054**
Keely Smith . . . . **Capitol T 1145**
Doris Day appeared in both *It's Magic* and *Starlift*.
Nominated for Academy Award 1948.

IT'S MY LIFE November 1965
Roger Atkins / Carl D'Errico
Screen Gems - Columbia Music . . . . USA
The Animals . . . . **Columbia DB 7741**

IT'S MY LIFE June 1990
Mark Hollis / Tim Friese-Green
Zomba Music . . . . UK
Talk Talk . . . . **Parlophone R 6254**

IT'S MY MOTHER'S BIRTHDAY TODAY 1935
Eddie Lisbona / Tommie Connor
Dash Music Ltd . . . . UK
Joe Petersen . . . . **Rex 8601**
Teddy Johnson . . . . **Columbia DB 2902**

IT'S MY PARTY July 1963
Herb Weiner / John Gluck Jnr. / Wally Gold
Aaron Schroeder Ltd. . . . . USA
Lesley Gore . . . . **Mercury AMT 1205**
Helen Shapiro . . . . **Columbia 33SX 1561**
Dave Stewart & Barbara Gaskin (1981) . . . . **Stiff BRO 2**

IT'S NEVER TOO LATE TO FALL IN LOVE May 1954
Sandy Wilson
Chappell & Co. Ltd. . . . . UK
Show(s): . . . . The Boy Friend
Film(s): . . . . The Boy Friend
Maria Charles & John Rutland . . . . **HMV DLP 1078**
Geoffrey Hibbert & Dilys Lay . . . . **RCA LOC 1018**
Max Adrian & Georgina Hale . . . . **MGM 1SE 32 ST**
Maria Charles & John Rutland appeared in the British production of
The Boy Friend.
Geoffrey Hibbert & Dilys Lay appeared in the American production of
The Boy Friend.
Max Adrian & Georgina Hale appeared in the film of *The Boy Friend*.

IT'S NICE TO GET UP IN THE MORNING 1913
Harry Lauder
Francis, Day & Hunter Ltd. . . . . UK
Harry Lauder . . . . **HMV 02484**
George Elrick . . . . **Beltona ABL 509**

IT'S NOT UNUSUAL March 1965
Les Reed / Gordon Mills
Leeds Music Ltd . . . . UK
Film(s): . . . . Lost Flight
Tom Jones . . . . **Decca F 12062**
Ivor Novello Award.

IT'S NOW OR NEVER December 1960
Aaron Schroeder / Wally Gold
Aberbach (London) Ltd. . . . . USA
Elvis Presley . . . . **RCA 1209**
Adapted from *O Sole Mio* by Eduardo Di Capua.

IT'S ONE OF THOSE NIGHTS April 1972
Tony Romeo
Screen Gems Music Ltd . . . . USA

The Partridge Family . . . . Bell 1203

IT'S ONLY A PAPER MOON   **1934**
Harold Arlen / E.Y. Harburg / Billy Rose
Chappell & Co. Ltd. . . . . USA
Film(s): . . . . .Take a Chance / Too Young to Know
Cliff Edwards (Ukulele Ike) . . . . **Fontana TFL 5037**
Perry Como . . . . **Camden CDN 110**
Morgana King . . . . **Mercury MPL 6515**
Nat King Cole Trio . . . . **Capitol LC 6569**
Cliff Edwards appeared in *Take a Chance.*

IT'S ONLY LOVE   **September 1980**
Mark James / Steve Tyrell
Screen Gems Music Ltd . . . . USA
Elvis Presley . . . . **RCA 4**
B.J. Thomas . . . . **Pye 7N 25487**

IT'S ONLY MAKE BELIEVE   **January 1959**
Conway Twitty / Jack Nance
Francis, Day & Hunter Ltd . . . . USA
Conway Twitty . . . . **MGM C 781**
Connie Francis . . . . **MGM C 804**
Billy Fury (1964) . . . . **Decca F 11939**
Glen Campbell (1970) . . . . **Capitol CL 15663**
Child (1978) . . . . **Ariola AHA 522**

IT'S ONLY ROCK AND ROLL   **August 1974**
Mick Jagger / Keith Richard
Essex Music Ltd. . . . . UK
The Rolling Stones . . . . **Rolling Stones RS 19114**

IT'S OVER   **June 1964**
Roy Orbison / Bill Dees
Acuff-Rose Publishing Co. Ltd . . . . USA
Roy Orbison . . . . **London HL 9882**

IT'S OVER   **July 1983**
Mandy Newton / Tony Williams
Rock Master Music . . . . UK
Funk Masters . . . . **Master Funk 7MP 004**

IT'S OVER   **October 1987**
Mark King / Walter Badarou / Philip Gould
Island Music . . . . France
Level 42 . . . . **Polydor POSP 900**

IT'S RAINING   **October 1981**
Naomi Neville
United Artists Music . . . . USA
Shakin' Stevens . . . . **Epic EPC A 1643**

IT'S RAINING   **September 1978**
Ian Collier
Magnet Music . . . . UK
The Darts . . . . **Magnet MAG 126**

IT'S RAINING MEN   **April 1984**
Paul Jabara / Paul Shaffer
Warner Chappell Music . . . . USA
The Weather Girls . . . . **CBS A 2924**

IT'S RAINING SUNBEAMS   **1937**
Sam Coslow / Frederick Hollander
Harms-Connelly Ltd. . . . . USA
Film(s): . . . . One Hundred Men and a Girl
Deanna Durbin . . . . **Brunswick 02486**
Deanna Durbin appeared in *One Hundred Men and a Girl.*

IT'S SO EASY   **September 1970**
Dor Lee / Dave Watkins
Valley Music . . . . UK
Andy Williams . . . . **CBS S 5113**

IT'S SO NICE TO HAVE A MAN
AROUND THE HOUSE   **April 1950**
Jack Elliot / Harold Spina
Edwin H. Morris & Co. Ltd . . . . USA
Ethel Merman & Ray Bolger . . . . **Brunswick 04491**
Eydie Gormé & Steve Lawrence . . . . **HMV CLP 1463**

IT'S STILL ROCK AND ROLL TO ME   **September 1980**
Billy Joel
April Music Ltd . . . . USA
Billy Joel . . . . **CBS 8753**

IT'S THE DARNDEST THING   **1931**
Dorothy Fields / Jimmy McHugh
Keith Prowse Music Publishing Co. Ltd. . . . . USA
Film(s): . . . . .Singin' the Blues
Red Nichols & his Orchestra . . . . **Brunswick 1275**

IT'S THE NATURAL THING TO DO   **1937**
Arthur Johnston / Johnny Burke
Campbell Connelly & Co. Ltd. . . . . USA
Film(s): . . . . .Double or Nothing
Bing Crosby . . . . **Brunswick Bing 3**
Petula Clark . . . . **Nixa NPL 18007**

IT'S THE SAME OLD DREAM   **1947**
Jule Styne / Sammy Cahn
Edwin H. Morris & Co. Ltd. . . . . USA
Film(s): . . . . .It Happened in Brooklyn
Frank Sinatra . . . . **Columbia DB 2296**
Artie Shaw & his Orchestra,
vocal Mel Tormé . . . . **Parlophone R 3067**
Frank Sinatra . . . . **Capitol LCT 6155**
Frank Sinatra appeared in *It Happened in Brooklyn.*

IT'S THE SAME OLD SONG   **October 1965**
Brian Holland / Eddie Holland / Lamont Dozier
Jobete Music (UK) Ltd. . . . . USA
The Four Tops . . . . **Tamla Motown TMG 528**
The Weathermen (1971) . . . . **B&C CB 139**
K.C. & The Sunshine Band . . . . **T.K. TKR 6037**

IT'S THE TALK OF THE TOWN   **1933**
Marty Symes / Al Neiburg / Jerry Livingston
Keith Prowse Music Publishing Co. Ltd. . . . . USA
Annette Hanshaw . . . . **Edison Bell Winner W 20**
Connee Boswell . . . . **Brunswick 01594**
Bing Crosby . . . . **Brunswick 04116**
Kay Starr . . . . **Capitol T 948**
Perry Como . . . . **RCA RD 27070**

IT'S TIME FOR LOVE   **October 1975**
Eugene Record
Burlington Music Co. Ltd . . . . USA
The Chi-Lites . . . . **Brunswick BR 25**

IT'S TIME TO SAY GOODNIGHT   **1934**
Henry Hall / Kate Gibson
Ascherberg, Hopwood & Crew Ltd. UK
The BBC Dance Orchestra,
conducted by Henry Hall . . . . **Columbia CB 716**
Henry Hall & his Orchestra,
vocal The Coronets . . . . **Columbia 33SX 1067**

IT'S TOO LATE   **September 1971**
Carole King / Toni Stern
Screen Gems Music Ltd . . . . USA
Carole King . . . . **A&M AMS 849**

IT'S TOO SOON TOO KNOW   **May 1958**
Deborah Chessler
Edwin H. Morris . . . . USA
Ella Fitzgerald . . . . **Brunswick 04051**
Pat Boone . . . . **London HLD 8574**

IT'S WONDERFUL   **November 1970**
James Dean / William Witherspoon
Jobete Music (UK) Ltd. . . . . USA
Jimmy Ruffin . . . . **Tamla Motown TMG 753**

IT'S YOU   **March 1974**
Larry Butler
London Tree Music Ltd. . . . . USA
Freddie Starr . . . . **Tiffany 6121501**
Pat Campbell (Spoken) . . . . **Major Minor MCP 5051**

IT'S YOU OR NO-ONE   **February 1949**
Jule Styne / Sammy Cahn
Campbell Connelly & Co. Ltd. . . . . USA
Film(s): . . . . .It's Magic
Doris Day . . . . **Columbia DB 2503**
Dakota Staton . . . . **Capitol T 1325**
Doris Day appeared in *It's Magic.*

IT'S YOUR LIFE   **August 1977**
Mike Chapman / Nicky Chinn
Rak Music Ltd . . . . UK

Smokie . . . . **Rak 260**

ITALIAN STREET SONG — 1910
Victor Herbert / Rida Johnson Young
B. Feldman & Co. Ltd . . . . USA
Show(s): . . . . Naughty Marietta
Film(s): . . . . Naughty Marietta
Jeanette MacDonald . . . . **HMV B 8320**
Nadine Connor . . . . **Philips NBE 11116**
Paul Britten & his Orchestra . . . . **MGM C 779**
Jeanette MacDonald appeared in the film *Naughty Marietta.*

ITALIAN THEME, THE (Mambo Caliente) — June 1956
Angelo Giacomazzi / Clyde Hamilton / Buddy Kaye
World Wide Music Co. Ltd. . . . . Italy
Cyril Stapleton & his Orchestra . . . . **Decca F 10703**
Dorothy Collins . . . . **Vogue Q 72198**

ITCHYCOO PARK — September 1967
Steve Marriott / Ronnie Lane
United Artists Music Co. Ltd. . . . . UK
The Small Faces . . . . **Immediate IM 057**
The Small Faces (1976) . . . . **Immediate IMS 102**

ITSY BITSY TEENIE WEENIE
YELLOW POLKA DOT BIKINI — August 1960
Lee Pockriss / Paul Vance
Campbell Connelly & Co. Ltd . . . . USA
Brian Hyland (1960) . . . . **London HLP 9161**
Paul Handford . . . . **Parlophone R 4680**
Bombalurina (1990) . . . . **Carpet CRP 1**

IVORY RAG — July 1951
Lou Busch / Jack Elliott
Macmelodies Ltd . . . . USA
Joe 'Fingers' Carr (piano) . . . . **Capitol T 1217**
Sid Philips & his Band, vocal Johnnie Eager . . . **HMV BD 6100**
Crazy Otto (piano) . . . . **Polydor LPH 45042**

IVORY TOWER — June 1956
Jack Fulton / Lois Steele
Chappell & Co. Ltd. . . . . USA
Cathy Carr . . . . **London HLH 8274**
Otis Williams . . . . **Parlophone MSP 6239**

J'ATTENDRAI — 1939
Bruce Sievier / Dino Olivieri / Nino Rastelli & L. Poterat
Francis, Day & Hunter Ltd. . . . . France
Tino Rossi . . . . **Columbia 33S 1008**
The Troubadours . . . . **London HAR 2249**
Patachou . . . . **Philips BBL 7423**
Jean Sablon . . . . **Brunswick 03858**
Theme song of Jean Sablon.

JA-DA — 1919
Bob Carelton
Francis, Day & Hunter Ltd. . . . . USA
Show(s): . . . . Bran Pie
Film(s):Rose of Washington Square / The Five Pennies / The Rat Race
The Two Bobs . . . . **Edison Bell Winner 3334**
Bob Crosby & his Band . . . . **Vogue LVA 9045**
Muggsy Spanier's Ragtime Band . . . . **Vogue EPV 1237**
Red Nichols & his Five Pennies . . . . **Capitol T 1297**
Johnny & The Hurricanes (1961) . . . . **London HL 9289**
The Two Bobs appeared in *Bran Pie.*

JACK AND JILL — May 1978
Ray Parker Jnr
Warner Brothers Music Ltd . . . . USA
Raydio . . . . **Arista 161**

JACK IN A BOX — April 1971
David Myers / John Worsley
Southern Music Publishing Co. Ltd . . . . UK
Clodagh Rodgers . . . . **RCA 2066**
United Kingdom entry for the 1971 Eurovision Song Contest (Placed Fourth).

JACK IN THE BOX — February 1977
Al Goodman / Harry Ray / Tony Keith
Sunbury Music Ltd . . . . USA
The Moments . . . . **All Platinum 6146318**

JACK THAT HOUSE BUILT, THE — May 1987
Ed Stratton / Vlad Naslas

Oval Music . . . . UK
Jack 'n' Chill . . . . **Oval TEN 174**

JACK YOUR BODY — January 1987
Steve Hurley
Unknown Publisher . . . . USA
Steve 'Silk' Hurley . . . . **London LON 117**

JACKIE WILSON SAID — October 1982
Van Morrison
Warner Brothers Music . . . . USA
Kevin Rowland & Dexy's Midnight Runners . . **Mercury DEXYS 10**

JAILHOUSE ROCK — January 1958
Jerry Leiber / Mike Stoller
Belinda (London) Ltd . . . . USA
Film(s): . . . . Jailhouse Rock
Elvis Presley . . . . **RCA RD 27159**
Elvis Presley appeared in *Jailhouse Rock.*

JAMAICAN RUMBA — February 1948
Arthur Benjamin
Boosey & Hawkes Music Publishers Ltd. . . . . UK
The London Symphony Orchestra,
conducted by Muir Mathieson . . . . **Decca K 1571**
The Eastman-Rochester 'Pops' Orchestra . . **Mercury MMA 11045**

JAMBALAYA (On The Bayou) — October 1952
Hank Williams
Chappell & Co. Ltd . . . . USA
Hank Williams . . . . **MGM D 137**
Joni James . . . . **MGM C 785**
Jo Stafford . . . . **Philips BBL 7395**
Brenda Lee . . . . **Brunswick LAT 8347**
The Carpenters (1974) . . . . **A&M AMS 7098**

JAMES BOND THEME, THE — December 1962
Monty Norman
United Artists Music Co. Ltd . . . . UK
Film(s): . . . . Doctor No
The John Barry Seven . . . . **Columbia DB 4898**
John Barry & his Orchestra (Sound Track) **United Artists ULP 1052**
Johnny & The Hurricanes . . . . **London REX 1414**

JAMMING — January 1978
Bob Marley
Rondor Music (London) Ltd . . . . UK
Bob Marley & The Wailers . . . . **Island WIP 6410**

JANETTE — 1928
Horatio Nicholls
Lawrence Wright Music Co. Ltd. . . . . UK
Jack Hylton & his Orchestra . . . . **HMV B 5422**

JANUARY — February 1975
Dave Patton
Robbins Music Ltd . . . . UK
Pilot . . . . **EMI 2255**

JANUARY FEBRUARY — April 1980
Alan Tarney
A.T.V. Music Ltd. . . . . UK
Barbara Dickson . . . . **Epic EPC 8115**
Ivor Novello Nomination.

JAPANESE BOY — August 1981
Bob Heatlie
EMI Music . . . . UK
Aneka . . . . **Ariola MANSA 5**

JAPANESE SANDMAN — 1920
Ray Egan / Richard A. Whiting
B. Feldman & Co. Ltd . . . . USA
Nora Bayes (Original artiste) . . . . **Columbia 3008**
Paul Whiteman & his Orchestra . . . . **HMV B 116**
The Andrews Sisters . . . . **Capitol T 9**
Connee Boswell . . . . **RCA RD 270**

JARROW SONG, THE — June
Alan Price
Keith Prowse Music Publishing Co. Ltd. . . . .
Alan Price . . . . **Warner Brothers K**

JAVA JIVE
Milton Drake / Ben Oakland

Chappell & Co. Ltd .... USA
The Ink Spots .... Brunswick 03197
The King Sisters .... Regal Zonophone MR 3403

JAWS   November 1976
Paul Williams
Leeds Music Ltd .... USA
Film(s): .... Jaws
Lalo Schifrin .... CTI CTSP 005
Orchestra conducted by Paul Williams
(Sound Track) .... MCA MCF 2716

JAZZ ME BLUES   1921
Tom Delaney
Herman Darewski Music Publising Co. Ltd .... USA
The Original Dixieland Jazz Band .... HMV B 1257
Bix Beiderbecke & his Gang .... Philips BBL 7356
Bob Crosby's Bob Cats .... Brunswick LAT 8050
Matty Matlock & The Paducah Patrol . Warner Brothers WM 4027

JE NE SAIS PAS, POURQUOI   November 1988
Mike Stock / Matt Aitken / Peter Waterman
All Boys Music .... UK
Kylie Minogue .... PWL PWL 21

JE T'AIME, MOI NON PLUS   October 1969
Serge Gainsbourg
Shapiro-Bernstein & Co. Ltd. .... France
Jane Birkin & Serge Gainsbourg .... Fontana 260196
Jane Birkin & Serge Gainsbourg ...... Major Minor MCP 5044
Judge Dread (1975) .... Cactus CT 65

JEALOUS   1924
Jack Little / Tommie Malie / Dick Finch
B. Feldman & Co. Ltd. .... USA
Film(s): .... The Feminine Touch / Somebody Loves Me
The International Novelty Orchestra .... HMV B 1891
The Andrews Sisters .... Brunswick 03268
Teresa Brewer .... Vogue LVA 9020
Pee Wee Hunt & his Orchestra .... Capitol T 1523

JEALOUS GUY   March 1981
John Lennon
Northern Songs .... UK
Roxy Music .... Polydor ROXY 2
Owen Gray .... Island WIP 6185
Frankie Miller .... Chrysalis CHR 1128

JEALOUS HEART   November 1949
Jennie Lou Carson
Chappell & Co. Ltd .... USA
Al Morgan .... London HAPB 1001
Tex Ritter .... Capitol CL 14900

JEALOUS MIND   March 1974
Peter Shelley
Magnet Music .... UK
Alvin Stardust .... Magnet MAGS 5

JEALOUSY   1927
Jacob Gade / Winifred May (English Lyrics) / Vera Bloom (American Lyrics)
Lawrence Wright Music Co. Ltd. .... Denmark
Film(s): ..... Anchors Aweigh / Painting the Clouds With Sunshine
Orchestra Da Ballo .... Regal G 9054
The Boston 'Pops' Orchestra .... RCA RCX 1013
Connie Francis .... MGM C 836
Lucille Norman .... Capitol CL 13679
Emmanuel Vardi & his Orchestra ...... Brunswick LAT 8112
Billy Fury (1961) .... Decca F 11384
Frankie Laine .... Columbia DB 2970
Kathryn Grayson .... MGM 130
Lucille Norman appeared in *Painting the Clouds with Sunshine.*
Kathryn Grayson appeared in *Anchors Aweigh.*

EAN GENIE, THE   February 1973
vid Bowie
ysalis Music Ltd. .... UK
'd Bowie .... RCA 2302

NIE   February 1962
Stanford / Norman Newell
Kassner Music Co. Ltd. .... UK
Villiams .... HMV POP 968

Russ Conway &The William Singers .... Columbia 33SX 1214
Ivor Novello Nomination.

JEANNINE, I DREAM OF LILAC TIME   1928
L. Wolfe Gilbert / Nat Shilkret
Francis, Day & Hunter Ltd .... USA
John McCormack .... HMV DA 1027
Ben Selvin & his Orchestra .... Columbia 5122
Layton & Johnstone .... Columbia 5239
**Louis Armstrong with Gordon Jenkins
& His Orchestra** .... Brunswick LA 8700

JEANS ON   August 1976
David Dundas / Roger Greenaway
Dick James Music Ltd .... UK
David Dundas .... Air CHS 2094

JEEPERS CREEPERS   1939
Harry Warren / Johnny Mercer
B. Feldman & Co. Ltd. .... USA
Film(s): .... Going Places
Nat Gonella & his Georgians .... Parlophone F 1376
The Mills Brothers .... Brunswick 02725
Mel Tormé .... Vogue LVA 9004
Louis Armstrong Orchestra .... Decca F 6990
Maxine Sullivan .... Parlophone PMC 7123
Louis Armstrong .... RCA ZL 71036
Louis Armstrong & Maxine Sullivan appeared in *Going Places.*
The RCA recording by Louis Armstrong is part of the soundtrack of
Going Places.
Nominated for an Academy Award 1938.

JEEPSTER   December 1971
Marc Bolan
Essex Music Ltd .... UK
T. Rex .... Fly BUG 16

JENNIFER ECCLES   May 1968
Allan Clarke / Graham Nash
Gralto Music Ltd. .... UK
The Hollies .... Parlophone R 5680

JENNIFER JUNIPER   April 1968
Donovan Leitch
Donovan Music Ltd. .... UK
Donovan .... Pye 7N 17457

JENNY   1943
Ira Gershwin / Kurt Weill
Chappell & Co. Ltd .... USA
Show(s): .... Lady in the Dark / Berlin to Broadway
Film(s): .... Lady in the Dark / Star
**Joe Loss & his Orchestra,
vocal Elizabeth Batey** .... HMV BD 5845
Hildegarde .... Brunswick 03512
Gertrude Lawrence .... HMV DLP 1099
Judy Lander, Jerry Lanning & Hal Watters . Paramount PAS 4000
Julie Andrews .... Stateside SL 10233
Gertrude Lawrence appeared in the show *Lady in the Dark.*
Judy Lander, Jerry Lanning & Hal Watters appeared in *Berlin To Broadway.*
Julie Andrews appeared in *Star.*

JERSEY BOUNCE   1942
Robert Plater / Edward Johnson / Tiny Bradshaw & Robert Wright
Sterling Music Publishing Co. Ltd .... USA
Film(s): .... Sweet and Lowdown / The Benny Goodman Story
Jimmy Dorsey & his Orchestra .... Brunswick 03348
Les Brown & his Band .... Vogue LVA 9002
Benny Goodman & his Orchestra ...... Brunswick LAT 8103
Benny Goodman Orchestra appeared in *Sweet and Lowdown.*

JET   March 1974
Paul McCartney
McCartney Music .... UK
Wings .... Apple R 5996

JEZEBEL   July 1951
Wayne Shanklin
Campbell Connelly & Co. Ltd .... USA
Film(s): .... Seven Hills of Rome
Frankie Laine .... Philips BBL 7331
Jim Lowe .... London HAD 2146
Mario Lanza .... RCA RA 13001
Mario Lanza appeared in *Seven Hills of Rome.*

JIG A JIG   **May 1971**
Uncle Doris Music Ltd. . . . .
East of Eden . . . . **Deram DM 297**

JILTED   **June 1954**
Bob Colby / Dick Manning
Sterling Music Co. . . . . USA
Red Foley . . . . **Brunswick 05307**
Joan Regan . . , ... **Decca F 10311**
Frankie Vaughan & Alma Cogan . . . . **HMV B 10712**

JILTED JOHN   **September 1978**
J.G. John
Sparta Music Ltd . . . . , ... UK
Jilted John . . . . **EMI INT 567**

JIM   **1942**
Caesar Petrillo / Edward Ross / Nelson Shawn
Peter Maurice Music Co. Ltd . . . . USA
Film(s): . . . . Yokel Boy
Dinah Shore . . . . **Regal Zonophone MR 3605**
Peggy Loe . . . . **Capitol T 1131**

JIMMY JIMMY   **June 1979**
John O'Neill
Warner Brothers Music Ltd. . . . . UK
The Undertones . . . . **Sire SIR 4015**

JIMMY UNKNOWN   **March 1956**
Ruth Roberts / Bill Katz
Yale Music Corporation Ltd. . . . . USA
Doris Day . . . . **Philips BBR 8094**
Lita Roza . . . . **Decca LF 1266**

JINGLE BELL ROCK   **November 1958**
Joe Beal / Jim Boothe
Essex Music Ltd . . . . USA
Max Bygraves . . . . , ... **Decca F 11176**
Teresa Brewer . . . . **Vogue LVA 9137**
Bobby Helms . . . . , . . . **Brunswick 05765**

JINGLE, JANGLE, JINGLE   **1942**
Joseph Lilley / Frank Loesser
Chappell & Co. Ltd . . . . , . . . USA
Film(s): . . . . The Forest Rangers
The Merry Macs . . . . **Brunswick LAT 8350**
Gene Autry . . . . **Regal Zonophone MR 3666**
Bill Shepherd & his Ocrhestra,
vocal The Beryl Stott Chorus . . . . **Pye NPL 16018**

JINGO   **January 1988**
Michael Olatunji
SBK Songs . . . . USA
Jellybean . . . . **Chrysalis JEL 2**

JIVE TALKIN'   **August 1975**
Barry Gibb / Robin Gibb / Maurice Gibb
Abigail Music . . . . UK
Film(s): . . . . Saturday Night Fever
The Bee Gees . . . . **RSO 2090160**
Boogie Box High (1987) . . . . **Hardback 7 BOSS 4**

JOAN OF ARC   **November 1981**
Andy McCluskey
Dinsong Ltd . . . . UK
Orchestral Manoeuvres In The Dark . . . . **Dindisc DIN 36**

JOANNA   **June 1968**
Tony Hatch / Jackie Trent
Welbeck Music Co. Ltd. . . . . , ... UK
Scott Walker . . . . **Philips BF 1662**

JOANNA   **March 1984**
Charles Smith / James Taylor / "Kool & The Gang"
Planetary-Nom Music . . . . UK
Kool & The Gang . . . . **Phonogram DE 16**

JOE LE TAXI   **March 1988**
Frank Langolff / Elienne Roda
Warner Chappell Music . . . . France
Vanessa Paradis . . , ... **Polydor POSP 902**

JOHN AND JULIE   **August 1955**
Philip Green

David Toff Music Publishing Co. Ltd. . . . . UK
Film(s): . . . . John and Julie
Eddie Calvert & his Orchestra . . . . **Columbia SEG 7627**
Ivor Novello Nomination.

JOHN I'M ONLY DANCING   **October 1972**
David Bowie
Chrysalis Music Ltd. . . . . UK
David Bowie . . . . **RCA 2263**
David Bowie (1980) . . . . **RCA BOW 4**

JOHNNY COME HOME   **July 1985**
David Steele / Roland Gift
Virgin Music . . . . UK
Fine Young Cannibals . . . . **London LON 68**

JOHNNY DOUGHBOY FOUND A ROSE IN IRELAND   **1943**
Al Goodhart / Kay Twomey
Sterling Music Publishing Co. Ltd . . . . USA
Film(s). Johnny Doughboy
Kenny Baker . . , ... **Brunswick 03336**
Guy Lombardo & his Royal Canadians . . . . . . **Brunswick 03344**

JOHNNY FEDORA   **1946**
Allie Wrubel / Ray Gilbert
Leeds Music Ltd. . . . . , ... USA
Film(s): . . . . Make Mine Music (cartoon)
The Andrews Sisters . . , ... **Brunswick 03627**

JOHNNY GUITAR   **July 1954**
Peggy Lee / Victor Young
Chappell & Co. Ltd. . . . . USA
Film(s): . . . . Johnny Guitar
Peggy Lee . . . . **Brunswick 05286**
Norman George . . . . **Pye NEP 24126**

JOHNNY IS THE BOY FOR ME   **May 1953**
Paddy Roberts / Marcel Stellman
Francis, Day & Hunter Ltd . . . . UK
Les Paul & Mary Ford . . . . **Capitol EAP 1-21045**
Adapted from the Romanian folk song *Sanie Cu Zurgalai*.

JOHNNY ONE NOTE   **1940**
Richard Rodgers / Lorenz Hart
Chappell & Co. Ltd . . . . USA
Show(s): . . . . Babes in Arms
Film(s): . . . . Words and Music
Judy Garland . . . . **MGM C 853**
Chris Connor . . . . **London LTZK 15151**
Ella Fitzgerald . . , ... **HMV CLP 1116**
Judy Garland appeared in *Words and Music.*

JOHNNY PEDLER   **1941**
Laurindo Almeida / U. Nasdan / Lew Brown
Francis, Day & Hunter Ltd . . , ... , ... USA
The Andrews Sisters . . . . **Brunswick 03104**

JOHNNY REGGAE   **December 1971**
Jonathan King
Jonjo Music Co. Ltd . . . . , . . . UK
The Piglets . . . . **Bell BLL 1180**

JOHNNY REMEMBER ME   **September 1961**
Geoffrey Goddard
Meridian Music Publishing Co. Ltd. . . . . UK
John Leyton . . . . **Top Rank JAR 577**

JOHNNY WILL   **January 19**
Fred Tobias / Paul Evans
Blossom Music Ltd. . . . .
Pat Boone . . . . **London HLD**

JOHNNY ZERO
Vee Lawnhurst / Mack David
Campbell Connelly & Co. Ltd
Ambrose & his Orchestra,
vocal Anne Shelton . . . .

JOHNSON RAG
Henry Kleinkauf / Jack Lawrence / Guy Hall
Francis, Day & Hunter Ltd . . . . , ...
The Merry Macs . . . . ,
Glenn Miller & his Orchestra . . . .
The Jack Teter Trio (1949) . . . .

Russ Morgan & his Orchestra (1949) .... Brunswick 04441
Red Nichols & his Five Pennies .... Capitol T 1297

JOIN TOGETHER
July 1972
Peter Townshend
Fabulous Music Ltd. .... UK
The Who .... Track 2094102

JOINT IS JUMPIN', THE
1938
Andy Razaf / Thomas Waller / James Johnson
.... USA
Fats Waller & his Rhythm .... HMV BD 1079
George Melly .... Warner Brothers K 46269
Teresa Brewer .... Doctor Jazz ASLD 85?

JOKER, THE
September 1990
Steve Miller / Ahmet Ertegun / Eddie Curtis
Warner Chappell Music .... USA
Steve Miller Band .... Capitol CL 583

JOLENE
June 1976
Dolly Parton
Carlin Music Corporation .... USA
Dolly Parton .... RCA 2675

JOLLITY FARM
1930
Leslie Sarony
Lawrence Wright Music Co. Ltd .... UK
Jack Payne & The BBC Dance Orchestra ..... Columbia 5729

JOLLY BROTHERS, THE (Lustige Bruder)
1933
Robert Volstedt
Herman Darewski Music Publishing Co. Ltd. .... Germany
The International Novelty Orchestra .... HMV C 1682
The Hodlars .... Columbia DC 707
Victor Sylvester's Harmony Music .... Parlophone R 1387
Albert Whelan .... Fontana TFL 5043
Theme tune of Albert Whelan.

JOLLY GOOD COMPANY
1931
Raymond Wallace
Campbell Connelly & Co. Ltd. .... UK
Jack & Claude Hulbert .... HMV B 4003
The Coronets .... Columbia SEG 7617
The Big Ben Banjo Band .... Columbia SCD 2121

JOLLY GOOD LUCK TO THE GIRL WHO LOVES A SOLDIER
1907
Fred W. Leigh / Kenneth Lyle
Francis, Day & Hunter Ltd. .... UK
Film(s): .... After the Ball
Vesta Tilley .... Regal G 7079

JONES BOY, THE
March 1954
Mann Curtis / Vic Mizzy
Bradbury Wood Ltd. .... USA
The Mills Brothers .... Brunswick 05240
Max Bygraves .... HMV 7M 180
The Mills Brothers .... London HAD 2319
Billy Cotton & his Band .... Decca F 10266

JOSEPH, JOSEPH
1938
Sammy Cahn / Saul Chaplin
Sterling Music Publishing Co. Ltd. .... USA
The Andrews Sisters .... Brunswick 02654

JOSH-U-AH
1910
George Arthurs / Bert Lee
Francis, Day & Hunter Ltd. .... UK
?ice Mayne & "That" .... HMV 03290
?ng at 'Jim's Inn' .... Piccadilly NPL 38002

?NEY TO A STAR, A
1944
?arren / Leo Robin
?Wood Ltd. .... USA
.... The Girls He Left Behind
?d .... Brunswick 03515
?ess .... Regal Zonophone MR 3726

October 1973
?td. .... UK
?arth Band .... Vertigo 6059083
? Movement (Jupiter-Bringer of Jollity) of "The
?" by Gustav Holst (1874 - 1934).

JUDY IN DISGUISE
March 1968
John Fred / Andrew Bernard
Jewel Music Publishing Co. Ltd. .... USA
John Fred & The Playboy Band .... ?e 7N 25442

JUDY TEEN
June 1974
Steve Harley
Rak Music Ltd. .... UK
Cockney Rebel .... EMI 2128

JUKE BOX ?VE
December 1974
Wayne ?ckerton / Tony Waddington
A.T.V. Music Ltd. .... UK
The Rubettes .... Polydor 2058529

JUKE BOX SATURDAY NIGHT
1945
Paul McGrane / Al Stillman
Chappell & Co. Ltd. .... USA
Show(s): .... Stars on Ice
Glenn Miller & his Orchestra, vocal Marion
Hutton, Tex Beneke and the Modernaires ..... RCA RCX 1034

JULIE DO YA LOVE ME
December 1970
Tom Bahler
Warner Brothers Music Ltd .... UK
White Plains .... Deram DM 315

JULIE-ANN
September 1975
Bill Martin / Phil Coulter
Martin-Coulter Music Ltd .... UK
Kenny .... Rak 214

JULIET
May 1964
Mike Wilsh / Fritz Fryer / Lionel Morton
Flamingo Music Ltd .... UK
The Four Pennies .... Philips BF 1322

JUMP
March 1984
Ted Templeton
Warner Brothers Music .... USA
Van Halen .... Warner Brothers W 9384

JUMP (For My Love)
July 1984
Marti Sharron / Steve Mitchell / Gary Skardina
MCA Music .... USA
The Pointer Sisters .... Planet RPS 106

JUMP TO THE BEAT
July 1980
Narada Michael Walden / Lisa Walden
Warner Brothers Music Ltd .... USA
Stacy Lattisaw .... Atlantic K 11496

JUMPING BEAN
January 1949
Robert Farnon
Chappell & Co. Ltd .... UK
The Kingsway Symphony Orchestra,
conducted by Robert Farnon .... Decca F 9038
Sidney Torch & his Orchestra .... Parlophone R 3161

JUMPING JACK FLASH
July 1968
Mick Jagger / Keith Richard
Mirage Music Ltd. .... UK
The Rolling Stones .... Decca F 12782

JUNE BROUGHT THE ROSES
1924
Ralph Stanley / John Openshaw
B. Feldman & Co. Ltd. .... USA
The Troubadours .... HMV B 1924

JUNE COMES AROUND EVERY YEAR
1945
Johnny Mercer / Harold Arlen
Edwin H. Morris & Co. Ltd. .... USA
Film(s): .... Out of This World
Bing Crosby .... Brunswick 03596

JUNE IN JANUARY
1935
Leo Robin / Ralph Rainger
Chappell & Co. Ltd .... USA
Film(s): .... Here is My Heart
Bing Crosby .... Brunswick Bing 1
Jo Stafford .... Philips BBL 7187
Dean Martin .... Capitol EAP 2-1285
Bing Crosby appeared in *Here Is My Heart*.

JUNE IS BUSTING OUT ALL OVER   June 1950
Richard Rodgers / Oscar Hammerstein II
Williamson Music Ltd . . . . USA
Show(s): . . . . Carousel
Film(s): . . . . Carousel
Christine Johnson & Jean Darling . . . . . **Brunswick LAT 8006**
Marion Ross & chorus . . . . **Columbia SED 5536**
Clara Mae Turner & Barbara Ruick . . . . . **Capitol LCT 6105**
Christine Johnson & Jean Darling appeared in the American production
of *Carousel.*
Marion Ross appeared in the British production of *Carousel.*
Clara Mae Turner & Barbara Ruick appeared in the film of *Carousel.*

JUNE NIGHT   1924
Cliff Friend / Abel Baer
Francis, Day & Hunter Ltd. . . . . USA
The Carolina Club Orchestra . . . . **Columbia 3446**
Frankie Vaughan . . . . **Philips BBL 7330**
The McGuire Sisters . . . . **Vogue LVA 9024**

JUNGLE ROCK   May 1976
Hank Mizell / James Bobo / Bob Collins / Eddie Simonton
Carlin Music Corporation . . . . USA
Hank Mizell . . . . **Charly CS 1005**

JUST A COTTAGE SMALL (By A Waterfall)   1926
Buddy De Sylva / James Hanley
Chappell & Co. Ltd. . . . . USA
John McCormack . . . . **HMV DA 765**
Guy Lombardo & his Royal Canadians . . . . . **Capitol LCT 6127**

JUST A GIGOLO   1930
Leanello Cassucci / Irving Caesar
Lawrence Wright Music Co. Ltd . . . . Austria
Bing Crosby . . . . **HMV 7EG 8139**
The Jonah Jones Quartet . . . . **Capitol T 1039**

JUST A GIRL THAT MEN FORGET   1923
Al Dubin / Fred Rath / Joe Garren
Lawrence Wright Music Co. Ltd . . . . USA
The Troubadours . . . . **HMV B 1730**
Max Bygraves with Ted Heath & His Music . . . . **Decca LK 4317**

JUST A KID NAMED JOE   1939
Mack David / Jerry Livingston
Francis, Day & Hunter Ltd. . . . . USA
Bing Crosby . . . . **Brunswick 02718**

JUST A LITTLE BIT BETTER   September 1965
Kenny Young
T.M. Music Ltd . . . . USA
Herman's Hermits . . . . **Columbia DB 7670**

JUST A LITTLE FOND AFFECTION   1945
Lewis Ilda / Elton Box / Desmond Cox
Dash Music Ltd. . . . . UK
Joe Loss & his Orchestra,
vocal Elizabeth Batey . . . . **HMV BD 5872**

JUST A LITTLE TOO MUCH   September 1959
Johnny Burnette
Chappell & Co. Ltd . . . . USA
Ricky Nelson . . . . **London HAP 2206**

JUST A MEMORY   1928
Buddy De Sylva / Lew Brown / Ray Henderson
Chappell & Co. Ltd. . . . . USA
Film(s):Look for the Silver Lining / The Best Things in Life are Free /
Both Ends of the Candle
Paul Whiteman & his Orchestra . . . . **HMV B 5374**
Jessie Matthews . . . . **Brunswick 135**
Gogi Grant . . . . **RCA RD 27054**
Pinky's Playboys . . . . **Warner Brothers WM 4035**

JUST A PRAYER AWAY   1945
Charles Tobias / Dave Kapp
Campbell Connelly & Co. Ltd. . . . . USA
Film(s): . . . . The Blonde From Brooklyn
Bing Crosby . . . . **Brunswick LA 8656**
Dorothy Squires . . . . **Parlophone F 2080**
Michael Holliday . . . . **Columbia 33SX 1262**

JUST A SONG AT TWI-LIGHT (See Love's Old Sweet Song)

JUST A WEE DEOCH AN' DORIS   1911
Harry Lauder / G. Grafton / R.F. Morrison / Whit Cunliffe
B.Feldman & Co. Ltd . . . . UK
Harry Lauder . . . . **Camden CDN 130**
George Elrick . . . . **Ace of Clubs ACL 1024**

JUST A-SITTIN' AND A-ROCKIN'   1942
Duke Ellington / Billy Strayhorn / Lee Gaines
Robbins Music Corporation Ltd . . . . USA
Duke Ellington & his Orchestra . . . . **RCA RD 27134**
Stan Kenton & his Orchestra,
vocal June Christy . . . . **Capitol CL 13030**
Ella Fitzgerald with Duke Ellington
& his Orchestra . . . . **HMV CLP 1214**

JUST A-WEARYIN' FOR YOU   1901
Carrie Jacobs-Bond / Frank Stanton
Campbell Connelly & Co. Ltd. . . . . USA
Paul Robeson (1938) . . . . **HMV CLP 1415**
Tony Brent . . . . **Columbia DB 4514**

JUST AN ECHO IN THE VALLEY   1933
Harry Woods / James Campbell / Reginald Connelly
Campbell Connelly & Co. Ltd. . . . . UK
Film(s): . . . . Going Hollywood
Bing Crosby . . . . **Brunswick LAT 8052**
Bing Crosby appeared in *Going Hollywood.*

JUST AN ILLUSION   April 1982
Tony Swain / Steve Jolly / Leee John & Ashley Ingram
Red Bus Music . . . . UK
Imagination . . . . **R&B RBS 208**

JUST AN OLD-FASHIONED GIRL   April 1957
Marve Fisher
Dash Music Ltd. . . . . USA
Eartha Kitt . . . . **HMV POP 309**

JUST ANOTHER DAY WASTED AWAY   1927
Roy Turk / Charles Tobias
Campbell Connelly & Co. Ltd. . . . . USA
The California Ramblers . . . . **Edison Bell 4714**
Rosemary Squires . . . . **MGM EP 640**
The Buster Bailey Quartet . . . . **Columbia 33SX 1218**

JUST AS MUCH AS EVER   September 1959
Charles Singleton / Larry Coleman
Campbell Connelly & Co. Ltd . . . . USA
Nat 'King' Cole . . . . **Capitol CL 15163**

JUST BE GOOD TO ME   May 1984
Terry Lewis / James Harris
CBS Songs . . . . USA
The S.O.S. Band . . . . **Epic A 3626**

JUST BUGGIN'   March 1986
Kid Kangol / Howie Tee
Intersong Music . . . . USA
Whistle . . . . **Champion CHAMP 12**

JUST CAN'T GET ENOUGH   October 1981
Vincent Clarke
Sonet Music . . . . UK
Depeche Mode . . . . **Mute MUTE 01**

JUST DON'T WANT TO BE LONELY   August 1
Vinnie Barratt / John Freeman / Bob Eli
Island Music . . . .
Freddie McGregor . . . . **Germa**

JUST FOR A WHILE (Nur Eine Nacht)
Oskar Geiger / Arthur Anderson
Keith Prowse Music Publishing Co. Ltd . . . .
Show(s): . . . .
Jose Collins
Bob Sharples & his Orchestra . . . .
Jose Collins appeared in *The Last Waltz.*

JUST FOR YOU
John Rossall / Gerry Shephard
Rock Artistes Music . . . .
The Glitter Band . . . .

JUST FRIENDS
John Klenner / Sam M. Lewis

Keith Prowse Music Publishing Co. Ltd. . . . . USA
Greta Keller . . . . **Decca F 2813**
Frank Sinatra . . . . **Capitol EAP 3-1221**

JUST GOT LUCKY   June 1983
Chris Bostock / Dig Wayne
Zomba Music . . . . UK
Jo Boxers . . . . **RCA BOX 2**

JUST HUMMING ALONG   1932
Montague Ewing / Sherman Myers
Cecil Lennox Music Co. Ltd. . . . . UK
The Durium Dance Band, vocal Cab Calloway . . **Durium EN 13**
Quentin MacLean (Organ) . . . . **Columbia DB 821**

JUST IMAGINE   1928
Buddy De Sylva / Lew Brown / Ray Henderson
Chappell & Co. Ltd. . . . . USA
Show(s): . . . . Good News
Film(s): . . . . Good News / The Best Things in Life are Free
Jean Goldkette & his Orchestra . . . . **HMV B 5531**
June Allyson . . . . **MGM EP 703**
Judy Garland . . . . **Capitol LCT 6121**
Helen Merrill . . . . **Mercury MMB 12000**
June Allyson appeared in the 1947 film of *Good News*.

JUST IN TIME   October 1957
Jule Styne / Betty Comden / Adolph Green
Chappell & Co. Ltd . . . . USA
Show(s): . . . . Bells Are Ringing
Film(s): . . . . Bells Are Ringing
Judy Holliday & Sydney Chaplin . . . . . **Philips BBL 7201**
Judy Holliday & Dean Martin . . . . **Capitol W 1435**
Judy Holliday appeared in the American production and the film of
Bells Are Ringing.
Sydney Chaplin appeared in the American production of *Bells Are Ringing*.
Dean Martin appeared in the film of *Bells Are Ringing*.

JUST KEEP ROCKIN'   June 1989
Leigh Guest / Michael Memson / Harry Johnson
Fiction Music . . . . UK
Double Trouble & The Rebel M.C. . . . . **Desire WANT 9**

JUST LIKE A BUTTERFLY   1927
Mort Dixon / Harry Woods
Francis, Day & Hunter Ltd. . . . . USA
The Savoy Orpheans . . . . **HMV B 5344**
Annette Hanshaw . . . . **Actuelle 11472**
Kay Starr . . . . **RCA RD 27056**

JUST LIKE A GIPSY   1919
Seymour Simons / Norah Bayes
B. Feldman & Co. Ltd. . . . . USA
Show(s): . . . . Ladies First
Maxine Sullivan . . . . **Brunswick 03246**

JUST LIKE A MELODY OUT OF THE SKY   1928
Walter Donaldson
Keith Prowse Music Publishing Co. Ltd. . . . . USA
Paul Whiteman & his Orchestra . . . . **Columbia 5007**
Jay Wilbur & his Orchestra, vocal Sam Browne . . . . . **Rex 9893**
Billy Daniels . . . . **HMV DLP 1174**
Theme song of *Jay Wilbur*.

'ST LIKE A THIEF   1923
*   atio Nicholls*
    nce Wright Music Co. Ltd . . . . UK
    ilton & his Orchestra . . . . **HMV B 1588**

E A WOMAN   September 1966

    Co. Ltd. . . . . USA
    . . . . **Fontana TF 730**
    . . . . **CBS 66012**

E   September 1963

    g Co. Ltd . . . . UK
    . . . . **Decca F 11693**

ES   February 1990
    ren
    . . . . USA
    . . . . **Geffen GEF 69**

(JUST LIKE) STARTING OVER   December 1980
John Lennon
Warner Brothers Music. . . . . UK
John Lennon & Yoko Ono . . . . **WEA K 79186**
Ivor Novello Nomination 1981.

JUST LIKE THE IVY   1902
A.J. Mills / Harry Castling
Francis, Day & Hunter Ltd. . . . . UK
Marie Kendall . . . . **Decca E 5169**
Dennis Bowen . . . . **Piccadilly NPL 38002**

JUST LOVING YOU   December 1967
Tom Springfield
Chappell & Co. Ltd. . . . . UK
Anita Harris . . . . **CBS 2724**

JUST MY IMAGINATION   July 1971
Norman Whitfield / Barrett Strong
Jobete Music (UK) Ltd. . . . . USA
The Temptations . . . . **Tamla Motown TMG 773**

JUST ONCE FOR ALL TIME   1932
Werner Heymann / Robert Gilbert / Rowland Leigh
Campbell Connelly & Co. Ltd. . . . . Germany
Film(s): . . . . Congress Dances
Lillian Harvey . . . . **Parlophone R 1088**
Cyril Stapleton & his Orchestra . . . . **Decca LK 4321**
Lillian Harvey appeared in *Congress Dances*.

JUST ONE LOOK   April 1964
Doris Payne / Gregory Carroll
T.S. Music Ltd . . . . USA
The Hollies . . . . **Parlophone R 5104**
Doris Troy . . . . **London HLK 9749**

JUST ONE MORE CHANCE   1931
Sam Coslow / Arthur Johnston
Victoria Music Co. Ltd. . . . . USA
Film(s): . . . . College Coach / The Stooge
Bing Crosby . . . . **Brunswick LAT 8251**
Jack Payne & The BBC Dance Orchestra . . . . **Columbia CB 356**
Billie Holiday . . . . **MGM C 792**
Jack Payne & his Orchestra . . . . **HMV CLP 1160**

JUST ONE MORE NIGHT   March 1978
Kenny Young
Heath Levy Music Ltd . . . . USA
Yellow Dog . . . . **Virgin VS 195**

JUST ONE OF THOSE THINGS   1941
Cole Porter
Chappell & Co. Ltd . . . . USA
Show(s): . . . . Jubilee
Film(s):Night and Day / Lullaby of Broadway, Young At Heart, The
Eddie Duchin Story, Can-Can / Panama Hattie
Bing Crosby . . . . **Brunswick LA 8513**
Lena Horne . . . . **RCA RD 27063**
Doris Day . . . . **Philips BBL 7175**
Peggy Lee . . . . **Brunswick OE 9282**
Frank Sinatra . . . . **Capitol W 582**
Frank Sinatra appeared in *Can-Can*.
Lena Horne appeared in *Panama Hattie*.
Doris Day appeared in *Lullaby of Broadway*.

JUST ONE SMILE   December 1966
Randy Newman
Schroeder Music Ltd. . . . . USA
Gene Pitney . . . . **Stateside SS 558**

JUST SAY I LOVE HER   December 1950
Martin Kalmanoff / Sam Ward / Jack Val / Jimmy Dale
Chappell & Co. Ltd . . . . USA
Edmund Hockridge . . . . **HMV 7EG 8175**
Vic Damone . . . . **Philips BBL 7234**
Carmen Cavallaro (piano) . . . . **Brunswick LAT 8156**
Connie Francis . . . . **MGM C 854**
Adapted from *Dicitencello Vuje* by Rudolfo Falvo.

JUST SAY NO   May 1986
Al Grogoni / George McManon
E.K.A. Music . . . . UK
Grange Hill Cast . . . . **BBC RESL 183**

JUST THE WAY YOU ARE — February 1979
Billy Joel
April Music Ltd. .... USA
Barry White .... 20th Century BTC 2380
Billy Joel .... CBS 5872

JUST WALKING IN THE RAIN — October 1956
Johnny Brag / Robert Riley
Frank Music Co. Ltd. .... USA
Johnnie Ray .... Philips BBL 7254

JUST WHAT I ALWAYS WANTED — October 1982
Teddy Johns
Warner Brothers Music .... UK
Mari Wilson .... London PINK 4

JUST WHAT I NEEDED — March 1979
Richard Ocasek
Carlin Music Corporation .... UK
Cars .... Elektra K 12312

JUST WHEN I NEEDED YOU MOST — September 1979
Randy Vanwarmer
Warner Brothers Music Ltd. .... USA
Randy Vanwarmer .... Island WIP 6516

JUST WHO IS THE FIVE O'CLOCK HERO — August 1982
Paul Weller
Chappell Music Co. .... UK
The Jam .... Polydor 2059 504

JUST YOU, JUST ME — 1930
Ray Klages / Jesse Greer
Robbins Music Corporation Ltd .... USA
Film(s): .... Marianne / This Could be the Night
Smith Ballew & his Orchestra,
vocal Smith Ballew .... Parlophone R 535
Benny Goodman & his Orchestra .... Parlophone R 3000
Louis Armstrong & his All Stars .... Brunswick LAT 8019
Ray Anthony & his Orchestra .... MGM C 761
Nat 'King' Cole .... Capitol T 1034
Ray Anthony appeared in This Could Be The Night.

JUSTIFY MY LOVE — December 1990
Madonna Ciccone / Lenny Kravitz
Virgin Music .... USA
Madonna .... Sire W 900

K-K-K-KATY — 1918
Geoffrey O'Hara
Francis, Day & Hunter Ltd. .... USA
Show(s): .... Buzz Buzz / The Glorious Days
Film(s): .... The Cockeyed World / Tin Pan Alley
Walter Williams & Dan O'Neill .... Columbia L 1294
Maurice Chevalier .... MGM C 860
Anna Neagle .... Philips PB 153
Anna Neagle appeared in Glorious Days.
Walter Williams & Dan O'Neill appeared in Buzz Buzz.

KALUA — 1922
Jerome Kern / Anne Caldwell
Chappell & Co. Ltd .... USA
Show(s): .... Good Morning Dearie / The Cabaret Girl
Film(s): .... Till the Clouds Roll By
Dorothy Dickson .... HMV C 2946
Paul Whiteman & his Orchestra .... HMV B 1397
Stanley Black & his Orchestra .... Ace of Clubs ACL 1031
Dorothy Dickson appears in The Cabaret Girl.

KARMA CHAMELEON — October 1983
George O'Dowd / John Moss / Michael Craig / Roy Hay / Philip Pickett
Virgin Music .... UK
Culture Club .... Virgin VS 612
Ivor Novello Award

KASHMIRI LOVE SONG (From The Four Indian Love Lyrics) — 1904
Amy Woodforde-Finden
Boosey & Hawkes Music Publishers Ltd. .... USA
Ivor Foster .... Odeon 0258
Peter Dawson .... HMV B 1686
Dennis Noble .... Argo EAF 5

KATY DID, KATY DIDN'T — 1942
Hoagy Carmichael / Frank Loesser
Victoria Music Co. Ltd .... USA
Film(s): .... Hoppity Goes to Town (cartoon)
George Formby .... Regal Zonophone MR 3619
The R.A.O.C. Blue Rockets Dance Orchestra .... HMV BD 5745

KAYLEIGH — June 1985
"Marillion"
Chappell Music Co. .... UK
Marillion .... EMI MARIL 3

KEEP AN EYE ON YOUR HEART — 1942
Milton Leeds / Henry Manners
Campbell Connelly & Co. Ltd .... USA
Harry Roy & his Band,
vocal Harry Roy .... Regal Zonophone MR 3696

(KEEP FEELING) FASCINATION — May 1983
Philip Oakey / Jo Callis
Virgin Music .... UK
Human League .... Virgin VS 569

KEEP ON — August 1968
Thomas Wayne
Shapiro-Bernstein & Co. Ltd. .... USA
Bruce Channel .... Bell BLL 1010

KEEP ON DANCIN' — March 1979
Eric Matthews / Gary Turnier
April Music Ltd .... USA
Gary's Gang .... CBS 7109

KEEP ON DANCING — October 1971
Allen Jones / Andrew Love / Richard Shann
Jewel Music Publishing Co. Ltd .... USA
The Bay City Rollers .... Bell BLL 1164
The Gentrys .... MGM 1284

KEEP ON LOVING YOU — May 1981
Kevin Cronin
Warner Brothers Music .... USA
REO Speedwagon .... Epic EPC 9544

KEEP ON MOVIN' — April 1989
Beresford Romeo
Virgin Music .... UK
Soul II Soul featuring Caron Wheeler .... 10 TEN 263

KEEP ON RUNNING — February 1966
Jackie Edwards
Island Music Ltd .... UK
The Spencer Davis Group .... Fontana TF 632

KEEP SEARCHIN' (We'll Follow The Sun) — February 1965
Del Shannon
Vicki Music Ltd .... USA
Del Shannon .... Stateside SS 368

KEEP SMILING AT TROUBLE — 1925
Lewis Gensier / Al Jolson / Buddy De Sylva
Chappell & Co. Ltd. .... USA
Show(s): .... Big Boy
Film(s): .... The Singing Fool
Al Jolson .... Brunswick LA 857*
The California Ramblers .... Riverside RLP 12-8*
Al Jolson appeared in Big Boy and The Singing Fool.

KEEP THE HOME FIRES BURNING
Ivor Novello / Lena Guilbert-Ford
Ascherberg, Hopwood & Crew Ltd. ....
Film(s): .... Vari
Stanley Kirkby .... R
Olive Gilbert & Chorus ....

KEEP YOUNG AND BEAUTIFUL
Al Dubin / Harry Warren
B. Feldman & Co. Ltd. ....
Film(s): ....
Florence Oldham
Carroll Gibbons & The Savoy Orpheans .

KEEP YOUR HANDS OFF MY BABY
Gerry Goffin / Carole King
Aldon Music Ltd. ....

Little Eva .... London HLU 9633
Helen Shapiro .... Columbia 33SX 1661

KEEP YOUR SKIRTS DOWN MARY ANN   1926
Andrew Sterling / Ray Henderson / Robert King
B. Feldman & Co. Ltd. .... USA
Olive Fox & Clarkson Rose .... Zonophone 2690
The Andrews Sisters .... Capitol T 973

KEEPING MYSELF FOR YOU   1930
Vincent Youmans / Sidney Clare
Campbell Connelly & Co. Ltd .... USA
Film(s): .... Hit the Deck
The High Hatters .... HMV B 5820
Ann Miller & Tony Martin .... MGM EP 525
Ann Miller & Tony Martin appeared in the 1955 film of *Hit The Deck.*

KEEPING THE DREAM ALIVE   January 1989
Aron Strobell / Curtis Biggs / Stefan Zauner
Chappell Music Co. .... Germany
Freiheit .... CBS 652989

KENTUCKY   1946
Henry Prichard
Campbell Connelly & Co. Ltd. .... USA
Geraldo & his Orchestra,
vocal Archie Lewis .... Parlophone F 2120
The Everly Brothers .... London HAA 2150

KENTUCKY LULLABY   1927
Irving Cohn
Francis, Day & Hunter Ltd. .... USA
Jean Goldkette & his Orchestra
with Jesse Crawford (Wurlitzer Organ) .... HMV B 5190

KENTUCKY WALTZ, THE   September 1951
Bill Monroe
Southern Music Co. .... USA
Tennessee Ernie Ford .... Capitol CL 13517
Rosemary Clooney .... Columbia DB 2895
Ernest Tubb & Red Foley .... Brunswick 04783

KEWPIE DOLL   June 1958
Sid Tepper / Roy Bennett
Leeds Music .... USA
Perry Como .... RCA 1055
Frankie Vaughan .... Philips PB 825

KICKING THE GONG AROUND   1932
Harold Arlen / Ted Koehler
Lawrence Wright Music Co. Ltd. .... USA
Film(s): .... The Big Broadcast
Cab Calloway & his Orchestra,
vocal Cab Calloway .... Brunswick 05022
Cab Calloway appeared in *The Big Broadcast.*

KID'S LAST FIGHT, THE   May 1954
Bob Merrill
Dash Music Co. .... USA
Frankie Laine .... Philips PB 258

KIDS IN AMERICA   March 1981
Marty Wilde / Ricky Wilde
Rak Music .... UK
Kim Wilde .... Rak RAK 327

⸺LARNY   1862
⸺ael Balfe / Edmund Falconer
.... Wings o' the Morning
⸺**Cormack** .... MRF LP 5
⸺**'rooks** .... Columbia DB 2337
⸺**'Dowda** .... Columbia 33SX 1185
.... Warner Brothers WM 4046
⸺ck appeared in *Wings o'the Morning.*

                                                May 1990
(Henry Samuel)
.... UK
.... MCA MCA 1400

⸺GE   October 1980
.... UK

Thin Lizzy .... Vertigo LIZZY 7

KILLER QUEEN   November 1974
Freddie Mercury
B. Feldman & Co. Ltd. .... UK
Queen .... EMI 2229
Ivor Novello Nomination.

KILLING ME SOFTLY WITH HIS SONG   April 1973
Norman Gimbel / Charles Fox
Essex Music Ltd. .... USA
Roberta Flack .... Atlantic K 10282

KILLING MOON, THE   February 1984
"Echo & The Bunnymen"
Warner Brothers Music .... UK
Echo & The Bunnymen .... Korova KOW 32

KILLING OF GEORGIE, THE   October 1976
Rod Stewart
Riva Music .... UK
Rod Stewart .... Riva 4

KIND OF MAGIC, A   April 1986
Roger Taylor
EMI Music .... UK
Queen .... EMI QUEEN 7
Ivor Novello Nomination

KING   April 1980
Robin Campbell / Ali Campbell / Michael Virtue & Earl Falconer
A.T.V. Music Ltd. .... UK
UB 40 .... Graduate GRAD 6

KING CREOLE   December 1959
Jerry Leiber / Mike Stoller
Seventeen Saville Row Ltd .... USA
Film(s): .... King Creole
Elvis Presley .... RCA RD 27088
Cliff Richard .... Parlophone PMC 1072
Elvis Presley appeared in *King Creole.*

KING FOR A DAY   1929
Ted Florito / Sam M. Lewis / Joe Young
Francis, Day & Hunter Ltd .... USA
Harry Richman .... Brunswick 3873
Ted Lewis & his Band .... Brunswick LA 8608
Steve Lawrence .... Parlophone R 3874

KING OF PAIN   February 1984
"Sting"
Virgin Music .... UK
The Police .... A&M AM 176

KING OF ROCK 'N' ROLL, THE   June 1988
Patrick McAloon
SBK Songs .... UK
Prefab Sprout .... CBS SK 37

KING OF THE COPS   January 1976
Roger Miller
Burlington Music Co. Ltd .... USA
Billy Howard .... Penny Farthing PEN 892
Parody of "King of the Road".

KING OF THE ROAD   May 1965
Roger Miller
Burlington Music Co. Ltd .... USA
Roger Miller .... Philips BF 1397

KING ROCKER   February 1979
Billy Idol / Tony James
Chrysalis Music Ltd. .... UK
Generation X .... Chrysalis CHS 2261

KING'S HORSES, THE   1930
Noel Gay / Harry Graham
Lawrence Wright Music Co. Ltd .... UK
Show(s): .... Folly to be Wise
The Big Four .... Columbia DB 403
Jack Hylton & his Orchestra .... HMV B 5875
Ted Heath & his Music,
vocal Dennis Lotis & The Stargazers .... Decca F 3694

KISSIN' COUSINS June 1964
Fred Wise / Randy Starr
December Music .... USA
Film(s): .... Kissin' Cousins
Elvis Presley .... **RCA 1404**
Elvis Presley appeared in *Kissin' Cousins*

KISSIN' IN THE BACK ROW OF THE MOVIES July 1974
Tony Macaulay / Roger Greenaway
Cookaway Music .... UK
The Drifters .... **Bell 1358**

KITES January 1968
Lee Pockriss / Hal Hackady
Robbins Music Ltd. .... USA
Simon Dupree & The Big Sound .... **Parlophone R 5646**

KITTEN ON THE KEYS 1922
Zez Confrey
Francis, Day & Hunter Ltd .... USA
Zez Confrey (piano) & Orchestra .... **HMV B 1385**
Lou Busch (piano) & Orchestra .... **Capitol LC 6572**

KITTY THE TELEPHONE GIRL 1912
A.J. Lawrence / Huntley Trevor / Tom Mellor / Harry Gifford
Francis, Day & Hunter Ltd. .... UK
Show(s): .... 5064 Gerard
Jack Norworth .... **Columbia 2539**
Jack Norworth appeared in *5064 Gerard.*

KNEE DEEP IN THE BLUES February 1957
Melvin Endsley
Leeds Music Ltd. .... USA
Tommy Steele .... **Decca DFE 6389**
Guy Mitchell .... **Philips BBR 8108**

KNEES UP MOTHER BROWN 1938
Harris Weston / Bert Lee / Irving Taylor
Peter Maurice Music Co. Ltd. .... UK
Elsie & Doris Waters .... **Decca F 7309**
Billy Cotton & his Band .... **Decca DFE 6224**
Ivor Raymonde & The Mike Sammes Singers .. **HMV CLP 1401**

KNICK KNACK PADDY WHACK (See This Old Man)

KNOCK KNOCK WHO'S THERE April 1970
John Carter / Geoff Stevens
See Saw Music .... UK
Mary Hopkin .... **Apple 26**
United Kingdom entry for the 1970 Eurovision Song Contest (Placed
Second).
Ivor Novello Nomination.

KNOCK ON WOOD April 1967
Eddie Floyd / Steve Cropper
Warner Brothers Music Ltd. .... USA
Eddie Floyd .... **Atlantic 584041**
Otis Redding & Carla Thomas .... **Stax 601 021**
David Bowie (1974) .... **RCA 2466**
Amii Stewart (1979) .... **Hansa K 11214**
Amii Stewart (1985) .... **Sedition EDIT 3303**

KNOCK THREE TIMES June 1971
Irwin Levine / L. Russell Brown
Martin Music Corporation .... USA
.... **Bell 1468**

KNOCK, KNOCK, WHO'S THERE 1936
... son / Bill Davies / Vincent Lopez & Johnny Morris
... & Hunter Ltd .... USA
... & his Orchestra .... Brunswick 02300
.... Regal Zonophone MR 2179
.... RCA 1137

... IN THE OLD KENT ROAD (See Wot Cher)

December 1979
... Britten
...d. .... UK
.... **Asylum K 12396**

... DOOR November 1973
.... USA
..... Pat Garrett & Billy the Kid

Bob Dylan .... **CBS 1762**

KNOWING ME, KNOWING YOU April 1977
Benny Andersson / Bjorn Ulvaeus / Stig Anderson
Bocu Music Ltd .... Sweden
Abba .... **Epic EPC 4955**

KON-TIKI October 1961
Michael Carr
B. Feldman & Co. Ltd. .... UK
The Shadows .... **Columbia DB 4698**

KUNG FU FIGHTING October 1974
Carl Douglas
Sibiddu Music .... UK
Carl Douglas .... **Pye 7N 45377**
Ivor Novello Award.

KYRIE March 1986
Richard Page / Steve George / John Lang
Warner Brothers Music .... USA
Mr Mister .... **RCA PB 49927**

L-L-LUCY October 1975
Ray Stiles / Rob Davis
Isalnd Music Ltd .... UK
Mud .... **Private Stock PVT 41**

LA BAMBA August 1987
Traditional
Carlin Music .... No origin
Los Lobos .... **Slash LASH 13**

LA DE DE, LA DE DA 1937
Sam M. Lewis / Peter De Rose
Francis, Day & Hunter Ltd. .... USA
'Fats' Waller & his Rhythm .... **HMV BD 5150**
Carroll Gibbons & his Boy Friends ... **Columbia FB 1698**

LA DEE DAH April 1958
Frank Slay / Bob Crewe
Cromwell Music Co. .... USA
Colin Hicks .... **Pye NIXA N 15125**
Jackie Dennis .... **Decca F 10992**
Billie & Lillie .... **London HLU 8564**

LA GOLONDRINA (The Swallow) 1909
Narcisco Serradell
Unknown Publisher .... Mexico
Film(s): .... Happy Days
Emilio De Gogorza .... **HMV DA 782**
The Melachrino Strings .... **RCA RD 27108**
The Emanuel Vardi Orchestra .... **Brunswick LAT 8112**

LA ISLA BONITA May 1987
Madonna Ciccone / Bruce Gaitsch
Warner Brothers Music .... USA
Madonna .... **Sire W 8378**

LA-DI-DA-DI-DA 1934
Noel Gay / Desmond Carter
Chappell & Co. Ltd. .... UK
Show(s): .... That's a Pretty Thing
Bobbie Comber .... **Broadcast 3359**
Ray Noble & his Orchestra, vocal Bobbie Comber . **HMV B 6432**
Bobbie Comber appeared in *That's a Pretty Thing.*

LABELLED WITH LOVE November 1981
Glen Tilbrook / Chris Difford
Illegal Music .... UK
Squeeze .... **A&M AMS 8166**

LABOUR OF LOVE August 1987
Patrick Kane / Gregory Kane
Chappell Music Co. .... UK
Hue & Cry .... **Circa YR 4**

LADIES NIGHT December 1979
George Brown
Planetary-Nom (London) Ltd. .... UK
Kool & The Gang .... **Mercury KOOL 712**

LADY January 1981
Lionel Richie
Warner Brothers Music .... USA

Kenny Rogers . . . . United Artists UP 635

LADY BARBARA   December 1970
Tony Wilson / Errol Brown / Giancarlo Bigazzi
Rak Music Ltd . . . . Italy
Peter Noone & Herman's Hermits . . . . **Rak 106**

LADY D'ARBANVILLE   August 1970
Cat Stevens
Freshwater Music . . . . UK
Cat Stevens . . . . **Island WIP 6086**

LADY DIVINE   1929
Richard Kounts / Nat Shilkret
B. Feldman & Co. Ltd . . . . USA
Film(s): . . . . The Lady Divine
Nat Shilkret & his Orchestra . . . . **HMV B 5642**

LADY ELEANOR   June 1972
Alan Hull
Crazy Music Ltd. . . . . UK
Lindisfarne . . . . **Charisma CB 153**

LADY GODIVA   November 1966
Mike Leander / Charlie Mills
Dean Street Music Ltd. . . . . UK
Peter & Gordon . . . . **Columbia DB 8003**

LADY IN RED   August 1986
Chris De Burgh
Rondor Music . . . . UK
Chris De Burgh . . . . **A&M AM 331**

LADY IN RED, THE   1935
Allie Wrubel / Mort Dixon
B. Feldman & Co. Ltd . . . . USA
Film(s): . . . . In Caliente
Ethel Merman . . . . **Brunswick 02087**
Xavier Cugat & his Orchestra . . . . **HMV BD 297**
Harry Roy & his Orchestra . . . . **Parlophone F 312**
The Hi-Lo's . . . . **Philips BBL 7288**
Winifred Shaw & Judy Canova . . . . . United Artists UAG 29644
Winifred Shaw & Judy Canova appeared in *In Caliente*.

LADY IS A TRAMP, THE   1940
Richard Rodgers / Lorenz Hart
Chappell & Co. Ltd . . . . USA
Show(s): . . . . Babes in Arms
Film(s): . . . . Words and Music / Pal Joey
Sophie Tucker . . . . **Brunswick LAT 8144**
Lena Horne . . . . **MGM C 853**
Frank Sinatra . . . . **Capitol LCT 6148**
Ella Fitzgerald . . . . **HMV CLP 1116**
Lena Horne appeared in *Words and Music*.
Frank Sinatra appeared in *Pal Joey*.

LADY LOVE ME (One More Time)   June 1983
David Paich / James Howard
Rocket Music . . . . USA
George Benson . . . . **Warner Brothers W 9614**

LADY LYNDA   July 1979
Alan Jardine / Ronald Altbach
Carlin Music Corporation . . . . UK
The Beach Boys . . . . **Caribou CRB 74271**
Based on "Jesu Joy of Man's Desiring" (Cantata No.147) by Johann Sebastian Bach (1685 - 1750).

LADY MADONNA   April 1968
John Lennon / Paul McCartney
Northern Songs Ltd. . . . . UK
The Beatles . . . . **Parlophone R 5675**

LADY MARMALADE (Voulez-vous Coucher Avec Moi Ce Soir)   April 1975
Bob Crewe / Kenny Nolan
Ardmore & Beechwood Ltd . . . . USA
Labelle . . . . **Epic EPC 2852**

LADY OF MADRID   1938
Tolchard Evans / Stanley Damerell / Robert Hargreaves
Southern Music Publishing Co. Ltd. . . . . UK
Ray Noble & his Orchestra, vocal Al Bowlly . . . . **HMV B 6510**
Geraldo & his Gaucho Tango Orchestra . . . **Columbia FB 2825**
David Whitfield . . . . **Decca DFE 6289**

LADY OF SPAIN   1931
Tolchard Evans / Robert Hargreaves / Harry Tilsley / Stanley Damerell
Peter Maurice Music Co. Ltd. . . . . UK
The New Mayfair Dance Orchestra, vocal Al Bowlly . **HMV B 5999**
Frank Chacksfield & his Orchestra . . . . **Decca LK 4168**

LADY OF THE EVENING   1923
Irving Berlin
Francis, Day & Hunter Ltd . . . . USA
Show(s): . . . . The Music Box Revue of 1922
Paul Whiteman & his Orchestra . . . . **HMV B 1650**
Billy Daniels . . . . **Vogue LAE 12021**
Fred Astaire . . . . **London HAR 2219**

LADY PLAY YOUR MANDOLIN   1931
Irving Caesar / Oscar Levant
Victoria Music Co. Ltd . . . . USA
Ambrose & his Orchestra, vocal Sam Browne . . . . **HMV B 5979**
The Jumping Jacks . . . . **Capitol CI 14597**

LADY ROSE   July 1971
Ray Dorset
Our Music . . . . UK
Mungo Jerry . . . . **Dawn DNX 2510**

LADY WHO DIDN'T BELIEVE IN LOVE, THE   1943
Jule Styne / Kim Gannon
B. Feldman & Co. Ltd . . . . USA
Film(s): . . . . Hello Beautiful
Ambrose & his Orchestra, vocal Anne Shelton . . **Decca F 8314**

LADY WILLPOWER   October 1968
Jerry Fuller
Dick James Music Ltd. USA
Gary Puckett & The Union Gap . . . . **CBS 3551**

LADY'S IN LOVE WITH YOU, THE   1939
Frank Loesser / Burton Lane
Victoria Music Co. Ltd. USA
Film(s): . . . . Some Like it Hot
Bob Hope & Shirley Ross . . . . **Brunswick 02822**
Sammy Davis . . . . **Brunswick LAT 8215**
Bob Hope & Shirley Ross appeared in *Some Like it Hot*.

LAMBADA   December 1989
De Oliverira
EMI Music
Kaoma . . . . **CBS 6555011**

LAMBETH WALK, THE   1938
Noel Gay / Douglas Furber / Arthur Rose
Cinephonic Music Co. Ltd. . . . . UK
Show(s): . . . . Me and My Girl
Film(s): . . . . Me and My Girl
Lupino Lane & Teddie St. Denis . . . . **HMV BD 596**
Pat Dodd & his Boys, vocal The Michael Sammes Singers . **HMV CLP 1401**
Lupino Lane appeared in both the show and the film of *Me and My Girl*.
Teddie St. Denis appeared in the show of *Me and My Girl*.

LAMP IS LOW   1940
Peter De Rose / Bert Shefter / Mitchell Parish
Francis, Day & Hunter Ltd . . . . US
Connee Boswell . . . . **Brunswick 02?**
Greta Keller . . . . **Decca F ?**
Doris Day . . . . **Philips BBL?**
Adapted from "Pavane Pour Une Infante Defunte" by Mauric?
(1875 - 1937).

LAMPLIGHT   Jan?
David Essex
Jeff Wayne Music . . . .
David Essex . . . .

LAMPLIGHTER'S SERENADE, THE
Hoagy Carmichael / Paul Francis Webster
Francis, Day & Hunter Ltd . . . .
Bing Crosby . . . .
Michael Holliday . . . .

LAND OF CONFUSION
Anthony Banks / Phil Collins / Michael
Hit & Run Music Ltd . . . .
Genesis . . . .

LAND OF HOPE AND GLORY   1902
Arthur Benson / Edward Elgar
Boosey & Hawkes Ltd . . . . UK
Dame Ciara Butt . . . . **HMV 03510**
Raymond Newell . . . . **Columbia FB 1589**
British Legion Festival Community Singing . **Columbia DX 561**
Based on "Pomp & Circumstance March No.1" by Edward Elgar

LAND OF MAKE BELIEVE   January 1982
Andy Hill / Peter Sinfield
Paper Music . . . . UK
Bucks Fizz . . . . **RCA RCA 163**
Ivor Novello Nomination

LANGUAGE OF LOVE, THE   January 1962
John D. Loudermilk
Acuff-Rose Publishing Co. Ltd. . . . . USA
John D. Loudermilk . . . . **RCA 1263**
The King Brothers . . . . **Parlophone R 4861**

LAROO LAROO LILLI BOLERO   June 1948
Sidney Lippman / Sylvia Dee / Elizabeth Moore
Dash Music Ltd. . . . . USA
Bing Crosby . . . . **Brunswick 03889**
Perry Como . . . . **HMV BD 1211**

LAST CHRISTMAS   January 1985
George Michael
Morrison Leahy Music . . . . UK
Wham . . . . **Epic A 4949**
Wham (1986) . . . . **Epic WHAM 1**

LAST FAREWELL, THE   September 1975
Roger Whittaker / Ronald Webster
Tembo Music . . . . UK
Roger Whittaker . . . . **EMI 2294**
Ivor Novello Nomination.

LAST KISS   March 1985
Alan Tarney / David Cassidy
Morrison Leahy Music . . . . UK
David Cassidy . . . . **Arista ARIST 589**

LAST MILE HOME, THE   September 1949
Walter Kent / Walton Farrar
Leeds Music Ltd . . . . USA
Bing Crosby . . . . **Brunswick LA 8565**
Ruby Murray . . . . **Columbia 33SX 1201**

LAST NIGHT A D.J. SAVED MY LIFE   February 1983
Michael Cleveland
Planetary-Nom Music . . . . USA
In Deep . . . . **Sound of New York SNY 1**

LAST NIGHT IN SOHO   August 1968
Howard Blaikley
Lynn Music Ltd. . . . . UK
Dave Dee, Dozy, Beaky, Mick & Tich . . . . **Fontana TF 953**

LAST NIGHT ON THE BACK PORCH   1923
Carl Schraubstader / Lew Brown
Keith Prowse Music Publishing Co. Ltd . . . . USA
Show(s): . . . . George White's Scandals of 1923
Paul Whiteman & his Orchestra . . . . **HMV B 1714**
Bing Crosby with Bob Scoby's Jazz Band . . . . **RCA RD 27032**
Andrews Sisters . . . . **Capitol T 973**
Cogan . . . . **HMV POP 573**

NIGHT WAS MADE FOR LOVE   July 1962
ing
Music Publishing Co. Ltd . . . . UK
. . . . **Decca F 11458**

OF SUMMER   1813
Richard Alfred Milliken
. . . . UK
Three Smart Girls Grow Up, The Great Caruso
. . . . **HMV 03062**
. . . . **HMV E 480**
. . . . **HMV B 9574**
. . . . **Brunswick 02803**
. . . . **Decca SXL 6793**
. . . . **HMV EL 27040**
ree Smart Girls Grow Up

LAST ROUNDUP, THE   1934
Billy Hill
Lawrence Wright Music Co. Ltd. . . . . USA
Show(s): . . . . The Ziegfeld Follies of 1934
Film(s): . . . . The Singing Hill / Don't Fence Me in
Bing Crosby . . . . **Brunswick 01608**
Gene Autry . . . . **Philips PB 169**
Bing Crosby . . . . **Fontana TFR 6000**
The Sons of The Pioneers . . . . **RCA RD 27016**
Gene Autry appeared in *The Singing Hill.*

LAST TIME I SAW PARIS, THE   1941
Jerome Kern / Oscar Hammerstein II
Chappell & Co. Ltd . . . . USA
Film(s): . . . . . Lady be Good / Till the Clouds Roll By / Paris Holiday
Noel Coward . . . . **HMV 7EG 8346**
The Troubadours . . . . **London HAR 2249**
Bob Hope . . . . **London HAT 2143**
Bob Hope appeared in *Paris Holiday.*
Academy Award winning song of 1941.

LAST TIME, THE   March 1965
Mick Jagger / Keith Richards
Mirage Music Ltd . . . . UK
The Rolling Stones . . . . **Decca F 12104**

LAST TRAIN TO SAN FERNANDO, THE   August 1957
Sylvester Devere / Randolph Padmore / 'Mighty Dictator'
Cromwell Music Ltd. . . . . USA
Johnny Duncan . . . . **Columbia SEG 7733**

LAST WALTZ, THE   November 1967
Les Reed / Barry Mason
Donna Music Ltd. . . . . UK
Engelbert Humperdinck . . . . **Decca F 12655**
Ivor Novello Award.

LATELY   April 1981
Stevie Wonder
Jobete Music . . . . USA
Stevie Wonder . . . . **Motown TMG 1226**

LAUGH AT ME   September 1965
Sonny Bono
West One Music Ltd . . . . USA
Sonny . . . . **Atlantic AT 4038**

LAUGH CLOWN LAUGH   1928
Sam M. Lewis / Joe Young / Ted Fiorito
Francis, Day & Hunter Ltd. USA
Fred Waring & his Pennsylvanians . . . . **HMV B 5479**
Gracie Fields . . . . **HMV B 2782**
Duke Ellington & his Orchestra . . . . **Philips BBL 7315**
Bobby Short . . . . **London HAE 2215**

LAUGHING GNOME, THE   October 1973
David Bowie
Essex Music Ltd. . . . . UK
David Bowie . . . . **Deram DM 123**

LAUGHING IRISH EYES   1936
Sidney Mitchell / Sammy Stept
Keith Prowse Music Publishing Co. Ltd . . . . USA
Film(s): . . . . Laughing Irish Eyes
Phil Regan . . . . **Brunswick 02227**
Jack Daly . . . . **Regal Zonophone MR 2144**
Phil Regan appeared in *Laughing Irish Eyes.*

LAUGHING ON THE OUTSIDE   1946
Ben Raleigh / Bernie Wayne
Campbell Connelly & Co. Ltd. . . . . USA
Dorothy Squires . . . . **Parlophone F 2165**
The Four Freshmen . . . . **Capitol T 763**

LAUGHING POLICEMAN, THE   1938
Billy Grey
Reynolds & Co. (Music Publishers) Ltd. . . . . UK
Charles Penrose . . . . **Columbia SEG 7743**
Charles Jolly . . . . **Regal G 9351**

LAURA   1945
Johnny Mercer / David Raksin
Robbins Music Corporation Ltd. . . . . USA
Film(s): . . . . Laura

Dick Haymes	Brunswick 03590
Woody Herman & his Orchestra	Parlophone R 2987
Frank Sinatra	Capitol LCT 6152
Frank Chacksfield & his Orchestra	Decca LK 4322

Lyric added after the release of the film.

LAVENDER September 1985
"Marillion"
Chappell Music Co. Ltd	UK
Marillion	EMI MARIL 4

LAVENDER BLUE May 1949
Larry Morey / Elliot Daniel
Francis, Day & Hunter Ltd	USA
Film(s):	So Dear to My Heart
Burl Ives	Brunswick 04066
Dinah Shore	Columbia DB 2529
Sammy Turner	London HAX 2246

Burl Ives appeared in *So Dear To My Heart*.
Nominated for an Academy Award 1949.

LAY ALL YOUR LOVE ON ME August 1981
Benny Andersson / Bjorn Ulvaeus
Bocu Music	Sweden
Abba	Epic EPC A 1314

LAY BACK IN THE ARMS OF SOMEONE April 1977
Mike Chapman / Nicky Chinn
Rak Music Ltd	UK
Smokie	Rak 251

LAY DOWN December 1972
Dave Cousins
Summerland Songs	UK
The Strawbs	A&M AMS 7035

LAY DOWN YOUR ARMS September 1956
Ake Gerhard / Leon Land / Paddy Roberts
Francis, Day & Hunter Ltd.	Sweden
Anne Shelton	Philips BBL 7422
The Chordettes	London HAA 2088

LAY LADY LAY October 1969
Bob Dylan
B.Feldman & Co. Ltd.	USA
Bob Dylan	CBS 4434

LAY YOUR HANDS ON ME December 1984
Tom Bailey / Alannah Currie / Joe Leeway
Point Music	UK
The Thompson Twins	Arista TWINS 6

LAY YOUR LOVE ON ME January 1979
Mike Chapman / Nicky Chinn
Rak Music Ltd.	UK
Racey	Rak 284

LAYLA September 1972
Eric Clapton / Jim Gordon
Throat Music	UK
Derek & The Dominoes	Polydor 2058130
Derek & The Dominoes (1982)	RSO RSO 87

LAZY COUNTRYSIDE January 1948
Bobby Worth
Francis, Day & Hunter Ltd.	USA
Film(s):	Fun and Fancy Free
Tony Martin	HMV B 9609

LAZY RIVER 1941
Hoagy Carmichael / Sidney Arodin
Southern Music Publishing Co. Ltd.	USA
Film(s):	The Best Years Our Lives / Hey Boy, Hey Girl
The Hoagy Carmichael Orchestra vocal Hoagy Carmichael	HMV B 6500
The Mills Brothers	Brunswick 05058
Roberta Sherwood	Brunswick LAT 8159
The Mills Brothers	London HAD 2192
Louis Prima & Keely Smith	Capitol T 1160
Bobby Darin (1961)	London HL 9303
Louis Prima & Keely Smith	

appeared in *Hey Boy! Hey Girl!*.

LAZY SUNDAY Lane May 1968
Steve Marriott /
Immediate Music	UK

The Small Faces	Immediate IM 064

LAZYBONES 1933
Hoagy Carmichael / Johnny Mercer
Lawrence Wright Music Co. Ltd.	USA
Hoagy Carmichael	HMV 7EG 8037
The Mills Brothers	Brunswick 01800
Louis Armstrong & Gary Crosby	Brunswick 05574
The Johnny Mann Singers	London HAG 2297
Max Bygraves	Decca LK 4360

LEADER OF THE PACK, THE February 1965
Ellie Greenwich / George Morton / Jeff Barry
Robert Mellin Ltd	USA
The Shangri-Las	Red Bird RB 10014
The Shangri-Las (1972)	Kama Sutra 2013024
The Shangri-Las (1976)	Charley CS 1009

LEAN ON ME December 1976
Bill Withers
United Artists Music Co. Ltd	USA
Mud	Private Stock PVT 85
Bill Withers	A&M AMS 7004
Club Nouveau (1987)	King Jay W 8430

LEAN ON ME October 1985
Simon Clark
Warner Brothers Music	UK
Red Box	Sire W 8926

LEANIN' 1926
Hugh Wright / Sterndale Bennett
Boosey & Hawkes Ltd	UK
Harry Dearth	HMV C 1344
Owen Brannigan	HMV CLP 1446
Ian Wallace	MFP MFP 50563

LEANING ON A LAMP POST 1937
Noel Gay
Cinephonic Music Co. Ltd	UK
Film(s):	Feather Your Nest / Me and My Girl
George Formby	Decca DFE 6328
George Formby	Columbia SEG 7550
The King Brothers	Parlophone R 4513
Robert Lindsay	Columbia EJ 240301

George Formby appeared in *Feather Your Nest*.
Theme song of George Formby.
Robert Lindsay appeared in *Me and My Girl*.
Song added to *Me and My Girl* (Revival) 1985.

LEAP UP AND DOWN August 1971
Keith Hancock
Jonjo Music Co. Ltd	UK
St. Cecilia	Polydor 2058104

LEARN TO CROON 1933
Sam Coslow / Arthur Johnston
Victoria Music Co. Ltd.	USA
Film(s):	College Humour
Bing Crosby	Fontana TFR 6000
Bing Crosby	Brunswick LAT 8251

Bing Crosby appeared in *College Humour*.

LEARNING THE BLUES August 1955
Dolores Vicki Silvers
Barton Music Co. Ltd.	
Frank Sinatra	Capitol LCT
Julie London	London HA

LEAVE A LIGHT ON November
Richard Nowells / Ellen Shipley
Virgin Music	
Belinda Carlisle	

LEAVE A LITTLE LOVE
Robin Conrad / Les Reed
Skidmore Music Ltd	
Lulu	

LEAVE ME ALONE
Michael Jackson
Warner Chappell Music	
Michael Jackson	

LET ME IN December 1973
Alan Osmond / Wayne Osmond / Merrill Osmond
Carlin Music Corporation . . . . USA
The Osmonds . . . . MGM 2006321

LET ME LOVE YOU TONIGHT (No Te Importe Saber) 1944
Mitchell Parish / Rene Saber
Sun Music Publishing Co. Ltd . . . . Cuba
Bing Crosby . . . . **Brunswick LAT 8331**
Jane Morgan . . . . **London HAR 2244**

LET ME SING AND I'M HAPPY 1930
Irving Berlin
Francis, Day & Hunter Ltd . . . . USA
Film(s): . . . . Mammy / The Jolson Story
Al Jolson . . . . **Brunswick LAT 8521**
Frankie Vaughan . . . . **Philips BBL 7482**
Brook Benton . . . . **Mercury MMC 14108**
Al Jolson appeared in *Mammy*.

LET ME TRY AGAIN (Laisse Moi Le Temps) May 1975
Vasori Caraveli / Michael Jourdan / Paul Anka & Sammy Cahn
Leeds Music Ltd . . . . France
Tammy Jones . . . . **Epic EPC 3211**
Frank Sinatra . . . . **Reprise K 44249**

LET THE CURTAIN COME DOWN 1940
Al Newman
Cinephonic Music . . . . UK
Turner Layton . . . . **Columbia FB 2439**
Joe Loss & his Orchestra . . . . **HMV BD 5588**
Clinton Ford . . . . **Columbia 33SX 1689**

LET THE GREAT BIG WORLD KEEP TURNING 1917
Nat. D. Ayer / Clifford Grey
B. Feldman & Co. Ltd. . . . . UK
Show(s): . . . . The Bing Girls are There
Violet Lorraine & chorus . . . . **HMV D 431**
Kathie Kay with the Billy Cotton Band . . . **Columbia 33SX 1278**
Violet Lorraine appeared in *The Bing Girls are There*.

LET THE HEARTACHES BEGIN January 1968
Tony Macaulay / John MacLeod
Schroeder Music Ltd. . . . . UK
Long John Baldry . . . . **Pye 7N 17385**

LET THE MUSIC PLAY January 1976
Barry White
Schroeder Music Ltd . . . . USA
Barry White . . . . **20th Century BTC 2265**

LET THE MUSIC PLAY March 1984
Chris Barbosa / Ed Chisholm
Heath Levy Music . . . . USA
Shannon . . . . **Phonogram LET 1**

LET THE PEOPLE SING 1940
Noel Gay / Ian Grant / Frank Eyton
Noel Gay Music Co. Ltd . . . . UK
Film(s): . . . . Lights Up / Let the People Sing
Evelyn Laye . . . . **Columbia DB 1895**
Russ Conway (piano) . . . . **Columbia SEG 7837**

LET THE REST OF THE WORLD GO BY 1919
Ernest Ball / J. Keirn Brennan
B. Feldman & Co. Ltd . . . . USA
Film(s): . . . . Irish Eyes Are Smiling
Eric Courtland & Walter Jefferies . . . . **HMV B 1098**
Dick Haymes (1945) . . . . **Brunswick 03590**
Pat & Shirley Boone . . . . **London HAD 2210**
Mitch Miller & The Gang . . . . **Philips BBL 7258**
Dick Haymes appeared in *Irish Eyes Are Smiling*.

LET THE SUNSHINE IN December 1968
Gerome Ragni / James Rado / Galt MacDermot
United Artists Music Co. Ltd. . . . . USA
Show(s): . . . . Hair
Film(s): . . . . Hair
James Rado, Lynn Kellogg,
Melba Moore & Chorus . . . . **RCA RD 7959**
Paul Nicholas, Annebel Leventon,
Marsha Hunt & The Tribe . . . . **Polydor 583043**
Cleavant Derricks-Carroll, Cheryl Barnes,
Annie Golden, Beverly D'Angelo, John Savage,
Don Dacus & Dorsey Wright . . . . **RCA BL 03274**

James Rado, Lynn Kellogg, Melba Moore & Chorus appeared in the
American production of *Hair*.
Paul Nicholas, Annebel Leventon, Marsha Hunt & The Tribe appeared
in the British production of *Hair*.
Cleavant Derricks-Carroll, Cheryl Barnes, Annie Golden, Beverly D'Ange-
lo, John Savage, Don Dacus & Dorsey Wright appeared in the film of *Hair*.

LET THERE BE DRUMS January 1962
Sandy Nelson
Commodore-Imperial Music Ltd. . . . . USA
Sandy Nelson & his Orchestra . . . . **London HLP 9466**

LET THERE BE LOVE 1941
Ian Grant / Lionel Rand
Chappell & Co. Ltd . . . . UK
Ambrose & his Orchestra,
vocal Anne Shelton & Sam Browne . . . . . . **Decca F 7876**
Julie London . . . . **London HAG 2280**
Nat 'King' Cole (1962) . . . . **Capitol CL 15257**

LET US BE SWEETHEARTS ALL OVER AGAIN 1937
Joseph Gilbert
Campbell Connelly & Co. Ltd. . . . . UK
Joe Loss & his Band . . . . **Regal Zonophone MR 2487**
Jack Harris & his Band . . . . **Rex 9128**
Eric Winstone & his Orchestra, vocal Les Howard . **HMV BD 6029**
Guy Mitchell . . . . **Philips PB 487**

LET YOUR LOVE FLOW June 1976
Larry Williams
EMI Music Ltd . . . . USA
The Bellamy Brothers . . . . **Warner Brothers K 16690**

LET YOUR YEAH BE YEAH September 1971
Jimmy Oliff
Island Music Ltd . . . . UK
The Pioneers . . . . **Trojan TRLS 172**
Jimmy Cliff . . . . **Island ICD 6/B**

LET YOURSELF GO 1936
Irving Berlin
Irving Berlin Ltd . . . . USA
Film(s): . . . . Follow the Fleet
Fred Astaire . . . . **Columbia DB 1633**
The Boswell Sisters . . . . **Brunswick 02165**
Ella Fitzgerald . . . . **HMV CLP 1183**
Fred Astaire appeared in *Follow the Fleet*.

LET'S ALL CHANT May 1978
Alvin Fields / Michael Zager
Carlin Music Corporation . . . . USA
Michael Zager Band . . . . **Private Stock PVT 143**

LET'S ALL CHANT May 1988
Mike Stock / Matt Aitken / Peter Waterman
All Boys Music . . . . UK
Mick 'N' Pat . . . . **PWL PWL 10**

LET'S ALL GO DOWN THE STRAND 1909
Harry Castling / C.W. Murphy
B. Feldman & Co. Ltd. . . . . UK
Harry Fay . . . . **Columbia 1210**
Stanley Holloway . . . . **Philips BBL 7273**

LET'S ALL GO TO MARY'S HOUSE 1926
Con Conrad / Harry Woods
Campbell Connelly & Co. Ltd. . . . . USA
Jay Whidden & The Midnight Follies Band . . . . **Columbia 4130**

LET'S ALL GO TO THE MUSIC HALL 1934
Ralph Butler / Harry Tilsley / Horatio Nicholls
Lawrence Wright Music . . . . UK
Harry Claff . . . . **Decca F 5200**
The BBC Dance Orchestra,
conducted by Henry Hall . . . . **Columbia CB 795**
Una McLean . . . . **Lismor LILP 5084**

LET'S ALL SING LIKE THE BIRDIES SING 1933
Robert Hargreaves / Stanley Damerell / Tolchard Evans
Campbell Connelly & Co. Ltd. . . . . UK
Ambrose & his Orchestra, vocal Sam Browne . . . **HMV B 6279**
The Bowman-Hydo Singers & Players . . **Parlophone PMC 1155**

LET'S BE BUDDIES 1941
Cole Porter

Chappell & Co. Ltd .... USA
Show(s): .... Panama Hattie / Black Vanities
Film(s): .... Panama Hattie
Ethel Merman & Joan Carroll .... **Brunswick LA 8569**
Flanagan & Allen .... **Decca F 7910**
Ethel Merman & Joan Carroll appeared in the American production of
Panama Hattie.
Flanagan & Allen appeared in *Black Vanities.*

LET'S CALL THE WHOLE THING OFF   1937
George Gershwin / Ira Gershwin
Chappell & Co. Ltd........................ USA
Film(s): .... Shall We Dance
Fred Astaire .... **Philips BBL 7052**
Mel Tormé .... **London LTZN 15076**
Fred Astaire .... **HMV CLP 1100**
Fred Astaire appeared in *Shall We Dance.*

LET'S DANCE   November 1962
Jim Lee
Edwin H. Morris & Co. Ltd .... USA
Chris Montez .... **London HL 9596**
Brian Poole & The Tremeloes .... **Ace of Clubs ACL 1146**
Chris Montez (1972) .... **London HL 10205**

LET'S DANCE   April 1983
David Jones
EMI Music .... UK
David Bowie .... **EMI EA 152**
Ivor Novello Award.

LET'S DANCE   July 1987
Chris Rea
Magnet Music .... UK
Chris Rea .... **Magnet MAG 299**

LET'S DO IT (Let's Fall In Love)   1929
Cole Porter
Chappell & Co. Ltd .... USA
Show(s): .... Paris / Wake Up and Dream
Film(s): .... Night and Day / Can Can
Leslie Hutchinson (Hutch) .... **Parlophone R 342**
Mary Martin .... **Brunswick 03229**
Dinah Shore & Buddy Clark .... **Columbia DC 447**
Eartha Kitt .... **RCA RD 27067**
Frank Sinatra & Shirley MacLaine .... **Capitol W 1301**
Frank Sinatra & Shirley MacLaine appeared in *Can Can.*

LET'S DO IT AGAIN   June 1950
Desmond O'Connor / Ray Hartley / Sam Browne
Cecil Lennox Music Co. Ltd .... UK
Donald Peers .... **HMV B 9915**
Marie Benson .... **Columbia DB 2707**
Margaret Whiting .... **Capitol CL 13353**

LET'S FACE THE MUSIC AND DANCE   1936
Irving Berlin
Irving Berlin Ltd .... USA
Film(s): .... Follow the Fleet
Fred Astaire .... **Columbia DB 1633**
Tony Martin .... **RCA RD 27003**
Ruth Brown .... **London LTZK 15187**
Fred Astaire appeared in *Follow the Fleet.*

LET'S FALL IN LOVE   1934
Ted Koehler / Harold Arlen
Francis, Day & Hunter Ltd................. USA
Film(s):Let's Fall in Love / Sunny Side of the Street / The Eddy Duchin
Story / Pepe
Annette Hanshaw .... **Edison Bell Winner W 94**
The Ray Charles Singers .... **Brunswick LAT 8342**
Frank Sinatra .... **Reprise R 1001**
Bing Crosby .... **Pye NPL 28015**
Bing Crosby appeared in *Pepe.*

LET'S GET AWAY FROM IT ALL   1942
Matt Dennis / Tom Adair
Francis, Day & Hunter Ltd .... USA
'Fats' Waller & his Rhythm .... **HMV 7EG 8054**
Della Reese .... **RCA RD 27167**
The Cliff Adams Singers .... **Columbia 33SX 1362**

LET'S GET LOST   1943
Jimmy McHugh / Frank Loesser

Victoria Music Co. Ltd .... USA
Film(s): .... Happy Go Lucky
Adelaide Hall .... **Decca F 8292**
Don Cornell .... **Vogue LVA 9037**

LET'S GET SERIOUS   June 1980
Stevie Wonder / Lee Garrett
Jobete Music (UK) Ltd. .... USA
Jermaine Jackson .... **Motown YMG 1183**

LET'S GET TOGETHER   November 1961
Richard M. Sherman / Robert B. Sherman
Walt Disney Music Co. Ltd. .... USA
Film(s): .... The Parent Trap
Hayley Mills .... **Decca F 21396**
The Vernons Girls .... **Parlophone R 4832**
Hayley Mills appeared in *The Parent Trap.*

LET'S GET TOGETHER   March 1970
Chet Powers
Essex Music Ltd. .... USA
The Dave Clark Five .... **Columbia DB 8660**
The Kingston Trio .... **Capitol T 2081**

LET'S GET TOGETHER AGAIN   November 1974
John Rossall / Gerry Shephard
Rock Artistes Music .... UK
Film(s): .... Never too Young To Rock
The Glitter Band .... **Bell 1383**
The Glitter Band appeared in *Never Too Young To Rock.*

LET'S GO ALL THE WAY   June 1986
Gary Cooper
EMI Music .... USA
Sly Fox .... **Capitol CL 403**

LET'S GO CRAZY   March 1985
"Prince"
Island Music .... USA
Prince & The Revolution .... **Warner Brothers W 2000**

LET'S GO DANCING   November 1982
"Kool & The Gang"
Planetary-Nom Music .... USA
Kool & The Gang .... **De Lite DE 9**

LET'S GO ROUND AGAIN   June 1980
Alan Gorrie
Island Music Ltd .... UK
The Average White Band .... **RCA AWB 1**

LET'S GO TO SAN FRANCISCO   October 1967
John Carter / Ken Lewis
Carter-Lewis Music Ltd. .... UK
The Flowerpot Men .... **Deram DM 142**

LET'S GROOVE   December 1981
Maurice White / Wayne Vaughan
April Music Ltd .... USA
Earth Wind & Fire .... **CBS A 1679**

LET'S HANG ON   November 1965
Bob Crewe / Sandy Linzer / Bob Gaudio & Denny Randell
Ardmore & Beechwood Ltd .... USA
The Four Seasons .... **Philips BF 1439**
Darts (1980) .... **Magnet MAG 174**
David & Jonathan .... **Columbia SX 6031**
Barry Manilow (1981) .... **Arista ARIST 429**

LET'S HAVE A JUBILEE   1935
Irving Mills / Alexander Hill
Lafleur & Co. Ltd .... USA
Alex Hill & his Hollywood Seplans,
vocal Alex Hill .... **Vocalion S 70**

LET'S HAVE A QUIET NIGHT IN   January 1978
Tony Macaulay
Macaulay Music......................... UK
David Soul .... **Private Stock PVT 130**

LET'S HAVE A TIDDLEY AT THE MILK BAR   1936
Noel Gay
Cinephonic Music Co. Ltd .... UK
Nellie Wallace .... **HMV B 8502**

Bing Crosby appeared in *Here Come the Waves*.

LET'S HAVE ANOTHER CUP O'COFFEE   1932
Irving Berlin
Chappell & Co. Ltd. .... USA
Show(s): .... Face the Music
The BBC Dance Orchestra,
conducted by Henry Hall .... **Columbia CB 474**
Burl Ives .... **HMV CLP 1410**

LET'S HAVE ANOTHER ONE   1940
Don Raye / Hughie Prince
Leeds Music Co. Ltd .... USA
The Andrews Sisters .... **Brunswick 02966**
The Mike Sammes Singers .... **Columbia SEG 7760**

LET'S HEAR IT FOR THE BOY   June 1984
Dean Pitchford / Eric Carmen
Famous Chappell Music Ltd. .... USA
Film(s): .... Footloose
Deniece Williams .... **CBS A 3419**
Nominated for an Academy Award 1984.

LET'S JUMP THE BROOMSTICK   April 1961
Charles Robbins
Aberbach (London) Ltd. .... USA
Brenda Lee .... **Brunswick 05823**

LET'S KEEP IT THAT WAY   1946
Desmond O'Connor / Jack Denby / Muriel Watson
Noel Gay Music Co. Ltd. .... UK
Paula Green .... **Columbia FB 3172**

LET'S PUT IT ALL TOGETHER   November 1974
Hugo Peretti / Luigi Creatore / George Weiss
Carlin Music Corporation .... USA
The Stylistics .... **Avco 6105032**

LET'S PUT OUT THE LIGHTS AND GO TO SLEEP   1933
Herman Hupfeld
Victoria Music Co. Ltd. .... USA
Show(s): .... George White's Music Hall Varieties
Bing Crosby .... **Fontana TFR 6000**
Lew Stone & his Orchestra,
vocal Al Bowlly & Mary Charles .... **Decca F 3270**
Lena Horne .... **RCA RD 27098**

LET'S SEE ACTION   December 1971
Peter Townshend
Fabulous Music Ltd .... UK
The Who .... **Track 2094012**

LET'S SPEND THE NIGHT TOGETHER   February 1967
Mick Jagger / Keith Richard
Mirage Music Ltd. .... UK
The Rolling Stones .... **Decca F 12456**

LET'S START THE NEW YEAR RIGHT   1942
Irving Berlin
Chappell & Co. Ltd .... USA
Film(s): .... Holiday Inn
Bing Crosby .... **Brunswick Bing 7**
Bing Crosby appeared in *Holiday Inn*.

LET'S STAY TOGETHER   February 1972
Willie Mitchell / Al Green / Al Jackson
Burlington Music Co. Ltd .... USA
Al Green .... **London HL 10348**
Tina Turner (1984) .... **Capitol CL 316**

LET'S STICK TOGETHER   July 1976
Wilbert Harrison
United Artists Music Co. Ltd .... USA
Bryan Ferry .... **Island WIP 6307**
See also "Lets Work Together".

LET'S TAKE AN OLD FASHIONED WALK   March 1956
Irving Berlin
Irving Berlin Ltd. .... USA
Show(s): .... Miss Liberty
Perry Como .... **Camden CDN 110**

LET'S TAKE THE LONG WAY HOME   1944
Harold Arlen / Johnny Mercer
Edwin H. Morris & Co. Ltd. .... USA
Film(s): .... Here Come the Waves
Bing Crosby .... **Brunswick Bing 9**

LET'S TALK ABOUT LOVE   **May 1962**
Norrie Paramor / Bunny Lewis
Lorna Music Co. Ltd. .... UK
Film(s): .... It's Trad Dad
Helen Shapiro .... **Columbia DB 4824**
Helen Shapiro appeared in *It's Trad Dad*.

LET'S TALK ABOUT MY SWEETIE   1926
Walter Donaldson / Gus Kahn
Francis, Day & Hunter Ltd. .... USA
The Savoy Orpheans .... **HMV B 5075**

LET'S THINK ABOUT LIVING   October 1960
Boudleaux Bryant
Acuff-Rose Publishing Co. Ltd .... USA
Bob Luman .... **Warner Brothers WM 4025**
Johnny Burnette .... **London HAG 2349**

LET'S TURKEY TROT   April 1963
Gerry Goffin / Carole King
Aldon Music Ltd. .... USA
Little Eva .... **London HL 9687**

LET'S TWIST AGAIN   April 1962
Kal Mann / Dave Appell
West One Music Ltd. .... USA
Chubby Checker .... **Columbia DB 4691**
The Ventures .... **London HAG 2429**
Chubby Checker (1976) .... **London HL 10512**
John Asher .... **Creole CR 112**

LET'S WAIT AWHILE   April 1987
James Harris / Terry Lewis / Janet Jackson & Renee Andrews
SBK Songs .... USA
Janet Jackson .... **Breakout USA 601**

LET'S WALK THAT-A-WAY   July 1953
Kay Twomey / Fred Wise / Ben Wiseman
Aberbach Music .... USA
Doris Day & Johnnie Ray .... **Philips PB 157**
Dennis Lotis .... **Decca F 10153**
The Malcolm Mitchell Trio .... **Parlophone R 3711**

LET'S WORK TOGETHER   March 1970
Wilbert Harrison
United Artists Music Co. Ltd. .... USA
Canned Heat .... **Liberty LBF 15302**
Wilbert Harrison .... **London HL 10307**
See also 'Let's Stick Together'.

LETTER FROM AMERICA   December 1987
Charles Reid / Craig Reid
Warner Brothers Music .... UK
The Proclaimers .... **Chrysalis CHS 3178**

LETTER FULL OF TEARS   March 1962
Don Covey
Belinda (London) Ltd. .... USA
Billy Fury .... **Decca F 11437**

LETTER SONG, THE   1909
Oscar Straus / Stanislaus Stange
B. Feldman & Co Ltd .... Germany
Show(s): .... The Chocolate Soldier
Film(s): .... The Chocolate Soldier
Evelyn D'Alroy & C.H. Workman .... **Odeon 0704**
Ann Ayars & Charles Fredericks .... **Camden CDN 134**
Evelyn D'Alroy & C.H. Workman appeared in the British production of
The Chocolate Soldier.

LETTER TO A SOLDIER   December 1956
Gee Langdon
David Toff Music Publishing Ltd. .... UK
Terry Burton .... **Philips PB 653**
Barbara Lyon .... **Columbia DB 3865**

LETTER TO YOU   October 1984
Dennis Linde
EMI Music .... USA
Shakin' Stevens .... **Epic A 4677**

LETTER, THE   November 1967
Wayne Thompson

B. Feldman & Co. Ltd. . . . . USA
The Boxtops . . . . **Stateside SS 2044**

'LEVEN-THIRTY SATURDAY NIGHT   **1930**
Earl Burtnett / Bill Grantham / Jess Kirkpatrick
Keith Prowse Music Publishing Co. Ltd . . . . USA
The Arcadians Dance Orchestra . . . . **Zonophone 5603**

LICENCE TO KILL   **June 1989**
Narada Michael Walden / Jeff Cohen / Walter Afanasieff
EMI Music . . . . USA
Film(s): . . . . Licence To Kill
Gladys Knight . . . . **MCA MCA 1339**

LIDO SHUFFLE   **June 1977**
Boz Scaggs / David Paich
Heath Levy Music Ltd . . . . USA
Boz Scaggs . . . . **CBS 5136**

LIES   **1932**
George Springer / Harry Barris
B. Feldman & Co. Ltd. . . . . USA
John Firman & his Band . . . . **Zonophone 6039**
Perry Como . . . . **HMV B 10431**
Paul Weston & his Orchestra . . . . **Capitol T 1361**

LIES   **January 1981**
Francis Rossi / Bernard Frost
Eaton Music . . . . UK
Status Quo . . . . **Vertigo QUO 4**

LIFE GET'S TEDIOUS, DON'T IT   **1948**
Carson Robison
. . . . USA
Peter Lind Hayes . . . . **Brunswick 04036**
Tex Williams . . . . **Capitol CL 13083**
Carson Robison . . . . **MGM 187**

LIFE IS A LONG SONG   **October 1971**
Ian Anderson
Chrysalis Music Ltd . . . . UK
Jethro Tull . . . . **Chrysalis WIP 6106**

LIFE IS A MINESTRONE   **May 1975**
Lol Creme / Eric Stewart
St. Annes Music Ltd . . . . UK
10 CC . . . . **Mercury 6008010**

LIFE IS A SONG   **1935**
Joe Young / Fred Ahlert
Francis, Day & Hunter Ltd . . . . USA
Bob Crosby & his Orchestra . . . . **Decca M 463**
Janette Scott & Jackie Rae . . . . **Fontana TFL 5102**

LIFE IS JUST A BOWL OF CHERRIES   **1931**
Lew Brown / Ray Henderson
Victoria Music Co. Ltd. . . . . USA
Show(s): . . . . George White's Scandals of 1931
Film(s): George White's Scandals / The Best Things in Life are Free
Ethel Merman . . . . **Brunswick 04334**
Roy Fox & his Orchestra, vocal Al Bowlly . . . . . . **Decca F 2682**
Billy Eckstine . . . . **MGM EP 548**
Janette Scott & Jackie Rae . . . . **Fontana TFL 5102**
Ethel Merman . . . . **Reprise R 6032**
Ethel Merman appeared in *George White's Scandals of 1931.*

LIFE IS NOTHING WITHOUT MUSIC   **1939**
Fred Hartley
World Wide Music Co. Ltd. . . . . UK
Leslie Hutchinson (Hutch) . . . . **Parlophone F 1476**
Jackie Rae . . . . **Fontana TFL 5102**
Fred Hartley Orchestra . . . . **Hartley CTPX 14256**
Theme tune of Fred Hartley.

LIFE IS TOO SHORT GIRL   **May 1976**
Herbert Watins
A.T.V. Music Ltd. . . . . UK
Sheer Elegance . . . . **Pye 7N 25703**

LIFE ON MARS   **August 1973**
David Bowie
Chrysalis Music Ltd. . . . . UK
David Bowie . . . . **RCA 2316**

LIFE'S DESIRE   **1932**
Tolchard Evans / Stanley Damerell / Robert Hargreaves
Cecil Lennox Music Co. Ltd. . . . . UK
Gracie Fields . . . . **HMV B 4000**
Harry Lawson . . . . **HMV B 10068**
Doris Day . . . . **Columbia DB 2888**

LIFE'S FULL OF CONSEQUENCES   **1944**
E.Y. Harburg / Harold Arlen
Robins Music Corporation . . . . USA
Film(s): . . . . Cabin in the Sky
Eddie 'Rochester' Anderson . . . **Hollywood Soundstage HS 5003**
Eddie Anderson appeared in *Cabin in the Sky.*

LIFELINE   **October 1982**
Gary Kemp
Reformation Music . . . . UK
Spandau Ballet . . . . **Chrysalis CHS 2642**

LIGHT MY FIRE   **November 1968**
John Densmore / Robert Krieger / Ray Manzarek & Jim Morrison
Campbell, Connelly & Co. Ltd. . . . . USA
Jose Feliciano . . . . **RCA 1715**
The Doors . . . . **Elektra EKSN 45014**

LIGHTERMAN TOM   **1907**
Francis J. Barron / W.H. Squire
Chappell & Co Ltd . . . . UK
Harry Dearth . . . . **Columbia DX 19**

LIGHTIN' STRIKES   **March 1966**
Lou Christie / Twyla Herbert
Debmar Music Ltd. . . . . USA
Lou Christie . . . . **MGM 1297**

LIGHTS OF CINCINNATI, THE   **July 1969**
Tony Macaulay / Geoff Stevens
Welbeck Music Co. Ltd. . . . . UK
Scott Walker . . . . **Philips BF 1793**
Ivor Novello Nomination.

LIGHTS OF LISBON, THE   **January 1958**
Werner Bochmann
Campbell Connelly & Co. Ltd . . . . Germany
Tony Osborne & his Dancing Strings . . . . **HMV POP 439**

LIGHTS OUT   **1936**
Billy Hill
Lawrence Wright Music Co. Ltd . . . . USA
Phylis Robins . . . . **Rex 8714**
Greta Keller . . . . **Decca LK 4126**
Billy Vaughan & his Orchestra . . . . **London HLD 8859**

LIKE A BABY   **February 1966**
John Madara / David White / Len Barry
Leeds Music . . . . USA
Len Barry . . . . **Brunswick 05949**

LIKE A BUTTERFLY   **October 1975**
Wayne Bickerton / Tony Waddington
A.T.V. Music Ltd. . . . . UK
Mac & Katie Kissoon . . . . **State STAT 9**

LIKE A PRAYER   **April 1989**
Madonna Ciccone / Patrick Leonard
No Publisher . . . . USA
Madonna . . . . **Sire W 7539**

LIKE A ROLLING STONE   **September 1965**
Bob Dylan
Blossom Music Ltd . . . . USA
Bob Dylan . . . . **CBS 201811**
The Surfaris . . . . **Brunswick LAT 8631**

LIKE A VIRGIN   **December 1984**
William Steinberg / Tom Kelly
Warner Brothers Music . . . . USA
Madonna . . . . **Sire W 9210**

LIKE CLOCKWORK   **August 1978**
Bob Geldof
Sewer Fire Hits . . . . UK
The Boomtown Rats . . . . **Ensign ENY 14**

LIKE I DO   February 1963
Dick Manning
Bourne Music Ltd . . . . USA
Maureen Evans . . . . **Oriole CB 1760**
Nancy Sinatra . . . . **Reprise R 20045**
Adapted from *Dance of the Hours* from Act 3 of *La Gioconda* by
Amilcare Ponchielli (1834 - 1886).
See also 'Hello Muddah, Hello Fadduh'.

LIKE I'VE NEVER BEEN GONE   March 1963
Paul Hampton / C. Monte
Skidmore Music Ltd . . . . USA
Billy Fury . . . . **Decca F 11582**

LIKE SISTER AND BROTHER   September 1973
Roger Cook / Roger Greenaway / Geoff Stevens
A.T.V. Music Ltd. . . . . UK
The Drifters . . . . **Bell 1313**
Ivor Novello Nomination.

LIKE STRANGERS   January 1961
Boudleaux Bryant
Acuff-Rose Publishing Co. Ltd . . . . USA
The Everly Brothers . . . . **London HL 9250**

LIKE TO GET TO KNOW YOU WELL   September 1984
Howard Jones
Warner Brothers Music . . . . UK
Howard Jones . . . . **WEA HOW 5**

LIL' DEVIL   May 1987
Ian Astbury / William Duffy
Chappell Music Co. . . . . UK
The Cult . . . . **Beggars Banquet BEG 188**

LILAC DOMINO, THE   1918
Charles Culliver / Robert B. Smith
B. Feldman & Co. Ltd. . . . . Germany
Show(s): . . . . The Lilac Domino
Clara Butterworth, Vincent Sullivan
& Jamieson Dodds . . . . **Columbia L 1239**
Aileen Cochrane . . . . **HMV 7EG 8525**
Clara Butterworth, Vincent Sullivan & Jamieson Dodds appeared in
the British production of *The Lilac Domino*.

LILACS IN THE RAIN   1940
Mitchell Parish / Peter De Rose
Robbins Music Corporation Ltd . . . . USA
Tony Martin . . . . **Decca F 7391**
Carmen McRae . . . . **Brunswick LAT 8147**

LILI MARLENE   1944
Norbert Schultze / Hans Leip / Tommie Connor
Peter Maurice Music Co. Ltd. Germany
Lale Anderson . . . . **HMV 7EG 8277**
Marlene Dietrich . . . . **Philips BBL 7322**
Anne Shelton . . . . **Decca F 8434**

LILY OF LAGUNA   1898
Leslie Stuart
Francis, Day & Hunter Ltd. . . . . UK
Film(s): . . . . Lilacs in the Spring / Variety Jubilee
Eugene Stratton . . . . **HMV C 556**
Bing Crosby & Mary Martin . . . . **Brunswick 03657**
Stanley Holloway . . . . **Pye NPL 18056**
Errol Flynn . . . . **Philips PB 380**
Errol Flynn appeared in *Lilacs in the Spring*.

LILY THE PINK   January 1969
Roger McGough / Mike McGear / John Gorman
Noel Gay Music Co. Ltd. . . . . UK
Scaffold . . . . **Parlophone R 5734**

LILY WAS HERE   March 1990
David A. Stewart
Eligible Music . . . . UK
David A. Stewart featuring Candy Dulfer . . . **Anxious ZB 43045**
Ivor Novello Nomination.

LIMEHOUSE BLUES   1922
Douglas Furber / Philip Braham
Ascherberg, Hopwood & Crew . . . . UK
Show(s): . . . . A to Z / Andre Charlot's Revue of 1924
Film(s): . . . . The Ziegfeld Follies / Star
Gertrude Lawrence . . . . **Brunswick 05001**

The 'Queens' Dance Orchestra . . . . **HMV B 1387**
The Mills Brothers . . . . **Brunswick 01943**
Rosemary Clooney . . . . **RCA RD 27218**
Julie Andrews . . . . **Stateside SL 10233**
Gertrude Lawrence appeared in *A to Z* and *Andre Charlot's Revue of
1924*.
Julie Andrews appeared in *Star*.

LIMELIGHT   July 1953
Charles Chaplin
Bourne Music Ltd . . . . USA
Film(s): . . . . Limelight
Frank Chacksfield & his Orchestra . . . **Ace of Clubs ACL 1034**
The Melachrino Strings . . . . **HMV 7EG 8601**
Victor Young & his Orchestra . . . . **Brunswick LAT 8029**
Ron Goodwin Orchestra . . . . **Parlophone R 3686**
See also 'Eternally'.

LINDA   1947
Jack Lawrence / Ann Ronell
Chappell & Co. Ltd. . . . . USA
Film(s): . . . . The Story of G.I. Joe
The Skyrockets Dance Orchestra,
vocal Dick James . . . . **HMV BD 5982**
Jimmy Young . . . . **Decca F 10064**
Perry Como . . . . **RCA RD 27154**
Nominated for an Academy Award 1945.

LINGER A LITTLE LONGER IN THE TWILIGHT   1932
Harry Woods / James Campbell / Reginald Connelly
Campbell Connelly & Co. Ltd. . . . . UK
Bing Crosby . . . . **Columbia DB 2142**

LINGER AWHILE   1924
Harry Owens / Vincent Rose
Francis, Day & Hunter Ltd . . . . USA
Film(s): . . . . Belles on Their Toes
Paul Whiteman & his Orchestra . . . . **HMV B 1771**
Sarah Vaughan . . . . **Philips BBL 7165**
Paul Weston & his Orchestra & Chorus . . . . . . **Capitol T 1361**

LINGER IN MY ARMS A LITTLE LONGER BABY   1946
Herb Magidson
New World Publishers Ltd. . . . . USA
Woody Herman & his Orchestra,
vocal Lynne Stevens . . . . **Parlophone R 3017**
Tony Henry & The Tom Boys . . . . **Decca F 8683**

LION SLEEPS TONIGHT, THE   January 1962
Traditional
The Tokens (1962) . . . . **RCA 1263**
Dave Newman . . . . **Pye 7N 45134**
Tight Fit (1982) . . . . **Jive JIVE 9**
See also 'Wimoweh'

LIPSTICK ON YOUR COLLAR   August 1959
Edna Lewis / George Goehring
Joy Music Ltd . . . . USA
Connie Francis . . . . **MGM C 804**
The Hunters . . . . **Fontana TFL 5140**

LIPSTICK, POWDER AND PAINT   November 1985
Jesse Stone
Carlin Music . . . . UK
Shakin' Stevens . . . . **Epic A 6610**

LIQUIDATOR, THE   January 1969
Harry Johnson
B & C Music . . . . Jamaica
Harry J All Stars . . . . **Trojan TRO 9063**

LISTEN TO ME   November 1968
Tony Hazzard
Sydney Bron Music Co. Ltd. . . . . UK
The Hollies . . . . **Parlophone R 5733**

LISTEN TO WHAT THE MAN SAID   June 1975
Paul McCartney
A.T.V. Music Ltd. . . . . UK
Wings . . . . **Apple R 6006**

LISTEN TO YOUR HEART   September 1990
Per Gessle / Matts Persson
EMI Music . . . . Sweden
Roxette . . . . **EMI EM 149**

LISZT, CHOPIN AND MENDELSSOHN　　　1932
Horatio Nicholls / Leo Towers / Harry Leon
Lawrence Wright Music Co. Ltd. UK
Ambrose & his Orchestra, vocal Sam Browne — **HMV B 6255**

LITTLE ANNIE ROONEY　　　1889
Michael Nolan
Francis, Day & Hunter Ltd. . . . . UK
Reg Grant . . . . **Parlophone E 6341**
Mitch Miller & The Gang . . . . **Philips BBL 7404**

LITTLE APRIL SHOWER　　　1942
Frank Churchill / Larry Morey
Campbell Connelly & Co. Ltd . . . . USA
Film(s): . . . . Bambi (cartoon)
Sound Track . . . . **Top Rank JKP 2032**

LITTLE ARROWS　　　November 1968
Albert Hammond / Mike Hazlewood
Shaftsbury Music Ltd. . . . . UK
Leapy Lee . . . . **MCA MU 1028**

LITTLE BIRD ON NELLIE'S HAT, THE　　　1906
Arthur Lamb / Alfred Solman
W. Paxton & Co. Ltd. . . . . USA
Film(s): . . . . Atlantic City
Maidie Scott . . . . **HMV C 616**

LITTLE BIRD TOLD ME, A　　　January 1949
Harvey Brooks
Bourne Music Ltd . . . . USA
Evelyn Knight . . . . **Brunswick OE 9428**

LITTLE BIT INDEPENDENT, A　　　1936
Edgar Leslie / Joe Burke
Francis, Day & Hunter Ltd . . . . USA
'Fats' Waller & his Rhythm . . . . **HMV BD 5012**
Dick Haymes . . . . **Brunswick 04589**
Eddie Fisher . . . . **Camden CDN 123**

LITTLE BIT MORE, A　　　August 1976
Bobby Gosh
Sunbury Music Ltd . . . . USA
Dr. Hook . . . . **Capitol CL 15871**

LITTLE BIT OF HEAVEN, A　　　1915
Ernest Ball / J. Keirn Brennan
B. Feldman & Co. Ltd. . . . . USA
Show(s): . . . . The Heart of Paddy Whack
Film(s): . . . . Irish Eyes Are Smiling
Dorothy Ward . . . . **Regal G 7170**
Ruby Murray . . . . **Columbia SEG 7952**

LITTLE BIT OF LOVE, A　　　July 1972
"Free"
Socks Music . . . . UK
Free . . . . **Island WIP 6129**

LITTLE BIT OF ME, A LITTLE BIT YOU, A　　　May 1967
Neil Diamond
Screen Gems Music Ltd. . . . . USA
The Monkees . . . . **RCA 1580**

LITTLE BIT OF SOAP　　　July 1978
Bert Russell
Sherwin Music Co. . . . . USA
Showaddywaddy . . . . **Arista 191**
The Jarmels . . . . **Top Rank JAR 580**
Jimmy Justice . . . . **Pye 7N 15376**
Gene McDaniels . . . . **Liberty LBY 1021**
First published 1961.

LITTLE BIT OFF THE TOP, A　　　1898
Fred Murray / Fred W. Leigh
Francis, Day & Hunter Ltd. . . . . UK
Reg Grant . . . . **Parlophone R 1518**
The Two Bills from Bermondsey . . . . **Parlophone R 3953**
Jimmy Hanley . . . . **Piccadilly NPL 38002**

LITTLE BITTY TEAR, A　　　February 1962
Hank Cochran
Acuff-Rose Publishing Co. Ltd. . . . . USA
Burl Ives . . . . **Brunswick 05863**
Miki & Griff . . . . **Pye 7N 15412**

LITTLE BOOGIE WOOGIE　　　August 1987
Mike Leander / Eddie Seagoy / Gary Glitter
MCA Music . . . . UK
Shakin' Stevens . . . . **Epic SHAKY 3**

LITTLE BOXES　　　March 1964
Malvina Reynolds
Essex Music Ltd . . . . USA
Pete Seeger . . . . **CBS AAG 187**
The Womenfolk . . . . **RCA RD 7651**
Nina & Frederik . . . . **Columbia DB 7400**

LITTLE BOY SAD　　　May 1961
Wayne P. Walker
Southern Music Publishing Co. Ltd . . . . USA
Johnny Burnette . . . . **London HL 9315**
Paul Preston . . . . **Pye 7N 25173**

LITTLE BOY THAT SANTA CLAUS FORGOT　　　1937
Tommie Connor / Jimmy Leach / Michael Carr
Peter Maurice Music Co. Ltd. UK
Phyllis Robins . . . . **Rex 9165**
Lita Roza . . . . **Decca F 10204**

LITTLE BROWN JUG　　　February 1976
Traditional, arranged by Bill Finnigan
Robbins Music Ltd . . . . USA
Film(s): . . . . Glenn Miller Story
Glenn Miller Orchestra . . . . **HMV B 10662**
Glenn Miller Orchestra . . . . **RCA 2644**
First published 1869.

LITTLE BY LITTLE　　　February 1966
Beatrice Verdi / E. Ginn / Buddy Kaye
Raintree Music Ltd . . . . USA
Dusty Springfield . . . . **Philips BF 1466**

LITTLE CHILDREN　　　April 1964
Mort Schuman / John McFarland
Belinda (London) Ltd . . . . USA
Billy J. Kramer . . . . **Parlophone R 5105**

LITTLE CO-OPERATION FROM YOU, A　　　1937
Samuel Lerner / Al Goodhard / Al Hoffman
Cinephonic Music Co. Ltd. . . . . UK
Show(s): . . . . Going Greek
Louise Brown & Roy Royston . . . . **HMV BD 462**
Louise Brown & Roy Royston appeared in *Going Greek*.

LITTLE CURLY HAIR IN A HIGH CHAIR　　　1940
Charles Tobias / Nat Simon
Francis, Day & Hunter Ltd . . . . USA
Film(s): . . . . Forty Little Mothers
Eddie Cantor . . . . **Fontana TFL 5037**
Jimmy Dorsey & his Orchestra,
vocal Helen O'Connell . . . . **Brunswick 03027**
Eddie Cantor appeared in *Forty Little Mothers*.

LITTLE DARLIN'　　　August 1957
Maurice Williams
Campbell Connelly & Co. Ltd. . . . . USA
The Diamonds . . . . **Mercury ZEP 10003**
Tommy Steele . . . . **Decca LK 4351**

LITTLE DEVIL　　　June 1961
Howard Greenfield / Neil Sedaka
Nevins-Kirshner Ltd . . . . USA
Neil Sedaka . . . . **RCA 1236**
Helen Shapiro . . . . **Columbia 33SX 1397**

LITTLE DEVIL (See also Lil'Devil)

LITTLE DOES SHE KNOW　　　January 1977
Will Birch / Graham Douglas / Paul Shuttleworth
Rock Artistes Music . . . . UK
The Kursaal Flyers . . . . **CBS 4689**

LITTLE DOLLY DAYDREAM　　　1897
Leslie Stuart
Francis, Day & Hunter Ltd. . . . . UK
Leslie Stuart (Piano) . . . . **Berliner 5509**
Eugene Stratton . . . . **HMV 02377**
The George Mitchell Minstrels . . . . **HMV CLP 1399**

LITTLE DONKEY December 1959
Eric Boswell
Chappell & Co. Ltd . . . . UK
The Beverley Sisters . . . . Ace of Clubs ACL 1048
Nina & Frederik (1960) . . . . Columbia SEG 8111
Gracie Fields . . . . Columbia DB 4360

LITTLE DRUMMER BOY, THE 1938
Art Noel / Don Pelosi
Dash Music Ltd. . . . . UK
Gracie Fields . . . . Rex 9308
Les Allen . . . . Columbia FB 1938
Lew Stone & his Orchestra, vocal Al Bowlly . . . . Decca F 6607

LITTLE DRUMMER BOY, THE March 1959
Harry Simeone / Henry Onorati / Katherine Davis
Bregmann, Vocco & Conn Ltd . . . . USA
The Beverley Sisters . . . . Ace of Clubs ACL 1048
Harry Simeone Chorale . . . . Ember S 118
The Mike Sammes Singers . . . . Fontana TFL 5070
The Band of The Royal Scots Dragoon Guards (1972) . RCA 2301
Bing Crosby & David Bowie (1982) . . . . RCA BOW 12

LITTLE DUTCH MILL 1934
Arthur Freed / Harry Barris
Campbell Connelly & Co. Ltd. . . . . USA
Bing Crosby . . . . Brunswick 01735
Billy Vaughan & his Orchestra . . . . London HAD 2241

LITTLE GIRL 1931
Madeline Hyde / Francis Henry
Campbell Connelly & Co. Ltd. . . . . USA
Joe Venuti's Blue Four, vocal Harold Arlen Parlophone R 1003
Nat 'King' Cole . . . . Capitol CL 13008
Al Jolson . . . . Brunswick LAT 8322
Marty Wilde (1961) . . . . Philips PB 1078
Vic Damone . . . . Capitol T 1748
Sam Cooke . . . . RCA RD 7539

LITTLE GIRL February 1963
Sonny Curtis
Cricket Music Ltd . . . . USA
The Crickets . . . . Liberty LIB 10067

LITTLE GIRL BLUE 1935
Richard Rodgers / Lorenz Hart
Chappell & Co. Ltd . . . . USA
Show(s): . . . . Jumbo
Film(s): . . . . Jumbo
Ella Fitzgerald . . . . HMV CLP 1116
Sarah Vaughan . . . . Mercury MMC 14024
Louis Armstrong . . . . HMV CLP 1388
Doris Day . . . . CBS BPG 62118
Doris Day appeared in the film *Jumbo*.

LITTLE GREEN APPLES May 1968
Bobby Russell
Peter Maurice Music Co. Ltd. . . . . USA
Roger Miller . . . . Mercury MF 1021
Tony Bennett . . . . CBS 63962

LITTLE GREY HOME IN THE WEST 1911
D. Eardley Wilmott / Herman Loehr
Chappell & Co. Ltd. . . . . UK
John McCormack . . . . HMV DA 299
Arthur Tracey (The Street Singer) . . . . Decca LF 1077

LITTLE IN LOVE, A February 1981
Alan Tarney
ATV Music . . . . UK
Cliff Richard . . . . EMI 5123

LITTLE KISS EACH MORNING, A 1930
Harry Woods
Chappell & Co. Ltd . . . . USA
Film(s): . . . . The Vagabond Lover
Rudy Vallee . . . . HMV B 5761
Bing Crosby . . . . Brunswick LAT 8138

LITTLE LADY MAKE BELIEVE 1938
Charles Tobias / Nat Simon
Chappell & Co. Ltd . . . . USA
Gracie Fields . . . . Rex 9354
Bing Crosby . . . . Brunswick 02618

Lew Stone & his Band, vocal Al Bowlly . . . . Decca F 6744

LITTLE LIES November 1987
Christine McVie / Eddy Quintela
Bright Music . . . . USA
Fleetwood Mac . . . . Warner Brothers W 8291

LITTLE LOVE AND UNDERSTANDING, A (Un Peu
D'amour Et D'amitie) May 1975
Gilbert Becaud / Marcel Stellman
A.T.V. Music Ltd. . . . . France
Gilbert Becaud . . . . Decca F 13537

LITTLE LOVE, A LITTLE KISS, A (Un Peu d'Amour) 1912
Lao Silesu / Adrian Ross / A.N. Fysher
Chappell & Co. Ltd. . . . . France
Show(s): . . . . The Ziegfeld Follies of 1913
John McCormack . . . . HMV DA 300
Arthur Tracey (The Street Singer) . . . . Decca LF 1077
Karl Denver (1962) . . . . Decca F 11470

LITTLE LOVIN', A May 1964
Russell Alquist
Jaep Music Ltd . . . . UK
The Fourmost . . . . Parlophone R 5128

LITTLE MAN October 1966
Sonny Bono
Belinda (London) Ltd. . . . . USA
Sonny & Cher . . . . Atlantic 584040

LITTLE MAN YOU'VE HAD A BUSY DAY 1934
Maurice Sigler / Mabel Wayne / Al Hoffman
Chappell & Co. Ltd. . . . . USA
Paul Robeson . . . . HMV B 8202
Phyllis Robins . . . . Rex 8247
Perry Como . . . . RCA RD 27078

LITTLE MISS LONELY August 1962
Mike Hawker / John Schroeder
Lorna Music Ltd . . . . UK
Helen Shapiro . . . . Columbia DB 4869

LITTLE MISS MELODY 1917
Lionel Monckton / Adrian Ross / Percy Greenbank
Chappell & Co. Ltd. . . . . UK
Show(s): . . . . The Boy
Nellie Taylor . . . . HMV C 833
Nellie Taylor appeared in *The Boy*.

LITTLE MORE LOVE, A February 1979
John Farrar
Rondor Music (London) Ltd. . . . . UK
Olivia Newton-John . . . . EMI 2879

LITTLE NELLIE KELLY I LOVE YOU 1923
George M. Cohan
B. Feldman & Co. Ltd . . . . USA
Show(s): . . . . Little Nellie Kelly / George M.
Film(s): . . . . Yankee Doodle Dandy / Little Nellie Kelly
The Mayfair Orchestra . . . . HMV C 1118
Stanley Black & his Orchestra . . . . Decca LK 4243
Joel Grey . . . . Columbia KOS 3200
Joel Grey appeared in *George M.*.

LITTLE OF WHAT YOU FANCY, A 1915
Fred W. Leigh / George Arthurs
Francis, Day & Hunter Ltd. . . . . UK
Film(s): . . . . Variety Jubilee
Marie Lloyd . . . . Regal G 7076
Alfred Lynch . . . . Decca F 11171
Marie Lloyd Jr. . . . . Broadcast 518
Georgia Brown . . . . Decca LK 4411
Marie Lloyd Jr. appeared in *Variety Jubilee*.

LITTLE OLD LADY 1937
Hoagy Carmichael / Stanley Adams
Chappell & Co. Ltd. . . . . USA
Show(s): . . . . The Show is on
Gracie Fields . . . . Rex 9166
Ray Noble & his Orchestra, vocal Al Bowlly . . . . HMV BD 5287
Hoagy Carmichael . . . . Brunswick LA 8663

LITTLE OLD MILL 1947
Don Pelosi / Lewis Ilda / Leo Towers

Dash Music Ltd. .... UK
Geraldo & his Orchestra, vocal Carol Carr . **Parlophone F 2234**

LITTLE ON THE LONELY SIDE, A   1945
Dick Robertson / James Cavanaugh / Frank Weldon
Bradbury Wood Ltd. .... USA
Geraldo & his Orchestra, vocal Carol Carr . **Parlophone F 2064**
Eve Boswell .... **Parlophone PMC 1038**

LITTLE PAL   1929
Buddy De Sylva / Lew Brown / Ray Henderson / Al Jolson
Campbell Connelly & Co. Ltd .... USA
Film(s): .... Say it With Songs
Al Jolson .... **Brunswick LAT 8220**
Paul Robeson .... **HMV B 3146**
Al Jolson appeared in *Say It With Songs*.

LITTLE PEACE, A (Ein Bisschen Frieden)   May 1982
Ralph Siegel / Paul Greedus
Carlin Music .... Germany
Nicole .... **CBS A 2365**
The German entry for the 1982 Eurovision Song Contest (Placed First).

LITTLE PINK PETTY FROM PETER   1907
Paul Rubens
Chappell & Co. Ltd. .... UK
Show(s): .... Miss Hook of Holland
Ruby Gray .... **Beka 40174**
The Pro Arte Orchestra .... **Pye CML 33003**

LITTLE RAIN MUST FALL, A   1940
Jack Little
Campbell Connelly & Co. Ltd .... USA
Al Bowlly .... **HMV BD 827**

LITTLE RED CORVETTE   February 1985
"Prince"
Island Music .... USA
Prince .... **Warner Brothers W 1999**

LITTLE RED MONKEY   March 1953
Jack Jordan / Stephen Gale
Robbins Music Corporation Ltd .... UK
Frank Chacksfield's Tunesmith's
with Jack Jordan (Clavioline) .... **Parlophone R 3658**
Joy Nichols, Jimmy Edwards
& Dick Bentley .... **Parlophone GEP 8509**
The Melanchrino Strings .... **HMV B 10461**
Rose Murphy .... **London L 1176**

LITTLE RED ROOSTER   December 1964
Willie Dixon
Jewel Music Publishing Co. Ltd .... USA
Sam Cooke .... **RCA 1367**
The Rolling Stones .... **Decca F 12014**

LITTLE RESPECT   October 1988
Vincent Clarke / Andrew Bell
Sonet Music .... UK
Erasure .... **Mute MUTE 85**
Ivor Novello Nomination.

LITTLE ROCK GETAWAY   1934
Joe Sullivan
Robbins Music Corporation Ltd. .... USA
Joe Sullivan (piano) .... **Columbia SEG 7652**
Les Paul (guitar) .... **Capitol EAP 1-20145**
Matty Matlock & The Paducah Patrol .. **Warner Brothers WM 4027**

LITTLE SERENADE (Piccolissima Serenata)   May 1958
Giovanni Ferrio / Antonio Amurri / Geoffrey Parsons & John Turner
Macmelodies Ltd .... Italy
Eddie Calvert (trumpet) .... **Columbia SEG 7891**
Roberto Murolo .... **Durium U 20037**
Percy Faith & his Orchestra .... **Philips BBL 7359**

LITTLE SHIRT MY MOTHER MADE FOR ME   1909
Harry Wincott
Darewski Music Co. .... UK
Stanley Holloway .... **Philips BBL 7237**
Montana Slim .... **London HAB 8264**
The Bards .... **Polydor POSP 310**

LITTLE SHOEMAKER, THE (Le Petit Cordonnier)   June 1954
Rudi Revil / Francis Lemarque / John Turner & Geoffrey Parsons

Bourne Music Ltd. .... France
Petula Clark .... **Nixa NPT 19002**
Tommy Kinsman & his Orchestra .... **Fontana TFL 5143**

LITTLE SIR ECHO   1939
Laura Smith / J.S. Fearis / Adele Girard & Joe Marsala
Francis, Day & Hunter Ltd. .... USA
Dick Todd .... **HMV BD 699**
Ambrose & his Orchestra,
vocal Vera Lynn & Denny Dennis .... **Decca F 7041**
Max Bygraves .... **HMV 7M 113**

LITTLE STREET WHERE OLD FRIENDS MEET, A   1933
Gus Kahn / Harry Woods
Campbell Connelly & Co. Ltd. .... USA
Gene Austin .... **Decca F 3392**
Jim Lowe .... **London HAD 2108**
Vera Lynn .... **MGM C 840**

LITTLE THINGS   April 1965
Bobby Goldboro
Dominion Music Co. Ltd .... USA
Dave Berry .... **Decca F 12103**
Bobby Goldsboro .... **United Artists UP 1079**

LITTLE THINGS MEAN A LOT   June 1954
Carl Stutz / Edith Lindeman
Robbins Music Corporation Ltd. .... USA
Kitty Kallen .... **Brunswick OE 9425**
Vera Lynn .... **Decca LK 4120**
Joan Regan .... **Pye NPL 18048**

LITTLE TIME, A   October 1990
Paul Heaton / David Rotheray
Go Disc Music .... UK
The Beautiful South .... **Go Disc GOD 47**

LITTLE TOWN FLIRT   February 1963
Del Shannon / Marion McKenzie
Vicki Music Ltd .... USA
Del Shannon .... **London HL 9653**

LITTLE VALLEY IN THE MOUNTAINS   1934
J. Dvoracek / K. Zeleny / Jimmy Kennedy
B. Feldman & Co. Ltd .... Czechoslovakia
Ray Noble & his Orchestra, vocal Al Bowlly ..... **HMV B 6512**

LITTLE WHITE BULL   December 1959
Lionel Bart / Michael Pratt / Jimmy Bennett
Peter Maurice Music Co. Ltd .... UK
Film(s): .... Tommy the Toreador
Tommy Steele .... **Decca DFE 6607**
The Michael Sammes Singers .... **HMV 7EG 126**
Tommy Steele appeared in *Tommy the Toreador*.
Ivor Novello Nomination.

LITTLE WHITE CLOUD THAT CRIED, THE   January 1952
Johnnie Ray
Larry Spier Lts .... USA
Johnnie Ray .... **Philips BBL 7264**
Jan Hoiland .... **Parlophone R 4810**

LITTLE WHITE DUCK   February 1951
Bernard Zaritzky / Walt Burrows
Southern Music Publishing Co. Ltd .... USA
Danny Kaye .... **Brunswick LAT 8350**

LITTLE WHITE GARDENIA, A   1935
Sam Coslow
Sterling Music Publishing Co. Ltd .... USA
Film(s): .... All the King's Horses
Carl Brisson .... **Decca F 6997**
Ronald Binge & his Orchestra .... **RCA RD 27157**
Carl Brisson appeared in *All The King's Horses*.

LITTLE WHITE LIES   1930
Walter Donaldson
Lawrence Wright Music Co. Ltd .... USA
Film(s): .... Lover Come Back to Me
Ted Wallace & his Orchestra .... **Columbia CB 137**
Dick Haymes (1948) .... **Brunswick OE 9428**
Mel Tormé .... **Parlophone R 3131**
Pat Boone .... **London HAD 2127**
Julie London .... **London HAU 2186**

LITTLE WILLY   July 1972
Mike Chapman / Nicky Chinn
Rak Music Ltd. . . . . UK
The Sweet . . . . **RCA 2225**

LITTLE WOODEN WHISTLE WOULDN'T WHISTLE, THE   1924
Harry Von Tilzer / Billy Curtis
Chappell & Co. Ltd. . . . . USA
The "S.S. Leviathan" Orchestra . . . . **HMV B 1848**

LITTLE YELLOW BIRD   1903
C.W. Murphy / William Hargreaves
Francis, Day & Hunter . . . . UK
Show(s): . . . . The Cherry Girl
Film(s): . . . . The Picture of Dorian Gray
Flo De Vere . . . . **HMV GC 3526**
Geraldo & his Orchestra, vocal Carol Carr . . . **Parlophone F 2093**

LIVE AND LET DIE   July 1973
Paul McCartney
United Artists Music Co. Ltd. . . . . UK
Film(s): . . . . Live and Let Die
Paul McCartney & Wings . . . . **Apple R 5987**
Nominated for an Academy Award 1973.

LIVE IS LIFE   August 1985
"Opus"
EMI Music . . . . Australia
Opus . . . . **Polydor POSP 743**

LIVE IT UP   March 1987
Greely Smith
Syray Music . . . . UK
Mental as Anything . . . . **Epic ANY 1**

LIVE TO TELL   May 1986
Madonna Ciccone / Patrick Leonard
Warner Brothers Music . . . . USA
Madonna . . . . **Sire W 8717**

LIVE, LAUGH AND LOVE   1932
Werner Heymann / Rowland Leigh
Campbell Connelly & Co. Ltd. . . . . Germany
Film(s): . . . . Congress Dances
Liddell Peddieson . . . . **Parlophone R 1088**
Sidney Kyte & his Piccadilly
Hotel Orchestra . . . . **Regal Zonophone MR 466**
The Vienna State Orchestra,
conducted by Robert Stolz . . . . **RCA RD 27152**
Liddell Peddieston appeared in *Congress Dances.*

LIVELY   November 1960
Peter Buchanan / Lonnie Donegan
Tyler Music Ltd . . . . UK
Lonnie Donegan . . . . **Pye 7N 15312**

LIVERPOOL LOU   June 1974
Dominic Behan
Coda Music Ltd. . . . . UK
The Scaffold . . . . **Warner Brothers K 16400**
Dominic Behan . . . . **Piccadilly 7N 35172**

LIVERY STABLE BLUES   1917
Ray Lopez / Marvin Lee / Alcide Nunez
Herman Darewski Music Publishing Co. Ltd. . . . . USA
The Original Dixieland Jazz Band . . . . **RCA RCX 1028**
Muggsy Spanier's Ragtime Band . . . . **RCA RD 27132**

LIVIN' THING   December 1976
Jeff Lynne
United Artists Music Co. Ltd . . . . UK
The Electric Light Orchestra . . . . **Jet UP 36184**

LIVING AFTER MIDNIGHT   April 1980
Glenn Tipton / Robert Halford / Kenneth Downing
Warner Brothers Music Ltd . . . . UK
Judas Priest . . . . **CBS 8379**

LIVING DAYLIGHTS, THE   July 1987
Pal Waaktaar / Magne Furholmen / John Barry
SBK Songs . . . . UK
Film(s): . . . . The Living Daylights
A-Ha . . . . **Warner Brothers W 8305**
Ivor Novello Nomination.

LIVING DOLL   August 1959
Lionel Bart
Mills Music Ltd . . . . UK
Film(s): . . . . Serious Charge
Cliff Richard . . . . **Columbia SEG 7895**
Cliff Richard & The Young Ones (1986) . . . . **WEA YZ 65**
Cliff Richard appeared in *Serious Charge.*
Ivor Novello Nomination 1986.

LIVING FOR THE CITY   February 1974
Stevie Wonder
Jobete Music (UK) Ltd. . . . . USA
Stevie Wonder . . . . **Tamla Motown TMG 881**

LIVING IN A BOX   May 1987
Marcus Vere / Steve Piggott
Empire Music . . . . UK
Living in a Box . . . . **Chrysalis LIB 1**
Ivor Novello Nomination.

LIVING IN AMERICA   February 1986
Dan Hartman / Charles Midnight
CBS Songs . . . . USA
James Brown . . . . **Scotti Brothers A 6701**

LIVING IN HARMONY   September 1972
Alan Tarney / Trevor Spencer
Mervyn Music . . . . UK
Cliff Richard . . . . **Columbia DB 8917**

LIVING IN THE PAST   July 1969
Ian Anderson
Chrysalis Music Ltd. . . . . UK
Jethro Tull . . . . **Island WIP 6056**

LIVING NEXT DOOR TO ALICE   January 1977
Mike Chapman / Nicky Chinn
Rak Music Ltd . . . . UK
Smokie . . . . **Rak 244**

LIVING ON A PRAYER   December 1986
Jon Bon Jovi / Richard Sambora / Desmond Child
CBS Songs . . . . UK
Bon Jovi . . . . **Vertigo VER 28**

LIVING ON AN ISLAND   December 1979
Richard Parfitt / Robert Young
Shawbury Music . . . . UK
Status Quo . . . . **Vertigo 6059248**

LIVING ON THE CEILING   December 1982
Neil Arthur / Steven Luscombe
Cherry Red Music . . . . UK
Blancmange . . . . **London BLANC 3**

LIVING ON THE FRONT LINE   July 1979
Eddy Grant
Intersong Music . . . . UK
Eddy Grant . . . . **Ensign ENY 26**

LIVING ON VIDEO   August 1985
Pascal Languirand
Memory Lane Music . . . . Canada
Tran-X . . . . **Polydor POSP 650**

LIVING YEARS   February 1989
Michael Rutherford / B.A. Robertson
Hit & Run Music . . . . UK
Mike & The Mechanics . . . . **WEA U 7717**
Ivor Novello Award.

LIZA (All The Clouds'll Roll Away)   1929
George Gershwin / Ira Gershwin
Chappell & Co. Ltd . . . . USA
Show(s): . . . . Show Girl
Film(s): Rhapsody in Blue / The Man I Love / George White's Scandals
of 1945 / The Jolson Story / An American in Paris / Starlift
Al Jolson . . . . **Brunswick LA 8509**
The Benny Goodman Sextet . . . . **Philips BBE 12189**
Ethel Smith (organ) . . . . **Brunswick 03612**
The Four Freshmen . . . . **Capitol T 844**
Ethel Smith appeared in *George White's Scandals of 1945.*

LIZA JOHNSON   1901
Edgar Bateman / George Le Brunn

Francis, Day & Hunter Ltd. .... UK
Film(s): .... No Trees in the Street
Stanley Holloway .... **Pye NEP 24097**
Stanley Holloway appeared in *No Trees in the Street*.

LOAD OF HAY, A   July 1950
Michael Feahy / Howard Barnes
John Fields Music Co. Ltd .... UK
Benny Lee .... **Decca F 9423**
Doris Day .... **Columbia SCM 5087**
Adapted from *Narcissus* by Ethelbert Nevin.

LOCO - MOTION, THE   October 1962
Gerry Goffin / Carole King
Aldon Music Ltd. .... USA
Little Eva .... **London HL 9581**
The Vernon Girls .... **London F 11495**
Little Eva (1972) .... **London HL 9581**
Kylie Minogue (1988) .... **P.W.L. PWL 14**

LOCO IN ACAPULCO   January 1989
Phil Collins / Lamont Dozier
.... USA
The Four Tops .... **Arista 111850**

LOCOMOTION   May 1984
"Orchestral Manoeuvres in the Dark"
Virgin Music .... UK
Orchestral Manoeuvres in the Dark .... **Virgin VS 660**

LOGICAL SONG, THE   May 1979
Rick Davies / Roger Hodgson
Rondor Music (London) Ltd. .... UK
Supertramp .... **A&M AMS 7427**
Ivor Novello Award.

LOLA   August 1970
Raymond Davies
Carlin Music Corporation .... UK
The Kinks .... **Pye 7N 17961**

LOLLIPOP   April 1958
Beverly Ross / Julius Dixon
Anglo-Pic Music Co. Ltd .... USA
Gary Miller .... **Pye NPT 19032**
Ray Martin & his Orchestra .... **RCA RD 27101**
The Mudlarks .... **Columbia DB 4099**

LONDON BY NIGHT   April 1951
Carroll Coates
Leeds Music Ltd .... USA
Frank Sinatra .... **Columbia LB 104**
Larry Cross .... **Parlophone R 3411**
Frank Sinatra .... **Reprise R 1006**

LONDON CALLING   January 1980
Joe Strummer / Mick Jones
Riva Music .... UK
The Clash .... **CBS 8087**

LONDON I LOVE, THE   1941
George Posford
Chappell & Co. Ltd .... UK
Ambrose & his Orchestra, vocal Sam Browne ... **Decca F 7827**
Frank Barber & his Orchestra .... **Columbia 33SX 1233**

LONDON NIGHTS   July 1989
Ralf Mave
Warner Chappell Music .... Germany
London Boys .... **Teldec YZ 393**

LONDON PRIDE   1941
Noel Coward
Chappell & Co. Ltd .... UK
Noel Coward .... **HMV 7EG 8300**
Julie Andrews .... **RCA RD 27061**

LONE RANGER, THE   June 1979
John Perry / James Morais / Edward Hine, Mark Warner & David Maciver
Chrysalis Music Ltd. .... UK
Quantum Jump .... **Electric WOT 33**

LONELY   October 1962
Norrie Paramor / Acker Bilk

Filmusic Publishing Co. Ltd .... UK
Film(s): .... Band of Thieves
Acker Bilk (clarinet) with
The Leon Young String Chorale .... **Columbia DB 4897**
Robert Earl .... **Philips 326556 BF**
Acker Bilk appeared in *Band of Thieves*.

LONELY BALLERINA   October 1954
Michael Carr 'Lambrecht'
Edward Kassner Music Co. Ltd. .... UK
The Mantovani Orchestra .... **Decca LK 4122**
The Vernon Girls .... **Parlophone PMC 1052**

LONELY BOY   August 1959
Paul Anka
Monarch Music Ltd .... USA
Film(s): .... Girl's Town
Paul Anka .... **Columbia 33SX 1282**
Paul Anka appeared in *Girl's Town*.

LONELY BOY   May 1977
Andrew Gold
Warner Brothers Music Ltd .... USA
Andrew Gold .... **Asylum K 13076**

LONELY CITY   July 1962
Geoffrey Goddard
Southern Music Publishing Co. Ltd .... USA
John Leyton .... **HMV POP 1014**

LONELY FOOTSTEPS   1945
Howard Barnes / Lucia Ravenge
Bradbury Wood Ltd. .... UK
The Sentimentalists .... **Decca F 8589**

LONELY GIRL (Non Seitu)   November 1974
Salvatore Adamo
Ardmore & Beechwood Ltd. .... Italy
Eddie Holman .... **ABC 4012**
Adamo (in Italian) .... **HMV 7MQ 1971**
Adamo (in English) .... **HMV CLP 3635**

LONELY PUP (In A Christmas Shop)   December 1960
Archie Alexander
Mills Music Ltd .... UK
Adam Faith .... **Parlophone R 4708**

LONELY THIS CHRISTMAS   December 1974
Mike Chapman / Nicky Chinn
Rak Music Ltd. .... UK
Mud .... **Rak 187**

LONESOME   February 1962
Bert Pellish
Essex Music Ltd. .... USA
Adam Faith .... **Parlophone R 4864**

LONESOME (Si Tu Vois Ma Mere)   June 1959
Sidney Bechet
Essex Music Ltd .... France
The Chris Barber Band .... **Columbia 33SX 1158**

LONESOME AND SORRY   1926
Con Conrad / Benny Davis
B. Feldman & Co. Ltd. .... USA
The Cliquot Club Eskimos .... **Columbia 4023**
The Alex Welsh Band .... **Columbia 33SX 1219**

LONESOME ROAD   1930
Gene Austin / Nat Shilkret
Campbell Connelly & Co. Ltd .... USA
Film(s): .... Show Boat
Gene Austin .... **HMV B 3018**
Paul Robeson .... **HMV B 3146**
Frank Sinatra .... **Capitol LCT 6135**
Julie London .... **London HAG 2280**

LONG AGO AND FAR AWAY   1944
Jerome Kern / Ira Gershwin
Chappell & Co. Ltd. .... USA
Film(s): .... Cover Girl / Till the Clouds Roll By
Bing Crosby .... **Brunswick LA 8505**
Michael Holliday .... **Columbia 33SX 1262**
Roberto Cardinali .... **HMV 7EG 8456**
Nominated for an Academy Award 1944.

LONG BEFORE I KNEW YOU   October 1957
Jule Styne / Betty Comden / Adolph Green
Chappell & Co. Ltd . . . . USA
Show(s): . . . . Bells Are Ringing
Film(s): . . . . Bells Are Ringing
Judy Holliday & Sydney Chaplin . . . . **Philips BBL 7201**
Petula Clark . . . . **Nixa N 15112**
Judy Holliday appeared in the American production and the film of
Bells Are Ringing.
Sydney Chaplin appeared in the American production of *Bells Are
Ringing.*

LONG HAIRED LOVER FROM LIVERPOOL   February 1973
Joe Young
Edwin H. Morris & Co. Ltd. . . . . USA
Little Jimmy Osmond . . . . **MGM 2006109**

LONG HOT SUMMER   August 1983
Paul Weller
EMI Music . . . . UK
The Style Council . . . . **Polydor TSC 3**

LONG LEGGED WOMAN DRESSED IN BLACK   May 1974
Ray Dorset
Chrysalis Music Ltd. . . . . UK
Mungo Jerry . . . . **Dawn DNS 1061**

LONG LIVE LOVE   June 1965
Chris Andrews
Glissando Music Ltd . . . . UK
Sandie Shaw . . . . **Pye 7N 15841**

LONG LIVE LOVE   April 1974
Valerie Avon / Harold Spiro
B. Feldman & Co. Ltd. . . . . UK
Olivia Newton-John . . . . **Pye 7N 25638**
United Kingdom entry for the 1974 Eurovision Song Contest (Placed
Fourth).

LONG TALL GLASSES   October 1974
David Courtney / Leo Sayer
Compass Music Ltd. . . . . UK
Leo Sayer . . . . **Chrysalis CHS 2052**

LONG TALL SALLY   June 1956
Enotris Johnson / Richard Penniman
Southern Music Publishing Co. Ltd. . . . . USA
Film(s): . . . . Don't Knock the Rock
Little Richard . . . . **London HAQ 2055**
Buzz Clifford . . . . **Fontana TFL 5147**
Little Richard appeared in *Don't Knock the Rock.*

LONGING FOR YOU   July 1955
Walter Dana / Bernard Jansen
Chappell & Co. Ltd. . . . . UK
Teresa Brewer . . . . **London L 1069**
Joe Loss & his Orchestra . . . . **HMV BD 6108**
Russ Morgan & his Orchestra,
vocal Russ Morgan . . . . **Brunswick 04792**
Sammy Kaye & his Orchestra,
vocal Tony Alamo & Chorus . . . . **Fortune Z 4005**
Adapted from 'A Waltz Dream' by Oskar Straus (1870 - 1954).

LOOK AROUND (And You'll Find Me There)   November 1971
Lowell Mark / Norman Simon / Francis Lai
Famous-Chappell . . . . USA
Film(s): . . . . Love Story
Vince Hill . . . . **Columbia DB 8804**
Sound Track Recording . . . . **Paramount SPFL 267**

LOOK AT THAT FACE   1964
Anthony Newley / Leslie Bricusse
Concord Music . . . . UK
Show(s): . . . The Roar of the Greasepaint - The Smell of the Crowd
Cyril Richard & Sally Smith . . . . **RCA LOC 1109**
Dennis Lotis . . . . **Decca F 10153**
Sammy Davis Jnr. . . . . **Reprise R 6169**
Cyril Richard & Sally Smith appeared in *The Roar of the Greasepaint
- The Smell of the Crowd.*

LOOK AT THAT GIRL   July 1953
Bob Merrill
Cinephonic Music Co. Ltd . . . . USA
Guy Mitchell . . . . **Philips BBL 7265**

LOOK AWAY   April 1986
Stuart Adamson
Ten Music . . . . UK
Big Country . . . . **Mercury BIG 1**

LOOK FOR A STAR   August 1960
Mark Anthony
Filmusic Publishing Co. Ltd . . . . UK
Film(s): . . . . Circus of Horrors
Gary Mills . . . . **Top Rank JKP 3001**
The Cambridge Strings . . . . **Ace of Clubs ACL 1087**

LOOK FOR THE SILVER LINING   1921
Jerome Kern / Buddy De Sylva
Chappell & Co. Ltd . . . . USA
Show(s): . . . . Sally / Wild Rose
Film(s): . . . Sally / Till the Clouds Roll By / Look for the Silver Lining
Dorothy Dickson & Gregory Stroud . . . . **Columbia F 1076**
Jessie Mathews . . . . **Columbia DB 2094**
Vera Lynn . . . . **MGM C 840**
Judy Garland . . . . **MGM C 886**
June Haver & Gordon MacRae . . . . **Titania 504**
Dorothy Dickson & Gregory Stroud appeared in the British production
of *Sally.*
Jessie Matthews appeared in *Wild Rose.*
Judy Garland appeared in *Till the Clouds Roll By.*

LOOK HOMEWARD ANGEL   March 1957
Wally Gold
Unit Music Publishing Co. Ltd. . . . . USA
Johnnie Ray . . . . **Philips BBL 7264**

LOOK MAMA   May 1985
Howard Jones
Warner Brothers Music . . . . UK
Howard Jones . . . . **WEA HOW 7**

LOOK OF LOVE   May 1967
Burt Bacharach / Hal David
Carlin Music Corporation . . . . USA
Film(s): . . . . Casino Royale
Dusty Springfield (Soundtrack) . . . . **RCA RD 7874**
Shani Wallis . . . . **London HAR 8338**
Sergio Mendez . . . . **A&M AMS 721**
Gladys Knight & the Pips (1973) . . . . . **Tamla Motown TMG 844**
Nominated for an Academy Award 1967.

LOOK OF LOVE   December 1987
Madonna Ciccone / Patrick Leonard
Warner Brothers Music . . . . USA
Madonna . . . . **Sire W 8115**

LOOK OF LOVE, THE   July 1982
A.B.C.
Virgin Music . . . . UK
A.B.C. . . . . **Phonogram NT 103**

LOOK THROUGH ANY WINDOW   October 1965
Graham Gouldman / Charles Silverman
B. Feldman & Co. Ltd. . . . . UK
The Hollies . . . . **Parlophone R 5322**

LOOK WOT YU DUN   March 1972
Neville Holder / James Lea / Donald Powell
Barn Music Ltd. . . . . UK
Slade . . . . **Polydor 2058195**

LOOK, THE   May 1989
Per Gilssle
EMI Music . . . . Sweden
Roxette . . . . **EMI EM 87**

LOOKING AFTER NUMBER ONE   September 1977
Bob Geldof
Sewer Fire Hits . . . . UK
The Boomtown . . . . **Rats Ensign ENY 4**

**LOOKING AT THE WORLD THROUGH ROSE COLOURED
GLASSES**   1927
Tommy Malie / Jimmy Steiger
Francis, Day & Hunter Ltd. . . . . USA
Ed Lowry & The Gilt Edged Four . . . . **Columbia 4422**
Nellie Lutcher . . . . **London HAU 2036**

LOOKING FOR A BOY — 1926
George Gershwin / Ira Gershwin
Chappell & Co. Ltd. . . . . USA
Show(s): . . . . Tip Toes
George Gershwin (piano) . . . . **Columbia 4065**
Dorothy Dickson . . . . **Columbia 4078**
Eartha Kitt . . . . **RCA RD 27084**
Shirley Abicair . . . . **Fontana TFE 17206**
Dorothy Provine . . . . **Warner Brothers WM 4053**
Dorothy Dickson appeared in the British production of *Tip Toes*.

LOOKING HIGH, HIGH, HIGH — February 1960
John Watson
Robbins Music Corporation Ltd . . . . UK
Bryan Johnson . . . . **Decca DFE 6664**
United Kingdom entry for the 1960 Eurovision Song Contest (Placed Second).

LOOKING THROUGH THE EYES OF LOVE — July 1965
Barry Mann / Cynthia Weill
Screen Gems - Columbia Music . . . . USA
Gene Pitney . . . . **Stateside SS 240**
The Partridge Family (1973) . . . . **Bell 1278**

LOOKING THROUGH THE WINDOWS — December 1972
Clifton Evans
Jobete Music (UK) Ltd. . . . . USA
The Jackson Five . . . . **Tamla Motown TMG 833**

LOOP DE LOOP — March 1963
Traditional, arranged by Teddy Van & Joe Dong
P.K. Music Ltd . . . . USA
Frankie Vaughan . . . . **Philips 3265566**

LOOP DI LOVE — November 1972
Traditional, an arrangement by Michael Schepior & Dieter Dierks
Intersong Music . . . . USA
Shag . . . . **UK 7**
See also 'Loop De Loop'

LORDS OF THE AIR — 1939
Davy Burnaby / Michael North
Noel Gay Music Co. Ltd. . . . . UK
Harold Williams . . . . **Columbia DB 1892**
Billy Cotton & his Band . . . . **Decca LF 1124**

LORELEI — September 1960
Jerry Leiber / Mike Stoller
Tyler Music . . . . USA
Lonnie Donegan . . . . **Pye 7N 15275**

LOSING YOU — December 1964
Tom Springfield / Clive Westlake
Springfield Music Ltd . . . . UK
Dusty Springfield . . . . **Philips BF 1369**
Ivor Novello Nomination.

LOSING YOU (Un Ange Est Renn) — May 1963
Jean Renard / Carl Sigman
Ivan Mogul Music Associates . . . . France
Brenda Lee . . . . **Brunswick 05886**
Al Martino . . . . **Capitol T 1914**
Doris Day . . . . **CBS BPG 62226**

LOST — 1936
Phil Ohman / Johnny Mercer / Macy Teetor
Francis, Day & Hunter . . . . USA
Ruth Etting . . . . **Brunswick 02218**
Bobby Britton . . . . **Decca F 10288**

LOST CHORD, THE — 1877
Adelaide Proctor / Arthur Sullivan
Boosey & Hawkes Ltd. . . . . UK
Enrico Caruso . . . . **HMV DB 133**
Dame Clara Butt . . . . **Columbia 7373**
Frederick Harvey . . . . **HMV CLP 1680**
Norma Proctor . . . . **Prelude PRS 2506**

LOST IN A FOG — 1934
Dorothy Fields / Jimmy McHugh
Francis, Day & Hunter Ltd. . . . . USA
Film(s): . . . . Have a Heart
Jane Froman . . . . **Brunswick 01902**
Ella Fitzgerald . . . . **HMV CLP 1383**

LOST IN FRANCE — December 1976
Ronnie Scott / Steve Wolfe
Rak Music Ltd . . . . UK
Bonnie Tyler . . . . **RCA 2734**

LOST IN MUSIC — September 1984
Nile Rodgers / Bernard Edwards
Warner Brothers Music . . . . UK
Sister Sledge . . . . **Atlantic B 9718**

LOST JOHN — May 1956
Traditional, arranged by Lonnie Donegan
Essex Music Ltd. . . . . UK
Lonnie Donegan . . . . **Pye NIXA 7N 15036**

LOT OF LIVING TO DO, A — August 1961
Charles Strouse / Lee Adams
Edwin H. Morris & Co. Ltd. . . . . USA
Show(s): . . . . Bye Bye Birdie
Film(s): . . . . Bye Bye Birdie
Dick Gautier, Susan Watson & chorus . . . . . **Fontana CFL 1073**
Marty Wilde & Sylvia Tysick . . . . **Philips ABL 3383**
Jess Pearson, Ann-Margaret & Bobby Rydell . . . **RCA RD 7580**
Dick Gautier & Susan Watson appeared in the American production of *Bye Bye Birdie*.
Marty Wilde & Sylvia Tysick appeared in the British production of *Bye Bye Birdie*.
Jess Pearson, Ann-Margaret & Bobby Rydell appeared in the film *Bye Bye Birdie*.

LOUISE — 1929
Leo Robin / Richard A. Whiting
Campbell Connelly & Co. Ltd . . . . USA
Film(s): . . . . Innocents of Paris / The Stooge
Paul Whiteman & his Orchestra,
vocal The Rhythm Boys . . . . **CBS BPG 62545**
Maurice Chevalier . . . . **RCA RCX 1057**
Frank Chacksfield & his Orchestra . . . . **Decca LK 4135**
Maurice Chevalier appeared in *Innocents of Paris*.
Theme song of Maurice Chevalier.

LOUISIANA — 1928
Andy Razaf / J.C. Johnson / Bob Schafer
Lawrence Wright Music Co. Ltd. . . . . USA
Paul Whiteman & his Orchestra,
vocal Bing Crosby . . . . **HMV DLP 1106**
Red Nichols & his Famous Pennies . . . . **Capitol T 775**
The Harry Edison Quartet . . . . **Columbia SEG 7934**

LOUISIANNA HAYRIDE — 1932
Howard Dietz / Arthur Schwartz
Chappell & Co. Ltd. . . . . USA
Show(s): . . . . Flying Colours / Please
Film(s): . . . . The Band Wagon
Leo Reisman & his Orchestra,
vocal Arthur Schwartz . . . . **HMV B 6419**
Nanette Fabray . . . . **MGM C 752**
Nanette Fabray appeared in *The Band Wagon*.

LOVE — 1947
Hugh Martin / Ralph Blane
Francis, Day & Hunter Ltd. . . . . USA
Film(s): . . . . Ziegfeld Follies
Ambrose & his Orchestra, vocal Rita Marlow . . . **Decca F 8648**
Judy Garland . . . . **Brunswick 03623**
Lena Horne . . . . **MGM 943**
Lena Horne appeared in *Ziegfeld Follies*.

LOVE (Your Magic Spell Is Everywhere) — 1929
Elsie Janis / Edmund Goulding
Francis, Day & Hunter Ltd . . . . USA
Film(s): . . . . The Trespasser
Gloria Swanson . . . . **HMV B 3168**
Johnny Mathis . . . . **Fontana TFL 5011**
Gloria Swanson appeared in *The Trespasser*.

LOVE ACTION (I Believe in Love) — August 1981
Philip Oakey / Ian Burden
Virgin Music . . . . UK
Human League . . . . **Virgin VS 435**

LOVE AND AFFECTION — November 1976
Joan Armatrading
Rondor Music (London) Ltd . . . . USA
Joan Armatrading . . . . **A&M AMS 7249**

LOVE AND MARRIAGE   January 1956
Sammy Cahn / Jimmy Van Heusen
Barton Music Co. Ltd. .... USA
Tony Martin .... **RCA RD 27003**
Joan Regan .... **Decca LF 1266**
Frank Sinatra .... **Capitol LCT 6123**

LOVE AND PRIDE   February 1985
Paul King / Mick Roberts
CBS Songs .... UK
King .... **CBS A 4988**

LOVE AND WINE   1911
Franz Lehar / Adrian Ross
Chappell & Co. Ltd .... Austria
Show(s): .... Gipsy Love
Peter Dawson .... **HMV B 318**

LOVE BITES   July 1988
"Def Leppard"
Zomba Music .... UK
Def Leppard .... **Phonogram LEP 5**

LOVE BUG WILL BITE YOU, THE   1937
Pinky Tomlin
Campbell Connelly & Co. Ltd. .... USA
'Fats' Waller & his Rhythm .... **HMV BD 5229**
Pinky Tomlin .... **Vocalion 544**
Henry Hall & The B.B.C. Dance Orchestra .. **Columbia FB 1687**
The Mills Brothers .... **Brunswick 02415**

LOVE CAN'T TURN AROUND   September 1986
Isaac Hayes
MCA Music .... USA
Farley 'Jackmaster' Funk .... **London LON 105**

LOVE CATS, THE   November 1983
Robert Smith
A.P.B. Music .... UK
The Cure .... **Fiction FICS 19**

LOVE CHANGES EVERYTHING   April 1988
Simon Climie / Rob Fisher / Dennis Morgan
Rondor Music .... UK
Climie Fisher .... **EMI EM 47**
Ivor Novello Award.

LOVE CHANGES EVERYTHING   March 1989
Don Black / Charles Hart / Andrew Lloyd Webber
Really Usefull Music .... UK
Show(s): .... Aspects of Love
Michael Ball .... **Really Usefull RUR 3**
Michael Ball appeared in *Aspects of Love*.

LOVE CHILD   January 1969
R. Dean Taylor / Pam Sawyer / Frank Wilson & Deke Richards
Jobete Music (UK) Ltd. .... USA
Diana Ross & The Supremes .... **Tamla Motown TMG 677**

LOVE COME DOWN   October 1982
"Kashif"
MCA Music .... USA
Evelyn King .... **RCA 249**

LOVE DON'T LIVE HERE ANYMORE   October 1978
Miles Gregory
Warner Brothers Music Ltd .... USA
Rose Royce .... **Whitfield K 17236**
Jimmy Nail (1985) .... **Virgin VS 764**

LOVE FOR SALE   1931
Cole Porter
Chappell & Co. Ltd. .... USA
Show(s): .... The New Yorkers
Jack Payne & The BBC Dance Orchestra .... **Columbia CB 318**
Patti Page .... **Emarcy EJL 1252**
Jane Morgan .... **London HAR 2137**
Boney M .... **Atlantic K 50385**

LOVE GROWS   March 1970
Barry Mason / Tony Macaulay
Schroeder Music Ltd. .... UK
Edison Lighthouse .... **Bell 1091**
Barry Mason .... **Magnet MAG 5012**
Ivor Novello Award.

LOVE HANGOVER   May 1976
Pam Sawyer / Marilyn McLeod
Jobete Music (UK) Ltd. .... USA
Diana Ross .... **Tamla Motown TMG 1024**

LOVE HERE IS MY HEART (Mon Coeur est Pour Toi) 1915
Adrian Ross / Lao Silesu
Ascherberg, Hopwood & Crew Ltd. .... France
Film(s): .... Young Eagles
John McCormack .... **HMV DA 300**
Richard Tauber .... **Parlophone RO 20535**
**Ambrose & his Orchestra,
vocal Anne Shelton** .... **Decca F 8488**
Charles Kullman .... **Columbia DB 1227**

LOVE HURTS   November 1975
Boudleaux Bryant
Acuff-Rose Publishing Co. Ltd .... USA
Jim Capaldi .... **Island WIP 6246**
The Everly Brothers .... **Warner Brothers WM 4028**
Nazareth .... **Mountain NAZ 1**

LOVE IN BLOOM   1934
Leo Robin / Ralph Rainger
Victoria Music Co. Ltd .... USA
Film(s): .... She Loves Me Not
Bing Crosby .... **Columbia DB 1802**
Jack Payne & his Orchestra ...... **HMV CLP 1160**
Bing Crosby .... **Brunswick LAT 8251**
Bing Crosby appeared in *She Loves Me Not*.
Nominated for an Academy Award 1934.
Theme song of Jack Benny.

LOVE IN THE FIRST DEGREE   November 1987
*Sarah Dallin / Siobhan Fahey / Keren Woodward, Mike Stock, Matt
Aitken & Peter Waterman*
All Boys Music .... UK
Bananarama .... **London NANA 14**

LOVE IN THE SUN   September 1975
Gerry Shephard / John Springate
Rock Artistes Music .... UK
The Glitter Band .... **Bell 1437**

LOVE IS A DANCING THING   1936
Howard Dietz / Arthur Schwarz
Chappell & Co. Ltd .... USA
Show(s): .... At Home Abroad / Follow the Sun
Hildegarde .... **Columbia FB 1266**
Arthur Schwarz (Piano) .... **Columbia FB 1269**
Jack Jackson & his Orchestra .... **HMV C 2833**

LOVE IS A GOLDEN RING   April 1957
Frank Miller / Rich Dehr / Terry Gilkyson
Montclare Music Co. Ltd. .... USA
Frankie Laine .... **Philips BBR 8108**
Terry Gilkyson & The Easy Riders ...... **London HAR 2301**

LOVE IS A MANY SPLENDOURED THING   November 1955
Sammy Fain / Paul Francis Webster
Robbins Music Corporation Ltd. .... USA
Film(s): .... Love is a Many Splendoured Thing / Grease
The Four Aces .... **Brunswick LAT 8203**
The Four Lads .... **Brunswick LAT 8249**
David Rose & his Orchestra .... **MGM 860**
Ray Conniff & his Orchestra & chorus ..... **Philips BBL 7310**
Shirley Bassey .... **Columbia 33SX 1382**
Sound Track of Grease .... **RSO 2479-211**
Used instrumentally in the film *Grease*.
Academy Award winning song for 1955.

LOVE IS A SONG   1942
Larry Morey / Frank Churchill
Campbell Connelly & Co. Ltd .... USA
Film(s): .... Bambi (cartoon)
Sound Track .... **Top Rank JKP 2032**
**The Walt Disney Studio Orchestra
& Chorus** .... **Disneyland DPL 39001**
Nominated for an Academy Award 1942.

LOVE IS A STRANGER   May 1983
Annie Lennox / David Stewart
Arnakata Music .... UK
Eurythmics .... **RCA DA 1**

LOVE IS ALL 1940
Pinky Tomlin / Harry Tobias
Sun Music Publishing Co. Ltd . . . . USA
Film(s): . . . . It's a Date
Deanna Durbin . . . . **Brunswick 03007**
Joe Loss & his Orchestra . . . . **HMV CLP 1473**
Deanna Durbin appeared in *It's A Date*.

LOVE IS ALL December 1969
Les Reed / Barry Mason
Donna Music Ltd . . . . UK
Malcolm Roberts . . . . **Major Minor MM 637**
Ivor Novello Award.

LOVE IS ALL AROUND December 1967
Reginald Presley
Dick James Music Ltd. . . . . UK
The Troggs . . . . **Page One POF 040**

LOVE IS BLUE (L'amour Est Bleu) May 1968
Andre Popp / Brian Blackburn
Shaftesbury Music Ltd. . . . . France
Jeff Beck . . . . **Columbia DB 8359**
Paul Mauriat Orchestra . . . . **Philips BF 1637**

LOVE IS CONTAGIOUS March 1988
Taja Sevelle
No Publisher . . . . USA
Taja Sevelle . . . . **Paisley Park W 8257**

LOVE IS IN THE AIR June 1978
Harry Vanda / George Young
EMI Music Ltd . . . . Australia
John Paul Young . . . . **Ariola ARO 117**

LOVE IS JUST AROUND THE CORNER 1935
Leo Robin / Lewis Gensler
Chappell & Co. Ltd . . . . USA
Film(s): . . . . Here is My Heart
Bing Crosby . . . . **Brunswick Bing 1**
Michael Holliday . . . . **Columbia 33SX 1170**
Bing Crosby appeared in *Here Is My Heart*.

LOVE IS LIFE September 1970
Errol Brown / Tony Wilson
Rak Music Ltd . . . . UK
Hot Chocolate . . . . **Rak 103**

LOVE IS LIKE A VIOLIN
(Mon Coeur Est Un Violin) September 1960
Miarka Laparcerie / Jimmy Kennedy
Keith Prowse Music Publishing Co. Ltd . . . . France
Film(s): . . . . Little Boy Lost
Lucienne Boyer . . . . **Decca C 16081**
Vicky Autier . . . . **HMV CLP 1150**
Bing Crosby . . . . **Brunswick Bing 15**
Jaqueline Francois . . . . **Philips BBL 7438**
Ken Dodd . . . . **Decca F 11248**
Bing Crosby appeared in *Little Boy Lost*.

LOVE IS LIKE OXYGEN March 1978
Scott Griffin / Andy Scott
Carlin Music Corporation . . . . UK
Film(s): . . . . The Stud
Sweet . . . . **Polydor POSP 1**

LOVE IS MY REASON 1945
Ivor Novello
Chappell & Co. Ltd. . . . . UK
Show(s): . . . . Perchance to Dream
Muriel Barron . . . . **Decca LF 1309**
Ivor Emmanuel & Julie Bryan . . . . **HMV CLP 1258**
Muriel Barron appeared in *Perchance to Dream*.

LOVE IS STRANGE November 1965
Mickey Baker / Ethel Smith
Cromwell Music Ltd . . . . USA
Lonnie Donegan . . . . **Nixa N 15087**
The Everly Brothers . . . . **Warner Brothers WB 5649**
The Crickets . . . . **Liberty LBY 1120**

LOVE IS SWEEPING THE COUNTRY 1932
George Gershwin / Ira Gershwin
Chappell & Co. Ltd. . . . . USA

Show(s): . . . . Of Thee I Sing
Ella Fitzgerald . . . . **HMV CLP 1348**

LOVE IS THE DRUG November 1975
Bryan Ferry / Andrew MacKay
E.G. Music . . . . UK
Roxy Music . . . . **Island WIP 6248**

LOVE IS THE SWEETEST THING 1932
Ray Noble
Francis, Day & Hunter Ltd. . . . . UK
Film(s): . . . . Say it With Music / Confidential Agent
Ray Noble & The New Mayfair Dance Orchestra HMV 7EG 8056
Jack Payne & his Orchestra . . . . **HMV CLP 1160**
Frankie Vaughan . . . . **Philips BBE 12247**
Mike Preston . . . . **Decca DFE 6635**
Jack Payne appeared in *Say it With Music*.

LOVE IS WHERE YOU FIND IT October 1948
Earl Brent / Nacio Herb Brown
Robbins Music Corporations Ltd. . . . . USA
Film(s): . . . . The Kissing Bandit
Kathryn Grayson . . . . **MGM 150**
The Everly Brothers . . . . **Warner Brothers WM 4052**
Kathryn Grayson appeared in *The Kissing Bandit*.

LOVE KILLS October 1984
Freddie Mercury / Giorgio Moroder
Queen Music . . . . UK
Film(s): . . . . Metropolis
Freddie Mercury . . . . **CBS A 4735**

LOVE LETTERS 1946
Edward Heyman / Victor Young
Famous Music . . . . USA
Film(s): . . . . Love Letters
Dick Haymes . . . . **Brunswick 03638**
Victor Young & his Orchestra . . . . . **Brunswick LAT 8034**
Peggy Lee . . . . **Brunswick LAT 8356**
Ketty Lester (1962) . . . . **London HL 9527**
Elvis Presley (1966) . . . . **RCA 1526**
Alison Moyet (1987) . . . . **CBS MOYET 5**
Nominated for an Academy Award 1945.

LOVE LETTERS IN THE SAND 1931
J. Fred Coots / Nick Kenny / Charles Kenny
Francis, Day & Hunter Ltd. USA
Layton & Johnston . . . . **Columbia DB 740**
Ambrose & his Orchestra, vocal Sam Browne . . **HMV BD 6110**
Joan Savage . . . . **Columbia DB 3968**
Pat Boone (1957) . . . . **London HAD 2098**
Vince Hill . . . . **Columbia DB 8268**
Tom T. Hall . . . . **Mercury 824 508-1**

LOVE LIKE A MAN August 1970
Alvin Lee
Chrysalee Music . . . . UK
Ten Years After . . . . **Deram DM 299**

LOVE LIKE YOU AND ME, A May 1975
Gary Glitter / Mike Leander
Rock Artistes Music . . . . UK
Gary Glitter . . . . **Bell 1423**

LOVE LIKE YOURS, A December 1966
Brian Holland / Eddie Holland / Lamont Dozier
Jobete Music (UK) Ltd. . . . . USA
Ike & Tina Turner . . . . **London HL 10083**

LOVE MACHINE February 1976
Warren Moore / William Griffin
Jobete Music (UK) Ltd. . . . . USA
The Miracles . . . . **Tamla Motown TMG 1015**

LOVE MAKES THE WORLD GO ROUND August 1958
Ollie Jones
Chappell & Co. Ltd . . . . USA
Perry Como . . . . **RCA 1086**
Vera Lynn . . . . **Decca F 11106**

LOVE ME December 1976
Barry Gibb / Robin Gibb
RSO Group . . . . UK
Yvonne Elliman . . . . **RSO 2090205**

LOVE ME AND THE WORLD IS MINE 1906
Ernest Ball / Dave Reed
B. Feldman & Co. Ltd. . . . . USA
Film(s): . . . . Irish Eyes Are Smiling
William T. Evans . . . . **HMV GC 3-2953**
Joseph Locke . . . . **Columbia DB 3221**

**LOVE ME AS THOUGH THERE
WERE NO TOMORROW** October 1956
Harold Adamson / Jimmy McHugh
Robbins Music Corporation Ltd. . . . . USA
Nat 'King' Cole . . . . **Capitol LCT 6142**
Malcolm Vaughan . . . . **HMV POP 250**

LOVE ME DO November 1962
John Lennon / Paul McCartney
Northern Songs Ltd . . . . UK
The Beatles . . . . **Parlophone R 4949**

LOVE ME FOR A REASON September 1974
Johnny Bristol / Wade Brown / David Jones
Jobete Music (UK) Ltd. . . . . USA
The Osmonds . . . . **MGM 2006458**
Johnny Bristol . . . . **MGM 2315303**

LOVE ME FOREVER 1935
Victor Schertzinger / Gus Kahn
Sterling Music Publishing Co. Ltd . . . . USA
Film(s): . . . . .On Wings of Song
Grace Moore . . . . **Brunswick LAT 8025**
Maria Perilli . . . . **Philips BBE 14236**
Grace Moore appeared in *On Wings of Song.*

LOVE ME FOREVER February 1958
Gary Lynes / Beverly Guthrie
Unit Music Publishing Co. Ltd . . . . USA
Marion Ryan . . . . **Nixa NEP 24079**

LOVE ME LIKE I LOVE YOU April 1976
Eric Faulkner / Stuart Wood
Carlin Music Corporation . . . . UK
The Bay City Rollers . . . . **Bell 1477**

LOVE ME LOVE MY DOG April 1975
Peter Shelley / Marty Wilde
Intune Ltd . . . . UK
Peter Shelley . . . . **Magnet MAG 22**

LOVE ME NOW 1923
Leo Fall / Clare Kummer / Harry Graham
Ascherberg, Hopwood & Crew Ltd . . . . Germany
Show(s):. Madame Pompadour
Evelyn Laye . . . . **Columbia 966**
Hilde Gueden . . . . **Decca LXT 5033**
Evelyn Laye appeared in the British production of *Madame Pompa-
dour.*

LOVE ME OR LEAVE ME 1929
Gus Kahn / Walter Donaldson
Keith Prowse Music Publishing Co. Ltd . . . . USA
Show(s):. . . . . .Whoopee
Film(s): . . . . I'll See You in My Dreams / Love Me or Leave Me
Ruth Etting . . . . **Columbia 5553**
Kay Starr . . . . **London HLU 2039**
Doris Day . . . . **Philips BBL 7297**
Sammy Davis Jnr. (1955) . . . . **Brunswick 05428**
Billie Holiday . . . . **Columbia 33SX 10092**
Ruth Etting appeared in *Whoopee.*
Doris Day appeared in both *I'll See You in My Dreams* and *Love Me
or Leave Me.*

LOVE ME TENDER December 1956
Elvis Presley / Vera Matson
Aberbach (London) Ltd. . . . . USA
Film(s): . . . . Love Me Tender
Elvis Presley . . . . **RCA RB 16069**
The Ray Conniff Orchestra & chorus . . . . **Philips BBL 7439**
Richard Chamberlain (1962) . . . . **MGM 1173**
Elvis Presley appeared in *Love Me Tender.*
Based on 'Aura Lee' by George Poulton.

LOVE ME TONIGHT (Alla Fine Della Strada) June 1969
Daniele Pace / Lorenzo Pilat / Mario Panzeri & Barry Mason
Valley Music . . . . Italy
Tom Jones . . . . **Decca F 12924**

**LOVE ME WITH ALL OF YOUR HEART (Caundo Caliente
El Sol)** May 1966
Michael Vaughn / Carlos Riguel
Southern Music Publishing Co. Ltd. . . . . Mexico
Karl Denver . . . . **Decca F 11905**
The Bachelors . . . . **Decca F 12351**

LOVE MISSILE F1-11 March 1986
Martin Degville / James Whitmore / Neal Whitmore
Sputnik Songs . . . . UK
Sigue Sigue Sputnik . . . . **Parlophone R 555 1**

LOVE NEST 1921
Otto Harbach / Louis Hirsch
Chappell & Co. Ltd . . . . USA
Show(s): . . . . .Mary
Film(s): . . . . Both Ends of the Candle
John Steele . . . . **HMV B 1187**
**Frankie Trumbauer & his Orchestra,
vocal Martin Hunt** . . . . **Parlophone R 2645**
Gogi Grant . . . . **RCA RD 27054**
Gogi Grant dubbed the singing voice of Ann Blyth who appeared in
the film *Both Ends of the Candle.*

LOVE OF MY LIFE February 1953
Hans May / Michael Reine
Michael Reine Music Co. Ltd . . . . UK
Vera Lynn . . . . **Decca DFE 6042**

LOVE OF MY LIFE December 1977
Ben Findon / Mike Myers
Heath Levy Music Ltd . . . . UK
The Dooleys . . . . **GTO GT 110**

LOVE OF THE COMMON PEOPLE August 1970
John Hurley / Ronnie Wilkins
London Tree . . . . USA
Nicky Thomas . . . . **Trojan TR 7750**
Sandy Posey . . . . **MGM C 8051**
Paul Young (1983) . . . . **CBS A 3583**

LOVE ON A MOUNTAIN TOP January 1974
Buzz Cason / Mac Gayden
Keith Prowse Music Publishing Co. ltd. . . . . USA
Robert Knight . . . . **Monument MNT 1875**

LOVE ON THE ROCKS January 1981
Gilbert Becaud / Neil Diamond
Chappell Music Co. . . . . France
Neil Diamond . . . . **Capitol CL 16173**

LOVE ON YOUR SIDE March 1983
Tom Bailey / Alannah Currie / Joe Leeway
A.T.V. Music . . . . UK
The Thompson Twins . . . . **Arista ARIST 504**

LOVE PLUS ONE March 1982
Nick Heyward
Bryan Music . . . . UK
Haircut 100 . . . . **Arista CLIP 2**
Ivor Novello Nomination.

LOVE REALLY HURTS WITHOUT YOU April 1976
Ben Findon
Black Sheep Music . . . . UK
Billy Ocean . . . . **GTO GT 52**

LOVE RESURRECTION July 1984
Alison Moyet / Tony Swain / Steve Jolley
Rondor Music . . . . UK
Alison Moyet . . . . **CBS A 4497**

LOVE SENDS A LITTLE GIFT OF ROSES 1919
John Openshaw / Leslie Cooke
Francis, Day & Hunter Ltd . . . . UK
Walter Glynne . . . . **HMV B 1142**
Eddie Fisher . . . . **HMV DLP 1074**
Kenneth McKellar . . . . **Decca DFE 6576**

LOVE SHACK April 1990
*Catherine Pearson / Freddie Schneider / Julie Strickland / Cynthia
Wilson*
Rondor Music . . . . USA
B 52's . . . . **Reprise W 9917**

LOVE SOMEBODY   October 1948
Alex Cramer / Joan Whitney
Bradbury Wood Ltd . . . . USA
Doris Day & Buddy Clark . . . . **Columbia DB 2449**
Eddie Fisher . . . . **HMV DLP 1074**

LOVE STEALS YOUR HEART   1946
Hans May / Alan Stranks
Chappell & Co. Ltd. . . . . UK
Film(s): . . . . The Wicked Lady
The Mantovani Orchestra . . . . **Decca F 8622**
Anne Ziegler & Webster Booth . . . . **HMV B 9489**

LOVE THY NEIGHBOUR   1934
Mack Gordon / Harry Revel
Victoria Music Co. Ltd. . . . . USA
Film(s): . . . . We're Not Dressing
Bing Crosby . . . . **Brunswick LAT 8251**
Lillian Roth . . . . **Philips BBL 7079**
Bing Crosby appeared in *We're Not Dressing.*

LOVE TIMES LOVE (Love x Love)   November 1980
Rodney Temperton
Rodsongs Ltd. . . . . USA
George Benson . . . . **Warner Brothers K 17699**

LOVE TO LOVE YOU BABY   February 1976
Giorgio Moroder / Pete Bellotte / Donna Summer
Louvigny-Marquee Music Co. . . . . USA
Donna Summer . . . . **GTO GT 17**

LOVE TOWN   June 1983
Bob Elli / Len Barry
A.T.V. Music . . . . USA
Booker Newberry . . . . **Polydor POSP 613**

LOVE TRAIN   April 1973
Kenny Gamble / Leon Huff
Carlin Music Corporation . . . . USA
The O'Jays . . . . **CBS 1181**

LOVE TRAIN   February 1989
Holly Johnson
Warner Chappell Music . . . . UK
Holly Johnson . . . . **MCA 1306**

LOVE WALKED IN   1938
George Gershwin / Ira Gershwin
Chappell & Co. Ltd. . . . . USA
Film(s): . . . . The Goldwyn Follies / Rhapsody in Blue
Kenny Baker . . . . **Brunswick 03711**
Hildegarde . . . . **Columbia FB 1992**
Johnny Mathis . . . . **Fontana TFL 5039**
Ella Fitzgerald . . . . **HMV CLP 1348**
Kenny Baker appeared in *The Goldwyn Follies.*

LOVE WILL FIND A WAY   1917
Harold Fraser-Simpson / Harry Graham
Ascherberg, Hopwood & Crew Ltd. . . . . UK
Show(s): . . . . The Maid of the Mountains
Jose Collins . . . . **Columbia L 1155**
Mary Thomas . . . . **HMV 7EG 8413**
Jose Collins appeared in the British production of *The Maid of the Mountains.*

LOVE WILL SAVE THE DAY   June 1988
Toni Colandreo
House of Fun Music . . . . USA
Whitney Houston . . . . **Arista 111516**

LOVE WILL TEAR US APART   July 1980
"Joy Division"
Fractured Music . . . . UK
Joy Division . . . . **Factory FAC 23**

LOVE WORTH WAITING FOR, A   April 1984
Garry Sulch / Stuart Leatherwood
Shaky Music . . . . UK
Shakin' Stevens . . . . **Epic A 4291**

LOVE YOU FUNNY THING   1932
Roy Turk / Fred Ahlert
Francis, Day & Hunter Ltd. . . . . USA
Bing Crosby . . . . **Brunswick 01304**
Kate Smith . . . . **Columbia DB 871**
Mel Tormé . . . . **MGM EP 562**

LOVE YOU SAVE, THE   August 1970
"The Corporation"
Jobete Music (UK) Ltd. . . . . USA
The Jackson Five . . . . **Tamla Motown TMG 746**

LOVE'S BEEN GOOD TO ME   November 1969
Rod McKuen
Ambassador Music Ltd. . . . . USA
Frank Sinatra . . . . **Reprise RS 20852**
Rod McKuen . . . . **Capitol T 2079**

LOVE'S GARDEN OF ROSES   1914
Haydn Wood / Ruth Rutherford
Chappell & Co. Ltd. . . . . UK
Hubert Eisdell (1915) . . . . **HMV C 746**
Hubert Eisdell (1931) . . . . **Columbia DB 751**
Ann Ziegler & Webster Booth . . . . **HMV B 9177**

LOVE'S GOTTA HOLD ON ME   September 1979
David Van Day / Thereze Bazar
Warner Brothers Music Ltd. . . . . UK
Dollar . . . . **Carrere CAR 122**

LOVE'S GREAT ADVENTURE   November 1984
Warren Cann / Bill Currie / James Ure & Chris Allen
B.M.G. Music . . . . UK
Ultravox . . . . **Chrysalis UV 3**

LOVE'S JUST A BROKEN HEART   February 1966
Mort Shuman / Kenny Lynch
Belinda (London) Ltd . . . . UK
Cilla Black . . . . **Parlophone R 5395**

LOVE'S LAST WORD IS SPOKEN
(Le Chaland Qui Passe)   1934
C.A. Bixio / Bruce Sievier
Ascherberg, Hopwood & Crew Ltd. . . . . France
Lys Gauty . . . . **Columbia DB 1328**
Arthur Tracey (The Street Singer) . . . . **Decca F 7143**
Guiseppe Di Stefano . . . . **Decca LXT 5485**

LOVE'S OLD SWEET SONG   1884
G. Clifton Bingham / James L. Molloy
Boosey & Hawkes Ltd. . . . . UK
John McCormack . . . . **HMV DB 1200**
Anne Ziegler & Webster Booth . . . . **HMV B 9070**
Jo Stafford & Gordon MacRae . . . . **Capitol CL 13548**
The Cliff Adams Singers . . . . **Ronco RON 7**

LOVE'S THEME   March 1974
Barry White / Aaron Schroeder
Schroeder Music Ltd. . . . . USA
The Love Unlimited Orchestra . . . . **Pye 7N 25635**

LOVELIEST NIGHT OF THE YEAR   July 1951
Juventino Rosas / Paul Francis Webster
Robbins Music Corporation . . . . Mexico
Film(s): . . . . The Great Caruso
Mario Lanza . . . . **RCA RB 16113**
Ann Blyth . . . . **MGM 391**
Connie Francis . . . . **MGM C 854**
Mario Lanza & Ann Blyth appeared in *The Great Caruso.*
Adapted from *Over the Waves* by Juventino Rosas.

LOVELY DAY   February 1978
Bill Withers / Skip Scarborough
Chappell & Co. Ltd . . . . USA
Bill Withers . . . . **CBS 5773**
Bill Withers (1988) . . . . **CBS 653001**

LOVELY LADY   1936
Ted Koehler / Jimmy McHugh
Francis, Day & Hunter Ltd . . . . USA
Show(s): . . . . Glorious Days
Film(s): . . . . King of Burlesque
Bing Crosby . . . . **Brunswick 02179**
Anna Neagle & chorus . . . . **Philips PB 153**
Frank Chacksfield & his Orchestra . . . . **Decca LK 4172**
Anna Neagle appeared in *Glorious Days.*

LOVELY TO LOOK AT   1935
Jerome Kern / Dorothy Fields / Jimmy McHugh
Chappell & Co. Ltd . . . . USA
Film(s): . . . . Roberta / Lovely to Look at
Irene Dunne . . . . **Columbia DB 1805**

Turner Layton . . . . **Columbia DB 1574**
Howard Keel . . . . **MGM D 141**
Sammy Davis . . . . **Brunswick LAT 8330**
Irene Dunne appeared in *Roberta.*
Howard Keel appeared in *Lovely To Look At.*
Nominated for an Academy Award 1935.

LOVELY WAY TO SPEND AN EVENING, A   1944
Harold Adamson / Jimmy McHugh
Victoria Music Co. Ltd. . . . . USA
Film(s): . . . . Higher and Higher
Frank Sinatra . . . . **Fontana TFE 17042**
June Christy . . . . **Capitol T 725**
Shirley Bassey . . . . **Columbia 33SX 1382**
Frank Sinatra appeared in *Higher and Higher.*

LOVER   1933
Richard Rodgers / Lorenz Hart
Chappell & Co. Ltd. . . . . USA
Film(s):Love Me Tonight / Words & Music / The Jazz Singer / The Rat Race
Jeanette MacDonald . . . . **Conifer CHD 133**
Greta Keller . . . . **Decca F 3601**
Les Paul (guitar) (1949) . . . . **Capitol T 1438**
Peggy Lee . . . . **Brunswick OE 9282**
Jeanette MacDonald appeared in *Love Me Tonight.*
Peggy Lee appeared in *The Jazz Singer.*

LOVER COME BACK TO ME   1929
Sigmund Romberg / Oscar Hammerstein II
Chappell & Co. Ltd . . . . USA
Show(s): . . . . The New Moon
Film(s): . . . . The New Moon / Deep in My Heart
Evelyn Laye . . . . **Columbia 9751**
Jeanette MacDonald . . . . **RCA RCX 1051**
Tony Martin . . . . **MGM C 755**
John Hanson . . . . **Oriole EP 7009**
Evelyn Laye appeared in the British production of *The New Moon.*
Jeanette MacDonald appeared in the 1940 film of *The New Moon.*
Tony Martin appeared in *Deep In My Heart.*

LOVER MAN (Oh Where Can You Be)   1942
Jimmy Davis / Roger Ramirez / Jimmy Sherman
Pickwick Music . . . . USA
Film(s): . . . . Lady Sings The Blues
Billy Holiday . . . . **Brunswick 04389**
Anne Shelton . . . . **Decca F 8842**
Lena Horne . . . . **MGM C 943**
Dianna Ross . . . . **Taml Motown 11311-2**
Crystal Gayle . . . . **CBS 84529**
Dianna Ross appeared in *Lady Sings The Blues*

LOVERBOY   February 1985
Keith Alexander / Leslie Charles / Robert Lange
Zomba Music . . . . UK
Billy Ocean . . . . **Jive 80**

LOVERS CONCERTO   December 1965
Sandy Linzer / Denny Randell
Ardmore & Beechwood Ltd . . . . USA
The Toys . . . . **Stateside SS 460**
Adapted from *Minuet in G* by Johann Sebastian Bach (1685 - 1750).

LOVERS OF THE WORLD UNITE   September 1966
Roger Cook / Roger Greenaway
Mills Music Ltd. . . . . UK
David & Jonathan . . . . **Columbia DB 7950**

LOVES UNKIND   January 1978
Donna Summer / Pete Bellotte / Giorgio Moroder
Heath Levy Music Ltd . . . . USA
Donna Summer . . . . **GTO GT 113**

LOVESICK BLUES   May 1951
Irving Mills / Clifford Friend
Lawrence Wright Music Co. Ltd . . . . USA
Hank Williams . . . . **MGM C 893**
Kay Starr . . . . **Capitol CL 13511**
Slim Whitman . . . . **London HLP 8459**
Frank Ifield (1962) . . . . **Columbia DB 4913**
Clinton Ford . . . . **Oriole CB 1516**
First Published 1922.

LOVIN' THINGS   July 1968
Arthur Schroeck / Jet Loring

Gallico Music Ltd. . . . . USA
Marmalade . . . . **CBS 3412**

LOVING AND FREE   October 1976
Kiki Dee
Rocket Publishing . . . . UK
Kiki Dee . . . . **Rocket ROKN 515**

LOVING YOU   July 1957
Jerry Leiber / Mike Stoller
Belinda (London) Ltd. . . . . USA
Film(s): . . . . Loving You
Elvis Presley . . . . **RCA RD 27159**
Elvis Presley appeared in *Loving You.*

LOVING YOU   May 1975
Minnie Riperton / Richard Rudolph
April Music Ltd . . . . USA
Minnie Riperton . . . . **Epic 3121**

LOW RIDER   February 1976
Jerry Goldstein
Carlin Music Corporation . . . . USA
War . . . . **Island WIP 6267**

LUCILLE   October 1960
Albert Collins / Richard W. Penniman
Duchess Music Ltd . . . . USA
The Everly Brothers . . . . **Warner Brothers WM 4028**
Little Richard . . . . **London HAU 2126**

LUCILLE   June 1977
Roger Bowling / Hal Bynum
Campbell Connelly & Co. Ltd . . . . USA
Film(s): . . . . Convoy
Kenny Rogers . . . . **United Artists UP 36242**

LUCK BE A LADY TONIGHT   June 1953
Frank Loesser
Edwin H. Morris & Co. Ltd . . . . USA
Show(s): . . . . Guys and Dolls
Film(s): . . . . Guys and Dolls
Robert Alda . . . . **Brunswick LAT 8022**
Jerry Wayne . . . . **Philips PD 146**
Edmund Hockridge . . . . **Parlophone R 3696**
Marlon Brando . . . . **Brunswick OE 9241**
Robert Alda appeared in the American production of *Guys and Dolls.*
Jerry Wayne & Edmund Hockridge appeared in the British production
of *Guys and Dolls.*
Marlon Brando appeared in the film *Guys and Dolls.*

LUCKY DAY   1927
Buddy De Sylva / Lew Brown / Ray Henderson
Chappell & Co. Ltd. . . . . USA
Show(s): . . . . George White's Scandals / Shake Your Feet
Film(s): . . . . The Best Things in Life are Free
Layton & Johnstone . . . . **Columbia 4548**
Petula Clark . . . . **Nixa N 15182**
Ronnie Hilton . . . . **HMV CLP 1295**

LUCKY FIVE   July 1960
Trevor Stanford
Clover-Conway Music Co. Ltd . . . . UK
Russ Conway (piano) . . . . **Columbia DB 4457**

LUCKY IN LOVE   1928
Buddy De Sylva / Lew Brown / Ray Henderson
Chappell & Co. Ltd. . . . . USA
Show(s): . . . . Good News
Film(s): . . . . Good News / The Best Things in Life Are Free
George Olsen & his Music . . . . **HMV B 5495**
Dinah Shore . . . . **Capitol T 1354**
June Allyson, Peter Lawford & Pat Marshall . . . . **MGM 166**
Sarah Vaughan . . . . **Mercury MMC 14024**
George Olsen & his Music appeared in the American production of
Good News.
June Allyson, Peter Lawford & Pat Marshall appeared in the 1947 film
of *Good News.*

LUCKY LIPS   June 1963
Jerry Leiber / Mike Stoller
Cromwell Music Ltd . . . . USA
Cliff Richard . . . . **Columbia DB 4034**
Alma Cogan . . . . **HMV POP 317**

LUCKY LUCKY LUCKY ME — January 1951
Milton Berle / Buddy Arnold
Dash Music Ltd .... USA
Evelyn Knight .... **Brunswick 04631**

LUCKY NUMBER — March 1979
Lene Lovich / Leslie Chappell
Oval Music .... UK
Lene Lovich .... **Stiff BUY 42**

LUCKY STARS — November 1978
Dean Friedman
Heath Levy Music Ltd .... USA
Dean Friedman .... **Lifesong LS 402**

LUCY IN THE SKY WITH DIAMONDS — December 1974
John Lennon / Paul McCartney
Northern Songs Ltd. .... UK
Show(s): .... John, Paul, George, Ringo & Bert
Elton John .... **DJM DJS 340**
The Beatles .... **Parlophone PMC 7027**
Barbara Dickson .... **RSO 2394141**
Barbara Dickson appeared in *John, Paul, George, Ringo & Bert.*

LULLABY IN RHYTHM — 1938
Edgar Sampson / Benny Goodman / Walter Hirsch & Clarence Profit
Francis, Day & Hunter Ltd. .... USA
Film(s): ....The Benny Goodman Story
Harry James & his Orchestra .... **Columbia DB 5040**
Peggy Lee .... **Capitol T 1049**

LULLABY OF BIRDLAND — November 1952
George Shearing / B.Y. Forster
Good Music Ltd .... USA
George Shearing (piano) .... **MGM 571**
Ella Fitzgerald .... **Brunswick LAT 8115**
George Shearing (piano) .... **Capitol T 1524**

LULLABY OF BROADWAY — 1935
Al Dubin / Harry Warren
B. Feldman & Co. Ltd .... USA
Show(s): .... Forty Second Street (Revival)
Film(s): ..... Gold Diggers of 1935 / Lullaby of Broadway
Dick Powell .... **Decca F 5548**
The Boswell Sisters .... **Brunswick 02043**
Eddie Fisher .... **HMV CLP 1095**
Doris Day .... **Philips BBL 7175**
Dick Powell & Winifred Shaw ..... **United Artists UAG 29421**
Winifred Shaw .... **RCA ZL 70136**
Frankie Vaughan .... **Creole FVLP 3**
Dick Powell & Winifred Shaw appeared in *Gold Diggers of 1935.*
Doris Day appeared in *Lullaby of Broadway.*
Frankie Vaughan appeared in the britisg production of *Forty Second Street.*
Academy Award winning song of 1935.

LULLABY OF THE LEAVES — 1932
Bernice Petkere / Joe Young
Francis, Day & Hunter Ltd. .... USA
Layton & Johnstone .... **Columbia DB 889**
Roy Fox & his Orchestra, vocal Al Bowlly ...... **Decca F 3029**
Billy Eckstine .... **Mercury MMB 12002**
The Ray Charles Singers .... **MGM EP 653**

LULU'S BACK IN TOWN — 1935
Al Dubin / Harry Warren
B. Feldman & Co. Ltd .... USA
Film(s): .... Broadway Gondolier
Dick Powell .... **Decca F 5694**
Mel Tormé .... **London LTZN 15009**
Dick Powell .... **RCA ZL 70136**
Dick Powell appeared in *Broadway Gondolier.*

LUXEMBOURG POLKA — January 1954
Emile Reisdorff
Dash Music Ltd. .... Germany
The Mantovani Orchestra .... **Decca LK 4079**
Winifred Atwell (piano) .... **Decca LK 4376**

LYDIA THE TATTOOED LADY — 1939
E.Y. Harburg / Harold Arlen
Francis, Day & Hunter Ltd. .... USA
Film(s): ....At The Circus

Groucho Marx .... **A&M AMLS 6003**
Burl Ives .... **Brunswick LAT 8321**
Stubby Kaye .... **Polydor NN 66827**
Groucho Marx appeared in *At The Circus.*

MA BAKER — August 1977
Frank Farian / George Reyam / Fred Jay
A.T.V. Music Ltd. .... Germany
Boney M .... **Atlantic K 10965**

MA BELLE MARGUERITA — 1947
A.P. Herbert / Vivian Ellis
Chappell & Co. Ltd. .... UK
Show(s): .... Bless the Bride
George Guetary .... **Columbia SEG 7551**
George Guetary appeared in *Bless the Bride.*

MA BLUSHIN' ROSIE — 1918
Edgar Smith / John Stromberg
B. Feldman & Co. Ltd. .... USA
Film(s):The Jolson Story / Broadway to Hollywood / Daughter of Rosie O'Grady
Al Jolson .... **Brunswick LAT 8322**

MA CURLY HEADED BABBY — 1932
George H. Clutsam
Edwin Ashdown Ltd. .... UK
Paul Robeson .... **HMV CLP 1415**

MA! HE'S MAKING EYES AT ME — 1922
Sidney Clare / Con Conrad
B. Feldman & Co. Ltd .... USA
Show(s): .... The Midnight Rounders of 1921
The Benson Orchestra of Chicago .... **HMV B 1294**
Eddie Cantor .... **Brunswick LA 8658**
Marie Adams (1958) .... **Capitol CL 14794**
Lena Zavaroni (1974) .... **Philips 6006367**
Eddie Cantor appeared in *The Midnight Rounders of 1921.*

MA, I MISS YOUR APPLE PIE — 1942
Carmen Lombardo / John J. Loeb
Dash Music Ltd .... USA
The R.A.O.C. Blue Rockets Dance Orchestra ... **HMV BD 5743**
Jimmy Boyd .... **Philips PB 315**

MACARTHUR PARK — July 1968
Jim Webb
Carlin Music Corporation .... USA
Richard Harris .... **RCA 1699**
Donna Summer (1978) .... **Casablanca CAN 131**

MACK THE KNIFE — June 1956
Kurt Weill / Bertholt Brecht / Mark Blitzstein
Arcadia Music Publishing Co. Ltd. .... Germany
Show(s): .... Dreigroschenoper / The Threepenny Opera
Film(s): .... Satchmo the Great
Dick Hyman Trio .... **MGM 890**
Maria Remusat .... **Felsted SD 80042**
Eddie Barclay & his Orchestra .... **Felsted PDL 85025**
Louis Armstrong (1956) (Nov 1959) .... **Philips BBL 7216**
Bobby Darin (Oct 1959) .... **London HAE 2172**
Maria Remusat appeared in the British production of *The Threepenny Opera.*
Louis Armstrong appeared in *Satchmo the Great.*

MACUSHLA — 1911
Joephine V. Rowe / Dermot MacMurrough
Boosey & Hawkes Music Publishers Ltd .... UK
John McCormack .... **Camden CDN 1002**
Kenneth McKellar .... **Decca LK 4338**

MAD ABOUT THE BOY — 1932
Noel Coward
Chappell & Co. Ltd. .... UK
Show(s): ....Words and Music / Set to Music
Gertrude Lawrence .... **Decca F 3214**
Jeri Southern .... **Brunswick LA 8699**
Julie London .... **London HAU 2171**
Gertrude Lawrence appeared in *Words and Music.*

MAD ABOUT YOU — August 1972
Bruce Ruffin
Creole Music .... UK
Bruce Ruffin .... **Rhino RNO 101**

MAD DOGS AND ENGLISHMEN   **1932**
Noel Coward
Chappell & Co. Ltd. .... UK
Show(s): .... The Third Litttle Show / Words and Music
Noel Coward .... **HMV 7EG 8300**
Danny Kaye .... **Brunswick LA 8507**

MAD PASSIONATE LOVE   **October 1958**
Dick Sherman / Dave Coleman
Duchess Music .... USA
Bernard Bresslaw .... **HMV POP 522**

MAD WORLD   **November 1982**
Roland Orzabel
D.J.M. Music .... UK
Tears For Fears .... **Mercury IDEA 3**

MADAM BUTTERFLY (Un Bel Di Verdremo)   **September 1984**
Malcolm McLaren / Steve Mague / Walter Turbitt
CBS Songs .... UK
Malcolm McLaren .... **Charisma MALC 5**
Based on an original composition by Giacomo Puccini (1958-1924).

MADE YOU   **June 1960**
John Barry
Robbins Music Corporation Ltd .... UK
Film(s): .... Beat Girl
Adam Faith .... **Parlophone R 4665**
Adam Faith .... **Columbia 33SX 1225**
Adam Faith appeared in *Beat Girl*.

MADELON (QUAND MADELON)   **1918**
Louis Bousquet / Camille Robert / Ray Sonin
Lafleur & Co. Ltd. .... France
Show(s): .... Hullo America
The Palace Theatre Orchestra .... **HMV C 877**
Maurice Chevalier .... **MGM C 860**

MADEMOISELLE DE PARIS   **May 1951**
Paul Durand / Henri Contet / Eric Maschwitz
Peter Maurice Music Co. Ltd .... France
Teddy Johnson .... **Columbia DB 1211**
Stanley Black & his Orchestra .... **Decca LK 4212**
Bing Crosby .... **Brunswick LA 8645**

MADEMOISELLE FROM ARMENTIERES   **1919**
Harry Carlton / Joseph Tunbridge
B. Feldman & Co. Ltd. .... UK
Jack Charman .... **Guarsman 954**
The Big Ben Banjo Band .... **Columbia SEG 7825**

MAGGIE MAY   **November 1971**
Rod Stewart / Martin Quittenton
Chappell & Co. Ltd .... UK
Rod Stewart .... **Mercury 73224**

MAGGIE MURPHY'S HOME   **1891**
David Barham / Edward Harrigan
Francis, Day & Hunter Ltd. .... USA
Show(s): .... Reilly & The 400
Reg Grant .... **Parlophone E 6372**
Harry Davidson & his Orchestra .... **Columbia DX 1570**

MAGGIE! YES MA?   **1923**
Leslie Moore / Johnny Tucker
Francis, Day & Hunter Ltd .... USA
Olive Fox & Clarkson Rose .... **Zonophone 2419**
Lisa Noble .... **Decca F 11006**

MAGIC   **November 1974**
Bill Lyall / David Patton
Robbins Music Ltd. .... UK
Pilot .... **EMI 2217**
Ivor Novello Nomination.

MAGIC FLY   **September 1977**
Ecema'
Heath Levy Music Ltd .... France
Space .... **Pye 7N 25746**

MAGIC IS THE MOONLIGHT (Te Quiero Dijiste)   **1936**
Maria Grever / Charles Pasquale
Southern Music Publishing Co. Ltd .... Mexico
Film(s): .... Nancy Goes To Rio / Bathing Beauty
Geraldo & his Gaucho Tango Orchestra .... **Decca F 6317**

Ann Sothern & Jane Powell .... **MGM 313**
Connie Francis .... **MGM C 836**
Ann Sothern & Jane Powell appeared in *Nancy Goes To Rio*.
See also Echo of a Serenade.

MAGIC MOMENTS   **January 1958**
Burt Bacharach / Hal David
Chappell & Co. Ltd .... USA
Perry Como .... **RCA RD 27100**

MAGIC TOUCH   **May 1956**
Buck Ram
Southern Music Publishing Co. Ltd. .... USA
The Platters .... **Mercury MEP 9504**
Buck Ram & his Orchestra ...... **Mercury ZEP 10072**

MAGNOLIA   **1927**
Buddy De Sylva / Lew Brown / Ray Henderson
Campbell Connelly & Co. Ltd. .... USA
Paul Whiteman & his Orchestra,
vocal Bing Crosby & The Rhythm Boys ... **HMV B 5317**
George Melly .... **Decca F 10840**

MAGNOLIAS IN THE MOONLIGHT   **1937**
Victor Schertzinger / Walt Bullock
Keith Prowse Music Publishing Co. Ltd .... USA
Film(s): .... Follow Your Heart
Frank Tanner & his Rhythm Kings .. **Regal Zonophone MR 2304**
Carroll Gibbons & his Boy Friends .... **Columbia FB 2281**
Roy Fox & his Orchestra, vocal Barry Gray ..... **HMV BD 5148**

MAH NA MAH NA   **May 1977**
Piero Umiliani
Lorna Music Co. Ltd .... Italy
Film(s): .... Sweden Heaven and Hell
Piero Umiliani .... **EMI INT 530**
The Muppets .... **Pye NSPH 19**

MAHAHAJAH OF MAGADOR, THE   **January 1949**
John L. Loeb / Lewis Harris
Chappell & Co. Ltd .... USA
The Squadronaires Dance Orchestra,
vocal Jimmy Miller .... **Decca F 9067**
Vaughn Monroe & Orch, vocal Ziggy Talent ..... **HMV BD 6031**

MAID OF ORLEANS, THE   **February 1982**
Andy McClusky
Dinsong Music .... UK
Orchestral Manoevres In the Dark .... **Dindisc 40**

MAIGRET THEME, THE   **February 1961**
Ron Grainer
Merit Music Ltd. .... UK
Ron Grainer & his Orchestra .... **Warner Brothers WB 24**
Joe Loss & his Orchestra .... **HMV POP 995**
Theme of the television production *Maigret*.
Ivor Novello Award.

MAIN ATTRACTION, THE   **December 1962**
Pat Boone / Jeff Cory
Spoone Music Ltd .... USA
Film(s): .... The Main Attraction
Pat Boone .... **London HL 9620**
Pat Boone appeared in *The Main Attraction*.

MAIRZY DOATS AND DOZY DOATS   **1944**
Milton Drake / Al Hoffman / Jerry Livingston
Robbins Music Corporation Ltd. .... USA
Johnny Dennis & his Novelty Quartet,
vocal Johnny Dennis .... **Decca F 8417**
Beverley Kenny .... **Vogue VA 160141**
The Mark IV .... **Mercury AMT 1060**

MAIS QUI   **July 1960**
Carlo Donida / 'Pinchi' / Mann Curtis
Leeds Music Ltd .... Italy
The King Brothers .... **Parlophone GEP 8838**

MAJORCA   **February 1956**
Louis Gaste / Johnny Lehmann / George Bunnett
Mills Music Ltd. .... Italy
Petula Clark .... **Nixa NPT 19002**

MAKE BELIEVE   **1928**
Jerome Kern / Oscar Hammerstein II

Chappell & Co. Ltd. . . . . USA
Show(s): . . . . Show Boat
Film(s): . . . . Show Boat / Till the Clouds Roll By
Edith Day & Howett Worster . . . . Columbia 9428
Allan Jones . . . . HMV 7EG 8231
Kathryn Grayson & Tony Martin . . . . MGM D 143
Kathryn Grayson & Howard Keel . . . . MGM D 104
Edith Day & Howett Worster appeared in the British production of
Show Boat.
Allan Jones appeared in the 1936 film of *Show Boat.*
Kathryn Grayson appeared in both the 1951 film of *Show Boat* and
Till the Clouds Roll By.
Tony Martin appeared in *Till the Clouds Roll By.*
Howard Keel appeared in the 1951 film of *Show Boat.*

MAKE IT EASY ON YOURSELF   September 1965
Burt Bacharach / Hal David
Chappell & Co. Ltd . . . . USA
Jerry Butler . . . . Stateside SS 121
The Walker Brothers . . . . Philips BF 1428
Dionne Warwick . . . . Pye NEP 44024
Kenny Lynch . . . . HMV CLP 1635

MAKE IT SOON
Henri Salvador / Maurice Pon / William Enguick
Campbell Connelly & Co. Ltd. . . . . France
Tony Brent . . . . Columbia DB 3187

MAKE IT WITH YOU   September 1970
David Gates
Screen Gems Music Ltd . . . . USA
Bread . . . . Elektra 2101010
Andy Williams . . . . CBS S 64127
The Nolan Sisters . . . . Target TGS 502

MAKE LOVE TO ME   March 1954
Alan Copeland / Bill Norvas
Edwin H. Morris & Co. Ltd. . . . . USA
Alma Cogan . . . . HMV 7M 196
Connee Boswell . . . . RCA RD 27017
Jo Stafford . . . . Philips BBL 7395
Based on 'Tin Roof Blues' by Paul Mares, George Brunies, Mel Stitzel,
Leon Rappalo, Ben Pollack & Walter Melrose.

MAKE ME AN ISLAND   August 1969
Albert Hammond / Mike Hazlewood
Shaftesbury Music Ltd. . . . . UK
Joe Dolan . . . . Pye 7N 17731

MAKE ME SMILE (Come Up And See Me)   March 1975
Steve Harley
Rak Music Ltd . . . . UK
Steve Harley & Cockney Rebel . . . . EMI 2263

MAKE MINE MUSIC   1946
Ken Darby / Eliot Daniels
Southern Music Publishing Co. Ltd. . . . . USA
Film(s): . . . . Make Mine Music (cartoon)
Frank Weir & his Orchestra,
vocal Denny Vaughan . . . . Decca F 8628

MAKE SOMEONE HAPPY   November 1961
Betty Comden / Adolph Green / Jule Styne
Chappell & Co. Ltd. . . . . USA
Show(s): . . . . Do-Re-Mi
John Reardon . . . . RCA RD 27228
Steve Arlen & Jan Waters . . . . Decca LK 4413
John Reardon appeared in the American production of *Do-Re-Mi.*
Steve Arlen & Jan Waters appeared in the British production of *Do-Re-Mi.*

MAKE THE WORLD GO AWAY   May 1966
Hank Cochran
Acuff-Rose Music Ltd. . . . . USA
Eddie Arnold . . . . RCA 1496
Ray Price . . . . CBS AAG 20033
Timi Yuro . . . . Liberty LIB 55587
Donny & Marie Osmond . . . . MGM 2006523

MAKE YOURSELF A HAPPINESS PIE   1931
Steve Nelson / Frank Perkins
Lawrence Wright Music Co. Ltd . . . . USA
The New Mayfair Dance Orchestra, vocal Al Bowlly . . HMV B 5967

MAKE YOURSELF COMFORTABLE   January 1955
Bob Merrill

Dash Music Ltd. . . . . USA
Steve Lawrence & Eydie Gormé . . . . Coral FEP 2017
Sarah Vaughan . . . . Mercury MPT 7503

MAKIN' LOVE   October 1959
Floyd Robinson
Chappell & Co. Ltd . . . . USA
Floyd Robinson . . . . RCA RD 27166
The King Brothers . . . . Parlophone R 4577

MAKIN' WHOOPEE   1929
Walter Donaldson / Gus Kahn
Keith Prowse Music Publishing Co. Ltd . . . . USA
Show(s): . . . . Whoopee
Film(s):Whoopee / Show Business / I'll See You in My Dreams / The
Eddie Cantor Story
Eddie Cantor . . . . Capitol EAP 1-20113
Steve Lawrence . . . . Coral FEP 2012
Janette Scott & Jackie Rae . . . . Fontana TFE 17023
Eddie Cantor appeared in both the show and the film of *Whoopee* and
also the film of *Show Business.*
Theme song of Eddie Cantor.

MAKING PLANS FOR NIGEL   November 1979
Colin Moulding
Virgin Music (Publishers) Ltd. . . . . UK
X.T.C. . . . . Virgin VS 282

MAKING THE BEST OF EACH DAY   1935
Charles Tobias / Sidney Clare / Murray Mencher
Francis, Day & Hunter Ltd . . . . USA
Film(s): . . . . Kid Millions
Eddie Cantor . . . . Decca F 6748
Eddie Cantor appeared in *Kid Millions.*

MAKING UP AGAIN   July 1978
Dave Black / Peter MacDonald
Essex Music Ltd . . . . UK
Goldie . . . . Bronze BRO 50

MAKING YOUR MIND UP   April 1981
Andy Hill / John Danter
RCA Music . . . . UK
Bucks Fizz . . . . RCA 56
United Kindom entry for the 1981 Eurovision Song Contest. Placed
First.

MALAGUENA   1930
Ernesto Lecuona / Marion Banks
Campbell Connelly & Co. Ltd . . . . Cuba
Ernesto Lecuona (piano) & his Orchestra . . . . HMV 7EG 8143
Caterina Valente (1955) . . . . Polydor LPHM 46065
Charles Marqulis & his Orchestra . . . . London HAL 2154
The Ted Heath & Edmundo Ros Orchestras . . Decca PFS 4033

MALE STRIPPER   March 1987
Miki Zone
Passion Music . . . . USA
Man to Man . . . . Bolts BOLTS 4

MALT AND BARLEY BLUES   June 1971
Bernard Gallagher / Graham Lyle
Gallagher & Lyle Music . . . . UK
McGuiness Flint . . . . Capitol CL 15682

MAM'SELLE   1947
Mack Gordon / Edmund Goulding
Robbins Music Corporation Ltd. . . . . USA
Film(s): . . . . The Razor's Edge
Dick Haymes . . . . Brunswick 03803
Frank Sinatra . . . . Capitol W 1417

MAMA   July 1955
C.A. Bixio / R. Cherubini / Geoffrey Parsons & John Turner
Macmelodies Ltd. . . . . Italy
Beniamino Gigli . . . . HMV DA 5397
David Whitfield (1955) . . . . Decca F 10515
Connie Francis (1960) . . . . MGM C 821
First Published in Italy in 1940.

MAMA   September 1966
Mark Charron
Francis, Day & Hunter Ltd. . . . . USA
Dave Berry . . . . Decca F 12435

MAMA   September 1983
Anthony Banks / Phil Collins / Mike Rutherford
Hit & Run Music .... UK
Genesis .... **Virgin MAMA 1**

MAMA DOLL SONG, THE   December 1954
Nat Simon / Charles Tobias
Leeds Music Ltd. .... USA
Lita Roza .... **Decca F 10393**
Patti Page .... **Mercury MB 3161**
The Beverley Sisters .... **Philips BBR 8052**

MAMA DON'T WANT NO PEAS, AN' RICE, AN' COCONUT OIL   1934
L. Wolfe Gilbert / Charles Lofthouse
Campbell Connelly & Co. Ltd .... USA
Cleo Brown .... **Brunswick 02047**
Count Basie & his Orchestra,
vocal Jimmy Rushing .... **Brunswick 02668**
Burl Ives .... **Brunswick LAT 8381**

MAMA GOES WHERE PAPA GOES   1924
Jack Yellen / Milton Ager
Lawrence Wright Music Co. Ltd .... USA
The David H. Silverman Orchestra .... **HMV B 1774**
Kay Starr .... **Capitol LC 6574**
The Girls .... **Warner Brothers WM 4053**

MAMA I WANNA MAKE RHYTHM   1938
Richard Jerome / Richard Byron / Walter Kent
Campbell Connelly & Co. Ltd. .... USA
Film(s): .... Manhattan Music Box
Lew Stone & his Orchestra, vocal Al Bowlly .... **Decca F 6664**

MAMA INEZ   1931
Eliseo Grenet / L. Wolfe Gilbert
Lawrence Wright Music Co. Ltd .... Cuba
The Havana Novelty Orchestra .... **HMV B 6028**
Maurice Chevalier .... **Camden CDN 152**
George Barnes & his Orchestra .... **Mercury MMC 14076**

MAMA LOVES PAPA - PAPA LOVES MAMA   1924
Cliff Friend / Abel Baer
Francis, Day & Hunter Ltd. .... USA
The Original Capitol Orchestra .... **Zonophone 2436**
Bing Crosby .... **RCA RD 27032**
Nancy Sinatra .... **Reprise RLP 6239**

MAMA MIA   February 1976
Benny Andersson / Stig Anderson
Bocu Music Ltd .... Sweden
Abba .... **Epic EPC 3790**

MAMA TOLD ME NOT TO COME   September 1970
Randy Newman
Schroeder Music Ltd .... USA
Three Dog Night .... **Stateside SS 8052**
P.J. Proby .... **Liberty LBL 83045**
Randy Newman .... **Reprise RSLP 6373**

MAMA USED TO SAY   June 1982
Norman Giscombe / Robert Carter
EMI Music .... UK
Junior .... **Mercury MER 98**

MAMA WEER ALL CRAZEE NOW   September 1972
Neville Holder / James Lea
Barn Publishing Ltd. .... UK
Slade .... **Polydor 2058274**

MAMA YO QUIERO (I Want My Mama)   1941
Jararaca Paiva / Vincente Paiva / Al Stillman
Robbins Music Corporation Ltd .... Brazil
Show(s): .... Earl Carroll's Vanities
Film(s): .. Down Argentine Way / Babes on Broadway / Ladies' Man
Carmen Miranda .... **Brunswick 03111**
Carmen Miranda appeared in *Down Argentine Way.*

MAMBO ITALIANO   January 1955
Bob Merrill
Campbell Connelly & Co. Ltd. .... USA
Rosemary Clooney .... **Philips BBL 7301**

MAMBO JAMBO   June 1950
Perez Prado

Southern Music Publishing Co. Ltd .... Mexico
Perez Prado & his Orchestra .... **RCA RCX 1001**
Geoff Love & his Orchestra .... **Columbia 33SX 1186**
Edmundo Ros & his Orchestra .... **Decca DFE 6045**

MAMMA GAVE BIRTH TO THE SOUL CHILDREN   April 1990
David Jolicoeur / Kelvin Mercer / Dana Owens & Paul Prince
MCA Music .... USA
Queen Latifah & De La Soul .... **Tommy Boy GEE 26**

MAMMY O'MINE   1919
Maceo Pinkard / William Tracey
B. Feldman & Co. Ltd .... USA
The Original Dixieland Jazz Band ...... **Columbia 33S 1087**
Sid Philips & his Band .... **HMV DLP 1194**
The Alex Welsh Band .... **Columbia 33SX 1219**

MAMMY'S LITTLE COAL BLACK ROSE   1918
Ray Egan / Richard A. Whiting
B. Feldman & Co. Ltd. .... USA
Lee White .... **Edison Bell Winner 3181**

MAN (Uh-Huh)   March 1954
Eddy McKean / Dick Gleason
Blue Ribbon Music .... USA
Rosemary Clooney .... **Philips PB 220**
See also Woman.

MAN AND HIS DREAM, A   1939
Jimmy Monaco / Johnny Burke
Campbell Connelly & Co. Ltd. .... USA
Film(s): .... The Star Maker
Bing Crosby .... **Brunswick Bing 5**
Bing Crosby appeared in *The Star Maker.*

MAN FROM LARAMIE, THE   September 1955
Ned Washington / Lester Lee
Chappell & Co. Ltd. .... USA
Film(s): .... The Man from Laramie
Jimmy Young .... **Decca LF 1265**

MAN I LOVE, THE   1928
George Gershwin / Ira Gershwin
Chappell & Co. Ltd. .... USA
Show(s): .... Will o' the Whispers
Film(s):Rhapsody in Blue / The Man I Love / Sincerely Yours / Young at Heart / The Eddy Duchin Story / Both Ends of the Candle / Lady Sings the Blues
Sophie Tucker .... **Columbia SEG 7766**
Paul Whiteman & his Orchestra,
vocal Vaughn De Leath .... **CBS BPG 62545**
Eddy Duchin (piano) .... **Philips BBL 7081**
Liberace (piano) .... **Philips BBL 7063**
Lena Horne .... **MGM EP 643**
Gogi Grant .... **RCA RD 27054**
Diana Ross .... **Tamla Motown STML 11311-2**
Liberace appeared in *Sincerely Yours.*
Diana Ross appeared in *Lady Sings the Blues.*

MAN OF MYSTERY   December 1960
Michael Carr
B. Feldman & Co. Ltd .... UK
The Shadows .... **Columbia SEG 8094**
Bobby Glen Orchestra .... **Oriole PS 40009**

MAN OF THE WORLD, A   June 1969
Peter Green
Fleetwood Music .... UK
Fleetwood Mac .... **Immediate IM 080**

MAN ON FIRE   October 1957
Sammy Fain / Paul Francis Webster
Robbins Music Corporation Ltd .... USA
Film(s): .... Man on Fire
Bing Crosby .... **Capitol CL 14761**
Frankie Vaughan .... **Philips BBL 7233**
Bing Crosby appeared in *Man on Fire.*

MAN ON THE FLYING TRAPEZE, THE   1933
George Leybourne / Alfred Lee
B. Feldman & Co. Ltd. .... UK
Film(s): .... Two Many Blondes
Eddie Cantor .... **Broadcast 4011**
Mitch Miller & The Gang .... **Philips BBL 7382**
Originally published in 1868.

MAN THAT GOT AWAY, THE   March 1955
Ira Gershwin / Harold Arlen
Edwin H. Morris & Co. Ltd. . . . . USA
Film(s): . . . . A Star is Born
Judy Garland . . . . **Philips PB 366**
Judy Garland appeared in *A Star is Born*.
Nominated for an Academy Award 1954.

MAN TO MAN   July 1976
Errol Brown
Rak Music Ltd . . . . UK
Hot Chocolate . . . . **Rak 238**

MAN WHO BROKE THE BANK AT MONTE CARLO, THE   1892
Fred Gilbert
Francis, Day & Hunter Ltd. . . . . UK
Film(s): . . . . Variety Jubilee
Charles Coborn . . . . **Columbia 5665**
Bing Crosby & Friends   **Warner Brothers WM 4046**
Charles Coborn appeared in *Variety Jubilee*.

MAN WHO SOLD THE WORLD, THE   March 1974
David Bowie
Chrysalis Music Ltd. . . . . UK
Lulu . . . . **Polydor 2001490**
David Bowie . . . . **Mercury 6338041**

MAN WITH THE CHILD IN HIS EYES   July 1978
Kate Bush
EMI Music Ltd . . . . UK
Kate Bush . . . . **EMI 2806**
Ivor Novello Award.

MAN WITH THE GOLDEN ARM   May 1956
Elmer Bernstein
Victoria Music Co. Ltd . . . . USA
Film(s): . . . . Man With the Golden Arm
Billy May Orchestra (1956) . . . . **Capitol CL 14551**
Jet Harris (guitar) (1962) . . . . **Decca F 11488**

MAN WITH THE MANDOLIN, THE   1939
James Cavanaugh / John Redmond / Frank Weldon
Campbell Connelly & Co. Ltd. . . . . USA
Frances Langford . . . . **Brunswick 02829**

MAN WITHOUT LOVE, A   March 1966
Robin Conrad / Cyril Ornadel
Skidmore Music Ltd. . . . . UK
Kenneth McKeller . . . . **Decca F 12341**
United Kingdom entry for the 1966 Eurovision Song Contest (Placed
Seventh).

MAN WITHOUT LOVE, A (Quando M'innamoro)   June 1968
Barry Mason / Robert Livraghi
Valley Music . . . . Italy
Engelbert Humperdinck . . . . **Decca F 12770**

MANAGUA NICARAGUA   1947
Albert Gamse / Irving Fields
Leeds Music Ltd. . . . . USA
Edmundo Ros & his Orchestra . . . . **Decca F 8815**
Guy Lombardo & his Royal Canadians . . **Brunswick LAT 8063**

MANANA - IS SOON ENOUGH FOR ME   May 1948
Peggy Lee / Dave Barbour
Campbell Connelly & Co. Ltd. . . . . USA
Peggy Lee . . . . **Capitol T 1366**
The Mills Brothers . . . . **London HAD 2319**
Theme song of Peggy Lee.

MANCHILD   June 1989
Neneh Cherry / Cameron McVey / Hobert Delnaja
Virgin Music . . . . UK
Neneh Cherry . . . . **Circa YR 30**

MANDOLIN SERENADE   September 1957
Charles Chaplin / John Turner / Geoffrey Parsons
Bourne Music Ltd . . . . UK
Film(s): . . . . A King in New York
Charles Chaplin & his Orchestra . . . . **HMV POP 370**
Norrie Paramor & his Orchestra . . . . **Columbia SEG 7720**
The Mantovani Orchestra . . . . **Decca DFE 6431**

MANDOLINS IN THE MOONLIGHT   October 1958
George Weiss / Aaron Schroeder

Yale Music Corporation Ltd . . . . USA
Perry Como . . . . **RCA 1086**
Vera Lynn . . . . **Decca F 11106**

MANDY   1919
Irving Berlin
Francis, Day & Hunter Ltd. . . . . USA
Show(s):Yip Yip Yaphank / The Ziegfeld Follies of 1919 / This is the
Army
Film(s): . . . . Kid Millions / White Christmas
Eddie Cantor . . . . **Rex 8390**
Bing Crosby & Danny Kaye . . . . **Brunswick LA 8044**
Bing Crosby & Danny Kaye appeared in *White Christmas*.
Eddie Cantor appeared in *Kid Millions*.

MANDY   March 1975
Scott English / Richard Kerr
Graphle Music Ltd . . . . UK
Barry Manilow . . . . **Arista 1**
This song has the same melody as *Brandy*.

MANDY (See also Panse, La)

MANDY MAKE UP YOUR MIND   1925
George Meyer / Roy Turk / Grant Clarke / Arthur Johnson
Francis, Day & Hunter Ltd. . . . . USA
Show(s): . . . . Dixie to Broadway
Fletcher Henderson & his Orchestra . . . . **London AL 3547**
Muggsy Spanier's Ragtime Band . . . . **RCA RD 27132**

MANEATER   November 1982
Daryl Hall / John Oates / Sara Allen
April Music . . . . USA
Daryl Hall & John Oates . . . . **RCA 290**

MANGOS   May 1957
Dee Libbey / Sid Wayne
Sydney Bron Music Co. Ltd. . . . . USA
Rosemary Clooney . . . . **Philips BBL 7301**
Marion Ryan . . . . **Columbia DB 4448**

MANHATTAN   1925
Richard Rodgers / Lorenz Hart
Francis, Day & Hunter Ltd. . . . . USA
Show(s): . . . . Garrick Gaieties
Film(s): . . . . Words and Music / Two Tickets to Broadway
The California Ramblers . . . . **Riverside RPL 12-801**
Paul Whiteman & his Orchestra . . . . . . **HMV HMV B 2175**
Tony Martin . . . . **RCA RD 27003**
Mickey Rooney . . . . **MGM C 853**
Ella Fitzgerald . . . . **HMV CLP 1116**
Mel Tormé . . . . **Parlophone PMC 1114**
Tony Martin appeared in *Two Tickets to Broadway*.
Mickey Rooney appeared in *Words and Music*.

MANIC MONDAY   March 1986
Jamie Starr
Island Music . . . . USA
The Bangles . . . . **CBS A 6796**

MANY HAPPY RETURNS OF THE DAY   1931
Al Dubin / Joe Burke
B. Feldman & Co. Ltd. . . . . USA
Bing Crosby . . . . **Brunswick LA 8741**

MANY RIVERS TO CROSS   January 1984
Jimmy Cliff
Island Music . . . . UK
UB40 . . . . **Virgin DEP 9**

MANY YEARS AGO   February 1961
Winfield Scott
Roosevelt Music Ltd . . . . USA
Connie Francis . . . . **MGM 1111**

MAPLE LEAF RAG   1899
Scott Joplin
Herman Darewski Music Publishing Co. Ltd. . . . . USA
Scott Joplin (Piano Roll) . . . . **Riverside RLP 12-110**
The New Orleans Rhythm Kings . . . . **Brunswick 02209**
Red Nichols & his Famous Pennies . . . . **Capitol T 775**

MARCH HARE, THE   July 1956
Philip Green
David Toff Music Publishing Co. Ltd. . . . . UK

Joseph McNally with Philip Green
& his Orchestra . . . . Oriole CB 1326
Billy Cotton & his Band . . . . Decca F 10730
Ron Goodwin & his Orchestra . . . . Parlophone R 4186
Ivor Novello Award.

MARCH OF THE GRENADIERS   1929
Victor Schertzinger / Clifford Grey
Campbell Connelly & Co. Ltd . . . . USA
Film(s): . . . . The Love Parade
Jeanette MacDonald . . . . HMV B 3289
David Whitfield . . . . Decca LK 4270
Jeanette MacDonald appeared in The Love Parade.

MARCH OF THE MODS   December 1964
Tony Carr
Laurel Music Co. Ltd . . . . UK
The Executives . . . . Columbia DB 7323
Joe Loss & his Orchestra . . . . HMV POP 1351
Ivor Novello Award.

MARCH OF THE SIAMESE CHILDREN, THE   March 1962
Richard Rodgers
Williamson Music Ltd. . . . . USA
Show(s): . . . . The King and I
Film(s): . . . . The King and I
Kenny Ball's Jazzmen . . . . Pye 7NJ 2051
Orchestra (USA Show), conducted
by Reginald Dvonch . . . . Brunswick 05170
Orchestra (UK Show), conducted
by Reginald Burston . . . . Philips BBL 7002
Orchestra (Soundtrack), conducted
by Alfred Newman . . . . Capitol LCT 6108

MARCH OF THE TOYS, THE   1903
Victor Herbert / Glen MacDonough
B. Feldman & Co. Ltd. . . . . USA
Show(s): . . . . Babes in Toyland
Film(s): . . . . Babes in Toyland / The Great Victor Herbert
Victor Young & his Orchestra . . . . Brunswick 02939
The Frederick Fennell Orchestra . . . . Mercury MMC 14070

MARCH WINDS AND APRIL SHOWERS   1935
Walter G. Samuels / Leonard Whitcup / Teddy Powell
Lawrence Wright Music Publishing Co. Ltd. . . . . USA
Wingy Manone & his Orchestra . . . . Vocalion 3
Phyllis Robins . . . . Rex 8504

MARCHÉTA   1923
Victor Schertzinger
Chappell & Co. Ltd . . . . USA
John McCormack . . . . HMV DA 606
Bing Crosby . . . . Brunswick 03044
Perry Como . . . . Camden CDN 110
Thomas L. Thomas . . . . Decca LXT 5247
The Karl Denver Trio (1961) . . . . Decca F 11360

MARCHING ALONG TOGETHER   1932
Franz Steininger / Eddie Pola
Peter Maurice Music Co. Ltd. . . . . UK
Jack Hylton & his Orchestra . . . . Decca F 7232

MARCHING STRINGS   September 1952
Marshall Ross
Cecil Lennox Music Co. Ltd . . . . UK
Film(s): . . . . It's Great to be Young
Ray Martin & his Orchestra . . . . Columbia SEG 7736

MARGIE   1921
Benny Davis / Con Conrad / J. Russell Robinson
B. Feldman & Co. Ltd . . . . USA
Show(s): . . . . The Midnight Rounders of 1921
Film(s): . . . . Margie / The Eddie Cantor Story
The Original Dixieland Jazz Band . . . . HMV B 1199
Eddie Cantor . . . . Columbia DB 1935
Maurice Chevalier . . . . MGM C 860
Eddie Cantor . . . . Capitol LC 6652
Eddie Cantor appeared in The Midnight Rounders of 1921.

MARGUERITA TIME   January 1984
Francis Rossi / Bernard Frost
Eaton Music . . . . UK
Status Quo . . . . Vertigo QUO 14

MARIA   June 1959
Leonard Bernstein / Stephen Sondheim
Chappell & Co. Ltd . . . . USA
Show(s): . . . . West Side Story
Film(s): . . . . West Side Story
Larry Kert . . . . CBS BPG 62060
Don McKay . . . . HMV 7EG 8429
Johnny Mathis . . . . Fontana H 272
Jim Bryant . . . . CBS BPG 62058
P.J. Proby (1965) . . . . Liberty LIB 10218
Don McKay appeared in the British production of West Side Story.
Richard Beymer appeared in the film of West Side Story (voice
dubbed by Jim Bryant).
Larry Kert appeared in the American production of West Side Story.

MARIA ELENA   1941
Lorenzo Barcelata / S.K. Russell
Southern Music Publishing Co. Ltd . . . . Mexico
Jimmy Dorsey & his Orchestra,
vocal Bob Eberly . . . . Brunswick 03210
Jimmy Dorsey & his Orchestra,
vocal Tommy Mercer . . . . HMV CLP 1132
Bob Eberly with Lou Busch
& his Orchestra . . . . Warner Brothers WM 4033
Los Indios Tabajaros (1963) . . . . RCA 1365

MARIANDL-ANDL-ANDL   July 1951
Hans Lang / Eric Maschwitz
Bourne Music Ltd . . . . Germany
Donald Peers . . . . HMV B 10089
Geraldo & his Orchestra, vocal
Eve Boswell & Derrick Francis . . . . Parlophone F 2464

MARIANNE   April 1957
Terry Gilkyson / Frank Miller / Richard Dehr
Montclare Music . . . . USA
The Hilltoppers . . . . London HLD 8381
Terry Gilkyson & The Easy Riders
vocal Richard Dehr . . . . Philips PB 670
The King Brothers . . . . Parlophone R 4288

MARIE   1929
Irving Berlin
Francis, Day & Hunter Ltd . . . . USA
Film(s):The Awakening / Alexander's Ragtime Band / The Fabulous
Dorseys
The Rhythmic Eight . . . . Zonophone 5498
Tommy Dorsey & his Orchestra,
vocal Jack Leonard . . . . RCA RCX 1002
Pete Rugolo & his Orchestra . . . . Mercury MMC 14065

MARIGOLD   1928
Billy Mayerl
Keith Prowse Music Publishing Co. Ltd. . . . . UK
Billy Mayerl (piano) . . . . Columbia 4783
Billy Mayerl's Forte Fingers . . . . Decca F 8250
Billy Mayerl & his Rhythm Ensemble . . . Parlophone GEP 8583
Theme tune of Billy Mayerl.

MARRY ME   March 1961
Lawrence Jacks
Lawrence Wright Music Co. Ltd . . . . UK
Mike Preston . . . . Decca F 11335

MARRYING FOR LOVE   April 1952
Irving Berlin
Irving Berlin Ltd . . . . USA
Show(s): . . . . Call Me Madam
Film(s): . . . . Call Me Madam
Ethel Merman . . . . Brunswick LAT 8016
Billie Worth & Anton Walbrook . . . . Columbia 33SX 1002
George Sanders . . . . Brunswick LA 8603
Ethel Merman appeared in the American production of Call Me
Madam and also the film Call Me Madam.
Billie Worth & Anton Walbrook appeared in the British production of
Call Me Madam
George Sanders appeared in the film Call Me Madam.

MARTA   1932
L. Wolfe Gilbert / Moises Simons
Lawrence Wright Music Co. Ltd. . . . . Cuba
Film(s): . . . . The Big Broadcast
Arthur Tracey (The Street Singer) . . . . Decca F 8870
David Whitfield . . . . Decca F 10062
Bing Crosby . . . . MGM C 868

Arthur Tracy appeared in *The Big Broadcast.*
Theme song of Arthur Tracy.

MARTHA'S HARBOUR   August 1988
Tim Bricheno / Andy Cousin / Julianne Regan
B.M.G. Music . . . . UK
AllAbout Eve . . . . **Mercury EVEN 8**

MARY   1920
Hugo Frey
G. Riordi & Co. (London) Ltd . . . . USA
Joseph C. Smith's Orchestra . . . . **HMV B 1100**

MARY ANNE   March 1965
Jerry Lordan
Francis, Day & Hunter Ltd . . . . UK
The Shadows . . . . **Columbia DB 7476**

MARY HAD A LITTLE LAMB   June 1972
Paul McCartney / Linda McCartney
Northern Songs Ltd. . . . . UK
Wings . . . . **Apple R 5949**
Based on the traditional nursery rhyme.

MARY LOU   1927
George Waggner / J. Russel Robinson / Abe Lyman
B. Feldman & Co. Ltd. . . . . USA
Show(s): . . . . High Time
The Ipana Troubadours . . . . **Columbia 4182**
The Merry Macs . . . . **Decca F 7960**
Johnny Maddox & his Orchestra . . . . **London HAD 2101**

MARY LOU   April 1959
Dick Hurran
Francis, Day & Hunter Ltd . . . . UK
Jerry Angelo . . . . **Parlophone R 4548**
Frankie Vaughan . . . . **Philips BBE 12412**

MARY OF THE FOURTH FORM   December 1977
Bob Geldof
Sewer Fire Hits . . . . UK
The Boomtown Rats . . . . **Ensign ENY 9**

MARY ROSE   1933
Harry Parr-Davies
Francis, Day & Hunter Ltd. . . . . UK
Film(s): . . . . This Week of Grace
Gracie Fields . . . . **HMV B 4476**
Gracie Fields appeared in *This Week of Grace.*

MARY'S A GRAND OLD NAME   1905
George M. Cohan
B. Feldman & Co. Ltd. . . . . USA
Show(s): . . . . Forty-Five Minutes From Broadway
Film(s):Yankee Doodle Dandy / Eddie Foy and the Seven Little Foys
Bing Crosby (1943) . . . . **Brunswick LA 8620**
James Cagney . . . . **HMV DLP 1088**
Mickey Rooney . . . . **RCA RD 27038**
James Cagney appeared in *Yankee Doodle Dandy* and *Eddie Foy and the Seven Little Foys.*

MARY'S BOY CHILD   November 1957
Jester Hairston
Bourne Music Ltd. . . . . USA
Harry Belafonte (1958) . . . . **RCA 1022**
Gracie Fields . . . . **Columbia SEG 7759**
Nina & Frederik (1959) . . . . **Columbia SEG 8111**
Boney M (1978) . . . . **Atlantic K 11221**

MARY'S PRAYER   May 1988
Gary Clark
Warner Chappell Music . . . . UK
Danny Wilson . . . . **Virgin VS 934**
Ivor Novello Nomination.

MASQUERADE   1932
John Jacob Loeb / Paul Francis Webster
Francis, Day & Hunter Ltd. . . . . USA
Ambrose & his Orchestra, vocal Sam Browne . . . . **HMV B 6321**
The Melachrino . . . . **HMV DLP 1014**
Ken Griffin (organ) . . . . **Philips BBL 7515**

MASQUERADE   June 1979
Richard Jobson / Stuart Adamson
Virgin Music (Publishers) Ltd. . . . . UK

The Skids . . . . **Virgin VS 262**

MASQUERADE IS OVER, THE   1939
Herb Magidson / Allie Wrubel
Bradbury Wood Ltd. . . . . USA
Dick Robertson . . . . **Panachord 26030**
Sarah Vaughan . . . . **Emarcy EJL 1258**
Patti Page . . . . **Mercury MMC 14064**

MASSACHUSSETTS   November 1967
Maurice Gibb / Barry Gibb / Robin Gibb
Abigail Music . . . . UK
The Bee Gees . . . . **Polydor 56192**

MASTER AND SERVANT   September 1984
Martin Gore
Sonet Music . . . . UK
Depeche Mode . . . . **Mute 7 Bong 6**

MASTERBLASTER (Jammin')   October 1980
Stevie Wonder
Jobete Music (UK) Ltd. . . . . USA
Stevie Wonder . . . . **Motown TMG 1204**

MATCHMAKER, MATCHMAKER   October 1967
Sheldon Harnick / Jerry Bock
Chappell & Co. Ltd. . . . . USA
Show(s): . . . . Fiddler on the Roof
Film(s): . . . . Fiddler on the Roof
Joanna Merlin, Julia Migenes & Tanya Everett . . **RCA RD 7843**
Rosemary Nicols, Linda Gardner & Caryl Little . **CBS BRG 70030**
Nerva Small, Michele Marsh
& Patience Collier . . . . **United Artists UP 35307**
Joanna Merlin, Julia Migenes & Tanya Everett appeared in the American production of *Fiddler on the Roof.*
Rosemary Nicols, Linda Gardner & Caryl Little appeared in the British production of *Fiddler on the Roof.*
Nerva Small, Michele Marsh & Patience Collier appeared in the film *Fiddler on the Roof.*

MATCHSTALK MEN AND MATCHSTALK CATS AND
DOGS   April 1978
Michael Coleman / Brian Burke
EMI Music Ltd . . . . UK
Brian & Michael . . . . **Pye 7N 46035**
Ivor Novello Award 1977.
Ivor Novello Nomination 1978.

MATE O' MINE   1914
Leslie Cooke / Percy Elliott
Ascherberg, Hopwood & Crew Ltd. . . . . UK
Clarence Whitehill . . . . **HMV DA 380**
Morris Stephens . . . . **Decca F 5953**

MATELOT   1945
Noel Coward
Chappell & Co. Ltd. . . . . UK
Show(s): . . . . Sigh No More
Noel Coward . . . . **HMV B 9434**
Graham Payne . . . . **Decca F 8562**
Graham Payne appearde in *Sigh No More.*

MATERIAL GIRL   March 1985
Peter Brown / Robert Rans
Minong Publishing . . . . USA
Madonna . . . . **Sire W 9083**

MATINEE   July 1948
Carl Sigman / Bob Russell
Edwin H. Morris & Co. Ltd. . . . . USA
Bob Eberly . . . . **Brunswick 03921**

MATTHEW AND SON   February 1967
Cat Stevens
Cat Music . . . . UK
Cat Stevens . . . . **Deram DM 110**

MATTINATA (Tis The Day)   1904
Ruggiero Leoncavallo / Edward Teshemacher
. . . . Italy
Film(s): . . . . The Great Caruso / Yes Giorgio
Enrico Caruso . . . . **HMV DA 546**
Beniamino Gigli . . . . **HMV DA 1454**
Giuseppe Di Stefano . . . . **HMV ALP 1902**
Mario Lanza . . . . **HMV DB 21302**

Luciano Pavarotti .... Decca YG 1
Mario Lanza appeared in *The Great Caruso*.
Luciano Pavarotti appeared in *Yes Giorgio*.

MAXIM'S   1907
Franz Lehar / Adrian Ross
Chappell & Co. Ltd. .... Austria
Show(s): .... The Merry Widow
Film(s): .... The Merry Widow
Herbert Ernst Groh .... Parlophone R 2651
Erich Kunz .... Columbia 33CX 1051
Fernando Lamas .... MGM D 107
Per Grunden and the Vienna
State Opera Orchestra .... Decca LXT 5448
Fernando Lamas appeared in the 1952 film of *The Merry Widow*.

MAXINA   1919
M. Boissonade / W.F. Hurndall
Francis, Day & Hunter Ltd. .... UK
The Mayfair Dance Orchestra .... HMV C 891
Harry Davidson & his Orchestra .... Columbia SCD 2016

MAY EACH DAY   May 1966
Mort Green / George Wyle
Robbins Music Corporation Ltd. .... USA
Andy Williams .... CBS 202042

MAY I   1934
Mack Gordon / Harry Revel
Victoria Music Co. Ltd. .... USA
Film(s): .... We're Not Dressing
Bing Crosby .... Brunswick LAT 8251
Dennis Lotis .... Columbia 33SX 1089
Michael Holliday .... Columbia DB 4121
Bing Crosby appeared in *We're Not Dressing*.

MAY I HAVE THE NEXT DREAM WITH YOU   December 1968
Harry Tobias / Charles Tobias / Henry Tobias
Cyril Shane Music .... USA
Malcolm Roberts .... Major Minor MM 581

MAY I HAVE THE NEXT ROMANCE WITH YOU   1937
Mack Gordon / Harry Revel
Cinephonic Music Co. Ltd. .... USA
Film(s): .... Head Over Heels
Jessie Matthews .... Decca F 6287
Jessie Matthews appeared in *Head Over Heels*.

MAY KWAY O MAY KWAY (See Rose Rose I Love You)

MAY MORNING, A   1907
Luigi Denza / Frederick E. Weatherly
Chappell & Co. Ltd. .... Italy
Ernest Pike .... Zonophone 817
Elsie Suddaby .... HMV B 3719

MAY THE GOOD LORD BLESS AND KEEP YOU February 1951
Meredith Wilson
Pickwick Music Ltd .... USA
Bing Crosby .... Brunswick 04657
Perry Como .... RCA RD 27106

MAY YOU ALWAYS   June 1959
Larry Markes / Dick Charles
Colby Music Ltd .... USA
Joan Regan .... HMV POP 593
The McGuire Sisters .... Coral LVA 9115

MAYBE   1927
George Gershwin / Ira Gershwin
Chappell & Co. Ltd. .... USA
Show(s): .... Oh Kay
George Gershwin (piano) .... Columbia 4539
Gertrude Lawrence & Harold French .... Columbia 4618
Bing Crosby .... Brunswick LA 8666
Ella Fitzgerald .... Brunswick LA 8648
Gertrude Lawrence appeared in both the American and British pro-
ductions of *Oh Kay*.
Harold French appeared in the British production of *Oh Kay*.

MAYBE   1941
Frank Madden / Allan Flynn
Robbins Music Corporation Ltd .... USA
The Ink Spots .... Brunswick 03075
Cliffie Stone & his Orchestra & Chorus ..... Capitol CL 14982

Dean Martin .... Capitol CL 15064

MAYBE   July 1979
Thom Pace
Unknown Publisher .... USA
Thom Pace .... RSO 34

MAYBE - WHO KNOWS   1929
Ruth Etting / Joe Schuster / Johnny Tucker
B. Feldman & Co. Ltd .... USA
Show(s): .... Whoopee
Ted Lewis & his Band, vocal Ted Lewis .... Columbia 5540
The Dorsey Brothers Orchestra .... Parlophone R 464
Kate Smith .... CBS BPG 62547

MAYBE BABY   March 1958
Norman Petty / Buddy Holly
Southern Music Publishing Co. Ltd .... USA
Buddy Holly .... Vogue LVA 9105
The Crickets .... Vogue LVA 9081

MAYBE IT'S BECAUSE   November 1949
Johnny Scott / Harry Ruby
Victoria Music Co. Ltd .... USA
Show(s): .... Along Fifth Avenue
Dick Haymes .... Brunswick 04350
Andy & Della Russell .... Capitol CL 13154
Louis Armstrong .... Brunswick LA 8679

MAYBE IT'S BECAUSE I'M A LONDONER   May 1949
Hubert Gregg
Francis, Day & Hunter Ltd .... UK
Billy Cotton & his Band .... Ace of Clubs ACL 1041
The Big Ben Banjo Band,
vocal Michael Sammes Singers .... Columbia 33SX 1367

MAYBE THIS YEAR   August 1959
Ronald Waldey / Marcel Stellman
Lawrence Wright Music Co. Ltd .... UK
Edna Savage .... Parlophone R 4572
Ivor Novello Nomination.

MAYBE YOU'LL BE THERE   1947
Rube Bloom / Sammy Gallop
Victoria Music Co. Ltd. .... USA
Steve Conway .... Columbia FB 3439
Gordon Jenkins & his Orchestra .... Brunswick LA 8543
Joni James .... MGM C 777
Pat Boone .... London HAD 2204

MAZIE   1921
Eli Dawson / Sidney Caine / Lew Gold
Chappell & Co Ltd .... USA
The All Star Trio .... HMV D 1204

McNAMARA'S BAND   1917
Shamus O'Connor / John J. Stamford
Edwin Ashdown Ltd. .... UK
Film(s): .... I'll Get By
Bing Crosby & The Jesters .... Brunswick LAT 8106

ME   1931
Irving Berlin
Francis, Day & Hunter Ltd. .... USA
The Knickerbockers .... Columbia CB 360

ME AND JANE IN A PLANE   1927
Edgar Leslie / Joe Gilbert
Lawrence Wright Music Co. Ltd. .... UK
Jack Hylton & his Orchestra .... HMV B 5336
The Cliff Adams Singers .... Columbia 33SX 1362

ME AND MRS JONES   February 1973
Kenny Gamble / Leon Huff / Don Gilbert
Carlin Music Corporation .... USA
Billy Paul .... Epic 1055

ME AND MY DOG   1936
Vivian Ellis
Chappell & Co. Ltd .... UK
Film(s): .... Public Nuisance No. 1
Frances Day .... HMV BD 323

ME AND MY GIRL   1938
Noel Gay / Douglas Furber

Cinephonic Music Co. Ltd. . . . . UK
Show(s): . . . . Me and My Girl
Film(s): . . . . Me and My Girl
Lupino Lane & Teddie St. Denis . . . . **HMV BD 506**
Lupino Lane appeared in both the show and the film of *Me and My Girl*.
Teddie St. Denis appeared in the show of *Me and My Girl*.

ME AND MY IMAGINATION   October 1950
Bob Merrill / Al Hoffman
Campbell Connelly & Co. Ltd . . . . USA
The Stargazers . . . . **Decca F 9535**
Betty Brewer . . . . **Brunswick 04575**

ME AND MY LIFE   November 1970
Alan Blaikley / Len Hawkes
Gale Music Ltd . . . . UK
The Tremeloes . . . . **CBS 5139**

ME AND MY SHADOW   1927
Dave Dreyer / Al Jolson / Billy Rose
Francis, Day & Hunter Ltd. . . . . UK
Film(s): . . . . Hold That Ghost
Jack Smith . . . . **HMV B 2496**
Rose Murphy (1950) . . . . **Brunswick 04493**
The Mills Brothers . . . . **London RED 1215**

ME AND THE MAN IN THE MOON   1928
Jimmy Monaco / Edgar Leslie
Keith Prowse Music Publishing Co. Ltd . . . . USA
Arnold Johnston & His Orchestra . . . . **Brunswick 3917**

ME AND THE MOON   1936
Walter Hirsch / Lou Handman
Campbell Connelly & Co. Ltd . . . . USA
Bing Crosby . . . . **Brunswick OE 9472**
Guy Mitchell . . . . **Philips BBL 7246**

ME AND THE OLD FOLKS AT HOME   1935
Rodd Arden / Leo Towers / Harry Leon
Dash Music Ltd . . . . UK
The New Mayfair Dance Orchestra . . . . **HMV BD 180**

ME AND YOU AND A DOG NAMED BOO   August 1971
Kent Lavoie
Chappell & Co. Ltd . . . . USA
Lobo . . . . **Philips 6073801**

ME THE PEACEFUL HEART   April 1968
Tony Hazzard
Sydney Bron Music Co. Ltd. . . . . UK
Lulu . . . . **Columbia DB 8295**
Tony Hazzard . . . . **CBS 563608**

ME TOO   1926
Harry Woods / Charles Tobias / Al Sherman
Keith Prowse Music Publishing Co. Ltd. . . . . USA
The Denza Dance Band (California Ramblers) . **Columbia 4133**
The Andrews Sisters . . . . **Capitol T 973**
Kay Starr . . . . **Capitol CL 13760**

MEADOWLARK   1927
Ted Fiorito / Hal Keidel
Francis, Day & Hunter Ltd. . . . . USA
Correll & Gosden . . . . **HMV B 2412**
The Red Heads . . . . **Philips BBL 7434**

MEAN STREAK   JUN 1959
Ian Samwell
Kalith Music . . . . UK
Cliff Richard . . . . **Columbia DB 4290**

MEAN TO ME   1929
Roy Turk / Fred Ahlert
Campbell Connelly & Co. Ltd . . . . USA
Film(s): . . . . Love Me or Leave Me / Lady Sings the Blues
Ruth Etting . . . . **Columbia 5446**
Doris Day . . . . **Philips BBL 7047**
Debbie Reynolds . . . . **London HAD 2200**
Diana Ross . . . . **Tamla Motown STML 11311-2**
Doris Day appeared in *Love Me or Leave Me*.
Diana Ross appeared in *Lady Sings the Blues*.

MEET ME IN ST. LOUIS   1904
Andrew Sterling / Kerry Mills

Sun Music Publishing Co. Ltd. . . . . USA
Film(s): . . . . Meet Me In St.Louis
Judy Garland (1945) . . . . **Ace of Hearts AH 11**
Bing Crosby . . . . **Warner Brothers WM 4021**
Mitch Miller & the Gang . . . . **Philips BBL 7419**
Dorothy Provine . . . . **Warner Brothers WM 8109**
Judy Garland appeared in *Meet Me in St. Louis*.

MEET ME JENNY WHEN THE SUN GOES DOWN   1907
Harry Castling / Fred Godfrey
B. Feldman & Co. Ltd. . . . . UK
The Pavement Artists . . . . **Regal Zonophone MR 614**

MEET ME ON THE CORNER   November 1955
Peter Hart / Paddy Roberts
Berry Music Ltd. . . . . UK
Max Bygraves . . . . **HMV 7EG 8203**

MEET ME ON THE CORNER   April 1972
Rod Clements
Crazy Music Ltd. . . . . UK
Lindisfarne . . . . **Charisma CB 173**
Ivor Novello Nomination.

MEET ME TONIGHT IN DREAMLAND   1909
Beth Slater-Whitson / Leo Friedman
Francis, Day & Hunter Ltd. . . . . USA
Film(s): . . . . In the Good Old Summertime
Ernest Pike . . . . **Zonophone 720**
The Mills Brothers . . . . **Brunswick 04449**
Judy Garland . . . . **MGM EP 568**
Judy Garland appeared in *In the Good Old Summertime*.

MEET MISTER CALLAGHAN   June 1952
Eric Spear
David Toff Music Publishing Co. Ltd . . . . UK
Show(s): . . . . Meet Mister Callaghan
Film(s): . . . . Meet Mister Callaghan
Frank Chacksfield's Tunesmiths . . . . **Oriole CB 1107**
Kurt Edelhagen & his Orchestra . . . . **Polydor LPHM 46345**

MEET THE SUN HALF WAY   1940
Jimmy Monaco / Johnny Burke
Campbell Connelly & Co. Ltd . . . . USA
Film(s): . . . . If I Had My Way
Bing Crosby . . . . **Brunswick Bing 5**
Guy Mitchell . . . . **Philips BBL 7465**
Bing Crosby appeared in *If I Had My Way*.

MEGABLAST   September 1988
Tim Simenon / Pascal Gabriel
Rhythm King Music . . . . UK
Bomb The Bass . . . . **Rhythm King DOOD 2**

MEGAMIX   October 1990
Eric Martin / Jo Bogaert / Thomas De Quincy / Manuela Kamos
Brothers Organisation . . . . Belgium
Technotronic . . . . **Swanyard SYR 17**

MELBA WALTZ, THE   September 1953
Mischa Spoliansky / Norman Newell
Chappell & Co. Ltd. . . . . UK
Film(s): . . . . Melba
Patrice Munsel . . . . **HMV B 10532**
Ron Goodwin & his Orchestra . . . . **Parlophone PMD 1014**
Victor Young & his Singing Strings . . . . . **Brunswick LAT 8028**
Patrice Munsel appeared in *Melba*.

MELISANDS IN THE WOOD   1902
Alma Goetz / Ethel Clifford
Chappell & Co. Ltd. . . . . UK
Essie Ackland . . . . **HMV B 3128**

MELLO CELLO   1921
Harry Williams / Neil Moret
Francis, Day & Hunter Ltd . . . . USA
Joseph C. Smith's Orchestra . . . . **HMV B 1255**
Victor Sylvester & his Orchestra . . . . **Columbia FB 3679**

MELLOW YELLOW   March 1967
Donovan Leitch
Donovan Music Ltd . . . . UK
Donovan . . . . **Pye 7N 17267**

MELODIE D'AMOUR (Maladie d'Amour)　　　June 1957
Henri Salvador / Leo Johns / Marcel Stellman
Imperia Music Co. Ltd. .... France
Henri Salvador .... **Philips PB 754**
Jane Morgan .... **London HAR 2110**
Nina & Frederik .... **Columbia 33SX 1314**

MELODY FROM THE SKY, A　　　1936
Sidney Mitchell / Louis Alter
Victoria Music Co. Ltd .... USA
Film(s): ....The Trail of the Lonesome Pine
Frances Langford .... **Brunswick 02216**
Nominated for an Academy Award 1936.

MELODY OF LOVE　　　1917
Tom Glazer / Harry Engelman
Campbell Connelly & Co. Ltd. .... USA
The Mayfair Orchestra .... **HMV B 783**
The Four Aces .... **Brunswick OE 9090**
Pat Boone .... **London HAD 2210**
The Ink Spots (1955) .... **Parlophone R 6152**
Stanley Black Orchestra .... **Decca F 10462**

MELTING POT　　　January 1970
Roger Cook / Roger Greenaway
Cookaway Music .... UK
Blue Mink .... **Philips BF 1818**
Ivor Novello Award.

MEMORIES　　　1915
Gus Kahn / Egbert Van Alstyne
Francis, Day & Hunter Ltd. .... USA
Film(s): .... I'll See You in My Dreams
The Mayfair Dance Orchestra .... **HMV C 926**
Sidney Thompson & his Orchestra ...... **Parlophone R 3358**
Al Jolson .... **Brunswick LAT 8220**
Bing Crosby .... **Brunswick 04386**

MEMORIES ARE MADE OF THIS　　　February 1956
Rich Dehr / Frank Miller / Terry Gilkyson
Montclare Music Co. Ltd. .... USA
Film(s): .... The Seven Hills of Rome
Dave King .... **Decca LF 1266**
Dean Martin .... **Capitol T 949**
Bing Crosby .... **Brunswick LAT 8138**
Mario Lanza .... **RCA RA 13001**
Val Doonican (1967) .... **Decca F 12566**
Mario Lanza appeared in The Seven Hills of Rome.

MEMORIES LIVE LONGER THAN DREAMS　　　1940
Ross Parker
Dash Music Ltd .... UK
Vera Lynn .... **Decca F 7654**

MEMORIES OF YOU　　　1931
Eubie Blake / Andy Razaf
Lawrence Wright Music Co. Ltd .... USA
Show(s): .... Blackbirds of 1930
Film(s): .... The Benny Goodman Story / Drum Crazy
Louis Armstrong & his Orchestra .... **Parlophone R 854**
The Casa Loma Orchestra ...... **Brunswick 02690**
The Ink Spots .... **Brunswick 02981**
The Benny Goodman Sextet ...... **Columbia SEGC 9**
Rosemary Clooney with
The Benny Goodman Trio .... **Philips BBR 8084**
Matt Monro .... **Ace of Clubs ACL 1069**
Anita O'Day .... **HMV CLP 1352**
Anita O'Day appeared in Drum Crazy.

MEMORY　　　July 1981
Andrew Lloyd Webber / T.S. Elliot / Trevor Nunn
Really Usefull Music Co. .... UK
Show(s): .... Cats
Elaine Page .... **Polydor CATX 001**
Betty Buckley .... **Geffen GEF 8815**
Elaine Page appeared in the British production of Cats.
Betty Buckley appeared in the American production of Cats.
Ivor Novello Award.

MEMORY LANE　　　1924
Buddy De Sylva / Larry Spier / Con Conrad
Chappell & Co. Ltd. .... USA
Fred Waring & his Pennsylvanians .... **HMV B 1851**
Kate Smith .... **MGM D 145**

Connee Boswell .... **Brunswick 02828**

MEMPHIS BLUES　　　1913
William C. Handy
Campbell Connelly & Co. Ltd. .... USA
Fletcher Henderson & his Orchestra ... **Brunswick 02119**
Ted Lewis & his Band .... **Columbia 4609**
Duke Ellington Orchestra .... **HMV B 9690**
Humphrey Lyttelton & his Band .. **Parlophone R 3257**
Nat 'King' Cole .... **Capitol LCT 6156**
Nat 'King' Cole appeared in St. Louis Blues.
Duke Ellington Orchestra appeared in Belle of the Nineties.

MEMPHIS TENNESSEE　　　November 1963
Chuck Berry
Jewel Music Publishing Co. Ltd .... USA
Chuck Berry .... **Pye 7N 25218**
Dave Berry & The Cruisers ..... **Decca F 11374**

MER, LA　　　1947
Charles Trenet
Chappell & Co. Ltd. .... France
Show(s): .... Together Again
Charles Trenet .... **Columbia 33S 1008**
The Montovani Orchestra ...... **Decca LK 4297**
Theme song of Charles Trenet.

MERRILY WE ROLL ALONG　　　1938
Raymond Wallace / Michael Carr
Peter Maurice Music Co. Ltd. .... UK
Billy Cotton & his Band .... **Rex 9326**
The Nick Nack Kids .... **Top Rank 25-005**

MERRY CHRISTMAS EVERYONE　　　December 1985
Bob Heatlie
FMI Music .... UK
Shakin' Stevens .... **Epic A 6769**

MERRY XMAS EVERYBODY　　　December 1973
Noddy Holder / Jimmy Lea
Barn Publishing Ltd. .... UK
Slade .... **Polydor 2058422**
Slade (1983) .... **Polydor 2058**
Ivor Novello Nomination.

MERRY-GO-ROUND BROKE DOWN, THE　　　1937
Cliff Friend / Dave Franklin
Victoria Music Co. Ltd. .... USA
Dick Robertson & his Orchestra,
vocal Dick Robertson .... **Panachord 25928**
Eddy Duchin & his Orchestra ...... **HMV BD 5232**

MESS OF BLUES, A　　　August 1960
Doc Pomus / Mort Shuman
Belinda (London) Ltd .... USA
Elvis Presley .... **RCA 1194**

MESSAGE, THE　　　September 1982
Edward Fletcher / Melvin Glover / Sylvia Robinson / Clifton Chase
Four Hills Music .... USA
Grand Master Flash, Melle Mel
& The Furious Five .... **Sugarhill SHL 117**

MESSAGE IN A BOTTLE　　　October 1979
"Sting"
Virgin Music (Publishers) Ltd. .... UK
Police .... **A&M AMS 7474**

MESSAGE TO MARTHA　　　December 1964
Burt Bacharach / Hal David
Sea-Lark Music Ltd .... USA
Adam Faith .... **Parlophone R 5201**
Lou Johnson .... **London HLX 9929**

MESSAGE TO YOU RUDY (See Rudy-a Message To Rudy)

MESSAGE UNDERSTOOD　　　October 1965
Chris Andrews
Glissando Music Ltd .... UK
Sandie Shaw .... **Pye 7N 15940**

METAL GURU　　　June 1972
Marc Bolan
Wizard Music .... UK

T. Rex . . . . T. Rex MARC 1

MEXICALI ROSE   **1925**
Jack Teeney / Helen Stone
Francis, Day & Hunter Ltd. . . . . USA
Film(s): . . . . Rhythm on the Range / Mexicali Rose
Dick Foran . . . . **Decca F 6296**
Bing Crosby (1939) . . . . **Brunswick LAT 8152**
Slim Whitman . . . . **London HAP 2139**
The Karl Denver Trio (1961) . . . . **Decca F 11395**
Bing Crosby appeared in *Rhythm on the Range.*

MEXICO   **November 1968**
Tony Macaulay / John MacLeod / Anthony Instone & John Allen
Welbeck Music Co. Ltd. . . . . UK
Long John Baldry . . . . **Pye 7N 17563**

MIA BELLA ROSA   **1929**
Ted Koehler / Frank Magine
B. Feldman & Co. Ltd . . . . USA
The New Mayfair Dance Orchestra . . . . **HMV B 5639**

MIAMI VICE   **October 1985**
Jan Hammer
MCA Music . . . . USA
Jan Hammer . . . . **MCA T 1000**
Theme of television series *Miami Vice.*

MICHAEL CAINE   **February 1984**
Charles Smythe / Mark Woodgate
Warner Brothers Music . . . . UK
Madness . . . . **Stiff BUY 196**

MICHAEL ROW THE BOAT ASHORE   **October 1961**
Traditional
An edition by Essex Music Ltd. . . . . USA
Lonnie Donegan . . . . **Pye 7N 15371**
The Highwaymen . . . . **HMV POP 910**

MICHELLE   **February 1966**
John Lennon / Paul McCartney
Northern Songs Ltd. . . . . UK
David & Jonathan . . . . **Columbia DB 7800**
The Overlanders . . . . **Pye 7N 17034**
The Beatles . . . . **Parlophone PMC 1267**
Ivor Novello Award.

MICKEY   **May 1982**
Mike Chapman / Nicky Chinn
Rak Music . . . . UK
Toni Basil . . . . **Radialchoice TIC 4**

MIDAS TOUCH, THE   **November 1986**
Wade Watson
Chappell & Co. Ltd. . . . . USA
Midnight Star . . . . **Solar MCA 1096**

MIDNIGHT DYNAMOS   **June 1980**
Steve Bloomfield
Magnet Music . . . . UK
Matchbox . . . . **Magnet MAG 169**

MIDNIGHT IN MOSCOW (Moscow Nights)   **December 1961**
Vassili Soloviev-Sedoi / Adapted by Kenny Ball
An edition by Tyler Music Ltd. . . . . UK
Kenny Ball's Jazzmen . . . . **Pye 7NJ 2049**

MIDNIGHT RIDER   **January 1976**
Greg Allman
Shapiro-Bernstein & Co. Ltd . . . . USA
Paul Davidson . . . . **Tropical ALO 56**

MIDNIGHT TRAIN TO GEORGIA   **June 1976**
Jim Weatherly
Keith Prowse Music Publishing Co. Ltd . . . . USA
Gladys Knight & The Pips . . . . **Buddah BDS 444**

MIFANWY   **1910**
Dorothy Foster / Frederick E. Weatherly
Chappell & Co. Ltd. . . . . UK
Alice Wilna . . . . **HMV 3952**
Webster Booth . . . . **HMV B 8413**

MIGHTY LAK' A ROSE   **1901**
Ethelbert Nevin / Frank Stanton

Boosey & Hawkes Music Publishers Ltd. . . . . USA
Lilian Nordica . . . . **Columbia 74024**
Paul Robeson . . . . **HMV DLP 1165**
Bing Crosby . . . . **Brunswick 03939**

MIGHTY QUINN   **March 1968**
Bob Dylan
B. Feldman & Co. Ltd. . . . . USA
Manfred Mann . . . . **Fontana TF 897**
Bob Dylan . . . . **CBS S 64086**

MILK AND ALCOHOL   **February 1979**
Nick Lowe / John Mayo
Rock Artistes Music . . . . UK
Dr. Feelgood . . . . **United Artists UP 36468**

MILKMAN KEEP THOSE BOTTLES QUIET   **1944**
Don Raye / Gene De Paul
Chappell & Co. Ltd. . . . . USA
Film(s): . . . . Broadway Rhythm
The R.A.F. Dance Orchestra, vocal Beryl Davis . **Decca F 8477**

MILORD   **August 1959**
Marguerite Monnot / Georges Moustacki / Bunny Lewis
Aberbach (London) Ltd. . . . . France
Edith Piaf . . . . **Columbia 33SX 1276**
Frankie Vaughan . . . . **Philips BBE 12412**

MIMI   **1933**
Richard Rodgers / Lorenz Hart
Victoria Music Co. Ltd. . . . . USA
Film(s): . . . . Love Me Tonight / Pepe
Maurice Chevalier (1932) . . . . **RCA RCX 1057**
Maurice Chevalier (1958) . . . . **MGM C 771**
Enoch Light & his Orchestra & chorus . . . . . **London HAZ 2385**
Maurice Chevalier appeared in *Love Me Tonight* and *Pepe.*

MIND BLOWING DECISIONS   **July 1978**
Johnnie Wilder
Unknown . . . . USA
Heatwave . . . . **GTO GT 226**

MINER'S DREAM OF HOME, THE   **1891**
Will Godwin / Leo Dryden
Francis, Day & Hunter Ltd. . . . . UK
Frank Williams . . . . **Zonophone 78**
Peter Dawson . . . . **HMV B 3543**
David Kossoff . . . . **Oriole MG 20043**

MINNIE FROM TRINIDAD   **1941**
Roger Edens
Francis, Day & Hunter Ltd . . . . USA
Film(s): . . . . The Ziegfeld Girl
Ambrose & his Orchestra, vocal Anne Shelton . . **Decca F 7934**
Adelaide Hall . . . . **Decca F 8031**
Xavier Cugat & his Waldorf
Astoria Orchestra . . . . **Parlophone DP 11**

MINNIE THE MOOCHER   **1932**
Clarence Gaskill / Cab Calloway / Irving Mills
Lawrence Wright Music Co. Ltd. . . . . USA
Film(s): . . . . The Big Broadcast
Cab Calloway & his Orchestra,
vocal Cab Calloway . . . . **Fontana TFE 17216**
Danny Kaye . . . . **Fontana TFE 17180**
Cab Calloway appeared in *The Big Broadcast.*
Theme song of Cab Calloway.

MINUTE OF YOUR TIME, A   **January 1969**
Clive Westlake
Carlin Music Corporation . . . . UK
Tom Jones . . . . **Decca F 12854**

MINUTE YOU'RE GONE, THE   **April 1965**
Jimmy Gateley
Jewel Music Publishing Co. Ltd . . . . USA
Cliff Richard . . . . **Columbia DB 7496**

MIRACLE OF LOVE, THE   **November 1956**
Bob Merrill
Cinephonic Music Co. Ltd. . . . . USA
Marion Ryan . . . . **Pye N 15078**

MIRROR IN THE BATHROOM   **May 1980**
Roger Charlery / Andy Cox / Everett Morton / David Steele / David

Wakeling
Zomba Music Publishers . . . . UK
The Beat . . . . **Go-Feet FEET 2**

MIRROR MAN   December 1982
Philip Oakey / John Callis / Ian Burden
Ten Music . . . . UK
The Human League . . . . **Virgin VS 522**

MIRROR MIRROR   February 1966
Anthony Newman
King Music . . . . UK
Pinkerton's Assorted Colours . . . . **Decca F 12307**

MIRROR MIRROR (Mon Amour)   January 1982
Trevor Horn / Bruce Wooley
Carlin Music . . . . UK
Dollar . . . . **WEA BUCK 2**

MISERY FARM   1929
C. Jay Wallis
Campbell Connelly & Co. Ltd . . . . UK
Tommy Handley . . . . **Piccadilly 222**

MISFIT   July 1987
"Curiosity Killed The Cat"
Warner Brothers Music . . . . UK
Curiosity Killed The Cat . . . . **Mercury CAT 4**

MISIRLOU   1941
N. Roubanis / Milton Leeds / S.K. Russell. Fred Wise
Campbell Connelly & Co. Ltd . . . . Greece
The Nicholas Matthey Oriental Orchestra . . . . . . **Decca F 7762**
Jan August (piano) (1947) . . . . **Brunswick 03952**
Dante Varela & his Orchestra . . . . **Brunswick LAT 8192**
Martin Denny & his Orchestra . . . . **London HAG 2387**

MISS ANNABELLE LEE   1928
Sidney Clare / Lew Pollack / Harry Richman
Francis, Day & Hunter Ltd. . . . . USA
Show(s): . . . . Will o' the Whispers
Film(s): . . . . Gentlemen Marry Brunettes
The California Ramblers . . . . **Riverside RLP 12-801**
Jack Smith . . . . **HMV B 2666**
Jack Jackson & his Orchestra . . . . **HMV B 6550**
Joe Loss & his Orchestra . . . . **HMV DLP 1103**
Jack Smith appeared in *Will O' the Whispers*.

MISS OTIS REGRETS   1934
Cole Porter
Chappell & Co. Ltd . . . . USA
Show(s): . . . . Hi Diddle Diddle
Film(s): . . . . Night and Day
Douglas Byng . . . . **Decca F 5249**
The Mills Brothers . . . . **Brunswick 01887**
Ella Fitzgerald . . . . **HMV CLP 1083**
Jim Lowe . . . . **London HAD 2146**
Nat Gonella & his Georgians,
vocal Nat Gonella . . . . **Columbia 33SX 1380**
Douglas Byng appeared in *Hi Diddle Diddle*.

MISS YOU   1929
Charles Tobias / Harry Tobias
Campbell Connelly & Co. Ltd . . . . USA
Film(s): . . . . Strictly in the Groove
Ben Selvin & his Orchestra . . . . **Columbia 5704**
Bing Crosby (1942) . . . . **Brunswick 03312**
Malcolm Vaughan . . . . **HMV 7EG 8377**
The Four Aces . . . . **Brunswick LAT 8221**
Jimmy Young (1963) . . . . **Columbia DB 7119**

MISS YOU   July 1978
Mick Jagger
EMI Music Ltd . . . . UK
The Rolling Stones . . . . **EMI 2802**

MISS YOU LIKE CRAZY   June 1989
Michael Masser / Gerry Goffin / Preston Glass
Rondor Music . . . . USA
Natalie Cole . . . . **EMI USA MT 63**

MISS YOU NIGHTS   March 1976
Dave Townsend
Island Music Ltd . . . . UK

Cliff Richard . . . . **EMI 2376**
Ivor Novello Nomination.

MISSING YOU   November 1984
John Waite / Charles Sandford / Mark Leonard
Carlin Music . . . . UK
John Waite . . . . **EMI EA 182**

MISSING YOU   December 1988
Chris De Burgh
Rondor Music . . . . UK
Chris De Burgh . . . . **A&M AM 474**

MISSISSIPPI   1917
Harry Tierney / Bert Hanlon / Benny Ryan
Chappell & Co. Ltd. . . . . USA
Show(s): . . . . Hitchy-Koo / The Beauty Spot
Anna Wheaton . . . . **Columbia 2851**

MISSISSIPPI   September 1950
Curley Williams / Billy Simmons
Edward Kassner Music Co. Ltd . . . . USA
Ella Fitzgerald . . . . **Brunswick 04583**
Kay Starr . . . . **Capitol CL 13330**
Clare Hogan & Bobby Wayne . . . . **London L 593**

MISSISSIPPI   November 1976
Werner Theuissen
Noon Music . . . . Germany
Pussycat . . . . **Sonet SON 2077**

MISSISSIPPI MUD   1927
James Cavanaugh / Harry Barris
Campbell Connelly & Co. Ltd. . . . . USA
Film(s): . . . . The King of Jazz
Paul Whiteman & his Orchestra,
vocal The Rhythm Boys . . . . **HMV B 2562**
Frankie Trumbauer & his Orchestra,
vocal Bing Crosby & Frankie Trumbauer . . **Fontana TFE 17060**
Bing Crosby . . . . **Brunswick LAT 8251**
The McGuire Sisters . . . . **Vogue LVA 9024**
Bobby Darin & Johnny Mercer . . . . **London HAK 2363**
Paul Whiteman & his Orchestra appeared in *The King of Jazz*.

MISSOURI WALTZ, THE   1918
J.R. Shannon / Frederick Logan / John Eppell
Chappell & Co. Ltd. . . . . USA
The London Dance Orchestra . . . . **Columbia 732**
Joe Reisman & his Orchestra . . . . **Columbia SEG 8020**
Glenn Miller & his Orchestra . . . . **HMV BD 5644**
Bing Crosby . . . . **Brunswick 02809**
Teddy Johnson & Pearl Carr . . . . **Columbia DB 4260**
Cyril Stapleton & his Orchestra . . . . **Decca LK 4206**

MISTAKES   1928
Horatio Nicholls / Edgar Leslie
Lawrence Wright Music Co. Ltd . . . . UK
The Rhythmic Eight . . . . **Zonophone 5232**
Frank Froba & his Orchestra . . . . **Brunswick 04653**
Vera Lynn . . . . **Decca LK 4305**
Al Morgan (1952) . . . . **Brunswick 04913**

MISTER AND MRS IS THE NAME   1934
Mort Dixon / Alfie Wrubel
B. Feldman & Co. Ltd . . . . USA
Film(s): . . . . Flirtation Walk
Dick Powell . . . . **Decca F 5650**
Dick Powell appeared in *Flirtation Walk*.

MISTER BLUE   November 1959
Dewayne Blackwell
Edwin H. Morris & Co. Ltd . . . . USA
Mike Preston . . . . **Decca F 11167**
David Macbeth . . . . **Nixa N 15231**
Bobby Vee . . . . **London HAG 2320**
The Fleetwoods . . . . **Top Rank JAR 202**

MISTER BLUE SKY   March 1978
Jeff Lynne
United Artists Music Co. Ltd . . . . UK
The Electric Light Orchestra . . . . **Jet UP 36342**

MISTER CUCKOO (Cuculino)   July 1956
Willy Mattes / Walter Brandin / Geoffrey Parsons & John Turner

Macmelodies Ltd. . . . . Germany
Edmundo Ros & his Orchestra . . . . **Decca LF 1297**

MISTER FIVE BY FIVE 1943
Don Raye / Gene De Paul
Peter Maurice Music Ltd . . . . USA
Film(s): . . . . Off the Beaten Track / Always a Bridesmaid
The Andrews Sisters . . . . **Brunswick 03416**
Benny Goodman & his Orchestra,
vocal Jimmy Rushing . . . . **Philips BBL 7300**
The Andrews Sisters appeared in *Always the Bridesmaid.*

MISTER GALLAGHER AND MISTER SHEAN 1923
Ed Gallagher / Al Shean
Lawrence Wright Music Co. Ltd . . . . USA
Show(s): . . . . The Ziegfeld Follies of 1922
Film(s): . . . . The Ziegfeld Girl / Atlantic City
The Two Gilberts . . . . **Regal G 7989**
Bing Crosby & Johnny Mercer . . . . **Brunswick LAT 8306**
Al Shean appeared in *Atlantic City.*

MISTER MEADOWLARK 1940
Walter Donaldson / Johnny Mercer
Edwin H. Morris & Co. Ltd . . . . USA
Bing Crosby & Johnny Mercer . . . . **Brunswick 03171**
Glenn Miller & his Orchestra . . . . **HMV CLPC 5**

MISTER MOON YOU'VE GOT A MILLION SWEETHEARTS 1946
Charlie Chester / Ken Morris
Lawrence Wright Music Co. Ltd. . . . . UK
Charlie Chester & his Gang . . . . **Decca F 8720**
The Skyrockets Dance Orchestra,
vocal Doreen Lundy . . . . **HMV BD 5952**

MISTER RAFFLES (Man It Was Mean) June 1975
Steve Harley
Rak Music Ltd . . . . UK
Steve Harley & Cockney Rebel . . . . **EMI 2299**

MISTER SANDMAN February 1955
Pat Ballard
Edwin H. Morris & Co. Ltd. . . . . USA
Dickie Valentine . . . . **Decca LF 1211**
The Four Aces . . . . **Brunswick OE 9090**
The Cordettes . . . . **Columbia DB 3553**
Dorothy Collins . . . . **Coral LVA 9137**

MISTER SNOW July 1950
Richard Rodgers / Oscar Hammerstein II
Williamson Music Ltd . . . . USA
Show(s): . . . . Carousel
Film(s): . . . . Carousel
Jan Clayton & Jean Darling . . . . **Brunswick LAT 8006**
Eric Mattson & Margot Mosser . . . . . . **Columbia SED 5536**
Barbara Ruick . . . . **Capitol LCT 6105**
Jan Clayton & Jean Darling appeared in the American production of
Carousel.
Eric Mattson & Margot Mosser appeared in the British production of
Carousel.
Barbara Ruick appeared in the film of *Carousel.*

MISTER SOFT September 1974
Steve Harley
Rak Music Ltd. . . . . UK
Cockney Rebel . . . . **EMI 2191**

MISTER TAMBOURINE MAN July 1965
Bob Dylan
Blossom Music Ltd . . . . USA
The Byrds . . . . **CBS S 7596**

MISTER TAP-TOE September 1953
Rich Dehr / Frank Miller / Terry Gilkyson
Montclare Music Co. Ltd. . . . . USA
Doris Day . . . . **Columbia SCM 5062**

MISTER WONDERFUL April 1957
Larry Holofcener / George Weiss / Jerry Bock
Valando Music Co. Ltd. . . . . USA
Show(s): . . . . Mr. Wonderful
Olga James . . . . **Brunswick LAT 8184**
Peggy Lee . . . . **Brunswick LAT 8287**
Joni James . . . . **MGM C 865**
Olga James appeared in *Mr. Wonderful.*

MISTLETOE AND WINE December 1988
Leslie Stewart / Jeremy Paul / Keith Strachan
Southern Music Co. . . . . UK
Cliff Richard . . . . **EMI EM 78**
Ivor Novello Award.

MISTY January 1960
Erroll Garner / Johnny Burke
Bregmann, Vocco & Conn Ltd . . . . USA
The Erroll Garner Trio . . . . **Fontana FJL 103**
Johnny Mathis . . . . **Fontana H 219**
Chris Connor . . . . **London LTZK 15195**
Sarah Vaughan . . . . **Mercury MMC 14011**
Ray Stevens (1975) . . . . **Janus 6146204**

MISTY BLUE August 1976
Bob Montgomery
Intersong Music . . . . USA
Dorothy Moore . . . . **Contempo CS 2087**
Eddy Arnold . . . . **RCA RD 7852**

MISTY ISLANDS OF THE HIGHLANDS 1935
Jimmy Kennedy / Michael Carr
Peter Maurice Music Co. Ltd . . . . UK
Arthur Tracey (The Street Singer) . . . . **Decca F 5713**
Father Sidney MacEwan . . . . **Philips ABL 3263**

MOANIN' LOW 1931
Howard Dietz / Ralph Rainger
Chappell & Co. Ltd . . . . USA
Show(s): . . . . The Little Show
Annette Hanshaw . . . . **Parlophone R 850**
Ella Fitzgerald . . . . **Brunswick LAT 8091**
Lee Morse . . . . **CBS BPG 62547**

MOBILE February 1955
Bob Wells / David Holt
Leeds Music Ltd. . . . . USA
Ray Burns . . . . **Columbia SEG 7594**
Bob Scobey's Frisco Band,
vocal Clancy Hayes . . . . **Vogue LAG 12116**

MOCKING BIRD HILL May 1951
Vaughan Horton
Southern Music Publishing Co. Ltd . . . . USA
Russ Morgan & his Orchestra . . . . **Brunswick 04668**
Patti Page . . . . **Oriole CB 1079**
Les Paul & Mary Ford . . . . **Capitol T 1476**
Burl Ives . . . . **Brunswick LAT 8381**
The Migil Five (1964) . . . . **Pye 7N 15597**

MODEL, THE February 1982
Ralf Hutter / Karl Bartos / Emil Schult
EMI Music . . . . Germany
Kraftwerk . . . . **EMI 5207**

MODERN GIRL September 1980
Dominic Bugatti / Frank Musker
Chappell & Co. Ltd . . . . UK
Sheena Easton . . . . **EMI 5042**

MODERN LOVE October 1983
David Bowie
Mainman Music . . . . UK
David Bowie . . . . **EMI EA 158**

MOLLY 1930
Edmund Goulding / Dan Dougherty
Lawrence Wright Music Co. Ltd . . . . USA
Film(s): . . . . The Grand Parade
Donald Novis . . . . **HMV B 3362**
Donald Novis appeared in *The Grand Parade.*

MOLLY O! 1894
William Scanlan
Francis, Day & Hunter Ltd. . . . . USA
Show(s): . . . . Mavourneen
William Kennedy . . . . **Regal MR 1615**
John Fogarty . . . . **Decca F 5423**

MOLLY O'MORGAN 1909
William Letters / Fred Godfrey
B. Feldman & Co. Ltd. . . . . UK
Florrie Forde . . . . **Zonophone X 43201**

Ella Retford .... Jumbo A 28096

MOMENT I SAW YOU, THE   1931
Howard Dietz / Arthur Schwartz
Chappell & Co. Ltd .... USA
Show(s): .... Three's a Crowd / The Co-Optimists of 1930
Film(s): .... Spring in Park Lane
Stuart Ross & Joe Sargent .... **Parlophone R 653**
Ray Starita & The Ambassadors Orchestra ... **Columbia CB 59**

MOMENTS TO REMEMBER   December 1955
Robert Allen / Al Stillman
Larry Spier Ltd. .... USA
Louis Armstrong .... **Brunswick 05512**
Bing Crosby .... **Brunswick OE 9466**
The Four Lads .... **Philips BBE 12044**

MONA   July 1990
Ella McDaniel
Jewel Music .... USA
Craig McLachlan & Check 1-2 .... **Epic 6557847**

MONA LISA   1932
Henry Sullivan / Desmond Carter
Chappell & Co. Ltd. .... UK
Show(s): .... Bow Bells
Binnie Hale & Andre Randall .... **Columbia DB 743**
Jack Hylton & his Orchestra .... **Decca F 2757**
The New Mayfair Dance Orchestra .... **HMV C 2342**
Binnie Hale & Andre Randall appeared in *Bow Bells*.

MONA LISA   July 1950
Jay Livingston / Ray Evans
New World Publishers Ltd .... USA
Film(s): .... After Midnight
Allan Jones .... **HMV B 9989**
Nat 'King' Cole .... **Capitol T 946**
Bing Crosby .... **Brunswick LAT 8138**
Conway Twitty (1050) .... **MGM C 781**
Academy Award winning song for 1950.

MONDAY MONDAY   July 1966
John Phillips
Dick James Music Ltd. .... USA
The Mamas & The Papas .... **RCA 1516**

MONEY (That's What I Want)   December 1963
Janie Bradford / Berry Gordy Jnr.
Dominion Music Co. Ltd .... USA
Bern Elliott & The Fenmen .... **Decca F 11770**
The Searchers .... **Pye NPL 18066**
The Beatles .... **Parlophone PMC 1206**
The Flying Lizards (1979) .... **Virgin VS 276**

MONEY FOR NOTHING   August 1985
Mark Knopfler'Sting'
Rondor Music .... UK
Dire Straits .... **Vertigo DSTR 10**
Ivor Novello Nomination.

MONEY HONEY   December 1975
Eric Faulkner / Stuart Wood
Carlin Music Corporation .... UK
The Bay City Rollers .... **Bell 1461**

MONEY IN MY POCKET   March 1979
Joe Gibbs / Denis Brown
Lightening Music .... UK
Dennis Brown .... **Atlantic LV 5**

MONEY IS THE ROOT OF ALL EVIL   1946
Joan Whitney / Alex Kramer
Pickwick Music Ltd. .... USA
Show(s): .... High Time
The Andrews Sisters .... **Brunswick 03627**
The Viscounts .... **Pye 7N 15323**

MONEY MONEY MONEY   December 1976
Benny Andersson / Bjorn Ulvaeus
Bocu Music Ltd .... Sweden
Abba .... **Epic 4713**

MONEY SONG, THE   May 1968
John Kander / Fred Ebb

Valando Music Co. Ltd. .... USA
Show(s): .... Cabaret
Film(s): .... Cabaret
Joel Grey .... **Columbia KOL 6640**
Barry Dennen .... **CBS 70039**
Liza Minelli .... **ABC ABCD 752**
Joel Grey appeared in the american production of *Cabaret*.
Barry Dennen appeared in the British production of *Cabaret*.
Liza Minelli appeared in the film of *Cabaret*.

MONKEY   July 1988
George Michael
Morrison Leany Music .... UK
George Michael .... **Epic EMU 6**

MONKEY AND THE ORGAN GRINDER, THE   July 1949
Peter Tinturin
Bradbury Wood Ltd .... USA
Allan Jones .... **HMV B 9780**

MONKEY SPANNER   August 1971
Winston Riley
B&C Music .... UK
Dave & Ansil Collins .... **Technique TE 914**

MONOTONOUS   November 1954
Arthur Siegel / June Carroll
Campbell Connelly & Co. Ltd. .... USA
Show(s): .... New Faces of 1952
Film(s): .... New Faces
Eartha Kitt .... **RCA RCX 138**
Eartha Kitt appeared in both the show and the film.

MONSIEUR DUPONT   March 1969
Christian Bruhn / Peter Callander
Carlin Music Corporation .... Germany
Sandie Shaw .... **Pye 7N 17675**

MONSTER MASH   October 1973
Gary Paxton / Bobby Pickett
Carlin Music Corporation .... USA
Bobby Pickett & The Crypt Kickers .... **London HL 10320**

MONTEGO BAY   October 1970
Jeff Dany / Bobby Bloom
United Artists Music Co. Ltd .... USA
Bobby Bloom .... **Polydor 2058051**
Amazulu (1986) .... **Island IS 293**

MONY MONY   August 1968
Bobby Bloom / Ritchie Cordell / Tommy James / Bo Gentry
Planetary-Nom (London) Ltd. .... USA
Tommy James & The Shondells ...... **Major Minor MM 567**
Billy Idol (1987) .... **Chrysalis IDOL 11**
Amazulu .... **EMI EM 32**

MOOD INDIGO   1931
Duke Ellington / Irving Mills / Albany Bigard
Lawrence Wright Music Co. Ltd .... USA
Duke Ellington & his Orchestra (1930) .... **Philips BBE 12405**
Duke Ellington & his Orchestra (1954) ..... **Philips BBL 7229**
Duke Ellington & his Orchestra,
vocal Rosemary Clooney .... **Philips BBL 7090**
Ella Fitzgerald .... **HMV CLP 1227**

MOODY BLUE   March 1977
Mark James
Screen Gems Music Ltd .... USA
Elvis Presley .... **RCA PB 0857**

MOODY RIVER   July 1961
Gary Bruce
Shapiro-Bernstein & Co. Ltd. .... USA
Pat Boone .... **London HL 9350**

MOON   1932
Michael Caleo / Jack Miles
Dash Music Ltd. .... USA
Melville Gideon .... **HMV B 4329**
Ralph Flanagan & his Orchestra .... **HMV 7M 150**

MOON AND THE WILLOW TREE, THE   1940
Victor Schertzinger / Johnny Burke
Campbell Connelly & Co. Ltd .... USA
Film(s): .... Road to Singapore

Bing Crosby . . . . Brunswick Bing 5
Dorothy Lamour . . . . HMV B 9049
Bing Crosby and Dorothy Lamour appeared in *Road to Singapore*.

MOON AT SEA   1937
Harry Pease / Vincent Rose / Larry Stock
Cinephonic Music Co. Ltd. . . . . USA
Shep Fields & his Rippling Rhythm . . Regal Zonophone MR 2614
Les Allen . . . . Columbia FB 1782

MOON GOT IN MY EYES, THE   1937
Arthur Johnston / Johnny Burke
Campbell Connelly & Co. Ltd. . . . . USA
Film(s): . . . . Double or Nothing
Bing Crosby . . . . Brunswick Bing 3
Jackie Rae . . . . Fontana H 242
Bing Crosby appeared in *Double or Nothing*.

MOON IS LOW   1931
Arthur Freed / Nacio Herb Brown
Robbins Music Corporation Ltd . . . . USA
Film(s): . . . . Montana Moon
George Metaxa . . . . HMV B 3660
'Fats' Waller & his Rhythm . . . . RCA RD 7552
Bonnie Guitar . . . . London HAD 2122

MOON LOVE   1923
P.G. Wodehouse / Jerome Kern
Chappel & Co. Ltd. . . . . USA
Show(s): . . . . Beauty Prize
Jack Hylton Orchestra . . . . HMV B 1743
Victor Sylvester Orchestra . . . . Pye NSPL 18350

MOON OF MANAKOORA, THE   1937
Alfred Newman / Frank Loesser
Victoria Music Co. Ltd. . . . . USA
Film(s): . . . . The Hurricane
Dorothy Lamour . . . . Brunswick 04492
Bing Crosby . . . . Ace of Hearts AH 1
The Arthur Lyman Group . . . . Vogue VA 160174
Dorothy Lamour appeared in *The Hurricane*.

MOON RIVER   November 1961
Henry Mancini / Johnny Mercer
Chappell & Co. Ltd. . . . . USA
Film(s): . . . . Breakfast at Tiffany's
Danny Williams . . . . HMV POP 932
Henry Mancini & his Orchestra & chorus . . . . . . RCA 1256
Jane Morgan . . . . London RED 1331
Greyhound (1972) . . . . Trojan TR 7848
Academy Award winning song for 1961.

MOON SONG (That Wasn't Meant for Me)   1933
Sam Coslow / Arthur Johnston
Victoria Music Co. Ltd. . . . . USA
Film(s): . . . . Hello Everybody
Morton & Ridley (vocal duet) . . . . Parlophone R 1503
Annette Hanshaw . . . . Panachord 25413
Mel Tormé . . . . HMV CLP 1445
Sue Raney . . . . Capitol T 964

MOON WAS YELLOW, THE   1935
Fred Ahlert / Edgar Leslie
Francis, Day & Hunter Ltd . . . . USA
Bing Crosby . . . . Brunswick OE 9472
Jane Morgan . . . . London HAR 2244

MOONBEAM KISS HER FOR ME   1927
Harry Woods / Mort Dixon
Francis, Day & Hunter Ltd . . . . USA
Jim Miller & Charlie Farrell . . . . HMV B 2456

MOONBURN   1936
Hoagy Carmichael / Edward Heyman
Chappell & Co. Ltd . . . . USA
Film(s): . . . . Anything Goes
Bing Crosby . . . . Brunswick Bing 2
Bing Crosby appeared in *Anything Goes*.

MOONGLOW   1934
Will Hudson / Eddie Le Lange / Irving Mills
Lafleur & Co. Ltd . . . . USA
Show(s): . . . . Blackbirds of 1934
Film(s): . . . . Picnic / The Benny Goodman Story

Ethel Waters . . . . Brunswick 03026
The Benny Goodman Quartet . . . . HMV 7EG 8003
Benny Goodman & his Orchestra . . . . Brunswick LAT 8103
The Columbia Pictures Orchestra,
conducted by Morris Stoloff . . . . Brunswick LAT 8177
The Cliff Adams Singers . . . . Columbia 33SX 1362

MOONLIGHT   1921
Con Conrad
B. Feldman & Co. Ltd . . . . USA
Paul Whiteman & his Orchestra . . . . HMV B 1251
Richard Hayes & his Orchestra . . . . Oriole CB 1227
Eddie Dexter . . . . Capitol CL 14371

MOONLIGHT AND ROSES   1926
Edwin Lemare / Neil Moret / Ben Black
Francis, Day & Hunter Ltd. . . . . USA
Film(s): . . . . Tin Pan Alley
The Savoy Havana Band . . . . HMV B 2171
Bonnie Guitar . . . . London HAD 2122
Adapted from "Andantino in D Flat Major" by Lemare.

MOONLIGHT AND SHADOWS   1937
Frederick Hollander / Leo Robin
Victoria Music Co. Ltd. . . . . USA
Film(s): . . . . Jungle Princess
Dorothy Lamour . . . . Brunswick 02416
Bing Crosby . . . . Brunswick LA 8514
Bonnie Guitar . . . . London HAD 2122
Dorothy Lamour appeared in *Jungle Princess*.

MOONLIGHT BAY   1912
Edward Madden / Percy Wenrich
B. Feldman & Co. Ltd . . . . USA
Film(s): . . . . Tin Pan Alley / On Moonlight Bay
Herbert Payne . . . . Zonophone 935
Alice Faye . . . . Reprise R 6029
The Mills Brothers . . . . Brunswick 04453
Bing Crosby . . . . Brunswick OE 9027
The George Mitchell Singers . . . . HMV CLP 1399
Alice Faye appeared in *Tin Pan Alley*.

MOONLIGHT BECOMES YOU   1942
Johnny Burke / Jimmy Van Heusen
Victoria Music Co. Ltd . . . . USA
Film(s): . . . . Road to Morocco
Bing Crosby . . . . Brunswick Bing 8
Jimmy Young . . . . Columbia 33SX 1102
Bing Crosby appeared in *Road to Morocco*.

MOONLIGHT COCKTAIL   1942
C. Luckeyth Roberts / Kim Gannon
Chappell & Co. Ltd . . . . USA
Film(s): . . . . A Night in Casablanca
Glenn Miller & his Orchestra, vocal
Ray Eberle & The Modernaires . . . . RCA RCX 1040
Bing Crosby . . . . Brunswick LA 8620
C. Luckeyth (Lucky) Roberts (piano) . . . . . London HBU 1057
Ray Eberle & The Modernaires . . . . Vogue LVA 9103
Adapted from "Ripples of the Nile" by C. Luckeyth Roberts.

MOONLIGHT GAMBLER, THE   February 1957
Phil Springer / Bob Hilliard
Edwin H. Morris & Co. Ltd. . . . . USA
Frankie Laine . . . . Philips BBE 12130

MOONLIGHT IN VERMONT   November 1950
Karl Suessdorf / John Blackburn
Chappell & Co. Ltd . . . . USA
Margaret Whiting . . . . Capitol T 9103
Chris Connor . . . . London LTZK 15151
Mel Tormé . . . . HMV CLP 1445

MOONLIGHT MADONNA (See My Moonlight Madonna)

MOONLIGHT ON THE ALSTER   1935
Osacar Fetras
Bosworth & Co. Ltd . . . . Germany
Orchestre Mascotte . . . . Parlophone R 1880
Albert Sandler & his Orchestra . . . . Columbia FB 1688
The Vienna State Opera Orchestra . . . . . . Vanguard PVL 7067

MOONLIGHT ON THE COLORADO   1931
Robert King / Billy Moll

Campbell Connelly & Co. Ltd .... USA
Nat Shilkret & his Orchestra .... HMV B 5919
Bonnie Guitar .... London HAD 2122

MOONLIGHT ON THE GANGES 1926
Chester Wallace / Sherman Myers
Campbell Connelly & Co. Ltd. .... UK
The Savoy Havana Band .... HMV B 5094
The Sauter-Finigan Orchestra .... HMV CLP 1469

MOONLIGHT ON THE RIVER 1932
Bud Green
Dash Music Ltd. .... USA
Melville Gideon .... HMV B 4265

MOONLIGHT SAVING TIME 1931
Irving Kahal / Harry Richman
Francis, Day & Hunter Ltd. .... USA
Ruth Etting .... Columbia DB 571
Blossom Dearie .... Felsted SDL 86034

MOONLIGHT SERENADE 1939
Glenn Miller / Mitchell Parish
Robbins Music Corporation Ltd. .... USA
Film(s): .... The Glenn Miller Story
Glenn Miller & his Orchestra .... RCA RCX 1003
Henry Jerome & his Orchestra .... Brunswick LAT 8379
The Universal International Studio Orchestra . Brunswick LA 8647
Glenn Miller Orchestra (1976) .... RCA 2644
The Universal International Studio Orchestra appeared in *The Glenn Miller Story*.
Theme tune of Glenn Miller.

MOONLIGHT SHADOW July 1983
Mike Oldfield
Virgin Music .... UK
Mike Oldfield .... Virgin VS 586
Ivor Novello Nomination.

MOONLIGHTING October 1975
Leo Sayer / Frank Farrell
Compass Music Ltd .... UK
Leo Sayer .... Chrysalis CHS 2076

MOONLIGHTING March 1987
Al Jarreau / Lee Holdridge
Minder Music .... USA
Al Jarreau .... WEA U 8407
Theme of the television series *Moonlighting*.

MOONSHINE SALLY July 1975
Mike Chapman / Nicky Chinn
Chinnichap Music .... UK
Mud .... Rak 208

MOONSTRUCK 1909
Ivan Caryll / Lionel Monckton
Chappell & Co. Ltd. .... UK
Show(s): .... Our Miss Gibbs
Gertie Millar .... HMV 03215
Gwen Catley .... Pye CCT 31006
Gertie Millar appeared in *Our Miss Gibbs*.

MOONSTRUCK 1933
Sam Coslow / Arthur Johnston
Victoria Music Co. Ltd. .... USA
Film(s): .... College Humour
Bing Crosby .... Brunswick 01562
Al Bowlly .... Decca F 3627
Bing Crosby appeared in *College Humour*.

MORE September 1956
Alex Alstone / Tom Glazer
Berry Music Ltd. .... USA
Jimmy Young .... Decca DFE 6404

MORE June 1963
Nino Oliviero / Riz Ortolani / Norman Newell
Ardmore & Beechwood Ltd .... Italy
Film(s): .... Mondo Cane
Danny Williams .... HMV POP 1150
The Mantovani Orchestra .... Decca LK 4640
Andy Williams .... CBS BPG 62372
Nancy Wilson .... Capitol T 2351
Perry Como .... HMV POP 240

Robert Earl .... Philips PB 622
Nominated for an Academy Award 1963

MORE AND MORE 1945
Jerome Kern / E.Y. Harburg
Chappell & Co. Ltd. .... USA
Film(s): .... Can't Help Singing
Deanna Durbin .... Brunswick 03570
Deanna Durbin appeared in *Can't Help Singing*.
Nominated for an Academy Award 1945.

MORE I SEE YOU, THE 1945
Mack Gordon / Harry Warren
Bregman, Vocca & Conn Ltd. .... USA
Film(s): .... The Diamond Horseshoe
Dick Haymes .... Brunswick 03582
Julie London .... London HAW 2229
Dick Haymes .... Capitol LC 6823
Joy Marshall (1966) .... Decca F 12422
Chris Montez (1966) .... Pye 7N 25369
Dick Haymes appeared in *The Diamond Horseshoe*.

MORE LIKE THE MOVIES April 1978
Shel Silverstein
Essex Music Ltd .... USA
Dr Hook .... Capitol CL 15967

MORE MORE MORE May 1976
Greg Diamond
Intersong Music .... USA
Andrea True Connection .... Buddah BDS 442

MORE THAN A WOMAN June 1978
Robin Gibb / Maurice Gibb / Barry Gibb
Chappell & Co. Ltd .... UK
Film(s): .... Saturday Night Fever
Tavares .... Capitol CL 15977

MORE THAN I CAN SAY June 1961
Jerry Allison / Sonny Curtis
Southern Music Publishing Co. Ltd .... USA
The Crickets .... Coral LVA 9142
Bobby Vee .... London HL 9316
Leo Sayer (1980) .... Chrysalis CHS 2442

MORE THAN IN LOVE June 1981
Barry Leng / Simon May
A.T.V. Music .... UK
Kate Robbins .... RCA 69

MORE THAN LOVE September 1966
Norman Newell / Ernest Ponticelli
Keith Prowse Music Publishing Co. Ltd. .... UK
Ken Dodd .... Columbia DB 7976
Adapted from the Second Movement of 'The Sonata for Piano No. 8 in C. Minor, Opus 13' by Ludwig Van Beethoven (1770-1827).

MORE THAN THIS April 1982
Brian Ferry
E.G. Music .... UK
Roxy Music .... Polydor ROXY 3

MORE THAN YOU KNOW 1930
Vincent Youmans / Edward Eilscu / Billy Rose
Campbell Connelly & Co. Ltd .... USA
Show(s): .... Great Day
Film(s): .... Hit the Deck / Encore / Both Ends of the Candle
Helen Morgan .... HMV B 3534
Layton & Johnstone .... Columbia DB 315
Mildred Bailey .... Brunswick LA 8692
Perry Como (1947) .... HMV BD 1156
Jane Froman .... Capitol LC 6605
Tony Martin .... MGM EP 526
Gogi Grant .... RCA RD 27054
Gale Storm .... London HAD 2104
Barbra Streisand .... Arista ARTY 101
Helen Morgan appeared in *Great Day*. Tony Martin appeared in the 1955 film of *Hit The Deck*.
Barbra Streisand appeared in *Funny Lady*.

MORE WE ARE TOGETHER, THE 1926
Irving King
Campbell Connelly & Co. Ltd. .... UK
Jack Hylton & his Orchestra .... HMV B 5183
Russ Morgan & his Orchestra .... Brunswick 03892

The Bowman-Hyde Singers & players .. Parlophone PMC 1155

MORNING January 1972
Bill Graham
M.A.M. (Music Publishing) Ltd .... USA
Val Doonican .... **Philips 6006177**

MORNING HAS BROKEN January 1972
Eleanor Farjeon
Freshwater Music .... UK
Cat Stevens .... **Island WIP 6121**
Based on the melody of *Bunessan*

MORNINGSIDE OF THE MOUNTAIN, THE February 1975
Dick Manning / Larry Stock
Warner Brothers Music Ltd .... USA
Donny & Marie Osmond .... **MGM 2006474**
Tommy Edwards .... **MGM 436**
Larry Cross .... **Parlophone R 3443**

MORNINGTOWN RIDE February 1967
Malvina Reynolds
Compass Music Ltd. .... USA
The Seekers .... **Columbia DB 8060**

MOSES 1952
Roger Edens / Betty Comden / Adolph Green
Francis, Day & Hunter Ltd. .... USA
Show(s): .... Singin' in the Rain
Film(s): .... Singin' in the Rain
Gene Kelly & Donald O'Connor .... **MGM 491**
Tommy Steele & Roy Castle .... **Safari RAIN 1**
Gene Kelly & Donald O'Connor appeared in the film *Singin' in the Rain.*
Tommy Steele & Roy Castle appeared in the show *Singin' in the Rain.*

MOST BEAUTIFUL GIRL IN THE WORLD 1935
Richard Rodgers / Lorenz Hart
Chappell & Hart Co Ltd .... USA
Show(s): .... Jumbo
Film(s): .... Jumbo
The New York Philharmonic Orchestra, conductor Richard Rodgers .... **Philips BBL 7097**
Guy Lombardo & his Royal Canadians .. **Brunswick LAT 8063**
The Living Strings, conducted by Hill Bowen .. **RCA RD 27188**
Jimmy Durante .... **CBS BPG 62118**
Jimmy Durante appeared in the film *Jumbo.*

MOST BEAUTIFUL GIRL, THE April 1974
Rory Bourke / Billy Sherrill / Norris Wilson
Gallico Music Ltd. .... USA
Charlie Rich .... **Epic 1897**
Engelbert Humperdinck .... **Decca SKL 5163**

MOST GENTLEMEN DON'T LIKE LOVE 1939
Cole Porter
Chappell & Co. Ltd. .... USA
Show(s): .... Leave it to Me / Black Velvet
Pat Kirkwood .... **HMV BD 785**
Bill Savill & his Orchestra .... **Decca LK 4285**
Pat Kirkwood appeared in *Black Velvet.*

M-O-T-H-E-R 1915
Theodore F. Morse / Howard Johnson
Ascherberg, Hopwood & Crew Ltd. .... USA
Bobby Breen .... **Decca F 6177**
Andy Cole .... **Major Minor SMPC 5011**
The Adams Singers .... **Pye NPL 28013**

MOTHER AND CHILD REUNION March 1972
Paul Simon
Pattern Music Ltd .... USA
Paul Simon .... **CBS 7793**

MOTHER MACHREE 1910
Ernest Ball / Rida Johnson Young / Chauncey Olcott
B. Feldman & Co. Ltd. .... USA
Show(s): .... Barry of Ballimore
Film(s): .... Doughboys in Ireland
John McCormack .... **Camden CDN 1002**
Eileen Donaghy .... **Fontana TFL 5036**
Theme song of John McCormack.

MOTHER NATURE AND FATHER TIME August 1953
Kay Twomey / Fred Wise / Ben Wiseman

Aberbach Music Ltd. .... USA
Nat King Cole .... **Capitol CL 13912**
Dick James .... **Parlophone R 3706**
Ray Burns .... **Columbia DB 3306**

MOTHER O' MINE 1903
Frank Tours / Rudyard Kipling
Chappell & Co. Ltd. .... UK
Richard Crooks .... **Camden CDN 1019**

MOTHER OF MINE March 1972
Bill Parkinson
Chappell & Co. Ltd .... UK
Neil Reid .... **Decca F 13264**

MOTOR BIKING September 1975
Chris Spedding
Island Music Ltd .... UK
Chris Spedding .... **Rak 210**

MOULDY OLD DOUGH November 1972
Nigel Fletcher / Robert Woodward
Campbell, Connelly & Co. Ltd. .... UK
Lieutenant Pigeon .... **Decca F 13278**
Ivor Novello Award.

MOUNTAIN GREENERY 1927
Richard Rodgers / Lorenz Hart
Chappell & Co. Ltd. .... USA
Show(s): .... Garrick Gaieties / The Girl Friend
Film(s): .... Words and Music
The Roger Wolfe Kahn Orchestra .... **HMV B 5313**
Frank Crumit .... **HMV B 2526**
Mel Tormé (1956) .... **Vogue LVA 9098**
Ella Fitzgerald .... **HMV CLP 1117**

MOUNTAINS OF MOURNE 1910
Traditional
An edition by Keith Prowse Music Publishing Co. Ltd. .... UK
Browning Mummary .... **Zonophone 484**
Joe Lynch .... **Beltona EBL 525**

MOUNTIES, THE 1925
Rudolf Frimi / Otto Harbach / Oscar Hammerstein II
Chappell & Co. Ltd. .... USA
Show(s): .... Rose Marie
Film(s): .... Rose Marie
John Dunsmure & Chorus .... **Columbia 3639**
Nelson Eddy .... **RCA RCX 1051**
Howard Keel .... **MGM D 128**
John Dunsmure appeared in the British production of *Rose Marie.*
Nelson Eddy appeared in the 1936 film of *Rose Marie.*
Howard Keel appeared in the 1954 film of *Rose Marie.*

MOVE AWAY March 1986
George O'Dowd / Roy Hay / John Moss, Michael Craig & Phil Pickett
Virgin Music .... UK
Culture Club .... **Virgin VS 845**

MOVE CLOSER May 1985
Phyllis Nelson
Lawrence Welk Music .... USA
Phyllis Nelson .... **Carrere CAR 337**

MOVE IT September 1985
Ian Samwell
Bradbury Wood Music .... UK
Cliff Richard .... **Columbia DB 4178**

MOVE ON UP September 1971
Curtis Mayfield
Camad Publishers .... USA
Curtis Mayfield .... **Buddah 2318015**

MOVE OVER DARLING April 1964
Terry Melcher / Hal Kanter / Joe Lubin
California Music Ltd .... USA
Film(s): .... Move Over Darling
Doris Day .... **CBS AAG 183**
Frank Chacksfield & his Orchestra .... **Decca DFE 8572**
Helen Shapiro .... **Columbia 33SX 1661**
Tracy Ullman (1983) .... **Stiff BUY 195**
Doris Day appeared in *Move Over Darling.*

MOZART 40   **May 1971**
Ellis Rich / Ben Kelsey
B. Feldman & Co. Ltd ....
Wadlo De Los Rios .... **A&M AMLS 2014**
Adapted from 1st Movement (Allegro Moito) of *Symphony No. 40 in
G Minor (K550)* by Wolfgang Amadeus Mozart (1756 - 1791).

MRS WORTHINGTON   **1935**
Noel Coward
Chappell & Co. Ltd .... UK
Noel Coward .... **HMV CLP 1050**
Lucie Mannheim .... **Columbia DB 1600**

**MRS. BROWN YOU'VE GOT A
LOVELY DAUGHTER**   **August 1965**
Trevor Peacock
Good Music Ltd .... UK
Herman's Hermits .... **Columbia 33SX 1727**
Ivor Novello Nomination.

MRS. ROBINSON   **August 1968**
Paul Simon
Pattern Music Ltd. .... USA
Film(s): .... The Graduate
Simon & Garfunkel .... **CBS 3443**

Ms GRACE   **January 1975**
John Hall / Johanne Hall
Intersong Music .... USA
The Tymes .... **RCA 2493**

MUCKING ABOUT THE GARDEN   **1929**
Q. Cumber (Leslie Sarony)
Lawrence Wright Music Co. Ltd .... UK
**Jack Payne & The BBC Dance Orchestra,
vocal Leslie Sarony & Tommy Handley** ...... **Columbia 5555**
George Buck .... **Decca F 1545**

MUDDY WATER   **1927**
Jo Trent / Peter De Rose / Henry Richman
Lawrence Wright Music Co. Ltd. .... USA
**Gene Austin, piano accompaniment
by Peter De Rose** .... **HMV B 2529**
Bessie Smith .... **Parlophone R 2478**
Bing Crosby .... **Brunswick LAT 8251**

MULE TRAIN   **November 1949**
Johnny Lange / Hy Heath / Fred Glickman
Chappell & Co. Ltd .... USA
Film(s): .... Mule Train / Singing Guns
Vaughn Monroe .... **RCA RCX 1043**
Bing Crosby .... **Brunswick LAT 8052**
Frankie Laine .... **Philips BBL 7468**
Vaughn Monroe appeared in *Singing Guns*.
Nominated for an Academy Award 1950.

MULL OF KINTYRE   **January 1978**
Paul McCartney / Denny Laine
A.T.V. Music Ltd. .... UK
Wings .... **Parlophone R 6018**
Ivor Novello Award 1977.
Ivor Novello Nomination 1978.

MULTIPLICATION   **January 1962**
Bobby Darin
Barton Music Co. Ltd. .... USA
Film(s): .... Come September
Bobby Darin .... **London HL 9476**
Bobby Darin appeared in *Come September*.

'MURDER' HE SAYS   **1943**
Jimmy McHugh / Frank Loesser /
Chappell & Co. Ltd .... USA
Film(s): .... Happy Go Lucky / Jam Session
**Jimmy Dorsey & his Orchestra,
vocal Helen O'Connell** .... **Brunswick 03443**
Teddy Powell & his Orchestra .. **Hollywood Soundstage HS 5014**
Dinah Shore .... **HMV BD 1058**
Teddy Powell & his Orchestra appeared in *Jam Session*.

MUSCLE BOUND   **May 1981**
Gary Kemp
Reformation Music .... UK
Spandau Ballet .... **Chrysalis CHS 2509**

MUSIC   **April 1976**
John Miles
Rak Music Ltd .... UK
John Miles .... **Decca F 31267**
Ivor Novello Award.

MUSIC AND LIGHTS   **July 1982**
Tony Swain / Steve Jolly / Lee John / Ashley Ingram
Red Bus Music .... UK
Imagination .... **R&B RBS 210**

MUSIC GOES 'ROUND AND 'ROUND, THE   **1936**
Edward Farley / Michael Riley / 'Red' Hodgson
Campbell Connelly & Co. Ltd .... USA
Film(s): .... The Music Goes 'Round / The Five Pennies
Farley & Riley's Onyx Club Boys .... **Brunswick RL 325**
The Boswell Sisters .... **Brunswick 02142**
Henry Hall & his Orchestra ...... **Columbia 33SX 1067**
The Johnny Mann Singers .... **London HAG 2297**
Danny Kaye & Louis Armstrong .... **London HAU 2189**
Danny Kaye & Louis Armstrong appeared in *The Five Pennies*.

MUSIC MAESTRO PLEASE   **1938**
Herb Magidson / Allie Wrubel
Chappell & Co. Ltd. .... USA
Show(s): .... These Foolish Things
Frances Day .... **HMV B 8793**
Flanagan & Allen .... **Columbia 33S 1010**
Lew Stone & his Band, vocal Al Bowlly ..... **Decca DFE 6574**
Jeri Southern .... **Columbia 33SX 1155**
The Clark Sisters .... **London HAD 2128**
Frances Day & Flanagan & Allen appeared in *These Foolish Things*.
Theme song of The Harry Leader Orchestra.

MUSIC MAKERS, THE   **1941**
Don Raye / Harry James
Chappell & Co. Ltd .... USA
Harry James & his Orchestra .... **Capitol I C 6800**
The Clark Sisters .... **London HAD 2128**

MUSIC OF THE NIGHT   **February 1987**
Andrew Lloyd Webber / Charles Hart / Richard Stilgoe
Really Usefull Music .... UK
Show(s): .... Phantom of the Opera
Michael Crawford .... **Polydor POSP 803**
Michael Crawford appeared in both the British and American produc-
tion of *Phantom of the Opera*.

MUSIC STOPPED, THE   **1944**
Harold Adamson / Jimmy McHugh
Victoria Music Co. Ltd. .... USA
Film(s): .... Higher and Higher
Frank Sinatra .... **Fontana SET 303B**
Frank Sinatra appeared in *Higher and Higher*.

MUSIC TO WATCH GIRLS BY   **June 1967**
Tony Velona / Sidney Ramin
Keith Prowse Music Publishing Co. Ltd. .... USA
Andy Williams .... **CBS 2675**

MUSIC, MUSIC, MUSIC   **February 1950**
Stephen Weiss / Bernie Baum
Leeds Music Ltd .... USA
Teresa Brewer .... **London L 604**
Ronnie Aldrich & The Dreamers ...... **Ace of Clubs ACL 1051**
Teresa Brewer .... **Vogue LVA 9020**

MUSKRAT   **October 1961**
Merle Travis / Harold Hensley / Tex Ann
Campbell Connelly & Co. Ltd. .... USA
The Everly Brothers ...... **Warner Brothers WB 50**

MUSKRAT RAMBLE   **1926**
Edward 'Kid' Ory / Ray Gilbert
Herman Darewski Music Publishing Co. Ltd. .... USA
Louis Armstrong & his Hot Five .... **Parlophone PMC 1140**
Bob Crosby & his Orchestra .... **Decca F 6067**
Bing Crosby & Louis Armstrong .... **MGM C 844**

MUST BE MADISON   **December 1962**
Jack Woodman
Baton Music Ltd .... UK
Joe Loss & his Orchestra .... **HMV POP 1075**

MUST TO AVOID, A February 1966
Steve Barri / P.F. Sloan
Dick James Music Ltd. . . . . USA
Film(s): . . . . Hold on
Herman's Hermits . . . . **Columbia DB 7791**
Herman's Hermits appeared in *Hold On*.

MUSTAFA May 1960
Bob Azzam / Bob Merrill
Leeds Music Ltd . . . . France
Bob Azzam & his Orchestra . . . . **Decca F 21235**
Clinton Ford . . . . **Oriole CB 1551**
The Four Lads . . . . **Philips PB 1051**

MY ADOBE HACIENDA 1947
Louise Massey / Lee Penny
Southern Music Publishing Co. Ltd. . . . . USA
Film(s): . . . . The Big Sombrero
Kenny Baker . . . . **Brunswick 03816**
The Browns . . . . **RCA RCX 187**

MY AIN FOLK 1904
Wilfred Mills / Laura G. Lemon
Boosey & Hawkes Music Publishers Ltd. . . . . UK
Dame Clara Butt . . . . **Columbia X 341**
Kenneth McKellar . . . . **Decca DFE 6576**

MY BABY JUST CARES FOR ME 1930
Walter Donaldson / Gus Kahn
Francis, Day & Hunter Ltd . . . . USA
Show(s): . . . . Whoopee
Film(s): . . . . Whoopee
Ambrose & his Orchestra, vocal Sam Browne . . . . **HMV B 5916**
Pat Boone . . . . **London HAD 2144**
Maurice Chevalier . . . . **MGM C 826**
Nina Simone (1987) . . . . **Charly CYZ 7112**

MY BABY LOVES LOVIN' March 1970
Roger Cook / Roger Greenaway
Cookaway Music . . . . UK
White Plains . . . . **Deram DM 280**

MY BEAUTIFUL LADY 1912
Ivan Caryll / C.M.S. McLellan
Chappell & Co. Ltd . . . . USA
Show(s): . . . . The Pink Lady
Film(s): . . . . The Actress
Idelle Patterson . . . . **Columbia 1817**
Lucy Isabel Marsh . . . . **HMV GC 3888**
Philip Green & his Orchestra . . . . **Parlophone MSP 6071**
Harry Davidson Orchestra . . . . **Columbia S 1045**
Frank Chacksfield Orchestra . . . . **Decca LK 4198**

MY BEST FRIEND'S GIRL December 1978
Rik Okasek
Carlin Music Corporation . . . . USA
Cars . . . . **Elektra K 12301**

MY BLACKBIRDS ARE BLUEBIRDS NOW 1929
Irving Caesar / Cliff Friend
Francis, Day & Hunter Ltd . . . . USA
Show(s): . . . . Whoopee
Film(s): . . . . Lucky Boy
The Hollywood Dance Orchestra . . . . **Edison Bell Winner 4881**

MY BLUE HEAVEN 1927
Walter Donaldson / George Whiting
Francis, Day & Hunter Ltd. . . . . USA
Show(s): . . . . Will o' the Whispers
Film(s): My Blue Heaven / Love Me or Leave Me / The Five Pennies
Paul Whiteman & his Orchestra,
vocal Bing Crosby . . . . **HMV B 5366**
Gene Austin . . . . **HMV B 2644**
Jack Smith . . . . **HMV B 2665**
Gene Austin . . . . **RCA RCX 113**
Bing Crosby . . . . **Brunswick LAT 8138**
Jack Smith appeared in *Will o' the Whispers*.
Theme song of Gene Austin.

MY BOOMERANG WON'T COME BACK October 1961
Max Diamond / Charlie Drake
Kaye Music Co. Ltd. . . . . UK
Charlie Drake . . . . **Parlophone R 4824**

MY BOY December 1974
Bill Martin / Phil Coulter
Mews Music . . . . UK
Elvis Presley . . . . **RCA 2458**
Richard Harris . . . . **Probe PRO 540**

MY BOY LOLLIPOP May 1964
Johnny Roberts / Morris Levy
Planetary Nom (London) Ltd . . . . USA
Millie . . . . **Fontana TF 449**
See also 'My Girl Lollipop'

MY BRITISH BUDDY 1943
Irving Berlin
Irving Berlin Ltd . . . . USA
Film(s): . . . . This is the Army
Irving Berlin . . . . **HMV B 9355**
Carroll Gibbons & his Orchestra,
vocal Leslie Douglas . . . . **Columbia FB 2986**
Irving Berlin appeared in the British production of *This is the Army*.

MY BROTHER JAKE June 1971
Andy Fraser / Paul Rodgers
Blue Mountain Music . . . . UK
Free . . . . **Island WIP 6100**

MY BUDDY 1923
Gus Kahn / Walter Donaldson
Francis, Day & Hunter Ltd . . . . USA
Film(s): . . . . I'll See You in My Dreams
The International Novelty Orchestra . . . . **HMV B 1558**
Bing Crosby . . . . **Brunswick 04740**
Teresa Brewer . . . . **Vogue LVA 9020**
Dinah Shore . . . . **Capitol T 1296**
Doris Day . . . . **Caliban 6008**
Doris Day appeared in *I'll See You in My Dreams*.

MY CAMERA NEVER LIES April 1982
Andy Hill / Nicholas Martin
Paper Music . . . . UK
Bucks Fizz . . . . **RCA 202**

MY CASTLE ON THE NILE 1901
James Weldon Johnson / Bob Cole / J. Rosamond Johnson
Campbell Connelly & Co. Ltd. . . . . USA
The Deep River Boys . . . . **HMV B 10633**

MY CHERIE AMOUR September 1969
Stevie Wonder / Henry Cosby / Sylvia Moy
Jobete Music (UK) Ltd. USA
Stevie Wonder . . . . **Tamla Motown TMG 690**

MY COLOURING BOOK February 1963
John Kander / Frederick Ebb
Valando Music Co. Ltd . . . . USA
Nana Mouskouri . . . . **Fontana TE 17420**
Kitty Kallen . . . . **RCA 1324**
Maureen Evans . . . . **Oriole PS 40046**
Brenda Lee . . . . **Brunswick LAT 8530**
Jackie Trent . . . . **Pye NPL 18125**

MY COO-CA-CHOO January 1973
Peter Shelley
Magnet Music . . . . UK
Alvin Stardust . . . . **Magnet MAG 1**

MY CROONY MELODY 1914
E. Ray Goetz / Joe Goodwin
B. Feldman & Co. Ltd. USA
Alfred Collins & Byron G. Hanlan . . . . **HMV B 515**

MY CURLY HEADED BABBY (See Ma Curly Headed Babby)

MY CUTIES DUE AT TWO TO TWO TODAY 1927
Albert Von Tilzer / Leo Robin
Lawrence Wright Music Co. Ltd. . . . . USA
Ted Weems & his Orchestra, vocal Parker Gibbs . . . **HMV B 5145**
Betty Hutton . . . . **Capitol CL 14117**
Bobby Darin & Johnny Mercer . . . . **London HAK 2363**

MY DARLING 1933
Edward Heyman / Richard Myers
Chappell & Co. Ltd. . . . . USA
Show(s): . . . . Earl Carroll's Vanities

Elsie Carlisle .... **Decca F 3507**
Roger Coleman .... **Brunswick 05072**

MY DARLING, MY DARLING   May 1949
Frank Loesser
Edwin H. Morris & co. Ltd .... USA
Show(s): .... Where's Charley
Film(s): .... Where's Charley
Terence Cooper & Pamela Gale .... **Columbia 33SX 1085**
Sarah Vaughan .... **Mercury MMC 14024**
Paul Weston & his Orchestra .... **Capitol T 1563**
Terence Cooper & Pamlea Gale appeared in the British production of
Where's Charley.

MY DEAR LITTLE CINGALEE   1904
Lionel Monckton / Adrian Ross / Percy Greenbank
Chappell & Co. Ltd. .... UK
Show(s): .... The Cingalee
Stanley Kirby .... **HMV GC 3-2110**

MY DEAREST DEAR   1939
Ivor Novello / Christopher Hassall
Chappell & Co. Ltd. .... UK
Show(s): .... The Dancing Show
Mary Ellis & Ivor Novello .... **HMV DLP 1028**
Teddy Johnson & Pearl Carr .... **Columbia DB 4603**
Mary Ellis & Ivor Novello appeared in *The Dancing Years.*

MY DEFENSES ARE DOWN   1947
Irving Berlin
Irving Berlin Ltd. .... USA
Show(s): .... Annie Get Your Gun
Film(s): .... Annie Get Your Gun
Ray Middleton .... **Brunswick LA 8002**
Bill Johnson .... **Columbia SEG 7711**
Howard Keel .... **MGM D 146**
Ray Middleton appeared in the American production of *Annie Get
Your Gun.*
Bill Johnson appeared in the British production of *Annie Get Your Gun.*
Howard Keel appeared in the film of *Annie Get Your Gun.*

MY DEVOTION   1943
Roc Hillman / Johnny Napton
Campbell Connelly & Co. Ltd .... USA
Film(s): .... Follow The Band
Eric Winstone & his Orchestra,
vocal Julie Dawn .... **Regal Zonophone MR 3677**
Glenn Miller & his Orchestra .... **HMV CLPC 4**
The Four Aces .... **Brunswick LA 8614**
Tab Hunter .... **London HLD 9381**

MY DING-A-LING   December 1972
Chuck Berry
Carlin Music Corporation .... USA
Chuck Berry .... **Chess 6415019**

MY DIXIE DARLING   December 1957
A.P. Carter
Southern Music Publishing Co. Ltd .... USA
The Carter Family .... **Brunswick OE 9168**
Lonnie Donegan .... **Nixa NPL 18034**

MY DREAM IS YOURS   October 1949
Harry Warren / Ralph Blane
B. Feldman & Co. Ltd .... USA
Film(s): .... My Dream is Yours
Doris Day .... **Philips BBE 12167**
Earl Grant .... **Brunswick LAT 8351**
Doris Day appeared in *My Dream is Yours.*

MY DREAM OF LOVE   1909
Adrian Ross / Leo Fall
Ascherberg, Hopwood & Crew Ltd. .... USA
Show(s): .... The Dollar Princess
Alfred Reeves .... **Columbia 1269**

MY DREAMS ARE GETTING BETTER ALL THE TIME   1945
Mann Curtis / Vic Mizzy
Campbell Connelly & Co. Ltd. .... USA
Film(s): .... In Society
Lou Preager & his Orchestra,
vocal Edna Kaye .... **Regal Zonophone MR 3751**
Art Mooney & his Orchestra .... **MGM 1042**
Guy Mitchell .... **Philips BBL 7465**

MY EVER CHANGING MOODS   May 1984
Paul Weller
EMI Music .... UK
Style Council .... **Polydor TSC 5**

MY EYES ADORED YOU   March 1975
Bob Crewe / Kenny Nolan
Jobete Music (UK) Ltd. .... USA
Frankie Valli .... **Private Stock PVT 1**

MY FATE IS IN YOUR HANDS   1930
Andy Razaf / Thomas Waller
Campbell Connelly & Co. Ltd .... USA
Gene Austin, piano accompaniment 'Fats' Waller . **HMV B 3297**
Pearl Bailey .... **Columbia 33SX 1269**

MY FAVOURITE THINGS   July 1961
Richard Rodgers / Oscar Hammerstein II
Williamson Music Ltd. .... USA
Show(s): .... Sound of Music
Film(s): .... Sound of Music
Mary Martin & Patricia Neway .... **Philips ABL 3370**
Jean Bayless & Constance Shacklock .... **HMV CLP 1453**
Julie Andrews .... **RCA RB 6616**
Mary Martin & Patricia Neway appeared in the American production
of *Sound of Music.*
Jean Bayless & Constance Shacklock appeared in the British produc-
tion of *Sound of Music.*
Julie Andrews appeared in the film *Sound of Music.*

MY FAVOURITE WASTE OF TIME   July 1986
Marshall Crenshaw
Warner Brothers Music .... UK
Owen Paul .... **Epic A 7125**

MY FIRST LOVE, MY LAST LOVE FOR ALWAYS   1947
Billy Reid
Dash Music .... UK
Dorothy Squires .... **Parlophone F 2244**
Arthur Tracy (The Street Singer) .... **Decca F 8811**
Monte Ray .... **Columbia FB 3356**
Joe Loss Orchestra .... **HMV BD 5988**

MY FIRST THRILL   1936
Maurice Sigler / Al Hoffman / Al Goodhart
Cinephonic Music Co. Ltd .... UK
Film(s): .... She Shall Have Music
Jack Hylton & his Band .... **HMV BD 5018**
Jack Hylton appeared in *She Shall Have Music.*

MY FOOLISH HEART   May 1950
Ned Washington / Victor Young
Francis, Day & Hunter Ltd .... USA
Film(s): .... My Foolish Heart
Steve Conway .... **Columbia SEG 7573**
Victor Young & his Singing Strings ...... **Brunswick LAT 8283**
Billy Eckstine .... **MGM D 151**
Carmen McRae .... **Brunswick LAT 8147**
Sam Cooke .... **HMV CLP 1273**
Jane Morgan .... **London HAR 2371**
Nominated for an Academy Award 1949.

MY FRIEND   July 1954
Ervin Drake / Jimmy Shirl
Chappell & Co. Ltd. .... USA
Eddie Fisher .... **HMV B 10729**
Frankie Laine .... **Philips BBL 7263**

MY FRIEND STAN   October 1973
Noddy Holder / Jimmy Lea
Barn Publishing Ltd. .... UK
Slade .... **Polydor 2058407**

MY FRIEND THE SEA   December 1961
Ron Goodwin / Jack Fishman
Sydney Bron Music Co. Ltd. .... UK
Petula Clark .... **Pye 7N 15389**

MY FUNNY VALENTINE   1937
Richard Rodgers / Lorenz Hart
Chappell & Co. Ltd. .... USA
Show(s): .... Babes in Arms
Film(s): .... Gentlemen Marry Brunettes / Pal Joey
Gordon Jenkins & his Orchestra,
vocal Charles La Vere .... **Brunswick LA 8543**

Anita Ellis & Alan Young .... **Vogue LVA 9003**
Kim Novak .... **Capitol LCT 6148**
Ella Fitzgerald .... **HMV CLP 1117**
Anita Ellis & Alan Young appeared in *Gentlemen Marry Brunettes*.
Kim Novak appeared in *Pal Joey*.

MY FUTURE JUST PASSED   1931
George Marion / Richard A. Whiting
Chappell & Co. Ltd .... USA
Film(s): ....Safety in Numbers
Charles 'Buddy' Rogers .... **Columbia DB 242**
Carmen McRae .... **Brunswick LAT 8133**
Charles 'Buddy' Rogers appeared in *Safety In Numbers*.

MY GAL SAL   1906
Paul Dresser
Francis, Day & Hunter Ltd. .... USA
Film(s): .... My Gal Sal / The Jazz Singer
The Mills Brothers (1943) .... **Brunswick 04448**
Al Jolson .... **Brunswick LAT 8322**
Bobby Darin .... **London HAK 2235**
Al Jolson appeared in *The Jazz Singer*.

MY GENERATION   December 1965
Peter Townshend
Fabulous Music Ltd .... UK
The Who .... **Brunswick 05944**

MY GIRL   February 1966
William Robinson / Ronald White
Belinda (London) Ltd. .... USA
Otis Reading .... **Atlantic AT 4050**
The Temptations .... **Stateside SS 395**

MY GIRL   February 1980
Michael Barson
Warner Brothers Music Ltd .... UK
Madness .... **Stiff BUY 62**

MY GIRL LOLLIPOP   August 1982
Johnny Roberts / Morris Levy
Planetary-Nom Music .... USA
Bad Manners .... **Magnet MAG 232**
See also 'My Boy Lollipop'

MY GIRL'S A YORKSHIRE GIRL   1908
C.W. Murphy / Dan Lipton
Francis, Day & Hunter Ltd. .... UK
Herbert Foreman .... **Zonophone 91**
George Elrick .... **Decca F 10318**

MY GOLDEN BABY   August 1949
Alfred Grunwald / Paul Abraham / Fritz Lohner-Beda
Chappell & Co. Ltd .... Germany
Marek Weber & his Orchestra,
vocal The Comedy Harmonists .... **HMV C 2329**
Donald Peers .... **HMV B 9808**

MY GUY   June 1964
William Robinson
Belinda (London) Ltd .... USA
Mary Wells .... **Stateside SS 288**
Helen Shapiro .... **Columbia 33SX 1661**
Joy Marshall .... **Decca LK 4678**
Mary Wells (1972) .... **Tamla Motown TMG 820**

MY GUY'S COME BACK   1945
Mel Powell / Ray McKinley
Peter Maurice Music Co. Ltd. .... UK
Benny Goodman & his Orchestra,
vocal Liza Morrow .... **Parlophone R 3000**
Bruce Turner's Jump Band .... **Melodisc 1551**

MY HAPPINESS   June 1948
Betty Peterson / Borney Bergantine
Chappell & Co. Ltd. .... USA
Ella Fitzgerald .... **Brunswick LAT 8370**
Connie Francis (1959) .... **MGM C 831**

MY HAT'S ON THE SIDE OF MY HEAD   1933
Harry Woods / Claude Hulbert
Cinephonic Music Co. Ltd. .... UK
Film(s): .... Jack Ahoy
Jack Hulbert .... **HMV BD 278**
Jack Hulbert appeared in *Jack Ahoy*.

MY HEART AND I   1943
Frederick Tysh / Richard Tauber / Walter Ellis
Lawrence Wright Music Co. Ltd .... UK
Show(s): .... Old Chelsea
Richard Tauber .... **Parlophone PMB 1009**
Kenneth McKellar .... **Decca F 11091**
David Whitfield .... **Decca LK 4348**
Richard Tauber appeared in *Old Chelsea*.

MY HEART BELONGS TO DADDY   1939
Cole Porter
Chappell & Co. Ltd. .... USA
Show(s): .... Leave it to Me / Black Velvet
Film(s): .... Love Thy Neighbour / Night and Day / Let's Make Love
Mary Martin .... **Parlophone F 1619**
Pat Kirkwood .... **HMV BD 785**
Peggy Lee .... **Brunswick LA 8629**
Eartha Kitt .... **RCA RD 27067**
Marilyn Monroe .... **Philips BBL 7414**
Mary Martin appeared in the show *Leave it to Me* and the films *Love Thy Neighbour* and *Night and Day*.
Pat Kirkwood appeared in *Black Velvet*.
Marilyn Monroe appeared in *Let's Make Love*.
Theme song of Mary Martin.

MY HEART BELONGS TO YOU   June 1953
Frank Daniels / Dorothy Daniels
Edward Kassner Music Co. Ltd .... USA
June Christy .... **Capitol T 1006**
Larry Hovis .... **Capitol CL 15083**

MY HEART CRIES FOR YOU   February 1951
Percy Faith / Carl Sigman
Edwin H. Morris & Co. Ltd .... USA
Guy Mitchell .... **Philips BBL 7265**
Evelyn Knight & Red Foley .... **Brunswick 04644**

MY HEART GOES CRAZY   1946
Johnny Burke / Jimmy Van Heusen
Edwin H. Morris & Co. Ltd .... USA
Film(s): .... London Town
The London Town Orchestra .... **Decca F 8673**
Bing Crosby .... **Brunswick 04745**

MY HEART HAS A MIND OF IT'S OWN   November 1960
Howard Greenfield / Jack Keller
Nervins-Kirshner Ltd .... USA
Connie Francis .... **MGM EP 742**

MY HEART IS AN OPEN BOOK   November 1958
Lee Pockriss / Hall David
Sheldon Music Ltd .... USA
Michael Holliday .... **Columbia DB 4216**
Carl Dobkins .... **Brunswick LAT 8329**

MY HEART IS TAKING LESSONS   1938
Jimmy Monaco / Johnny Burke
Campbell Connelly & Co. Ltd. .... USA
Film(s): .... Doctor Rhythm
Bing Crosby .... **Brunswick Bing 4**
Bing Crosby appeared in *Doctor Rhythm*.

MY HEART ISN'T IN IT   1946
Jack Lawrence
Leeds Music Ltd. .... USA
Film(s): .... Stars on Parade
Beryl Davis .... **Decca F 8658**
Betty Brewer .... **Brunswick 04575**

MY HEART SINGS   1945
'Jamblan' / Henri Herpin / Harold Rome
Peter Maurice Music Co. Ltd. .... France
Film(s): .... Anchors Aweigh
Geraldo & his Orchestra,
vocal Carol Carr .... **Parlophone F 2097**
Kathryn Grayson .... **MGM EP 636**
Julie Dawn .... **Columbia 33SX 1124**
Paul Anka (1959) .... **Columbia 33SX 1196**
Kathryn Grayson appeared in *Anchors Aweigh*.

MY HEART STOOD STILL   1927
Richard Rodgers / Lorenz Hart
Chappell & Co. Ltd. .... USA
Show(s): ...One Damn Thing After Another / A Connecticut Yankee

Film(s): . . . . A Connecticut Yankee / Words and Music
Edith Baker (piano) . . . . **Columbia 9217**
Jessie Matthews . . . . **Brunswick 135**
Peggy Lee . . . . **Capitol T 864**
Edith Baker & Jessie Matthews appeared in *One Damn Thing After Another*.

MY HEART TELLS ME   **1944**
Mack Gordon / Harry Warren
Bregman, Vocco & Conn Ltd . . . . USA
Film(s): . . . . Sweet Rosie O'Grady
Stephane Grapelli's Quartet, vocal
Dave Fullerton with George Shearing (piano) . . . **Decca F 8392**
Joni James . . . . **MGM C 777**

MY HERO   **1908**
Oscar Straus / Stanislaus Stange
B. Feldman & Co. Ltd. . . . . Germany
Show(s): . . . . The Chocolate Soldier
Film(s): . . . . The Chocolate Soldier / Two Weeks with Love
Evelyn D'Alroy . . . . **Odeon 0706**
Rise Stevens & Nelson Eddy . . . . **Philips 11090**
Jane Powell . . . . **MGM EP 633**
Ralph Flanagan & his Orchestra . . . . **HMV B 9972**
Evelyn D'Alroy appeared in the British production of *The Chocolate Soldier*.
Rise Stevens & Nelson Eddy appeared in the film of *The Chocolate Soldier*.
Jane Powell appeared in *Two Weeks In Love*.

MY HONEY'S LOVIN' ARMS   **1922**
Herman Ruby / Joseph Meyer
B. Feldman & Co. Ltd . . . . USA
Ladds Black Aces . . . . **London AL 3556**
Bing Crosby & The Mills Brothers with
The Dorsey Brothers Orchestra . . . . **Philips BBE 12142**
Barbara Lee . . . . **Esquire 32-043**

MY HOUSE IS YOUR HOUSE (Mi Casa, Su Casa)   **March 1957**
Al Hoffman / Dick Manning
Leeds Music Ltd. . . . . USA
Perry Como . . . . **RCA RD 27100**

MY IDEAL   **1931**
Leo Robin / Richard A. Whiting / Newell Chase
Chappell & Co. Ltyd . . . . USA
Film(s): . . . . Playboy of Paris
Maurice Chevalier . . . . **HMV B 3684**
Maxine Sullivan . . . . **Brunswick 03531**
Jeri Southern . . . . **Brunswick LAT 8209**

MY IRISH MOLLY-O   **1905**
William Jerome / Jean Schwartz
Francis, Day & Hunter Ltd. . . . . USA
Show(s): . . . . Sergeant Brue
Madge Lessing . . . . **Beka 8316**
The Flanagan Brothers . . . . **Regal Zonophone MR 1741**

MY ISLE OF GOLDEN DREAMS   **1919**
Gus Kahn / Walter Blaufuss
B. Feldman & Co. Ltd . . . . USA
The Ex-Serviceman's Band
(with Ted Heath (trombone)) . . . . **Edison Bell Winner 3549**
Bing Crosby . . . . **Brunswick LAT 8334**
The Troubadours . . . . **London HAA 2121**
The Outriggers . . . . **Warner Brothers WEP 6027**

MY KID'S A CROONER   **1935**
Marion Harris / Reg Montgomery
Lawrence Wright Music Co. Ltd . . . . UK
Phyllis Robins . . . . **Rex 8378**

MY KIND OF GIRL   **April 1961**
Leslie Bricusse
Essex Music Ltd . . . . UK
Matt Monro . . . . **Parlophone R 4755**
Frank Sinatra . . . . **Reprise R 21048**
Frank Ifield . . . . **Columbia 33SX 1534**
Ivor Novello Award.

MY KINDA LIFE   **April 1977**
Chris East
Heath Levy Music Ltd . . . . UK
Cliff Richard . . . . **EMI 2584**

MY KINDA LOVE   **1929**
Jo Trent / Louis Alter
Francis, Day & Hunter Ltd . . . . USA
Show(s): . . . . Americana of 1928
The Dorsey Brothers Orchestra,
vocal Bing Crosby . . . . **Parlophone R 2475**
Bing Crosby . . . . **Brunswick LAT 8251**
Sarah Vaughan . . . . **MGM EP 605**

MY LIFE   **February 1979**
Billy Joel
April Music Ltd. . . . . USA
Billy Joel . . . . **CBS 6821**

MY LIFE BELONGS TO YOU   **1939**
Ivor Novello / Christopher Hassall
Chappell & Co. Ltd. . . . . UK
Show(s): . . . . The Dancing Years
Mary Ellis & Dunstan Hart . . . . **HMV DLP 1028**
Evelyn Laye . . . . **Columbia DB 1867**
Webster Booth . . . . **HMV C 4081**
Mary Ellis & Dunstan Hart appeared in *The Dancing Years*.

MY LITTLE BUCKAROO   **1937**
Jack Scholl / M.K. Jerome
B. Feldman & Co. Ltd. . . . . USA
Film(s): . . . Strange Laws / The Cherokee Strip / Don't Fence Me in
Bing Crosby . . . . **Brunswick LAT 8152**
The Diamonds . . . . **Mercury MMC 14039**

MY LITTLE CORNER OF THE WORLD   **August 1960**
Lee Pockriss / Bob Hilliard
Edward-Kassner Music Co. Ltd . . . . USA
Anita Bryant . . . . **London HAL 2381**
Maureen Evans . . . . **Oriole CB 1563**

MY LITTLE DIETCHER GIRL   **1907**
Bert Lee
B. Feldman & Co. Ltd. . . . . UK
William Bard . . . . **Jumbo 255**

MY LITTLE LADY (Non Illuderti Mai)   **October 1968**
Daniele Pace / Mario Panzeri / Lorenzo Pilat, Alan Blaikley & Leonard Hawks
Cyril Shane Music . . . . Italy
The Tremeloes . . . . **CBS 3680**

MY LOVE   **March 1966**
Tony Hatch
Welbeck Music Co. Ltd. . . . . UK
Petula Clark . . . . **Pye 7N 17038**

MY LOVE   **May 1973**
Paul McCartney
McCartney Music . . . . UK
Wings . . . . **Apple R 5985**
Ivor Novello Nomination.

MY LOVE   **September 1988**
Stevie Wonder
Jobete Music . . . . USA
Julio Inglesias . . . . **CBS Julio 2**

MY LOVE AND DEVOTION   **November 1951**
Milton Carson
Manor Music Co. Ltd . . . . UK
Teddy Johnson . . . . **Columbia DB 3183**
Perry Como . . . . **Camden CDN 149**
Doris Day (1952) . . . . **Columbia DB 3157**

MY LOVE FOR YOU   **November 1960**
Abner Silver / Sid Wayne
Johnny Mathis Music Ltd . . . . USA
Johnny Mathis . . . . **Fontana TFE 17334**

MY LOVE PARADE   **1930**
Victor Schertzinger / Clifford Grey
Campbell Connelly & Co. Ltd . . . . USA
Film(s): . . . . The Love Parade
Maurice Chevalier . . . . **Camden CDN 152**

MY LOVE, MY LIFE, MY HAPPINESS   **October 1953**
Milton Carson
John Fields Music Co. Ltd. . . . . USA
Vera Lynn . . . . **Decca F 10184**
The Ames Brothers . . . . **HMV 7M 153**

MY MAMMY 1921
Sam M. Lewis / Joe Young / Walter Donaldson
Francis, Day & Hunter Ltd . . . . USA
Show(s): . . . . Sinbad
Film(s):The Jazz Singer / Rose of Washington Square / The Jolson Story / Jolson Sings Again
Paul Whiteman & his Orchestra . . . . **HMV B 1233**
Al Jolson . . . . **Brunswick LA 8512**
Connie Francis . . . . **MGM C 861**
Al Jolson appeared in *Sinbad, The Jazz Singer* and *The Rose Of Washington Square.*
Theme song of Al Jolson.

MY MAN (Mon Homme) 1921
Maurice Yvain / Jacques Charles / Albert Willemetz / Channing Pollock
Ascherberg, Hopwood & Crew Ltd . . . . France
Show(s): . . The Ziegfeld Follies of 1921 / Greenwich Village Follies
Film(s):My Man / The Great Ziegfeld / Rose of Washington Square / Funny Girl / Lady Sings the Blues
Fanny Brice . . . . **HMV B 2975**
Judy Garland . . . . **Capitol LCT 6103**
Jane Morgan . . . . **London HAR 2133**
Barbra Streisand . . . . **CBS BPG 62534**
Diana Ross . . . . **Tamla Motown STML 11311-2**
Fanny Brice appeared in both *The Ziegfeld Follies Of 1921* and *My Man.*
Barbra Streisand appeared in *Funny Girl.*
Diana Ross appeared in *Lady Sings the Blues.*

MY MELANCHOLY BABY 1912
Ernie Burnett / George Norton
Francis, Day & Hunter Ltd. . . . . USA
Film(s): Birth of the Blues / A Star is Born / Both Ends of the Candle
Bing Crosby . . . . **Brunswick Bing 6**
The Dorsey Brothers, vocal Seger Ellis . . . . . **Philips BBL 7431**
Al Bowlly . . . . **HMV BD 228**
Judy Garland . . . . **Philips BBL 7007**
Tommy Edwards . . . . **MGM 1020**
Gogi Grant . . . . **RCA RD 27054**
Bing Crosby appeared in *Birth of the Blues.*
Judy Garland appeared in *A Star is Born.*

MY MESSAGE 1911
Jacob Gade / Guy D' Hardelot
Chappell & Co Ltd . . . . France
Marion Beeley . . . . **HMV 3914**
Nelson Eddy . . . . **Columbia DC 483**
The Hon. W. Brownlow . . . . **Columbia DB 1650**

MY MIND'S EYE December 1966
Steve Marriott / Ronnie Lane
Robbins Music Corporation Ltd. . . . . UK
The Small Faces . . . . **Decca F 12500**

MY MONDAY DATE 1935
Earl Hines / Sid Robin
Leeds Music Ltd . . . . USA
Louis Armstrong & his Hot Five, vocal Louis Armstrong & Earl Hines . . . . **Parlophone PMC 1146**
Louis Armstrong's All Stars . . . . **Brunswick LAT 8214**

MY MOONLIGHT MADONNA 1933
William Scotti / Paul Francis Webster
Keith Prowse Music Publishing Co. Ltd. . . . . USA
Paul Whiteman & his Orchestra . . . . **HMV B 6399**
David Whitfield . . . . **Decca LK 4384**
Adapted from 'Poeme' by Zdenek Fibich (1850-1900).

MY MOTHER'S EYES 1929
L. Wolfe Gilbert / Abel Baer
Francis, Day & Hunter Ltd . . . . USA
Film(s): . . . . Lucky Boy
George Jessel . . . . **HMV B 3049**
Nellie Lutcher . . . . **Capitol EAP 20066**
Kenny Ball & his Jazzmen, vocal Kenny Ball . . . . **Pye 7NJ 2049**
George Jessel appeared in *Lucky Boy.*

MY NAME IS JACK July 1968
John Simon
B. Feldman & Co. Ltd. . . . . USA
Film(s): . . . . You Are What You Eat
Manfred Mann . . . . **Fontana TF 943**
John Simon . . . . **CBS 70045**
John Simon appeared in *You Are What You Eat.*

MY OH MY December 1983
Neville Holder / James Lea
Wild John Music . . . . UK
Slade . . . . **RCA 373**

MY OHIO HOME 1928
Walter Donaldson / Gus Kahn
Francis, Day & Hunter Ltd. . . . . USA
The Swinging Sophomores . . . . **Columbia 4866**
Frankie Laine . . . . **Philips BBR 8068**

MY OLD DUTCH 1893
Albert Chevalier / Charles Ingle
Reynolds & Co. (Music Publishers) Ltd. . . . . UK
Albert Chevalier . . . . **HMV D 373**
Stanley Holloway . . . . **Philips BBL 7237**
Peter Sellers . . . . **Parlophone PMC 1111**

MY OLD FLAME 1934
Sam Coslow / Arthur Johnston
Victoria Music Co. Ltd . . . . USA
Film(s): . . . . Belle of the Nineties
Duke Ellington Orchestra, vocal Ivie Anderson . . **HMV B 8404**
Mary Ann McCall . . . . **Coral FEP 2041**
Spike Jones & his City Slickers (comedy version) . . **HMV BD 1200**
Duke Ellington appeared in *Belle of the Nineties.*

MY OLD MAN'S A DUSTMAN April 1960
Lonnie Donegan
Tyler Music Ltd. . . . . UK
Lonnie Donegan . . . . **Pye NEP 24134**

MY OLD PIANO October 1980
Bernard Edwards / Nile Rodgers
Warner Brothers Music Ltd . . . . USA
Diana Ross . . . . **Motown TMG 1202**

MY ONE AND ONLY 1928
George Gershwin / Ira Gershwin
Chappell & Co. Ltd . . . . USA
Show(s): . . . . Funny Face
Film(s): . . . . Funny Face
George Gershwin (piano) . . . . **Columbia 5109**
Fred Astaire . . . . **Columbia 5173**
Ella Fitzgerald . . . . **HMV CLP 1338**
Fred Astaire appeared in both the American and British productions and also the film of *Funny Face.*

MY ONE AND ONLY HIGHLAND FLING September 1949
Harry Warren / Ira Gershwin
Francis, Day & Hunter Ltd . . . . USA
Film(s): . . . . The Barkleys of Broadway
Fred Astaire & Ginger Rogers . . . . **MGM 211**
Mel Tormé . . . . **Philips BBL 7205**
Fred Astaire & Ginger Rogers appeared in the *Barkleys of Broadway.*

MY ONE AND ONLY LOVE June 1953
Guy Wood / Robert Mellin
Robert Mellin Ltd . . . . USA
Frank Sinatra . . . . **Capitol LCT 6123**
Mary Kay . . . . **HMV CLP 1490**
Adapted from *Romance* by Anton Rubenstein (1829 - 1894).

MY ONE TEMPTATION June 1988
Michael Leeson / Peter Vale / Miles Walters
Warner Chappell Music . . . . UK
Mica Paris . . . . **4th & Broadway BRW 85**

MY OWN 1939
Harold Adamson / Jimmy McHugh
Frances, Day & Hunter Ltd. . . . . USA
Film(s): . . . . That Certain Age
Deanna Durbin . . . . **Brunswick 02705**
Frank Chacksfield & his Orchestra . . . . **Decca LK 4138**
Deanna Durbin appeared in *That Certain Age.*
Nominated for an Academy Award 1938.

MY OWN TRUE LOVE September 1954
Max Steiner / Mack David
B. Feldman & Co. Ltd. . . . . USA
Margaret Whiting . . . . **Capitol CL 14213**
Lee Lawrence . . . . **Decca F 10422**
Nick Noble . . . . **Mercury MB 3199**
Based on 'Tara's Theme'.

MY OWN WAY   December 1981
"Duran Duran"
Carlin Music . . . . UK
Duran Duran . . . . **EMI 5254**

MY PARADISE   1942
Harry Parr-Davies
Chappell & Co. Ltd . . . . UK
Show(s): . . . . Gangway
Anne Ziegler & Webster Booth . . . . **HMV B 9247**
Anne Ziegler & Webster Booth appeared in *Gangway*.

MY PERFECT COUSIN   May 1980
Damian O'Neil / Michael Bradley
Warner Brothers Music . . . . UK
The Undertones . . . . **Sire SIR 4038**

MY PET   1928
Jack Yellen / Milton Ager
Lawrence Wright Music Co. Ltd. . . . . USA
Paul Whiteman & his Orchestra,
vocal Bing Crosby & The Rhythm Boys . . . . **HMV B 5504**
Frankie Trumbauer & his Orchestra . . . . . . **Fontana TFE 17252**
Sophie Tucker . . . . **CBS BPG 62547**

MY PRAYER   1939
Georges Boulanger / Jimmy Kennedy
World Wide Music Co. Ltd. France
The Ink Spots . . . . **Brunswick 02935**
Vera Lynn . . . . **Decca F 7120**
Ronnie Hilton . . . . **HMV 7EG 8198**
The Platters (1956, 1957) . . . . **Mercury MT 120**
Gerry Monroe (1970) . . . . **Chapter One CH 132**
Adapted from 'Avant de Mourir' by Georges Boulanger.

MY PREROGATIVE   February 1989
Gene Griffin / Ted Riley / Bobby Brown
MCA Music . . . . USA
Bobby Brown . . . . **MCA 1299**

MY PRETTY ONE   July 1987
Alan Tarney
Morrison Leahy Music . . . . UK
Cliff Richard . . . . **EMI EM 4**

MY RAINBOW VALLEY   June 1968
Buzz Cason / Mac Gayden
Peter Maurice Music Co. Ltd. . . . . USA
The Love Affair . . . . **CBS 3366**

MY RESISTANCE IS LOW   May 1951
Hoagy Carmichael / Harold Adamson
Chappell & Co. Ltd . . . . USA
Film(s): . . . . Las Vegas Story
Hoagy Carmichael . . . . **Brunswick 04710**
Robin Sarstedt (1976) . . . . **Decca F 13624**
Hoagy Carmichael appeared in *Las Vegas Story*.

MY ROMANCE   1941
Richard Rodgers / Lorenz Hart
Chappell & Co. Ltd . . . . USA
Show(s): . . . . Jumbo
Film(s): . . . . Jumbo
Ambrose & his Orchestra, vocal Sam Browne . . **Decca F 7704**
Carmen McRae . . . . **London HAR 2185**
Doris Day . . . . **CBS BPG 62118**
Doris Day appeared in *Jumbo*.

MY SENTIMENTAL FRIEND   May 1969
John Stephens / John Carter
Monique Music Ltd. . . . . UK
Herman's Hermits . . . . **Columbia DB 8563**

MY SEPTEMBER LOVE   March 1956
Tolchard Evans / Richard Mullen
Hit Songs Ltd. . . . . UK
David Whitfield . . . . **Decca LK 4242**
Ivor Novello Award

MY SHARONA   July 1979
Doug Fieger / Berton Averre
Chappell & Co. Ltd . . . . USA
The Knack . . . . **Capitol CL 16087**

MY SHINING HOUR   1943
Harold Arlen / Johnny Mercer
Chappell & Co. Ltd . . . . USA
Film(s): . . . . The Sky's the Limit
Glen Gray & The Casa Loma Orchestra,
vocal Eugene Baird . . . . **Brunswick 03493**
Ella Fitzgerald . . . . **HMV CLP 1479**
Nominated for an Academy Award 1943.

MY SHIP   1942
Kurt Weill / Ira Gershwin
Chappell & Co. Ltd . . . . USA
Show(s): . . . . Lady in the Dark
Film(s): . . . . Star
Gertrude Lawrence . . . . **HMV DLP 1099**
Doris Day . . . . **Philips BBL 7495**
Julie Andrews . . . . **Stateside SL 10233**
Gertrude Lawrence appeared in the show *Lady in the Dark*.
Julie Andrews appeared in *Star*.

MY SHIP IS COMING IN   February 1966
Joey Brooks
Schroeder Music Ltd. . . . . USA
The Walker Brothers . . . . **Philips BF 1454**

MY SILENT LOVE   1932
Dana Suesse / Edward Heymann
Victoria Music Co. Ltd. . . . . USA
Victor Young & his Orchestra . . . . **Brunswick 0107**
Sue Raney . . . . **Capitol T 964**

MY SIMPLE HEART   December 1979
Dominic Bugatti / Frank Musker
Chappell & Co. Ltd. . . . . USA
The Three Degrees . . . . **Ariola ARO 202**

MY SIN   1929
Buddy De Sylva / Lew Brown / Ray Henderson
Campbell Connelly & Co. Ltd . . . . USA
Film(s): . . . . The Best Things in Life are Free
Jack Hylton & his Orchestra . . . . **HMV B 5637**
Dick Haymes & The Andrews Sisters . . . . **Brunswick 03860**
Julia Lee & her Boy Friends . . . . **Capitol T 1057**

MY SISTER AND I   1941
Hy Zaret / Joan Whitney / Alex Kramer
Campbell Connelly & Co Ltd . . . . USA
Vera Lynn . . . . **Decca F 8014**

MY SON, MY SON   October 1954
Eddie Calvert / Melville Farley / Bob Howard
Edward Kassner Music Co. Ltd. . . . . UK
Eddie Calvert (trumpet) . . . . **Columbia SCM 5129**
Vera Lynn . . . . **Decca LK 4120**

MY SONG GOES ROUND THE WORLD   1933
Hans May / Ernst Neubach / Jimmy Kennedy
B. Feldman & Co. Ltd. . . . . Germany
Film(s): . . . . My Song Goes Round the World
Josef Schmidt . . . . **Parlophone GEP 8632**
Leo Fuld . . . . **Decca F 9434**
Cavan O'Connor . . . . **Regal Zonophone MR 1157**
Josef Schmidt appeared in *My Song Goes Round the World*.

MY SONG OF LOVE   1931
Robert Stolz / Ralph Benatzky / Harry Graham
Chappell & Co. Ltd. . . . . Germany
Show(s): . . . . White Horse Inn
Winnie Melville & Derek Oldham . . . . **HMV B 3854**
Mary Thomas & Andy Cole . . . . **HMV CLP 1205**

MY SONG OF THE NILE   1929
Alfred Bryan / George Meyer
B. Feldman & Co. Ltd . . . . USA
Film(s): . . . . Parasites
Layton & Johnstone . . . . **Columbia 5650**

MY SPECIAL ANGEL   December 1957
Jimmy Duncan
Hit Songs Ltd . . . . USA
Malcolm Vaughan . . . . **HMV 7EG 8377**
Bobby Helms . . . . **Brunswick LAT 8250**
Connie Francis . . . . **MGM C 812**

MY SUNNY TENNESSEE   1921
Bert Kalmar / Harry Ruby / Herman Ruby
B. Feldman & Co. Ltd . . . . USA
Show(s): . . . . Midnight Rounders
Film(s): . . . . Three Little Words
The Benson Orchestra of Chicago . . . . **HMV B 1294**
Fred Astaire & Red Skelton . . . . **MGM D 139**
Fred Astaire & Red Skelton appeared in *Three Little Words*.

(MY SWEET) HORTENSE   1923
Walter Donaldson / Joe Young / Sam M. Lewis
Francis, Day & Hunter Ltd . . . . USA
Jack Hylton & his Orchestra . . . . **HMV B 1438**
The Tuneful Twenties Dance Orchestra . . . **Parlophone R 3350**

MY SWEET LORD   March 1971
George Harrison
Harrisongs Ltd . . . . UK
George Harrison . . . . **Apple R 5884**
Ivor Novello Award.

MY SWEETHEART'S THE MAN IN THE MOON   1892
James Thornton / Frank Harding
Unknown Publisher . . . . USA
Frank Luther & Zora Layman . . . . **Decca F 6791**
Frances Wyatt . . . . **Fontana TFL 5019**
Bing Crosby . . . . **Warner Brothers WM 4034**

MY SWEETIE WENT AWAY   1923
Roy Turk / Lou Handman
B. Feldman & Co. Ltd . . . . USA
Joe Raymond & his Orchestra . . . . **HMV B 1704**
Frankie Vaughan . . . . **HMV 7EG 8245**

MY THANKS TO YOU   April 1950
Norman Newell / Noel Gay
Noel Gay Music Ltd . . . . UK
Steve Conway . . . . **Columbia DB 2669**
Vera Lynn . . . . **Decca F 9382**
Connie Francis . . . . **MGM C 782**

MY TIME IS YOUR TIME   1924
Eric Little / Leo Dance
Ascherberg, Hopwood & Crew Ltd. . . . . UK
Rudy Vallee & his Connecticut Yankees . . . . **Camden CDN 170**
The Hi-Lo's . . . . **Philips BBL 7177**
Rudy Vallee . . . . **Capitol LC 6698**
Theme song of Rudy Vallee.

MY TOOT TOOT   July 1985
Sidney Simien
Flyright Music . . . . USA
Denise La Salle . . . . **Epic A 6334**

MY TRUE LOVE   November 1958
Jack Scott
Southern Music Co. . . . . USA
Jack Scott . . . . **London HLU 8626**

MY TRULY TRULY FAIR   August 1951
Bob Merrill
Dash Music Ltd . . . . USA
Guy Mitchell . . . . **Philips BBL 7265**

MY TWO FRONT TEETH   December 1949
Don Gardner
B. Feldman & Co. Ltd . . . . USA
Danny Kaye & The Andrews Sisters . . . . **Brunswick 04399**
Nat 'King' Cole . . . . **Capitol T 9030**
Spike Jones & his City Slickers . . . . **HMV B 9855**

MY UNFINISHED SYMPHONY   September 1956
Milton Carson
JohnFields Music Co. Ltd. . . . . UK
David Whitfield . . . . **Decca LK 4242**
Ivor Novello Nomination.

MY VERY GOOD FRIEND THE MILKMAN   1935
Joe Burke / Harold Spina
Campbell Connelly & Co. Ltd . . . . USA
'Fats' Waller & his Rhythm . . . . **HMV DLP 1056**
Joy & Dave . . . . **Decca F 11291**
Ted Heath & his Music, vocal Lita Rosa . . . . **Decca F 9540**

MY WAY   June 1969
Jacques Ravaux / Claude Francois / Gillis Thibout & Paul Anka
Shapiro-Bernstein & Co. Ltd. . . . . France
Frank Sinatra (1970 & 1971) . . . . **Reprise RS 20817**
Dorothy Squires . . . . **President PT 305**
Elvis Presley (Jan 1978) . . . . **RCA PB 1165**
The Sex Pistols (Aug 1978) . . . . **Virgin VS 220**

MY WAY OF THINKING   July 1980
Randy Newman
A.T.V. Music Ltd. . . . . USA
UB 40 . . . . **Graduate GRAD 8**

MY WHITE BICYCLE   July 1975
Keith Hopkins / Ken Burgess
Getaway Music . . . . UK
Nazareth . . . . **Mooncrest 47**
Tomorrow . . . . **Parlophone R 5597**

MY WILD IRISH ROSE   1899
Chauncey Olcott
B. Feldman & Co. Ltd. . . . . USA
Show(s): . . . . Romance of Athlone
Film(s): . . . . My Wild Irish Rose
John McCormack . . . . **HMV DA 474**
Kenny Baker . . . . **HMV 7EG 8099**
Mitch Miller & The Gang . . . . **Philips BBL 7334**
Kenny Baker appeared in *My Wild Irish Rose*.

MY WORD YOU DO LOOK QUEER   1922
R.P. Weston / Bert Lee
Francis, Day & Hunter Ltd . . . . UK
Ernest Hastings . . . . **HMV C 1095**
Stanley Holloway . . . . **Philips BBL 7237**

MY WORLD   March 1972
Barry Gibb / Robin Gibb
Abigail Music . . . . UK
The Bee Gees . . . . **Polydor 2058185**

MY WORLD   April 1980
David Cairns
Bryan Morrison Music . . . . UK
Secret Affair . . . . **I Spy SEE 5**

MY YIDDISHE MOMME   1928
Jack Yellen / Lew Pollack
Lawrence Wright Music Co. Ltd. . . . . USA
Sophie Tucker (1928) . . . . **Columbia SEG 7766**
Sophie Tucker (1951) . . . . **Brunswick LAT 8144**
Anne Shelton . . . . **Philips BBL 7393**
Connie Francis . . . . **MGM C 845**

MYSTERY   1920
Joseph Cirina / Howard Johnson
Herman Darewski Music Publishing Co. Ltd . . . . USA
The Happy Six, vocal Jack Kaufman . . . . **Columbia 2999**

MYSTERY GIRL   March 1961
Trevor Peacock
Jack Good Music Publishing Co. Ltd . . . . UK
Jess Conrad . . . . **Decca F 11315**

MYSTERY SONG, THE   August 1976
Richard Parfitt / Robert Young
Shawbury Music . . . . UK
Status Quo . . . . **Vertigo 6059146**

'N' EVERYTHING   1919
Al Jolson / Buddy De Sylva / Gus Khan
B. Feldman & Co. Ltd. . . . . USA
Show(s): . . . . Tails Up / Sinbad
Film(s): . . . . Star
Davy Burnaby . . . . **HMV B 1011**
John Watt's 'Songs from the Shows' . . . . **Decca F 3408**
Jacob's Trocaderians . . . . **Columbia 2867**
Gareth Lewis . . . . **Stateside SL 10233**
Gareth Lewis appeared in *Star*.

NA NA HEY HEY KISS HIM GOODBYE   March 1970
Garry De Carlo / Dale Frashuer / Paul Leka
Chappell & Co. Ltd. . . . . USA
Steam . . . . **Fontana TF 1058**
Bananarama (1983) . . . . **London NANA 4**

NA NA IS THE SADDEST WORD December 1975
Hugo Peretti / Luigi Creatore / George Weiss
Cyril Shane Music . . . . USA
The Stylistics . . . . Avco 6105041

NA NA NA September 1974
John Cameron
Rak Music Ltd. . . . . UK
Cozy Powell . . . . Rak 180

NAGASAKI 1928
Mort Dixon / Harry Warren
Francis, Day & Hunter Ltd. . . . . USA
The Trix Sisters accompanied by
The Gilt-Edged Four . . . . Columbia 5300
The Mills Brothers . . . . Brunswick 01800
The Albert Ammons Rhythm Kings . . . . . Brunswick OE 9325
Bobby Short . . . . London HAE 2215
Nat Gonella & his Band . . . . Columbia 33SX 1380

NAIROBI April 1958
Bob Merrill
Leeds Music . . . . USA
Tommy Steele . . . . Decca F 10991
Bob Merrill . . . . Columbia DB 4086

NAKED IN THE RAIN August 1990
Martin Glover / Durga McBroom
E.G. Music . . . . UK
Blue Pearl . . . . Big Life BLR 23

NAME OF THE GAME November 1977
Benny Andersson / Bjorn Ulvaeus
Bocu Music Ltd . . . . Sweden
Abba . . . . Epic EPC 5750

NANCY (With the Laughing Face) 1946
Phil Silvers / Jimmy Van Heusen
Chappell & Co. Ltd. . . . . USA
Frank Sinatra . . . . Philips BBL 7331
The Four Freshmen . . . . Capitol T 1255

NARCISSUS 1891
Ethelbert Nevin
. . . . USA
Orchestre Mascotte . . . . Parlophone F 1468
The Casa Loma Orchestra . . . . Brunswick 01984
Norman Wisdom & Joyce Grenfell . . . . Columbia DB 3161
Ronald Binge Orchestra . . . . RCA RD 27157
Adapted from the 'Water Scenes Suite opus 13, no.4' by Ethelbert
Nevin (1862 - 1901)

NASTY MAN 1934
Ray Henderson / Jack Yellen / Irving Caesar
Keith Prowse Music Publishing Co. Ltd. . . . . USA
Film(s): . . . . George White's Scandals of 1934
Frances Langford . . . . Rex 8231
Ray Noble & his Orchestra, vocal Dorothy Carless . . HMV B 6499

NATHAN JONES October 1971
Kathy Wakefield / Leonard Caston
Jobete Music (UK) Ltd. . . . . USA
The Supremes . . . . Tamla Motown TMG 782
Bananarama (1988) . . . . London NANA 18

NATIVE NEW YORKER February 1978
Sandy Linzer / Denny Randell
Chappell & Co. Ltd . . . . USA
Odyssey . . . . RCA PB 1129

NATURAL BORN BUGIE September 1969
Steve Marriott
Immediate Music Ltd. . . . . UK
Humble Pie . . . . Immediate IM 082

NATURAL SINNER August 1970
Andy Fairweather Low
Amen Music . . . . UK
Fair Weather . . . . RCA 1977

NATURAL THING March 1990
Mark Jolley / Anna Jolley / Brian Harris
MCA Music . . . . UK
Innocence . . . . Cool Tempo COOL 201

NATURE BOY May 1948
Eden Ahbez
Edwin H. Morris & Co. Ltd. . . . . USA
Nat 'King' Cole . . . . Capitol EAP 20053
Garry Miller . . . . Nixa NPL 18008

NAUGHTY LADY OF SHADY LANE, THE January 1955
Sid Tepper / Roy C. Bennett
Chappell & Co. Ltd. . . . . USA
The Beverley Sisters . . . . Philips BBR 8052
Dean Martin . . . . Capitol T 1007
Jim Lowe . . . . London HAD 2146
The Ames Brothers . . . . RCA RCX 1047

NEANDERTHAL MAN September 1970
Kevin Godley / Lawrence Creme / Eric Stewart
Kennedy Street Music Ltd . . . . UK
Hotlegs . . . . Fontana 6007019

NEAR YOU 1947
Francis Craig / Kermit Goell
Bregman, Vocco & Conn Ltd. . . . . USA
Francis Craig & his Orchestra,
vocal Bob Lamm . . . . Brunswick 03876
Edna Savage . . . . Parlophone R 4489
The Andrews Sisters . . . . Brunswick 03823
Roger Williams & his Orchestra . . . . London HAR 2303
Theme song of Francis Craig.

NEARNESS OF YOU, THE 1940
Ned Washington / Hoagy Carmichael
Victoria Music Co. Ltd . . . . USA
Film(s): . . . . Romance In The Dark
Elisabeth Welch . . . . HMV BD 889
Pat Boone . . . . London HAD 2204
Shirley Bassey . . . . Columbia 33SX 1382

'NEATH THE SOUTHERN MOON 1910
Victor Herbert / Rida Johnson Young /
B Feldman & Co Ltd . . . . USA
Show(s): . . . . Naughty Marietta
Film(s): . . . . Naughty Marietta
Nelson Eddy . . . . HMV DA 1419
Nelson Eddy & Nadine Connor . . . . Philips NBE 11116
The Paul Britten Orchestra & Chrous . . . . MGM C 779
Nelson Eddy appeared in the film *Naughty Marietta*.

NEED YOU TONIGHT November 1988
Andrew Farriss / Michael Hutchence
MCA Music . . . . Australia
INXS . . . . Mercury INXS 12

NEEDLES AND PINS February 1964
Jack Nitzche / Sonny Bono
Metric Music Ltd . . . . USA
Jackie De Shannon . . . . Liberty LIB 55563
The Searchers . . . . Pye 7N 15594
Smokie (1977) . . . . RAK 263

NELLIE DEAN 1905
Harry Armstrong
B. Feldman & Co. Ltd. . . . . USA
Gertie Gitana . . . . Ariel 1973
The Four Singing Waiters . . . . Parlophone PMC 1127

NELLIE KELLY I LOVE YOU (See Little Nelly Kelly I Love You)

NELLIE THE ELEPHANT October 1956
Peter Hart / Ralph Butler
Dash Music Ltd. . . . . UK
Mandy Miller . . . . Parlophone GEP 8776
The Toy Dolls (1984) . . . . Volume VOL 11
Ivor Novello Award.

NELSON MANDELA April 1984
Jerry Dammers
Plangent Visions Music . . . . UK
The Special AKA . . . . 2 Tone CHSTT 26

NESSUN DORMA July 1990
Giacomo Puccini
Ricordi . . . . Italy
Luciano Pavarotti . . . . Decca PAVO 3
From Act 3 of the opera *Turandot*.

NEVER   April 1952
Elliot Daniels / Lionel Newman
Robbins Music Corporation . . . . USA
Film(s): . . . . The Golden Girl
Toni Arden . . . . **Columbia DB 2998**
Lee Lawrence . . . . **Decca F 9833**
Bob Eberly . . . . **Capitol CL 13613**
Dennis Day . . . . **HMV B 10242**
Nominated for an Academy Award 1951.

NEVER   March 1988
Holly Knight / Gene Bloch'Connie'
Warner Chappell Music . . . . USA
Heart . . . . **Capitol CL 482**

NEVER CAN SAY GOODBYE   February 1975
Clifton Davis
Jobete Music (UK) Ltd. . . . . USA
Gloria Gaynor . . . . **MGM 2006463**
The Communards (1987) . . . . **London LON 158**

NEVER DO A TANGO WITH AN ESKIMO   January 1956
Tommie Connor
Michael Reine Music Co. Ltd. . . . . UK
Alma Cogan . . . . **HMV 7M 337**

NEVER ENDING SONG OF LOVE   September 1971
Delaney Bramlett
United Artists Music Co. Ltd . . . . USA
The New Seekers . . . . **Philips 6006125**
Delaney & Bonnie . . . . **Atlantic 2400119**

NEVER ENDING STORY   November 1984
Giorgio Moroder / Keith Forsey
Moroder Music . . . . UK
Limahl . . . . **EMI LML 3**

NEVER GONNA GIVE YOU UP   March 1983
Frederick Waite / Dennis Seaton
Ten Music . . . . UK
Musical Youth . . . . **MCA YOU 3**

NEVER GONNA GIVE YOU UP   September 1987
Mike Stock / Matt Aitken / Peter Waterman
All Boys Music . . . . UK
Rick Astley . . . . **RCA PB 41447**
Ivor Novello Award.

NEVER GOODBYE   April 1962
Jimmy Kennedy
Palace Music Ltd. . . . . UK
Karl Denver . . . . **Decca F 11431**

NEVER HAD A DREAM COME TRUE   May 1970
Sylvia Moy / Stevie Wonder / Henry Cosby
Jobete Music (UK) Ltd. . . . . USA
Stevie Wonder . . . . **Tamla Motown TMG 731**

NEVER IN A MILLION YEARS   1937
Mack Gordon / Harry Revel
Francis, Day & Hunter Ltd. . . . . USA
Film(s): . . . . Wake Up and Live
Alice Faye . . . . **Columbia DB 1831**
Joan Regan . . . . **Decca LK 4151**
Alice Faye . . . . **Reprise R 6029**
Alice Faye appeared in *Wake Up and Live.*

NEVER KNEW LOVE LIKE THIS BEFORE   November 1980
James Mtume / Reggie Lucas
Fresh Air Music . . . . USA
Stephanie Mills . . . . **20th Century TC 2406**

NEVER LET HER SLIP AWAY   May 1978
Andrew Gold
Warner Brothers Music Ltd . . . . UK
Andrew Gold . . . . **Asylum K 13112**

NEVER MIND   May 1959
Ian Samwell
Kalith Music Ltd . . . . UK
Cliff Richard . . . . **Columbia DB 4290**

NEVER NEVER   December 1983
Vincent Clarke
Sonet Music . . . . UK

Assembly . . . . **Mute TINY 1**

NEVER NEVER LAND   July 1954
Gerhard Froboess / Ralph Butler / Sy Cromwell & S.A. Beecher Stevens
Keith Prowse Music Publishing Co. Ltd. . . . . UK
Diana Decker . . . . **Columbia SCM 5123**
Peter Sellers . . . . **HMV B 10724**

NEVER ON SUNDAY   October 1960
Manos Hadjidakis / Billy Towne
United Artists Music Ltd . . . . Greece
Film(s): . . . . Never on Sunday
Melina Mercouri . . . . **HMV 7EG 8701**
Lyn Cornell . . . . **Decca F 11277**
Don Costa & his Orchestra & chorus . . . . **HMV 7EG 8701**
Academy Award winning song for 1960.

NEVER SAY GOODBYE   1943
Harry Parr-Davies / Harold Purcell
Chappell & Co. Ltd . . . . UK
Show(s): . . . . Lisbon Story
Film(s): . . . . Lisbon Story
Patricia Burke . . . . **Columbia DB 2118**
Richard Tauber . . . . **Parlophone RO 20545**
Patricia Burke appeared in the show *Lisbon Story.*
Richard Tauber appeared in the film *Lisbon Story.*

NEVER TOO LATE   November 1989
Mike Stock / Matt Aitken / Peter Waterman
All Boys Music . . . . UK
Kylie Minogue . . . . **P.W.L. PWL 45**

NEVER TRUST A STRANGER   October 1988
Kim Wilde / Ricky Wilde
Rickim Music . . . . UK
Kim Wilde . . . . **MCA KIM 9**

**NEVER TURN YOUR BACK ON
MOTHER EARTH**   November 1974
Ron Mael
Island Music Ltd. . . . . UK
Sparks . . . . **Island WIP 6211**

NEVER, NEVER, NEVER (Grande, Grande, Grande)   April 1973
Alberto Testa / Tony Renis / Norman Newell
Southern Music Publishing Co. Ltd. . . . . Italy
Shirley Bassey . . . . **United Artists UP 35490**
Vikki Carr (in Italian) . . . . **CBS 8438**

NEVERTHELESS   1931
Bert Kalmar / Harry Ruby
Victoria Music Co. Ltd. . . . . USA
Film(s): . . . . Three Little Words
Ambrose & his Orchestra, vocal Sam Browne . . . **HMV B 6061**
The Mills Brothers . . . . **Brunswick 04639**
Fred Astaire, Red Skelton & Anita Ellis . . . . **MGM D 139**
The Mills Brothers . . . . **London HAD 2196**
Gordon MacRae . . . . **Capitol T 1050**
Frankie Vaughan (1967) . . . . **Columbia DB 8354**
Fred Astaire, Red Skelton & Anita Ellis appeared in *Three Little Words.*

NEVR BE ANYONE ELSE BUT YOU   May 1959
Baker Knight
Commodore Imperial Music . . . . USA
Ricky Nelson . . . . **London HLP 8817**

NEW BEGINNING   June 1986
Mike Myers / Tony Gibber
Tasty Music . . . . UK
Bucks Fizz . . . . **Polydor POSP 794**

NEW ENGLAND   February 1985
Billy Bragg
Chappell Music Co. . . . . UK
Kirsty McColl . . . . **Stiff BUY 216**

NEW FANGLED TANGO, A   August 1957
Matt Dubey / Harold Karr
Chappell & Co. Ltd. . . . . USA
Show(s): . . . . Happy Hunting
Lena Horne . . . . **RCA RD 27021**
Maurice Chevalier . . . . **MGM C 783**

NEW LIFE   **August 1981**
Vincent Clarke
Sonet Music . . . . UK
Depeche Mode . . . . **Mute 014**

NEW MOON AND AN OLD SERENADE, A   **1939**
Abner Silver / Martin Block / Sam Coslow
Chappell & Co. Ltd. . . . . USA
Adelaide Hall   **Decca F 7095**

NEW MOON ON MONDAY   **February 1984**
"Duran Duran"
Carlin Music . . . . UK
Duran Duran . . . . **EMI DURAN 1**

NEW ORLEANS   **1939**
Hoagy Carmichael
Southern Music Publishing Co. Ltd. . . . . USA
Ella Logan & Hoagy Carmichael . . . . **Parlophone R 2611**
Hoagy Carmichael . . . . **Vogue VA 160112**
Louis Armstrong & The
Dukes of Dixieland . . . . **Audio Fidelity AFLP 1924**

NEW ORLEANS   **February 1961**
Frank Guida / Joseph Royster
Dominion Music Ltd . . . . USA
Gary U.S. Bonds . . . . **Top Rank JAR 527**
Harley Quinne . . . . **Bell 1255**
Bern Elliott & The Fen Men . . . . **Decca F 11852**
Gillan (1981) . . . . **Virgin VS 406**

NEW SONG   **October 1983**
Howard Jones
Warner Brothers Music . . . . UK
Howard Jones . . . . **WEA HOW 1**

NEW SUN IN THE SKY, A   **1932**
Howard Dietz / Arthur Schwartz
Chappell & Co. Ltd. . . . . USA
Show(s): . . . . Band Wagon
Film(s): . . . . Band Wagon / Dancing in the Dark
Fred & Adele Astaire . . . . **RCA RD 7756**
Fred Astaire . . . . **HMV CLP 1304**
Keeley Smith . . . . **Reprise R 6086**
Bing Crosby . . . . **Philips 6359013**
Inidia Adams (Dubbed for Cyd Charisse) . . . . . . **MGM 686**
Fred & Adele Astaire appeared in the show *Band Wagon*.
Fred Astaire appeared in the film *Band Wagon*.
Cyd Charisse appeared in the film *Dancing in the Dark*.

NEW WORLD IN THE MORNING, A   **November 1970**
Roger Whittaker
Tembo Music . . . . UK
Roger Whittaker . . . . **Columbia DB 8718**

NEW YEARS DAY   **February 1983**
"U2"
Blue Mountain Music . . . . UK
U2 . . . . **Island UWIP 6848**

NEW YORK CITY   **August 1975**
Marc Bolan
Wizard Music . . . . UK
T. Rex . . . . **EMI MARC 10**

NEW YORK GROOVE   **November 1975**
Russ Ballard
Island Music Ltd . . . . UK
Hello . . . . **Bell 1438**

NEW YORK MINING DISASTER 1941, THE   **May 1967**
Barry Gibb / Maurice Gibb / Robin Gibb
Abigail Music . . . . UK
The Bee Gees . . . . **Polydor 56 161**

NEW YORK, NEW YORK   **October 1949**
Betty Comden / Adolph Green / Leonard Bernstein
Warner Brothers Music Ltd . . . . USA
Show(s): . . . . On the Town
Film(s): . . . . On the Town
Franklin Kiser, Don McKay & Elliot Gould . . . . **CBS APG 60005**
Betty Comden & Adolph Green . . . . **Capitol LCT 6186**
Frank Sinatra, Gene Kelly & Jules Munshin . . . . . . **Caliban 6023**
Franklin Kiser, Don McKay & Elliot Gould appeared in the British
production of *On The Town*.

Frank Sinatra, Gene Kelly & Jules Munshin appeared in the film *On
the Town*.

NEW YORK, NEW YORK   **March 1986**
John Kander / Fred Ebb
United Partnership Music Co. . . . . USA
Film(s): . . . . New York New York
Liza Minelli . . . . **Silver Screen 154 99290**
Frank Sinatra . . . . **Reprise K 14502**
Liza Minelli appeared in *New York New York*.

NEXT TIME   **February 1963**
Buddy Kaye / Philip Springer
Elstree Music Ltd . . . . UK
Film(s): . . . . Summer Holiday
Cliff Richard . . . . **Columbia DB 4950**
Cliff Richard appeared in *Summer Holiday*.

NICE CUP OF TEA, A   **1937**
A.P. Herbert / Henry Sullivan
B. Feldman & Co. Ltd. . . . . UK
Show(s): . . . . Home and Beauty
Binnie Hale . . . . **Columbia DB 1686**
Binnie Hale appeared in *Home and Beauty*.

NICE ONE CYRIL   **March 1973**
Harold Spiro / Helen Clarke
Belwin-Mills Music Ltd. . . . . UK
The Cockerel Chorus . . . . **Young Blood YB 1017**
Ivor Novello Award.

NICE PEOPLE   **1938**
Nat Mills / Fred Malcolm
Francis, Day & Hunter Ltd. . . . . UK
Show(s): . . . . These Foolish Things
Flanagan & Allen . . . . **Columbia 33S 1010**
Flanagan & Allen appeared in *These Foolish Things*

NICE TO KNOW YOU CARE   **October 1948**
Norman Newell / Leslie Baguley
Unit Music Publishing Co. Ltd . . . . UK
Leslie Hutchinson (Hutch) . . . . **HMV B 9629**
Tony Brent . . . . **Columbia S 1125**
The Radio Revellers . . . . **Columbia FB 3415**

NICE WORK IF YOU CAN GET IT   **1938**
George Gershwin / Ira Gershwin
Chappell & Co. Ltd. . . . . USA
Film(s): . . . . A Damsel in Distress / An American in Paris
Fred Astaire . . . . **Philips DDL 7052**
Dinah Shore . . . . **RCA RD 27072**
Mel Tormé . . . . **Parlophone GEP 8830**
Doris Day . . . . **Philips BBL 7248**
Fred Astaire appeared in *A Damsel in Distress*.

NICOLA   **May 1962**
Steve Race
Mills Music Ltd. . . . . UK
Chaquito & his Orchestra . . . . **Fontana TFL 5111**
Steve Race (Piano with Rhythm accomp.) . . . . . . **Gala GSP 811**
Steve Race Orchestra . . . . **Parlophone R 4894**
Manuel & his Music of The Mountains . . . **Columbia 33SX 1538**
Steve Race Orchestra . . . . **HMV CLP 1583**
The King Brothers . . . . **Parlophone R 4947**
Theme tune of Steve Race.
Ivor Novello Award.

NIGHT AND DAY   **1933**
Cole Porter
Chappell & Co. Ltd. . . . . USA
Show(s): . . . . The Gay Divorce
Film(s):The Gay Divorcee / Night and Day / Reveille with Beverly /
Lady on a Train
Leo Reisman & his Orchestra, vocal Fred Astaire . . . **HMV B 6398**
Fred Astaire . . . . **Columbia DB 1215**
Ella Fitzgerald . . . . **HMV CLP 1084**
Fred Astaire . . . . **HMV CLP 1100**
Steve Lawrence . . . . **HMV CLP 1462**
Al Hibbler . . . . **Brunswick LAT 8140**
Frank Sinatra . . . . **RCA RD 27104**
Fred Astaire appeared in both the American and British productions
of *The Gay Divorce* and also *The Gay Divorcee*.
Frank Sinatra appeared in *Reveille with Beverly*.

NIGHT BIRDS   May 1982
William Sharpe / Roger O'Dell
Skratch Music .... UK
Shakatak .... **Polydor POSP 407**

NIGHT CHICAGO DIED, THE   June 1974
Mitch Murray / Peter Callander
Intune Ltd. .... UK
Paper Lace .... **Bus Stop BUS 1016**
Ivor Novello Award.

NIGHT FEVER   June 1978
Robin Gibb / Maurice Gibb / Barry Gibb
Chappell & Co. Ltd .... UK
Film(s): .... Saturday Night Fever
The Bee Gees .... **RSO 002**
Ivor Novello Award.

NIGHT GAMES   April 1981
Ed Hamilton
Eaton Music .... UK
Graham Bonnet .... **Vertigo VER 1**

NIGHT HAS A THOUSAND EYES, THE   March 1963
Ben Weisman / Dottie Wayne / Marilyn Garrett
Aberbach (London) Ltd. .... USA
Film(s): .... Just For Fun
Bobby Vee .... **Liberty LIB 10069**
Jimmy Justice .... **Pye NPL 18085**

NIGHT IS FILLED WITH MUSIC, THE   1938
Irving Berlin
Irving Berlin Ltd. .... USA
Film(s): .... Carefree
Harry Roy & his Orchestra .... **Parlophone F 1259**
Victor Sylvester & his Silver Strings . **Columbia 33SX 1109**

NIGHT IS YOUNG AND YOU'RE SO BEAUTIFUL, THE   1937
Billy Rose / Irving Kahal / Dana Suesse
Chappell & Co. Ltd. .... USA
Show(s): .... And on We Go
Harry Richman .... **Columbia DB 1698**
Mario Lanza .... **RCA RB 16085**

NIGHT OF FEAR   February 1967
Roy Wood
Essex Music Ltd. .... UK
The Move .... **Deram DM 109**
Adapted from the 1812 Overture by Peter Ilyitch Tchaikovsky (1840 - 1893).

NIGHT ON THE DESERT   1934
Billy Hill
Peter Maurice Music Co. Ltd. .... USA
Ted Hanson's Hotel Normandie
Orchestra .... **Regal Zonophone MR 1365**

NIGHT OWL   July 1979
Gerry Rafferty
Island Music Ltd. .... UK
Gerry Rafferty .... **United Artists UP 36512**

NIGHT THE FLOOR FELL IN, THE   June 1950
Ken Wheeley
Southern Music Publishing Co. Ltd .... UK
Billy Cotton & his Band, vocal
Alan Breeze & The Bandits .... **Decca F 9458**

NIGHT THEY DROVE OLD DIXIE DOWN, THE   November 1971
Jamie Robertson
Island Music Ltd .... USA
Joan Baez .... **Vanguard VRS 35138**

NIGHT THEY INVENTED CHAMPAGNE, THE   1958
Alan J Lerner / Frederick Loewe
Chappell Music Co. Ltd. .... USA
Film(s): .... Gigi
Leslie Caron, Louis Jourdan & Hermoine Gingold   **MGM C 770**
Leslie Caron, Louis Jourdan & Hermoine Gingold appeared in *Gigi*.
Betty Wand dubbed the singing voice of Leslie Caron.

NIGHT TO REMEMBER, A   July 1982
Donna Meyers / Charmaine Sylvers / Nidra Beard
Chappell Music Co. .... USA
Shalamar .... **Solar K 13162**

NIGHT WAS MADE FOR LOVE, THE   1932
Jerome Kern / Otto Harbach
Chappell & Co. Ltd. .... USA
Show(s): .... The Cat and the Fiddle
Film(s): .... The Cat and the Fiddle
Peggy Wood .... **Columbia DB 797**
Doreen Hume & Dennis Quiley .... **Fontana TFL 5028**
Peggy Wood appeared in the British production of *The Cat and the Fiddle*.

NIGHT WE CALLED IT A DAY, THE   September 1955
Matt Dennis / Tom Adair
Dorsey Brothers Music Ltd. .... USA
Film(s): .... Sing a Jingle
Frank Sinatra .... **RCA RD 27104**
Chris Connor .... **London LTZK 15151**

NIGHT, THE   May 1975
Bob Gaudio / Al Ruzicka
Jobete Music (UK) Ltd. .... USA
Frankie Valli & The Four Seasons ..... **Mowest MW 3024**

NIGHTINGALE   1943
Xavier Cugat / George Rosner / Fred Wise
Campbell Connelly & Co. Ltd .... USA
Ambrose & his Orchestra, vocal Anne Shelton .. **Decca F 8242**
Xavier Cugat & his Orchestra .... **Mercury MMC 14967**
Ann Richards .... **Capitol T 1087**

NIGHTINGALE SANG IN BERKELEY SQUARE, A   1940
Eric Maschwitz / Jack Strachey / Manning Sherwin
Peter Maurice Music Co. Ltd .... UK
Show(s): .... New Faces
Leslie Hutchinson (Hutch) .... **Parlophone F 1736**
Bing Crosby .... **Brunswick 03127**
Anita O'Day .... **HMV CLP 1085**
Mark Murphy .... **Brunswick LAT 8172**

NIGHTS IN THE WOOD (Les Nuits Du Bois)   1924
Harold De Bozi / L. Lemarchand / William Helmore
Keith Prowse Music Publishing Co. Ltd .... France
The Savoy Havana Band .... **Columbia 3357**

NIGHTS IN WHITE SATIN   January 1967
Justin Hayward
Tyler Music ltd. .... UK
The Moody Blues .... **Deram DM 161**
The Moody Blues (1972) .... **Deram DM 161**
The Moody Blues (1979) .... **Deram DM 161**

NIGHTS OF GLADNESS   1912
Charles Ancliff
Boosey & Hawkes Music Publishers Ltd .... UK
The Peerless Orchestra .... **Zonophone 970**
Charles Ancliff & his Orchestra ..... **Columbia DB 339**
Sidney Thompson & his Orchestra .... **Parlophone GEP 8512**

NIGHTS ON BROADWAY   September 1977
Robin Gibb / Barry Gibb / Maurice Gibb
Abigail Music .... UK
Candi Staton .... **Warner Brothers K 16972**

NIGHTSHIFT   March 1985
Walter Orange / Dennis Lambert / Frannie Golde
EMI Music .... USA
The Commodores .... **Motown TMG 1371**

NIKITA   November 1985
Elton John / Bernie Taupin
Big Pig Music .... UK
Elton John .... **Rocket EJS 9**
Ivor Novello Award (1985).
Ivor Novello Nomination (1986).

NINA   1945
Noel Coward
Chappell & Co. Ltd. .... UK
Show(s): .... Sigh No More
Noel Coward (1945) .... **HMV B 9434**
Noel Coward (1956) .... **Philips BBL 7108**

NINE TIMES OUT OF TEN   October 1960
Otis Blackwell / Waldense Hall
Aberbach (London) Ltd. .... USA
Cliff Richard .... **Columbia SEG 8050**

NINE TO FIVE　　　　　　　　　**September 1980**
Florrie Palmer
Chappell & Co. Ltd .... UK
Sheena Easton .... **EMI 5066**

NINE TO FIVE　　　　　　　　　**April 1981**
Charles Fox
Unknown Publisher .... USA
Film(s): ....Nine to Five
Dolly Parton (Soundtrack) .... **20th Century Fox T 627**
Dolly Parton .... **RCA 25**
Nominated for an Acadmey Award 1980.

NINETEEN　　　　　　　　　　**May 1985**
Paul Hardcastle / William Couturie / Mike Oldfield / Jonas McCord
Oval Music .... UK
Paul Hardcastle .... **Chrysalis CHS 2860**
Ivor Novello Award.

NINETEENTH NERVOUS BREAKDOWN　　**March 1966**
Mick Jagger / Keith Richard
Mirage Music Ltd. .... UK
The Rolling Stones .... **Decca F 12331**

NINETY-NINE OUT OF A HUNDRED　　**1931**
Al Lewis / Al Sherman
Keith Prowse Music Publishing Co. Ltd .... USA
Ben Selvin & his Orchestra .... **Columbia CB 279**

NINETY-NINE RED BALLOONS　　　**March 1984**
Jorn-Uwe Fahrenkrog-Petersen / Carlos Karges / Kevin McAlea
CBS Songs .... Germany
Nena .... **Epic A 4074**

NINETY-NINE WAYS　　　　　　**May 1957**
Charlie Grace / Anthony September
Good Music Ltd. .... USA
Charlie Gracie .... **Parlophone GEP 8630**
Tab Hunter .... **London RED 1134**

NIRVANA　　　　　　　　　　**1900**
Stephen Adams / Frederick E. Weatherly
Boosey & Hawkes Ltd. .... UK
Sidney Coltham .... **Zonophone Twin A 150**
John McCormack .... **HMV DB 633**
Richard Crooks .... **HMV DB 1951**
Vernon Midgley .... **MVM MVM 6680**

NO ARMS CAN EVER HOLD YOU　　**January 1965**
Art Grafer / Jimmy Nebb
Burlington Music Co. Ltd .... USA
Jimmy Young .... **Decca F 10597**
The Bachelors .... **Decca F 12034**
Pat Boone .... **London HLD 8197**
Connie Francis .... **MGM C 930**

NO CAN DO　　　　　　　　　**1946**
Charles Tobias / Nat Simon
Francis, Day & Hunter Ltd. .... USA
Joe Loss & his Orchestra, vocal Elizabeth Batey ... **HMV BD 5915**
Kurt Edelhagen & his Orchestra .... **Philips BBR 8007**
Guy Lombardo & his Royal Canadians .. **Brunswick LAT 8063**

NO CHARGE　　　　　　　　　**June 1976**
Harlan Howard
London Tree Music Ltd .... USA
J.J. Barrie .... **Power Exchange PX 209**

NO DOUBT ABOUT IT　　　　　　**June 1980**
Dave Most / Steven Glen / Michael Burns
Rak Music Ltd .... UK
Hot Chocolate .... **Rak 310**

NO GREATER LOVE　　　　　　**1936**
Isham Jones / Marty Symes
Keith Prowse Music Publishing Co. Ltd .... USA
Duke Ellington & his Orchestra .... **Brunswick 02194**
Woody Herman & his Four Chips,
vocal Woody Herman (1947) .... **Columbia DB 2356**
Billie Holiday .... **Brunswick LA 8676**
Monty Babson .... **London HAJ 2212**
Adapted from 'Concerto No. 1' by Peter Ilyitch Tchaikovsky 91840-1893).

NO HONESTLY　　　　　　　　**November 1974**
Lynsey De Paul

Standard Music .... UK
Lynsey De Paul .... **Jet 747**
Theme of the TV series "No Honestly".
Ivor Novello Award.

NO LOVE, NO NOTHING　　　　　**1944**
Harry Warren / Leo Robin
Bradbury Wood Ltd. .... USA
Film(s): .... The Girls He Left Behind
Alice Faye .... **Reprise R 6029**
Dorothy Carless .... **Regal Zonophone MR 3726**
Jo Stafford .... **Philips BBL 7290**
Alice Faye appeared in *The Girls He Left Behind.*

NO MATTER HOW I TRY　　　　**January 1972**
Gilbert O'Sullivan
April Music Ltd .... UK
Gilbert O'Sullivan .... **MAM 53**
Ivor Novello Award.

NO MATTER WHAT　　　　　　**February 1971**
Peter Ham
Apple Pubishing .... UK
Badfinger .... **Apple 31**

NO MILK TODAY　　　　　　　**November 1966**
Graham Gouldman
Hournew Music Ltd. .... UK
Herman's Hermits .... **Columbia DB 8012**

NO MOON AT ALL　　　　　　**1949**
Redd Evans / Dave Mann
.... USA
King Cole Trio .... **Capitol EST 23480**
Jerry Vale .... **CBS CBS 32411**
Robert Goulet .... **CBS BPG 62500**

NO MORE HEROES　　　　　　**October 1977**
"The Stranglers"
April Music Ltd .... UK
The Stranglers .... **United Artists UP 36300**

NO MORE LONELY NIGHTS　　　**November 1984**
Paul McCartney
M.P.L. Publishing .... UK
Paul McCartney .... **Parlophone R 6080**

NO MORE MISTER NICE GUY　　**May 1973**
Alice Cooper / Mike Bruce
Warner Brothers Music Ltd. .... USA
Alice Cooper .... **Warner Brothers K 16262**

NO MORE TEARS (Enough is Enough)　**December 1979**
Paul Jabara / Bruce Roberts
Sunbury Music Ltd. .... USA
Donna Summer & Barbra Streisand .... **CBS 800**
Donna Summer & Barbra Streisand .... **Casablanca CAN 174**

NO MORE THE FOOL　　　　　**January 1987**
Russ Ballard
Virgin Music .... UK
Elkie Brooks .... **Legend LM 4**

NO ONE BUT YOU　　　　　　**September 1954**
Nicholas Brodszky / Jack Lawrence
Robbins Music Corporation Ltd. .... USA
Film(s): .... The Flame and the Flesh
Billy Eckstine .... **MGM D 138**
Al Martino .... **Capitol CL 14202**
The Beverley Sisters .... **Columbia 33SX 1285**

NO ONE CAN MAKE MY SUNSHINE SMILE　**November 1962**
Gerry Goffin / Jack Keller
Aldon Music Ltd. .... USA
The Everly Brothers .... **Warner Brothers WB 79**

NO ORCHIDS FOR MY LADY　　**September 1948**
Jack Strachey / Alan Stranks
Edward Kassner Music Co. Ltd. .... UK
Show(s): .... Bolton's Revue
The Ink Spots .... **Brunswick 04057**
Peter Yorke & his Orchestra,
vocal Steve Conway .... **Columbia DB 2452**
Billy Eckstine .... **MGM EP 690**

NO OTHER LOVE August 1950
Paul Weston / Bob Russell
Walt Disney Music Co. Ltd . . . . USA
Jo Stafford with Paul Weston &
his Orchestra . . . . **Capitol CL 14030**
Ronnie Hilton . . . . **HMV POP 198**
Paul Weston & his Orchestra . . . . **Capitol T 1563**
Adapted from *Etude in E Major* by Frederic Chopin (1810 - 1849).

NO OTHER LOVE April 1956
Richard Rodgers / Oscar Hammerstein II
Williamson Music Ltd. . . . . USA
Show(s): . . . . Me and Juliet / Cinderella
Perry Como . . . . **RCA RCX 1018**
Bing Crosby . . . . **Brunswick LAT 8281**
Bruce Trent . . . . **Decca LK 4303**
Bruce Trent appeared in *Cinderella*. Adapted from 'Beneath the
Southern Cross' by Richard Rodgers (from the TV Serial 'Victory at
Sea').

NO PARTICULAR PLACE TO GO June 1964
Chuck Berry
Jewel Music Publishing Co. Ltd . . . . USA
Chuck Berry . . . . **Pye 7N 25242**
Jerry Lee Lewis . . . . **Philips BL 7650**

NO REGRETS 1936
Harry Tobias / Roy Ingraham
Keith Prowse Music Publishing Co. Ltd . . . . USA
Billie Holiday . . . . **Vocalion S 24**
Johnnie Ray . . . . **Philips BBE 12217**
The Hilltoppers . . . . **London RED 1099**

NO REGRETS February 1976
Tom Rush
Essex Music Ltd . . . . USA
The Walker Brothers . . . . **GTO GT 42**
Tom Rush . . . . **Elektra EKL 4018**
Shirley Bassey . . . . **United Artists UAG 29471**
Olivia Newton-John . . . . **Pye NSPL 28155**
Midge Ure (1982) . . . . **Chrysalis CHS 2618**

NO REGRETS (Non Je Ne Regrette Rien) March 1961
Charles Dumont / Michel Vaucaire / Hal David
Shapiro-Bernstein & Co. Ltd . . . . France
Edith Piaf (in French) . . . . **Columbia DB 4596**
Kay Starr . . . . **Capitol CL 15308**
Shirley Bassey (1965) . . . . **Columbia DB 7535**

NO STRINGS 1936
Irving Berlin
Irving Berlin Ltd . . . . USA
Film(s): . . . . Top Hat
Fred Astaire . . . . **HMV 7EG 8463**
Ginger Rogers . . . . **Decca F 5746**
Fred Astaire & Ginger Rogers appeared in *Top Hat*.

NO TWO PEOPLE December 1952
Frank Loesser
Edwin H. Morris & Co. Ltd . . . . USA
Show(s): . . . . Hans Andersen
Film(s): . . . . Hans Christian Andersen
Danny Kaye & Jane Wyman . . . . **Brunswick LA 8572**
Eydie Gormé & Steve Lawrence . . . . **HMV CLP 1372**
Tomme Steele & Colette Gleeson . . . . **Pye NSPL 18451**
Danny Kaye appeared in *Hans Christian Andersen*.
Tommy Steele & Colette Gleeson appeared in *Hans Andersen*

NO WOMAN NO CRY July 1981
Vincent Ford
Rondor Music . . . . USA
Bob Marley & The Wailers . . . . **Island WIP 6244**

NO! NO! A THOUSAND TIMES NO 1935
Abner Silver / Al Sherman / Al Lewis
Francis, Day & Hunter Ltd . . . . USA
Ambrose & his Orchestra,
vocal Elsie Carlisle & Sam Browne . . . . **Decca F 6926**
Jean Campbell & The Steve Race Four . . **Columbia 33SX 1124**

NO-ONE IS INNOCENT July 1978
Paul Cook / Steve Jones / Ronald Biggs
Warner Brothers Music Ltd . . . . UK
The Sex Pistols . . . . **Virgin VS 220**

NOBODY DOES IT BETTER September 1977
Carole Bayer Sager / Marvin Hamilisch
United Artists Music Co. Ltd . . . . USA
Film(s): . . . . The Spy Who Loved Me
Carly Simon . . . . **Elektra K 12261**

NOBODY I KNOW June 1964
John Lennon / Paul McCartney
Northern Songs Ltd . . . . UK
Peter & Gordon . . . . **Columbia DB 7292**

NOBODY KNOWS 1920
Irving Berlin
Herman Darewski Music Publising Co. Ltd . . . . USA
Will Strong (pseudonym for Peter Dawson) . . . . . **HMV B 1119**
Eddie Condon & Jack Teagarden . . . . **Brunswick LA 8542**

NOBODY KNOWS WHAT A
RED-HEAD MAMA CAN DO 1925
Irving Mills / Al Dubin / Sammy Fain
Lawrence Wright Music Co. Ltd. . . . . USA
Sophie Tucker . . . . **HMV B 2223**

NOBODY KNOWS YOU WHEN YOU'RE DOWN AND OUT 1931
Jimmy Cox
B. Feldman & Co. Ltd. . . . . USA
Bessie Smith . . . . **Philips BBL 7020**
Ottie Patterson . . . . **Decca DFE 6303**

NOBODY LIED (When They Said That I Cried Over You) 1922
Edwin J. Weber
B. Feldman & Co. Ltd . . . . USA
The Virginians . . . . **HMV B 1421**
Norah Blaney & Gwen Farrar . . . . **HMV B 1585**

NOBODY LOVES A FAIRY WHEN SHE'S FORTY 1934
Arthur Le Clerq
Lawrence Wright Music Co. Ltd . . . . UK
Tessie O'Shea . . . . **Decca F 5336**

NOBODY NEEDS YOUR LOVE August 1966
Randy Newman
Schroeder Music Ltd. . . . . USA
Gene Pitney . . . . **Stateside SS 518**

NOBODY TOLD ME February 1984
John Lennon
Warner Brothers Music . . . . UK
John Lennon . . . . **Polydor POSP 700**

NOBODY'S CHILD November 1969
Cy Coben
Acuff-Rose Publishing Co. Ltd. . . . . USA
Karen Young . . . . **Major Minor MM 625**

NOBODY'S DARLIN' BUT MINE 1935
Jimmy Davis
Southern Music Publishing Co. Ltd . . . . USA
Bing Crosby (1949) . . . . **Brunswick 04123**
Patti Page . . . . **Mercury MPL 6524**
Frank Ifield (1963) . . . . **Columbia DB 7007**
Les Allen . . . . **Columbia FB 1624**

NOBODY'S DIARY June 1983
Alison Moyet
Sonet Music . . . . UK
Yazoo . . . . **Mute YAZ 003**

NOBODY'S FOOL September 1982
Nick Heyward
Brian Morrison Music . . . . UK
Haircut 100 . . . . **Arista CLIP 4**

NOBODY'S SWEETHEART 1924
Gus Kahn / Ernie Erdman / Elmer Schoebel / Billy Meyers
Lawrence Wright Music Co. Ltd. . . . . USA
Film(s):Red Headed Woman / I'll See You in My Dreams / Cuban Love
Song / I'm Nobody's Sweetheart Now / Atlantic City
Charles Dornberg & his Orchestra . . . . **HMV B 1920**
Harry Roy & his Orchestra . . . . **Parlophone R 1734**
Connee Boswell . . . . **Brunswick 03231**
Bing Crosby . . . . **Brunswick LAT 8228**
Paul Whiteman &
his Orchestra . . . . **CBS BPG 62545**

NOBODY'S USING IT NOW 1930
Victor Schertzinger / Clifford Grey
Campbell Connelly & Co. Ltd . . . . USA
Film(s): . . . . The Love Parade
Maurice Chevalier . . . . **HMV B 3332**
Maurice Chevalier appeared in *The Love Parade*.

NOLA 1915
Felix Arndt
Keith Prowse Music Publishing Co. Ltd. . . . . USA
Film(s): . . . . That's the Spirit / The Big Broadcast
Vincent Lopez & his Orchestra . . . . **Parlophone E 5133**
The Revellers . . . . **HMV B 2680**
Ted Weems & his Orchestra . . . . **Brunswick 03806**
Liberace (piano) . . . . **Philips BBL 7160**
The Deep River Boys . . . . **Top Rank JAR 172**
Les Paul (guitar) . . . . **Capitol CL 13332**

NON DIMENTICAR (T'Ho Voluto Bene) April 1953
P.G. Redi / Michele Galdieri / Shelly Dobbins
Southern Music Publishing Co. Ltd . . . . Italy
Film(s): . . . . Anna
Silvana Mangano . . . . **MGM 624**
Nat 'King' Cole . . . . **Capitol CL 14937**
Connie Francis . . . . **MGM C 821**
Silvano Mangano appeared in *Anna*.

NORA MALONE (Call Me By Phone) 1909
Albert Von Tilzer / Junie McRee
Francis, Day & Hunter Ltd. . . . . USA
Film(s): . . . . The Naughty Nineties
Herbert Payne . . . . **Zonophone 935**
Teresa Brewer . . . . **Vogue LVA 9020**

NORMAN February 1962
John D. Loudermilk
Acuff-Rose Publishing Co. Ltd. . . . . USA
Sue Thompson . . . . **Polydor NH 66973**
Carol Deene . . . . **HMV POP 973**

NORTH TO ALASKA February 1961
Mike Philips
United Artists Music . . . . USA
Film(s): . . . . North to Alaska
Johnny Horton . . . . **Philips PB 1062**

NORTHERN LIGHTS August 1978
Michael Dunford / Betty Thatcher
Warner Brothers Music Ltd . . . . UK
Renaissance . . . . **Warner Brothers K 17177**

NOT FADE AWAY March 1964
Norman Potty / Charles Hardin
Southern Music Publishing Co. Ltd . . . . USA
The Crickets . . . . **Vogue Q 72298**
The Rolling Stones . . . . **Decca F 11845**

NOT MINE 1943
Victor Schertzinger / Johnny Mercer
Victoria Music Co. Ltd . . . . USA
Film(s): . . . . The Fleet's In
Jimmy Dorsey & his Orchestra,
vocal Bob Eberly & Helen O'Connell . . . . **Brunswick 03369**
Lita Roza . . . . **Pye NPL 18030**
Jimmy Dorsey, Bob Eberly & Helen O'Connell appeared in *The Fleet's in*.

NOT UNTIL THE NEXT TIME May 1965
Gail Tally
Burlington Music Co. Ltd . . . . USA
Jim Reeves . . . . **RCA 1446**

NOTHING CAN DIVIDE US October 1988
Mike Stock / Matt Aitken / Peter Waterman
All Boys Music . . . . UK
Jason Donovan . . . . **P.W.L. PWL 17**

NOTHING COMES EASY June 1966
Chris Andrews
Glissando Music Ltd. . . . . UK
Sandie Shaw . . . . **Pye 7N 17086**

NOTHING COMPARES 2 U February 1990
"Prince"
Warner Chappell Music . . . . USA

Sinead O'Connor . . . . **Ensign ENY 630**

NOTHING EVER HAPPENS February 1990
Justin Currie
Polygram Music . . . . UK
Del Amitri . . . . **A&M AM 536**
Ivor Novello Nomination.

NOTHING HAS BEEN PROVED March 1989
Neil Tennant / Chris Lowe
10 Music . . . . UK
Film(s): . . . . Scandal
Dusty Springfield & The Pet Shop Boys . . . **Parlophone R 6207**
Ivor Novello Nomination.

NOTHING RHYMED January 1971
Gilbert O'Sullivan
M.A.M. (Music Publishing) Ltd . . . . UK
Gilbert O'Sullivan . . . . **MAM 3**

NOTHING SERIOUS JUST BUGGIN' (See Just Buggin')

NOTHING'S GONNA CHANGE MY LOVE FOR YOU July 1988
Michael Masser / Gerry Goffin
Rondor Music . . . . USA
Glenn Madieros . . . . **London LON 184**

NOTHING'S GONNA STOP ME NOW June 1987
Mike Stock / Matt Aitken / Peter Waterman
All Boys Music . . . . UK
Samantha Fox . . . . **Jive FOXY 5**

NOTHING'S GONNA STOP US NOW May 1987
Dianne Warren / Albert Hammond
S.B.K. Songs . . . . UK
Film(s): . . . . Mannequin
Starship . . . . **Grunt FB 49757**
Nominated for an Academy Award 1987.

NOTORIOUS November 1986
John Taylor / Nick Rhodes / Simon Le Bon
EMI Music . . . . UK
Duran Duran . . . . **EMI DDN 45**

NOW February 1953
Joe Priolo / Pat Noto / Andrew Perri
Dash Music . . . . USA
Al Martino . . . . **Capitol CL 13835**
Julie Dawn . . . . **Columbia DB 3227**
Dick James . . . . **Parlophone R 3629**

NOW AND FOREVER (Oh Heideroslein) September 1954
Walter Rothenberg / Gerhard Winkler / Johnny May
New World Publishers Ltd. Germany
Vera Lynn . . . . **Decca F 10361**

NOW I HAVE TO CALL HIM FATHER 1908
Charles Collins / Fred Godfrey
Francis, Day & Hunter LKtd. . . . . UK
Vesta Victoria . . . . **HMV GC 3896**
Florrie Forde . . . . **Regal T 160**

NOW I KNOW 1944
Ted Koehler / Harold Arlen
Sterling Music Publishing Co. Ltd. . . . . USA
Film(s): . . . . Up in Arms
Dinah Shore . . . . **HMV BD 1084**
Anne Shelton . . . . **Philips BBL 7188**
Frank D'Rone . . . . **Mercury MMC 14053**
Dinah Shore appeared in *Up in Arms*.
Nominated for an Academy Award 1944.

NOW I'M HERE February 1975
Brian May
B. Feldman & Co. Ltd . . . . UK
Queen . . . . **EMI 2256**

NOW IS THE HOUR (Hearere Ra) 1947
Maewa Kaihau / Dorothy Scott
Keith Prowse Music Publishing Co. Ltd. . . . . New Zealand
Ana Hato . . . . **Parlophone R 3355**
Gracie Fields . . . . **Ace of Clubs ACL 1042**
Bing Crosby . . . . **Brunswick LAT 8370**
Connie Francis . . . . **MGM C 782**
First Published 1913.

NOW IS THE TIME   August 1976
Biddu'
Chappell & Co. Ltd . . . . UK
Jimmy James & The Vagabonds . . . . **Pye 7N 45606**

NOW IT CAN BE TOLD   1938
Irving Berlin
Chappell & Co. Ltd. . . . . USA
Film(s): . . . . Alexander's Ragtime Band
Bing Crosby . . . . **Brunswick 02646**
Dennis Lotis . . . . **Columbia 33SX 1089**
Nominated for an Academy Award 1938.

NOW THAT I NEED YOU   December 1949
Frank Loesser
Victoria Music Ltd . . . . USA
Film(s): . . . . Red, Hot and Blue
Betty Hutton . . . . **Capitol CL 13195**
Fran Warren . . . . **HMV B 9835**
Petula Clark . . . . **Pye NPL 18039**
Betty Hutton appeared in *Red, Hot and Blue.*

NOW THAT WE'VE FOUND LOVE   October 1978
Kenny Gamble / Leon Huff
Carlin Music Corporation . . . . USA
Third World . . . . **Island WIP 6457**

NOW THOSE DAYS ARE GONE   July 1982
Andy Hill / Nicola Martin
RCA Music . . . . UK
Bucks Fizz . . . . **RCA 241**

NOWS THE TIME TO FALL IN LOVE   1932
Al Sherman / Al Lewis
Victoria Music Co. Ltd. . . . . USA
Film(s): . . . . The Eddie Cantor Story
**Ambrose & his Orchestra,
vocal Sam Browne** . . . . **HMV B 6140**
Eddie Cantor . . . . **Brunswick LA 8658**

NUMBER ONE SONG IN HEAVEN, THE   June 1979
Ron Mael / Russell Mael
Heath Levy Music ltd. . . . . UK
The Sparks . . . . **Virgin VS 244**

NUMBER SOMETHING FAR AWAY LANE   1943
Howard Barnes / Hedley Grey / Ord Hamilton
Lawrence Wright Music Co. Ltd . . . . UK
Joe Loss & his Orchestra, vocal Harry Kaye . . . **HMV BD 5826**

NUMERO UNO   September 1989
Mirko Limoni / Daniela Davoli / Valerio Semplici
Warner Chappell Music . . . . Italy
Starlight . . . . **Beggars Banquet CBE 742**

NUNC DIMITTIS   December 1979
Traditional, arranged by Geoffrey Burgon
J. & W. Chester . . . . UK
Paul Phoenix . . . . **Different 20**
Theme of the TV production *Tinker, Tailor, Soldier, Spy.*
Ivor Novello Award.

NURSIE   1939
Art Noel / Don Pelosi
Chappell & Co. Ltd. . . . . UK
Elsie Carlisle . . . . **Rex 9693**

NUT ROCKER   June 1962
Arranged by Kim Fowley
Ardmore & Beechwood Ltd . . . . USA
B. Bumble & The Stingers . . . . **Top Rank JAR 611**
Adapted from the March from *Casse-Noisette Suite Op. 71a* by Peter
Ilyitch Tchaikovsky (1840 - 1893).

NUTBUSH CITY LIMITS   October 1973
Tina Turner
United Artists Music Co. Ltd. . . . . USA
Ike & Tina Turner . . . . **United Artists UP 35582**

O DRY THOSE TEARS   1901
Teresa Del Riego
Chappell & Co. Ltd. . . . . USA
Webster Booth . . . . **HMV B 9562**
Essie Ackland . . . . **HMV C 1885**

O FLOWER DIVINE   1914
Edward Teschemacher / Hadyn Wood
Chappell & Co. Ltd. . . . . UK
Doris Vane . . . . **Columbia 3879**

O MEIN PAPA   May 1953
Paul Burhard / Geoffrey Parsons / John Turner
Peter Maurice Music Co. Ltd . . . . Switzerland
Lys Assia . . . . **Decca F 10097**
Eddie Calvert (trumpet) . . . . **Columbia 33S 1020**
Connie Francis . . . . **MGM C 845**
Eddie Fisher . . . . **Camden CDN 167**

O SUPERMAN   October 1981
Laurie Anderson
Warner Brothers Music . . . . USA
Laurie Anderson . . . . **Warner Brothers K 17870**

O' L'AMOUR   February 1988
Vincent Clarke / Andrew Bell
Sonet Music . . . . UK
Dollar . . . . **London LON 146**

O.K. FRED   November 1979
John Holt / Monty Babson / Terry Creamer
Sparta Music Ltd. . . . . UK
Errol Dunkley . . . . **Scope SC 6**

O.K.?   June 1977
Howard Schuman / Andy MacKay
E.G. Music . . . . UK
**Julie Covington, Rula Lenska,
Charlotte Cornwell & Sue Jones-Davies** . . . . **Polydor 200 1714**

OB-LA-DI OB-LA-DA   January 1969
John Lennon / Paul McCartney
Northern Songs Ltd. . . . . UK
Marmalade . . . . **CBS 3892**
The Bedrocks . . . . **Columbia DB 8516**
The Beatles . . . . **Apple PMC 7067**
Ivor Novello Award.

OBJECT OF MY AFFECTION, THE   1934
Coy Poe / Jimmy Grier / Pinky Tomlin
Victoria Music Co. Ltd. . . . . USA
Film(s): . . . . Times Square Lady / The Fabulous Dorseys
The New Mayfair Dance Orchestra . . . . **HMV BD 111**
The Boswell Sisters . . . . **Brunswick 01961**
Dean Martin . . . . **Capitol T 849**

OBSESSION   June 1985
Holly Knight / Des Barnes
Zomba Music . . . . UK
Animotion . . . . **Mercury PH 34**

OCCASIONAL MAN, AN   1956
Hugh Martin / Ralph Blane
Frank Music Ltd. . . . . USA
Film(s): . . . . Girl Rush
Jeri Southern . . . . **Capitol CL 14376**
Marion Ryan . . . . **Columbia DB 4857**
Julie London . . . . **London HAG 2405**

OCTOBER TWILIGHT   August 1948
Henry Hadley / Guy Wood
Dash Music Ltd. . . . . USA
Anne Shelton . . . . **Decca F 8950**
Steve Conway . . . . **Columbia FB 3416**

ODE TO BILLY JOE   October 1967
Bobbie Gentry
Compass Music Ltd. . . . . USA
Bobbie Gentry . . . . **Capitol CL 15511**

OF THEE I SING   1931
George Gershwin / Ira Gershwin
Chappell & Co. Ltd. . . . . USA
Show(s): . . . . Of Thee I Sing
Sarah Vaughan . . . . **Mercury MPL 6525**
The Andrews Sisters . . . . **Capitol LCT 6145**

OFF THE WALL   December 1979
Rodney Temperton
Rondor Music (London) Ltd. . . . . USA
Michael Jackson . . . . **Epic EPC 8045**

Ivor Novello Nomination.

OGO-POGO, THE 1925
Ralph Butler / Mark Strong / Cumberland Clark
Box & Cox (Publications) Ltd. .... UK
The Savoy Havana Band .... **Columbia 3461**

OH BABE WHAT WOULD YOU SAY June 1972
Eileen Smith
Chappell & Co. Ltd. .... UK
Hurricane Smith .... **Columbia DB 8878**
Ivor Novello Award.

OH BOY February 1958
Norman Petty / Bill Tilghman / Sunny West
Southern Music Publishing Co. Ltd .... USA
The Crickets .... **Vogue LVA 9105**
Mud (1975) .... **RAK 201**

OH BOY (The Mood I'm In) April 1977
Tony Romeo
A.T.V. Music Ltd. .... USA
Brotherhood of Man .... **Pye 7N 45656**

OH BOY, WHAT JOY WE HAD IN BAREFOOT DAYS 1923
James Brennan / Al Wilson
Herman Darewski Music Publishinig Co. Ltd .... USA
Show(s): ....Bombo
The Five Smith Brothers .... **Parlophone R 3414**
Art Mooney & his Orchestra .... **MGM SP 1088**
Song added to *Bombo* in 1923.

OH BUT I DO 1947
Arthur Schwartz / Leo Robin
B. Feldman & Co. Ltd. .... USA
Film(s): .... The Time, the Place and the Girl
Ambrose & his Orchestra, vocal Bette Roberts .... **Decca F 8765**
Bing Crosby .... **Brunswick 03775**
Doris Day .... **Philips BBL 7248**

OH BY JINGO, OH BY GEE 1919
Albert Von Tilzer / Lew Brown
Francis, Day & Hunter Ltd .... USA
Show(s): ....Linger Longer Letty
Film(s): ....Incendiary Blonde
Violet Loraine .... **HMV D 487**
Bonnie Alden .... **Columbia 33S 1123**
Danny Kaye .... **Brunswick 04007**
Clinton Ford .... **Oriole EP 7027**

OH CAROL October 1959
Howard Greenfield / Neil Sedaka
Nevins-Kirshner Ltd .... USA
Neil Sedaka .... **RCA 1152**

OH CAROL June 1978
Mike Chapman / Nicky Chinn
Rak Music Ltd .... UK
Smokie .... **Rak 276**
Smokie (1987) .... **Rak 276**

OH DIANE February 1983
Lindsey BuckinghamRica
Intersong Publishing .... USA
Fleetwood Mac .... **Warner Brothers FLEET 1**

OH DONNA CLARA 1930
J. Petersburski / Jimmy Kennedy
B. Feldman & Co. Ltd .... Austria
Show(s): ....Wonder Bar
Dol Dauber & his Tango Orchestra .... **HMV B 5905**
George Metaxa .... **HMV B 3714**
Joe Loss & his Orchestra .... **HMV DLP 1129**
Stanley Black & his Orchestra .... **Decca LK 4325**

OH GEE, OH GOSH, OH GOLLY, I'M IN LOVE 1924
Ole Olsen / Chic Johnson / Ernest Breuer
B. Feldman & Co. Ltd. .... USA
Show(s): ....The Ziegfeld Follies of 1923
Eddie Cantor .... **Brunswick 04298**
Eddie Cantor appeared in *The Ziegfeld Follies of 1923*.

OH HAPPY DAY March 1953
Don Howard Koplow / Nancy Binns Reed

Bregman, Vocco & Conn Ltd .... USA
David Carey .... **Columbia SCM 5030**
Dick Todd .... **Brunswick 05061**
Johnston Brothers .... **Decca F 10071**

OH HAPPY DAY June 1969
Edwin Hawkins
Kama Sutra Music Ltd. .... USA
Edwin Hawkins Singers .... **Buddah 201048**

OH HOW I HATE TO GET UP IN THE MORNING 1918
Irving Berlin
B. Feldman & Co. Ltd. .... USA
Show(s): .... Yip Yip Yaphank / This is the Army
Film(s): ....Alexander's Ragtime Band / This is the Army
Irving Berlin .... **Brunswick 03492**
The Ray Charles Singers .... **Brunswick LAT 8310**
Irving Berlin appeared in Yip Yip Yaphank and both the American and
British productions and the film of *This is the Army*.

OH HOW I LAUGH WHEN I THINK HOW I CRIED ABOUT
YOU 1919
Roy Turk / Willy White / George Jessel
B. Feldman & Co. Ltd. .... USA
Violet Loraine .... **HMV D 494**

OH HOW I MISS YOU TONIGHT 1925
Joe Burke / Benny Davis / Mark Fisher
Francis, Day & Hunter Ltd. .... USA
The Benson Orchestra of Chicago .... **HMV B 2074**
Perry Como .... **RCA RCX 108**
Bing Crosby .... **Brunswick 04128**

OH HOW SHE COULD YACKI
HACKI WICKI WACKI WOO 1916
Albert Von Tilzer / Stanley Murphy / Charles McCarron
Francis, Day & Hunter Ltd. .... USA
Show(s). .... The Ziegfeld Follies of 1916 / Houp-La
Murray's Savoy Quartette .... **HMV B 830**
Ida Adams .... **HMV 03542**

OH IT'S A LOVELY WAR 1917
John P. Long / Maurice Scott
B. Feldman & Co. Ltd. .... UK
Show(s): ....Oh What a Lovely War
Film(s): ....Star
Ella Shields .... **Columbia 2850**
Chorus & Orchestra of Oh What a Lovely War .. **Decca LK 4542**
Julie Andrews .... **Stateside SL 10233**
Julie Andrews appeared in *Star*.

OH JULIE January 1982
Shakin' Stevens
Shaky Music .... UK
Shakin' Stevens .... **Epic EPCA 1742**
Ivor Novello Nomination.

OH LADY BE GOOD 1926
George Gershwin / Ira Gershwin
Chappell & Co. Ltd. .... USA
Show(s): .... Lady Be Good
Film(s): .... Lady Be Good / Rhapsody in Blue
Fred Astaire .... **London HAR 2219**
William Kent .... **Columbia 3980**
Buddy Lee .... **Columbia 3981**
Ella Fitzgerald .... **Brunswick LAT 8115**
Fred Astaire appeared in both the American and British productions
of *Lady Be Good*.
William Kent & Buddy Lee appeared in the British production of *Lady Be Good*.

OH LONESOME ME November 1962
Don Gibson
Acuff-Rose Publishing Co. Ltd .... USA
Craig Douglas .... **Decca F 11523**
Don Gibson .... **RCA RCX 110**
Johnny Burnette .... **London HAG 2349**

OH LOOK AT ME NOW January 1952
Joe Bushkin / John De Vries
Dorsey Brothers Music ITD .... USA
Film(s): .... Disc Jockey
Tommy Dorsey & his Orchestra, vocal Frank Sinatra & Connie
Haines .... **RCA RD 27069**
Frank Sinatra .... **Capitol LCT 6135**
Carmen McRae .... **Mercury AMT 1122**

OH LORD
August 1977
Billy Alessi / Bobby Alessi
Alessi Music .... USA
Alessi .... **A&M AMS 7289**

OH MAIDEN MY MAIDEN
1930
Franz Lehar / Harry S. Pepper
Chappell & Co. Ltd .... Austria
Show(s): .... Frederica
Joseph Hislop .... **HMV B 3590**
Richard Tauber .... **Parlophone PMB 1006**
Harry Secombe .... **Philips BBL 7387**
Joseph Hislop appeared in *Frederica.*

OH MAMA (The Butcher Boy)
1938
Rudy Vallee / Lew Brown / Paolo Citorello
Francis, Day & Hunter Ltd. .... Italy
Betty Driver .... **HMV BD 575**
The Andrews Sisters .... **Brunswick 02610**
Max Bygraves .... **Decca LK 4360**

OH MAMMA MIA
1940
Roma Campbell-Hunter / Freddy Grant
Dash Music Ltd .... UK
Monte Ray .... **Parlophone F 1710**

OH MONAH
1932
Ted Weems / Country Washburn
Southern Music Publishing Co. Ltd. .... USA
Roy Fox & his Orchestra, vocal Nat Gonella .. **Decca DFE 6272**
The Washboard Novelty Quartette .... **Rex 8053**
The Dinning Sisters .... **Capitol CL 13192**
Theme song of Lew Stone.

OH MR PORTER
1893
Thomas Le Brun / George Le Brun
Ascherberg, Hopwood & Crew Ltd. .... UK
Norah Blaney .... **Columbia DB 568**
Leon Cortez & his Coster Pals ... **Regal MR 2307**
Ray Wallace .... **Parlophone R 1190**

OH MUKI MUKI OH
1934
Billy Hill / Peter De Rose
Dash Music Co. Ltd .... USA
Al Shaw's Hawaiian Beachcombers .. **Regal Zonophone MR 1422**
Brian Lawrence .... **Decca F 5725**

OH NICHOLAS DON'T BE SO RIDICULOUS
1939
Jimmy Kennedy / Harry Castling
B. Feldman & Co. Ltd. .... UK
Tommy Trinder .... **Regal Zonophone MR 2930**
Billy Cotton & his Band, vocal Alan Breeze ..... **Decca F 9360**

OH NO NOT MY BABY
May 1965
Gerry Goffin / Carole King
Screen Gems - Columbia Music .... USA
Maxine Brown .... **Pye 7N 25272**
Manfred Mann .... **HMV POP 1413**
Rod Stewart (1973) .... **Mercury 6052371**

OH OH ANTONIO
1908
C.W. Murphy / Dan Lipton
Francis, Day & Hunter .... UK
Florrie Forde .... **Columbia 9780**
George Formby Snr .... **Pathé 77720**
The Coronets .... **Columbia SEG 7617**

OH OH I'M FALLING IN LOVE AGAIN
April 1958
Al Hoffman / Dick Manning / Mark Maxwell
Chappell & Co. .... USA
Marion Ryan .... **Nixa N 15130**
Donald Peers .... **Oriole CB 1431**
Marty Wilde .... **Philips PB 804**

OH PRETTY WOMAN
October 1964
Roy Orbison / Bill Dees
Acuff-Rose Publishing Co. Ltd .... USA
Roy Orbison .... **London HL 9919**

OH PROMISE ME
1889
Reginald De Koven / Clement Scott
Ascherberg, Hopwood & Crew Ltd. .... USA
Show(s): .... Robin Hood
Maurice D'Oisly .... **Odeon Talking 66683**

Nelson Eddy .... **Camden CDN 157**
Paul Robeson .... **HMV B 9059**

OH SO WUNDERBAR
February 1960
Wener Scharfenberger / Aldo Von Pinelli / Buddy Kaye
Edward Kassner Music Co. Ltd .... Germany
Robert Earl .... **Philips BBL 6394**
Malcolm Vaughan .... **HMV POP 700**

OH STAR OF EVE
1922
Hubert W. David / Ed Bryant
Lawrence Wright Music Co. Ltd .... UK
The Broadway Five .... **Columbia 3237**

OH THE PITY OF IT ALL
1943
Leo Robin / Ralph Rainger
Sun Music Publishing Co. Ltd. .... USA
Film(s): .... My Gal Sal
Martha Ray .... **Brunswick 03424**
Harry Roy & his Band,
vocal Harry Roy .... **Regal Zonophone MR 3671**

OH THEY'RE TOUGH MIGHTY TOUGH IN THE WEST
1937
Clive Erard / Frank Trafford
Dash Music Ltd. .... USA
Billy Cotton & his Band .... **Rex 9138**
Bob Mallin .... **Rex 9093**

OH WELL
November 1969
Peter Green
Fleetwood Music .... UK
Fleetwood Mac .... **Reprise REP 44138**

OH WHAT A BEAUTIFUL MORNING
1947
Richard Rodgers / Oscar Hammerstein II
Williamson Music Ltd. .... USA
Show(s): .... Oklahoma
Film(s): .... Oklahoma
Alfred Drake .... **Brunswick LAT 8001**
Harold Keel .... **HMV 7EP 7023**
Gordon MacRae .... **Capitol LCT 6100**
Alfred Drake appeared in the American production of *Oklahoma.*
Harold Keel appeared in the British production of *Oklahoma.*
Gordon MacRae appeared in the film of *Oklahoma.*

OH WHAT A CIRCUS
September 1978
Tim Rice / Andrew Lloyd Webber
Leeds Music Ltd .... UK
Show(s): .... Evita
David Essex & Elaine Paige ...... **MCA MCG 3527**
Mandy Patinkin & Patti Lupone .... **MCA MCA2 11007**
David Essex .... **Mercury 6007185**
David Essex & Elain Paige appeared in the British production of *Evita*
Mandy Patinkin & Patti Lupone appeared in the American production of *Evita.*

OH WHAT A PAL WAS MARY
1920
Pete Wendling / Edgar Leslie / Bert Kalmar
B. Felman & CVo. Ltd .... USA
William Thomas .... **Regal G 7481**
Florrie Forde .... **Regal MR 2198**

OH WHAT A SHAME
June 1975
Doreen Chanter / Herbie Flowers
Mews Music .... UK
Roy Wood .... **Jet JET 754**

OH WHAT A SURPRISE FOR THE DUCE (Evviva La Torre Di Pisa)
1940
Nino Rastelli / Nino Casirolli / Phil Park
Chappell & Co. Ltd .... Italy
Florence Desmond .... **HMV B 9133**
Bertha Wilmot .... **Decca F 7692**
Billy Cotton & his Band .... **Rex 9906**

OH WHAT IT SEEMED TO BE
1946
Bennie Benjamin / George Weiss / Frankie Garle
Sun Music Publishing Co. Ltd. .... USA
Frank Sinatra .... **Philips BBL 7168**
Geraldo & his Orchestra, vocal Dick James ... **Parlophone F 2144**
Brook Benton .... **Mercury MMC 14060**

OH YEAH
August 1980
Bryan Ferry
E.G. Music .... UK

Roxy Music . . . . **Polydor 2001972**

OH YES YOU'RE BEAUTIFUL　　　　　December 1974
Gary Glitter / Mike Leander
Leeds Music Ltd. . . . . UK
Gary Glitter . . . . **Bell 1391**

OH YOU BEAUTIFUL DOLL　　　　　　　　　1911
Seymour Brown / Nat.D. Ayer
B. Feldman & Co. Ltd . . . . USA
Film(s):Wharf Angel / The Story of Vernon & Irene Castle / For Me
and My Gal / Oh You Beautiful Doll
The Original Ragtime Octet . . . . **HMV B 370**
Ida Barr . . . . **Fontana TFL 5043**
Mel Tormé . . . . **Capitol CL 13292**
Verdi . . . . **Decca LK 4290**

OH YOU HAVE NO IDEA　　　　　　　　　　1928
Phil Ponce / Dan Dougherty
Lawrence Wright Music Co. Ltd . . . . USA
Paul Whiteman & his Orchestra . . . . **Columbia 4956**
Sophie Tucker . . . . **Parlophone R 197**

OH YOU PRETTY THING　　　　　　　　June 1971
David Bowie
Chrysalis Music Ltd . . . . UK
Peter Noone . . . . **Rak 114**
David Bowie . . . . **RCA INTS 5064**

OH YOU SWEET ONE　　　　　　　　　　July 1950
Moe Jaffe / Dick Hardt
Southern Music Publishing Co. Ltd . . . . USA
Geraldo & his Orchestra . . . . **Parlophone F 2415**
Donald Peers . . . . **HMV B 9933**
The Andrews Sisters . . . . **Brunswick 04262**

OII!　　　　　　　　　　　　　　　　　　1920
Byron Gay / Arnold Johnston
Francis, Day & Hunter Ltd . . . . USA
Pee Wee Hunt & his Orchestra . . . . **Capitol T 953**
Benny Lee . . . . **Decca F 10155**
Billy Vaughan & his Orchestra . . . . **London HAD 2209**

OH! I MUST GO HOME TONIGHT　　　　　　1909
William Hargreaves
B. Feldman & Co. Ltd . . . . UK
The Pavement Artists . . . . **Regal Zonophone MR 614**
Stanley Holloway . . . . **Philips BBL 7237**

OH! IF I ONLY HAD YOU　　　　　　　　　1927
Gus Kahn / Cliff Friend
Francis, Day & Hunter Ltd. . . . . USA
Ted Weems & his Orchestra . . . . **HMV B 5145**

OH! JOHNNY OH!　　　　　　　　　　　　1917
Abe Olman / Ed Rose
Francis, Day & Hunter Ltd. . . . . USA
Show(s): . . . . Follow Me
Dick Robertson & his Orchestra,
vocal Dick Robertson . . . . **Decca F 7393**
The Andrews Sisters . . . . **Brunswick 02874**
Peggy Lee . . . . **Capitol T 1131**

OH, KATHARINA　　　　　　　　　　　　1925
L. Wolfe Gilbert / Richard Fall
Francis, Day & Hunter Ltd. . . . . Austria
The International Novelty Orchestra . . . . **HMV B 2047**
Carmen Cavallaro & his Orchestra,
vocal Bob Lido . . . . **Brunswick 04472**
Pee Wee Hunt & his Band . . . . **Capitol T 783**

'OI' SONG, THE　　　　　　　　　　　　1933
Harry Carlton / / /
Peter Maurice Music Co. Ltd. . . . . UK
Flanagan & Allen . . . . **Columbia 33S 1010**

OKAY　　　　　　　　　　　　　　　July 1967
Howard Blaikley
Lynn Music Ltd. . . . . UK
Dave Dee, Dozy, Beaky, Mick & Tich . . . . **Fontana TF 830**

OKAY TOOTS　　　　　　　　　　　　　1935
Walter Donaldson / Gus Kahn
Francis, Day & Hunter Ltd . . . . USA
Film(s): . . . . Kid Millions

Eddie Cantor . . . . **Rex 8391**
Harry Roy & his Band . . . . **Parlophone F 126**
Eddie Cantor appeared in *Kid Millions.*

OKLAHOMA　　　　　　　　　　　　　　1947
Richard Rodgers / Oscar Hammerstein II
Williamson Music Ltd. . . . . USA
Show(s): . . . . Oklahoma
Film(s): . . . . Oklahoma
Alfred Drake & chorus . . . . **Brunswick LAT 8001**
Harold Keel & chorus . . . . **HMV 7EP 7023**
Entire Company of the Film . . . . **Capitol LCT 6100**
Alfred Drake appeared in the American production of *Oklahoma.*
Harold Keel appeared in the British production of *Oklahoma.*

OL' BUTTERMILK SKY　　　　　　　　　　1947
Hoagy Carmichael / Jack Brooks
Edwin H. Morris & Co. Ltd. . . . . USA
Film(s): . . . . Canyon Passage
Hoagy Carmichael . . . . **Brunswick LAT 8369**
Nellie Lutcher . . . . **London HAU 2036**
Gary Crosby . . . . **HMV 7EG 8573**
Hoagy Carmichael appeared in *Canyon Passage.*
Nominated for an Academy Award 1946.

OL' FAITHFUL　　　　　　　　　　　　　1934
Jimmy Kennedy / Michael Carr
Dash Music Ltd . . . . UK
The Hillbillies . . . . **Regal Zonophone MR 1408**
Les Allen . . . . **Columbia DB 1469**
Rex Allen . . . . **Brunswick LAT 8198**
Jimmy Rodgers . . . . **Columbia 33SX 1217**

OL' MACDONALD　　　　　　　　　November 1960
Traditional
Barton Music Co. Ltd . . . . USA
Frank Sinatra . . . . **Capitol CL 15168**

OL' MAN RIVER　　　　　　　　　　　　1928
Jerome Kern / Oscar Hammerstein II
Chappell & Co. Ltd. . . . . USA
Show(s): . . . . Show Boat
Film(s): . . . . Show Boat / Till the Clouds Roll By
Norris Smith . . . . **Columbia 9426**
Paul Robeson . . . . **HMV B 8497**
Frank Sinatra . . . . **Fontana TFL 5030**
William Warfield . . . . **MGM D 104**
Paul Robeson appeared in the British production of *Show Boat* and
also the 1936 film of *Show Boat.*
Frank Sinatra appeared in *Till the Clouds Roll By.*
William Warfield appeared in the 1951 film of *Show Boat.*

OLD BRIGADE, THE　　　　　　　　　　　1881
Frederick E. Weatherly / Odoardo Barri
Reynolds Music Co. . . . . UK
Peter Dawson . . . . **HMV B 8158**
Raymond Newell . . . . **Decca LK 4026**
The Chelsea Pensioner . . . . **Marble Arch MALS 1283**
The Band of the Irish Guards . . . . **Ember EMB 3399**

OLD FASHIONED WAY, THE
(Les Plaisirs Demodes)　　　　　　November 1973
Charles Aznavour / George Garvarentz
Chappell Music Co. . . . . France
Charles Aznavour . . . . **Barclay BAR 20**

OLD FATHER THAMES　　　　　　　　　　1933
Raymond Wallace / Betsy O'Hogan
Lawrence Wright Music Co. Ltd. UK
Roy Fox & his Orchestra, vocal Denny Dennis . . **Decca F 3417**
Peter Dawson . . . . **HMV B 4374**
Gracie Fields . . . . **Rex 9302**
John Hanson . . . . **Oriole MG 20015**

OLD KITCHEN KETTLE, THE　　　　　　　1932
Harry Woods / James Campbell / Reginald Connelly
Campbell Connelly & Co. Ltd. . . . . UK
Jack Hylton & his Orchestra . . . . **Decca F 3222**
The Bowman-Hyde Singers & Players . . **Parlophone PMC 1155**

OLD LAMPLIGHTER, THE　　　　　　　　1946
Charles Tobias / Nat Simon
Dash Music Ltd. . . . . USA
Lou Preager & his Orchestra,
vocal Paul Rich . . . . **Columbia FB 3273**

The Squadronaires Dance Orchestra,
conducted by Jimmy Miller .... Decca F 8747
Kenny Baker .... Brunswick 03711
The Browns .... RCA 1176

OLD MAN MOSE 1938
Louis Armstrong / Zilner Trenton Randolph
Campbell Connelly & Co. Ltd. .... USA
Louis Armstrong's All Stars .... Brunswick LAT 8085
Connie Francis .... MGM C 870
Terry Lightfoot & his
New Orleans Jazzmen .... Columbia 33SX 1353

OLD MAN OF THE MOUNTAIN, THE 1933
George Brown / Victor Young
Campbell Connelly & Co. Ltd. .... USA
Doris Hare .... Regal 6265
The Mills Brothers .... Brunswick 01346
The Carlyle Cousins .... Columbia DB 977

OLD MASTER PAINTER, THE March 1950
Haven Gillespie / Beasley Smith
Robbins Music Corporation Ltd .... USA
Geraldo & his Orchestra,
vocal Cyril Grantham .... Parlophone F 2406
Lou Preager & his Orchestra,
vocal Rusty Hurren .... Columbia FB 3554
Frank Sinatra .... Columbia DB 2664
Peggy Lee & Mel Tormé .... Capitol CL 13241

OLD MUSIC MASTER, THE 1943
Hoagy Carmichael / Johnny Mercer
Victoria Music Co. Ltd .... USA
Film(s): .... True To Life
Hoagy Carmichael .... Brunswick LA 8663
Paul Whiteman & his Orchestra,
vocal Johnny Mercer & Jack Teagarden .... Capitol CL 13845

OLD PI-ANNA RAG, THE January 1956
Don Philips / Elizabeth Brice
Lawrence Wright Music Co. Ltd. .... UK
Dickie Valentine .... Decca F 10645
Billie Anthony .... Columbia DB 3698
The Big Ben Banjo Band .... Columbia SX 1653

OLD PIANO ROLL BLUES, THE June 1950
Cy Coben
Leeds Music Ltd .... USA
The Jubalaires .... Capitol CL 13278
Al Jolson & The Andrews Sisters .... Brunswick LA 8705
Bonnie Alden .... Columbia 33S 1123

OLD RAG BLUES October 1983
Alan Lancaster / Keith Lamb
Eaton Music .... UK
Status Quo .... Vertigo QUO 11

OLD RUSTIC BRIDGE BY THE MILL 1881
J.P. Skelly
Francis, Day & Hunter Ltd. .... USA
Walter Glynne .... HMV B 8078
Eileen Donaghy .... Fontana TL 5197
Foster & Allen .... Ritz RITZ 0012

OLD SHEP November 1959
Arthur 'Red' Foley
Lawrence Wright Music .... USA
Elvis Presley .... HMV CLP 1105
Clinton Ford .... Piccadilly NPL 38028

OLD SHIP OF MINE 1935
Don Pelosi / Rodd Arden
Dash Music Ltd .... UK
Lou Preager & his Band .... Panachord 25827

OLD SOFT SHOE, THE February 1952
Roy Jordan / Sid Bass
Francis, Dau & Hunter Ltd .... USA
G.H. Elliott & Dorothy Squires .... Columbia DB 3046
Dinah Shore & Tony Martin .... HMV B 10167

OLD SPINNING WHEEL, THE 1935
Billy Hill
Campbell Connelly & Co. Ltd .... USA
Derickson & Brown .... HMV B 4436

Bob Crosby & his Orchestra .... Vogue LAV 9045
Bessley Smith Orchestra & chorus ..... London HLD 8273

OLD TIMER 1935
Lewis Ilda / Michael Carr
Dash Music Ltd .... UK
Geraldo & his Accordion Band .... Columbia FB 1038
Teddy Joyce & his Orchestra .... HMV BD 139

OLDEST SWINGER IN TOWN, THE February 1981
Edward Pickford
Rocket Music .... UK
Fred Wedlock .... Rocket Xpres 46

OLE OLA June 1978
Rod Stewart / Philip Chen / Evaldo Gouveia / Jair Amorim
Chappell & Co. Ltd. .... USA
Rod Stewart .... Riva RIVA 15

OLGA PULLOFFSKI (The Beautiful Spy) 1935
R.P. Weston / Bert Lee
Francis, Day & Hunter Ltd. .... UK
Jack Hylton & his Orchestra .... HMV BD 163

OLIVER'S ARMY March 1979
Elvis Costello
Plangent Visions Music .... UK
Elvis Costello & The Attractions ... Radar ADA 31

OMAHA 1919
Horatio Nicholls / Worton David
Lawrence Wright Music Co. Ltd. .... UK
Leslie Stone .... Columbia 3016
The New Mayfair Orchestra .... HMV B 3944

ON A CAROUSEL April 1967
Graham Nash / Tony Hicks / Allan Clarke
Gralto Music Ltd. .... UK
The Hollies .... Parlophone R 5562

ON A CLEAR DAY YOU CAN SEE FOREVER 1966
Alan Jay Lerner / Burton Lane
Chappell Music Co. .... USA
Show(s): ....On a Clear Day You Can See Forever
Film(s): ....On a Clear Day You Can See Forever
John Cullum .... RCA LOCD 2006
Yves Montand .... CBS S 70075
Barbra Streisand .... CBS S 70075
Robert Goulet .... CBS 202034
John Cullum appeared in the show *On a Clear Day You Can See Forever*.
Barbra Streisand & Yves Montand appeared in the film *On a Clear Day You Can See Forever*.

ON A LITTLE BALCONY IN SPAIN 1931
Saul Klein / Jack Le Soir / Ray Doll
Lawrence Wright Music Co. Ltd .... USA
Jack Payne & his Orchestra .... Columbia CB 228
George Metaxa .... HMV B 3822
Tony Brent .... Columbia SEG 7689

ON A LITTLE BAMBOO BRIDGE 1937
Al Sherman / Archie Fletcher
Campbell Connelly & Co. Ltd. .... USA
Roy Smeck & his Hawaiian Serenaders,
vocal Donald King .... Decca F 6297
Turner Layton .... Columbia FB 1692
Louis Armstrong & his Orchestra .... Decca F 6393

ON A LITTLE STREET IN SINGAPORE 1940
Billy Hill / Peter De Rose
Francis, Day & Hunter Ltd .... USA
Kenny Baker (1938) .... HMV BD 838
Jimmy Dorsey & his Orchestra,
vocal Bob Eberly .... Brunswick 02934
Glenn Miller & his Orchestra, vocal Ray Eberle ... HMV CLPC 3
Manhattan Transfer (1978) .... Atlantic K 11136

ON A SLOW BOAT TO CHINA December 1948
Frank Loesser
Edwin H. Morris & Co. Ltd .... USA
Kay Kyser & his Orchestra .... Columbia FB 3450
The Merry Macs .... Decca F 9038
Al Nevins & his Orchestra .... RCA RD 27007
Emile Ford (1960) .... Pye NEP 24124
Bing Crosby & Rosemary Clooney .... RCA RD 27105

ON A STEAMER COMING OVER 1934
Lou Handman / Joe Goodwin / Henry Bergman
Campbell Connelly & Co. Ltd. . . . . USA
Elsie Carlisle . . . . **Decca F 3812**
Ray Noble & his Orchestra . . . . **HMV B 6440**
Dick James . . . . **Parlophone GEP 8643**

ON A STREET OF CHINESE LANTERNS 1927
James Campbell / Reginald Connelly
Campbell Connelly & Co. Ltd. . . . . UK
The Savoy Orpheans . . . . **HMV B 5338**

ON A SUNDAY AFTERNOON 1903
Andrew B. Sterling / Harry Von Tilzer
. . . . USA
Frank Crumit . . . . **Decca F 5257**
Dorothy Provine . . . . **Warner Brothers WM 8109**

ON A SUNDAY AFTERNOON 1936
Arthur Freed / Nacio Herb Brown
Robbins Music Corporation Ltd . . . . USA
Film(s): . . . . Broadway Melody of 1936
Jack Payne & his Orchestra . . . . **Rex 8706**

ON DAYS LIKE THESE 1969
Quincy Jones
Famous Music Co. . . . . USA
Film(s): . . . . The Italian Job
Matt Monro . . . . **Capitol CL 15603**
Quincy Jones Orchestra (Sound Track) . . **Paramount SPFL 256**

ON MIAMI SHORE 1920
Victor Jacobi / William Le Baron
Chappell & Co. Ltd . . . . USA
The Joseph C. Smith Orchestra . . . . **HMV B 1102**
The Paradise Island Trio . . . . **Rex 9968**
Felix Mendelsohn & his Hawaiian Serenaders . . . Columbia FB 2871

ON MOBILE BAY 1910
Earle Jones / Charles Daniels
B. Feldman & Co. Ltd . . . . USA
Herbert Payne . . . . **Zonophone Twin 775**

ON MOTHER KELLY'S DOORSTEP 1925
G.A. Stevens
Francis, Day & Hunter Ltd. . . . . UK
Frankie Vaughan . . . . **Philips BBL 7482**
Barbara Windsor . . . . **HMV POP 1884**
Clinton Ford . . . . **Oriole CB 1884**

ON MY OWN May 1986
Burt Bacharach / Carole Bater Sager
MCA Music . . . . USA
Patti La Belle & Michael McDonald . . . . **MCA 1045**

ON MY RADIO November 1979
Noel Davies
Fairwood Music . . . . UK
Selector . . . . **2 Tone CHSTT 4**

ON MY WORD July 1965
Chip Taylor
Aaron Schroeder Ltd. . . . . USA
Cliff Richard . . . . **Columbia DB 7617**

ON OUR OWN August 1989
L.A. Reid / Daryl Simmons'Babyface'
MCA Music . . . . UK
Bobby Brown . . . . **MCA 1350**

ON THE AIR 1932
Carroll Gibbons
Campbell Connelly & Co. Ltd. . . . . UK
Carroll Gibbons & The Savoy Orpheans . . . . **Columbia CB 525**
**Matt Malneck (Violin) with
Carroll Gibbons & his Boy Friends** . . . . **Columbia DB 1001**
Carroll Gibbons & The Savoy Orpheans . . **Columbia 33S 1094**
Ian Stewart (Piano) . . . . **Fontana TFE 17140**
Theme song of Carroll Gibbons.

ON THE ALAMO 1922
Isham Jones / Gilbert Keys / Joe Lyons
Francis, DFay & Hunter Ltd . . . . USA
Red Nichols & his Five Pennies . . . . **Brunswick 01856**
Bing Crosby . . . . **Brunswick LAT 8217**

Benny Goodman & his Orchestra,
vocal Art Lund . . . . **Parlophone R 3018**
Isham Jones & his Orchestra,
vocal Kurt Massey . . . . **Capitol LC 6350**

ON THE ATCHISON, TOPEKA AND THE SANTA FE 1946
Harry Warren / Johnny Mercer
Robbins Music Corporation Ltd. . . . . USA
Film(s): . . . . The Harvey Girls
Judy Garland . . . . **Ace of Hearts AH 128**
Bing Crosby . . . . **Brunswick 03650**
Paula Green . . . . **Columbia FB 3172**
The Four Freshmen . . . . **Capitol T 1543**
Judy Garland appeared in *The Harvey Girls*.
Academy Award winning song for 1946.

ON THE BANKS OF THE WABASH 1899
Paul Dresser
B. Feldman & Co. Ltd. . . . . USA
Film(s):My Gal Sal / The Jolson Story / Wait Till the Sun Shines Nellie
The American Quartette . . . . **Zonophone Twin 1228**
The Mills Brothers (1943) . . . . **Brunswick 04453**
Bing Crosby . . . . **Warner Brothers WM 4021**

ON THE BEACH September 1964
Bruce Welch / Hank B. Marvin / Cliff Richard
Elstree Music Ltd . . . . UK
Film(s): . . . . Wonderful Life
Cliff Richard . . . . **Columbia DB 7305**
Cliff Richard appeared in *Wonderful Life*.

ON THE BEACH AT BALI BALI 1936
Al Sherman / Jack Meskill / Abner Silver
Campbell Connelly & Co. Ltd . . . . USA
Connee Boswell . . . . **Brunswick 02235**
**Felix Mendelsohn & his
Hawaiian Serenaders** . . . . **Columbia FB 2644**
Frank Chacksfield & his Orchestra . . . . **Decca LK 4174**

ON THE BEACH AT WAIKIKI 1919
G.H. Stover / Henry Kailimai
B. Feldman & Co. Ltd. . . . . Hawaii
Show(s): . . . . The Bird of Paradise
The Hawaiians . . . . **HMV B 1068**
**Felix Mendelsohn & his
Hawaiian Serenaders** . . . . **Columbia FB 2501**
The King Sisters . . . . **Capitol T 808**
Les Paul & Mary Ford . . . . **Philips BBL 7306**
The Hawaiians appeared in *The Bird Of Paradise*.

ON THE BRIDGE OF SIGHS 1938
Harry Freed / Victor Royal
Campbell Connelly & Co. Ltd. . . . . USA
Geraldo & his Orchestra . . . . **Decca F 6609**
Primo Scala's Accordion Band . . . . **Rex 9250**

ON THE BUMPY ROAD TO LOVE 1938
Al Hoffman / Al Lewis / Murray Mencher
Robbins Music Corporation Ltd. . . . . USA
Film(s): . . . . Listen Darling
'Fats' Waller & his Rhythm . . . . **HMV BD 5431**
The Merry Macs . . . . **Capitol T 850**

ON THE FIVE FORTY-FIVE April 1949
Mark Warren
Strauss-Miller Musisc Co. Ltd . . . . USA
Joy Nichols & Benny Lee . . . . **Decca F 9094**
Donald Peers . . . . **HMV B 9772**

ON THE FIVE-FIFTEEN 1914
Stanley Murphy / Henry Marshall
Francis, Day & Hunter Ltd. . . . . USA
Show(s): . . . . 5064 Gerard
Lee White & Jack Morrison . . . . **Columbia 527**
Harry Fay & Herbert Payne . . . . **Regal 1471**
Lee White & Jack Morrison appeared in *5064 Gerard*.

ON THE GOOD SHIP LOLLIPOP 1935
Richard A. Whiting / Sidney Clare
Sam Fox Publishing Co. (London) Ltd . . . . USA
Film(s): . . . . Bright Eyes / You're My Everything
Shirley Temple . . . . **Top Rank JKR 8003**
Rosemary Clooney . . . . **Philips BBL 7191**
Shirley Temple appeared in *Bright Eyes*.

ON THE GOOD SHIP YACKI HICKI DOO LA　　　1917
Billy Merson
Francis, Day & Hunter Ltd. . . . . USA
Billy Merson . . . . **Decca F 2653**
Billy Costello (Popeye) . . . . **Rex 9238**

ON THE ISLE OF MAY　　　1941
Andre Kostelanetz / Mack David
Chappell & Co. Ltd . . . . USA
**Kay Kyser & his Orchestra,
vocal Ginny Simms & Harry Babbitt** . . . . . . **Parlophone F 1750**
Connee Boswell . . . . **Brunswick 03005**
Cyril Stapleton & his Orchestra . . . . **Decca LK 4162**
Adapted from "The Quartet In D Major opus 11" by Peter Ilych
Tchaikovsky (1840 - 1893).

ON THE LEVEL YOU'RE A LITTLE DEVIL　　　1918
Jean Schwartz / Joe Young
B. Feldman & Co. Ltd. . . . . USA
Show(s): . . . . Hullo America
Maurice Chevalier . . . . **HMV B 1024**
The Mayfair Dance Orchestra . . . . **HMV C 921**

ON THE OUTSIDE LOOKING IN　　　1939
Michael Carr
Peter Maurice Music Co. Ltd. . . . . UK
Show(s): . . . . The Little Dog Laughed
Flanagan & Allen . . . . **Decca LF 1125**
Lew Stone & his Orchestra, vocal James Brown . . . **Decca F 7169**
Flanagan & Allen appeared in *The Little Dog Laughed.*

ON THE REBOUND　　　May 1961
Floyd Cramer
Acuff-Rose Publishing Co. Ltd . . . . USA
Floyd Cramer (piano) . . . . **RCA 1231**
Ken Jones & his Orchestra . . . . **Parlophone R 4763**

ON THE ROAD AGAIN　　　September 1968
Allen Wilson / Floyd Jones
Southern Music Publishing Co. Ltd. . . . . USA
Canned Heat . . . . **Liberty LBS 15090**

ON THE ROAD AGAIN　　　November 1980
Willie Nelson
Planetary Nom (London) Ltd. . . . . USA
Film(s): . . . . Honeysuckle Rose
Willie Nelson . . . . **CBS 70193**
Nominated for an Academy Award 1980.

ON THE ROAD TO MANDALAY　　　1907
Rudyard Kipling / Oley Speaks
Boosey & Hawkes Music Publishers Ltd. . . . . UK
Peter Dawson . . . . **HMV DLP 1180**
Owen Brannigan . . . . **HMV CLP 1446**
The poem by Rudyard Kipling written in 1892.

ON THE SENTIMENTAL SIDE　　　1938
Johnny Burke / Jimmy Monaco
Campbell Connelly & Co. Ltd. . . . . USA
Film(s): . . . . .Doctor Rhythm
Bing Crosby . . . . **Brunswick Bing 4**
Billie Holiday . . . . **Parlophone R 2566**
Bing Crosby appeared in *Doctor Rhythm.*

ON THE STREET WHERE YOU LIVE　　　April 1958
Alan Jay Lerner / Frederick Loewe
Chappell & Co. ltd . . . . USA
Show(s): . . . . My Fair Lady
Film(s): . . . . My Fair Lady
John Michael King . . . . **Philips RBL 1000**
Leonard Weir . . . . **CBS 70005**
Ronnie Hilton . . . . **HMV 7EG 8352**
Vic Damone . . . . **Philips BBL 7331**
Jeremy Brett . . . . **CBS BRG 72237**
David Whitfield . . . . **Decca F 11018**
John Michael King appeared in the American production of *My Fair Lady.*
Leonard Weir appeared in the Brirish production of *My Fair Lady.*
Jeremy Brett appeared in the film *My Fair Lady.*

ON THE SUNNY SIDE OF THE STREET　　　1931
Jimmy McHugh / Dorothy Fields
Lawrence Wright Music Co. Ltd . . . . USA
Show(s): . . . . The International Revue
Film(s):Is Everybody Happy / Swing Parade of 1946 / The Sunny Side

of the Street / The Benny Goodman Story / The Eddy Duchin Story /
Both Ends of the Candle
Ted Lewis & his Band . . . . **Columbia CB 74**
**Tommy Dorsey & his Orchestra, vocal
The Sentimentalists (1945)** . . . . **HMV 7EG 8011**
The Clark Sisters . . . . **London HAD 2128**
**Benny Goodman & his Orchestra,
vocal Peggy Lee** . . . . **Philips BBE 12172**
Gogi Grant . . . . **RCA RD 27054**
Ted Lewis appeared in *Is Everybody Happy.*

ON THE WINGS OF LOVE　　　August 1984
Peter Schless / Jeffrey Osbourne
Rondor Music . . . . USA
Jeffrey Osbourne . . . . **A&M AM 198**

ON TOP OF OLD SMOKEY　　　June 1951
Traditional, arranged by Pete Seeger
Leeds Music Co. Ltd . . . . USA
The Weavers (1951) . . . . **Brunswick OE 9427**
The Weavers (1958) . . . . **Vanguard PPL 11011**

ON TREASURE ISLAND　　　1935
Edgar Leslie / Joe Burke
Campbell Connelly & Co. Ltd . . . . USA
Val Rosing . . . . **Regal Zonophone MR 1924**
Bing Crosby . . . . **Brunswick 02100**
Teresa Brewer . . . . **Vogue LVA 9075**

ON YOUR TOES　　　1937
Richard Rodgers / Lorenz Hart
Chappell & Co. Ltd. . . . . USA
Show(s): . . . . On Your Toes
Film(s): . . . . Words and Music
Jack Whiting . . . . **Columbia DB 1687**
**The BBC Dance Orchestra,
conducted by Henry Hall** . . . . **Columbia FB 1609**
Kay Coulter, Bobby Van & Joshua Shelley . **Brunswick LAT 8061**
Jack Whiting appeared in the British production of *On Your Toes.*
Kay Coulter, Bobby Van & Joshua Shelley appeared in the 1954
American production of *On Your Toes.*

ONCE A YEAR DAY　　　October 1955
Richard Adler / Jerry Ross
Frank Music Co. Ltd. . . . . USA
Show(s): . . . . The Pajama Game
Film(s): . . . . The Pajama Game
John Raitt & Janis Paige . . . . **Philips BBL 7050**
Edmund Hockridge & Joy Nichols . . . . . . **HMV CLP 1062**
John Raitt & Doris Day . . . . **Philips BBL 7197**
Janis Paige appeared in the American production of *The Pajama Game.*
Edmund Hockridge & Joy Nichols appeared in the British produc-
tion of *The Pajama Game.*
Doris Day appeared in the film of *The Pajama Game.*
John Raitt appeared in both the American production and film of *The
Pajama Game.*

ONCE BITTEN TWICE SHY　　　May 1975
Ian Hunter
April Music Ltd . . . . UK
Ian Hunter . . . . **CBS 3194**

ONCE IN A LIFETIME　　　March 1981
Brian Emo / David Byrne
Warner Brothers Music . . . . UK
Talking Heads . . . . **Sire SIR 4048**

ONCE IN A WHILE　　　1938
Bud Green / Michael Edwards
Robbins Music Corporation Ltd. USA
Film(s): . . . . .I'll Get By
Frances Langford . . . . **Brunswick 02563**
The Dinning Sisters . . . . **Capitol T 9103**
The Mills Brothers . . . . **London HAD 2250**

ONCE IN LOVE WITH AMY　　　March 1949
Frank Loesser
Edwin H. Morris Co. Ltd . . . . USA
Show(s): . . . . Where's Charley
Film(s): . . . . Where's Charley
Norman Wisdom . . . . **Columbia 33SX 1085**
Ray Bolger . . . . **Brunswick 04972**
Frank Sinatra . . . . **Philips BBL 7180**
Norman Wisdom appeared in the British production of *Where's Char-
ley.*

Ray Bolger appeared in both the American production and the film of *Where's Charley.*

ONCE UPON A DREAM   August 1962
Norrie Paramor / Richard Rowe
Filmusic Publishing Co. Ltd . . . . UK
Film(s): . . . . Play it Cool
Billy Fury . . . . **Decca F 11485**
Billy Fury appeared in *Play It Cool.*

ONCE UPON A LONG AGO   December 1987
Paul McCartney
M.P.L. Music Ltd. . . . . UK
Paul McCartney . . . . **Parlophone R 6170**

ONCE UPON A WINTERTIME   May 1948
Johnny Brandon / Ray Martin
Cinephonic Music Ltd. . . . . UK
Vera Lynn . . . . **Decca F 8883**
The Skyrockets Dance Orchestra . . . . **HMV BD 6000**
Geraldo & his Orchestra . . . . **Parlophone F 2296**

ONE   May 1989
James Hetfield / Lars Ulrich
Polygram Music . . . . USA
Metallica . . . . **Vertigo METAL 5**

ONE ALONE   1927
Sigmund Romberg / Otto Harbach / Oscar Hammerstein II
Chappell & Co. Ltd. . . . . ⸲ . . . . USA
Show(s): . . . . The Desert Song
Film(s): . . . . The Desert Song / Deep in My Heart
Harry Welchman . . . . **Columbia 4387**
Gordon MacRae . . . . **Capitol LCT 6114**
Kathryn Grayson & Tony Martin . . . . **HMV DLP 1029**
Edmund Hockridge . . . . **HMV CLP 1274**
Harry Welchman appeared in the British production *The Desert Song.*
Kathryn Grayson & Gordon MacRae appeared in the 1953 film of *The Desert Song.*

ONE AND ONE IS ONE   June 1973
John Fiddler
Biscuit Music . . . . UK
Medicine Head . . . . **Polydor 2001432**

ONE BROKEN HEART FOR SALE   March 1963
Otis Blackwell / Winifred Scott
Seventeen Saville Row Ltd . . . . USA
Film(s): . . . . It Happened At The World's Fair
Elvis Presley . . . . **RCA 1337**
Elvis Presley appeared in *It Happened At The World's Fair*

ONE DAY AT A TIME   November 1979
Marijon Wilkin / Chris Kristofferson
Valentine Music Group . . . . USA
Lena Martell . . . . **Pye 7N 46021**

ONE DAY I'LL FLY AWAY   October 1980
Joe Sample / Will Jennings
Leeds Music Ltd . . . . USA
Randy Crawford . . . . **Warner Brothers K 17680**

ONE DAY IN YOUR LIFE   June 1981
Samuel Brown / Renee Armand
Jobete Music . . . . USA
Michael Jackson . . . . **Motown TMG 976**

ONE DAY WHEN WE'RE YOUNG   1939
Johann Strauss / Oscar Hammerstein II
Chappell & Co. Ltd. . . . . USA
Film(s): . . . . The Great Waltz
Militza Korjus . . . . **HMV B 8863**
Adele Leigh . . . . **Philips BBE 12379**
Richard Tauber . . . . **Parlophone PMB 1009**
Militza Korjus appeared in *The Great Waltz.*

ONE DOZEN ROSES   1942
Roger Lewis / Country Washburn / Dick Jurgens & Walter Donovan
Victoria Music Co. Ltd . . . . USA
Oscar Rabin & his Band,
vocal Diane & Benny Lee . . . . **Decca F 8165**
The Mills Brothers . . . . **Brunswick LAT 8235**

ONE GIRL   1933
Vincent Youmans / Melville Gideon

Campbell Connelly & Co. Ltd. . . . . USA
Show(s): . . . . One Girl
The London Hippodrome Orchestra . . . . . . **Parlophone R 1471**

ONE I LOVE BELONGS TO SOMEBODY ELSE, THE   1924
Gus Kahn / Isham Jones
Francis, Day & Hunter Ltd. . . . . USA
Film(s): . . . . . . I'll Soo You in My Dreams / Both Ends of the candle
Doc Cook's Dreamland Orchestra . . . . **London AL 3557**
Al Jolson . . . . **Brunswick LAT 8322**
Gogi Grant . . . . **RCA RD 27054**
Dinah Shore . . . . **Capitol T 1247**

ONE IN TEN   September 1981
"UB40"
A.T.V. Music . . . . UK
UB40 . . . . **Dep DEP 2**

ONE KISS   1929
Sigmund Romberg / Oscar Hammerstein II
Chappell & Co. Ltd . . . . USA
Show(s): . . . . The New Moon
Film(s): . . . . The New Moon
Evelyn Laye . . . . **Columbia 9751**
Jeanette MacDonald . . . . **HMV DA 1721**
Elizabeth Larner . . . . **HMV CLP 1148**
Evelyn Laye appeared in the British production of *The New Moon.*
Jeanette MacDonald appeared in the 1940 film of *The New Moon.*

ONE LOVE   May 1984
Bob Marley
. . . . UK
Bob Marley & The Wailers . . . . **Island IS 169**

ONE LOVE   July 1990
John Squire / Ian Brown
Zomba Music . . . . UK
The Stone Roses . . . . **Silvertone ORE 17**

ONE LOVE FOREVER   1942
Jimmy Dyrenforth / Kenneth Leslie-Smith
Boosey & Hawkes Music Publishers Ltd . . . . UK
John McCormack . . . . **HMV DA 1820**
Jo Stafford & David Hughes . . . . **Philips PB 251**

ONE MAN BAND   July 1974
Leo Sayer / David Courtney
Blandell Music . . . . UK
Leo Sayer . . . . **Chrysalis CHS 2045**
Roger Daltrey . . . . **Track 2106107**

ONE MEAT BALL   1945
Hy Zaret / Lou Singer
Leeds Music Ltd. . . . . USA
The Andrews Sisters . . . . **Brunswick 03576**
Josh White . . . . **Vogue B 10**

ONE MOMENT IN TIME   October 1988
Albert Hammond / John Bettis
Warner Chappell Music . . . . USA
Whitney Houston . . . . **Arista 111613**

ONE MORE DANCE   July 1968
Traditional
This Edition by Sparta Music Ltd. . . . . UK
Esther & Abi Ofarim . . . . **Philips BF 1678**

ONE MORE KISS   1942
Morton Morrow
Peter Maurice Music Co. Ltd . . . . UK
Vera Lynn . . . . **Decca F 8169**
Jay Wilbur & his Band, vocal Anne Trevor . . . . **Rex 10147**

ONE MORE NIGHT   May 1985
Phil Collins
Hit & Run Music . . . . UK
Phil Collins . . . . **Virgin VS 755**

ONE MORE SUNRISE (Morgen)   October 1959
Peter Moesser / Noel Sherman
Dominion Music Co. Ltd . . . . Germany
Dickie Valentine . . . . **Pye NEP 24120**
Vera Lynn . . . . **Decca F 11155**
Eddie Calvert (trumpet) . . . . **Columbia DB 4342**

ONE MORE TRY　　　　　　　　　　**May 1988**
George Michael
Morrison Leany Music .... UK
George Michael .... **Epic EMU 5**

ONE MORNING IN MAY　　　　　　　　**1934**
Hoagy Carmichael / Mitchell Parish
Campbell Connelly & Co. Ltd. .... USA
Ray Noble & his Orchestra .... **HMV B 6478**
Dick Todd .... **HMV BD 796**
Turner Layton .... **Columbia DB 1387**
Matt Monroe .... **Parlophone PMC 1185**

ONE NATION UNDER A GROOVE　　**January 1979**
George Clinton / Gary Shider / Walter Morrison
Warner Brothers Music Ltd. .... USA
Funkadelic .... **Warner Brothers K 17246**

ONE NIGHT　　　　　　　　　　**February 1959**
Dave Bartholomew / Pearl Kink
Commodore Imperial Music .... USA
Elvis Presley .... **RCA 1100**

ONE NIGHT IN BANKOK　　　　　**December 1984**
Benny Andersson / Bjorn Ulvaeus / Tim Rice
Bocu Music .... UK
Show(s): ....Chess
Murray Head .... **RCA CHESS 1**
Murray Head appeared in *Chess*.

ONE NIGHT OF LOVE　　　　　　　　**1934**
Victor Schertzinger / Gus Kahn
Sterling Music Publishing Co. Ltd .... USA
Film(s): .... One Night of Love
Grace Moore .... **Philips SBF 200**
Maria Perilli .... **Philips BBE 12436**
Mario Lanza .... **HMV ALP 1186**
Grace Moore appeared in *One Night of Love*.

ONE NOTE SAMBA (Samba De Uma Nota So)　**March 1963**
Antonio Carlos Jobim / John Hendricks
Leeds Music Ltd .... Brazil
Stan Getz (tenor saxophone)
& Charlie Byrd (guitar) .... **Verve VLP 9013**
Pat Thomas .... **MGM C 922**
Quincy Jones & his Orchestra .... **Mercury MMC 14125**
Peggy Lee .... **Capitol T 1857**

ONE O'CLOCK JUMP　　　　　　　　**1941**
William 'Count' Basie / Harry James
Robbins Music Corporation Ltd. .... USA
Film(s):Reveille With Beverly / The Benny Goodman Story / Hello Beautiful
Count Basie & his Orchestra .... **Brunswick LAT 8028**
Harry James & his Orchestra .... **Columbia 33S 1014**
Benny Goodman & his Orchestra .... **Philips BBL 7441**
Duke Ellington & his Orchestra .... **Capitol LCT 6008**
The Clark Sisters .... **London HAD 2177**
Count Basie & his Orchestra appeared in *Reveille With Beverly*.
Benny Goodman Orchestra appeared in *Hello Beautiful*.
Theme tune of Count Basie.

**ONE OF THE RUINS THAT CROMWELL KNOCKED
ABOUT A BIT (See It's A Bit Of A Ruin That Cromwell
Knocked About A Bit)**

ONE OF US　　　　　　　　　　**December 1981**
Benny Andersson / Bjorn Ulvaeus
Bocu Music .... Sweden
Abba .... **Epic EPCA 1740**

ONE ROAD　　　　　　　　　　**March 1969**
Philip Goodhand-Tait
Dick James Music Ltd. .... UK
The Love Affair .... **CBS 3994**

ONE ROSE (That's Left In My Heart)　　**1936**
Del Lyon / Lani McIntire
Campbell Connelly & Co Ltd .... Hawaii
The Parade Isle Trio .... **Panachord 25996**
Bing Crosby .... **Brunswick LAT 8368**
Patti Page .... **Mercury MMC 14013**

ONE SONG　　　　　　　　　　**1938**
Larry Morey / Frank Churchill

Walt Disney Music Co. Ltd. .... USA
Film(s): .... Snow White and the Seven Dwarfs
Sound Track .... **HMV BD 515**
Sound Track .... **Disneyland DLP 39003**

ONE STEP BEYOND　　　　　　　**December 1979**
Cecil Campbell
Melodisc Music .... UK
Madness .... **Stiff BUY 56**
Prince Buster & The All Stars .... **Blue BEAT 324**

ONE STEP FURTHER　　　　　　　　**May 1982**
Simon Jeffries
Chappell Music Ltd. .... UK
Bardo .... **Epic EPCA 2265**
United Kingdom entry for the 1982 Eurovision Song Contest (Placed Seventh).

ONE SUMMER NIGHT　　　　　　　　**1927**
Sam Coslow / Larry Spier
Campbell Connelly & Co. Ltd. .... USA
The Roger Wolfe Kahn Orchestra .... **HMV B 5339**
Layton & Johnstone .... **Columbia 4598**

ONE SWEET LETTER FROM YOU　　　**1940**
Harry Warren / Lew Brown / Sidney Clare
Campbell Connelly & Co Ltd .... USA
**Benny Goodman & his Orchestra,
vocal Louise Tobin** .... **Columbia DB 5077**
Bing Crosby .... **Brunswick 03794**
Michael Holliday .... **Columbia 33SX 1262**

ONE TWO THREE　　　　　　　　**December 1965**
John Madara / David White / Leonard Borisoff
Leeds Music Ltd .... USA
Len Barry .... **Brunswick 05942**

ONE TWO THREE　　　　　　　　**November 1988**
Gloria Estefan
S.B.K. Songs .... USA
Gloria Estefan & The Miami Sound Machine .... **Epic 6529587**

ONE VISION　　　　　　　　　　**December 1985**
"Queen"
EMI Music .... UK
Queen .... **EMI QUEEN 6**

ONE WAY LOVE　　　　　　　　**October 1964**
Bert Russell / Norman Meade
Robert Mellin Ltd .... UK
Cliff Bennett & The Rebel Rousers .... **Parlophone R 5173**
The Drifters .... **London HLK 9886**

ONE WAY TICKET　　　　　　　　**May 1979**
Jack Keller / Hank Hunter
Robert Mellin Ltd. .... USA
Eruption .... **Atlantic K 11266**

ONE, TWO, BUTTON YOUR SHOE　　**1937**
Arthur Johnston / Johnny Burke
Campbell Connelly & Co. Ltd. .... USA
Film(s): .... Pennies From Heaven
Bing Crosby .... **Brunswick Bing 2**
Les Allen .... **Columbia FB 1624**
Dickie Valentine .... **Decca LK 4269**
Bing Crosby appeared in *Pennies From Heaven*.

ONE-TWO-THREE O'LEARY　　　　**December 1968**
Michael Carr / Barry Mason
Patricia Music .... UK
Des O'Connor .... **Columbia DB 8492**

ONEDIN LINE, THE　　　　　　　**January 1972**
Aram Khatchaturian
Burlington Music Co. Ltd .... UK
**Vienna Philharmonic Orchestra,
conducted by Aram Khacaturian** .... **Decca F 13259**
An arrangement by Anthony Isaacs of the Adagio from *Spartacus & Phrygia* by Aram Khatchaturian (1903 - 1978) and used as the theme of the T.V. series *The Onedin Line*.

ONION SONG, THE　　　　　　　**December 1969**
Nicholas Ashford / Valerie Simpson
Jobete Music (UK) Ltd. .... USA
Marvin Gaye & Tammi Terrell .... **Tamla Motown TMG 715**

ONLY A ROSE   **1927**
Rudolf Friml / Brian Hooker
B.Feldman & Co.Ltd. . . . . USA
Show(s):. . . . . The Vagabond King
Film(s):. . . . . The Vagabond King
Winnie Melville & Derek Oldham   **HMV B 2570**
Anne Ziegler & Webster Booth   **HMV B 9065**
Jane Fyffe & John Hanson   **Pye NPL 18046**
Oreste & Jean Fenn   **HMV ALP 1378**
Winnie Melville & Derek Oldham appeared in the British production
of *The Vagabond King.*
Oreste appeared in the 1956 film of *The Vagabond King.*

ONLY FOOLS   **April 1952**
David Heneker / Tommy Duggan
Sun Music . . . . UK
Jimmy Young   **Polygon P 1017**
Lee Lawrence   **Decca F 9833**
Camarata & his Music   **Brunswick 04873**
David Hughes   **HMV B 10208**

ONLY FOREVER   **1941**
Johnny Burke / Jimmy Monaco
Campbell Connelly & Co. Ltd . . . . USA
Film(s):. . . . . Rhythm on the River
Bing Crosby   **Brunswick Bing 6**
Vera Lynn   **Decca F 7693**
Dean Martin   **Capitol T 849**
Bing Crosby appeared in *Rhythm on the River.*
Nominated for an Academy Award 1940.

ONLY LOVE   **February 1986**
Vladimir Cosma / Norman Gimble
Unknown Publisher . . . . France
Nana Mouskouri   **Carrere CAR 376**
Theme of the television series *Mistral's Daughter.*

ONLY MAN ON THE ISLAND, THE   **JULY 1958**
Bob Hilliard / Dave Mann
Bron Music Co. . . . . USA
Tommy Steele   **Decca F 11041**
Vic Damone   **Philips PB 837**
Dennis Lotis   **Columbia DB 4158**

ONLY ONE I KNOW, THE   **June 1990**
"The Charlatans"
Warner Chappell Music . . . . UK
The Charlatans   **Situation Two SIT 70**

ONLY ONE WOMAN   **November 1968**
Robin Gibb / Maurice Gibb / Barry Gibb
Abigail Music . . . . UK
The Marbles   **Polydor 56272**

ONLY RHYME THAT BITES, THE   **July 1990**
Nicky Lockett / Graham Massey
Warner Chappell Music . . . . UK
MC Tunes Versus 808 State   **ZTT ZANG 3**

ONLY SIXTEEN   **September 1959**
Barbara Campbell
Ardmore & Beechwood Ltd . . . . USA
Craig Douglas   **Top Rank JAR 159**
Sam Cooke   **HMV POP 642**
Al Saxon   **Fontana H 205**

ONLY THE LONLEY   **October 1960**
Roy Orbison / Joe Melson
Acuff-Rose Publishing Co. Ltd . . . . USA
Roy Orbison   **London HAU 2342**

ONLY WAY IS UP, THE   **August 1988**
George Jackson / John Henderson
B.M.G. Music . . . . USA
Yazz & The Plastic Population   **Big Life BLR 4**

ONLY WAY OUT, THE   **August 1982**
Richard Martinez
Warner Brothers Music . . . . UK
Cliff Richard   **EMI 5318**

ONLY WHEN YOU LEAVE   **June 1984**
Gary Kemp
Reformation Music . . . . UK
Spandau Ballet   **Chrysalis SPAN 3**

ONLY WHEN YOU'RE IN MY ARMS   **1939**
Bert Kalmar / Con Conrad / Herman Ruby
Chappell & Co. Ltd. . . . . USA
Film(s): . . . . .The Story of Vernon & Irene Castle
Jack Harris & his Orchestra   **HMV BD 5504**
Leslie Hutchinson (Hutch)   **Parlophone F 1485**

ONLY WOMEN BLEED   **January 1978**
Alice Cooper / Dick Wagner
Warner Brothers Music Ltd . . . . USA
Julie Covington   **Virgin VS 196**

ONLY YESTERDAY   **May 1975**
Richard Carpenter / John Bettis
Rondor Music (London) Ltd . . . . USA
The Carpenters   **A&M AMS 7159**

ONLY YOU   **June 1956**
Buck Ram / Ande Rand
Sherwin Music Co. Ltd. . . . . USA
Film(s): . . . . Rock Around the Clock
The Platters   **Mercury MT 117**
The Hilltoppers   **London HAD 2071**
Billy Eckstine   **MGM MGM 830**
Annie Ross   **Decca F 10680**

ONLY YOU   **May 1982**
Vincent Clarke
Sonet Music . . . . UK
Yazoo   **Mute 020**
The Flying Pickets (1983)   **Mute 020**
Ivor Novello Nomination 1983.

ONLY YOU CAN   **March 1975**
Kenny Young
Chrysalis Music Ltd . . . . UK
Fox   **GTO GT 8**

OO! WHAT YOU DO TO ME   **August 1953**
Kay Twomey / Fred Wise / Ben Weisman
Dash Music Ltd . . . . USA
Patti Page   **Oriole CB 1190**
Lita Roza   **Decca F 10144**

OOH LA LA LA (Let's Go Dancing) (See Let's Go Dancing)

OOH THAT KISS   **1932**
Mort Dixon / Joe Young / Harry Warren
Chappell & Co. Ltd. . . . . USA
Show(s):. . . . . The Laugh Parade
Frances Day   **HMV B 4266**
Peggy Lee   **Brunswick LAT 8205**

OOH TO BE AH   **April 1983**
Chris Hamill / Stuart Neale / Jerry Strode / Stephen Askent / Nick Beggs
Tritec Music . . . . UK
Kajagoogoo   **EMI 5383**

OOH WHAT A LIFE   **September 1979**
Alex Francfort / Daniel Vangarde
Blue Mountain Music . . . . France
The Gibson Brothers   **Island WIP 6503**

OOH-WAKKA-DOO-WAKKA-DAY   **July 1972**
Gilbert O'Sullivan
M.A.M. (Music Publishing) Ltd. . . . . UK
Gilbert O'Sullivan   **MAM 78**

OOPS UP SIDE YOUR HEAD   **August 1980**
*Lonnie Simmons / Robert Wilson / Ronnie Wilson / Charles Wilson
/ R. Taylor*
Leosong Copyright Services Ltd . . . . USA
The Gap Band   **Mercury MER 22**

OPEN THE DOOR RICHARD   **1947**
Dusty Fletcher / Jack McVea / John Manson & Dan Howell
Leeds Music Ltd. . . . . USA
Dusty Fletcher   **Parlophone R 3037**
Louis Jordan & his Tympany Five   **Brunswick 03778**

OPEN UP YOUR HEART   **March 1955**
Stuart Hamblen
Duchess Music Ltd. . . . . USA
Tony Brent & Anne Warren   **Columbia SCM 5170**
Beverley Bunt   **HMV 7EG 8483**

OPEN YOUR HEART   October 1981
Philip Oakey / John Callis
Virgin Music . . . . UK
Human League . . . . **Virgin VS 453**

OPEN YOUR HEART   January 1987
Madonna Ciccone / Gardner Cole / Peter Rafelson
Warner Brothers Music . . . . USA
Madonna . . . . **Sire W 8480**

OPPORTUNITIES   June 1986
Neil Tennant / Chris Lowe
10 Music . . . . UK
The Pet Shop Boys . . . . **Parlophone R 6129**

OPPOSITES ATTRACT   May 1990
Oliver Leiber
Virgin Music . . . . USA
Paula Abdul . . . . **Siren SRN 124**

OPUS NUMBER ONE   1945
Sy Oliver
Peter Maurice Music Co. Ltd. . . . . USA
Tommy Dorsey & his Orchestra . . . . **RCA RCX 1002**
Gene Krupa & his Orchestra,
vocal Anita O'Day . . . . **Columbia 33S 1064**
Gene Krupa & his Orchestra,
vocal Anita O'Day . . . . **HMV CLP 1087**
The Clark Sisters . . . . **London HAD 2128**
Ted Heath & his Music . . . . **Decca F 8512**

ORANGE BLOSSOM SPECIAL   June 1962
Ervin Rousse
Leeds Music . . . . USA
Johnny Cash . . . . **CBS BPG 62501**
The Spotnicks (1962) . . . . **Oriole CB 1724**
First Published 1938.

ORANGE BLOSSOM TIME   1929
Joe Goodwin / Gus Edwards
Robbins Music Corporation Ltd . . . . USA
Film(s): . . . . Hollywood Revue
Cliff Edwards (Ukulele Ike) . . . . **Columbia 5559**
Paul Whiteman & his Orchestra . . . . **Columbia 5560**
Jack Hylton & his Orchestra . . . . **HMV B 5700**
Cliff Edwards appeared in *Hollywood Revue.*

ORANGE COLOURED SKY   November 1950
Milton De Lugg / Willie Stein
Edwin H. Morris & Coi. Ltd . . . . USA
Nat 'King' Cole . . . . **Capitol CI 13392**
Doris Day . . . . **Columbia DB 2750**

ORCHIDS IN THE MOONLIGHT   1933
Vincent Youmans / Gus Kahn / Edward Eliscu
Chappell & Co. Ltd. . . . . USA
Film(s): . . . . Flying Down to Rio
Rudy Vallee & his Connecticut Yankees . . . . **HMV B 6466**
The Platters . . . . **Mercury MMC 14072**

ORGAN GRINDERS SWING   1936
Mitchell Parish / Irving Mills / Will Hudson
Campbell Connelly & Co. Ltd . . . . USA
Connie Russell . . . . **HMV B 383**
Hudson-Delange Orchestra . . . . **Vocalion 508**
The Mills Brothers . . . . **Brunswick 02460**
The Four Aces . . . . **Brunswick 05127**

ORIGINAL DIXIELAND ONE-STEP   1917
Nick La Rocca / Jimmy Dale
Peter Maurice Music . . . . USA
Original Dixieland Jazz Band (1917) . . . . **RCA RD 7919**
Original Dixieland Jazz Band (1936) . . . . **HMV B 8648**
Bob Crosby Orchestra . . . . **Brunswick 04398**
The Dutch Swing College Band . . . . **Philips BBR 8018**

ORINOCO FLOW   November 1988
Nick Ryan / Roma Ryan'Enya'
S.B.K. Songs . . . . UK
Enya . . . . **East West YZ 312**

ORVILLE'S SONG   January 1983
Bobby Crush
EMI Music . . . . UK
Keith Harris & 'Orville' . . . . **B.B.C. RESL 124**

OSSIE'S DREAM (The Way To Wembley)   May 1981
Charles Hodges / David Peacock
Campbell Connelly & Co. . . . . UK
Spurs F.A. Cup Final Squad . . . . **Shelf 1**

OTHER MAN'S GRASS, THE   February 1968
Tony Hatch / Jackie Trent
Welbeck Music Co. Ltd. . . . . UK
Petula Clark . . . . **Pye 7N 17416**

OTHER PEOPLE'S BABIES   1934
Vivian Ellis / A.P. Herbert
Chappell & Co. Ltd . . . . UK
Show(s): . . . . Streamline
Norah Howard . . . . **Columbia DX 617**
Vivian Ellis . . . . **Decca LF 1331**
Norah Howard appeared in *Streamline.*

OTHER SIDE OF LOVE, THE   December 1982
Vincent Clarke / Alison Moyet
Sonet Music . . . . UK
Yazoo . . . . **Mute YAZ 002**

OUR DAY WILL COME   February 1963
Mort Garson / Bob Hilliard
Francis, Day & Hunter Ltd . . . . USA
Ruby & The Romantics . . . . **London HLR 9679**
Mary May . . . . **Fontana 267266**
Percy Faith & his Orchestra . . . . **CBS BPG 62330**

OUR FAVOURITE MELODIES   July 1962
Bob Elgin / Kay Rogers / Wes Farrell
Roosevelt Music Ltd . . . . USA
Craig Douglas . . . . **Columbia DB 4854**
Gary Criss . . . . **Stateside SS 104**

OUR HOUSE   December 1982
Carl Smith / Christopher Foreman
Warner Brothers Music . . . . UK
Madness . . . . **Stiff BUY 163**
Ivor Novello Award.

OUR LANGUAGE OF LOVE   November 1958
Marguerite Monnot / Alxandre Breffort / Julian More / David
Heneker & Monty Norman
Trafalgar Music Ltd . . . . France
Show(s): . . . . Irma La Douce
Elizabeth Seal & Keith Michell . . . . **Philips BBL 7274**
Millicent Martin . . . . **Columbia DB 4171**
Elizabeth Seal and Keith Michell appeared in both the American and
British productions of *Irma La Douice.*

OUR LIPS ARE SEALED   May 1983
Terence Hall / Jane Weidlin
Chappell Music Co. . . . . USA
Fun Boy Three . . . . **Chrysalis FUNB 1**

OUR LODGER'S SUCH A NICE YOUNG MAN   1897
Fred Murray / Laurence Barclay
Francis, Day & Hunter Ltd. . . . . UK
Norah Blaney . . . . **Columbia DB 568**
Leon Cortez & his Costa Pals . . . . **Regal Zonophone MR 3214**
The Variety Singers . . . . **Columbia SEG 7744**

OUR LOVE AFFAIR   1941
Arthur Freed / Roger Edens
Robbins Music Corporation Ltd . . . . USA
Film(s): . . . . Strike Up the Band
Judy Garland . . . . **Brunswick 03128**
Frances Langford & Tony Martin . . . . **Decca F 7725**
Tommy Dorsey & his Orchestra,
vocal Frank Sinatra . . . . **RCA RD 27069**
Judy Garland appeared in *Strike Up the Band.*
Nominated for and Academy Award 1940.

OUR LOVE IS HERE TO STAY   February 1952
George Gershwin / Ira Gershwin
Chappell & Co. Ltd . . . . USA
Film(s):Goldwyn Follies / An American in Paris / Lady Sings the Blues
Kate Smith . . . . **Capitol T 854**
Ella Fitzgerald . . . . **HMV CLP 1348**
Gene Kelly . . . . **MGM D 133**
Diana Ross . . . . **Tamla Motown STML 11311-2**
Gene Kelly appeared in *An American in Paris.*
Diana Ross appeared in *Lady Sings the Blues.*

OUR LOVE STORY   **August 1949**
Normal Newell / William Harrison
Carolin Music .... UK
Dorothy Squires .... **Columbia DB 2573**
Bill Johnson .... **Columbia DB 2539**
Vera Lynn .... **Decca F 9221**

OUR VERY OWN   **July 1951**
Jack Elliot / Victor Young
Bradbury Wood Music Ltd. .... USA
Victor Young Orchestra v Don Cherry ...... **Brunswick 04621**
Jo Stafford .... **Capitol CL 13444**
Teddy Johnson .... **Columbia DB 2870**

OUR WORLD   **October 1970**
Herbie Flowers / Kenneth Pickett
In-Music Ltd .... UK
Blue Mink .... **Philips 6006042**

OURS IS A NICE 'OUSE OURS IS   **1921**
Herbert Rule / Fred Holt
Herman Darewski Music Publishing Co.Ltd .... UK
Show(s): .... Fun of the Fayre
Alfred Lester .... **Columbia 887**
Alfred Lester appeared in *Fun of the Fayre*.

OUT HERE ON MY OWN   **November 1982**
Michael Gore / Lesley Gore
Warner Chappell Music .... USA
Film(s): .... Fame
Irene Cara .... **RSO RSO 66**
Irene Cara appeared in *Fame*.
Nominated for an Academy Award 1980.

OUT IN THE COLD AGAIN   **1935**
Ted Koehler / Rube Bloom
Peter Maurice Music Co. Ltd .... USA
The Dorsey Brothers Orchestra ...... **Brunswick 01899**
The BBC Dance Orchestra,
conducted by Henry Hall .... **Columbia CB 7798**
Johnny Ray .... **Columbia DB 3241**
Kay Starr .... **Capitol T 1468**

OUT IN THE COLD COLD SNOW   **1934**
W.E. Haines / J. Harper
Cameo Music Publishing Co. .... UK
Film(s): .... Love, Life and Laughter
Gracie Fields .... **Regal Zonophone MR 1878**
Gracie Fields appeared in *Love, Life and Laughter*.

OUT IN THE FIELDS   **June 1985**
Gary Moore
10 Music .... UK
Gary Moore & Phil Lynott .... **10 TEN 49**

OUT OF A CLEAR BLUE SKY   **April 1950**
Gene Piller / Ruth Roberts
Kassner Music Co. .... USA
Donald Peers .... **HMV B 9903**
Tommy Tucker Orchestra .... **MGM 268**

OUT OF MY DREAMS   **1947**
Richard Rodgers / Oscar Hammerstein II
Williamson Music Co. Ltd. .... USA
Show(s): .... Oklahoma
Film(s): .... Oklahoma
Joan Roberts .... **Brunswick LAT 8001**
Betty Jane Watson .... **HMV 7EP 7023**
Shirley Jones .... **Capitol LCT 6100**
Joan Roberts appeared in the American production of *Oklahoma*.
Betty Jane Watson appeared in the British production of *Oklahoma*.
Shirley Jones appeared in the film of *Oklahoma*.

OUT OF NOWHERE   **1931**
Edward Heyman / Johnny Green
Chappell & Co. Ltd. .... USA
Film(s): .... Dude Ranch / You Came Along / The Rat Race
Ruth Etting .... **Columbia DB 546**
Bing Crosby (1945) .... **Brunswick LAT 8251**
The R.A.F. Dance Orchestra,
vocal Dorothy Carless .... **Decca F 8572**
Vic Damone .... **Philips BBL 7259**

OUT OF THE NIGHT   **1945**
Eddie Lisbona / Bob Musel

Southern Music Publishing Co. Ltd. .... USA
Monte Ray .... **Columbia FB 3162**
Anne Shelton .... **Decca F 8588**
Based on 'Ay Ay Ay' by Osman Perez Freire.

OUT OF THIS WORLD   **1945**
Harold Arlen / Johnny Mercer
Edwin H. Morris & Co. Ltd. .... USA
Film(s): .... Out of This World
Bing Crosby .... **Brunswick Bing 10**
Helen Forrest .... **Capitol LC 6834**
Buddy Rich .... **HMV CLP 1092**
Tony Bennett .... **Philips BBL 7452**

OUT OF TIME   **August 1966**
Mick Jagger / Keith Richard
Mirage Music Ltd. .... UK
Chris Farlowe .... **Immediate IM 023**

OUT OF TOWN   **April 1956**
Leslie Bricusse / Robin Beaumont
Edward Kassner Music Co. Ltd. .... UK
Film(s): .... Charley Moon
Max Bygraves .... **HMV 7EG 8203**
Dickie Valentine .... **Decca F 10752**
Max Bygraves appeared in *Charley Moon*.
Ivor Novello Nomination.

OUTSIDE OF HEAVEN   **February 1953**
Sammy Gallop / Chester Conn
Bradbury Wood Music Co. .... USA
Margaret Whiting .... **Capitol CL 13826**
Eddie Fisher .... **HMV B 10362**
David Carey .... **Columbia DB 3200**

OVER MY SHOULDER   **1934**
Harry Woods
Cinophonic Music Co. Ltd .... UK
Film(s): .... Evergreen
Jessie Matthews .... **Columbia DB 1404**
Ray Noble & his Orchestra .... **HMV B 6504**
Jessie Matthews appeared in *Evergreen*.

OVER ON THE SUNNY SIDE   **1934**
Allan Flynn / Jack Egan
Lawrence Wright Music Co. Ltd. .... USA
Aileen Stanley .... **Brunswick 01706**
Ray Noble & his Orchestra .... **HMV B 6463**

OVER THE GARDEN WALL   **1930**
Leslie Sarony / Cecil Harrington
Campbell Connelly & Co. Ltd .... UK
The BBC Dance Orchestra, conducted
by Jack Payne, vocal Jack Payne ...... **Columbia CB 132**
Gracie Fields .... **HMV B 3600**
Tommy Handley .... **Piccadilly 674**

OVER THE RAINBOW   **1940**
Harold Arlen / E.Y. Harburg
Robbins Music Corporation Ltd. .... USA
Film(s): .... The Wizard of Oz
Judy Garland .... **MGM C 757**
Judy Garland .... **Capitol T 1118**
Sarah Vaughan .... **Emarcy EJL 100**
Judy Vaughan .... **Brunswick LA 8725**
Judy Garland appeared in *The Wizard of Oz*.
Theme song of Judy Garland.
Academy Award winning song for 1939.

OVER THERE   **1918**
George M. Cohan
Chappell & Co. Ltd. .... USA
Show(s): .... Zig-Zag
Film(s): .... The Cockeyed World / Yankee Doodle Dandy
Shirley Kellog .... **Columbia L 1222**
Enrico Caruso .... **RCA RB 16128**
Fred Waring & his Pennsylvanians ...... **Brunswick 03408**
Shirley Kellog appeared in *Zig-Zag*.

OVER UNDER SIDEWAYS DOWN   **July 1966**
Jeff Beck / James McCarty / Chris Dreja, Keith Relf & Paul Samwell-Smith
Yardbird Music Ltd. .... UK
The Yardbirds .... **Columbia DB 7928**

OVER YOU — March 1964
Derek Quinn / Alan Jones
Kennedy Street Music Ltd . . . . UK
Freddie & The Dreamers — Columbia DB 7214

OVER YOU — June 1980
Bryan Ferry / Phil Manzanera
E.G. Music . . . . UK
Roxy Music — Polydor POSP 93

OVERJOYED — March 1986
Stevie Wonder
Jobete Music . . . . USA
Stevie Wonder — Motown ZB 40567

OXYGENE — September 1977
Jean Michel Jarre
Black Neon Music . . . . France
Jean Michel Jarre — Polydor 2001721

P.S. I LOVE YOU — 1934
Gordon Jenkins / Johnny Mercer
Campbell Connelly & Co. Ltd . . . . USA
Lew Stone & his Band, vocal Alan Kane . . . . Decca F 5241
Cyril Stapleton & his Orchestra, vocal Pearl Carr . . . Decca F 8946
Gordon Jenkins & his Orchestra,
vocal Don Burke — Brunswick 05187

PABLO THE DREAMER — 1945
Julio Sanders / Roberto Lopez
Southern Music Publishing Co. Ltd. . . . . Argentina
Carroll Gibbons & The Savoy Orpheans,
vocal Paul Carpenter — Columbia FB 3122
Anne Shelton — Decca F 8538
Monte Ray — Columbia FB 3119
Based on "Adios Muchachos".

PACIFIC — December 1989
"808 State"
Perfect Songs . . . . UK
808 State — ZTT ZANG 1

PACK UP YOUR TROUBLES IN YOUR OLD KIT BAG — 1915
Felix Powell / George Asaf
Francis, Day & Hunter Ltd. . . . . UK
Show(s): . . . . Her Soldier Boy
Film(s): . . . . Wait Till the Sun Shines Nellie
Murray Johnson . . . . HMV B 605
Florrie Forde — Columbia 9780
Dick Haymes & The Andrews Sisters . . . . Brunswick 04199

PADAM, PADAM — September 1952
Norbert Glanzberg / Henri Contet / Mann Holiner & Alberta Nichols
Leeds Music Ltd . . . . France
Edith Piaf — Columbia 33SX 5
Vera Lynn . . . . Decca F 9936
Tony Martin — HMV B 10318

PADDLIN' MADELIN' HOME — 1925
Harry Woods
Lawrence Wright Music Co. Ltd. . . . . USA
Jack Hylton & his Orchestra . . . . HMV B 2163
Layton & Johnstone — Columbia 3793
Max Bygraves — Decca LK 4317
Bobby Darin & Johnny Mercer — London HAK 2363

PADDY McGINTY'S GOAT — 1917
R.P. Weston / Bert Lee
Francis, Day & Hunter Ltd. . . . . UK
David McAlpin . . . . Regal Zonophone MR 72

PAGAN LOVE SONG, THE — 1929
Arthur Freed / Nacio Herb Brown
Robbins Music Corporation Ltd . . . . USA
Film(s): . . . . The Pagan / Pagan Love Song
Ramon Navaro — HMV C 2778
Nat Gonella & his Georgians . . . . Parlophone R 832
Howard Keel — MGM D 146
Bing Crosby — MGM C 868
Ramon Navaro appeared in *The Pagan*.
Howard Keel appeared in *Pagan Love Song*.

PAGAN MOON — 1932
Al Dubin / Al Bryan / Joe Burke
B. Feldman & Co. Ltd. . . . . USA

Ray Noble & his Orchestra . . . . HMV B 6219

PAINT IT BLACK — June 1966
Mick Jagger / Keith Richard
Mirage Music Ltd. . . . . UK
The Rolling Stones — Decca F 12395

PAINTER MAN — April 1979
Kenny Pickett / Eddie Philips
Dominion Music . . . . UK
Boney M — Hansa K 11351
The Creation (1966) — Planet PLF 119

PAINTING THE CLOUDS WITH SUNSHINE — 1930
Al Dubin / Joe Burke
B. Feldman & Co. Ltd . . . . USA
Film(s):Gold Diggers of Broadway / Little Johnny Jones / Painting the
Clouds With Sunshine
Nick Lucas — ASV AJA 5022
Layton & Johnstone — Columbia 5708
Jack Hylton & his Orchestra . . . . HMV B 5722
Larry Cross — Parlophone R 3504
George Greeley & his Orchestra & Chorus . . Capitol CL 13680
Nick Lucas appeared in *Gold Diggers of Broadway*.
George Greeley appeared in *Painting The Clouds With Sunshine*.

PAIR OF SILVER WINGS, A — 1941
Michael Carr / Eric Maschwitz
Peter Maurice Music . . . . UK
Frances Day . . . . Decca F 7854
Anne Shelton — Rex 9984
The New Mayfair Dance Orchestra,
vocal Alan Kane . . . . HMV BD 5673

PAL OF MY CRADLE DAYS — 1925
Al Piantadosi / Marshall Montgomery
Francis, Day & Hunter Ltd. . . . . USA
Paul Whiteman & his Orchestra — HMV B 2099
Thomas Jackson . . . . Regal G 8735

PALE MOON — 1920
Jesse Glick / Frederick Logan
Francis, Day & Hunter Ltd . . . . USA
Hubert Eisdell . . . . Columbia DB 1392
Bing Crosby & The Merry Macs — Brunswick OE 9473

PALE SHELTER — May 1983
Roland Orzabel / Curt Smith
Polygram Music . . . . UK
Tears For Fears . . . . Mercury IDEA 5

PALESTEENA — 1921
Con Conrad / J. Russel Robinson
Francis, Day & Hunter Ltd . . . . USA
The Original Dixieland Jazz Band . . . . RCA RD 7919
Bob Crosby's Bob Cats, vocal Nappy Lamare . . Decca F 6874

PAMELA PAMELA — February 1967
Graham Gouldman
Hournew Music Ltd. . . . . UK
Wayne Fontana . . . . Fontana TF 770

PANDORA'S BOX — September 1975
Keith Reid / Gary Brooker
Blue Beard Music . . . . UK
Procul Harum — Chrysalis CHS 2073

PANIC — August 1986
Steven Morrisey / John Marr
Warner Brothers Music . . . . UK
The Smiths . . . . Rough Trade RT 193

PANSÉ, LA (Mandy) — December 1957
Furio Rendine / Gigi Pisano / Jack Elliot
Peter Maurice Music Co. Ltd . . . . Italy
Marino Marini Quartet . . . . Durium DLU 96034
Edmundo Ros & his Orchestra . . . . Decca F 10954
The Gaylords — Mercury ZEP 10021
Eddie Calvert (Trumpet) & his Orchestra
(this version entitled 'Mandy') — Columbia DB 3956

PAPA DON'T PREACH — July 1986
Madonna Ciccone / Brian Elliot
Warner Brothers Music . . . . USA
Madonna . . . . Sire W 8636

PAPA LOVES MAMBO   November 1954
Al Hoffman / Dick Manning / Bix Reichner
Macmelodies Ltd. .... USA
Perry Como .... RCA RD 27100
Johnny Ray .... Philips BBR 8062

PAPA WAS A ROLLING STONE   February 1973
Norman Whitfield / Barrett Strong
Jobete Music (UK) Ltd. .... USA
The Temptations (1973) .... Tamla Motown TMG 839
Was Not Was (1990) .... Fontana WAS 7

PAPA WON'T YOU DANCE WITH ME   December 1948
Jule Styne / Sammy Cahn
Edwin H. Morris & Co. Ltd .... USA
Show(s): .... High Button Shoes
Guy Lombardo & his Royal Canadians ..... Brunswick 03998
Doris Day .... Columbia SCM 5059

PAPA'S GOT A BRAND NEW PIGBAG   May 1982
"Pigbag"
Warner Brothers Music .... UK
Pigbag .... Y Records Y 10

PAPER DOLL   1915
Johnny Black
Peter Maurice Music Co. Ltd. .... USA
Film(s): .... Hi Good Lookin'
The Mills Brothers .... Brunswick LA 8728
Bing Crosby .... Brunswick LAT 8138
The Mills Brothers .... London HAD 2192
Theme song of The Mills Brothers.

PAPER KISSES   March 1955
John Jerome
John Fields Music Co. Ltd. .... UK
Alma Cogan .... HMV 7M 286

PAPER PLANE   February 1973
Francis Rossi / Robert Young
Valley Music .... UK
Status Quo .... Vertigo 6059071

PAPER ROSES   September 1960
Fred Spielman / Janice Torre
Leeds Music Ltd .... USA
The Kaye Sisters .... Philips BBL 7422
Anita Bryant .... London HLL 9114
Maureen Evans .... Oriole CB 1550
Marie Osmond (1973) .... MGM 2006315

PAPER SUN   July 1967
Steve Winwood / Jim Capaldi
Island Music Ltd. .... UK
Traffic .... Island WIP 6002

PAPERBACK WRITER   July 1966
John Lennon / Paul McCartney
Northern Songs Ltd. .... UK
The Beatles .... Parlophone R 5452

PARADE OF THE WOODEN SOLDIERS   1922
Ballard MacDonald / Leon Jessel
Boosey & Hawkes Music Publishers Ltd .... Germany
Show(s): .... Chauve Souris
Orchestre Mascotte .... Parlophone E 11160
The Andrews Sisters .... Brunswick 04669
Russ Garcia & his Orchestra .... London HAU 2102
First Published 1906.

PARADISE   1933
Nacio Herb Brown / Gordon Clifford
Keith Prowse Music Publishing Co. Ltd. .... USA
Film(s): ....A Woman Commands / The Five Pennies
Bing Crosby .... Brunswick 1308
Peggy Wood .... Columbia DB 884
Bing Crosby .... Brunswick LAT 8251
Frank Sinatra (1946) .... Fontana TFL 5001
Frank Ifield .... Columbia DB 7655

PARADISE CITY   April 1989
"Guns 'n' Roses"
Warner Chappell Music .... USA
Guns 'n' Roses .... Geffen GEF 50

PARADISE FOR TWO, A   1917
James W. Tate / Clifford Harris / Arthur Valentine
Francis, Day & Hunter Ltd. .... UK
Show(s): .... The Maid of the Mountains
Jose Collins & Thorpe Bates .... Columbia L 1157
Anne Ziegler & Webster Booth .... HMV B 8982
Mary Thomas & Barry Kent .... HMV CLP 1311
Jose Collins & Thorpe Bates appeared in the British production of *The
Maid of the Mountains.*

PARALYSED   April 1957
Otis Blackwell
Aberbach (London) Ltd. .... USA
Elvis Presley .... RCA RCX 175

PARANOID   October 1970
Tony Iommi / Bill Ward / Geezer Butler & Ozzy Osborne
Essex Music Ltd .... UK
Black Sabbath .... Vertigo 6059010
Black Sabbath (1980) .... Nems BSS 101

PARDON ME PRETTY BABY   1931
Ray Klages / Jack Meskill / Vincent Rose
Lawrence Wright Music Co. Ltd .... USA
Jack Smith .... Imperial 2600
Layton & Johnstone .... Columbia SEG 7778
Jimmy Parkinson .... Columbia 33S 1109

PARIS IN THE SPRING   1935
Mack Gordon / Harry Revel
Victoria Music Co. Ltd .... USA
Film(s): ....Paris Love Song
Maurice Winnick & his Orchestra ..... Decca F 5617
Michel Legrand & his Orchestra ...... Philips BBL 7481

PARIS STAY THE SAME   1930
Victor Schertzinger / Clifford Grey
Campbell Connelly & Co. Ltd .... USA
Film(s): .... The Love Parade
Maurice Chevalier .... Camden CDN 152
Jaqueline Francois .... Philips BBL 7438
Maurice Chevalier appeared in *The Love Parade.*

PARISIAN PIERROT   1924
Noel Coward
Keith Prowse Music Publishing Co. Ltd. .... UK
Show(s): .... London Calling / Andre Charlot's Revue 1924
Film(s): ....Star
Noel Coward .... HMV CLP 1050
Gertrude Lawrence .... Ace of Clubs ACL 1171
The Romaine Orchestra .... HMV B 1803
Julie Andrews .... Stateside SL 10233
Noel Coward appeared in *London Calling.*
Gertrude Lawrence appeared in both *London Calling* and *Andre
Charlot's Revue of 1924.*
Julie Andrews appeared in *Star.*

PARISIENNE WALKWAYS   June 1979
Gary Moore / Phil Lynott
Chappell & Co. Ltd. .... UK
Gary Moore .... MCA 419

PARROT ON THE FORTUNE TELLER'S HAT, THE   1946
Zequinha Abreu
Latin-American Music Publishing Co. Ltd. .... Brazil
Ethel Smith (organ) .... Brunswick LA 8504
Howard Lanin & his Orchestra .... Brunswick LAT 8279
Edmundo Ros & his Orchestra .... Decca F 8598

PART OF THE UNION   March 1973
John Ford / Richard Hudson
Essex Music Ltd. .... UK
The Strawbs .... A&M AMS 7047

PART TIME LOVE   December 1978
Elton John / Gary Osborne
Big Pig Music .... UK
Elton John .... Rocket XPRES 1

PART TIME LOVER   September 1985
Stevie Wonder
Jobete Music .... USA
Stevie Wonder .... Motown ZB 40351

PARTY October 1957
Jessie Mae Robinson
Belinda (London) Ltd .... USA
Film(s): ....Loving You
Elvis Presley .... **RCA RC 24001**
Wanda Jackson .... **Capitol EAP 1-1041**
Elvis Presley appeared in *Loving You*.

PARTY'S OVER, THE December 1957
Jule Styne / Betty Comden / Adolph Green
Chappell & Co. Ltd .... USA
Show(s): ....Bells Are Ringing
Film(s): ....Bells Are Ringing
Judy Holliday .... **Capitol W 1345**
Betty Comden & Adolph Green .... **Capitol LCT 6186**
Doris Day .... **Philips PB 758**
Lonnie Donegan (1962) .... **Pye 7N 15424**
Judy Holliday appeared in the American production and the film of *Bells Are Ringing*.

PASADENA (See Home In Pasadena)

PASS THE DUTCHIE October 1982
Jackie Mitto / Fitzroy Simpson / Robbie Lynn / Lloyd Ferguson / Leroy Sibbles / Headley Bennett
Sparta Music .... UK
Musical Youth .... **MCA YOU 1**

PASSENGERS September 1984
Elton John / Bernie Taupin / David Johnson & Phineas McHize
Big Pig Music .... UK
Elton John .... **Rocket EJS 5**

PASSING BREEZE November 1960
Trevor Stanford
Clover-Conway Music Co. Ltd .... UK
Ross Conway (piano) .... **Columbia DB 4508**
Danny Williams .... **HMV CLP 1521**

PASSING BY 1890
Robert Herrick / Edward Purcell
Edwin Ashdown Ltd................................ UK
Walter Glynne .... **HMV B 1103**
Dennis Noble .... **Columbia DB 1016**
Alvar Liddell .... **HMV B 9233**

PASSING STRANGERS November 1957
Mel Mitchell / Rita Mann
Francis, Day & Hunter Ltd .... USA
Sarah Vaughan & Billy Eckstine ..... **Mercury MT 164**
Ruby Murray .... **Columbia DB 3994**
Sarah Vaughan & Billy Eckstine (1969) ..... **Mercury 6463041**

PATCHES November 1970
General Johnson / Ronald Dunbar
Ardmore & Beechwood Ltd .... USA
Clarence Carter .... **Atlantic 2091030**

PATIENCE AND FORTITUDE 1947
Billy Moore Jnr. / Blackie Warren
Leeds Music Ltd................................. USA
Film(s): .... Freddie Steps Out
Geraldo & his Orchestra, vocal Carol Carr . **Parlophone F 2161**
The Andrews Sisters .... **Brunswick 03750**
Count Basie & his Orchestra,
vocal Jimmy Rushing .... **Fontana TFL 5046**

PATIENTLY SMILING 1931
Franz Lehar / Harry Graham
Chappell & Co. Ltd........................... Austria
Show(s): ....Land of Smiles
Richard Tauber (in German) ..... **Parlophone RO 20107**
Richard Tauber .... **Parlophone BSP 3002**
Charles Craig .... **HMV CLP 1286**
Richard Tauber appeared in the British production of *Land of Smiles*.

PATRICIA July 1958
Perez Prado
Southern Music Publishing Co. Ltd .... USA
Film(s): .... La Dolce Vita
Perez Prado & his Orchestra .... **RCA RD 27102**
David Carroll & his Orchestra .... **Mercury MMC 14061**
Sound Track of La Dolce Vita .... **RCA RD 27202**

PAVANNE 1940
Morton Gould
Campbell Connelly & Co. Ltd .... USA
The Boston Promenade Orchestra .... **HMV 7EG 8066**
Morton Gould & his Orchestra .... **Columbia DCX 102**
Glenn Miller & his Orchestra .... **HMV DLP 1081**

PAVEMENTS OF PARIS, THE (Sur Le Pavé) December 1954
George Auric / Sonny Miller / S.A. Beecher Stevens
Keith Prowse Music Publishing Co. Ltd. .... France
Film(s): .... La Fete A Henriette
Jean Sablon .... **HMV 7M 272**
The Melachrino Orchestra .... **HMV 7EG 8206**

PEACHES July 1977
"The Stranglers"
April Music Ltd .... UK
The Stranglers .... **United Artists UP 36248**

PEANUT VENDOR, THE (El Manisero) 1931
Moises Simons / L. Wolfe Gilbert / Marion Sunshine
Lawrence Wright Music Co. Ltd .... Cuba
Film(s): .... Cuban Love Song / A Star is Born
Don Azpiazu's Havana Casino Orchestra ..... **HMV DLP 1072**
Xavier Cugat & his Orchestra .... **Columbia 33S 1061**
Judy Garland .... **Philips BBL 7007**
Stan Kenton & his Orchestra (1949) .... **Capitol LCT 6109**
Percy Faith & his Orchestra .... **Philips BBL 7311**
Judy Garland appeared in *A Star Is Born*.

PEARL IN THE SHELL June 1984
Howard Jones
Warner Brothers Music .... UK
Howard Jones .... **WEA HOW 4**

PEARL OF SWEET CEYLON, THE 1904
Lionel Monckton / Adrian Ross / Percy Greenbank
Chappell & Co. Ltd. .... UK
Show(s): .... The Cingalee
Charles Holland .... **Zonophone X 42079**

PEARL'S A SINGER May 1977
Gerry Leiber / Mike Stoller / Ralph Dino & John Sembello
Carlin Music Corporation .... USA
Elkie Brooks .... **A&M AMS 7275**

PECKIN' 1938
Ben Pollack / Harry James
Cinephonic Music Co. Ltd. .... USA
Film(s): .... New Faces of 1937
Ozzie Nelson & his Orchestra .... **HMV BD 5240**
Benny Goodman & his Orchestra .... **Camden CDN 112**
Jimmy Dorsey & his Orchestra,
vocal Bing Crosby .... **Brunswick 02481**

PEDRO THE FISHERMAN 1943
Harry Parr-Davies / Harold Purcell
Chappell & Co. Ltd .... UK
Show(s): .... Lisbon Story
Film(s): .... Lisbon Story
Vincent Tildsley's Mastersingers .... **Parlophone F 1993**
Gracie Fields .... **Decca LK 4182**
Richard Tauber .... **Parlophone PMB 1010**
The Spinners .... **Columbia DB 4267**
Vincent Tildsley's Mastersingers appeared in the show *Lisbon Story*.
Richard Tauber appeared in the film *Lisbon Story*.

PEEK A BOO March 1967
Geoff Stevens / John Carter
Monique Music Ltd. .... UK
The New Vaudeville Band .... **Fontana TF 784**

PEG O' MY HEART 1913
Alfred Bryan / Fred Fisher
Ascherberg, Hopwood & Crew Ltd. .... USA
Show(s): .... The Ziegfeld Follies of 1913
Film(s): .... Oh You Beautiful Doll
The Metropolitan Band .... **HMV C 357**
Red Nichols & his Five Pennies .... **Brunswick 01019**
Glenn Miller & his Orchestra .... **Brunswick 03807**
Art Lund .... **MGM 106**
Max Bygraves with
Ted Heath & his Music .... **Decca LK 4317**

PEGGY O'NEIL   **1922**
Gilbert Dodge / Ed G. Nelson / Harry Pease
Francis, Day & Hunter Ltd . . . . USA
Robert Woodville . . . . **Regal 2252**
Pamela Baselow . . . . **HMV B 1391**
Tony Williams . . . . **Mercury MMC 14027**
Bing Crosby . . . . **Warner Brothers WM 4021**

PEGGY SUE   **November 1957**
Norman Petty / Jerry Allison / Buddy Holly
Southern Music Publishing Co. Ltd . . . . USA
Buddy Holly . . . . **Vogue LVA 9126**

PEGGY SUE GOT MARRIED   **September 1959**
Buddy Holly
Southern Music Publishing Co. Ltd . . . . USA
Buddy Holly . . . . **Coral LVA 9127**
The Crickets . . . . **Coral Q 72417**

PENNIES FROM HEAVEN   **1937**
Arthur Johnston / Johnny Burke
Campbell Connelly & Co. Ltd. . . . . USA
Film(s): . . . . Pennies From Heaven / Pepe
Bing Crosby . . . . **Brunswick Bing 2**
Bing Crosby, Louis Armstrong
& Frances Langford . . . . **Brunswick 0134**
Doris Day . . . . **Philips BBL 7248**
Frank Sinatra . . . . **Capitol LCT 6106**
The MacGuire Sisters . . . . **Coral LVA 9146**
Bing Crosby . . . . **Pye NPL 28015**
Bing Crosby appeared in *Pennies From Heaven* and *Pepe*.
Nominated for an Academy Award 1936.

PENNSYLVANIA POLKA   **1943**
Lester Lee / Zeke Manners
Francis, Day & Hunter Ltd . . . . USA
Film(s): . . . . Give Out Sisters
The Andrews Sisters . . . . **Brunswick 03368**
The Tommy Dorsey Orchestra,
conducted by Warren Covington . . . . **Brunswick LAT 8380**
The Andrews Sisters appeared in *Give Out Sisters*.

PENNSYLVANIA SIX-FIVE-THOUSAND   **1940**
Carl Sigman / Jerry Gray
Sun Music Publishing Co. Ltd . . . . USA
Film(s): . . . . The Glenn Miller Story
Glenn Miller & his Orchestra . . . . **RCA RCX 1024**
The Andrews Sisters . . . . **Brunswick 03089**
The Universal International
Studio Orchestra . . . . **Brunswick LA 8647**
The Universal International Studio Orchestra appeared in *The Glenn Miller Story*.

PENNY A KISS, A PENNY A HUG, A   **January 1951**
Buddy Kaye / Ralph Clare
Leeds Music Ltd . . . . USA
Dinah Shore & Tony Martin . . . . **HMV B 10034**
The Andrews Sisters . . . . **Brunswick 04665**
Dick Lee . . . . **MGM 1013**

PENNY LANE   **April 1967**
John Lennon / Paul McCartney
Northern Songs Ltd. . . . . UK
Show(s): . . . . John, Paul, George, Ringo and Bert
The Beatles . . . . **Parlophone R 5570**
Barbara Dickson . . . . **RSO 2394 141**
Barbara Dickson appeared in *John, Paul, George, Ringo & Bert*.

PENNY SERENADE, THE   **1939**
Melle Weersma / Hal Halifax
World Wide Music Co. Ltd. . . . . UK
Lew Stone & his Orchestra, vocal Al Bowlly . . . . **Decca F 6890**
Brian Lawrence . . . . **Rex 9445**
Vic Damone . . . . **Philips PB 914**
Ronnie Hilton . . . . **HMV CLP 1295**

PENNY WHISTLE SONG, THE   **February 1953**
Leroy Anderson
Mills Music Ltd . . . . USA
Leroy Anderson & his Concert Orchestra . . . **Beunswick LA 8613**
The Eastman-Rochester 'Pops' Orchestra,
conducted by Frederick Fennell . . . . **Mercury MMA 11059**

PEOPLE   **June 1966**
Bob Merrill / Jule Styne

Chappell & Co. Ltd. . . . . USA
Show(s): . . . . Funny Girl
Film(s): . . . . Funny Girl
Barbra Streisand . . . . **Capitol W 2059**
Lisa Shane . . . . **Pye NEP 24257**
Barbra Streisand . . . . **CBS 70044**
Barbara Streisand appeared in the American & British production and the film of *Funny Girl*.
Lisa Shane appeared in the British production of *Funny Girl*.

PEOPLE ARE PEOPLE   **April 1984**
Martin Gore
Sonet Music . . . . UK
Depeche Mode . . . . **Mute 7 BONG 5**

PEOPLE HOLD ON   **April 1989**
Matthew Black / Jonathan More / Lisa Stansfield
Block & Gilbert Music . . . . UK
Coldcut Featuring Lisa Stansfield . . . **Ahead Of Our Time CCUT 5**

PEOPLE LIKE YOU AND ME   **1943**
Mack Gordon / Harry Warren
Chappell & Co. Ltd . . . . USA
Film(s): . . . . Orchestra Wives
Glenn Miller & his Orchestra . . . . **HMV DLP 1059**
Glenn Miller appeared in *Orchestra Wives*.

PEOPLE LIKE YOU AND PEOPLE LIKE ME   **March 1976**
Gerry Shephard / John Springate
Rock Artistes Music . . . . UK
The Glitter Band . . . . **Bell 1471**

PEOPLE WILL SAY WE'RE IN LOVE   **1947**
Richard Rodgers / Oscar Hammerstein II
Williamson Music Co. Ltd. . . . . USA
Show(s): . . . . Oklahoma
Film(s): . . . . Oklahoma
Alfred Drake & Joan Roberts . . . . **Brunswick LAT 8001**
Betty Jane Watson . . . . **HMV 7EP 7023**
Gordon MacRae & Shirley Jones . . . . **Capitol LCT 6100**
Alfred Drake & Joan Roberts appeared in the American production of *Oklahoma*.
Betty Jane Watson appeared in the British production of *Oklahoma*.
Gordon MacRae & Shirley Jones appeared in the film of *Oklahoma*.

PEPE   **January 1961**
Hans Wittstatt / Dory Langdon
Edward Kassner Music Co. Ltd . . . . Germany
Film(s): . . . . Pepe
Duane Eddy (guitar) . . . . **London HL 9257**
Russ Conway (piano) . . . . **Columbia DB 4564**
Shirley Jones . . . . **Pye 7N 25067**
Shirley Jones appeared in *Pepe*.

PEPPER BOX   **November 1974**
Peter Arpadys / Mat Camison
Instant Music . . . . France
The Peppers . . . . **Spark SRL 1100**

PERDIDO   **1943**
Juan Tizol / Harry Lenk / Ervin Drake
Campbell Connelly & Co. Ltd . . . . USA
Duke Ellington & his Famous Orchestra . . . . **RCA RD 27134**
Sammy Davis . . . . **Brunswick LAT 8215**
Sarah Vaughan . . . . **Columbia 33SX 1360**

PERFECT   **May 1988**
Mark Nevin
MCA Music . . . . UK
Fairground Attraction . . . . **RCA PB 41845**
Ivor Novello Nomination.

PERFECT DAY, A   **1910**
Carrie Jacobs-Bond
Boosey & Hawkes Music Publishers Ltd . . . . USA
Alma Gluck & Chorus . . . . **HMV DA 232**
Bing Crosby . . . . **Brunswick 04657**
Thomas L. Thomas . . . . **Decca LXT 5247**

PERFIDIA   **1941**
Alberto Dominguez / Milton Leeds
Southern Music Publishing Co. Ltd . . . . Mexico
Film(s): . . . . Stardust on the Sage
Glenn Miller & his Orchestra,
vocal Dorothy Clare & The Modernaires . . . . . . **HMV DLP 1149**

Jane Morgan . . . . London HAR 2244
The Modernaires . . . . Vogue LVA 9103
Trio Los Panchos . . . . Philips BBL 7527
The Ventures (1961) . . . . London HL 9232

PERHAPS YOU'LL THINK OF ME   1927
Edgar Leslie / Billy Stone
Lawrence Wright Music Co. Ltd. . . . . USA
The Sylvians Orchestra . . . . HMV B 5243
Vera Lynn . . . . Decca LK 4305

PERHAPS, PERHAPS, PERHAPS
(Quizas, Quizas, Quizas)   February 1949
Osvaldo Farres / Joe Davis
Southern Music Publishing Co. Ltd . . . . Mexico
Jan Mazurus . . . . Decca F 9099
Jean Caval . . . . HMV B 9744
The Stargazers . . . . Decca LK 4309
Nat 'King' Cole . . . . Capitol LCT 6166

PERSIAN ROSEBUD   1928
Horatio Nicholls
Lawrence Wright Music Co. Ltd. . . . . UK
Jack Hylton & his Orchestra . . . . HMV B 5391

PERSIAN RUG   1928
Neil Moret / Gus Kahn
Francis, Day & Hunter Ltd. . . . . USA
The Louisiana Sugar Babies . . . . HMV 7EG 8215
The Jack Teagarden Group . . . . Brunswick LAT 8229

PERSONALITY   July 1959
Lloyd Price / Harold Logan
Leeds Music Ltd . . . . USA
Lloyd Price . . . . HMV CLP 1314
Anthony Newley . . . . Decca F 11422
Pat Boone . . . . London HAD 2345

PESSIMISTIC CHARACTER, THE
(With The Crab Apple Face)   1940
Jimmy Monaco / Johnny Burke
Campbell Connelly & Co. Ltd . . . . USA
Film(s): . . . . If I Had My Way
Bing Crosby . . . . Brunswick Bing 5
Bing Crosby appeared in *If I Had My Way.*

PETER GUNN   July 1959
Henry Mancini
Chappell & Co. Ltd . . . . USA
The Henry Mancini Orchestra . . . . RCA RD 27123
Duane Eddy (guitar) . . . . London HAW 1291
Ray Anthony Orchestra . . . . Capitol EAP 1-1181
Ted Heath & his Music . . . . Decca F 11111
The Art of Noise & Duane Eddy (1986) . . . . China WOK 6
Theme of the TV production *Peter Gunn.*

PETITE FLEUR   April 1959
Sidney Bechet
Essex Music Ltd . . . . France
Chris Barber's Jazz Band . . . . Nixa NJT 505
Sidney Bechet with The Claude Luter Orchestra Vogue EPV 1062
David Carroll & his Orchestra . . . . Mercury MMC 14082

PETITE WALTZ, THE   December 1950
Joe Heyne / E.A. Ellington / Phyllis Claire
Leeds Music Ltd . . . . Belgium
Joe Heyne & his Orchestra . . . . Esquire 5-009
Billy Cotton & his Band . . . . Decca F 9564
Guy Lombardo & his Royal Canadians . . Brunswick LAT 8063
David Carroll & his Orchestra . . . . Mercury MMC 14082

PETTIN' IN THE PARK   1933
Al Dubin / Harry Warren
B. Feldman & Co. Ltd. . . . . USA
Film(s): . . . . Gold Diggers of 1933
Dick Powell . . . . Broadcast 3339
Matty Matlock & the Paducah Patrol . Warner Brothers WM 4043
Dick Powell appeared in *Gold Diggers of 1933.*

PHANTOM OF THE OPERA, THE   February 1986
Andrew Lloyd Webber / Charles Hart / Richard Stilgoe
Really Usefull Music . . . . UK
Show(s): . . . . The Phantom Of The Opera
Sarah Brightman & Steve Harley . . . . Polydor POSP 800

Sarah Brightman & Steve Harley appeared in *The Phantom Of The Opera.*

PHIL THE FLUTER'S BALL   1912
Percy French
Keith Prowse Music Publishing Co. Ltd . . . . UK
Albert Whelan . . . . Jumbo 509
Kenneth McKellar . . . . Decca LK 4203
Billy Cotton Band . . . . Rex 9383

PHILADELPHIA FREEDOM   April 1975
Elton John / Bernie Taupin
Big Pig Music . . . . UK
The Elton John Band . . . . DJM DJS 354

PHILOMEL   1919
Andre Messager / Adrian Ross
Ascherberg, Hopwood & Crew Ltd. . . . . France
Show(s): . . . . Monsieur Beaucaire
Maggie Teyte . . . . Columbia L 1310
Gwen Catley . . . . Pye CCT 31006
Maggie Teyte appeared in *Monsieur Beaucaire.*

PHOTO OF THE GIRL I LEFT BEHIND, THE   1911
Billy Merson
Francis, Day & Hunter Ltd. . . . . UK
Billy Merson (1911) . . . . Zonophone 621
Billy Merson (1928) . . . . Broadcast 165

PHOTOGRAPH   December 1973
Richard Starkey / George Harrison
Wobble Music . . . . UK
Ringo Starr . . . . Apple R 5992

PHYSICAL   November 1981
Steve Kipner / Terry Shaddick
A.T.V. Music . . . . UK
Olivia Newton-John . . . . EMI 5234

PHYSICIAN, THE   1933
Cole Porter
Chappell & Co. Ltd. . . . . USA
Show(s): . . . . Nymph Errant
Film(s): . . . . Star
Gertrude Lawrence . . . . HMV DLP 1099
Pearl Bailey . . . . Columbia 33S 1126
Julie Andrews, Bruce Forsyth & Beryl Reid . . Stateside SL 10233
Gertrude Lawrence appeared in *Nymph Errant.*
Julie Andrews, Bruce Forsyth & Beryl Reid appeared in *Star.*

PICCOLINO, THE   1935
Irving Berlin
Irving Berlin Ltd . . . . USA
Film(s): . . . . Top Hat
Fred Astaire . . . . Brunswick RL 298
Ginger Rogers . . . . Decca F 5747
Mel Tormé . . . . London LTZN 15076
Fred Astaire & Ginger Rogers appeared in *Top Hat.*

PICCOLO PETE   1929
Phil Baxter
Chappell & Co. Ltd . . . . USA
Film(s): . . . . The Vagabond Lover
Jack Hylton & his Orchestra . . . . HMV B 5742
Ted Weems & his Orchestra, vocal Parker Gibbs . . HMV BD 1172
The Andrews Sisters . . . . Brunswick LA 8599

PICK A BALE OF COTTON   September 1962
Traditional, arranged by Huddie Leadbetter & Alan Lomax
Kensington Music Ltd . . . . USA
Lonnie Donegan . . . . Pye 7N 15455

PICK UP THE PIECES   September 1973
Richard Hudson / John Ford
Arnakata Music . . . . UK
Hudson-Ford . . . . A&M AMS 7078

PICK UP THE PIECES   March 1975
Nalcom Duncan / Robbie McIntosh / Roger Ball / Hamish Stewart /
Alan Gorrie & Onnie McIntyre
A.W.B. Entertainments . . . . UK
The Average White Band . . . . Atlantic K 10489

PICK YOURSELF UP   1936
Jerome Kern / Dorothy Fields
Chappell & Co. Ltd . . . . USA

Film(s): .... Swing Time
Fred Astaire .... **Vocalion 501**
Anita O'Day .... **HMV DLP 1169**
Debbie Reynolds .... **London HAD 2326**
Fred Astaire appeared in *Swing Time*.

PICKIN' A CHICKEN   January 1956
Garfield De Mortimer / Derek Bernfield / Paddy Roberts
Berry Music Ltd. .... South Africa
Eve Boswell .... **Parlophone GEP 8601**

PICTURE NO ARTIST CAN PAINT, A   1903
Fred J. Helf
B. Feldman & Co. Ltd. .... USA
Show(s): .... Hodge Podge and Co.
Mac & Bob .... **Decca F 3785**

PICTURE OF YOU, A   July 1962
Johnny Beveridge / Peter Oakman
Michael Reine Music Co. Ltd .... UK
Joe Brown & The Bruvers .... **Piccadilly 7N 35047**
Paul Evans .... **London RER 1349**

PICTURE THIS   September 1978
Chris Stein / Deborah Harry
EMI Music Ltd .... UK
Blondie .... **Chrysalis CHS 2242**

PICTURES OF LILY   June 1967
Peter Townshend
Fabulous Music Ltd. .... UK
The Who .... **Track 604002**

PICTURES OF MATCHSTICK MEN   March 1968
Francis Rossi
Valley Music .... UK
Status Quo .... **Pye 7N 17449**

PIE JESU   March 1985
Andrew Lloyd Webber
Really Usefull Music .... UK
Sarah Brightman & Paul Miles-Kingston .... **EMI WEBBER 1**

PIED PIPER, THE   May 1966
Artie Kornfeld / Steve Doboff
Robbins Music Corporation Ltd. .... USA
Crispian St. Peters .... **Decca F 12359**
Bob & Marcia (1971) .... **Trojan TR 7818**

PIERETTE & PIERROT   1911
Franz Lehar / Robert Bodansky / A.M. Willner
Chappell & Co Ltd .... Austria
Show(s): .... The Count of Luxembourg
May De Sousa .... **HMV 03248**
May De Sousa appeared in the British production of *The Count of Luxembourg*.

PIG GOT UP AND SLOWLY WALKED AWAY, THE   1935
Benjamin Burt
Dash Music .... USA
Frank Crumit .... **Decca F 5325**
Rudy Vallee .... **Capitol LC 6698**
Clinton Ford .... **Pye NPL 18210**

PIGALLE   February 1949
George Ulmer / George Koger / Jimmy Kennedy
Campbell Connelly & Co. Ltd .... France
George Ulmer .... **Columbia 33S 1099**
Johnny Desmond .... **MGM 318**
Patachou .... **Philips BBL 7423**
The Troubadours .... **London HAR 2249**

PILLOW TALK   August 1973
Michael Burton / Sylvia Robinson
Burlington Music Co. Ltd. .... USA
Sylvia .... **London HL 10415**

PINBALL WIZARD   May 1969
Peter Townshend
Fabulous Music Ltd. .... UK
Film(s): .... Tommy
The Who .... **Track 613014**
The New Seekers (1973) .... **Polydor 2058338**
Elton John (1976) .... **DJM DJS 652**
Elton John appeared in *Tommy*.

PINK CADILLAC   May 1988
Bruce Springsteen
Zomba Music .... USA
Natalie Cole .... **Manhattan MT 35**

PINK CHAMPAGNE   April 1951
Robert Wright / George Forrest
Mills Music Ltd .... USA
Film(s): .... Rainbow 'Round My Shoulder
Henri René & his Orchestra .... **HMV 7EG 8024**
Martinas & his Music .... **Columbia 33SX 1242**

PINK ELEPHANTS   1933
Harry Woods / Mort Dixon
Francis, Day & Hunter Ltd. .... USA
Joe Venuti & Eddie Lang's Blue Five .... **Columbia SEG 7695**
Zaidee Jackson .... **Parlophone R 1481**

PINK LADY (See My Beautiful Lady)

PINK PETTY FROM PETER, A (See Little Pink Petty From Peter, A)

PIPELINE   June 1963
Bob Spickard / Brian Carman
World Wide Music Co. Ltd .... USA
The Chantays .... **London HL 9696**
Al Caiola (guitar) .... **United Artists ULP 1045**

PIPES OF PAN, THE   1909
Lionel Monckton / Arthur Wimperis / Howard Talbot
Chappell & Co. Ltd. .... UK
Show(s): .... The Arcadians
Florence Smithson .... **Columbia 542**
Gwen Catley .... **HMV B 9704**
June Bronhill .... **Columbia TWO 233**
Florence Smithson appeared in *The Arcadians*.

PIPES OF PEACE, THE   January 1984
Paul McCartney
MPL Music publishing .... UK
Paul McCartney .... **Parlophone R 6064**
Ivor Novello Nomination 1983.

PISTOL PACKIN' MAMA   1943
Al Dexter
Edwin H. Morris & Co. Ltd .... USA
Bing Crosby & The Andrews Sisters ..... **Brunswick LAT 8055**
Jim Lowe .... **London HAD 2146**
Gene Vincent (1960) .... **Capitol CL 15136**

PLAY A SIMPLE MELODY   1915
Irving Berlin
Irving Berlin Ltd. .... USA
Show(s): .... Watch Your Step
Film(s): .... There's No Business Like Show Business
Ethel Levey & Blanche Tomlin .... **HMV C 611**
Dinah Shore .... **Columbia DB 2751**
Bing & Gary Crosby (1950) .... **Brunswick LAT 8051**
Ethel Merman & Dan Dailey .... **Brunswick LAT 8059**
Ethel Levey & Blanche Tomlin appeared in the British production of *Watch Your Step*
Ethel Merman & Dan Dailey appeared in *There's No Business Like Show Business*.

PLAY FIDDLE PLAY   1933
Emery Deutsch / Jack Lawrence / Arthur Altman
Campbell Connelly & Co. Ltd. .... USA
The New Mayfair Dance Orchestra,
vocal Al Bowlly .... **HMV B 6318**
The Troubadours .... **London HAR 2106**

PLAY ME LIKE YOU PLAY YOUR GUITAR   April 1975
Keith Potger / Tony Macaulay
Carlin Music Corporation .... UK
Duane Eddy & The Rebelettes .... **GTO GT 11**

PLAY ORCHESTRA PLAY   1936
Noel Coward
Chappell & Co. Ltd .... UK
Show(s): .... Tonight at Eight-Thirty
Noel Coward & Gertrude Lawrence .... **HMV CLP 1050**
Noel Coward .... **Philips BBL 7108**
Noel Coward & Gertrude Lawrence appeared in the British production of *Tonight at Eight-Thirty*.

PLAY THAT BARBERSHOP CHORD　　　　　　**1910**
Lewis Muir / William Tracey / Ballard MacDonald
B. Feldman & Co. . . . . USA
Film(s): . . . . In the Good Old Summertime
Judy Garland . . . . **MGM 243**
Evelyn Knight & Foster Carling . . . . **Brunswick 04381**
Judy Garland appeared in *In the Good Old Summertime*.

PLAY THAT FUNKY MUSIC　　　　**November 1976**
Robert Parissi
Chappell & Co. Ltd . . . . USA
Wild Cherry . . . . **Epic EPC 4593**

PLAY THE GAME　　　　　　　　**July 1980**
Freddie Mercury
EMI Music Ltd . . . . UK
Queen . . . . **EMI 5076**

PLAY TO ME GIPSY　　　　　　　　**1934**
Karel Vacek / Jimmy Kennedy
B. Feldman & Co. Ltd. . . . . UK
Gracie Fields . . . . **HMV B 8130**
Jack Jackson & his Orchestra,
vocal Sam Costa . . . . **HMV B 6448**
Frank Chacksfield & his Orchestra . . . **Ace of Clubs ACL 1060**

PLAYMATES　　　　　　　　　　　**1940**
Saxie Dowell
Campbell Connelly & Co. Ltd . . . . USA
Hal Kemp & his Orchestra . . . . **HMV BD 5594**
The Fontane Sisters . . . . **London HAD 2053**

PLAYTHINGS　　　　　　　　　　　**1921**
Horatio Nicholls / Worton David
Lawrence Wright Music Co. Ltd . . . . UK
Gwyn Ellis . . . . **HMV B 1288**

PLEASE　　　　　　　　　　　　　**1933**
Leo Robin / Ralph Rainger
Victoria Music Co. Ltd. . . . . USA
Film(s): . . . . The Big Broadcast
Bing Crosby . . . . **Philips BBE 12142**
Bing Crosby . . . . **Brunswick LAT 8251**
Noel Harrison . . . . **Philips BBL 7399**
Bing Crosby appeared in *The Big Broadcast*.

PLEASE BE KIND　　　　　　　　　**1938**
Sammy Cahn / Saul Chaplin
Chappell & Co. Ltd. . . . . USA
Maxine Sullivan . . . . **HMV B 8749**
Johnny Mathis . . . . **Fontana TFL 5050**
Sarah Vaughan . . . . **Mercury MMC 14011**

PLEASE BELIEVE ME　　　　　　　**1936**
Al Jacobs / Larry Yoell
Keith Prowse Music Publishing Co. Ltd . . . . USA
Jane Froman . . . . **Brunswick 02174**

PLEASE DO IT AGAIN　　　　　　　**1922**
George Gershwin / Buddy De Sylva
Chappell & Co. Ltd . . . . USA
Show(s): . . . . The French Doll / Mayfair and Montmartre
Film(s): . . . . Rhapsody in Blue / Thoroughly Modern Millie
Alice Delysia . . . . **Columbia DX 523**
Mary Martin . . . . **Brunswick 03253**
Trudi Richards . . . . **Capitol T 838**
Mel Tormé . . . . **Parlophone R 3138**
Judy Garland . . . . **Capitol T 1036**
Carol Channing . . . . **Brunswick LAT 8685**
Alice Delysia appeared in *Mayfair and Montmartre*.
Carol Channing appeared in *Thoroughly Modern Millie*.

PLEASE DON'T FALL IN LOVE　　**December 1983**
Mike Batt
CBS Songs . . . . UK
Cliff Richard . . . . **EMI 5437**

PLEASE DON'T GO　　　　　　　**March 1969**
Les Reed / Jackie Rae
Donna Music Ltd. . . . . UK
Donald Peers . . . . **Columbia DB 8502**
Adapted from the 'Barcarolle' from 'The Tales of Hoffmann' by Jac-
ques Offenbach (1819 - 1880).

PLEASE DON'T GO　　　　　　　**February 1980**
Richard Finch
April Music Ltd . . . . UK
K.C. & The Sunshine Band . . . . **T.K. TKR 7558**

PLEASE DON'T MAKE ME CRY　　**November 1983**
Winston Tucker
Intersong Music . . . . UK
UB40 . . . . **Virgin DEP 8**

PLEASE DON'T TALK ABOUT ME WHEN I'M GONE　**1931**
Sammy Stept / Sidney Clare
Francis, Day & Hunter Ltd. . . . . USA
Film(s): . . . . Lullaby of Broadway
Gene Austin . . . . **HMV B 3936**
The Mills Brothers . . . . **Brunswick 04685**
Doris Day . . . . **Columbia 33S 1038**
Maurice Chevalier . . . . **MGM C 826**
Doris Day appeared in *Lullaby of Broadway*.

PLEASE DON'T TEASE　　　　　**August 1960**
Bruce Welch / Peter Chester
Belinda (London) Ltd . . . . UK
Cliff Richard . . . . **Columbia SEG 8050**

PLEASE HELP ME I'M FALLING　　**October 1960**
Don Robertson / Hal Blair
Aberbach (London) Ltd. . . . . USA
Hank Locklin . . . . **RCA RD 27201**

PLEASE MISTER SUN　　　　　**February 1952**
Ray Getzov / Sid Frank
Chappell & Co. Ltd . . . . USA
Johnnie Ray . . . . **Columbia DB 3006**
Perry Como . . . . **HMV B 10232**
Tommy Edwards . . . . **MGM C 774**

PLEASE MR. HEMINGWAY (See Pu-leeze Mr. Hemingway)

PLEASE MR. POSTMAN　　　　　**March 1975**
Brian Holland / Freddy Gorman
Dominion Music Co. Ltd . . . . USA
The Carpenters . . . . **A&M AMS 7141**
The Beatles . . . . **Parlophone PCS 3045**

PLEASE PLEASE ME　　　　　　**March 1963**
John Lennon / Paul McCartney
Dick James Music Ltd . . . . UK
The Beatles . . . . **Parlophone R 4983**
Keely Smith . . . . **Reprise R 6142**
David Cassidy (1974) . . . . **Bell 1371**

PLEASE TELL HIM THAT I SAID HELLO　**March 1975**
Mike Sheptone / Peter Dibbens
Chrysalis Music Ltd . . . . UK
Dana . . . . **GTO GT 6**
Sheptone & Dibbens . . . . **Polydor 2001528**

PLENTY GOOD LOVIN'　　　　**September 1959**
Connie Francis
Francon Music Ltd . . . . USA
Connie Francis . . . . **MGM C 831**

PLINK, PLANK, PLUNK　　　　**December 1952**
Leroy Anderson
Mills Music Ltd . . . . USA
Leroy Anderson & his Orchestra . . . . **Brunswick LAT 8337**
The Boston Promenade Orchestra . . . . **HMV DLP 1142**
The Spectacular Harmonicas . . . . **MGM C 851**

POETRY IN MOTION　　　　　**December 1960**
Paul Kaufman / Mike Anthony
Edwin H. Morris & Co. Ltd . . . . USA
Johnny Tillotson . . . . **London HAA 2388**
Bobby Vee . . . . **London HAZ 2352**

POINCIANA　　　　　　　　　　　**1944**
Nat Simon / Buddy Bernier
Francis, Day & Hunter Ltd. . . . . Cuba
Bing Crosby . . . . **Brunswick 03510**
David Rose & his Orchestra . . . . **HMV B 9379**
Ethel Smith (organ) . . . . **Brunswick LAT 8134**

POINT OF NO RETURN, THE　　　**January 1960**
John Harris / Derek New

Essex Music Ltd .... UK
Diana Dors .... **Pye NPL 18044**
Chris Martin .... **HMV POP 692**

POISON   **August 1989**
Alice Cooper / Desmond Child / John McCurry
EMI Music .... USA
Alice Cooper .... **Epic 6550617**

POISON ARROW   **March 1982**
"A.B.C."
Virgin Music .... UK
A.B.C. .... **Phonogram NT 102**

POISON IVY   **October 1959**
Jerry Lieber / Mike Stoller
Carlin Music Corporation .... USA
The Coasters .... **London HLE 8938**
The Lambrettas (1980) .... **Rocket 25**

POLICEMAN'S HOLIDAY, THE   **1911**
Montague Ewing / Earl Berwick
Silvester Music Co. Ltd .... UK
The Crazy Star Band .... **Regal Zonophone MR 660**
The New Light Symphony Orchestra .... **HMV B 8005**
The Keynotes .... **Decca F 9389**
Lyric added in 1932.

POLKA DOTS AND MOONBEAMS   **1941**
Johnny Burke / Jimmy Van Heusen
Chappell & Co. Ltd .... USA
Glenn Miller & his Orchestra, vocal Ray Erble .... **HMV DLP 1145**
Tommy Dorsey & his Orchestra,
vocal Frank Sinatra .... **RCA RD 27069**
Nelson Riddle & his Orchestra .... **Capitol T 915**

POLLY PERKINS OF PADDINGTON GREEN   **1912**
Harry Clifton
Hopwood & Crew Ltd .... UK
The Victorian Quartet .... **Regal Zonophone MR 967**
Archie Harradine .... **Columbia DB 2917**
Jack Train & The Michael
Sammes Orchestra & Chorus .... **Columbia SEG 8014**
Originally published circa 1864.

POMPTON TURNPIKE   **1946**
Will Osborne / Dick Rogers
Campbell Connelly & Co. Ltd. .... USA
Charlie Barnet & his Orchestra .... **RCA RCX 1008**
The Tommy Dorsey Orchestra,
conducted by Warren Covington .... **Brunswick LAT 8311**

POOL HALL RICHARD   **January 1974**
Rod Stewart / Ron Wood
Warner Brothers Music Ltd. .... UK
Faces .... **Warner Brothers K 16341**

POOR BUTTERFLY   **1916**
John Golden / Raymond Hubbell
Francis, Day & Hunter Ltd. .... USA
Show(s): .... The Big Show
Film(s): .... Thoroughly Modern Millie
G.H. Elliott .... **Columbia 2789**
Helen Traubel .... **London HAD 2117**
Sarah Vaughan .... **Mercury MMC 14026**
Julie Andrews .... **Brunswick LAT 8685**
Julie Andrews appeared in *Thoroughly Modern Millie.*

POOR JENNY   **June 1959**
Felice Bryant / Boudleaux Bryant
Acuff-Rose Publishing Co. Ltd .... USA
The Everly Brothers .... **London HAA 2266**

POOR JOHN   **1906**
Fred W. Leigh / Henry Pether
Francis, Day & Hunter Ltd. .... UK
Film(s): .... Cover Girl
Florrie Forde .... **Regal X 43143**
Vesta Victoria .... **Regal Zonophone MR 414**

POOR LITTLE ANGELINE   **1936**
Will Grosz / Jimmy Kennedy
Peter Maurice Music Co. Ltd .... UK
Roy Fox & his Orchestra, vocal Sid Buckman .. **HMV BD 5075**
The New Mayfair Orchestra .... **HMV C 3033**

Victor Sylvester & his Orchestra .... Columbia 33SX 1126

POOR LITTLE FOOL   **October 1958**
Sharron Sheeley
Commodore-Imperial Music .... USA
Ricky Nelson .... **London HLP 8670**

POOR LITTLE RICH GIRL   **1925**
Noel Coward / Philip Braham
Ascherberg, Hopwood & Crew Ltd. .... UK
Show(s): .... On With the Dance / Charlot's Revue of 1926
Alice Delysia .... **HMV B 2070**
Noel Coward .... **HMV 7EG 8300**
Chris Connor .... **London LTZK 15195**
Alice Delysia appeared in *On with the Dance.*

POOR MAN'S SON   **June 1965**
Joannie Bratton / Bob Hamilton / Ronnie Savoy & Steve Venet
Essex Music Ltd .... USA
The Rocking Berries .... **Piccadilly 7N 35236**

POOR ME   **March 1960**
Les Vandyke
Mills Music Ltd .... USA
Adam Faith .... **Parlophone 8811**

POOR PAPA (He's Got Nothing At All)   **1926**
Harry Woods / Billy Rose
Francis, Day & Hunter Ltd. .... USA
Jack Smith .... **HMV B 2310**
Kay Starr .... **Capitol CL 13309**

POOR PEOPLE OF PARIS, THE   **March 1956**
Marguerite Monnot / Rene Rouzaud / Jack Lawrence
Berry Music Ltd. .... France
Edith Piaf .... **Columbia 33S 1099**
Eddie Barclay & his Orchestra .... **Felsted SD 80022**
Winifred Atwell (piano) .... **Decca LF 1266**
Les Baxter & his Orchestra .... **Capitol T 780**
Maurice Chevalier .... **Philips BBL 7182**

POP GOES THE WEASEL   **June 1961**
Traditional, new lyric by George Hackney
Essex Music Ltd .... UK
Anthony Newley .... **Decca F 11362**

POP MUZIK   **May 1979**
Robin Scott
Pop Muzik Ltd. .... UK
M .... **MCA 413**

POPCORN   **September 1972**
Gershon Kingsley
Bourne Music Ltd. .... USA
Hot Butter .... **Pye 7N 25583**

POPPA JOE   **March 1972**
Mike Chapman / Nicky Chinn
Rak Music Ltd .... UK
The Sweet .... **RCA 2164**

POPPA PICCOLONO (Papaveri E Papere)   **August 1953**
Vittorio Masheroni / Nino Rastelli / Mario Panzeri / Bob Musel
Chappell & Co. Ltd .... Italy
Diana Decker .... **Columbia DB 3325**
Billy Cotton & his Band .... **Decca F 10179**
David Whitfield .... **Decca LK 4270**
The Beverly Sisters .... **Philips PB 166**
Allan Jones .... **HMV B 10588**

PORTRAIT OF A FLIRT   **March 1948**
Robert Farnon
Chappell & Co. Ltd. .... UK
The Queens Hall Light Orchestra,
conducted by Sidney Torch .... **Columbia DB 2436**
The Kingsway Symphony Orchestra,
conducted by Robert Farnon .... **Decca F 9038**
David Rose & his Orchestra .... **MGM 323**

PORTRAIT OF MY LOVE, A   **February 1961**
Norman Newell / Cyril Ornadel
Edward Kassner Music Co. Ltd .... UK
Matt Monro .... **Parlophone R 4714**
Cyril Ornadel & The Starlight Symphony Orchestra .. **MGM 1090**
Perry Como .... **RCA RD 27232**

Ivor Novello Award 1960.
Ivor Novello Nomination 1961.

PORTSMOUTH January 1977
Traditional
Virgin Music (Publishers) Ltd . . . . UK
Mike Oldfield . . . . **Virgin VS 163**

PORTUGUESE WASHERWOMEN, THE (Les Lavandieres
Du Portugal) September 1955
Andre Popp / Roger Lucchesi
Blossom Music Ltd. . . . . France
Luis Mariano . . . . **HMV CLP 1222**
August Alguero Jr. & his Orchestra . . . . **RCA RD 27164**
Joe 'Fingers' Carr (1956) . . . . **Capitol CL 14587**

POSITIVELY FOURTH STREET November 1965
Bob Dylan
Blossom Music Ltd . . . . USA
Bob Dylan . . . . **CBS 201824**

POWDER YOUR FACE WITH SUNSHINE January 1949
Stanley Rochinski / Carmen Lombardo
Chappell & Co. Ltd . . . . USA
Film(s): . . . . Cow Town
Evelyn Knight . . . . **Brunswick 04033**
Donald Peers . . . . **HMV B 9764**
Dean Martin . . . . **Capitol CL 13058**
Craig Douglas . . . . **Top Rank 35-103**

POWER OF LOVE, THE December 1984
Holly Johnson / Mark O'Toole / Peter Gill & Brian Nash
Perfect Songs . . . . UK
Frankie Goes to Hollywood . . . . **Island ZTAS 5**

POWER OF LOVE, THE September 1985
Huey Lewis / John Hayes / John Colla
Chrysalis Music . . . . USA
Film(s): . . . . Back to the Future
Huey Lewis & The News . . . . **Chrysalis HUEY 1**
Nominated for an Acadmey Award 1985.

POWER OF LOVE, THE October 1985
Candy De Rouge / Gunter Mende / Jennifer Rush & Susan Applegate
CBS Songs . . . . Germany
Jennifer Rush . . . . **CBS A 5003**

POWER TO ALL OUR FRIENDS April 1973
Guy Fletcher / Doug Flett
Chrysalis Music Ltd. . . . . UK
Cliff Richard . . . . **EMI 2012**
United Kingdom entry for the 1973 Eurovision Song Contest (Placed Third).
Ivor Novello Award.

POWER TO THE PEOPLE April 1971
John Lennon
Northern Songs Ltd . . . . UK
John Lennon & The Plastic Ono Band . . . . **Apple R 5892**

POWER, THE April 1990
Benito Benites / John Garrett
Warner Chappell Music . . . . Germany
Snap . . . . **Arista 113133**

PRAISE THE LORD AND PASS THE AMMUNITION 1943
Frank Loesser
Chappell & Co. Ltd . . . . USA
The Merry Macs . . . . **Decca F 8249**
Joe Loss & his Orchestra . . . . **HMV BD 5786**

PRAYING FOR TIME September 1990
George Michael
Morrison Leahy Music . . . . UK
George Michael . . . . **Epic GEO 1**

PREACHER AND THE BEAR 1907
Joseph Arzonia
Francis, Day & Hunter . . . . USA
Albert Whelan . . . . **Jumbo 572**
Phil Harris (1947) . . . . **Camden CDN 124**

PRECIOUS LITTLE THING CALLED LOVE, A 1929
J. Fred Coots / Lou Davis
Francis, Day & Hunter Ltd . . . . USA
Film(s): . . . . Shopworn Angel

The Ipana Troubadours . . . . **Columbia 5391**
The Frank Petty Trio . . . . **MGM 312**

PRETEND September 1953
Lew Douglas / Cliff Parman / Frank Levere
Leeds Music Ltd. . . . . USA
Nat 'King' Cole . . . . **Capitol T 952**
Vera Lynn . . . . **Decca F 10164**
Johnny Preston . . . . **Mercury MMC 14051**
Alvin Stardust (1981) . . . . **Stiff BUY 124**

PRETENDING February 1947
Marty Symes / Al Sherman
Bradbury Wood Music . . . . USA
Lou Preager Orchestra . . . . **Columbia FB 3250**
Geraldo & his Orchestra . . . . **Parlophone F 2179**
Bing Crosby . . . . **Brunswick 03800**

PRETTY BABY 1916
Egbert Van Alstyne / Gus Kahn / Tony Jackson
Francis, Day & Hunter Ltd. . . . . USA
Show(s): . . . . The Passing Show of 1916 / Houp-La
Film(s): Rose of Washington Square / Is Everybody Happy / Broadway Rhythm
/ Jolson Sings Again / I'll See You in my Dreams / The Eddie Cantor Story
Gertie Millar . . . . **HMV 03541**
Al Jolson . . . . **Brunswick LA 8541**
Doris Day . . . . **Philips BBE 12167**
Eddie Cantor . . . . **Capitol LC 6652**
Gertie Millar appeared in *Houp-La.*
Al Jolson appeared in *Rose of Washington Square.*
Doris Day appeared in *I'll See You in my Dreams.*

PRETTY BLUE EYES March 1960
Teddy Randazzo / Bob Weistein
Maxana Music Ltd . . . . USA
Craig Douglas . . . . **Top Rank JAR 268**
Steve Lawrence . . . . **HMV POP 689**

PRETTY EYED BABY June 1951
Mary Lou Williams / William Johnson / Leo Mosley
Pickwick Music Ltd . . . . USA
Jo Stafford & Frankie Laine . . . . **Columbia DB 2883**
Margaret Whiting . . . . **London HAD 2321**

PRETTY FLAMINGO June 1966
Mark Barkan
Shapiro-Bernstein & Co. Ltd. . . . . USA
Manfred Mann . . . . **HMV POP 1523**

PRETTY GIRL IS LIKE A MELODY, A 1919
Irving Berlin
Irving Berlin Ltd. . . . . USA
Show(s): . . . . The Ziegfeld Follies of 1919
Film(s): The Great Ziegfeld / Alexander's Ragtime Band / Blue Skies
/ There's No Business Like Show Business
Red Nichols & his Five Pennies . . . . **Brunswick 01854**
Tony Martin . . . . **Decca F 8901**
Pat Boone . . . . **London HAD 2082**

PRETTY KITTY BLUE EYES 1945
Mann Curtis / Vic Mizzy
Campbell Connelly & Co. Ltd. . . . . USA
Film(s): . . . . Kansas City Kitty
The Merry Macs . . . . **Brunswick 03553**

PRETTY LITTLE ANGEL EYES December 1978
Tommy Boyce / Curtis Lee
Belinda (London) Ltd . . . . USA
Showaddywaddy . . . . **Arista ARIST 222**
Curtis Lee . . . . **London HLX 9397**

PRETTY LITTLE BLACK EYED SUSIE April 1953
Kay Twomey / Fred Wise / Ben Weisman
Campbell Connelly & Co. Ltd . . . . USA
Guy Mitchell . . . . **Philips BBL 7265**

PRETTY PAPER December 1964
Willie Nelson
Acuff-Rose Publishing Co. Ltd . . . . USA
Roy Orbison . . . . **London HL 9930**

PRETTY VACANT August 1977
Steve Jones / Glen Matlock / Paul Cook / Johnny Rotten
Warner Brothers Music Ltd . . . . UK
The Sex Pistols . . . . **Virgin VS 184**

PRICE OF LOVE, THE June 1965
Phil Everly / Don Everly
Acuff-Rose Publishing Co. Ltd .... USA
The Everly Brothers .... **Warner Brothers WB 161**

PRIDE (In The Name Of Love) September 1984
Larry Mullen / David Evans / Adam Clayton & Paul Hewson
Blue Mountain Music .... UK
U2 .... **Island S 202**

PRIMROSE 1939
Ivor Novello / Christopher Hassall
Chappell & Co. Ltd. .... UK
Show(s): ....The Dancing Years
Roma Beaumont .... **HMV DLP 1028**
Roma Beaumont appeared in *The Dancing Years*.

PRIMROSE HILL 1946
Charlie Chester / Ken Morris / Everett Lynton
Lawrence Wright Music Co. Ltd. .... UK
The Skyrockets Dance Orchestra, conducted
by Paul Fenoulhet, vocal Doreen Lundy .... **HMV BD 5938**

PRINCE CHARMING October 1981
Adam Ant / Marco Pirroni
EMI Music .... UK
Adam & The Ants .... **CBS A 1408**

PRINCESS IN RAGS December 1965
Helen Miller / Roger Atkins
Screen Gems - Columbia Music .... USA
Gene Pitney .... **Stateside SS 471**

PRISONER OF LOVE 1931
Leo Robin / Con Conrad / Clarence Gaskill / Russ Columbo
Edwin H. Morris & Co. Ltd. .... USA
Russ Columbo .... **HMV 7EG 8139**
The Ink Spots .... Brunswick 03736
Perry Como (1947) .... **RCA RD 27100**
Bing Crosby .... **Brunswick LAT 8138**

PRISONER'S SONG, THE 1925
Guy Massey
Lawrence Wright Music Co. Ltd. .... USA
The Singing Mountaineers .... **Regal Zonophone MR 1078**
Bunny Berigan & his Orchestra (1937) .... **RCA RCX 1005**
Mitch Miller & The Gang .... **Philips BBL 7494**

PRIVATE INVESTIGATIONS September 1982
Mark Knopfler
Rondor Music .... UK
Dire Straits .... **Phonogram DSTR 1**
Ivor Novello Award.

PRIVATE NUMBER January 1969
Booker T. Jones / William Bell
Fous-Chappell .... USA
Judy Clay & William Bell .... **Stax 101**

PRIZE OF GOLD April 1955
Ned Washington / Lester Lee
Victoria Music Co. Ltd. .... USA
Film(s): ....Prize of Gold
Joan Regan .... **Decca DFE 6278**

PROBLEMS February 1959
Felice Bryant / Boudleaux Bryant
Acuff-Rose Publishing Co. Ltd .... USA
The Everly Brothers .... **London HAA 2266**

PROMISED LAND, THE February 1975
Chuck Berry
Jewel Music Publishing Co. Ltd .... USA
Elvis Presley .... **RCA PB 10074**
Chuck Berry .... **Pye 7N 25285**

PROMISED YOU A MIRACLE May 1982
"Simple Minds"
EMI Music .... UK
Simple Minds .... **Virgin VS 488**

PROMISES August 1966
Tom Springfield / Norman Newell
Springfield Music Ltd. .... UK
Ken Dodd .... **Columbia DB 7914**

PROUD MARY July 1969
John Fogerty
Burlington Music Co. Ltd. .... USA
Film(s): .... Dog Soldiers
Creedence Clearwater Revival .... **Liberty LBF 15223**
Checkmates Ltd. .... **A&M AMS 769**

PROUD ONE, THE June 1975
Bob Crewe / Bob Gaudio
Ardmore & Beechwood Ltd .... USA
The Osmonds .... **MGM 2006520**

PROVE YOUR LOVE April 1988
Arnie Roman / Seth Swirsky
Jobete Music .... USA
Taylor Dayne .... **Arista 109830**

PU-LEEZE MR. HEMINGWAY 1933
Milton Drake / Walter Kent / Abner Silver
Peter Maurice Music Co. Ltd. .... USA
Gracie Fields .... **HMV B 4366**

PUB WITH NO BEER, THE March 1959
Gordon Parsons
Good Music Ltd .... Australia
Slim Dusty .... **Columbia DB 4212**

PUBLIC IMAGE November 1978
James Walke / John Lydon / Jah Wobble & Keith Levine
Virgin Music (Publishers) Ltd .... UK
Public Image Ltd .... **Virgin VS 228**

PUFF THE MAGIC DRAGON May 1963
Peter Yerrow / Leonard Lipton
Blossom Music Ltd .... USA
Peter, Paul & Mary .... **Warner Brothers WB 95**
Nina & Frederik .... **Columbia DB 7172**

PULL UP TO THE BUMPER February 1986
Grace Jones / Dana Mano / Nookoo Baya
Island Music .... UK
Grace Jones .... **Island S 240**

PUMP UP THE JAM October 1989
Manuel Kamosi / Thomas De Quincey
Brothers Organisation .... Belgium
Technotronic .... **Swanyard SYR 4**

PUMP UP THE VOLUME October 1987
Steve Young / Andrew Biggs
Blue Mountain Music .... UK
M.A.R.R.S. .... **4 A.D. AD 70**

PUPPET ON A STRING July 1967
Phil Coulter / Bill Martin
Peter Maurice Music Co. Ltd. .... UK
Sandie Shaw .... **Pye 7N 17272**
United Kingdom entry for the 1967 Eurovision Song Contest (Placed First).
Ivor Novello Award.

PUPPY LOVE April 1960
Paul Anka
MAM .... USA
Paul Anka .... **Columbia DB 4434**
Donny Osmond (1972) .... **MGM 2006104**

PURELY BY COINCIDENCE February 1975
Des Parton
Mr & Mrs Music .... UK
Sweet Sensation .... **Pye 7N 45421**

PURPLE HAZE May 1967
Jimi Hendrix
Sea-Lark Music Ltd. .... USA
Jimi Hendrix Experience .... **Track 604001**

PURPLE PEOPLE EATER, THE June 1958
Sheb Wooley
Peter Maurice Music Co. Ltd .... USA
Sheb Wooley .... **MGM 981**
Judy Garland .... **Capitol T 1118**

PURPLE RAIN October 1984
"Prince"

Island Music .... USA
Film(s): .... Purple Rain
Prince & The Revolution .... **Warner Brothers W 9174**
Prince & The Revolution appeared in *Purple Rain*

PUSH IT   **July 1988**
Herb Azor
Intersong Music .... USA
Salt 'n' Pepa .... **Champion CHAMP 51**

PUSHBIKE SONG, THE   **April 1971**
Idriss Jones / Evan Jones
Carlin Music Corporation .... USA
The Mixtures .... **Polydor 2058083**

PUSS 'N' BOOTS   **November 1983**
Adam Ant / Marco Pirroni
EMI Music .... UK
Adam & The Ants .... **CBS A 3614**

PUT 'EM IN A BOX   **February 1949**
Jule Styne / Sammy Cahn
Campbell Connelly & Co. Ltd .... USA
Film(s): .... It's Magic
Doris Day .... **Columbia DB 2493**
Danny Kaye & The Andrews Sisters .... **Brunswick 04032**
Doris Day appeared in *It's Magic.*

PUT A LIGHT IN THE WINDOW   **March 1958**
Rhoda Roberts / Kenny Jacobson
Dominion Music .... USA
The Four Lads .... **Philips PB 776**
Gary Miller .... **Nixa N 15120**
The King Brothers .... **Parlophone R 4389**

PUT IT THERE PAL   **1946**
Johnny Burke / Jimmy Van Heusen
Edwin H. Morris & Co. Ltd. .... USA
Film(s): .... Road to Utopia
Bing Crosby & Bob Hope .... **Brunswick Bing 9**
Bing Crosby & Bob Hope appeared in *Road to Utopia.*

PUT ME AMONG THE GIRLS   **1907**
C.W. Murphy / Dan Lipton
B. Feldman & Co. Ltd. .... UK
Maurice Harvey .... **Odeon 0613**
"Charlie" .... **Piccadilly NPL 38002**

PUT ON A HAPPY FACE   **September 1961**
Charles Strouse / Lee Adams
Edwin H. Morris & Co. Ltd. .... USA
Show(s): .... Bye Bye Birdie
Film(s): .... Bye Bye Birdie
Dick Van Dyke .... **Fontana CFL 1073**
Peter Marshall .... **Philips ABL 3383**
Dick Van Dyke & Janet Leigh .... **RCA RD 7580**
Dick Van Dyke appeared in the American production and the film of
Bye Bye Birdie.
Peter Marshall appeared in the British production of *Bye Bye Birdie.*
Janet Leigh appeared in the film of *Bye Bye Birdie.*

PUT ON AN OLD PAIR OF SHOES   **1935**
Dedette Lee Hill / Billy Hill
Lawrence Wright Music Co. Ltd .... USA
Jack Hylton & his Orchestra .... **HMV BD 142**
The Browns .... **RCA RD 27153**

PUT ON YOUR OLD GRAY BONNET   **1909**
Stanley Murphy / Percy Wenrich
B. Feldman & Co. Ltd. .... USA
Ozzie Nelson & his Orchestra .... **Decca F 3822**
Jimmy Lunceford & his Orchestra .... **Brunswick 02476**
Jimmy Durante & Helen Traubel .... **Brunswick LAT 8218**
Pee Wee Hunt & his Orchestra .... **Capitol T 1523**

PUT ON YOUR TAT-TA LITTLE GIRLIE   **1910**
Fred W. Leigh
Francis, Day & Hunter Ltd. .... UK
Clarice Mayne .... **HMV C 2331**
The George Mitchell Minstrels .... **HMV CLP 1460**

PUT THE BLAME ON MAME   **1946**
Allan Roberts / Doris Fisher
Chappell & Co. Ltd. .... USA
Film(s): .... Betty Co-ed / Gilda

Nat Gonella & his Georgians, vocal Nat Gonella ... **Decca F 8663**
Jim Lowe .... **London HAD 2146**

PUT YOUR ARMS AROUND ME HONEY   **1910**
Albert Von Tilzer / Junie McCree
Francis, Day & Hunter Ltd. .... USA
Film(s):Coney Island / Louisiana Hayride / In the Good Old Summertime
Beth Tate .... **Columbia 1917**
Jean Goldkette & his Orchestra,
vocal Debbie & the Diplomats .... **Camden CDN 154**
Dick Haymes .... **Brunswick 03497**
Judy Garland .... **MGM C 886**
Judy Garland appeared in *In the Good Old Summertime.*

PUT YOUR HANDS TOGETHER   **January 1990**
*Dany Poku / Kenneth Gamble / Leon Huff / Charles Scarlet /
George Stennet*
Warner Chappell Music .... USA
D Mob .... **London F 124**

PUT YOUR HEAD ON MY SHOULDER   **November 1959**
Paul Anka
Spanka Music Ltd .... USA
Paul Anka .... **Columbia 33SX 1282**

PUT YOUR LOVE IN ME   **December 1977**
Errol Brown
Rak Music Ltd .... UK
Hot Chocolate .... **Rak 266**

PUT YOUR SHOES ON LUCY   **May 1949**
Hank Fort
Bourne Music Ltd .... USA
Anne Shelton .... **Decca F 9102**
Russ Morgan & his Orchestra .... **Brunswick 04086**

PUTTIN' ON THE RITZ   **1930**
Irving Berlin
Francis, Day & Hunter Ltd .... USA
Film(s): .... Puttin' on the Ritz / Blue Skies / Idiot's Delight
Fred Astaire .... **Columbia DB 96**
Leo Reisman & his Orchestra .... **HMV B 5810**
Fred Astaire .... **Brunswick LA 8602**
Judy Garland .... **Capitol W 1569**
Fred Astaire appeared in *Blue Skies.*

PUTTIN' ON THE STYLE   **June 1957**
Traditional, New arrangement & lyric by Norman Cazden
An edition by Essex Music Ltd. .... UK
Lonnie Donegan .... **Nixa N 15093**
The Vipers Skiffle Group .... **Parlophone R 4356**
Dickie Valentine .... **Decca F 10906**

PYJAMARAMA   **April 1973**
Bryan Ferry
E.G. Music .... UK
Roxy Music .... **Island WIP 6159**

QUANDO, QUANDO, QUANDO   **July 1962**
Arturo Testa / Tony Renis / Pat Boone
Blossom Music Ltd .... Italy
Pat Boone .... **London HLD 9543**
The Marino Marini Quartet .... **Durium U 20078**
Tony Renis .... **HMV POP 1036**
Joe Loss & his Orchestra .... **HMV POP 1059**

QUARTER TO THREE   **August 1961**
Gene Barge / Frank Guida / Gary Anderson & Joe Royster
Ardmore & Beechwood Ltd. .... USA
Gary (U.S.) Bonds .... **Top Rank JAR 575**
Don Lang .... **Ace of Clubs ACL 1111**

QUE SERA MI VIDA (If You Should Go)   **December 1979**
Daniel Vangarde / Jean Kluger / Nelly Byl
Blue Mountain Music .... France
The Gibson Brothers .... **Island WIP 6525**

QUE SERA, SERA   **June 1956**
Jay Livingston / Ray Evans
Melcher Music Ltd. .... USA
Film(s): .... The Man Who Knew too Much
Doris Day .... **Philips BBL 7297**
The Four Aces .... **Brunswick LAT 8249**
Doris Day appeared in *The Man Who Knew Too Much.*
Academy Award winning song for 1956.

QUEEN OF CLUBS, THE　　　September 1974
H.W. Casey / Willie Clark
Southern Music Publishing Co. Ltd. . . . . USA
K.C. & The Sunshine Band . . . . **Jayboy BOY 88**

QUEEN OF HEARTS　　　October 1979
Hank Devito
Heath Levy Music Ltd. . . . . USA
Dave Edmunds . . . . **Swansong SSK 19419**

QUEEN WAS IN THE PARLOUR, THE　　　1931
Sherman Myers
Cecil Lennox Music Co. Ltd. . . . . UK
Ambrose & his Orchestra, vocal Sam Browne . . . **HMV B 6075**

QUESTION　　　June 1970
Justin Hayward
Tyler Music Ltd. . . . . UK
The Moody Blues . . . . **Threshold TH 4**

QUESTION AND ANSWER (Demande et Response)　　1943
Samuel Coleridge-Taylor / Stanley Arthur
Boosey & Hawkes Publishing Ltd . . . . UK
Anne Shelton . . . . **Decca F 8279**
Oscar Rabin Orchestra . . . . **Decca F 8248**
Adapted from "Petite Suite de Concert" Opus 77 by Samuel Coleridge-Taylor.

QUICKSILVER　　　March 1950
Irving Taylor / George Wyle / Eddie Pola
Edwin H. Morris & Co. Ltd . . . . USA
Doris Day . . . . **Columbia DB 2656**
Bing Crosby . . . . **Brunswick 04454**

QUIET NIGHTS OF QUIET STARS (Corcovado)　July 1964
Gene Lees / Antonio Carlos Jobim
Leeds Music Ltd . . . . Brazil
Tony Bennett . . . . **CBS BPG 62149**
Astrud Gilberto . . . . **Verve V 8545**
Nancy Wilson . . . . **Capitol T 2155**
Perry Como . . . . **RCA RD 7802**
Frank Sinatra . . . . **Reprise RLP 1021**
The Four Tops . . . . **Tamla Motown TML 11037**

RABBIT　　　January 1981
Charles Hodges / David Peacock
Chasdave Music . . . . UK
Chas & Dave . . . . **Rockney 9**

RACE WITH THE DEVIL　　　December 1960
Adrian Gurvitz
Pop Gun Music . . . . UK
Gun . . . . **CBS 3764**

RACE, THE　　　September 1988
Boris Blank / Dieter Meier
Warner Chappell Music . . . . Germany
Yello . . . . **Mercury YELLO 1**

RACHEL　　　August 1953
Tom Lavello / Harry Pressman
Southern Music Co. . . . . USA
Al Martino . . . . **Capitol CL 13878**

RADANCER　　　May 1972
Hugh Nicholson
Catrine Music . . . . UK
Marmalade . . . . **Decca F 13297**

RADAR LOVE　　　February 1974
George Kooymans / Barry Hay
Louvigny-Marquee Music Co. Holland
Golden Earring . . . . **Track 2094116**

RADIO GA GA　　　February 1984
Roger Taylor
EMI Music . . . . UK
Queen . . . . **EMI QUEEN 1**

RAG DOLL　　　October 1964
Bob Crewe / Bob Gaudio
Ardmore & Beechwood Ltd . . . . USA
The Four Seasons . . . . **Philips BF 13447**
The Fenmen . . . . **Decca F 11955**

RAG MAMA RAG　　　May 1970
J.R. Robertson
B. Feldman & Co. Ltd. . . . . UK
The Band . . . . **Capitol CL 15629**

RAG MOP　　　March 1950
Johnny Lee Wills / Deacon Anderson
Victoria Music Co. Ltd . . . . USA
Film(s): . . . . Honeychile
Lionel Hampton & his Orchestra . . . . **Brunswick 04457**
The Ames Brothers . . . . **Vogue LVA 9126**

RAGAMUFFIN MAN　　　June 1969
Mitch Murray / Peter Callander
Intune Ltd. . . . . UK
Manfred Mann . . . . **Fontana TF 1013**

RAGE HARD　　　September 1986
Peter Gill / Holly Johnson / Brian Nash & Mark O'Toole
Perfect Songs . . . . UK
Frankie Goes To Hollywood . . . . **ZTT ZTAS 22**

RAGS TO RICHES　　　December 1953
Richard Adler / Jerry Ross
Chappell & Co. Ltd. . . . . USA
Tony Bennett . . . . **Philips PB 216**
David Whitfield . . . . **Decca LF 1165**
Elvis Presley (1971) . . . . **RCA 2084**

RAGS, BOTTLES OR BONES　　　1938
Stanley Holloway / Harry S. Pepper
Dix Ltd. . . . . UK
Syd Walker . . . . **HMV BD 637**
Brian Lawrence . . . . **Decca F 6087**
Theme song of Syd Walker.

RAGTIME COWBOY JOE　　　1912
Grant Clarke / Lewis Muir / Maurice Abrahams
Francis, Day & Hunter Ltd. . . . . USA
Film(s): . . . . Hello 'Frisco Hello / Incendiary Blonde
The Two Bobs (1913) . . . . **Columbia 2087**
Geraldo & his Orchestra,
vocal Dorothy Carless (1943) . . . . **Parlophone F 1998**
Jo Stafford . . . . **Capitol EAP 1-20154**
David Seville Orchestra and
the Chipmunks (1959) . . . . **London HAU 2205**

RAIN　　　1928
Eugene Ford
Francis, Day & Hunter Ltd. . . . . USA
Don Voorhees & his Orchestra . . . . **Columbia 4684**
Bing Crosby . . . . **Brunswick 05790**
The Sauter-Finegan Orchestra . . . . **HMV CLP 1469**
The King Sisters . . . . **Capitol T 1333**

RAIN　　　July 1966
John Lennon / Paul McCartney
Northern Songs Ltd. . . . . UK
The Beatles . . . . **Parlophone R 5452**

RAIN　　　May 1971
Jose Feliciano
Ivan Mogul Music Associates . . . . USA
Bruce Ruffin . . . . **Trojan TBLS 172**
Jose Feliciano . . . . **RCA SF 8188**

RAIN　　　March 1976
Rick Parfitt
Shawbury Music . . . . UK
Status Quo . . . . **Vertigo 6059133**

RAIN　　　January 1987
Vincent Bell
Island Music . . . . UK
Oran 'Juice' Jones . . . . **De Jam A 7303**

RAIN OR SHINE　　　October 1986
Bill Livsey / Peter Sinfield
Virgin Music . . . . UK
Five Star . . . . **Tent PB 40970**

RAIN, RAIN, RAIN　　　November 1954
Jay McConologue
Larry Speir Ltd. . . . . USA
Frankie Laine . . . . **Philips BBL 7111**

RAINBOW　　　　　　　　　　　　　　**April 1957**
Ronald Hulme
Robbins Music Corporation Ltd. . . . . UK
Russ Hamilton . . . . **Oriole EP 7005**
Floyd Robinson . . . . **RCA RD 27166**

RAINBOW　　　　　　　　　　　　**September 1970**
William Campbell / Thomas McAleese
Walrus Music . . . . UK
Marmalade . . . . **Decca F 13035**

RAINBOW ON THE RIVER　　　　　　　　　　　**1936**
Louis Alter / Paul Francis Webster
Francis, Day & Hunter Ltd . . . . USA
Film(s): . . . . Rainbow on the River
Bobby Breen . . . . **Decca F 6301**
Bobby Breen appeared in *Rainbow on the River*.

RAINDROPS KEEP FALLING ON MY HEAD　**March 1970**
Burt Bacharach / Hal David
Jac Music . . . . USA
Film(s): . . . . .Butch Cassidy and the Sundance Kid
Satcha Distel . . . . **Warner Brothers 7345**
B.J. Thomas (Sound Track) . . . . **A&M AMLS 963**
Bobbie Gentry . . . . **Capitol CL 15626**
Academy Award winning song for 1969.

RAINY DAY REFRAIN, A (Schnürlregen)　**November 1950**
Heino Gaze / Eric Maschwitz
Peter Maurice Music Co. Ltd . . . . Germany
Mindy Carson . . . . **HMV B 9986**
The Andrews Sisters . . . . **Brunswick 04599**

RAINY DAY WOMAN Nos. 12 & 35　　　　**July 1966**
Bob Dylan
B. Feldman & Co. Ltd. . . . . USA
Bob Dylan . . . . **CBS 202307**

RAINY NIGHT IN RIO, A　　　　　　　　　　　**1947**
Arthur Schwartz / Leo Robin
B. Feldman & Co. Ltd. . . . . USA
Film(s): . . . . The Time, the Place and the Girl
The Andrews Sisters . . . . **Brunswick 03789**

RAMBLING ROSE　　　　　　　　　　**August 1948**
Joseph McCarthy / Joe Burke
Dash Music Ltd. . . . . USA
**The Skyrockets Dance Orchestra,
vocal Doreen Lundy** . . . . **HMV BD 6016**

RAMBLING ROSE　　　　　　　　　**November 1962**
Joe Sherman / Noel Sherman
Comet Music Ltd . . . . USA
Nat 'King' Cole . . . . **Capitol CL 15270**
The Wilburn Brothers . . . . **Brunswick LAT 8555**

RAMONA　　　　　　　　　　　　　　　　　**1928**
Mabel Wayne / L. Wolfe Gilbert
Francis, Day & Hunter Ltd. . . . . USA
Paul Whiteman & his Orchestra . . . . **HMV B 5476**
Mabel Wayne . . . . **Columbia DX 672**
Gene Austin . . . . **RCA RCX 113**
Brian Grey . . . . **Columbia DB 4237**
Bing Crosby . . . . **MGM C 868**
The Bachelors (1964) . . . . **Decca F 11910**

RANCHO GRANDE, EL　　　　　　　　　　　**1939**
Silvano Ramos / J. Del Morales / Emilio Uranga & Bartley Costello
World Wide Music Co. Ltd. . . . . Mexico
Film(s): . . . . Mexicali Rose
Gene Autry . . . . **Regal Zonophone MR 3497**
Al Bowlly . . . . **HMV BD 805**
Bing Crosby . . . . **Brunswick LAT 8382**
Trio Los Panchos . . . . **Philips BBL 7469**
Gene Autry appeared in *Mexicali Rose*.

RANDY　　　　　　　　　　　　　　**August 1973**
Roger Cook / Roger Greenaway / Herbie Flowers
Cookaway Music . . . . UK
Blue Mink . . . . **EMI 2028**

RANGERS' SONG, THE　　　　　　　　　　　**1930**
Joseph McCarthy / Harry Tierney
Francis, Day & Hunter Ltd . . . . USA
Show(s): . . . . Rio Rita
Film(s): . . . . Rio Rita
Geoffrey Gwyther . . . . **Columbia DX 54**
The Light Opera Company . . . . **HMV C 1780**
Geoffrey Gwyther appeared in the British production of *Rio Rita*.

RAPPER'S DELIGHT　　　　　　　　**December 1979**
Bernard Edwards / Nile Rodgers
Warner Brothers Music Ltd. . . . . USA
The Sugarhill Gang . . . . **Sugarhill SHL 101**

RAPTURE　　　　　　　　　　　　**February 1981**
Deborah Harry / Christopher Stein
Chrysalis Music . . . . UK
Blondie . . . . **Chrysalis CHS 2485**

RASPUTIN　　　　　　　　　　　　**October 1978**
Frank Farian / George Reyam / Fred Jay
A.T.V. Music Ltd. . . . . Germany
Boney M . . . . **Atlantic K 11192**

RAT RACE　　　　　　　　　　　　　**June 1980**
Roddy Radiation
Plangent Visions Music . . . . UK
The Specials . . . . **2-Tone CHSTT 11**

RAT TRAP　　　　　　　　　　　　**November 1978**
Bob Geldof
Sewer Fire Hits . . . . UK
The Boomtown Rats . . . . **Ensign ENY 16**
Ivor Novello Nomination.

RAUNCHY　　　　　　　　　　　　　**March 1958**
Bill Justice / Sid Manker
Aberbach Music Ltd. . . . . USA
Billy Vaughan Orchestra . . . . **London HLD 8522**
Ken Mackintosh Orchestra . . . . **HMV POP 426**
Bill Justice (saxophone) . . . . **London HLS 8517**

RAVE ON　　　　　　　　　　　　　　**July 1958**
Norman Petty / Bill Tilghman / Sunny West
Southern Music Co. . . . . USA
Buddy Holly . . . . **Coral Q 72325**

RAWHIDE　　　　　　　　　　　　**December 1959**
Dimitri Tiomkin / Ned Washington
Leeds Music Ltd . . . . USA
Frankie Laine . . . . **Philips BBL 7468**
Sheb Wooley . . . . **MGM C 859**
Theme of the Television production *Rawhide*.

RAZZLE DAZZLE　　　　　　　　　　**January 1957**
Charles E. Calhoun
Robert Mellin Ltd. . . . . USA
Bill Haley & his Comets . . . . **Brunswick LAT 8117**
Tommy Steele . . . . **Decca LF 1287**

**REACH FOR THE STARS (Woner Ich Auch Komm, Wohin
Ich Auch Geh)**　　　　　　　　　　**September 1961**
Udo Jurgens / David West
Edward Kassner Music Co. Ltd. . . . . Germany
Shirley Bassey . . . . **Columbia DB 4685**
Mark Wynter . . . . **Decca LK 4409**

REACH OUT I'LL BE THERE　　　　　**November 1966**
Brian Holland / Eddie Holland / Lamont Dozier
Belinda (London) Ltd. . . . . USA
The Four Tops . . . . **Tamla Motown TMG 579**
Gloria Gaynor . . . . **MGM 2006499**
The Four Tops (1988) . . . . **Motown ZB 41943**

REACHING FOR THE MOON　　　　　　　　　**1931**
Irving Berlin
Francis, Day & Hunter Ltd. . . . . USA
Ed Lloyd & his Orchestra . . . . **Parlophone R 874**
Lillian Davies . . . . **HMV B 3807**
Ella Fitzgerald . . . . **HMV CLP 1184**

READY FOR THE RIVER　　　　　　　　　　　**1929**
Gus Kahn / Neil Moret
Francis, Day & Hunter Ltd . . . . USA
The Goofus Five . . . . **Parlophone R 218**

READY, WILLING AND ABLE　　　　　**March 1955**
Al Rinker / Floyd Huddlestone / Dick Gleason

California Music Ltd. . . . . USA
Film(s): . . . . Young at Heart
Doris Day . . . . **Philips BBL 7297**
Doris Day appeared in *Young at Heart*.

REAL GONE KID   November 1988
Ricky Ross
A.T.V. Music . . . . UK
Deacon Blue . . . . **CBS DEAC 7**

REAL THING, THE   October 1987
Arnie Roman / C. Toni
Warner Chappell Music . . . . USA
Jellybean, Featuring Steven Dante . . . . **Chrysalis CHS 3167**

REAL WILD CHILD   January 1987
Johnny O'Keefe / David Owens / Johnny Greenan
Southern Music Co. . . . . Australia
Iggy Pop . . . . **A&M AM 368**

REALLY SAYING SOMETHING (See He Was Really Saying Something)

REASONS TO BE CHEERFUL   September 1979
Ian Dury / Davey Payne / Charles Jankel
Blackhill Music . . . . UK
Ian Dury & The Blockheads . . . . **Stiff BUY 50**

REBEL REBEL   March 1974
David Bowie
Chrysalis Music Ltd. . . . . UK
David Bowie . . . . **RCA LPBO 5009**

REBEL YELL   October 1985
Billy Idol / Steve Stevens
Chrysalis Music . . . . UK
Billy Idol . . . . **Chrysalis IDOL 6**

RED BALLOON   October 1968
Raymond Froggatt
Edwin H. Morris & Co. Ltd. . . . . USA
The Dave Clark Five . . . . **Columbia DB 8465**
Raymond Froggatt . . . . **Polydor 56249**

RED DRESS   June 1974
Peter Shelley
Magnet Music . . . . UK
Alvin Stardust . . . . **Magnet MAG 8**

RED HOT MAMMA   1925
Gilbert Wells / Bud Cooper / Fred Rose
Francis, Day & Hunter Ltd. . . . . USA
The California Club Orchestra . . . . **Columbia 3446**
Joe 'Fingers' Carr (piano) . . . . **Capitol T 1151**

RED LIGHT SPELLS DANGER   April 1977
Ben Findon / Les Charles
Heath Levy Music Ltd . . . . UK
Billy Ocean . . . . **GTO GT 85**

RED MOON   1923
Lew Brown / John Traver / Max Kortlander / Henri De Martini
Francis, Day & Hunter Ltd . . . . USA
The Serenaders . . . . **HMV B 1561**

RED RED WINE   October 1983
Neil Diamond
Warner Brothers Music . . . . USA
UB40 . . . . **D.E.P. DEP 7**

RED RIVER ROCK   November 1959
Tom King / Ira Mack / Fred Mendelsohn
Burlington Music Co. Ltd . . . . USA
Johnny & The Hurricanes . . . . **London HA 2227**
An arrangement of *Red River Valley*.

RED RIVER VALLEY   1931
Traditional
. . . . USA
Peterson's Hobo Orchestra . . . . **Panachord 25062**
The Rocky Mountaineers . . . . **Columbia FB 1249**
The Andrews Sisters . . . . **Brunswick 03750**
Bing Crosby . . . . **RCA RD 27196**
The Sons of The Pioneers . . . . **RCA RD 27016**

RED ROSES FOR A BLUE LADY   June 1949
Sid Tepper / Roy Brodsky
Lawrence Wright Music Co. Ltd . . . . USA
Vaughn Monroe . . . . **HMV BD 1247**
Bryan Johnson . . . . **Decca LK 4362**
Bert Kaempfert & his Orchestra (1965) . . **Polydor LPMH 46446**
Lorne Gibson . . . . **Decca F 12102**
Vic Dana . . . . **Liberty LIB 10190**

RED SAILS IN THE SUNSET   1935
Hugh Williams / Jimmy Kennedy
Peter Maurice Music Co. Ltd . . . . UK
Show(s): . . . . Province Town Follies
Al Bowlly . . . . **HMV BD 295**
Bing Crosby . . . . **Brunswick 02101**
Gracie Fields . . . . **Decca LK 4182**
Perry Como . . . . **RCA RD 27078**
Theme song of Suzette Tarri.

RED WING   1907
Thurland Chattaway / Kerry Mills
B. Feldman & Co. Ltd. . . . . USA
Herbert Payne . . . . **Zonophone 479**
The Rocky Mountaineers . . . . **Columbia 1124**
Les Brown & his Band of Renown . . . . **Vogue LVA 9043**
Terry Lightfoot's Jazzmen . . . . **Encore ENC 124**

REELIN' AND ROCKIN'   April 1965
Chuck Berry
Jewel Music Publishing Co. Ltd . . . . USA
Dave Clark Five . . . . **Columbia DB 7503**
Chuck Berry (1973) . . . . **Chess 6145020**

REET PETITE   January 1958
Tyran Carlo / Berry Gordy Jnr.
Burlington Music Co. Ltd . . . . USA
Jackie Wilson . . . . **Coral Q 72290**
Darts . . . . **Magnet MAG 160**
Jackie Wilson (1987) . . . . **SMP SKM 3**

REFLECTIONS   October 1967
Brian Holland / Eddie Holland / Lamont Dozier
Carlin Music Corporation . . . . USA
Diana Ross & The Supremes . . . . **Tamla Motown TMG 616**

REFLECTIONS IN THE WATER   1933
John Jacob Loeb / Paul Francis Webster
Francis, Day & Hunter Ltd. . . . . USA
Bob & Alf Pearson . . . . **Rex 8037**
The Platters . . . . **Mercury MMC 14045**

REFLECTIONS OF MY LIFE   February 1970
William Campbell / Thomas McAleese
Walrus Music . . . . UK
Marmalade . . . . **Decca F 12982**

REFLECTIONS ON THE WATER   April 1948
Billy Reid
Peter Maurice Music Co. Ltd. . . . . UK
Dorothy Squires . . . . **Columbia DB 2418**
Dorothy Squires . . . . **Pye NPL 18015**

REFLEX, THE   May 1984
Simon Le Bon / John Taylor / Andy Taylor / Roger Taylor / Nick Rhodes
Carlin Music . . . . UK
Duran Duran . . . . **EMI DURAN 2**
Ivor Novello Award.

REGGAE FOR IT NOW   September 1979
Bill Lovelady / Aubrey Cash
Louvigny-Marquee Music Co. . . . . UK
Bill Lovelady . . . . **Charisma CB 337**

REGGAE TUNE   October 1974
Andy Fairweather Low
Rondor Music (London) Ltd. . . . . UK
Andy Fairweather Low . . . . **A&M AMS 7129**

REGIMENT OF FROCK AND FRILLS, THE   1905
Percy Greenbank / Andre Messanger
Chappell Music Co. . . . . France
Show(s) . . . . The Little Michus
Stanley Kirkby . . . . **Zonophone X 43222**

RELAX   **February 1984**
Peter Gill / Holly Johnson / Mark O'Toole
Perfect Songs . . . . UK
Frankie Goes To Hollywood . . . . **Island ZTAS 1**
Ivor Novello Nornination.

RELEASE ME   **May 1967**
Eddie Miller / W.S. Stevenson / Bob Harris
Palace Music Co. Ltd. . . . . USA
Esther Phillips . . . . **Stateside SS 140**
Engelbert Humperdinck . . . . **Decca F 12541**
Dean Martin . . . . **Reprise RLP 6250**
Eddy Arnold . . . . **RCA LSA 3166**

RELICAIRO, EL   **1920**
Jose Padilla
Ascherberg, Hopwood & Crew Ltd . . . . Spain
De Groot & his Picadilly Orchestra . . . . **HMV B 1124**
Emilio De Gogriza . . . . **HMV DA 998**
Emmanuel Vardi & his Orchestra . . . . . . **Brunswick LAT 8112**
The Troubadours . . . . **London HAR 2095**

REMEMBER   **1925**
Irving Berlin
Francis, Day & Hunter Ltd. . . . . USA
Show(s): . . . . The Co-Optimists
Film(s):Alexander's Ragtime Band / There's No Business Like Show
Business
Melville Gideon . . . . **HMV B 2119**
Connee Boswell . . . . **Brunswick 02645**
Pat Boone . . . . **London HAD 2082**
Dinah Shore . . . . **Capitol T 1296**
Melville Gideon appeared in *The Co-Optimists*.

REMEMBER (SHA-LA-LA)   **March 1974**
Bill Martin / Phil Coulter
Martin-Coulter Music ltd. . . . . UK
The Bay City Rollers . . . . **Bell 1338**

REMEMBER (Walking In The Sand)   **November 1964**
George Morton
Robert Mellin Ltd . . . . USA
The Shangri-Las . . . . **Red Bird RB 10008**

REMEMBER ME   **1934**
Sonny Miller / Syd Seymour
B. Feldman & Co. Ltd . . . . UK
Michael Regan . . . . **Rex 8234**

REMEMBER ME   **1938**
Al Dubin / Harry Warren
B. Feldman & Co. Ltd. . . . . USA
Film(s): . . . . Mr Dodd Takes the Air / Never Say Goodbye
Lew Stone & his Orchestra, vocal Sam Costa . . **Decca F 6566**
Bing Crosby . . . . **Brunswick 02534**
The Norman Luboff Choir . . . . **Philips BBL 7302**
Nominated for an Academy Award 1938.

REMEMBER ME   **May 1971**
Nicholas Ashford / Valerie Simpson
Jobete Music (UK) Ltd. . . . . USA
Diana Ross . . . . **Tamla Motown TMG 768**

REMEMBER ME THIS WAY   **April 1974**
Gary Glitter / Mike Leander
Leeds Music Ltd. . . . . UK
Gary Glitter . . . . **Bell 1349**

REMEMBER YOU'RE A WOMBLE   **May 1974**
Mike Batt
Batt Songs . . . . UK
The Wombles . . . . **CBS 2241**

REMEMBER YOU'RE MINE   **October 1957**
Kal Mann / Bernie Lowe
Belinda Music . . . . USA
Pat Boone . . . . **London HLD 8479**

REMINISCING   **October 1962**
Sonny Curtis
Southern Music Publishing Co. Ltd . . . . USA
Buddy Holly . . . . **Coral Q 72455**

RENT   **November 1987**
Neil Tennant / Chris Lowe

TEN Music . . . . UK
The Pet Shop Boys . . . . **Parlophone R 6158**

REQUIEM   **May 1989**
Ralf Mave
Warner Chappell Music . . . . Germany
The London Boys . . . . **Teldec YZ 345**

RESCUE ME   **January 1966**
Carl Smith / Raynard Miner
Jewel Music Publishing Co. Ltd . . . . USA
Fontella Bass . . . . **Chess CRS 8023**

RESPECT   **July 1967**
Otis Redding
Shapiro-Bernstein & Co. Ltd. . . . . USA
Aretha Franklin . . . . **Atlantic 584 115**

RESPECT YOURSELF   **March 1987**
Mack Rice / Luther Ingram
Rondor Music . . . . USA
Bruce Willis . . . . **Motown ZB 41117**

RESPECTABLE   **April 1987**
Mike Stock / Matt Aitken / Peter Waterman
All Boys Music . . . . UK
Mel & Kim . . . . **Supreme SUPE 111**
Ivor Novello Nomination.

RESSURRECTION SHUFFLE, THE   **March 1971**
Tony Ashton
B. Feldman & Co. Ltd . . . . USA
Ashton, Gardner & Dyke . . . . **Capitol CL 15565**

RETURN OF DJANGO, THE   **November 1969**
Lee Perry
Island Music Ltd . . . . Jamaica
The Upsetters . . . . **Trojan TRLS 176**

RETURN OF THE LOS PALMAS SEVEN, THE   **February 1981**
Michael Barson / Daniel Woodgate / Mark Bedford
Warner Brothers Music . . . . UK
Madness . . . . **Stiff BUY 108**

RETURN TO ME (Ritorna Ame)   **August 1958**
Danny Di Minno / Carmen Lombardo
Southern Music Publishing Co. Ltd . . . . USA
Dean Martin . . . . **Capitol T 1047**
Connie Francis . . . . **MGM C 854**

RETURN TO SENDER   **December 1962**
Otis Blackwell / Winfield Scott
Manor Music Co. Ltd . . . . USA
Film(s): . . . . Girls, Girls, Girls
Elvis Presley . . . . **RCA 1320**
Elvis Presley appeared in *Girls, Girls, Girls*

REUNITED   **June 1979**
Dino Fekaris / Freddie Perren
A.T.V. Music Ltd. . . . . USA
Peaches & Herb . . . . **Polydor POSP 43**

REWARD   **February 1981**
Alan Gill / David Balfe
Warner Brothers Music . . . . UK
Teardrop Explodes . . . . **Vertigo TEAR 2**

RHAPSODY IN BLUE   **1925**
George Gershwin
Chappell & Co. Ltd. . . . . USA
Film(s): . . . . The King of Jazz / Rhapsody in Blue
Paul Whiteman & his Orchestra
with George Gershwin (piano) . . . . **HMV C 1395**
The Mantovani Orchestra with
Julius Katchen (piano) . . . . **Decca LXT 5069**
Paul Whiteman & his Orchestra appeared in *The King of Jazz*.
Theme tune of Paul Whiteman.

RHINESTONE COWBOY, THE   **November 1975**
Larry Weiss
Keith Prowse Music Publishing Co. Ltd . . . . USA
Glen Campbell . . . . **Capitol CL 15824**

RHYMES   **1931**
Leslie Sarony

Lawrence Wright Music Co. Ltd. . . . . UK
Jack Hylton & his Orchestra . . . . **Zonophone 5997**
Jimmy Edwards . . . . **Fontana TFE 17296**

RHYTHM IS OUR BUSINESS 1935
Jimmy Lunceford / Saul Kaplan / Sammy Cahn
Peter Maurice Music Co. Ltd . . . . USA
Film(s): . . . . It's Great to be Young
Jimmy Lunceford & his Orchestra . . . . **Brunswick 01965**
Billy May & his Orchestra, vocal Willie Smith . . . **Capitol T 924**

RHYTHM OF LIFE November 1967
Dorothy Fields / Cy Coleman
Campbell, Connelly & Co. Ltd. . . . . USA
Show(s): . . . . Sweet Charity
Film(s): . . . . Sweet Charity
Arnold Soboloff, Eddie Gasper
& Harold Pierson . . . . **Columbia KOL 6500**
Fred Evan, Roger Finch, Ken Walsh
& The Worshippers . . . . **CBS BRG 70035**
Sammy Davis Jnr. . . . . **MCA MUCS 133**
Arnold Soboloff, Eddie Gasper & Harold Pierson appeared in the
American production of *Sweet Charity*.
Fred Evan, Roger Finch & Ken Walsh appeared in the British produc-
tion of *Sweet Charity*.
Sammy Davis Jnr. appeared in the film *Sweet Charity*.

RHYTHM OF THE NIGHT May 1985
Diane Warren
EMI Music . . . . USA
Debarge . . . . **Motown TMG 1376**

RHYTHM OF THE RAIN 1935
Jack Meskill / Jack Stern
Francis, Day & Hunter Ltd . . . . USA
Film(s): . . . . The Man From the Folies Bergere
Maurice Chevalier . . . . **HMV B 8305**
The Dorsey Brothers Orchestra . . . . **Gala GLP 307**
Maurice Chevalier appeared in *The Man From The Folies Bergere*.

RHYTHM OF THE RAIN April 1963
John Gummoe
Edwin H. Morris & Co. Ltd . . . . USA
The Cascades . . . . **Warner Brothers WB 88**
Percy Faith & his Orchestra . . . . **CBS BPG 62330**

RHYTHM ON THE RIVER 1941
Johnny Burke / Jimmy Monaco
Victoria Music Co. Ltd . . . . USA
Film(o): . . . . Rhythm on the River
Bing Crosby . . . . **Brunswick Bing 6**
Bing Crosby appeared in *Rhythm on the Range*.

RICKERTY RICKSHAW MAN, THE March 1947
Ervin Drake
Southern Music Co. . . . . USA
The Skyrockets Dance Orchestra . . . . **HMV BD 5970**
Geraldo & his Orchestra . . . . **Parlophone F 2213**

RICOCHET January 1954
Larry Coleman / Joe Darion / Norman Gimbel
Sheldon Music Ltd. . . . . USA
Vicky Young . . . . **Capitol CL 13996**
Joan Regan . . . . **Decca LF 1182**
Teresa Brewer . . . . **Vogue LVA 9131**

RIDDLE, THE December 1984
Nik Kershaw
Rondor Music . . . . UK
Nik Kershaw . . . . **MCA NIK 6**

RIDE A WHITE SWAN January 1971
Marc Bolan
Essex Music Ltd . . . . UK
T. Rex . . . . **Fly BUG 1**

RIDE A WILD HORSE November 1975
Kenny Nolan
April Music Ltd . . . . USA
Dee Clark . . . . **Chelsea 2005037**

RIDE COSSACK, RIDE 1940
Robert Wright / George Forrest / Herbert Stothart
Francis, Day & Hunter . . . . USA
Film(s): . . . . Balalaika

Nelson Eddy . . . . **Columbia DB 1911**
Bruce Low . . . . **HMV 7EG 8385**
Nelson Eddy appeared in *Balalaika*.

RIDE ON TIME October 1989
Dan Hartman / Mirko Limoni / Daniel Davoli & Valerio Semplici
Warner Chappell Music . . . . Italy
Black Box . . . . **RCA PB 43055**

RIDE, TENDERFOOT, RIDE 1938
Richard A. Whiting / Johnny Mercer
B. Feldman & Co. Ltd. . . . . USA
Film(s): . . . . Romance and Rhythm, Ride, Tenderfoot, Ride
Dick Powell . . . . **Decca F 6784**
Les Allen . . . . **Columbia FB 2078**
Dick Powell appeared in *Romance and Rhythm*.

RIDIN' AROUND IN THE RAIN 1934
Gene Austin / Carmen Lombardo
Campbell Connelly & Co. Ltd. . . . . USA
Bing Crosby . . . . **Fontana TFR 6000**
Guy Mitchell . . . . **Philips BBL 7465**

RIDIN' HIGH 1941
Cole Porter
Chappell & Co. Ltd . . . . USA
Show(s): . . . . Red Hot and Blue
Carroll Gibbons & The Savoy Orpheans . . . . **Columbia FB 2565**
Peggy Lee . . . . **Capitol T 1049**

RIDING ON A TRAIN October 1988
"The Pasadenas"
SBK Songs . . . . UK
The Pasadenas . . . . **CBS PASA 2**

RIFF SONG, THE 1927
Sigmund Romberg / Otto Harbach / Oscar Hammerstein II
Chappell & Co. Ltd . . . . USA
Show(s): . . . . The Desert Song
Film(s): . . . . The Desert Song
Harry Welchman . . . . **Columbia 4387**
Raymond Newell . . . . **Regal G 8878**
Wilbur Evans . . . . **Brunswick LA 8501**
Gordon MacRae . . . . **Capitol LCT 6114**
Harry Welchman appeared in the British production *The Desert Song*.
Gordon MacRae appeared in the 1953 film of *The Desert Song*.

RIGHT BACK WHERE WE STARTED FROM November 1975
Pierre Tubbs / Vince Edwards
A.T.V. Music Ltd. . . . . UK
Film(s): . . . . The World is Full of Married Men
Maxine Nightingale . . . . **United Artists UP 36015**
Maxine Nightingale . . . . **Ronco RTD 2038**
Sinitta (1989) . . . . **Fanfare FAN 18**
Maxine Nightingale appeared in *The World is Full of Married Men*.

RIGHT BY YOUR SIDE December 1983
Annie Lennox / David Stewart
RCA Music . . . . UK
Eurythmics . . . . **RCA DA 4**

RIGHT HERE WAITING October 1989
Richard Marks
EMI Music . . . . USA
Richard Marks . . . . **EMI USA MT 72**

RIGHT NOW August 1983
Herbie Mann / Carl Sigman
. . . . USA
The Creatures . . . . **Polydor SHE 2**

RIGHT SAID FRED August 1962
Ted Dicks / Myles Rudge
Noel Gay Music Co. Ltd . . . . UK
Bernard Cribbens . . . . **Parlophone R 4923**

RIGHT THING, THE March 1987
Mick Hucknall
SBK Songs . . . . UK
Simply Red . . . . **WEA YZ 103**

RING DEM BELLS 1931
Duke Ellington / Irving Mills
Chappell & Co. Ltd . . . . USA
Film(s): . . . . Check and Double Check

Duke Ellington & his Orchestra,
vocal Cootie Williams . . . . **Parlophone PMC 1154**
Ted Heath & his Music . . . . **Decca LK 4347**
Duke Ellington appeared in *Check and Double Check.*

RING MY BELL   June 1979
Frederic Knight
Island Music Ltd. . . . . USA
Anita Ward . . . . **T.K. TKR 7543**

RING OF FIRE   August 1961
Duane Eddy
Twangy Music Ltd. . . . . USA
Film(s): . . . . Ring of Fire
Duane Eddy (guitar) . . . . **London HL 9370**

RIO   December 1982
"Duran Duran"
Carlin Music . . . . UK
Duran Duran . . . . **EMI 5346**

RIO RITA   1930
Joseph McCarthy / Harry Tierney
Francis, Day & Hunter Ltd . . . . USA
Show(s): . . . . Rio Rita
Film(s): . . . . Rio Rita
Bebe Daniels . . . . **Decca F 7803**
Geoffrey Gwyther & Edith Day . . . . **Columbia DX 55**
Edmund Hockridge . . . . **Pye NPL 18040**
Geoffrey Gwyther & Edith Day appeared in the British production of *Rio Rita.*
Bebe Daniels appeared in the film of *Rio Rita.*

RIP IT UP   December 1956
Bob Blackwell / John Marascalco
Peter Maurice Music . . . . USA
Bill Haley & his Comets . . . . **Brunswick 05615**

RIP IT UP   April 1983
Edwyn Collins
Zomba Music . . . . UK
Orange Juice . . . . **Polydor POSP 547**

RISE   February 1986
John Lydon / William Laswell
EMI Music . . . . UK
Public Image Ltd. . . . . **Virgin VS 841**

RISE 'N' SHINE   1936
Vincent Youmans / Buddy De Sylva
Chappell & Co. Ltd . . . . USA
Show(s): . . . . Take a Chance / Rise and Shine
Film(s): . . . . Take a Chance
Abe Lyman & his Orchestra,
vocal Paul Smith . . . . **Brunswick 02219**
Carroll Gibbons &
The Savoy Hotel Orpheans . . . . **Columbia FB 1399**
Sydney Kyte & his Piccadilly Orchestra . . . . **Decca F 5979**
The Jay & Kai Trombone Octet . . . . **Fontana TFL 5022**

RISE AND FALL OF FLINGLE BUNT   June 1964
Bruce Welsh / Hank B. Marvin / John Rostill & Brian Bennett
Shadows Music Ltd . . . . UK
The Shadows . . . . **Columbia DB 7261**

RISE TO THE OCCASION   January 1988
Simon Climie / Rob Fisher / Dennis Morgan
Rondor Music . . . . UK
Climie Fisher . . . . **EMI EM 33**

RISING SUN, THE   September 1973
John Fiddler
Biscuit Music . . . . UK
Medicine Head . . . . **Polydor 2058389**

RIVER DEEP, MOUNTAIN HIGH   July 1966
Jeff Barry / Ellie Greenwich / Phil Spector
Belinda (London) Ltd. . . . . USA
Ike & Tina Turner . . . . **London HL 10046**
The Supremes & The Four Tops . . . . . **Tamla Motown TMG 777**

RIVER KWAI MARCH   January 1958
Malcolm Arnold
Campbell Connelly & Co. Ltd . . . . UK
Film(s): . . . . The Bridge on the River Kwai

Ron Goodwin & his Orchestra . . . . **Parlophone GEP 8722**
Based on *Colonel Bogey March* by Kenneth Alford.

RIVER OF NO RETURN, THE   July 1954
Lionel Newman / Ken Darby
Francis, Day & Hunter Ltd. . . . . USA
Film(s): . . . . The River of No Return
Marilyn Monroe . . . . **HMV 7M 232**
Michel Legrand & his Orchestra,
vocal Christine Legrand . . . . **Philips BBL 7304**
Marilyn Monroe appeared in *The River of No Return.*

RIVER STAY 'WAY FROM MY DOOR   1931
Mort Dixon / Harry Woods
B. Feldman & Co. Ltd. . . . . USA
Paul Robeson . . . . **HMV B 3956**
Frank Sinatra (1960) . . . . **Capitol CL 15135**

RIVER, THE (Le Colline Sono In Fiore)   January 1966
Renato Angiolini'Calibi' / Bob Shuman
Peter Maurice Music Co. Ltd . . . . Italy
The New Christy Minstrels . . . . **CBS 201758**
Ken Dodd . . . . **Columbia DB 7706**

RIVERS OF BABYLON, THE   June 1978
Frank Farian / George Reyam / Brent Dowe & Trevor McNaughton
A.T.V. Music Ltd. . . . . Germany
Boney M . . . . **Atlantic K 11120**

RIVIERA ROSE   1924
Horatio Nicholls
Lawrence Wright Music Co. Ltd. . . . . UK
Jack Hylton & his Orchestra . . . . **HMV B 1808**

RO-RO-ROLLIN' ALONG   1930
Harry Richman / Billy Moll / Murray Mencher
Lawrence Wright Music Co. Ltd . . . . USA
Film(s): . . . . Near The Rainbow's End
Jack Hylton & his Orchestra . . . . **HMV B 5840**

ROAD TO HELL, THE   November 1989
Chris Rea
Magnet Music . . . . UK
Chris Rea . . . . **WEA YZ 43**

ROAD TO MANDALAY, THE (See On The Road To Mandalay)

ROAD TO MOROCCO, THE   1942
Johnny Burke / Jimmy Van Heusen
Victoria Music Co. Ltd . . . . USA
Film(s): . . . . Road to Morocco
Bing Crosby & Bob Hope . . . . **Brunswick Bing 8**
Bing Crosby & Bob Hope appeared in *Road to Morocco.*

ROAD TO NOWHERE   November 1985
David Byrne / Chris Frantz / Tina Weymouth & Jerry Harrison
Warner Brothers Music . . . . UK
Talking Heads . . . . **EMI 5530**

ROAMIN' IN THE GLOAMIN'   1911
Harry Lauder
Francis, Day & Hunter Ltd. . . . . UK
Harry Lauder . . . . **HMV DLP 1089**
George Elrick . . . . **Beltona ABL 509**
Kenneth McKellar . . . . **Decca LK 4295**

ROAMIN' TO WYOMIN'   1924
Walter Donaldson
Francis, Day & Hunter Ltd . . . . USA
Paul Whiteman & his Orchestra . . . . **HMV 1771**

ROBBER'S CHORUS   1916
Frederick Norton / Oscar Asche
Keith Prowse Music Publishing Co. Ltd. . . . . UK
Show(s): . . . . Chu Chin Chow
Film(s): . . . . Chu Chin Chow
The Columbia Vocal Gems Company . . . . **Columbia 659**
Inia Te Wiata & Chorus . . . . **HMV CLP 1269**

ROBERT DE NIRO'S WAITING   April 1984
Tony Swain / Steve Jolly / Sarah Dalin / Siobhan Fahey / Keren Woodward
Rondor Music . . . . UK
Bananarama . . . . **London NANA 6**

ROBIN HOOD   **March 1956**
Carl Sigman
Chappell & Co. Ltd. . . . . USA
Dick James . . . . **Parlophone R 4117**
Gary Miller . . . . **Nixa NPT 19015**
Billy Cotton & his Band, vocal Doreen
Stephens, Alan Breeze & The Bandits . . . . **Decca DFE 6338**
Theme of the TV Programme.

ROBINS AND ROSES   **1936**
Edgar Leslie / Joe Burke
Victoria Music Co. Ltd . . . . USA
Bing Crosby . . . . **Brunswick 02223**
Pat Boone . . . . **London HAD 2144**

ROBINSON CRUSOE'S ISLE   **1922**
Robert Stolz / Harry Graham
Ascherberg, Hopwood & Crew Ltd . . . . Germany
Show(s) . . . . Whirled into Happiness
The 'Queens' Dance Orchestra,
conductor Jack Hylton . . . . **HMV B 1389**

ROBOT   **April 1963**
Joe Meek
Ivy Music Ltd . . . . UK
The Tornados . . . . **Decca F 11606**

ROBOT MAN   **July 1960**
Sylvia Dee / G. Goehring
Joy Music Ltd . . . . USA
Connie Francis . . . . **MGM C 831**

ROCK 'N' ME   **December 1976**
Steve Miller
Heath Levy Music Ltd . . . . USA
The Steve Miller Band . . . . **Mercury 6078804**

ROCK AND ROLL PART I & 2   **August 1972**
Gary Glitter / Mike Leander
Leeds Music Ltd. . . . . UK
Gary Glitter . . . . **Bell 1216**

ROCK AND ROLL WALTZ   **February 1956**
Shorty Allen / Dick Ware
United Artists Music Co. Ltd. . . . . USA
Kay Starr . . . . **HMV 7M 371**
Bob Bain & his Music . . . . **Capitol T 965**

ROCK AND ROLL WINTER   **May 1974**
Roy Wood
Carlin Music Corporation . . . . UK
Wizzard . . . . **Warner Brothers K 16357**

ROCK AROUND THE CLOCK   **December 1955**
Jimmy De Knight / Max Freedman
Myers Music Ltd. . . . . USA
Film(s): . . . . The Blackboard Jungle / Rock Around the Clock
Bill Haley & his Comets . . . . **Brunswick LAT 8117**
Chubby Checker . . . . **Columbia 33SX 1341**
Bill Haley appeared in *Rock Around the Clock*.

ROCK ISLAND LINE   **January 1956**
Traditional, additional Lyrics Lonnie Donnegan
Essex Music Ltd. . . . . USA
Lonnie Donegan & his Skiffle Group . . **Ace of Clubs ACL 1037**
Huddie Leadbetter . . . . **Melodisc MLP 511**

ROCK ME AMADEUS   **May 1986**
Robert Bolland / Ferdinand Bolland
Island Music . . . . Holland
Falco . . . . **A&M AM 278**

ROCK ME GENTLY   **October 1974**
Andy Kim
Intersong Music . . . . USA
Andy Kim . . . . **Capitol CL 15787**

ROCK OF GIBRALTAR   **January 1952**
Terry Gilkyson
Dash Music Ltd . . . . USA
Frankie Laine . . . . **Columbia DB 3113**

ROCK ON   **September 1973**
David Essex
Jeff Wayne Music . . . . UK

David Essex . . . . **CBS 1693**

ROCK THE BOAT   **August 1974**
Wally Holmes
Warner Brothers Music Ltd. . . . . USA
The Hues Corporation . . . . **RCA APBO 0232**
Forrest (1983) . . . . **CBS A 3163**

ROCK THE BOAT   **February 1987**
Joey Tempest
EMI Music . . . . Holland
Europe . . . . **Epic EUR 1**

ROCK THE HOUSE (See Rok Da House)

ROCK THIS TOWN   **March 1981**
Brian Setzer
Zomba Music . . . . UK
Stray Cats . . . . **Arista SCAT 2**

ROCK WITH THE CAVEMEN   **March 1957**
Michael Pratt / Lionel Bart / Tommy Steele
Robbins Music Corporation Ltd. . . . . UK
Tommy Steele . . . . **Decca F 10795**

ROCK WITH YOU   **March 1980**
Rodney Temperton
Rondor Music (London) Ltd . . . . USA
Michael Jackson . . . . **Epic EPC 8206**

ROCK YOUR BABY   **August 1974**
H.W. Casey / Richard Finch
Southern Music Publishing Co. Ltd. . . . . USA
George McRae . . . . **Jayboy BOY 85**

ROCK 'N' ROLL   **December 1981**
Francis Rossi / Bernard Frost
Eaton Music . . . . UK
Status Quo . . . . **Vertigo QUO 6**

ROCK 'N' ROLL LADY   **September 1974**
"Showaddywaddy"
Bailey Music Publishing . . . . UK
Showaddywaddy . . . . **Bell 1374**

ROCK-A-BEATIN' BOOGIE   **December 1954**
Bill Halley
Edward Kassner Music Co. Ltd. . . . . USA
Bill Haley & his Comets . . . . **Brunswick LAT 8117**

ROCK-A-BILLY   **May 1957**
Woody Harris / Eddie Deane
Joy Music Ltd. . . . . USA
Guy Mitchell . . . . **Philips BBL 7265**

ROCK-A-BYE YOUR BABY WITH A DIXIE MELODY   **1918**
Sam M. Lewis / Joe Young / Jean Schwartz
B. Feldman & Co. Ltd. . . . . USA
Show(s): . . . . Sinbad
Film(s):Show of Shows / Rose of Washington Square / The Jolson
Story / Jolson Sings Again
Al Jolson . . . . **Brunswick LAT 8267**
Judy Garland . . . . **Capitol EAP 20051**
Jerry Lewis . . . . **Brunswick LAT 8371**
Al Jolson appeared in *Sinbad* and *Rose of Washington Square*.

ROCK-A-DOODLE DOO   **July 1973**
Linda Lewis
Warner Brothers Music Ltd. . . . . UK
Linda Lewis . . . . **Raft RA 18502**

ROCK-A-HULA BABY   **March 1962**
Fred Wise / Dolores Fuller / Ben Wiseman
Belinda (London) Ltd. . . . . USA
Film(s): . . . . Blue Hawaii
Elvis Presley . . . . **RCA 1270**
Elvis Presley appeared in *Blue Hawaii*.

ROCKARIA   **March 1977**
Jeff Lynne
United Artists Music Co. Ltd . . . . UK
The Electric Light Orchestra . . . . **Jet UP 36209**

ROCKET   **August 1974**
Mike Chapman / Nicky Chinn

Chinnichap Music . . . . UK
Mud . . . . **Rak 178**

ROCKET MAN   **June 1972**
Elton John / Bernie Taupin
Dick James Music Ltd. . . . . UK
Elton John . . . . **DJM DJX 501**

ROCKIN' ALL OVER THE WORLD   **November 1977**
John Fogerty
Intersong Music . . . . USA
Status Quo . . . . **Vertigo 6059184**

ROCKIN' AROUND THE CHRISTMAS TREE   **December 1962**
Johnny Marks
Chappell & Co. Ltd . . . . USA
Brenda Lee . . . . **Brunswick 05880**
Mel Smith & Kim Wilde (1987) . . . . **Virgin TEN 2**

ROCKIN' CHAIR   **1931**
Hoagy Carmichael
Southern Music Publishing Co. Ltd. . . . . USA
Hoagy Carmichael & his Orchestra . . . . **HMV DLP 1106**
Hoagy Carmichael . . . . **Vogue VA 160112**
Jack Teagarden, Louis Armstrong
& The All Stars . . . . **RCA RCX 1007**

ROCKIN' GOOD WAY, A   **February 1984**
Brook Benton / Clyde Otis / Luchi Dejesus
Campbell, Connelly & Co. . . . . USA
Shaky & Bonnie
(Shakin' Stevens & Bonnie Tyler) . . . . **Epic A 4071**

ROCKIN' IN RHYTHM   **1931**
Duke Ellington / Harry Carney / Irving Mills
Lawrence Wright Music Co. Ltd . . . . USA
Duke Ellington & his Orchestra . . . . **Coral LRA 10027**
The Chris Barber Jazz Band . . . . **Pye NJL 17**

ROCKIN' OVER THE BEAT   **August 1990**
Manuela Kamosi / Jo Bogaert
Brothers Organisation . . . . Belgium
Technotronic . . . . **Swanyard SYR 14**

ROCKIN' ROBIN   **July 1972**
Jimmy Thomas
Carlin Music Corporation . . . . USA
Michael Jackson . . . . **Tamla Motown TMG 816**

ROCKIN' ROLL BABY   **February 1974**
Thomas Bell / Linda Creed
Gamble-Huff Music . . . . USA
The Stylistics . . . . **Avco 6105026**

ROCKIN' THROUGH THE RYE   **October 1956**
Bill Halley / Arret 'Rusty' Keefer
Chappell & Co. Ltd. . . . . USA
Bill Haley & his Comets . . . . **Brunswick LAT 8139**

ROCKING GOOSE   **December 1960**
T. King / J. Mack / T.J. Fowler
Vicki Music Ltd . . . . USA
Johnny & The Hurricanes . . . . **London HLX 9190**

ROCKIT   **August 1983**
Herbie Hancock / Bill Laswell / Michael Beinhorn
Carlin Music . . . . USA
Herbie Hancock . . . . **CBS A 3577**

ROCKSTEADY CREW, THE (See HEY YOU, THE ROCK-STEADY CREW)

RODRIGO'S CONCERTO (Aranjuez Mon Amour) **March 1976**
Joaquin Rodrigo
Critico Music Co. . . . . Spain
Manuel & The Music of the Mountains . . . . **EMI 2383**
An arrangement of the 2nd movement of "The Concerto for Guitar and Orchestra in D Major" by Joaquin Rodrigo (1901 -).

ROGUE SONG, THE   **1932**
Clifford Grey / Herbert Stothart
Francis, Day & Hunter Ltd. . . . . USA
Film(s): . . . . The Rogue Song
Lawrence Tibbett . . . . **HMV DA 1101**
Lawrence Tibbett appeared in *The Rogue Song.*

ROK DA HOUSE   **February 1988**
Debbie Pryce / Susan Banfield / Manda Glanfield, Paul Carter & Richard Walmsley
Virgin Music . . . . UK
The Beatmasters . . . . **Rhythm King LEFT 11**

ROLL ALONG COVERED WAGON   **1935**
Jimmy Kennedy
Peter Maurice Music Co. Ltd . . . . UK
Film(s): . . . . The Arizonians
The Hillbillies . . . . **Regal Zonophone Mr 1548**
Roy Fox & his Orchestra . . . . **Decca F 5391**

ROLL ALONG KENTUCKY MOON   **1933**
Bill Halley
Lawrence Wright Music Co. Ltd. USA
Debroy Somers & his Band, vocal Dan Donovan **Columbia CB 563**
Bonnie Guitar . . . . **London HAD 2122**

ROLL ALONG PRAIRIE MOON   **1935**
Ted Fiorito / Albert Von Tilzer / Harry MacPherson
Francis, Day & Hunter Ltd . . . . USA
Film(s): . . . . Here Comes the Band
Henry Allen & his Orchestra . . . . **Vocalion S 29**
Al Bowly . . . . **HMV BD 295**
Bonnie Guitar . . . . **London HA 2122**

ROLL AWAY CLOUDS   **1928**
Jack Waller / Joe Tunbridge
Chappell & Co. Ltd. . . . . UK
Show(s): . . . . Virginia
Paul Robeson & chorus . . . . **HMV C 1591**

ROLL AWAY THE STONE   **January 1973**
Ian Hunter
Island Music Ltd. . . . . UK
Mott the Hoople . . . . **CBS 1895**

ROLL ME OVER   **1944**
Desmond O'Connor
Peter Maurice Music Co. Ltd. . . . . UK
Billy Cotton & his Band . . . . **Decca F 9430**
Bob Cort . . . . **Decca LK 4301**

ROLL OVER BEETHOVEN   **March 1973**
Chuck Berry
Jewel Music Publishing Co. Ltd. USA
Electric Light Orchestra . . . . **Harvest HAR 5063**
Chuck Berry . . . . **London HLU 8428**
The Beatles . . . . **Parlophone PMC 1206**

ROLL OVER LAY DOWN   **June 1975**
Francis Rossi / Robert Young / Alan Lancaster / Rick Parfitt & John Coghlan
Valley Music . . . . UK
Status Quo . . . . **Vertigo QUO 13**

ROLLIN' HOME   **June 1986**
John David
Warner Brothers Music . . . . UK
Status Quo . . . . **Vertigo QUO 18**

ROLLING HOME   **1934**
Billy Hill / Peter De Rose
Campbell Connelly & Co. Ltd . . . . USA
Lew Stone & his Orchestra, vocal Al Bowlly . . . . . **Decca F 5172**

ROLLING ROUND THE WORLD   **1926**
Scott Sanders
Francis, Day & Hunter Ltd. . . . . UK
Donald Peers (1949) . . . . **HMV B 9817**
Eric Winstone Orchestra, vocal Les Howard . . . . **MGM 223**
Billy Cotton & his Band . . . . **Decca F 9182**
The Big Ben Banjo Band,
vocal Michael Sammes Singers . . . . . . **Columbia 33SX 1367**
Max Bygraves . . . . **Pye NPL 18151**

ROLLING STONE   **August 1975**
David Essex
April Music Ltd . . . . UK
David Essex . . . . **CBS 3425**

ROMANTICA   **June 1960**
Renato Rascel / Dino Verde
Peter Maurice Music Co. Ltd . . . . Italy
Aurelio Fierro . . . . **Durium TLU 97026**

ROMANY (Vivere) 1939
"Bixio" / Roma Campbell-Hunter
Peter Maurice Music Co. Ltd. .... Italy
Joe Loss & his Band .... **Regal Zonophone MR 2990**
Jack Harris & his Orchestra .... **HMV BD 5460**
Lew Stone & his Band .... **Decca F 7017**

ROMANY LIFE 1898
Harry B. Smith / Victor Herbert
B. Feldman & Co. .... USA
Show(s): .... The Fortune Teller
Jeanette MacDonald .... **HMV B 9550**
Andre Kostelanetz Orchestra .... **Philips BBL 7372**
Peter Yorke Orchestra .... **Brunswick LAT 8130**

ROMANY ROSE 1924
Horatio Nicholls
Lawrence Wright Music Co. Ltd .... UK
The Albany Dance Orchestra .... **HMV B 1745**

ROMEO August 1961
Robert Stolz / Jimmy Kennedy
Herman Darewski Music Publishing Co. Ltd. .... Germany
Petula Clark .... **Pye 7N 15361**
See also 'Salome'.

ROMEO March 1977
Edward Carter / Jeffrey Pain
EMI Music Ltd .... UK
Mr. Big .... **EMI 2567**

ROMEO AND JULIET February 1981
Mark Knopfler
Rondor Music .... UK
Dire Straits .... **Vertigo MOVIE 1**

RONDE DE L'AMOUR, LA September 1951
Oscar Straus / Louis Ducreaux / Harold Purcell
Cinephonic Music Co. Ltd .... France
Film(s): .... La Ronde
Anton Walbrook .... **Parlophone MSP 6002**
Teddy Johnson .... **Columbia DB 2914**
Vicky Autier .... **HMV CLP 1150**
The Mantovani Orchestra .... **Decca LK 4051**
Anton Walbrook appeared in *La Ronde*.

ROOM FIVE HUNDRED AND FOUR 1941
Eric Maschwitz / George Posford
Chappell & Co. Ltd .... UK
Binnie Hale .... **Columbia FB 2676**
Leslie Hutchinson (Hutch) .... **HMV BD 913**
Frank Barber & his Orchestra .... **Columbia 33SX 1200**

ROOM FULL OF ROSES, A October 1949
Tim Spencer
Rumbalero Ltd .... USA
Film(s): .... Mule Train
Dick Haymes .... **Brunswick 04254**
The Mills Brothers .... **Brunswick LAT 8235**

ROOM IN YOUR HEART November 1989
Marcus Vere / Richard Darbyshire / Albert Hammond
Warner Chappell Music .... UK
Living in a Box .... **Chrysalis LIB 7**
Ivor Novello Nomination.

ROOM WITH A VIEW 1928
Noel Coward
Chappell & Co. Ltd. .... UK
Show(s): .... This Year of Grace
Noel Coward .... **HMV B 2719**
Julie London .... **London HAU 2083**
Noel Coward .... **Philips BBL 7108**
Noel Coward appeared in the American production of *This Year of Grace*.

ROSALIE 1938
Cole Porter
Chappell & Co. Ltd .... USA
Film(s): .... Rosalie
Artie Shaw & his Orchestra, vocal Tony Pastor Camden CDN 127
Maurice Winnick & his Orchestra, vocal Al Bowlly .. **Decca F 6605**
Bing Crosby .... **Brunswick LA 8513**
Jimmy Rushing .... **Philips BBL 7252**
The Ray Conniff Singers & Orchestra ...... **Philips BBL 7354**

ROSANNA May 1983
David Paitch
April Music .... USA
Toto .... **CBS A 2079**

ROSARY, THE 1898
Ethelbert Nevin / Robert C. Rogers
Boosey & Hawkes Music Publishers Ltd. .... USA
Sir Charles Santley .... **Columbia 360**
Nelson Eddy .... **Camden CDN 157**
Perry Como .... **RCA RCX 161**

ROSE 1921
Frank Magine / Paul Biese / Arthur Sizemore
B. Feldman & Co. Ltd .... USA
F.W. Ramsey .... **Regal G 7641**
Wayne King &
his Orchestra .... **Brunswick LAT 8151**

ROSE GARDEN April 1971
Joe South
Chappell & Co. Ltd .... USA
Lynn Anderson .... **CBS 5360**
New World .... **Rak 111**
Joe South .... **Capitol E-T 108**

ROSE HAS TO DIE, A October 1978
Ben Findon
Heath Levy Music Ltd .... UK
The Dooleys .... **GTO GT 229**

ROSE I BRING YOU, THE February 1950
Tommie Connor / Michael Reine
Box & Cox (Publications) Ltd .... UK
Lee Lawrence .... **Decca F 9350**
Based on "Angels Serenade" by Gaetano Braga.

ROSE IN A GARDEN OF WEEDS, A November 1949
R.B. Saxe / Hubert W. David
Box & Cox (Publications) Ltd .... UK
Donald Peers .... **HMV B 9817**
The Five Smith Brothers .... **Parlophone R 3258**

ROSE IN HER HAIR, THE 1935
Al Dubin / Harry Warren
B. Feldman & Co. Ltd .... USA
Film(s): .... The Broadway Gondolier
Dick Powell .... **Decca F 5694**
Edmundo Ros & his Orchestra .... **Decca LK 4236**
Bing Crosby .... **MGM C 868**
Dick Powell appeared in *The Broadway Gondolier*.

ROSE IN THE BUD 1907
Dorothy Foster / P.J. Barrow
Chappell & Co. Ltd. .... UK
Eleanor Jones-Hudson .... **HMV 3791**
Harry Dawson & The Stargazers ...... **Decca F 9681**

ROSE MARIE 1925
Rudolf Frimi / Otto Harbach / Oscar Hammerstein II
Chappell & Co. Ltd. .... USA
Show(s): .... Rose Marie
Film(s): .... Rose Marie
Derek Oldham .... **Columbia 9038**
Nelson Eddy .... **RCA RCX 1051**
Howard Keel .... **MGM D 128**
Earl Wrightson .... **Philips BBL 7522**
Slim Whitman (1955) .... **London HL 8061**
Derek Oldham appeared in the British production of *Rose Marie*.
Nelson Eddy appeared in the 1936 film of *Rose Marie*.
Howard Keel appeared in the 1954 film of *Rose Marie*.

ROSE O'DAY 1942
Charles Tobias / Al Lewis
Chappell & Co. Ltd .... USA
Flanagan & Allen .... **Ace of Clubs ACL 1092**
Mel Tormé .... **Vogue LVA 9032**

ROSE OF ENGLAND 1938
Ivor Novello / Christopher Hassall
Chappell & Co. Ltd .... UK
Show(s): .... Crest of the Wave
Edgar Elmes .... **HMV B 8624**
Olive Gilbert .... **HMV C 3521**

Ivor Emmanuel .... HMV CLP 1258
Edgar Elmes & Olive Gilbert appeared in *Crest of the Wave.*

ROSE OF MY HEART   1911
Herman Lohr
Chappell & Co Ltd .... UK
Sydney Coltham .... HMV B 1646

ROSE OF THE RIO GRANDE   1923
Edgar Leslie / Harry Warren / Ross Gorman
Francis, Day & Hunter Ltd .... USA
The Virginans Orchestra,
conducted by Ross Gorman .... HMV B 1592
Eddie Condon & his Band,
vocal Jack Teagarden .... Brunswick LAT 8229

ROSE OF TRALEE, THE   1912
Charles Glover / Mordaunt Spencer
Keith Prowse Music Publishing Co. Ltd .... UK
Film(s): .... Song o' My Heart
William Thomas .... Regal G 6277
John McCormack .... Camden CDN 1002
Bing Crosby .... Brunswick LAT 8278
John McCormack appeared in *Song o' My Heart.*

ROSE OF WASHINGTON SQUARE   1920
Ballard MacDonald / James Hanley
B. Feldman & Co. Ltd .... USA
Show(s): .... The Ziegfeld's Midnight Frolics
Film(s): .... Rose of Washington Square
All Star Trio .... HMV B 1155
Bob Crosby & his Orchestra, vocal Bob Crosby .. Decca F 7128
Max Bygraves with Ted Heath & His Music .... Decca LK 4317
Alice Faye .... Reprise R 6029
Kaye Ballard .... MGM EP 700
Alice Faye appeared in *Rose of Washington Square.*

ROSE ROOM   1919
Harry Williams / Art Hickman
Herman Darewski Music Publishing Co. Ltd. .... USA
Film(s): .... Somebody Loves Me / The Strip
Prince's Band .... Columbia 767
Duke Ellington & his Orchestra .... Brunswick 01292
The Benny Goodman Sextet .... Fontana TFL 5067
Glenn Miller & his Orchestra .... RCA RD 27147
Louis Armstrong & his Orchestra ..... Brunswick LAT 8084
Louis Armstrong Orchestra appeared in *The Strip.*

ROSE ROSE I LOVE YOU (May Kway O May Kway) April 1951
Traditional, English Lyrics by Wilfred Thomas
Chappell & Co Ltd .... UK
Hue Lee (in Chinese) .... Columbia DB 2837
Frank Chacksfield & his Orchestra ...... Decca LK 4231
Benny Lee .... Decca F 9679
Frankie Laine .... Philips BBL 7263
Based on a traditional Chinese melody.

ROSE TATTOO, THE   January 1956
Harry Warren / Jack Brooks
Maddox Music Co. Ltd. .... USA
Perry Como .... Camden CDN 149
Helmut Zacharias & his Magic Violins ... Polydor LPHM 46346

ROSES   August 1986
Michael Leeson / Peter Vale
Chappell Music Co. .... UK
Haywoode .... CBS A 7224

ROSES ARE RED   September 1962
Al Byron / Paul Evans
Leeds Music Ltd .... USA
Ronnie Carroll .... Philips 326532 BF
Bobby Vinton .... Columbia DB 4878

ROSES ARE RED   July 1988
L.A. Reid / Kenny Edmonds
Warner Chappell Music .... USA
Macband .... MCA MCA 1264

ROSES FOR REMEMBRANCE   1927
Gus Kahn / Loyal Curtis
Campbell Connelly & Co. Ltd. .... USA
Maurice J. Gunsky .... Zonophone 5336

ROSES IN DECEMBER   1938
Herb Magidson / George Jessel / Ben Oakland
Chappell & Co. Ltd. .... USA
Film(s): .... Life of the Party
Dick Robertson & his Orchestra ...... Panachord 25953
Dick Powell .... Decca F 6569
Bunny Berigan & his Orchestra ...... HMV B 8680
Benny Carter & his Orchestra ..... London LTZT 15169

ROSES OF PICARDY   1916
Frederick E. Weatherly / Haydn Wood
Chappell & Co. Ltd. .... UK
Sydney Coltham .... Zonophone 1851
Al Jolson .... Brunswick LAT 8220
Perry Como .... Camden CDN 142
Vince Hill (1967) .... Columbia DB 8185

ROSES REMIND ME OF YOU   1926
Benny Davis / Joe Burke / Al Sherman
Francis, Day & Hunter Ltd. .... USA
The Savoy Orpheans .... HMV B 5104
Sy Oliver & his Orchestra ..... Brunswick LAT 8302

ROSETTA   1933
Earl Hines
Chappell & Co. Ltd. .... USA
Earl Hines & his Orchestra, vocal Earl Hines . Brunswick 01559
The Earl Hines Quartet .... MGM C 833
Ray Charles .... HMV CLP 1449

ROSETTA   May 1971
Mike Snow
St. George Music Ltd .... UK
Georgie Fame & Alan Price .... CBS S 7108
Ivor Novello Nomination.

ROSEWOOD SPINET, A   April 1949
Charles Tobias / Nat Simon
Dash Music Ltd .... USA
Dick Haymes .... Brunswick 04061
Joe Loss & his Orchestra, vocal Howard Jones . HMV BD 6041
Kate Smith .... MGM 193

ROSIE   April 1968
Don Partridge
Essex Music Ltd. .... UK
Don Partridge .... Columbia DB 8330
Ivor Novello Nomination.

ROSIE (Make It Rosy For Me)   1921
Grant Clarke / J.L. Merkur
B. Feldman & Co. Ltd .... USA
Paul Whiteman & his Orchestra ...... HMV B 1214

ROSITA, LA   1924
Paul Dupont / Allan Stuart
Sam Fox Publishing Co.(London) Ltd. .... USA
The International Novelty Orchestra ...... HMV B 1772
The Four Aces .... Brunswick LA 8614
Mel Tormé .... HMV CLP 1315

ROULETTE   July 1959
Trevor Stanford
Mills Music Ltd .... UK
Russ Conway (piano) .... Columbia DB 4298

ROUND AND ROUND   June 1957
Lou Stallman / Joe Shapiro
Rush Music Ltd. .... USA
Perry Como .... RCA RD 27

ROUND AND ROUND   December 1984
Gary Kemp
Reformation Music .... UK
Spandau Ballet .... Chrysalis SPAN 6

ROUND AND ROUND   July 1985
Derek Bramble
D.J.A. Publishing .... UK
Jaki Graham .... EMI JAKI 4

ROUND THE BEND OF THE ROAD   1932
Sam M. Lewis / John Klenner
B. Feldman & Co. Ltd. .... USA
Paul Robeson .... HMV B 4352

'ROUND THE MARBLE ARCH   **1932**
Noel Gay / Ralph Butler
Francis, Day & Hunter Ltd. .... UK
Henry Hall & his Orchestra,
vocal The Coronets .... **Columbia 33SX 1067**
Ambrose & his Orchestra .... **HMV B 6179**

ROUTE SIXTY-SIX   **1947**
Bobby Troup
Chappell & Co. Ltd. .... USA
Bing Crosby & The Andrews Sisters .... **Brunswick 04132**
Perry Como .... **RCA RD 27133**
Nat King Cole Trio .... **Capitol LCT 6133**
The Four Freshmen .... **Capitol T 1295**

ROVING KIND, THE   **March 1951**
Jessie Cavanaugh / Arnold Stanton
Leeds Music Ltd .... USA
Film(s): ....Disc Jockey
Guy Mitchell .... **Philips BBL 7265**
The Wilcox Three .... **Camden CDN 158**

ROW, ROW, ROW   **1912**
Jimmy Monaco / William Jerome
Francis, Day & Hunter Ltd. .... USA
Show(s): ....The Ziegfeld Follies of 1912
Film(s): .... Incendiary Blonde / Two Weeks with Love /
Eddie Foy and the Seven Little Foys
The Metropolitan Band .... **HMV B 193**
Bing Crosby .... **Brunswick 04947**
Carleton Carpenter & Debbie Reynolds .... **MGM EP 633**
Bob Hope .... **HMV DLP 1088**
Carleton Carpenter & Debbie Reynolds appeared in *Two Weeks with Love.*
Bob Hope appeared in *Eddie Foy and the Seven Little Foys.*

ROXANNE   **May 1979**
"Sting"
Virgin Music (Publishers) Ltd .... UK
The Police .... **A&M AMS 7348**

ROYAL EVENT   **March 1960**
Trevor Stanford
Noel Gay Music Co. Ltd .... UK
Russ Conway .... **Columbia DB 4418**

ROYAL GARDEN BLUES   **1919**
Spencer Williams / Clarence Williams
Francis, Day & Hunter Ltd .... USA
Film(s): .... Jazz Dance / Drum Crazy
The Original Dixieland Jazz Band, vocal Al Bernard   **HMV B 8500**
The Wolverines Orchestra .... **Riverside RLP 12-123**
Ted Lewis & his Band, vocal Fats Waller ... **Philips BBE 12106**
George Chisholm & The Tradsters .... **Philips BBL 7461**
Gene Krupa & his Orchestra .... **HMV CLP 1352**
Gene Krupa & his Orchestra appeared in *Drum Crazy.*

RUBBER BALL   **February 1961**
Anne Orlowski / Aaron Schroeder
B. Feldman & Co. Ltd .... USA
Bobby Vee .... **London HL 9255**
Marty Wilde .... **Philips PB 1101**
The Avons .... **Columbia DB 4569**

RUBBER BAND MAN, THE   **November 1976**
Linda Creed / Thomas Bell
Carlin Music Corporation .... USA
The Detroit Spinners .... **Atlantic K 10807**

RUBBER BULLETS   **July 1973**
Kevin Godley / Lol Creme / Graham Gouldman
St. Annes Music Ltd. .... UK
10 CC .... **UK 36**
Ivor Novello Award.

RUBY   **September 1953**
Heinz Roemheld / Mitchell Parish
Leo Feist Music Ltd. .... USA
Film(s): .... Ruby Gentry
Victor Young Orchestra .... **Brunswick 05110**
Max Geldray (harmonica) .... **Columbia DB 3301**
Ethel Smith (organ) .... **Brunswick 05145**
Les Baxter Orchestra .... **Capitol CL 13933**

RUBY (Don't Take Your Love To Town)   **December 1969**
Mel Tillis
Southern Music Publishing Co. Ltd .... USA
Kenny Rogers & The First Edition .... **Reprise RS 20829**
Roger Miller .... **Philips BL 7822**

RUBY TUESDAY   **February 1967**
Mick Jagger / Keith Richard
Mirage Music Ltd .... UK
The Rolling Stones .... **Decca F 12546**
Melanie (1970) .... **Buddah 2011038**

RUDOLPH THE RED NOSED REINDEER   **November 1950**
Johnny Marks
Chappell & Co. Ltd .... USA
Gene Autry .... **Columbia FB 3576**
Perry Como .... **RCA RD 27082**
Pinky & Perky .... **Columbia SEG 8122**

RUDY - A MESSAGE TO YOU   **November 1979**
Robert Thompson
Chappell & Co. Ltd .... UK
The Specials .... **2-Tone CHSTT 5**

RUM AND COCA-COLA   **1945**
Morey Amsterdam / Jeri Sullivan / Paul Baron
Francis, Day & Hunter Ltd. .... USA
The Andrews Sisters .... **Brunswick OE 9426**
The Andrews Sisters .... **Capitol LCT 6132**

RUMOURS ARE FLYING   **1947**
Bennie Benjamin / George Weiss
Francis, Day & Hunter Ltd. .... USA
The Andrews Sisters .... **Brunswick LAT 8369**
Issy Bonn .... **Decca F 8707**

RUN BABY RUN   **December 1971**
Joe Melson / Donald Grant
Acuff-Rose Publishing Co. Ltd .... USA
The Newbeats .... **London HLE 10341**

RUN FOR HOME   **July 1978**
Alan Hull
Crazy Music Ltd. .... UK
Lindisfarne .... **Mercury 6007177**

RUN LITTLE RAINDROP RUN   **1943**
Mack Gordon / Harry Warren
Sun Music Publishing Co. Ltd .... USA
Film(s): .... Springtime in the Rockies
Guy Lombardo &
his Royal Canadians .... **Brunswick 03445**

RUN RABBIT RUN   **1939**
Noel Gay / Ralph Butler
Noel Gay Music Co. Ltd. .... UK
Film(s): .... The Little Dog Laughed
Flanagan & Allen .... **Decca LF 1125**
Billy Cotton & his Band .... **Rex 9633**
The Cliff Adams Singers .... **Columbia 33SX 1362**
Flanagan & Allen appeared in *The Little Dog Laughed.*

RUN RUN AWAY   **March 1984**
Neville Holder / James Lee
Wild John Music .... UK
Slade .... **RCA 385**

RUN RUN RUN   **May 1972**
Jay Feruson / Matthew Andes
Rondor Music (London) Ltd .... USA
Jo Jo Gunne .... **Asylum AYM 501**

RUN TO HIM   **February 1962**
Gerry Goffin / Jack Keller
Aldon Music Ltd. .... USA
Bobby Vee .... **London HL 9470**
Little Eva .... **London HAU 8036**

RUN TO ME   **September 1972**
Robin Gibb / Maurice Gibb / Barry Gibb
Abigail Music .... UK
The Bee Gees .... **Polydor 2058255**

RUN TO THE HILLS   **March 1982**
Stephen Harris

Zomba Music .... UK
Iron Maiden .... **EMI 5263**

RUN TO YOU   **February 1985**
Bryan Adams / Jim Vallance
Rondor Music .... Canada
Bryan Adams .... **A&M AM 224**

RUNAROUND SUE   **December 1961**
Dion Di Mucci / Ernest Maresca
Dominion Music Co. Ltd. .... USA
Dion .... **Top Rank JAR 586**
Doug Sheldon .... **Decca F 11398**
Chubby Checker .... **Columbia 33SX 1445**
Racey (1980) .... **RAK 325**

RUNAWAY   **July 1961**
Del Shannon / Max Crook
Vicki Music Ltd. .... USA
Del Shannon .... **London HL 9317**
The Hunters .... **Fontana TFL 5175**

RUNAWAY BOYS   **January 1981**
Brian Setzer / James McDonnell
Zomba Music .... UK
Stray Cats .... **Arista SCAT 1**

RUNAWAY TRAIN, THE   **1931**
Carson Robison / R.E. Massey
B. Feldman & Co. .... USA
Vernon Dalhart .... **Regal MR 346**
Michael Holliday .... **Columbia DB 3813**
Bryan Chalker .... **Chapter One CMS 1020**

RUNNER, THE   **April 1979**
Sheila Fergus / Giorgio Moroder
Heath Levy Music Ltd. .... USA
The Three Degrees .... **Ariola ARO 154**

RUNNIN' WILD   **1923**
Joseph Grey / A. Harrington-Gibbs / Leo Wood
Francis, Day & Hunter Ltd .... USA
Film(s): ...... Running Wild / Some Like it Hot / The Five Pennies
The Great White Way Orchestra ...... **HMV B 1673**
Norah Blaney & Gwen Farrar .... **HMV BD 254**
The Benny Goodman Quartet .... **HMV B 8568**
Marilyn Monroe .... **London HAT 2176**
Red Nichols & his Five Pennies .... **London HAT 2189**
Sid Philips & his Band .... **HMV CLP 1198**
Marilyn Monroe appeared in *Some Like It Hot*.
Red Nichols' Five Pennies appeared in *The Five Pennies*.

RUNNING BEAR   **March 1960**
J. P. Richardson
Southern Music Co. Ltd .... USA
Johnny Preston .... **Mercury MMC 14051**
Pat Boone .... **London HAD 2354**

RUNNING IN THE FAMILY   **March 1987**
Mark King / Wally Badarou / Roland Gould
Island Music .... UK
Level 42 .... **Polydor POSP 842**

RUNNING SCARED   **June 1961**
Roy Orbison / Joe Melson
Acuff-Rose Publishing Co. Ltd .... USA
Roy Orbison .... **London HLU 9342**

RUNNING UP THAT HILL   **August 1985**
Kate Bush
EMI Music .... UK
Kate Bush .... **EMI KB 1**
Ivor Novello Nomination.

RUNNING WITH THE NIGHT   **January 1984**
Lionel Richie / Cynthia Weil
Warner Brothers Music .... USA
Lionel Richie .... **Motown TMG 1324**

RUPERT   **February 1971**
Ronald Roker / Frank Weston
ATV Music Ltd .... UK
Jackie Lee .... **Pye 7N 45003**

RUSH HOUR   **September 1988**
Jane Wiedlin / Peter Rafelson
B.M.G. Music .... USA
Jane Wiedlin .... **Manhattan MT 36**

RUSSIAN LULLABY   **1927**
Irving Berlin
Francis, Day & Hunter Ltd. .... USA
Film(s): .... Blue Skies
Harold Leonard's Waldorf Astoria Orchestra .. **Columbia 4602**
The Mantovani Orchestra .... **Decca LF 1259**

RUSSIAN RAG   **1918**
George L. Cobb
Francis, Day & Hunter Ltd. .... USA
The Mayfair Dance Orchestra .... **HMV C 924**
Sid Philips & his Band .... **HMV 7EG 8425**
Based on 'Prelude in C sharp minor' by Serge Rachmaninoff (1873-1943).

S'POSIN'   **1929**
Paul Denniker / Andy Razaf
Lawrence Wright Music Co. Ltd .... USA
Paul Whiteman & his Orchestra,
  vocal Bing Crosby .... **Columbia 5520**
Bing Crosby .... **Brunswick LA 8514**
Debbie Reynolds .... **London HAD 2200**

S'WONDERFUL   **1928**
George Gershwin / Ira Gershwin
Chappell & Co. Ltd .... USA
Show(s): .... Funny Face
Film(s): Rhapsody in Blue / An American in Paris / Starlift / Funny Face
Adele Astaire & Bernard Clifton .... **Columbia 5175**
Gene Kelly & George Guetary .... **MGM C 789**
Fred Astaire & Audrey Hepburn .... **HMV CLP 1119**
Adele Astaire appeared in both the American and British productions
of *Funny Face*.
Bernard Clifton appeared in the British production of *Funny Face*.
Gene Kelly & George Guetary appeared in *An American In Paris*.
Audrey Hepburn appeared in the film *Funny Face*.
Fred Astaire appeared in both the American and British productions
and the film of *Funny Face*.

S-S-S-SINGLE BED   **May 1976**
Kenny Young
Chrysalis Music Ltd .... USA
Fox .... **GTO GT 57**

S.O.S.   **October 1975**
Benny Andersson / Bjorn Ulvaeus / Stig Anderson
Bocu Music Ltd .... Sweden
Abba .... **Epic EPC 3576**

SABRE DANCE   **August 1948**
Allan Roberts / Lester Lee
Leeds Music Ltd. .... USA
The Andrews Sisters .... **Brunswick 03916**
Freddy Martin & his Orchestra .... **HMV B 9683**
The Love Sculpture (1969) .... **Parlophone R 5744**
Adapted from 'Gayaneh Ballet' by Aram Khachaturian (1903 - 1978).

SACRIFICE   **July 1990**
Bernie Taupin / Elton John
Big Pig Music .... UK
Elton John .... **Rocket EJS 22**
Ivor Novello Award.

SAD SONGS (SAY SO MUCH)   **June 1984**
Elton John / Bernie Taupin
Big Pig Music .... UK
Elton John .... **Rocket PH 7**

SAD SWEET DREAMER   **October 1974**
Desmond Parton
Mr & Mrs Music .... UK
Sweet Sensation .... **Pye 7N 45385**
Ivor Novello Nomination.

SADDLE UP   **September 1982**
Jack Robinson / James Bolden
Warner Chappell Music .... France
David Christie .... **K.R. 9**

SADDLE YOUR BLUES TO A WILD MUSTANG   **1936**
George Whiting / Buddy Bernier / Billy Haid

Peter Maurice Music Co. Ltd . . . . USA
Bob Mallin . . . . **Decca F 5969**
The Rocky Mountaineers . . . . **Columbia FB 1348**

SADIE'S SHAWL   **August 1956**
Nico Carsten / Sam Lorraine
John Fields Music Co. Ltd. . . . . South Africa
Frank Cordell & his Orchestra . . . . **HMV POP 229**
Bob Sharples & his Orchestra . . . . **Decca F 10748**

SAFETY DANCE   **November 1983**
Ivan Doroschuk
Tactic Music . . . . Canada
Men Without Hats . . . . **Statik TAK 1**

SAHARA   **1924**
Horatio Nicholls / Jean Frederick
Lawrence Wright Music Co. Ltd. . . . . UK
Jack Hylton & his Orchestra, vocal Jack Hylton . . **HMV B 1925**

SAIL ALONG SILVERY MOON   **1938**
Percy Wenrich / Harry Tobias
Cinephonic Music Co. Ltd. . . . . USA
Bing Crosby . . . . **Brunswick LAT 8334**
Andy Williams . . . . **London HAA 2203**

SAIL ON   **October 1979**
Lionel Richie
Jobete Music (UK) Ltd. . . . . USA
The Commodores . . . . **Motown TMG 1155**

SAILING   **September 1975**
Gavin Sutherland
Island Music Ltd . . . . UK
Rod Stewart . . . . **Warner Brothers K 16600**
Rod Stewart (1976) . . . . **Warner Brothers K 16600**
Ivor Novello Nomination.

SAILING DOWN CHESAPEAKE BAY   **1913**
Jean Havez / George Botsford
Francis, Day & Hunter Ltd. . . . . USA
Ella Retford . . . . **Jumbo 1109**
Bing Crosby . . . . **Ace of Hearts AH 164**
Des O'Connor . . . . **Columbia DB 4011**

SAILOR (Seeman Deine Heimat Ist Das Meer) **February 1961**
Fini Busch / Werner Scharfenberger / David West
Leeds Music Ltd . . . . Austria
Petula Clark . . . . **Pye 7N 15314**
Anne Shelton . . . . **Philips PB 1096**

SAILOR WHO ARE YOU DREAMING OF TONIGHT   **1944**
Stanley Damerell / Reg Butler / Tolchard Evans
Lawrence Wright Music Co. Ltd. . . . . UK
Billy Cotton & his Band . . . . **Rex 10193**

SAILOR WITH THE NAVY BLUE EYES, THE   **1940**
Irving Taylor / Vic Mizzy / Al Hoffman
Campbell Connelly & Co. Ltd . . . . USA
The King Sisters . . . . **Regal Zonophone MR 3350**
Ambrose & his Orchestra, vocal Sam Browne . . **Decca F 8115**

SAINT JAMES' INFIRMARY   **1935**
Joe Primrose
Lawrence Wright Music Co. Ltd . . . . USA
Show(s): . . . . Blackbirds of 1934
Film(s): . . . . The Birth of the Blues
Louis Armstrong & his Savoy
Ballroom Five, vocal Louis Armstrong . . **Parlophone PMC 1150**
Jack Teagarden & his Orchestra,
vocal Jack Teagarden . . . . **Brunswick 03264**
Jack Teagarden . . . . **Saga XIC 4005**
Jack Teagarden appeared in *The Birth of the Blues*.

SAINT LOUIS BLUES   **1914**
William C. Handy
Francis, Day & Hunter Ltd. . . . . USA
Film(s):Saint Louis Blues / Is Everybody Happy / The Birth of the Blues
Bessie Smith . . . . **Philips BBL 7019**
Bessie Smith . . . . **Riverside RLP 12-121**
Ciro's Club Coon Orchestra . . . . **Columbia 699**
Ted Lewis & his Orchestra . . . . **Brunswick 02715**
Nat 'King' Cole . . . . **Capitol LCT 6156**
Bing Crosby . . . . **Columbia DX 898**
Louis Armstrong & his Orchestra . . . . **Parlophone R 618**

Bessie Smith appeared in the 1928 film of *Saint Louis Blues*.
Ted Lewis appeared in both 1929 and 1943 films of *Is Everybody Happy*.
Nat 'King' Cole appeared in the 1958 film of *Saint Louis Blues*.

SAINT MARY'S IN THE TWILIGHT   **1941**
Jimmy Kennedy
Campbell Connelly & Co. Ltd . . . . UK
Anne Shelton . . . . **Rex 10040**

SAINT THERESE OF THE ROSES   **November 1956**
Art Strauss / Remus Harris
Dash Music Ltd. . . . . USA
Malcolm Vaughan . . . . **HMV 7EG 8272**

SAINTS ROCK AND ROLL   **June 1956**
Bill Haley / Luther Presley
Leeds Music . . . . USA
Bill Haley & his Comets . . . . **Brunswick 05565**

SALLY   **1931**
Will Haines / Harry Leon / Leo Towers
Keith Prowse Music Publishing Co. Ltd. . . . . UK
Film(s): . . . . Sally in Our Alley
Gracie Fields . . . . **HMV 7EG 8071**
Eileen Donaghy . . . . **Fontana TFL 5144**
Gerry Monroe (1970) . . . . **Chapter One CH 122**
Gracie Fields appeared in *Sally in Our Alley*.
Theme song of Gracie Fields.

SALLY, YOU BROUGHT THE SUNSHINE TO OUR ALLEY   **1922**
Wynn Stanley / Andrew Allen
Lawrence Wright Music Co. Ltd . . . . UK
Victor Vorzanger's Broadway Band . . . . **Scala 536**

SALOME   **1921**
Robert Stolz
Herman Darewski Music Publishing Co. Ltd . . . . Germany
The 'Queens' Dance Orchestra . . . . **HMV B 1259**
Willy Mattes & Chorus (in German) . . . . . . **Columbia SEG 7680**
Robert Stoltz & The Zurich Tonhalle Orchestra . **Decca LK 4013**

SAM   **July 1977**
John Farrar / Hank Marvin / Don Black
Rondor Music (London) Ltd . . . . UK
Olivia Newton-John . . . . **EMI 2616**
Ivor Novello Nomination.

SAM THE OLD ACCORDION MAN   **1927**
Walter Donaldson
Francis, Day & Hunter Ltd. . . . . USA
Film(s): . . . . . . Glorifying the American Girl / Love Me or Leave Me
Jack Hylton & his Orchestra . . . . **HMV B 5236**
Doris Day . . . . **Philips BBL 7047**
Doris Day appeared in *Love Me or Leave Me*.

SAM YOU MADE THE PANTS TOO LONG   **1941**
Sam Lewis / Victor Young / Fred Whitehouse & Milton Berle
Campbell Connelly & Co. . . . . USA
Barbra Streisand . . . . **CBS BPG 62675**
Parody of 'Lord You Made the Night Too Long'.

SAM'S SONG   **July 1950**
Lew Quadling / Jack Elliott
Sterling Music Publishing Ltd . . . . USA
Bing & Gary Crosby . . . . **Brunswick LAT 8051**
The Big Ben Banjo Band . . . . **Columbia 33SX 1367**

SAME THING, THE   **November 1990**
Richard Howells / Ellen Shipley
Virgin Music . . . . USA
Belinda Carlisle . . . . **Virgin VS 1291**

SAN   **1921**
Lindsay McPhail / Walter Michels
Herman Darewski Music Publishing Co. Ltd . . . . USA
The Benson Orchestra of Chicago . . . . **HMV B 1271**
Paul Whiteman & his Orchestra . . . . **RCA RD 27225**
Frank Chacksfield & his Orchestra . . . . **Decca LK 4231**
The Kid Ory - Red Allen Group . . . . **HMV CLP 1422**

SAN ANTONIO ROSE   **1941**
Bob Wills
Victoria Music Co. Ltd . . . . USA
Film(s): . . . . San Antonio Rose

Bing Crosby . . . . Brunswick OE 9424
Pat Boone . . . . London HAD 2265

SAN BERNADINO November 1970
Christie'
Christabel Music . . . . UK
Christie . . . . **CBS 5169**

SAN FERNANDO VALLEY 1944
Gordon Jenkins
Chappell & Co. Ltd. . . . . USA
Film(s): . . . . San Fernando Valley
Roy Rogers . . . . **Regal Zonophone MR 3807**
Ambrose & his Orchestra, vocal Anne Shelton . . **Decca F 8465**
Bing Crosby . . . . **Brunswick LAT 8055**
Roy Rogers appeared in *San Fernando Valley*.

SAN FRANCISCAN NIGHTS November 1967
Eric Burdon / Vic Briggs / John Weider, Barry Jenkins & Danny McCulloch
Aaron Schroeder Music . . . . USA
Eric Burdon . . . . **MGM 1359**

SAN FRANCISCO 1936
Bronislaw Kaper / Gus Kahn / Walter Jurmann
Francis, Day & Hunter Ltd . . . . USA
Film(s): . . . . San Francisco
Jeanette MacDonald . . . . **RCA RCX 1051**
Ben Bernie & his Orchestra, vocal Billy Wilson . **Brunswick 02278**
Judy Garland . . . . **Capitol WBO 1569**
Jeanette MacDonald appeared in *San Francisco*.

SAN FRANCISCO September 1967
John Phillips
Dick James Music Ltd. . . . . USA
Scott McKenzie . . . . **CBS 2816**

SANCTIFY YOURSELF March 1986
"Simple Minds"
EMI Music . . . . UK
Simple Minds . . . . **Virgin SM 1**

SANCTUARY 1919
Edward Lockton / Thomas Hewitt
Keith Prowse Music Ltd. . . . . UK
Essie Ackland . . . . **HMV B 8512**
Rosa Ponselle . . . . **V.A. 67**

SAND DUNES 1919
Byron Gay
Francis, Day & Hunter Ltd. . . . . USA
The Mayfair Dance Orchestra . . . . **HMV C 923**

SAND IN MY SHOES 1941
Victor Schertzinger / Frank Loesser
Victoria Music Co. Ltd . . . . USA
Film(s): . . . . Kiss The Boys Goodbye
Connee Boswell . . . . **Brunswick 03239**
Leslie Hutchinson (Hutch) . . . . **HMV BD 992**
Bobby Short . . . . **London HAK 2123**
Connee Boswell appeared in *Kiss the Boys Goodbye*.

SANDY November 1978
Louis St. Louis / Scott Simon
Famous-Chappell . . . . USA
Film(s): . . . . Grease
John Travolta . . . . **RSO 2479-210**
John Travolta appeared in *Grease*.

SANTA BRING MY BABY BACK TO ME December 1957
Aaron Schroeder / Claud Demetrius
Belinda Music Ltd. . . . . USA
Elvis Presley . . . . **RCA 1025**

SANTA CLAUS IS COMING TO TOWN 1934
Haven Gillespie / J. Fred Coots
Francis, Day & Hunter Ltd . . . . USA
Harry Reser & his Orchestra . . . . **Decca F 5324**
Bing Crosby & The Andrews Sisters . . . . . **Brunswick LA 8686**
Pat Boone . . . . **London RED 1128**
Bruce Springsteen (1985) . . . . **CBS A 6773**

SANTO NATALE December 1954
Belle Nardone / Al Hoffman / Dick Manning
Larry Spier Ltd. . . . . USA

David Whitfield . . . . Decca DFE 6408
Johnny Desmond . . . . Coral LVA 9137

SARAWAKI 1935
Val Gordon
Peter Maurice Music Co. Ltd . . . . UK
Harry Roy & his Orchestra . . . . **Parlophone R 2013**
The Coronets . . . . **Columbia 33SX 1124**

SARIE MARAIS 1945
Traditional arranged by Reg Owen & Garfield De Mortimer
Berry Music Ltd. . . . . South Africa
Anne Shelton . . . . **Decca F 8510**
Eve Boswell . . . . **Parlophone PMD 1039**

SATISFACTION September 1965
Mick Jagger / Keith Richards
Mirage Music Ltd . . . . UK
The Rolling Stones . . . . **Decca F 12220**

SATURDAY January 1986
James Harris / Terry Lewis
CBS Songs . . . . USA
Cherrelle with Alexander O'Neal . . . . **Tabu A 6829**

SATURDAY NIGHT AT THE MOVIES June 1972
Barry Mann / Cynthia Weill
Screen Gems Music Ltd. . . . . USA
The Drifters . . . . **Atlantic K 10148**

SATURDAY NIGHT IS THE LONELIEST NIGHT OF THE WEEK 1945
Sammy Cahn / Jule Styne
Chappell & Co. Ltd. . . . . USA
Frank Sinatra . . . . **Fontana TFL 5074**
Frank Sinatra . . . . **Capitol LCT 6179**

SATURDAY NIGHT'S ALRIGHT FOR FIGHTING August 1973
Elton John / Bernie Taupin
Dick James Music Ltd. . . . . UK
Elton John . . . . **DJM DJX 502**

SATURDAY RAG April 1952
John Jerome / Hal Biddy
John Fields Music . . . . UK
The Five Smiths Brothers . . . . **Parlophone R 3522**
The Tanner Sisters . . . . **HMV B 10215**
Les Howard & The Stargazers . . . . **Decca F 9875**

SAVAGE, THE November 1961
Norrie Paramor
Harms-Whitmark Ltd. . . . . UK
Film(s): . . . . The Young Ones
The Shadows . . . . **Columbia DB 4726**
The Shadows appeared in *The Young Ones*.

SAVE A PRAYER September 1982
"Duran Duran"
Carlin Music . . . . UK
Duran Duran . . . . **EMI 5327**

SAVE ME January 1967
Ken Howard / Alan Blaikley
Lynn Music Ltd. . . . . UK
Dave Dee, Dozy, Beaky, Mick & Tich . . . . **Fontana TF 775**

SAVE THE LAST DANCE FOR ME December 1960
Doc Pomus / Mort Shuman
Manor Music Co. Ltd . . . . USA
The Drifters . . . . **London REK 1282**
Dion . . . . **HMV 7EG 8745**

SAVE YOUR KISSES FOR ME May 1976
Tony Hiller / Martin Lee / Lee Sheridan
A.T.V. Music Ltd. . . . . UK
Brotherhood of Man . . . . **Pye 7N 45569**
United Kingdom entry for the 1976 Eurovision Song Contest (Placed First).
Ivor Novello Award.

SAVE YOUR LOVE December 1982
John Edwards / Susanne Edwards
Hollywood Music . . . . UK
Renee & Renato . . . . **Hollywood HWD 003**

SAVE YOUR SORROW FOR TOMORROW 1925
Al Sherman / Buddy De Sylva
Lawrence Wright Music Co. Ltd. .... USA
The New Princes Toronto Band .... Columbia 3786
Bing Crosby .... Brunswick 04748
The Mary Kaye Trio .... Brunswick LAT 8293

SAVED BY THE BELL August 1969
Robin Gibb
Saharet Music .... UK
Robin Gibb .... Polydor 56337

SAVING ALL MY LOVE FOR YOU December 1985
Michael Masser / Gerry Goffin
Warner Brothers Music .... USA
Whitney Houston .... Arista ARIST 640

SAW MILL RIVER ROAD, THE 1923
Harry Tierney / Joseph McCarthy
Francis, Day & Hunter Ltd .... USA
Show(s): .... Glory
The Great White Way Orchestra .... HMV B 1695

SAY A LITTLE PRAYER December 1988
Burt Bacharach / Hal David
MCA Music .... USA
Bomb the Bass featuring Maureen ..... Rhythm King DOOD 3

SAY A PRAYER FOR THE BOYS OVER THERE 1944
Herb Magidson / Jimmy McHugh
Southern Music Publishing Co. Ltd. .... USA
Film(s): .... Hers to Hold
Deanna Durbin .... Brunswick 03500
Deanna Durbin appeared in Hers to Hold.
Nominated for an Academy Award 1943.

SAY 'AU REVOIR' BUT NOT 'GOODBYE' 1893
Harry Kennedy
.... USA
John McCormack .... Ember GVC 51

SAY, HAS ANYBODY SEEN MY SWEET GYPSY ROSE September 1973
Irwin Levine / L. Russell Brown
Schroeder Music Ltd. .... USA
Dawn .... Bell 1322

SAY HELLO, WAVE GOODBYE February 1982
Marc Almond / David Ball
Warner Brothers Music .... UK
Soft Cell .... Phonogram BZ 57

SAY I WON'T BE THERE May 1963
Tom Springfield
Chappell & Co Ltd .... UK
The Springfields .... Philips 326577 BF

SAY I'M YOUR NUMBER ONE August 1985
Mike Stock / Matt Aitken / Peter Waterman
All Boys Music .... UK
Princess .... Supreme SUPE 101

SAY IT 1940
Frank Loesser / Jimmy McHugh
Victoria Music Co. Ltd .... USA
Film(s): .... Buck Benny Rides Again
Frances Langford .... Brunswick 03022
Tommy Dorsey & his Orchestra, vocal Frank Sinatra RCA RD 27069

SAY IT AGAIN 1926
Harry Richman / Abner Silver
Francis, Day & Hunter Ltd. .... USA
Jack Smith .... HMV B 2319
Margareta Kjelberg .... Decca LM 4545

SAY IT AGAIN February 1988
Bunny Siegler / Carol Davis
SBK Songs .... USA
Jermaine Stewart .... 10 TEN 188

SAY IT ISN'T SO 1933
Irving Berlin
Francis, Day & Hunter Ltd. .... USA
Rudy Vallee .... Columbia CB 524
Pat Boone .... London HAD 2082

Julie London .... London HAU 2005
Perry Como .... RCA RD 27032

SAY IT WHILE DANCING 1923
Benny Davis / Abner Silver
B. Feldman & Co. Ltd .... USA
The Benson Orchestra of Chicago .... HMV B 1654
The Ballyhooligans .... HMV BD 5198

SAY IT WITH A UKULELE 1924
Art Conrad
B. Feldman & Co. Ltd. .... USA
Show(s): ....Leap Year
The Romaine Orchestra .... HMV B 1792

SAY IT WITH MUSIC 1922
Irving Berlin
Francis, Day & Hunter Ltd .... USA
Show(s): .... The Music Box Revue / Mayfair and Montmartre
Film(s): .... Alexander's Ragtime Band
Paul Whiteman & his Orchestra .... HMV B 1306
Jane Morgan .... London HAR 2136
Jack Payne & his Orchestra .... HMV CLP 1160
Theme song of Jack Payne.

SAY NOT LOVE IS A DREAM 1911
Franz Lehar / Basil Hood / Adrian Ross
Chappell & Co Ltd. .... Austria
Show(s): ....The Count of Luxembourg
Elsie Fox-Bennett & Philip Cummings .... Jumbo 636
Orchestre Mascotte .... Parlophone R 2592
Anne Ziegler .... HMV C 4125
Mantovani & his Orchestra .... Decca LK 4347
Lisa Della Casa .... Decca LM 4520

SAY SAY SAY November 1983
Paul McCartney / Michael Jackson
M.P.L. Music .... UK
Paul McCartney & Michael Jackson ...... Parlophone R 6062

SAY "SI SI" (Para Vigo Me Voy) 1937
Ernesto Lecuona / Francia Luban / Al Stillman
Lawrence Wright Music Co. Ltd. .... Cuba
The Lecuona Cuban Boys .... HMV DLP 1205
Xavier Cugat & his Waldorf Astoria Orchestra . Camden CDN 111
The Andrews Sisters .... Brunswick 02996
The George Shearing Quintet .... Capitol T 1567

SAY WONDERFUL THINGS April 1963
Norman Newell / Phillip Green
Mutual Music Ltd .... UK
Ronnie Carroll .... Philips 326574 BB
Julie London .... Liberty BBY 1185
United Kingdom entry for the 1963 Eurovision Song Contest (Placed Fourth).

SAY YOU'RE MINE AGAIN July 1953
Charles Nathan / Dave Heisler
E.H. Morris Ltd. .... USA
Dolores Grey .... Brunswick 05111
Jimmy Young .... Decca F 10132
Perry Como .... HMV B 10511
June Hutton .... Capitol CL 13918

SAY YOU, SAY ME December 1985
Lionel Richie
Warner Brothers Music .... USA
Film(s): ....White Nights
Lionel Richie .... Motown ZB 40421
Academy Award winning song for 1985.

SAYS MY HEART 1938
Frank Loesser / Burton Lane
B. Feldman & Co. Ltd. .... USA
Film(s): .... The Cocoanut Grove
The Andrews Sisters .... Brunswick 02629
Tony Brent .... Columbia SEG 7824

SCARLET RIBBONS February 1950
Jack Segal / Evelyn Danzig
Mills Music Ltd .... USA
Harry Belafonte .... RCA RCX 1049
Jeri Southern .... Brunswick LAT 8100
Jane Morgan .... London HAR 2316

SCARLETT O'HARA June 1963
Jerry Lordan
Francis, Day & Hunter Ltd . . . . UK
Jet Harris & Tony Meehan . . . . Decca F 11644
Lawrence Welk & his Orchestra . . . . London HAD 8123
Ivor Novello Nomination.

SCATTERBRAIN 1940
Johnny Burke / Frankie Masters / Kahn Keene / Carl Bean
Francis, Day & Hunter Ltd . . . . USA
Film(s): . . . . That's Right, You're Wrong / Scatterbrain
The Milt Herth Trio . . . . Brunswick 02954
Joe Loss & his Orchestra,
vocal Chick Henderson . . . . Regal Zonophone MR 3199
Guy Lombardo & his Royal Canadians . . . . . Brunswick 02956
Max Bygraves . . . . Decca LK 4360
Alan Fielding . . . . Decca F 11404

SCHOOL DAYS 1907
Will Cobb / Gus Edwards
Francis, Day & Hunter Ltd. USA
Show(s): . . . . School Days
Bing Crosby . . . . Brunswick 02841
Dick Todd . . . . HMV BD 750

SCHOOL LOVE April 1974
Barry Blue / Lynsey De Paul
A.T.V. Music Ltd. . . . . UK
Barry Blue . . . . Bell 1345

SCHOOLS OUT August 1972
Alice Cooper / Michael Bruce
Carlin Music Corporation . . . . USA
Film(s): . . . . Rock and Roll High School
Alice Cooper . . . . Warner Brothers K 16188

SCOTCH ON THE ROCKS October 1975
Bill Bates
Southern Music Publishing Co. Ltd . . . . UK
The Band of the Black Watch . . . . Spark SRL 1128

SCOTTISH SAMBA, THE January 1950
Tomme Connor / Johnnie Reine
Sun Music Ltd. . . . . UK
Edmundo Ros & his Rumba Band . . . . Decca F 9306
Roberto Inglez Orchestra . . . . Parlophone R 3259
Ethel Smith (organ)
with Guy lombardo & his Royal Canadians . Brunswick 04500

SCRUB ME MAMA WITH A BOOGIE BEAT 1941
Don Raye
Leeds Music Ltd . . . . USA
The Andrews Sisters . . . . Brunswick 03157

SEA OF LOVE October 1959
G. Khoury / P. Baptiste
Southern Music Publishing Co. Ltd . . . . USA
Marty Wilde . . . . Philips BBL 7380
Phil Philips . . . . Mercury AMT 1059

SEA WEED 1905
Fred Earle
Francis, Day & Hunter Ltd. UK
Alf Gordon . . . . Columbia 25923

SEALED WITH A KISS September 1962
Peter Udell / Gary Geld
Sheldon Music Ltd . . . . USA
Brian Hyland . . . . HMV POP 1051
Brian Hyland (1975) . . . . ABC 4059
Jason Donovan (1989) . . . . PWL PWL 39

SEARCHIN' October 1963
Jerry Leiber / Mike Stoller
Progressive Music Ltd . . . . USA
The Hollies . . . . Parlophone R 5052
The Coasters . . . . London HA 8189
Wanda Jackson . . . . Capitol T 2030

SEARCHIN' June 1984
Ian Stevens
Ramalam Music . . . . UK
Hazel Dean . . . . Pronto ENA 109

SEASIDE SHUFFLE August 1972
Jona Lewie
Sonet Publishing . . . . UK
Terry Dactyll & The Dinosaurs . . . . UK 5

SEASONS IN THE SUN (Le Moribond) April 1974
Jacques Brel / Rod McKuen
Francis, Day & Hunter Ltd. France
Terry Jacks . . . . Bell 1344
Rod McKuen . . . . Ember NR 5018
Jacques Brel (In French) . . . . Philips P 77863

SECOND HAND ROSE 1922
Grant Clarke / James Hanley
Keith Prowse Music Publishing Co. Ltd . . . . USA
Show(s): . . . . The Ziegfeld Follies of 1921
Film(s): . . . . My Man / Funny Girl
Norah Blaney & Gwen Farrer . . . . HMV B 1513
Barbra Streisand (1966) . . . . CBS 202025
Barbra Streisand appeared in *Funny Girl.*

SECOND STAR TO THE RIGHT, THE June 1953
Sammy Fain / Sammy Cahn
Walt Disney Music Co. Ltd . . . . USA
Film(s): . . . . Peter Pan
Don Cherry . . . . Brunswick 05087
Sound Track of Peter Pan . . . . Top Rank JKP 2034
Doris Day . . . . Columbia SCM 5054

SECOND TIME AROUND October 1961
Sammy Cahn / Jimmy Van Heusen
Robbins Music Corporation Ltd. . . . . USA
Film(s): . . . . High Time
Bing Crosby . . . . MGM 1098
Frank Sinatra . . . . Reprise R 30001
Jane Morgan . . . . London HAR 2377
Bing Crosby appeared in *High Time.*
Nominated for an Academy Award 1960.

SECRET LOVE February 1954
Sammy Fain / Paul Francis Webster
Campbell Connelly & Co. Ltd. . . . . USA
Film(s): . . . . .Calamity Jane
Doris Day . . . . Philips BBL 7175
Bing Crosby . . . . Brunswick LA 8674
Joni James . . . . MGM C 839
Kathy Kirby (1963) . . . . Decca F 11759
Doris Day appeared in *Calamity Jane.*
Academy Award winning song for 1953.

SECRET LOVERS April 1986
David Lewis / Wayne Lewis
Rondor Music . . . . USA
Atlantic Starr . . . . A&M AM 307

SECRET OF HAPPINESS, THE June 1958
Hoyt Curtin / Carl Sigmund
Cromwell Music Ltd . . . . USA
Kathie Kay . . . . HMV POP 485
Tony Osborne & his Orchestra . . . . HMV POP 483

SECRETS THAT YOU KEEP, THE March 1975
Mike Chapman / Nicky Chinn
Rak Music Ltd . . . . UK
Mud . . . . Rak 194

SEE EMILY PLAY July 1967
Roger Barrett
Essex Music Ltd. . . . . UK
Pink Floyd . . . . Columbia DB 8214

SEE MY BABY JIVE June 1973
Roy Wood
Carlin Music Corporation . . . . UK
Wizzard . . . . Harvest HAR 5070

SEE MY FRIEND September 1965
Ray Davies
Edward Kassner Music Co. Ltd . . . . UK
The Kinks . . . . Pye 7N 15919

SEE THE DAY December 1985
Dee C. Lee
EMI Music . . . . UK
Dee C. Lee . . . . CBS A 6570

SEE YOU   **March 1982**
Martin Gore
Sonet Music . . . . UK
Depeche Mode . . . . **Mute 018**

SEINE, LA   **May 1949**
F. Monod / Guy Lafarge / Geoffrey Parsons
Peter Maurice Music Co. Ltd . . . . France
Show(s): . . . . Sauce Tartare
Jean Caval . . . . **HMV B 9815**
Jane Morgan . . . . **London HAR 2086**
Doris Day . . . . **Columbia DB 2629**
Josephine Baker . . . . **RCA RD 27177**

SELF CONTROL   **September 1984**
Gampiero Bigazzi / Raffaele Riefoli / Andrea Piccolo
MCA Music . . . . Italy
Laura Branigan . . . . **Atlantic A 9676**

SEMI-DETACHED SUBURBAN MR JAMES December 1966
Geoff Stevens / John Carter
Carter-Lewis Music Ltd. . . . . UK
Manfred Mann . . . . **Fontana TF 757**

SEMINOLA   **1925**
Harry Warren / Robert King
B. Feldman & Co. Ltd. . . . . USA
The Savoy Orpheans . . . . **HMV B 2052**

SEND IN THE CLOWNS   **June 1975**
Stephen Sondheim
Chappell & Co. Ltd . . . . USA
Show(s): . . . . A Little Night Music
Glynis Johns . . . . **CBS S 31515**
Jean Simmons . . . . **RCA LRL 15090**
Judy Collins . . . . **Elektra 12177**
Glynis Johns appeared in the American production of *A Little Night Music*.
Jean Simmons appeared in the British production of *A Little Night Music*.

**SEND ME THE PILLOW THAT
YOU DREAM ON**   **November 1962**
Hank Locklin
Cecil Lennox Music . . . . USA
Hank Locklin . . . . **RCA RCX 115**
Johnny Tillotson . . . . **London HLA 9598**
Dean Martin . . . . **Reprise R 6146**
Connie Francis & Hank Williams Jnr. . . . . **MGM C 1003**
Dolly Parton . . . . **RCA RCALP 6080**

SENORA   **October 1950**
George Tobias / Ramaz Idriss
Dash Music Ltd . . . . USA
The Ray Ellington Quartet . . . . **Decca F 9496**
The Mike Cotton Jazzmen . . . . **Columbia DB 4697**
Jack Smith . . . . **Capitol CL 13403**

SENSES WORKING OVERTIME   **February 1982**
Andre Partridge
Virgin Music . . . . UK
X.T.C. . . . . **Virgin VS 462**

SENTIMENTAL GENTLEMAN FROM GEORGIA, A   **1932**
Frank Perkins / Mitchell Parish
Lawrence Wright Music Co. Ltd. . . . . USA
The Boswell Sisters . . . . **Brunswick 01379**
The Dinning Sisters . . . . **Capitol CL 13294**

SENTIMENTAL JOURNEY   **1945**
Les Brown / Ben Homer / Bud Green
Edwin H. Morris & Co. Ltd. . . . . USA
**Les Brown & his Band,
vocal Doris Day** . . . . **Philips BBL 7297**
Ella Fitzgerald . . . . **Brunswick LAT 8223**
Frank Sinatra . . . . **Capitol W 1594**

SENTIMENTAL ME   **May 1950**
Jim Morehead / Jimmy Cassin
Cinephonic Music Co. Ltd . . . . USA
Steve Conway . . . . **Columbia DB 2724**
The Ames Brothers . . . . **Vogue LVA 9126**
Elvis Presley . . . . **RCA RD 27224**

SEPARATE LIVES   **December 1985**
Stephen Bishop
EMI Music Ltd. . . . . UK

Film(s): . . . . White Nights
Phil Collins & Marilyn Martin . . . . **Virgin VS 818**
Nominated for an Academy Award 1985.

SEPTEMBER   **February 1979**
Maurice White / Al McKay / Allee Willis
Rondor Music (London) Ltd. . . . . USA
Earth Wind & Fire . . . . **CBS 6922**

SEPTEMBER IN THE RAIN   **1937**
Al Dubin / Harry Warren
B. Feldman & Co. Ltd. . . . . USA
Film(s): . . . . Melody for Two
James Melton . . . . **Decca F 6404**
Dick Robertson . . . . **Panachord 25920**
Sarah Vaughan . . . . **Mercury MPL 6542**
Bing Crosby . . . . **HMV CLP 1088**
James Melton . . . . **RCA ZL 70136**
James Melton appeared in *Melody for Two*.

SEPTEMBER SONG   **1946**
Maxwell Anderson / Kurt Weill
Chappell & Co. Ltd. . . . . USA
Show(s): . . . . Knickerbocker Holliday
Film(s): . . . . Knickerbocker Holliday / September Affair / Pepe
Walter Huston . . . . **Fontana TFL 5037**
Bing Crosby . . . . **Brunswick LA 8624**
Maurice Chevalier . . . . **Pye NPL 28015**
Tony Martin . . . . **London HAD 2341**
Walter Huston appeared in the show *Knickerbocker Holliday*.
Maurice Chevalier appeared in *Pepe*.

SERENADE   **August 1956**
Sammy Cahn / Nicholas Brodszky
Blossom Music Co. . . . . USA
Film(s): . . . . Serenade
Mario Lanza . . . . **HMV DA 2085**
Slim Whitman . . . . **London HLU 8287**
Mario Lanza appeared in *Serenade*.

SERENADE   **1922**
Jonny Heykens
B. Feldman & Co. . . . . Germany
Albert Sandler Orchestra . . . . **Columbia DB 469**
Mantovani & his Orchestra . . . . **Decca F 7718**
Max Jaffa Orchestra . . . . **Columbia 33S 1104**
James Last Orchestra . . . . **Polydor 2371190**

SERENADE   **1926**
Sigmund Romberg / Dorothy Donnelly
Chappell & Co. Ltd. . . . . USA
Show(s): . . . . The Student Prince
Film(s): . . . . The Student Prince / Deep in My Heart
Harry Welchman . . . . **Columbia 9057**
**Allan Prior, Raymond Marlowe, Paul Clemon
& Olaf Olson** . . . . **Columbia 9083**
Richard Crooks . . . . **HMV DA 1142**
Mario Lanza . . . . **RCA RB 16113**
David Whitfield . . . . **Decca LK 4348**
Harry Welchman, Allan Prior, Raymond Marlowe, Paul Clemon & Olaf Olson appeared in the British production of *The Student Prince*.
Mario Lanza dubbed the singing voice of Edmund Purdom who appeared in the 1954 film of *The Student Prince*.

SERENADE FRASQUITA (Farewell My Love, Farewell) 1925
Franz Lehar / Reginald Arkell
Ascherberg, Hopwood & Crew Ltd. . . . . Austria
Show(s): . . . . Frasquita
Jose Collins . . . . **Decca K 730**
Richard Tauber . . . . **Parlophone PMB 1006**
The Mantovani Orchestra . . . . **Decca LK 4347**
Jose Collins appeared in the British production of *Frasquita*.

SERENADE IN BLUE   **1942**
Mack Gordon / Harry Warren
Victoria Music Co. Ltd . . . . USA
Film(s): . . . . Orchestra Wives
Glenn Miller & his Orchestra (Sound Track) . **Top Rank TR 5003**
**Glenn Miller & his Orchestra, vocal
Ray Eberle & The Modernaires** . . . . **RCA RCX 1024**
Ray Eberle, Tex Beneke & The Modernaires . **Vogue LVA 9103**
Glenn Miller appeared in *Orchestra Wives*.

SERENADE IN THE NIGHT 1936
C.A. Bixio / B. Cherubini / Jimmy Kennedy
Peter Maurice Music Co. Ltd . . . . Italy
Roy Fox & his Orchestra . . . . **HMV BD 5126**
Tino Rossi . . . . **Columbia DB 1656**
Vic Damone . . . . **Philips BBL 7234**
Adapted from *Violino Tzigano* by Bixio & Cherubini.

SERENADE OF THE BELLS January 1948
Al Urbano / Kay Twomey / Al Goodhart
Edwin H. Morris & Co. Ltd. . . . . USA
Dick Haymes . . . . **Brunswick 03890**
Billy Vaughan & his Orchestra . . . . **London RED 1330**

SERIOUS May 1987
Lou Pace / Donna Allen / Gary King, Embridge Jones & 'Blitz'
EMI Music . . . . USA
Donna Allen . . . . **Portrait PRT 650744**

SET ME FREE June 1986
Derek Bramble
Virgin Music . . . . UK
Jaki Graham . . . . **EMI JAKI 7**

SET ME FREE June 1965
Ray Davies
Edward Kassner Music Co. Ltd . . . . UK
The Kinks . . . . **Pye 7N 15854**

SETTIN' THE WOODS ON FIRE January 1953
Ed Nelson / Fred Rose
New World Music Ltd. . . . . USA
Jo Stafford & Frankie Laine . . . . **Columbia DB 3168**
Hank Williams . . . . **MGM 566**
Ted Heath & his Music,
vocal Lita Rosa & Dennis Lotis . . . . **Decca F 10027**

(SEXUAL) HEALING November 1982
Marvin Gaye / Odell Brown
CBS Songs . . . . USA
Marvin Gaye . . . . **CBS A 2855**

SEVEN DRUNKEN NIGHTS May 1967
Traditional
This edition by Scott Solomon Music . . . . UK
The Dubliners . . . . **Major Minor MM 506**

SEVEN FOUR SEVEN (Strangers in the Night) July 1980
Peter Byford / Steven Dawson / Peter Gill / Graham Oliver & Paul Quinn
Heath Levy Music Ltd . . . . UK
Saxon . . . . **Carrere CAR 151**

SEVEN LITTLE GIRLS SITTING
IN THE BACK SEAT December 1959
Lee Pockriss / Bob Hilliard
Sheldon Music Co. Ltd . . . . USA
The Avons . . . . **Columbia DB 4363**
Paul Evans . . . . **London HAL 2248**
Al Saxon & The Lana Sisters . . . . **Fontana H 221**

SEVEN LONELY DAYS May 1953
Alden Shuman / Earl Shuman / Marshall Brown
Robbins Music Corporation Ltd . . . . USA
Gisele MacKenzie . . . . **Capitol CL 13920**
Bonnie Lou . . . . **Parlophone MSP 6021**
The Teddy Bears . . . . **London HAP 2183**

SEVEN ROOMS OF GLOOM July 1967
Brian Holland / Eddie Holland / Lamont Dozier
Carlin Music Corporation . . . . USA
The Four Tops . . . . **Tamla Motown TMG 612**

SEVEN SEAS OF RHYE, THE April 1974
Freddie Mercury
Trident Music . . . . UK
Queen . . . . **EMI 2121**

SEVEN TEARS April 1982
Wolff Stein / Wolfgang Jass
Southern Music Co. . . . . Germany
The Goombay Dance Band . . . . **Epic EPC A 1242**

SEVEN YEARS WITH THE WRONG WOMAN 1933
Bob Miller

Lawrence Wright Music Co. Ltd. USA
Show(s): . . . . On With the Show
Ray Noble & his Orchestra, vocal Al Bowlly . . . . **HMV B 6364**
Jimmy Campbell & his Band . . . . **Rex 8007**
Something Smith & The Redheads . . . . . **Fontana TFR 6005**
Jimmy Campbell appeared in *On With the Show.*

SEVENTEEN November 1955
John F. Young Jnr. / Chuck Gorman / Boyd Bennet
World Wide Music Co. Ltd. . . . . USA
Frankie Vaughan . . . . **Philips BBE 12022**
The Fontane Sisters . . . . **London HAD 2053**

SEVENTEEN February 1980
Martin Sheller / Damian Pew
EMI Music Ltd . . . . UK
The Regents . . . . **Rialto TREB 111**

SEVENTEEN CANDLES 1940
Art Strauss / Bob Dale / Sonny Miller
Lawrence Wright Music Co. Ltd . . . . UK
Ken Johnson & his Orchestra . . . . **HMV BD 5559**

SEVENTH HEAVEN 1937
Sidney Mitchell / Lew Pollack
Keith Prowse Music Publishing Co. Ltd. . . . . USA
Film(s): . . . . Seventh Heaven
Phil Regan . . . . **Decca F 6486**

SEVENTY-SIX TROMBONES May 1961
Meredith Wilson
Frank Music Co. Ltd . . . . USA
Show(s): . . . . Music Man
Film(s): . . . . Music Man
Robert Preston . . . . **Capitol W 990**
Van Johnson . . . . **HMV CLP 1444**
Robert Preston . . . . **Warner Brothers WM 4066**
The King Brothers . . . . **Parlophone R 4737**
Robert Preston appeared in the American production and the film of
Music Man
Van Johnson appeared in the British production of *Music Man.*

SEWING MACHINE, THE 1947
Frank Loesser
Famous Music Ltd. . . . . USA
Film(s): . . . . The Perils of Pauline
Betty Hutton . . . . **Capitol CL 13005**
Betty Hutton appeared in *The Perils of Pauline.*

SEX CRIME (NINETEEN EIGHTY FOUR) December 1984
Annie Lennox / David Stewart
RCA Music . . . . UK
Eurythmics . . . . **Virgin VS 728**

SEXUAL HEALING (See Healing)

SEXY EYES April 1980
Robert Mather / Keith Stegall / Chris Waters
April Music Ltd . . . . USA
Dr Hook . . . . **Capitol CL 16127**

SH-BOOM October 1954
Carl Feaster / Claude Feaster / James Keyes / J. Edwards / Floyd McRae
Aberbach (London) Ltd. . . . . USA
The Crew Cuts . . . . **Mercury MPT 7501**
The Chordcats . . . . **London HAE 2167**

SHA LA LA November 1964
Robert Taylor / Robert Mosely
Ludix Music Ltd . . . . USA
The Shirelles . . . . **Pye 7N 25240**
Manfred Mann . . . . **HMV POP 1346**

SHA LA LA LA LEE April 1966
Mort Shuman / Kenny Lynch
Belinda (London) Ltd. . . . . USA
The Small Faces . . . . **Decca F 12317**

SHADDUP YOU FACE February 1981
Joe Dolce
April Music . . . . Australia
Joe Dolce . . . . **Epic EPC 9518**

SHADE OF THE PALM, THE   1900
Leslie Stuart / Owen Hall
Francis, Day & Hunter Ltd. . . . . UK
Show(s): . . . . Florodora
Sydney Barraclough . . . . **Berliner 2932**
Edgar Coyle . . . . **Columbia 2441**
Victor Mixed Chorus . . . . **HMV B 9097**

SHADOW OF YOUR SMILE   February 1966
Paul Francis Webster / Johnny Mandel
United Artists Music Ltd. . . . . USA
Film(s): . . . . The Sandpiper
Tony Bennett . . . . **CBS 202084**
Nancy Wilson . . . . **Capitol T 2495**
Soundtrack . . . . **Mercury MCL 20065**
Academy Award winning song for 1965.

SHADOW WALTZ, THE   1933
Al Dubin / Harry Warren
B. Feldman & Co. Ltd. . . . . USA
Film(s): . . . . Gold Diggers of 1933
Dick Powell . . . . **Broadcast 3340**
Bing Crosby . . . . **Brunswick 02413**
Joe Loss & his Orchestra . . . . **HMV 7EG 8473**
The Mantovani Orchestra . . . . **Decca LK 4074**
The Tommy Dorsey Orchestra,
conducted by Warren Covington . . . . **Brunswick LAT 8353**
Dick Powell & Ruby Keeler . . . . **United Artists UAG 29421**
Dick Powell & Ruby Keeler appeared in *Gold Diggers of 1933*.

SHADRACK   1938
Robert MacGimsey
Keith Prowse music Publishing Co. Ltd. . . . . USA
Film(s): . . . . The Strip
Louis Armstrong & The
Lynn Murray Chorus . . . . **Brunswick LAT 8368**
Jack Teagarden . . . . **Capitol EAP 3-820**
The Golden Gate Quartet . . . . **Fontana TFR 6009**
Louis Armstrong appeared in *The Strip*.

SHAFT (Theme From)   December 1971
Isaac Hayes
Island Music Ltd . . . . USA
Film(s): . . . . Shaft
Isaac Hayes . . . . **Stax 2369001**
Academy Award winning song for 1971.

SHAKE DOWN THE STARS   1940
Jimmy Van Heusen / Edgar De Lange
Cavendish Music Co. Ltd . . . . USA
Tommy Dorsey & his Orchestra,
vocal Frank Sinatra . . . . **HMV BD 5601**
Jeri Southern . . . . **Columbia 33SX 1155**

SHAKE YOU DOWN   December 1986
Gregory Abbott
CBS Songs . . . . USA
Gregory Abbott . . . . **CBS A 7326**

SHAKE YOUR BODY (Down To The Ground)   May 1979
Randy Jackson / Michael Jackson
Carlin Music Corporation . . . . USA
Film(s): . . . . Because They're Young
The Jacksons . . . . **Epic EPC 7181**

SHAKE YOUR LOVE   February 1988
Debbie Gibson
EMI Music . . . . USA
Debbie Gibson . . . . **Atlantic A 9187**

SHAKE, RATTLE AND ROLL   October 1954
Charles E. Calhoun
Campbell Connelly & Co. Ltd. . . . . USA
Bill Haley & his Comets . . . . **Ace of Hearts AH 13**
Chubby Checker . . . . **Columbia 33SX 1341**

SHAKIN' ALL OVER   August 1960
Johnny Kidd
Mills Music Ltd . . . . UK
Johnny Kidd . . . . **HMV 7EG 8628**

SHAKING THE BLUES AWAY   1928
Irving Berlin
Irving Berlin Ltd. . . . . USA
Show(s): . . . . The Ziegfeld Follies of 1927

Film(s): . . . . Easter Parade / Love Me or Leave Me
Paul Whiteman & his Orchestra . . . . **HMV B 5415**
Ann Miller . . . . **MGM D 140**
Doris Day . . . . **Philips BBL 7047**
Ann Miller appeared in *Easter Parade*.
Doris Day appeared in *Love Me or Leave Me*.

SHALL WE DANCE   September 1953
Richard Rodgers / Oscar Hammerstein II
Williamson Music Ltd. . . . . USA
Show(s): . . . . The King and I
Film(s): . . . . The King and I
Gertrude Lawrence & Yul Brynner . . . . . **Brunswick LAT 8026**
Valerie Hobson & Herbert Lom . . . . **Philips BBL 7002**
Deborah Kerr & Yul Brynner . . . . **Capitol LCT 6108**
Gertrude Lawrence appeared in the American production of *The King and I*.
Yul Brynner appeared in the American production and the film of *The King and I*.
Valerie Hobson & Herbert Lom appeared in the British production of *The King and I*.
Deborah Kerr appeared in the film of *The King and I*.
The Singing voice of Deborah Kerr was dubbed by Marni Nixon.

SHAME SHAME SHAME   March 1975
Sylvia Robinson
Sunbury Music Ltd . . . . USA
Shirley & Company . . . . **All Platinum 6146301**

SHANG-A-LANG   May 1974
Bill Martin / Phil Coulter
Martin-Coulter Music Ltd. . . . . UK
The Bay City Rollers . . . . **Bell 1355**

SHANGHAI   September 1951
Bob Hilliard / Milton De Lugg
Campbell Connelly & Co. Ltd . . . . France
Doris Day . . . . **Columbia DB 2909**

SHANGHAI   1925
Horatio Nicholls
Lawrence Wright Music Co. Ltd. . . . . UK
The Savoy Orpheans . . . . **HMV B 1981**

SHAPES OF THINGS   April 1966
Keith Relf / James McCarty / Paul Samwell-Smith
B. Feldman & Co. Ltd. . . . . UK
The Yardbirds . . . . **Columbia DB 7848**

SHARING YOU   July 1962
Gerry Goffin / Carole King
Aldon Music Ltd. . . . . USA
Bobby Vee . . . . **Liberty LIB 554541**

SHATTERED DREAMS   June 1987
Clark Datchler
Virgin Music . . . . Holland
Johnny Hates Jazz . . . . **Virgin VS 948**

SHAZAM   May 1960
Duane Eddy / Lee Hazlewood
Burlington Music Co. Ltd . . . . USA
Film(s): . . . . Because They're Young
Duane Eddy (guitar) . . . . **London HAW 2325**
Duane Eddy appeared in *Because They're Young*.

SHE   July 1974
Charles Aznavour / Herbert Kretzmer
Standard Music . . . . France
Charles Aznavour . . . . **Barclay BAR 26**
Theme from the TV series 'The Seven Faces of Woman'.

SHE BROKE MY HEART IN THREE PLACES   1945
Milton Drake / Al Hoffman / Jerry Livingston
B. Feldman & Co. Ltd. . . . . USA
Film(s): . . . . Swing in the Saddle
The Hoosier Hot Shots . . . . **Brunswick 03549**
The Hoosier Hot Shots appeared in *Swing in the Saddle*.

SHE DIDN'T SAY "YES"   1932
Jerome Kern / Otto Harbach
Chappell & Co. Ltd. . . . . USA
Show(s): . . . . The Cat and the Fiddle
Film(s): . . . . The Cat and the Fiddle / Till the Clouds Roll By
Peggy Wood . . . . **Columbia DB 796**

Peggy Lee . . . . **Capitol LC 6578**
Eydie Gormé & Steve Lawrence . . . . **HMV CLP 1463**
Peggy Wood appeared in the British production of *The Cat and the Fiddle.*

SHE DON'T WANNA   1928
Jack Yellen / Milton Ager
Lawrence Wright Music Co. Ltd. . . . . USA
Harry Reser's Jazz Pilots,
vocal Tom Stacks . . . . **Parlophone E 5970**
The California Humming Birds . . . . **HMV B 2550**

SHE DRIVES ME CRAZY   February 1989
David Steele / Roland Gift
Virgin Music . . . . UK
Fine Young Canibals . . . . **London LON 199**
Ivor Novello Award.

SHE IS MA DAISY   1905
Harry Lauder / J.D. Harper
Francis, Day & Hunter Ltd. . . . . UK
Harry Lauder . . . . **Zonophone X 42351**
George Elrick . . . . **Ace of Clubs ACL 1024**

SHE IS THE BELLE OF NEW YORK   1898
Gustave Kerker / Hugh Morton
Ascherberg, Hopwood & Crew Ltd. . . . . USA
Show(s): . . . . .The Belle of New York
Film(s): . . . . .The Belle of New York
The Columbia Light Opera Company . . . . **Columbia 9925**
Barry Kent & The Rita Williams Singers . . . . . . **HMV 7EG 8442**

SHE LOVES ME   June 1964
Jerry Bock / Sheldon Harnick
Valando Music Co. Ltd . . . . USA
Show(s): . . . . She Loves Me
Daniel Massey . . . . **MGM C 973**
Gary Raymond . . . . **HMV CLP 1745**
Shirley Bassey . . . . **Columbia DB 1691**
Daniel Massey appeared in the American production of *She Loves Me*
Gary Raymond appeared in the British production of *She Loves Me.*

SHE LOVES YOU   November 1963
John Lennon / Paul McCartney
Northern Songs Ltd . . . . UK
Film(s): . . . . A Hard Day's Night
The Beatles . . . . **Parlophone R 5055**
The Beatles appeared in *A Hard Day's Night.*
Ivor Novello Award.

SHE MAKES MY DAY   November 1988
Robert Palmer
Island Music . . . . UK
Robert Palmer . . . . **EMI EM 65**

SHE MEANS NOTHING TO ME   March 1983
John David
Warner Brothers Music . . . . UK
Phil Everly & Cliff Richard . . . . **Capitol CL 276**

SHE SELLS SANCTUARY   July 1985
Ian Astbury / William Duffy
Chappell Music Co. . . . . UK
The Cult . . . . **Beggars Banquet BEG 135**

SHE SELLS SEA SHELLS   1908
Terry Sullivan / Harry Gifford
Francis, Day & Hunter LKtd. . . . . UK
Wilkie Bard . . . . **Jumbo 253**
Laurie London . . . . **Parlophone GEP 8689**

SHE WANTS TO DANCE WITH ME   October 1988
Rick Astley
All Boys Music . . . . UK
Rick Astley . . . . **RCA PB 42189**

SHE WAS ONE OF THE EARLY BIRDS   1895
T.W. Conner
Francis, Day & Hunter Ltd. . . . . UK
The Pavement Artists . . . . **Regal Zonophone MR 563**
The Variety Singers . . . . **Columbia SEG 7712**
The George Mitchell Singers . . . . **HMV CLP 1399**

SHE WEARS MY RING   April 1968
Felice Bryant / Boudleaux Bryant
Acuff-Rose Publishing Co. Ltd. . . . . USA
Solomon King . . . . **Columbia DB 8325**

SHE WEARS RED FEATHERS   February 1953
Bob Merrill
Dash Music Ltd . . . . USA
Guy Mitchell . . . . **Philips BBL 7265**

SHE'D RATHER BE WITH ME   August 1967
Gerry Bonner / Alan Gordon
Robbins Music Ltd. . . . . USA
The Turtles . . . . **London HLU 10135**

SHE'S A GREAT GIRL   1928
Harry Woods
Keith Prowse Music Publishing Co. Ltd . . . . USA
The Roger Wolfe Kahn Orchestra . . . . **HMV B 5514**

SHE'S A HOME GIRL   August 1949
Benny Davis / Abner Silver
Peter Maurice Music Co. Ltd . . . . USA
Mel Tormé . . . . **Capitol CL 13131**

SHE'S A LADY   February 1971
Paul Anka
M.A.M. (Music Publishing) Ltd . . . . USA
Tom Jones . . . . **Decca F 13113**
Paul Anka . . . . **Buddah 2318049**

SHE'S A LADY   December 1950
Cy Coben
Edward Kassner Music Co. Ltd . . . . USA
Perry Como & Betty Hutton . . . . **HMV B 9997**
Ted Heath & his Music, vocal Lita Roza,
Jack Parnell & Denis Lotis . . . . **Decca F 9620**

SHE'S A LASSIE FROM LANCASHIRE   1907
C.W. Murphy / Dan Lipton / John Neat
B. Feldman & Co. Ltd. . . . . UK
Florrie Forde . . . . **Zonophone X 43147**
Max Bygraves . . . . **HMV 7EG 8271**

SHE'S A LATIN FROM MANHATTAN   1935
Al Dubin / Harry Warren
B. Feldman & Co. Ltd . . . . USA
Film(s): . . . . Casino de Paris / The Jolson Story
Reva Reyes . . . . **HMV BD 223**
Johnnie Green & his Orchestra . . . . **Columbia FB 1103**
Al Jolson . . . . **Brunswick LAT 8267**
Al Jolson appeared in *Casino de Paris.*

SHE'S A WINNER   August 1974
Kenny Gamble / Leon Huff
Gamble & Huff Music . . . . USA
The Intruders . . . . **Philadelphia PIR 2212**

SHE'S FUNNY THAT WAY   1929
Richard A. Whiting / Neil Moret
Francis, Day & Hunter Ltd . . . . USA
Film(s):The Postman Always Rings Twice / Rainbow 'Round My Shoulder / Meet Danny Wilson
Ted Lewis & his Orchestra . . . . **Columbia 5268**
Nat 'King' Cole . . . . **Capitol LCT 6176**
Alma Cogan with The Billy Cotton Band . **Columbia 33SX 1388**
Billy Daniels . . . . **Fontana TFL 5000**
Billy Daniels appeared in *Rainbow 'Round My Shoulder.*

SHE'S GOT CLAWS   September 1981
Gary Numan
Numan Music . . . . UK
Gary Numan . . . . **Beggars Banquet BEG 62**

SHE'S IN LOVE WITH YOU   November 1979
Mike Chapman / Nicky Chinn
Rak Music Ltd. . . . . UK
Suzi Quatro . . . . **Rak 299**

SHE'S LEAVING HOME   June 1988
John Lennon / Paul McCartney
Northern Songs Ltd. . . . . UK
Billy Bragg . . . . **Childline CHILD 1**

SHE'S MY LOVELY   1937
Vivian Ellis
Victoria Music Co. Ltd. .... UK
Show(s): .... Hide and Seek
Bobby Howes .... HMV B 8675
Philip Green & his Orchestra .... Columbia 33S 1096
Billy Ternant & his Orchestra .... Decca LK 4356
Bobby Howes appeared in *Hide and Seek*.
Theme song of Billy Ternant.

SHE'S NOT THERE   September 1964
Rod Argent
Marquis Music Ltd .... UK
The Zombies .... Decca F 11940
Santana (1977) .... CBS 5671

SHE'S NOT YOU   October 1962
Doc Pomus / Jerry Leiber / Mike Stoller
Hill & Range Songs (London) Ltd .... USA
Elvis Presley .... RCA 1303

SHE'S ON IT   August 1987
Rick Rubin / Adam Horovitz
Island Music .... UK
The Beastie Boys .... Def Jam BEAST 2

SHE'S OUT OF MY LIFE   May 1980
Tom Bahler
Sunbury Music Ltd .... USA
Michael Jackson .... Epic EPC 8384

SHE'S SO BEAUTIFUL   September 1985
Hans Poulsen
Spurs Music .... UK
Show(s): .... Time
Clif Richard .... EMI 5531
Cliff Richard appeared in *Time*.

SHE'S SO MODERN   May 1978
Bob Geldof / Johnnie Fingers
Zomba Music Publishers .... UK
The Boomtown Rats .... Ensign ENY 13

SHE'S SUCH A COMFORT TO ME   1930
Douglas Furber / Donovan Parsons / Arthur Schwartz
Chappell Music Co. .... UK
Show(s): .... The House That Jack Built
Jack Hulbert .... Columbia 5689
Jack Hulbert appeared in *The House That Jack Built*.

SHEIK OF ARABY, THE   1922
Harry B. Smith / Ted Snyder / Francis Wheeler
B. Feldman & Co. Ltd .... USA
Show(s): .... Make it Snappy
Film(s): .... Tin Pan Alley
The Club Royal Orchestra .... HMV B 1331
Jack Teagarden & his Music, vocal Jack Teagarden Capitol T 721
**The Kid Ory Band,
vocal Kid Ory & Marty Marsala** .... Columbia 33CX 10134
Eddie Condon's All Stars .... Brunswick LAT 8229

SHEILA TAKE A BOW   May 1987
Steven Morrisey / John Marr
Warner Brothers Music .... UK
The Smiths .... Rough Trade RT 196

SHELIA   October 1962
Tommy Roe
Robert Mellin Ltd .... USA
Tommy Roe .... HMV POP 1060

SHEPHERD OF THE HILLS   1927
Horatio Nicholls / Edgar Leslie
Lawrence Wright Music Co. Ltd. .... UK
Jack Hylton & his Orchestra .... HMV B 5207
The Stargazers .... Decca F 9872
The Cliff Adams Singers .... Columbia 33SX 1362

SHERRY   November 1962
Robert Gaudio
Ardmore & Beechwood Ltd .... USA
The Four Seasons .... Stateside SS 122
Adrian Baker (1975) .... Magnet MAG 34

SHIFTING, WHISPERING SANDS   December 1955
Jack Gilbert / Mary Hadler
Peter Maurice Music Co. Ltd. .... USA
Eamonn Andrews .... Parlophone R 4106
Rusty Draper .... Mercury MPT 7000
Billy Vaughan .... London HLD 8205

SHIM-ME-SHA-WABBLE   1918
Spencer Williams
Keith Prowse Music Publishing Co. Ltd. .... USA
The New Orleans Rhythm Kings .... London AL 3552
McKinney's Cotton Pickers .... HMV B 9228
Eddie Condon's Chicagoans ..... Warner Brothers WM 4009

SHINANIKI DA   1929
Harry Carlton
Lawrence Wright Music Co. Ltd .... UK
Jack Hylton & his Orchestra .... HMV B 5629

SHINDIG   October 1963
Hank B. Marvin / Bruce Welch
Shadows Music Ltd .... UK
The Shadows .... Columbia DB 7106

SHINE   1924
Lew Brown / Cecil Mack / Ford Dabney
Lawrence Wright Music Co. Ltd. .... USA
Film(s):Birth of the Blues / The Benny Goodman Story / The Eddy
Duchin Story / Cabin in the Sky
The Virginians .... HMV B 1850
The Savoy Orpheans .... Columbia 2459
Bing Crosby & the Mills Brothers (1941) .. Philips BBE 12142
The Original Barnstormers Spasm Band ..... Tempo EXA 95
Bing Crosby appeared in *Birth of the Blues*.

SHINE A LITTLE LOVE   June 1979
Jeff Lynne
United Artists Music Co. Ltd. .... UK
The Electric Light Orchestra .... Jet 144

SHINE ON HARVEST MOON   1908
Jack Norworth / Nora Bayes
Francis, Day & Hunter Ltd. .... USA
Show(s):The Ziegfeld Follies of 1908 / Miss Innocence / The Ziegfeld
Follies of 1931
Film(s):Ever Since Eve / Nancy Goes to Rio / Shine on Harvest Moon
/ The Eddy Duchin Story / The Great Ziegfeld
The Boswell Sisters .... Brunswick 01218
Flanagan & Allen .... Ace of Clubs ACL 1092
Al Jolson (1945) .... Brunswick LAT 8387
Eddy Duchin (piano) .... Philips BBI 7081
Carmen Cavallaro & his Orchestra ..... Brunswick LAT 8119
Theme song of Nora Hayes.

SHINE ON VICTORY MOON   1944
Joseph Gilbert
Campbell Connelly & Co. Ltd. .... UK
Issy Bonn .... Rex 10214

SHINE ON YOUR SHOES, A   1932
Howard Dietz / Arthur Schwartz
Chappell & Co. Ltd. .... USA
Show(s): .... Flying Colours
Film(s): .... The Band Wagon
Donald Peers .... HMV B 10609
Fred Astaire .... MGM C 752
Mel Tormé .... MGM 1144
Fred Astaire appeared in *The Band Wagon*.

SHINE THROUGH MY DREAMS   1935
Ivor Novello / Christopher Hassell
Chappell & Hart Co. Ltd .... UK
Show(s): .... Glamorous Night
Film(s): .... Glamorous Night
Trefor Jones .... HMV DLP 1095
Harry Secombe .... Philips BBR 8133
Trefor Jones appeared in both the show and the film of *Glamorous Night*.

SHIP AHOY   1909
A.J. Mills / Bennett Scott
B. Feldman & Co. Ltd. .... UK
Ella Retford .... Regal Zonophone MR 205
Frank Williams .... Regal 214

| Hetty King | Fontana TFL 5043 |
| Paddie O'Neil | Decca LK 4026 |

SHIP OF FOOLS — March 1988
Vincent Clarke / Andrew Bell
Sonet Music .... UK
Erasure .... **Mute MUTE 74**

SHIP WITHOUT A SAIL, THE — 1930
Richard Rodgers / Lorenz Hart
Chappell & Co. Ltd .... USA
Show(s): .... Heads Up
Film(s): .... Heads Up
Spike Hughes & his Orchestra ...... **Decca F 1748**
Sarah Vaughan .... **Mercury MMC 14026**

SHIPMATES O' MINE — 1913
Wilfred Sanderson
Boosey & Hawkes Music Ltd. .... UK
Robert Radford .... **HMV 4-2494**
Peter Dawson .... **HMV B 3839**
Sidney Burchall .... **Decca F 7779**

SHIRALEE — June 1957
Tommy Steele
Robbins Music Corporation Ltd. .... UK
Film(s): .... Shiralee
Tommy Steele .... **Decca LK 4351**

SHIRLEY — April 1982
John Fred
.... USA
Shakin' Stevens (1982) .... **Epic EPC A 2087**
John Fred & The Playboys (1968) ...... **CBS 3475**

SHISH KEBAB — July 1957
David Carroll / George Stone
Good Music Ltd. .... USA
David Carroll & his Orchestra .. **Mercury MMC 14066**
Ted Heath & his Music .... **Decca DFE 6432**

SHOE SHINE BOY — 1936
Saul Chaplin / Sammy Cahn
Lawrence Wright Music Co. Ltd .... USA
Fletcher Henderson & his Orchestra .. **RCA RCX 1027**
Bing Crosby .... **Ace of Hearts AH 1**
The Mills Brothers .... **Brunswick 02245**
Frankie Vaughan .... **Philips BBL 7198**

SHOEMAKER'S SERENADE, THE — March 1948
Joe Lubin / Eddie Lisbona
Kassner Music Ltd. .... UK
Lou Preager Orchestra .... **Columbia FB 3368**
Roberto Inglez Orchestra ...... **Parlophone F 2269**
The Five Smith Orchestra ...... **Parlophone F 2282**

SHOES WITH WINGS ON — September 1949
Harry Warren / Ira Gershwin
Francis, Day & Hunter Ltd .... USA
Film(s): .... The Barkleys of Broadway
Fred Astaire .... **MGM 212**
Fred Astaire appeared in the *Barkleys of Broadway*.

SHOO FLY PIE AND APPLE PAN DOWDY — 1946
Sammy Gallop / Guy Woods
Chappell & Co. Ltd. .... USA
Dinah Shore .... **Columbia DB 2228**
Stan Kenton & his Orchestra,
vocal June Christy .... **Capitol CL 13419**

SHOO SHOO BABY — 1944
Phil Moore
Leeds Music Ltd. .... USA
Film(s): ...... Follow the Boys / Beautiful But Broke / Trocadero
The Andrews Sisters .... **Brunswick 03502**
Glenn Miller & his Orchestra ..... **RCA RD 27090**
The Andrews Sisters .... **Capitol LCT 6132**
The Andrews Sisters appeared in *Follow the Boys*.

SHOOTING STAR — January 1979
David Courtney
Heath Levy Music Ltd. .... UK
Dollar .... **Carrere EMI 2871**

SHORES OF MINNETONKA — 1923
Percy Wenrich / Gus Khan
B. Feldman & Co. Ltd .... USA
Jack Hylton & his Orchestra ...... **HMV B 1653**

SHORT'NIN' BREAD — 1928
Traditional, arranged by Jacques Wolfe
An edition by Campbell Connelly & Co. Ltd. ..... USA
Film(s): .... Jericho
Paul Robeson (1937) .... **HMV DLP 1165**
The Viscounts .... **Pye NEP 24132**
Paul Robeson appeared in *Jericho*.

SHOT GUN BOOGIE — June 1951
Ernie Ford
Campbell Connelly & Co. Ltd .... USA
'Tennessee' Ernie Ford .... **Capitol T 1380**
Tex Williams .... **Capitol T 1463**

SHOTGUN WEDDING — June 1966
Roy Hammond
Sparta Music Ltd. .... USA
Roy C. .... **Island WI 273**
Roy C. (1972) .... **UK 19**

SHOULD I — 1930
Arthur Freed / Nacio Herb Brown
Robbins Music Corporation Ltd .... USA
Film(s): .... Lord Byron of Broadway / Singin' in the Rain
Paul Whiteman & his Orchestra,
vocal Bing Crosby .... **Columbia 5724**
Frank Sinatra .... **Capitol W 1491**
Tommy Sands .... **Capitol T 1123**

SHOUT — June 1964
O'Kelly Isley / Ronald Isley / Rudolph Isley
Dominion Music Ltd .... USA
The Isley Brothers .... **RCA 1149**
Lulu & The Luvvers (1964) ...... **Decca F 11884**
Chubby Checker .... **Columbia 33SX 1445**
Lulu (1986) .... **London SHOUT 1**

SHOUT — January 1985
Roland Orzabal / Ian Stanley
Ten Music .... UK
Tear For Fears .... **Mercury IDEA 8**
Ivor Novello Nomination.

SHOUT BROTHER SHOUT — 1941
Herman Fairbanks / Deke Watson
.... USA
The Ink Spots .... **Brunswick 03377**

SHOUT TO THE TOP — November 1984
Paul Weller
EMI Music .... UK
The Style Council .... **Polydor TSC 7**

SHOW ME HEAVEN — October 1990
Maria McKee / Jay Rifkin / Eric Rackin
Warner Chappell Music .... USA
Film(s): .... Days of Thunder
Maria McKee .... **Epic 6563037**

SHOW ME THE WAY — June 1976
Peter Frampton
Rondor Music (London) Ltd .... UK
Peter Frampton .... **A&M AMS 7218**

SHOW ME THE WAY TO GO HOME — 1925
Irving King
Campbell Connelly & Co. Ltd. .... UK
Ella Shields .... **Columbia 3646**
Michael Holliday .... **Columbia SEG 7892**
The Andrews Sisters .... **Capitol T 973**

SHOW ME YOU'RE A WOMAN — December 1975
Phil Wainman / John Goodison
Utopia Music .... UK
Mud .... **Private Stock PVT 45**

SHOW MUST GO ON, THE — February 1974
Leo Sayer / Dave Courtney
Compass Music Ltd. .... UK
Leo Sayer .... **Chrysalis CHS 2023**

SHOW YOU THE WAY TO GO   July 1977
Kenny Gamble / Leon Huff
Carlin Music Corporation .... USA
The Jacksons .... **Epic EPC 5266**

SHOW, THE   December 1985
Douglas Davis / Rick Walters
EMI Music Ltd. .... USA
Doug E. Fresh & The Get Fresh Crew .... **Chrysalis COOL 116**

SHOWDOWN   November 1973
Jeff Lynne
Carlin Music Corporation .... UK
The Electric Light Orchestra .... **Harvest HAR 5077**

SHOWING OUT   November 1986
Mike Stock / Matt Aitken / Peter Waterman
All Boys Music .... UK
Mel & Kim .... **Supreme SUPE 107**

SHRIMP BOATS   December 1951
Mason Howard / Paul Weston
Walt Disney Music Co. Ltd .... USA
Jo Stafford .... **Philips BBL 7395**

SHRINE OF ST. CECILIA, THE (Min Soldat)   1942
Carroll Loveday / "Jokern"
Victoria Music Co. Ltd .... Sweden
Joe Loss & his Orchestra, vocal Harry Kaye .... **HMV BD 5741**
Faron Young .... **Capitol CL 14735**

SHUFFLE OFF TO BUFFALO   1933
Al Dubin / Harry Warren
B. Feldman & Co. Ltd. .... USA
Film(s): .... Forty-Second Street / Footlight Parade
The Boswell Sisters .... **Brunswick 01516**
Ray Ellis & his Orchestra .... **Fontana TFL 5027**
Ruby Keeler, Clarence Nordstrom, Una Merkel
& Ginger Rogers .... **United Artists UAG 29644**
Ruby Keeler, Clarence Nordstrom, Una Merkel & Ginger Rogers
appeared in *Forty Second Street*.

SHUFFLE, THE   June 1977
Van McCoy
Warner Brothers Music Ltd .... USA
Van McCoy .... **H&L 6105076**

SHUFFLIN' ALONG   1922
Nat. D. Ayer / Ralph Stanley
B. Feldman & Co. Ltd .... UK
Show(s): .... Snap
The 'Queens' Dance Orchestra,
director Jack Hylton .... **HMV B 1403**
Ennis Parkes (Mrs Jack Hylton) .... **HMV B 1400**

SHUT UP   October 1981
Graham McPherson / Christopher Forman
Warner Brothers Music .... UK
Madness .... **Stiff BUY 126**

SHUT UP YOUR FACE (See SHADDUP YOU FACE)

SHY BOY   July 1982
Tony Swain / Steve Jolley
Red Bus Music .... UK
Bananarama .... **London NANA 2**

SHY SERENADE   1938
George Scott-Wood
Lawrence Wright Music Co. Ltd. .... UK
The Albert Sandler Trio .... **Columbia FB 2098**
The New Mayfair Novelty Orchestra .... **HMV BD 702**

SIBONEY   1931
Ernesto Lecuona / Dolly Morse
Francis, Day & Hunter Ltd. .... Cuba
Film(s): .... Get Hep to Love
Enric Madriguera & his Orchestra .... **Columbia CB 354**
Bing Crosby .... **Brunswick LAT 8331**
Edmundo Ros Orchestra .... **Decca LK 4175**

SIDE BY SIDE   1927
Harry Woods
Lawrence Wright Music Co. Ltd. .... USA
Paul Whiteman & his Orchestra, vocal Bing Crosby   **HMV B 5318**

Kay Starr (1953) .... **Capitol T 950**
Pat & Shirley Boone .... **London HAD 2210**

SIDE SADDLE   April 1959
Trevor Stanford
Mills Music Ltd .... UK
Russ Conway (piano) .... **Columbia SEG 7905**
Ivor Novello Award.

SIDE SHOW   February 1977
Barry Biggs
Famous-Chappell .... UK
Barry Biggs .... **Dynamic DYN 118**

SIDEWALKS OF CUBA   1935
Ben Oakland / Mitchell Parish / Irving Mills
Keith Prowse Music Publishing Co. Ltd .... USA
Lew Stone & his Orchestra .... **Regal Zonophone MR 1583**
Ted Heath & his Music .... **Decca LK 4204**

SIDEWALKS OF NEW YORK, THE   1894
James W. Blake / Charles B. Lawler
Herman Darewski Music Publishing Co. Ltd. .... USA
Film(s): .... Beau James
Joe Green & his Novelty Orchestra .. **Edison Bell Winner 1161**
The Justin Ring Orchestra .... **Panachord 26020**
Duke Ellington & his Orchestra .... **RCA RCX 1006**
Bob Hope & Jimmy Durante .... **London HAP 2056**
Bob Hope appeared in *Beau James*.

SIERRA SUE   1940
Joseph Carey
Francis, Day & Hunter Ltd .... USA
Film(s): .... Sierra Sue
Gene Autry .... **Regal Zonophone MR 3404**
Bing Crosby .... **Brunswick 03044**
Gene Autry appeared in *Sierra Sue*.

SIGN O' THE TIMES   March 1987
"Prince"
Warner Brothers Music .... USA
Prince .... **Paisley Park W 8399**

SIGN OF THE TIMES   February 1983
Stella Barker / Clare Hurst / Miranda Joyce / Sarah Owen / Judy Parsons / Lesley Shone / Jenny McKeown
Chrysalis Music .... UK
The Belle Stars .... **Stiff BUY 167**

SIGN YOUR NAME   February 1088
Terence Trent D'Arby
Virgin Music .... UK
Terence Trent D'Arby .... **CBS TRENT 4**

SIGNED, SEALED, DELIVERED, I'M YOURS   August 1970
Stevie Wonder / Lee Garrett / Syreeta Wright / Lula Hardaway
Jobete Music (UK) Ltd. .... USA
Stevie Wonder .... **Tamla Motown TMG 744**

SILENCE IS GOLDEN   July 1967
Bob Crewe / Bob Gaudio
Ardmore & Beechwood Ltd. .... USA
The Tremeloes .... **CBS 2723**

SILENZIO, IL   October 1965
N.R. Celeste / G. Brezza
Peter Maurice Music Co. Ltd .... Italy
Nino Rosso (trumpet) with Orchestra ..... **Durium DRS 54000**
Eddie Calvert (trumpet) with Orchestra .... **Columbia DB 7646**

SILHOUETTES   March 1965
Frank Slay / Bob Crewe
Sylvester .... USA
Herman's Hermits .... **Columbia DB 7475**
Cliff Richard (1990) .... **EMI EM 152**

SILLY GAMES   July 1979
Diana Bovell / John Myatt
Intersong Music .... UK
Janet Kay .... **Scope SC2**

SILLY LOVE SONGS   June 1976
Paul McCartney
A.T.V. Music Ltd. .... UK
Wings .... **Parlophone R 6014**

275

SILLY THING   April 1979
Paul Cook / Steve Jones
Warner Brothers Music Ltd. .... UK
The Sex Pistols .... **Virgin VS 256**

SILVER BELL   1910
Edward Madden / Percy Wenrich
B. Feldman & Co. Ltd. .... USA
Gertie Gitana .... **Ariel 1973**
The International Novelty Quartet . **Regal Zonophone MR 1215**

SILVER DOLLAR   April 1950
Clark Van Ness / Jack Palmer
Anglo-Pic Music Co. Ltd. .... USA
Eve Young .... **London L 858**
Turk Murphy's Jazz Band .... **Philips BBL 7088**
'Something' Smith & The Red Heads .... **MGM C 872**

SILVER DREAM MACHINE   May 1980
David Essex
April Music Ltd .... UK
Film(s): .... Silver Dream Racer
David Essex .... **Mercury BIKE 1**
David Essex appeared in *Silver Dream Racer*
Ivor Novello Nomination.

SILVER HAIR AND HEART OF GOLD   1932
Peter Maurice / Joe Gilbert
Peter Maurice Music Co. Ltd. .... UK
Layton & Johnstone .... **Columbia DB 989**
David Whitfield .... **Decca DFE 6601**

SILVER LADY   October 1977
Tony Macaulay
Dick James Music Ltd .... UK
David Soul .... **Private Stock PVT 115**

SILVER MACHINE   September 1972
Robert Calvert / S. MacManus
United Artists Music Co. Ltd. .... UK
Hawkwind .... **United Artists UP 3581**

SILVER ROSE   1927
George Meyer
Ascherberg, Hopwood & Crew Ltd. .... USA
Show(s): .... Blackbirds
The Plantation Orchestra .... **Columbia 4185**
The Plantation Orchestra appeared in *Blackbirds*.

SILVER STAR   May 1976
Bob Gaudio / Judy Parker
Jobete Music (UK) Ltd. .... USA
The Four Seasons .... **Warner Brothers K 16742**

SILVER THREADS AMONG THE GOLD   1874
Eben Rexford / Hart Pease Danks
Ascherberg, Hopwood & Crew Ltd. .... USA
Arthur Gray & Quartet .... **Zonophone 188**
Bing Crosby .... **Brunswick 03839**
Clinton Ford .... **Oriole CB 1578**

SILVER WINGS IN THE MOONLIGHT   1942
Sonny Miller / Hugh Charles / Leo Towers
Dash Music Ltd .... UK
Anne Shelton .... **Decca F 8352**

SIMILAU   July 1949
Harry Coleman / Arden Clare
Edward Kassner Music Co. Ltd .... USA
Edmundo Ros & his Orchestra .... **Decca LK 4104**
Peggy Lee .... **Capitol CL 13111**
Sallie Blair .... **Parlophone PMC 1083**

SIMON SAYS   May 1968
Elliot Chiprut
Carlin Music Corporation .... USA
The 1910 Fruitgum Company .... **Pye 7N 25447**

SIMON SMITH & HIS AMAZING DANCING BEAR   May 1967
Randy Newman
Aaron Schroeder Music Ltd. .... USA
The Alan Price Set .... **Decca F 12570**
Randy Newman .... **Reprise R 44185**

SIMON TEMPLAR   July 1980
Martin Everest / Peter Neil / Terence Dale
A.T.V. Music Ltd. .... UK
Splodgenessabounds .... **Deram BUM 1**
Based on the theme of the TV serial "Return of the Saint" by Irving
Martin & Brian Dee.

SIMPLE GAME   November 1971
Mike Pinder
Sparta Music Ltd .... UK
The Four Tops .... **Tamla Motown TMG 785**
Ivor Novello Award.

SIN   January 1952
George Hoven / Chester R. Shull
Edwin H.Morris & Co. Ltd .... USA
The Four Knights .... **Capitol T 950**
Teddy Johnson .... **Columbia DB 2996**
Jimmy Young .... **Polygon P 1032**
Brook Benton .... **Mercury MMC 14022**

SINCE I FOUND YOU   1927
Sidney Clare / Harry Woods
B. Feldman & Co. Ltd. .... USA
The Ipana Troubadours .... **Columbia 4339**
Jim Miller & Charlie Farrell .... **HMV B 2456**

SINCE YESTERDAY   February 1985
Jill Bryson / Rose McDowall
Warner Brothers Music .... UK
Strawberry Switchblade .... **Korva KOW 38**

SINCE YOU'VE BEEN GONE   October 1979
Russ Ballard
Island Music Ltd. .... UK
Rainbow .... **Polydor POSP 70**

SINCERELY   March 1955
Harvey Fuqua / Alan Freed
Dash Music Ltd. .... USA
Muriel Smith .... **Philips PB 422**
The McGuire Sisters .... **Vogue LVA 9133**
Connie Francis .... **MGM C 804**

SING A LITTLE JINGLE   1931
Harry Warren / Mort Dixon
Victoria Music Co. Ltd. .... USA
Show(s): .... Crazy Quilt
Victor Young & his Orchestra,
vocal The Boswell Sisters .... **Brunswick 01193**

SING A SONG OF FREEDOM   December 1971
Guy Fletcher / Doug Flett
Big Secret Music .... UK
Cliff Richard .... **Columbia DB 8836**

SING A SONG OF SUNBEAMS   1939
Jimmy Monaco / Johnny Burke
Campbell Connelly & Co. Ltd. .... USA
Film(s): .... East Side of Heaven
Bing Crosby .... **Brunswick Bing 4**
Bing Crosby appeared in *East Side of Heaven*.

SING AS WE GO   1934
Harry Parr-Davies / Gracie Fields
Francis, Day & Hunter Ltd .... UK
Film(s): .... Sing as We Go
Gracie Fields (1934) .... **HMV B 8209**
Gracie Fields (1959) .... **Columbia 33SX 1198**
Gracie Fields appeared in *Sing as We Go*.

SING BABY SING   1937
Lew Pollack / Jack Yellen
Francis, Day & Hunter Ltd. .... USA
Film(s): .... Sing Baby Sing
Ambrose & his Orchestra .... **Decca F 6187**
The Peters Sisters .... **Columbia 33SX 1288**
Jack Hylton Orchestra v Alice Mann ... **World Records SH 190**

SING BABY SING   June 1975
Hugo Peretti / Luigi Creatore / George Weiss
Cyril Shane Music .... USA
The Stylistics .... **Avco 6105036**

SING FOR YOUR SUPPER — 1939
Richard Rodgers / Lorenz Hart
Sterling Music Publishing Co. Ltd. . . . . USA
Show(s): . . . . The Boys From Syracuse / Up and Doing
Film(s): . . . . The Boys From Syracuse
Count Basie & his Orchestra,
vocal Helen Hume . . . . **Brunswick 02940**
Frank Cordell & his Orchestra . . . . **HMV CLP 1341**
Mel Tormé . . . . **London LTZN 15009**
Lynn Kennington, Paula Hendrix
& Maggie Fitzgibbon . . . . **Decca LK 4564**
Lynn Kennington, Paula Hendrix & Maggie Fitzgibbon appeared in
the British production of *The Boys from Syracuse*.

SING JOYOUS BIRD — 1914
Norah Usher / Montague Phillips
Chappell Music Co. . . . . UK
Elsa Stralia . . . . **Columbia 7137**
Felicity Palmer . . . . **Argo ZK 97**

SING LITTLE BIRDIE — May 1959
Stan Butcher / Syd Cordell
Good Music Ltd . . . . UK
Teddy Johnson & Pearl Carr . . . . **Columbia DB 4275**
United Kingdom entry for the 1959 Eurovision Song Contest (Placed
Second).

SING ME — March 1977
John Greenslade / June Greenslade
Intune Ltd . . . . UK
The Brothers . . . . **Bus Stop BUS 1054**

SING ME A SONG OF THE ISLANDS — 1943
Harry Owens / Mack Gordon
Chappell & Co. Ltd . . . . USA
Film(s): . . . . Song of the Islands
Bing Crosby . . . . **Brunswick 03355**
Harry Owens & his Royal Hawaiians,
vocal Gil Mershon . . . . **Columbia SEG 7557**
The Hawaiian Hula Boys . . . . **Columbia 33SX 1101**

SING OUR OWN SONG — August 1986
"*UB40*"
A.T.V. Music . . . . UK
UB40 . . . . **Virgin DEP 23**

SING SOMETHING SIMPLE — 1930
Herman Hupfeld
Chappell & Co. Ltd . . . . USA
Show(s): . . . . The Second Little Show
The Revellers . . . . **HMV B 3704**
Maxine Sullivan . . . . **HMV JO 101**
Debbie Reynolds . . . . **London HAD 2326**

SING YOU SINNERS — 1930
Sam Coslow / Franke Harling
Chappell & Co. Ltd . . . . USA
Film(s): . . . . Honey / I'll Cry Tomorrow
Smith Ballew & his Orchestra,
vocal Smith Ballew . . . . **Parlophone R 724**
Susan Hayward . . . . **MGM EP 555**
Rosemary Clooney . . . . **Coral LVA 9112**
Susan Hayward appeared in *I'll Cry Tomorrow*.

SING, EVERYBODY SING — 1942
John P. Long
Francis, Day & Hunter Ltd . . . . UK
Donald Peers . . . . **Decca F 8170**

SING, SING, SING — 1937
Louis Prima
Keith Prowse Music Publishing Co. Ltd. . . . . USA
Film(s): . . . . Strike Up the Band / The Benny Goodman Story
Benny Goodman & his Orchestra (1936) . . . . . . **RCA RCX 1026**
Benny Goodman & his Orchestra . . . . **Brunswick LAT 8103**
The Clark Sisters . . . . **London HAD 2128**

SINGIN' IN THE RAIN — 1929
Arthur Freed / Nacio Herb Brown
Robbins Music Corporation . . . . USA
Show(s): . . . . Singin' in the Rain
Film(s): . . . Hollywood Revue / Little Nellie Kelly / Singin' in the Rain
Cliff Edwards (Ukulele Ike) . . . . **Columbia 5559**
Cliff Edwards (Ukulele Ike) (1959) . . . . . . **Disneyland WBL 3003**
Gene Kelly . . . . **MGM C 789**

Michael Holliday . . . . **Columbia 33SX 1354**
Shelia B. Devotion . . . . **Carrere 2751**
Tommy Steele . . . . **Safari RAIN 1**
Cliff Edwards appeared in *Hollywood Revue*.
Gene Kelly appeared inthe film *Singin' in the Rain*.
Tommy Steele appeared in the show *Singin' in the Rain*.

SINGIN' THE BLUES — 1931
Dorothy Fields / Jimmy McHugh
Keith Prowse Music Publishing Co. Ltd. . . . . USA
Show(s): . . . . Singin' the Blues
Red Nichols & his Five Pennies . . . . **Brunswick 01276**

SINGIN' THE BLUES (Till My Daddy Comes Home) — 1921
J. Russell Robinson / Con Conrad
B. Feldman & Co. Ltd . . . . USA
Frankie Trumbauer & his Orchestra . . . . . . **Philips BBL 12125**
Connee Boswell & The Original Memphis Five . **RCA RD 27017**
The Original Dixieland Jazz Band . . . . **HMV B 1199**

SINGING A VAGABOND SONG — 1930
Sam Messenheimer / Harry Richman / Val Burton
Campbell Connelly & Co. Ltd . . . . USA
Film(s): . . . . Puttin' on the Ritz
Harry Richman . . . . **Brunswick 03959**
Ted Lewis & his Band, vocal Ted Lewis . . . . . **Columbia CB 74**
Harry Richman appeared in *Puttin' On The Ritz*.

SINGING HILLS, THE — 1940
Mack David / Dick Sanford / Mammy Mysels
Campbell Connelly & Co. Ltd . . . . USA
Bing Crosby . . . . **Brunswick LAT 8253**
Slim Whitman . . . . **London HAP 2199**

SINGING IN THE BATHTUB — 1930
Ned Washington / Herb Magisdon / Michael Cleary
B. Feldman & Co. Ltd . . . . USA
Film(s): . . . . Show of Shows
Gracie Fields . . . . **HMV 7EG 8299**
The Girls . . . . **Warner Brothers WM 4053**

SINGING PIANO, THE — October 1959
Tolchard Evans
Sydney Bron Music Co. Ltd . . . . UK
Tolchard Evans (piano) . . . . **Decca F 11173**

SINGING THE BLUES — December 1956
Melvin Endsley
Frank Music Co. Ltd. . . . . USA
Guy Mitchell . . . . **Philips BBL 7265**
Tommy Steele . . . . **Decca LF 1299**
Marty Robbins . . . . **Fontana TFL 5086**

SINGLE GIRL — February 1967
Martha Sharp
Combine Music . . . . USA
Sandy Posey . . . . **MGM 1330**

SINK RED SUN — 1909
Teresa Del Riego
Chappell & Co. Ltd. . . . . UK
Phyllis Lett . . . . **HMV D 249**
Muriel Brunskill . . . . **Columbia 4259**

SINNER KISSED AN ANGEL, A — 1942
Mack David / Ray Joseph
Chappell & Co. Ltd . . . . USA
Tommy Dorsey & his Orchestra,
vocal Frank Sinatra . . . . **HMV BD 5739**
The R.A.F. Dance Orchestra, vocal Jimmy Miller . . **Decca F 8049**
Sarah Vaughan . . . . **Emarcy EJL 1258**
Louis Armstrong & his Orchestra,
vocal Louis Armstrong . . . . **Brunswick LAT 8210**

SIOUX CITY SUE — 1946
Dick Thomas / Roy Freedman
Edwin H. Morris & Co. Ltd. . . . . USA
Film(s): . . . . Sioux City Sue
Bing Crosby & The Jesters . . . . **Brunswick LAT 8053**
Bryan Johnson . . . . **Decca LK 4362**

SIPPIN' SODA — November 1953
Paul Campbell
Cinephonic Music Co. Ltd. . . . . USA
Guy Mitchell & Children's Chorus . . . . **Philips PB 210**

SIR DUKE   May 1977
Stevie Wonder
Jobete Music (UK) Ltd. . . . . USA
Stevie Wonder . . . . **Motown TMG 1068**

SISTER JANE   June 1972
Mike Chapman / Nicky Chinn
Rak Music Ltd. . . . . UK
New World . . . . **Rak 130**

SISTER SUSIE'S SEWING SHIRTS FOR SOLDIERS   1914
R.P. Weston / Herman Darewski
Francis, Day & Hunter Ltd. . . . . UK
Jack Norworth . . . . **Columbia 2526**

SISTERS ARE DOING IT FOR THEMSELVES   Nov 1985
Annie Lennox / Dave Stewart
RCA Music . . . . UK
The Eurythmics & Aretha Franklin . . . . **RCA PB 40339**

SIT DOWN YOU'RE ROCKING THE BOAT   July 1953
Frank Loesser
Edwin H. Morris & Co. Ltd . . . . USA
Show(s): . . . . Guys and Dolls
Film(s): . . . . Guys and Dolls
Stubby Kaye . . . . **Brunswick LAT 8022**
Sammy Davis . . . . **Brunswick OE 9209**
Stubby Kaye appeared in both the American and British productions,
and the film of, *Guys and Dolls.*

SITTING IN THE PARK   February 1967
Billy Stewart
Jewel Music Publishing Co. Ltd. USA
Georgie Fame . . . . **Columbia DB 8096**

SITTING ON A BACK-YARD FENCE   1934
Irving Kahal / Sammy Fain
B. Feldman & Co. Ltd. . . . . USA
Film(s): . . . . Footlight Parade
Paul Whiteman & his Orchestra . . . . **HMV B 6434**
Adrian Rollini & his Orchestra . . . . **Decca F 3827**

SITTING ON A FIVE BARRED GATE   1931
Stanley Damerell / Reginald Hargreaves
Cecil Lennox Music Co. Ltd . . . . UK
Jack Payne & The BBC Dance Orchestra . . . **Columbia CB 197**

SIX LESSONS FROM MADAME LA ZONGA   1940
Charles Newman / Jimmy Monaco
Lafleur & Co. Ltd . . . . USA
Film(s): . . . . Six Lessons From Madame La Zonga
Jimmy Dorsey & his Orchestra,
vocal Helen O'Connell . . . . **Brunswick 03037**
The King Sisters . . . . **Regal Zonophone MR 3350**
Mel Tormé . . . . **HMV CLP 1315**

SIX TEENS, THE   July 1974
Mike Chapman / Nicky Chinn
Chinnichap Music . . . . UK
Sweet . . . . **RCA LPBO 5037**

SIX TIMES A WEEK AND TWICE ON SUNDAYS   April 1950
Lew Porter / 'Teepee' Mitchell
Chappell & Co. ltd . . . . USA
Margaret Whiting & Jimmy Wakely . . . . . . **Capitol CL 13245**

SIXTEEN BARS   September 1976
Hugo Peretti / Luigi Creatore
Cyril Shane Music . . . . USA
The Stylistics . . . . **H&L 6105059**

SIXTEEN REASONS   June 1960
Bill Post / Doree Post
Campbell Connelly & Co. Ltd . . . . USA
Connie Stevens . . . . **Warner Brothers WB 3**
Marion Ryan . . . . **Columbia DB 4448**

SIXTEEN TONS   January 1956
Merle Travis
Campbell Connelly & Co. Ltd. . . . . USA
Tennessee Ernie Ford . . . . **Capitol T 841**
Frankie Laine . . . . **Philips BBL 7357**

SIXTY SECONDS GOT TOGETHER   1938
Mack David / Jerry Livingston

Campbell Connelly & Co. Ltd. . . . . USA
Ambrose & his Orchestra, vocal Denny Dennis . **Decca F 6868**

SKIING IN THE SNOW   April 1975
Sandy Linzer / Denny Randell
A&B Music . . . . UK
Wigans Ovation . . . . **Spark SRL 1122**

SKIN DEEP   April 1954
Louis Belson
United Artists Music . . . . USA
Louis Belson Orchestra . . . . **Columbia SEB 10050**
Duke Ellington Orchestra . . . . **Philips PB 243**
Ted Heath & his Music . . . . **Decca F 10246**

SKIRTS   1933
Joe Roberts / Slatz Randall
B. Feldman & Co. Ltd. . . . . USA
Billy Cotton & his Band,
vocal Alan Breeze . . . . **Regal Zonophone MR 866**
Eddy Howard & his Orch, vocal Eddy Howard . **Oriole CB 1240**

SKOKIAAN   August 1954
August Msarugwa / Tom Glazer
Peter Maurice Music Co. Ltd. . . . . South Africa
The Bulawayo Sweet Rhythm Band . . . . . . **Decca F 10350**
Louis Armstrong . . . . **Brunswick 05332**
Horst Wende & his Orchestra . . . . . . **Polydor LPHM 46531**

SKWEEZE ME PLEEZE ME   July 1973
Noddy Holder / Jimmy Lea
Barn Publishing Ltd. . . . . UK
Slade . . . . **Polydor 2058377**

SKY BLUE SHIRT AND A RAINBOW TIE, A   September 1954
Jack Berch / John Redmond
Lawrence Wright Music Co. Ltd. USA
Jack Parnell & his Orchestra . . . . . . **Parlophone MSP 6138**
The Hedley Ward Trio . . . . **Melodisc 1298**
Norman Brooks . . . . **London REP 1004**

SKY HIGH   November 1975
Clive Scott / Des Dyer
Leeds Music Ltd . . . . UK
Film(s): . . . . The Man From Hong Kong
Jigsaw . . . . **Splash CPI 1**
Ivor Novello Nomination.

SKYE BOAT SONG, THE   December 1986
Traditional, arranged by Roger Whittaker & Colin Keyes
Tembo Music . . . . UK
Roger Whittaker . . . . **Tembo TML 119**

SKYLARK   1942
Hoagy Carmichael / Johnny Mercer
Chappell & Co. Ltd . . . . USA
Bing Crosby . . . . **Brunswick 03326**
Hoagy Carmichael . . . . **Vogue VA 160112**
Jackie Paris . . . . **Vogue LVA 9098**
Dinah Shore . . . . **Capitol T 1354**

SKYLINER   1946
Charlie Barnet
Peter Maurice Music Co. Ltd. . . . . USA
Charlie Barnet & his Orchestra . . . . . . **Brunswick LAT 8094**
Jackie Gleason & his Orchestra . . . . **Capitol LCT 6153**
Theme tune of Charlie Barnet.

SLAP THAT BASS   1938
George Gershwin / Ira Gershwin
Chappell & Co. Ltd . . . . USA
Film(s): . . . . Shall We Dance
Fred Astaire . . . . **Fontana TFL 5037**
The Ink Spots . . . . **Brunswick 02440**
Ella Fitzgerald . . . . **HMV CLP 1340**
Fred Astaire appeared in *Shall We Dance.*

SLAUGHTER ON TENTH AVENUE   1937
Richard Rodgers
Chappell & Co. Ltd. . . . . USA
Show(s): . . . . On Your Toes
Film(s): . . . . On Your Toes / Words and Music
Paul Whiteman & his Orchestra . . . . **HMV C 2884**
The New York Philharmonic Orchestra, conductor Richard
Rodgers . . . . **Philips BBL 7097**

The Warner Brothers Orchestra ... Warner Brothers WM 4002

SLAVE TO LOVE, A   June 1985
Bryan Ferry
E.G. Music .... UK
Bryan Ferry .... **Polydor FERRY 1**

SLAVE TO THE RHYTHM   November 1985
Bruce Woolley / Simon Darow / Stephen Lipon & Trevor Horn
CBS Songs .... UK
Grace Jones .... **Island IS 206**

SLEDGEHAMMER   May 1986
Peter Gabriel
Cliofine Music Ltd. .... UK
Peter Gabriel .... **Virgin PGS 1**
Ivor Novello Nomination.

SLEEP   1924
Earl Lebieg
Herman Darewski Music Publishing Co. Ltd .... USA
The Romancers .... **Columbia 3310**
Fred Waring's Glee Club .... **Capitol LCT 6143**
Pat Boone .... **London HAD 2382**
Theme tune of Fred Waring.

SLEEP MY BABY SLEEP   1935
Eddie Pola / Franz Vienna
Keith Prowse Music Publishing Co. Ltd .... USA
Leo Fuld .... **Decca F 9224**
Judy Garland .... **Brunswick 02611**

SLEEP MY LITTLE ONE   1936
Selma Hautzik / Hugo Riesenfeld
Francis, Day & Hunter Ltd .... USA
Film(s): .... Let's Sing Again
Kitty Masters .... **Regal Zonophone MR 2181**

SLEEP WALK   September 1959
Ann Farina / Johnny Farina / Santo Farina
Frank Music Co. Ltd .... USA
The Sleepwalkers .... **Parlophone R 4580**
Chet Atkins (guitar) .... **RCA RD 27168**

SLEEPY SERENADE   1941
Lou Singer / Mort Greene
Leeds Music Ltd .... USA
Film(s): .... Hold That Ghost
The Andrews Sisters .... **Brunswick 03215**
Jack Pleis & his Orchestra ... **Brunswick LAT 8304**
Cyril Stapleton & his Orchestra ...... **Decca F 8752**
The Andrews Sisters appeared in *Hold That Ghost*.
Theme song of Cyril Stapleton.

SLEEPY SHORES   January 1972
Johnny Pearson
Keith Prowse Music Publishing Co. Ltd .... UK
Johnny Pearson & Orchestra ..... **Penny Farthing PEN 778**
Theme of the T.V. series *Owen M.D.*
Ivor Novello Nomination.

SLEEPY TIME GAL   1926
Richard A. Whiting / Ray Egan / Joseph Alden / Ange Lorenzo
Francis, Day & Hunter Ltd. .... USA
Film(s): .... Sleepy Time Gal / Never a Dull Moment
The Denza Dance Band .... **Columbia 3913**
Bing Crosby .... **Brunswick LA 8673**
Art Lund .... **MGM 106**

SLEEPY VALLEY   1929
Andrew Sterling / James Hanley
Chappell & Co. Ltd .... USA
Film(s): .... The Rainbow Man
The Cavaliers .... **Columbia 5558**

SLEIGH RIDE   June 1950
Leroy Anderson / Mitchell Parish
Mills Music Ltd .... USA
Leroy Anderson & his Orchestra .. **Brunswick LAT 8337**
Bing Crosby .... **Brunswick 05014**
Ella Fitzgerald .... **HMV CLP 1397**

SLIGHTEST TOUCH   May 1987
Michael Jay / Marvin Morrow
MCA Music .... UK

Five Star .... **Tent PB 41265**

SLIPPING AROUND   December 1949
Floyd Tillman
Southern Music Publishing Co. Ltd .... USA
Margaret Whiting & Jimmy Wakely ..... **Capitol CL 13220**
Ernest Tubb .... **Brunswick LAT 8313**

SLOOP JOHN B, THE   June 1966
Brian Wilson
Immediate Music Ltd. .... USA
The Beach Boys .... **Capitol CL 15441**

SLOW COACH   March 1952
Pee Wee King / Redd Stewart / Chilton Price
Chappell & Co. Ltd .... USA
Pee Wee King & his Golden West Cowboys,
vocal Redd Stewart .... **HMV B 10203**
The Radio Revellers .... **Columbia DB 3027**
Helen O'Connell .... **Capitol CL 13657**
Kenny Lynch .... **HMV POP 786**

SLOW DOWN   July 1977
Bob Marshall / John Miles
Rondor Music (London) Ltd .... UK
John Miles .... **Decca F 13709**

SLOW HAND   September 1981
John Bettis / Michael Clark
Warner Brothers Music .... USA
The Pointer Sisters .... **Planet K 12530**

SLUMMING ON PARK AVENUE   1937
Irving Berlin
Irving Berlin Ltd. .... USA
Film(s): .... On the Avenue
Alice Faye .... **Brunswick 02454**
Petula Clark .... **Pye NPL 18007**
Alice Faye appeared in *On the Avenue*.

SMALL FRY   1938
Hoagy Carmichael / Frank Loesser
Victoria Music Co. Ltd. .... USA
Film(s): .... Sing You Sinners
Bing Crosby & Johnny Mercer ..... **Brunswick Bing 3**
June Christy .... **Capitol T 1398**
Bing Crosby appeared in *Sing You Sinners*.

SMALL TOWN BOY   July 1984
Larry Steinbachek / Steve Bronski
Bronski Music .... UK
Bronski Beat .... **London BITE 1**

SMARTY PANTS   September 1973
Norman Harris / Alan Felder
Carlin Music Corporation .... USA
First Choice .... **Bell 1324**

SMILE   August 1954
Charles Chaplin / John Turner / Geoffrey Parsons
Bourne Music Ltd. .... USA
Petula Clark .... **Nixa NPT 19002**
Nat 'King' Cole .... **Capitol EAP 1-20108**
Perry Como .... **RCA RD 27232**

SMILE   August 1986
Audrey Hall
Beverley Music .... UK
Audrey Hall .... **Germain DG 15**

SMILE RIGHT BACK AT THE SUN   1947
Johnny Burke / Jimmy Van Heusen
Edwin H. Morris & Co. Ltd. .... USA
Film(s): .... Welcome Stranger
Bing Crosby .... **Brunswick Bing 11**
Bing Crosby appeared in *Welcome Stranger*.

SMILE WILL GO A LONG, LONG WAY, A   1924
Benny Davis / Harry Akst
B. Feldman & Co. Ltd. .... USA
Ted Weems & his Orchestra .... **HMV B 1863**
The Andrews Sisters .... **Capitol T 973**

SMILE, DARN YA SMILE   1931
Charles O'Flynn / Jack Meskill / Max Rich

Victoria Music Co. Ltd. . . . . USA
Roy Fox & his Band, vocal Al Bowlly . . . . **Decca F 2580**
The Big Ben Banjo Band . . . . **Columbia 33SX 1108**

SMILES   1918
Lee Roberts / Will Callahan
Francis, Day & Hunter Ltd. . . . . USA
Show(s): . . . . The Passing Show of 1918
Film(s):The Dolly Sisters / Somebody Loves Me / Wait Till the Sun
Shines Nellie / The Eddy Duchin Story / Applause / For Me and My
Gal
Elsie Janis . . . . **HMV 03645**
Jo Stafford . . . . **Capitol CL 13302**
Gordon MacRae . . . . **Capitol T 1251**

SMILIN' THROUGH   1918
Arthur Penn
B. Feldman & Co. Ltd. . . . . USA
Walter Glynne . . . . **HMV B 1250**
John McCormack . . . . **HMV DA 1805**
Thomas L. Thomas . . . . **Decca LXT 5247**

SMITHS AND THE JONESES, THE   1943
Kay Twomey / Al Goodhart / Irwin S. Nelson
Chappell & Co. Ltd . . . . USA
Show(s): . . . . Hi-De-Hi
Flanagan & Allen . . . . **Decca F 8325**
Flanagan & Allen appeared in *Hi-De-Hi*.

SMOKE GETS IN YOUR EYES   1934
Jerome Kern / Otto Harbach
Sterling Music Publishing Co. Ltd . . . . USA
Show(s): . . . . Roberta
Film(s): . . . . . . Roberta / Till the Clouds Roll By / Lovely to Look at
Ruth Etting . . . . **Brunswick 01879**
Irene Dunne . . . . **Brunswick 03340**
Kathryn Grayson . . . . **MGM EP 703**
The Platters (1959) . . . . **Mercury MMC 14014**
Ronnie Hilton . . . . **HMV CLP 1295**
Bryan Ferry (1974) . . . . **Island WIP 6205**
Irene Dunne appeared in the film of *Roberta*.
Kathryn Grayson appeared in *Lovely to Look at*.

SMOKE RINGS   1932
Gene Gifford / Ned Washington
Lafleur & Co Ltd. . . . . USA
The Casa Loma Orchestra . . . . **Brunswick 01311**
The Mills Brothers . . . . **Brunswick 02782**
Glenn Miller & his Orchestra . . . . **RCA RD 27146**
Henry Mancini & his Orchestra . . . . **RCA RD 27195**
Theme song of Glen Gray & The Casa Loma Orchestra.

SMOKE, SMOKE, SMOKE (That Cigarette)   February 1948
Tex Williams / Merle Travis
Campbell Connelly & Co. Ltd. . . . . USA
Phil Harris . . . . **HMV BD 1195**
Tex Williams . . . . **Capitol T 1463**

SMOOTH CRIMINAL   December 1988
Michael Jackson
Warner Chappell Music . . . . USA
Michael Jackson . . . . **Epic 653026**

SMURF SONG, THE   July 1978
Pierre Kartner
Burlington Music Co. Ltd . . . . Holland
Father Abraham . . . . **Decca F 13759**

SNAKE CHARMER, THE   1938
Teddy Powell / Leonard Whitcup / Larry Clinton
Peter Maurice Music Co. Ltd. . . . . USA
Ben Pollack's Pic-A-Rib Boys . . . . **Brunswick 02557**

SNOOKER LOOPY   June 1986
Charles Hodges / Dave Peacock
Chasdave Music . . . . UK
The Matchroom Mob & Chas 'n' Dave . . . . . . **Rockney POT 147**

SNOOKY OOKUMS   1913
Irving Berlin
B. Feldman & Co. Ltd. . . . . USA
Show(s): . . . . Hullo Ragtime
Film(s): . . . . Easter Parade
Lew Hearn & Bonita . . . . **HMV C 557**

Judy Garland & Fred Astaire . . . .   **MGM D 140**
Lew Hearn & Bonita appeared in *Hullo Ragtime*.
Judy Garland & Fred Astaire appeared in *Easter Parade*.

SNOOPY VERSUS THE RED BARON   February 1967
Philip Gernhard / Dick Holler
Robert Mellin Ltd. . . . . USA
The Royal Guardsmen . . . . **Stateside SS 574**
The Hot Shots (1973) . . . . **Mooncrest MOON 5**

SNOW COACH   November 1959
Trevor Stanford
B. Feldman & Co. Ltd . . . . UK
Russ Conway (piano) . . . . **Columbia DB 4368**

SNOWBALL   1933
Hoagy Carmichael
Lawrence Wright Music Co. Ltd. . . . . USA
Mildred Bailey . . . . **Brunswick 01593**
Elsie Carlisle . . . . **Decca F 3696**
Louis Armstrong & his Orchestra . . . . **RCA RD 27230**
Hoagy Carmichael . . . . **HMV 7EG 8037**

SNOWY WHITE SNOW AND JINGLE BELLS   Dec 1949
Billy Reid
Billy Reid Music Ltd . . . . UK
Dorothy Squires with Orchestra,
conducted by Billy Reid . . . . **Columbia DB 2605**

SNUGGLED ON YOUR SHOULDER   1932
Joe Young / Carmen Lombardo
Francis, Day & Hunter Ltd. . . . . USA
Bing Crosby . . . . **Brunswick 01285**
Julie London . . . . **London HAU 2083**

SO AM I   1926
George Gershwin / Ira Gershwin
Chappell & Co. Ltd. . . . . USA
Show(s): . . . . Lady Be Good
Adele Astaire & George Voltaire . . . . **Columbia 3979**
George Bassman & his Orchestra . . . . **Brunswick LAT 8315**

SO BEATS MY HEART FOR YOU   1930
Pat Ballard / Charles Henderson / Tom Waring
Victoria Music Co. Ltd . . . . USA
Layton & Johnstone . . . . **Columbia DB 346**
The Charles Henderson Singers . . . . **Brunswick LAT 8365**

SO BLUE   1927
Buddy De Sylva / Lew Brown / Ray Henderson
Campbell Conelly & Co. Ltd. . . . . USA
Annette Hanshaw . . . . **Actuelle 11409**
Paul Whiteman & his Orchestra . . . . **HMV B 5319**
Vera Lynn . . . . **Decca LK 4305**
Based on a theme by Helen Crawford.

SO COLD THE NIGHT   December 1986
James Somerville / Richard Coles
Rocket Music . . . . UK
Communards . . . . **London LON 110**

SO DEEP IS THE NIGHT (Tristesse)   1940
Lyrics by Sonny Miller
Keith Prowse Music Publishing Co. Ltd. . . . . USA
John McCormack . . . . **HMV DA 1730**
Ann Ziegler & Webster Booth . . . . **HMV B 9247**
Adapted from 'Etude in E Minor, Opus 10, No. 3' by Frederic Chopin
(1810-1849).

SO DO I   1937
Arthur Johnston / Johnny Burke
Campbell Connelly & Co. Ltd. . . . . USA
Film(s): . . . . Pennies From Heaven
Bing Crosby . . . . **Brunswick Bing 2**
Bing Crosby & Frances Langford . . . . **Brunswick 0134**
Guy Mitchell . . . . **Philips BBL 7246**
Bing Crosby appeared in *Pennies From Heaven*.

SO DO I (Bet Ami)   September 1962
Theo Mackeban / Hans Fritz Beckman / Ian Grant
Peter Maurice Music Co. Ltd . . . . Germany
Kenny Ball & his Jazzmen . . . . **Pye 7NJ 2056**

SO EMOTIONAL   December 1987
William Steinberg / Tom Kelly

Warner Brothers Music . . . . USA
Whitney Houston . . . . **Arista RIS 43**

SO GOOD TO BE BACK HOME   March 1980
Peet Coombs
Arnakata Music . . . . UK
The Tourists . . . . **Logo TOUR 1**

SO IN LOVE   March 1951
Cole Porter
Chappell & Co. Ltd . . . . USA
Show(s): . . . . .Kiss Me Kate
Film(s): . . . . .Kiss Me Kate
Patricia Morison & Alfred Drake . . . . **Philips BBL 7224**
Bill Johnson . . . . **Columbia SEG 7721**
Kathryn Grayson & Howard Keel . . . . **MGM C 789**
Patricia Morison appeared in both the American & British productions
of *Kiss Me Kate*.
Alfred Drake appeared in the American production of *Kiss Me Kate*.
Bill Johnson appeared in the British production of *Kiss Me Kate*.
Kathryn Grayson & Howard Keel appeared in the film *Kiss Me Kate*.

SO IS YOUR OLD LADY   1926
Joe Burke / Al Dubin
Lawrence Wright Music Co. Ltd. . . . . USA
The Denza Dance Band . . . . **Columbia 4068**

SO LONELY   March 1980
"Sting"
Virgin Music (Publishers) Ltd . . . . UK
Police . . . . **A&M AMS 7402**

SO LONG BABY   December 1961
Del Shannon
Vicki Music Ltd. . . . . USA
Del Shannon . . . . **London HL 9462**

SO LONG MARY   1905
George M. Cohan
B. Feldman & Co. Ltd. . . . . USA
Show(s): . . . . Forty-Five Minutes from Broadway
Film(s): . . . . Yankee Doodle Dandy
Corinne Morgan & Chorus . . . . **HMV GC 3818**
Bing Crosby . . . . **Warner Brothers WM 4034**

SO LONG, IT'S BEEN GOOD TO KNOW YOU   January 1951
Woody Guthrie
Leeds Music Ltd . . . . USA
The Weavers . . . . **Brunswick LAT 8357**
Tommy Steele . . . . **Decca LK 4351**
Woody Guthrie . . . . **RCA RD 7642**
First Published 1939.

SO LONG, OO-LONG (How Long You Gonna Be Gone)   1920
Bert Kalmar / Harry Ruby
B. Feldman & Co. Ltd . . . . USA
Film(s): . . . . Three Little Words
The Savoy Quartet, vocal Joe Wilbur . . . . **HMV B 1153**
Fred Astaire & Red Skelton . . . . **MGM D 139**
Fred Astaire & Red Skelton appeared in *Three Little Words*.

SO MACHO   August 1986
James Hargreaves
Sigh Music . . . . USA
Sinitta . . . . **Fanfare FAN 7**

SO MANY MEMORIES   1938
Harry Woods
Campbell Connelly & Co. Ltd. . . . . USA
Frances Langford . . . . **Brunswick 02537**
Vera Lynn . . . . **Decca F 6602**

SO MANY WAYS   December 1959
Bobby Stevenson
Southern Music Publishing Co. Ltd . . . . USA
Brook Benton . . . . **Mercury MMC 14042**

SO RARE   1937
Jack Sharpe / Jerry Herst
Keith Prowse Music Publishing Co. Ltd. . . . . USA
Vera Lynn . . . . **Rex 9153**
Jimmy Dorsey & his Orchestra . . . . **HMV CLP 1132**
Vera Lynn . . . . **Decca LF 1022**
Don Cherry . . . . **Philips BBL 7128**
Ella Fitzgerald . . . . **HMV CLP 1383**

Closing theme of The Jimmy Dorsey Orchestra.

SO SAD   October 1960
Don Everly
Acuff-Rose Publishing Co. Ltd . . . . USA
The Everly Brothers . . . . **Warner Brothers WM 4012**

SO STRONG   May 1987
Labi Siffre
Xavier Music . . . . UK
Labi Siffre . . . . **China WOK 2**
Ivor Novello Award.

SO THIS IS ROMANCE   October 1981
David Grant / Peter Martin
B.M.G. Music . . . . UK
Linx . . . . **Chrysalis CHS 2546**

SO TIRED   1928
George Little / Art Sizemore
B. Feldman & Co. Ltd. . . . . USA
Jean Goldkette & his Orchestra,
vocal Hoagy Carmichael . . . . **HMV B 5479**
Gracie Fields . . . . **HMV B 2739**
Florence Oldham . . . . **Columbia 4777**
The Hilltoppers . . . . **London HAD 2029**

SO TIRED   June 1948
Russ Morgan / Jack Stuart
Campbell Connelly & Co. Ltd. . . . . USA
Russ Morgan & his Orchestra,
vocal Russ Morgan . . . . **Brunswick LAT 8370**
Kay Starr . . . . **Capitol T 1358**
Frankie Vaughan (1967) . . . . **Columbia DB 8298**
Theme song of Russ Morgan.

SO WILL I   1927
Lew Brown / Cliff Friend
Francis, Day & Hunter Ltd. . . . . USA
Jack Smith . . . . **HMV B 2435**

SO WOULD I   1946
Johnny Burke / Jimmy Van Heusen
E.H. Morris Music . . . . USA
Steve Conway . . . . **Columbia FB 3243**
Bing Crosby with The Russ Morgan Orch. . . . . **Brunswick 04747**

SO YOU WIN AGAIN   July 1977
Russ Ballard
Island Music Ltd . . . . UK
Hot Chocolate . . . . **Rak 259**

SOBBIN' BLUES   1924
Art Kassel / Vic Burton
Herman Darewski Music Publising Co. Ltd . . . . USA
King Oliver's Creole Jazz Band . . . . **Philips BBL 7181**
Papa Bue's Viking Jazz Band . . . . **Parlophone PMC 1141**

SOBBIN' WOMEN   November 1954
Johnny Mercer / Gene De Paul
Robbins Music Corporation Ltd. . . . . USA
Film(s): . . . . Seven Brides for Seven Brothers
Howard Keel . . . . **MGM C 853**
Howard Keel appeared in *Seven Brides for Seven Brothers*.

SOFT LIGHTS AND SWEET MUSIC   1932
Irving Berlin
Francis, Day & Hunter Ltd. . . . . USA
Show(s): . . . . .Face the Music
Henry Hall & the B.B.C. Dance Orchestra . . . **Columbia CB 474**
Dick Haymes . . . . **Brunswick LA 8516**
Pat Boone . . . . **London HAD 2082**

SOFT SHOE SHUFFLE, THE   1942
Spencer Williams / Maurice Burman
Peter Maurice Music Co. Ltd . . . . UK
Geraldo & his Orchestra . . . . **Parlophone F 1901**
Jack Simpson & his Sextette, vocal Betty Kent . . . . . **Rex 10004**
Jan Garber & his Orchestra . . . . **Capitol LC 6815**

SOFTLY AS I LEAVE YOU (Piano)   March 1962
Alfredo De Vita / Hal Shaper
Robbins Music Corporation Ltd. . . . . Italy
Matt Monro . . . . **Parlophone R 4868**
Doris Day . . . . **CBS BPG 62226**

SOFTLY AS IN A MORNING SUNRISE 1929
Sigmund Romberg / Oscar Hammerstein II
Chappell & Co. Ltd . . . . USA
Show(s): . . . . The New Moon
Film(s): . . . . The New Moon / Deep in My Heart
Ben Williams & Chorus . . . . **Columbia 9753**
Nelson Eddy . . . . **Columbia 33S 1012**
Bruce Trent . . . . **Fontana TFL 5112**
Helen Traubel . . . . **MGM C 755**
Ben Williams appeared in the British production of *The New Moon*.
Nelson Eddy appeared in the 1940 film of *The New Moon*. Helen
Traubel appeared in *Deep In My Heart*.

SOFTLY WHISPERING I LOVE YOU January 1972
Roger Greenaway / Roger Cook
Maribus Music Ltd . . . . UK
The Congregation . . . . **Columbia DB 8830**

SOFTLY, SOFTLY February 1955
Pierre Dudan / Paddy Roberts / Mark Paul
Cavendish Music Co. Ltd. . . . . UK
Ruby Murray . . . . **Encore ENC 104**
Fele Sowande & his Quiet Rhythm . . . . **Decca LK 4383**

SOLDIER BLUE September 1971
Buffy Saint-Marie
Compass Music Ltd . . . . USA
Film(s): . . . . Soldier Blue
Buffy Saint-Marie . . . . **RCA 2081**

SOLDIERS IN THE PARK, THE 1898
Lionel Monckton / Ivan Caryll
Chappell & Co. Ltd. . . . . UK
Show(s): . . . . A Runaway Girl
The Georgia Glee Singers . . . . **Berliner 4107**
George Baker . . . . **Decca F 1950**
Debroy Somers & his Band . . . . **Columbia DX 305**
The Band of H.M. Coldstream Guards . . . . **HMV B 9258**
Barbara Windsor . . . . **Parlophone PMC 1127**

SOLDIERS OF THE QUEEN 1895
Leslie Stuart
Francis, Day & Hunter Ltd. . . . . UK
Albert Christian (1899) . . . . **Berliner 2400**
Charles Young . . . . **Parlophone PMC 1127**

SOLEY SOLEY January 1972
Miro Arbex
Sunbury Music Ltd . . . . UK
Middle of the Road . . . . **RCA 2151**

SOLID February 1985
Nicholas Ashford / Valerie Simpson
Nik-O-Val Music . . . . USA
Ashford & Simpson . . . . **Capitol CL 345**

SOLID GOLD EASY ACTION January 1973
Marc Bolan
Wizard Music . . . . UK
T. Rex . . . . **EMI MARC 3**
Ivor Novello Nomination.

SOLITAIRE February 1974
Neil Sedaka / Phil Cody
Campbell, Connelly & Co. Ltd. . . . . USA
Andy Williams . . . . **CBS 1824**
Neil Sedaka . . . . **RCA SF 8324**

SOLITUDE 1936
Eddie De Lange / Duke Ellington / Irving Mills
Lafleur & Co. Ltd . . . . USA
Duke Ellington & his Orchestra . . . . **Philips BBE 12404**
The Mills Brothers . . . . **Brunswick OE 9060**
Duke Ellington & his Orchestra . . . . **RCA RCX 1006**
The Mills Brothers . . . . **London HAD 2250**
Tony Bennett . . . . **Philips BBL 7308**

SOLOMON 1933
Cole Porter
Chappell & Co. Ltd. . . . . USA
Show(s): . . . . Nymph Errant
Elizabeth Welch . . . . **HMV B 8031**
Virginia Somers . . . . **Decca LF 1213**
Elizabeth Welch appeared in *Nymph Errant*.

SOLSBURY HILL May 1977
Peter Gabriel
Hit and Run Music . . . . UK
Peter Gabriel . . . . **Charisma CB 301**

SOME DAY 1927
Rudolf Frimi / Brian Hooker
B. Feldman & Co. Ltd. . . . . USA
Show(s): . . . . The Vagabond King
Film(s): . . . . The Vagabond King
Bernice Claire . . . . **Decca K 739**
Barbara Leigh . . . . **Columbia SEG 7930**
Mario Lanza & Judith Raskin . . . . **RCA RB 16264**

SOME DAY I'LL FIND YOU 1930
Noel Coward
Chappell & Co. Ltd . . . . UK
Show(s): . . . . Private Lives
Film(s): . . . . Star
Noel Coward & Gertrude Lawrence . . . . **HMV C 2043**
Gertrude Lawrence . . . . **Brunswick 05001**
Hilde Gueden . . . . **Decca LK 4196**
Julie Andrews . . . . **Stateside SL 10233**
Noel Coward & Gertrude Lawrence appeared in the British production
of *Private Lives*. Julie Andrews appeared in *Star*.

SOME DAY I'LL MEET YOU AGAIN 1944
Max Steiner / Ned Washington
B. Feldman & Co. Ltd. . . . . USA
Film(s): . . . . Passage to Marseilles
The Ink Spots . . . . **Brunswick 03524**
The Warner Brothers Orchestra,
conducted by Max Steiner . . . . **Warner Brothers WM 4044**

SOME DAY MY HEART WILL AWAKE September 1949
Ivor Novello
Chappell & Co. Ltd . . . . UK
Show(s): . . . . King's Rhapsody
Film(s): . . . . King's Rhapsody
Vanessa Lee . . . . **HMV DLP 1010**
Hilde Gueden . . . . **Decca LK 4196**
Vanessa Lea appeared in the show of *King's Rhapsody*.

SOME DAY MY PRINCE WILL COME 1938
Larry Morey / Frank Churchill
Walt Disney Music Co. Ltd. . . . . USA
Film(s): . . . . Snow White and the Seven Dwarfs
Sound Track . . . . **HMV BD 516**
Sound Track . . . . **Disneyland DLP 39003**

SOME DAY SOON 1944
Jimmy Leach
Campbell Connelly & Co. Ltd . . . . UK
Ambrose & his Orchestra, vocal Anne Shelton . . **Decca F 8398**

SOME DAY SWEETHEART 1920
John Spikes / Benjamin Spikes
B. Feldman & Co. Ltd . . . . USA
Ted Lewis & his Band, vocal Ted Lewis . . . . . **Columbia CB 215**
Muggsy Spanier's Ragtime Band . . . . **RCA RD 27132**
Bing Crosby . . . . **Ace of Hearts AH 1**

SOME DAY WE'LL BE TOGETHER January 1970
Robert Beavers / Johnny Bristol / Harvey Faqua
Jobete Music (UK) Ltd. . . . . USA
Diana Ross & The Supremes . . . . **Tamla Motown TMG 721**

SOME DAY WE'RE GONNA LOVE AGAIN August 1964
Sharon McMahan
Toby Music Ltd . . . . UK
The Searchers . . . . **Pye 7N 15670**

SOME DAY YOU'LL BE SORRY December 1954
Louis Armstrong
Campbell Connelly & Co. Ltd. . . . . USA
Film(s): . . . . The Beat Generation
Louis Armstrong . . . . **Brunswick LAT 8243**
Louis Armstrong appeared in *The Beat Generation*.

SOME ENCHANTED EVENING November 1951
Richard Rodgers / Oscar Hammerstein II
Williamson Music Ltd . . . . USA
Show(s): . . . . South Pacific
Film(s): . . . . South Pacific

Ezio Pinza	Philips BBL 7157
Wilbur Evans	Columbia SEG 7668
Giorgio Tozzi	RCA RB 16065

Ezio Pinza appeared in the American production of *South Pacific*.
Wilbur Evans appeared in the British production of *South Pacific*.
Giorgio Tozzi dubbed the singing voice for Rossano Brazzi in the film
South Pacific.

SOME GIRLS — May 1979
Mike Chapman / Nicky Chinn

| Rak Music Ltd. | UK |
| Racey | Rak 291 |

SOME GUYS HAVE ALL THE LUCK — September 1984
Jeff Fortang

Warner Brothers Music	USA
Rod Stewart	Warner Brothers W 9204
Maxi Priest (1987)	10 TEN 198

SOME KINDA FUN — November 1962
Chris Montez / Jim Lee

| E.H. Morris Music | USA |
| Chris Montez | London HLU 9650 |

SOME OF THESE DAYS — 1910
Shelton Brooks

Francis, Day & Hunter Ltd ... USA
Film(s):Animal Crackers / Broadway / Follow the Boys / Broadway
Melody of 1938 / All That Jazz

Sophie Tucker	HMV B 3720
The Original Dixieland Jazz Band	Parlophone PMC 1171
Lorne Lesley	Parlophone R 4518
Rosemary Clooney	RCA RD 27218

Sophie Tucker appeared in *Follow the Boys* and *Broadway Melody of
1938*.
Theme song of Sophie Tucker.

SOME OF YOUR LOVIN' — October 1965
Gerry Goffin / Carole King

| Screen Gems - Columbia Music | USA |
| Dusty Springfield | Philips BF 1430 |

SOME PEOPLE — September 1987
Alan Tarney

| Warner Brothers Music | UK |
| Cliff Richard | EMI EM 18 |

SOME SUNDAY MORNING — 1918
Gus Kahn / Ray Egan / Richard A. Whiting

| B. Feldman & Co. Ltd. | USA |
| The Savoy Quartet, vocal Joe Wilbur | HMV B 895 |

SOME SUNDAY MORNING — 1946
Ted Koehler / M.K. Jerome / Ray Heindorf

Vistoria Music Co. Ltd.	USA
Film(s):	San Antonio
Dick Haymes & Helen Forrest	Brunswick 03637

Nominated for an Academy Award 1945.

SOME SUNNY DAY — 1922
Irving Berlin

Francis, Day & Hunter Ltd	USA
Paul Whiteman & his Orchestra	HMV B 1384
Bing Crosby with Bob Scoby's Frisco Band	RCA RD 27032

SOME SUNNY DAY — 1942
Sam Kern / Reg Morgan

Lawrence Wright Music Co. Ltd	USA
Joe Loss & his Orch., vocal Chick Henderson	HMV BD 5723
Anne Shelton	Rex 10104
The R.A.F. Dance Orchestra, vocal Jimmy Miller	Decca F 8049

SOME SWEET DAY — 1927
Ed Rose / Tony Jackson / Abe Olman

| Francis, Day & Hunter Ltd. | USA |
| Miff Mole's Molers | Philips BBL 7432 |

SOMEBODY — July 1954
Joe Henderson

Bourne Music Ltd.	UK
Petula Clark	Pye NPT 19002
Joe 'Mr. Piano' Henderson & his Friends	Pye NPL 18053

SOMEBODY BAD STOLE DE WEDDING BELL — April 1954
Bob Hilliard / David Mann

Edwin H. Morris & Co. Ltd.	USA
Georgia Gibbs	Oriole CB 1270
Eartha Kitt	HMV 7M 198
Caterina Valente	Polydor EPH 21516

SOMEBODY ELSE IS TAKING MY PLACE — 1937
Dick Howard / Bob Ellsworth / Russ Morgan

B. Feldman & Co.	USA
Film(s):	Strictly in the Groove
Al Martino	Capitol CL 15390
Russ Morgan Orchestra v Russ Morgan	MCA 24036
Dinah Washington	Columbia SX 1705
Connie Francis	MGM C 8086
Ozzie Nelson Orchestra	London HMP 5041

Ozzie Nelson & his Orchestra appeared in *Strictly in the Groove*.

SOMEBODY ELSE'S GUY — May 1984
Jocelyn Brown / Fred Linton

| Warner Brothers Music | UK |
| Jocelyn Brown | Island BRW 5 |

SOMEBODY HELP ME — May 1966
Jackie Edwards

| Island Music Ltd. | UK |
| The Spencer Davis Group | Fontana TF 679 |

SOMEBODY LOVES ME — 1924
George Gershwin / Buddy De Sylva

Chappell & Co. Ltd. ... USA
Show(s): ... George White's Scandals of 1924
Film(s):Rhapsody in Blue / Lullaby of Broadway / Somebody Loves
Me / Pete Kelly's Blues / Broadway Rhythm

Paul Whiteman & his Orchestra	HMV B 1889
Peggy Lee	Brunswick LAT 8078
Julie London	London HAU 2112
Dorothy Provine	Warner Brothers WM 4053

Peggy Lee appeared in *Pete Kelly's Blues*.

SOMEBODY LOVES YOU — 1932
Peter De Rose / Charles Tobias

Campbell Connelly & Co. Ltd.	USA
Layton & Johnstone	Columbia DB 819
Kathy Linden	Felsted GEP 1004

SOMEBODY STOLE MY GAL — 1924
Leo Wood

Francis, Day & Hunter Ltd	USA
Aileen Stanley	Brunswick 01722
Billy Cotton & his Band, vocal Alan Breeze	Regal Zonophone MR 598
Harry Roy & his Band	Parlophone F 100
Johnnie Ray (1953)	Philips PB 123

Theme song of Billy Cotton.

SOMEBODY TO LOVE — December 1976
Freddie Mercury

| EMI Music Ltd | UK |
| Queen | EMI 2565 |

SOMEBODY'S THINKING OF YOU TONIGHT — 1938
Marty Symes / Teddy Powell / Ira Schuster

Southern Music Publishing Co. Ltd.	USA
Dick Robertson & his Orchestra	Panachord 25977
Maurice Winnick & his Sweet Music	Decca F 6695

SOMEBODY'S WATCHING ME — May 1984
"Rockwell"

| Jobete Music | USA |
| Rockwell | Motown TMG 1331 |

SOMEDAY ONE DAY — May 1966
Paul Simon

| Lorna Music Ltd. | USA |
| The Seekers | Columbia DB 7867 |

SOMEDAY YOU'LL WANT ME TO WANT YOU — 1946
Jimmy Hodges

Leeds Music Ltd.	USA
Joe Loss & his Orchestra, vocal Howard Jones	HMV BD 5949
The Mills Brothers	Brunswick 04335
The Four Preps	Capitol T 1216
Jodi Sands (1958)	HMV POP 533
Ricky Nelson (1958)	London HAP 2119

SOMEONE September 1959
Bill Tennyson
Johnny Mathis Music Ltd . . . . USA
Johnny Mathis . . . . **Fontana TFL 5083**

SOMEONE ELSE MAY BE THERE WHEN I'M GONE 1919
Irving Berlin
B. Feldman & Co. Ltd. . . . . USA
Show(s): . . . . Bran Pie
Beatrice Lillie . . . . **Columbia F 1011**
Al Jolson . . . . **Brunswick LA 8575**
Beatrice Lillie appeared in *Bran Pie*.

SOMEONE ELSE'S BABY May 1960
Les Vandyke / Perry Ford
Mills Music Ltd . . . . UK
Adam Faith . . . . **Parlophone GEP 8811**

SOMEONE ELSE'S ROSES June 1954
Milton Carson
John Fields Music . . . . USA
Vivian Blaine . . . . **Parlophone R 3822**
Joan Regan . . . . **Decca F 10257**
Joe Loss Orchestra . . . . **HMV BD 6171**
Doris Day . . . . **Philips PB 302**

SOMEONE LIKE YOU October 1949
Harry Warren / Ralph Blane
B. Feldman & Co. Ltd . . . . USA
Film(s): . . . . My Dream is Yours
Doris Day . . . . **Columbia DB 2590**
Ella Fitzgerald . . . . **Brunswick 04351**
The Four Freshmen . . . . **Capitol T 763**
Doris Day appeared in *My Dream is Yours*.

SOMEONE STOLE GABRIEL'S HORN 1934
Edgar Hayes / George Washington / Irving Mills
Lafleur & Co. Ltd. . . . . USA
Bing Crosby . . . . **Columbia DB 1894**
The Humphrey Lyttelton Band . . . . **Parlophone PMD 1049**

SOMEONE TO WATCH OVER ME 1927
George Gershwin / Ira Gershwin
Chappell & Co. Ltd. . . . . USA
Show(s): . . . . Oh Kay
Film(s):Rhapsody in Blue / Young at Heart / Three for the Show / Beau
James / Both Ends of the Candle / Star
Gertrude Lawrence . . . . **Columbia 4618**
Frances Langford . . . . **Brunswick 02994**
Frank Sinatra (1947) . . . . **Fontana TFL 5082**
Vera Miles . . . . **London HAP 2056**
Gogi Grant . . . . **RCA RD 27054**
Julie Andrews . . . . **Stateside SL 10233**
Gertrude Lawrence appeared in both the British and American pro-
ductions of *Oh Kay*.
Frank Sinatra appeared in *Young at Heart*.
Vera Miles appeared in *Beau James*.Julie Andrews appeared in *Star*.
Gogi Grant dubbed the singing voice of Ann Blyth who appeared in
the film *Both Ends of the Candle*.

SOMEONE'S LOOKING AT YOU February 1980
Bob Geldof
Zomba Music Publishers . . . . UK
The Boomtown Rats . . . . **Ensign ENY 34**

SOMEONE'S ROCKING MY DREAMBOAT 1942
Leon Rene / Otis Rene / Emerson Scott
Chappell & Co. Ltd . . . . USA
Film(s): . . . . Juke Girl
The Ink Spots . . . . **Brunswick LA 8710**
Al Nevins & his Orchestra . . . . **RCA RD 27005**

SOMEONE, SOMEONE June 1964
Violet Petty / Edwin Greines
Burlington Music Co. Ltd . . . . USA
The Crickets . . . . **Coral Q 72365**
Brian Poole & The Tremeloes . . . . **Decca F 11893**

SOMETHIN' ELSE November 1959
Sharron Sheeley / Eddie Cochran
Burlington Music Co. Ltd . . . . USA
Eddie Cochran . . . . **London HLU 8944**
The Sex Pistols (1979) . . . . **Virgin VS 240**

SOMETHIN' STUPID June 1967
Carson Parks
Montclare Music Co. Ltd. . . . . USA
Nancy & Frank Sinatra . . . . **Reprise RS 23166**

SOMETHING November 1969
George Harrison
Harrisongs Ltd . . . . UK
The Beatles . . . . **Apple R 5814**
Peggy Lee . . . . **Capitol ST 21543**
Shirley Bassey (1970) . . . . . . **United Artists UP 35125**
Ivor Novello Award.

SOMETHING 'BOUT YOU BABY I LIKE May 1981
Richard Supa
Screen Gems Music . . . . USA
Status Quo . . . . **Vertigo QUO 5**

SOMETHING ABOUT YOU November 1985
*Michael Lindup / Philip Gould / Rowland Gould, Mark King & Wally
Badarou*
Island Music . . . . UK
Level 42 . . . . **Polydor POSP 759**

SOMETHING BETTER CHANGE September 1977
"The Stranglers"
April Music Ltd . . . . UK
The Stranglers . . . . **United Artists UP 36277**

SOMETHING HERE IN MY HEART May 1968
John MacLeod / Tony Macaulay
Schroeder Music Ltd. . . . . UK
The Paper Dolls . . . . **Pye 7N 17456**

SOMETHING IN THE AIR July 1969
John Keene
Fabulous Music Ltd. . . . . UK
Thunderclap Newman . . . . **Track 2409205**

SOMETHING INSIDE SO STRONG (See So Strong)

SOMETHING OLD, SOMETHING NEW April 1971
Tony Macaulay / Roger Greenaway / Roger Cook
Cookaway Music . . . . UK
The Fantastics . . . . **Bell 1141**

SOMETHING SEEMS TINGLE-INGLE-ING 1916
Rudolf Frimi / Otto Harbach
Francis, Day & Hunter Ltd. . . . . USA
Show(s): . . . . High Jinks
Peter Gawthorne & Chorus . . . . **HMV C 720**
Peter Gawthorne appeared in the British production of *High Jinks*.

SOMETHING TELLS ME December 1971
Roger Greenaway / Roger Cook
Cookaway Music . . . . UK
Cilla Black . . . . **Parlophone R 5924**

SOMETHING TO REMEMBER YOU BY 1930
Howard Dietz / Arthur Schwartz
Chappell & Co. Ltd . . . . USA
Show(s): . . . . Three's a Crowd
Film(s):Dancing in the Dark / Both Ends of the Candle / The Band Wagon
Leo Reisman & his Orchestra . . . . **HMV B 5953**
Dinah Shore (1944) . . . . **HMV BD 1058**
Dick Haymes & Helen Forrest . . . . **Brunswick 04366**
Dinah Shore . . . . **Capitol T 1296**
Gogi Grant . . . . **RCA RD 27054**

SOMETHING'S BURNING April 1970
Mac Davis
Carlin Music Corporation . . . . USA
Kenny Rogers & The First Edition . . . . **Reprise RS 20888**

SOMETHING'S COMING July 1959
Leonard Bernstein / Stephen Sondheim
Chappell & Co. Ltd . . . . USA
Show(s): . . . . West Side Story
Film(s): . . . . West Side Story
Larry Kert . . . . **CBS BPG 62060**
Andy Cole . . . . **Saga STP 1028**
Jim Bryant . . . . **CBS BPG 62058**
Larry Kert appeared in the American production of *West Side Story*.
Richard Beymer appeared in the film of *West Side Story* (singing voice
dubbed by Jim Bryant).

SOMETHING'S GOTTA GIVE   September 1957
Johnny Mercer
Essex Music Ltd . . . . USA
Film(s): . . . . Daddy Long Legs
Sammy Davis . . . . **Brunswick LAT 8296**
Fred Astaire . . . . **London HAR 2219**
Fred Astaire appeared in *Daddy Long Legs*.

SOMETHING'S GOTTEN HOLD OF MY HEART   Dec 1967
Roger Cook / Roger Greenaway
Polygram Music Ltd. . . . . UK
Gene Pitney . . . . **Stateside SS 2060**
Marc Almond & Gene Pitney (1989) . . . . **Parlophone R 6201**
Ivor Novello Nomination 1989.

SOMETHING'S HAPPENING (Luglio)   January 1969
Ricca Del Turco / Giancar Bigazzi / Jack Fishman
Cyril Shane Music . . . . Italy
Herman's Hermits . . . . **Columbia DB 8504**

SOMETIME   1925
Ted Fiorito / Gus Khan
Francis, Day & Hunter Ltd. . . . . USA
The Xylo-Rimba Orchestra . . . . **Columbia 3850**
Jo Stafford (1950) . . . . **Capitol CL 13372**

SOMETIMES   December 1986
Vincent Clarke / Andy Bell
Sonet Music . . . . UK
Erasure . . . . **Mute MUTE 51**

SOMETIMES I'M HAPPY   1927
Vincent Youmans / Clifford Grey / Irving Caesar
Chappell & Co. Ltd. . . . . USA
Show(s): . . . . Hit the Deck
Film(s): . . . . Hit the Deck
Stanley Holloway & Ivy Tresmand . . . . **Columbia 4651**
Mildred Bailey . . . . **Brunswick LA 8602**
Dorothy Collins . . . . **Vogue LVA 9058**
Jane Powell . . . . **MGM EP 525**
Stanley Holloway & Ivy Tresmand appeared in the British production
of *Hit the Deck*.
Jane Powell appeared in the 1955 film of *Hit the Deck*.

SOMETIMES WHEN WE TOUCH   April 1978
Dan Hill / Barry Mann
A.T.V. Music Ltd. . . . . USA
Dan Hill . . . . **20th Century BTC 2355**

SOMEWHERE   January 1965
Stephen Sondheim / Leonard Bernstein
Chappell & Co. Ltd . . . . USA
Show(s): . . . . West Side Story
Film(s): . . . . West Side Story
Reri Grist . . . . **CBS BPG 62060**
Maureen Fulham . . . . **Saga STP 1028**
Marni Nixon & Jim Bryant . . . . **CBS BPG 62058**
P.J. Proby . . . . **Liberty LIB 10182**
Reri Grist appeared in the American production of *West Side Story*.
Natalie Wood & Richard Beymer appeared in the film *West Side Story*
(singing voices dubbed by Marni Nixon & Jim Bryant)

SOMEWHERE A VOICE IS CALLING   1911
Eileen Newton / Arthur Tate
Francis, Day & Hunter Ltd. . . . . UK
Francis Alda . . . . **HMV DA 138**
John McCormack . . . . **Camden CDN 1002**
Harry Secombe . . . . **Philips BBL 7349**

SOMEWHERE ALONG THE WAY   July 1952
Sammy Gallop / Kurt Adams
Magna Music Co. Ltd . . . . USA
Nat 'King' Cole . . . . **Capitol EAP 1-20108**
The Four Preps . . . . **Capitol T 1216**

SOMEWHERE IN FRANCE WITH YOU   1918
James W. Tate / A. Anderson / Arthur Valentine
Francis, Day & Hunter Ltd. . . . . UK
Herbert Payne & Chorus . . . . **Zonophone 1870**
Leslie Hutchinson (Hutch) . . . . **Parlophone F 1614**
Ambrose & his Orchestra, vocal Vera Lynn . . . . . **Decca F 7326**
Arthur Tracey (The Street Singer) . . . . **Decca F 7394**

SOMEWHERE IN MY HEART   June 1988
Roddy Frame

Warner Chappell Music . . . . UK
Aztec Camera . . . . **WEA YZ 181**

SOMEWHERE IN OLD WYOMING   1931
Will Havlin / S. Lesser
Campbell Connelly & Co. Ltd . . . . USA
Bud Billington & Carson Robison . . . . **Zonophone 5809**

SOMEWHERE MY LOVE (LARA'S THEME) September 1966
Paul Francis Webster / Maurice Jarre
Robbins Music Corporation Ltd. . . . . USA
Film(s): . . . . Dr Zhivago
MGM Studio Orch., conducted by Maurice Jarre . . . **MGM 1417**
Al Martino . . . . **Capitol T 2592**
Connie Francis . . . . **MGM 1320**
The Mike Sammes Singers (1966 & 1967) . . . . . **HMV POP 1546**

SOMEWHERE OUT THERE   August 1987
James Horner / Barry Mann / Cynthia Weil
MCA Music Ltd. . . . . USA
Film(s): . . . . An American Tail
Linda Ronstadt & James Ingram . . . . . . **MCA MCA 1132**
Nominated for an Academy Award 1987.

SOMEWHERE THE SUN IS SHINING   1906
Charles.K. Harris
B. Feldman & Co. Ltd . . . . USA
Florrie Forde . . . . **Imperial 2892**

SON OF A PREACHER MAN   January 1969
John Hurley / Ronnie Wilkins
London Tree . . . . USA
Dusty Springfield . . . . **Philips BF 1730**

SON OF HICKORY HOLLER'S TRAMP, THE   July 1968
Dallas Frazier
Burlington Music Co. Ltd. . . . . USA
O. C. Smith . . . . **CBS 0040**

SON OF MY FATHER   March 1972
Georgio Moroder / Pete Bellotte / Michael Holme
A.T.V. Music Ltd. . . . . USA
Chicory Tip . . . . **CBS 7737**

SON, THIS IS SHE   January 1962
Geoffrey Goddard
Southern Music publishing Co. Ltd. . . . . UK
John Leyton . . . . **HMV POP 956**

SONG FOR GUY   January 1979
Elton John
Big Pig Music . . . . UK
Elton John . . . . **Rocket XPRES 5**
Ivor Novello Award.

SONG FOR WHOEVER   July 1989
Paul Heaton / Dave Rotheray
Go Disc Music . . . . UK
The Beautiful South . . . . **Go Disc GOD 32**

SONG I LOVE, THE   1928
Buddy De Sylva / Lew Brown / Ray Henderson
Campbell Connelly & Co. Ltd . . . . USA
Jack Smith . . . . **HMV B 2871**

SONG IS ENDED, THE   1928
Irving Berlin
Francis, Day & Hunter Ltd. . . . . USA
Show(s): . . . . Will o' the Whispers
Jack Smith . . . . **HMV B 2665**
The Mills Brothers . . . . **Brunswick 02648**
Reg Owen & his Orchestra . . . . **RCA RD 27059**
Jack Smith appeared in *Will O' the Whispers*.

SONG IS YOU, THE   1932
Jerome Kern / Oscar Hammerstein II
Chappell & Co. Ltd. . . . . USA
Show(s): . . . . Music in the Air
Film(s): . . . . Music in the Air
Mary Ellis . . . . **Columbia DB 1139**
Vanessa Lee . . . . **HMV 7EG 8702**
Ronnie Hilton . . . . **HMV CLP 1295**
Mary Ellis appeared in the British production of *Music in the Air*.

SONG OF CAPRI, THE   September 1949
Mischa Spoliansky / Norman Newell
Chappell & Co. Ltd . . . . UK
Film(s): . . . . .That Dangerous Age
Harry Dawson . . . . **HMV B 9845**
The Queens Hall Light Orchestra . . . . **Columbia DB 2564**

SONG OF DELILAH, THE   February 1951
Victor Young / Jerry Livingston / Ray Evans
Victoria Music Co. Ltd . . . . USA
Film(s): . . . . Samson and Delilah
Paramount Symphony Orchestra,
conducted by Victor Young . . . . **Brunswick LA 8517**
Frank Chacksfield & his Orchestra . . . **Ace of Clubs ACL 1094**

SONG OF INDIA   1923
Nikolai Rimsky-Korsakov
Boosey & Hawkes Music Publishers . . . . Russia
Film(s): . . . . Drum Crazy
Paul Whiteman & his Orchestra . . . . **HMV B 1657**
Tommy Dorsey & his Orchestra . . . . **RCA RCX 1002**
The Tommy Dorsey Orchestra,
conducted by Warren Covington . . . . **Brunswick LAT 8282**
The Clark Sisters . . . . **London HAD 2177**
Sound Track recording of *Drum Crazy* . . . . . . **HMV CLP 1352**
Tommy Dorsey Orchestra appeared in *Gay City*.
Adapted from *Chanson Indoue* by Nikolai Rimsky-Korsakov (1844-1908).

SONG OF LOVE   1922
Sigmund Romberg / Dorothy Donnelly
Chappell & Co. Ltd . . . . USA
Show(s): . . . . Blossom Time
Earl Wrightson & Lois Hunt . . . . **Philips BBL 7329**

SONG OF SONGS, THE   1914
Maurice Vaucaire / Clarence Lucas / Stella Moya
Chappell & Co. Ltd. . . . . USA
Richard Crooks . . . . **HMV DA 999**
Frank Titterton . . . . **Decca F 2371**
Harry Secombe . . . . **Philips BBE 12236**

SONG OF THE DAWN   1930
Jack Yellen / Milton Ager
Lawrence Wright Music Co. Ltd . . . . USA
Film(s): . . . . The King of Jazz
John Boles . . . . **HMV B 3456**
Paul Whiteman & his Orchestra,
vocal Bing Crosby . . . . **Columbia CB 87**
Frank Chacksfield & his Orchestra . . . . . . **Decca LK 4135**
John Boles & Paul Whiteman appeared in *The King of Jazz*.

SONG OF THE DREAMER   October 1955
Eddie Curtis
Essex Music . . . . USA
Johnnie Ray . . . . **Philips PB 516**

SONG OF THE ISLANDS (Na Lei O Hawaii)   1930
Charles E. King
Keith Prowse Music Publishing Co. Ltd . . . . USA
Film(s): . . . . .Melody Lane / Ice Capades Revue
Louis Armstrong & his Orchestra . . . . **Parlophone R 909**
Bing Crosby . . . . **Brunswick LAT 8053**
Danny Stewart . . . . **London HAU 2014**
The Arthur Lyman Group . . . . **Vogue VA 160171**
Felix Mendelsohn & his
Hawaiian Serenaders . . . . **Columbia FB 2690**

SONG OF THE MOUNTAINS, THE (La Montanara)   May 1949
Toni Ortelli / Luigi Pigarelli
Keith Prowse Music Publishing Co. Ltd . . . . Italy
Film(s): . . . . The Glass Mountain
Tito Gobbi . . . . **HMV 7P 240**
Tito Gobbi appeared in *The Glass Mountain*.

SONG OF THE TREES, THE   1935
Tolchard Evans / Stanley Damerell / Robert Hargreaves
Cecil Lennox Music Co. Ltd . . . . UK
Jack Payne & his Orchestra,
vocal Billy Scott-Coomber . . . . **Rex 8438**
Dickie Valentine . . . . **Decca F 10667**
Frank Chacksfield & his Orchestra . . . . . . **Decca LK 4160**

SONG OF THE VAGABONDS, THE   1927
Rudolf Frimi / Brian Hooker

B. Feldman & Co. Ltd. . . . . USA
Show(s): . . . . The Vagabond King
Film(s): . . . . The Vagabond King
Dennis King . . . . **HMV B 2426**
Derek Oldham . . . . **HMV C 2510**
Oreste . . . . **HMV ALP 1378**
David Whitfield . . . . **Decca LK 4270**
Gordon MacRae . . . . **Capitol T 1510**
Dennis King appeared in the American production of *The Vagabond King*.
Derek Oldham appeared in the British production of *The Vagabond King*.
Oreste appeared in the 1956 film of *The Vagabond King*.

SONG OF THE WANDERER, THE   1927
Neil Moret
Francis, Day & Hunter Ltd. USA
Paul Whiteman & his Orchestra,
vocal Bing Crosby . . . . **HMV B 5311**
Annette Hanshaw . . . . **Actuelle 11409**
Kid Ory's Creole Jazz Band . . . . **Columbia 33CX 10134**
Margaret Whiting . . . . **London HAD 2109**

SONG SUNG BLUE   July 1972
Neil Diamond
Ardmore & Beechwood Ltd. . . . . USA
Neil Diamond . . . . **Uni UN 538**

SONNY BOY   1929
Buddy De Sylva / Lew Brown / Ray Henderson / Al Jolson
Campbell Connelly & Co. Ltd . . . . USA
Film(s):The Singing Fool / Jolson Sings Again / The Best Things in
Life are Free
Al Jolson . . . . **Brunswick 01364**
The Andrews Sisters . . . . **Ace of Hearts AH 21**
Al Jolson . . . . **Ace of Hearts AH 33**
Al Jolson appeared in *The Singing Fool*.

SONS OF THE SEA   1897
Felix McGlennon
Herman Darewski Music Publishing Co. Ltd. . . . . UK
Arthur Reece . . . . **HMV C 2795**
The Pavement Artists . . . . **Regal Zonophone MR 530**
Billy Cotton & his Band . . . . **Regal Zonophone MR 1686**

SONYA (Yup Alay Yup)   1925
Bob Schaefer
Francis, Day & Hunter Ltd. USA
Paul Whiteman & his Orchestra,
vocal Billy Murray . . . . **HMV B 2112**
Frank Crumit . . . . **HMV B 2170**

SOON   1930
George Gershwin / Ira Gershwin
Chappell & Co. Ltd . . . . USA
Show(s): . . . . Strike Up the Band
Connee Boswell . . . . **Brunswick 02991**
Ella Fitzgerald . . . . **Brunswick LA 8648**
Doris Day . . . . **Philips BBL 7247**

SOON - THERE'LL JUST BE TWO OF US   1935
Richard Rodgers / Lorenz Hart
Victoria Music Co. Ltd . . . . USA
Film(s): . . . . Mississippi
Bing Crosby . . . . **Brunswick Bing 1**
Bing Crosby appeared in *Mississippi*.

SOON IT WILL BE SUNDAY   1946
James Bunting / Peter Hart
Lawrence Wright Music Co. Ltd. . . . . UK
Joe Loss & his Orchestra, vocal Howard Jones . . **HMV B 5915**

SOONER OR LATER   1947
Ray Gilbert / Charles Wolcott
Sun Music Publishing Co. Ltd. . . . . USA
Film(s): . . . . Song of the South
Dinah Shore . . . . **Columbia DB 2276**

SOPHISTICATED LADY   1933
Duke Ellington / Irving Mills / Mitchell Parish
Lawrence Wright Music Co. Ltd. . . . . USA
Duke Ellington & his Orchestra . . . . . . **Columbia SEG 7677**
Dinah Shore . . . . **Camden CDN 105**
Stanley Black & his Orchestra . . . . **Decca LK 4170**

SORROW   July 1966
Bob Feldman / Gerry Goldstein / Richard Gottehrer
Dominion Music Co. Ltd. .... USA
The Merseys .... **Fontana TF 694**
David Bowie (1973) .... **RCA 2424**

SORRY I'M A LADY   February 1978
Rolf Soja / Frank Dostal
Louvigny Marquee Music Co. .... Germany
Baccara .... **RCA PB 5555**

SORRY SUZANNE   April 1969
Tony Macaulay / Geoff Stevens
A.T.V. Music Ltd. .... UK
The Hollies .... **Parlophone R 5765**

SOUND AND VISION   March 1977
David Bowie
Chrysalis Music Ltd .... UK
David Bowie .... **RCA PB 0905**

SOUND OF MUSIC, THE   July 1961
Richard Rodgers / Oscar Hammerstein II
Williamson Music Ltd. .... USA
Show(s): .... Sound of Music
Film(s): .... Sound of Music
Mary Martin .... **Philips ABL 3370**
Jean Bayless .... **HMV CLP 1453**
Julie Andrews .... **RCA RB 6616**
Mary Martin appeared in the American production of *Sound of Music.*
Jean Bayless appeared in the British production of *Sound of Music.*
Julie Andrews appeared in the film of *Sound of Music.*

SOUND OF SILENCE, THE   May 1966
Paul Simon
Lorna Music Ltd. .... USA
Simon & Garfunkel .... **CBS 1977**
The Bachelors .... **Decca F 12351**
Paul Simon .... **CBS BPG 62579**

SOUND OF THE SUBURBS   March 1979
Nick Tesco / Jean Carroll
Virgin Music (Publishers) Ltd. .... UK
The Members .... **Virgin VS 242**

SOUTH   1928
Benny Moten / Thomas Hayes
Southern Music Publishing Co. Ltd .... USA
Benny Moten's Kansas City Orchestra .... **HMV DLP 1057**
Bob Scobey's Frisco Band .... **Vogue LAG 12284**
Kid Ory's Creole Jazz Band .... **Vogue LAG 12104**

SOUTH AMERICA, TAKE IT AWAY   1947
Harold Rome
B. Feldman & Co. Ltd. .... USA
Show(s): .... Call Me Mister / Starlight Roof
Film(s): .... Call Me Mister
Betty Garrett .... **Brunswick LA 8523**
Bing Crosby & The Andrews Sisters .... **Brunswick LAT 8053**
Pearl Bailey .... **Columbia 33SX 1065**
Betty Garrett appeared in the show of *Call Me Mister.*

SOUTH AMERICAN JOE   1935
Cliff Friend / Irving Caeser
Chappell & Co. Ltd .... USA
Larry Adler (harmonica) .... **Rex 8598**
Jack Hylton & his Orchestra .... **HMV BD 203**

SOUTH AMERICAN WAY   1941
Al Dubin / Jimmy McHugh
Chappell & Co. Ltd .... USA
Show(s): .... The Streets of Paris
Film(s): .... Down Argentine Way
Carmen Miranda .... **Brunswick 03178**
The Andrews Sisters .... **Brunswick 03157**
Carmen Miranda appeared in both *The Streets of Paris* and *Down Argentine Way.*

SOUTH OF THE BORDER   1939
Michael Carr / Jimmy Kennedy
Peter Maurice Music Co. Ltd. .... UK
Film(s): .... Pepe
Al Bowlly .... **HMV BD 706**

Perry Como .... **RCA RD 27035**
The Mills Brothers .... **Brunswick 02823**
Patti Page .... **Mercury MMC 14000**
The Stargazers .... **Decca LK 4309**
Bing Crosby & Cantinflas .... **Pye NPL 28015**
Bing Crosby & Cantinflas appeared in *Pepe.*

SOUTH RAMPART STREET PARADE   1940
Ray Bauduc / Bob Haggart / Bob Crosby
Robbins Music Corporation Ltd .... USA
Bing Crosby & his Orchestra .... **Brunswick LAT 8368**
Bing Crosby & The Andrews Sisters .... **Brunswick 05019**
Papa Bue's Viking Jazz Band .... **Parlophone PMC 1168**

SOUTH SEA ISLAND MAGIC   1936
Lysle Tomerlin / Andy Iona Long
Lafleur & Co. Ltd .... USA
Bing Crosby .... **Brunswick LA 8730**
Wout Steenhuis (guitar) .... **Columbia 33SX 1695**
Tony Osborne & his Orchestra .... **Nixa NPL 18009**

SOUTHERN FREEEZ   March 1981
Andrew Stennet / Peter Mass / John Roca
Pereman & Co. Ltd. .... UK
Freeez .... **Beggers Banquet BEG 51**

SOUVENIR   September 1981
Phil Humphries / Martin Cooper
Dinsong Music Co. .... UK
Orchestral Manoeuvres in the Dark .... **Dindisc DIN 24**

SOUVENIR D'ITALIE   February 1956
G. Scarnicci / R. Tarabusi / Lelio Luttazzi & Carl Sigman
Leeds Music Ltd. .... Italy
Flo Sandon .... **Durium TLU 97009**
Bob Sharples & his Orchestra .... **Decca LK 4287**

SOWING THE SEEDS OF LOVE   September 1989
Roland Orzabel / Curt Smith
Virgin Music .... UK
Tears for Fears .... **Fontana IDEA 12**

SPACE JUNGLE, THE   October 1990
Adam Tinley / Otis Blackwell / Elvis Presley
MCA Music .... USA
Adamski .... **MCA MCA 1435**

SPACE ODDITY   November 1969
David Bowie
Essex Music Ltd .... UK
David Bowie .... **Philips BF 1801**
David Bowie (1975) .... **RCA 2593**
Ivor Novello Award.

SPACER   February 1980
Bernard Edwards / Nile Rogers
Warner Brothers Music Ltd .... UK
Shelia B. Devotion .... **Carrere CAR 128**

SPAIN   1924
Gus Kahn / Isham Jones
Francis, Day & Hunter Ltd. .... USA
Paul Whiteman & his Orchestra .... **HMV B 1847**
Bob Crosby's Bob Cats .... **Decca F 7587**
The Big Ben Banjo Band .... **Columbia 33SX 1356**

SPANIARD THAT BLIGHTED MY LIFE, THE   1911
Billy Merson
Francis, Day & Hunter Ltd. .... UK
Film(s): .... The Singing Fool / The Jolson Story
Billy Merson .... **Columbia 1757**
Al Jolson .... **RCA INTS 1077**
Bing Crosby & Al Jolson .... **Brunswick LAT 8306**
Stanley Holloway .... **Philips BBL 7237**
Al Jolson appeared in *The Singing Fool.*

SPANISH EYES (Moon Over Naples)   September 1973
Berthold Kaempfert / Charles Singleton / Eddie Snyder
Carlin Music Corporation .... USA
Al Martino .... **Capitol CL 15430**
Bert Kaempfert Orchestra .... **Polydor LPHM 46456**
Engelbert Humperdinck .... **Decca SKL 4939**
Andy Williams .... **CBS SS 62884**

287

SPANISH FLEA — May 1966
Julius Wechter
Burlington Music Co. Ltd. . . . . USA
Herb Alpert & his Tijuana Brass . . . . **Pye 7N 25335**

SPANISH HARLEM — August 1962
Jerry Leiber / Phil Spector
Carlin Music Corporation . . . . USA
Jimmy Justice . . . . **Pye 7N 15457**
Manuel & his Music of The Mountains . . . **Columbia 33SX 1538**
Herb Alpert & his Tijuana Brass . . . . **Stateside SL 10072**
Aretha Franklin (1971) . . . . **Atlantic 2091138**

SPARROW IN THE TREETOP — April 1951
Bob Merrill
Cinephoneic Music Co. Ltd. . . . . USA
Guy Mitchell . . . .

SPARROW, THE — November 1979
Maurice Jordan
St. Annes Music Ltd. . . . . UK
The Ramblers . . . . **Decca F 13860**

SPEAK LIKE A CHILD — April 1983
Paul Weller
EMI Music . . . . UK
Style Council . . . . **Polydor TSC 1**

SPEAK LOW — September 1950
Kurt Weill / Ogden Nash
Chappell & Co. Ltd . . . . USA
Show(s): . . . . One Touch of Venus
Film(s): . . . . One Touch of Venus
Fran Warren . . . . **MGM EP 617**
Vic Damone . . . . **Philips BBL 7476**
Carmen McRae . . . . **Brunswick LAT 8133**
Mary Martin & Kenny Baker . . . . **Decca DL 9122**
Mary Martin & Kenny Baker appeared in the show *One touch of Venus*.

SPEAK TO ME OF LOVE (Parlez Moi d'Amour) — 1931
Jean Lenoir / Bruce Sievier
Ascherberg, Hopwood & Crew Ltd. . . . . France
Film(s): . . . . Both Ends of the Candle
Lucienne Boyer . . . . **Columbia 33S 1043**
Gogi Grant . . . . **RCA RD 27054**
Jane Morgan . . . . **London HAR 2133**
Maurice Chevalier . . . . **MGM C 826**
Theme song of Lucienne Boyer.

SPEAK TO ME PRETTY — May 1962
Henry Vars / 'By' Dunham
Macmelodies Ltd. . . . . USA
Film(s): . . . . Two Little Bears
Brenda Lee . . . . **Brunswick 05867**
Brenda Lee appeared in *Two Little Bears*.

SPECIAL BREW — November 1980
"Bad Manners"
Magnet Music . . . . UK
Bad Manners . . . . **Magnet MAG 180**

SPECIAL YEARS, THE — February 1965
Martha Sharp
Shapiro-Bernstein & Co. Ltd . . . . USA
Val Doonican . . . . **Decca F 12049**

SPEEDY GONZALES — August 1962
Buddy Kaye / David Hill / Ethel Lee
Budd Music Co. Ltd . . . . USA
Pat Boone . . . . **London HL 9573**

SPEND THE NIGHT — April 1985
Stephen McIntosh
Zomba Music . . . . UK
The Cool Notes . . . . **Abstract AD 3**

SPIDERS AND SNAKES — May 1974
Jim Stafford / David Bellamy
Famous-Chappell . . . . USA
Jim Stafford . . . . **MGM 2006374**

SPIES LIKE US — December 1985
Paul McCartney
MPL Music . . . . UK
Paul McCartney . . . . **Parlophone R 6118**

SPIRIT IN THE SKY — May 1970
Norman Greenbaum
Great Honesty Music . . . . USA
Norman Greenbaum . . . . **Reprise RS 20885**
Dr. & The Medics (1986) . . . . **MCA IRM 113**

SPIRITS IN THE MATERIAL WORLD — December 1981
"Sting"
Virgin Music . . . . UK
Police . . . . **A&M AM 8194**

SPLISH SPLASH — September 1958
Bobby Darin / Jean Murray
Good Music Ltd . . . . USA
Bobby Darin . . . . **London HLE 8666**
Charlie Drake . . . . **Parlophone R 4461**
Barbra Streisand . . . . **CBS 86104**

SPOONFUL OF SUGAR, A — February 1965
Richard M. Sherman / Robert B. Sherman
Walt Disney Music Co. Ltd . . . . USA
Film(s): . . . . Mary Poppins
Julie Andrews . . . . **HMV CLP 1794**
Julie Andrews appeared in *Mary Poppins*.

SPREAD A LITTLE HAPPINESS — 1929
Vivian Ellis / Richard Myers / Greatrex Newman
Chappell & Co. Ltd . . . . UK
Show(s): . . . . Mister Cinders
Binnie Hale . . . . **Columbia 5334**
Cleo Laine . . . . **Esquire EP 102**
Sting (1982) . . . . **A&M AMS 8242**
Binnie Hale appeared in *Mister Cinders*.

SPRING IS HERE — May 1954
Richard Rodgers / Lorenz Hart
Francis, Day & Hunter Ltd. USA
Show(s): . . . . I Married an Angel
Film(s): . . . . I Married an Angel
Jo Stafford . . . . **Columbia 22S 1024**
Julie London . . . . **London HAU 2186**
First Published 1942.

SPRING WILL BE A LITTLE LATE THIS YEAR — 1944
Frank Loesser
Chappell & Co. Ltd. . . . . USA
Film(s): . . . . Christmas Holiday
Deanna Durbin . . . . **Brunswick LAT 8285**
Jeri Southern . . . . **Columbia 33SX 1134**
Ella Fitzgerald . . . . **HMV CLP 1383**
Deanna Durbin appeared in *Christmas Holiday*.

SPRING, SPRING, SPRING — January 1955
Johnny Mercer / Gene De Paul
Robbins Music Corporation Ltd. . . . . USA
Film(s): . . . . Seven Brides for Seven Brothers
The Brothers & The Girls . . . . **MGM C 853**
The Ray Charles Singers . . . . **MGM EP 748**
The Brothers & The Girls appeared in *Seven Brides for Seven Brothers*.

SPRINGTIME REMINDS ME OF YOU (Deine Mutter Bleibt Immer Bei Mir) — 1931
Fritz Rotter / Walter Jurmann / Desmond Cadter
Chappell & Co. Ltd. . . . . Germany
Richard Tauber (in German) . . . . . **Parlophone RO 20155**
Jack Payne & The BBC Dance Orchestra,
vocal Jack Payne . . . . **Columbia CB 318**

SQUEEZE BOX — February 1976
Peter Townshend
Eel Pie Publishing Ltd . . . . UK
The Who . . . . **Polydor 2121275**

SQUEEZE ME PLEASE ME (See Skweeze Me Pleeze Me)

ST. ELMO'S FIRE (Man in Motion) — October 1985
David Foster / John Parr
CBS Songs . . . . UK
Film(s): . . . . St. Elmo's Fire
John Parr . . . . **London LON 73**

STACCATO'S THEME — January 1960
Elmer Bernstein
Peter Maurice Music Co. Ltd . . . . USA

Elmer Bernstein & his Orchestra . . . . Capitol EAP 1-1287
Buddy Morrow & his Orchestra . . . . RCA 1167
Theme of the TV production *Johnny Staccato*.

STAGE COACH 1942
Eric Winstone
Campbell Connelly & Co. Ltd . . . . UK
Eric Winstone & his Band . . . . Regal Zonophone MR 3595
Theme song of Eric Winstone.

STAGGER LEE March 1959
Lloyd Price / Harold Logan
Sheldon Music Ltd . . . . USA
Lloyd Price . . . . HMV CLP 1285
Bill Haley . . . . Warner Brothers WEP 6001
Pat Boone . . . . London HAD 2354

STAIRWAY OF LOVE June 1958
Sid Tepper / Roy C. Bennett
Leeds Music Ltd . . . . USA
Michael Holliday . . . . Columbia SEG 7818

STAIRWAY TO HEAVEN June 1960
Neil Sedaka / Howard Greenfield
Nevins-Kirshner Ltd . . . . USA
Neil Sedaka . . . . RCA RCX 186

STAIRWAY TO HEAVEN November 1985
Robert Plant / Jimmy Page
Warner Brothers Music . . . . USA
Led Zepplin (1971) . . . . Atlantic 2401012
Far Corporation . . . . Arista ARIST 639

STAIRWAY TO THE STARS 1939
Mitchell Parish / Matty Malneck / Frank Signorelli
Robbins Music Corporation Ltd. . . . . USA
Ella Fitzgerald . . . . Ace of Hearts AH 16
Ella Fitzgerald . . . . HMV CLP 1383

STAND AND DELIVER May 1981
Adam Ant / Marco Pirroni
EMI Music . . . . UK
Adam & The Ants . . . . CBS A 1065
Ivor Novello Award.

STAND BY ME August 1961
Ben E. King / Jerry Leiber / Mike Stoller
Trio Music Ltd. . . . . USA
Ben E. King . . . . London HLK 9358
Kenny Lynch . . . . HMV POP 1280
John Lennon . . . . Apple R 6005
Ben E. King (1987) . . . . Atlantic A 9361

STAND BY YOUR MAN June 1975
Billy Sherrill / Tammy Wynette
Keith Prowse Music Publishing Co. Ltd . . . . USA
Tammy Wynette . . . . Epic EPC 7137

STAND UP FOR YOUR LOVE RIGHTS November 1988
Yasmin Evans / Tim Parry
Big Life Music . . . . UK
Yazz . . . . Big Life BLR 5

STANDING IN THE ROAD September 1972
Thomas Farmer / David Farmer / Edward Golga / Alan Jones
B. Feldman & Co. Ltd. . . . . UK
Blackfoot Sue . . . . DJM JAM 13

STANDING IN THE SHADOWS OF LOVE February 1967
Brian Holland / Eddie Holland / Lamont Dozier
Jobete Music . . . . USA
The Four Tops . . . . Tamla Motown TMG 589

STANDING ON THE CORNER April 1960
Frank Loesser
Frank Music Co. Ltd . . . . USA
Show(s): . . . . Most Happy Fella
American Stage Cast . . . . Philips BBL 7374
British Stage Cast . . . . HMV CLP 1365
The King Brothers . . . . Parlophone GEP 8838

STANLEY STEAMER, THE January 1949
Ralph Blane / Harry Warren
Sun Music Publishing Co. Ltd . . . . USA
Film(s): . . . . Summer Holiday

Dinah Shore & The Modernaires . . . . Columbia DB 2494

STAR June 1990
Vincent Clarke / Andrew Bell
Sony Music . . . . UK
Erasure . . . . Mute MUTE 111

STAR EYES 1943
Don Raye / Gene De Paul
Francis, Day & Hunter Ltd . . . . USA
Film(s): . . . . I Dood it
Jimmy Dorsey & his Orchestra,
vocal Bob Eberly & Kitty Kallen . . . . Brunswick 03498
Carmen McRae . . . . Brunswick LAT 8133
Jimmy Dorsey, Bob Eberly & Kitty Kallen appeared in *I Dood It*.

STAR FELL OUT OF HEAVEN, A 1936
Mack Gordon / Harry Revel
Chappell & Co. Ltd . . . . USA
Ben Bernie & his Orchestra . . . . Brunswick 02278
Eddy Duchin & his Orchestra . . . . HMV BD 5111
Turner Layton . . . . Columbia FB 1502

STAR OF HOPE January 1952
Philip Boutelje / Harry Tobias
Ascherberg, Hopwood & Crew Ltd. . . . . USA
Jo Stafford . . . . Columbia DB 3014
Margaret Whiting & Jimmy Wakely . . . . Capitol CL 13716
Don Cherry & Eileen Wilson . . . . Brunswick 04915
Adapted from 'Tres Jolie' by Emile Waldteufel (1837-1915)

STAR ON A TV SHOW March 1975
Hugo Peretti / Luigi Creatore / George Weiss
Cyril Shane Music . . . . USA
The Stylistics . . . . Avco 6105035

STAR TREKKIN' June 1987
Graham Lister / John O'Connor
Bark Music . . . . UK
The Firm . . . . Bark TREK 1

STAR WARS THEME October 1977
John Williams
Chappell & Co. Ltd . . . . USA
Film(s): . . . . Star Wars
Meco . . . . RCA XB 1028
The London Symphony Orchestra,
conducted by John Williams . . . 20th Century BTD 541

STARDUST 1931
Hoagy Carmichael / Mitchell Parish
Lawrence Wright Music Co. Ltd . . . . USA
Film(s): . . . . The Eddy Duchin Story
Bing Crosby . . . . Brunswick LAT 8251
The Mills Brothers . . . . Brunswick 02741
Hoagy Carmichael . . . . Brunswick LA 8663
The Mills Brothers . . . . London HAD 2250
David Essex (1975) . . . . CBS 2828

STARLIGHT SERENADE 1941
Hans May / Frederick Tysh / Sonny Miller
Keith Prowse Music Publishing Co. Ltd . . . . UK
Joe Loss & his Orchestra,
vocal Chick Henderson . . . . HMV BD 5708

STARMAKER October 1982
Bruce Roberts / Carol Bayer-Sager
Carlin Music . . . . USA
The Kids From Fame . . . . RCA 280
The Kids From Fame appeared in the television series *Fame*.

STARMAN August 1972
David Bowie
Chrysalis Music Ltd. . . . . UK
David Bowie . . . . RCA 2199

STARRY EYED February 1960
Earl Shuman / Mort Garson
Lawrence Wright Music Co. Ltd . . . . USA
Michael Holliday . . . . Columbia DB 4378

STARS AND STRIPES FOREVER, THE 1897
John Philip Sousa
Boosey & Hawkes Music Co. . . . . USA
The Philadelphia Orchestra,

conducted Leopold Stokowski . . . . **HMV B 8095**
The Silver Stars Band . . . . **Regal G 7088**
The Band of the Irish Guards . . . . **Decca MW 51**
Roland Shaw Orchestra . . . . **Decca SKL 4125**
Boston Symphony Orchestra . . . . **Philips 9500692**

STARS FELL ON ALABAMA   1934
Mitchell Parish / Ray Perkins
Campbell Connelly & Co. Ltd . . . . USA
Jack Teagarden & his Orchestra (1934) . . . . . **Brunswick 01913**
Jack Teagarden & his Orchestra (1956) . . . . **Capitol T 721**
Doris Day . . . . **Philips BBL 7211**

STARS IN MY EYES   1937
Fritz Kreisler / Dorothy Fields
Chappell & Co. Ltd. . . . . USA
Film(s): . . . . The King Steps Out
Grace Moore . . . . **Brunswick LAT 8025**
Jane Morgan . . . . **London HAR 2086**
Bob Sharples & The Living Strings . . . . **RCA RD 27187**
Grace Moore appeared in *The King Steps Out.*

STARS SHINE IN YOUR EYES   August 1955
Nino Rota / Geoffrey Parsons / John Turner
Peter Maurice Music Co. Ltd. . . . . Italy
Film(s): . . . . La Strada
Ronnie Hilton . . . . **HMV 7EG 8121**
Eddie Barclay & his Orchestra . . . . **Felsted PDL 85024**

STARS WILL REMEMBER, THE   1946
Don Pelosi / Leo Towers
B. Feldman & Co. Ltd. . . . . UK
Film(s): . . . . Smart Girls Don't Talk
Steve Conway . . . . **Columbia FB 3256**

START   September 1980
Paul Weller
Bryan Morrison Music . . . . UK
The Jam . . . . **Polydor 2059266**

START ME UP   September 1981
Mick Jagger / Keith Richard
EMI Music . . . . UK
The Rolling Stones . . . . **EMI RSR 108**

START MOVIN'   August 1957
David Hill / Bobby Stevenson
Bradbury Wood Ltd. . . . . USA
Larry Page . . . . **Columbia DB 3965**

START THE DAY RIGHT   1939
Charles Tobias / Maurice Spitalny / Al Lewis
Sterling Music Publishing Co. Ltd. . . . . USA
Show(s): . . . . Haw Haw
Bing Crosby & Connee Boswell . . . . **Brunswick LA 8558**
Bebe Daniels & Ben Lyon . . . . **Decca F 7349**
Bebe Daniels & Ben Lyon appeared in *Haw Haw.*

STARTING TOGETHER   March 1986
Bill Buckley
Bill Buckley Music . . . . UK
Su Pollard . . . . **Rainbow RBR 4**

STATELY HOMES OF ENGLAND, THE   1938
Noel Coward
Chappell Music Co. . . . . UK
Show(s): . . . . Operette/Set to Music
Noel Coward . . . . **HMV B 8722**
His Majesty's Theatre Orchestra (Part of Medley) . . . . **HMV C 2999**

STAY   January 1961
Maurice Williams
Lorna Music Co. Ltd . . . . USA
Maurice Wiliams & The Zodiacs . . . . **Top Rank JAR 526**
The Hollies (1964) . . . . **Parlophone R 5077**
Jackson Brown (1978) . . . . **Asylum K 13128**

STAY AS SWEET AS YOU ARE   1934
Mack Gordon / Harry Revel
Victoria Music Co. Ltd . . . . USA
Film(s): . . . . College Rhythm
Kate Smith . . . . **Brunswick 0-1970**
Nat 'King' Cole . . . . **Capitol T 986**
Mel Tormé . . . . **Parlophone GEP 8773**

STAY AWHILE   March 1964
Mike Hawker / Ivor Raymonde
Flamingo Music Ltd . . . . UK
Dusty Springfield . . . . **Philips BF 1313**

STAY ON THE RIGHT SIDE OF THE ROAD   1933
Rube Bloom / Ted Koehler
Campbell Connelly & Co. Ltd. . . . . USA
Film(s): . . . . Love Me or Leave Me
Bing Crosby . . . . **Columbia DB 1964**
Doris Day . . . . **Philips BBL 7047**
Doris Day appeared in *Love Me or Leave Me.*

STAY ON THESE ROADS   April 1988
Pal Waaktaar / Magne Furnholmen / Morten Harket
A.T.V. Music . . . . UK
A-Ha . . . . **Warner Brothers W 7936**

STAY OUT OF MY LIFE   February 1987
Denise Pearson
Chrysalis Music . . . . UK
Five Star . . . . **Tent PB 41131**

STAY OUT OF THE SOUTH   1928
Mort Dixon / Harry Woods
Lawrence Wright Music Co. Ltd. . . . . USA
The Coon-Sanders Orchestra . . . . **HMV B 5463**
Sophie Tucker . . . . **Columbia 4941**
The Saints Jazz Band, vocal Fred Fydler . . **Parlophone PMC 1067**

STAY WITH ME   February 1972
Ron Wood / Rod Stewart
Warner Brothers Music Ltd . . . . UK
The Faces . . . . **Warner Brothers K 16136**

STAYIN' ALIVE   March 1978
Robin Gibb / Maurice Gibb / Barry Gibb
R.S.O. Group . . . . UK
Film(s): . . . . Saturday Night Fever
The Bee Gees . . . . **RSO 2090257**
Ivor Novello Award.

STEAM HEAT   September 1955
Richard Adler / Jerry Ross
Frank Music Co. Ltd. . . . . USA
Show(s): . . . . The Pajama Game
Film(s): . . . . The Pajama Game
Carol Haney, Buzz Miller & Peter Gennaro . . . **Philips BBL 7050**
Elizabeth Seal, Ivor Meggido & Johnny Greenland . . **HMV CLP 1062**
Carol Haney, Buzz Miller & Kenneth Leroy . . **Philips BBL 7197**
Elizabeth Seal, Ivor Meggido & Johnny Greenland appeared in the
British production of *The Pajama Game.*
Kenneth Leroy appeared in the film of *The Pajama Game.*
Carol Haney & Buzz Miller appeared in both the American produc-
tion and the film of *The Pajama Game.*
Peter Gennaro appeared in the American production of *The Pa-
jama Game.*

STEAMBOAT BILL   1910
Ren Shields / Bert Leighton / Frank Leighton
Francis, Day & Hunter Ltd . . . . USA
Paul Tremaine & his Orchestra,
vocal Paul Tremaine . . . . **Columbia CB 138**
The Big Ben Banjo Band . . . . **Columbia 33SX 1188**

STEIN SONG, THE   1911
Lincoln Colcord / E.A. Fenstad
Keith Prowse Music Publishing Co. Ltd . . . . USA
Film(s): . . . . With a Song in My Heart
Harold Williams . . . . **Columbia DB 118**
Rudy Vallee & his Connecticut Yankees (1930) . . . **HMV B 5834**
Michael Holliday . . . . **Columbia DB 3657**

STELLA BY STARLIGHT   1945
Victor Young / Ned Washington
Victoria Music Co. Ltd. . . . . USA
Film(s): . . . . The Uninvited
Frank Sinatra . . . . **Fontana TFL 5107**
Dick Haymes . . . . **Brunswick 03824**
Al Hibbler . . . . **Brunswick LAT 8140**
Caterina Valente . . . . **RCA RD 27216**
Used as the main theme of *The Uninvited.*

STEP BACK IN TIME   November 1990
Mike Stock / Matt Aitken / Peter Waterman

All Boys Music . . . . UK
Kylie Minogue . . . . **PWL PWL 64**

STEP BY STEP
July 1973
Raeford Gerald
Intersong Music . . . . USA
Joe Simon . . . . **Mojo 2093030**

STEP INSIDE LOVE
April 1968
John Lennon / Paul McCartney
Northern Songs Ltd. . . . . UK
Cilla Black . . . . **Parlophone R 5706**

STEP OFF
January 1985
Kenny Gamble / Leon Huff
Island Music . . . . USA
Grandmaster Melle Mel . . . . **Sugarhill SH 139**

STEP ON
April 1990
John Kongos / Chris Demetriou
Tapestry Music . . . . UK
The Happy Mondays . . . . **Factory FAC 2727**

STEPHANIE GAVOTTE, THE
1880
Alphons Czibulka Circa (1842-1894)
. . . . Hungary
The International Novelty Quartet . . . . **Regal T 6020**
Harry Davidson Orchestra . . . . **Columbia DX 1265**
Peter Katin (piano) . . . . **Pickwick PLD 8007**

STEPPIN' OUT
December 1981
Ronald Bell / Taylor
Planetary-Nom Music Co. . . . . USA
Kool & The Gang . . . . **Delite DE 4**

STEPPIN' OUT
January 1983
Joe Jackson
Albion Music . . . . UK
Joe Jackson . . . . **A&M AM 8262**

STEPPING IN SOCIETY
1925
Harry Akst / Alex Gerber
Lawrence Wright Music Co. Ltd. . . . . USA
The Denza Dance Orchestra . . . . **Columbia 3714**
Sid Philips & his Band . . . . **HMV DLP 1206**

STEPPING OUT WITH MY BABY
February 1949
Irving Berlin
Irving Berlin Ltd . . . . USA
Film(s): . . . . Easter Parade
Fred Astaire . . . . **MGM D 140**
Garry Miller with The Kenny Ball Jazz Band . . . **Pye NPL 18059**
Fred Astaire appeared in *Easter Parade*.

STEREOTYPE
October 1980
Jerry Dammers / Neville Staples
Plangent Visions Music Co. UK
The Specials . . . . **2 Tone CHSTT 13**

STILL
September 1963
Bill Anderson
Macmelodies Ltd . . . . USA
Bill Anderson . . . . **Brunswick 05887**
Karl Denver . . . . **Decca F 11720**
Ken Dodd . . . . **Columbia DB 7094**

STILL
December 1979
Lionel Richie
Jobete Music (UK) Ltd. . . . . USA
The Commodores . . . . **Motown TMG 1166**

STILL I'M SAD
November 1965
Paul Samwell-Smith / James McCarty
Yardbirds Music Ltd . . . . UK
The Yardbirds . . . . **Columbia DB 7706**

STILL WATER
November 1970
William Robinson / Frank Wilson
Jobete Music (UK) Ltd. . . . . USA
The Four Tops . . . . **Tamla Motown TMG 752**

STINGRAY
June 1965
Claus Ogerman
Ambassador Music . . . . USA
The Shadows . . . . **Columbia DB 7588**

Claus Ogerman Orchestra . . . . **RCA RD 7784**

STIR IT UP
May 1972
Bob Marley
Rondor Music (London) Ltd . . . . UK
Johnny Nash . . . . **CBS 7800**
Bob Marley . . . . **Island ISLD 11/A**

STOMP
April 1980
Louis Johnson / George Johnson / Valerie Johnson & Rod Temperton
Sunbury Music Ltd . . . . USA
The Brothers Johnson . . . . **A&M AMS 7509**

STOMPIN' AT THE SAVOY
1936
Benny Goodman / Andy Razaf / Edgar Sampson / Chick Webb
Francis, Day & Hunter Ltd . . . . USA
Film(s): . . . . The Benny Goodman Story
Chick Webb's Savoy Orchestra . . . . **Parlophone R 2088**
Benny Goodman & his Orchestra . . . . **RCA RCX 1033**
Judy Garland . . . . **Brunswick 03352**
The Johnny Mann Singers . . . . **London HAG 2297**
Edgar Sampson & his Orchestra . . . . **Vogue LVA 9039**

STONED LOVE
March 1971
Frank Wilson / Yennik Somoht
Jobete Music (UK) Ltd. . . . . USA
The Supremes . . . . **Tamla Motown TMG 760**

STOOL PIGEON
August 1982
August Darnell
Island Music . . . . USA
Kid Creole & The Coconuts . . . . **Island WIP 6793**

STOP
March 1989
Samantha Brown / Greg Sutton / Bruce Brody
Rondor Music . . . . UK
Sam Brown . . . . **A&M AM 440**

STOP AND SHOP AT THE CO-OP SHOP
1930
R.P. Weston / Bert Lee
Francis, Day & Hunter Ltd . . . . USA
Gracie Fields . . . . **HMV 7EG 8299**

STOP HER ON SIGHT
February 1969
Al Hamilton / Richard Morris / Charles Hatcher
Essex Music Ltd. . . . . USA
Edwin Starr . . . . **Polydor 56753**

STOP IN THE NAME OF LOVE
April 1965
Brian Holland / Eddie Holland / Lamont Dozier
Manor Music Co. Ltd . . . . USA
The Supremes . . . . **Tamla Motown TMG 501**

STOP ME (If You've Heard It All Before)
December 1976
Ben Findon / Les Charles / Michael Myers
Black Sheep Music . . . . UK
Billy Ocean . . . . **GTO GT 72**

STOP STOP STOP
November 1966
Tony Hicks / Alan Clarke / Graham Nash
Gralto Music Ltd. . . . . UK
The Hollies . . . . **Parlophone R 5508**

STOP THE CAVALRY
December 1980
Jona Lewie
Street Music . . . . UK
Jona Lewie . . . . **Stiff BUY 104**
Ivor Novello Award.

STOP YOUR TICKLING JOCK
1904
Harry Lauder / Frank Folley
Francis, Day & Hunter Ltd. . . . . UK
Harry Lauder (1901) . . . . **Berliner 2-2420**
Harry Lauder (1926) . . . . **HMV DLP 1089**
George Elrick . . . . **Ace of Clubs ACL 1024**

STORM IN A TEACUP
March 1972
Ronald Roker / Lynsey Rubin
A.T.V. Music Ltd. . . . . UK
The Fortunes . . . . **Capitol CL 15707**

STORMY WEATHER
1933
Ted Koehler / Harold Arlen
Lawrence Wright Music Co. Ltd. . . . . USA

Show(s): . . . . On With the Show
Film(s): . . . . Stormy Weather / Swing Parade of 1946
Leo Reisman & his Orchestra, vocal Harold Arlen . . HMV B 6349
Ethel Waters . . . . **Brunswick 01524**
Jimmy Campbell & his Orchestra . . . . **Rex 8007**
Lena Horne . . . . **HMV JO 201**
Connee Boswell . . . . **Brunswick LA 8665**
Frank Sinatra . . . . **Fontana SET 303B**
Judy Garland . . . . **Capitol WBO 1569**
Jimmy Campbell appeared in *On With the Show.*
Lena Horne appeared in *Stormy Weather.*
Connee Boswell appeared in *Swing Parade of 1946.* Theme song of
Lena Horne.

STORY OF A STARRY NIGHT, THE   1942
Mann Curtis / Al Hoffman / Jerry Livingston
Chappell & Co. Ltd . . . . USA
Glenn Miller & his Orchestra, vocal Ray Eberle . . HMV 7EG 8043
Bob Sharples & The Living Strings . . . . **RCA RD 27187**
Based on the first movement of Symphony no. 6 by Peter Ilych
Tchaikovsky (1840 - 1893).

STORY OF MY LIFE, THE   January 1958
Burt Bacharach / Hal David
Chappell & Co. Ltd . . . . USA
Michael Holliday . . . . **Columbia SEG 7818**
Dave King . . . . **Decca DFE 6514**
Gary Miller . . . . **Pye N 15120**
Alma Cogan . . . . **HMV POP 433**

STORY OF THE BLUES   February 1983
Peter Wylie
Warner Brothers Music . . . . UK
Wah . . . . **Eternal JF 1**

STORY OF TINA, THE (Dio Prasina Matia)   July 1954
K. Kioussi Katrivanou / Christopher Hassall
Macmelodies Ltd. . . . . Greece
Ronnie Harris . . . . **Columbia DB 3499**
Ronald Binge & his Orchestra . . . . **RCA RD 27117**
Stanley Black Orchestra . . . . **Decca LK 4243**
Al Martino . . . . **Capitol CL 14163**
Lee Lawrence . . . . **Decca F 10367**

STOUT HEARTED MEN   1929
Sigmund Romberg / Oscar Hammerstein II
Chappell & Co. Ltd . . . . USA
Show(s): . . . . The New Moon
Film(s): . . . . The New Moon / Deep in My Heart
Howett Worster & Ben Williams . . . . **Columbia 9753**
Nelson Eddy . . . . **RCA RCX 1044**
Helen Traubel . . . . **MGM C 755**
Howett Worster & Ben Williams appeared in the British production of
The New Moon.
Nelson Eddy appeared in the 1940 film of *The New Moon.*
Helen Traubel appeared in *Deep In My Heart.*

STOWAWAY   June 1955
Jerry Livingston / Carolyn Leigh
Edwin H. Morris 7 Co. Ltd. . . . . USA
Barbara Lyon . . . . **Columbia DB 3619**

STRAIGHT AHEAD   January 1984
James Taylor'Kool & The Gang'
Planetary-Nom Music Co. . . . . UK
Kool & The Gang . . . . **De Lite DE 5**

STRAIGHT UP   April 1989
Elliot Wolf
Virgin Music . . . . USA
Paula Abdul . . . . **Siren SRN 111**

STRAIGHTEN UP AND FLY RIGHT   1945
Nat Cole / Irving Mills
Sterling Music Publishing Co. Ltd. . . . . USA
Film(s): . . . . Here Comes Elmer / On Stage Everybody
The Andrews Sisters . . . . **Brunswick 03548**
Nat 'King' Cole . . . . **Capitol EMTV 9**
Colin James & Keith Cooper . . . . **Pye 7N 25084**
The Andrews Sisters appeared in *On Stage Everybody.*
Nat King Cole appeared in *Here Comes Elmer.*
Theme song of Nat 'King' Cole.

STRANGE BAND   October 1970
Richard Whitney / Roger Chapman

Carlin Music Corporation . . . . UK
Family . . . . **Reprise RS 27009**

STRANGE KIND OF WOMAN, A   April 1971
Jon Lord / Ian Pace / Ritchie Blackmore / Ian Gillan & Roger Glover
Hec Music . . . . UK
Deep Purple . . . . **Harvest SHSP 4122**

STRANGE LADY IN TOWN   August 1955
Ned Washington / Dimitri Tiomkin
Chappell Music Co. . . . . USA
Film(s): . . . . Strange Lady in Town
Frankie Laine . . . . **Philips PB 478**

STRANGE LITTLE GIRL   July 1982
*Jet Black / Jean Burnel / Hugh Cornwell / David Greenfield / Harns
Warmling*
EMI Music . . . . UK
The Stranglers . . . . **Liberty BP 412**

STRANGE MUSIC   1946
Robert Wright / George Forrest
Chappell & Co. Ltd. . . . . USA
Show(s): . . . . Song of Norway
Film(s): . . . . Song of Norway
Lawrence Brooks & Helena Bliss . . . . **MCA 2032**
John Hargreaves & Janet Hamilton-Smith . . . **HMV B 9479**
Toralv Maurstad . . . . **ABCS OC 14**
Bing Crosby . . . . **Brunswick 03647**
Harry Secombe . . . . **Philips 6006103**
John Lawrenson & Norma Hughes . . . . **HMV CLP 1313**
Lawrence Brooks & Helena Bliss appeared in the American produc-
tion of *Song of Norway.*
John Hargreaves & Janet Hamilton-Smith appeared in the British
production of *Song of Norway.*
Toralv Maurstad appeared in the film of *Song of Norway.*
Adapted from "Wedding Day in Troldhaugen" by Edvard Grieg (1843-
1907).

STRANGER IN PARADISE   April 1955
Robert Wright / George Forrest
Frank Music Co. Ltd. . . . . USA
Show(s): . . . . Kismet
Film(s): . . . . Kismet
Doretta Morrow & Richard Kiley . . . . **Philips BBL 7023**
Ann Blyth & Vic Damone . . . . **MGM C 758**
The Four Aces . . . . **Brunswick OE 9431**
Tony Martin . . . . **HMV B 10849**
Tony Bennett . . . . **Philips BBR 8051**
Doretta Morrow appeared in both the American and British produc-
tions of *Kismet.*
Richard Kiley appeared in the American production of *Kismet.*
Ann Blyth & Vic Damone appeared in the film *Kismet.*
Adapted from a theme of the 'Polovtsian Dances' by Alexander
Borodin.

STRANGER ON THE SHORE   January 1962
Acker Bilk / Robert Mellin
Sherwin Music Co. . . . . UK
**Acker Bilk (clarinet) with The
Leon Young String Chorale** . . . . **Columbia DB 4750**
The Drifters . . . . **London HLK 9554**
Andy Williams . . . . **CBS AAG 20016**
Theme of the TV series "Stranger on the Shore".
Ivor Novello Nomination 1961.
Ivor Novello Award 1962.

STRANGER, THE   November 1960
Bill Crompton / Morgan Jones
Tin Pan Alley Music Co. Ltd . . . . UK
The Shadows . . . . **Columbia SEG 8094**

STRANGERS IN THE NIGHT   August 1966
Charles Singleton / Eddie Snyder / Bert Kaempfert
Welbeck Music Co. Ltd. . . . . USA
Film(s): . . . . A Man Could Get Killed
Frank Sinatra . . . . **Reprise R 23052**
Bert Kaempfert Orchestra . . . . **Polydor 84053**

STRAWBERRY FAIR   December 1960
Traditional, new lyric by Nolly Clapton
Essex Music Ltd . . . . UK
Anthony Newley . . . . **Decca F 11295**

STRAWBERRY FIELDS FOREVER   April 1967
John Lennon / Paul McCartney

Northern Songs Ltd. . . . . UK
The Beatles (1967) . . . . **Parlophone R 5570**
Candy Flip (1990) . . . . **Debut DEBT 3092**

STRAWBERRY MOON IN A BLUEBERRY SKY, A   June 1949
Bob Hilliard / Sammy Mysels
Yale Music Corporation Ltd. . . . . USA
Donald Peers . . . . **HMV B 9773**
Joy Nichols & Benny Lee . . . . **Decca F 9105**
Bob & Alf Pearson . . . . **Parlophone F 2371**
Anita O'Day . . . . **Columbia 33C 9020**

STRAY CAT STRUT   May 1981
Brian Setzer
Zomba Music . . . . UK
The Stray Cats . . . . **Arista SCAT 3**

STREAK, THE   June 1974
Ray Stevens
Peter Maurice Music Co. Ltd. . . . . USA
Ray Stevens . . . . **Janus 6146201**

STREET DANCE   March 1984
Jacques Morali / Fred Zarr / Henri Belolo & Keith Rogers
Leosong Ltd. . . . . USA
Break Machine . . . . **Record Shack SOHO 13**

STREET LIFE   January 1974
Bryan Ferry
E.G. Music . . . . UK
Roxy Music . . . . **Island WIP 6173**

STREET LIFE   September 1979
Joe Sample / William Jennings
Rondor Music (London) Ltd. . . . . USA
The Crusaders . . . . **MCA 513**

STREET OF DREAMS   1933
Sam M. Lewis / Victor Young
Francis, Day & Hunter Ltd. . . . . USA
Bing Crosby . . . . **Columbia DB 2085**
The Ink Spots . . . . **Brunswick LA 8710**
The Four Freshmen . . . . **Capitol LC 6685**
The King Sisters . . . . **Capitol T 1333**

STREET TUFF   November 1989
Leigh Guest / Michael Menson / Michael West
Fiction Songs Ltd. . . . . UK
Rebel MC . . . . **Desire WANT 18**

STREETS OF LAREDO, THE   July 1949
Jay Livingston / Ray Evans
Victoria Muoic Co. Ltd . . . . UK
Film(s): . . . . The Streets Of Lorado
Dick Haymes . . . . **Brunswick 04254**
Bob Cort & his Skiffle Group . . . . **Decca LK 4222**

STREETS OF LONDON, THE   January 1975
Ralph McTell
Essex Music Ltd. . . . . UK
Ralph McTell . . . . **Reprise K 14380**
Ivor Novello Award.

STRING OF PEARLS, A   1942
Eddie De Lange / Jerry Gray
Bradbury Wood Ltd . . . . USA
Film(s): . . . . The Glenn Miller Story
Glenn Miller & his Orchestra . . . . **RCA RD 27068**
The Clark Sisters . . . . **London HAD 2128**
The Universal International Studio
Orchestra . . . . **Brunswick LA 8647**
The Universal Studio Orchestra appeared in *The Glenn Miller Story.*

STRIPPER, THE   June 1962
David Rose
Bregman, Vocco & Conn Ltd . . . . USA
David Rose & his Orchestra . . . . **MGM 1158**
Billy Vaughan & his Orchestra . . . . **London HAD 8506**

STROLLIN'   July 1959
Ralph Reader
Reynolds & Co (Music Publishers) Ltd . . . . UK
Bud Flanagan . . . . **Columbia DB 4265**
Kim Cordell . . . . **Columbia 33SX 1678**
Max Bygraves . . . . **Pye NPL 18183**

STRUT YOUR FUNKY STUFF   October 1979
James Robinson / Vivien Robinson / James Bolden
Carlin Music Corporation . . . . USA
Frantique . . . . **Philadelphia PIR 7728**

STRUTTIN' WITH SOME BARBECUE   1928
Lillian Hardin Armstrong / Don Raye
Leeds Music Ltd. . . . . USA
Louis Armstrong Hot Five with
Lill Hardin (piano) . . . . **Parlophone PMC 1146**
Louis Armstrong's All Stars . . . . **Ace of Hearts AH 18**

STUCK ON YOU   April 1960
Aaron Schroeder / Leslie MacFarland
Belinda (London) Ltd . . . . USA
Elvis Presley . . . . **RCA 1187**

STUCK ON YOU   July 1984
Lionel Richie
Warner Brothers Music . . . . USA
Trevor Walters (August 1984) . . . . **Sanity IS 002**
Lionel Richie . . . . **Motown TMG 1341**

STUCK WITH YOU   October 1986
Huey Lewis
Chrysalis Music . . . . USA
Huey Lewis & The News . . . . **Chrysalis HUEY 5**

STUMBLING   1922
Zez Confrey
Francis, Day & Hunter Ltd . . . . USA
Film(s): . . . . Mother Wore Tights
Paul Whiteman & his Orchestra . . . . **HMV B 1382**
Bob Scobey's Band,
vocal Clancy Hayes . . . . **Columbia 33CX 10089**
Bob Crosby's Bob Cats . . . . **Vogue LVA 9083**

STUPID CUPID   September 1958
Neil Sedaka / Howard Greenfield
Aldon Music Ltd. . . . . USA
Connie Francis . . . . **MGM C 831**
Neil Sedaka . . . . **RCA RD 27140**

STUTTER RAP   January 1988
Tony Hawks / Geoff Grange
Rondor Music . . . . UK
Morris Minor & The Majors . . . . **Virgin TEN 203**

SUBSTITUTE   May 1966
Peter Townshend
Fabulous Music Ltd. . . . . UK
The Who . . . . **Reaction 591001**
The Who (1976) . . . . **Polydor 2058803**

SUBSTITUTE   August 1978
W.H. Wilson
A.T.V. Music Ltd. . . . . USA
Clout . . . . **EMI 2788**

SUBSTITUTE   July 1980
Adrian Baker / Eddie Seago
Leeds Music Ltd . . . . UK
Liquid Gold . . . . **Polo POLO 4**

SUBTERRANEAN HOMESICK BLUES   May 1965
Bob Dylan
Blossom Music Ltd . . . . USA
Bob Dylan . . . . **CBS 201753**

SUBURBIA   October 1986
Neil Tennant / Chris Lowe
Cage Music . . . . UK
The Pet Shop Boys . . . . **Parlophone R 6140**

SUCH A NIGHT   April 1954
Lincoln Chase
Chappell & Co. Ltd. . . . . USA
Johnnie Ray . . . . **Phillips BBL 7264**
Elvis Presley . . . . **RCA RD 27171**
Elvis Presley (1964) . . . . **RCA 1411**

SUCU SUCU   September 1961
Tarateno Rosas
Peter Maurice Music Co. Ltd. Argentina
Laurie Johnson & his Orchestra . . . . **Pye 7N 15383**

Nina & Frederik . . . . **Columbia DB 4632**
Theme of the TV production "Top Secret".

SUDDENLY   **1935**
Billy Rose / Vernon Duke / E.Y. Harburg
Peter Maurice Music Co. Ltd . . . . USA
Show(s): . . . . The Ziegfeld Follies of 1934
Vivian Blaine . . . . **Mercury MPL 6518**

SUDDENLY   **1955**
Dorcas Cochrane / Richard Heuberger
Bosworth & Co. Ltd. . . . . USA
Tony Bennett . . . . **Philips BBL 7413**
Adapted from 'Im Chambre Separee' by Richard Heuberger (1850-
1914). See also Kiss in your Eyes.

SUDDENLY   **June 1985**
Billy Ocean / Keith Diamond
Zomba Music . . . . UK
Billy Ocean . . . . **Jive 90**

SUDDENLY   **December 1988**
Garry Anderson / Andrew Cichon / Kevin Beamish
Island Music . . . . Australia
Angry Anderson . . . . **Food For Thought YUM 113**

SUDDENLY IT'S SPRING   **1945**
Johnny Burke / Jimmy Van Heusen
Chappell & Co. Ltd. . . . . USA
Film(s): . . . . Lady in the Dark
Hildegarde . . . . **Brunswick 03523**
Chris Connor . . . . **London HAK 2066**

SUDDENLY THERE'S A VALLEY   **November 1955**
Chuck Meyer / Biff Jones
Aberbach (London) Ltd. . . . . USA
Kathie Kay . . . . **HMV 7M 335**
Lee Lawrence . . . . **Columbia SCM 5201**
Gogi Grant . . . . **London HAB 2032**

SUDDENLY YOU LOVE ME (Uno Tranquillo)   **March 1968**
Daniele Pace / Lorenzo Pilat / Mario Panzeri & Peter Callander
Shapiro-Bernstein & Co. Ltd. Italy
The Tremeloes . . . . **CBS 3234**

SUEDEHEAD   **March 1988**
Stephen Street / Steven Morrissey
Warner Brothers Music . . . . UK
Morrissey . . . . **HMV POP 1618**

SUGAR   **1928**
Sidney Mitchell / Edna Alexander / Maceo Pinkard
Francis, Day & Hunter Ltd. . . . . USA
Film(s): . . . . Pete Kelly's Blues
Paul Whiteman & his Orchestra . . . . **HMV B 8931**
Peggy Lee . . . . **Brunswick LAT 8078**
Bing Crosby & Louis Armstrong . . . . **MGM C 844**
Peggy Lee appeared in *Pete Kelly's Blues.*

SUGAR AND SPICE   **November 1963**
Fred Nightingale
Welbeck Music Co. Ltd . . . . UK
The Searchers . . . . **Pye 7N 15566**

SUGAR BABY LOVE   **June 1974**
Wayne Bickerton / Tony Waddington
A.T.V. Music Ltd. . . . . UK
The Rubettes . . . . **Polydor 2058442**

SUGAR BLUES   **1935**
Clarence Williams / Lucy Fletcher
Southern Music Publishing Co. Ltd . . . . USA
Clarence Williams & his Orchestra,
vocal Chick Bullock . . . . **Columbia SEG 7545**
Clyde McCoy & his Orchestra . . . . **Brunswick OE 9420**
The Clyde McCoy Dixieland Band . . . . **London HAU 2232**
The Clark Sisters . . . . **London HAD 2177**
Theme tune of Clyde McCoy.

SUGAR BUSH   **October 1952**
Joseph Marais
Chappell & Co. Ltd . . . . South Africa
Eve Boswell . . . . **Parlophone GEP 8601**
Doris Day & Frankie Laine . . . . **Columbia DB 3123**

SUGAR CANDY KISSES   **February 1975**
Wayne Bickerton / Tony Waddington
A.T.V. Music Ltd. . . . . UK
Mac & Katie Kissoon . . . . **Polydor 2058531**

SUGAR ME   **September 1972**
Lynsey De Paul / Barry Green
A.T.V. Music Ltd. . . . . UK
Lynsey De Paul . . . . **MAM 81**

SUGAR MOON   **July 1958**
Danny Wolfe
Frank Music Co. . . . . USA
Pat Boone . . . . **London HLD 8640**

SUGAR SUGAR   **December 1969**
Jeff Barry / Andy Kim
Don Kirschner Music . . . . USA
The Archies . . . . **RCA 1872**
Sakkarin (1971) . . . . **RCA 2064**

SUGAR TOWN   **February 1967**
Lee Hazlewood
Lorna Music Co. Ltd. . . . . USA
Nancy Sinatra . . . . **Reprise RS 20527**

SUGARTIME   **February 1958**
Charlie Phillips / Odis Echols
Southern Music Publishing Co. Ltd . . . . USA
Alma Cogan . . . . **HMV POP 450**
The McGuire Sisters . . . . **Vogue LVA 9133**
Kitty Wells . . . . **Brunswick LAT 8361**

SUICIDE IS PAINLESS   **June 1980**
Mike Altman / Johnny Mandell
Chappell & Co. Ltd . . . . USA
Film(s): . . . . M.A.S.H.
The Mash . . . . **CBS 8536**
First published 1970.

SUKIYAKI (Ueo Muite Aruku)   **February 1963**
El Rohsuke / Hachidai Nakamura
Welbeck Music Co. Ltd . . . . Japan
Kenny Ball Jazz Band (February) . . . . **Pye 7NJ 2062**
Kyu Sakamoto (August) . . . . **HMV POP 1171**

SULTANA   **October 1971**
"Titanic"
April Music Ltd . . . . France
Titanic . . . . **CBS 5365**

SULTANS OF SWING   **April 1979**
Mark Knopfler
Rondor Music (London) Ltd. . . . . UK
Dire Straits . . . . **Vertigo 6059206**

SUMMER (The First Time)   **September 1973**
Bobby Goldsboro
United Artists Music Co. Ltd. USA
Bobby Goldsboro . . . . **United Artists UP 35558**

SUMMER EVENING IN SANTA CRUZ, A   **1939**
Fred Hartley / Jose Payan
Peter Maurice Music Co. Ltd. . . . . UK
Maxwell Stewart's Ballroom Melody,
vocal Pat O'Regan . . . . **Rex 9620**

SUMMER HOLIDAY   **March 1963**
Bruce Welch / Brian Bennett
Elstree Music Ltd . . . . UK
Film(s): . . . . Summer Holiday
Cliff Richard . . . . **Columbia DB 4977**
Cliff Richard appeared in *Summer Holiday.*

SUMMER IN THE CITY   **August 1966**
John Sebastian / Mark Sebastian / Steve Boon
Robbins Music Corporation Ltd. . . . . USA
The Lovin' Spoonful . . . . **Kama Sutra KAS 200**

SUMMER IS A-COMIN' IN   **May 1958**
Leslie Bricusse
Unit Music Publishing Co. Ltd . . . . UK
Kathie Kay . . . . **HMV POP 485**

SUMMER KNOWS, THE   September 1975
Michel Legrand
Warner Brothers Music Ltd . . . . USA
Film(s): . . . . Summer of '42
The Biddu Orchestra . . . . **Epic EPC 3318**
Michel Legrand . . . . **Warner Brothers WB 7486**

SUMMER LOVE SENSATION   August 1974
Bill Martin / Phil Coulter
Martin-Coulter Music Ltd. . . . . UK
The Bay City Rollers . . . . **Bell 1369**

SUMMER NIGHT CITY   October 1978
Benny Andersson / Bjorn Ulvaeus
Bocu Music Ltd . . . . Sweden
Abba . . . . **Epic EPC 6595**

SUMMER NIGHTS   August 1965
Brian Henderson / Liza Strike
Ardmore & Beechwood Ltd . . . . UK
Marianne Faithull . . . . **Decca F 12193**

SUMMER NIGHTS   October 1978
Warren Casey / Jimmy Jacobs
Chappell & Co. Ltd . . . . USA
Film(s): . . . . Grease
John Travolta & Olivia Newton-John . . . . **RSO 2479-210**
John Travolta & Olivia Newton-John appeared in *Grease*.

SUMMER OF MY LIFE, THE   November 1976
Simon May
A.T.V. Music Ltd. . . . . UK
Simon May . . . . **Pye 7N 45627**

SUMMER PLACE, A   April 1960
Max Steiner
Blossom Music Ltd . . . . USA
Film(s): . . . . A Summer Place
Percy Faith & his Orchestra . . . . **Philips BBL 7488**
Vera Lynn . . . . **MGM C 855**

SUMMER SET   March 1960
Acker Bilk / David Collett
Allegro Music Ltd. . . . . UK
Mr Acker Bilk & his Paramount Jazz Band . . **Columbia 33SX 1205**

SUMMERTIME   1938
George Gershwin / Ira Gershwin
Chappell & co. Ltd. . . . . USA
Show(s): . . . . Porgy and Bess
Film(s): . . . . Porgy and Bess
Anne Brown & chorus . . . . **Brunswick LAT 8021**
Helen Jessop & chorus . . . . **HMV DB 3396**
Carmen McRae . . . . **Brunswick LAT 8308**
Sound Track recording of *Porgy and Bess* . . **Philips ABL 3282**
Fun Boy Three (1982) . . . . **Chrysalis CHS 2629**
Anne Brown appeared in the American production of *Porgy and Bess*.

SUMMERTIME CITY   September 1975
Mike Batt
April Music Ltd . . . . UK
Mike Batt . . . . **Epic EPC 3460**

SUMMERTIME IN VENICE   July 1955
'Icini' / Carl Sigman
Pickwick Music Ltd. . . . . Italy
Film(s): . . . . Summer Madness
Ron Goodwin & his Concert Orchestra . . . **Parlophone GEP 8555**
The Mantovani Orchestra . . . . **Decca LK 4200**
Connie Francis . . . . **MGM C 854**
Frank Chacksfield & his Orchestra . . . . **Ace of Clubs ACL 1080**

SUN AIN'T GONNA SHINE ANYMORE, THE   April 1966
Bob Crewe / Bob Gaudio
Ardmore & Beechwood Ltd. . . . . USA
The Walker Brothers . . . . **Philips BF 1473**

SUN ALWAYS SHINES ON T.V., THE   February 1986
Pal Waaktaar
A.T.V. Music . . . . UK
A-Ha . . . . **Warner Brothers W 8846**

SUN AND THE RAIN, THE   December 1983
Michael Barson

Warner Brothers Music . . . . UK
Madness . . . . **Stiff BUY 192**

SUN ARISE   December 1962
Rolf Harris / Harry Butler
Ardmore & Beechwood Ltd . . . . Australia
Rolf Harris . . . . **Columbia DB 4888**

SUN GOES DOWN, THE   September 1983
Walter Badarou / Mark King / Philip Gould / Michael Lindup
A.T.V. Music . . . . UK
Level 42 . . . . **Polydor POSP 622**

SUN HAS GOT HIS HAT ON, THE   1932
Noel Gay / Ralph Butler
B. Feldman & Co. Ltd. . . . . UK
Show(s): . . . . Me and My Girl (Revival)
The B.B.C. Dance Orchestra,
conducted by Henry Hall, vocal Val Rosing . **Columbia CB 472**
Ambrose & his Orchestra vocal Sam Browne . . . . **HMV B 6210**
Robert Longden . . . . **Columbia EJ 24031**
Robert Longden appeared in the 1985 revival of *Me and My Girl*.

SUNBONNET BLUE, A   1935
Irving Kahal / Sammy Fain
B. Feldman & Co. Ltd . . . . USA
Teddy Wilson & his Orchestra,
vocal Billie Holiday . . . . **Brunswick 02066**

SUNBONNET SUE   1908
Will Cobb / Gus Edwards
Francis, Day & Hunter . . . . USA
Film(s): . . . . The Star Maker / Sunbonnet Sue
Bing Crosby . . . . **Brunswick Bing 5**
Dick Todd . . . . **HMV BD 750**
Bing Crosby appeared in *The Star Maker*.

SUNDAY   1927
Chester Conn / Ned Miller / Jules Stein / Benny Krueger
Francis, Day & Hunter Ltd. . . . . USA
Cliff Edwards (Ukulele Ike) . . . . **CBS BPG 62546**
Jean Goldkette & his Orchestra,
vocal The Keller Sisters & Lynch . . . . . . **RCA RD 27225**
Frank Sinatra . . . . **Capitol W 587**
Teresa Brewer . . . . **Vogue LVA 9020**

SUNDAY GIRL   June 1979
Chris Stein
EMI Music Ltd. . . . . UK
Blondie . . . . **Chrysalis CHS 2320**

SUNDAY KIND OF LOVE, A   1947
Barbara Belle / Anita Leonard / Stan Rhodes & Louis Prima
Peter Maurice Music Co. Ltd. . . . . USA
Ella Fitzgerald . . . . **Brunswick 03805**
Claude Thornhill Orchestra . . . . **Columbia DB 2517**
Stan Kenton & his Orchestra . . . . **Capitol T 1068**

SUNDAY, MONDAY OR ALWAYS   1943
Johnny Burke / Jimmy Van Heusen
Edwin H. Morris & Co. Ltd . . . . USA
Film(s): . . . . Dixie
Bing Crosby . . . . **Brunswick Bing 8**
Nat 'King' Cole . . . . **Capitol W 1574**
Bing Crosby appeared in *Dixie*.

SUNDOWN IN LITTLE GREEN HOLLOW   1934
Richard A. Whiting / Billy Baskette
B. Feldman & Co. Ltd. . . . . USA
The Broadway Brothers . . . . **Parlophone R 1600**
Roy Fox & his Orchestra . . . . **Decca F 3834**

SUNNY   1926
Otto Harbach / Jerome Kern / Oscar Hammerstein II
Chappell & Co. Ltd. . . . . USA
Show(s): . . . . Sunny
Film(s): . . Sunny / Till the Clouds Roll By / Look for the Silver Lining
Jack Hobbs & Chorus . . . . **Columbia 4142**
Jack Hylton & his Orchestra . . . . **HMV B 5129**
Melville Gideon & Doris Bentley . . . . **HMV C 2378**
Maurice Chevalier . . . . **MGM C 860**
Jack Hobbs appeared in the British production of *Sunny*.

SUNNY   November 1966
Bobby Hebb

Campbell Connelly & Co. Ltd. . . . . USA
Bobby Hebb . . . . **Philips BF 1503**
Cher . . . . **Liberty LIB 12083**
Georgie Fame . . . . **Columbia DB 8015**
Boney M (1977) . . . . **Atlantic K 10892**

SUNNY AFTERNOON   August 1966
Ray Davies
Belinda (London) Ltd. . . . . UK
The Kinks . . . . **Pye 7N 17125**

SUNNY DAYS   1931
Reginald Connelly / Will Jason / Val Burton
Campbell Connelly & Co. Ltd . . . . UK
The New Mayfair Dance Orchestra, vocal Al Bowlly . . **HMV B 5956**

SUNNY DISPOSISH   1927
Phil Charig / Ira Gershwin
Chappell & Co. Ltd. . . . . USA
Show(s): . . . . Americana
Jean Goldkette & his Orchestra,
vocal Lewis James & chorus . . . . **HMV B 5293**
Benny Goodman & his Orchestra . . . . **Philips BBL 7009**
Bob Scobey's Frisco Band . . . . **RCA RD 27031**

SUNNY HAVANA   1925
Horatio Nicholls
Lawrence Wright Music Co. Ltd. . . . . UK
Cyril Newton . . . . **HMV B 2151**

SUNNY HONEY GIRL   February 1971
Roger Greenaway / Roger Cook / John Goodison & Tony Hiller
Cookaway Music . . . . UK
Cliff Richard . . . . **Columbia DB 8747**

SUNNY SIDE UP   1930
Buddy De Sylva / Lew Brown / Ray Henderson
Campbell Connelly & Co. Ltd . . . . USA
Film(s): . . . . Sunny Side Up / The Best Things in Life are Free
Frankie Trumbauer & his Orchestra,
vocal Smith Ballew . . . . **Parlophone R 499**
Ben Selvin & his Orchestra . . . . **Columbia 5679**
The Big Ben Banjo Band,
vocal Michael Sammes Singers . . . . **Columbia 33SX 1367**

SUNRISE AND YOU   1918
Arthur Penn
B. Feldman & Co. Ltd. . . . . USA
The Justin Ring Orchestra,
vocal Jack Palmer . . . . **Panachord 26033**
Thomas L. Thomas . . . . **Decca LXT 5247**

SUNRISE SERENADE   1939
Frankie Carle / Jack Lawrence
Herman Darewski Music Publishing Co. Ltd. . . . . USA
Frankie Carle & his Orchestra . . . . **Columbia FB 3239**
Glenn Miller & his Orchestra . . . . **RCA RD 27057**
The Sauter-Finegan Orchestra . . . . **RCA RD 27093**
Theme song of Frankie Carle Orchestra.

SUNRISE SUNSET   September 1967
Sheldon Harnick / Jerry Bock
Chappell & Co. Ltd. . . . . USA
Show(s): . . . . Fiddler on the Roof
Film(s): . . . . Fiddler on the Roof
Zero Mostel & Maria Karnilova . . . . **RCA RD 7843**
Topol & Miriam Karlin . . . . **CBS BRG 70030**
Topol & Norma Crane . . . . **United Artists UP 35307**
Zero Mostel & Maria Karnilova appeared in the American production
of *Fiddler on the Roof.*
Topol & Miriam Karlin appeared in the British production of *Fiddler*
on the Roof.
Topol & Norma Crane appeared in the film *Fiddler on the Roof.*

SUNSET TRAIL, THE   1936
Jimmy Kennedy / Michael Carr
Peter Maurice Music Co. Ltd . . . . UK
Ambrose & his Orchestra . . . . **Decca F 5860**
The Rocky Mountaineers . . . . **Columbia FB 1314**

SUNSHINE   1928
Irving Berlin
Francis, Day & Hunter Ltd. . . . . USA
Jack Smith . . . . **HMV B 2706**

SUNSHINE AFTER THE RAIN   October 1977
Ellie Greenwich
United Artists Music Co. Ltd . . . . USA
Elkie Brooks . . . . **A&M AMS 7306**

SUNSHINE CAKE   May 1950
Johnny Burke / Jimmy Van Huesen
Victoria Music Co. Ltd . . . . USA
Film(s): . . . . Riding High
Bing Crosby & Carole Richards . . . . **Brunswick Bing 12**
Bing Crosby appeared in *Riding High.*

SUNSHINE GIRL   August 1968
John Carter / Geoff Stevens
Monique Music Ltd. . . . . UK
Herman's Hermits . . . . **Columbia DB 8446**

SUNSHINE OF YOUR LOVE, THE   November 1968
Eric Clapton / Jack Bruce / Peter Brown
Dratleaf Music . . . . UK
The Cream . . . . **Polydor 56286**

SUNSHINE OF YOUR SMILE, THE   1913
Leonard Cooke / Lilian Ray
Francis, Day & Hunter Ltd. . . . . USA
Show(s): . . . . Business as Usual
Julie Dolaro . . . . **Regal G 6832**
Derek Oldham . . . . **HMV B 8682**
Lester Ferguson . . . . **Parlophone R 3384**
Mike Berry (1980) . . . . **Polydor 2059261**

SUNSHINE SUPERMAN   January 1967
Donovan Leitch
Donovan Music Ltd. . . . . UK
Donovan . . . . **Pye 7N 17241**

SUPER TROUPER   December 1980
Benny Andersson / Bjorn Ulvaeus
Bocu Music Ltd . . . . Sweden
Abba . . . . **Epic EPC 9089**

SUPERCALIFRAGILISTICEXPIALIDOCIOUS   January 1965
Richard M. Sherman / Robert B. Sherman
Walt Disney Music Co. Ltd . . . . USA
Film(s): . . . . Mary Poppins
Julie Andrews & Dick Van Dyke . . . . **HMV CLP 1794**
Julie Andrews & Dick Van Dyke appeared in *Mary Poppins.*

SUPERFLY GUY   August 1988
Mark Moore / Pascal Gabriel
Rhythm King Music . . . . UK
S-Express . . . . **Rhythm King LEFT 28**

SUPERMAN (Gioca Jouer)   October 1983
Claudio Cecchetto / Claudio Simonetti
Arretta Music . . . . Italy
Black Lace . . . . **Flair FLA 105**

SUPERNATURE   September 1978
Marc Cerrone / Alain Wisniak
Panache . . . . France
Cerrone . . . . **Atlantic K 11089**

SUPERSTAR   February 1972
Tim Rice / Andrew Lloyd Webber
Leeds Music Ltd . . . . UK
Show(s): . . . . Jesus Christ - Superstar
Film(s): . . . . Jesus Christ - Superstar
Stephen Tate & Chorus . . . . **MCA MCF 2503**
Carl Anderson . . . . **MCA MDKS 8013**
Murray Head . . . . **MCA MMKS 5077**
Stephen Tate appeared in the British production of *Jesus Christ -*
Superstar.
Carl Anderson appeared in the film *Jesus Christ - Superstar.*
Ivor Novello Award.

SUPERSTITION   March 1973
Stevie Wonder
Jobete Music (UK) Ltd. . . . . USA
Stevie Wonder . . . . **Tamla Motown TMG 841**

SUPERWOMAN   July 1989
L.A. Reid / Daryl Simmons'Babyface'
Warner Chappell Music . . . . UK
Karyn White . . . . **Warner Brothers W 2920**

SURRENDER   1946
Bennie Benjamin / George Weiss
Sun Music Publishing Co. Ltd. .... USA
Perry Como .... **HMV BD 1153**

SURRENDER   June 1961
Doc Pomus / Mort Shuman
Aberbach (London) Ltd. .... USA
Elvis Presley .... **RCA 1227**
Adapted from *Torna A Surriento* by Ernesto De Curtis.
See also 'Come Back To Sorrento'.

SURRENDER   December 1971
Nicholas Ashford / Valerie Simpson
Jobete Music (UK) Ltd. .... USA
Diana Ross .... **Tamla Motown TMG 792**

SURRENDER   July 1987
"Swing Out Sister"
10 Music .... UK
Swing Out Sister .... **Mercury SWING 3**

SURREY WITH THE FRINGE ON TOP, THE   1947
Richard Rodgers / Oscar Hammerstein II
Williamson Music Ltd. .... USA
Show(s): .... Oklahoma
Film(s): .... Oklahoma
Alfred Drake & Lee Dixon .... **Brunswick LAT 8001**
Harold Keel .... **HMV 7EP 7023**
Gordon MacRae, Shirley Jones &
Charlotte Greenwood .... **Capitol LCT 6100**
Alfred Drake & Lee Dixon appeared in the American production of
Oklahoma.
Harold Keel appeared in the British production of *Oklahoma.*
Gordon MacRae, Shirley Jones & Charlotte Greenwood appeared in
the film of *Oklahoma.*

SURROUND YOURSELF WITH SORROW   March 1969
Bill Martin / Phil Coulter
Peter Maurice Music Co. Ltd. .... UK
Cilla Black .... **Parlophone R 5759**

SUSPICION   February 1977
Doc Pomus / Mort Shuman
Carlin Music Corporation .... USA
Elvis Presley .... **RCA 2768**
Terry Stafford .... **London HLU 9871**

SUSPICIOUS MINDS   January 1970
Mark James
Screen Gems Music Ltd. .... USA
Elvis Presley .... **RCA 1900**
Dee Dee Warwick .... **Atlantic 2091092**
Candi Staton .... **Sugarhill SH 112**
Fine Young Cannibals (1986) .... **London LON 82**

SUSSEX BY THE SEA   1907
W. Ward-Higgs
Herman Darewski Music Publishing Co. Ltd. .... UK
The R.A.F. Band and Male Chorus .... **Columbia SEG 7633**
The Band of H.M. Grenadier Guards .... **Decca LK 4181**

SUSSUDIO   February 1985
Phil Collins
Hit & Run Music .... UK
Phil Collins .... **Virgin VS 736**

SUZANNE BEWARE OF THE DEVIL   September 1972
Mulby Thompson
Trojan Music .... UK
Dandy Livingstone .... **Horse HOSS 6**

SWAMP FIRE   1937
Hal Mooney
Lafleur & Co. Ltd. .... USA
Les Brown & his Duke University Blue Devils . **Brunswick 02442**
Hal Mooney & his Orchestra .... **Mercury MMC 14078**

SWANEE   1919
George Gershwin / Irving Caesar
Francis, Day & Hunter Ltd .... USA
Show(s): .... Sinbad / Jigsaw / The Glorious Days
Film(s):Rhapsody in Blue / The Jolson Story / Jolson Sings Again /
Sincerely Yours / A Star is Born
Al Jolson .... **Columbia 2974**

Al Jolson .... **Brunswick LA 8554**
Bing Crosby .... **Brunswick LA 8687**
Anna Neagle .... **Philips PB 153**
Judy Garland .... **Philips BBL 7007**
Dorothy Provine .... **Warner Brothers WM 4053**
Al Jolson .... **RCA ZL 70136**
Al Jolson appeared in *Sinbad* and *Rhapsody in Blue.*
Anna Neagle appeared in *The Glorious Days.*
Judy Garland appeared in *A Star Is Born.*

SWANEE RIVER MOON   1922
H. Pitman Clarke
Francis, Day & Hunter Ltd .... USA
The Original Novelty Orchestra .... **HMV B 1389**
The Gilberts .... **Regal G 7849**

SWAY (Quien Sera)   May 1954
Pablo Beltran Ruiz / Norman Gimbel
Southern Music Publishing Co. Ltd. .... Mexico
Roberto Inglez & his Mambo Orchestra ... **Parlophone R 3876**
Dean Martin .... **Capitol CL 14138**
Connie Francis .... **MGM C 836**
Bobby Rydell (1961) .... **Columbia DB 4545**

SWEDISH POLKA, THE   September 1957
Hugo Alfven
Lawrence Wright Music Co. Ltd .... Sweden
Hugo Alfven & his Orchestra .... **Philips PB 737**
Zacharias & his Magic Violins .... **Polydor LPHM 46064**

SWEDISH RHAPSODY   October 1953
Hugo Alfven
Campbell Connelly & Co. Ltd. .... Sweden
The Mantovani Orchestra .... **Decca LK 4079**
Percy Faith & his Orchestra .... **Philips BBE 12034**
Ray Martin Orchestra .... **Columbia DB 3346**
Frank Chacksfield .... **Ace of Clubs ACL 1080**

SWEEPING THE CLOUDS AWAY   1930
Sam Coslow
Chappell & Co. Ltd .... USA
Film(s): .... Paramount on Parade
Maurice Chevalier .... **HMV B 3480**
Charles 'Buddy' Rogers .... **CBS BPG 62546**
Maurice Chevalier appeared in *Paramount on Parade.*

SWEET ADELINE   1903
Harry Armstrong / Richard Gerard
B. Feldman & Co. Ltd. .... USA
Joe Green & his Novelty Orchestra .. **Edison Bell Winner 1161**
The Columbia Light Opera Company ...... **Columbia DB 962**
The Mills Brothers .... **Brunswick 04447**
Mitch Miller & The Gang .... **Philips BBL 7334**

SWEET AND GENTLE (Me Lo Dijo Adela)   July 1955
Otilio Portal / George Thorn
Southern Music Publishing Co. Ltd. .... Cuba
Eartha Kitt .... **HMV B 10892**
Alan Dale .... **Vogue LVA 9098**
Norrie Paramor & his Orchestra ...... **Columbia 33SX 1162**

SWEET AND LOVELY   1931
Gus Arnheim / Harry Tobias / Jules Lemare
Keith Prowse Music Publishing Co. Ltd. .... USA
Film(s): .... Two Girls and a Sailor
The Savoy Orpheans .... **Columbia CB 376**
Bing Crosby .... **Brunswick LAT 8251**
Roy Fox & his Orchestra, vocal Al Bowlly ...... **Decca F 2514**
Stan Kenton & his Orchestra .... **Capitol T 1533**
Theme song of Russ Columbo.

SWEET AND LOW   1920
Charles L. Johnson / Stanley Royce
Francis, Day & Hunter Ltd .... USA
The 'Queens' Dance Orchestra .... **HMV B 1287**

SWEET AND LOWDOWN   1925
George Gershwin / Ira Gershwin
Chappell & Co. Ltd. .... USA
Show(s): .... Tip Toes
Laddie Cliff & Peggy Beatty .... **Columbia 4079**
George Gershwin (piano) .... **Columbia 4065**
George Bassman & his Orchestra .... **Brunswick LAT 8315**
Laddie Cliff & Peggy Beatty appeared in the British production of *Tip Toes.*

SWEET CAROLINE   March 1971
Neil Diamond
ATV Music Ltd .... USA
Neil Diamond .... **United Artists UN 531**

SWEET CHILD (I'm Wild About You)   1926
Richard A. Whiting / Al Lewis / Howard Simons
Francis, Day & Hunter Ltd. .... USA
Paul Whiteman & his Orchestra .... **HMV B 5039**

SWEET CHILD O' MINE   June 1989
"Guns 'n' Roses"
Warner Chappell Music .... USA
Guns 'n' Roses .... **Geffen GEF 35**

SWEET DREAM   November 1969
Ian Anderson
Chrysalis Music Ltd .... UK
Jethro Tull .... **Chrysalis WIP 6070**

SWEET DREAMS (Are Made of This)   March 1983
Annie Lennox / Dave Stewart
RCA Music .... UK
Eurythmics .... **RCA DA 2**
Ivor Novello Nomination.

SWEET DREAMS SWEETHEART   1945
M.K. Jerome / Ted Koehler
B. Feldman & Co. Ltd. .... USA
Film(s): .... Hollywood Canteen
Jimmy Dorsey & his Orchestra .... **Brunswick 03560**
Geraldo & his Orchestra .... **Parlophone F 2065**
Kitty Carlisle .... **Curtain Call 100/11**
Joan Leslie .... **Curtain Call 100/11**
Kitty Carlisle, Joan Leslie & Jimmy Dorsey & his Orchestra appeared
in *Hollywood Canteen*.
Nominated for an Academy Award 1944.

SWEET FREEDOM   October 1986
Rodney Temperton
Rondor Music .... UK
Michael McDonald .... **MCA 1073**
Ivor Novello Award.

SWEET GENEVIEVE   1869
Henry Tucker / George Cooper
Boosey, Hawkes Music Publishers Ltd. .... USA
Ernest Pike & Peter Dawson .... **Zonophone X 44093**
The Mills Brothers .... **Brunswick 04451**
Bing Crosby & Chorus .... **Warner Brothers WM 4046**

SWEET GEORGIA BROWN   1925
Maceo Pinkard / Ben Bernie / Kenneth Casey
Francis, Day & Hunter Ltd. .... USA
Film(s): .... Broadway / Follow the Boys / Some Like it Hot
Oliver Naylor & his Orchestra .... **HMV B 2078**
The Ohio Novelty Band .... **ACO G 15750**
Jean Goldkette & his Orchestra .... **Camden CDN 154**
Bing Crosby .... **Fontana TFR 6012**
The Mills Brothers .... **Brunswick 01995**
The Chris Barber Band .... **Nixa NJT 505**
The Ohio Novelty Band is a pseudonym for Ben Bernie's Hotel
Roosevelt Orchestra.

SWEET HEARTACHE   1937
Ned Washington / Sammy Stept
Campbell Connelly & Co. Ltd. .... USA
Film(s): .... Hit Parade
Frances Langford .... **Brunswick 02430**
Phil Regan .... **Decca F 6414**
'Fats' Waller & his Rhythm .... **HMV DLP 1056**
Frances Langford & Phil Regan appeared in *Hit Parade*.

SWEET ILLUSION   June 1973
Junior Campbell
Camel Music .... UK
Junior Campbell .... **Deram DM 387**

SWEET INDIANA HOME   1923
Walter Donaldson
B. Feldman & Co. Ltd .... USA
The Club Royal Orchestra .... **HMV B 1652**

SWEET INSPIRATION   September 1970
John Cameron

Keith Prowse Music Publishing Co. Ltd .... UK
Johnny Johnson & The Bandwagon .... **Bell 1111**

SWEET JENNY LEE   1931
Walter Donaldson
Francis, Day & Hunter Ltd .... USA
Ted Wallace & his Campus Boys .... **Columbia CB 205**
Johnny Maddox & his Orchestra .... **London HAD 2101**

SWEET LEILANI   1937
Harry Owens
Campbell Connelly & Co. Ltd. .... USA
Film(s): .... Waikiki Wedding
Bing Crosby .... **Brunswick Bing 3**
Harry Owens & his Royal Hawaiians .... **Capitol CL 13134**
Andy Williams .... **London HAA 2203**
The "Hawaiia Calls" Orchestra,
vocal Haunani Kahalewai .... **Capitol T 1229**
Bing Crosby appeared in *Waikiki Wedding*.
Academy Award winning song for 1937.

SWEET LITTLE MYSTERY   August 1987
Graham Clark / Tom Cunningham / Neil Mitchell & Marti Pellow
Precious Music .... UK
Wet Wet Wet .... **Precious JEWEL 4**

SWEET LORRAINE   1934
Cliff Burwell / Mitchell Parish
Lawrence Wright Music Co. Ltd. .... USA
Joe Venuti & his Blue Six .... **Columbia SEG 7663**
The 'King' Cole Trio .... **Brunswick LAT 8123**
Maurice Chevalier .... **MGM C 860**

SWEET MAN   1926
Roy Turk / Maceo Pinkard
Francis, Day & Hunter Ltd. .... USA
Isham Jones & his Orchestra .... **Brunswick 2970**
The California Ramblers .... **Riverside RLP 12-801**

SWEET MUSIC   March 1975
"Showaddywaddy"
Dick James Music Ltd .... UK
Showaddywaddy .... **Bell 1403**

SWEET NOTHINS   May 1960
Ronnie Self
Peter Maurice Music Co. Ltd .... USA
Brenda Lee .... **Brunswick LAT 8347**
Helen Shapiro .... **Columbia 33SX 1397**

SWEET OLD FASHIONED GIRL   August 1956
Bob Merrill
Campbell Connelly & Co. Ltd. .... USA
Teresa Brewer .... **Vogue LVA 9131**

SWEET POTATO PIPER   1940
Jimmy Monaco / Johnny Burke
Campbell Connelly & Co. Ltd .... USA
Film(s): .... Road to Singapore
Bing Crosby .... **Brunswick Bing 5**
Bing Crosby appeared in *Road to Singapore*.

SWEET ROSIE O'GRADY   1896
Maud Nugent
B. Feldman & Co. Ltd. .... USA
Marie Kendall .... **Decca F 5169**
Cavan O'Connor .... **Regal Zonophone MR 114**
Guy Lombardo & his Royal Canadians ... **Brunswick LA 8612**
Bing Crosby .... **Warner Brothers WM 4034**

SWEET SOUL MUSIC   June 1967
Otis Redding / Arthur Conley / Sam Cooke
Kags Music Ltd. .... USA
Arthur Conley .... **Atlantic 584083**

SWEET SUE-JUST YOU   1928
Victor Young / Will J. Harris
Campbell Connelly & Co. Ltd. .... USA
Film(s): .... Rhythm Parade
Paul Whiteman & his Orchestra,
vocal Jack Fulton .... **Columbia 9572**
The Mills Brothers .... **Brunswick 02764**
Pat Boone .... **London HAD 2144**
The Mills Brothers appeared in *Rhythm Parade*.

SWEET SURRENDER   October 1989
Graham Clark / Tom Cunningham / Neil Mitchell & Marti Pellow
Chrysalis Music .... UK
Wet Wet Wet .... **Precious JEWEL 12**

SWEET TALKIN' GUY   June 1966
Douglas Morris / Elliot Greenburg
Sunbury Music Ltd. .... USA
The Chiffons .... **Stateside SS 512**
The Chiffons (1972) .... **London HL 10271**

SWEET TALKIN' WOMAN   October 1978
Jeff Lynne
United Artists Music Co. Ltd .... UK
The Electric Light Orchestra .... **Jet 121**

SWEET VIOLETS   1931
Cy Coben / Charles Grean
An edition by Edwin H. Morris & Co. Ltd .... USA
Bob Dickson .... **Zonophone 6102**
Mitch Miller & The Gang .... **Philips BBL 7258**
Dinah Shore .... **HMV B 10115**
The Radio Revellers .... **Columbia DB 2922**
Billy Cotton & his Band .... **Decca F 9760**
Based on an original composition by J.K. Emmet (Circa 1880).

SWEETEST MUSIC THIS SIDE OF HEAVEN, THE   1935
Carmen Lombardo / Cliff Friend
Victoria Music Co. Ltd .... USA
Film(s): .... Many Happy Returns
Maurice Winnick & his Orchestra .... **Parlophone F 321**
Reilly & Comfort .... **Decca F 5334**
Theme song of Maurice Winnick.

SWEETEST SMILE   July 1987
Colin Vearncombe
Rondor Music .... UK
Black .... **A&M AM 394**

SWEETEST SONG IN THE WORLD, THE   1938
Harry Parr-Davies
Francis, Day & Hunter Ltd. .... UK
Film(s): .... We're Going to be Rich
Gracie Fields .... **Ace of Clubs ACL 1107**
Gracie Fields appeared in We're Going to be Rich.

SWEETEST SOUNDS, THE   March 1964
Richard Rodgers
Williamson Music Ltd .... USA
Show(s): .... No Strings
Diahann Carroll & Richard Kiley .... **Capitol W 1695**
Beverly Todd & Art Lund .... **Decca LK 4576**
Diahann Carroll & Richard Kiley appeared in the American production
of No Strings.
Beverly Todd & Art Lund appeared in the British production of No
Strings.

SWEETHEART DARLING   1933
Gus Kahn / Herbert Stothart
Campbell Connelly & Co. Ltd. .... USA
Film(s): .... Peg o' My Heart
Danny Malone .... **HMV B 4489**
Annette Hanshaw .... **Panachord 25551**
Dennis Martin .... **Parlophone R 3189**

SWEETHEART OF ALL MY DREAMS   1929
Art Fitch / Kay Fitch / Bert Lowe
Lawrence Wright Music Co. Ltd .... USA
Film(s): .... Thirty Seconds Over Tokyo / Applause
Jack Hylton & his Orchestra .... **HMV B 5627**
Joe Loss & his Orchestra,
vocal Elizabeth Batey (1945) .... **HMV BD 5890**
Charlie Spivak & his Orchestra (1945) .... **HMV BD 5903**
Ruby Murray .... **Columbia DB 4497**

SWEETHEART OF SIGMA CHI   1912
Byron.D. Stokes / F. Dudleigh Vernon
B. Feldman & Co. Ltd .... USA
Film(s): .... The Sweetheart of Sigma Chi
Fred Waring & his Pennsylvanians .... **HMV B 5414**
Gene Austin .... **RCA RCX 113**
Bing Crosby .... **Brunswick 04738**

SWEETHEART WE NEED EACH OTHER   1930
Joseph McCarthy / Harry Tierney

Francis, Day & Hunter Ltd .... USA
Show(s): .... Rio Rita
Film(s): .... Rio Rita
Ben Pollack & his Orchestra,
vocal 'Scrappy' Lambert .... **HMV B 5729**

SWEETHEART, LET'S GROW OLD TOGETHER   1936
John W. Bratton / Leo Edwards
Dash Music Ltd .... USA
Turner Layton .... **Columbia FB 1422**
Hughie Green .... **Rex 8869**

SWEETHEART, WE'LL NEVER GROW OLD   1946
Jack Denby / Muriel Watson
Strauss-Miller Music Co. Ltd. .... UK
Doreen Harris .... **HMV BD 1146**

SWEETHEARTS   1914
Victor Herbert / Robert B. Smith
Chappell & Co. Ltd. .... USA
Show(s): .... Sweethearts
Film(s): Sweethearts / The Great Victor Herbert / The Great Caruso
Jeanette MacDonald .... **HMV B 9510**
Alan Jones .... **HMV B 8999**
George Melachrino & his Orchestra .... **RCA RD 27200**
Dorothy Kirsten .... **Glendale GL 9002**
Jeanette MacDonald appeared in the film Sweethearts.
Alan Jones appeared in The Great Victor Herbert.
Dorothy Kirsten appeared in The Great Caruso.

SWEETS FOR MY SWEET   August 1963
Doc Pomus / Mort Shuman
Hill & Range Songs (London) Ltd .... USA
The Searchers .... **Pye 7N 15533**
The Drifters .... **London HLK 9427**

SWING HIGH, SWING LOW   1938
Ralph Freed / Burton Lane
Victoria Music Co. Ltd .... USA
Film(s): .... Swing High, Swing Low
Dorothy Lamour .... **Brunswick 02421**
Tempo King & his Kings of Tempo . **Regal Zonophone MR 2439**
Dorothy Lamour appeared in Swing High, Swing Low.

SWING SONG   1904
Andre Messager / Lilian Eldee / Percy Greenbank
Chappell & Co. Ltd. .... France
Show(s): .... Veronique
Carmen Hill & Marcus Thomas .... **HMV 04127**
Anne Ziegler & Webster Booth .... **HMV B 9870**

SWING YOUR DADDY   April 1975
Kenny Nolan
April Music Ltd .... USA
Jim Gilstrap .... **Chelsea 2005021**

SWINGIN' DOWN THE LANE   1923
Gus Kahn / Isham Jones
Francis, Day & Hunter Ltd .... USA
Film(s): .... Greenwich Village / Mother Wore Tights
The Great White Way Orchestra .... **HMV B 1676**
Bing Crosby .... **RCA RD 27035**
Frank Sinatra .... **Capitol LCT 6106**
Isham Jones & his Orchestra,
vocal Kurt Massey .... **Capitol LC 6350**

SWINGING ON A STAR   1944
Johnny Burke / Jimmy Van Heusen
Edwin H. Morris & Co. Ltd. .... USA
Film(s): .... Going My Way
Bing Crosby .... **Brunswick BING 8**
Eddie Fisher .... **HMV CLP 1095**
Big Dee Irwin (1964) .... **Colpix PX 11010**
Bing Crosby appeared in Going My Way.
Academy Award winning song 1944.

SWINGING SHEPHERD BLUES   January 1958
Rhoda Roberts / Kenny Jacobson / Moe Koffman
Robert Mellin Ltd .... USA
Ted Heath & his Music .... **Decca DFE 6487**
The Moe Koffman Quartet .... **London REJ 1103**
Ella Fitzgerald .... **HMV POP 486**
Cyril Stapleton & his Orchestra ...... **Ace of Clubs ACL 1058**

SWISS MAID November 1962
Roger Miller
Burlington Music Co. Ltd . . . . USA
Del Shannon . . . . **London HL 9609**

SWORDS OF A THOUSAND MEN May 1981
Eddie Tudorpole
Warner Brothers Music . . . . UK
Tenpole Tudor . . . . **Stiff BUY 109**

SYLVIA 1914
Clinton Scollard / Oley Speaks
Boosey & Hawkes Music Publishers Ltd. . . . . USA
Walter Glynne . . . . **HMV B 4491**
Allan Jones . . . . **HMV B 9234**
Mario Lanza . . . . **Camden CDN 115**

SYLVIA March 1973
Thijs Van Leer
Radio-Tele Music . . . . Holland
Focus . . . . **Polydor 2001422**

SYLVIA'S MOTHER August 1972
Shel Silverstein
Essex Music Ltd. . . . . USA
Dr. Hook & The Medicine Show . . . . **CBS 7929**

SYMPATHY 1917
Rudolf Frimi / Otto Harbach / Gus Kahn
Chappell & Co. Ltd. . . . . USA
Show(s): . . . . The Firefly
Film(s): . . . . The Firefly
Louis Leigh & Charles Nelson . . . . **HMV B 709**
Rudolf Frimi (Piano Solo) . . . . **Brunswick LA 8557**
Bob Sharples & his Orchestra . . . . **Decca LK 4213**
Paul Britten & his Orchestra . . . . **MGM C 779**

SYMPHONY 1945
Andre Tabet / Roger Bernstein / Alex Alstone & Jack Lawrence
Chappell & Co. Ltd. . . . . France
Jean Sablon . . . . **Brunswick 03630**
Jean Caval . . . . **HMV B 9444**
Bing Crosby . . . . **Brunswick 03624**
Ed Townsend . . . . **Capitol T 1140**

SYSTEM ADDICT February 1986
Bill Livsey / Garry Bell
Chrysalis Music . . . . UK
Five Star . . . . **RCA PB 40515**

T'AINT NOBODY'S BIZNESS IF I DO 1922
Clarence Williams / Porter Granger / Graham Prince
Lawrence Wright Music Co. . . . . USA
Film(s): . . . . .Lady Sings the Blues
Ladds Black Aces . . . . **Fountain FJ 111**
Billie Holliday . . . . **Brunswick 04374**
Kay Starr . . . . **Capitol CL 13354**
Jimmy Witherspoon . . . . **London LTZK 15150**
Marian Montgomery . . . . **Brunswick LAT 8661**
Diana Ross . . . . **Tamla Motown STML 11311-2**
Diana Ross appeared in *Lady Sings the Blues.*

T'AINT WHAT YOU DO 1939
Sy Oliver / James Young
Leeds Music Co. Ltd. . . . . USA
Jimmy Lunceford & his Orchestra . . . . **Parlophone R 2647**
Louis Armstrong . . . . **Brunswick LAT 8084**
Ella Fitzgerald . . . . **Brunswick 02777**
Fun Boy Three & Bananarama (1982) . . . . **Chrysalis CHS 2570**

TA-RA-RA-BOOM-DER-E 1892
Richard Morton
C. Sheard & Co. . . . . USA
The Big Four . . . . **Columbia DX 288**
The Pavement Artists . . . . **Regal Zonophone MR 530**
Bing Crosby . . . . **Warner Brothers WM 4021**

TABOO 1942
Margarita Leucona / Bob Russell
Southern Music Publishing Co. Ltd . . . . Cuba
Edmundo Ros & his Rumba Band . . . . . **Parlophone F 1883**
Tony Martin . . . . **Decca F 8024**
Xavier Cugat & his Waldorf Astoria Orchestra . **HMV DLP 1072**
Percy Faith & his Orchestra . . . . **Philips BBL 7311**

TAHITI October 1983
David Essex / Richard Crane
Mutiny Music . . . . UK
Show(s): . . . . Mutiny
David Essex . . . . **Mercury BOUNT 1**
David Essex appeared in *Mutiny.*

TAINTED LOVE September 1981
Ed Cobb
Burlington Music . . . . USA
Soft Cell . . . . **Bizarre BZS 2**

TAKE A CHANCE ON ME March 1978
Benny Andersson / Bjorn Ulvaeus
Bocu Music Ltd . . . . Sweden
Abba . . . . **Epic EPC 5950**

TAKE A LOOK AROUND May 1972
Norman Whitfield / Barrett Strong
Jobete Music (UK) Ltd. . . . . USA
The Temptations . . . . **Tamla Motown TMG 808**

TAKE A NUMBER FROM ONE TO TEN 1935
Mack Gordon / Harry Revel
Victoria Music Co. Ltd . . . . USA
Film(s): . . . . College Rhythm
Lyda Roberti . . . . **Parlophone R 2016**
Johnnie Davis . . . . **Brunswick 01935**

TAKE FIVE November 1961
Paul Desmond / Lola Brubeck
Burlington Music Co. Ltd. . . . . USA
The Dave Brubeck Orchestra . . . . **Fontana H 339**
Si Zentner & his Orchestra . . . . **Liberty LBY 1007**
Carmen McRae . . . . **Fontana TFE 17395**

TAKE GOOD CARE OF MY BABY December 1961
Gerry Goffin / Carole King
Nevins-Kirshner Ltd. . . . . USA
Bobby Vee . . . . **London HL 9438**
Dion . . . . **HMV CLP 1539**

TAKE GOOD CARE OF YOURSELF May 1975
Kenny Gamble / Leon Huff
Carlin Music Corporation . . . . USA
The Three Degrees . . . . **Philadelphia PIR 3177**

TAKE HER TO JAMAICA
(Where The Rum Comes From) October 1950
Irving Fields / Jack Edwards
Campbell Connelly & Co. Ltd . . . . USA
Edmundo Ros & his Orchestra . . . . **Decca F 9484**
The Shaw Park Calypso Band . . . . **London W 91034**

TAKE IT EASY 1944
Vic Mizzy / Albert De Bru / Irving Taylor
Campbell Connelly & Co. Ltd. . . . . USA
Film(s): . . . . Two Girls and a Sailor
Virginia O'Brian . . . . **Caliban 6022**
Ambrose & his Orchestra, vocal Anne Shelton . . **Decca F 8411**
Guy Lombardo & his Royal Canadians . . . . . **Brunswick 03526**
Virginia O'Brian appeared in *Two Girls and a Sailor.*

TAKE IT TO THE LIMIT April 1976
Randy Meisner / Don Henley / Glen Frey
Warner Brothers Music Ltd . . . . USA
The Eagles . . . . **Asylum K 13029**

TAKE ME BACK 'OME July 1972
Neville Holder / James Lea
Barn Publishing Ltd. . . . . UK
Slade . . . . **Polydor 2058231**

TAKE ME BACK TO DEAR OLD BLIGHTY 1916
A.J. Mills / Fred Godfrey / Bennett Scott
B. Feldman & Co. Ltd. . . . . UK
Dorothy Ward . . . . **Regal G 7398**
Ella Retford . . . . **Regal Zonophone MR 205**
Florrie Forde . . . . **Regal 1725**
Verdi . . . . **Decca LK 4290**

TAKE ME GIRL I'M READY February 1973
Johnny Bristol / Laverne Ware / Pam Sawyer
Jobete Music (UK) Ltd. . . . . USA
Junior Walker & The All Stars . . . . **Tamla Motown TMG 840**

TAKE ME HOME COUNTRY ROADS   February 1973
John Denver / Bill Danoff / Taffy Nivert
Cherry Lane Music . . . . USA
Olivia Newton-John . . . . **Pye 7N 25599**

TAKE ME OUT TO THE BALL GAME   1908
Jack Norworth / Albert Von Tilzer
Francis, Day & Hunter . . . . USA
Film(s): . . . . Everybody's Cheering
Dan Dailey & The Andrews Sisters . . . . **Brunswick 04085**
Gene Kelly & Betty Garrett . . . . **MGM 213**
Bing Crosby . . . . **Warner Brothers WM 4021**
Gene Kelly & Betty Garret appeared in *Everybody's Cheering.*

TAKE ME TO THE MARDI GRAS   July 1973
Paul Simon
Pattern Music Ltd. . . . . USA
Paul Simon . . . . **CBS 1578**

TAKE ME TO YOUR HEART   December 1988
Mike Stock / Matt Aitken / Peter Waterman
All Boys Music . . . . UK
Rick Astley . . . . **RCA PB 42573**

TAKE ME TO YOUR HEART AGAIN
(La Vie en Rose)   September 1948
R.S. Louiguy / Edith Piaf / Frank Eyton
Noel Gay Music Co. Ltd. . . . . France
Film(s): . . . . To the Victor / The Eddy Duchin Story
Edith Piaf . . . . **Columbia 33S 1008**
Bing Crosby . . . . **Brunswick LA 8645**
Paul Weston & his Orchestra . . . . **Capitol T 1192**
Vince Hill (1966) . . . . **Columbia DB 7781**
Theme song of Edith Piaf.

TAKE MY BREATH AWAY   December 1986
Giorgio Morodor / Tom Whitlock
Famous Music . . . . USA
Film(s): . . . . Top Gun
Berlin (1986) . . . . **CBS A 7320**
Berlin (1990) . . . . **CBS 6563617**
Academy Award winning song for 1986.

TAKE MY HEART   August 1952
Bill Borrelli / Pat Genaro
Dash Music Ltd . . . . USA
Al Martino . . . . **Capitol EAP 1-405**
Dennis Lotis . . . . **Polydor P 1045**

TAKE ON ME   November 1985
Pal Waaktaar / Magne Furholmen / Morton Harket
A.T.V. Music . . . . UK
A-Ha . . . . **Warner Brothers W 9006**

TAKE ON THE WORLD   February 1979
Glenn Tipton / Robert Halford
CBS Songs . . . . UK
Judas Priest . . . . **CBS 6915**

TAKE THAT LOOK OFF YOUR FACE   March 1980
Don Black / Andrew Lloyd Webber
Really Useful Music Ltd . . . . UK
Show(s): . . . . Song and Dance
Sarah Brightman . . . . **MCA BL 70480**
Marti Webb (1980) . . . . **Polydor PODV 4**
Sarah Brightman & Marti Webb appeared in *Song and Dance.*
Ivor Novello Award 1980.

TAKE THE 'A' TRAIN   1944
Billy Strayhorn
Campbell Connelly & Co. Ltd . . . . USA
Film(s): . . . . Reveille With Beverly
Duke Ellington & his Orchestra . . . . **RCA RD 27134**
Harry James & his Orchestra . . . . **MGM C 830**
The Clark Sisters . . . . **London HAD 2177**
Theme tune of Duke Ellington.
Duke Ellington appeared in *Reveille with Beverly.*

TAKE THESE CHAINS FROM HEART   July 1963
Hy Heath / Fred Rose
Acuff-Rose Publishing Co. Ltd . . . . USA
Ray Charles . . . . **HMV POP 1161**
Tommy Edwards . . . . **MGM C 791**

TAKE YOUR GIRL   August 1949
Ivor Novello / Christopher Hassall
Chappell & Co. Ltd . . . . UK
Show(s): . . . . King's Rhapsody
Film(s): . . . . King's Rhapsody
Olive Gilbert . . . . **HMV DLP 1010**
The New Symphony Orchestra . . . . **Parlophone R 4080**
John Hanson . . . . **Philips BBL 7654**
Olive Gilbert appeared in the show of *King's Rhapsody.*

TAKE YOUR TIME   May 1990
Curtis Khaleel / John Rodriguez
MCA Music . . . . USA
Mantronix featuring Wondress . . . . **Capitol CL 573**

TAKES TWO TO TANGO   January 1953
Al Hoffman / Dick Manning
Francis, Day & Hunter Ltd . . . . USA
Fran Warren . . . . **MGM 559**
Louis Armstrong . . . . **Brunswick LAT 8243**
Hermione Gingold & Gilbert Harding . . . . **Philips PB 104**

TAKING A CHANCE ON LOVE   1942
John Latouche / Vernon Duke / Ted Fetter
Robbins Music Corporation Ltd . . . . USA
Show(s): . . . . Cabin in the Sky
Film(s):Cabin in the Sky / By Hook or By Crook / I'll Get By / The Benny
Goodman Story / This Could be the Night
Ambrose & his Orchestra, vocal Anne Shelton . . **Decca F 8313**
Ella Fitzgerald . . . . **Brunswick LAT 8091**
Frankie Laine . . . . **Philips BBL 7080**
Dinah Shore . . . . **Capitol T 1247**
Julie Wilson . . . . **MGM C 761**
Julie Wilson appeared in *This Could Be The Night.*

TALK OF THE TOWN   May 1980
Chrissie Hynde
A.T.V. Music Ltd. . . . . UK
Film(s): . . . . Times Square
The Pretenders . . . . **Real ARE 12**

TALK TO THE ANIMALS   November 1967
Leslie Bricusse
Robbins Music Ltd. . . . . USA
Film(s): . . . . Doctor Dolittle
Rex Harrison . . . . **Stateside SL 10214**
Bobby Darin . . . . **Atlantic 587089**
Bing Crosby . . . . **Stateside SL 10257**
Rex Harrison appeared in *Doctor Dolittle.*
Academy Award winning song for 1967.

TALKING IN YOUR SLEEP   October 1978
Roger Cook / Bobby Woods
Goal Music . . . . USA
Crystal Gayle . . . . **United Artists UP 36422**

TALKING LOUD AND CLEAR   July 1984
Andy McCluskey / Paul Humphreys / Martin Cooper
Virgin Music . . . . UK
Orchestral Manoeuvres in the Dark . . . . **Virgin VS 685**

TAMMY   September 1957
Jay Livingston / Ray Evans
Macmelodies Ltd . . . . USA
Film(s): . . . . Tammy and the Bachelor
Debbie Reynolds . . . . **Vogue LVA 9096**
The Four Aces . . . . **Brunswick LAT 8249**
The Beverley Sisters . . . . **Columbia 33SX 1285**
Debbie Reynolds appeared in *Tammy and the Bachelor.*
Nominated for an Academy Award 1957.

TAMPICO   1946
Allan Roberts / Doris Fisher
Chappell & Co. Ltd. . . . . USA
Edmundo Ros & his Rumba Band . . . . **Decca F 8649**
Stan Kenton & his Orchestra,
vocal June Christy . . . . **Capitol LO 6676**

TANGERINE   1942
Victor Schertzinger / Johnny Mercer
Victoria Music Co. Ltd . . . . UK
Film(s): . . . . The Fleet's In
Jimmy Dorsey & his Orchestra,
vocal Bob Eberly & Helen O'Connell . . . . **Brunswick 03328**

Anne Shelton . . . . **Philips BBL 7188**
Bob Eberly & Helen O'Connell . . . . **Warner Brothers WM 4033**
Jimmy Dorsey, Bob Eberly & Helen O'Connell appeared in *The Fleet's In.*

TAP TURNS ON THE WATER   October 1971
John Cameron / Alexis Korner
Rak Music Ltd . . . . UK
C.C.S. . . . . **Rak 119**

TARA'S THEME   August 1954
Max Steiner
Chappell & Co. Ltd. . . . . USA
Film(s): . . . . Gone With the Wind
Victor Young & his Orchestra . . . . **Brunswick LA 8672**
The Sinfonia of London . . . . **Warner Brothers WM 4019**
See also My Own True love.

TARZAN BOY   September 1985
Naimy Hackett / Maurizio Bassil
EMI Music . . . . Ireland
Baltimora . . . . **Columbia DB 9102**

TASTE OF HONEY, A   February 1963
Bobby Scott / Ric Marlow
Ambassador Music Ltd . . . . USA
Acker Bilk (clarinet) with
The Leon Young String Chorale . . . . **Columbia DB 4949**

TASTE OF YOUR TEARS   November 1985
Paul King
King Songs Ltd. . . . . UK
King . . . . **CBS A 6618**

TEA FOR TWO   1925
Vincent Youmans / Irving Caesar / Otto Harbach
Chappell & Co. Ltd. . . . . USA
Show(s): . . . . No No Nanette
Film(s):No No Nanette / Tea for Two / With a Song in My Heart /
Sincerely Yours / Jazz on a Summers Day
Binnie Hale & Seymour Beard . . . . **Columbia 3630**
Edna Savage & Michael Holliday . . . . **Columbia SEG 7836**
Doris Day . . . . **Philips BBL 7175**
Jane Froman . . . . **Capitol CL 13719**
Liberace (piano) . . . . **Philips BBL 7063**
The Tommy Dorsey Orchestra (Cha Cha Version) (1959), con-
ductor Warren Covington . . . . **Brunswick LAT 8286**
Anita O'Day . . . . **HMV POP 821**
Binnie Hale & Seymour Beard appeared in the British Production of
No No Nanette.
Doris Day appeared in *Tea For Two.*
Jane Froman dubbed the singing voice of Susan Hayward who
appeared in the film *With a Song in My Heart.*
Liberace appeared in *Sincerely Yours.*
Anita O'Day appeared in *Jazz on a Summers Day.*

TEACH ME HOW TO KISS   1898
Gustave Kerker / Hugh Morton
Ascherberg, Hopwood & Crew Ltd. . . . . USA
Show(s): . . . . The Belle of New York
The Columbia Light Opera Company . . . . **Columbia 9925**
Mary Thomas . . . . **HMV 7EG 8442**

TEACH ME TONIGHT   March 1955
Sammy Cahn / Gene De Paul
Leeds Music Ltd. . . . . USA
Jo Stafford . . . . **Philips BBR 8057**
Nat 'King' Cole . . . . **Capitol CL 14207**
Sarah Vaughan & Joe Williams . . . . **Columbia DB 4511**

TEAR FELL, A   April 1956
Eugene Randolf / Dorian Burton
Robbins Music Corporation Ltd. . . . . USA
Teresa Brewer . . . . **Vogue LVA 9131**
Edna Savage . . . . **Parlophone R 4159**
Lita Roza . . . . **Decca F 10752**

TEARDROPS   December 1984
Shakin' Stevens
Shaky Music . . . . UK
Shakin' Stevens . . . . **Epic A 4882**

TEARDROPS   October 1988
Linda Womack / Cecil Womack
Zomba Music . . . . USA

Womack & Womack . . . . **4th & Broadway BRW 10**

TEARS   October 1965
Frank Capano / Billy Uhr
Keith Prowse Music Publishing Co. Ltd . . . . USA
Albert Sandler & his Orchestra . . . . **Columbia DB 475**
Ken Todd . . . . **Columbia DB 7659**

TEARS I CRIED, THE   May 1975
Gerry Shephard
Rock Artistes Music . . . . UK
The Glitter Band . . . . **Bell 1416**

TEARS OF A CLOWN, THE   October 1970
William Robinson / Henry Cosby / Stevie Wonder
Jobete Music (UK) Ltd. . . . . USA
Smokey Robinson & The Miracles . . . **Tamla Motown TMG 745**
The Beat (1980) . . . . **Two Tone CHSTT 6**

TEARS ON MY PILLOW   1939
Max Nesbitt / Harry Nesbitt
J. Norris Music Publishing Co. Ltd. UK
Les Allen . . . . **Columbia FB 2183**
Denny Dennis . . . . **Rex 9536**

TEARS ON MY PILLOW   August 1975
Ernie Smith
A.T.V. Music Ltd. . . . . USA
Johnny Nash . . . . **CBS 3220**

TEARS ON MY PILLOW   February 1990
Mike Stock / Matt Aitken / Peter Waterman
Sterling Music Co. . . . . UK
Film(s): . . . . The Delinquents
Kylie Minogue . . . . **PWL PWL 47**
Kylie Minogue appeared in *The Delinquents.*

TEASE ME   May 1960
Keith Kelly
Meridan Music Publishing Co. Ltd . . . . UK
Keith Kelly . . . . **Parlophone R 4640**

TEASING   1904
Albert Von Tilzer / Cecil Mack
Francis, Day & Hunter Ltd. . . . . USA
Show(s): . . . . The Catch of the Season
Herbert Payne . . . . **HMV GC 3-2211**
The Naughty Nineties Singers . . . . **Columbia FB 2590**
Frankie Vaughan . . . . **Philips BBL 7482**

TEDDY BEAR   July 1957
Kal Mann / Bernie Lowe
Belinda (London) Ltd. . . . . USA
Film(s): . . . . Loving You
Elvis Presley . . . . **RCA RD 27159**
Elvis Presley appeared in *Loving You.*

TEDDY BEAR   June 1981
Red Sovine / Dale Royal / Tommy Hill & Billy Burnett
Southern Music Co. . . . . USA
Red Sovine . . . . **Starday SD 142**

TEDDY BEAR'S PICNIC, THE   1907
John Bratton / Jimmy Kennedy
B. Feldman & Co. Ltd. . . . . UK
The International Novelty Quartet . . . . **Regal T 5524**
Henry Hall & his Orchestra . . . . **Columbia FB 2816**
Bing Crosby . . . . **Brunswick 04581**
Max Bygraves . . . . **Decca LK 4333**
Lyric added in 1932.

TEEN BEAT   November 1959
Sandy Nelson / Arthur Egnoian
Leeds Music Ltd . . . . USA
Sandy Nelson & his Orchestra . . . . **Top Rank JKP 2060**

TEENAGE RAMPAGE   February 1974
Mike Chapman / Nicky Chinn
Chinnichap Music . . . . UK
Sweet . . . . **RCA LPBO 5004**

TEENAGER IN LOVE, A   July 1959
Doc Pomus / Mort Shuman
West One Music Ltd . . . . USA
Marty Wilde . . . . **Philips BBL 7380**

| Craig Douglas | Top Rank JAR 133 |
| Dion & The Belmonts | London HAU 2194 |

TELEGRAM SAM February 1972
Marc Bolan
Wizard Music .... UK
T. Rex .... T. Rex 101

TELEPHONE LINE July 1977
Jeff Lynne
United Artists Music Co. Ltd .... UK
The Electric Light Orchestra .... Jet UP 36254

TELEPHONE MAN October 1977
Meri Wilson
Campbell Connelly & Co. Ltd .... USA
Meri Wilson .... Pye 7N 25747

TELL HER ABOUT IT January 1984
Billy Joel
CBS Songs .... USA
Billy Joel .... CBS A 3655

TELL HIM March 1963
Bert Russell
Robert Mellin Ltd .... USA
Alma Cogan .... Columbia DB 4965
Billie Davis .... Decca F 11572
Hello (1974) .... Bell 1377

TELL IT TO MY HEART February 1988
Seth Swirsky / Ernie Gold
Chappell Music Co. .... USA
Taylor Dayne .... Arista 109616

TELL LAURA I LOVE HER October 1960
Jeff Barry / Ben Raleigh
Lawrence Wright Music Co. Ltd .... USA
Ricky Valence .... Columbia DB 4493
Ray Peterson .... RCA 1195

TELL ME 1919
Max Kortlander / J. Will Callahan
B. Feldman & Co. Ltd .... USA
Film(s): .... On Moonlight Bay
The Original Dixieland Jazz Band ...... Columbia 33S 1087
Bing Crosby .... RCA RD 27032
Doris Day .... Columbia DB 3033
Doris Day appeared in *On Moonlight Day.*

TELL ME A STORY June 1953
Terry Gilkyson
Cinephonic Music Ltd. .... USA
Frankie Laine & Jimmy Boyd .... Philips PB 126

TELL ME I'M FORGIVEN 1930
Robert Katscher / Roland Leigh
Ascherberg, Hopwood & Crew Ltd .... Germany
Show(s): .... Wonder Bar
Carl Brisson .... Decca F 2128
Gwen Farrar .... Columbia DB 983
Carl Brisson & Gwen Farrar appeared in the British production of
Wonder Bar.

TELL ME LITTLE GIPSY 1920
Irving Berlin
Francis, Day & Hunter Ltd .... USA
Show(s): .... The Ziegfeld Follies of 1920
Joseph C. Smith's Orchestra .... HMV C 1002
Paul Whiteman's Wood-Winds ...... Brunswick 02858

TELL ME MARIANNE (A Media Luz) 1939
Edgardo Donato / Bob Musel
Southern Music Publishing Co. Ltd. .... Argentina
Pancho & his Orchestra .... Columbia FB 3302
Monte Rey .... Columbia FB 3302
Rita Williams .... Columbia FB 3320

TELL ME PRETTY MAIDEN 1900
Leslie Stuart / Owen Hall
Francis, Day & Hunter Ltd. .... UK
Show(s): .... Florodora
The Lyric Theatre Chorus with
Leslie Stuart (piano) .... Berliner 4524
The Light Opera Company .... HMV C 2090

| The Victor Mixed Chorus | HMV B 2097 |
| The George Mitchell Singers | HMV CLP 1460 |

TELL ME TONIGHT 1932
Mischa Spoliansky / Frank Eyton
Chappell & Co. Ltd. .... USA
Film(s): .... Tell Me Tonight
Jan Kepura .... Parlophone GEP 8639
Richard Crooks .... HMV DA 1284
Lee Lawrence .... Decca LF 1132
Mario Lanza .... HMV ALP 1405
Jan Kepura appeared in *Tell me Tonight.*

TELL ME WHAT HE SAID March 1962
Jeff Barry
Ardmore & Beechwood Ltd. .... USA
Helen Shapiro .... Columbia DB 4782

TELL ME WHEN April 1964
Geoff Stevens / Les Reed
Southern Music Publishing Co. Ltd .... UK
The Applejacks .... Decca F 11833
Troy Dante .... Fontana TF 445

TELL ME WHY April 1952
Al Albert / Marty Gold
Edwin H. Morris & Co. Ltd .... USA
The Four Aces .... Brunswick OE 9426

TELL ME WHY December 1965
Titus Turner
Southern Music Publishing Co. Ltd .... USA
Elvis Presley .... RCA 1489
Gale Storm .... London HLD 8311

TELL ME WHY December 1974
Peter Shelley
Magnet Music .... UK
Alvin Stardust .... Magnet MAG 19

TELL ME YOU'RE MINE (Per Un Bacio D'Amor) April 1953
Ronald Fredianelli / Domenico Ravasini
Chappell & Co. Ltd .... Italy
Vic Damone .... Philips BBL 7234
Tony Dallera .... Columbia SEG 7887
Joni James .... MGM C 809
The Gaylords .... Oriole CB 1164

TELSTAR November 1962
Joe Meek
Ivy Music Ltd .... UK
The Tornados .... Decca F 11494
Billy Vaughan & his Orchestra ...... London HAD 8056
Ivor Novello Award.

TEMMA HARBOUR February 1970
Philamore Lincoln
Rak Music Ltd. .... USA
Mary Hopkin .... Apple 22

TEMPLE BELL, THE 1911
Lionel Monckton / Arthur Wimperis
Chappell & Co. Ltd .... UK
Show(s): .... The Mousme
Florence Smithson .... HMV C 531
Geraldo & his Orchestra .... Columbia DX 679
The Pro Arte Orchestra,
conducted by Stanford Robinson .... Pye CML 33003
Florence Smithson appears in *The Mouse.*

TEMPTATION 1933
Nacio Herb Brown / Arthur Freed
Robbins Music Corporation Ltd. .... USA
Show(s): .... Singin' in the Rain
Film(s):Going Hollywood / Kiss Them for Me / Written on the Wind /
The Seven Hills of Rome
Bing Crosby .... Fontana TFR 6000
Perry Como (1946) .... RCA RD 27100
Bing Crosby .... Brunswick LAT 8251
Mario Lanza .... RCA RA 13001
The King Sisters .... Capitol T 1333
The Everly Brothers (1961) .... Warner Brothers WB 42
Sarah Payne & Tommy Steele .... Safari RAIN 1
Bing Crosby appeared in *Going Hollywood.*

Mario Lanza appeared in *The Seven Hills of Rome*.
Sarah Payne & Tommy Steele appeared in the show *Singin' in the Rain*.

TEMPTATION   May 1983
Guen Gregory / Ian Marsh / Martyn Ware
Virgin Music .... UK
Heaven 17 .... **Virgin VS 570**

TEMPTATION RAG   1909
Henry Lodge / Louis Weslyn
B. Feldman & Co. .... USA
Harry Roy Band .... **Parlophone F 102**
Benny Goodman Sextet .... **Columbia DB 3315**
Petula Clark .... **Polygon 1057**
Kenny Ball & his Jazzmen .... **Pye NJL 51**

TEN CENTS A DANCE   1931
Richard Rodgers / Lorenz Hart
Chappell & Co. Ltd. .... USA
Show(s): .... Simple Simon
Film(s): ....Ten Cents a Dance / Love Me or Leave Me
Ruth Etting .... **Columbia DB 440**
Doris Day .... **Philips BBL 7047**
Ella Fitzgerald .... **HMV CLP 1117**
Ruth Etting appeared in *Simple Simon*. Doris Day appeared in *Love Me or Leave Me*.

TEN PRETTY GIRLS   1937
Will Grosz / Jimmy Kennedy
Peter Maurice Music Co. Ltd. .... UK
Jay Wilbur & his Band, vocal Sam Costa .... **Rex 9103**
Max Bygraves .... **Decca LK 4360**

TEN THOUSAND FIVE HUNDRED AND THIRTY EIGHT
OVERTURE   August 1972
Jeff Lynn
April Music .... UK
Electric Light Orchestra .... **Harvest HAR 5053**

TENDER TRAP, THE   March 1956
Sammy Cahn / Jimmy Van Heusen
Barton Music Co. Ltd. .... USA
Film(s): .... The Tender Trap / This Could Be the Night
Frank Sinatra .... **Capitol LCT 6123**
Patti Lewis .... **Philips PB 541**
Debbie Reynolds .... **MGM EP 670**
Ray Anthony & his Orchestra .... **MGM C 761**
Frank Sinatra appeared in *The Tender Trap*.
Ray Anthony appeared in *This Could Be the Night*.
Nominated for an Academy Award 1955.

TENDERLY   July 1948
Jack Lawrence / Walter Gross
Edwin H. Morris & Co. Ltd. .... USA
Film(s): .... Torch Song
Randy Brooks & his Orchestra .... **Brunswick LAT 8370**
Billy Eckstine .... **MGM D 126**
The McGuire Sisters .... **Vogue LVA 9082**
Rosemary Clooney .... **Philips BBR 8073**
Nat 'King' Cole (1954) .... **Capitol CL 14061**
The Mantovani Orchestra .... **Decca LK 4339**
Theme song of Rosemary Clooney.

TENEMENT SYMPHONY, THE   1944
Sid Kuller / Hal Borne / Ray Golden
Robbins Music Corporation Ltd .... USA
Film(s): .... The Big Store
Tony Martin .... **HMV 7EG 8124**
Edmund Hockridge .... **Nixa NPL 18021**
Tony Martin appeared in *The Big Store*.

TENNESSEE WALTZ, THE   January 1951
Redd Stewart / Pee Wee King
Cinephonic Music Co. Ltd .... USA
Teddy Johnson .... **Columbia DB 2799**
Patti Page .... **Mercury MEP 9502**
Johnny Duncan .... **Columbia SEG 7850**

TENNESSEE WIG-WALK, THE   November 1953
Norman Gimbel / Larry Coleman
Francis, Day & Hunter Ltd. .... USA
Bonnie Lou .... **Parlophone PMD 1064**
Suzi Miller .... **Decca F 10264**

TEQUILA   March 1958
Chuck Rio
Leeds Music Ltd .... USA
The Champs .... **London HAH 2152**
Don Lang .... **HMV POP 465**
Ted Heath & his Music .... **Decca DFE 6487**

TERESA   March 1948
Jack Hoffman / Babe Russin
Leeds Music .... USA
Dick Haymes & The Andrews Sisters .... **Brunswick 03860**
Geraldo & his Orchestra .... **Parlophone F 9647**
Joe Loss Orchestra .... **HMV BD 6008**

TERRY   January 1965
'Twinkle'
Favourite Music Ltd .... UK
Twinkle .... **Decca F 12013**

THANK GOD FOR A GARDEN   1915
Teresa Del Riego
Chappell & Co. Ltd. .... UK
John McCormack .... **HMV DA 320**
Alfred Piccaver .... **Decca M 449**

THANK HEAVEN FOR LITTLE GIRLS   March 1959
Alan Jay Lerner / Frederick Loewe
Chappell & Co. Ltd .... USA
Film(s): .... Gigi
Maurice Chevalier .... **MGM C 770**
The King Brothers .... **Parlophone R 4513**
Maurice Chevalier appeared in *Gigi*.

THANK U VERY MUCH   January 1968
Mike McGear
Noel Gay Music Co. Ltd. .... UK
Scaffold .... **Parlophone R 5643**

THANKS   1933
Sam Coslow / Arthur Johnston
Victoria Music Co. Ltd. .... USA
Film(s): .... Too Much Harmony
Bing Crosby .... **Columbia 33S 1036**
Ray Noble & Orchestra .... **HMV B 6413**
Bing Crosby .... **Brunswick LAT 8251**
Bing Crosby appeared in *Too Much Harmony*.

THANKS FOR THE BUGGY RIDE   1926
Jules Buffano
Francis, Day & Hunter Ltd. .... USA
Frank Crumit .... **HMV B 2325**

THANKS FOR THE MEMORY   1938
Leo Robin / Ralph Rainger
Victoria Music Co. Ltd. .... USA
Film(s): .... The Big Broadcast of 1938
Bob Hope & Shirley Ross .... **Brunswick 02697**
Turner Layton .... **Columbia FB 1963**
Bing Crosby .... **Brunswick LAT 8138**
Ray Conniff & his Orchestra & chorus ...... **Philips BBL 7310**
Bob Hope & Shirley Ross appeared in *The Big Broadcast of 1938*.
Theme song of Bob Hope.
Academy Award winning song for 1938.

THANKS FOR THE MEMORY (Wham Bam Thank You
Mam)   May 1975
Jimmy Lea / Noddy Holder
Barn Publishing Ltd .... UK
Slade .... **Polydor 2058585**

THAT CERTAIN FEELING   1926
George Gershwin / Ira Gershwin
Chappell & Co. Ltd. .... USA
Show(s): .... Tip Toes
Film(s): .... That Certain Feeling
Dorothy Dickson & Allen Kearns .... **Columbia 9129**
Paul Whiteman & his Orchestra .... **HMV B 5109**
Mitzi Gaynor .... **HMV CLP 1319**
Dorothy Dickson & Allen Kearns appeared in both American and British productions of *Tip Toes*.

THAT CERTAIN PARTY   1926
Gus Kahn / Walter Donaldson
Francis, Day & Hunter Ltd. .... USA
Ted Lewis & his Band .... **Columbia 3932**

Al Jolson . . . . Brunswick LAT 8322
Doris Day & Buddy Clark . . . . Columbia DB 2483

THAT DEAR OLD GENTLEMAN December 1956
Paddy Roberts
Berry Music Ltd. . . . . UK
Max Bygraves . . . . HMV POP 262

THAT DOGGIE IN THE WINDOW March 1953
Bob Merrill
Campbell Connelly & Co. Ltd . . . . USA
Patti Page . . . . Oriole CB 1156
Lita Roza . . . . Decca LF 1297

THAT GIRL BELONGS TO YESTERDAY April 1964
Keith Richards / Mick Jagger
Pakkamak Music Ltd . . . . UK
Gene Pitney . . . . United Artists UP 1045

THAT INTERNATIONAL RAG (see International Rag)

THAT LOVELY WEEKEND 1942
Ted Heath / Moira Heath
Bradbury Wood Ltd . . . . UK
Leslie Hutchinson (Hutch) . . . . HMV BD 982
Geraldo & his Orchestra,
vocal Dorothy Carless . . . . Parlophone F 1881
Dennis Lotis . . . . Nixa NPL 18002

THAT LUCKY OLD SUN November 1949
Haven Gillespie / Beasley Smith
Robbins Music Corporation Ltd . . . . USA
Vaughn Monroe . . . . HMV B 9836
Frankie Laine . . . . Mercury MPT 7007
'Bumps' Blackwell & his Orchestra . . . . . . HMV CLP 1261
Pat Boone . . . . London HAD 2030

THAT MYSTERIOUS RAG 1911
Irving Berlin / Ted Snyder
B. Feldman & Co. Ltd . . . . USA
Albert Whelan . . . . Jumbo A 28286
The Peerless Orchestra . . . . Zonophone 1002
Harry Roy & his Orchestra . . . . Decca F 9145

THAT NAUGHTY WALTZ 1920
Solomon Levy / Edwin Stanley
Francis, Day & Hunter Ltd . . . . USA
Joseph C. Smith's Orchestra . . . . HMV B 1100
The Andrews Sisters . . . . Capitol T 973

THAT NIGHT IN ARABY 1927
Ted Snyder / Billy Rose
B. Feldman & Co. Ltd. . . . . USA
The Denza Dance Band . . . . Columbia 4206
Jack Hylton's Kit Kat Band . . . . HMV B 5142

THAT OLD BLACK MAGIC 1943
Harold Arlen / Johnny Mercer
Victoria Music Co. Ltd . . . . USA
Film(s):Star Spangled Rhythm / Radio Stars on Parade / Here Come
the Waves / Meet Danny Wilson.
Judy Garland . . . . Brunswick 03446
Glenn Miller & his Orchestra . . . . HMV BD 5811
Doris Day . . . . Philips BBL 7247
Frank Sinatra . . . . Philips BBL 7137
Billy Daniels (1952) . . . . Oriole CB 1095
Mark Murphy . . . . Capitol T 1177
Frank Sinatra appeared in *Meet Danny Wilson.*
Theme song of both Billy Daniels and Stanley Black.
Nominated for an Academy Award 1943.

THAT OLD DEVIL CALLED LOVE March 1985
Allan Roberts / Doris Fisher
MCA Music . . . . USA
Alison Moyet . . . . CBS A 6044

THAT OLD DEVIL CONSEQUENCE (See Life's Full Of Consequences)

THAT OLD FASHIONED MOTHER OF MINE 1919
Horatio Nicholls / Worton David
Lawrence Wright Music Co. Ltd. . . . . UK
Joe Petersen . . . . Decca F 10247
David Whitfield . . . . Decca DFE 6601

THAT OLD FEELING 1937
Sammy Fain / Lew Brown
Sun Music Publishing Co. Ltd. . . . . USA
Film(s): . . . . Vogues of 1938 / With a Song in My Heart
Connee Boswell . . . . Brunswick 02474
Shep Fields & his Orchestra . . . . . . Regal Zonophone MR 2557
Frank Sinatra . . . . Philips BBL 7180
Ray Conniff & his Orchestra & chorus . . . . . Philips BBL 7281
Nominated for an Academy Award 1937.

THAT OLD GANG OF MINE March 1949
Billy Rose / Ray Henderson / Mort Dixon
B. Feldman & Co. Ltd . . . . USA
Perry Como . . . . Brunswick 04018
Al Morgan . . . . London HAPB 1003
Mitch Miller & The Gang . . . . Philips BBL 7258
First Published 1923.

THAT RED HEAD GAL 1923
Henry Lodge / Gus Van / Joe Schenk
B. Feldman & Co. Ltd . . . . USA
The Original Memphis Five . . . . Actuelle 10546
The Pavilion Players . . . . Edison Bell 3874

THAT SAME OLD FEELING April 1970
Tony Macaulay / John MacLeod
Welbeck Music Co. Ltd. . . . . UK
Pickettywitch . . . . Pye 7N 17887

THAT SLY OLD GENTLEMAN (From Featherbed Lane) 1940
Jimmy Monaco / Johnny Burke
Campbell Connelly & Co. Ltd . . . . USA
Film(s): . . . . East Side of Heaven
Bing Crosby . . . . Brunswick Bing 4
Kay Kyser & his Orchestra . . . . Parlophone F 1494
Jack Hylton & his Orchestra . . . . HMV BD 5503
Bing Crosby appeared in *East Side of Heaven.*

THAT'LL BE THE DAY October 1957
Norman Petty / Buddy Holly
Southern Music publishing Co. Ltd . . . . USA
The Crickets . . . . Vogue LVA 9081
Buddy Holly . . . . Ace of Hearts AH 3
Cliff Richard . . . . Columbia 33SX 1147

THAT'S A PLENTY 1929
Lew Pollack / Ray Gilbert
Campbell Connelly & Co. Ltd . . . . USA
Miff Mole & his Little Molers . . . . Philips BBL 7432
The New Orleans Rhythm Kings . . . . Brunswick 02208
Bing Crosby & Connee Boswell . . . . Brunswick LAT 8228
Phil Harris . . . . HMV B 9918

THAT'S ALL December 1983
Anthony Banks / Phil Collins / Mike Rutherford
Hit & Run Music . . . . UK
Genesis . . . . Virgin TATA 1

THAT'S AMORE December 1953
Harry Warren / Jack Brooks
Victoria Music Co. Ltd. . . . . USA
Film(s): . . . . The Caddy
Dean Martin . . . . Capitol T 946
Connie Francis . . . . MGM C 854
Dean Martin appeared in *The Caddy.*
Theme song of Dean Martin.
Nominated for an Academy Award 1953.

THAT'S ENTERTAINMENT 1953
Howard Dietz / Arthur Schwartz
Chappell Music Co. . . . . USA
Film(s): . . . . The Band Wagon
Fred Astaire, Nanette Fabray, Jack Buchanan
& Cyd Charisse . . . . MGM C 752
The King Brothers . . . . Parlophone PMC 1060
Dolores Gray . . . . Philips BL 7566
Sammy Davis Jnr. . . . . MGM 2315309
Arthur Schwartz . . . . RCA RS 1029
Fred Astaire, Nanette Fabray, Jack Buchanan & Cyd Charisse appeared in *The Band Wagon.*
The voice for Cyd Charisse was dubbed by India Adams.

THAT'S FOR ME 1941
Johnny Burke / Jimmy Monaco

Victoria Music Co. Ltd . . . . USA
Film(s): . . . . Rhythm on the River
Bing Crosby . . . . **Brunswick Bing 6**
Gary Miller . . . . **Nixa NPL 18008**
Bing Crosby appeared in *Rhythm on the Range*.

THAT'S FOR ME   1946
Richard Rodgers / Oscar Hammerstein II
Williamson Music Ltd. . . . . USA
Film(s): . . . . State Fair
Dick Haymes . . . . **Brunswick 03620**
Teddi King . . . . **Coral FEP 2051**
Gordon MacRae . . . . **Capitol T 1353**
Dick Haymes appeared in *State Fair*.

THAT'S HOW A LOVE SONG WAS BORN   August 1955
Norman Newell / Philip Green
Chappell & Co. Ltd. . . . . UK
Frankie Vaughan . . . . **Philips PB 438**

THAT'S LIVING ALRIGHT   February 1984
David Mackay / Ken Ashby
Sabre Music . . . . UK
Joe Fagin . . . . **Towerbell TOW 46**
Theme of the television series *Auf Wiedersehen Pet*.
Ivor Novello Award 1983.

THAT'S MY DESIRE   January 1948
Carol Loveday / Helmy Kresa
B. Feldman & Co. Ltd. . . . . USA
Maurice Elwin . . . . **Decca F 2714**
Woody Herman & his Four Chips . . . . **Columbia DB 2356**
Frankie Laine . . . . **Brunswick 03951**
Louis Armstrong . . . . **Brunswick LAT 8018**

THAT'S MY HOME   September 1961
Sid Robin
Leeds Music Ltd. . . . . USA
Louis Armstrong's All Stars . . . . **Brunswick LAT 8211**
Acker Bilk . . . . **Columbia DB 4673**

THAT'S MY WEAKNESS NOW   1928
Bud Green / Sammy Stept
Lawrence Wright Music Co. Ltd. . . . . USA
Film(s): . . . . Applause
Helen Kane (Original artiste) . . . . **MGM EP 649**
Paul Whiteman & his Orchestra . . . . **Columbia 5006**
Vera Lynn . . . . **Decca LK 4305**
Bobby Short . . . . **London HAE 2215**

THAT'S THE BEGINNING OF THE END   1947
Joan Whitney / Alex Kramer
Victoria Music Co. Ltd. . . . . USA
Leslie Hutchinson (Hutch) . . . . **HMV BD 1163**
Perry Como . . . . **HMV BD 1167**
Lita Roza . . . . **Nixa NPL 18020**

THAT'S THE MOON MY SON   1942
Art Kassel / Sammy Gallop / Norman Litman
Leeds Music Ltd . . . . USA
Film(s): . . . . Private Buckaroo
The Andrews Sisters . . . . **Brunswick 03402**
Anne Shelton . . . . **Decca F 8279**
The Andrews Sisters appeared in *Private Buckaroo*.

THAT'S THE WAY   September 1965
Howard Blaikley
Lynn Music Ltd . . . . UK
The Honeycombs . . . . **Pye 7N 15890**

THAT'S THE WAY (I Like It)   September 1975
H.W. Casey / Robert Finch
Sunbury Music Ltd . . . . USA
Film(s): . . . . The Stud
K.C. & The Sunshine Band . . . . **Jayboy BOY 99**

THAT'S THE WAY GOD PLANNED IT   July 1969
Billy Preston
Apple Publishing . . . . USA
Billy Preston . . . . **Apple 12**

THAT'S THE WAY IT IS   March 1988
Mike Stock / Matt Aitken / Peter Waterman
All Boys Music . . . . UK

Mel & Kim . . . . **Supreme SUPE 117**

THAT'S THE WAY LOVE IS   February 1989
Herbert Lawson / Byron Burke / Byron Stingily
SBK Songs . . . . UK
Ten City . . . . **Atlantic A 8963**

THAT'S WHAT A RAINY DAY IS FOR   June 1954
Vic Mizzy / Mann Curtis
Robbins Music Corporation Ltd. . . . . USA
Film(s): . . . . Easy to Love
Tony Martin . . . . **HMV B 10686**
Gary Miller . . . . **Pye NPL 18008**
Tony Martin appeared in *Easy to Love*.

THAT'S WHAT FRIENDS ARE FOR   September 1977
Deniece Williams / Clarence McDonald / Lani Groves & Fritz Basket
V.I.P. Music . . . . USA
Deniece Williams . . . . **CBS 5432**
Deniece Williams & Johnny Mathis . . . . **CBS 86068**

THAT'S WHAT FRIENDS ARE FOR   December 1985
Burt Bacharach / Carole Bayer Sager
Island Music . . . . USA
Dionne Warwick . . . . **Arista ARIST 638**

THAT'S WHAT I LIKE ABOUT THE SOUTH   1947
Andy Razaf
Southern Music Publishing Co. Ltd. . . . . USA
Phil Harris . . . . **Camden CDN 124**
Theme song of Phil Harris.

THAT'S WHAT LOVE WILL DO   March 1963
Trevor Peacock
Jack Good Music Publishing Co. Ltd . . . . UK
Joe Brown & The Bruvers . . . . **Pye 7N 35106**

THAT'S WHAT MAKES PARIS PAREE   August 1953
Sammy Cahn / Vernon Duke
Harms-Connelly Ltd. . . . . USA
Film(s): . . . . April in Paris
Doris Day . . . . **Columbia SCM 5039**
Julie Dawn . . . . **Columbia 33SX 1124**
Doris Day appeared in *April in Paris*.

THAT'S WHY   December 1952
Bob Merrill
Campbell Connelly & Co. Ltd . . . . USA
Mindy Carson & Guy Mitchell . . . . **Columbia SCM 5022**
Ted Heath & his Music, vocal Litz Roza
& Dennis Lotis . . . . **Decca F 10027**

THAT'S WHY DARKIES WERE BORN   1931
Ray Henderson / Lew Brown
Victoria Music Co. Ltd. . . . . USA
Show(s): . . . . George White's Scandals of 1931
Film(s): . . . . George White's Scandals
Layton & Johnstone . . . . **Columbia DB 678**
Paul Robeson . . . . **HMV B 8973**

THAT'S YOU   June 1960
Sammy Gallop / Chester Conn / Nelson Riddle
Bregman, Vocco & Conn Ltd. . . . . USA
Nat 'King' Cole . . . . **Capitol CL 15129**

THAT'S YOU BABY   1929
Con Conrad / Sidney Mitchell / Archie Gottler
Campbell Connelly & Co. Ltd . . . . USA
Film(s): . . . . Fox Movietone Follies of 1929
Jack Hylton & his Orchestra . . . . **HMV B 5658**
Annette Hanshaw . . . . **Columbia 5425**

THEM THERE EYES   1931
Maceo Pinkard / William Tracey / Doris Tauber
Francis, Day & Hunter Ltd. . . . . USA
Film(s): . . . . Lady Sings the Blues
Louis Armstrong & his Orchestra . . . . **Parlophone R 1286**
Bing Crosby with Gus Arnheim & his Orchestra . . **RCA RD 27075**
The McGuire Sisters . . . . **Vogue LVA 9024**
Peggy Lee . . . . **Capitol T 1743**
Diana Ross . . . . **Tamla Motown STML 11311-2**
Diana Ross appeared in *Lady Sings the Blues*.

THEME FOR A DREAM   March 1961
Mort Garson / Earl Shuman

Leeds Music Ltd .... USA
Cliff Richard .... **Columbia DB 4593**
Bobby Vee .... **Liberty LBY 1139**

THEME FOR YOUNG LOVERS   **April 1964**
Bruce Welch
Elstree Music Ltd .... UK
Film(s): ....Wonderful Life
The Shadows .... **Columbia DB 7231**
The Shadows appeared in *Wonderful Life*.

THEME FROM DIXIE   **May 1961**
Traditional, arranged by Duane Eddy
Twangy Music Ltd .... USA
Duane Eddy (guitar) .... **London HL 9324**

THEME FROM S-EXPRESS   **May 1988**
Mark Moore / Pascal Gabriel
Rhythm King Music .... UK
S-Express .... **Rhythm King LEFT 21**

THEME FROM THE APARTMENT, THE   **March 1960**
Adolph Deutsch
United Artists Music Ltd .... USA
Film(s): .... The Apartment
The Hollywood Studio Symphony Orchestra . **London HAT 2287**
Percy Faith & his Orchestra .... **Philips BBL 7488**

THEN HE KISSED ME   **October 1963**
Phil Spector / Ellie Greenwich / Jeff Barry
Seventeen Saville Row Ltd .... USA
The Crystals .... **London HL 9773**
See also 'Then I Kissed Her'

THEN I KISSED HER   **June 1967**
Phil Spector / Ellie Greenwich / Jeff Barry
Belinda (London) Ltd. .... USA
The Beach Boys .... **Capitol CL 15502**

THEN I'LL BE HAPPY   **1926**
Cliff Friend / Sidney Clare / Lew Brown
Francis, Day & Hunter Ltd. .... USA
Jack Smith .... **HMV B 2260**
Eddie Fisher .... **HMV 7EG 8156**
The Four Freshmen .... **Capitol T 1103**

THERE AIN'T NO MAYBE IN MY BABY'S EYES   **1927**
Gus Kahn / Walter Donaldson / Ray Egan
Francis, Day & Hunter Ltd. .... USA
Jack Smith .... **HMV B 2414**
The New York Syncopators .... **Parlophone E 5769**
Max & Harry Nesbitt .... **HMV B 2625**

THERE ARE ANGELS OUTSIDE HEAVEN   **1943**
Frederick Tysh / Richard Tauber / Walter Ellis
Lawrence Wright Music Co. Ltd .... UK
Show(s): .... Old Chelsea
Richard Tauber, Carloe Lynn
& Nancy Browne .... **Parlophone RO 20519**
Leslie Hutchinson (Hutch) .... **HMV BD 1038**
Richard Tauber, Carole Lynn & Nancy Browne appeared in *Old Chelsea*.

THERE ARE FAIRIES AT THE BOTTOM
OF OUR GARDEN   **1917**
Rose Fyleman / Liza Lehmann
Chappell Music Co. .... UK
Doris Vane .... **Columbia 3878**
Beatrice Lillie .... **Decca LK 4129**
Carole Rosen .... **Hyperion A 66063**

THERE ARE MORE QUESTIONS THAN
ANSWERS   **November 1972**
Johnny Nash
Rondor Music (London) Ltd. .... USA
Johnny Nash .... **CBS 8351**

THERE ARE SUCH THINGS   **1943**
Stanley Adams / George Meyer / Abel Baer
Sterling Music Publishing Co. Ltd .... USA
Ambrose & his Orchestra, vocal Denny Dennis . **Decca F 8267**
Tommy Dorsey & his Orchestra,
vocal Frank Sinatra .... **RCA RD 27069**
Anne Shelton .... **Decca F 8291**
Al Hibbler .... **Brunswick LAT 8140**

Patti Page .... **Mercury MMC 14007**

THERE BUT FOR FORTUNE   **August 1965**
Phil Ochs
Harmony Music .... USA
Joan Baez .... **Fontana TF 587**

THERE GOES MY EVERYTHING   **August 1967**
Dallas Frazier
Burlington Music Co. Ltd. .... USA
Engelbert Humperdinck .... **Decca F 12610**
Elvis Presley (1971) .... **RCA 2060**

THERE GOES MY FIRST LOVE   **October 1975**
Roger Greenaway / Barry Mason
Cookaway Music .... UK
The Drifters .... **Bell 1433**

THERE GOES THAT SONG AGAIN   **1945**
Jule Styne / Sammy Cahn
Francis, Day & Hunter Ltd. .... USA
Film(s): .... Carolina Blues
Russ Morgan & his Orchestra,
vocal Russ Morgan .... **Brunswick 03551**
Adelaide Hall .... **Decca F 8517**

THERE I'VE SAID IT AGAIN   **1945**
Redd Evans / Dave Mann
Campbell Connelly & Co. Ltd. .... USA
Vaughn Monroe .... **HMV BD 5899**
Nat 'King' Cole .... **Capitol LCT 6003**
Jimmy Young .... **Columbia DB 4211**
Vaughn Monroe .... **RCA RCX 1043**
The Four Aces .... **Brunswick LAT 8221**

THERE IS A MOUNTAIN   **December 1967**
Donovan Leitch
Donovan Music Ltd. .... UK
Donovan .... **Pye 7N 17403**

THERE IS NOTHING LIKE A DAME   **December 1951**
Richard Rodgers / Oscar Hammerstein II
Williamson Music Ltd .... USA
Show(s): .... South Pacific
Film(s): .... South Pacific
Men's Chorus (from American production) . **Philips BBL 7157**
Ray Walston .... **RCA RB 16065**
Ray Walston appeared in the film *South Pacific*.

THERE ISN'T ANY LIMIT TO MY LOVE   **1936**
Maurice Sigler / Al Hoffman / Al Goodhart
Cinephonic Music Co. Ltd .... UK
Film(s): .... This'll Make You Whistle
Jack Buchanan .... **Brunswick 02347**
Jack Hylton & his Orchestra .... **HMV BD 5037**
Jack Buchanan appeared in *This'll Make You Whistle*.

THERE IT IS   **October 1982**
Dana Meyers / Charmaine Sylvers / Nidra Beard
Chappell Music Co. .... USA
Shalamar .... **Sola K 13194**

THERE MUST BE A REASON   **September 1954**
Benny Davis / Ted Murray
Campbell Connelly & Co. Ltd. .... USA
Frankie Laine .... **Philips PB 306**
Vera Lynn .... **Decca F 10339**

THERE MUST BE A WAY   **April 1959**
Sammy Gallop / David Saxon / Robert Cook
Bradbury Wood Ltd .... USA
Joni James .... **MGM MGM 1002**
Frankie Vaughan (1967) .... **Columbia DB 8248**
Al Martino .... **Capitol T 1975**

THERE MUST BE AN ANGEL PLAYING
WITH MY HEART   **August 1985**
Annie Lennox / David Stewart
RCA Music .... UK
Eurythmics .... **RCA PB 40247**

THERE SHE GOES   **November 1990**
Lee Mavers
Go Disc Music .... UK
The La's .... **Go Disc GOLAS 5**

THERE THERE MY DEAR   August 1980
Kevin Rowland / Kevin Archer
EMI Music Ltd .... UK
Dexy's Midnight Runners .... **Parlophone R 6038**

THERE WILL NEVER BE ANOTHER YOU   1943
Harry Warren / Mack Gordon
Edwin H. Morris & Co. Ltd .... USA
Film(s): .... Iceland / I'll Get By
The Andrews Sisters .... **Brunswick 04572**
Gogi Grant .... **London HAB 2032**
Tony Brent .... **Columbia 33SX 1200**
Ernestine Anderson .... **Mercury MMC 14016**

THERE WON'T BE MANY COMING HOME   December 1966
Roy Orbison / Bill Dees
Acuff-Rose Music Ltd. .... USA
Roy Orbison .... **London HL 10096**

THERE'LL ALWAYS BE AN ENGLAND   1939
Ross Parker / Hugh Charles
Dash Music Ltd. .... UK
Dennis Noble .... **HMV B 8971**
Vincent Tildsley's Mastersingers ... **Parlophone F 1497**
Ross Parker & Hugh Charles .... **Decca F 7356**
Vera Lynn .... **HMV CLP 1591**

**THERE'LL BE A HOT TIME IN THE
OLD TOWN TONIGHT**   1896
Theodore Metz / Joe Hayden
Francis, Day & Hunter Ltd. .... USA
Bessie Smith .... **Philips BBL 7042**
**The Chris Barber Jazz Band,
vocal Ottile Patterson** .... **Columbia SEG 7915**
Lavern Baker .... **London LTZK 15139**

THERE'LL BE SOME CHANGES MADE   1929
W. Benton Overtstreet / Billy Higgins
Herman Darewksi Music Publishing Co. Ltd .... USA
Film(s): .... Designing Women / The Blue Veil / All That Jazz
**The Dorsey Brothers Orchestra,
vocal The Boswell Sisters** .... **Brunswick 01306**
**Benny Goodman & his Orchestra,
vocal Louise Tobin** .... **Parlophone R 2916**
Dolores Gray .... **Capitol CL 14732**
Teresa Brewer .... **Vogue LVA 9020**
Dolores Gray appeared in *Designing Women*.

**THERE'S A BLUE RIDGE ROUND
MY HEART, VIRGINIA**   1929
Alfred Bryan / Ira Schuster / Fred Philips
Lawrence Wright Music Co. Ltd. .... USA
Sophie Tucker .... **Columbia 4942**
Leslie Sarony .... **Victory 56**
Betty Smith .... **Decca DFE 6446**

THERE'S A BOY COMING HOME ON LEAVE   1940
Jimmy Kennedy
Peter Maurice Music Co. Ltd .... UK
Ambrose & his Orchestra, vocal Jack Cooper ... **Decca F 7440**
**Maurice Winnick & his Orchestra,
vocal Al Bowlly** .... **HMV BD 5583**

THERE'S A CABIN IN THE PINES   1933
Billy Hill
Lawrence Wright Music Co. Ltd. .... USA
Show(s): .... On With the Show
Bing Crosby .... **Brunswick 01557**
Jimmy Campbell & his Band .... **Rex 8007**
Al Bowlly .... **Decca F 3638**
Jimmy Campbell appeared in *On With the Show*.

THERE'S A GHOST IN MY HOUSE   June 1974
Eddie Holland / Brian Holland / Lamont Dozier & R. Dean Taylor
Jobete Music (UK) Ltd. .... UK
R. Dean Taylor .... **Tamla Motown TMG 896**

THERE'S A GIRL IN THE HEART OF MARYLAND 1914
Ballard MacDonald / Harry Carroll
Francis, Day & Hunter Ltd. .... USA
Harry MacDonough .... **Zonophone Twin 1232**

THERE'S A GOLD MINE IN THE SKY   1939
Nick Kenny / Charles Kenny
Victoria Music Co. Ltd. .... USA

Film(s): .... Gold Mine in the Sky / An Affair to Remember
Bing Crosby .... **Brunswick LAT 8152**
Pat Boone .... **London HAD 2098**

THERE'S A GOOD TIME COMING   1930
Ralph Butler / Raymond Wallace
Campbell Connelly & Co. Ltd .... UK
Jack Payne & The BBC Dance Orchestra .... **Columbia CB 132**
Harry Davidson & his Orchestra .... **Columbia 33S 1080**

THERE'S A HARBOUR OF DREAMBOATS   1943
Nat Burton / Arthur Altman / Al Sherman
Francis, Day & Hunter Ltd. .... USA
Ambrose & his Orchestra, vocal Anne Shelton .. **Decca F 8306**
Joe Loss & his Orchestra, vocal Harry Kaye .... **HMV BD 5799**

THERE'S A HEARTACHE FOLLOWING ME   December 1964
Ray Baker
Burlington Music Co. Ltd .... USA
Jim Reeves .... **RCA 1423**

THERE'S A KIND OF HUSH   April 1967
Les Reed / Geoff Stevens
Donna Music Ltd. .... UK
Herman's Hermits .... **Columbia DB 8123**

THERE'S A LAND OF BEGIN AGAIN   1942
Ross Parker / Hugh Charles
Dash Music Ltd .... UK
Vera Lynn .... **Decca F 8028**
Jay Wilbur & his Band, vocal Jack Cooper .... **Rex 10066**

**THERE'S A LITTLE BIT OF BAD IN EVERY GOOD LITTLE
GIRL**   1916
Grant Clarke / Fred Fisher
Ascherberg, Hopwood & Crew Ltd. .... USA
Pearl Bailey .... **Columbia 33CX 1247**

THERE'S A LONG LONG TRAIL   1913
Stoddard King / Joe Elliott
B. Feldman & Co. Ltd. .... UK
Ernest Pike .... **Zonophone 1590**
Vaughn Monroe .... **RCA RD 27049**

THERE'S A LOVELY LAKE IN LONDON   1935
Tolchard Evans / Stanley Damerell / Ralph Butler
Campbell Connelly & Co. Ltd .... UK
Gracie Fields .... **Rex 8592**
Vanessa Lee .... **Oriole MG 20015**
The Michael Sammes Singers .... **Columbia 33SX 1193**

THERE'S A LULL IN MY LIFE   1937
Mack Gordon / Harry Revel
Francis, Day & Hunter Ltd. .... USA
Film(s): .... Wake Up and Live
Alice Faye .... **Brunswick 02435**
Ruth Etting .... **Brunswick 02446**
Kay Starr .... **London HAU 2039**
Anne Shelton .... **Philips BBL 7188**
Alice Faye appeared in *Wake Up and Live*.

THERE'S A PAWNSHOP ON THE CORNER   May 1952
Bob Merrill
Cinephonic Music Co. Ltd .... USA
Guy Mitchell .... **Philips BBL 7265**

THERE'S A RAINBOW 'ROUND MY SHOULDER   1929
Billy Rose / Dave Dreyer / Al Jolson
Francis, Day & Hunter Ltd .... USA
Film(s):The Singing Fool / The Jolson Story / Rainbow 'Round My
Shoulder
Al Jolson .... **Brunswick 1364**
Al Jolson .... **Brunswick LA 8575**
Frankie Laine .... **Columbia DB 3148**
Al Jolson appeared in *The Singing Fool*.
Frankie Lane appeared in *Rainbow 'Round My Shoulder.*

THERE'S A SMALL HOTEL   1937
Richard Rodgers / Lorenz Hart
Chappell & Co. Ltd. .... USA
Show(s): .... On Your Toes
Film(s): .... Words and Music / Pal Joey
Jack Whiting .... **Columbia DB 1687**
Greta Keller .... **Decca F 6256**
Frank Sinatra .... **Capitol LCT 6148**

Petula Clark . . . . Pye NPL 18039
Betty Garrett . . . . MGM C 853
Bobby Van & Kay Coulter . . . . Brunswick LAT 8061
Jack Whiting appeared in the British production of *On Your Toes.*
Frank Sinatra appeared in *Pal Joey.* Betty Garrett appeared in *Words and Music.*
Bobby Van & Kay Coulter appeared in the 1954 American production of *On Your Toes.*

THERE'S A WHOLE LOT OF LOVING   April 1975
Chris Arnold / David Martin / Geoff Morrow
Ammo-James Music . . . . UK
Guys & Dolls . . . . Magnet MAG 20

THERE'S ALWAYS ROOM AT OUR HOUSE   December 1951
Bob Merrill
Campbell Connelly & Co. Ltd . . . . USA
Guy Mitchell . . . . Philips BBL 7265
Billy Cotton & his Band . . . . Decca F 9827

THERE'S ALWAYS SOMETHING THERE TO REMIND ME
(See Always Something There To Remind Me)

THERE'S ALWAYS TOMORROW   1931
Phil Charig / Vivian Ellis / Douglas Furber
Chappell & Co. Ltd. . . . . UK
Show(s):. . . . . Stand Up and Sing
Jack Buchanan & Elsie Randolph . . . . Columbia SEG 7767
Jack Buchanan & Elsie Randolph appeared in *Stand Up and Sing.*

THERE'S DANGER IN YOUR EYES CHERIE   1930
Jack Meskill / Pete Wendling / Harry Richman
Francis, Day & Hunter Ltd . . . . USA
Film(s): . . . . Puttin' on the Ritz / Rich, Young and Pretty
Leslie Hutchinson (Hutch) . . . . Parlophone R 695
Trudy Edwards . . . . Capitol T 838

THERE'S EVERYTHING NICE ABOUT YOU   1928
Pete Wendling / Alfred Bryan / Arthur Terker
B. Feldman & Co. Ltd. . . . . USA
Nat Shilkret & his Orchestra . . . . HMV B 5319

THERE'S NEVER BEEN A NIGHT   October 1958
Irwin Schuster / Bob Davie
Leeds Music ltd . . . . USA
The Mudlarks . . . . Columbia SEG 7854
Alma Cogan . . . . HMV POP 531

THERE'S NO BUSINESS LIKE SHOW BUSINESS   1947
Irving Berlin
Irving Berlin Ltd. . . . . USA
Show(s): . . . . Annie Get Your Gun
Film(s):Annie Get Your Gun / There's no Business Like Show Business
Chorus & Orchestra of the American
production of Annie Get Your Gun . . . . . . Brunswick LAT 8002
Chorus & Orchestra of the British
production of Annie Get Your Gun . . . . Columbia SEG 7711
Howard Keel, Betty Hutton,
Louis Calhern & Keenan Wynn . . . . MGM CD 1
Ethel Merman . . . . Brunswick LAT 8059
Howard Keel, Betty Hutton, Louis Calhern & Keenan Wynn appeared in the film of *Annie Get Your Gun.*
Ethel Merman appeared in *There's No Business Like Show Business.*

THERE'S NO ONE BUT YOU   1946
Austen Croom-Johnson / Redd Evans
Dash Music Ltd. . . . . USA
Doreen Harris . . . . HMV BD 1140
The Mills Brothers . . . . Brunswick 03737
The Four Freshmen . . . . Capitol T 844

THERE'S NO TOMORROW   October 1951
Leo Corday / Al Hoffman / Leon Carr
G. Ricordi & Co. (London) Ltd . . . . USA
Film(s): . . . . Two Tickets To Broadway
Tony Martin . . . . HMV B 9967
Johnny Desmond . . . . Vogue LVA 9035
Tony Martin appeared in *Two Tickets to Broadway.*
Based on *O Sole Mio* by Eduardo De Capua.

THERE'S NO TWO WAYS ABOUT LOVE   1943
James P. Johnson / Ted Koehler / Irving Mills
Lawrence Wright Music Co. Ltd . . . . USA
Film(s): . . . . Stormy Weather

Harry Roy & his Band,
vocal Marjorie Kingsley . . . . Regal Zonophone MR 3716
Billy Ternent & his Orchestra,
vocal Sid Buckman . . . . Decca F 8369

THERE'S NO YOU   1945
Tom Adair / Hal Hopper / George Durgom
Ascherberg, Hopwood & Crew Ltd. . . . . USA
Frank Sinatra . . . . Columbia DB 2190
June Christy . . . . Capitol T 725
Frank Sinatra . . . . Capitol LCT 6152

THERE'S NOTHING ROUGHER THAN LOVE   September 1949
Jule Styne / Sammy Cahn
B. Feldman & Co. Ltd . . . . USA
Film(s): . . . . .It's a Great Feeling
Lita Roza . . . . Pye NPL 18020

THERE'S SOMETHING ABOUT A SOLDIER   1935
Noel Gay
Lawrence Wright Music Co. Ltd . . . . UK
Film(s): . . . . Me and Marlborough
Cicely Courtneidge . . . . HMV B 4418
Cicely Courtneidge appeared in *Me and Marlborough.*

THERE'S SOMETHING IN THE AIR   1937
Jimmy McHugh / Harold Adamson
Francis, Day & Hunter Ltd. . . . . USA
Film(s): . . . . A Banjo on My Knee
Ray Noble & his Orchestra, vocal Al Bowlly . . . . . HMV BD 5153
Anthony Martin . . . . Vocalion 528
The R.A.F. Dance Orchestra . . . . Decca F 8062

THERE'S SOMETHING IN YOUR EYES   1932
Franz Grothe
Campbell Connelly & Co. Ltd. . . . . Germany
Geraldo & his Tango Orchestra . . . . Columbia FB 1343
Cliff Connolly . . . . Decca F 2526

THERE'S SOMETHING SPANISH IN YOUR EYES   1929
Irving Caesar / Cliff Friend
Francis, Day & Hunter Ltd . . . . USA
Show(s): . . . . George White's Scandals
Sophie Tucker . . . . Columbia 4941

THERE'S YES! YES! IN YOUR EYES   1924
Joseph Santly / Cliff Friend
Francis, Day & Hunter Ltd. . . . . USA
Paul Whiteman & his Orchestra . . . . HMV B 1876
Kay Starr . . . . Capitol CL 13167
Teresa Brewer . . . . Coral LVA 9138
The Girls . . . . Warner Brothers WM 4053

THESE BOOTS ARE MADE FOR WALKING   April 1966
Lee Hazlewood
Lorna Music Co. Ltd. . . . . USA
Nancy Sinatra . . . . Reprise R 20432

THESE FOOLISH THINGS   1936
Holt Marvell / Jack Strachey / Harry Link
Boosey & Hawkes Music Publishers Ltd . . . . UK
Show(s): . . . . Spread it Abroad
Film(s): . . . . .The Ghost Catchers
Dorothy Dickson . . . . HMV C 2946
Leslie Hutchinson (Hutch) . . . . Parlophone F 373
Dinah Shore . . . . RCA RD 27062
Leslie Hutchinson (Hutch) . . . . Decca LF 1207
Dorothy Dickson appeared in *Spread it Abroad.*

THEY ALL FOLLOW ME   1898
Gustave Kerker / Hugh Morton
Ascherberg, Hopwood & Crew Ltd. . . . . USA
Show(s): .The Belle of New York
Edna May . . . . Berliner 3192
The Columbia Light Opera Company . . . . Columbia 9925
Mary Thomas . . . . HMV 7EG 8442

THEY ALL LAUGHED   1937
George Gershwin / Ira Gershwin
Chappell & Co. Ltd. . . . . USA
Film(s): . . . . Shall We Dance
Fred Astaire . . . . Brunswick 02426
Dakota Staton . . . . Capitol T 1054
Fred Astaire . . . . HMV CLP 1100

Fred Astaire appeared in *Shall We Dance*.

THEY ALL WALK THE WIBBLY WOBBLY WALK   1912
Paul Pelham / James Long
B. Feldman & Co. .... UK
Mark Sheridan .... **Regal G 6506**
Reg Grant .... **Parlophone R 1332**
George Mitchell Minstrels .... **HMV CLP 1667**

THEY CALL THE WIND MARIA   April 1953
Alan Jay Lerner / Frederick Loewe
Chappell & Co. Ltd .... USA
Show(s): .... Paint Your Wagon
Film(s): .... Paint Your Wagon
Rufus Smith & chorus .... **HMV CLP 1005**
Joe Leader & chorus .... **Columbia DB 3288**
The Kingston Trio .... **Capitol T 1107**
Harve Presnell .... **Paramount PMS 1001**
Rufus Smith appeared in the American production of *Paint Your Wagon*
Joe Leader appeared in the British production of *Paint Your Wagon*.
Harve Presnell appeared in the film *Paint Your Wagon*.

THEY CAN'T BLACK-OUT THE MOON   1940
Art Strauss / Sonny Miller / Bob Dale
Lawrence Wright Music .... UK
Caroll Gibbons & his Savoy Hotel Orpheans . **Columbia FB 2326**
Jay Wilbur Band, vocal Sam Browne .... **Rex 9692**

THEY CAN'T TAKE THAT AWAY FROM ME   1937
George Gershwin / Ira Gershwin
Chappell & Co. Ltd. .... USA
Film(s): .... Shall We Dance / Barkleys of Broadway
Fred Astaire .... **Philips**
Fred Astaire .... **HMV**
Connee Boswell .... **Brunswick**
Peggy Lee .... **Brunswick LAT 8287**
Fred Astaire appeared in both *Shall We Dance* and *Barkleys of Broadway*.
Nominated for an Academy Award 1937.

THEY CUT DOWN THE OLD PINE TREE   1932
Edward Eliscu / Willie Raskin / George Brown
Campbell Connelly & Co. Ltd. .... USA
Frank Marvin .... **Panachord 25052**
Gene Autry .... **Rex 9462**

THEY DIDN'T BELIEVE ME   1914
Jerome Kern / Herbert Reynolds
Francis, Day & Hunter Ltd. .... USA
Show(s): .... The Girl from Utah / Tonight's the Night
Film(s): .... Till the Clouds Roll By / That Midnight Kiss
Haidee De Rance & George Grossmith .... **HMV C 578**
Julie Sanderson .... **Brunswick LA 8569**
Kathryn Grayson .... **MGM EP 639**
Julie London .... **London HAG 2280**
Mario Lanza .... **RCA RB 16223**
Haidee De Rance & George Grossmith appeared in *Tonight's the Night*.
Kathryn Grayson appeared in *Till the Clouds Roll By*.
Mario Lanza appeared in *That Midnight Kiss*.

THEY DON'T KNOW   October 1983
Kirsty MacColl
Chrysalis .... UK
Tracy Ullman .... **Stiff BUY 180**
Kirsty MacColl .... **Stiff BUY 47**

THEY GO WILD SIMPLY WILD OVER ME   1918
Fred Fisher / Joseph McCarthy
Francis, Day & Hunter Ltd. .... USA
Eddie Cantor .... **Brunswick 04298**
Jerry Lewis .... **Capitol LC 6591**

THEY SAY   1939
Edward Heyman / Paul Mann / Stephen Weiss
B. Feldman & Co. Ltd. .... USA
Geraldo & his Orchestra, vocal Al Bowlly ...... **HMV BD 5448**
Mildred Bailey & her Orchestra .... **Parlophone R 2994**
Les Allen .... **Columbia FB 2152**

THEY SAY IT'S WONDERFUL   1947
Irving Berlin
Irving Berlin Ltd. .... USA
Show(s): .... Annie Get Your Gun

Film(s): .... Annie Get Your Gun
Ethel Merman & Ray Middleton .... **Brunswick LAT 8002**
Dolores Gray & Bill Johnson .... **Columbia SEG 7711**
Betty Hutton & Howard Keel .... **MGM CD 1**
Ethel Merman & Ray Middleton appeared in the American production of *Annie Get Your Gun*.
Dolores Gray & Bill Johnson appeared in the British production of *Annie Get Your Gun*.
Betty Hutton & Howard Keel appeared in the film of *Annie Get Your Gun*.

THEY SHOOT HORSES DON'T THEY   March 1977
Gareth Mortimer
Chrysalis Music Ltd .... UK
Racing Cars .... **Chrysalis CHS 2129**

THEY WERE ALL OUT OF STEP BUT JIM   1918
Irving Berlin
B. Feldman & Co. Ltd. .... USA
The Two Bobs .... **Edison Bell Winner 3266**

THEY'RE COMING TO TAKE
ME AWAY HA-HAAAA!   September 1966
N. Bonaparte
ATV Music Ltd. .... USA
Napoleon XIV .... **Warner Brothers 5831**

THEY'RE EITHER TOO YOUNG OR TOO OLD   1944
Arthur Shwartz / Frank Loesser
B. Feldman & Co. Ltd .... USA
Film(s): .... Thank Your Lucky Stars / With a Song in My Heart
Jimmy Dorsey & his Orchestra,
vocal Kitty Kallen .... **Brunswick 03495**
Jane Froman .... **Capitol LC 6554**
Nominated for an Academy Award 1943.

THEY'RE WEARING 'EM HIGHER IN HAWAII   1916
Joe Goodwin / Halsey Mohr
B. Feldman & Co. Ltd .... USA
Film(s): .... Show Business
Murray's Savoy Quartette .... **HMV B 830**

THINE ALONE   1917
Victor Herbert / Henry Blossom
B. Feldman & Co. Ltd. .... USA
Show(s): .... Eileen
Film(s): .... The Great Victor Herbert
Allan Jones .... **HMV B 9032**
Bing Crosby .... **Brunswick LA 8600**
Mario Lanza .... **RCA RD 27200**
Alan Jones appeared in *The Great Victor Herbert*.

THING CALLED LOVE, A   May 1972
Jerry Hubbard
Valley Music .... USA
Johnny Cash .... **CBS 7797**

THING, THE   January 1951
Charles Randolf Green
Leeds Music Ltd .... USA
Film(s): .... The Wild Blue Yonder
Phil Harris .... **Camden CDN 124**
Danny Kaye .... **Brunswick 04635**
Phil Harris appeared in *The Wild Blue Yonder*.

THING-UMMY-BOB, THE   1942
Gordon Thompson / David Heneker
Francis, Day & Hunter Ltd. .... UK
Arthur Askey .... **HMV BD 989**

THINGS   September 1962
Bobby Darin
T.M. Music Ltd .... USA
Bobby Darin .... **London HL 9575**
Dean Martin .... **Reprise R 6130**

THINGS AIN'T WHAT THEY USED TO BE (See Fings Ain't What They Used To Be)

THINGS ARE LOOKING UP   1935
Noel Gay
Cinephonic Music Co. Ltd .... UK
Film(s): .... Things are Looking Up
Cicely Courtneidge .... **HMV BD 239**
Leslie Holmes .... **Rex 8400**

Cicley Courtneidge appeared in *Things Are Looking Up.*

THINGS CAN ONLY GET BETTER   February 1985
Howard Jones
Warner Brothers Music . . . . UK
Howard Jones . . . . **WEA HOW 6**

THINGS I LOVE, THE   1941
Harold Barlow / Lewis Harris
Chappell & Co. Ltd . . . . USA
Adelaide Hall . . . . **Decca F 7891**
Turner Layton . . . . **Columbia FB 2635**
Jeri Southern . . . . **Columbia 33SX 1155**
Based on 'Melodie in E Flat Major, opus 42 no.3' by Peter Ilych
Tchaikovsky (1840 - 1893).

THINGS WE DID LAST SUMMER, THE   1947
Jule Styne / Sammy Cahn
Edwin H. Morris & Co. Ltd. . . . . USA
Frank Sinatra . . . . **Fontana TFL 5048**
Jane Powell . . . . **HMV CLP 1131**
Vic Damone . . . . **Philips BBL 7347**

THINGS WE DO FOR LOVE, THE   January 1977
Eric Stewart / Graham Gouldman
St. Annes Music Ltd . . . . UK
10 CC . . . . **Mercury 6008002**

THINK I'M GONNA FALL IN LOVE WITH YOU   October 1977
Ben Findon / Mike Myers
Heath Levy Music Ltd . . . . UK
The Dooleys . . . . **GTO GT 95**

THINKING ABOUT THE WABASH   1944
Sammy Cahn / Jule Styne / Walter Bullock
Chappell & Co. LTd. . . . . USA
Film(s): . . . . Carolina Blues
Turner Layton . . . . **Columbia FB 3014**
Johnny Dennis & his Novelty Quartet . . . . **Decca F 8417**

THINKING OF YOU   1929
Bert Kalmar / Harry Ruby
Chappell & Co. Ltd . . . . USA
Show(s): . . . . The Five O'clock Girl
Film(s): . . . . Three Little Words
Jack Hylton & his Orchestra . . . . **HMV B 5612**
Barbara Lea . . . . **London HBU 10058**
Eddie Fisher . . . . **HMV B 10023**
Dorothy Provine . . . . **Warner Brothers WM 4053**

THINKING OF YOU   June 1984
Nile Rodgers / Bernard Edwards
Warner Brothers Music . . . . UK
Sister Sledge . . . . **Atlantic B 9744**
Maureen (1990) . . . . **Urban URB 55**

THINKING OF YOU   February 1985
Terry Hall / Toby Lyons
Plangent Visions Music . . . . UK
The Colourfield . . . . **Chrysalis COLF 3**

THIS CAN'T BE LOVE   1939
Richard Rodgers / Lorenz Hart
Chappell & Co. Ltd. . . . . USA
Show(s): The Boys From Syracuse / Funny Side Up / Up and Doing
Film(s): . . . . . The Boys From Syracuse / Words and Music / Jumbo
Frances Langford & Rudy Vallee . . . . **Brunswick 02883**
Patricia Burke . . . . **Columbia DB 1918**
Dick Bentley . . . . **Columbia FB 2355**
Rosemary Clooney . . . . **Vogue LVA 9112**
Bob Monkhouse & Paula Hendrix . . . . **Decca LK 4564**
Doris Day . . . . **CBS BPG 62118**
Patricia Burke appeared in *Up and Doing.*
Bob Monkhouse & Paula Hendrix appeared in the British production
of *The Boys From Syracuse.*
Doris Day appeared in the film of *Jumbo.*

THIS CORROSION   November 1987
Andrew Eldritch
EMI Music . . . . UK
The Sisters of Mercy . . . . **Merciful Release MR 39**

THIS DOOR SWINGS BOTH WAYS   July 1966
Don Thomas / Estelle Levitt
Dick James Music Ltd. . . . . UK

Herman's Hermits . . . . **Columbia DB 7947**

THIS FLIGHT TONIGHT   November 1973
Joni Mitchell
Warner Brothers Music Ltd. . . . . USA
Nazareth . . . . **Mooncrest MOON 14**
Joni Mitchell . . . . **Reprise K 44128**

THIS GUY'S IN LOVE WITH YOU   September 1968
Burt Bacharach / Hal David
Blue Seas Music . . . . USA
Herb Alpert . . . . **A&M AMS 727**

THIS HEART OF MINE   1946
Harry Warren / Arthur Freed
Bradbury Wood Ltd. . . . . USA
Film(s): . . . . The Ziegfeld Follies
Judy Garland . . . . **Brunswick 03623**
Turner Layton . . . . **Columbia FB 3212**
Johnny Mathis . . . . **Fontana TFL 5039**
Judy Garland appeared in *The Ziegfeld Follies.*

THIS IS ALWAYS   1947
Mack Gordon / Harry Warren
Bradbury Wood Ltd. . . . . USA
Film(s): . . . . Three Little Girls in Blue
Geraldo & his Orchestra, vocal Carol Carr . **Parlophone F 2187**
Dick Haymes . . . . **Brunswick 03690**
Teddi King . . . . **Vogue VA 160109**

THIS IS HOW IT FEELS   March 1990
"Inspiral Carpets"
Chrysalis Music . . . . UK
Inspiral Carpets . . . . **Cow DUNG 7**

THIS IS IT   June 1976
Van McCoy
Warner Brothers Music Ltd . . . . USA
Melba Moore . . . . **Buddah BDS 443**

THIS IS MY LOVELY DAY   1947
Vivian Ellis
Chappell & Co. Ltd. . . . . UK
Show(s): . . . . .Bless the Bride
Lizbeth Webb & George Guetary . . . . **Columbia SEG 7551**
Roberto Cardinali . . . . **HMV CLP 1311**
Kathryn Grayson . . . . **MGM 249**
Lizbeth Webb & George Guetary appeared in *Bless the Bride.*

THIS IS MY MOTHER'S DAY   December 1948
Billy Reid
Billy Reid Music Ltd . . . . UK
Dorothy Squires . . . . **Columbia DB 2455**
Vera Lynn . . . . **Decca F 9195**
Dorothy Squires . . . . **Pye NPL 18015**

THIS IS MY PRAYER (Non Ho L'Eta Per Amarti)   June 1964
Mario Panzeri / 'Nisa' / Buddy Kaye & Philip Springer
Chappell & Co. Ltd . . . . Italy
Dana Valery . . . . **Decca F 11881**
Gigiola Cinquetti . . . . **Decca F 21882**
Vera Lynn . . . . **HMV POP 1287**
Italian entry for the 1964 Eurovision Song Contest (Placed First).

THIS IS MY SONG   May 1967
Charles Chaplin
Leeds Music Ltd. . . . . USA
Film(s): . . . . .The Countess from Hong Kong
Petula Clark . . . . **Pye 7N 17258**
Harry Secombe . . . . **Philips BF 1539**
The melody was used as the theme for the film.
Ivor Novello Nomination.

THIS IS NO LAUGHING MATTER   1941
Van Loman / Martin Block / Al Frisch
Dash Music Ltd . . . . USA
Anne Shelton . . . . **Rex 10129**
Glenn Miller & his Orchestra, vocal Ray Eberle . . . **HMV DLP 1049**
Eydie Gormé . . . . **HMV CLP 1156**

THIS IS NOT A LOVE SONG   October 1983
John Lydon / Keith Levine
CBS Songs . . . . USA
P.I.L. (Public Image Limited) . . . . **Virgin VS 5291**

THIS IS THE ARMY MISTER JONES   1943
Irving Berlin
Irving Berlin Ltd . . . . USA
Show(s): . . . . This is the Army
Film(s): . . . . This is the Army / Blue Skies
Irving Berlin & Chorus . . . . **HMV B 9355**
The All Soldier Orchestra & Chorus . . . . **Brunswick 03489**
The Four Sergeants . . . . **HMV 7EG 8396**
The All Soldier Orchestra & Chorus appeared in the American production of *This Is The Army*.
Irving Berlin appeared in the British production of *This Is The Army*.

THIS IS TOMORROW   March 1977
Bryan Ferry
E.G. Music . . . . UK
Bryan Ferry . . . . **Polydor 2001704**

THIS IS WORTH FIGHTING FOR   1942
Eddie De Lange / Sammy Stept
Sterling Music Co. Ltd . . . . USA
Film(s): . . . . When Johnny Comes Marching Home
Donald Peers . . . . **Decca F 8202**
The Ink Spots . . . . **Brunswick 03404**
John McHugh . . . . **Columbia FB 2854**

THIS LITTLE BIRD   June 1965
John D. Loudermilk
Acuff-Rose Publishing Co. Ltd . . . . USA
Marianne Faithfull . . . . **Decca F 12162**

THIS NEARLY WAS MINE   November 1951
Richard Rodgers / Oscar Hammerstein II
Williamson Music Ltd . . . . USA
Show(s): . . . . South Pacific
Film(s): . . . . South Pacific
Ezio Pinza . . . . **Philips BBL 7157**
Wilbur Evans . . . . **Columbia SEG 7668**
Giorgio Tozzi . . . . **RCA RB 16065**
Ezio Pinza appeared in the American production of *South Pacific*. Wilbur Evans appeared in the British production of *South Pacific*. Giorgio Tozzi dubbed the singing voice for Rossino Brazzi who appeared in the film *South Pacific*.

THIS OLD HEART OF MINE   December 1968
Brian Holland / Eddie Holland / Lamont Dozier
Jobete Music (UK) Ltd. . . . . USA
The Isley Brothers . . . . **Tamla Motown TMG 555**
Rod Stewart (1975) . . . . **Riva 1**

THIS OLD MAN (Knick Knack Paddy Whack)   February 1959
Traditional, arranged by Malcolm Arnold
B. Feldman & Co. Ltd. . . . . UK
Film(s): . . . . The Inn of the Sixth Happiness
Cyril Stapleton Orchestra . . . . **Decca F 11094**
Mitch Miller Orchestra . . . . **Philips PB 893**

THIS OLE HOUSE   October 1954
Stuart Hamblen
Leeds Music Ltd. . . . . USA
Rosemary Clooney . . . . **Philips BBR 8047**
Billie Anthony . . . . **Columbia DB 3519**
Stuart Hamblen . . . . **HMV JO 413**
Shakin' Stevens (1981) . . . . **Epic EPC 9555**

THIS TIME (We'll Get It Right)   May 1982
Chris Norman / Peter Spencer
Rak Music . . . . UK
The England World Cup Squad . . . . **Rak ER 1**

THIS TIME I KNOW IT'S FOR REAL   April 1989
Mike Stock / Matt Aitken / Peter Waterman & Donna Summer
All Boys Music . . . . UK
Donna Summer . . . . **Warner Brothers U 7780**
Ivor Novello Award.

THIS TIME THE DREAM'S ON ME   1942
Harold Arlen / Johnny Mercer
Chappell & Co. Ltd . . . . USA
Film(s): . . . . Blues in the Night
Jeri Southern . . . . **Columbia 33SX 1134**
Helen Merrill . . . . **Mercury MMB 12000**
Tony Bennett . . . . **Philips BBL 7455**

THIS TOWN AIN'T BIG ENOUGH FOR THE BOTH OF US   June 1974
Ron Mael
Island Music Ltd. . . . . UK
Sparks . . . . **Island WIP 6193**

THIS WHEEL'S ON FIRE   June 1968
Bob Dylan / Rick Danko
B. Feldman & Co. Ltd. . . . . USA
Julie Driscoll & The Brian Auger Trinity . . . . **Marmalade 698006**

THIS YEAR'S KISSES   1937
Irving Berlin
Irving Berlin Ltd. . . . . USA
Film(s): . . . . On the Avenue
Dick Powell . . . . **Decca F 6453**
Alice Faye . . . . **Brunswick 02454**
June Christy . . . . **Capitol T 725**
Alice Faye . . . . **Reprise R 6029**
Alice Faye & Dick Powell appeared in *On The Avenue*.

THIS'LL MAKE YOU WHISTLE   1936
Maurice Sigler / Al Hoffman / Al Goodhart
Cinephonic Music Co. Ltd . . . . UK
Show(s): . . . . This'll Make You Whistle
Film(s): . . . . This'll Make You Whistle
Jack Buchanan & Elsie Randolph . . . . **Brunswick 02348**
Jack Hylton & his Orchestra . . . . **HMV BD 5037**
Jack Buchanan & Elsie Randolph appeared in both the show and the film of *This'll Make You Whistle*.

THORA   1905
Stephen Adams / Frederick E. Weatherly
Boosey & Hawkes Music Ltd. UK
John Harrison . . . . **HMV 02122**
Charles Kullman . . . . **Columbia DB 1439**
Stuart Burrows . . . . **Qualiton QEP 4041**
Robert White . . . . **RCA RL 25345**

THORN BIRDS (Love Theme)   February 1984
Henry Mancini
Warner Brothers Music . . . . USA
Juan Martin (Guitar) . . . . **WEA X 9518**
Henry Mancini Orchestra . . . . **Warner Brothers W 9697**
Theme of the television series *The Thorn Birds*.

THORN IN MY SIDE   October 1986
Annie Lennox / David Stewart
RCA Music . . . . UK
The Eurythmics . . . . **RCA DA 8**

THOROUGHLY MODERN MILLIE   December 1967
Sammy Cahn / James Van Heusen
Leeds Music Ltd. . . . . USA
Film(s): . . . . Thoroughly Modern Millie
Julie Andrews . . . . **Brunswick 05975**
Julie Andrews appeared in *Thoroughly Modern Millie*.
Nominated for an Academy Award 1967.

THOSE WERE THE DAYS   November 1968
Gene Raskin
Essex Music Ltd. . . . . USA
Mary Hopkin . . . . **Apple 2**

THOU ART MY ROSE   1903
Ivan Caryll / Frederick E. Weatherly
Chappell Music Co. . . . . UK
Show(s): . . . . The Earl and the Girl
Robert Evett . . . . **Odean 44165**
Robert Evett appeared in *The Earl and the Girl.*

THOU SWELL   1929
Richard Rodgers / Lorenz Hart
Chappell & Co. Ltd . . . . USA
Show(s):A Connecticut Yankee / A Yankee at the Court of King Arthur
Film(s): . . . . .A Connecticut Yankee / Words and Music
Bix Beiderbecke & his Orchestra . . . . **Fontana TFE 17059**
Leslie Hutchinson (Hutch) . . . . **Parlophone R 461**
June Allyson . . . . **MGM C 853**
Della Reese . . . . **RCA RD 27167**
June Allyson appeared in *Words And Music.*

THOUGHTLESS   1943
Jerry Livingston / Mack David

Chappell & Co. Ltd .... USA
Show(s): ....Bright Lights of 1944
The Ink Spots .... **Brunswick LA 8710**
Sam Browne .... **Decca F 8856**

THOUSAND STARS, A   February 1961
Eugene Pearson
B. Feldman & Co. Ltd .... USA
Billy Fury .... **Decca F 11311**
Linda Scott .... **Columbia 33SX 1386**

THREE BELLS, THE (Les Trois Cloches)   November 1948
Jean Villard / Bert Reisfield
Southern Music Publishing Co. Ltd. .... France
Edith Piaf & Les Compagnons
de la Chanson .... **Columbia 33S 1083**
Les Compagnons de la Chanson .... **Columbia SEG 7829**
The Browns (1959) .... **RCA RD 27153**

THREE CABALLEROS, THE (Ay Jalisco No Te Rajes)   1945
Manuel Esperon / Ray Gilbert
Southern Music Publishing Co. Ltd. .... Mexico
Film(s): .... The Three Caballeros (Cartoon)
The Andrews Sisters .... **Brunswick 03565**
Edmundo Ros & his Orchestra .... **Decca F 8549**
The Fleetwoods .... **Top Rank BUY 028**

THREE COINS IN THE FOUNTAIN   July 1954
Sammy Cahn / Jule Styne
Robbins Music Corporation Ltd. .... USA
Film(s): ....Three Coins in the Fountain
Frank Sinatra .... **Capitol LCT 6123**
The Four Aces .... **Brunswick LAT 8249**
Doris Day .... **Philips BBL 7248**
Academy Award winning song for 1954.

THREE GALLEONS, THE (Las Tres Carabelas)   July 1955
Augusto Alguego / G. Moreu / Paddy Roberts
B. Feldman & Co. Ltd. .... Spain
Robert Earl .... **Philips BBL 7394**
Les Howard .... **HMV B 10928**

THREE LITTLE FISHES   1939
Saxie Dowell
Campbell Connelly & Co. Ltd. .... USA
Bebe Daniels & Ben Lyon .... **Decca F 7101**
The Radio Revellers .... **Columbia FB 3394**
Guy Lombardo & his Royal Canadians .... **Brunswick 02767**
Beatrice Lillie .... **Decca LK 4293**
Frankie Howard .... **Harmony A 1001**

THREE LITTLE SISTERS   1942
Vic Mizzy / Irving Taylor
Campbell Connelly & Co. Ltd .... USA
Film(s): .... Private Buckaroo
The Andrews Sisters .... **Brunswick 03353**
Dinah Shore .... **HMV BD 1020**
Donald Peers .... **Decca F 8188**
The Andrews Sisters appeared in *Private Buckaroo*.

THREE LITTLE WORDS   1931
Bert Kalmar / Harry Ruby
Chappell & Co. Ltd .... USA
Show(s): .... Folly to be Wise
Film(s): .... Check and Double Check / Three Little Words
Duke Ellington & his Orchestra .... **HMV B 5945**
Fred Astaire .... **MGM D 139**
Patti Page .... **Mercury MMC 14036**
Duke Ellington appeared in *Check and Double Check*.
Fred Astaire appeared in *Three Little Words*.

THREE O'CLOCK IN THE MORNING   1922
Dorothy Terriss / Julian Robledo
B. Feldman & Co. Ltd .... USA
Show(s): .... Greenwich Village Follies of 1921
Film(s):Margie / Belles on Their Toes / The Eddy Duchin Story /
Presenting Lily Mars
Paul Whiteman & his Orchestra .... **HMV B 1420**
Ted Lewis & his Band .... **Brunswick 02756**
Vaughn Monroe .... **RCA RD 27049**
The Andrews Sisters .... **Brunswick 04034**
Judy Garland .... **Caliban 6038**
Judy Garland appeared in *Presenting Lily Mars*.

THREE POTS A SHILLING (See When The Summer Comes Again)

THREE STARS   June 1959
Tommy Dee
Campbell Connelly & Co. Ltd .... USA
Ruby Wright .... **Parlophone R 4556**
Tommy Dee .... **Melodisc 1516**

THREE STARS WILL SHINE TONIGHT   July 1962
Hal Winn / Gerry Goldsmith
Robbins Music Corporation Ltd. .... USA
Richard Chamberlain .... **MGM 1160**
Based on the theme of the TV series 'Doctor Kildare'.
Richard Chamberlain appeared in *Doctor Kildare*.

THREE STEP TO HEAVEN   June 1960
Eddie Cochran
Palace Music Ltd .... USA
Eddie Cochran .... **London HAG 2267**
Showaddywaddy (1975) .... **Bell 1426**

THREE TIMES A LADY   September 1978
Lionel Richie
Jobete Music (UK) Ltd. .... USA
The Commodores .... **Motown TMG 1113**

THREE'S A CROWD   1932
Harry Warren / Al Dubin / Irving Kahal
B. Feldman & Co. Ltd. .... USA
Film(s): .... The Crooner
Rudy Vallee & his Connecticut Yankees .... **Columbia CB 548**
Diana Clare .... **HMV B 4280**
Pee Wee Hunt & his Band .... **Capitol CL 14090**

THRILL IS GONE, THE   1932
Lew Brown / Ray Henderson
Victoria Music Co. Ltd. .... USA
Show(s): .... George White's Scandals of 1931
Film(s): .... The Best Things in Life are Free
Dinah Shore .... **Columbia DB 2284**
Carmen McRae .... **London HAR 2185**

THRILLER   December 1983
Rodney Temperton
Rondor Music .... UK
Michael Jackson .... **Epic A 3643**

THROUGH THE BARRICADES   November 1986
Gary Kemp
Reformation Music .... UK
Spandau Ballet .... **Reformation SPANS 1**

THROUGH THE YEARS   1937
Vincent Youmans / Edward Heyman
Campbell Connelly & Co. Ltd. .... USA
Show(s): .... Through the Years
Film(s): .... Smiling Through
Nelson Eddy .... **HMV DA 1520**
Eileen Farrell .... **Columbia 33CX 1553**

THROW DOWN A LINE   October 1969
Hank B. Marvin
Shadows Music Ltd. .... UK
Cliff Richard & Hank Marvin .... **Columbia DB 8615**

THUNDER IN THE MOUNTAINS   October 1981
Toyah Wilcox / Adrian Lee / Nigel Glockler
D.J.M. Music .... UK
Toyah .... **Safari SAFE 38**

TI-PI-TIN   1938
Maria Grever / Raymond Leveen
Robbins Music Corporation Ltd. .... Mexico
The Horace Heidt Orchestra .... **Vocalion 580**
Benny Goodman & his Orchestra .... **HMV B 8777**
The Andrews Sisters .... **Brunswick 02592**
The Andrews Sisters .... **Capitol LCT 6132**
Will Glahe & his Orchestra .... **Decca LF 1133**

TICKET TO RIDE   April 1965
John Lennon / Paul McCartney
Northern Songs Ltd .... UK
The Beatles .... **Parlophone R 5265**

TICKLE TOE, THE 1917
Otto Harbach / Louis Hirsch
B. Feldman & Co. Ltd. . . . . USA
Show(s): . . . . Going Up
Majorie Gordon & Henry De Bray . . . . **HMV 03614**
Majorie Gordon & Henry De Bray appeared in the British production of *Going Up*.

TICO TICO 1943
Zeguinha Abreu / Aloysio Oliviera / Ervin Drake
Southern Music Publishing Ltd . . . . Brazil
Film(s): Saludos Amigos (Cartoon) / Bathing Beauty / Copacabana
Ethel Smith (organ) . . . . **Brunswick LAT 8134**
The Andrews Sisters . . . . **Brunswick 03543**
Xavier Cugat & his Orchestra . . . . **Fontana TFL 5020**
Carmen Miranda . . . . **Brunswick 03588**
Dorothy Collins . . . . **Vogue LVA 9058**
Ethel Smith & Xavier Cugat appeared in *Bathing Beauty*.
Carmen Miranda appeared in *Copacabana*.

TIDE IS HIGH, THE December 1980
John Holt
Sparta Music Ltd . . . . UK
Blondie . . . . **Chrysalis CHS 2465**

TIE A STRING AROUND YOUR FINGER 1925
Vincent Youmans
Chappell & Co. Ltd. . . . . USA
Show(s): . . . . Mercenary Mary
June . . . . **Columbia 3809**
The Columbia Vocal Gems Orchestra . . . . **Columbia 9067**
Kathlyn Hilliard . . . . **HMV B 2195**
June appeared in the British production of *Mercenary Mary*.

TIE A YELLOW RIBBON May 1973
Irwin Levine / L. Russell Brown
Schroeder Music Ltd. . . . . USA
Dawn . . . . **Bell BELL 1287**

TIE ME KANGAROO DOWN SPORT September 1960
Rolf Harris
Ardmore & Beechwood Ltd . . . . Australia
Rolf Harris . . . . **Columbia DB 4483**

TIGER FEET February 1974
Mike Chapman / Nicky Chinn
Chinnichap Music . . . . UK
Mud . . . . **Rak 166**
Ivor Novello Award.

TIGER RAG 1919
"The Original Dixieland Jazz Band"
Herman Darewski Music Publishing Co. Ltd. . . . . USA
Film(s):Is Everybody Happy / The Big Broadcast / Birth of the Blues / Has Anybody Seen My Gal
The Original Dixieland Jazz Band . . . . **HMV B 8466**
Ted Lewis & his Band . . . . **Columbia 4309**
The Mills Brothers . . . . **Brunswick LAT 8728**
Kid Ory's Creole Jazz Band . . . . **Columbia 33CX 10134**
Harry Roy Band . . . . **Parlophone R 1505**
Ted Lewis appeared in *Everybody Happy*.
The Mills Brothers appeared in *The Big Broadcast*.

TIGGERTY BOO 1940
Hal Halifax
Peter Maurice Music Co. Ltd . . . . UK
Harry Roy & his band . . . . **Regal Zonphone MR 3335**
Elsie Carlisle . . . . **Rex 9847**

TILL October 1957
Carl Sigman / Charles Danvers
Chappell & Co. Ltd . . . . USA
Jane Morgan . . . . **London HAR 2110**
Colin Day . . . . **Parlophone PMC 1130**
Roger Williams & his Orchestra . . . . **London HLR 8516**
Tom Jones (1971) . . . . **Decca F 13236**

TILL ALL OUR DREAMS COME TRUE April 1949
H.C. Bonocini / Desmond O'Connor
Lawrence Wright Music Co. Ltd . . . . UK
Joe Loss & his Orchestra . . . . **HMV BD 6044**
Rita Williams . . . . **Columbia FB 3484**
Dick James . . . . **Decca F 9163**

'TIL I KISSED YOU October 1959
Don Everly
Acuff-Rose Publishing Co. Ltd . . . . USA
The Everly Brothers . . . . **london HLA 8934**

TILL I WALTZ AGAIN WITH YOU March 1953
Sidney Prosen
Francis, Day & Hunter Ltd . . . . USA
Jimmy Young . . . . **Decca F 10069**
Russ Morgan & his Orchestra . . . . **Brunswick LA 8662**
Teresa Brewer . . . . **Vogue LVA 9126**

TILL STARS FORGET TO SHINE 1944
Joe Lubin / Sonny Miller / Hugh Charles
Noel Gay Music Co. Ltd . . . . UK
Ambrose & his Orchestra . . . . **Decca F 8465**
Leslie Hutchinson (Hutch) . . . . **HMV BD 1087**

TILL THE CLOUDS ROLL BY 1919
Jerome Kern / P.G. Wodehouse
Francis, Day & Hunter Ltd. . . . . USA
Show(s): . . . . Oh Boy / Oh Joy
Film(s): . . . . Till the Clouds Roll By
Tom Powers & Beatrice Lillie . . . . **Columbia L 1285**
Bing Crosby . . . . **Brunswick LA 8505**
Mel Tormé . . . . **London HAN 2016**
Tom Powers & Beatrice Lillie appeared in *Oh Joy*.

TILL THE END OF THE DAY February 1966
Ray Davies
Belinda (London) Ltd. . . . . UK
The Kinks . . . . **Pye 7N 15981**

TILL THE END OF TIME 1946
Buddy Kaye / Ted Mossman
Campbell Connelly & Co. Ltd. USA
Film(s): . . . . Till the End of Time
Perry Como . . . . **RCA RD 27100**
Dick Haymes . . . . **Brunswick 03638**
Ed Townsend . . . . **Capitol T 1140**
Adapted from the 'Polonaise in A Flat Major, Opus 53 No.6' by Frederic Chopin (1810 - 1849).

TILL THE LIGHTS OF LONDON SHINE AGAIN 1940
Tommie Connor / Eddie Pola
B. Feldman & Co. Ltd . . . . UK
Lew Stone & his Band . . . . **Decca F 7296**
Vera Lynn . . . . **Decca F 7324**
Phyllis Robins . . . . **Parlophone F 1618**

TILL THE SANDS OF THE DESERT GROW COLD 1911
George Graff / Ernest Ball
B. Feldman & Co. Ltd. . . . . USA
Peter Dawson . . . . **HMV B 3023**
Robert Howe . . . . **Edison Bell Winner 2663**

TILL THEN 1946
Guy Wood / Eddie Seiler / Sol Marcus
Pickwick Music Ltd. . . . . USA
The Mills Brothers . . . . **Brunswick 03639**
The Four Knights . . . . **Capitol EAP 1-506**
The Mills Brothers . . . . **London HAD 2192**
The Barry Sisters . . . . **Decca F 11118**

TILL THERE WAS YOU June 1961
Meredith Wilson
Frank Music Co. Ltd . . . . USA
Show(s): . . . . Music Man
Film(s): . . . . Music Man
Robert Preston & Barbara Cook . . . . **Capitol W 990**
Van Johnson & Patricia Lambert . . . . **HMV CLP 1444**
Shirley Jones . . . . **Warner Brothers WM 4066**
The Beatles . . . . **Parlophone PCS 7214**
Robert Preston appeared in the American production of and the film of *Music Man*.
Barbara Cook appeared in the American production of *Music Man*
Van Johnson & Patricia Lambert appeared in the British prodution of *Music Man*
Shirley Jones appeared in the film of *Music Man*.

TILL THEY'VE ALL GONE HOME June 1953
Bob Hilliard / Alex Alstone
Edwin H. Morris & Co. Ltd . . . . USA
Alma Cogan . . . . **HMV B 10505**
Joan Regan . . . . **Decca DFE 6278**

Monty Norman . . . . Columbia DB 3305

TILL WE MEET AGAIN   **1918**
Richard A. Whiting / Egan
B. Feldman & Co. Ltd . . . . USA
Film(s): . . . . On Moonlight Bay / The Eddy Duchin Story
Herbert Payne . . . . **Zonophone 1944**
Florrie Forde . . . . **Rex 8222**
The Mills Brothers . . . . **Brunswick 04452**
Doris Day . . . . **Philips BBL 7175**
The Mills Brothers . . . . **London HAD 2250**
Mitch Miller & The Gang . . . . **Philips BBL 7528**
Doris Day appeared in *Moonlight Bay*.

TIME   **August 1961**
Buddy Kaye / Philip Springer
Edwin H. Morris & Co. Ltd. . . . . USA
Craig Douglas . . . . **Top Rank JAR 569**

TIME (Clock Of The Heart)   **December 1982**
George O'Dowd / Jonathan Moss
Virgin Music . . . . UK
Culture Club . . . . **Virgin VS 558**

TIME AFTER TIME   **1947**
Jule Styne / Sammy Cahn
Chappell & Co. Ltd. . . . . USA
Film(s): . . . . It Happened in Brooklyn
Frank Sinatra . . . . **Philips BBL 7168**
Tony Bennett . . . . **Philips BBL 7280**
Valerie Carr . . . . **Columbia 33S 1137**
Debbie Reynolds . . . . **London HAD 2200**
Frank Sinatra appeared in *It Happened in Brooklyn*.

TIME AFTER TIME   **July 1984**
Cyndi Lauper / Robert Hyman
EMI Music . . . . USA
Cyndi Lauper . . . . **Epic A 4290**

TIME DRAGS BY   **November 1966**
Hank B. Marvin / Bruce Welch / John Rostill & Brian Bennett
Shadows Music Ltd. . . . . UK
Cliff Richard . . . . **Columbia DB 8017**
Ivor Novello Nomination.

TIME HAS COME, THE   **December 1961**
Les Vandyke
Downbeat Publishing Co. Ltd. . . . . UK
Film(s): . . . . What a Whopper
Adam Faith . . . . **Parlophone R 4837**
Adam Faith appeared in *What a Whopper*.

TIME IS TIGHT   **July 1969**
Booker T. Jones
Famous-Chappell . . . . USA
Film(s): . . . . Uptight
Booker T. & The M.G.'s . . . . **Stax 119**

TIME MAY CHANGE   **July 1948**
Leigh Stafford / Hugh Wade
Campbell Connelly & Co. Ltd. . . . . UK
Show(s): . . . . Maid to Measure
Anne Shelton . . . . **Decca F 8898**
Archie Lewis . . . . **Parlophone F 2294**
Rita Williams . . . . **Columbia FB 3407**
Joe Loss Orchestra . . . . **HMV BD 6015**

TIME OF MY LIFE   **November 1987**
Frank Previte / John De Nicola / Donald Markowitz
EMI Music Ltd. . . . . USA
Film(s): . . . . Dirty Dancing
Bill Medley & Jennifer Warnes . . . . **RCA PB 49625**
Academy Award Winning Song 1987.

TIME ON MY HANDS   **1931**
Vincent Youmans / Harold Adamson / Mack Gordon
Campbell Connelly & Co. Ltd . . . . USA
Show(s): . . . . Smiles / One Girl
Film(s): . . . . Look For the Silver Lining / The Eddy Duchin Story
The New Mayfair Dance Orchestra . . . . **HMV B 5983**
Eddy Duchin (piano) . . . . **Philips BBL 7081**
Ray Noble & his Orchestra . . . . **Encore ENC 140**
Ronnie Hilton . . . . **HMV DLP 1109**
The Mills Brothers . . . . **London HAD 2250**

TIME WAITS FOR NO ONE   **1944**
Charles Tobias / Cliff Friend
B. Feldman & Co. Ltd. . . . . USA
Film(s): . . . . Shine on Harvest Moon
Helen Forrest . . . . **Brunswick 03559**
Geraldo & his Orchestra, vocal Len Camber . . **Parlophone F 2044**
Tony Brent . . . . **Columbia 33S 1125**

TIME WARP, THE   **September 1989**
Des Tong
Druidcrest Music . . . . UK
Damian . . . . **Jive JIVE 209**

TIME WAS (Duerme)   **1941**
Miguel Prado / Gabriel Luna / Bob Russell
Southern Music Publishing Co. Ltd . . . . Mexico
Ambrose & his Orchestra, vocal Sam Browne . . **Decca F 8086**
Jimmy Dorsey & his Orchestra,
vocal Bob Eberly & Helen O'Connell . . . . **Brunswick 03274**
The Four Freshmen . . . . **Capitol T 1074**
Bob Eberly & Helen O'Connell . . . . . **Warner Brothers WM 4033**
This song has the same melody as *Dreaming*.

TIME'S A WASTIN'   **1943**
Duke Ellington
Campbell Connelly & Co. Ltd . . . . USA
Film(s): . . . . Cabin in the Sky
Duke Ellington & his Orchestra . . . . **HMV B 9456**
Ted Heath & his Music . . . . **Decca F 8856**
Duke Ellington appeared in *Cabin in the Sky*.

TIMES THEY ARE A-CHANGIN', THE   **April 1965**
Bob Dylan
Blossom Music Ltd . . . . USA
Bob Dylan . . . . **CBS 201 751**

TIN SOLDIER   **January 1968**
Steve Marriott / Ronnie Lane
United Artists Music . . . . UK
The Small Faces . . . . **Immediate IM 062**

TINA   **1934**
Will Grosz / Hamilton Kennedy
Peter Maurice Music Co. Ltd . . . . UK
Primo Scala's Accordion Band . . . . **Rex 8337**
Frank Chacksfield & his Orchestra . . . . **Decca LK 4168**

TING-A-LING (The Waltz of the Bells)   **1927**
Jack Little / Andy Britt
B. Feldman & Co. Ltd. . . . . USA
The Piccadilly Revels Band . . . . **Columbia 4550**
Jesse Crawford (Organ) . . . . **HMV B 2401**
Gordon MacRae . . . . **Capitol CL 13189**

TIP OF MY FINGER, THE   **November 1970**
Bill Anderson
London Tree . . . . USA
Des O'Connor . . . . **Columbia DB 8713**
Eddy Arnold . . . . **RCA 1539**

TIP-TOE THROUGH THE TULIPS   **1930**
Al Dubin / Joe Burke
B. Feldman & Co. Ltd . . . . USA
Film(s):Gold Diggers of Broadway / Confidential Agent / Painting the
Clouds With Sunshine
Solemn & Gay . . . . **Regal Zonophone T 5496**
Layton & Johnstone . . . . **Columbia 5708**
Nick Lucas . . . . **Decca DEA 7-1**
The Midnight Minstrels . . . . **Regal Zonophone G 9452**
Edna Savage & Michael Holliday . . . . **Columbia SEG 7836**
Gisele MacKenzie . . . . **RCA RD 27033**
Dorothy Provine . . . . **Warner Brothers WM 4053**
Tiny Tim . . . . **Reprise RS 23258**
Nick Lucas appeared in *Gold Diggers of Broadway*.

TIRED OF BEING ALONE   **November 1971**
Al Green
Burlington Music Co. Ltd . . . . USA
Al Green . . . . **London HLU 10337**

TIRED OF WAITING FOR YOU   **February 1965**
Ray Davies
Edward Kassner Music Co. Ltd . . . . UK
The Kinks . . . . **Pye 7N 15759**

TIS THE LAST ROSE OF SUMMER (See Last Rose Of Summer)

TO A WILD ROSE   1896
Edward MacDowell
.... UK
Patricia Rossborough .... Parlophone F 669
Neddle Nash .... Columbia DB 1365
Julie Andrews .... RCA RD 27061
Andre Kostelanetz .... Columbia 33SX 1004
Part of the suite 'Woodland Sketches' opus 51 for piano.

TO BE LOVED   May 1958
Tyran Carlo / Berry Gordy Jnr. / Gwen Gordy
Duchess Music .... USA
Jackie Wilson .... Coral Q 72306
Malcolm Vaughan .... HMV POP 459
Ronnie Carroll .... Philips PB 801

TO BE OR NOT TO BE   June 1980
B.A. Robertson / Terry Britten
Myaxe Music .... UK
B.A. Robertson .... Asylum K 12449

TO BE WITH YOU AGAIN   May 1987
Mark King / Rowland Gould
Chappell Music Co. .... UK
Level 42 .... Polydor POSP 855

TO BE WORTHY OF YOU   May 1952
Ray Klages / Walter Gross
Dash Music Ltd .... USA
Frankie Laine .... Columbia 33S 1047
Alma Cogan .... HMV B 10280
Dorothy Squires .... Columbia DB 3086

TO BE YOUNG GIFTED AND BLACK   April 1970
Nina Simone / Weldon Irvine
Essex Music Ltd. .... USA
Bob & Marcia .... Harry J HJ 6605
Nina Simone .... RCA 1903

TO CUT A LONG STORY SHORT   December 1980
Gary Kemp
Reformation Music .... UK
Spandau Ballet .... Chrysalis CHS 2473

TO EACH HIS OWN   1946
Jay Livingston / Ray Evans
Victoria Music Co. Ltd. .... USA
The Ink Spots .... Brunswick OE 9426
The Platters .... Mercury AMT 1118
Tony Martin .... Mercury MPT 7005
Pat Boone .... London HAD 2127

TO KEEP MY LOVE ALIVE   1944
Richard Rodgers / Lorenz Hart
Chappell & Co. Ltd. .... USA
Show(s): .... A Connecticut Yankee (Revival)
Ella Fitzgerald .... HMV CLP 1116
Jim Lowe .... London HAD 2146

TO KNOW HIM IS TO LOVE HIM   February 1959
Phil Spector
Bourne Music Ltd .... USA
The Teddy Bears .... London HLU 8733
Evelyn Kingsley .... Capitol CL 14944
Emile Ford .... Pye NPL 18049
See also *To Know You Is To Love You.*

TO KNOW YOU IS TO LOVE YOU   July 1965
Phil Spector
Bourne Music Ltd .... USA
Peter & Gordon .... Columbia DB 7617
See also *To Know Him Is To Love Him.*

TO LOVE SOMEBODY   February 1969
Barry Gibb / Robin Gibb
Abigail Music .... UK
The Bee Gees .... Polydor 583012
Nina Simone .... RCA 1779
Jimmy Somerville (1990) .... London LON 281

TO MARY WITH LOVE   1937
Mack Gordon / Harry Revel

Francis, Day & Hunter Ltd. .... USA
Film(s): .... To Mary With Love
Eddy Duchin & his Orchestra .... HMV BD 5143
Geraldo & his Orchestra, vocal Cyril Grantham . Decca F 6250
Denny Dennis .... HMV BD 398

TO THE LAND OF MY OWN ROMANCE   1911
Victor Herbert / Harry B. Smith
B.Feldman & Co. Ltd .... USA
Show(s): .... The Enchantress
Film(s): .... The Great Victor Herbert
Richard Tauber .... Parlophone RO 20393
John McHugh .... Columbia FB 2870

TO WHOM IT CONCERNS   December 1965
Chris Andrews
Glissando Music Ltd .... UK
Chris Andrews .... Decca F 22285

TO-KAY   1929
Noel Coward
Chappell & Co. Ltd .... UK
Show(s): .... Bitter Sweet
Film(s): .... Bitter Sweet
The Columbia Light Opera Company .... Columbia 9900
Nelson Eddy .... Columbia DB 2022
John Hauxvell .... HMV CLP 1242
Nelson Eddy appeared in the 1940 film of *Bitter Sweet.*

TOBACCO ROAD   August 1964
John D. Loudermilk
Southern Music Publishing Co. Ltd .... USA
Frank Ifield .... Columbia DB 4658
The Nashville Teens .... Decca F 11930
John D. Loudermilk .... RCA RD 7515

TOCCATA   May 1980
Traditional, arranged by Kevin Peek
United Artists Music Co. Ltd .... UK
Sky .... Ariola ARO 300

TODAY I FEEL SO HAPPY   1931
Paul Abrahams / Desmond Carter / Frank Eyton
Chappell & Co. Ltd. .... Germany
Film(s): .... Sunshine Susie
Renata Muller .... Columbia DB 687
Jack Payne & The BBC Dance Orchestra,
vocal Jack Payne .... Columbia CB 356
Renata Muller appeared in *Sunshine Susie.*

TOGETHER   1928
Buddy De Sylva / Lew Brown / Ray Henderson
Campbell Connelly & Co. Ltd. .... USA
Film(s): .. Since You Went Away / The Best Things In Life Are Free
Melville Gideon .... HMV B 2741
Layton & Johnstone .... Columbia 4898
Dick Haymes & Helen Forrest (1945) .... Brunswick 03552
Betty Johnson .... London HAE 2163
Connie Francis (1961) .... MGM 1138
P.J. Proby (1964) .... Decca F 11967

TOGETHER FOREVER   March 1988
Mike Stock / Matt Aitken / Peter Waterman
All Boys Music .... UK
Rick Astley .... RCA PB 41817

TOGETHER IN ELECTRIC DREAMS   November 1984
Giorgio Moroder / Phil Oakey
Virgin Music .... UK
Film(s): .... Electric Dreams
Giorgio Moroder & Phil Oakey .... Virgin VS 713

TOGETHER WE ARE BEAUTIFUL   March 1980
Ken Leray
Brampton Music .... UK
Fern Kinney .... WEA K 7911

TOGETHERNESS   November 1960
Russ Faith
Debmar Music Ltd .... USA
Mike Preston .... Decca F 11287
Frankie Avalon .... HMV POP 794

TOKOLOSHE MAN   December 1971
John Kongos
Tapestry Music .... UK
John Kongos .... **Fly BUG 14**

TOKYO MELODY   November 1964
Helmut Zacharias / Heinz Hellmer / Lionel Bart
Francis, Day & Hunter Ltd .... Germany
Bert Weedon (guitar) .... **HMV POP 1355**
Helmut Zacharias & his Orchestra .... **Polydor NH 52341**

TOM DOOLEY   January 1959
Traditional
An edition by Essex Music Ltd .... USA
Lonnie Donegan .... **Pye NPT 19032**
The Kingston Trio .... **Capitol CL 14951**

TOM HARK   April 1958
Rupert Bopape
Southern Music Publishing Co. Ltd .... South Africa
Elias & his Zig Zag Jive Flutes .... **Columbia 33SX 1099**
Ted Heath & his Music .... **Decca F 11025**
The Pirhanas (1980) .... **Sire SIR 4044**
Theme of the television series *The Killing Game*.

TOM PILLIBI   June 1960
Pierre Cour / Andre Popp / Marcel Stellman
Chappell & Co. Ltd .... France
Jacqueline Boyer .... **Columbia 33SX 1259**
Julie Andrews .... **Decca F 11230**
French entry for the 1960 Eurovision Song Contest (Placed first).

TOM'S DINER   August 1990
Suzanne Vega
Rondor Music .... USA
D.N.A. featuring Suzanne Vega .... **A&M AM 592**

TOM-TOM TURNAROUND   August 1971
Mike Chapman / Micky Chinn
Chinnichap Music .... UK
The New World .... **Rak 117**

TOMBOY   April 1959
Joe Farrell / Jim Conway
John Fields Music Co. Ltd .... USA
Perry Como .... **RCA 1111**

TOMORROW   February 1955
Peter Hart / Bob Geraldson
Cavendish Music Co. Ltd. .... USA
Johnny Brandon .... **Nixa NEP 24003**
Max Bygraves .... **HMV 7EG 8123**
Lita Roza .... **Decca F 10479**

TOMORROW   March 1966
Chris Andrews
Glissando Music Ltd. .... UK
Sandie Shaw .... **Pye 7N 17036**

TOMORROW (I'LL BE IN MY DIXIE HOME AGAIN)   1924
Roy Turk / J. Russel Robinson
B. Feldman & Co. Ltd. .... USA
The Great White Way Orchestra .... **HMV B 1458**
The Harry Wood Dance Band .... **Regal G 7956**

TOMORROW NIGHT   March 1971
Vincent Crane
Westminster Music .... UK
Atomic Rooster .... **B&C CB 131**

TOMORROW'S JUST ANOTHER DAY   March 1983
Carl Smith / Michael Barson
Warner brothers Music .... UK
Madness .... **Stiff BUY 169**

TONIGHT   August 1961
Leonard Bernstein / Stephen Sondheim
Chappell & Co. Ltd. .... USA
Show(s): .... West Wide Story
Film(s): .... West Wide Story
Larry Kert & Carol Lawrence .... **CBS BPG 62060**
Marlys Watters & Don McKay .... **HMV 7EG 8429**
Marni Nixon & Jim Bryant .... **CBS BPG 62058**
Shirley Bassey .... **Columbia DB 4777**
Andy Williams .... **CBS AAG 20014**

Larry Kert & Carol Lawrence appeared in the American production of *West Side Story*.
Marlys Watters & Don McKay appeared in the British production of *West Side Story*.
Richard Beymer & Natalie Wood appeared in the film of *West Side Story* (singing voices dubbed by Marni Nixon & Jim Bryant).

TONIGHT   August 1971
Roy Wood
Roy Wood Music .... UK
The Move .... **Harvest HAR 5038**

TONIGHT   August 1974
Wayne Bickerton / Tony Waddington
A.T.V. Music Ltd. .... UK
The Rubettes .... **Polydor 2058499**

TONIGHT   September 1990
Maurice Starr / Alfredo Lancellotti
EMI Music .... USA
New Kids On The Block .... **CBS BLOCK 7**

TONIGHT I CELEBRATE MY LOVE   September 1983
Michael Masser / Gerald Goffin
Rondor Music .... USA
Peabo Bryson & Roberta Flack .... **Capitol CL 302**

TONIGHT I'M YOURS   November 1981
Rod Stewart / Jim Cregan / Kevin Savigar
Warner Brothers Music .... USA
Rod Stewart .... **Riva 33**

TONIGHT WE LOVE   1941
Ray Austin / Bobby Worth / Freddy Martin
Campbell Connelly & Co. .... USA
Freddy Martin Orchestra .... **HMV B 9694**
Tony Martin .... **Decca F 8205**
Caterina Valente .... **RCA RD 27240**
Lawrence Welk Orchestra .... **Coral Q 9111**
Adapted from the Piano Concerto no.1 in B flat minor, opus 23 by Peter Ilyich Tchaikovsky (1840-1893).

TONIGHT YOU BELONG TO ME   1927
Billy Rose / Lee David
B. Feldman & Co. Ltd. .... USA
The Tennessee Ramblers .... **Regal Zonophone ME 2**
Kay Starr .... **Capitol T 1468**
Frankie Laine .... **Columbia DB 3239**
Patience & Prudence (1956) .... **London HLU 8321**

TONIGHT'S MY NIGHT WITH BABY   1926
Irving Caesar / Joseph Meyer / Bobby Buttenuth
Francis, Day & Hunter Ltd. .... USA
Jack Smith .... **HMV B 2337**

TONIGHT'S THE NIGHT   July 1976
Rod Stewart
Riva Music .... UK
Rod Stewart .... **Riva 3**

TONY FROM AMERICA   1910
Lionel Monckton / Arthur Wimperis
Chappell & Co. Ltd .... UK
Show(s): .... The Quaker Girl
Gertie Millar .... **HMV C 530**
Celia Lipton .... **Columbia DB 2146**
Gertie Millar appeared in the British production of *The Quaker Girl*.

TOO BEAUTIFUL TO LAST   April 1972
Richard Rodney Bennett / Paul Francis Webster
Screen Gems Music Ltd .... USA
Engelbert Humperdinck .... **Decca F 13281**

TOO BUSY THINKING ABOUT MY BABY   September 1969
Norman Whitfield / Janie Bradford
Jobete Music (UK) Ltd. .... USA
Marvin Gaye .... **Tamla Motown TMG 705**
The Temptations .... **Tamla Motown TML 11035**
Mardi Gras (1972) .... **Bell 1226**

TOO CLOSE FOR COMFORT   May 1957
Jerry Bock / Larry Holofcener / George Weiss
Valando Music Co. Ltd. .... USA
Show(s): .... Mr. Wonderful
Sammy Davis .... **Brunswick LAT 8184**

Yana . . . . **HMV POP 340**
Peggy Lee . . . . **Capitol T 1401**
Sammy Davis appeared in *Mr. Wonderful*.

TOO DARN HOT   April 1951
Cole Porter
Chappell & Co. Ltd . . . . USA
Show(s): . . . . Kiss Me Kate
Film(s): . . . . Kiss Me Kate
Lorenzo Fuller, Fred Davis & Eddie Sledge . . **Philips BBL 7224**
Archie Savage . . . . **Columbia DX 1741**
Ann Miller . . . . **MGM C 753**
Lorenzo Fuller, Fred Davis & Eddie Sledge appeared in the American production of *Kiss Me Kate*.
Archie Savage appeared in the British production of *Kiss Me Kate*.
Ann Miller appeared in the film *Kiss Me Kate*.

TOO FAT POLKA   March 1948
Ross MacLean / Arthur Richardson
Francis, Day & Hunter Ltd. . . . . USA
Arthur Godfrey . . . . **Columbia DB 2397**
The Andrews Sisters . . . . **Brunswick 03841**

TOO GOOD TO BE FORGOTTEN   December 1974
Eugene Record / Barbara Acklin
Intersong Music . . . . USA
The Chi-Lites . . . . **Brunswick BR 13**
Amazulu (1986) . . . . **Island IS 284**

TOO HOT TO HANDLE   June 1977
Rodney Temperton
Rondor Music (London) Ltd . . . . UK
Heatwave . . . . **GTO GT 91**

TOO LATE FOR GOODBYES   November 1984
Julian Lennon
Chappell & Co. . . . . USA
Julian Lennon . . . . **Virgin JL 1**

TOO LATE NOW   June 1951
Alan Jay Lerner / Burton Lane
New World Publishers Ltd . . . . USA
Film(s): . . . . Wedding Bells
Jane Powell . . . . **MGM EP 635**
Billie Anthony . . . . **Columbia DB 4279**
Jimmy Young . . . . **Decca LK 4219**
Jane Powell appeared in *Wedding Bells*.
Nominated for an Academy Award 1951.

TOO MANY BROKEN HEARTS IN THE WORLD   April 1989
Mike Stock / Matt Aitken / Peter Waterman
All Boys Music . . . . UK
Jason Donovan . . . . **PWL PWL 32**
Ivor Novello Award.

TOO MANY IRONS IN THE FIRE   1946
J.S. Black
Campbell Connelly & Co. Ltd. . . . . USA
Lou Preager & his Orchestra,
vocal Paul Rich . . . . **Columbia FB 3260**
The Mills Brothers . . . . **Brunswick 03694**
Roy Fox & his Band,
vocal Jack O'Hagan & Bobby Joy . . . . **Decca F 8718**

TOO MANY RIVERS   September 1965
Harlan Howard
Acuff-Rose Publishing Co. Ltd . . . . USA
Brenda Lee . . . . **Brunswick 05936**

TOO MANY TEARS   1932
Al Dubin / Harry Warren
B. Feldman & Co. Ltd. . . . . USA
Ambrose & his Orchestra . . . . **HMV B 6181**
The Carlyle Cousins . . . . **Columbia DB 977**

TOO MARVELLOUS FOR WORDS   1938
Johnny Mercer / Richard A. Whiting
Chappell & Co. Ltd. . . . . USA
Film(s):Ready, Willing and Able / Young Man of Music / Sunny Side of the Street
Winifred Shaw, Ross Alexander,
Ruby Keeler & Lee Dixon . . . . **RCA ZL 70136**
Bing Crosby . . . . **Brunswick LA 8624**
Doris Day with The Harry James Quintet . **Columbia SEG 7572**
Frank Sinatra . . . . **Capitol LCT 6106**

Jeri Southern . . . . **Brunswick LAT 8100**
Winifred Shaw, Ross Alexander, Ruby Keeler & Lee Dixon appeared in *Ready Willing and Able*.
Doris Day appeared in *Young Man of Music* and *Sunny Side of the Street*.

TOO MUCH   June 1957
Bernard Weinman
Carlin Music . . . . USA
Elvis Presley . . . . **HMV POP 330**

TOO MUCH   August 1989
Matthew Goss / Luke Goss / Nicky Graham
Warner Chappell Music . . . . UK
Bros **CBS0ATOM 7**

TOO MUCH HEAVEN   January 1979
Robin Gibb / Maurice Gibb / Barry Gibb
U.N.I.C.E.F. . . . . UK
The Bee Gees . . . . **RSO 25**
Ivor Novello Nomination.

TOO MUCH TOO LITTLE TOO LATE   May 1978
Nat Kipner / John Vallins
Heath Levy Music Ltd . . . . USA
Johnny Mathis & Deniece Williams . . . . **CBS 6164**

TOO MUCH TOO YOUNG   February 1980
Jerry Dammers
Plangent Visions Music . . . . UK
The Specials . . . . **2-Tone CHSTT 7**

TOO NICE TO TALK TO   January 1981
"The Beat"
Zomba Music . . . . UK
The Beat . . . . **Go Feet FEET 4**

TOO ROMANTIC   1940
Jimmy Monaco / Johnny Burke
Victoria Music Co. Ltd . . . . USA
Film(s): . . . . Road to Singapore
Bing Crosby . . . . **Brunswick Bing 5**
Dorothy Lamour . . . . **HMV 04488**
Tommy Dorsey & his Orchestra,
vocal Frank Sinatra . . . . **Camden CDN 153**
Bing Crosby & Dorothy Lamour appeared in *Road To Singapore*.

TOO SHY   February 1983
Chris Hamill / Stuart Neal / Jeremy Strode / Stephen Asken / Nick Beggs
Tritec Music . . . . UK
Kajagoogoo . . . . **EMI 5359**

TOO SOON TO KNOW   November 1966
Don Gibson
Acuff-Rose Music Ltd. . . . . USA
Roy Orbison . . . . **London HLU 10067**

TOO YOUNG   August 1951
Sidney Lippman / Sylvia Dee
Sun Music Publishing Co. Ltd . . . . USA
Jimmy Young . . . . **Nixa N 15022**
Patty Andrews . . . . **Brunswick 04754**
Nat 'King' Cole . . . . **Capitol EAP 1-20108**
Donny Osmond (1972) . . . . **MGM 2006113**

TOO YOUNG TO GO STEADY   June 1956
Harold Adamson / Jimmy McHugh
Robbins Music Corporation Ltd. . . . . USA
Patti Page . . . . **Mercury MEP 9003**
Nat 'King' Cole . . . . **Capitol EAP 1040**
Anne Shelton . . . . **Philips BBL 7393**

TOO-RA-LOO-RA-LOO-RAL   1914
J.R. Shannon
B. Feldman & Co. Ltd. . . . . USA
Show(s): . . . . Shameen Dhu
Film(s): . . . . Going My Way
Bing Crosby . . . . **Brunswick Bing 8**
Ruby Murray . . . . **Columbia 33S 1079**
Bing Crosby appeared in *Going My Way*.

TOOLIE OOLIE DOOLIE   July 1948
Vaughan Horton / Arthur Beul
Southern Music Publishing Co. Ltd. . . . . Switzerland

Film(s): . . . . Riders of the Whistling Pines
The Andrews Sisters . . . . **Brunswick 03903**
The Five Smith Brothers . . . . **Parlophone F 2303**

TOOR-IE ON HIS BONNET, THE   1947
Noel Gay / George Brown
Clover Music Co. Ltd. . . . . UK
Billy Cotton & his Band . . . . **Rex 10225**
Sandy Glen . . . . **Parlophone F 3365**
Evelyn Knight . . . . **Brunswick LA 8538**

TOOT TOOT TOOTSIE GOODBYE   1923
Gus Kahn / Ernie Erdman / Dan Russo
Francis, Day & Hunter Ltd . . . . USA
Show(s): . . . . Bombo
Film(s):The Jazz Singer / Rose of Washington Square / The Jolson Story / Jolson Sings Again / I'll See You in My Dreams
The Benson Orchestra of Chicago . . . . **HMV B 1456**
Al Jolson . . . . **Brunswick LAT 8322**
Gary Miller . . . . **Pye NPL 18008**
Eydie Gormé . . . . **HMV CLP 1201**
Doris Day . . . . **Caliban 6008**
Al Jolson appeared in *Bombo*, *The Jazz Singer* and *Rose of Washington Square*. Song added to *Bombo* in 1922.
Doris Day appeared in *I'll See You in My Dreams*.

TOP HAT, WHITE TIE AND TAILS   1935
Irving Berlin
Irving Berlin Ltd . . . . USA
Film(s): . . . . Top Hat
Fred Astaire . . . . **Columbia DB 1825**
Ella Fitzgerald . . . . **HMV CLP 1183**
Fred Astaire . . . . **London HAR 2219**
Fred Astaire appeared in *Top Hat*.

TOP OF THE WORLD   November 1973
Richard Carpenter / John Bettis
Rondor Music (London) Ltd. . . . . USA
The Carpenters . . . . **A&M AMS 7086**

TORCH   June 1982
David Ball / Marc Almond
Warner Brothers Music . . . . UK
Soft Cell . . . . **Phonogram BZ 59**

TORERO   June 1958
Renato Carosone / 'Nisa' / Al Hoffman / Dick Manning
Leeds Music Ltd . . . . Italy
Renato Carosone . . . . **Parlophone GEP 8729**
Julius La Rosa . . . . **RCA 1063**
The Andrews Sisters . . . . **Capitol CL 14878**

TORN BETWEEN TWO LOVERS   April 1977
Peter Yarrow / Phillip Jarrell
Leosong Copyright Service Ltd . . . . USA
Mary MacGregor . . . . **Ariola AA 111**

TOSSING AND TURNING   July 1965
John Carter / Ken Lewis / Perry Ford
Southern Music Publishing Co. Ltd . . . . UK
The Ivy League . . . . **Piccadilly 7N 25251**

TOTAL ECLIPSE OF THE HEART   March 1983
Jim Steinman
Lost Boys Music . . . . USA
Bonnie Tyler . . . . **CBS TYLER 1**

TOUCH ME   February 1990
Pietro Rossin / Gianfranca Bortolotti
Supreme Songs . . . . Italy
49 ers . . . . **4th & Broadway BRW 157**

TOUCH ME (I Want Your Body)   April 1986
Mark Shreeve / Jon Astrop
Zomba Music . . . . UK
Samantha Fox . . . . **Jive FOXY 1**

TOUCH ME IN THE MORNING   August 1973
Ron Miller / Mike Masser
Jobete Music (UK) Ltd. . . . . USA
Diana Ross . . . . **Tamla Motown TMG 861**

TOUCH OF TEXAS   1943
Jimmy McHugh / Frank Loesser
Southern Music Publishing Co. Ltd . . . . USA

Film(s): . . . . Seven Days Leave / Moon Over Las Vegas
The Jack Simpson Sextet, vocal Betty Kent . . . . **Rex 10179**

TOUCH OF YOUR HAND, THE   1934
Jerome Kern / Otto Harbach
Chappell & Co. Ltd. . . . . USA
Show(s): . . . . Roberta
Film(s): . . . . Roberta / Lovely to Look at
Paul Whiteman & his Orchestra . . . . **HMV BD 194**
Leo Reisman & his Orchestra,
vocal Bernice Clare . . . . **Brunswick RL 278**
Kitty Carlisle & Alfred Drake . . . . **Brunswick LAT 8005**
Kathryn Grayson & Howard Keel . . . . **MGM D 141**
Sarah Vaughan . . . . **Mercury MPL 6522**
Kathryn Grayson & Howard Keel appeared in *Lovely to Look At.*

TOUCH OF YOUR LIPS   1936
Ray Noble
Campbell Connelly & Co. Ltd . . . . UK
Bing Crosby . . . . **Brunswick 03079**
Ray Noble & his Orchestra . . . . **HMV C 2887**
Sarah Vaughan . . . . **Mercury MPT 7503**
Vic Damone . . . . **Philips BBL 7144**

TOUCH TOO MUCH, A   June 1974
Mike Chapman / Nicky Chinn
Chinnichap Music . . . . UK
The Arrows . . . . **Rak RAK 171**

TOWER OF STRENGTH   December 1961
Burt Bacharach / Bob Hilliard
Chappell & Co. Ltd. . . . . USA
Frankie Vaughan . . . . **Philips PB 1195**
Gene McDaniels . . . . **Liberty LBY 1021**

TOWER OF STRENGTH   February 1988
Craig Adams / Mick Brown / Simon Hinkler & Wayne Hussey
B.M.G. Music . . . . UK
The Mission . . . . **Mercury MYTH 4**

TOWN CALLED MALICE, A   February 1982
Paul Weller
Chappell Music Co. . . . . UK
The Jam . . . . **Polydor POSP 400**

TOY BALLOONS   December 1961
Billy Mure
Jewel Music Publishing Co. Ltd. . . . . USA
Russ Conway (piano) . . . . **Columbia DB 4738**

TOY BOY   September 1987
Mike Stock / Matt Aitken / Peter Waterman
All Boys Music . . . . UK
Sinitta . . . . **Fanfare FAN 12**

TOY DRUM MAJOR, THE   1925
Horatio Nicholls
Lawrence Wright Music Co. Ltd. . . . . UK
The Savoy Orpheans . . . . **HMV B 2031**
The Tuneful Twenties Dance Orchestra . . . **Parlophone R 3045**

TOY SOLDIERS   August 1989
Mitch Miltenberg'Martika'
Famous Music Ltd. . . . . USA
Martika . . . . **CBS 655049**

TOY TOWN   1915
Lionel Monckton / Herman Finck
Chappell & Co. Ltd. . . . . UK
Show(s): . . . . Bric-a-Brac
Gertie Millar . . . . **HMV C 539**
The Palace Theatre Orchestra,
conducted by Herman Finck . . . . **HMV C 607**
Gertie Millar appeared in *Bric-A-Brac.*

TOY TRUMPET   1938
Raymond Scott / Lew Pollack / Sidney Mitchell
Cinephonic Music Co. Ltd. . . . . USA
Film(s): . . . . Rebecca of Sunnybrook Farm
Horace Heidt & his Orchestra . . . . **Vocalion 580**
The Boston Promenade Orchestra . . . . **HMV B 9045**

TOYLAND   1903
Victor Herbert / Glen MacDonough
B. Feldman & Co. Ltd. . . . . USA

Show(s): . . . . .Babes in Toyland
Film(s): . . . . .Babes in Toyland
Rudy Vallee . . . . **Brunswick 02852**
Jo Stafford . . . . **Philips BBL 7100**
Jane Morgan . . . . **London HAR 2136**

TRA LA LA SONG, THE (See Banana Splits)

TRACKS OF MY TEARS, THE   June 1969
Smokey Robinson / Warren Moore / Marv Tarplin
Belinda (London) Ltd. . . . . USA
Smokey Robinson & The Miracles . . . **Tamla Motown TMG 522**
Linda Ronstadt . . . . **Asylum K 13034**

TRACY   January 1970
Lee Pockriss / Paul Vance
Peter Maurice Music Co. Ltd. . . . . USA
The Cuff Links . . . . **MCA MU 1101**

TRADE WINDS   1941
Charles Tobias / Cliff Friend
Chappell & Co. Ltd . . . . USA
Bing Crosby . . . . **Brunswick 03073**
Kate Smith . . . . **Columbia FB 2356**
Tommy Dorsey & his Orchestra . . . . **HMV BD 5645**

TRAGEDY   March 1979
Robin Gibb / Maurice Gibb / Barry Gibb
Chappell & Co. Ltd. . . . . UK
The Bee Gees . . . . **RSO 27**

TRAIL OF THE LONESOME PINE   1913
Ballard MacDonald / Harry Carroll
Francis, Day & Hunter Ltd. . . . . USA
Film(s): . . . . Way Out West
Edna Brown & James Harrison . . . . **HMV 2-4154**
The Rocky Mountaineers . . . . **Columbia FB 1390**
Rex Allen . . . . **Brunswick LAT 8198**
Laurel & Hardy (1975) . . . . **United Artists UP 36026**
Laurel & Hardy appeared in *Way Out West.*

TRAIN OF THOUGHT   May 1986
Pal Waaktaar
A.T.V. Music . . . . UK
A-Ha . . . . **Warner Brothers W 8736**

TRAINS AND BOATS AND PLANES   June 1965
Hal David / Burt Bacharach
Seventeen Savile Row Ltd . . . . USA
Burt Bacharach & his Orchestra & chorus . . . **London HL 9968**
Billy J. Kramer . . . . **Parlophone R 5287**
Anita Harris . . . . **Pye 7N 15868**

TRAMP, TRAMP, TRAMP ALONG THE HIGHWAY   1910
Victor Herbert / Rida Johnson Young
B. Feldman & Co. Ltd . . . . USA
Show(s): . . . . Naughty Marietta
Film(s): . . . . Naughty Marietta
Nelson Eddy . . . . **Fontana TFE 17096**
Gordon MacRae . . . . **Capitol LCT 6114**
Paul Britten & his Orchestra . . . . **MGM C 779**
Nelson Eddy appeared in the film *Naughty Marietta.*

TRANSATLANTIC LULLABY   1939
Diana Morgan / Robert McDermott / Geoffrey Wright
Ascherberg, Hopwood & Crew Ltd. UK
Show(s): . . . . The Gate Revue
Turner Layton . . . . **Columbia FB 2197**
Eve Boswell . . . . **Parlophone R 3394**
Edmund Hockridge . . . . **Pye NPL 18004**

TRAPPED   October 1985
"Colonel Abrams"
MCA Music . . . . USA
Colonel Abrams . . . . **MCA 997**

TRAVELLIN' BAND   May 1970
John Fogerty
Burlington Music Co. Ltd. . . . . USA
Creedence Clearwater Revival . . . . **Liberty LBF 15310**

TRAVELLIN' LIGHT   November 1959
Sid Tepper / Roy C. Bennett
Kalith Music Ltd . . . . USA

Cliff Richard . . . . **Columbia SEG 8050**

TREBLE CHANCE   October 1959
Joe Henderson
Henderson Music Ltd . . . . UK
Joe 'Mr. Piano' Henderson . . . . **Nixa 7N 15224**

TREE IN A PARK, A   1927
Richard Rodgers / Lorenz Hart
Chappell & Co. Ltd. . . . . USA
Show(s): . . . . Peggy Ann
Harry Reser's Syncopaters . . . . **Columbia 4437**
Dorothy Dickson . . . . **Columbia 4540**
Sarah Vaughan . . . . **Mercury MMC 14024**
Dorothy Dickson appeared in the British production of *Peggy Ann.*

TREE IN THE MEADOW, A   February 1948
Billy Reid
Bevan Music Productions Ltd. . . . . UK
Sam Browne . . . . **Decca F 8830**
Dorothy Squires with Orchestra,
conducted by Billy Reid . . . . **Parlophone R 3092**
Al Jolson . . . . **Brunswick LAT 8267**
The Four Preps . . . . **Capitol T 1090**

TREES   1920
Oscar Rasbach / Joyce Kilmer
Chappell & Co. Ltd. . . . . USA
Film(s): . . . . The Big Broadcast
John Morel . . . . **Parlophone R 1236**
Donald Novis . . . . **Columbia DB 1807**
Paul Robeson . . . . **HMV DLP 1155**
Nelson Eddy . . . . **Camden CDN 157**
Helen Traubel . . . . **London HAD 2117**
Donald Novis appeared in *The Big Broadcast.*

TRIBUTE (Right On)   July 1988
Michael Milliner / David Milliner / Peter Wingfield & Andrew Bayfield
Island Music . . . . UK
The Pasadenas . . . . **CBS PASA 1**

TRIPLETS   1953
Howard Dietz / Arthur Schwartz
Chappell & Co. . . . . USA
Show(s): . . . . Between the Devil
Film(s): . . . . The Band Wagon
Fred Astaire, Jack Buchanan & Nanette Fabray . . . **MGM C 752**
Fred Astaire, Jack Buchanan & Nanette Fabray appeared in *The Band Wagon.*

TROLLEY SONG, THE   1944
Hugh Martin / Ralph Blane
Sun Music Publishing Co. Ltd . . . . USA
Film(s): . . . . Meet Me In St.Louis
Judy Garland . . . . **Brunswick LA 8725**
Lou Preager & his Orchestra,
vocal Edna Kaye . . . . **Regal Zonophone MR 3749**
Judy Garland . . . . **Capitol T 1118**
Judy Garland appeared in *Meet Me in St. Louis*
Nominated for an Academy Award 1944.

TROPICAL MAGIC   1942
Mack Gordon / Harry Warren
Cavendish Music Co. ltd . . . . USA
Film(s): . . . . Weekend in Havana
Jimmy Dorsey & his Orchestra,
vocal Bob Eberly . . . . **Brunswick 03274**
Frances Langford . . . . **Brunswick 03322**

TROUBLE   July 1961
Meredith Wilson
Frank Music Ltd. . . . . USA
Show(s): . . . . The Music Man
Film(s): . . . . The Music Man
Robert Preston (US cast) . . . . **Capitol W 990**
Van Johnson (UK cast) . . . . **HMV CLP 1444**
Robert Preston (Sound Track) . . . . . **Warner Brothers WM 4066**
Robert Preston appeared in the American production and the film of
The Music Man.
Van Johnson appeared in the British production of *The Music Man.*

TROUBLE IN PARADISE   1933
Milton Ager / Jean Schwartz / Ned Wever
Lawrence Wright Music Co. Ltd. . . . . USA
Ray Noble & his Orchestra . . . . **HMV B 6394**

Arthur Tracey (The Street Singer) . . . . **Decca F 3637**

TRUCK ON (Tyke)   December 1973
Marc Bolan
Wizard Music . . . . UK
T. Rex . . . . **EMI MARC 6**

TRUCKIN'   1935
Ted Koehler / Rube Bloom
Peter Maurice Music Co. Ltd . . . . USA
Film(s): . . . . The Big Broadcast of 1938
'Fats' Waller & his Rhythm . . . . **HMV BD 262**
Duke Ellington & his Orchestra,
vocal Ivie Anderson . . . . **Columbia SEG 7563**
The King Brothers . . . . **Parlophone PMC 1060**
Mel Tormé . . . . **HMV CLP 1382**

TRUDIE   July 1958
Joe Henderson
Henderson Music Ltd . . . . UK
Joe 'Mr. Piano' Henderson . . . . **Nixa NPT 19032**
Harry Grove & his Music . . . . **Decca F 11050**
Ivor Novello Award.

TRUE   May 1983
Gary Kemp
Reformation Music . . . . UK
Spandau Ballet . . . . **Chrysalis SPAN 1**
Ivor Novello Nomination.

TRUE BLUE   October 1986
Madonna Ciccone / Stephen Bray
Island Music . . . . USA
Madonna . . . . **Sire W 8550**

TRUE COLOURS   October 1986
Tom Kelly / Bill Steinberg
Warner Brothers Music . . . . UK
Cyndi Lauper . . . . **Portrait 6500267**

TRUE FAITH   August 1987
"New Order"
Warner Brothers Music . . . . UK
New Order . . . . **Factory FAC 183**

TRUE LOVE   December 1956
Cole Porter
Chappell & Co. Ltd. . . . . USA
Film(s): . . . . High Society
Bing Crosby & Grace Kelly . . . . **Capitol LCT 6116**
Ronnie Hilton . . . . **HMV 7EG 8198**
Pat Boone . . . . **London HAD 2204**
Bing Crosby & Grace Kelly appeared in *High Society*.
Nominated for an Academy Award 1956.

TRUE LOVE WAYS   May 1965
Norman Petty / Buddy Holly
Southern Music Publishing Co. Ltd . . . . USA
Buddy Holly . . . . **Coral Q 72397**
Peter & Gordon . . . . **Columbia DB 7524**
Cliff Richard (1983) . . . . **EMI 5385**

TRULY   December 1982
Lionel Richie
Brockman Music Co. . . . . USA
Lionel Richie . . . . **Motown TMG 1284**

TRUMPETER, THE   1904
Airlie Dix / Francis Barron
Boosey & Hawkes Music Ltd. . . . . UK
John McCormack . . . . **HMV DB 329**
Peter Dawson . . . . **HMV DLP 1180**
Owen Brannigan . . . . **HMV CLP 3639**

TRUST IN ME   1937
Milton Ager / Jean Schwartz / Ned Wever
Lawrence Wright Music Co. Ltd. . . . . USA
Mildred Bailey & her Orchestra . . . . **Vocalion S 67**
Connee Boswell . . . . **Brunswick 02401**
Eddie Fisher (1952) . . . . **HMV B 10247**
Patti Page . . . . **Mercury MMC 14043**
David Whitfield . . . . **Decca DFE 6601**

TRY A LITTLE TENDERNESS   1933
Harry Woods / James Campbell / Reginald Connelly

Campbell Connelly & Co. Ltd. . . . . UK
Ruth Etting . . . . **Imperial 2840**
Bing Crosby . . . . **Columbia SEG 7522**
Frank Sinatra (1947) . . . . **Fontana TFL 5000**
Jack Payne & his Orchestra . . . . **HMV CLP 1160**
Valerie Carr . . . . **Columbia 33S 1137**

TRY AGAIN JOHNNIE   1902
Lionel Monckton / Adrian Ross
Chappell & Co. Ltd. . . . . UK
Show(s): . . . . A Country Girl
Evie Greene . . . . **HMV GC 3411**
Ann Welch, Norton Collyer & Victor Conway . . . . **Decca F 2554**
Evie Greene appeared in the British production of *Country Girl*.

TU-LI-TULIP TIME   1938
Maria Grever / Jack Lawrence
Sterling Music Publishing Co. Ltd. . . . . Mexico
Roy Smeck & his Hawaiian Serenders,
vocal Donald King . . . . **Rex 9430**
The Andrews Sisters . . . . **Brunswick 02654**
The Andrews Sisters . . . . **Capitol LCT 6132**

TUBBY THE TUBA   May 1948
George Kleinsinger / Paul Tripp
Leeds Music Ltd. . . . . USA
Danny Kaye . . . . **Brunswick OE 9022**

TULANE   September 1977
Chuck Berry
Carlin Music Corporation . . . . USA
The Steve Gibbons Band . . . . **Polydor 2058889**
Chuck Berry . . . . **Contour CN 2019**

TULIPS AND HEATHER   September 1951
Milton Carson
John Fields . . . . USA
Fred Waring & his Pennsylvanians . . . . **Brunswick 04099**
Joe Loss Orchestra . . . . **HMV BD 6110**
Daphne & Benny Lee . . . . **Decca F 9734**
Bob & Alf Pearson . . . . **Parlophone F 2471**

TULIPS FROM AMSTERDAM   May 1958
Ralf Arnie / Gene Martyn
Hans Sikorski Ltd . . . . Germany
Max Bygraves . . . . **Decca DFE 6581**
Vera Lynn . . . . **MGM C 840**

TUMBLING DICE   May 1972
Mick Jagger / Keith Richard
Essex Music Ltd . . . . UK
The Rolling Stones . . . . **Rolling Stones RS 19103**

TUMBLING TUMBLEWEEDS   1941
Bob Nolan
Bradbury Wood Ltd . . . . USA
Film(s):Tumbling Tumbleweeds / Don't Fence Me In / Hollywood Canteen
The Sons of The Pioneers . . . . **Panachord 25925**
Bing Crosby . . . . **Brunswick LAT 8253**
The Sons of The Pioneers . . . . **RCA RD 27016**
The Sons of The Pioneers appeared in *Hollywood Canteen*.
Theme song of The Sons of the Pioneers.

TUNNEL OF LOVE, THE   March 1983
"Fun Boy Three"
Plangent Visions Music . . . . UK
Fun Boy Three . . . . **Chrysalis CHS 2678**

TURN 'ERBERTS FACE TO THE WALL MOTHER   1935
William Ellis / Max Kester / Ronald Hill
Lawrence Wright Music Ltd . . . . UK
Gracie Fields . . . . **Rex 8557**

TURN BACK THE CLOCK   December 1987
Clark Datchler
Virgin Music . . . . UK
Johnny Hates Jazz . . . . **Virgin VS 1017**

TURN BACK THE HANDS OF TIME   February 1952
Jimmy Eaton / Larry Wagner / Con Hammond
Chappell & Co. Ltd . . . . USA
Eddie Fisher . . . . **HMV B 10190**
Jimmy Young . . . . **Polydor P 1035**

TURN IT ON AGAIN   April 1980
Phil Collins / Mike Rutherford / Tony Banks
Hit and Run Music .... UK
Genesis .... **Charisma CB 356**

TURN THE MUSIC UP   April 1979
Laural Dann / Christopher Hills
.... USA
The Players Association .... **Vanguard VS 5001**

TURNING JAPANESE   March 1980
David Fenton
EMI Music Ltd .... UK
The Vapours .... **United Artists BP 334**

TURNTABLE SONG, THE   1947
Leo Robin / Johnny Green
Francis, Day & Hunter Ltd. .... USA
Film(s): .... Something in the Wind
Deanna Durbin .... **Brunswick LAT 8285**
The Andrews Sisters .... **Brunswick 03815**
Deanna Durbin appeared in *Something in the Wind.*

TURTLE POWER   August 1990
James Alpern / Richard Usher
EMI Music .... USA
Film(s) ....Teenage Mutant Ninja Turtles
Partners In Kryme .... **SBK TURTLE 1**

TUSK   November 1979
Lindsey Buckingham
Bright Music Ltd. .... USA
Fleetwood Mac .... **Warner Brothers K 17468**

TUTTI FRUTTI   March 1957
Dorothy La Bostrie / Richard Penniman / Joe Lubin
Burlington Music .... USA
Film(s): .... Don't Knock the Rock
Little Richard .... **London HLO 8366**
Elvis Presley .... **HMV POP 213**
Pat Boone .... **London HLD 8253**
Little Richard appeared in *Don't Knock the Rock.*

TUXEDO JUNCTION   1940
Julian Dash / William Johnson / Erskin Hawkins & Buddy Feyne
Lafleur & Co. Ltd .... USA
Film(s): ....The Glenn Miller Story
Glenn Miller & his Orchestra .... **RCA RD 27068**
Erskin Hawkins & his Orchestra .... **Vogue LVA 9099**
The Andrews Sisters .... **Brunswick 03011**
The Universal International Studio Orchestra . **Brunswick LA 8647**
Quincy Jones & his Orchestra .... **Mercury AMT 1037**
Manhatten Transfer (1976) .... **Atlantic K 10670**
The Universal International Studio Orchestra appeared in *The Glenn Miller Story.*

TWEEDLE DEE   April 1955
Winfield Scott
Robbins Music Ltd. .... USA
Georgia Gibbs .... **Mercury MB 3196**
Frankie Vaughan .... **Philips PB 423**
Jimmy Osmond (1973) .... **MGM 2006 175**

TWEEDLE DEE TWEEDLE DUM   October 1971
Harold Stott / Mario Cupano / Giosy Cupano
Sunbury Music Ltd .... Italy
Middle of the Road .... **RCA PM 3580**

TWELFTH OF NEVER   October 1964
Paul Francis Webster / Jerry Livingston
Frank Music Co. Ltd .... USA
Cliff Richard .... **Columbia DB 7372**
Donny Osmond (1973) .... **MGM 2006 199**

TWELFTH STREET RAG   1921
Euday Bowman
Chappell Music Co. Ltd .... USA
Abe Lyman's Sharps & Flats .... **Brunswick 01340**
'Fats' Waller & his Rhythm .... **HMV BD 262**
Pee Wee Hunt & his Orchestra (1949) ..... **Capitol CL 13002**
Del Wood (piano) .... **RCA RD 27011**

TWELVE O'CLOCK AT NIGHT   1924
Herman Ruby / Lou Hamdman / Billy Rose

Lawrence Wright Music Co. Ltd .... USA
The Savoy Orpheans .... **Columbia 3431**
Phil Green & his Orchestra .... **Decca MW 91**

TWENTIETH CENTURY BLUES   1931
Noel Coward
Chappell & Co. Ltd. .... UK
Film(s): ....Cavalcade
Noel Coward .... **HMV C 2431**
The New Mayfair Dance Orchestra .... **HMV B 4001**
Noel Coward .... **Philips BBL 7167**
Geoff Love & his Orchestra ...... **Columbia 33SX 1060**

TWENTIETH CENTURY BOY   March 1973
Marc Bolan
Wizard Music .... UK
T. Rex. .... **EMI MARC 4**

TWENTY FIVE OR SIX TO FOUR   September 1970
Robert Lamm
Island Music Ltd .... USA
Chicago .... **CBS S 63943**

TWENTY TINY FINGERS   October 1955
Sid Tepper / Roy C. Bennett
Francis, Day & Hunter Ltd. .... USA
Marie Benson .... **Philips PB 512**
The Stargazers .... **Decca LF 1297**
Alma Cogan .... **HMV POP 129**

TWENTY-FOUR HOURS FROM TULSA   January 1964
Hal David / Burt Bacharach
Aaron Schroeder Ltd. .... USA
Gene Pitney .... **United Artists UP 1035**
Dusty Springfield .... **Philips BL 7594**

TWENTY-FOUR HOURS OF SUNSHINE   August 1949
Peter De Rose / Carl Sigman
B. Feldman & Co. Ltd .... USA
Donald Peers .... **HMV B 9801**
Gordon MacRae .... **Capitol CL 13144**

TWILIGHT IN TURKEY   1937
Raymond Scott
Cinephonic Music Co. Ltd. .... USA
Film(s): ....Ali Baba Goes to Town
Tommy Dorsey's Clambake Seven .... **HMV B 8596**
The Raymond Scott Quintet .... **Columbia DB 2300**
Stuff Smith & his Onyx Club Boys .... **Brunswick 02450**
Jack Parnell & his Orchestra ...... **Parlophone GEP 8564**

TWILIGHT ON THE TRAIL   1937
Louis Alter / Sidney Mitchell
Chappell & Co. Ltd. .... USA
Film(s): .... The Trail of the Lonesome Pine
Bing Crosby .... **Brunswick LAT 8253**
Rex Allen .... **Brunswick LAT 8198**
Perry Como .... **RCA RD 27078**

TWILIGHT TIME   1946
Buck Ram / Morty Nevins / Al Nevins & Artie Dunn
Victoria Music Co. Ltd. .... USA
The Three Suns .... **HMV B 9969**
The Buck Ram Orchestra .... **Mercury ZEP 10037**
Jimmy Dorsey & his Orchestra,
vocal Teddy Walters .... **Brunswick 03724**
Andy Williams .... **London HAA 2203**
The Platters (1958) .... **Mercury MT 214**

TWIST AND SHOUT   August 1963
Philip Medley / Bert Russell
Sherwin Music Co. .... USA
Brian Poole & The Tremeloes .... **Decca F 11694**
The Beatles .... **Parlophone GEP 8882**
Salt 'n' Pepa (1988) .... **London FFR 16**

TWIST, THE   January 1962
Hank Ballard
Lois Music Ltd. .... USA
Hank Ballard .... **Parlophone R 4688**
Chubby Checker .... **Columbia DB 4503**
Dion .... **Stateside SL 10034**
The Fat Boys with Chubby Checker (1988) ... **Polydor URB 20**

TWISTIN' THE NIGHT AWAY   April 1962
Sam Cooke
Kags Music Ltd. . . . . USA
Bobby Rydell   **Cameo-Parkway C 1019**
Sam Cooke . . . . **RCA 1277**

TWISTING BY THE POOL   February 1983
Mark Knopfler
Rondor Music . . . . UK
Dire Straits . . . . **Vertigo DSTR 2**

TWIXT TWELVE AND TWENTY   July 1959
Aaron Schroeder / Fredda Gold
Spoone Music Ltd . . . . USA
Pat Boone . . . . **London HLD 8910**

TWO CIGARETTES IN THE DARK   1934
Lew Pollock / Paul Francis Webster
Sterling Music Publishing Co. Ltd . . . . USA
Bing Crosby . . . . **Brunswick 01874**
Layton & Johnstone . . . . **Columbia DB 1449**
Morton Downey . . . . **Rex 8307**
April Ames . . . . **Vogue VA 160152**

TWO DIFFERENT WORLDS   November 1956
Sid Wayne / Al Frisch
Larry Spier Ltd. . . . . USA
Jane Morgan . . . . **London HAR 2086**
Ronnie Hilton . . . . **HMV POP 274**
David Hughes . . . . **Philips PB 642**

TWO FOUR SIX EIGHT MOTORWAY   November 1977
Tom Robinson
Konkwest Music Ltd . . . . UK
The Tom Robinson Band . . . . **EMI 2715**

TWO HEARTS   December 1988
Phil Collins / Lamont Dozier
Hit & Run Music . . . . , . UK
Film(s): . . . . Buster
Phil Collins . . . . **Virgin VS 1141**
Nominated for an Academy Award 1988.
Ivor Novello Award.
Phil Collins appeared in the film *Buster*.

TWO HEARTS IN THREE QUARTER TIME   1931
Robert Stolz / Joe Young
Campbell Connelly & Co. Ltd. . . . . Germany
Film(s): . . . . Two Hearts in Waltz Time
Marek Weber & his Orchestra . . . . **HMV B 6007**
Carl Brisson . . . . **Decca F 3968**
The Vienna State Orchestra,
conducted by Robert Stolz . . . . **RCA RD 27152**

TWO KINDS OF TEARDROPS   June 1963
Del Shannon / Marion McKenzie
Vicki Music Ltd . . . . USA
Del Shannon . . . . **London HL 0710**

TWO LITTLE BLUE BIRDS   1926
Otto Harbach / Jerome Kern / Oscar Hammerstein II
Chappell & Co. Ltd. . . . . USA
Show(s): . . . . Sunny
Film(s): . . . . Sunny
Kitty Reidy & Howett Worster . . . . **Vocalion X 9905**
Elsie Randolph & Claude Hulbert . . . . **Columbia 4140**
Jack Buchanan . . . . **HMV 7EG 8307**
Kitty Reidy & Howett Worster appear in the American production of
Sunny.
Elsie Randolph, Claude Hubert & Jack Buchanan appeared in the
British production of *Sunny*.

TWO LITTLE BOYS   February 1970
Theodore F. Morse / Edward Madden
Herman Darewski Music Publishing Co. Ltd. . . . . USA
Rolf Harris . . . . **Columbia DB 8630**
Slodgenessabounds (1980) . . . . **Deram ROLF 1**
First Published 1903.

TWO LITTLE GIRLS IN BLUE   1894
Charles Graham
Francis, Day & Hunter Ltd. USA
Marie Kendall . . . . **Decca F 5169**
Gerald Adams . . . . **Regal Zonophone MR 57**

TWO OF US, THE   1936
Van Philips / James Campbell / Reginald Connelly
Campbell Connelly & Co. Ltd . . . . UK
Emmie Joyce & Hal Chambers . . . . **Columbia FB 1587**
Doreen Stephens & Alan Kane . . . . **Decca F 9010**

**TWO PINTS OF LAGER AND A PACKET OF CRISPS
PLEASE**   July 1980
Max Splodge
Tony Roberts Music Ltd . . . . UK
Splodgenessabounds . . . . **Deram BUM 1**

TWO SILHOUETTES   1946
Charles Wolcott / Ray Gilbert
Southern Music Publishing Co. Ltd. . . . . USA
Film(s): . . . . Make Mine Music (cartoon)
Dinah Shore . . . . **Columbia DB 2271**

TWO SLEEPY PEOPLE   1939
Hoagy Carmichael / Frank Loesser
Victoria Music Co. Ltd. . . . . USA
Film(s): . . . . Thanks for the Memory
Bob Hope & Shirley Ross . . . . **Brunswick 02697**
Jeri Southern . . . . **Columbia 33SX 1155**
Julie London . . . . **London HAW 2229**
Dean Martin & Line Renaud . . . . . . **Capitol EAP 1-20060**
Bob Hope & Shirley Ross appeared in *Thanks for the Memory*.

TWO STEP, SIDE STEP   December 1954
Murray Wilson
Francis, Day & Hunter Ltd. USA
Bonnie Lou . . . . **Parlophone MSP 6132**
Suzi Miller . . . . **Decca F 10423**

TWO THOUSAND MILES   December 1983
Chrissie Hynde
A.T.V. Music . . . . UK
The Pretenders . . . . **Real ARE 20**

TWO TRIBES   August 1984
Holly Johnson / Peter Gill / Mark O'Toole
Perfect Song . . . . UK
Frankie Goes To Hollywood . . . . **Island ZTAS 3**
Ivor Novello Award.

TZENA, TZENA, TZENA   September 1950
Issach Miron / Julius Grossman / Mitchell Parish
Francis, Day & Hunter Ltd . . . . Israel
The Mitch Miller Orchestra & chorus . . . . . . **Columbia DB 2726**
**Gordon Jenkins & his Orchestra,
vocal The Weavers** . . . . **Brunswick 04552**
The Weavers . . . . **Brunswick 04563**
The Weavers . . . . **Vanguard PPL 11011**

U CAN'T TOUCH THIS   August 1990
Rick James / Alonzo Miller / M.C. Hammer
Jobete Music Ltd. (UK) . . . . USA
M.C. Hammer . . . . **Capitol CL 578**

U GOT THE LOOK   September 1987
"Prince"
Warner Brothers Music . . . . USA
Sheena Easton & Prince . . . . . . **Paisley Park W 8289**

UGLY DUCKLING, THE   January 1953
Frank Loesser
Edwin H. Morris & Co. Ltd . . . . USA
Show(s): . . . . Hans Andersen
Film(s): . . . . Hans Christian Anderson
Danny Kaye . . . . **Brunswick 05031**
Mike Reid . . . . **Pye 7N 45434**
Tommy Steele . . . . **Pye NSPL 18451**
Danny Kaye appeared in *Hans Christian Andersen*.
Tommy Steele appeared in *Hans Andersen*

UKULELE LADY   1925
Gus Kahn / Richard A. Whiting
Francis, Day & Hunter Ltd. USA
Norah Blaney & Gwen Farrar . . . . . . **Columbia 3788**
The Denza Dance Band . . . . **Columbia 3730**
Ethel Merman . . . . **Brunswick 04661**
**Peter Sellers with The
Temperance Seven** . . . . **Parlophone PMC 1131**

UM UM UM UM UM UM November 1964
Curtis Mayfield
Ivan Mogul Music Associates . . . . USA
Major Lance . . . . **Columbia DB 7205**
Wayne Fontana & The Mindbenders . . . . **Fontana TF 497**

UMBRELLA MAN, THE 1939
Vincent Rose / Larry Stock / James Cavanaugh
Chappell & Co. Ltd. . . . . USA
Show(s): . . . . These Foolish Things
Film(s): . . . . Garden of the Moon
Flanagan & Allen . . . . **Columbia 33S 1010**
The King Brothers . . . . **Parlophone GEP 8760**
Flanagan & Allen appeared in *These Foolish Things.*

UN PEU D'AMOUR (See Little Love, A Little Kiss, A)

UNA PALOMA BLANCA October 1975
Hans J. Bouwens
Noon Music . . . . Belgium
Jonathan King . . . . **UK 105**
George Baker Selection . . . . **Warner Brothers K 16541**
See also 'I Am a Cider Drinker'

UNBELIEVABLE December 1990
*James Atken / Ian Dench / Zachary Foley / Mark Decloedt / Deran
Brownson*
Warner Chappell Music . . . . UK
EMF . . . . **Parlophone R 6273**
Ivor Novello Nomination.

UNCHAINED MELODY June 1955
Alex North / Hy Zaret
M.P.L. . . . . USA
Film(s): . . . . Unchained
Jimmy Young (1955) . . . . **Decca LF 1244**
Les Baxter Orchestra . . . . **Capitol CL 14257**
Al Hibbler . . . . **Brunswick 05420**
Frank Ifield . . . . **Columbia DB 4464**
The Righteous Brothers (1990) . . . . **Verve PO 101**
Nominated for an Academy Award 1955.

UNDECIDED 1939
Sid Robin / Charlie Shavers
Leeds Music Co. Ltd. . . . . USA
**John Kirby & his Onyx Club Boys
with Charlie Shavers (Trumpet)** . . . . **Vocalion S 220**
**Ella Fitzgerald with Chick Webb
& his Orchestra** . . . . **Ace of Hearts AH 16**
Humphrey Lyttleton & his Band . . . . **Columbia 33SX 1305**
The Ames Brothers . . . . **Vogue LVA 9098**

UNDER A BLANKET OF BLUE 1933
Marty Symes / Al Neiburg / Jerry Livingston
Keith Prowse Music Publishing Co. Ltd. . . . . USA
Connee Boswell . . . . **Brunswick 01555**
Dinah Shore . . . . **RCA RD 27072**

UNDER MY THUMB January 1975
Mick Jagger / Keith Richard
Essex Music Ltd. . . . . UK
Wayne Gibson . . . . **Pye DDS 2001**
The Rolling Stones . . . . **Decca SKL 5101**
The Who . . . . **Track 604006**

UNDER PARIS SKIES (Sous Le Ciel De Paris) August 1952
Hubert Giraud / Jean Drejec
Cinephonic Music Co. Ltd . . . . France
Juliette Greco . . . . **Philips BBL 7425**
Ray Martin & his Orchestra . . . . **Columbia 33S 1011**
The Troubadours . . . . **London HAR 2249**

UNDER PRESSURE November 1981
David Bowie / "Queen"
EMI Music . . . . UK
David Bowie & Queen . . . . **EMI 5250**

UNDER THE BAMBOO TREE 1902
J. Rosamond Johnson / Bob Cole
Campbell Connelly & Co. Ltd. . . . . USA
Show(s): . . . . Sally in Our Alley
Film(s): . . . . Meet Me in St.Louis
Louis Bradfield . . . . **HMV GC2-2945**
Judy Garland & Margaret O'Brian . . . . **MCA 2-11002**

Kid Ory's Creole Jazz Band,
vocal Budd Scott . . . . **Vogue LAG 12104**
Mitch Miller & The Gang . . . . **Philips BBL 7497**
Clinton Ford . . . . **Oriole CB 1747**
Judy Garland & Margaret O'Brian appeared in *Meet Me in St.Louis.*

UNDER THE BOARDWALK July 1987
Art Resnick / Kenny Young
T.M. Music . . . . USA
Bruce Willis . . . . **Motown ZB 41349**

**UNDER THE BRIDGES OF PARIS (Sous les Ponts de
Paris)** 1931
Vincent Scotto / Jean Rodor / Dorcas Cochran
Southern Music Publishing Co. Ltd. . . . . France
Orchestre Mascotte . . . . **Parlophone R 969**
Eartha Kitt (1955) . . . . **RCA RD 27067**
Frank Chacksfield & his Orchestra . . . . **Ace of Clubs ACL 1080**
Patachou . . . . **Philips BBL 7423**
Dean Martin (1955) . . . . **Capitol CL 14255**

UNDER THE DEODAR 1902
Lionel Monckton / Adrian Ross
Chappell & Co. Ltd. . . . . UK
Show(s): . . . . A Country Girl
L. Henri . . . . **HMV GC 3247**
The Columbia Light Opera Company . . . . **Columbia DX 73**

UNDER THE LILAC BOUGH 1922
Adrian Ross / George Clutsam
Chappel Music Ltd. . . . . UK
Show(s): . . . . Lilac Time
Courtice Pounds & Percy Heming . . . **Reolian Vocalion K 05065**
**Thomas Round, John Cameron, Barry Kent,
Kenneth Tudor & Eric Wilson-Hyde** . . . . . **HMV CLP 1248**
Courtice Pounds & Percy Heming appeared in *Lilac Time.*
Based on the music of Franz Schubert (1797-1828)

UNDER THE MOON 1928
Ted Snyder / Francis Wheeler / Ev. E. Lyn
B. Feldman & Co. Ltd. . . . . USA
Fred Elizalde & his Music . . . . **Brunswick 143**

UNDER THE MOON OF LOVE December 1976
Tommy Boyce / Curtis Lee
Carlin Music Corporation . . . . USA
Showaddywaddy . . . . **Bell 1495**

**UNDER THE ROOFS OF PARIS
(Sous Les Toits De Paris)** 1929
Raoul Moretti / Rene Nazelles / Bruce Sievier / Irving Caeser
Ascherberg, Hopwood & Crew Ltd . . . . France
Alexander's Accordions . . . . **Columbia 33S 1008**
The Mantovani Orchestra . . . . **Decca LK 4105**
Jaqueline Francois . . . . **Philips BBL 7438**

UNDER YOUR THUMB October 1981
Kevin Godley / Lol Creme
St. Annes Music . . . . UK
Godley & Creme . . . . **Polydor POSP 322**

UNDERNEATH THE ARCHES 1932
Bud Flanagan / Chesney Allen
Campbell Connelly & Co. Ltd. . . . . UK
Flanagan & Allen . . . . **Columbia 33S 1010**
The Andrews Sisters . . . . **Brunswick 03969**
Max Bygraves . . . . **Decca LK 4360**

UNDERNEATH THE HARLEM MOON 1932
Mack Gordon / Harry Revel
Victoria Music Co. Ltd. . . . . USA
Fletcher Henderson & his Orchestra . . . . **Columbia CB 548**
Werner Muller & his Orchestra . . . . **Polydor LPHM 46007**

UNDERNEATH THE MELLOW MOON 1923
Wendell Hall
Francis, Day & Hunter Ltd . . . . USA
Paul Whiteman & his Orchestra . . . . **HMV B 1639**
**The Green Brothers Marimba Orchestra,
vocal Donald King** . . . . **Rex 9367**

UNDERNEATH THE RUSSIAN MOON 1929
James Kendis / Frank Samuels / Meyer Gusman
Campbell Connelly & Co. Ltd . . . . USA
Ruddy Vallee & his Connecticut Yankees . . . . . . **HMV B 5667**

UNDERNEATH THE STARS 1915
Herbert Spencer / F. Brown
Francis, Day & Hunter Ltd. . . . . UK
Odette Myrtle . . . . Columbia L 1051
Sydney Bowman & his Orchestra . . . . . Ace of Clubs ACL 1089

UNFORGETTABLE October 1951
Irving Gordon
Bourne Music Ltd . . . . USA
Nat 'King' Cole . . . . Capitol T 944
Teddi King . . . . Coral FEP 2052
Cleo Laine . . . . Piccadilly 7N 35020

UNFORGETTABLE FIRE, THE July 1985
"U2"
Blue Mountain Music . . . . UK
U2 . . . . Island IS 220

UNION CITY BLUES December 1979
Deborah Harry / Nigel Harrison
EMI Music Ltd. . . . . UK
Blondie . . . . Chrysalis CHS 2400

UNION OF THE SNAKE November 1983
"Duran Duran"
Carlin Music Ltd. . . . . UK
Duran Duran . . . . EMI 5429

UNITED WE STAND March 1970
Tony Hiller / Peter De Simmons
Mills Music Ltd. . . . . UK
The Brotherhood of Man . . . . Deram DM 284
Ivor Novello Nomination.

UNIVERSAL August 1968
Steve Marriott / Ronnie Lane
Immediate Music Ltd. . . . . UK
The Small Faces . . . . Immediate IM 069

UNIVERSAL SOLDIER October 1965
Buffy Saint-Marie
Monique Music Ltd . . . . USA
Donovan . . . . Pye NEP 24219
Glen Campbell . . . . Capitol CGB 1010
Buffy Saint-Marie . . . . Fontana TFL 6040

UNLESS 1934
Tolchard Evans / Hobert Hargreaves / Stanley Damerell
Cecil Lennox Music Co. Ltd. . . . . UK
Lew Stone & his Band, vocal Al Bowlly . . . . Decca F 3883
Tolchard Evans (piano) . . . . Rex 8364
Guy Mitchell (1951) . . . . Columbia DB 2871
David Whitfield . . . . Decca LK 4270
Eddie Fisher . . . . HMV B 10099
Bill Snyder Orchestra, vocal by Stuart Foster . . London L 1075

UNSQUARE DANCE, THE June 1962
Dave Brubeck
Burlington Music Co. Ltd . . . . USA
The Dave Brubeck Quartet . . . . CBS AAG 102

UNSUSPECTING HEART January 1955
Joe Beal / Bob Singer / Freddy James & Joe Shank
Berry Music Ltd. . . . . USA
Frankie Vaughan . . . . HMV 7M 298

UNTIL 1911
Edward Teschemacher / Wilfred Sanderson
Boosey & Hawkes Music Publishers Ltd . . . . UK
Kennedy Rumford . . . . Columbia L 1123
John McCormack . . . . HMV DA 309
Dennis Noble . . . . Argo RG 53

UNTIL IT'S TIME FOR YOU TO GO May 1972
Buffy Saint-Marie
Essex Music Ltd . . . . USA
Elvis Presley . . . . RCA 2188
Buffy Saint-Marie . . . . Fontana TF 574

UNTIL MY LUCK COMES ROLLING ALONG 1923
George M. Cohan
B. Feldman & Co. Ltd . . . . USA
Show(s): . . . . Little Nellie Kelly
Paul Whiteman & his Orchestra . . . . HMV B 1642

UNTIL THE REAL THING COMES ALONG 1936
Saul Chaplin / Sammy Cahn / Mann Holiner & Alberta Nichols
Sterling Music Publishing Co. Ltd . . . . USA
Leo Reisman & his Orchestra . . . . Vocalion 504
The Ink Spots . . . . Ace of Hearts AH 2
'Fats' Waller & his Rhythm . . . . RCA RCX 1010
June Christy . . . . Capitol T 1006

UNTIL WE MEET AGAIN 1917
Lilian Shirley
Lawrence Wright Music Co. Ltd. . . . . UK
Ernest Pike & Peter Dawson . . . . Zonophone 1811

UP AROUND THE BEND July 1970
John Fogerty
Burlington Music Co. Ltd. . . . . USA
Creedence Clearwater Revival . . . . Liberty LBF 15354

UP IN THE CLOUDS 1929
Bert Kalmar / Harry Ruby
Chappell & Co. Ltd . . . . USA
Show(s): . . . . The Five O'clock Girl
Jack Hylton & his Orchestra . . . . HMV B 5612

UP ON THE ROOF January 1963
Gerry Goffin / Carole King
Aldon Music Ltd. . . . . USA
Kenny Lynch . . . . HMV POP 1090
The Drifters . . . . London HLK 9626

UP THE JUNCTION July 1979
Christopher Difford / Glenn Tilbrook
Rondor Music (London) Ltd. . . . . UK
Squeeze . . . . A&M AMS 7444

UP THE LADDER TO THE ROOF June 1970
Vincent Dimirco / Frank Wilson
Jobete Music (UK) Ltd. . . . . USA
The Supremes . . . . Tamla Motown TMG 735

UP TOWN TOP RANKING February 1978
Errol Thompson / Althia Forrest / Donna Reid & Joe Gibbs
Carlin Music Corporation . . . . Jamaica
Althia & Donna . . . . Lightning LIG 506

UP UP AND AWAY September 1967
Jim Webb
Carlin Music Corporation . . . . USA
The Johnny Mann Singers . . . . Liberty LIB 55972
Andy Williams . . . . CBS 63311
Nancy Sinatra . . . . Reprise RLP 6277

UP WHERE WE BELONG February 1983
Jack Nitzche / William Jennings / Buffy Sainte-Marie
Famous Music Ltd. . . . . USA
Film(s): . . . . An Officer and a Gentleman
Joe Cocker & Jennifer Warnes . . . . Island WIP 6830
Academy Award winning song for 1982.

UPSIDE DOWN August 1980
Nile Rodgers / Bernard Edwards
Warner Brothers Music Ltd . . . . USA
Diana Ross . . . . Motown TMG 1195

UPTOWN GIRL December 1983
Billy Joel
CBS Songs . . . . USA
Billy Joel . . . . CBS A 3775

USE IT UP AND WEAR IT OUT August 1980
Sandy Linzer / Russell Brown
Chappell & Co. Ltd . . . . USA
Odyssey . . . . RCA PC 1962

USE TA BE MY GIRL July 1978
Kenny Gamble / Nicky Chinn
Carlin Music Corporation . . . . USA
The O'Jays . . . . Philadelphia PIR 6332

VACATION August 1962
Hank Hunter / Connie Francis / Gary Weston
Merna Music Lts . . . . USA
Connie Francis . . . . MGM 1165

VALENCIA 1926
Jose Padilla / Lucien Boyer / Jacques Charles / Clifford Grey
B.Feldman & Co. Ltd. . . . . France
Show(s): . . . . Great Temptation
Henri Leoni . . . . **Columbia 3935**
The Savoy Havana Band, vocal Raymon Newton . **HMV B 2272**
Tito Schipa . . . . **HMV DA 821**
Mario Lanza . . . . **RCA RC 16085**
Frank Chacksfield & his Orchestra . . . . **Decca LK 4168**

VALENTINE 1929
Henri Christine / Herbert Reynolds
B. Feldman & Co. Ltd . . . . France
Film(s): . . . . Innocents of Paris
Maurice Chevalier (1929) . . . . **RCA RCX 1057**
David Carroll & his Orchestra . . . . **Mercury MMC 14082**
Maurice Chevalier (1958) . . . . **MGM C 771**
Maurice Chevalier appeared in *Innocents of Paris*.

VALENTINE February 1988
Ronald Rogers / Carol Decker
Virgin Music . . . . UK
T'Pau . . . . **Siren SRN 69**

VALETA 1905
Arthur Morris
Francis, Day & Hunter Ltd. . . . . UK
The Bohemian Orchestra . . . . **Regal MR 167**
Tommy Kinsman Orchestra . . . . **Fontana TFL 5068**
Sydney Thompson Orchestra . . . . . **Sydney Thompson PDR 3**

VAMP, THE 1920
Byron Gay
Francis, Day & Hunter Ltd . . . . USA
The Savoy Quartet, vocal Joe Wilbur . . . . **HMV B 1082**
Tommy Hamilton & his Orchestra . . . . **Capitol CL 13359**

VAMPING ROSE 1921
Ed Violinsky / Ira Schuster / Bert Hanlan / Ben Ryan
Francis, Day & Hunter Ltd . . . . USA
The All Star Trio & Orchestra (Ed Violinsky (violin)) . . **HMV B 1272**
Victor Vorzanger's Famous Broadway Band,
vocal Al Young . . . . **Scala 539**

VARSITY DRAG 1928
Buddy De Sylva / Lew Brown / Ray Henderson
Chappell & Co. Ltd. . . . . USA
Show(s): . . . . Good News
Film(s): . . . . Good News
Zelma O'Neal . . . . **Brunswick 3832**
Jean Goldkette & his Orchestra,
vocal The Debs . . . . **Camden CDN 154**
Cass Hagan & his Orchestra . . . . **CBS BPG 62545**
June Allyson & Peter Lawford . . . . **MGM E 3771**
Zelma O'Neal appeared in both the American and British productions
of *Good News*.
June Allyson & Peter Lawford appeared in the 1947 film *Good News*.

VAYA CON DIOS September 1953
Larry Russell / Inez James / Buddy Pepper
Edwin H. Morris & Co. Ltd. . . . . USA
Les Paul & Mary Ford . . . . **Capitol T 946**
Bing Crosby . . . . **Brunswick LAT 8331**
Perry Como . . . . **RCA RD 27078**
Miki & Griff . . . . **Pye NPL 18058**
Millican & Nesbitt (1973) . . . . **Pye 7N 45310**

VENETIAN MOON 1920
Phil Goldberg / Frank Magine
B. Feldman & Co. Ltd . . . . USA
The Savoy Quartet, vocal Joe Wilbur . . . . **HMV B 1153**

VENI-VIDI-VICI December 1954
Paul Francis Webster / Jerry Livingston
Dash Music Ltd. . . . . USA
Ronnie Hilton . . . . **HMV B 10785**
Ray Martin & his Orchestra . . . . **Columbia SCM 5150**

VENUS February 1959
Ed Marshall
Essex Music Ltd. . . . . USA
Dickie Valentine . . . . **Nixa NEP 24120**
Frankie Vaughan . . . . **Philips BBE 12288**
Sam Cooke . . . . **RCA RD 27215**

VENUS March 1970
Robert Van Leeuwen
Page Full of Hits . . . . Holland
Shocking Blue . . . . **Penny Farthing PEN 913**
Bananarama (1986) . . . . **London NANA 10**
Don Pablo's Animals (1990) . . . . **Rumour RUMA 18**

VENUS IN BLUE JEANS November 1962
Howard Greenfield / Jack Keller
Aldon Music Ltd. . . . . USA
Mark Wynter . . . . **Pye 7N 15466**
Jimmy Clanton . . . . **Stateside SS 120**

VENUS WALTZ, THE 1913
Ivan Caryll / C.M.S. McLellan
Chappell & Co. Ltd. . . . . USA
Show(s): . . . . Oh! Oh! Delphine
Dorothy Jardon . . . . **HMV C 568**
Dorothy Jardon appeared in *Oh! Oh! Delphine*.

VERY PRECIOUS LOVE, A March 1958
Sammy Fain / Paul Francis Webster
Blossom Music Ltd . . . . USA
Film(s): . . . . Marjorie Morningstar
Doris Day . . . . **Philips BBL 6297**
Gene Kelly . . . . **RCA RCA 1068**
The Mantovani Orchestra . . . . **Decca LK 4339**
Gene Kelly appeared in *Marjorie Morningstar*.
Nominated for an Academy Award 1958.

VERY THOUGHT OF YOU, THE 1934
Ray Noble
Campbell Connelly & Co. Ltd. . . . . UK
Film(s): . . . . Young Man of Music
Ray Noble & his Orchestra, vocal Al Bowlly . . **HMV 7EG 8186**
Bing Crosby . . . . **Brunswick 03078**
Jeri Southern . . . . **Brunswick LA 8699**
The Johnny Mann Singers . . . . **London HAG 2297**
Doris Day . . . . **Columbia DB 2680**
Doris Day appeared in *Young Man of Music*.
Opening theme of The Ray Noble Orchestra.

VICTIM OF LOVE June 1987
Vincent Clarke / Andrew Bell
Sonet Music . . . . UK
Erasure . . . . **Mute MUTE 61**

VICTIMS December 1983
George O'Dowd / Jonathan Moss / Roy Hay & Michael Craig
Virgin Music . . . . UK
Culture Club . . . . **Virgin VS 641**

VICTORY POLKA 1944
Sammy Cahn / Jule Styne
Chappell & Co. Ltd. . . . . USA
Film(s): . . . . Jam Session
Bing Crosby & The Andrews Sisters . . . . **Brunswick 03494**

VICTORY TEST MATCH, THE July 1950
Egbert Moore
Unknown . . . . UK
'Lord' Beginner (Egbert Moore) . . . . **Melodisc 1133**
The Holder-McKenzie Calypso Kings . . . . **EMI 2534**

VIDEO KILLED THE RADIO STAR October 1979
Bruce Woolley / Trevor Horn / Geoff Fownes
Island Music Ltd. . . . . UK
Buggles . . . . **Island WIP 6524**
Ivor Novello Nomination.

VIENI, VIENI 1937
George Koger / H. Varna / Vincent Scotto / Sonny Miller
Keith Prowse Music Publishing Co. Ltd. . . . . France
Rudy Vallee . . . . **Columbia DB 1703**
Ronnie Munro & his Orchestra, vocal Al Bowlly . **HMV BD 5242**
Kurt Edelhagen & his Orchestra . . . . **Polydor LPHM 46365**

VIENNA February 1981
William Currie / Christopher Cross / Warren Cann & Midge Ure
Island Music . . . . UK
Ultravox . . . . **Chrysalis CHS 2481**
Ivor Novello Nomination.

VIENNA CALLING   June 1986
Robert Bolland / Ferdinand Bolland / Johann Hoelzel
Island Music . . . . Holland
Falco . . . . **A&M AM 318**

VIENNA, CITY OF MY DREAMS   1931
Rudolph Sieczynski / Edward Lockton
Ascherberg, Hopwood & Crew Ltd. . . . . Austria
Film(s): . . . . .Heart's Desire
Richard Tauber . . . . **Parlophone PMB 1006**
David Whitfield . . . . **Decca LK 4270**
Harry Secombe . . . . **Philips BBE 12131**
Richard Tauber appeared in *Heart's Desire.*

VIEW TO A KILL   June 1985
John Barry / "Duran Duran"
CBS Songs . . . . UK
Film(s): . . . . A View to a Kill
Duran Duran . . . . **Parlophone DURAN 007**
Ivor Novello Nomination.

VILIA   1907
Franz Lehar / Adrian Ross
Chappell & Co. Ltd. . . . . Austria
Show(s): . . . . The Merry Widow
Film(s): . . . . The Merry Widow
Jeanette MacDonald . . . . **HMV 7EG 8059**
Fernando Lamas . . . . **MGM D 107**
Elaine Mallin . . . . **Camden CDN 107**
Jeanette MacDonald appeared in the 1934 film of *The Merry Widow.*
Fernando Lamas appeared in the 1952 film of *The Merry Widow.*
New lyrics written by Lorenz Hart for the 1934 film.

VILLAGE OF SAINT BERNADETTE, THE   December 1959
Eula Parker
Francis, Day & Hunter Ltd . . . . UK
Anne Shelton . . . . **Philips BBL 7393**
Rosemary June . . . . **London HLA 9014**
Ivor Novello Award.

VINCENT   June 1972
Don McLean
United Artists Music Co. Ltd. . . . . USA
Don McLean . . . . **United Artists UP 35359**

VIOLIN SONG, THE   1915
Paul Rubens / Percy Greenbank
Chappell & Co. Ltd. . . . . UK
Show(s): . . . . Tina
Phyllis Dare . . . . **HMV C 633**
Gwen Catley . . . . **Pye CEC 32001**
Phyllis Dare appeared in *Tina.*

VIPER'S DRAG   1936
Thomas Waller
Unknown Publisher . . . . USA
Fats Waller & his Rhythm . . . . **HMV B 8784**
The Quintette of the Hot Club of France . . . . . . **HMV CLP 1244**
Ralph Sutton (Piano) . . . . **Columbia 33S 1025**

VIRGINIA PLAIN   September 1972
Bryan Ferry
E.G. Music . . . . UK
Roxy Music . . . . **Island WIP 6144**
Roxy Music (1977) . . . . **Polydor 2001739**

VISION OF LOVE   September 1990
Mariah Carey / Bob Margulies
Sony Music . . . . USA
Mariah Carey . . . . **CBS 6559320**

VISIONS   August 1966
Paul Ferris
Joaneline Ltd. . . . . UK
Cliff Richard . . . . **Columbia DB 7968**

VIVA BOBBY JOE   September 1969
Edmond Grant
Edward Kassner Music Co. Ltd. . . . . UK
The Equals . . . . **President PT 260**

VOGUE   May 1990
Madonna Ciccone / Shep Pettibone
Warner Chappell Music . . . . USA
Madonna . . . . **Sire W 9851**

VOICE IN THE OLD VILLAGE CHOIR, THE   1932
Harry Woods / Gus Kahn
Campbell Connelly & Co. Ltd. . . . . USA
Ambrose & his Orchestra, vocal Sam Browne . . . . **HMV B 6178**
The Bowman-Hyde Singers & Players . . **Parlophone PMC 1155**

VOICE IN THE WILDERNESS, A   January 1960
Norrie Paramor / Bunny Lewis
Chappell & Co. Ltd . . . . UK
Film(s): . . . . .Expresso Bongo
Cliff Richard . . . . **Columbia SEG 7971**
Cliff Richard appeared in *Expresso Bongo.*

VOLARE (Nel Blu Dipinto Di Blu)   August 1958
Franco Migliacci / Domenico Modungo / Mitchell Parish
Robbins Music Corporation . . . . Italy
The Marino Marini Quartet . . . . **Durium DLU 96034**
Domenico Modungo . . . . **Oriole MG 10023**
Dean Martin . . . . **Capitol T 1047**
Lita Roza . . . . **Nixa NPT 19032**
Italian entry for the 1958 Eurovision Song Contest (Placed Third).

VOLUNTEER ORGANIST, THE   1893
William Grey / Henry Lamb
Paxton & Co. Ltd. . . . . USA
Arthur Reeves . . . . **Regal G 6291**
Peter Dawson . . . . **HMV B 3630**
Benjamin Luxon . . . . **Argo ZFB 96**

VOODOO CHILE   December 1970
Jimi Hendrix
Schroeder Music Ltd . . . . UK
Jimi Hendrix . . . . **Track 613008**

VOODOO MOON (See Enlloro)

VOULEZ-VOUS   August 1979
Benny Andersson / Bjorn Ulvaeus
Bocu Music Ltd. . . . . Sweden
Abba . . . . **Epic EPC 7499**

VOYAGE VOYAGE   June 1988
Jean Rivat / Dominique Dubois
Minder Music . . . . France
Desireless . . . . **CBS DES 2**

WABASH BLUES   1922
Dave Ringle / Fred Meinken
Francis, Day & Hunter Ltd . . . . USA
The Charleston Chasers . . . . **Philips BBL 7433**
Pee Wee Hunt & his Orchestra . . . . **Capitol CL 13098**
Shirley Bassey . . . . **Philips BBR 8130**
Billy Vaughan & his Orchestra . . . . **London HAD 2241**

WABASH CANNON BALL   1940
A.P. Carter
Southern Music Publishing Co. Ltd . . . . USA
Kay Starr . . . . **Capitol EAP 1-20063**
The Riverboat Five . . . . **Mercury MMC 14029**
Gail Davis . . . . **RCA RCX 159**
Roy Acuff . . . . **Philips BBL 7410**

WAGON WHEELS   1934
Billy Hill / Peter De Rose
B. Feldman & Co. Ltd. . . . . USA
Show(s): . . . . The Ziegfeld Follies of 1934
Turner Layton . . . . **Columbia DB 1352**
Paul Robeson . . . . **HMV DLP 1165**
Gordon MacRae . . . . **Capitol T 834**
Adapted from part of the second movement of the Symphony no.9 in
E minor, opus 95 by Antonin Dvorak (1841 - 1904).

WAIT   1916
Guy D'Hardelot
Chappell & Co. Ltd. . . . . UK
Peter Dawson . . . . **Zonophone Twin 1810**
Alfred Piccaver . . . . **Decca M 465**
Nancy Evans . . . . **HMV B 9015**

WAIT   February 1989
Robert Howard
Warner Chappell Music . . . . UK
Robert Howard & Kym Mazelle . . . . **RCA PB 42595**

WAIT AND SEE 1946
Harry Warren / Johnny Mercer
Robbins Music Corporation Ltd. .... USA
Film(s): .... The Harvey Girls
Kenny Baker .... **Brunswick 03625**
Leslie Hutchinson (Hutch) .... **HMV BD 1129**
Joni James .... **MGM C 777**
Kenny Baker appeared in *The Harvey Girls.*

WAIT FOR ME (Ti Diro) June 1959
G. D'Anzi / A. Bracchi
Chappell & Co. Ltd .... Italy
Malcolm Vaughan .... **HMV 7EG 8453**
Marion Ryan .... **Nixa N 15184**
Kevin Scott .... **Parlophone R 4520**

WAIT FOR ME DARLING October 1954
Albert Hague / Bill Barr
Lafleur & Co. Ltd. .... USA
Joan Regan .... **Decca DFE 6235**
Bonnie Lou .... **Parlophone MSP 6177**

WAIT FOR ME MARY 1943
Nat Simon / Charles Tobias / Harry Tobias
B. Feldman & Co. Ltd .... USA
Film(s): .... Winged Victory
Dick Haymes .... **Brunswick 03478**
Gracie Fields .... **Decca F 8356**
Pat Boone .... **London HAD 2305**

WAIT TILL THE SUN SHINES NELLIE 1905
Andrew Sterling / Harry Von Tilzer
B. Feldman & Co. Ltd. .... USA
Film(s):Birth of the Blues / Rhythm Parade / In the Good Old Sum-
mertime / Wait Till the Sun Shines Nellie
Bing Crosby & Mary Martin .... **Brunswick Bing 6**
The Jesters .... **Decca F 8101**
The Sing-along Minstrels .... **Ace of Clubs ACL 1090**
Bing Crosby and Mary Martin appeared in *Birth of the Blues.*

**WAITER AND THE PORTER AND THE UPSTAIRS MAID,
THE** 1942
Johnny Mercer
Victoria Music Co. Ltd .... USA
Film(s): .... Birth of the Blues
Bing Crosby, Mary Martin & Jack Teagarden ... **Brunswick Bing 6**
The King Brothers .... **Parlophone PMC 1060**
Bing Crosby, Mary Martin & Jack Teagarden appeared in *Birth of The
Blues.*

WAITING AT THE CHURCH 1906
Fred W. Leigh / Henry Pether
Francis, Day & Hunter .... UK
Film(s): .... Birth of the Blues / I Thank You
Vesta Victoria (Original Artiste) .... **Regal Zonophone MR 414**
Florrie Forde .... **Zonophone X 43100**
The Jesters .... **Decca F 8101**
Joe 'Mr. Piano' Henderson & his Friends ..... **Pye NPL 18053**

WAITING FOR A GIRL LIKE YOU January 1982
Mick Jones / Lou Gramm
Warner Brothers Music .... France
Foreigner .... **Atlantic K 11696**

WAITING FOR A STAR TO FALL January 1989
George Merrill / Sharron Rubicam
Rondor Music .... UK
Boy Meets Girl .... **RCA PB 49519**

WAITING FOR A TRAIN June 1983
Harry Vanda / George Young
Chappell Music Ltd. .... USA
Flash and the Pan .... **Ensign EASY 1**

WAITING FOR AN ALIBI March 1979
Phil Lynott
Chappell & Co. Ltd. .... UK
Thin Lizzy .... **Vertigo LIZZY 3**

WAITING FOR THE ROBERT E. LEE 1913
L. Wolfe Gilbert / Lewis Muir
Francis, Day & Hunter Ltd. .... USA
Film(s):The Story of Vernon & Irene Castle / The Jolson Story / The
Jazz Singer / Applause / Babes on Broadway
The Metropolitan Band .... **HMV C 289**

Harry Roy & his Tiger Ragamuffins .... **Parlophone R 115**
Al Jolson .... **Brunswick LA 8509**
Dean Martin .... **Encore 103**
Judy Garland & Mickey Rooney .... **MCA 2-11002**
Al Jolson appeared in *The Jazz Singer.*
Judy Garland & Mickey Rooney appeared in *Babes on Broadway.*

WAITING FOR THE TRAIN TO COME IN 1946
Martin Block / Sunny Skylar
Francis, Day & Hunter Ltd. .... USA
Harry Roy & his Band, vocal Harry Roy .... **Parlophone F 2136**
**Jack Simpson & his Sextette,
vocal Maureen Morton** .... **Parlophone F 2138**

WAKE ME UP BEFORE YOU GO GO June 1984
George Michael
Morrison Leany Music .... UK
Wham .... **Epic A 4440**
Ivor Novello Nomination.

WAKE UP AND LIVE 1937
Mack Gordon / Harry Revel
Francis, Day & Hunter Ltd. .... USA
Film(s): .... Wake Up and Live
Alice Faye .... **Brunswick 02435**

WAKE UP LITTLE SUSIE November 1957
Felice Bryant / Boudleaux Bryant
Acuff-Rose Publishing Co. Ltd .... USA
The Everly Brothers .... **London HAE 2081**
The King Brothers .... **Parlophone R 4367**

WALK AWAY (Warum Nur Warum) November 1964
Don Black / Udo Jurgens
Ardmore & Beechwood Ltd .... Germany
Matt Monro .... **Parlophone R 5171**
Frank Chacksfield & his Orchestra .... **Decca LK 4666**

WALK AWAY FROM LOVE February 1976
Charles Kipps
EMI Music Ltd. .... USA
David Ruffin .... **Tamla Motown TMG 1017**

WALK AWAY RENEE February 1968
Mike Brown / Tony Sansone / Bob Calilli
Flamingo Music Ltd. .... USA
The Four Tops .... **Tamla Motown TMG 634**

WALK DON'T RUN October 1960
Johnny Smith
Planetary Nom (London) Ltd .... USA
The John Barry Seven .... **Columbia DB 4554**
The Ventures .... **London HAG 2308**

WALK HAND IN HAND May 1956
Johnny Cowell
Republic Music Ltd. .... USA
Ronnie Hilton .... **Philips BBE 12088**
Vera Lynn .... **Decca DFE 6397**
Tony Martin .... **HMV POP 222**
Andy Williams .... **London REA 1102**
Gerry & The Pacemakers (1965) .... **Columbia DB 7738**

WALK IN LOVE April 1978
David Batteau / John Klemmer
Rondor Music (London) Ltd .... USA
Manhattan Transfer .... **Atlantic K 11075**

**WALK IN THE BLACK FOREST
(Eine Schwarzwaldfahrt)** September 1965
Horst Jankowski
Intersong Music Ltd .... Germany
Horst Jankowski & his Orchestra .... **Mercury MF 861**

WALK IN THE NIGHT October 1972
Johnny Bristol / Marilyn McLeod
Jobete Music (UK) Ltd. .... USA
Junior Walker & The All Stars ..... **Tamla Motown TMG 824**

WALK LIKE A MAN April 1963
Bob Crewe / Bob Gaudio
Peter Maurice Music Co. Ltd .... USA
The Four Seasons .... **Stateside SS 169**

WALK LIKE AN EGYPTIAN　　　　November 1986
Liam Sternberg
Southern Music Co. . . . . USA
Bangles . . . . **CBS 650071**

WALK OF LIFE　　　　February 1986
Mark Knopfler
Rondor Music . . . . UK
Dire Straits . . . . **Vertigo DSTR 12**

WALK ON BY　　　　May 1964
Burt Bacharach / Hal David
Carlin Music Ltd. . . . . USA
Dionne Warwick (1964) . . . . **Pye 7N 25241**
Helen Shapiro . . . . **Columbia 33SX 1661**
Sybil (1990) . . . . **PWL PWL 48**

WALK ON BY　　　　May 1964
Kendall Hayes
Carlin Music Ltd. . . . . USA
Leroy Van Dyke . . . . **Mercury AMT 1166**
Johnny Burnette . . . . **Liberty LBY 1006**
Kay Starr . . . . **Capitol T 1795**

WALK ON THE WILD SIDE　　　　June 1973
Lou Reed
Oakfield Avenue Music . . . . USA
Lou Reed . . . . **RCA 2303**

WALK RIGHT BACK　　　　April 1961
Sonny Curtis
Leeds Music Ltd . . . . USA
The Everly Brothers . . . . **Warner Brothers WB 33**
Bobby Vee . . . . **Liberty LBY 1147**

WALK RIGHT IN　　　　March 1963
Gus Cannon / Hosie Woods
Southern Music Publishing Co. Ltd . . . . USA
The Rooftop Singers . . . . **Fontana 271700 TF**
Bobby Darin . . . . **Capitol T 1942**
First Published 1929.

WALK RIGHT NOW　　　　August 1981
Michael Jackson / Randy Jackson / Jackie Jackson
Carlin Music . . . . USA
The Jacksons . . . . **Epic EPC A 1294**

WALK TALL　　　　January 1965
Don Wayne
Shapiro-Bernstein & Co. Ltd . . . . USA
Val Doonican . . . . **Decca F 11982**

WALK THE DINOSAUR　　　　October 1987
David Weiss / Don Fagenson / Randell Jacobs
MCA Music . . . . USA
Was Not Was . . . . **Fontana WAS 3**

WALK THIS WAY　　　　September 1986
Steven Tyler / Joe Perry
Chappell Music Ltd. . . . . UK
Run D.M.C. . . . . **London LON 104**

WALK WITH ME　　　　November 1966
Tom Springfield
Springfield Music Ltd. . . . . UK
The Seekers . . . . **Columbia DB 8000**

WALKIN'　　　　April 1971
Donovan Leitch
Donovan Music Ltd . . . . UK
C.C.S. . . . . **Rak 109**

WALKIN' IN THE RAIN WITH THE ONE I LOVE　　July 1972
Barry White
Schroeder Music Ltd. . . . . USA
Love Unlimited . . . . **Uni UN 539**

WALKIN' IN THE SUNSHINE　　　　October 1981
"Bad Manners"
Magnet Music . . . . UK
Bad Manners . . . . **Magnet MAG 197**

WALKIN' MIRACLE, A　　　　May 1974
Hugo Peretti / Luigi Creatore / George Weiss & Adam Levy
Planetary-Nom (London) Ltd. . . . . USA

Limmie & The Family Cookin' . . . . **Avco 6105027**
The Essex . . . . **Columbia DB 7122**

WALKIN' MY BABY BACK HOME　　　　1931
Roy Turk / Fred Ahlert / Harry Richman
Victoria Music Co. Ltd . . . . USA
Layton & Johnstone . . . . **Columbia DB 532**
Louis Armstrong & his Orchestra . . . . **Parlophone R 2365**
Nat 'King' Cole . . . . **Capitol CL 13774**
Johnnie Ray (1952) . . . . **Philips BBL 7264**

WALKIN' THRU MOCKIN' BIRD LANE　　　　1940
Clarence Jones / Lowell Peters / John Turner
Peter Maurice Music Co. Ltd . . . . USA
Barney Gilbraith's Coconut Grove Quartet . . **Parlophone F 1691**
Elsie Carlisle . . . . **Rex 9775**
Al Bowlly . . . . **HMV BD 834**

WALKIN' TO MISSOURI　　　　September 1952
Bob Merrill
Dash Music Ltd . . . . USA
Tony Brent . . . . **Columbia SEG 7612**
Lita Roza . . . . **Decca F 9988**

WALKING AND WHISTLING BLUES　　　　August 1951
Les Paul
Dash Music Ltd . . . . USA
Les Paul (guitar) . . . . **Capitol LC 6806**
The Four Knights . . . . **Capitol CL 13687**

WALKING BACK TO HAPPINESS　　　　November 1961
Mike Hawker / John Schroeder
Filmusic Publishing Co. Ltd. . . . . UK
Helen Shapiro . . . . **Columbia DB 4715**
Ivor Novello Award.

WALKING IN THE AIR　　　　December 1985
Howard Blake
Faber & Faber Ltd. . . . . UK
Aled Jones . . . . **EMI ALED 1**
Theme of the television programme *The Snowman*.
Ivor Novello Nomination 1983.

WALKING IN THE RAIN　　　　September 1983
David Jaymes / Michael Mullins
CBS Songs . . . . UK
Modern Romance . . . . **WEA X 9733**

WALKING ON SUNSHINE　　　　September 1982
Eddy Grant
Intersong Music Ltd. . . . . UK
Rockers Revenge . . . . **London LON 11**

WALKING ON SUNSHINE　　　　June 1985
Kimberly Rew
Screen Gems Music . . . . USA
Katrina & The Waves . . . . **Capitol CL 354**

WALKING ON THE MOON　　　　December 1979
"Sting"
Virgin Music (Publishers) Ltd. . . . . UK
Police . . . . **A&M AMS 7494**

WALKING THE FLOOR OVER YOU　　　　1943
Ernest Tubb
Campbell Connelly & Co. Ltd . . . . USA
Bing Crosby . . . . **Brunswick LAT 8228**
Ernest Tubb . . . . **Brunswick LAT 8313**
Pat Boone . . . . **London RED 1255**

WALKING WITH SUSIE　　　　1929
Con Conrad / Sidney Mitchell / Archie Gottler
Campbell Connelly & Co. Ltd . . . . USA
Film(s): . . . . Fox Movietone Follies of 1929
George Olsen & his Music . . . . **HMV B 5655**
Ambrose & his Orchestra . . . . **Decca M 37**
Jack Hylton & his Orchestra . . . . **HMV B 5658**

WALL STREET SHUFFLE　　　　July 1974
Eric Stuart / Graham Gouldman
St. Annes Music Ltd. . . . . UK
10 CC . . . . **UK UK 69**

WALLS COME TUMBLING DOWN　　　　May 1985
Paul Weller

EMI Music . . . . UK
The Style Council . . . . **Polydor TSC 8**

WALTER, WALTER (Lead Me To The Altar)   **1937**
W.E. Haines / J. Harper / Eugene Butler
Campbell Connelly & Co. Ltd. UK
Gracie Fields . . . . **Rex 9307**
Gracie Fields . . . . **Ace of Clubs ACL 1042**

WALTZ DREAM, THE   **1908**
Oscar Straus / Adrian Ross
Chappell & Co. Ltd. . . . . Austria
Show(s): . . . . A Waltz Dream
Ernest Pike & Alan Turner . . . . **HMV GC 4456**
Richard Tauber . . . . **Parlophone PMB 1007**
June Bronhill & David Hughes . . . . **HMV CLP 1390**

WALTZ IN SWING TIME   **1936**
Jerome Kern / Dorothy Fields
Chappell & Co. Ltd . . . . USA
Film(s): . . . . Swing Time
Johnny Green & his Orchestra . . . . . **Brunswick 02383**
The BBC Dance Orchestra,
conducted by Henry Hall . . . . **Columbia FB 1527**
Geraldo & his Orchestra, vocal Cyril Grantham . . **Decca K 851**
The Skip Martin Orchestra . . . . **Capitol LC 6679**

WALTZ ME ROUND AGAIN WILLIE   **1906**
Will Cobb / Ren Shields
B. Feldman & Co. Ltd. . . . . USA
Show(s): . . . . His Honour the Mayor
Florrie Forde . . . . **Regal X 43114**
Herman Darewski & his Ballroom Orchestra . . **Parlophone F 653**

WALTZ OF MY HEART   **1939**
Ivor Novello / Christopher Hassall
Chappell & Co. Ltd. . . . . UK
Show(s): . . . . The Dancing Years
Film(s): . . . . The Dancing Years
Mary Ellis . . . . **HMV DLP 1028**
Sound Track . . . . **HMV B 9966**
Hilde Gueden . . . . **Decca LK 4196**
Mary Ellis appeared in the show *The Dancing Years*.

WALTZ SONG, THE (See Venus Waltz, The)

WALTZING CAT, THE   **June 1951**
Leroy Anderson
Mills Music Ltd . . . . USA
Leroy Anderson & his Orchestra . . . **Brunswick LA 8553**
The Boston Promenade Orchestra . . . . **HMV DLP 1142**

WALTZING IN THE CLOUDS   **1941**
Robert Stolz / Gus Kahn
B. Feldman & Co. Ltd . . . . USA
Film(s): . . . . Spring Parade
Deanna Durbin . . . . **Brunswick 03125**
Ambrose & his Orchestra, vocal Anne Shelton . . **Decca F 7742**
Deanna Durbin appeared in *Spring Parade*.
Nominated for an Academy Award 1940.

WANA (When I Wana, You No Wana)   **1922**
Cliff Friend
Lawrence Wright Music Co. Ltd . . . . USA
The Club Royal Orchestra . . . . **HMV B 1385**
Clinton Ford . . . . **Oriole EP 7027**

WANDERER, THE   **March 1962**
Ernest Maresca
Dominion Music Co. Ltd. . . . . USA
Dion . . . . **HMV POP 971**
Status Quo (1984) . . . . **Phonogram QUO 16**
Adam Faith . . . . **Parlophone PMC 1213**

WANDERERS   **1937**
Felix Barnard / Paul Francis Webster
Keith Prowse Music Publishing Co. Ltd. . . . . USA
The Hillbillies . . . . **Regal Zonophone MR 2371**
Lew Stone & his Band . . . . **Decca F 6349**

WANDERIN' STAR   **March 1970**
Alan Jay Lerner / Fredrick Loewe
Chappell & Co. Ltd. . . . . USA
Show(s): . . . . Paint Your Wagon

Film(s): . . . . Paint Your Wagon
James Barton . . . . **HMV CLP 1005**
Bobby Howes . . . . **Columbia DB 3288**
Lee Marvin (1970) . . . . **Paramount PMC 1001**
James Barton appeared in the American production of *Paint Your Wagon*.
Bobby Howes appeared in the British production of *Paint Your Wagon*.
Lee Marvin appeared in the film *Paint Your Wagon*.

WANDERING EYES   **September 1957**
Kal Mann / Bernie Lowe / Hal Norton
Sydney Bron Music Co. Ltd . . . . USA
Frankie Vaughan . . . . **Philips BBL 7233**
Charlie Gracie . . . . **London HL 8467**

WANG WANG BLUES, THE   **1921**
Henry Busse / 'Buster' Johnson / Gus Mueller
Francis, Day & Hunter Ltd . . . . USA
Film(s): . . . . Somebody Loves Me / The Rat Race
The Jungle Band . . . . **Brunswick 1088**
Ted Lewis & his Band . . . . **Columbia 3072**
Henry Busse & his Orchestra . . . . **Brunswick 03791**
Eydie Gormé . . . . **HMV CLP 1392**

WANNA BE STARTIN' SOMETHING   **July 1983**
Michael Jackson
Warner Chappell Music . . . . USA
Michael Jackson . . . . **Epic A 3427**

WANTED   **June 1954**
John Fulton / Lois Steele
Harms-Connelly Ltd. . . . . USA
Perry Como . . . . **RCA RD 27100**
Al Martino . . . . **Capitol CI 14128**
Gary Miller . . . . **Philips PB 278**

WANTED   **August 1979**
Ben Findon / Mike Myers / Robert Puzey
Black Sheep Music . . . . UK
The Dooleys . . . . **GTO GT 249**

WANTED DEAD OR ALIVE   **April 1987**
Jon Bon Jovi / Richard Sambora
Polygram Music . . . . UK
Bon Jovi . . . . **Vertigo JOV 1**

WANTING YOU   **1929**
Sigmund Romberg / Oscar Hammerstein II
Chappell & Co. Ltd . . . . USA
Show(s): . . . . The New Moon
Film(s): . . . . The New Moon
Evelyn Laye & Howett Worster . . . . **Columbia 9752**
Lawrence Tibbett . . . . **HMV DA 1200**
Nelson Eddy . . . . **Columbia 33S 1012**
Elizabeth Larner & Andy Cole . . . . . **HMV CLP 1148**
Evelyn Laye & Howett Worster appeared in the British production of
The New Moon.
Lawrence Tibbett appeared in the 1930 film of *The New Moon*.
Nelson Eddy appeared in the 1940 film of *The New Moon*.

WAP-BAM-BOOGIE   **July 1988**
Mark Reilly / Mark Fisher
Fishy Songs . . . . UK
Matt Bianco . . . . **WEA YZ 188R**

WAR   **November 1970**
Norman Whitfield / Barrett Strong
Jobete Music (UK) Ltd. . . . . USA
Edwin Starr . . . . **Tamla Motown TMG 968**

WAR BABY   **July 1983**
Tom Robinson
Blue Mountain Music . . . . UK
Tom Robinson . . . . **Panic NIC 2**

WAR SONG, THE   **October 1984**
"Culture Club"
Virgin Music . . . . UK
Culture Club . . . . **Virgin VS 694**

WARPAINT   **May 1961**
Barry Mann / Howard Greenfield
Nevins-Kirshner Ltd . . . . USA
The Brook Brothers . . . . **Pye 7N 15333**
Barry Mann . . . . **HMV CLP 1559**

WARSAW CONCERTO, THE   1942
Richard Addinsell
Keith Prowse Music Publishing Co. Ltd . . . . UK
Film(s): . . . . Dangerous Moonlight
The London Symphony Orchestra,
conducted by Muir Mathieson . . . . **Columbia SEG 7600**
Victor Young & his Concert Orchestra . . . . . . **Brunswick 03378**
The Mantovani Orchestra
(Rawicz & Landauer (pianos)) . . . . **Decca LK 4154**

WAS IT A DREAM   1928
Sam Coslow / Larry Spier / Addy Britt
Campbell Connelly & Co. Ltd. . . . . USA
Brian Thomas . . . . **Columbia 4693**
The Dorsey Brothers Concert Orchestra . . . **Parlophone R 226**
Ronald Binge & his Orchestra . . . . **RCA RD 27042**

WAS IT RAIN   1937
Lou Handman / Walter Hirsh
Campbell Connelly & Co. Ltd. . . . . USA
Film(s): . . . . Hit Parade
Frances Langford . . . . **Brunswick 02430**
Phil Regan . . . . **Decca F 6414**
Artie Shaw & his Orchestra . . . . **Vocalion 548**
Guy Mitchell . . . . **Philips BBL 7246**
Frances Langford & Phil Regan appeared in *Hit Parade*.

WAS THAT THE HUMAN THING TO DO   1932
Joe Young / Sammy Fain
B. Feldman & Co. Ltd. . . . . USA
The Boswell Sisters . . . . **Brunswick 1284**
Don Cornell . . . . **HMV 7EG 8105**
Kay Starr . . . . **Capitol LC 6574**

WASH YOUR FACE IN MY SINK   August 1990
Louie King / Richard Rodwell / Andrew Gooden
MCA Music . . . . Canada
Dream Warriors . . . . **4th & Broadway BRW 183**

WASHING ON THE SIEGFRIED LINE   1939
Jimmy Kennedy / Michael Carr
Peter Maurice Music Co. Ltd. . . . . UK
Ambrose & his Orchestra, vocal Jack Cooper . . **Decca F 7245**
Billy Cotton & his Band . . . . **Rex 9636**
Flanagan & Allen . . . . **Decca F 7265**

WATCH THE BIRDIE   1942
Don Raye / Gene De Paul
Leeds Music Ltd . . . . USA
Film(s): . . . . Hellzapoppin
Johnny Claes & his Clae Pigeons . . . . **Columbia FB 2771**
Jack Simpson & his Sextette, vocal Betty Kent . . . **Rex 10132**

WATCHING THE DETECTIVES   December 1977
Elvis Costello
Street Music . . . . UK
Elvis Costello . . . . **Stiff BUY 20**

WATCHING YOU, WATCHING ME   September 1983
Derek Bramble
D.J.A. Publishing . . . . UK
David Grant . . . . **Chrysalis GRAN 2**

WATERFALLS   July 1980
Paul McCartney
McCartney Music . . . . UK
Paul McCartney . . . . **Parlophone R 6037**

WATERLOO   July 1959
John D. Loudermilk / Marijohn Wilkin
Cedarwood Music Ltd . . . . USA
The Mudlarks . . . . **Columbia DB 4331**
Bob Cort . . . . **Decca F 11145**

WATERLOO   May 1974
Benny Andersson / Bjorn Ulvaeus / Stig Anderson
United Artists Music Co. Ltd. . . . . Sweden
Abba . . . . **Epic EPC 2240**
Swedish entry for the 1974 Eurovision Song Contest (Placed First).

WATERLOO SUNSET   June 1967
Raymond Davies
Belinda (London) Ltd. . . . . UK
The Kinks . . . . **Pye 7N 17321**

WAY BACK HOME   1935
Al Lewis / Tom Waring
Magna Music Co. Ltd . . . . USA
The Boswell Sisters . . . . **Brunswick 02033**
Bing Crosby . . . . **Brunswick 04433**
Teresa Brewer & Bobby Wayne . . . . **London L 562**

WAY DOWN   September 1977
Laying Martin Jnr
A.T.V. Music Ltd. . . . . USA
Elvis Presley . . . . **RCA PB 0998**

WAY DOWN YONDER IN NEW ORLEANS   1923
Henry Creamer / Turner Layton
Lawrence Wright Music Co. Ltd . . . . USA
Show(s): . . . . Spices of 1922
Film(s): . Is Everybody Happy / Somebody Loves Me / Drum Crazy
Paul Whiteman & his Orchestra . . . . **HMV B 1649**
The Andrews Sisters . . . . **Capitol T 933**
Sound Track recording of *Drum Crazy* . . . . **HMV CLP 1352**
Freddy Cannon (1960) . . . . **Top Rank JAR 247**
Betty Hutton . . . . **Motion Picture Tracks MPT 5**
Betty Hutton appeared in *Somebody Loves Me.*

WAY IT USED TO BE, THE   March 1969
Franco Cassano / Corrado Conti / Roger Cook & Roger Greenaway
Maribus Music Ltd. . . . . Italy
Engelbert Humperdinck . . . . **Decca F 12879**

WAY OF LIFE, THE   July 1969
Roger Cook / Roger Greenaway
Cookaway Music . . . . UK
The Family Dogg . . . . **Bell BLL 1055**

WAY WE WERE, THE   June 1975
Marvin Hamlisch / Alan Bergman / Marilyn Bergman
Screen Gems Music Ltd . . . . USA
Film(s): . . . . The Way We Were
Barbra Streisand . . . . **CBS S 70132**
Gladys Knight & the Pips . . . . **Buddah BDS 428**
Barbra Streisand appeared in *The Way We Were.*

WAY YOU LOOK TONIGHT, THE   1936
Jerome Kern / Dorothy Fields
Chappell & Co. Ltd . . . . USA
Film(s): . . . . Swing Time
Fred Astaire . . . . **Columbia DB 1828**
Bing Crosby & Dixie Lee . . . . **Brunswick 02291**
Fred Astaire . . . . **HMV CLP 1304**
Tony Bennett . . . . **Philips BBL 7280**
Fred Astaire appeared in *Swing Time.*
Academy Award winning song for 1936.

WAY YOU MAKE ME FEEL, THE   December 1987
Michael Jackson
Warner Brothers Music . . . . USA
Michael Jackson . . . . **Epic 651275**

WAYWARD WIND, THE   July 1956
Stan Lebowsky / Herb Newman
Lafleur & Co. Ltd. . . . . USA
Tex Ritter . . . . **Capitol CL 14581**
Gogi Grant . . . . **London HAB 2032**
Bill Monroe . . . . **Brunswick LAT 8338**
Shirley Bassey . . . . **Philips BBE 12088**
Frank Ifield (1963) . . . . **Columbia DB 4960**
The Everly Brothers . . . . **Warner Brothers WM 4052**

WE ALL FOLLOW MAN. UNITED   June 1985
Katrine Wallis / Dave Melia / Mike Timoney
SRS Music Co. . . . . UK
Manchester United Football Club . . . . **Columbia DB 9107**

WE ALL GO THE SAME WAY HOME   1911
C.W. Murphy / Harry Castling
Francis, Day & Hunter Ltd. . . . . UK
Charles Whittle . . . . **Columbia 1726**
Fred Douglas . . . . **Regal G 1715**
The George Mitchell Minstrels . . . . **Columbia SCX 6528**

WE ALL HAVE A SONG IN OUR HEARTS   April 1950
Carl Yale / Roger Yale
Grosvenor Music Ltd . . . . UK
Geraldo & his Orchestra . . . . **Parlophone F 2385**

Josef Locke . . . . Columbia DB 2636
Bing Crosby . . . . Brunswick 04868

WE ALL STAND TOGETHER   December 1984
Paul McCartney
MPL . . . . UK
Paul McCartney . . . . **Parlophone R 6068**
Ivor Novello Award.

WE ALL WALKED INTO THE SHOP   1904
A.J. Mills / Harry Castling
Francis, Day & Hunter . . . . USA
Walter Miller . . . . **HMV GC 3-2283**

WE ALL WENT UP UP THE MOUNTAIN   1933
Elton Box / Desmond Cox
Keith Prowse Music Publishing Co. Ltd. . . . . UK
The Midnight Minstrels . . . . **Regal Zonophone MR 1208**

WE ARE DETECTIVE   May 1983
Tom Bailey / Alannah Currie / Joe Leeway
ATV Music . . . . UK
The Thompson Twins . . . . **Arista ARIST 526**

WE ARE FAMILY   June 1979
Bernard Edwards / Nile Rodgers
Warner Brothers Music Ltd. . . . . USA
Sister Sledge . . . . **Atlantic K 11293**

WE ARE GLASS   June 1980
Gary Numan
Numan Music Ltd . . . . UK
Gary Numan . . . . **Beggars Banquet BEG 35**

WE ARE IN LOVE   January 1964
Chris Andrews
Glissando Music Ltd . . . . UK
Adam Faith . . . . **Parlophone R 5091**

WE ARE THE CHAMPIONS   November 1977
Freddie Mercury
EMI Music Ltd . . . . UK
Queen . . . . **EMI 2708**

WE ARE THE WORLD   April 1985
Michael Jackson / Lionel Richie
Warner Brothers Music . . . . USA
U.S.A. for Africa . . . . **CBS USAID 1**

WE BUILT THIS CITY   December 1985
Bernie Taupin / Martin Page / Dennis Lambert & Peter Wolf
Zomba Music . . . . UK
Starship . . . . **RCA FB 49929**

WE CALL IT ACIEED   October 1988
Gary Haisman
SBK Songs . . . . UK
D. Mob & Gary Haisman . . . . **London FFR 13**

WE CAN DO IT   June 1977
Wayne Bickerton / Tony Waddington
A.T.V. Music Ltd. . . . . UK
The Liverpool Football Team . . . . **State STAT 50**

WE CAN WORK IT OUT   December 1965
John Lennon / Paul McCartney
Northern Songs Ltd . . . . UK
Show(s): . . . . John, Paul, George, Ringo and Bert
The Beatles . . . . **Parlophone R 5389**
Stevie Wonder . . . . **Tamla Motown TMG 772**
Barbara Dickson . . . . **RSO 2394141**
The Four Seasons . . . . **Warner Brothers K 16845**
Barbara Dickson appeared in *John, Paul, George, Ringo & Bert.*
Ivor Novello Award.

WE CLOSE OUR EYES   April 1985
Peter Cox / Richard Drummie
ATV Music . . . . UK
Go West . . . . **Chrysalis CHS 2850**

**WE COULD MAKE SUCH BEAUTIFUL MUSIC
TOGETHER**   1947
Robert Sour / Henry Manners
Campbell Connelly & Co. Ltd. . . . . USA
Vaughn Monroe & his Orchestra,

vocal Vaughn Monroe & Betty Norton . . . . **HMV BD 1175**
Barbara Lea . . . . **Esquire 32-063**

WE DIDN'T START THE FIRE   October 1989
Billy Joel
EMI Music . . . . USA
Billy Joel . . . . **CBS JOEL 1**

WE DO IT   February 1976
Russell Stone
Rondor Music (London) Ltd . . . . UK
R & J Stone . . . . **RCA 2616**
Ivor Novello Nomination.

**WE DON'T HAVE TO TAKE OUR CLOTHES
OFF**   September 1986
Preston Glass / Narada Michael Walden
Island Music . . . . USA
Jermaine Stewart . . . . **10 TEN 96**

WE DON'T NEED ANOTHER HERO   August 1985
Terry Britten / Graham Lyle
Rondor Music . . . . UK
Tina Turner . . . . **Capitol CL 364**
Ivor Novello Award.

WE DON'T TALK ANYMORE   September 1979
Alan Tarney
A.T.V. Music Ltd. . . . . UK
Cliff Richard . . . . **EMI 2975**
Ivor Novello Award.

WE HAVE A DREAM   May 1982
B.A. Robertson
ATV Music . . . . UK
The Scottish World Cup Squad . . . . **WEA K 19145**

WE JUST COULDN'T SAY GOODBYE   1932
Harry Woods
Francis, Day & Hunter Ltd. . . . . USA
Annette Hanshaw . . . . **Panachord 25270**
The Boswell Sisters . . . . **Brunswick 1347**
Patti Page . . . . **Mercury MMC 14017**

WE KISS IN THE SHADOW   November 1953
Richard Rodgers / Oscar Hammerstein II
Williamson Music Ltd. . . . . USA
Show(s): . . . . The King and I
Film(s): . . . . The King and I
Doretta Morrow & Larry Douglas . . . . **Brunswick LAT 8026**
Doreen Duke & Jan Mazurus . . . . **Philips BBL 7002**
Rita Moreno & Carlos Rivas . . . . **Capitol LCT 6106**
Doretta Morrow & Larry Douglas appeared in the American production
of *The King and I.*
Doreen Duke & Jan Mazurus appeared in the British production of
The King and I.
Rita Moreno & Carlos Rivas appeared in the film of *The King and I.*

WE LOVE YOU   August 1967
Mick Jagger / Keith Richard
Westminster Music . . . . UK
The Rolling Stones . . . . **Decca F 12654**

WE MUSN'T SAY GOODBYE   1943
Al Dubin / Jimmy Monaco
Victoria Music Co. Ltd . . . . USA
Film(s): . . . . Stage Door Canteen
Ambrose & his Orchestra, vocal Anne Shelton . . **Decca F 8358**
Jo Stafford . . . . **Philips BBL 7290**
Nominated for an Academy Award 1943.

WE PARTED ON THE SHORE   1906
Harry Lauder
Francis, Day & Hunter Ltd . . . . UK
Sir Harry Lauder . . . . **HMV DLP 1089**
George Elrick . . . . **Ace of Clubs ACL 1024**

WE RUN THEM IN (See Gendarmes Duet, The)

WE SAW THE SEA   1936
Irving Berlin
Irving Berlin Ltd . . . . USA
Film(s): . . . . Follow the Fleet
Fred Astaire . . . . **Columbia DB 1634**
Skip Martin & his Orchestra . . . . **Capitol LC 669**

Fred Astaire appeared in *Follow the Fleet.*

WE TAKE MYSTERY TO BED　　　　　**July 1982**
Gary Numan
Numan Music .... UK
Gary Numan .... **Beggars Banquet BEG 77**

WE THREE (My Echo, My Shadow And Me)　**1941**
Dick Robertson / Sammy Mysels / Nelson Cogane
Edwin H. Morris & Co. Ltd .... USA
The Ink Spots .... **Brunswick 03109**
Tommy Dorsey & his Orchestra,
vocal Frank Sinatra .... **RCA RD 27104**
Patti Page .... **Mercury MMC 14036**

WE WILL　　　　　　　　**September 1971**
Gilbert O'Sullivan
M.A.M. (Music Publishing) Ltd .... UK
Gilbert O'Sullivan .... **MAM 30**

WE WILL MAKE LOVE　　　　　**June 1957**
Ronald Hulme
David Toff Music Publishing Co. Ltd. .... UK
Russ Hamilton .... **Oriole MG 20031**
Ivor Novello Award.

WE WON'T LIVE IN A CASTLE　　**April 1952**
Bob Merrill
Campbell Connelly & Co. Ltd .... USA
Eve Boswell .... **Parlophone R 3501**
Guy Mitchell .... **Philips BBL 7265**

WE'LL ALL GO RIDING ON A RAINBOW　**1934**
Harry Woods
Cinephonic Music Co. Ltd. .... USA
Film(s): .... Aunt Sally
Cicely Courtneidge .... **HMV B 8067**
The 'Sing it Again' Ensemble .. **Columbia 33SX 1124**
Cicely Courtniedge appeared in *Aunt Sally*.

WE'LL BE TOGETHER AGAIN　　**August 1948**
Carl Fischer / Frankie Laine
Dash Music Ltd. .... USA
Frankie Laine .... **Mercury MPT 7513**
Carmen McRae .... **Brunswick LAT 8133**
Louis Armstrong .... **HMV CLP 1388**
Theme song of Frankie Laine.

WE'LL BRING THE HOUSE DOWN　**February 1981**
Noddy Holder / Jimmy Lee
Wild John Music .... UK
Slade .... **Cheapskate CHEAP 16**

WE'LL GATHER LILACS　　　　　**1945**
Ivor Novello
Chappell & Co. Ltd. .... UK
Show(s): .... Perchance to Dream
Film(s): .... Lilacs in the Spring
Olive Gilbert & Muriel Barron ...... **Decca LF 1309**
Errol Flynn & Patrice Wymore ..... **Philips PB 380**
Marian Grimaldi .... **HMV CLP 1258**
Olive Gilbert & Muriel Barron appeared in *Perchance to Dream*.
Errol Flynn & Patrice Wymore appeared in *Lilacs in the Spring.*

**WE'LL HAVE A JUBILEE IN MY OLD KENTUCKY
HOME**　　　　　　　　　　**1915**
Walter Donaldson / E. Ray Goetz
B. Feldman & Co. Ltd. .... USA
Lee White & Beatrice Lillie ..... **Columbia 2632**
George Elliott .... **Regal 7235**
Billy Cotton & his Band .... **Rex 9405**

WE'LL KEEP A WELCOME　　　　**July 1949**
Mai Jones / Lyn Joshua / James Harper
Lawrence Wright Music Co. Ltd .... UK
Harry Secombe .... **Philips BBL 7387**
The Lyrian Singers .... **HMV 7P 278**
The Morriston Orpheus Choir ...... **Decca LK 4203**

WE'LL MAKE HAY WHILE THE SUN SHINES　**1934**
Arthur Freed / Nacio Herb Brown
Francis, Day & Hunter Ltd. .... USA
Film(s): .... Going Hollywood
Bing Crosby .... **Brunswick 01668**
Bing Crosby appeared in *Going Hollywood.*

WE'LL MEET AGAIN　　　　　　**1939**
Ross Parker / Hugh Charles
Dash Music Ltd. .... UK
Vera Lynn (1939) .... **Decca F 7268**
The Ink Spots .... **Ace of Hearts AH 2**
Vera Lynn (1960) .... **MGM C 840**
Sammy Davis .... **Brunswick LAT 8274**

WE'RE ALL ALONE　　　　　**August 1977**
Boz Scaggs
Heath Levy Music Ltd .... USA
Rita Coolidge .... **A&M AMS 7295**

WE'RE IN THE MONEY　　　　　**1933**
Al Dubin / Harry Warren
B. Feldman & Co. Ltd. .... USA
Film(s): . Gold Diggers of 1933 / Painting the Clouds With Sunshine
Dick Powell .... **Broadcast 3339**
Ginger Rogers .... **RCA ZL 70136**
Boswell Sisters .... **Brunswick 01556**
Jack Hylton Orchestra .... **Decca F 3672**
Ginger Rogers .... **United Artists USD 311**
Ginger Rogers & Dick Powell appeared in *Gold Diggers of 1933.*

WE'RE OFF TO SEE THE WIZARD　　**1940**
Harold Arlen / E.Y. Harburg
Robbins Music Corporation Ltd. .... USA
Film(s): .... The Wizard of Oz
Judy Garland .... **MGM C 757**
Judy Garland appeared in *The Wizard of Oz.*

WE'RE THROUGH　　　　　　**October 1964**
Lee Rainsford
Maribus Music Ltd .... UK
The Hollies .... **Parlophone R 5178**

WE'VE GOT TO KEEP UP WITH THE JONESES　**1935**
Leslie Elliot / Robert Rutherford
Francis, Day & Hunter Ltd .... UK
Gracie Fields (1935) .... **Rex 8592**
Gracie Fields (1959) .... **Columbia 33SX 1198**

WE'VE GOTTA GET OUT OF THIS PLACE　**August 1965**
Barry Mann / Cynthia Weill
Screen Gems - Columbia Music Ltd .... USA
The Animals .... **Columbia DB 7639**

WEAK IN THE PRESENCE OF BEAUTY　**April 1987**
Michael Ward / Rob Clarke
Virgin Music .... UK
Alison Moyet .... **CBS MOYET 2**

WEAR MY RING (Around Your Neck)　**August 1958**
Bert Carroll / Russell Moudy
Belinda Music .... USA
Elvis Presley .... **RCA 1058**

WEARY RIVER　　　　　　　　**1929**
Louis Silvers / Grant Clarke
Francis, Day & Hunter Ltd .... USA
Film(s): .... Weary River
Joe Venuti & his Concert Orchestra,
vocal Smith Ballew .... **Parlophone R 341**
Jack Teagarden's Dixieland Band,
Jack Teagarden .... **Capitol T 1095**

WEDDING BELL BLUES　　　　**February 1970**
Laura Nyro
Tuna Fish Music .... USA
The Fifth Dimension .... **Liberty LBF 15288**

WEDDING BELLS　　　　　　**January 1982**
Kevin Godley / Lol Creme
St. Annes Music .... UK
Godley & Creme .... **Polydor POSP 369**

WEDDING BELLS (Hochzeitsglocken)　**April 1955**
Robert Mellin / Herbert Jarczyk
Robert Mellin Music Ltd. .... Germany
Eddie Fisher .... **HMV B 10839**

**WEDDING BELLS ARE BREAKING UP THAT OLD GANG
OF MINE**　　　　　　　　　　**1929**
Sammy Fain / Irving Kahal / Willie Raskin
B. Feldman & Co Ltd .... USA

Nat Shilkret & his Orchestra .... HMV B 5668
Kay Starr .... RCA RD 27056

WEDDING GLIDE, THE   1912
Louis Hirsch
B. Feldman & Co. Ltd. .... USA
Show(s): .... The Passing Show of 1912 / Hullo Ragtime
Shirley Kellog & Gerald Kirby .... HMV C 558
Billy Cotton & his Band .... Regal Zonophone MR 2273
Shirley Kellog & Gerald Kirby appeared in *Hullo Ragtime*.

WEDDING O' SANDY McNAB   1908
Harry Lauder
Francis, Day & Hunter .... UK
Harry Lauder (1908) .... HMV 02132
Harry Lauder (1926) .... HMV DLP 1089

WEDDING OF LILLI MARLENE, THE   August 1949
Michael Reine / Tommie Connor
Box & Cox (Publications) Ltd .... UK
Anne Shelton .... Decca F 9148

WEDDING OF MR MICKEY MOUSE   1933
Eddie Pola / Franz Vienna
Keith Prowse Music Publishing Co. Ltd. .... UK
Henry Hall & The B.B.C. Dance Orchestra ... Columbia CB 662

WEDDING OF THE PAINTED DOLL, THE   1929
Arthur Freed / Nacio Herb Brown
Keith Prowse Music Publishing Co. Ltd .... USA
Film(s): .... Broadway Melody / Singin' in the Rain
Jack Hylton & his Orchestra, vocal Sam Browne .. HMV B 5637
Frank Chacksfield & his Orchestra .... Decca LK 4135
Johnny Gregory & his Orchestra .... Fontana TFL 5171

WEDDING RING   October 1957
Ronald Hulme
David Toff Music Publishing Co. Ltd .... UK
Russ Hamilton .... Oriole MG 20031

WEDDING SAMBA, THE   September 1949
Abraham Ellesein / Joseph Liebowitz / Alan Small
Leeds Music Ltd .... USA
Film(s): .... On an Island With You
Edmundo Ros & his Orchestra .... Decca LK 4110
The Andrews Sisters .... Brunswick 04436

WEDDING, THE (La Novia)   October 1964
Fred Jay / Jonquin Prieto
Peter Maurice Music Co. Ltd .... Argentina
Malcolm Vaughan .... HMV POP 923
Julie Rogers .... Mercury MF 820
Clinton Ford .... Columbia DB 7307

WEE RULE   October 1988
Samantha Lawrence / Sandra Lawrence / Ian MacDonald & Charles Cochrane
Zomba Music .... UK
Wee Papa Girl Rappers .... Jive 185

WEEKEND   July 1961
Bill Post / Dore Post
Cross Music Ltd. .... USA
Eddie Cochran .... London HL 9362

WEEP NO MORE MY LADY   1943
Alex Kramer / Joan Whitney
Southern Music Publishing Ltd .... USA
Film(s): .... South of Dixie
**The Stephane Grapelli Quintet, vocal Beryl Davis with
George Shearing (piano)** .... Decca F 8333

WEEPING WILLOW LANE   1922
F. Henri Klickman / Harold G. Frost
Chappell & Co. Ltd .... USA
Walter Glynne .... HMV B 1315

WELCOME HOME (Vivre)   August 1973
Jan Dupre / Stanislas Beldone / Bryan Blackburn
Shaftesbury Music .... France
Peters & Lee .... Philips 6006307

WELCOME TO MY DREAM   1946
Johnny Burke / Jimmy Van Heusen
Edwin H. Morris & Co. Ltd. .... USA

Film(s): .... Road to Utopia
Bing Crosby .... Brunswick Bing 9
Bing Crosby appeared in *Road to Utopia*.

WELCOME TO MY WORLD   July 1963
Ray Winkler / John Hitchcock
One Four Two Music Ltd .... USA
Jim Reeves .... RCA 1342

WELCOME TO THE PLEASURE DOME   April 1985
Peter Gill / Holly Johnson / Brian Nash / Mark O'Toole
Perfect Songs .... UK
Frankie Goes to Hollywood .... ZTT ZTT 7

WELL ALL RIGHT   1939
Frances Faye / Don Raye / Dan Howell
Leeds Music Ltd. .... USA
The Andrews Sisters (1938) .... Brunswick 02769
The Andrews Sisters (1957) .... Capitol LCT 6132

WELL I ASK YA   August 1961
Les Vandyke
Essex Music Ltd. .... UK
Eden Kane .... Decca F 11353
Kay Starr .... Capitol EAP 1-20210

WELL, DID YOU EVAH?   December 1956
Cole Porter
Chappell & Co. Ltd. .... USA
Show(s): .... Dubarry Was a Lady
Film(s): .... High Society
Bing Crosby & Frank Sinatra .... Capitol LCT 6116
Bing Crosby & Frank Sinatra appeared in *High Society*.

WERE YOU SINCERE   1931
Vincent Rose / Jack Meskill
Keith Prowse Music Publishing Co. Ltd. .... USA
Bing Crosby .... Brunswick 01155
Gene Autry .... Regal Zonophone ME 11

WEST END GIRLS   January 1986
Neil Tennant / Chris Lowe
10 Music .... UK
The Pet Shop Boys .... Parlophone R 6115
Ivor Novello Award.

WEST OF ZANZIBAR (Jambo)   August 1954
Jack Fishman
Bluebird Music Co. Ltd. .... UK
Film(s): .... West of Zanzibar
Anthony Steele .... Nixa N 15023
Anthony Steele appeared in *West of Zanzibar*.

WESTMINSTER WALTZ   May 1956
Robert Farnon
Chappell & Co. Ltd. .... UK
Robert Farnon & his Orchestra .... Decca F 10818
Wally Stott & his Orchestra .... Philips BBL 7255
Ivor Novello Award.

WEYMOUTH CHIMES, THE   1905
J.S. Howgill
Chappell & Co. Ltd. .... UK
The Black Diamonds Band .... Zonophone 596
The R.A.F. Band .... Regal G 7011

WHAM RAP (Enjoy What You Do)   February 1983
George Michael / Andrew Ridgeley
Morrison Leany Music .... UK
Wham .... Innervision IVL A 2442

WHAT   September 1982
H.B. Barnum
Warner Brothers Music .... USA
Soft Cell .... Phonogram BZS 11

WHAT A DIFFERENCE A DAY MADE   1934
Maria Grever / Stanley Adams
Peter Maurice Music Co. Ltd .... Mexico
**The Dorsey Brothers Orchestra,
vocal Bob Crosby** .... Brunswick 01956
The Four Aces .... Brunswick OE 9157
Jane Morgan .... London HAR 2244
Dinah Washington .... Mercury MMC 14030
Esther Phillips (1975) .... Kudu 925

WHAT A LITTLE MOONLIGHT CAN DO   1934
Harry Woods
Cinephonic Music Co. Ltd .... USA
Film(s): .... Road House / Lady Sings the Blues
Lew Stone & his Band, vocal Al Bowlly .... **Decca F 5270**
Bing & Gary Crosby .... **Brunswick 05224**
Teddy Wilson & his Orchestra,
vocal Billie Holiday .... **Fontana TFE 17214**
Tony Brent .... **Columbia 33SX 1200**
Diana Ross .... **Tamla Motown STML 11311-2**
Diana Ross appeared in *Lady Sings the Blues*.

WHAT A MOUTH   1906
R.P. Weston
Francis, Day & Hunter Ltd .... UK
The Two Bills from Bermondsey .... **Parlophone R 3953**
Tommy Steele .... **Decca LK 4351**

WHAT A PERFECT COMBINATION   1933
Bert Kalmar / Harry Ruby / Harry Akst
Victoria Music Co. Ltd. .... USA
Film(s): .... The Kid from Spain
Eddie Cantor .... **Columbia DB 1047**
Eddie Cantor appeared in *The Kid from Spain*.

WHAT A WASTE   June 1978
Ian Dury
Blackhill Music .... UK
Ian Dury .... **Stiff BUY 27**

WHAT A WONDERFUL WORLD   May 1968
George Weiss / George Douglas
Valando Music Co. Ltd. .... USA
Louis Armstrong .... **HMV POP 1615**

WHAT AM I GONNA DO   September 1983
Rod Stewart / Jay David / Tony Brock
Carlin Music .... USA
Rod Stewart .... **Warner Brothers W 9564**

WHAT AM I GONNA DO WITH YOU   April 1975
Barry White
Schroeder Music Ltd .... USA
Barry White .... **20th Century BTC 2177**

WHAT ARE YOU DOING SUNDAY   September 1971
Toni Wine / Irwin Levine
Carlin Music Corporation .... USA
Dawn .... **Bell SBLL 142**

WHAT ARE YOU DOING THE REST OF
YOUR LIFE   April 1970
Alan Bergman / Marilyn Bergman / Michel Legrand
United Artists Music Ltd. .... USA
Film(s): .... Happy Ending
Michael Dees (Soundtrack) .... **United Artists UAS 29084**
Shirley Bassey .... **United Artists UAS 29100**
Scott Walker .... **Philips 6308035**
Nominated for an Academy Award 1969.

WHAT BECOMES OF THE BROKENHEARTED   Dec 1966
James Dean / Paul Riser / William Witherspoon
Belinda (London) Ltd. .... USA
Jimmy Ruffin .... **Tamla Motown TMG 577**
Jimmy Ruffin (1974) .... **Tamla Motown TMG 911**
Dave Stewart (1981) .... **Stiff BROKEN 1**

WHAT CAN I SAY   March 1977
Boz Scaggs
Heath Levy Music Ltd .... USA
Boz Scaggs .... **CBS 4869**

(WHAT CAN I SAY) AFTER I SAY I'M SORRY   1926
Abe Lyman / Walter Donaldson
Francis, Day & Hunter Ltd. .... USA
Film(s): .... Pete Kelly's Blues
Jack Blake .... **Columbia 4128**
The Savoy Orpheans .... **HMV B 5075**
Peggy Lee .... **Brunswick LAT 8078**
Matt Monro .... **Decca LF 1276**
Peggy Lee appeared in *Pete Kelly's Blues*.

WHAT CAN YOU GIVE A NUDIST ON HIS BIRTHDAY 1934
Arthur Le Clerq

Cameo Music Publishing Co. ltd .... UK
Gracie Fields .... **HMV B 8232**

WHAT CHER (Knocked 'Em In the Old Kent Road) (See WOT CHER

WHAT DID I DO TO BE SO BLACK AND BLUE   1933
Andy Hazat / Thomas Waller / Harry Brooks
Lawrence Wright Music Co. Ltd. .... USA
Show(s): .... Hot Chocolates
Film(s): .... Satchmo the Great
Ethel Waters .... **CBS BPG 62547**
Louis Armstrong & his Orchestra ...... **Philips BBL 7218**
Muggsy Spanier's Ragtime Band .... **RCA RD 27132**
Louis Armstrong appeared in *Satchmo the Great*.

WHAT DIFFERENCE DOES IT MAKE   February 1984
Steve Morrisey / John Marr
Warner Brothers Music .... UK
The Smiths .... **Rough Trade RT 146**

WHAT DO I CARE WHAT SOMEBODY SAID   1927
Harry Woods / Sidney Clare
Campbell Connelly & Co. Ltd. .... USA
Jan Garber & his Orchestra, vocal Charlie Warren .. **HMV B 5349**

WHAT DO I DO   March 1984
Phil Fearon
Handle Music Ltd. .... UK
Phil Fearon & Galaxy .... **Island ENY 510**

WHAT DO WE DO ON A DEW-DEW-DEWY DAY   1927
Howard Johnson / Charles Tobias / Al Sherman
Francis, Day & Hunter Ltd. .... USA
Jack Hylton & his Orchestra .... **HMV B 5371**

WHAT DO YOU WANT   December 1959
Les Vandyke
Mills Music Ltyd .... UK
Adam Faith .... **Parlophone GEP 8811**
Ivor Novello Award.

WHAT DO YOU WANT TO MAKE THOSE EYES AT ME
FOR   1916
Joseph McCarthy / Jimmy Monaco / Howard Johnson
Francis, Day & Hunter Ltd. .... USA
Show(s): .... The Better 'Ole
Film(s): .... Incendiary Blonde
The London Revue Orchestra .... **Columbia 2814**
Walter Jefferies .... **HMV B 842**
Sophie Tucker .... **Mercury MPL 0000**
Betty Hutton .... **Capitol LC 6639**
Emile Ford (1959) .... **Nixa NEP 24124**
Shakin' Stevens (1987) .... **Epic SHAKY 5**
Betty Hutton appeared in *Incendiary Blonde*.

WHAT DOES IT MATTER   1927
Irving Berlin
Francis, Day & Hunter Ltd. .... USA
Melville Gideon .... **HMV B 2359**
Roberta Sherwood .... **Brunswick LAT 8064**

WHAT DOES IT TAKE (To Win Your Love)   November 1969
Johnny Bristol / Harvey Fuqua / Vernon Bullock
Jobete Music (UK) Ltd. .... USA
Junior Walker & The All Stars .... **Tamla Motown TMG 712**

WHAT HAVE I DONE TO DESERVE THIS September 1987
Neil Tennant / Chris Lowe / Allee Willis
10 Music .... UK
The Pet Shop Boys & Dusty Springfield .. **Parlophone R 6153**
Ivor Novello Nomination.

WHAT HAVE THEY DONE TO THE RAIN   January 1965
Malvina Reynolds
Cromwell Music Ltd .... USA
Joan Baez .... **Fontana TF 428**
The Searchers .... **Pye 7N 15739**
Marianne Faithfull .... **Decca LK 4689**

WHAT HAVE YOU DONE FOR ME LATELY   May 1986
James Harms / Terry Lewis
CBS Songs .... USA
Janet Jackson .... **A&M AM 308**

WHAT HO SHE BUMPS   1899
A.J. Mills / Harry Castling
Francis, Day & Hunter Ltd. . . . . UK
Herbert Danby . . . . **Berliner 2948**

WHAT I'VE GOT IN MIND   September 1976
Jack Clement
A.T.V. Music Ltd. . . . . USA
Billie Jo Spears . . . . **United Artists UP 36118**

WHAT IN THE WORLD'S COME OVER YOU   March 1960
Jack Scott
Southern Music Publishing Co. Ltd . . . . USA
Jack Scott . . . . **Top Rank JKP 3002**

WHAT IS LIFE   April 1972
George Harrison
Harrisongs Ltd . . . . UK
Olivia Newton-John . . . . **Pye 7N 25575**
George Harrison . . . . **Parlophone STCH 639/3**

WHAT IS LOVE   January 1984
John Jones / William Bryant
Warner Brothers Music . . . . UK
Howard Jones . . . . **WEA HOW 2**

WHAT IS THIS THING CALLED LOVE   1929
Cole Porter
Chappell & Co. Ltd . . . . USA
Show(s): . . . . Wake Up and Dream
Film(s):Wake Up and Dream / Night and Day / Starlift / The Eddy
Duchin Story
George Metaxa . . . . **HMV B 3016**
Tommy Dorsey & his Orchestra . . . . **HMV BD 5791**
Julie London . . . . **London HAU 2166**
Mel Tormé . . . . **HMV CLP 1382**
Artie Shaw & his Orchestra . . . . **HMV B 8959**
George Metaxa appeared in the British production of *Wake Up And
Dream*.

WHAT KIND OF FOOL AM I   September 1961
Leslie Bricusse / Anthony Newley
Essex Music Ltd. . . . . UK
Show(s): . . . . Stop the World - I Want to Get Off
Film(s): . . . . Stop the World - I Want to Get Off
Anthony Newley . . . . **Decca LK 4404**
Sammy Davis . . . . **Reprise R 20048**
Shirley Bassey . . . . **Columbia DB 4974**
Geoff Love & his Orchestra . . . . **Columbia SX 1600**
Tony Tanner . . . . **Warner Brothers B 1643**
Anthony Newley appeared in the British and American production of
Stop the World - I Want to Get Off.
Tony Tanner appeared in the film *Stop the World - I Want to Get Off*.
Ivor Novello Award.

WHAT KINDA BOY YOU LOOKIN' FOR GIRL   June 1983
Errol Brown
Rak Music . . . . UK
Hot Chocolate . . . . **RAK 357**

WHAT MAKES THE SUNSET   1945
Jule Styne / Sammy Cahn
Robbins Music Corporation Ltd. . . . . USA
Film(s): . . . . Anchors Aweigh
Frank Sinatra . . . . **Fontana SET 303A**
Dennis Lotis . . . . **Columbia 33SX 1089**
Frank Sinatra appeared in *Anchors Aweigh*.

WHAT MORE CAN I SAY   1942
Art Noel
Cinephonic Music Co. Ltd . . . . UK
Lew Stone & his Orchestra, vocal Benny Lee . . . . **Decca F 8083**
Flanagan & Allen . . . . **Decca F 8067**

WHAT NOW MY LOVE (Et Maintenant)   October 1962
Gilbert Becaud / Pierre Delanoe / Carl Sigman
Blossom Music Ltd . . . . France
Jane Morgan . . . . **London HLR 9528**
Shirley Bassey . . . . **Columbia DB 4870**
Gilbert Becaud . . . . **HMV POP 1334**
Sonny & Cher (1966) . . . . **Atlantic AT 4069**

WHAT TIME IS LOVE   September 1990
James Cauty / William Drummond
Warner Chappell Music . . . . UK

The KLF . . . . **KLF Communications KLF 004**

WHAT WILL I TELL MY HEART   1937
Peter Tinturin / Jack Lawrence
Chappell & Co. Ltd. . . . . USA
Bing Crosby . . . . **Brunswick 02402**
Andy Kirk & his Orchestra . . . . **Brunswick 02377**
Ella Fitzgerald . . . . **HMV CLP 1166**

WHAT WOULD I BE   December 1966
Jackie Trent
Darren Music Ltd. . . . . UK
Val Doonican . . . . **Decca F 12505**
Ivor Novello Nomination.

WHAT YOU'RE PROPOSING   November 1980
Francis Rossi / Bernie Frost
Eaton Music . . . . UK
Status Quo . . . . **Vertigo QUO 3**
Ivor Novello Nomination.

WHAT'CHA GONNA DO ABOUT IT   October 1965
Doris Payne
T.S. Music Ltd . . . . USA
Doris Troy . . . . **Atlantic AT 4011**
The Small Faces . . . . **Decca F 12208**
Cilla Black . . . . **Parlophone PMC 1243**

WHAT'D I SAY   July 1959
Ray Charles
Progressive Music Ltd . . . . USA
Ray Charles . . . . **London HAE 2226**
Cliff Richard . . . . **Columbia SX 1320**
Jerry Lee Lewis (1961) . . . . **London HLS 9335**

WHAT'LL I DO   1924
Irving Berlin
Francis, Day & Hunter Ltd. . . . . USA
Show(s): . . . . .The Music Box Revue / The Punch Bowl
Film(s): . . . . .Alexander's Ragtime Band
Norah Blaney & Gwen Farrar . . . . **HMV BD 254**
Walter Pidgeon . . . . **HMV B 1882**
Pat Boone . . . . **London HAD 2082**
Burl Ives . . . . **HMV CLP 1470**
Norah Blaney & Gwen Farrar appeared in *The Punch Bowl*.

WHAT'S ANOTHER YEAR   May 1980
Shay Healey
Bocu Music Ltd . . . . Ireland
Johnny Logan . . . . **Epic EPC 8572**
Irish entry for the 1980 Eurovision Song Contest (Placed First).

WHAT'S LOVE GOT TO DO WITH IT   August 1984
Terry Britten / Graham Lyle
Rondor Music . . . . UK
Tina Turner . . . . **Capitol CL 334**

WHAT'S NEW   1939
Bob Haggart / Johnny Burke
B. Feldman & Co. Ltd. . . . . USA
Bob Crosby & his Orchestra . . . . **Brunswick LA 8567**
Bing Crosby . . . . **Ace of Hearts AH 17**
Gogi Grant . . . . **London HAB 2032**
Bob Crosby & The Bob Cats . . . . **London HAD 2293**
Billy Butterfield Orchestra . . . . **Capitol LC 6684**
Originally written as an instrumental entitled *I'm Free*.
Theme tune of Billy Butterfield.

WHAT'S NEW PUSSYCAT   September 1965
Burt Bacharach / Hal David
United Artists Music Co. Ltd . . . . USA
Film(s): . . . . .What's New Pussycat
Tom Jones . . . . **Decca F 12203**
Nominated for an Academy Award 1965.

WHAT'S THE COLOUR OF MONEY   August 1986
Mark Rodgers / Leroy Rose
Island Music . . . . UK
Hollywood Beyond . . . . **WEA YZ 76**

WHAT'S THE GOOD WORD MISTER BLUEBIRD   1943
Al Hoffman / Allan Roberts / Jerry Livingston
Sterling Music Publishing Co. Ltd . . . . USA
Harry Roy & his Band . . . . **Regal Zonophone MR 3703**

WHAT'S THE USE OF DREAMING   1906
Joe Howard
B. Feldman & Co. Ltd. .... USA
Danny Kaye   **Brunswick 04068**

WHATEVER I DO (WHEREVER I GO)   **July 1984**
Mike Stock / Matt Aitken
All Boys Music .... UK
Hazel Dean .... **Pronto ENA 119**

WHATEVER LOLA WANTS   **April 1957**
Richard Adler / Jerry Ross
Frank Music Co. Ltd. .... USA
Show(s): .... Damn Yankees
Film(s): .... What Lola Wants
Gwen Verdon .... **HMV CLP 1108**
Gwen Verdon .... **RCA RD 27103**
Eartha Kitt .... **MGM C 878**
Gwen Verdon appeared in the American production of *Damn Yankees*
and also *What Lola Wants*.

WHATEVER YOU WANT   **October 1979**
Richard Parfitt / Andrew Brown
EMI Music Ltd. .... UK
Status Quo .... **Vertigo 6059242**

WHEEL OF FORTUNE, THE   **May 1952**
Bennie Benjamin / George Weiss
Valando Music Co. Ltd .... USA
Kay Starr .... **Capitol T 949**
Lavern Baker .... **London HAK 2422**
Theme song of Kay Starr.

WHEEL OF THE WAGON IS BROKEN, THE   1935
Elton Box / Desmond Cox / Michael Carr
Dash Music Ltd .... UK
The Rocky Mountaineers .... **Columbia FB 1113**
The Bowman-Hyde Singers & Players .. **Parlophone PMC 1155**

WHEELS   **March 1961**
Norman Petty
Petford Music Co. Ltd .... USA
The Stringalongs .... **London HL 9278**
Max Harris & his Group .... **Fontana H 296**
Johnny Spence Orchestra .... **Parlophone R 4736**
Joe Loss & his Orchestra (Cha cha version) .... **HMV POP 880**

WHEEZY ANNA   1933
Leslie Sarony
Dach Music Ltd. .... UK
Leslie Sarony .... **Imperial 2831**
Ray Noble & his Orchestra .... **HMV B 6316**
The Bowman-Hyde Singers & Players .. **Parlophone PMC 1155**

WHEN   **July 1958**
Paul Evans / Jack Reardon
Southern Music Publishing Co. Ltd .... USA
The Kalin Twins .... **Brunswick OE 9383**
The Kaye Sisters .... **Philips BBE 12256**
Showaddywaddy (1977) .... **Arista 91**

WHEN A CHILD IS BORN (Soleado)   **December 1976**
'Zacar' / Fred Jay
Armore & Beechwood Ltd .... Italy
Johnny Mathis .... **CBS 4599**

WHEN A LADY MEETS A GENTLEMAN DOWN SOUTH 1936
Dave Oppenheim / Michael Cleary / Jaques Krakeur
Chappell & Co. Ltd .... USA
Benny Goodman & his Orchestra,
vocal Helen Ward .... **Camden CDN 148**

WHEN A MAID COMES KNOCKING AT YOUR HEART   1913
Rudolf Frimi / Otto Harbach
Chappell & Co. Ltd .... USA
Show(s): .... Firefly
Film(s): .... Firefly
Jeanette MacDonald .... **Caliban 6027**
Paul Britten Orchestra .... **MGM C 779**
Jeanette MacDonald appeared in the film *Firefly*.

WHEN A MAN LOVES A WOMAN   **July 1966**
Calvin Lewis / Andrew Wright
Bolinda (London) Ltd. .... USA
Percy Sledge .... **Atlantic 584001**

Percy Sledge (1987) .... **Atlantic YZ 96**

WHEN A SOLDIER'S ON PARADE   1934
Leslie Sarony
Lawrence Wright Music Co. Ltd. .... UK
Show(s): .... On With the Show
Debroy Somers & his Band,
vocal Raymond Newell .... **Columbia FB 1362**

WHEN APRIL SINGS   1941
Robert Stolz / Gus Kahn
B. Feldman & Co. Ltd .... USA
Film(s): .... Spring Parade
Deanna Durbin .... **Brunswick LAT 8285**
Robert Stoltz & his Orchestra .... **MGM C 815**
Deanna Durbin appeared in *Spring Parade*.

WHEN AUTUMN LEAVES ARE FALLING   1926
Abner Silver / Sam Coslow
Francis, Day & Hunter Ltd. .... USA
Jack Smith (piano accompaniment Abner Silver) . **HMV B 2333**

WHEN BUDDHA SMILES   1922
Nacio Herb Brown / Arthur Freed / King Zany
Chappell & Co. Ltd .... USA
Paul Whiteman & his Orchestra .... **HMV B 1332**
Benny Goodman & his Orchestra ...... **Columbia 33CX 1529**

WHEN DAY IS DONE   1928
Robert Katscher / Buddy De Sylva
B. Feldman & Co. Ltd. .... Austria
Show(s): .... Will o' the Whispers
Jack Smith .... **HMV B 2666**
Paul Whiteman & his Orchestra .... **HMV C 2823**
Ambrose & his Orchestra .... **Decca K 749**
Bing Crosby .... **Brunswick 03875**
The Clark Sisters .... **London HAD 2177**
Jack Smith appeared in *Will O' the Whispers*.
Theme song of Ambrose.

WHEN DID YOU LEAVE HEAVEN   1937
Walter Bullock / Richard A. Whiting
Robbins Music Ltd. .... USA
Film(s): .... Sing Baby Sing
Tony Martin .... **Decca F 6102**
Les Allen .... **Columbia FB 1584**
Nancy Wilson .... **Capitol T 1934**
Tony Martin appeared in *Sing Baby Sing*.

WHEN DOVES CRY   **August 1984**
"Prince"
Island Music .... USA
Prince .... **Warner Brothers WB 9286**

WHEN FATHER PAPERED THE PARLOUR   1909
R.P. Weston / F.J. Barnes
Francis, Day & Hunter Ltd. .... UK
Billy Williams .... **Zonophone 407**
David Kossoff .... **Oriole MG 20043**

WHEN FOREVER HAS GONE   **October 1976**
Barry Mason / Stynianos Vlavianos
Mason Music Ltd .... France
Demis Roussos .... **Philips 6042186**

WHEN HE SHINES   **June 1981**
Florrie Palmer / Dominic Bugatti
Warner Brothers Music .... UK
Sheena Easton .... **EMI 5166**
Ivor Novello Nomination.

WHEN HEARTS ARE YOUNG   1923
Sigmund Romberg / Cyrus Wood / Alfred Goodman
Chappell & Co. Ltd .... USA
Show(s): .... The Lady in Ermine
Paul Specht & his Orchestra .... **Columbia 3292**
Perry Como .... **RCA RD 27206**

WHEN I FALL IN LOVE   **November 1952**
Edward Heyman / Victor Young
Chappell & Co. Ltd. .... USA
Film(s): .... One Minute to Zero / Istanbul
Jeri Southern .... **Brunswick 04978**
Doris Day .... **Columbia DB 3157**

Nat 'King' Cole (1957)	Capitol LCT 6129
Julie London	London HAW 2229
Donny Osmond (1973)	MGM 2006365
Rick Astley (1987)	RCA PB 41683

WHEN I GROW TOO OLD TO DREAM 1935
Sigmund Romberg / Oscar Hammerstein II

Francis, Day & Hunter Ltd . . . . USA
Film(s): . . . . The Night is Young / Deep in My Heart

Irene Dunne	Columbia DB 1805
Evelyn Laye	HMV B 8297
Jose Ferrer	MGM C 755

Evelyn Laye appeared in *The Night is Young.*
Jose Ferrer appeared in *Deep in My Heart.*

WHEN I LEAVE THE WORLD BEHIND 1915
Irving Berlin

B. Feldman & Co. Ltd. . . . . USA

Gertie Gitana	Regal G 7293
Cavan O'Connor	Rex 10146
Al Jolson	Brunswick LA 8575
Teresa Brewer	Vogue LVA 9020

WHEN I LOST YOU 1912
Irving Berlin

B. Feldman & Co. Ltd. . . . . USA

Bing Crosby	Brunswick LAT 8334
Kate Smith	MGM D 145

WHEN I LOVE, I LOVE 1942
Mack Gordon / Harry Warren

Cavendish Music Co. Ltd . . . . UK
Film(s): . . . . Weekend in Havana

Carmen Miranda	Brunswick 03272
The George Mitchell Minstrels	HMV CLP 1460

Carmen Miranda appeared in *Weekend in Havana.*

WHEN I NEED YOU March 1977
Albert Hammond / Carole Bayer Sager

Chappell & Co. Ltd . . . . USA

Leo Sayer	Chrysalis CHS 2127

WHEN I SEE AN ELEPHANT FLY 1941
Ned Washington / Oliver Wallace

Chappell & Co. Ltd . . . . USA
Film(s): . . . . Dumbo (cartoon)

Sound Track	Top Rank JKP 2031
Bill Hayes	HMV 7EG 8355
Bruce Forsyth	Parlophone PMC 1132

WHEN I TAKE MY MORNING PROMENADE 1910
A.J. Mills / Bennett Scott

B. Feldman & Co. . . . . UK

Marie Lloyd	Regal 1026
Patricia Rowlands	Decca LK 4628
George Mitchell Minstrels	Columbia SX 6373

WHEN I TAKE MY SUGAR TO TEA 1931
Irving Kahal / Sammy Fain / Pierre Norman

Chappell & Co. Ltd. . . . . USA
Film(s): . . . . Monkey Business

The Boswell Sisters	Brunswick 01113
Bing Crosby	Brunswick LAT 8217
Frank Sinatra	Reprise R 1001

WHEN I THINK OF YOU September 1986
James Harris / Terry Lewis

CBS Songs . . . . USA

Janet Jackson	A&M AM 337

WHEN I'M CLEANING WINDOWS 1936
George Formby / Fred E. Cliffe / Harry Gifford

Lawrence Wright Music Co. Ltd . . . . UK
Film(s): . . . . Keep Your Seats Please

George Formby	Decca DFE 6328
George Formby	Columbia SEG 7550

George Formby appeared in *Keep Your Seats Please.*

WHEN I'M DEAD AND GONE January 1971
Bernard Gallagher / Graham Lyle

Gallagher & Lyle Music . . . . UK

McGuiness Flint	Capitol CL 15662

Ivor Novello Nomination.

WHEN I'M LOOKING AT YOU 1930
Clifford Grey / Herbert Stothart

Chappell & Co. Ltd . . . . USA
Film(s): . . . . The Rogue Song

Lawrence Tibbett	HMV DA 1102

Lawrence Tibbett appeared in *The Rogue Song.*

WHEN I'M SIXTY-FOUR August 1967
John Lennon / Paul McCartney

Northern Songs Ltd. . . . . UK
Film(s): . . . . Yellow Submarine

Kenny Ball & his Jazzmen	Pye 7N 17348
The Beatles	Parlophone PMC 7027

The Beatles appeared in *Yellow Submarine.*

WHEN I'M WITH YOU 1937
Mack Gordon / Harry Revel

Robbins Music Corporation Ltd. . . . . USA
Film(s): . . . . Poor Little Rich Girl

Phyllis Robins	Rex 8950
Turner Layton	Columbia FB 1415
Hildegarde	Columbia FB 1523
Jack Payne & his Band	Rex 8875

WHEN IRISH EYES ARE SMILING 1912
George Graff / Ernest Ball / Chauncey Olcott

B. Feldman & Co. Ltd. . . . . USA
Show(s): . . . . The Isle of Dreams
Film(s): . . . . . . Irish Eyes Are Smiling / Doughboys in Ireland

John McCormack	Camden CDN 1002
Bing Crosby	Brunswick LAT 8278
Max Bygraves	HMV POP 277
Eileen Donaghy	Fontana TFL 5036

WHEN IT'S APPLE BLOSSOM TIME IN NORMANDY 1912
Harry Gifford / Huntley Trevor / Tom Mellor

Francis, Day & Hunter Ltd. . . . . UK
Film(s): . . . . Shine On Harvest Moon

Marguerite Dunlap & Harry MacDonough	HMV B 343

WHEN IT'S LAMP LIGHTING TIME IN THE VALLEY 1933
Joe Lyons / Sam C. Hart

B. Feldman & Co. Ltd. . . . . USA

The Musketeers	Columbia DB 1127
Mac Wiseman	London HAD 2217

WHEN IT'S NIGHT TIME IN DIXIELAND 1914
Irving Berlin

B. Feldman & Co. Ltd. . . . . USA

The Mayfair Orchestra	HMV B 811

WHEN IT'S NIGHT TIME IN ITALY, IT'S WEDNESDAY OVER HERE 1924
James Kendis / Lew Brown

Lawrence Wright Music Co. Ltd . . . . USA

The Two Gilberts	Regal G 8092
The Girls From 'Club 16' with Joe 'Fingers' Carr	Warner Brothers WM 4049

WHEN IT'S SLEEPY TIME DOWN SOUTH 1932
Leon & Otis Rene / Clarence Muse

Lawrence Wright Music Co. Ltd . . . . USA

Paul Robeson	HMV B 4058
Louis Armstrong & his Orchestra	Ace of Hearts AH 7
Louis Armstrong & his Orchestra	Parlophone R 1034
Ruby Braff & his Orchestra	Vogue LAE 12051

Theme song of Louis Armstrong.

WHEN IT'S SPRINGTIME IN THE ROCKIES 1930
Robert Sauer / Mary Woolsey

Francis, Day & Hunter Ltd . . . . USA
Film(s): . . . . Silver Spurs

Hobo Jack Turner	Columbia DB 218
Slim Whitman	London HA 2139
Gene Autry	Philips PB 169

WHEN JESAMINE GOES October 1968
F. Manston / Jack Gellar

Mills Music Ltd. . . . . UK

The Casuals	Decca F 22784

Ivor Novello Nomination.

WHEN JOHNNY COMES MARCHING HOME July 1960
Patrick Gilmore

Filmusic Publishing Co. Ltd . . . . USA
Film(s): . . . . Never Let Go
Adam Faith . . . . **Parlophone GEP 8811**
Adam Faith appeared in *Never Let Go*.First published 1863.

WHEN JULIE COMES AROUND   May 1970
Lee Pockriss / Paul Vance
Peter Maurice Music Co. Ltd. . . . . USA
The Cuff Links . . . . **MCA MU 1112**

WHEN JUNE COMES ALONG WITH A SONG   1923
George M. Cohan
B. Feldman & Co. Ltd . . . . USA
The Great White Way Orchestra . . . . **HMV B 1728**

WHEN LIGHTS ARE LOW   1936
Benny Carter / Spencer Williams
Peter Maurice Music Co. Ltd . . . . UK
Benny Carter & his Swing Quartet,
vocal Elizabeth Welch . . . . **Decca LK 4221**
June Christy . . . . **Capitol T 1076**

WHEN MEXICO GAVE UP THE RUMBA   October 1956
Gale Jones
Robbins Music Corporation Ltd. . . . . USA
Mitchell Torok . . . . **Brunswick 05586**
The Mudlarks . . . . **Columbia DB 4636**

WHEN MOTHER NATURE SINGS HER LULLABY   1938
Glen Brown / Larry Yoell
Campbell Connelly & Co. Ltd. . . . . USA
Geraldo & his Orchestra, vocal Al Bowlly . . . . . . **HMV BD 5427**
Ambrose & his Orchestra . . . . **Decca F 6855**
Al Bowlly . . . . **Decca F 6877**

WHEN MY BABY SMILES AT ME   1921
Andrew Sterling / Ted Lewis / Bill Munro
Herman Darewski Music Publishing Co. Ltd . . . . USA
Show(s): . . . . Greenwich Village Follies of 1920
Film(s): . . . . When My Baby Smiles at Me
Art Hickman's London Five . . . . **HMV B 1200**
Ted Lewis & his Band . . . . **Brunswick LAT 8601**
Bing Crosby . . . . **Brunswick LAT 8138**
Max Bygraves . . . . **Decca LK 4317**
Ted Lewis appeared in *When My Baby Smiles at Me.*
Theme song of Ted Lewis.

WHEN MY DREAMBOAT COMES HOME   1937
Cliff Friend / Dave Franklin
B. Feldman & Co. Ltd. . . . . USA
Bing Crosby . . . . **Brunswick LAT 8228**
Max Bygraves . . . . **Decca LK 4360**

WHEN MY DREAMS COME TRUE   1929
Irving Berlin
Francis, Day & Hunter Ltd . . . . USA
Film(s): . . . . The Cocoanuts
Paul Whiteman & his Orchestra,
vocal Austin 'Skin' Young . . . . **Columbia 5484**
Norah Blaney . . . . **Columbia 5614**

WHEN MY LITTLE GIRL IS SMILING   May 1962
Gerry Goffin / Carole King
Aldon Music Ltd. . . . . USA
Jimmy Justice . . . . **Pye 7N 15421**
Craig Douglas . . . . **Top Rank JAR 610**
The Drifters . . . . **London HLK 9522**

WHEN MY SHIP COMES IN   1935
Walter Donaldson / Gus Kahn
Francis, Day & Hunter Ltd . . . . USA
Film(s): . . . . Kid Millions
Eddie Cantor . . . . **Rex 8391**
Kate Smith . . . . **Brunswick 01970**
Eddie Cantor appeared in *Kid Millions.*

WHEN MY SUGAR WALKS DOWN THE STREET   1925
Jimmy McHugh / Irving Mills / Gene Austin
Lawrence Wright Music Co. Ltd. . . . . USA
Aileen Stanley & Gene Austin . . . . **HMV B 2006**
The Four Aces . . . . **Brunswick LAT 8221**
Peggy Lee . . . . **Capitol T 979**

WHEN SANTA GOT STUCK UP THE CHIMNEY   Dec 1953
Jimmy Grafton

Michael Reine Music . . . . UK
Billy Cotton Band . . . . **Decca F 10217**

WHEN SHALL WE MEET AGAIN   1922
Richard A. Whiting / Raymond Egan
B. Feldman & Co. Ltd . . . . USA
The Hackel-Berge Orchestra . . . . **HMV B 1340**

WHEN SHE WAS MY GIRL   November 1981
Marc Blatt / Larry Gottlieb
Leeds Music . . . . USA
The Four Tops . . . . **Casablanca CAN 1005**

WHEN SMOKEY SINGS   July 1987
Martin Fry / Mark White
10 Music . . . . UK
A.B.C. . . . . **Neutron NT 111**

WHEN SOMEBODY THINKS YOU'RE WONDERFUL   1936
Harry Woods
B. Feldman & Co. Ltd . . . . USA
'Fats' Waller & his Rhythm . . . . **RCA 1189**
Gary Miller with the Kenny Ball Jazzmen . . . . . **Pye NPL 18059**

WHEN THAT MAN IS DEAD AND GONE   1941
Irving Berlin
Chappell & Co. Ltd . . . . USA
Al Bowlly & Jimmy Mesene (guitar) . . . . **HMV BD 922**
Ambrose & his Orchestra, vocal Anne Shelton . . **Decca F 7791**

WHEN THE ANGELUS IS RINGING   1914
Joe Young / Bert Grant
B. Feldman & Co. Ltd. . . . . USA
Show(s): . . . . Business as Usual
Henri Leoni . . . . **Columbia 2485**
Vaughn Monroe & his Orchestra, vocal Vaughan Monroe &
The Moon Maids . . . . **HMV BD 5961**
Henri Leoni appeared in *Business as Usual.*

WHEN THE BLOOM IS ON THE SAGE   1931
Fred Howard / Nat Vincent
Keith Prowse Music Publishing Co. Ltd. . . . . USA
Peterson's Hobo Orchestra . . . . **Panachord 25060**
Bing Crosby . . . . **Brunswick LAT 8152**

WHEN THE BOYS TALK ABOUT THE GIRLS   May 1958
Bob Merrill
Lawrence Wright Music Co. Ltd . . . . USA
Valerie Carr . . . . **Columbia SEG 7860**
The Beverley Sisters . . . . **Columbia 33SX 1285**

WHEN THE GIRL IN YOUR ARMS   November 1961
Sid Teppor / Roy Bennett
Eugene Music Ltd. . . . . USA
Film(s): . . . . The Young Ones
Cliff Richard . . . . **Columbia DB 4716**
Cliff Richard appeared in *The Young Ones.*

WHEN THE GOING GETS TOUGH, THE TOUGH GET GOING   March 1986
Wayne Braithwaite / Barry Eastmond / Bob Lange & Billy Ocean
ATV Music . . . . UK
Billy Ocean . . . . **Jive JIVE 114**

WHEN THE GUARDS ARE ON PARADE   1931
Horatio Nicholls / Leslie Sarony
Lawrence Wright Music Co. Ltd. . . . . UK
Flotsam & Jetsam . . . . **Columbia DB 535**
Alyn Ainsworth & his Orchestra . . . . **Parlophone R 4419**

WHEN THE GUARDSMAN STARTED CROONING ON PARADE   1936
Eddie Lisbona / Tommie Connor
B. Feldman & Co. Ltd . . . . UK
Bobby Comber . . . . **Rex 8679**

WHEN THE GYPSY PLAYED   1935
Ivor Novello / Christopher Hassall
Chappell & Co. Ltd . . . . UK
Show(s): . . . . Glamorous Night
Film(s): . . . . Glamorous Night
Mary Ellis . . . . **HMV DLP 1095**
Mary Ellis appeared in both the show and the film of *Glamorous Night.*

WHEN THE HARVEST MOON IS SHINING 1920
George Stevens
Michael Reine Music Co. Ltd . . . . USA
Will Strong & Chorus . . . . **HMV B 1138**
Sid Philips & his Band, vocal Johnnie Eager . . . **HMV BD 6081**

WHEN THE LEAVES COME TUMBLING DOWN 1923
Richard Howard
Chappell & Co. Ltd . . . . USA
The Clyde Doer Orchestra . . . . **HMV B 1457**
Paul Specht & his Orchestra . . . . **Columbia 3293**
The Ballyhooligans . . . . **HMV BD 5211**

WHEN THE LIGHTS GO ON AGAIN 1942
Eddie Seiler / Sol Marcus / Bennie Benjamin
Dash Music Ltd . . . . USA
Vera Lynn . . . . **Decca F 8241**
The Four Sergeants & Rose Marie . . . . **HMV 7EG 8396**

**WHEN THE MIDNIGHT CHOO-CHOO LEAVES
FOR ALABAM'** 1912
Irving Berlin
B. Feldman & Co. Ltd. . . . . USA
Film(s):Alexander's Ragtime Band / Easter Parade / There's No
Business Like Show Business
The Victor Military Band . . . . **HMV C 289**
Tommy Dorsey & his Orchestra . . . . **HMV B 8809**
The Andrews Sisters . . . . **Brunswick 04204**
Judy Garland & Fred Astaire . . . . **MGM D 140**
Ethel Merman & Dan Dailey . . . . **Brunswick LAT 8059**
Ethel Merman & Dan Dailey appeared in *There's No Business Like
Show Business.*
Judy Garland & Fred Astaire appeared in *Easter Parade.*

WHEN THE MOON COMES OVER MADISON SQUARE 1941
Johnny Burke / Jimmy Monaco
Campbell Connelly & Co. Ltd . . . . USA
Film(s): . . . . Rhythm on the River
Bing Crosby . . . . **Brunswick Bing 6**
Bing Crosby appeared in *Rhythm on the Range.*

WHEN THE MOON COMES OVER THE MOUNTAIN 1931
Harry Woods / Howard Johnson / Kate Smith
Keith Prowse Music Publishing Co. Ltd. . . . . USA
Film(s): . . . . The Big Broadcast
Kate Smith . . . . **Columbia DB 683**
Jack Hylton & his Orchestra . . . . **HMV B 6027**
Kitty Wells . . . . **Brunswick LAT 8361**
Kate Smith appeared in *The Big Broadcast.*
Theme song of Kate Smith.

WHEN THE ORGAN PLAYED "O PROMISE ME" 1938
Al Sherman / Abner Silver / Jack Meskill
Campbell Connelly & Co. Ltd. . . . . USA
Bing Crosby . . . . **Brunswick 02604**
Al Bowlly . . . . **HMV BD 565**

WHEN THE ORGAN PLAYED AT TWILIGHT 1930
Raymond Wallace / Jimmy Campbell / Reginald Connelly
Campbell Connelly & Co. Ltd . . . . UK
Jack Hylton & his Orchestra (with Cinema Organ) . **HMV B 6763**
Dennis Day . . . . **Capitol T 741**

WHEN THE POPPIES BLOOM AGAIN 1936
Don Pelosi / Leo Towers / Morton Morrow
Dash Music Ltd . . . . UK
The Mantovani Tipica Orchestra . . . . **Columbia FB 1557**
Ambrose & his Orchestra . . . . **Decca F 6097**
Leslie Hutchinson (Hutch) . . . . **Parlophone F 586**
Jack Daly . . . . **Regal Zonophone MR 2271**

**WHEN THE RED RED ROBIN (Comes Bob Bob Bobbin'
Along)** 1926
Harry Woods
Francis, Day & Hunter Ltd. USA
Film(s):The Jolson Story / Has Anybody Seen My Gal / I'll Cry
Tomorrow
Jack Smith . . . . **HMV B 2337**
Lillian Roth . . . . **Philips BBL 7079**
Al Jolson . . . . **Brunswick LAT 8575**
Susan Hayward . . . . **MGM EP 555**
Susan Hayward appeared in *I'll Cry Tomorrow.*

WHEN THE SERGEANT MAJOR'S ON PARADE 1925
Ernest Longstaffe

Chappell & co. Ltd. . . . . UK
Peter Dawson . . . . **HMV B 8158**
Kenneth Walters . . . . **Regal G 1041**

**WHEN THE SUMMER COMES AGAIN (Three Pots a Shill-
ing)** 1895
Harry Bedford
Francis, Day & Hunter Ltd. UK
Elsa Lanchester . . . . **HMV CLP 1417**

WHEN THE SUN COMES OUT 1941
Ted Koehler / Harold Arlen
Cavendish Music Co. Ltd . . . . USA
**Jimmy Dorsey & his Orchestra,
vocal Helen O'Connell** . . . . **Brunswick 03189**
Helen O'Connell . . . . **Warner Brothers WM 4033**

WHEN THE SUN GOES DOWN 1938
Leroy Carr
Francis, Day & Hunter Ltd. USA
The Ink Spots . . . . **Brunswick 02637**
**Huddie Leadbetter with
Sonny Terry (harmonica)** . . . . **Melodisc MLP 12-107**
Eartha Kitt . . . . **London HAR 2207**

WHEN THE SUN GOES DOWN 1922
Melville Gideon
Francis, Day & Hunter Ltd . . . . UK
Show(s): . . . . The Co-Optimists
Melville Gideon . . . . **Zonophone 2322**
Melville Gideon . . . . **HMV C 2441**

**WHEN THE SWALLOWS COME BACK TO
CAPISTRANO** 1940
Leon Rene
B. Feldman & Co. Ltd . . . . USA
Dick Todd . . . . **HMV BD 869**
The Ink Spots . . . . **Brunswick LA 8590**
Pat Boone . . . . **London HAD 2098**

WHEN THE WORLD WAS YOUNG February 1952
Philippe Gerard / Johnny Mercer
Macmelodies Ltd . . . . France
Edith Piaf . . . . **Columbia DCF 66**
Peggy Lee . . . . **Ace of Hearts AH 5**
Helen Merrill . . . . **MGM EP 699**

WHEN THERE ISN'T A GIRL ABOUT 1906
Harry Castling / Charles Collins
B. Feldman & Co. . . . . UK
The Pavement Artists . . . . **Regal MR 643**
The Michael John Singers . . . . **Line L 2032**

WHEN THEY ASK ABOUT YOU 1944
Sammy Stept
Bradbury Wood Ltd. . . . . USA
Film(s): . . . . Stars on Parade
**Jimmy Dorsey & his Orchestra,
vocal Kitty Kallen** . . . . **Brunswick 03544**

WHEN THEY SOUND THE LAST ALL CLEAR 1941
Hugh Charles / Louis Elton
Dash Music Ltd . . . . UK
Vera Lynn . . . . **Decca F 7977**

WHEN WE WERE YOUNG July 1983
Warren Bacall
RCA Music . . . . UK
Bucks Fizz . . . . **RCA 342**

WHEN WE'RE ALONE (Penthouse Serenade) 1932
Will Jason / Val Burton
Victoria Music Co. Ltd. . . . . USA
Film(s): . . . . Beau James
Layton & Johnstone . . . . **Columbia DB 820**
Bob Hope & Shirley Ross . . . . **Brunswick 02822**
Imogene Lynn . . . . **London HAP 2056**
Bob Hope appeared in *Beau James.*

**WHEN WE'VE WOUND UP THE WATCH
ON THE RHINE** 1914
Herman Darewski / E.V. Lucas / Albert De Courville
Francis, Day & Hunter Ltd. UK
Show(s): . . . . Business as Usual
Violet Lorraine & Ambrose Thorne . . . . . . **Columbia 2484**

Violet Lorraine .... **HMV C 2357**
Violet Lorraine & Ambrose Thorne appeared in *Business As Usual.*

WHEN WILL I BE FAMOUS   February 1988
Nicky Graham / Tom Watkins
Virgin Music .... UK
Bros .... CBS ATOM 2

WHEN WILL I BE LOVED   August 1960
Phil Everly
Acuff-Rose Publishing Co. Ltd .... USA
The Everly Brothers .... London HAA 2266

WHEN WILL I SEE YOU AGAIN   August 1974
Kenny Gamble / Leon Huff
Carlin Music Corporation .... USA
Film(s): .... Black Joy
The Three Degrees .... Philadelphia PIR 2155
The Three Degrees appeared in *Black Joy.*

WHEN WILL THE GOOD APPLES FALL   November 1967
Kenny Young
United Artists Music Co. Ltd. .... USA
The Seekers .... Columbia DB 8273

WHEN WILL YOU SAY I LOVE YOU   June 1963
Alan Fielding
Jack Good Music Publishing Co. Ltd .... UK
Billy Fury .... Decca F 11655

WHEN YOU AND I WERE DANCING   1924
H.M. Tennent / Graham Jones
Ascherberg, Hopwood & Crew Ltd .... UK
Jack Hylton & his Orchestra .... HMV B 1743
Al Collins & his Orchestra .... Regal G 8120

WHEN YOU AND I WERE SEVENTEEN   1925
Gus Kahn / Charles Rosoff
Francis, Day & Hunter Ltd. .... USA
The Savoy Orpheans .... HMV B 2002
Julie Dawn & Roy Edwards .... Columbia 33SX 1271

WHEN YOU AND I WERE YOUNG, MAGGIE   1866
George Johnson / James Butterfield
Unknown Publisher .... USA
John McCormack .... RCA RB 6632
The Five Smith Brothers .... Parlophone R 2293
Debbie Reynolds & Carleton Carpenter .... MGM 400
Andy Stewart .... Top Rank 35-116
Foster & Allen (1983) .... Ritz 026

WHEN YOU ARE A KING   July 1971
John Hill / Roger Hill
A.I.R. Music .... UK
White Plains .... Deram DM 333
Ivor Novello Nomination.

WHEN YOU ARE IN LOVE   1912
Lionel Monckton / Percy Greenbank
Chappell & Co. Ltd .... UK
Show(s): .... The Dancing Mistress
The Light Opera Company .... HMV C 520
The Pro Arte Orchestra,
conducted by Stanford Robinson .... Pye CML 33003

WHEN YOU ASK ABOUT LOVE   October 1980
Jerry Allison / Sonny Curtis
Acuff-Rose Music Ltd. .... USA
Matchbox (1980) .... Magnet MAG 191
The Crickets .... Coral Q 72382
Julie Grant .... Pye 7N 15483

WHEN YOU COME BACK TO ME   January 1990
Mike Stock / Matt Aitken / Peter Waterman
All Boys Music .... UK
Jason Donovan .... PWL PWL 46

WHEN YOU KNOW YOU'RE NOT FORGOTTEN   1943
Elton Box / Desmond Cox
Francis, Day & Hunter Ltd .... UK
Carroll Gibbons & The Savoy Hotel Orpheans,
vocal Edna Kaye .... Columbia FB 2931

WHEN YOU LOOK IN THE HEART OF A ROSE   1917
Marian Gillespie / Florence Methven

Francis, Day & Hunter Ltd. .... UK
Show(s): .... The Better 'Ole
John McCormack .... HMV DA 315

WHEN YOU LOSE THE ONE YOU LOVE   October 1955
Don Pelosi / Rodd Arden / Jimmy Harper
Bradbury Wood Ltd. .... UK
Dorothy Squires .... Nixa NPT 19015
David Whitfield .... Decca LF 1266
Joanne, Johnny & Hal .... Capitol CL 15126

WHEN YOU PLAYED THE ORGAN AND I SANG "THE ROSARY"   1927
Edgar Leslie / Joseph Gilbert
Lawrence Wright Music Co. Ltd. .... UK
Jack Hylton & his Orchestra .... HMV B 5316

WHEN YOU WALK IN THE ROOM   November 1964
Jackie De Shannon
Metric Music Ltd .... USA
Jackie De Shannon .... Liberty LIB 55645
The Searchers .... Pye 7N 15694

WHEN YOU WERE SWEET SIXTEEN   1898
James Thornton
B. Feldman & Co. Ltd. .... USA
Film(s): .... A Man Called Sullivan / The Jolson Story
Steve Conway (1948) .... Columbia FB 3398
The Mills Brothers (1941) .... Brunswick 03139
Al Jolson (1948) .... Brunswick LAT 8322
Perry Como .... RCA RD 27100
The Fureys & Davey Arthur (1981) .... Ritz 003

WHEN YOU WISH UPON A STAR   1940
Ned Washington / Leigh Harline
Chappell & Co. Ltd .... USA
Film(s): .... Pinocchio (Cartoon)
Sound Track (voice of Cliff Edwards) .... Top Rank JKP 2033
June Christy .... Capitol T 1398
Academy Award winning song for 1940.

WHEN YOU WORE A TULIP   1916
Percy Wenrich / Jack Mahoney
Ascherberg, Hopwood & Crew Ltd. .... USA
Film(s): .For Me & My Gal / Belles on Their Toes / Grenwich Village
Corbett & Walker .... HMV B 621
Judy Garland & Gene Kelly .... Ace of Hearts AH 11
Michael Holliday .... Columbia 33SX 1354
Judy Garland & Gene Kelly appeared in *For Me and My Gal.*

WHEN YOU'RE A LONG LONG WAY FROM HOME   1914
George Meyer / Sam M. Lewis
Francis, Day & Hunter Ltd. .... USA
Charles Nelson & Harry Talbot .... HMV B 710
Bing Crosby .... Brunswick LAT 8334

WHEN YOU'RE ALL DRESSED UP AND NO PLACE TO GO   1913
Silvio Hein / Benjamin Burt
Francis, Day & Hunter Ltd. .... USA
Show(s): .... The Beauty Shop / Mr. Manhattan
Raymond Hitchcock .... HMV D 413
Frank Norris .... Columbia 606
Raymond Hitchcock appeared in both *The Beauty Shop* and *Mr. Manhattan.*

WHEN YOU'RE AWAY   1914
Victor Herbert / Henry Blossom
B. Feldman & Co. Ltd. .... USA
Show(s): .... The Only Girl
Film(s): .... His Butler's Sister
Grace Kerns .... Columbia 615
Richard Crooks .... Camden CDN 1019
Jackie Gleason & his Orchestra .... Capitol T 967
Deanna Durbin .... MCA MCL 1668
Deanna Durbin appeared in *His Butler's Sister.*

WHEN YOU'RE HAIR HAS TURNED TO SILVER   1931
Charles Tobias / Peter De Rose
Campbell Connelly & Co. Ltd .... USA
Carl Brisson .... Decca F 2251
Bob Eberly & Monica Lewis .... Brunswick 03915
David Whitfield .... Decca DFE 6601

WHEN YOU'RE IN LOVE March 1952
Carl Fischer / Frankie Laine
Campbell Connelly & Co. Ltd .... USA
Frankie Laine and The Norman Luboff Choir
with Carl Fischer (piano) .... **Columbia DB 3057**
Freddie Shaw .... **Columbia DB 4091**

WHEN YOU'RE IN LOVE September 1948
Desmond O'Connor / Harold Fields / Dominic John
Bradbury Wood Ltd. .... UK
Reggie Goff .... **Decca F 8941**
Robert Earl .... **Philips PB 1209**
Based on 'La Golondrina' by Narcisco Serradell.

WHEN YOU'RE IN LOVE WITH A
BEAUTIFUL WOMAN November 1979
Even Stevens
A.T.V. Music Ltd. .... USA
Dr. Hook .... **Capitol CL 16039**

WHEN YOU'RE SMILING 1929
Mark Fisher / Joe Goodwin / Larry Shay
B. Feldman & Co. Ltd .... USA
Film(s): .... Meet Danny Wilson
Louis Armstrong & his Orchestra .... **Parlophone R 1286**
Nat Gonella & his Band .... **Parlophone F 1084**
Perry Como .... **Camden CDN 142**
Frank Sinatra .... **Capitol W 1491**
Doris Day .... **Philips BBL 7377**
George Elrick .... **Regal Zonophone MR 3801**
Frank Sinatra appeared in *Meet Danny Wilson*.
Theme song of George Elrick.

WHEN YOU'RE YOUNG AND IN LOVE May 1984
Van McCoy
Campbell Connelly & Co. .... USA
The Flying Pickets .... **Ten Records TEN 20**

WHEN YOU'VE GOT A LITTLE SPRINGTIME IN YOUR
HEART 1934
Harry Woods
Cinephonic Music Co. Ltd .... USA
Film(s): .... Evergreen
Jessie Matthews .... **Columbia DB 1404**
Jessie Matthews appeared in *Evergreen*.

WHEN YOUR LOVER HAS GONE 1931
E.A. Swan
Francis, Day & Hunter Ltd. .... USA
Film(s): .... Blonde Crazy
Louis Armstrong & his Orchestra .... **Parlophone R 1034**
Maxine Sullivan .... **Brunswick 03531**
Frank Sinatra .... **Encore ENC 101**
Sue Raney .... **Capitol T 1533**

WHEN YUBA PLAYS THE RUMBA ON THE TUBA 1932
Herman Hupfeld
Victoria Music Co. Ltd. .... USA
Show(s): .... The Third Little Show
The Revellers .... **HMV B 4164**
Rudy Vallee .... **HMV C 2802**
The Three Suns .... **HMV DLP 1149**

WHENEVER YOU NEED SOMEBODY November 1987
Mike Stock / Matt Aitken / Peter Waterman
All Boys Music .... UK
Rick Astley .... **RCA PB 41567**

WHERE ARE YOU 1937
Jimmy McHugh / Harold Adamson
Francis, Day & Hunter Ltd. .... USA
Film(s): .... Top of the Town
Gertrude Niesen .... **Brunswick 02429**
Al Hibbler .... **Brunswick LAT 8140**
Pat Boone .... **RCA RD 27062**
Gertrude Niesien appeared in *Top of the Town*.

WHERE ARE YOU BABY September 1990
Alison Clarkson
Rhythm King Music .... UK
Betty Boo .... **Rhythm King LEFT 43**

WHERE ARE YOU NOW MY LOVE May 1965
Tony Hatch / Jackie Trent
Welbeck Music Co. Ltd .... UK

Jackie Trent .... **Pye 7N 15776**
Ivor Novello Nomination.

WHERE DID MY SNOWMAN GO November 1952
Freddie Poser / Geoffrey Venis
Polyphone Music Ltd .... UK
Petula Clark .... **Pye NEP 24006**

WHERE DID OUR LOVE GO October 1964
Brian Holland / Eddie Holland / Lamont Dozier
Belinda (London) Ltd .... USA
The Supremes .... **Stateside SS 327**
Donnie Elbert (1972) .... **London HL 10352**

WHERE DID ROBINSON CRUSOE GO WITH FRIDAY ON
SATURDAY NIGHT 1916
Sam M. Lewis / Joe Young / George W. Meyer
B. Feldman & Co. Ltd. .... USA
Show(s): .... Robinson Crusoe Jr. / Follow the Crowd
Al Jolson .... **Brunswick LAT 8294**
Ethel Levey .... **HMV 03478**
Al Jolson appeared in *Robinson Crusoe Jr.*.
Ethel Levey appeared in *Follow the Crowd*.

WHERE DID YOU GET THAT HAT 1890
James Rolmaz
Francis, Day & Hunter Ltd. .... UK
Reg Grant .... **Parlophone E 6293**
Stanley Holloway .... **Pye NPL 18056**

WHERE DO BROKEN HEARTS GO April 1988
Frank Wildhorn / Chuck Jackson
Chrysalis Music .... USA
Whitney Houston .... **Arista 109793**

WHERE DO I BEGIN May 1971
Carl Sigman / Francis Lai
Famous - Chappell .... USA
Film(s): .... Love Story
Andy Williams .... **CBS S 65151**
Francis Lai Orchestra .... **Paramount PARA 3010**

WHERE DO YOU GO TO MY LOVELY March 1969
Peter Sarstedt
Mortimer Music Co. .... UK
Peter Sarstedt .... **United Artists UP 2262**
Ivor Novello Award.

WHERE HAVE ALL THE FLOWERS GONE July 1961
Pete Seeger
Harmony Music Ltd. .... USA
The Kingston Trio .... **Capitol CL 15242**
Marlene Dietrich .... **HMV POP 1379**
Pete Seeger .... **CBS BPG 62217**

WHERE IN THE WORLD 1942
Paul Herrick / Freddy Martin / Ray Austin
Bradbury Wood Ltd .... USA
Ambrose & his Orchestra, vocal Anne Shelton .. **Decca F 8184**
Tony Osborne & his Orchestra .... **Nixa NPL 18009**

WHERE IS YOUR HEART (Moulin Rouge Theme) May 1953
George Auric / William Engvick
Campbell Connelly & Co. Ltd .... France
Film(s): .... Moulin Rouge
The Mantovani Orchestra .... **Decca LK 4079**
Connie Francis .... **MGM C 875**
Ron Goodwin Orchestra .... **Parlophone R 3686**
Line Renaud .... **Columbia DB 3328**
Jean Sablon .... **HMV B 10946**

WHERE MY CARAVAN HAS RESTED 1909
Edward Teschemacher / Herman Loehr
Chappell & Co. Ltd. .... UK
Sydney Coltham .... **Zonophone 1223**
Bing Crosby .... **Brunswick 03938**
Kenneth McKellar .... **Decca DFE 6576**

WHERE OR WHEN 1940
Richard Rodgers / Lorenz Hart
Chappell & Co. Ltd. .... USA
Show(s): .... Babes in Arms
Film(s): .... Babes in Arms / Words and Music
Jeri Southern .... **Columbia 33SX 1155**

Al Hibbler	Brunswick LAT 8140
Lena Horne	MGM C 853
Dinah Shore	Capitol T 1247

Lena Horne appeared in *Words and Music.*

WHERE THE BLACK EYED SUSANS GROW — 1917
Richard A. Whiting / Dave Radford
B. Feldman & Co. Ltd. .... USA
Show(s): .... Robinson Crusoe Jr. / Cheep
Al Jolson .... Brunswick LA 8575
Beatrice Lillie (1917) .... Columbia L 1192
Beatrice Lillie (1958) .... Decca LK 4293
Al Saxon .... Fontana H 138
Al Jolson appeared in *Robinson Crusoe Jr..*
Beatrice Lillie appeared in *Cheep.*

WHERE THE BLUE OF THE NIGHT — 1932
Roy Turk / Fred Ahlert / Bing Crosby
Victoria Music Co. Ltd. .... USA
Film(s): .... The Big Broadcast
Bing Crosby .... Brunswick LAT 8334
Jane Morgan .... London HAR 2138
Bing Crosby appeared in *The Big Broadcast.*
Theme song of Bing Crosby.

WHERE THE BOYS ARE — April 1961
Howard Greenfield / Neil Sedaka
Robbins Music Corporation Ltd .... USA
Film(s): .... Where the Boys Are
Connie Francis .... MGM 1121
Leroy Holmes & his Orchestra .... MGM C 880
Connie Francis appeared in *Where the Boys Are.*

WHERE THE LAZY DAISIES GROW — 1925
Cliff Friend / Lew Brown
Francis, Day & Hunter Ltd. .... USA
Jean Goldkette & his Orchestra .... HMV B 1849

WHERE THE MORNING GLORIES GROW — 1917
Gus Kahn / Raymond Egan / Richard A. Whiting
B. Feldman & Co. .... USA
Bing Crosby .... London SHU 8489

WHERE THE RIVER SHANNON FLOWS — 1905
James Russell
B. Feldman & Co. .... USA
Joe Green .... Eddison Bell W 116
Cavan O'Connor .... Rex 10208
Bing Crosby .... Brunswick 03651
Patrick O'Hagen .... Emerald GES 1182

WHERE THE SHY LITTLE VIOLETS GROW — 1929
Harry Warren / Gus Kahn
Francis, Day & Hunter Ltd .... USA
Guy Lombardo & his Royal Canadians .... Columbia 5542

WHERE THE STREETS HAVE NO NAME — October 1987
"U2"
Blue Mountain Music .... UK
U2 .... Island IS 340

WHERE THE SUNSET TURNS THE OCEAN'S BLUE TO GOLD — 1902
Henry W. Petrie / Eva Buckner
Herman Darewski Music Publishing Co. Ltd. .... USA
Ernest Pike .... Zonophone 493
Tom McLeod & Chorus .... Parlophone E 6218

WHERE THE WATERS ARE BLUE — 1942
Hugh Charles / Sonny Miller
Dash Music Ltd .... UK
Joe Loss & his Orchestra, vocal "Maureen" .. HMV BD 5773
Leslie Hutchinson (Hutch) .... HMV BD 1027

WHERE THE WIND BLOWS — October 1953
Terry Gilkyson
Dash Music Ltd. .... USA
Frankie Laine .... Philips PB 167

WHERE WILL THE DIMPLE BE — May 1955
Bob Merrill / Al Hoffman
Cinephonic Music Co. Ltd. .... USA
Rosemary Clooney .... Philips BBL 7301

WHERE'D YOU GET THOSE EYES — 1926
Walter Donaldson
Francis, Day & Hunter Ltd. .... USA
Ted Lewis & his Orchestra, vocal Ted Lewis ... Columbia 4089

WHERE'S MY SWEETIE HIDING — 1925
Jack Little / Dick Finch / Tommie Malie / Addy Britt
B. Feldman & Co. Ltd. .... USA
The Arcadia Peacock Orchestra,
vocal Chick Harvey .... Parlophone E 5325
The Savoy Orpheans .... HMV B 1973

WHERE'S THAT RAINBOW — 1927
Richard Rodgers / Lorenz Hart
Chappell & Co. Ltd. .... USA
Show(s): .... Peggy Ann
Film(s): .... Words and Music
Dorothy Dickson .... Columbia 4540
Ann Sothern .... MGM C 853
Dorothy Dickson appeared in the British production of *Peggy Ann.*
Ann Sothern appeared in *Words and Music.*

WHEREVER I LAY MY HAT (That's My Home) — August 1983
Marvin Gaye / Norman Whitfield
Jobete Music .... USA
Paul Young .... CBS A 3371
Marvin Gaye .... Stateside SL 10100

WHICH WAY YOU GOIN' BILLY? — October 1970
Terry Jacks
Burlington Music Co. Ltd .... Canada
Susan Jacks & The Poppy Family .... Decca F 22976

WHIFFENPOOF SONG, THE — 1937
Meade Minnigerode / Tod Galloway / George Pomeroy
Magna Music Co. Ltd. .... USA
Film(s): .... Winged Victory
Rudy Vallee (1937) .... Columbia DB 1703
Bing Crosby (1948) .... Brunswick LAT 8052
Slim Whitman .... London HAP 2199
Perry Como .... RCA RD 27078

WHILE A CIGARETTE WAS BURNING — 1938
Nick Kenny / Charles Kenny
Sterling Music Publishing Co. Ltd. .... USA
Geraldo & his Orchestra, vocal Al Bowlly ...... HMV BD 5437
Patti Page .... Mercury MPL 6521

WHILE THE ANGELUS WAS RINGING — March 1949
Jean Villard / Dick Manning
Southern Music publishing Co. Ltd .... France
Anne Shelton .... Decca F 9076
Dick Haymes .... Brunswick 04061
Allan Jones .... HMV B 9828
Based on "Les Trois Cloches" by Jean Villard.

WHILE WE DANCED AT THE MARDI GRAS — 1932
Johnny Mercer / Alfred Opler
Campbell Connelly & Co. Ltd. .... USA
George Olsen & his Music .... HMV B 6246
Pete Fountain & his Rhythm .... Coral LVA 9128

WHIP-POOR-WILL — 1921
Buddy De Sylva / Jerome Kern
Chappell Music Ltd. .... USA
Show(s): .... Sally
Dorothy Dickson & Gregory Stroud .... Columbia F 1077
Jessie Matthews .... Columbia DB 2094
Dorothy Dickson & Gregory Stroud appeared in *Sally.*

WHISKY IN THE JAR — March 1973
Traditional, arranged by Philip Lynott, additional lyrics by Eric Bell & Brian Donney
Pippin the Friendly Ranger Music .... UK
Thin Lizzy .... Decca F 13355

WHISPER TO ME — 1917
Lionel Monckton / Herman Finck / Adrian Ross
Chappell & Co. Ltd. .... UK
Show(s): .... Airs and Graces
Gertie Millar & Ernest Pike .... HMV 04208
Gertie Millar & Ernest Pike appeared in *Airs and Graces.*

WHISPERING — 1920
John Schonberger / Vincent Rose / Richard Coburn

Herman Darewski Music Publishing Co. Ltd . . . . USA
Film(s):The Ziegfeld Girl / Belles on Their Toes / The Eddy Duchin
Story / Greenwich Village
Paul Whiteman & his Orchestra (1920) . . . . **HMV B 1160**
Jack Smith . . . . **HMV B 2706**
Roy Fox & his Band . . . . **Decca F 2469**
Paul Whiteman & his Orchestra (1955) . . . . **Coral Q 2015**
Bing Crosby . . . . **RCA RD 27032**
Carmen Cavallaro . . . . **Brunswick LAT 8119**
The Bachelors (1963) . . . . **Decca F 11712**
Nino Tempo & April Stevens . . . . **London HLK 9829**
Theme song of Roy Fox.

WHISPERING GRASS   1941
Fred Fisher / Doris Fisher
Campbell Connelly & Co. Ltd . . . . USA
The Ink Spots (1941) . . . . **Ace of Hearts AH 2**
The Ink Spots (1959) . . . . **Gala GLP 305**
The Hilltoppers . . . . **London HAD 2029**
Windsor Davis & Don Estelle (1975) . . . . **EMI 2290**

WHISPERING HOPE   1912
Alice Hawthorne
Ardmore & Beechwood Ltd . . . . USA
Alma Gluck & Louise Homer . . . . **HMV DA 158**
The Andrews Sisters . . . . **Brunswick 04373**
Pat Boone . . . . **London HAD 2092**

WHISPERING PINES OF NEVADA, THE   1927
Horatio Nicholls
Lawrence Wright Music Co. Ltd . . . . UK
The Savoy Havana Band . . . . **HMV B 5300**
Eric Batty's Jazz Band . . . . **Esquire 32-015**

WHISTLE DOWN THE WIND   April 1983
Nick Heyward
Bryan Morrison Music . . . . UK
Nick Heyward . . . . **Arista HEY 1**

WHISTLE WHILE YOU WORK   1938
Larry Morey / Frank Churchill
Walt Disney Music Ltd. . . . . USA
Film(s): . . . . Snow White and the Seven Dwarfs
Sound Track . . . . **Top Rank JKP 2029**
Sound Track . . . . **Disneyland DLP 39003**
David Seville & The Chipmunks . . . . **London HAU 2205**

WHISTLER AND HIS DOG, THE   1905
Arthur Pryor
Chappell & Co. Ltd. . . . . USA
The Arthur Pryor Band . . . . **HMV B 2373**
Mitch Miller & The Gang . . . . **Philips BBL 7473**

WHISTLER'S MOTHER-IN-LAW, THE   1942
Bert Stevens / Larry Wagner
Southern Music Publishing Co. Ltd . . . . USA
Bing Crosby & Muriel Lane . . . . **Brunswick 03289**

WHISTLING IN THE DARK   1931
Dana Suesse / Allen Boretz
Campbell Connelly & Co. Ltd. . . . . USA
Ambrose & his Orchestra, vocal Sam Browne . . . . **HMV B 6032**
Guy Lombardo & his Royal Canadians . . **Brunswick LAT 8063**

WHISTLING RUFUS   1899
Kerry Mills
B. Feldman & Co. Ltd. . . . . USA
Olly Oakley (Banjo) . . . . **HMV B 138**
The Barnstormers Spasm Band . . . . **Parlophone R 4416**
The Chris Barber Jazz Band . . . . **Pye GGL 0075**

WHISTLING WALTZ, THE   1936
Harry Woods
Cinephonic Music Co. Ltd . . . . USA
Film(s): . . . . Limelight
Arthur Tracey (The Street Singer) . . . . **Decca F 5880**
Arthur Tracey appeared in the 1936 film *Limelight*.

WHITE CHRISTMAS   1942
Irving Berlin
Irving Berlin Ltd . . . . USA
Film(s): . . . . Holiday Inn / Blue Skies / White Christmas
Bing Crosby . . . . **Brunswick Bing 7**
Johnny Mathis . . . . **Fontana TFL 5031**

Bing Crosby, Peggy Lee, Danny Kaye &
Trudie Richards . . . . **Brunswick LAT 8044**
Rosemary Clooney . . . . **Philips BBR 8022**
Mantovani & his Orchestra (1952) . . . . **Decca F 10017**
Bing Crosby (1977) . . . . **MCA 111**
Bing Crosby appeared in *Holiday Inn, Blue Skies* and *White Christ-mas*.
Peggy Lee, Danny Kaye & Trudie Richards appeared in *White Christ-mas*.
Academy Award winning song for 1942.

WHITE CLIFFS OF DOVER, THE   1942
Nat Burton / Walter Kent
B. Feldman & Co. Ltd . . . . USA
Vera Lynn . . . . **Decca F 8110**
Glenn Miller & his Orchestra, vocal Ray Eberle . **HMV DLP 1049**
The Acker Bilk Jazz Band . . . . **Columbia 33SX 1248**

WHITE DOVE, THE   1930
Franz Lehar / Clifford Grey
Chappell & Co. Ltd . . . . Austria
Film(s): . . . . The Rogue Song
Lawrence Tibbett . . . . **HMV DA 1102**
David Whitfield . . . . **Decca LK 4348**
Lawrence Tibbett appeared in *The Rogue Song*.

WHITE HORSE INN, THE   1931
Robert Stolz / Ralph Benatzky / Harry Graham
Chappell & Co. Ltd. . . . . Germany
Show(s): . . . . White Horse Inn
Greta Hoffmann . . . . **Edison Bell Winner 5279**
The Tonhalle Orchestra of Zurich,
conducted by Robert Stolz . . . . **Decca LK 4013**
Andy Cole . . . . **HMV CLP 1205**
Harry Secombe . . . . **Philips BBL 7550**
Greta Hoffmann appeared in the British production of *White Horse Inn.*

WHITE HORSES   May 1968
Michael Carr / Ben Nisbet
Gerrard Music . . . . UK
Jacky . . . . **Philips BF 1674**

WHITE LINES (Don't Don't Do It)   August 1984
Sylvia Robinson / Mel Glover
Heath Levy Music . . . . USA
Grandmaster Flash & Melle Mel &
The Furious Five . . . . **Sugar Hill SH 130**

WHITE SILVER SANDS   October 1957
Charles G. Matthews
Southern Music Publishing Co. Ltd . . . . USA
Don Lang . . . . **HMV POP 382**
The Four Preps . . . . **Capitol T 1090**

WHITE SPORT COAT, A (And a Pink Carnation)   June 1957
Marty Robbins
Acuff-Rose Publishing Co. Ltd. . . . . USA
Marty Robbins . . . . **Philips BBR 8113**
The King Brothers . . . . **Parlophone R 4310**
Terry Dene . . . . **Decca DFE 6411**

WHITE SUIT SAMBA, THE   September 1951
Jack Parnell / T.E.B. Clarke
Chappell & Co. Ltd . . . . UK
Film(s): . . . . The Man in the White Suit
Jack Parnell & his Orchestra . . . . **Parlophone R 3435**

WHITE WEDDING   August 1985
Billy Idol
Chrysalis Music . . . . UK
Billy Idol . . . . **Chrysalis IDOL 5**

WHITER SHADE OF PALE, A   August 1967
Keith Richard / Gary Brooker
Essex Music Ltd. . . . . UK
Procol Harum . . . . **Deram DM 126**
Procol Harum (1972) . . . . **Magic Fly ECHO 101**
Ivor Novello Award.

WHO   1926
Otto Harbach / Jerome Kern / Oscar Hammerstein II
Chappell & Co. Ltd. . . . . USA
Show(s): . . . . Sunny
Film(s): . . Sunny / Till the Clouds Roll By / Look for the Silver Lining

Binnie Hale & Jack Buchanan . . . . Columbia SEG 7767
Jean Goldkette & his Orchestra,
vocal Lou Hurst . . . . Camden CDN 54
Jack Buchanan . . . . HMV 7EG 8307
Tommy Dorsey & his Orchestra,
vocal Jack Leonard . . . . RCA RCX 1023
Dinah Shore . . . . Capitol T 1354
Binnie Hale appeared in the British production of *Sunny*.

WHO AM I   1931
Gordon Clifford / Al Milne / Alfred Newman
Campbell Connelly & Co. Ltd. . . . . USA
The Savoy Orpheans, vocal Al Bowlly . . . . . . Columbia CB 377

WHO AM I   March 1961
Les Vandyke
Mills Music Ltd . . . . UK
Adam Faith . . . . Parlophone R 4735
Bobby Vee . . . . Liberty LBY 1004

WHO ARE WE   May 1956
Jerry Livingston / Paul Francis Webster
Bourne Music Ltd. . . . . USA
Vera Lynn . . . . Decca DFE 6397
Ronnie Hilton . . . . HMV POP 221
Gogi Grant . . . . London HAB 2032
Shirley Bassey . . . . Columbia 33SX 1382

WHO CAN I TURN TO   1964
Anthony Newley / Leslie Bricusse
Concord Music . . . . UK
Show(s): . . . . The Roar of the Greaspaint - The Smell of the Crowd
Anthony Newley . . . . RCA LOC 1109
Tony Bennett . . . . CBS BPG 62486
Dickie Valentine . . . . Philips BBL 7771
Shirley Bassey . . . . Columbia 33SX 1787
Anthony Newley appeared in *The Roar of the Greasepaint - The Smell of the Crowd*.

WHO CARES   1923
Jack Yellen / Milton Ager
Lawrence Wright Music Co. Ltd . . . . USA
Show(s): . . . . Bombo
The Regal Novelty Orchestra . . . . Regal G 8004
The Savoy Havana Band . . . . Columbia 3341

WHO COULD BE BLUER   May 1960
Jerry Lordan
Francis, Day & Hunter Ltd . . . . UK
Jerry Lordan . . . . Parlophone R 4627

WHO DAT UP DERE   1945
Walter Kent / Bob Russell
Chappell & Co. Ltd. . . . . USA
Film(s): . . . . The Earl Carroll Vanties
Woody Herman & his Orchestra,
vocal Woody Herman . . . . Brunswick LAT 8092
The Hedley Ward Trio . . . . Melodisc 1344
Woody Herman & his Orchestra appeared in *The Earl Carroll Vanities*.

WHO DO YOU LOVE   April 1970
Elias McDaniel
Jewel Music Publishing Co. Ltd. . . . . USA
Juicy Lucy . . . . Vertigo VO 2
Bo Diddley . . . . Pye 7N 25193

WHO FOUND WHO   December 1987
Paul Gurrvitz / Nicky Chin
Chrysalis Music . . . . UK
Jellybean featuring Elisa Fiorrillo . . . . Chrysalis JEL 1

WHO LOVES YOU   October 1975
Bob Gaudio / Judy Parker
Jobete Music (UK) Ltd. . . . . USA
The Four Seasons . . . . Warner Brothers K 16602

WHO PAYS THE FERRYMAN   January 1978
Yan Markopoulus
Chappell & Co. Ltd . . . . UK
Yannis Markopoulus . . . . BBC RESL 51
Theme of the TV series "Who Pays The Ferryman".

WHO PUT THE LIGHTS OUT   May 1971
Paul Ryan
Intersong Music . . . . UK

Dana . . . . Rex R 11062

**WHO TAKES CARE OF THE CARETAKER'S
DAUGHTER**   1925
Chick Endor / Paul Revere
Francis, Day & Hunter Ltd. . . . . USA
Whitney Kaufmann's Original
Pennsylvania Serenaders . . . . HMV B 2061
Percival Mackey & his Orchestra . . . . Columbia 3687
Bobby Darin & Johnny Mercer . . . . London HAK 2363

WHO WALKS IN (When I Walk Out)   1933
Ralph Freed / Al Goodhart / Al Hoffman
Peter Maurice Music Co. Ltd. . . . . USA
Ray Noble & his Orchestra, vocal Al Bowlly . . . . . . HMV B 6453
The Firehouse Five Plus Two . . . . Vogue LAG 12089

WHO WANTS TO BE A MILLIONAIRE   November 1956
Cole Porter
Chappell & Co. Ltd. . . . . USA
Film(s): . . . . High Society
Frank Sinatra & Celeste Holm . . . . Capitol LCT 6116
Bill Savill & his Orchestra . . . . Ace of Clubs ACL 1053
Frank Sinatra & Celeste Holm appeared in *High Society*.

WHO WERE YOU WITH IN THE MOONLIGHT   June 1979
David Courtney
Brighton Rock Productions . . . . UK
Dollar . . . . Carrere CAR 110

WHO WERE YOU WITH LAST NIGHT   1912
Fred Godfrey / Mark Sheridan
B. Feldman & Co. Ltd . . . . UK
Mark Sheridan . . . . Regal G 6506
The Coronets . . . . Columbia SEG 7617

WHO WOULDN'T LOVE YOU   1943
Bill Carey / Carl Fischer
Chappell & Co. Ltd . . . . USA
The Ink Spots . . . . Brunswick 03404
Steve Lawrence & Eydie Gormé . . . . HMV CLP 1404

WHO'LL BUY MY VIOLETS (La Violetera)   1924
Jose Padilla / E. Ray Goetz
Ascherberg, Hopwood & Crew Ltd . . . . Spain
Show(s): . . . . Little Miss Bluebeard
Film(s): . . . . City Lights
Raguel Miller (in Spanish) . . . . Parlophone R 1334
The Troubadours . . . . London HAR 2095

WHO'S AFRAID OF THE BIG BAD WOLF   1933
Ann Ronell / Frank Churchill
Francis, Day & Hunter Ltd. . . . . USA
Film(s): . . . . Three Little Pigs (cartoon)
Sound Track recording of Three Little Pigs . . . . . . HMV BD 387
Ray Noble & his Orchestra . . . . HMV B 6411
Duke Ellington & his Orchestra . . . . Philips BBL 7315

WHO'S BEEN POLISHING THE SUN   1935
Noel Gay
Cinephonic Music Co. Ltd . . . . UK
Film(s): . . . . The Camels are Coming
Jack Hulbert . . . . HMV BD 273
Leslie Holmes . . . . Rex 8359
Jack Hulbert appeared in *The Camels are Coming*.

WHO'S IN THE HOUSE   May 1989
Paul Carter / Manda Glanfield / Richard Walmsley
Zomba Music . . . . UK
The Beatmasters with Merlin . . . . Rhythm King LEFT 31

WHO'S LEAVING WHO   April 1988
Mike Stock / Matt Aitken / Peter Waterman
All Boys Music . . . . UK
Hazell Dean . . . . EMI EM 45

WHO'S SORRY NOW   1923
Bert Kalmar / Harry Ruby / Ted Snyder
B. Feldman & Co. Ltd . . . . USA
Film(s): . . . . A Night in Casablanca / Three Little Words
The Original Memphis Five . . . . HMV B 1663
Gloria De Haven . . . . MGM D 139
Jane Morgan . . . . London HAR 2133
Connie Francis (1958) . . . . MGM EP 658

Johnnie Ray (1956) .... **Philips PB 546**
Gloria De Haven appeared in *Three Little Words*.

WHO'S TAKING YOU HOME TONIGHT   1940
Manning Sherwin / Tommie Connor
Francis, Day & Hunter Ltd .... UK
Show(s): .... Shephard's Pie
Turner Layton .... **Columbia FB 2347**
Joe Loss & his Orchestra .... **HMV CLP 1470**

WHO'S THAT GIRL   August 1983
Annie Lennox / Dave Stewart
RCA Music .... UK
The Eurythmics .... **RCA DA 3**

WHO'S THAT GIRL   July 1987
Madonna Ciccone / Patrick Leonard
Warner Brothers Music .... USA
Madonna .... **Sire W 8341**

WHO'S YOUR LITTLE WHO-ZIS   1932
Al Goering / Ben Bernie / Walter Hirsch
Victoria Music Co. Ltd. .... USA
Film(s): .... The Stooge
The Knickerbockers .... **Columbia CB 424**
Dean Martin .... **Capitol T 950**
Dean Martin appeared in *The Stooge*.

WHODUNIT   May 1977
Kenny St Louis / Freddie Perren
A.T.V. Music Ltd. .... UK
Tavares .... **Capitol CL 15914**

WHOLE LOTTA LOVE   November 1970
Jimmy Page / Robert Plant / John Bonham & John Paul Jones
Warner Brothers Music Ltd .... UK
C.C.S. .... **Rak 104**
Led Zeppelin .... **Atlantic K 40037**

WHOLE LOTTA SHAKIN' GOIN' ON   October 1957
Dave Williams / Sonny David
Robert Mellin Music .... USA
Jerry Lee Lewis .... **London HLS 8457**

WHOLE LOTTA WOMAN, A   March 1958
Marvin Rainwater
Sheldon Music Ltd .... USA
Marvin Rainwater .... **MGM 974**
The Most Brothers .... **Decca F 10998**

WHOLE WORLD IS SINGING MY SONG   1947
Vic Mizzy / Mann Curtis
Francis, Day & Hunter Ltd. .... USA
**Jimmy Dorsey & his Orchestra,
vocal Bob Carroll** .... **Brunswick 03705**
Patti Page .... **Mercury MMC 14000**

WHOSE BABY ARE YOU   1921
Jerome Kern / Anne Caldwell
Chappell & Co. Ltd .... USA
Show(s): .... The Night Boat / Fun of The Fayre
Joseph C. Smith's Orchestra .... **HMV B 1130**
Louise Leigh & Will Strong .... **HMV B 1305**
The Big Ben Banjo Band .... **Columbia 33SX 1108**

WHY   February 1960
Robert Marcucci / Peter De Angelis
Debmar Music Ltd .... USA
Anthony Newley .... **Decca DFE 6629**
Frankie Avalon .... **HMV POP 688**
Donny Osmond (1972) .... **MGM 2006119**

WHY   October 1982
Bernard Edwards / Nile Rodgers
Warner Brothers Music .... USA
Carly Simon .... **WEA K 79300**

WHY   October 1984
James Somerville / Larry Steinbachek / Steve Bronski
William A. Bong Music .... UK
Bronski Beat .... **London BITE 2**

WHY AM I ALWAYS THE BRIDESMAID   1917
Fred W. Leigh / Charles Collins
Francis, Day & Hunter Ltd. .... UK

Lily Morris .... **Regal G 8987**

WHY CAN'T THIS BE LOVE   May 1986
Michael Anthony / David Landee / Alex Van Halen & Edward Van Halen
Warner Brothers Music .... USA
Van Halen .... **Warner Brothers W 8740**

WHY CAN'T WE LIVE TOGETHER   March 1973
Timmy Thomas
Southern Music Publishing Co. Ltd. .... UK
Timmy Thomas .... **Mojo 2027012**

WHY CAN'T YOU BEHAVE   May 1951
Cole Porter
Chappell & Co. Ltd .... USA
Show(s): .... Kiss Me Kate
Film(s): .... Kiss Me Kate
Lisa Kirk & Harold Lang .... **Philips BBL 7224**
Julie Wilson .... **Columbia DB 2848**
Ann Miller .... **MGM C 753**
Lisa Kirk & Harold Lang appeared in the American production of *Kiss Me Kate*.
Julie Wilson appeared in the British production of *Kiss Me Kate*.
Ann Miller appeared in the film *Kiss Me Kate*.

WHY DID I KISS THAT GIRL   1924
Robert King / Lew Brown / Ray Henderson
Keith Prowse Music Publishing Co. Ltd. .... USA
**Paul Whiteman & his Orchestra,
vocal Billy Munday** .... **HMV B 1814**

WHY DID I LEAVE MY LITTLE BACK ROOM   1898
A.J. Mills / Frank W. Carter
Francis, Day & Hunter Ltd. .... UK
Reg Grant .... **Parlophone E 6373**

WHY DID SHE FALL FOR THE LEADER OF THE BAND   1936
Jimmy Kennedy / Michael Carr
Peter Maurice Music Co. Ltd .... UK
Film(s): .... She Shall Have Music
Jack Hylton & his Orchestra .... **HMV BD 5023**
Gracie Fields .... **Rex 8768**
The Big Ben Banjo Band .... **Columbia 33SX 1254**
Jack Hylton Orchestra appeared in *She Shall Have Music*.

WHY DID YOU DO IT   November 1975
'Kirby'
Rachel Music .... UK
Stretch .... **Anchor ANC 1021**

WHY DO FOOLS FALL IN LOVE   July 1956
Frankie Lymon / George Goldner
Chappell & Co. Ltd. .... USA
The Teenagers .... **Columbia SEG 7662**
Diana Ross (1981) .... **Capitol CL 226**

WHY DO I LOVE YOU   1928
Jerome Kern / Oscar Hammerstein II
Chappell & Co. Ltd. .... USA
Show(s): .... Show Boat
Film(s): .... Show Boat
Edith Day & Howett Worster .... **Columbia 9428**
Allan Jones .... **HMV 7EG 8231**
Kathryn Grayson & Howard Keel .... **MGM D 104**
Edith Day & Howett Worster appeared in the British production of *Show Boat*.
Allan Jones appeared in the 1936 film of *Show Boat*.
Kathryn Grayson & Howard Keel appeared in the 1951 film of *Show Boat*.

WHY DON'T THEY UNDERSTAND   February 1958
Jack Fishman / Joe Henderson
Henderson Music Ltd .... UK
The Zodiacs .... **Oriole CB 1383**
George Hamilton IV .... **HMV POP 429**
Petula Clark .... **Pye NPL 18123**

WHY DON'T WE DO THIS MORE OFTEN   1941
Charles Newman / Allie Wrubel
Cavendish Music Co. Ltd .... USA
The Andrews Sisters .... **Brunswick 03257**
**Geraldo & his Orchestra, vocal Dorothy Carless & Jackie
Hunter** .... **Parlophone F 1874**
Doris Day .... **Philips BBL 7296**

WHY DON'T YOU BELIEVE ME   February 1953
Lew Douglas / King Laney / Roy Rodde
Francis, Day & Hunter Ltd . . . . USA
Jimmy Young . . . . **Decca F 10036**
Pat Boone . . . . **London HAD 2204**
Joni James . . . . **MGM EP 504**

WHY DON'T YOU DO RIGHT   1943
Joe McCoy
Edwin H. Morris & Co. Ltd . . . . USA
Film(s): . . . . Stage Door Canteen
Benny Goodman & his Orchestra,
vocal Peggy Lee . . . . **Parlophone R 2564**
Ruth Brown . . . . **London LTZK 15187**
Julie London . . . . **London HAG 2405**
Benny Goodman & his Orchestra appeared in *Stage Door Canteen*.

WHY DON'T YOU FALL IN LOVE WITH ME   1943
Al Lewis / Mabel Wayne
Chappell & Co. Ltd . . . . USA
Show(s): . . . . Hi-De-Hi
Film(s): . . . . Honeymoon Lodge
Geraldo & his Orchestra,
vocal Dorothy Carless . . . . **Parlophone F 1982**
Ambrose & his Orchestra, vocal Anne Shelton . . **Decca F 8306**
Connee Boswell . . . . **Brunswick 03392**

WHY IS THE BACON SO TOUGH   1929
Reginald Arkell / Charles Prentice
Ascherberg, Hopwood & Crew Ltd . . . . UK
Tommy Handley . . . . **Piccadilly 171**
Winning song of the 1928 Daily Mail Write-A-Song Contest.

WHY OH WHY OH WHY   December 1973
Gilbert O'Sullivan
M.A.M. (Music Publishing) Ltd. . . . . UK
Gilbert O'Sullivan . . . . **MAM 111**

WHY WAS I BORN   1930
Jerome Kern / Oscar Hammerstein II
Chappell & Co. Ltd . . . . USA
Show(s): . . . . Sweet Adeline
Film(s):Sweet Adeline / Till the Clouds Roll By / The Man I Love / Both
Ends of the Candle
Ambrose & his Orchestra . . . . **Decca F 5653**
Frank Sinatra . . . . **Philips BBR 8038**
Dick Haymes . . . . **Brunswick 04445**
Gogi Grant . . . . **RCA RD 27054**
Gogi Grant dubbed the singing voice of Ann Blyth who appeared in
the film *Both Ends of the Candle*.

WHY WASTE YOUR TEARS   1922
Val Holstius
Keith Prowse Music Publishing Ltd. . . . . USA
Lew Stone & his Orchestra, vocal Al Bowlly . . . . **Decca F 3233**
Gracie Fields . . . . **HMV B 4281**

WHY WORRY   January 1952
Ralph Edwards / John Sexton
Macmelodies Ltd . . . . UK
Billy Cotton & his Band . . . . **Ace of Clubs ACL 1085**

WICHITA LINEMAN   March 1969
Jim Webb
Carlin Music Corporation . . . . USA
Glen Campbell . . . . **Ember EMBS 261**
Tom Jones . . . . **Decca LK 5007**
The London Pops Orchestra,
conducted by Johnny Arthey . . . . **Pye NSPL 18332**

WIDE BOY   April 1985
Nik Kershaw
Rondor Music . . . . UK
Nik Kershaw . . . . **MCA NIK 7**

WIDE EYED AND LEGLESS   January 1976
Andy Fairweather Low
Rondor Music (London) Ltd . . . . UK
Andy Fairweather Low . . . . **A&M AMS 7202**

WIG-WAM BAM   October 1972
Mike Chapman / Nicky Chinn
Rak Music Ltd . . . . UK
The Sweet . . . . **RCA 2260**

WILD BOYS, THE   November 1984
*John Taylor / Andy Taylor / Roger Taylor, Nick Rhodes & Simon Le
Bon*
Tritec Music . . . . UK
Duran Duran . . . . **Parlophone DURAN 3**

WILD HORSES   April 1953
K.C. Rogan
Edwin H. Morris & Co. Ltd . . . . USA
Perry Como . . . . **HMV 7M 124**
David Hughes . . . . **Philips PB 120**
Based on *Wilder Reiter* by Robert Schumann (1810   1856).

WILD IN THE COUNTRY   September 1961
Hugo Peretti / George Weiss / Luigi Creatore
Seventeen Savile Row Ltd. . . . . USA
Film(s): . . . . Wild in the Country
Elvis Presley . . . . **RCA 1244**
Elvis Presley appeared in *Wild in the Country*.

WILD ONE   March 1960
Bernie Lowe / Kal Mann / Dave Appell
Belinda (London) Ltd . . . . USA
Bobby Rydell . . . . **Columbia 33SX 1243**

WILD ONE, THE   November 1974
Mike Chapman / Nicky Chinn
Chinnichap Music . . . . UK
Suzi Quatro . . . . **Rak 185**

WILD ROSE   1921
Jerome Kern / Clifford Grey
Chappell & Co. Ltd . . . . USA
Show(s): . . . . Sally / Wild Rose
Film(s): . . . . Sally / Look for the Silver Lining
Dorothy Dickson . . . . **Columbia F 1074**
Bessie Jones . . . . **HMV B 1273**
The New Mayfair Dance Orchestra . . . . **HMV C 2719**
Dorothy Dickson appeared in the British production of *Sally*.

WILD SIDE OF LIFE, THE   January 1977
William Warren / Arlie Carter
Pickwick Music Ltd . . . . USA
Status Quo . . . . **Vertigo 6059153**

WILD THING   June 1966
Chip Taylor
April Music Co. Ltd. . . . . USA
The Troggs . . . . **Fontana TF 689**

WILD WEST HERO   August 1978
Jeff Lynne
United Artists Music Co. Ltd . . . . UK
The Electric Light Orchestra . . . . **Jet 109**

WILD WIND   October 1961
Geoffrey Goddard
Meridian Music Publishing Co. Ltd. . . . . UK
John Leyton . . . . **Top Rank JAR 585**

WILD WORLD   September 1970
Cat Stevens
Freshwater Music . . . . UK
Jimmy Cliff . . . . **Island WIP 6087**
Cat Stevens . . . . **Island ILPS 0135**
Maxi Priest (1988) . . . . **10 TEN 22**

**WILD, WILD WOMEN ARE MAKING A WILD MAN OUT OF
ME, THE**   1917
Al Piantadosi / Al Wilson
Francis, Day & Hunter Ltd. . . . . USA
The Savoy Quartet, vocal Joe Wilbur . . . . **HMV B 962**
Freddie 'Schnichelfritz' Fisher & his Band,
vocal Stan Fritts . . . . **Brunswick 04752**

WILHELMINA   May 1950
Mack Gordon / Joseph Myrow
Francis, Day & Hunter Ltd . . . . USA
Film(s): . . . . Wabash Avenue
Danny Kaye . . . . **Brunswick 04485**
Nominated for an Academy Award 1950.

WILL I WHAT   September 1962
Johnny Powell / Nick Shakespear / Ken Hawker
Southern Music Publishing Co. Ltd . . . . UK

Mike Sarne . . . . Parlophone R 4932

WILL YOU   **June 1981**
Hazel O'Connor
Albion Music . . . . UK
Hazel O'Connor . . . . **A&M AM 8131**

WILL YOU LOVE ME IN DECEMBER
(As You Do in May)   **1906**
Ernest Ball / James Walker
B. Feldman & Co. Ltd. . . . . USA
Film(s): . . . . The Eddy Duchin Story / Beau James
Norman Blair . . . . **Panachord 25312**
Bob Hope . . . . **London HAP 2056**
Bob Hope appeared in *Beau James.*

WILL YOU LOVE ME TOMORROW   **March 1961**
Gerry Goffin / Carole King
Nevins-Kirshner Ltd . . . . USA
The Shirelles . . . . **Top Rank JAR 540**
The Raindrops . . . . **Oriole CB 1595**
Brenda Lee . . . . **Brunswick LAT 8376**
Helen Shapiro . . . . **Columbia 33SX 1397**

WILL YOU REMEMBER (Sweetheart)   **1917**
Sigmund Romberg / Rida Johnson Young
Chappell & Co. Ltd. . . . . USA
Show(s): . . . . Maytime
Film(s): . . . . Maytime / Deep in My Heart
Jeanette MacDonald & Nelson Eddy (1937) . . . **RCA RCX 1020**
Jane Powell & Vic Damone . . . . **MGM C 755**
Jeanette MacDonald & Nelson Eddy appeared in the film of *Maytime.*
Jane Powell & Vic Damone appeared in *Deep in My Heart.*

WILLIE CAN   **April 1956**
Felice Bryant / Boudleaux Bryant
Acuff-Rose Publishing Co. Ltd. . . . . USA
Alma Cogan . . . . **HMV 7EG 8169**

WILLINGLY (Melodie Perdue)   **March 1959**
Hubert Giraud / Jean Brousolle / Carl Sigman
Macmelodies Ltd. . . . . France
Johnny Desmond . . . . **Philips PB 890**
David Whitfield . . . . **Decca F 11101**
Malcolm Vaughan . . . . **HMV POP 590**

WILLOW WEEP FOR ME   **1933**
Ann Ronell
Francis, Day & Hunter Ltd. . . . . USA
Film(s): . . . . Love Happy
Paul Whiteman & his Orchestra,
vocal Mildred Bailey . . . . **HMV B 6314**
Andy Williams . . . . **London HAA 2238**
Ella Fitzgerald . . . . **HMV CLP 1383**

WIMMIN (I Gotta Have 'Em That's All)   **1922**
Eddie Cantor / Fred Fisher
B. Feldman & Co. Ltd . . . . USA
Show(s): . . . . The Midnight Rounders
The Club Royal Orchestra . . . . **HMV B 1343**

WIMOWEH   **March 1952**
Traditional, arranged by Paul Campbell
Southern Music Publishing Co. Ltd . . . . USA
The Weavers . . . . **Brunswick LAT 8357**
See also 'The Lion Sleeps Tonight'.

WIMOWEH   **March 1962**
Traditional, arranged by Karl Denver
An edition by Essex Music Ltd. . . . . UK
Karl Denver . . . . **Decca F 11420**
See also 'The Lion Sleeps Tongiht'.

WINCHESTER CATHEDRAL   **November 1966**
Geoff Stevens
Meteor Music Ltd. . . . . UK
The New Vaudeville Band . . . . **Fontana TF 741**
Ivor Novello Award.

WIND BENEATH MY WINGS   **August 1989**
Larry Henley / Jeff Silbar
Warner Chappell Music . . . . USA
Bette Midler . . . . **Atlantic A 8972**

WIND CRIES MARY, THE   **June 1967**
Jimi Hendrix
Schroeder Music Ltd. . . . . USA
Jimi Hendrix Experience . . . . **Track 604004**

WIND ME UP (Let Me Go)   **December 1965**
John Talley / Bob Montgomery
Ardmore & Beechwood Ltd . . . . USA
Cliff Richard . . . . **Columbia DB 7745**

WINDMILL IN OLD AMSTERDAM, A   **March 1965**
Ted Dicks / Myles Rudge
Essex Music Ltd . . . . UK
Ronnie Hilton . . . . **HMV POP 1378**
Ivor Novello Award.

WINDMILLS OF YOUR MIND   **April 1969**
Michel Legrand / Alan Bergman / Marilyn Bergman
United Artists Music Co. Ltd. . . . . USA
Film(s): . . . . The Thomas Crown Affair
Noel Harrison . . . . **Reprise 20758**
Michel Legrand Orchestra . . . . . **United Artists ULP 1218**
Dusty Springfield . . . . **Philips SBL 7889**
Lois Lane . . . . **Mercury MF 1092**
Academy Award winning song for 1968.

WINDOWS OF PARIS   **August 1959**
Tony Osborne
Mason Music Ltd . . . . UK
Tony Osborne & his Orchestra . . . . **HMV POP 633**
Victor Sylvester & his Orchestra . . . **Columbia DB 4372**
Ivor Novello Award.

WINDSOR WALTZ, THE   **April 1953**
Hans May / Michael Reine
Michael Reine Music Co. Ltd . . . . UK
Gerry Brereton . . . . **Parlophone R 3671**
Vera Lynn . . . . **Ace of Clubs ACL 1045**

WINE OF FRANCE   **1903**
Ivan Caryll
Chappell & Co. Ltd. . . . . UK
Show(s): . . . . The Duchess of Dantzig
The Light Opera Company (1909) . . . . . . **HMV 04535**
The Light Opera Company (1909) . . . . . . **HMV C 2262**

WINE, WOMAN AND SONG   **1898**
Gustave Kerker / Hugh Morton
Ascherberg, Hopwood & Crew Ltd. . . . . USA
Show(s): . . . . The Belle of New York
Barry Kent . . . . **HMV 7EG 8442**

WINGS OF A DOVE   **September 1983**
Charles Smythe / Graham McPherson
Warner Brothers Music . . . . UK
Madness . . . . **Stiff BUY 181**

WINGS OVER THE NAVY   **1939**
Harry Warren / Johnny Mercer
B. Feldman & Co. Ltd. . . . . USA
Film(s): . . . . Wings of the Navy
Billy Cotton & his Band . . . . **Rex 9665**
The Band of H.M. Grenadier Guards . . . . . . **Columbia DC 456**

WINNER TAKES IT ALL   ♦   **August 1980**
Benny Andersson / Bjorn Ulvaeus
Bocu Music Ltd . . . . Sweden
Abba . . . . **Epic EPC 8835**

WINTER WONDERLAND   **1935**
Felix Bernard / Dick Smith
Francis, Day & Hunter Ltd . . . . USA
Ted Weems & his Orchestra . . . . . . **Columbia FB 1009**
Johnny Mathis . . . . **Fontana TFL 5031**
Perry Como . . . . **RCA RD 27082**
The Ray Charles Singers . . . . **MGM EP 630**

WINTER WORLD OF LOVE   **December 1969**
Les Reed / Barry Mason
Donna Music Ltd. . . . . UK
Engelbert Humperdinck . . . . **Decca F 12980**

WINTER'S TALE, A   **January 1983**
Mike Batt / Tim Rice

Warner Brothers Music . . . . UK
David Essex . . . . **Mercury MER 127**

WIPE OUT   **August 1963**
"The Surfaris"
Ambassador Music Ltd . . . . USA
The Surfaris . . . . **London HL 9751**
The Ventures . . . . **Liberty LBY 1169**
Fat Boys & The Beach Boys (1987) . . . . **Urban URB 5**

WIRED FOR SOUND   **September 1981**
Alan Tarney / B.A. Robertson
ATV Music . . . . UK
Cliff Richard . . . . **EMI 5221**
Ivor Novello Nomination.

WISDOM OF A FOOL, THE   **March 1957**
Abner Silver / Roy Alfred
Leeds Music Ltd. . . . . USA
Ronnie Hilton . . . . **HMV POP 291**
Ronnie Carroll . . . . **Philips BBE 12114**

WISH ME LUCK AS YOU WAVE ME GOODBYE   **1939**
Harry Parr-Davies / Phil Park
Chappell & Co. Ltd. . . . . UK
Film(s): . . . . .Shipyard Sally
Gracie Fields . . . . **Regal Zonophone MR 3118**
Winifred Atwell (piano) . . . . **Decca LK 4360**
Gracie Fields appeared in *Shipyard Sally.*

WISH YOU WERE HERE   **October 1953**
Harold Rome
Chappell & Co. Ltd. . . . . USA
Show(s): . . . . Wish You Were Here
Bruce Trent . . . . **Philips PB 200**
Eddie Fisher . . . . **HMV B 10564**
Peggy Lee . . . . **Capitol T 1290**
Bruce Trent appeared in the British production of *Wish You Were Here.*

WISHFUL THINKING   **February 1984**
Gary Daley / Eddie London
Virgin Music . . . . UK
China Crisis . . . . **Virgin VS 647**

WISHIN' AND HOPIN'   **August 1964**
Burt Bacharach / Hal David
Belinda (London) Ltd . . . . USA
Dionne Warwick . . . . **Stateside SS 191**
The Merseybeats . . . . **Fontana TF 482**

WISHING   **1939**
Buddy De Sylva
Bradbury Wood Ltd. . . . . USA
Film(s): . . . . Love Affair / George White's Scandals
Vera Lynn . . . . **Decca F 7120**
Connee Boswell . . . . **Brunswick 02770**
Glenn Miller & his Orch, vocal Ray Eberle . . . . . **HMV DLP 1049**
Tony Brent . . . . **Columbia 33S 1124**
Nominated for an Academy Award 1939.

WISHING   **September 1963**
Buddy Holly / Bob Montgomery
Palace Music Ltd . . . . USA
Buddy Holly . . . . **Coral Q 72466**

WISHING (If I Had a Photograph of You)   **December 1982**
Michael Score / Alister Score / Paul Reynolds / Francis Maudsley
Zomba Music . . . . UK
Flock Of Seagulls . . . . **Jive 25**

WISHING I WAS LUCKY   **June 1987**
Marti Pellow / Graham Clarke / Neil Mitchell & Tom Cunningham
Precious Music . . . . UK
Wet Wet Wet . . . . **Phonogram Jewel 3**

WISHING ON A STAR   **March 1978**
Billie Calvin
Warner Brothers Music Ltd . . . . USA
Rose Royce . . . . **Warner Brothers K 17060**

WISHING WELL   **February 1973**
Paul Rodgers / Simon Kirke / Tetsu Yamauchi, John Bundrick & Paul Kossoff
Island Music Ltd. . . . . UK

Free . . . . **Island WIP 6146**

WISHING WELL   **July 1987**
Terence Trent D'Arby / Shaun Oliver
Virgin Music . . . . UK
Terence Trent D'Arby . . . . **CBS TRENT 2**

WITCH DOCTOR   **June 1958**
Ross Bagdasarian
Bourne Music Ltd . . . . USA
David Seville & his Orchestra,
vocal The Chipmunks . . . . **London HAU 2153**
Don Lang . . . . **HMV POP 488**

WITCH QUEEN OF NEW ORLEANS   **November 1971**
Pat Vegas / Lolly Vegas
April Music Ltd . . . . USA
Redbone . . . . **Epic EPC 7351**

WITCH, THE   **November 1970**
Herbert Hildebrandt
Hans Sikorski Ltd . . . . Germany
The Rattles . . . . **Decca F 23058**

WITCHCRAFT   **January 1958**
Carolyn Leigh / Cy Coleman
Edwin H. Morris & Co. Ltd . . . . USA
Frank Sinatra . . . . **Capitol EAP 1-1013**
Chris Connor . . . . **London LTZK 15185**

WITCHES PROMISE   **February 1970**
Ian Anderson
Chrysalis Music Ltd. . . . . UK
Jethro Tull . . . . **Chrysalis WIP 6077**

WITH A GIRL LIKE YOU   **August 1966**
Reginald Presley
Dick James Music Ltd. . . . . UK
The Troggs . . . . **Fontana TF 717**

WITH A LITTLE BIT OF LUCK   **April 1958**
Alan Jay Lerner / Frederick Loewe
Chappell & Co. Ltd . . . . USA
Show(s): . . . . My Fair Lady
Film(s): . . . . My Fair Lady
Stanley Holloway, Gordon Dilworth &
Rod McHennan . . . . **Philips RBL 1000**
Stanley Holloway, Alan Dudley & Bob Chisholm . . . **CBS 70005**
Stanley Holloway & chorus . . . . **CBS BRG 72237**
Stanley Holloway, Gordon Dilworth & Rod McHennan appeared in the American production of *My Fair Lady.*
Stanley Holloway, Alan Dudley & Bob Chisholm appeared in the British production of *My Fair Lady.*
Stanley Holloway appeared in the film *My Fair Lady.*

WITH A LITTLE HELP FROM MY FRIENDS   **July 1967**
John Lennon / Paul McCartney
Northern Songs Ltd. . . . . UK
Show(s): . . . . John, Paul, George, Ringo & Bert
Film(s):Yellow Submarine / Woodstock / Stardust / All This and World War II / Sgt. Pepper's Lonely Hearts Club Band
The Beatles . . . . **Parlophone R 6022**
Barbara Dixon . . . . **RSO 2394141**
Young Ideas (1967) . . . . **Columbia DB 8205**
Joe Cocker (1968) . . . . **Regal Zonophone RZ 3013**
Jeff Lynn & The London Symphony Orchestra . . . **Riva RVLP 2**
Peter Frampton & The Bee Gees . . . . **A&M AMLS 66600**
Wet Wet Wet (1988) . . . . **Childline CHILD 1**
Barbara Dickson appeared in *John, Paul, George, Ringo & Bert.*
The Beatles appeared in *Yellow Submarine.*
Joe Cocker appeared in both *Woodstock* and *Stardust.*
Jeff Lynn appeared in *Woodstock.*
Peter Frampton & The Bee Gees appeared in *Sgt. Pepper's Lonely Hearts Club Band.*

WITH A LITTLE LUCK   **April 1978**
Paul McCartney
A.T.V. Music Ltd. . . . . UK
Wings . . . . **Parlophone R 6019**

WITH A SMILE AND A SONG   **1938**
Larry Morey / Frank Churchill
Walt Disney Music Co. Ltd. . . . . USA
Film(s): . . . . Snow White and the Seven Dwarfs
Sound Track . . . . **HMV BD 514**
Sound Track . . . . **Disneyland DLP 39003**

WITH A SONG IN MY HEART   **1930**
Richard Rodgers / Lorenz Hart
Chappell & Co. Ltd . . . . USA
Show(s): . . . . Spring is Here / Cochrane's 1930 Revue
Film(s):Spring is Here / This Is the Life / Words and Music / Young Man
of Music / Painting the Clouds with Sunshine / With a Song in My Heart
Arthur Roseberry & his Band . . . . **Parlophone R 609**
Leslie Hutchinson (Hutch) . . . . **Parlophone R 639**
Jane Froman . . . . **Capitol LC 6654**
Doris Day . . . . **Columbia SEG 7572**
Ella Fitzgerald . . . . **HMV CLP 1116**
Doris Day appeared in *Young Man of Music.*
Jane Froman dubbed the singing voice of Susan Hayward who
appeared in the film *With a Song in My Heart.*

WITH ALL MY HEART   **1936**
Gus Kahn / Jimmy McHugh
Francis Day & Hunter Ltd . . . . USA
Film(s): . . . . Her Master's Voice
Ray Noble & his Orchestra, vocal Al Bowlly . . . . **HMV BD 5028**

WITH ALL MY HEART   **July 1957**
Peter De Angelis / Robert Marcucci
Sydney Bron Music Co. Ltd. . . . . USA
Petula Clark . . . . **Nixa NPT 19021**
Frankie Avalon . . . . **HMV CLP 1440**

WITH EVERY BREATH I TAKE   **1935**
Leo Robin / Ralph Rainger
Victoria Music Co. Ltd . . . . USA
Film(s): . . . . Here is My Heart
Bing Crosby . . . . **Brunswick Bing 1**
The Hilltoppers . . . . **London HAD 2100**
Billy Eckstine . . . . **Columbia 33SX 1249**
Bing Crosby appeared in *Here Is My Heart.*

WITH HER HEAD TUCKED UNDERNEATH HER ARM   **1934**
R.P. Weston / Bert Lee
Francis, Day & Hunter Ltd . . . . UK
Fred Vernon . . . . **Decca F 5295**
Stanley Holloway . . . . **Columbia DX 603**
Billy Cotton & his Band . . . . **Regal Zonophone MR 1474**

WITH MY EYES WIDE OPEN I'M DREAMIN'   **1934**
Mack Gordon / Harry Revel
Victoria Music Co. Ltd . . . . USA
Film(s): . . . . Shoot the Works / The Stooge
Lew Stone & his Band, vocal Al Bowlly . . . . **Decca F 5172**
The Ink Spots . . . . **Brunswick 04474**
Patti Page . . . . **Mercury ZEP 10032**

WITH MY SHILLELAGH UNDER MY ARM   **1937**
Billy O'Brien / Raymond Wallace
Lawrence Wright Music Co. Ltd. . . . . UK
Jack Daly . . . . **Regal Zonophone MR 2271**
Bing Crosby . . . . **Brunswick LAT 8106**

WITH OR WITHOUT YOU   **April 1987**
"U2"
Blue Mountain Music . . . . UK
U2 . . . . **Island S 319**

WITH PLENTY OF MONEY AND YOU   **1937**
Al Dubin / Harry Warren
Chappell & Co. Ltd. . . . . USA
Film(s): . . . . Gold Diggers of 1937
Dick Powell . . . . **Decca F 6394**
Tony Bennett . . . . **Columbia 33SX 1174**
Dick Powell . . . . **RCA ZL 70136**
Dick Powell appeared in *Gold Diggers of 1937.*

WITH THE EYES OF A CHILD   **December 1969**
Guy Fletcher / Doug Flett
Abacus Music . . . . UK
Cliff Richard . . . . **Columbia DB 8641**

WITH THE WIND AND THE RAIN IN YOUR HAIR   **1940**
Jack Lawrence / Clara Edwards
Victoria Music Co. Ltd . . . . USA
Frances Langford . . . . **Brunswick 02977**
The Eligibles . . . . **Capitol T 1411**

WITH THESE HANDS   **July 1951**
Abner Silver / Benny Davis

Edward Kassner Music Co. Ltd . . . . USA
Lee Lawrence . . . . **Decca F 9590**
Roberto Cardinali . . . . **HMV 7EG 8456**
Shirley Bassey . . . . **Columbia SEG 8063**
Tom Jones (1965) . . . . **Decca F 12191**

WITH YOU I'M BORN AGAIN   **January 1980**
David Shire / Carol Connors
Jobete Music (UK) Ltd. . . . . USA
Film(s): . . . . Fast Break
Billy Preston & Syreeta . . . . **Motown TMG 1159**

WITH YOUR LOVE (Mes Mains)   **January 1956**
Gilbert Becaud / Pierre Delanoe / John Turner & Geoffrey Parsons
Macmelodies Ltd. . . . . France
Gilbert Becaud . . . . **HMV DLP 1173**
Vera Lynn . . . . **Decca F 10622**
Petula Clark . . . . **Pye NPT 19014**

WITHOUT A SONG   **1930**
Vincent Youmans / Edward Eliscu / Billy Rose
Campbell Connelly & Co. Ltd . . . . USA
Show(s): . . . . Great Day
Film(s): . . . . The Prodigal
Paul Whiteman & his Orch, vocal Bing Crosby   **Columbia CB 116**
Lawrence Tibbett . . . . **HMV DA 1206**
Nelson Eddy . . . . **Philips SBF 281**
Tommy Dorsey & his Orch, vocal Frank Sinatra . **HMV DLP 1123**
Lawrence Tibbett appeared in *The Prodigal.*

WITHOUT A WORD OF WARNING   **1935**
Mack Gordon / Harry Revel
Victoria Music Co. Ltd . . . . USA
Film(s): . . . . Two for Tonight
Bing Crosby . . . . **Brunswick Bing 1**
Edmundo Ros & his Orchestra . . . . **Decca LK 4146**
Bing Crosby appeared in *Two for Tonight.*

WITHOUT LOVE (There Is Nothing)   **January 1970**
Danny Small
Duchess Music Ltd. . . . . USA
Tom Jones . . . . **Decca F 12990**
Rose Brennan . . . . **HMV POP 302**
Ronnie Carroll . . . . **Philips PB 667**

WITHOUT YOU   **April 1972**
Peter Ham / Tony Evans
Apple Publishing . . . . UK
Nilsson . . . . **RCA 2165**
Badfinger . . . . **Apple SAPCOR 16**
Ivor Novello Award.

WITHOUT YOU (Tres Palabras)   **1946**
Osvaldo Farres / Ray Gilbert
Southern Music Publishing Co. Ltd. . . . . Mexico
Film(s): . . . . Make Mine Music (cartoon)
**Edmundo Ros & his Orchestra,
vocal Ronaldo Mazar** . . . . **Decca F 8636**

WOMAN   **February 1981**
John Lennon
Warner Brothers Music . . . . UK
John Lennon . . . . **Geffen K 79195**
Ivor Novello Award.

WOMAN (Uh-Huh)   **March 1954**
Dick Gleason
Leeds Music . . . . USA
Jose Ferrer . . . . **Philips PB 220**
See also Man (Uh-Huh).

WOMAN IN LOVE, A   **August 1956**
Frank Loesser
Edwin H. Morris & Co. Ltd. . . . . USA
Film(s): . . . . Guys and Dolls
Jean Simmons & Marlon Brando . . . . **Brunswick OE 9241**
The Four Aces . . . . **Brunswick LAT 8249**
Frankie Laine . . . . **Philips PB 617**
Ronnie Hilton . . . . **HMV 7EG 8202**
Jean Simmons & Marlon Brando appeared in the film *Guys and Dolls.*

WOMAN IN LOVE, A   **February 1979**
Dominic Bugatti / Frank Musker
Chappell & Co. Ltd. . . . . UK

The Three degrees . . . . **Ariola ARO 141**
Ivor Novello Award.

WOMAN IN LOVE, A   **November 1980**
Barry Gibb / Robin Gibb
Chappell & Co. Ltd . . . . UK
Barbra Streisand . . . . **CBS 8966**
Ivor Novello Award 1980.
Ivor Novello Nomination 1981.

WOMBLING MERRY CHRISTMAS   **December 1974**
Mike Batt
Batt Songs . . . . UK
The Wombles . . . . **CBS 2842**

WOMBLING SONG, THE   **March 1974**
Mike Batt
Batt Songs . . . . UK
The Wombles . . . . **CBS 1794**
Theme of the TV series "The Wombles of Wimbledon".
Ivor Novello Award.

WON'T GET FOOLED AGAIN   **August 1971**
Peter Townshend
Fabulous Music Ltd . . . . UK
The Who . . . . **Track 2094009**

WON'T SOMEBODY DANCE WITH ME   **November 1973**
Lynsey De Paul
A.T.V. Music Ltd. . . . . UK
Lynsey De Paul . . . . **MAM 109**
Ivor Novello Award.

WON'T TALK ABOUT IT   **May 1990**
Norman Cook / Billy Bragg
Go Disc Music . . . . UK
Beats International . . . . **Go Beat GOD 43**

WON'T YOU COME HOME BILL BAILEY   **1902**
Hughie Cannon
Herman Darewski Music Publishing Co. Ltd. . . . . USA
Film(s): . . . . The Five Pennies
Al Bernard . . . . **Panachord 25146**
Albert Pearce . . . . **HMV GC 2-2984**
Jimmy Durante . . . . **MGM EP 508**
Louis Armstrong . . . . **London HAU 2189**
Connie Francis . . . . **MGM C 861**
Louis Armstrong appeared in *The Five Pennies*.

WONDER BAR   **1934**
Al Dubin / Harry Warren
B. Feldman & Co. Ltd. . . . . USA
Film(s): . . . . Wonder Bar
Dick Powell . . . . **Decca F 3944**
Dick Powell appeared in *Wonder Bar*.

WONDER OF YOU, THE   **August 1959**
Baker Knight
Duchess Music Ltd . . . . USA
Ronnie Hilton . . . . **HMV POP 638**
Ray Peterson . . . . **RCA 1131**
Elvis Presley (1970) . . . . **RCA 1974**

WONDERFUL CHRISTMAS TIME   **December 1979**
Paul McCartney
A.T.V. Music Ltd. . . . . UK
Paul McCartney . . . . **Parlophone R 6029**

WONDERFUL COPENHAGEN   **December 1952**
Frank Loesser
Edwin H. Morris & Co. Ltd . . . . USA
Show(s): . . . . Hans Andersen
Film(s): . . . . Hans Christian Andersen
Danny Kaye . . . . **Ace of Hearts AH 20**
Connie Stevens . . . . **Warner Brothers WM 4060**
Tommy Steele . . . . **Pye NSPL 18451**
Danny Kaye appeared in *Hans Christian Andersen*.
Tommy Steele appeared in *Hans Andersen*.

WONDERFUL DAY LIKE TODAY, A   **1964**
Anthony Newley / Leslie Bricusse
Concord Music . . . . UK
Show(s): . . . . The Roar of the Greaspaint - The Smell of the Crowd
Cyril Richard . . . . **RCA LOC 1109**
Lena Horne . . . . **United Artists ULP 1114**

Sammy Davis Jnr. . . . . **Reprise R 6169**
Cyril Richard appeared in *The Roar of the Greaspaint - The Smell of
the Crowd.*

WONDERFUL DREAM (Tu Te Reconnaitras)   **May 1973**
Vline Buggy / Claude Morgan / Sidney Lawton
Louvigny-Marquee Music Co. . . . . France
Ann-Marie David (in French) . . . . **Epic 1446**
Ann-Marie David (in English) . . . . **Epic EPC 80148**
Luxembourg entry for the 1973 Eurovision Song Contest (Placed
First).

WONDERFUL EYES   **1914**
Paul Rubens / Percy Greenbank
Chappell & Co. Ltd. . . . . UK
Show(s): . . . . After the Girl
Natalie Hall & Monte Rey . . . . **Columbia DX 679**

WONDERFUL LAND   **April 1962**
Jerry Lordan
Francis, Day & Hunter Ltd. . . . . UK
The Shadows . . . . **Columbia DB 4790**
Ivor Novello Nomination.

WONDERFUL LIFE   **September 1987**
Colin Vearncombe
Rondor Music . . . . UK
Black . . . . **A&M AM 402**

WONDERFUL ONE   **1923**
Ferde Grofé / Paul Whiteman / Dorothy Terriss / Marshal Neilan
Francis, Day & Hunter Ltd . . . . USA
Film(s): . . . . Margie / Murder in The Music Hall
Paul Whiteman & his Orchestra . . . . **HMV B 1639**
Glenn Miller & his Orchestra . . . . **HMV CLPC 1**
Anne Rogers . . . . **HMV 7EG 8564**
Vera Lynn . . . . **Decca LK 4305**

WONDERFUL SECRET OF LOVE, THE   **March 1959**
Irving Gordon
Leeds Music . . . . USA
Robert Earl . . . . **Philips PB 891**

WONDERFUL TIME UP THERE   **March 1958**
Lee Roy Abernathy
Edwin H. Morris & Co. Ltd . . . . USA
Pat Boone . . . . **London HAD 2161**

WONDERFUL WONDERFUL   **August 1957**
Ben Raleigh / Sherman Edwards
Loods Music Ltd. . . . . USA
Gary Miller . . . . **Nixa NPT 19021**
Ronnie Hilton . . . . **HMV 7EG 8270**
Johnny Mathis . . . . **Philips BBR 8113**

WONDERFUL WONDERFUL DAY   **February 1955**
Johnny Mercer / Gene De Paul
Robbins Music Ltd. . . . . USA
Film(s): . . . . Seven Brides for Seven Brothers
Jane Powell & The Brothers . . . . **MGM C 853**
Jane Powell & The Brothers appeared in *Seven Brides for Seven
Brothers.*

WONDERFUL WORLD   **May 1965**
Barbara Campbell / Lou Adler / Herb Alpert
Ardmore & Beechwood Ltd . . . . USA
Herman's Hermits . . . . **Columbia DB 7546**
Sam Cooke . . . . **HMV POP 754**
Johnny Nash . . . . **Epic EPC 4294**
Sam Cooke (1986) . . . . **RCA PB 4987**

WONDERFUL WORLD OF THE YOUNG, THE **May 1962**
Sid Tepper / Roy C. Bennett
Leeds Music Ltd. . . . . USA
Danny Williams . . . . **HMV POP 1002**
Andy Williams . . . . **Philips PB 1232**

WONDERFUL WORLD, BEAUTIFUL PEOPLE **Nov 1969**
Jimmy Cliff
Island Music Ltd . . . . USA
Jimmy Cliff . . . . **Trojan TR 690**

WONDERLAND   **February 1984**
"Big Country"
Virgin Music . . . . UK

Big Country . . . . Mercury COUNT 5

WONDROUS STORIES October 1977
Jon Anderson
Warner Brothers Music Ltd . . . . UK
Yes . . . . Atlantic K 10999

WOOD BEEZ April 1984
"Green"
Chrysalis Music Ltd. . . . . UK
Scritti Politti . . . . Virgin VS 657

WOODCHOPPER'S BALL 1939
Joe Bishop / Woody Herman
Leeds Music Ltd. . . . . USA
Film(s): . . . . What's Cooking
Woody Herman & his Orchestra . . . . **Brunswick LAT 8092**
Joe Loss & his Orchestra . . . . **HMV DLP 1068**
Henry Jerome & his Orchestra . . . . **Brunswick LAT 8379**
Woody Herman appeared in *What's Cooking*.

WOODEN HEART March 1961
Berthold Kaempfert / Kay Twomey / Fred Wise & Ben Weisman
West One Music Ltd . . . . USA
Film(s): . . . . G.I. Blues
Elvis Presley . . . . **RCA 1226**
Elaine & Derek . . . . **Parlophone R 4829**
Elvis Presley appeared in *G.I. Blues*.
Adapted from the German folk song *Muss I Denn*.

WOODMAN, WOODMAN SPARE THAT TREE 1947
Irving Berlin / Vincent Bryan
Francis, Day & Hunter Ltd. . . . . USA
Show(s): . . . . Ziegfeld Follies of 1911
Bert Williams . . . . **Sunbeam P 506**
Phil Harris (1947) . . . . **Camden CDN 124**
Bert Williams appeared in *Ziegfeld Follies of 1911*.

WOODPECKERS SONG (Reginella Campagnola) 1940
Eldo Di Lazzaro / Harold Adamson
Francis, Day & Hunter Ltd . . . . Italy
Film(s): . . . . Ride Tenderfoot Ride
Tino Rossi (in Italian) . . . . **Columbia SEG 7529**
The Andrews Sisters . . . . **Brunswick 02996**
Joe Loss & his Orchestra,
vocal Chick Henderson . . . . **HMV BD 5589**

WOODSTOCK November 1970
Joni Mitchell
Warner Brothers Music Ltd . . . . UK
Film(s): . . . . Woodstock
Matthews Southern Comfort . . . . **Uni UNS 526**
Joni Mitchell . . . . **Reprise RS 20906**

WOODY WOODPECKER August 1948
George Tibbles / Ramey Idriss
Leeds Music Ltd. . . . . USA
Danny Kaye & The Andrews Sisters . . . . **Brunswick LAT 8350**
Mel Blanc . . . . **Brunswick OE 9397**
Kay Kyser & his Orchestra . . . . **Columbia FB 3434**

WOOLY BULLY July 1965
Domingo Samudio
Beckie Music Ltd . . . . USA
Sam The Sham & The Pharaohs . . . . **MGM 1269**

WORD GIRL, THE June 1985
Paul Strohmeyer / Dave Gamson
Warner Brothers Music . . . . UK
Scritti Politti . . . . Virgin VS 747

WORD UP October 1986
Larry Blackman / Tom Jenkins
Polygram Music . . . . USA
Cameo . . . . **Club JAB 38**

WORDS March 1968
Barry Gibb / Robin Gibb / Maurice Gibb
Abigail Music . . . . UK
The Bee Gees . . . . **Polydor 56229**

WORDS May 1983
Robert Fitoussi
Carrere Music . . . . France
F.R. David . . . . **Carrere CAR 248**

WORDS ARE IN MY HEART, THE 1935
Al Dubin / Harry Warren
B. Feldman & Co. Ltd . . . . USA
Film(s): . . . . Gold Diggers of 1935
Dick Powell . . . . **Decca F 5549**
Dick Powell appeared in *Gold Diggers of 1935*.

WORDY RAPPINGHOOD July 1981
Tina Weymouth
Island Music . . . . USA
Tom Tom Club . . . . **Island WIP 6694**

WORK THAT BODY July 1982
Diana Ross / Raymond Chew
Carlin Music . . . . USA
Diana Ross . . . . **Capitol CL 241**

WORKING IN THE COALMINE September 1966
Allen Toussaint
Ardmore & Beechwood Ltd. . . . . USA
Lee Dorsey . . . . **Stateside SS 528**

WORKING MAN November 1990
Rita MacNeil
Unknown Publisher . . . . Canada
Rita MacNeil . . . . **Polydor PO 98**

WORKING MY WAY BACK TO YOU April 1980
Sandy Linzer / Denny Randell
Ardmore & Beechwood Ltd . . . . USA
The Detroit Spinners . . . . **Atlantic K 11432**

WORLD January 1968
Robin Gibb / Barry Gibb / Maurice Gibb
Abigail Music . . . . UK
The Bee Gees . . . . **Polydor 56220**

WORLD IN MOTION June 1990
*Bernard Sumner / Stephen Morris / Keith Allen / Gillian Gilbert /
Peter Hook*
EMI Music . . . . UK
New Order & The 1990 England
World Cup Team . . . . **Factory FAC 2937**
Ivor Novello Nomination.

WORLD IS MINE TONIGHT, THE 1935
George Posford / Holt Marvell
Keith Prowse Music Publishing Co. Ltd . . . . UK
Film(s): . . . . The Gay Desperado
Charles Kullman . . . . **Columbia DB 1579**
Sammy Davis . . . . **Brunswick LAT 8157**
Frank Barber & his Orchestra . . . . **Columbia 33SX 1233**

WORLD IS WAITING FOR THE SUNRISE, THE 1922
Eugene Lockhart / Ernest Seltz
Chappell & Co. Ltd . . . . USA
Film(s): . . . . Sweet and Lowdown
John Steele . . . . **HMV B 1359**
The Benson Orchestra of Chicago . . . . **HMV B 1521**
Les Paul & Mary Ford (1951) . . . . **Capitol T 1438**
Benny Goodman Orchestra . . . . **Capitol LC 6526**

WORLD OF OUR OWN, A May 1965
Tom Springfield
Springfield Music Ltd . . . . UK
The Seekers . . . . **Columbia DB 7532**

WORLD OUTSIDE, THE February 1959
Richard Addinsell / Carl Sigman
Keith Prowse Music . . . . UK
The Four Aces . . . . **Brunswick 05767**
Ronnie Hilton . . . . **HMV POP 559**
Russ Conway (Piano) with
the Rita Williams Singers . . . . **Columbia DB 4234**
Based on the melody of the Warsaw Concerto by Richard Addinsell
(1904-1977).

WORLD WITHOUT LOVE, A April 1964
John Lennon / Paul McCartney
Northern Songs Ltd . . . . UK
Peter & Gordon . . . . **Columbia DB 7225**
Keely Smith . . . . **Reprise R 6142**

WORRIED MAN BLUES February 1957
Traditional

An edition by Leeds Music Ltd. . . . . USA
Bob Cort Skiffle Group . . . . **Decca F 10831**
Charles McDevitt Skiffle Group . . . . **Oriole EP 7002**

WOT CHER   1891
Albert Chevalier / Charles Ingle
Reynolds & Co. (Music Publishers) Ltd. . . . . UK
Louis Bradfield . . . . **Berliner 2917**
Stanley Holloway . . . . **Pye NPL 18056**

WOULD I LOVE YOU   June 1951
Harold Spina / Bob Russell
Walt Disney Music . . . . USA
Tony Martin . . . . **HMV B 10051**
Steve Conway . . . . **Columbia DB 2841**
Doris Day with the Harry James Orchestra . **Columbia DB 2862**
Jimmy Young . . . . **Polygon P 1010**

WOULD YOU   1936
Arthur Freed / Nacio Herb Brown
Francis, Day & Hunter Ltd . . . . USA
Film(s): . . . . .San Francisco
Bing Crosby . . . . **Ace of Hearts AH 1**
Gracie Fields . . . . **Rex 8840**
Alma Cogan . . . . **HMV B 10280**

WOULD YOU LIKE TO TAKE A WALK   1931
Mort Dixon / Harry Warren / Billy Rose
Francis, Day & Hunter Ltd. . . . . USA
Show(s): . . . . Sweet and Low / Crazy Quilt
Film(s): . . . . You're My Everything
Frank Crumit & Julia Sanderson . . . . **HMV B 3833**
Eydie Gormé & Steve Lawrence . . . . **HMV CLP 1463**
Pat Boone . . . . **London HAD 2030**
Frank Crumit & Julia Sanderson appeared in *Sweet and Low.*

WOULDN'T CHANGE A THING   August 1989
Mike Stock / Matt Aitken / Peter Waterman
All Boys Music . . . . UK
Kylie Minogue . . . . **P.W.L. PWL 42**

WOULDN'T IT BE GOOD   March 1984
Nik Kershaw
Rondor Music . . . . UK
Nik Kershaw . . . . **MCA NIK 2**

WOULDN'T IT BE LUVERLY   May 1958
Alan Jay Lerner / Frederick Loewe
Chappell & Co. Ltd . . . . USA
Show(s): . . . . My Fair Lady
Film(s): . . . . My Fair Lady
Julie Andrews (USA) . . . . **Philips BBL 1000**
Julie Andrews (UK) . . . . **CBS 70005**
Eydie Gormé & Steve Lawrence . . . . **HMV CLP 1463**
Audrey Hepburn . . . . **CBS BRG 72237**
Julie Andrews appeared in the American and British productions of
My Fair Lady.
Marni Nixon dubbed the singing voice of Audrey Hepburn who ap-
peared in the film of *My Fair Lady.*

WOW   April 1979
Kate Bush
EMI Music Ltd. . . . . UK
Kate Bush . . . . **EMI 2911**

WRAP YOUR TROUBLES IN DREAMS   1931
Ted Koehler / Harry Barris / Billy Moll
Campbell Connelly & Co. Ltd. . . . . USA
Film(s): . . . . .Rainbow Round My Shoulder
Bing Crosby (1931) . . . . **RCA RD 27075**
Bing Crosby (1936) . . . . **Brunswick LAT 8251**
Frankie Laine . . . . **Mercury ZEP 10062**
Frankie Laine appeared in *Rainbow 'Round My Shoulder.*

WRAP YOURSELF IN COTTON WOOL   1942
Val Guest / Manning Sherwin
Francis, Day & Hunter Ltd . . . . UK
Show(s): . . . . Get a Load of This
Celia Lipton . . . . **Columbia FB 2735**
Hatchett's Swingtette, vocal Billie Campbell . . . . **Decca F 8054**
Celia Lipton appeared in *Get A Load Of This.*

WRAPPED AROUND YOUR FINGER   August 1983
"Sting"

Virgin Music . . . . UK
Police . . . . **A&m AM 127**

WRECK OF THE ANTOINETTE, THE   October 1968
Howard Blaikley
Lynn Music Ltd. . . . . UK
Dave Dee, Dozy, Beaky, Mick & Tich . . . . **Fontana TF 971**

WUNDERBAR   March 1951
Cole Porter
Chappell & Co. Ltd . . . . USA
Show(s): . . . . Kiss Me Kate
Film(s): . . . . Kiss Me Kate
Patricia Morison & Alfred Drake . . . . **Philips BBL 7224**
Patricia Morison & Bill Johnson . . . . **Columbia SEG 7721**
Kathryn Grayson & Howard Keel . . . . **MGM C 753**
Patricia Morison appeared in both the American & British productions
of *Kiss Me Kate.*
Alfred Drake appeared in the American production of *Kiss Me Kate.*
Bill Johnson appeared in the British production of *Kiss Me Kate*
Kathryn Grayson & Howard Keel appeared in the film *Kiss Me Kate..*

WUTHERING HEIGHTS   April 1978
Kate Bush
EMI Music Ltd . . . . UK
Kate Bush . . . . **EMI 2719**
Ivor Novello Nomination.

WYOMING   1920
Gene Williams
Lawrence Wright Music Co. Ltd . . . . UK
The Mayfair Dance Orchestra . . . . **HMV C 946**
The Mantovani Orchestra . . . . **Decca LK 4105**
Robert Farnon & his Orchestra . . . . **MGM C 808**

WYOMING LULLABY   1920
Gene Williams
Lawrence Wright Music . . . . UK
Oscar Rabin Band . . . . **Decca F 7719**
Alma Cogan . . . . **HMV B 10370**
The Beverley Sisters . . . . **Columbia DB 3184**

XANADU   July 1980
Jeff Lynne
April Music Ltd . . . . UK
Film(s): . . . . Xanadu
Olivia Newton-John & The Electric Light Orchestra . . . **Jet 185**
Olivia Newton-John & The Electric Light Orchestra appeared in *Xanadu*
Ivor Novello Award.

Y VIVA ESPANA   September 1974
Leo Caertz / Eddie Rosensrtaten
Sonet Publishing . . . . Belgium
Sylvia . . . . **Sonet SON 2037**

Y.M.C.A.   January 1979
Jacques Morali / Henri Belolo / John Willis
Zomba Music Publishers . . . . France
The Village People . . . . **Mercury 6007**

YA YA TWIST   August 1962
Lee Dorsey / Clarence Lewis / Morgan Robinson
Essex Music Ltd . . . . USA
Petula Clark . . . . **Pye 7N 15448**
Rufus Thomas . . . . **London HAK 8183**

YACKA HULA HICKEY DULA   1917
Pete Wendling / Ray Goetz / Joe Young
B. Feldman & Co. Ltd. . . . . USA
Show(s): . . . . Robinson Crusoe Jr.
Film(s): . . . . Applause
Stanley Kirby . . . . **Regal G 7362**
Elsie Janis . . . . **HMV 03511**
Al Jolson . . . . **Columbia 2711**
Al Jolson . . . . **Brunswick LAT 8267**
Al Jolson appeared in *Robinson Crusoe Jr..*

YAH-TA-TA, YAH-TA-TA   1946
Johnny Burke / Jimmy Van Heusen
Edwin H. Morris & Co. Ltd. . . . . USA
Bing Crosby & Judy Garland . . . . **Brunswick LAT 8054**

YAKITY YAK   August 1958
Jerry Leiber / Mike Stoller
Progressive Music Ltd . . . . USA

The Coasters . . . . **London HAK 2237**
Don Lang . . . . **Ace of Clubs ACL 1111**

YAM, THE 1938
Irving Berlin
Irving Berlin Ltd. . . . . USA
Film(s): . . . . Carefree
Fred Astaire with Ray Noble & his Orch . . . **Columbia DB 1810**
Ginger Rogers . . . . **HMV B 8822**
Fred Astaire & Ginger Rogers appeared in *Carefree*.

YAMA YAMA MAN, THE 1908
Karl Hoschna / George Davis
B. Feldman & Co. Ltd. . . . . USA
Show(s): . . . . The Three Twins
Film(s):The Story of Vernon & Irene Castle / Look for the Silver Lining
Louis Levy & his Orchestra . . . . **HMV BD 721**
The Chris Barber Jazz Band . . . . **Nixa NJL 6**

YANKEE DOODLE BOY 1904
George M. Cohan
B. Feldman & Co. Ltd. . . . . USA
Show(s): . . . . Little Johnny Jones
Film(s):Little Johnny Jones / Yankee Doodle Dandy / Eddie Foy and
the Seven Little Foys
Burt Shepard . . . . **HMV GC 3-2405**
Bob Hope & James Cagney . . . . **HMV DLP 1088**
Mickey Rooney . . . . **RCA RD 27038**
Fred Waring & his Pennsylvanians . . . . **Brunswick 03426**
James Cagney . . . . **RCA ZL 70136**
Bob Hope appeared in *Eddie Foy and the Seven Little Foys*.
James Cagney appeared in *Yankee Doodle Dandy* and *Eddie Foy
and the Seven Little Foys*.

YEAR OF DECISION May 1974
Kenny Gamble / Leon Huff
Carlin Music Corporation . . . . USA
The Three Degrees . . . . **Philadelphia PIR 2073**

YEARNING (Just For You) 1925
Joe Burke / Benny Davis
Francis, Day & Hunter Ltd. . . . . USA
Film(s): . . . . Sweethearts on Parade
The Salon Orchestra . . . . **HMV B 2138**
Jack Hylton & his Orchestra . . . . **HMV B 2056**
The Four Aces . . . . **Brunswick LAT 8299**
Vera Lynn . . . . **Decca LK 4305**

YEARS MAY COME, YEARS MAY GO March 1970
Andre Popp / Jack Fishman
Cyril Shane Music . . . . France
Herman's Hermits . . . . **Columbia DB 8656**
Andre Popp Orchestra . . . . **Polydor 2383142**

YEH YEH January 1965
John Hendricks / Roger Grant / Pat Patrick
B. Feldman & Co. Ltd . . . . USA
Dave Lambert, John Hendricks & Yolanda Bevan RCA RD 7594
Georgie Fame . . . . **Columbia DB 7428**

YELLOW DOG BLUES 1929
William C. Handy
Francis, Day & Hunter Ltd . . . . USA
Film(s): . . . . St. Louis Blues
Bessie Smith . . . . **Philips BBL 7042**
Duke Ellington & his Orchestra . . . . **Vogue LRA 10028**
Nat 'King' Cole . . . . **Capitol LCT 6156**
Nat 'King' Cole appeared in *St. Louis Blues*.

YELLOW RIVER June 1970
Jeff Christie
Gale Music Ltd. . . . . UK
Christie . . . . **CBS S 4911**
Ivor Novello Award.

YELLOW ROSE OF TEXAS, THE October 1955
Don George
Valando Music Co. Ltd. . . . . USA
Gary Miller . . . . **Nixa NEP 24013**
Mitch Miller . . . . **Philips BBR 8121**

YELLOW SUBMARINE October 1966
John Lennon / Paul McCartney
Northern Songs Ltd. . . . . UK

Film(s): . . . . Yellow Submarine
The Beatles . . . . **Parlophone R 5493**
The Beatles appeared in *Yellow Submarine*.
Ivor Novello Award.

YEOMAN OF ENGLAND, THE 1902
Edward German / Basil Hood
Chappell & Co. Ltd. . . . . UK
Show(s): . . . . Merrie England
Henry Lytton . . . . **HMV GC2-2654**
Dennis Noble . . . . **HMV 7EG 8319**
Frederick Harvey . . . . **HMV CLP 1594**
Henry Lytton appeared in *Merrie England*.

YES INDEED 1943
Sy Oliver
Campbell Connelly & Co. Ltd . . . . USA
Tommy Dorsey & his Orchestra,
vocal Sy Oliver & Jo Stafford . . . . **HMV B 9344**
Bing Crosby & Connee Boswell . . . . **Brunswick LAT 8054**
Peggy Lee . . . . **Capitol CL 15209**

YES MISTER BROWN 1933
Paul Abrahams / Robert Gilbert / Douglas Furber / A. Robinson
Chappell & Co. Ltd. . . . . Germany
Film(s): . . . . Yes Mister Brown
Ray Noble & his Orchestra . . . . **HMV B 6285**
Jack Buchanan . . . . **HMV B 4398**
Jack Buchanan appeared in *Yes Mister Brown*.

YES MY DARLING DAUGHTER 1941
Albert Sirmay / Jack Lawrence
Chappell & Co. Ltd . . . . USA
Elsie Carlisle . . . . **Rex 9989**
The Andrews Sisters . . . . **Ace of Hearts AH 21**
Eydie Gormé (1962) . . . . **CBS AAG 105**

YES SIR I CAN BOOGIE November 1977
Rolf Soja / Frank Dostal
Louvigny-Marquee Music Co. . . . . Germany
Baccara . . . . **RCA PB 5526**

YES SIR, THAT'S MY BABY 1925
Gus Kahn / Walter Donaldson
Francis, Day & Hunter Ltd. . . . . USA
Show(s): . . . . Broadway
Film(s): . . . . The Eddie Cantor Story
The Denza Dance Band . . . . **Columbia 3730**
Eddie Cantor . . . . **Brunswick LA 8658**
The Sensations . . . . **London HAE 2167**
Blossom Seeley . . . . **CBS BPG 62547**

YES TONIGHT JOSEPHINE May 1957
Winfield Scott / Dorothy Goodman
Berry Music Ltd. . . . . USA
Johnnie Ray . . . . **Philips BBL 7264**

YES WE HAVE NO BANANAS 1923
Frank Silver / Irving Cohn
Lawrence Wright Music Co. Ltd . . . . USA
The Great White Way Orchestra . . . . **HMV B 1672**
Johnny Desmond . . . . **Vogue LVA 9059**
The Pied Pipers . . . . **Capitol CL 13105**
The 'Sing It Again' Ensemble . . . . **Columbia 33SX 1187**

YESTER-ME YESTER-YOU YESTERDAY December 1969
Ron Miller / Bryan Wells
Jobete Music (UK) Ltd. . . . . USA
Stevie Wonder . . . . **Tamla Motown 717**

YESTERDAY November 1965
John Lennon / Paul McCartney
Northern Songs Ltd . . . . UK
The Beatles . . . . **Parlophone PMC 1255**
Matt Monro . . . . **Parlophone R 5348**
Marianne Faithfull . . . . **Decca F 12268**
The Beatles (1976) . . . . **Apple R 6013**
Ivor Novello Nomination.

YESTERDAY HAS GONE July 1968
Teddy Randazzo / Victoria Pike
Franklin Boyd Music . . . . USA
Cupid's Inspiration . . . . **Nems 563500**

YESTERDAY MAN — November 1965
Chris Andrews
Glissando Music Ltd .... UK
Chris Andrews .... Decca F 12236

YESTERDAY ONCE MORE — August 1973
Richard Carpenter / John Bettis
Rondor Music (London) Ltd. .... USA
The Carpenters .... A&M AMS 7073

YESTERDAYS — 1934
Jerome Kern / Otto Harbach
Chappell & Co. Ltd. .... USA
Show(s): .... Roberta
Film(s): .... Roberta / Till the Clouds Roll By / Lovely to Look at
Joan Merrill .... HMV BD 986
Kathryn Grayson .... MGM D 141
Jeri Southern .... Columbia 33SX 1134
Frank D'Rone .... Mercury AMT 1040
Kathryn Grayson appeared in *Lovely to Look at.*

YIDDLE ON YOUR FIDDLE — 1909
Irving Berlin
B. Feldman & Co. Ltd .... USA
Show(s): .... Ziegfeld Follies of 1910
Film(s): .... The Great Ziegfeld
Harry Fay .... Regal 415
Albert Whelan .... World Records H 222
Charles Lester .... Edison Bell 265

YING TONG SONG, THE — August 1973
Spike Milligan
Unknown Publisher .... UK
The Goons .... Decca F 13414

YIP I ADDY AY — 1908
Will Cobb / John Flynn
Chappell & Co. Ltd. .... USA
Show(s): .... Our Miss Gibbs
Film(s): .... New York Town / Sunbonnet Sue
George Grossmith Jr .... HMV 02219
Florrie Forde .... Regal 174
Guy Lombardo & his Royal Canadians ... Brunswick LA 8612
Eileen Donaghy .... Fontana TFL 5144
George Grossmith Jr. appeared in *Our Miss Gibbs.*

YOU — 1936
Harold Adamson / Walter Donaldson
Sun Music Publishing Co. Ltd .... USA
Film(s): .... The Great Ziegfeld
Turner Layton .... Columbia FB 1475
Ruth Etting .... Rex 8852
Kate Smith .... Capitol T 854

YOU AIN'T HEARD NOTHING YET — 1920
Al Jolson / Gus Kahn / Buddy De Sylva
B. Feldman & Co. Ltd .... USA
Al Jolson .... Columbia 2974
All Star Trio .... HMV B 1155

YOU AIN'T SEEN NOTHING YET — December 1974
Randy Bachman
Screen Gems Music Ltd. .... USA
The Bachman-Turner Overdrive .... Mercury 6167025

YOU ALWAYS HURT THE ONE YOU LOVE — 1946
Allan Roberts / Doris Fisher
Pickwick Music Ltd. .... USA
The Mills Brothers .... Brunswick LAT 8369
Spike Jones & his City Slickers .... HMV BD 1139
The Mills Brothers .... London HAD 2192
Connie Francis (1958) .... MGM C 861
Clarence 'Frogman' Henry (1961) .... Pye 7N 25089

YOU AND ME TONIGHT — May 1986
James Randolph / Eban Kelly
Intersong Music .... UK
Aurra .... 10 TEN 71

YOU AND THE NIGHT AND THE MUSIC — 1935
Howard Deitz / Arthur Schwartz
Chappell & Co. Ltd .... USA
Show(s): .... Revenge With Music / Stop Press
Film(s): .... The Band Wagon

Tony Martin .... HMV 7EG 8006
Gracie Fields .... Regal Zonophone MR 1792
Rise Stevens & Robert Merrill ...... HMV DLP 1135
Ruth Brown .... London LTZK 15187

YOU ARE BEAUTIFUL — May 1960
Richard Rodgers / Oscar Hammerstein II
Williamson Music Ltd .... USA
Show(s): .... Flower Drum Song
Film(s): .... Flower Drum Song
Gary Miller .... Nixa NEP 24123
Ed Kenny & Juanita Hall .... Philips ABL 3302
Johnny Mathis .... Fontana TFL 5083
Kevin Scott & Ida Shepley .... HMV CLP 1359
James Shigeta .... Brunswick LAT 8392
Ed Kenny & Juanita Hall appeared in the American production of *Flower Drum Song.*
Kevin Scott & Ida Shepley appeared in the British production of *Flower Drum Song.*
James Shigeta appeared in the film of *Flower Drum Song.*

YOU ARE EVERYTHING — April 1974
Thomas Bell / Linda Creed
Carlin Music Corporation .... USA
Diana Ross & Marvin Gaye .... Tamla Motown TMG 890

YOU ARE MY DESTINY — June 1951
Sidney Baynes / Harry Ralton
Swan & Co. Ltd. .... UK
Harry Dawson .... Decca F 9685
Lester Ferguson .... Parlophone R 3384
See also Destiny Waltz.

YOU ARE MY DESTINY — February 1958
Paul Anka
Robert Mellin Ltd .... USA
Paul Anka .... Columbia 33SX 1282

YOU ARE MY FIRST LOVE — August 1956
Lester Powell / Paddy Roberts
Unit Music Publishing Co. Ltd. .... UK
Film(s): .... It's Great to be Young
Ruby Murray .... Columbia SEG 7636
Nat 'King' Cole .... Capitol CL 14688
Ivor Novello Nomination.

YOU ARE MY HEART'S DELIGHT — 1931
Franz Lehar / Harry Graham
Chappell & Co. Ltd. .... Austria
Show(s): .... Land of Smiles
Richard Tauber .... Parlophone PMD 1006
Harry Secombe .... Philips BBR 8099
Richard Tauber appeared in *Land of Smiles.*

YOU ARE MY LOVE — July 1976
William Kinsley
Warner Brothers Music Ltd .... UK
Liverpool Express .... Warner Brothers K 16743

YOU ARE MY LUCKY STAR — 1936
Arthur Freed / Nacio Herb Brown
Robbins Music Corporation Ltd .... USA
Show(s): .... Singin' in the Rain
Film(s):Broadway Melody of 1936 / Babes in Arms / Born to Sing / Three Little Words / Singin' in the Rain
Eleanor Powell with Tommy Dorsey & his Orch .. HMV B 8396
Debbie Reynolds & Gene Kelly .... MGM D 140
Gisele MacKenzie .... RCA RD 27033
Tommy Steele .... Safari RAIN 1
Eleanor Powell appeared in *Broadway Melody of 1936.*
Debbie Reynolds & Gene Kelly appeared in the film *Singin' In The Rain.*
Tommy Steele appeared in the show *Singin' in the Rain.*

YOU ARE MY SUNSHINE — 1942
Jimmy Davis / Charles Mitchell
Southern Music Publishing Co. Ltd .... USA
Film(s): ...... Take Me Back To Oklahoma / Strictly in the Groove
Gene Autry .... Regal Zonophone MR 3588
Bing Crosby .... Brunswick LAT 8055

YOU ARE THE ONE — January 1989
Pal Waaktaar / Magne Furholmen
ATV Music .... UK
A-Ha .... Warner Brothers W 7636

YOU ARE THE SUNSHINE OF MY LIFE   June 1973
Stevie Wonder
Jobete Music (UK) Ltd. . . . . USA
Stevie Wonder . . . . **Tamla Motown TMG 852**
Frank Sinatra . . . . **Reprise K 54031**

YOU ARE TOO BEAUTIFUL   1946
Richard Rodgers / Lorenz Hart
Chappell & Co. Ltd. . . . . USA
Film(s): . . . . Hallelujah I'm a Tramp
Al Jolson . . . . **Brunswick 01507**
Frank Sinatra (1946) . . . . **Columbia DB 2224**
Al Jolson appeared in *Hallelujah I'm a Tramp*.

YOU BELONG TO ME   October 1952
Pee Wee King / Rod Stewart / Chilton Price
Chappell & Co. Ltd . . . . USA
Jo Stafford . . . . **Philips BBL 7395**
Pat Boone . . . . **London HAD 2204**

YOU BELONG TO MY HEART   1944
Augustin Lara / Ray Gilbert
Southern Music Publishing Co. Ltd. . . . . Mexico
Film(s):The Three Caballeros (Cartoon) / Gay Ranchero / You Belong
to My Heart
Bing Crosby with Xavier Cugat &
his Waldorf Astoria Orchestra . . . . **Brunswick LAT 8331**
Enzio Pinza . . . . **HMV 7EB 6024**
Charles Wolcott & his Orchestra,
vocal Ray Gilbert . . . . **Brunswick 03578**
Jane Morgan . . . . **London HAR 2244**
Enzio Pinza appeared in *You Belong to My Heart*.

YOU BETTER GO NOW   1936
Irving Graham / Bix Reichner
Chappell & Co. Ltd . . . . USA
Film(s): . . . . New Faces of 1936
Walsh & Barker . . . . **Columbia DB 1816**
Keely Smith . . . . **Capitol CL 14739**
Jeri Southern . . . . **Capitol T 1278**

YOU BETTER YOU BET   May 1981
Peter Townshend
Eel Pie Music . . . . UK
The Who . . . . **Polydor WHO 4**

YOU BROUGHT A NEW KIND OF LOVE TO ME   1930
Irving Kahal / Sammy Fain / Pierre Norman
Chappell & Co. Ltd . . . . USA
Film(s): . . . . The Big Pond / Monkey Business
Maurice Chevalier . . . . **Camden CDN 152**
Frank Sinatra . . . . **Capitol LCT 6106**
Maurice Chevalier . . . . **MGM C 771**
Maurice Chevalier appeared in *The Big Pond*.

YOU CALL EVERYBODY DARLING   November 1948
Sam Martin / Ben Trace / Clem Watts
Edwin H. Morris & Co. Ltd. . . . . USA
The Andrews Sisters . . . . **Brunswick 03969**
Benny Lee . . . . **Decca F 8970**
Patti Page . . . . **Mercury MMC 14017**

YOU CALL IT MADNESS   1932
Con Conrad / Russ Columbo / Gladys Du Bois / Paul Gregory
Victoria Music Co. Ltd. . . . . USA
Kate Smith . . . . **Columbia DB 709**
Jackie Gleason & his Orchestra . . . . **Capitol LC 6813**
Eddie Fisher . . . . **HMV DLP 1040**

YOU CAME   August 1988
Kim Wilde
Rickim Music . . . . UK
Kim Wilde . . . . **MCA KIM 8**

YOU CAN CALL ME AL   October 1986
Paul Simon
Pattern Music . . . . USA
Paul Simon . . . . **Warner Brothers W 8667**

YOU CAN DEPEND ON ME   1938
Charles Carpenter / Louis Dunlap / Earl Hines
Southern Music Publishing Co. Ltd. . . . . USA
Fletcher Henderson & his Orchestra . . . . **HMV B 8647**
The Three Keys . . . . **Brunswick 01612**

Kay Starr . . . . **HMV 7EG 8165**

YOU CAN DO MAGIC   September 1973
Sandy Linzer
Intersong Music . . . . USA
Limmie & The Family Cooking . . . . **Avco 6104019**

YOU CAN GET IT IF YOU REALLY WANT IT   October 1970
Jimmy Cliff
Island Music Ltd . . . . UK
Desmond Dekker . . . . **Trojan TRLS 176**
Jimmy Cliff . . . . **Island ILPS 9202**

YOU CAN MAKE ME DANCE SING
OR ANYTHING   January 1975
*Rod Stewart / Ron Wood / Kenny Jones/ Tetsuo Yamauchi & Ian
McLagan*
Island Music Ltd . . . . UK
The Faces . . . . **Warner Brothers K 16494**

YOU CAN NEVER STOP ME LOVING YOU   August 1963
Ian Samwell / Jean Slater
Klynch Music Ltd . . . . UK
Kenny Lynch . . . . **HMV POP 1165**

YOU CAN'T BE TRUE DEAR
(Du Lannst Nicht Treu Sein)   June 1948
Hans Otten / Gerhard Ebeler / Hal Cotton & Ken Griffen
Chappell & Co. Ltd. . . . . Germany
Vera Lynn . . . . **Decca F 8883**
Dick Haymes . . . . **Brunswick 03905**
Pat & Shirley Boone . . . . **London HAD 2210**

YOU CAN'T BE TRUE TO TWO   May 1956
Al Hoffman / Dick Manning
Dash Music Ltd. . . . . USA
Dave King . . . . **Decca DFE 6385**
Mindy Carson . . . . **Philips PB 579**

YOU CAN'T DO THAT THERE 'ERE   1935
Raymond Wallace / Jack Rolls
Peter Maurice Music Co. Ltd . . . . UK
The Corona Babes . . . . **Rex 8717**
Jack Payne & his Band . . . . **Rex 8657**

YOU CAN'T GET A MAN WITH A GUN   1947
Irving Berlin
Irving Berlin Ltd. . . . . USA
Show(s): . . . . Annie Get Your Gun
Film(s): . . . . Annie Get Your Gun
Ethel Merman . . . . **Brunswick LAT 8002**
Dolores Gray . . . . **Columbia SEG 7711**
Betty Hutton . . . . **MGM CD 1**
Ethel Merman appeared in the American production of *Annie Get Your
Gun*.
Dolores Gray appeared in the British production of *Annie Get Your Gun*.
Betty Hutton appeared in the film of *Annie Get Your Gun*.

YOU CAN'T GET MANY PIMPLES ON A POUND OF
PICKLED PORK   1914
Fred Terry
Francis, Day & Hunter Ltd. . . . . UK
Ernie Mayne . . . . **Edison Bell Winner 2680**

YOU CAN'T HAVE EVERYTHING   1937
Mack Gordon / Harry Revel
Robbins Music Corporation Ltd. USA
Film(s): . . . . You Can't Have Everything
Judy Garland . . . . **Brunswick 02488**
Doris Day . . . . **Philips BBL 7377**
Alice Faye . . . . **Reprise R 6029**
Alice Faye appeared in *You Can't Have Everything*.

YOU CAN'T HURRY LOVE   October 1966
Brian Holland / Eddie Holland / Lamont Dozier
Belinda (London) Ltd. . . . . USA
The Supremes . . . . **Tamla Motown TMG 575**
Phil Collins (1983) . . . . **Virgin VS 531**

YOU CAN'T KEEP A GOOD DREAMER DOWN   1946
Johnny Burke / Jimmy Van Heusen
Edwin H. Morris & Co. Ltd. . . . . USA
Film(s): . . . . London Town
Sid Field . . . . **Decca F 8672**
Sid Field appeared in *London Town*.

YOU CAN'T STOP ME FROM DREAMING   1938
Cliff Friend / Dave Franklin
B. Feldman & Co. Ltd. .... USA
Dick Robertson .... **Panachord 25950**
Maurice Winnick & his Orchestra .... **Decca F 6542**
The Playmates .... **Columbia DB 4084**

YOU DIE IF YOU WORRY   1930
Stanley Damerell / Robert Hargreaves
Cecil Lennox Music Co. Ltd .... UK
Jack Payne & The BBC Dance Orchestra .... **Columbia CB 76**

YOU DO SOMETHING TO ME   1929
Cole Porter
Chappell & Co. Ltd .... USA
Show(s): .... Fifty Million Frenchmen
Film(s): .. Night and Day / Starlift / Because You're Mine / Can-Can
Frank Sinatra .... **Fontana TFE 17273**
Doris Day .... **Philips BBL 7211**
Sammy Davis .... **Brunswick LAT 8088**
Mario Lanza .... **HMV DA 2020**
Louis Jordan .... **Capitol W 1301**
Doris Day appeared in *Starlift.*
Mario Lanza appeared in *Because You're Mine.*
Louis Jourdan appeared in *Can-Can.*

YOU DON'T BRING ME FLOWERS   January 1979
Neil Diamond
A.T.V. Music Ltd. .... USA
Barbra Streisand & Neil Diamond .... **CBS 6803**

YOU DON'T HAVE TO BE A BABY TO CRY   Sep 1963
Bob Merrill / Terry Shand
Frank Music Ltd .... USA
Tennessee Ernie Ford .... **Capitol CL 14500**
The Caravelles .... **Decca F 11697**
Bill Anderson .... **Brunswick LAT 8569**

YOU DON'T HAVE TO GO   September 1976
Eugene Record / Barbara Acklin
Burlington Music Co. Ltd .... USA
The Chi-Lites .... **Brunswick BR 34**

YOU DON'T HAVE TO KNOW THE LANGUAGE April 1948
Johnny Burke / Jimmy Van Heusen
Edwin H. Morris & Co. Ltd. .... USA
Film(s): ....Road to Rio
Bing Crosby & The Andrews Sisters ..... **Brunswick Bing 11**
Lena Horne .... **RCA RD 27141**
Bing Crosby & The Andrews Sisters appeared in *Road to Rio.*

YOU DON'T HAVE TO SAY YOU LOVE ME
(Lo Che Non Vivo)   June 1966
Vicki Wickham / Simon Napier-Bell / Pino Donaggio
B. Feldman & Co. Ltd. .... Italy
Dusty Springfield .... **Philips BF 1482**
Elvis Presley (1971) .... **RCA 2046**
Guys 'n' Dolls (1976) .... **Magnet MAG 50**

YOU DON'T HAVE TO TELL ME, I KNOW   1941
Don Pelosi / Art Noel
Francis, Day & Hunter Ltd .... UK
Joe Petersen .... **Rex 10013**
Harry Roy & his Band,
vocal Jean Farrar .... **Regal Zonophone MR 3514**
Stevie Marsh .... **Decca F 11209**

YOU DON'T KNOW   August 1961
Mike Hawker / John Schroeder
Lorna Music Co. Ltd. .... UK
Helen Shapiro .... **Columbia DB 4670**

YOU DON'T KNOW ME   October 1962
Cindy Walker / Eddy Arnold
Aberbach (London) Ltd. .... USA
Ray Charles .... **HMV POP 1064**
Carmen McRae .... **Brunswick 05588**

YOU DON'T OWE ME A THING   February 1957
Marty Robbins
Acuff Rose Music .... USA
Johnnie Ray .... **Philips PB 655**

YOU DON'T STOP WORDY RAPPINGHOOD (See Wordy Rappinghood)

YOU DRIVE ME CRAZY   May 1981
Ronnie Harwood
Quarry Music .... UK
Shakin' Stevens .... **Epic EPC 1165**
Ivor Novello Award.

YOU FORGOT YOUR GLOVES   1932
Edward Eliscu / Ned Lehak
Keith Prowse Music Publishing Co. Ltd. .... USA
Show(s): ....The Third Little Show
Jack Buchanan .... **HMV B 4005**
Binnie Hale .... **Columbia DB 698**
Jeri Southern .... **Brunswick LAT 8209**

YOU GAVE ME LOVE   June 1980
Ida Reid
Planetary-Nom (London) Ltd .... UK
Crown Heights Affair .... **Mercury MER 9**

YOU GO TO MY HEAD   1938
J. Fred Coots / Haven Gillespie
B. Feldman & Co. Ltd. .... USA
Leslie Hutchinson (Hutch) .... **Parlophone F 1362**
Frank Sinatra (1946) .... **Fontana TFL 5030**
Frank Sinatra .... **Capitol W 1417**
Patti Page .... **Mercury MPL 6521**
Bryan Ferry .... **Island WIP 6234**

YOU GOT IT   February 1989
Jeff Lynne / Roy Orbison / Tom Petty
SBK Songs .... USA
Roy Orbison .... **Virgin VS 1166**

YOU GOT IT (The Right Stuff)   December 1989
Maurice Starr
EMI Music .... USA
New Kids on the Block .... **CBS BLOCK 2**

YOU GOT SOUL   February 1969
Margaret Nash
Rondor Music (London) Ltd. .... USA
Johnny Nash .... **Major Minor MM 586**

YOU GOT THE LOOK (See U Got The Look)

YOU GOT WHAT IT TAKES   March 1960
Gwen Gordy / Raquel Davis / Berry Gordy Jnr.
Leeds Music Ltd .... USA
Marv Johnson .... **London HLT 9013**
Janet Richmond .... **Top Rank JAR 288**
Showaddywaddy (1977) .... **Arista 126**

YOU GROW SWEETER AS THE YEARS GO BY   1939
Johnny Mercer
B. Feldman & Co. Ltd. .... USA
Denny Dennis .... **Rex 9621**
Connee Boswell .... **Brunswick 02785**

YOU HIT THE SPOT   1936
Mack Gordon / Harry Revel
Chappell & Co. Ltd .... USA
Film(s): ....The Charm School
Frances Langford .... **Brunswick 02156**
Ella Fitzgerald .... **HMV CLP 1267**
Frances Langford appeared in *The Charm School.*

YOU JUST MIGHT SEE ME CRY   July 1976
Barry Mason / Roger Greenaway
Cookaway Music .... UK
Our Kid .... **Polydor 2058729**

YOU JUST YOU   1932
Robert Stolz / Desmond Carter
Chappell & Co. Ltd .... Germany
Show(s): .... Wild Violets
Heddle Nash .... **Columbia DB 979**
Olive Groves .... **Decca F 3212**
Barbara Leigh & Kevin Scott .... **HMV 7EG 8467**
David Whitfield .... **Decca LK 4348**

YOU KEEP COMING BACK LIKE A SONG   1946
Irving Berlin
Irving Berlin Ltd. .... USA
Film(s): .... Blue Skies

Bing Crosby .... **Brunswick Bing 10**
Paul Fenoulhet & The Skyrockets Dance Orch .. **HMV BD 5945**
Ella Fitzgerald .... **HMV CLP 1184**
Bing Crosby appeared in *Blue Skies*.
Nominated for an Academy Award 1946.

YOU KEEP IT ALL IN   October 1989
Paul Heaton / Dave Rotheray
Go Disc Music .... UK
The Beautiful South .... **Go Disc GOD 36**

YOU KEEP ME HANGIN' ON   December 1966
Brian Holland / Eddie Holland / Lamont Dozier
Jobete Music (UK) Ltd. .... USA
The Supremes .... **Tamla Motown TMG 585**
Vanilla Fudge (1967) .... **Atlantic 584123**
Kim Wilde (1986) .... **MCA KIM 4**

YOU LIGHT UP MY LIFE   December 1977
Joseph Brooks
Bocu Music Ltd .... USA
Film(s): .... You Light Up My Life
Debbie Boone .... **Warner Brothers K 17043**
Academy Award winning song for 1977.

YOU LITTLE THIEF   February 1986
Belmont Tench
Blue Gator Music .... UK
Fergal Sharkey .... **Virgin VS 840**

YOU LITTLE TRUSTMAKER   November 1974
Christopher Mark Jackson
Carlin Music Corporation .... USA
The Tymes .... **RCA 2456**

YOU MADE ME CARE WHEN I WASN'T IN LOVE   1940
Joseph George Gilbert
J. Norris Music Publishing Co. Ltd .... UK
Ambrose & his Orchestra, vocal Vera Lynn .... **Decca F 74561**
Leslie Hutchinson (Hutch) .... **Parlophone F 1714**
Lorrie Mann .... **Top Rank JAR 148**

YOU MADE ME LOVE YOU   1913
Joseph McCarthy / Jimmy Monaco
Francis, Day & Hunter Ltd. .... USA
Film(s):Wharf Angel / Broadway Melody of 1938 / Syncopation / The
Jolson Story / Jolson Sings Again / Love Me or Leave Me
Grace La Rue .... **HMV 03343**
Judy garland .... **Brunswick LA 8725**
Al Jolson .... **Brunswick LAT 8322**
Harry James & his Orchestra .... **Parlophone R 2869**
Doris Day .... **Philips BBL 7047**
Harry James & his Orchestra .... **Capitol T 947**
Doris Day appeared in *Love Me or Leave Me*.
Judy Garland appeared in *Broadway Melody of 1938*.

YOU MAKE ME FEEL (Mighty Real)   October 1978
James Wirrick / James Sylvester
I.Q. Music .... USA
Sylvester .... **Fantasy FTC 160**
Jimmy Somerville (1990) .... **London LON 249**

YOU MAKE ME FEEL BRAND NEW   August 1974
Thomas Bell / Linda Creed
Carlin Music Corporation .... USA
The Stylistics .... **Avco 6105 C28**

YOU MAKE ME FEEL LIKE DANCING   December 1976
Leo Sayer / Vincent Poncia
Chrysalis Music Ltd .... UK
Leo Sayer .... **Chrysalis CHS 2119**

YOU MAKE ME FEEL SO YOUNG   1947
Mack Gordon / Joseph Myrow
Chappell & Co. Ltd. .... USA
Film(s): .... Three Little Girls in Blue / I'll Get By
Dick Haymes .... **Brunswick LA 03690**
Frank Sinatra .... **Capitol LCT 6106**
Chris Connor .... **London HAK 2020**

YOU ME AND US   January 1957
John Jerome
Mistletoe Melodies Ltd. .... UK
Alma Cogan .... **HMV POP 284**
Adapted from "Cielito Lindo" by Sebastian Yradier.

YOU MIGHT NEED SOMEBODY   July 1981
Tom Snow / Nan O'Byrne
Rondor Music .... USA
Randy Crawford .... **Warner Brothers K 17803**

YOU MUST HAVE BEEN A BEAUTIFUL BABY   1939
Harry Warren / Johnny Mercer
B. Feldman & Co. Ltd. .... USA
Film(s): . The Eddie Cantor Story / My Dream is Yours / Hard to Get
Bing Crosby .... **Brunswick 02694**
Eddie Cantor .... **Capitol LC 6652**
The Ray Charles Singers .... **MGM C 766**
Bobby Darin (1961) .... **London HL 9429**
Dick Powell .... **RCA ZL 70136**
Dick Powell appeared in *Hard to Get*.

YOU MY LOVE   July 1955
Mack Gordon / Jimmy Van Heusen
Dash Music Ltd. .... USA
Doris Day .... **Philips PB 402**
Victor Young Orchestra .... **Brunswick 05386**
Frank Sinatra .... **Capitol CL 14240**

YOU NEED HANDS   April 1958
Roy Irwin
Lakeview Music Publishing Co .... UK
Max Bygraves .... **Decca DFE 6505**
Eydie Gormé .... **HMV POP 493**
Ivor Novello Nomination.

YOU ONLY LIVE TWICE   August 1967
Leslie Bricusse / John Barry
United Artists Music Co. Ltd. .... UK
Film(s): .... You Only Live Twice
Nancy Sinatra .... **Reprise RS 20595**

YOU OUGHT TO SEE SALLY ON SUNDAY   1934
Harry Woods
Cinephonic Music Co. Ltd. .... USA
Film(s): .... Aunt Sally
Val Rosing .... **Rex 8075**
Ray Noble & his Orchestra .... **HMV B 6440**

YOU OUGHTA BE IN PICTURES   1935
Edward Heyman / Dana Suesse
Chappell & Co. Ltd .... USA
Film(s): .... New York Town / Starlift
Ray Noble & his Orchestra .... **HMV B 6477**
The Boswell Sisters with
The Dorsey Brothers Orchestra ..... **Brunswick 01751**
Monty Babson .... **London HAJ 2212**

YOU RASCAL YOU   1932
Sam Theard
Lawrence Wright Music Co. Ltd. .... USA
Connie's Inn Orchestra .... **Brunswick 1281**
Louis Armstrong's All Stars .... **Brunswick LAT 8212**
Louis Prima .... **Capitol T 755**

YOU REALLY GOT ME   September 1964
Ray Davies
Edward Kassner Music Co. Ltd .... UK
The Kinks .... **Pye 7N 15673**

YOU REMIND ME OF MY MOTHER   1923
George M. Cohan
B. Feldman & Co. Ltd .... USA
Show(s): .... Little Nellie Kelly
Herman Finck & his Orchestra .... **Columbia 933**
Paul Whiteman & his Orchestra .... **HMV B 1650**
The Mayfair Orchestra .... **HMV C 1118**

YOU RHYME WITH EVERYTHING THAT'S BEAUTIFUL 1943
Mickey Stoner / Bert Reisfeld
Bradbury Wood Ltd .... USA
Leslie Hutchinson (Hutch) .... **HMV BD 1054**
Ambrose & his Orchestra, vocal Anne Shelton .. **Decca F 8344**

YOU SANG MY LOVE SONG TO SOMEBODY ELSE   1946
Allan Roberts / Doris Fisher
Pickwick Music Ltd. .... USA
Bing Crosby & The Jesters .... **Brunswick LA 8724**

YOU SAY THE SWEETEST THINGS BABY   1941
Harry Warren / Mack Gordon
Robbins Music Corporation Ltd . . . . USA
Film(s): . . . . .Tin Pan Alley
Alice Faye . . . . **Caliban 6003**
Ambrose & his Orchestra, vocal Anne Shelton . . **Decca F 7771**
The Savoy Hotel Orpheans,
conducted by Carroll Gibbons . . . . **Columbia FB 2593**
Alice Faye appeared in *Tin Pan Alley.*

YOU SEE THE TROUBLE WITH ME   April 1976
Barry White
Scroeder Music Ltd . . . . USA
Barry White . . . . **20th Century BTC 2277**

YOU SEND ME   October 1974
Sam Cooke
Kags Music Ltd. . . . . USA
Rod Stewart . . . . **Mercury 6167033**
Sam Cooke . . . . **London HLU 8506**

YOU SEXY THING   December 1975
Tony Wilson / Errol Brown
Rak Music Ltd . . . . UK
Hot Chocolate . . . . **Rak 221**
Hot Chocolate (1987) . . . . **EMI 15592**

YOU SHOULD BE DANCING   August 1976
Barry Gibb / Robin Gibb / Maurice Gibb
Abigail Music . . . . UK
Film(s): . . . . Saturday Night Fever
The Bee Gees . . . . **RSO 2090195**
Ivor Novello Nomination.

YOU SPIN ME 'ROUND (Like a Record)   March 1985
"Dead or Alive"
Chappell & Co. . . . . UK
Dead or Alive . . . . **Epic A 4861**

YOU STARTED SOMETHING   1941
Leo Robin / Ralph Rainger
Francis, Day & Hunter Ltd . . . . USA
Film(s): . . . . Moon Over Miami
The R.A.F. Dance Orchestra,
conducted by Jimmy Miller . . . . **Decca F 7994**
Harry Roy & his Band, vocal
Harry Roy & Marjorie Kingsley . . . **Regal Zonophone MR 3547**

YOU STEPPED OUT OF A DREAM   1941
Nacio Herb Brown / Gus Kahn
Robbins Music Corporation Ltd . . . . USA
Film(s): . . . . The Ziegfeld Girl
Tony Martin . . . . **Decca F 7954**
Leslie Hutchinson (Hutch) . . . . **HMV BD 971**
Vic Damone . . . . **Philips BBL 7144**
The King Sisters . . . . **Capitol T 1333**
Tony Martin appeared in *The Ziegfeld Girl.*

YOU TAKE ME UP   April 1984
Tom Bailey / Alannah Currie / Joe Leeway
Point Music . . . . UK
The Thompson Twins . . . . **Arista TWINS 4**

YOU TAUGHT ME HOW TO LOVE   1909
Jack Drislane / George Meyer / Alfred Bryan
Francis, Day & Hunter . . . . USA
Bob & Alf Pearson . . . . **Rex 8210**

YOU TELL ME YOUR DREAM   1940
Charles N. Daniel / Gus Kahn
Francis, Day & Hunter Ltd . . . . USA
The Mills Brothers . . . . **Brunswick LAT 8368**
Mitch Miller & The Gang . . . . **Philips BBL 7334**
First Published Circa 1908.

YOU TO ME ARE EVERYTHING   July 1976
Ken Gold / Michael Denne
Screen Gems Music Ltd . . . . USA
The Real Thing . . . . **Pye /N 25709**
The Real Thing (1986) . . . . **PRT 7P 349**

YOU TOO   1931
Robert Stolz / Ralph Benatzky / Harry Graham
Chappell & Co. Ltd. . . . . Germany
Show(s): . . . . White Horse Inn

Bruce Trent & Doreen Hume . . . . **Fontana TFL 5112**
Peter Regan & Rita Williams . . . . **HMV CLP 1205**

YOU TOOK ADVANTAGE OF ME   1929
Richard Rodgers / Lorenz Hart
Chappell & Co. Ltd . . . . USA
Show(s): . . . . Present Arms / On Your Toes
Film(s): . . . . Present Arms / A Star is Born
Paul Whiteman & His Orchestra,
vocal Bing Crosby . . . . **RCA RD 27225**
Judy Garland . . . . **Philips BBL 7007**
Miff Mole & his Little Molers . . . . **CBS BPG 62545**
Steve Lawrence . . . . **Coral FEP 2010**
Ella Fitzgerald . . . . **HMV CLP 1116**
Elaine Stritch . . . . **Brunswick LAT 8061**
Judy Garland appeared in *A Star is Born.*
Elaine Stritch appeared in *On Your Toes.*
Title added to the 1954 American revival of *On Your Toes.*

YOU TURNED THE TABLES ON ME   1937
Sidney Mitchell / Louis Alter
Keith Prowse Music Publishing Co. Ltd. . . . . USA
Film(s):Sing Baby Sing / The Benny Goodman Story / Kiss Them for
Me
Benny Goodman & his Orchestra,
vocal Helen Ward . . . . **HMV B 8516**
Benny Goodman & his Orchestra,
vocal Martha Tilton . . . . **Brunswick LAT 8102**
Ella Fitzgerald . . . . **Brunswick LAT 8264**
Teresa Brewer . . . . **Coral LVA 9129**
Alice Faye . . . . **Reprise R 6029**
Alice Faye appeared in *Sing Baby Sing.*

YOU WALK BY   1942
Bernie Wayne / Ben Raleigh
Campbell Connelly & Co. Ltd . . . . USA
Kenny Baker . . . . **HMV BD 932**
Anne Shelton . . . . **Decca F 0221**
Patti Page . . . . **Mercury MPL 6521**

YOU WANT IT YOU GOT IT   June 1973
Abrim Tilman
Carlin Music Corporation . . . . USA
The Detroit Emeralds . . . . **Westbound 6146103**

YOU WEAR IT WELL   September 1972
Rod Stewart / Martin Quittenton
H.G. Music . . . . UK
Rod Stewart . . . . **Mercury 6052171**

YOU WENT AWAY AND LEFT ME   1947
Jennie Parker
Box & Cox Music Ltd. . . . . UK
Jack Simpson Sextet . . . . **Parlophone F 2221**
Lou Preager Orchestra . . . . **Columbia FB 3304**
The Sentimentals . . . . **Decca F 8785**

YOU WERE MADE FOR ME   December 1963
Mitch Murray
B. Feldman & Co. Ltd . . . . UK
Freddie & The Dreamers . . . . **Columbia DB 7147**

YOU WERE MEANT FOR ME   1929
Arthur Freed / Nacio Herb Brown
Francis, Day & Hunter Ltd . . . . USA
Film(s):Broadway Melody / Hollywood Revue / Show of Shows / You
Were Meant for Me / Singin' in the Rain
Layton & Johnstone . . . . **Columbia 5392**
Nat Shilkret & his Orchestra . . . . **HMV B 5635**
Gene Kelly . . . . **MGM D 140**
Bing Crosby . . . . **Warner Brothers WM 4021**
Gene Kelly appeared in *Singin' in the Rain.*

YOU WERE NEVER LOVELIER   1943
Jerome Kern / Johnny Mercer
Chappell & Co. Ltd . . . . USA
Film(s): . . . . You Were Never Lovelier
Fred Astaire . . . . **Brunswick 03427**
Geraldo & his Orchestra . . . . **Camden CDN 136**
Fred Astaire appeared in *You Were Never Lovelier.*

YOU WERE ON MY MIND   March 1966
Sylvia Fricker
Blossom Music Ltd. . . . . USA
Crispian St. Peters . . . . **Decca F 12287**

YOU WERE THERE   1936
Noel Coward
Chappell & Co. Ltd . . . . UK
Show(s): . . . . Tonight at Eight-Thirty
Noel Coward & Gertrude Lawrence . . . . **HMV CLP 1050**
Roy Fox & his Orchestra, vocal Cathy Dennis . . . **Decca F 5851**
Noel Coward & Gertrude Lawrence appeared in the British production
of *Tonight at Eight-Thirty*.

YOU WILL REMEMBER VIENNA   1931
Sigmund Romberg / Oscar Hammerstein II
B. Feldman & Co. Ltd . . . . USA
Show(s): . . . . Viennese Night / Deep in My Heart
Richard Crooks . . . . **HMV DA 1174**
John Hanson . . . . **Oriole EP 7037**
Helen Traubel . . . . **MGM C 755**
Helen Traubel appeared in *Deep in My Heart*.

YOU WIN AGAIN   October 1987
Barry Gibb / Robin Gibb / Maurice Gibb
Chappell Music Co. . . . . UK
The Bee Gees . . . . **Warner Brothers W 8351**
Ivor Novello Award.

YOU WON'T BE SATISFIED   1946
Larry Stock / Freddy James
New World Publishers Ltd. . . . . USA
Perry Como . . . . **Camden CDN 110**
Debbie Reynolds . . . . **London HAD 2200**

YOU WON'T FIND ANOTHER FOOL LIKE ME   Jan 1974
Tony Macaulay / Geoff Stevens
A.T.V. Music Ltd. . . . . UK
The New Seekers . . . . **Polydor 2058421**
Ivor Novello Award.

YOU YOU YOU   September 1974
Peter Shelley
Magnet Music . . . . UK
Alvin Stardust . . . . **Magnet MAG 13**

YOU'D BE SO NICE TO COME HOME TO   1943
Cole Porter
Victoria Music Co. Ltd . . . . USA
Film(s): . . . . Something to Shout ABout
Dinah Shore . . . . **HMV BD 1048**
Eric Winstone & his Band . . . . **Regal Zonophone MR 3703**
Frank Sinatra . . . . **Capitol LCT 6135**
Sarah Vaughan . . . . **Mercury MMC 14001**
Nominated for an Academy Award 1943.

YOU'D BE SURPRISED   1920
Irving Berlin
Irving Berlin Ltd . . . . USA
Show(s): . . . . The Ziegfeld Follies of 1919 / Afgar
Film(s): . . . . . Blue Skies / There's No Business Like Show Business
Eddie Cantor . . . . **Brunswick 04284**
Alice Delysia . . . . **Columbia F 1043**
Marilyn Monroe . . . . **HMV 7EG 8090**
Vivian Blaine . . . . **Mercury MPL 6518**
Eddie Cantor appeared in *The Ziegfeld Follies of 1919*.
Alice Delysia appeared in *Afgar*.

YOU'LL ANSWER TO ME   October 1961
Sherman Edwards / Hal David
Shapiro-Bernstein & Co. Ltd. . . . . USA
Cleo Laine . . . . **Fontana H 326**

**YOU'LL NEVER FIND ANOTHER LOVE
LIKE MINE**   September 1976
Kenny Gamble / Leon Huff
Carlin Music Corporation . . . . USA
Lou Rawls . . . . **Philadelphia PIR 4372**

YOU'LL NEVER KNOW   1943
Mack Gordon / Harry Warren
Victoria Music Co. Ltd . . . . USA
Film(s): . . . . Hello 'Frisco Hello
Frank Sinatra . . . . **Philips BBL 7168**
Dick Haymes . . . . **Brunswick OE 9429**
Ella Fitzgerald . . . . **Brunswick LAT 8091**
Eve Boswell . . . . **Parlophone PMC 1038**
Alice Faye . . . . **Reprise R 6029**
Shirley Bassey (1961) . . . . **Columbia DB 4643**

Alice Faye appeared in *Hello 'Frisco Hello*.
Academy Award winning song for 1943.

YOU'LL NEVER KNOW   September 1981
Giulian Salerni / Bernard Diggs
Peterman & Co. . . . . USA
Hi Gloss . . . . **Epic EPC A 1387**

YOU'LL NEVER STOP ME LOVING YOU   August 1989
Mike Stock / Matt Aitken / Peter Waterman
All Boys Music . . . . UK
Sonia . . . . **Chrysalis CHS 3385**

YOU'LL NEVER WALK ALONE   July 1950
Richard Rodgers / Oscar Hammerstein II
Williamson Music Ltd . . . . USA
Show(s): . . . . Carousel
Film(s): . . . . Carousel
Christine Johnson & Jan Clayton . . . . **Brunswick LAT 8006**
Marion Ross . . . . **Columbia SED 5536**
Shirley Jones . . . . **Capitol LCT 6105**
Gerry & The Pacemakers (1963) . . . . **Columbia DB 7126**
The Crowd (1985) . . . . **Spartan BRAD 1**
Christine Johnson & Jan Clayton appeared in the American produc-
tion of *Carousel*.
Marion Ross appeared in the British production of *Carousel*.
Shirley Jones appeared in the film of *Carousel*.

YOU'RE A LADY   November 1972
Peter Skellern
Warner Brothers Music Ltd. . . . . UK
Peter Skellern . . . . **Decca F 13333**

YOU'RE A PINK TOOTHBRUSH   December 1953
Ralph Ruvin / Bob Halfin / Harold Irving
Sydney Bron Music Co. Ltd. . . . . UK
Max Bygraves . . . . **HMV 7EG 8006**
Max Bygraves . . . . **Decca LK 4333**

YOU'RE A SWEETHEART   1938
Harold Adamson / Jimmy McHugh
Francis, Day & Hunter Ltd. . . . . USA
Film(s): . . . . You're a Sweetheart / Meet Danny Wilson
**The Adrian Rollini Quartet,
vocal Sonny Schuyler** . . . . **Brunswick 02579**
Lew Stone & his Band, vocal Al Bowlly . . . . **Decca F 6606**
Gordon MacRae . . . . **Capitol T 875**
Tommy Edwards . . . . **MGM C 824**
Alice Faye . . . . **Reprise R 6029**
Alice Faye appeared in *You're a Sweetheart*.

YOU'RE AN OLD SMOOTHIE   1933
Nacio Herb Brown / Buddy De Sylva / Richard A. Whiting
Chappell & Co. Ltd. . . . . USA
Show(s): . . . . Take a Chance / Nice Goings On
Paul Whiteman & his Orchestra . . . . **HMV B 8008**
Jack Hylton & his Orchestra . . . . **Decca F 3670**
Ella Fitzgerald . . . . **HMV CLP 1267**
Ethel Merman . . . . **Reprise R 6032**
Ethel Merman appeared in *Take a Chance*.

YOU'RE AS PRETTY AS A PICTURE   1939
Harold Adamson / Jimmy McHugh
Francis, Day & Hunter Ltd. . . . . USA
Film(s): . . . . That Certain Age
Millicent Philips . . . . **Parlophone R 2615**
Gene Krupa & his Orchestra, vocal Irene Daye . . **HMV BD 5444**
Deanna Durbin . . . . **MCA MCA 6007**
Deanna Durbin appeared in *That Certain Age*.

YOU'RE BLASÉ   1932
Bruce Sievier / Ord Hamilton
Chappell & Co. Ltd. . . . . UK
Show(s): . . . . Bow Bells
Binnie Hale . . . . **Columbia DB 743**
Peggy Lee . . . . **Brunswick LAT 8171**
Binnie Hale appeared in *Bow Bells*.

YOU'RE BREAKING MY HEART   October 1949
Pat Genaro / Sunny Skylar
Chappell & Co. Ltd . . . . USA
Allan Jones . . . . **HMV B 9841**
**Oscar Rabin & his Band,
vocal Marjorie Daw** . . . . **Parlophone F 2382**
Vico Torriani . . . . **Decca LF 1320**

Joni James . . . . **MGM C 809**

YOU'RE DANCING ON MY HEART   **1932**
Al Bryan / George Meyer
B. Feldman & Co. Ltd. . . . . USA
Victor Sylvester & his Orchestra . . . . **Parlophone F 240**
Eric Jupp & his Orchestra . . . . **Columbia 33S 1097**
Theme song of Victor Silvester.

YOU'RE DRIVING ME CRAZY   **1931**
Walter Donaldson
Francis, Day & Hunter Ltd . . . . USA
Show(s): . . . . Smiles
Film(s): . . . . Gentlemen Marry Brunettes
Rudy Vallee & his Connecticut Yankees . . . . **HMV B 5951**
Bing Crosby . . . . **Brunswick LAT 8217**
Jane Russell & Anita Ellis . . . . **Vogue LVA 9003**
Max Bygraves . . . . **Decca LK 4360**
The Clark Sisters . . . . **London HAD 2128**
The Temperance Seven (1961) . . . . **Parlophone R 4757**
Jane Russell & Anita Ellis appeared in *Gentlemen Marry Brunettes.*

YOU'RE GETTING TO BE A HABIT WITH ME   **1933**
Al Dubin / Harry Warren
B. Feldman & Co. Ltd. . . . . USA
Film(s): . . . . Forty-Second Street / Lullaby of Broadway
Bebe Daniels . . . . **United Artists UAG 29644**
Bing Crosby . . . . **Brunswick 1480**
Frank Sinatra . . . . **Capitol LCT 6106**
Peggy Lee . . . . **Capitol T 1049**
Doris Day . . . . **Columbia 33S 1038**
Bebe Daniels appeared in *Forty-Second Street.*
Doris Day appeared in *Lullaby of Broadway.*

YOU'RE GONNA GET NEXT TO ME   **July 1977**
Bo Kirkland / Ruth Davis / Hense Powell
Sunbury Music Ltd . . . . USA
Bo Kirkland & Ruth Davis . . . . **EMI INT 532**

YOU'RE HERE AND I'M HERE   **1914**
Jerome Kern / Harry Smith
Francis, Day & Hunter Ltd. . . . . USA
Show(s): . . . . The Laughing Husband / The Passing Show
Elsie Janis & Basil Hallam . . . . **HMV 2-4201**
A. Kimball & Charles Harrison . . . . **Columbia 2443**
Elsie Janis & Basil Hallam appeared in *The Passing Show.*

YOU'RE HISTORY   **August 1989**
Siobhan Fahey / Richard Feldman / Marcy Levy & Pat Seymour
Warner Chappell Music . . . . UK
Shakespeare's Sister . . . . **London F 112**

YOU'RE IN KENTUCKY SURE AS YOU'RE BORN   **1924**
George Little / Larry Shay / Haven Gillespie
Lawrence Wright Music Co. Ltd. . . . . USA
The Garber-Davis Orchestra . . . . **HMV B 1810**
The Savoy Orpheans . . . . **Columbia 3430**
Max Bygraves with Ted Heath & his Music . . . . **Decca LK 4317**

YOU'RE IN MY HEART   **November 1977**
Rod Stewart
Riva Music . . . . UK
Rod Stewart . . . . **Riva 11**

YOU'RE IN THE ARMY NOW   **November 1986**
Robert Bolland / Ferdinand Bolland
Island Music . . . . Holland
Staus Quo . . . . **Vertigo QUO 201**

YOU'RE JUST IN LOVE   **March 1952**
Irving Berlin
Irving Berlin Ltd . . . . USA
Show(s): . . . . Call Me Madam
Film(s): . . . . Call Me Madam
Ethel Merman & Dick Haymes . . . . **Brunswick LAT 8016**
Jeff Warren & Billie Worth . . . . **Columbia 33SX 1002**
Ethel Merman & Donald O'Connor . . . . . . **Brunswick LA 8603**
Ethel Merman appeared in the American production of *Call Me Madam* and also the film *Call Me Madam.*
Jeff Warren & Billie Worth appeared in the British production of *Call Me Madam.*
Donald O'Connor appeared in the film *Call Me Madam.*

YOU'RE LAUGHING AT ME   **1938**
Irving Berlin

Irving Berlin Ltd. . . . . USA
Film(s): . . . . On the Avenue
Dick Powell . . . . **Decca F 6454**
Lew Stone & his Band, vocal Sam Costa . . . . . . **Decca F 6451**
Ella Fitzgerald . . . . **HMV CLP 1183**
Dick Powell appeared in *On the Avenue.*

**YOU'RE MORE THAN A NUMBER IN MY LITTLE RED
BOOK**   **February 1977**
Tony Macaulay / Roger Greenaway
Cookaway Music . . . . UK
The Drifters . . . . **Arista 78**

YOU'RE MOVING OUT TODAY   **July 1977**
Carole Bayer Sager / Bette Midler / Bruce Roberts
Chappell & Co. Ltd . . . . USA
Carole Bayer Sager . . . . **Elektra K 12257**

YOU'RE MY BABY   **1912**
Nat. D. Ayer / A. Seymour Brown
B. Feldman & Co. Ltd. . . . . USA
Show(s): . . . . Hullo Ragtime
Lew Hearn & Bonita . . . . **HMV C 558**
Harry Roy & his Orchestra, vocal Harry Roy . . . . **Decca F 9450**
Lew Hearn & Bonita appeared in *Hullo Ragtime.*

YOU'RE MY BEST FRIEND   **July 1976**
John Deacon
B. Feldman & Co. Ltd . . . . UK
Queen . . . . **EMI 2494**

YOU'RE MY EVERYTHING   **1932**
Mort Dixon / Joe Young / Harry Warren
Chappell & Co. Ltd. . . . . USA
Show(s): . . . . The Laugh Parade
Film(s):You're My Everything / Painting the Clouds with Sunshine /
The Eddy Duchin Story
George Metaxa . . . . **HMV B 4234**
Eddy Duchin (piano) . . . . **Philips BBL 7081**
Gisele MacKenzie . . . . **RCA RD 27033**
Louis Prima & Keely Smith . . . . **London HAD 2243**
Carmen Cavallaro . . . . **Brunswick LAT 8119**

YOU'RE MY WORLD (Il Mio Mondo)   **June 1964**
Umberto Bindi / Gino Paoli / Carl Sigman
Aberbach (London) Ltd. . . . . Italy
Cilla Black . . . . **Parlophone R 5133**

YOU'RE NO GOOD   **July 1964**
Clint Ballard
Edwin H. Morris & Co. Ltd . . . . USA
Betty Everett . . . . **Stateside SS 259**
The Swinging Blue Jeans . . . . **HMV POP 1304**

YOU'RE NOBODY 'TILL SOMEBODY LOVES YOU   **1946**
James Cavanaugh / Larry Stock / Russ Morgan
Southern Music Publishing Co. Ltd. USA
Russ Morgan & his Orchestra . . . . **Brunswick OE 9068**
Steve Conway . . . . **Columbia FB 3243**
Paula Green . . . . **Columbia FB 3236**
Dean Martin . . . . **Capitol T 1442**

YOU'RE READY NOW   **February 1971**
Bob Crewe / Bob Gaudio
Ardmore & Beechwood Ltd . . . . USA
Frankie Valli . . . . **Philips BF 1512**

YOU'RE SIXTEEN   **February 1961**
Dick Sherman / Bob Sherman
Jewel Music Publishing Co. Ltd . . . . USA
Johnny Burnette . . . . **London HL 9254**
Ringo Starr (1974) . . . . **Apple R 5995**

YOU'RE SO VAIN   **February 1973**
Carly Simon
Essex Music Ltd. . . . . USA
Carly Simon . . . . **Elektra K 12077**

YOU'RE SUCH A GOOD LOOKING WOMAN   **April 1970**
Albert Hammond / Mike Hazlewood
Shaftesbury Music . . . . UK
Joe Dolan . . . . **Pye 7N 17891**

YOU'RE THE CREAM IN MY COFFEE   **1929**
Buddy De Sylva / Lew Brown / Ray Henderson

Chappell & Co. Ltd .... USA
Show(s): .... Hold Everything
Film(s): ... The Cockeyed World / The Best Things in Life are Free
Dorothy Dickson .... **HMV C 2946**
Sam Lanin's Troubadours .... **Dominion A 133**
Layton & Johnstone .... **Columbia 5493**
Jack Hylton & his Orchestra .... **HMV B 5650**
Gordon MacRae .... **Capitol LCT 6119**
Dorothy Dickson appeared in the British production of *Hold Every-thing.*

YOU'RE THE DEVIL IN DISGUISE   August 1963
Bill Giant / Bernie Baum / Florence Kaye
West One Music Ltd .... USA
Elvis Presley .... **RCA 1355**

YOU'RE THE FIRST, THE LAST, MY
EVERYTHING   December 1974
Barry White / Tony Sepe / P.S. Radcliffe
Schroeder Music Ltd. .... USA
Barry White .... **20th Century BTC 2133**

YOU'RE THE ONE THAT I WANT   July 1978
John Farrar
Chappell & Co. Ltd .... UK
Film(s): .... Grease
John Travolta & Olivia Newton-John .... **RSO 2479210**
Hilda Baker & Arthur Mullard (comedy version) .. **Pye 7N 46121**
John Travolta & Olivia Newton-John appeared in *Grease.*

YOU'RE THE ONLY GOOD THING THAT'S
HAPPENED TO ME   December 1961
Jack Toombs
Palace Music Ltd. .... USA
Jim Reeves .... **RCA 1261**

YOU'RE THE ONLY STAR IN MY BLUE HEAVEN   1939
Gene Autry
B. Feldman & Co. Ltd. .... USA
Film(s): .... The Old Barn Dance / Mexicali Rose
Dick Todd .... **HMV BD 719**
Doye O'Dell .... **London HBB 1073**
Gene Autry .... **RCA RD 7839**

YOU'RE THE TOP   1935
Cole Porter
Chappell & Co. Ltd .... USA
Show(s): .... Anything Goes
Film(s): ....Anything Goes / Night and Day
Ethel Merman .... **Brunswick LA 8636**
Jeanne Aubert & Jack Whiting .... **Columbia DX 697**
Cole Porter .... **HMV B 8332**
Bing Crosby & Mitzi Gaynor .... **Brunswick Bing 15**
Ella Fitzgerald .... **HMV CLP 1084**
Anita O'Day .... **HMV CLP 1085**
Ethel Merman .... **Reprise R 6032**
Ethel Merman appeared in the American production and the 1936 film of *Anything Goes.*
Jeanne Aubert & Jack Whiting appeared in the British production of *Anything Goes.*
Bing Crosby appeared in both the 1936 and 1956 films of *Anything Goes.*
Mitzi Gaynor appeared in the 1956 film of *Anything Goes.*

YOU'RE THE VOICE   July 1987
Anita Quinta / Chris Thompson / Keith Reid & Maggie Ryder
Rondor Music .... UK
John Farnham .... **Wheatley PB 41093**

YOU'VE CHANGED   July 1948
Bill Carey / Carl Fischer
Southern Music Publishing Co. Ltd. .... USA
Film(s): ....Lady Sings the Blues
Anne Shelton .... **Decca F 8907**
Lita Roza .... **Decca LK 4171**
Julie London .... **London HAG 2280**
Diana Ross .... **Tamla Motown STML 11311-2**
Diana Ross appeared in *Lady Sings the Blues.*

YOU'VE DONE SOMETHING TO MY HEART   1940
Noel Gay / Ian Grant / Frank Eyton
Noel Gay Music Co. Ltd .... UK
Film(s): .... Lights Up
Evelyn Laye .... **Columbia DB 1895**
Dennis Lotis .... **Pye NPL 18002**

Evelyn Laye appeared in *Lights Up.*

YOU'VE GOT A FRIEND   October 1971
Carole King
Screen Gems Music Ltd .... USA
James Taylor .... **Warner Brothers WS 2561**
Carole King .... **A&M AMLS 2025**

YOU'VE GOT A FRIEND   July 1990
Mike Stock / Matt Aitken / Peter Waterman
All Boys Music .... UK
Big Fun & Sonia .... **Jive CHILD 90**

YOU'VE GOT ME CRYING AGAIN   1933
Isham Jones / Charles Newman
Chappell & Co. Ltd. .... USA
Connee Boswell .... **Brunswick 02785**
Bing Crosby .... **Brunswick 01503**
Dean Martin .... **Capitol T 849**
The Four Freshmen .... **Capitol T 1008**

YOU'VE GOT ME DANGLING ON A STRING   Dec 1970
Ronald Dunbar / Edith Wayne
Ardmore & Beechwood Ltd .... USA
Chairmen of the Board .... **Invictus INV 504**

YOU'VE GOT ME THIS WAY   1941
Johnny Mercer / Jimmy McHugh
Lafleur & Co. Ltd .... USA
Film(s): ..... You'll Find Out / When Willie Comes Marching Home
Jimmy Dorsey & his Orchestra,
vocal Helen O'Connell .... **Brunswick 03140**
Glenn Miller & his Orchestra,
vocal Marion Hutton .... **HMV 7EG 8224**

YOU'VE GOT ME WHERE YOU WANT ME   1944
Johnny Mercer / Harry Warren
Sterling Music Publishing Co. Ltd .... USA
Bing Crosby & Judy Garland .... **Brunswick 03597**

YOU'VE GOT THAT THING   1930
Cole Porter
Chappell & Co. Ltd .... USA
Paul Whiteman & his Orchestra .... **HMV C 2606**
Leslie Hutchinson (Hutch) .... **Parlophone E 11385**
Dorothy Provine .... **Warner Brothers WM 4053**

YOU'VE GOT THE WRONG RUMBA   1936
Maurice Sigler / Al Hoffman / Al Goodhart
Cinephonic Music Co. Ltd .... USA
Film(s): .... This'll Make You Whistle
Elsie Randolph .... **Brunswick 02349**
Elsie Randolph appeared in *This'll Make You Whistle.*

YOU'VE GOT TO HIDE YOUR LOVE AWAY   October 1965
John Lennon / Paul McCartney
Northern Songs Ltd .... UK
Film(s): .... Help
The Beatles .... **Parlophone PMC 1255**
Silkie .... **Fontana TF 603**
The Beatles appeared in *Help.*

YOU'VE GOT TO SEE MAMMA EVERY NIGHT   1923
Con Conrad / Billy Rose
Francis, Day & Hunter Ltd .... USA
Show(s): .... Dover Street to Dixie
The Two Gilberts .... **Regal G 8114**
The Tennessee Ten .... **HMV B 1677**
Peggy Lee .... **Brunswick LAT 8287**
Kay Starr .... **Capitol EAP 1-20063**

YOU'VE GOT YOUR TROUBLES   August 1965
Roger Greenaway / Roger Cook
Mills Music Ltd .... UK
The Fortunes .... **Decca F 12173**

YOU'VE LOST THAT LOVIN' FEELIN'   February 1965
Phil Spector / Barry Mann / Cynthia Weill
Screen Gems - Columbia Music .... USA
Film(s): ....Stardust
The Righteous Brothers .... **London HL 9943**
Cilla Black .... **Parlophone R 5225**
The Righteous Brothers (1969) .... **London HLU 9943**
Nancy Wilson .... **Capitol T 2321**

YOU'VE NEVER BEEN IN LOVE LIKE THIS BEFORE   June 1965
Tommy Moeller / Brian Parker
Apollo Music Ltd .... UK
Unit Four Plus Two .... **Decca F 12144**

YOU'VE NOT CHANGED   November 1967
Chris Andrews
Carnaby Music... UK
Sandie Shaw .... **Pye 7N 17378**

YOU, FASCINATING YOU   1945
P. Fruslaci / Pamela Smalley
Peter Maurice Music Co. Ltd. .... Italy
Geraldo & his Orch, vocal Len Camber .... **Parlophone F 2051**
Donald Peers .... **Decca F 8495**

YOU, YOU, YOU   November 1953
Robert Mellin / Lotar Olias
Robert Mellin Ltd. .... USA
The Stargazers .... **Decca F 10170**
Ken Remo .... **MGM SP 1063**
The Ames Brothers .... **HMV B 10543**

YOUNG AND FOOLISH   February 1956
Arnold Horwitt / Albert Hague
Chappell & Co. Ltd. .... USA
Show(s):.. Plain and Fancy
Gloria Marlow & David Daniels .... **Capitol LCT 6102**
Grace O'Connor & Jack Drummond .... **Oriole MG 10009**
Edmund Hockridge .... **Nixa NPT 19015**
Gloria Marlow & David Daniels appeared in the American production of *Plain and Fancy*.
Grace O'Connor & Jack Drummond appeared in the British production of *Plain and Fancy*.

YOUNG AND HEALTHY   1933
Al Dubin / Harry Warren
B. Foldman & Co. Ltd. .... USA
Film(s): .... Forty-Second Street
Bing Crosby .... **Columbia DB 2027**
Roy Fox & his Band .... **Decca F 3497**
Woolf Philips & his Orchestra .... **Decca LK 4137**
Dick Powell .... **United Artists UAG 29644**
Dick Powell appeared in *Forty-Second Street*.

YOUNG AT HEART   April 1954
Carolyn Leigh / Johnny Richards
Valando Music Co. Ltd. .... USA
Film(s): .... Young at Heart
Frank Sinatra .... **Capitol LCT 0123**
Patti Page .... **Mercury MMC 14013**
Bing Crosby .... **Brunswick OE 9003**
Frank Sinatra appeared in *Young at Heart*.

YOUNG AT HEART   July 1984
Robert Hodgens / Siobhan Fahey / Karen Woodwards / Sarah Dallin
ATV Music .... UK
The Bluebells .... **London LON 49**

YOUNG GIRL   June 1968
Jerry Fuller
Dick James Music Ltd. .... USA
Gary Puckett & The Union Gap .... **CBS 3365**
Gary Puckett & The Union Gap .... **CBS 8202**

YOUNG GUNS (Go For It)   December 1982
George Michael
Morrison Leany Music .... UK
Wham .... **Innervision IVL 2766**

YOUNG HEARTS RUN FREE   July 1976
Dave Crawford
Warner Brothers Music Ltd .... USA
Candi Staton .... **Warner Brothers K 16730**

YOUNG LOVE   February 1957
Carole Joyner / Ric Cartey
Cromwell Music Ltd. .... USA
Tab Hunter .... **London RED 1134**
The Crew Cuts .... **Mercury MPT 7519**
Sonny James .... **Capitol CL 14683**
Connie Francis .... **MGM C 812**
Donny Osmond (1973) .... **MGM 2006 300**

YOUNG LOVERS   June 1963
Ray Hildebrand / Jill Jackson
Le Bill Music Ltd .... USA
Paul & Paula .... **Philips 304016 BF**

YOUNG MAN'S FANCY   1921
Jack Yellen / Milton Ager / John Murray Anderson
Herman Darewski Music Publishing Co. Ltd .... USA
Show(s): .... What's in a Name / League of Nations
Joseph C. Smith's Orchestra .... **HMV B 1196**
Margaret Whiting .... **Capitol LC 6811**
The Ray Charles Singers .... **MGM EP 594**

YOUNG NEW MEXICAN PUPPETEER   April 1972
Leon Carr / Earl Schuman
Ambassador Music Ltd .... USA
Tom Jones .... **Decca F 13298**

YOUNG ONES, THE   February 1962
Sid Tepper / Roy C. Bennett
Harms-Whitmark Ltd. .... USA
Film(s): .... The Young Ones
Cliff Richard .... **Columbia DB 4761**
Cliff Richard appeared in *The Young Ones*.

YOUNG PARISIANS   January 1981
Adam Ant
Ant Music .... UK
Adam & The Ants .... **Decca F 13803**

YOUNGER THAN SPRINGTIME   December 1951
Richard Rodgers / Oscar Hammerstein II
Williamson Music Ltd .... USA
Show(s): .... South Pacific
Film(s): .... South Pacific
William Tabbert .... **Philips BBL 7157**
Peter Grant .... **Columbia SEG 7668**
John Kerr .... **ΠOA ΠD 10066**
William Tabbert appeared in the American production of *South Pacific*.
Peter Grant appeared in the British production of *South Pacific*.
John Kerr appeared in the film *South Pacific*.

YOUR CHEATING HEART   March 1953
Hank Williams
Bradbury Wood Ltd .... USA
Joni James .... **MGM 603**
Frankie Laine .... **Philips BBR 8014**
Hank Williams .... **MGM EP 770**
Patsy Cline .... **Brunswick LAT 8510**
Ray Charles (1963) .... **HMV POP 1099**
Connie Francis .... **MGM C 812**

YOUR EYES   1931
Robert Stolz / Ralph Benatzky / Harry Graham
Chappell & Co. Ltd. .... Germany
Show(s): .... White Horse Inn
Winnie Melville & Derek Oldham .... **HMV B 3854**
David Whitfield .... **Decca LK 4348**
Rita Williams & Charles Young .... **HMV CLP 1205**

YOUR EYES HAVE TOLD ME SO   1919
Gus Kahn / Walter Blaufuss / Egbert Van Alstyne
B. Feldman & Co. Ltd. .... USA
Film(s): .... Sing Me a Love Song
Alfred Piccaver .... **Decca M 445**
Gordon MacRae & June Hutton .... **Capitol LC 6599**

YOUR FEET'S TOO BIG   1936
Ada Benson / Fred Fisher / The Four Ink Spots
Francis, Day & Hunter Ltd .... USA
The Ink Spots .... **HMV BD 146**
'Fats' Waller & his Rhythm .... **HMV BD 1008**

YOUR HEART AND MINE   1936
Johnny Mercer / Rube Bloom
Sun Music Publishing Co. Ltd .... USA
Show(s): .... Blackbirds of 1936
The Nicholas Brothers .... **HMV BD 373**
Leslie Hutchinson (Hutch) .... **Parlophone F 541**
Roy Fox & his Orchestra, vocal Denny Dennis .. **HMV BD 5096**
The Nicholas Brothers appeared in the British production of *Blackbirds of 1936*.

YOUR HEART AND MY HEART   June 1950
Ross Parker
Lawrence Wright Music Co. Ltd . . . . UK
Show(s): . . . . .Knights of Madness
Vera Lynn . . . . **Decca F 9448**
Harry Dawson . . . . **HMV B 9920**
Eve Boswell . . . . **Parlophone R 3311**

YOUR KING AND COUNTRY WANT YOU   1914
Paul Rubens
Chappell & Co. Ltd. . . . . UK
Edna Thornton . . . . **HMV 03390**
Maggie Teyte . . . . **Columbia 495**
Jack Hylton & his Orchestra . . . . **HMV C 2744**

YOUR KISS IS SWEET   March 1975
Stevie Wonder / Syreeta Wright
Jobete Music (UK) Ltd. . . . . USA
Syreeta . . . . **Tamla Motown TMG 933**

YOUR LOVE IS KING   March 1984
Adu Sade / Stuart Matthewman
Angel Music . . . . UK
Sade . . . . **Epic A 4137**

YOUR MOTHER AND MINE   February 1953
Sammy Cahn / Sammy Fain
Walt Disney Music Co. Ltd . . . . USA
Film(s): . . . . .Peter Pan
Doris Day . . . . **Columbia SEG 7515**
Carol Carr . . . . **HMV B 10436**
Jean Carson . . . . **Philips PB 130**

YOUR SOCKS DON'T MATCH   1944
Leon Carr / Leo Cordey
Dash Music Ltd. . . . . USA
'Fats' Waller & his Rhythm . . . . **HMV BD 1073**
Bing Crosby . . . . **Brunswick 03744**

YOUR SONG   February 1971
Elton John / Bernie Taupin
Dick James Music Ltd . . . . UK
Elton John . . . . **DJM DJS 233**
Ivor Novello Nomination.

YOURS (Quierme Mucho)   1941
Gonzalo Roig / Augustin Rodriguez / Jack Sherr
Macmelodies Ltd . . . . Cuba
Film(s): . . . . Orchestra Wives
Vera Lynn . . . . **Decca F 9959**
Jimmy Dorsey & his Orchestra, vocal Bob Eberly
& Helen O'Connell . . . . **Brunswick 03234**
Vera Lynn . . . . **Decca LK 4120**
Bob Eberly & Helen O'Connell . . . . **Warner Brothers WM 4033**
Julio Iglesias (1982) . . . . **CBS A 1939**

YUMMY YUMMY YUMMY   August 1968
Arthur Resnick / Joe Levine
T.M. Music Ltd. . . . . USA
Ohio Express . . . . **Pye 7N 25459**

Z CARS THEME   April 1962
Traditional, arranged by Bridget Fry
An edition by Essex Music Ltd. . . . . UK
Johnny Keating & his Orchestra . . . . **Pye 7N 35032**
Norrie Paramor & his Orchestra . . . . **Columbia DB 4789**
Adapted from the Northumbrian melody "Johnny Todd". Theme of the TV production "Z Cars".

ZABADAK   November 1967
Howard Blaikley
Lynn Music Ltd. . . . . UK
Dave Dee, Dozy, Beaky, Mick & Tich . . . . **Fontana TF 873**

ZAMBESI   January 1956
Nico Carsten / Anton De Waal / Bob Hilliard
Shapiro-Bernstein & Co. Ltd. . . . . South Africa
Lou Busch & his Orchestra . . . . **Capitol CL 14504**
The Stargazers . . . . **Decca F 10696**
The Piranhas Featuring Bob Grover (1982) . . . . . **Dakota DAK 6**

ZIGEUNER   1929
Noel Coward
Chappell & Co. Ltd . . . . UK
Show(s): . . . . .Bitter Sweet
Film(s): . . . . .Bitter Sweet
Peggy Wood . . . . **HMV B 3144**
Evelyn Laye . . . . **HMV DB 1870**
Noel Coward . . . . **HMV CLP 1050**
Hilde Gueden . . . . **Decca LK 4196**
Vanessa Lee . . . . **HMV CLP 1242**
Peggy Wood appeared in the British production of *Bitter Sweet*.
Noel Coward & Evelyn Laye appeared in the American production of *Bitter Sweet*.

ZING A LITTLE ZONG   October 1952
Harry Warren / Leo Robin
Maddox Music Co. Ltd . . . . USA
Film(s): . . . . Just For You
Bing Crosby & Jane Wyman . . . . **Brunswick LA 8563**
Helen O'Connell . . . . **Capitol CL 13788**
Bing Crosby & Jane Wyman appeared in *Just for You*.
Nominated for an Academy Award 1952.

ZING WENT THE STRINGS OF MY HEART   1935
James Hanley
Chappell & Co. Ltd . . . . USA
Show(s): . . . . .Thumbs Up
Film(s): . . . . Listen Darling / Lullaby of Broadway
Anona Winn . . . . **Rex 8257**
Judy Garland . . . . **Brunswick 02969**
The Tommy Watt Orchestra . . . . **Parlophone PMC 1068**
Judy Garland . . . . **Capitol T 1118**
Petula Clark . . . . **Pye NPL 18007**
Judy Garland appeared in *Listen Darling*.

ZIP-A-DEE-DOO-DAH   1947
Allie Wrubel / Ray Gilbert
Sun Music Publishing Co. Ltd. . . . . USA
Film(s): . . . . Song of the South
Geraldo & his Orchestra . . . . **Parlophone F 2200**
Eddie Fisher . . . . **HMV CLP 1095**
Debbie Reynolds . . . . **London HAD 2326**
Academy Award winning song for 1947.

ZOOM   October 1982
Len Barry / Bobby Eli
ATV Music . . . . USA
Fat Larry's Band . . . . **Virgin VS 546**

ZOOT SUIT, A   1942
Ray Gilbert / Bob O'Brien
Bradbury Wood Ltd . . . . USA
Bob Crosby & his Orchestra,
vocal Nappy Lamare . . . . **Decca F 8158**
The Andrews Sisters . . . . **Brunswick 03353**
The R.A.O.C. Blue Rockets Dance Orchestra . . . **HMV BD 5751**

ZORBA'S DANCE   September 1965
Mikis Theodorakis
Robbins Music Corporation Ltd . . . . USA
Film(s): . . . . Zorba the Greek
Marcello Minerbi & his Orchestra . . . . **Durium DRS 54001**
Sound Track Orchestra,
conducted by Mikis Theodorakis . . . . **Stateside SL 10127**

STAGE PRODUCTIONS

A list of stage shows, the theatre at which they were first performed and the date on which they were first performed

SHOW	THEATRE	DATE
5064 Gerrard	Alhambra Theatre, London	19th March 1915
A to Z	Prince of Wales Theatre, London	11th October 1921
Afgar	Pavilion Theatre, London	17th September 1919
Africana	Daley's Theatre, New York	11th July 1927
After the Girl	Gaiety Theatre, London	7th February 1914
Airs and Graces	Palace Theatre, London	21st June 1917
Aladdin and His Wonderful Lamp (Pantomime)	Palladium Theatre, London	22nd December 1964
All Clear	Queens Theatre, London	20th December 1939
All For Love	Mark Hellinger Theatre, New York	22nd January 1949
Allegro	Majestic Theatre, New York	10th October 1947
Along Fifth Avenue	Broadhurst Theatre, New York	13th January 1949
America's Sweetheart	Broadhurst Theatre, New York	10th February 1931
Americana (1st Edition)	Belmont Theatre, New York	26th July 1926
Americana (2nd Edition)	Lew Fields Theatre, New York	30th October 1928
Americana (3rd Edition)	Shubert Theatre, New York	5th October 1932
And on We Go	Savoy Theatre, London	21st April 1937
André Charlot's Revue of 1924	Times Square Theatre, New York	9th January 1924
Angel Face	Knickerbocker Theatre, New York	20th December 1919
Angel In the Wings	Coronet Theatre, New York	11th December 1947
Annie Get Your Gun	Imperial Theatre, New York	16th May 1946
	Coliseum Theatre, London	7th June 1947
Anything Goes	Alvin Theatre, New York	21st November 1934
	Palace Theatre, London	14th June 1935
Anything Goes (revival)	Saville Theatre, London	18th November 1969
Arcadians, The	Shaftesbury Theatre, London	28th April 1909
	Liberty Theatre, New York	17th January 1910
Artists and Models	Winter Garden Theatre, New York	15th November 1927
As Thousands Cheer	Music Box Theatre, New York	30th September 1933
As You Were	Pavilion Theatre, London	3rd August 1918
	Central Theatre, New York	27th January 1920
Aspects of Love	Prince of Wales Theatre, London	17th April 1989
	Broadhurst Theatre, New York	8th April 1990
At Home Abroad	Winter Garden Theatre, New York	19th September 1935
Babes in Arms	Shubert Theatre, New York	14th April 1937
Babes in Toyland	Majestic Theatre, New York	13th October 1903
Back Again	Ambassadors Theatre, London	2nd September 1919
Balalaika	Adelphi Theatre, London	22nd December 1936
Bandwagon, The	New Amsterdam Theatre, New York	3rd June 1931
Barry of Barrymore	Academy of Music Theatre, New York	30th January 1911
Beauty Prize, The	Winter Garden Theatre, London	5th September 1923
Beauty Shop, The	Astor Theatre, New York	13th April 1914
Beauty Spot, The	Gaiety Theatre, London	22nd December 1917
Belle of New York, The	Casino Theatre, New York	28th September 1897
	Shaftesbury Theatre, London	12th April 1898
Bells Are Ringing	Shubert Theatre, New York	29th November 1956
	Coliseum Theatre, London	14th November 1957
Best Foot Forward	Ethel Barrymore Theatre, New York	1st October 1941
Betsy	New Amsterdam Theatre, New York	28th December 1926

Better 'Ole, The	Oxford Theatre, London	4th August 1917
	Greenwich Village Theatre, New York	19th October 1918
Betty	Daly's Theatre, London	24th April 1915
Between the Devil	Imperial Theatre, New York	23rd December 1937
Big Boy	44th Street Theatre, New York	24th August 1925
Big Show, The	Hippodrome Theatre, New York	31st August 1916
Big Top	His Majesty's Theatre, London	8th May 1942
Billy Rose's Crazy Quilt	44th Street Theatre, New York	19th May 1931
Bing Boys Are Here, The	Alhambra Theatre, London	19th April 1916
Bing Boys on Broadway, The	Alhambra Theatre, London	16th February 1918
Bing Girls Are There, The	Alhambra Theatre, London	24th February 1917
Birds of Paradise, The	Lyric Theatre, London	11th September 1919
Bitter Sweet	His Majesty's Theatre, London	18th July 1929
	Ziegfeld Theatre, New York	5th November 1929
Black Vanities	Victoria Palace Theatre, London	24th April 1941
Black Velvet	Hippodrome Theatre, London	14th November 1939
Blackbirds	Pavilion Theatre, London	11th September 1926
Blackbirds of 1928, The	Liberty Theatre, New York	9th May 1928
Blackbirds of 1930, The	Royale Theatre, New York	22nd October 1930
Blackbirds of 1933, The	Apollo Theatre, New York	2nd December 1933
Blackbirds of 1934, The	Coliseum Theatre, London	25th September 1934
Blackbirds of 1936, The	Gaiety Theatre, London	9th July 1936
Bless the Bride	Adelphi Theatre, London	26th April 1947
Blossom Time	Ambassadors Theatre, New York	29th September 1921
Blue Paradise, The	Casino Theatre, New York	5th August 1915
Blue Skies	Vaudeville Theatre, London	27th June 1927
Bolton's Revue, The	St. James Theatre, London	9th March 1948
Bombo	Jolson's 59th Street Theatre, New York	6th October 1921
	Winter Garden Theatre, New York	14th May 1923
Bow Bells	Hippodrome Theatre, London	4th January 1932
Boy, The	Adelphi Theatre, London	14th September 1917
Boyfriend, The	Wyndham's Theatre, London	14th January 1954
	Royale Theatre, New York	30th September 1954
Boys From Syracuse, The	Alvin Theatre, New York	23rd November 1938
	Theatre Royal, Drury Lane, London	7th November 1963
Bran Pie	Prince of Wales Theatre, London	28th August 1919
Bric-a-Brac	Palace Theatre, London	18th September 1915
Brigadoon	Ziegfeld Theatre, New York	13th March 1947
	His Majesty's Theatre, London	14th April 1949
Bright Lights of 1944, The	Forrest Theatre, New York	16th September 1943
Bubbly	Comedy Theatre, London	5th May 1917
Business as Usual	Hippodrome Theatre, London	16th November 1914
Buzz Buzz	Vaudeville Theatre, London	20th December 1918
By Jupiter	Shubert Theatre, New York	3rd June 1942
Bye Bye Birdie	Martin Beck Theatre, New York	14th April 1960
	Her Majesty's Theatre, London	15th June 1961
Cabaret	Broadhurst Theatre, New York	20th November, 1966
	Palace Theatre, London	25th February, 1968
Cabaret Girl, The	Winter Garden Theatre, London	19th September 1922
Cabin in the Sky	Martin Beck Theatre, New York	25th October 1940
Cairo	His Majesty's Theatre, London	15th October 1921
Call Me Madam	Imperial Theatre, New York	12th October 1950
	Coliseum Theatre, London	15th March 1952

Call Me Mister	National Theatre, New York	18th April 1946
Camelot	Majestic Theatre, New York	3rd December 1960
	Theatre Royal, Drury Lane, London	19th August 1964
Can-Can	Shubert Theatre, New York	7th May 1953
	Coliseum Theatre, London	14th October 1954
Carmen Jones	Broadway Theatre, New York	2nd December 1943
Carnival in Flanders	New York	1953
Carousel	Majestic Theatre, New York	19th April 1945
	Theatre Royal, Drury Lane, London	7th June 1950
Cat and the Fiddle, The	Globe Theatre, New York	15th October 1931
	Palace Theatre, London	4th March 1932
Catch of the Season, The	Vaudeville Theatre, London	9th September 1904
	Daley's Theatre, New York	28th August 1905
Cats	New London Theatre, London	11th May 1981
	Winter Garden Theatre, New York	7th October 1982
Charlot Revue of 1926, The	Selwyn Theatre, New York	10th November 1925
Charlot Show of 1926, The	Prince of Wales Theatre, London	5th October 1926
Chauve-Souris	49th Street Theatre, New York	1st February 1922
Cheep	Vaudeville Theatre, London	26th April 1917
Cherry Girl, The	Vaudeville Theatre, London	21st December 1903
Chess	Prince Edward Theatre, London	14th May 1986
Chin Chin	Globe Theatre, New York	20th October 1914
Chocolate Soldier, The (Der Tapfere Soldat)	Theatre An Der Wien, Vienna	14th November 1908
	Lyric Theatre, New York	13th September 1909
	Lyric Theatre, London	10th September 1910
Chu Chin Chow	His Majesty's Theatre, London	31st August 1916
	Manhattan Opera House, New York	22nd October 1917
Cinderella	Coliseum Theatre, London	18th December 1958
Cinderella (Pantomime)	Palladium Theatre, London	20th December 1966
Cingalee, The	Daly's Theatre, London	5th March 1904
	Daly's Theatre, New York	24th October 1904
Clowns in Clover	Adelphi Theatre, London	1st December 1927
Co-Optimists of 1930, The	Hippodrome Theatre, London	4th April 1930
Co-Optimists, The	Royalty Theatre, London	27th June 1921
	Palace Theatre, London	2nd September 1924
	His Majesty's Theatre, London	26th August 1925
Cochran's 1930 Revue	Pavilion Theatre, London	27th March 1930
Connecticut Yankee, A	Vanderbilt Theatre, New York	3rd November 1927
Connecticut Yankee, A (revival)	Martin Beck Theatre, New York	17th November 1943
Continental Varieties	Little Theatre, New York	3rd October 1934
Conversation Piece	His Majesty's Theatre, London	16th February 1934
	44th Street Theatre, New York	23rd October 1934
Count of Luxembourg, The (Der Graf Von Luxemburg)	Theatre An Der Wien, Vienna	12th November 1909
	Daly's Theatre, London	20th May 1911
	New Amsterdam Theatre, New York	16th September 1912
Countess Maritza, The (Die Grafin Maritza)	Theatre An Der Wien, Vienna	26th March 1924
	Palace Theatre, London	6th July 1926
	Shubert Theatre, New York	18th September 1926
Country Girl, A	Daly's Theatre, London	18th January 1902
	Daly's Theatre, New York	22nd September 1902
Cousins From Nowhere, The (Der Vetter Aus Dingsda)	Theatre Am Nollendorfplatz, Berlin	15th April 1921

Cousins From Nowhere, The		
(Der Vetter Aus Dingsda)	Princes Theatre, London	24th February 1923
Crazy Quilt	*(see Billy Rose's Crazy Quilt)*	
Crest of the Wave	Theatre Royal, Drury Lane, London	1st September 1937
Dairymaids, The	Apollo Theatre, London	14th April 1906
	Criterion Theatre, New York	26th August 1907
Damn Yankees	46th Street Theatre, New York	5th May 1955
	Coliseum Theatre, London	28th March 1957
Dancing Around	Winter Garden Theatre, New York	10th October 1914
Dancing Mistress, The	Adelphi Theatre, London	19th October 1912
Dancing Years, The	Theatre Royal, Drury Lane, London	23rd March 1939
Dear Miss Phoebe	Phoenix Theatre, London	13th October 1950
Dearest Enemy	Knickerbocker Theatre, New York	18th September 1925
Defender, The	Herald Square Theatre, New York	3rd July 1902
Desert Song, The	Casino Theatre, New York	30th November 1926
	Theatre Royal, Drury Lane, London	7th April 1927
Dixie to Broadway	Broadhurst Theatre, New York	29th October 1924
Do Re Mi	St. James Theatre, New York	26th December 1960
	Prince of Wales Theatre, London	12th October 1961
Dollar Princess, The (Die Dollar Princessin)	Carl Theatre, Vienna	2nd November 1907
	Knickerbocker Theatre, New York	6th September 1909
	Daly's Theatre, London	25th September 1909
Dover Street To Dixie	Pavilion Theatre, London	31st May 1923
Dreigroschenoper	*(see Threepenny Opera, The)*	
Dreimaderlhaus, Das	*(see Lilac Time)*	
Dubarry, The (Grafin Dubarry)	Theatre An Der Wien, Vienna	31st October 1879
	His Majesty's Theatre, London	14th April 1932
	George M. Cohan Theatre, New York	22nd November 1932
Dubarry Was a Lady	46th Street Theatre, New York	6th December 1939
	His Majesty's Theatre, London	22nd October 1942
Duchess of Dantzig, The	Lyric Theatre, London	17th October 1903
Earl and the Girl, The	Adelphi Theatre, London	10th December 1903
Earl Carroll's Vanities	Earl Carroll Theatre, New York	27th August 1931
	Earl Carroll Theatre, New York	5th July 1932
	St. James Theatre, New York	13th January 1940
Eileen	Schubert Theatre, New York	19th March 1917
Enchantress, The	New York Theatre, New York	19th October 1911
Evergreen	Adelphi Theatre, London	3rd December 1930
Everybody's Doing It	Empire Theatre, London	14th February 1912
Everybody's Welcome	Shubert Theatre, New York	13th October 1931
Evita	Prince Edward Theatre, London	21st June 1978
	Broadway Theatre, New York	25th September 1979
Face the Music	New Amsterdam Theatre, New York	17th February 1932
Faust on Toast	Gaiety Theatre, London	19th April 1921
Fiddler on the Roof	Imperial Theatre, New York	22nd September 1964
	Her Majesty's Theatre, London	16th February 1967
Fifty Miles From Boston	Garrick Theatre, New York	3rd February 1908
Fifty Million Frenchmen	Lyric Theatre, New York	27th November 1929
Fine and Dandy	Erlanger's Theatre, New York	23rd September 1930
Fing's Ain't Wot They Used T' Be	Garrick Theatre, London	11th February 1960
Finian's Rainbow	46th Street Theatre, New York	10th January 1947
	Palace Theatre, London	21st October 1947
Firefly, The	Lyric Theatre, New York	2nd December 1912

Five O'Clock Girl, The	44th Street Theatre, New York	10th October 1927
	Hippodrome Theatre, London	21st March 1929
Fleet's Lit Up, The	Hippodrome Theatre, London	17th April 1938
Floradora	Lyric Theatre, London	11th November 1899
	Casino Theatre, New York	10th November 1900
Flower Drum Song	St. James Theatre, New York	1st December 1958
	Palace Theatre, London	24th March 1960
Flying Colours	Hippodrome Theatre, London	16th September 1916
	Imperial Theatre, New York	15th September 1932
Follow Me	Casino Theatre, New York	29th November 1916
Follow the Crowd	Empire Theatre, London	19th February 1916
Follow the Girls	New Century Theatre, New York	8th April 1944
	His Majesty's Theatre, London	25th October 1945
Follow the Sun	Adelphi Theatre, London	4th February 1936
Follow Through	46th Street Theatre, New York	9th January 1929
	Dominion Theatre, London	3rd October 1929
Folly to be Wise	Piccadilly Theatre, London	8th January 1931
For the Love of Mike	Saville Theatre, London	8th October 1931
Fortune Teller, The	Wallack's Theatre, New York	26th September 1898
Forty-Five Minutes From Broadway	New Amsterdam Theatre, New York	1st January 1906
Forty-Second Street	Winter Garden Theatre, New York	25th August, 1980
	Theatre Royal, Drury Lane	8th August 1984
Frasquita	Theatre An Der Wien, Vienna	12th May 1922
	Prince's Theatre, London	23rd April 1925
Frederica (Friederike)	Metropol Theatre, Berlin	4th October 1928
	Palace Theatre, London	9th September 1930
	Imperial Theatre, New York	4th February 1937
French Doll, The	Lyceum Theatre, New York	20th February 1922
Friederike	(see Frederica)	
Fun of the Fayre, The	Pavilion Theatre, London	17th October 1921
Funny Face	Alvin Theatre, New York	22nd November 1927
	Prince's Theatre, London	8th November 1928
Funny Girl	Winter Garden Theatre, New York	26th March 1964
	Prince of Wales Theatre, London	13th April 1966
Funny Side Up	His Majesty's Theatre, London	11th January 1940
Gangway	Palladium Theatre, London	17th December 1941
Garrick Gaieties, The (First Edition)	Garrick Theatre, New York	8th June 1925
Garrick Gaieties, The (Second Edition)	Garrick Theatre, New York	10th May 1926
Gate Revue, The	Ambassadors Theatre, London	9th March 1939
Gay Divorce	Ethel Barrymore Theatre, New York	29th November 1932
	Palace Theatre, London	2nd November 1933
Gay Paree	Shubert Theatre, New York	18th August 1925
Geisha	Daly's Theatre, London	25th April 1896
	Fifth Avenue Theatre, New York	9th September 1896
Genevieve de Brabant	Bouffes Parisien Theatre, Paris	19th November 1859
	Philharmonic Theatre, London	11th November 1871
Gentlemen Prefer Blondes	Ziegfeld Theatre, New York	8th December 1949
	Princes Theatre, London	20th August 1962
George M	Palace Theatre, New York	10th April 1968
George White's Music Hall Varieties	Casino Theatre, New York	22nd November 1932
George White's Scandals (4th Edition)	Globe Theatre, New York	28th August 1922
George White's Scandals (6th Edition)	Apollo Theatre, New York	30th June 1924
George White's Scandals (8th Edition)	Apollo Theatre, New York	14th June 1926

George White's Scandals (10th Edition)	Apollo Theatre, New York	23rd September 1929
George White's Scandals (11th Edition)	Apollo Theatre, New York	14th September 1931
George White's Scandals (13th Edition)	Alvin Theatre, New York	28th August 1939
Get A Load of This	Hippodrome Theatre, London	19th November 1941
Gipsy Love (Zigeunerliebe)	Carl Theatre, Vienna	8th January 1910
	Daly's Theatre, London	1st June 1912
Girl Behind the Counter, The	Wyndhams Theatre, London	21st April 1906
	Herald Square Theatre, New York	1st October 1907
Girl Crazy	Alvin Theatre, New York	14th October 1930
Girl From Utah, The	Knickerbocker Theatre, New York	24th August 1914
Girlfriend, The	Vanderbilt Theatre, New York	17th March 1926
	Palace Theatre, London	8th September 1927
Glamorous Night	Theatre Royal, Drury Lane, London	2nd May 1935
Glorious Days, The	Palace Theatre, London	28th February 1953
Glory	Vanderbilt Theatre, New York	22nd December 1922
Godspell	Cherry Lane Theatre, New York	17th May 1971
	Wyndhams Theatre, London	17th November 1971
Going Greek	Gaiety Theatre, London	16th September 1937
Going Up	Liberty Theatre, New York	25th September 1917
	Gaiety Theatre, London	22nd May 1918
Gondoliers, The	Savoy Theatre, London	7th December 1889
	Park Avenue Theatre, New York	7th January 1890
Good Boy	Hammerstein Theatre, New York	5th September 1928
Good Morning Dearie	Globe Theatre, New York	1st November 1921
Good News	46th Street Theatre, New York	6th September 1927
	Carlton Theatre, London	15th August 1928
Graf Von Luxemburg, Der	*(see Count of Luxembourg, The)*	
Grafin Dubarry	*(see Dubarry, The)*	
Grafin Maritza, Die	*(see Countess Maritza, The)*	
Grease	Eden Theatre, New York	14th February, 1972
	New London Theatre, London	26th June, 1973
Great Day	Cosmopolitan Theatre, New York	17th October 1929
Great Temptations	Winter Garden Theatre, New York	18th May 1926
Greenwich Village Follies, The (1st Edition)	Greenwich Village Theatre, New York	15th July 1919
Greenwich Village Follies, The (2nd Edition)	Greenwich Village Theatre, New York	30th August 1920
Greenwich Village Follies, The (4th Edition)	Shubert Theatre, New York	12th September 1922
Greenwich Village Follies, The (6th Edition)	Shubert Theatre, New York	16th September 1924
Guys and Dolls	46th Street Theatre, New York	24th November 1950
	Coliseum Theatre, London	28th May 1953
Gypsy	Broadway Theatre, New York	21st May 1959
	Piccadilly Theatre, London	29th May 1973
Hair	Biltmore Theatre, New York	29th April 1968
	Shaftesbury Theatre, London	27th September 1968
Half a Sixpence	Cambridge Theatre, London	21st March 1963
	Broadhurst Theatre, New York	25th April 1965
Hans Andersen	Palladium Theatre, London	17th December, 1974
Happy Day, The	Daly's Theatre, London	13th May 1916
Happy Hunting	Majestic Theatre, New York	6th December 1956
Haw-Haw	Holborn Empire Theatre, London	22nd December 1939
Hazel Flagg	Mark Hellinger Theatre, New York	11th February 1953
Heads Up	Alvin Theatre, New York	11th November 1929
	Palace Theatre, London	1st May 1930
Heart of Paddy Whack, The	Grand Opera House, New York	26th November 1914

Hello Dolly	St. James Theatre, New York	16th January 1964
	Theatre Royal, Drury Lane, London	2nd December 1965
Hellzapoppin'	46th Street Theatre, New York	22nd September 1938
Her Soldier Boy	Astor Theatre, New York	6th December 1916
Here and There	Empire Theatre, London	29th November 1917
Here's Howe	Broadhurst Theatre, New York	1st May 1928
Hi De Hi	Palace Theatre, London	3rd June 1943
Hi Diddle Diddle	Comedy Theatre, London	3rd October 1934
Hide and Seek	Hippodrome Theatre, London	14th October 1937
High Button Shoes	Century Theatre, New York	9th October 1947
	Hippodrome Theatre, London	22nd December 1948
High Jinks	Lyric Theatre, New York	10th December 1913
	Adelphi Theatre, London	24th August 1916
High Time	Palladium Theatre, London	20th April 1946
Higher and Higher	Shubert Theatre, New York	4th April 1940
His Honour the Mayor	New York Theatre, New York	28th May 1906
Hit the Deck	Belasco Theatre, New York	25th April 1927
	Hippodrome Theatre, London	3rd November 1927
Hitchy-Koo	Cohan & Harris Theatre, New York	7th June 1917
Hodge Podge & Co	Madison Square Theatre, New York	23rd October 1900
Hold Everything	Broadhurst Theatre, New York	10th October 1928
	Palace Theatre, London	12th June 1929
Home and Beauty	Adelphi Theatre, London	2nd February 1937
Hot Chocolates	Hudson Theatre, New York	20th June 1929
Houp La	St. Martins Theatre, London	23rd November 1916
House That Jack Built, The	Adelphi Theatre, London	8th November 1929
Hullo America	Palace Theatre, London	25th September 1918
Hullo Ragtime	Hippodrome Theatre, London	23rd December 1912
Hullo Tango	Hippodrome Theatre, London	23rd December 1913
I Married an Angel	Shubert Theatre, New York	11th May 1938
I'd Rather be Right	Alvin Theatre, New York	2nd November 1937
Im Weissen Rossl	(see White Horse Inn)	
International Revue, The	Majestic Theatre, New York	25th February 1930
Irene	Vanderbilt Theatre, New York	18th November 1919
	Empire Theatre, London	7th April 1920
Irma la Douce	Theatre Gramont, Paris	12th November 1956
	Lyric Theatre, London	17th July 1958
	Plymouth Theatre, New York	29th September 1960
Isle of Dreams, The	Grand Opera House, New York	27th January 1912
Jack and Jill	New York	22nd March 1923
Jesus Christ Superstar	Mark Hellinger Theatre, New York	12th October 1971
	Palace Theatre, London	9th August 1972
Jig Saw	Hippodrome Theatre, London	14th June 1920
Jill Darling	Saville Theatre, London	19th December 1934
John Murray Anderson's Almanac	(see Murray Anderson's Almanac)	
John, Paul, George, Ringo & Bert	Lyric Theatre, London	15th August 1974
Jolly Bachelors	Broadway Theatre, New York	6th January 1910
Joy Bells	Hippodrome Theatre, London	25th March 1919
Jubilee	Imperial Theatre, New York	12th October 1935
Jumbo	Hippodrome Theatre, New York	16th November 1935
June Love	New York	25th April 1921
Just Fancy	Vaudeville Theatre, London	26th March 1920
Katinka	44th Street Theatre, New York	23rd December 1915

Katinka	Shaftesbury Theatre, London	30th August 1923
Kid Boots	Earl Carroll Theatre, New York	31st December 1923
King and I, The	St. James Theatre, New York	29th March 1951
	Theatre Royal, Drury Lane, London	8th October 1953
King's Rhapsody	Palace Theatre, London	15th September 1949
Kismet	Ziegfeld Theatre, New York	3rd December 1953
	Stoll Theatre, London	20th April 1955
Kiss Me Kate	New Century Theatre, New York	30th December 1948
	Coliseum Theatre, London	8th March 1951
Knickerbocker Holiday	Ethel Barrymore Theatre, New York	19th October 1938
Knight of Madness	Victoria Palace Theatre, London	16th March 1950
Ladies First	Broadhurst Theatre, New York	24th October 1918
Lady Be Good	Liberty Theatre, New York	1st December 1924
	Empire Theatre, London	14th April 1926
Lady in Ermine, The	Ambassadors Theatre, New York	2nd October 1922
Lady in the Dark	Alvin Theatre, New York	23rd January 1941
Laffing Room Only	Winter Garden Theatre, New York	23rd December 1944
Land of Smiles (Das Land Des Lachelns)	Metropol Theatre, Berlin	10th October 1929
	Theatre Royal, Drury Lane, London	8th May 1931
Last Waltz, The (Der Letzte Walzer)	Berliner Theatre, Berlin	1920
	Century Theatre, New York	10th May 1921
	Gaiety Theatre, London	7th October 1922
Latin Quarter	Casino Theatre, London	19th March 1949
Laugh Parade, The	Imperial Theatre, New York	2nd November 1931
Laughing Husband, The	New Theatre, London	2nd October 1913
	Knickerbocker Theatre, New York	2nd February 1914
League of Notions, The	New Oxford Theatre, London	17th January 1921
Leap Year	Hippodrome Theatre, London	20th March 1924
Leave It To Me	Imperial Theatre, New York	9th November 1938
Letzte Walzer, Der	(see Last Waltz, The)	
Lew Leslie's Internation Revue	(see International Revue)	
Lido Lady	Gaiety Theatre, London	1st December 1926
Lights Up	Savoy Theatre, London	9th February 1940
Lilac Domino, The	Vienna	1912
	44th Street Theatre, New York	28th October 1914
	Empire Theatre, London	21st February 1918
Lilac Time (Das Dreimaderlhaus)	Raimund Theatre, Vienna	15th January 1916
	Lyric Theatre, London	22nd December 1922
Linger Longer Letty	Fulton Theatre, New York	20th November 1919
Lisbon Story, The	Hippodrome Theatre, London	17th June 1943
Little Dog Laughed, The	Palladium Theatre, London	11th October 1939
Little Jessie James	Longacre Theatre, New York	15th August 1923
Little Johnny Jones	Liberty Theatre, New York	7th November 1904
Little Michus, The	Daly's Theatre, London	29th April 1905
Little Miss Bluebird	Lyceum Theatre, New York	28th August 1923
Little Nellie Kelly	Liberty Theatre, New York	13th November 1922
	New Oxford Theatre, London	2nd July 1923
Little Night Music, A	Shubert Theatre, New York	25th February 1973
	Adelphi Theatre, London	15th April 1975
Little Show, The	Music Box Theatre, New York	30th April 1929
London Calling	Duke of York's Theatre, London	4th September 1923
London Rhapsody	Palladium Theatre, London	1st September 1937
Louisiana Purchase	Imperial Theatre, New York	28th May 1940

Love Lies	Gaiety Theatre, London	30th March 1929
Lucky Girl	Shaftesbury Theatre, London	14th November 1928
Lustige Witwe, Die	(see Merry Widow, The)	
Madame Pompadour	Carl Theatre, Vienna	2nd March 1920
	Daly's Theatre, London	20th December 1923
	Martin Beck Theatre, New York	11th November 1924
Madame Sherry	New Amsterdam Theatre, New York	30th August 1910
Maid of the Mountains, The	Daly's Theatre, London	10th February 1917
	Casino Theatre, New York	11th September 1918
Maid to Measure	Cambridge Theatre, London	20th May 1948
Make it Snappy	Winter Garden Theatre, New York	13th April 1922
Man of la Mancha	Washington Square Theatre, New York	22nd November 1965
	Piccadilly Theatre, London	24th April 1968
Maritza	(see Countess Maritza)	
Marrying Mary	Daly's Theatre, New York	27th August 1906
Mary	Knickerbocker Theatre, New York	18th October 1920
	Queen's Theatre, London	27th April 1921
Mavourneen	14th Street Theatre, New York	28th September 1892
Mayfair and Montmartre	New Oxford Theatre, London	9th March 1922
Maytime	Shubert Theatre, New York	16th August 1917
Me and Juliet	Majestic Theatre, New York	28th May 1953
Me and My Girl	Victoria Palace Theatre, London	16th December 1937
Me and My Girl (Revival)	Adelphi Theatre, London	12th February 1985
Meet Mister Callaghan	Garrick Theatre, London	27th May 1952
Meet the People	Mansfield Theatre, New York	25th December 1940
Mercenary Mary	Longacre Theatre, New York	13th April 1925
	Hippodrome Theatre, London	7th October 1925
Merrie England	Savoy Theatre, London	2nd April 1902
Merry Widow, The (Die Lustige Witwe)	Theatre An Der Wien, Vienna	30th December 1905
	Daly's Theatre, London	8th June 1907
	New Amsterdam Theatre, New York	21st October 1907
Metropolis	Piccadilly Theatre, London	8th March 1989
Mexican Hayride	Winter Garden Theatre, New York	28th January 1944
Midnight Rounders, The	Century Promenade Theatre, New York	5th February 1921
Midnight Sons, The	Broadway Theatre, New York	22nd May 1909
Mikado, The	Savoy Theatre, London	14th March, 1885
	Fifth Avenue Theatre, New York	18th August, 1885
Miss Hook of Holland	Prince of Wales Theatre, London	31st January 1907
	Criterion Theatre, New York	31st December 1907
Miss Innocence	New York Theatre, New York	30th November 1908
Miss Liberty	Imperial Theatre, New York	15th July 1949
Mister Cinders	Adelphi Theatre, London	11th February 1929
Mister Manhattan	Prince of Wales Theatre, London	30th March 1916
Mister Wonderful	Broadway Theatre, New York	22nd March 1956
Mlle. Modiste	Knickerbocker Theatre, New York	25th December 1905
Monsieur Beaucaire	Princes Theatre, London	19th April 1919
	New Amsterdam Theatre, New York	11th December 1919
Most Happy Fella, The	Imperial Theatre, New York	3rd May 1956
	Coliseum Theatre, London	21st April 1960
Mousme, The (The Maids of Japan)	Shaftesbury Theatre, London	9th September 1911
Murray Anderson's Almanac	Erlanger Theatre, New York	14th August 1929
Music Box Revue, The	Music Box Theatre, New York	26th September 1921
	Music Box Theatre, New York	23rd October 1922

Music Box Revue, The	Palace Theatre, London	15th May 1923
	Music Box Theatre, New York	1st December 1924
Music in the Air	Alvin Theatre, New York	8th November 1932
	His Majesty's Theatre, London	19th May 1933
Music Man, The	Majestic Theatre, New York	19th December 1957
	Adelphi Theatre, London	16th March 1961
Mutiny	Piccadilly Theatre, London	18th July 1985
My Fair Lady	Mark Hellinger Theatre, New York	15th March 1956
	Theatre Royal, Drury Lane, London	30th April 1958
Naughty Cinderella	Lyceum Theatre, New York	9th November 1925
Naughty Marietta	New York Theatre, New York	7th November 1910
New Faces	Comedy Theatre, London	11th April 1940
New Faces of 1936	Vanderbilt Theatre, New York	19th May 1936
New Faces of 1952	Royale Theatre, New York	16th May 1952
New Moon, The	Imperial Theatre, New York	19th September 1928
	Theatre Royal, Drury Lane, London	4th April 1929
New Yorkers, The	Broadway Theatre, New York	8th December 1930
Nice Goings On	Strand Theatre, London	13th September 1933
Night Boat, The	Liberty Theatre, New York	2nd February 1920
Nine-Fifteen Revue, The	George M. Cohan Theatre, New York	11th February 1930
No No Nanette	Palace Theatre, London	11th March 1925
	Globe Theatre, New York	16th September 1925
No Strings	54th Street Theatre, New York	15th March 1962
	Her Majesty's Theatre, London	30th December 1963
Nymph Errant	Adelphi Theatre, London	6th October 1933
Of Thee I Sing	Music Box Theatre, New York	26th December 1931
Oh Boy	Princess Theatre, New York	20th February 1917
Oh Joy	Kingsway Theatre, London	27th January 1919
Oh Kay	Imperial Theatre, New York	8th November 1926
	His Majesty's Theatre, London	21st September 1927
Oh Look	Vanderbilt Theatre, New York	7th March 1918
Oh Oh Delphine	Knickerbocker Theatre, New York	30th September 1912
	Shaftesbury Theatre, London	18th February 1913
Oh Please	Fulton Theatre, New York	17th December 1926
Oh What a Lovely War	Wyndham's Theatre, London	20th June 1963
Okay For Sound	Palladium Theatre, London	2nd September 1936
Oklahoma	St. James Theatre, New York	31st March 1943
	Theatre Royal, Drury Lane, London	30th April 1947
Old Chelsea	Princes Theatre, London	17th February 1943
Oliver	New Theatre, London	30th June 1960
	Imperial Theatre, New York	6th January 1963
On A Clear Day You Can See Forever	Mark Hellinger Theatre, New York	17th October 1965
On the Town	Adelphi Theatre, New York	28th December 1944
	Prince of Wales Theatre, London	30th May 1963
On With the Dance	Pavilion Theatre, London	30th April 1925
On With the Show	Princes Theatre, London	20th December 1933
On Your Toes	Imperial Theatre, New York	11th April 1936
	Palace Theatre, London	5th February 1937
	46th Street Theatre, New York	11th October 1954
One Damn Thing After Another	Pavilion Theatre, London	19th May 1927
One Girl, The	Hippodrome Theatre, London	24th February 1933
One Touch of Venus	Imperial Theatre, New York	7th October 1943
Only Girl, The	39th Street Theatre, New York	2nd November 1914

Only Girl, The	Apollo Theatre, London	25th September 1915
Operette	His Majesty's Theatre, London	16th March 1938
Orange Blossoms	Fulton Theatre, New York	19th September 1922
Our Miss Gibbs	Gaiety Theatre, London	23rd January 1909
	Knickerbocker Theatre, New York	29th August 1910
Paganini	Johann Strauss Theatre, Vienna	30th October 1925
	Lyceum Theatre, London	30th May 1937
Paint Your Wagon	Shubert Theatre, New York	12th November 1951
	His Majesty's Theatre, London	11th February 1953
Pajama Game, The	St. James Theatre, New York	13th May 1954
	Coliseum Theatre, London	13th October 1955
Pal Joey	Ethel Barrymore Theatre, New York	25th December 1940
	Princes Theatre, London	31st March 1954
Panama Hattie	46th Street Theatre, New York	30th October 1940
	Piccadilly Theatre, London	4th November 1943
Paris	Music Box Theatre, New York	8th October 1928
Parisian Model	New York	27th November 1906
Passing Show, The	Palace Theatre, London	20th September 1922
Passing Show of 1912, The	Winter Garden Theatre, New York	22nd July 1912
Passing Show of 1915, The	Palace Theatre, London	9th March 1915
Passing Show of 1916, The	Winter Garden Theatre, New York	22nd June 1916
Passing Show of 1918, The	Winter Garden Theatre, New York	25th July 1918
Passing Show of 1922, The	Winter Garden Theatre, New York	20th April 1914
Peggy Ann	Vanderbilt Theatre, New York	27th December 1926
	Daly's Theatre, London	27th July 1927
Perchance to Dream	Hippodrome Theatre, London	21st April 1945
Phantom of the Opera	Her Majesty's Theatre, London	9th October 1986
	Majestic Theatre, New York	26th January 1988
Piccadilly Hayride	Prince of Wales Theatre, London	11th October 1946
Pickwick	Saville Theatre, London	4th July 1963
	46th Street Theatre, New York	October 1965
Pink Lady, The	New Amsterdam Theatre, New York	13th March 1911
	Globe Theatre, London	11th April 1912
Plain and Fancy	Mark Hellinger Theatre, New York	27th January 1955
	Theatre Royal, Drury Lane, London	25th January 1956
Please	Savoy Theatre, London	16th November 1933
Pleasure Seekers, The	Winter Garden Theatre, New York	13th November 1913
Porgy and Bess	Alvin Theatre, New York	10th October 1935
	Stoll Theatre, London	9th October 1952
Pot Luck	Vaudeville Theatre, London	24th December 1921
Present Arms	Mansfield Theatre, New York	26th April 1928
Princess Caprice	Shaftesbury Theatre, London	11th May 1912
Princess Pat, The	Cort Theatre, New York	29th September 1915
Private Lives	Phoenix Theatre, London	24th September 1930
	Times Square Theatre, New York	27th January 1931
Promises Promises	Shubert Theatre, New York	1st December 1968
	Prince of Wales Theatre, London	2nd October 1969
Provincetown Follies, The	Provincetown Playhouse Theatre, New York	3rd November 1935
Punch Bowl, The	Duke of York's Theatre, London	21st May 1924
Push and Go	Hippodrome Theatre, London	10th May 1915
Quaker Girl, The	Adelphi Theatre, London	5th November 1910
	Park Theatre, New York	23rd October 1911
Ramblers, The	Lyric Theatre, New York	20th September 1926

Rebel Maid, The	Empire Theatre, London	12th March 1921
Red Hot and Blue	Alvin Theatre, New York	29th October 1936
Reilly and the 400	Harrigan's Theatre, New York	1890
Revenge With Music	New Amsterdam Theatre, New York	28th November 1934
Right This Way	46th Street Theatre, New York	5th January 1938
Rio Rita	Ziegfeld Theatre, New York	2nd February 1927
	Prince Edward Theatre, London	3rd April 1930
Rise and Shine	Theatre Royal, Drury Lane, London	7th May 1936
Roar of the Greasepaint -		
The Smell of the Crowd	Shubert Theatre, New York	16th May 1965
Roberta	New Amsterdam Theatre, New York	18th November 1933
Robin Hood	Standard Theatre, New York	28th September 1890
Robinson Crusoe Junior	Winter Garden Theatre, New York	17th February 1916
Roly-Boly Eyes	Knickerbocker Theatre, New York	25th September 1919
Romance of Athlone, A	14th Street Theatre, New York	9th January 1899
Rosalie	New Amsterdam Theatre, New York	10th January 1928
Rose Marie	Imperial Theatre, New York	2nd September 1924
	Theatre Royal, Drury Lane, London	20th March 1925
Runaway Girl, A	Gaiety Theatre, London	21st May 1898
	Daly's Theatre, New York	25th August 1898
Runnin' Wild	Colonial Theatre, New York	29th October 1923
Sally	New Amsterdam Theatre, New York	21st December 1920
	Winter Garden Theatre, London	10th September 1921
Sally in Our Alley	Broadway Theatre, New York	29th August 1902
Samples	Playhouse Theatre, London	30th November 1915
Sauce Tartare	Cambridge Theatre, London	18th May 1949
School Days	New York	14th September 1908
Second Little Show, The	Royale Theatre, New York	2nd September 1930
Sergeant Blue	Knickerbocker Theatre, New York	24th April 1905
Set to Music	Music Box Theatre, New York	18th January 1939
Seven Lively Arts	Ziegfeld Theatre, New York	7th December 1944
Shake Your Feet	Hippodrome Theatre, London	20th July 1927
Shameen Dhu	Grand Opera House, New York	2nd February 1914
She Loves Me	Eugene O'Neill Theatre, New York	23rd April 1963
	Lyric Theatre, London	29th April 1964
She's a Good Fellow	Globe Theatre, New York	5th May 1919
Shepherd's Pie	Princes Theatre, London	21st December 1939
Shop Girl	Gaiety Theatre, London	24th November 1894
Show Boat	Ziegfeld Theatre, New York	27th December 1927
	Theatre Royal, Drury Lane, London	3rd May 1928
Show Girl	Ziegfeld Theatre, New York	2nd July 1929
Show is on, The	Winter Garden Theatre, New York	25th December 1936
Shuffle Along	63rd Street Theatre, New York	23rd May 1921
Sigh no More	Piccadilly Theatre, London	22nd August 1945
Silk Stockings	Imperial Theatre, New York	24th February 1955
Simple Simon	Ziegfeld Theatre, New York	18th February 1930
Sinbad	Winter Garden Theatre, New York	14th February 1918
Sing Out the News	Music Box Theatre, New York	24th September 1938
Singin' in the Rain	Palladium Theatre, London	30th June 1983
Singin' the Blues	Liberty Theatre, New York	16th September 1931
Smiles	Ziegfeld Theatre, New York	18th November 1930
Snap	Vaudeville Theatre, London	11th August 1922
Some	Vaudeville Theatre, London	29th June 1916

Song and Dance	Palace Theatre, London	26th March 1982
Song of Norway, The	Imperial Theatre, New York	21st August 1944
	Palace Theatre, London	7th March 1946
Sound of Music, The	Lunt-fontanne Theatre, New York	16th November 1959
	Palace Theatre, London	18th May 1961
South Pacific	Majestic Theatre, New York	7th April 1949
	Theatre Royal, Drury Lane, London	1st November 1951
Spices of 1922, The	Winter Garden Theatre, New York	6th July 1922
Spread it Abroad	Saville Theatre, London	1st April 1936
Spring is Here	Alvin Theatre, New York	11th March 1929
St. Louis Woman	Martin Beck Theatre, New York	30th March 1946
Stand up and Sing	Hippodrome Theatre, London	5th March 1931
Star and Garter	Music Box Theatre, New York	24th June 1942
Starlight Express	Apollo Theatre, London	27th March 1984
	Gershwin Theatre, New York	15th March 1987
Starlight Roof	Hippodrome Theatre, London	23rd October 1947
Stars on Ice	Centre Theatre, New York	2nd July 1942
Stop Flirting	Shaftesbury Theatre, London	30th May 1923
Stop Look Listen	Globe Theatre, New York	25th December 1915
Stop Press	Adelphi Theatre, London	21st February 1935
Stop the World - I Want to Get Off	Queens Theatre, London	20th July 1961
	Shubert Theatre, New York	3rd October 1962
Streamline	Palace Theatre, London	28th September 1934
Streets of Paris, The	Broadhurst Theatre, New York	19th June 1939
Strike up the Band	Times Square Theatre, New York	14th January 1930
Student Prince, The	Jolson Theatre, New York	2nd December 1924
	His Majesty's Theatre, London	3rd February 1926
Sunny	New Amsterdam Theatre, New York	22nd September 1925
	Hippodrome Theatre, London	7th October 1926
Sunshine Girl, The	Gaiety Theatre, London	24th February 1912
	Knickerbocker Theatre, New York	3rd February 1913
Sweet Adeline	Hammerstein's Theatre, New York	3rd September 1929
Sweet and Low	46th Street Theatre, New York	17th November 1930
Sweet Charity	Palace Theatre, New York	29th January 1966
	Prince of Wales Theatre, London	11th October 1967
Sweethearts	New Amsterdam Theatre, New York	8th September 1913
Swingin' the Dream	Centre Theatre, New York	29th November 1939
Tails Up	Comedy Theatre, London	1st June 1918
Take A Chance	Apollo Theatre, New York	26th November 1932
Tanz Ins Gluck, Der	(see Whirled Into Happiness)	
Tapfere Soldat, Der	(see Chocolate Soldier, The)	
That's a Good Girl	Hippodrome Theatre, London	5th June 1928
That's a Pretty Thing	Daly's Theatre, London	22nd November 1933
These Foolish Things	Palladium Theatre, London	28th September 1938
Third Little Show, The	Music Box Theatre, New York	1st June 1931
This is the Army	Broadway Theatre, New York	4th July 1942
	Palladium Theatre, London	10th November 1943
This Year of Grace	Pavilion Theatre, London	22nd March 1928
	Selwyn Theatre, New York	7th November 1928
This'll Make You Whistle	Palace Theatre, London	15th September 1936
Three Graces, The	Empire Theatre, London	26th January 1924
Three Twins, The	Herald Square Theatre, New York	15th June 1908
Three's a Crowd	Selwyn Theatre, New York	15th October 1930

Threepenny Opera, The (Dreigroschenoper)	Theatre Am Schiffbauerdamm, Berlin	29th January 1928
	Empire Theatre, New York	13th April 1933
	Royal Court Theatre, New York	9th February 1956
Through the Years	Manhattan Theatre, New York	28th January 1932
Thumbs Up	St. James Theatre, New York	27th December 1934
Time	Dominion Theatre, London	9th April 1986
Tina	Adelphi Theatre, London	2nd November 1915
Tip-Toes	Liberty Theatre, New York	28th December 1925
	Winter Garden Theatre, London	31st August 1926
Together Again	Victoria Palace Theatre, London	7th April 1947
Tonight at Eight-Thirty	Phoenix Theatre, London	9th January 1936
	National Theatre, New York	24th November 1936
Tonight's the Night	Gaiety Theatre, London	28th April 1915
Too Many Girls	Imperial Theatre, New York	18th October 1939
Tree Grows in Brooklyn, A	Alvin Theatre, New York	19th April 1951
Trip to Chinatown, A	Madison Square Theatre, New York	9th November 1891
Twirly Whirly	Weber & Fields Theatre, New York	18th September 1902
Two for the Show	Booth Theatre, New York	8th February 1940
U.S.	Ambassadors Theatre, London	28th November 1918
Up and Doing	Saville Theatre, London	17th April 1940
Up and Down Broadway	Casino Theatre, New York	18th July 1910
Up in Central Park	Century Theatre, New York	27th January 1945
Up With The Lark	Adelphi Theatre, London	25th August 1927
Vagabond King, The	Casino Theatre, New York	21st September 1925
	Winter Garden Theatre, London	19th April 1927
Vanderbilt Revue, The	Vanderbilt Theatre, New York	5th November 1930
Vera Violetta	Winter Garden Theatre, New York	20th November 1911
Veronique	Theatre Des Bouffes-Parisiens, Paris	20th November 1898
	Apollo Theatre, London	18th May 1904
	Broadway Theatre, New York	30th October, 1905
Very Warm For May	Alvin Theatre, New York	17th November 1939
Vetter Aus Dingsda, Der	(See Cousin From Nowhere, The)	
Virginia	Palace Theatre, London	24th October 1928
Wake up and Dream	Pavilion Theatre, London	27th March 1929
	Selwyn Theatre, New York	30th December 1929
Walk a Little Faster	St. James Theatre, New York	7th December 1932
Waltz Dream, A (Ein Waltzertraum)	Carl Theatre, Vienna	2nd March 1907
	Broadway Theatre, New York	27th January 1908
	Hicks Theatre, London	7th March 1908
Watch Your Step	New Amsterdam Theatre, New York	8th December 1914
	Empire Theatre, London	4th May 1915
Wenn Die Kleinen Veilchen Bluhen	(see Wild Violets)	
West Side Story	Winter Garden Theatre, New York	26th September 1957
	Her Majesty's Theatre, London	12th December 1958
What's in a Name	Maxine Elliott's Theatre, New York	19th March 1920
Where's Charley	St. James Theatre, New York	11th October 1948
	Palace Theatre, London	20th February 1958
Whirled Into Happiness (Der Tanz Ins Gluck)	Raimund Theatre, Vienna	23rd December 1920
	Lyric Theatre, London	18th May 1922
White Horse Inn (Im Weissen Rossl)	Grosses Schauspielhaus Theatre, Berlin	8th November 1930
	Coliseum Theatre, London	8th April 1931
	Centre Theatre, New York	1st October 1936
Whooppee	New Amsterdam Theatre, New York	4th December 1928

Wild Cat	Alvin Theatre, New York	16th December 1960
Wild Rose	Princes Theatre, London	6th August 1942
Wild Violets		
(Wenn Die Kleinen Veilchen Bluhen)	Princesse Schouwburg Theatre, The Hague	1st April 1932
	Theatre Royal, Drury Lane, London	31st October 1932
Will O' the Whispers	Shaftesbury Theatre, London	4th April 1928
Winged Victory	44th Street Theatre, New York	20th November 1943
Wish You Were Here	Imperial Theatre, New York	25th June 1952
	London Casino Theatre, London	10th October 1953
Wonder Bar	Savoy Theatre, London	5th December 1930
	Nora Bayes Theatre, New York	17th March 1931
Words and Music	Adelphi Theatre, London	16th September 1932
Yankee at the Court of King Arthur, A	Daly's Theatre, London	10th October 1929
Yip Yip Yaphank	Century Theatre, New York	19th August 1918
Yokel Boy	Majestic Theatre, New York	6th July 1939
You Never Know	Winter Garden Theatre, New York	21st September 1938
Ziegfeld Follies of 1908	Jardin De Paris Theatre, New York	15th June 1908
Ziegfeld Follies of 1909	Jardin De Paris Theatre, New York	14th June 1909
Ziegfeld Follies of 1911	Jardin De Paris Theatre, New York	26th June 1911
Ziegfeld Follies of 1912	Jardin De Paris Theatre, New York	21st October 1912
Ziegfeld Follies of 1913	New Amsterdam Theatre, New York	16th June 1913
Ziegfeld Follies of 1914	New Amsterdam Theatre, New York	6th January 1914
Ziegfeld Follies of 1915	New Amsterdam Theatre, New York	21st June 1915
Ziegfeld Follies of 1916	New Amsterdam Theatre, New York	12th June 1916
Ziegfeld Follies of 1919	New Amsterdam Theatre, New York	16th June 1919
Ziegfeld Follies of 1920	New Amsterdam Theatre, New York	22nd June 1920
Ziegfeld Follies of 1921	Globe Theatre, New York	21st June 1921
Ziegfeld Follies of 1922	New Amsterdam Theatre, New York	5th June 1922
Ziegfeld Follies of 1923	New Amsterdam Theatre, New York	20th October 1923
Ziegfeld Follies of 1927	New Amsterdam Theatre, New York	16th August 1927
Ziegfeld Follies of 1931	Ziegfeld Theatre, New York	1st July 1931
Ziegfeld Follies of 1934	Winter Garden Theatre, New York	4th January 1934
Ziegfeld Follies of 1936	Winter Garden Theatre, New York	14th September 1936
Ziegfeld Midnight Frolic	New Amsterdam Theatre, New York	15th March 1920
Zig-Zag	Hippodrome Theatre, London	31st January 1917
Zigeunerliebe	*(see Gipsy Love)*	

FILM	COMPANY	YEAR

Films are listed alphabetically with the name of the company which released or distributed the film and the year.

2001 A Space Odyssey	M.G.M.	1968
Actress, The	M.G.M.	1953
Adventures of Hajji Baba, The	20th Century Fox	1954
Adventures of Sherlock Holmes, The	20th Century Fox	1939
Affair in Trinidad, An	Columbia	1952
Affair to Remember, An	20th Century Fox	1957
After Midnight	Paramount	1950
After the Ball	Beaconsfield	1957
Alamo, The	United Artists	1960
Alexander's Ragtime Band	20th Century Fox	1938
Alfie	Paramount	1966
Ali Baba Goes To Town	Paramount	1937
All That Jazz	Columbia & 20th Century Fox	1979
All the King's Horses	Paramount	1935
Alligator Named Daisy, An	Rank	1955
Along the Navajo Trail	Republic	1945
Always in My Heart	Warner Brothers	1942
American Gigolo	Paramount	1980
American Graffiti	Universal	1973
American in Paris, An	M.G.M.	1951
American Tail, An	Universal	1987
Anchors Aweigh	M.G.M.	1945
And the Angels Sing	Paramount	1944
Andy Hardy Meets the Debutante	M.G.M.	1940
Animal Crackers	Paramount	1930
Anna	Lux	1951
Annie Get Your Gun	M.G.M.	1950
Anything Goes	Paramount	1936
	Paramount	1956
Apartment, The	Panavision	1959
Applause	Paramount	1929
April in Paris	Warner Brothers	1953
April Love	20th Century Fox	1957
April Showers	Warner Brothers	1948
Around the World in Eighty Days	United Artists	1956
Arthur	Warner Brothers	1981
At Long Last Love	20th Century Fox	1975
At the Circus	M.G.M.	1939
Athena	M.G.M.	1954
Atlantic City	Republic	1944
Aunt Sally	Gainsborough	1933
Awakening, The	United Artists	1929
Babes in Arms	M.G.M.	1939
Babes in Toyland	M.G.M.	1934
Babes on Broadway	M.G.M.	1942
Balalaika	M.G.M.	1939
Bambi	Disney	1942
Band of Thieves	Rank	1962
Band Wagon, The	M.G.M.	1953

Banjo on My Knee, A	20th Century Fox	1936
Barkleys of Broadway, The	M.G.M.	1949
Bathing Beauty	M.G.M.	1944
Be Mine Tonight (see Tell Me Tonight)		
Beat Generation, The	M.G.M.	1958
Beat Girl	Renown	1959
Beau James	Paramount	1957
Beautiful But Broke	Columbia	1944
Because They're Young	Columbia	1960
Because You're Mine	M.G.M.	1952
Behind the Eight Ball (see Off the Beaten Track)		
Belle of New York, The	M.G.M.	1952
Belle of The Nineties, The	Paramount	1934
Belles on Their Toes	20th Century Fox	1952
Bells Are Ringing	M.G.M.	1960
Bells of St. Mary's, The	R.K.O.	1945
Ben	Cinerama	1972
Benny Goodman Story, The	Universal International	1956
Bernadine	20th Century Fox	1957
Best Foot Forward	M.G.M.	1943
Best Things in Life Are Free, The	20th Century Fox	1956
Best Years of Our Lives, The	R.K.O.	1946
Betty Co-ed	Columbia	1946
Between Two Women	M.G.M.	1945
Bicyclettes de Belsize	British Lion	1968
Big Beat, The	Universal	1958
Big Broadcast of 1936, The	Paramount	1935
Big Broadcast of 1938, The	Paramount	1938
Big Broadcast, The	Paramount	1932
Big City, The	M.G.M.	1948
Big Pond, The	Paramount	1930
Big Sombrero, The	Columbia	1949
Big Store, The	M.G.M.	1941
Birds and the Bees, The	Paramount	1956
Birth of the Blues, The	Paramount	1941
Bitch, The	Rank	1979
Bitter Sweet	British & Dominion	1933
	M.G.M.	1940
Black Joy	Rank	1977
Blackboard Jungle, The	M.G.M.	1955
Blazing Sun, The	Columbia	1950
Blonde Crazy	Warner Brothers	1931
Blonde From Brooklyn, The	Columbia	1945
Blowing Wild	Warner Brothers	1953
Blue Angel, The	Paramount	1930
	20th Century Fox	1959
Blue Hawaii	Paramount	1960
Blue Skies	Paramount	1946
Blue Veil, The	R.K.O.	1951
Blues in the Night	Warner Brothers	1941
Body Rock	New World	1985
Born Free	Columbia	1960

Born to Dance	M.G.M.	1936
Born to Sing	M.G.M.	1942
Born Yesterday	Columbia	1951
Borsalino	Columbia	1971
Both Ends of the Candle	Warner Brothers	1957
Boyfriend, The	M.G.M.	1971
Boys From Syracuse, The	Universal	1940
Breakfast at Tiffany's	Paramount	1961
Bridge Over the River Kwai, The	Columbia	1957
Brigadoon	M.G.M.	1954
Bright Eyes	Fox	1934
Bright Lights	First National	1931
Bring Your Smile Along	Columbia	1955
Broadway	Universal	1942
Broadway Gondolier, The	Warner Brothers	1935
Broadway Melody	M.G.M.	1929
Broadway Melody of 1936	M.G.M.	1935
Broadway Melody of 1938	M.G.M.	1937
Broadway Melody of 1940	M.G.M.	1940
Broadway Rhythm	M.G.M.	1944
Broadway to Hollywood	M.G.M.	1933
Buck Benny Rides Again	Paramount	1940
Buck Privates	Universal	1941
Butch Cassidy and the Sundance Kid	20th Century Fox	1969
By Hook or By Crook	M.G.M.	1943
By the Light of the Silvery Moon	Warner Brothers	1953
Bye Bye Birdie	Columbia	1963
Cabaret	Allied Artists	1972
Cabin in the Sky	M.G.M.	1943
Caddy, The	Paramount	1953
Cain and Mabel	Warner Brothers	1936
Caine Mutiny, The	Columbia	1954
Calamity Jane	Warner Brothers	1953
Call Me Madam	20th Century Fox	1953
Call Me Mister	20th Century Fox	1951
Call of the Canyon, The	Republic	1942
Camelot	Warner Brothers	1967
Camels Are Coming, The	Exclusive	1934
Can-Can	20th Century Fox	1960
Can't Help Singing	Universal	1944
Canyon Passage	Universal	1946
Captain Carey, USA (see After Midnight)		
Carefree	R.K.O.	1938
Careless Lady	Fox	1932
Carmen Jones	20th Century Fox	1954
Carnival in Costa Rica	20th Century Fox	1947
Carolina Blues	Columbia	1944
Carousel	20th Century Fox	1956
Casa Manana	Monogram	1951
Casablanca	Warner Brothers	1943
Casbah	Universal	1948
Casino de Paris	First National	1935
Casino Royale	Columbia	1967

Cat and the Fiddle, The	M.G.M.	1934
Catch Us if You Can	Warner-Pathe	1965
Cavalcade	20th Century Fox	1933
Centennial Summer	20th Century Fox	1946
Certain Smile, A	20th Century Fox	1958
Chariots of Fire	Warner Brothers	1981
Charley Moon	British Lion	1956
Charm School, The	Paramount	1936
Chasing Rainbows	M.G.M.	1930
Check and Double Check	R.K.O.	1930
Cherokee Strip, The	Paramount	1940
Chitty Chitty Bang Bang	United Artists	1968
Chocolate Soldier, The	M.G.M.	1941
Christmas Holiday	Universal	1944
Chu Chin Chow	Gainsborough	1934
Cinderella	R.K.O.	1950
Cinderella Swings It	R.K.O.	1943
Circus of Horrors	Anglo-amalgamated	1959
City Lights	United Artists	1931
Clash By Night	R.K.O.	1952
Clock Strikes Eight, The	20th Century Fox	1946
Clock, The (see Under The Clock)		
Cockeyed Cavaliers, The	R.K.O.	1934
Cockeyed World	Fox	1929
Coconut Grove	Paramount	1938
Coconuts, The	Paramount	1929
College Coach	Warner Brothers	1933
College Humour	Paramount	1933
College Rhythm	Paramount	1934
College Scandal	Paramount	1935
College Swing (see Swing Teacher Swing)		
Collegiate (see Charm School, The)		
Come Back to Me	20th Century Fox	1945
Come Next Spring	Republic	1956
Come Out of the Pantry	Cinephonic	1935
Come September	Universal International	1961
Coney Island	20th Century Fox	1943
Confidential Agent	Warner Brothers	1945
Congress Dances	U.F.A.	1931
Connecticut Yankee, A	Fox	1931
Convoy	United Artists	1978
Cooley High	Brent Walker	1975
Copacabana	United Artists	1947
Copper Canyon	Paramount	1950
Countess From Hong Kong, The	Universal	1967
Courtneys of Curzon Street, The	British Lion	1947
Cover Girl	Columbia	1944
Cow Town	Columbia	1950
Cowboy From Brooklyn, The (see Romance And Rhythm)		
Crooner, The	First National	1932
Cuban Love Song	M.G.M.	1931
Cuban Pete	Universal	1946
Cuckoos, The	R.K.O.	1930

Curly Top	20th Century Fox	1935
D'ye Ken John Peel	Twickenham	1934
Daddy Long Legs	20th Century Fox	1955
Dam Busters, The	Warner Brothers	1955
Dames	Warner Brothers	1934
Damn Yankees (see What Lola Wants)		
Damsel in Distress, A	R.K.O.	1937
Dance Fools Dance	M.G.M.	1931
Dancing in the Park	20th Century Fox	1950
Dancing Lady, The	M.G.M.	1933
Dancing on a Dime	Paramount	1940
Dancing Sweeties	Warner Brothers	1930
Dancing Years, The	Associated British	1950
Dangerous Moonlight	R.K.O.	1941
Dark Sands	Buckingham	1938
Date With Judy, A	M.G.M.	1948
Daughter of Rosie O'Grady, The	Warner Brothers	1950
Davy Crockett, King of the Wild Frontier	Buena-Vista	1955
Day at the Races, A	M.G.M.	1937
Days of Wine and Roses, The	Warner Brothers	1963
Deep in My Heart	M.G.M.	1954
Deep, The	Columbia	1977
Deer Hunter, The	E.M.I.	1978
Deliverance	Warner Brothers	1972
Desert Song, The	Warner Brothers	1929
	Warner Brothers	1944
	Warner Brothers	1953
Designing Woman	M.G.M.	1934
Destry Rides Again	Universal	1939
Diamond Horseshoe, The	20th Century Fox	1945
Diamonds Are Forever	United Artists	1971
Dinner at Eight	M.G.M.	1933
Disc Jockey	Allied Artists	1951
Divine Lady, The	First National	1929
Dixie	Paramount	1943
Do You Love Me	20th Century Fox	1946
Doctor Doolittle	20th Century Fox	1967
Doctor No	United Artists	1962
Doctor Rhythm	Paramount	1938
Doctor Zhivago	M.G.M.	1966
Dog Soldiers, The	United Artists	1978
Dolce Vita, La	Columbia	1959
Doll Face (see Come Back to Me)		
Dolly Sisters, The	20th Century Fox	1945
Don't Fence Me In	Republic	1945
Don't Knock The Rock	Columbia	1957
Double Or Nothing	Paramount	1937
Doughboys in Ireland	Columbia	1943
Down Argentine Way	20th Century Fox	1940
Down Dakota Way	Republic	1949
Down the Wyoming Trail	Monogram	1939
Drag (see Parasites)		
Drum Crazy	Columbia	1959

Dubarry Was a Lady	M.G.M.	1943
Dude Ranch	Paramount	1931
Dumbo	R.K.O.	1941
Dynamite	M.G.M.	1929
East Side of Heaven, The	Universal	1939
Easter Parade	M.G.M.	1948
Easy to Love	M.G.M.	1953
Easy to Wed	M.G.M.	1946
Ebb Tide	Paramount	1938
Eddie Foy and the Seven Little Foys	Paramount	1955
Eddy Cantor Story, The	Warner Brothers	1953
Eddy Duchin Story, The	Columbia	1956
Electric Dreams	20th Century Fox	1984
Emperor Waltz, The	Paramount	1948
Encore	Paramount	1952
Escape to Happiness	United Artists	1939
Ever Since Eve	Warner Brothers	1937
Evergreen	Gaumont British	1937
Every Night at Eight	Paramount	1935
Everybody's Cheering	M.G.M.	1948
Everything I Have is Yours	M.G.M.	1952
Exodus	United Artists	1960
Expresso Bongo	Conquest	1959
Fabulous Dorseys, The	Universal	1947
Faithful in My Fashion	M.G.M.	1946
Fame	M.G.M.	1980
Fancy Pants	Paramount	1950
Farewell Performance	Rank	1963
Fast Break	Kings Road Productions	1978
Feather Your Nest	A.B.F.D.	1937
Feminine Touch, The	M.G.M.	1941
Ferdinand the Bull	R.K.O.	1939
Ferry Across the Mersey	United Artists	1964
Fete a Henriette, La	Gala	1952
Feudin' Fussin' and Fightin'	Universal	1948
Fiddler on the Roof	United Artists	1971
Fine and Dandy	Warner Brothers	1950
Finian's Rainbow	Warner Brothers	1968
Fire Down Below	Columbia	1957
Firefly	M.G.M.	1937
First a Girl	Gaumont British	1935
First Love	Universal	1939
Five Easy Pieces	Columbia	1970
Five Pennies, The	Paramount	1959
Flame and the Flesh, The	M.G.M.	1958
Flamingo Road	Warner Brothers	1949
Flashdance	Paramount	1983
Fleet's in, The	Paramount	1942
Flirtation Walk	First National	1934
Flower Drum Song, The	Universal	1961
Flying Down to Rio	R.K.O.	1933
Folies Bergere (see Man From the Folies Bergere, The)		
Follow That Dream	United Artists	1962

Follow the Band	Universal	1943
Follow the Boys	Universal	1944
Follow the Fleet	R.K.O.	1936
Follow Through	Paramount	1930
Follow Your Heart	Republic	1936
Footlight Parade	Warner Brothers	1933
Footloose	Paramount	1984
For Me and My Gal	M.G.M.	1942
For Your Eyes Only	United Artists	1981
Forest Rangers, The	Paramount	1942
Forty Little Mothers	M.G.M.	1940
Forty-Second Street	Warner Brothers	1933
Four Jills in a Jeep	20th Century Fox	1944
Fox Movietone Follies of 1929	Fox	1929
Freddie Steps Out	Monogram	1946
Friendly Persuasion	Allied Artists	1956
Frightened City, The	Anglo-amalgamated	1961
From Russia with Love	United Artists	1963
Fuehrer's Face, Der	R.K.O.	1943
Fun and Fancy Free	R.K.O.	1947
Fun at St. Fanny's	Advance	1955
Funny Face	Paramount	1957
Funny Girl	Columbia	1968
Galloping Major, The	Romulus	1951
Gang's All Here, The (see Girls He Left Behind, The)		
Gangway	Gaumont British	1937
Garden of the Moon, The	First National	1938
Gay City, The	Paramount	1941
Gay Desperado, The	United Artists	1936
Gay Divorcee, The	R.K.O.	1934
Gay Imposter, The	Warner Brothers	1938
Gay Ranchero, The	Republic	1948
Gene Krupa Story, The (see Drum Crazy)		
Gentlemen Marry Brunettes	United Artists	1955
Gentlemen Prefer Blondes	20th Century Fox	1953
George White's Scandals	20th Century Fox	1934
	R.K.O.	1945
Georgy Girl	Columbia	1966
Get Hep to Love	Universal	1942
Ghostbusters	Columbia	1984
G.I. Blues	Paramount	1960
Gigi	M.G.M.	1958
Gilda	Columbia	1946
Girl Can't Help It, The	20th Century Fox	1957
Girl Crazy	R.K.O.	1932
	M.G.M.	1943
Girl From Missouri, The	M.G.M.	1934
Girl Rush	Paramount	1955
Girl He Left Behind, The	20th Century Fox	1943
Girls, Les	M.G.M.	1957
Girls Town	M.G.M.	1959
Girls, Girls, Girls	Paramount	1962
Give Out Sisters	Universal	1942

Glad Rag Doll	Warner Brothers	1929
Glamorous Night	Associated British	1937
Glass Mountain, The	Eagle-Lion	1949
Glenn Miller Story, The	Universal International	1954
Glorifying the American Girl	Paramount	1929
Go Into Your Dance (see Casino De Paris)		
Godspell	Columbia	1973
Going Hollywood	M.G.M.	1933
Going My Way	Paramount	1944
Going Places	First National	1938
Gold Diggers of Broadway	Warner Brothers	1929
Gold Diggers of 1933	Warner Brothers	1933
Gold Diggers of 1935	First National	1935
Gold Diggers of 1937	First National	1937
Golden Earrings	Paramount	1947
Golden Girl, The	20th Century Fox	1951
Goldfinger	United Artists	1964
Goldmine in the Sky, A	Republic	1938
Goldwyn Follies, The	United Artists	1938
Gone With the Wind	M.G.M.	1939
Good Companions, The	Associated British	1956
Good News	M.G.M.	1930
	M.G.M.	1947
Good Time, The	Columbia	1967
Good, The Bad and the Ugly, The	United Artists	1966
Goodnight Vienna	Wilcox	1932
Grande Parade, The	R.K.O.	1929
Grease	Paramount	1978
Great American Broadcast, The	20th Century Fox	1941
Great Caruso, The	M.G.M.	1951
Great John L, The (see Man Called Sullivan, A)		
Great Schnozzle, The	United Artists	1934
Great Victor Herbert, The	Paramount	1939
Great Waltz, The	M.G.M.	1938
Great Ziegfeld, The	M.G.M.	1936
Greatest, The	Columbia	1977
Gullivers Travels	Paramount	1939
Guy Named Joe, A	M.G.M.	1944
Guys and Dolls	M.G.M.	195
Gypsy	Warner Brothers	1962
Hair	United Artists	1979
Half a Sixpence	Paramount	1967
Hallelujah I'm a Tramp	United Artists	1933
Hands Across the Border	Republic	1944
Hans Christian Andersen	R.K.O.	1952
Happy Anniversary	United Artists	1959
Happy Days	Fox	1930
Happy Ending, The	United Artists	1969
Happy Go Lucky	Paramount	1943
Hard Day's Night, A	United Artists	1964
Hard to Get	Warner Brothers	1938
Harlow	Paramount	1965
Harvey Girls, The	M.G.M.	1946

Has Anybody Seen My Gal	Universal	1952
Hats Off to Rhythm	Republic	1946
Have a Heart	M.G.M.	1934
Hawaii Calls	R.K.O.	1938
Head Over Heels	Gaumont British	1936
Heads Up	Paramount	1930
Heart of a Man, The	Rank	1959
Hearts Desire	B.I.P.	1935
Helen Morgan Story, The (see Both Ends of the Candle)		
Hello Beautiful	United Artists	1943
Hello Dolly	20th Century Fox	1969
Hello Everybody	Paramount	1933
Hello 'Frisco, Hello	20th Century Fox	1943
Hellzapoppin	Universal	1941
Help	United Artists	1965
Henriette (see Fete a Henriette, La)		
Her Highness and the Bellboy	M.G.M.	1945
Her Kind of Man	Warner Brothers	1946
Her Lucky Night	Universal	1945
Her Master's Voice	Paramount	1936
Here Come the Waves	Paramount	1944
Here Comes the Band	M.G.M.	1935
Here Comes the Groom	Paramount	1951
Here is my Heart	Paramount	1934
Here We Go 'Round the Mulberry Bush	United Artists	1967
Here's to Romance	20th Century Fox	1935
Hers to Hold	Universal	1943
Hey Boy, Hey Girl	Columbia	1959
Hi Beautiful	Universal	1944
Hi Good Lookin'	Universal	1944
Hi Neighbour	Republic	1942
High and the Mighty, The	Warner Brothers	1954
High Noon	United Artists	1952
High School Confidential	M.G.M.	1958
High Society	M.G.M.	1957
High Society Blues	Fox	1930
High Time	20th Century Fox	1960
High Wide and Handsome	Paramount	1937
Higher and Higher	R.K.O.	1943
His Butler's Sister	Universal	1943
Hit Parade	Republic	1937
Hit the Deck	R.K.O.	1929
	M.G.M.	1955
Hold on	M.G.M.	1966
Hold that Ghost	Universal	1941
Hole in the Head, A	United Artists	1959
Holiday Inn	Paramount	1942
Hollywood Canteen	Warner Brothers	1944
Hollywood Hotel	Warner Brothers	1938
Hollywood Party	M.G.M.	1934
Hollywood Revue	M.G.M.	1929
Holy Terror	Fox	1931
Honey	Paramount	1930

Honeychile	Republic	1951
Honeymoon Lodge	Universal	1943
Hoppity Goes to Town	Paramount-fleischer	1941
Hurricane, The	United Artists	1937
I Can't Give You Anything But Love, Baby	Universal	1940
I Could Go on Singing	United Artists	1963
I Dood it (see By Hook or By Crook)		
I Dream Too Much	R.K.O.	1935
I Love a Band Leader (see Memory For Two)		
I Married an Angel	M.G.M.	1942
I See Ice	Associated British	1938
I Thank You	Gaumont British	1941
I Wonder Who's Kissing Her Now	20th Century Fox	1947
I'd Rather Be Rich	United Artists	1964
I'll Be Seeing You	United Artists	1945
I'll Be Your Sweetheart	Gainsborough	1945
I'll Be Yours	Universal	1947
I'll Cry Tomorrow	M.G.M.	1957
I'll Get By	20th Century Fox	1950
I'll Remember April	Universal	1945
I'll See You in My Dreams	Warner Brothers	1952
I'll Take Romance	Columbia	1937
I'm Nobody's Sweetheart Now	Universal	1940
Ice Capades Revue	Republic	1942
Iceland	20th Century Fox	1942
Idaho	Republic	1943
Idiot's Delight	M.G.M.	1939
Idle on Parade	Warwick	1958
If I Had My Way	Universal	1940
If I'm Lucky	20th Century Fox	1946
If You Feel Like Singing	M.G.M.	1950
Illegal	Warner Brothers	1955
In Caliente	First National	1935
In Society	Universal	1944
In the Good Old Summertime	M.G.M.	1949
Incendiary Blonde	Paramount	1945
Indian Territory	Columbia	1950
Inn of the Sixth Happiness, The	20th Century Fox	1958
Innocents of Paris	Paramount	1929
Intermezzo (see Escape to Happiness)		
Irene	R.K.O.	1940
Irish Eyes are Smiling	20th Century Fox	1944
Is Everybody Happy?	Warner Brothers	1929
	Columbia	
Island in the Sun	20th Century Fox	1957
Istanbul	Universal	1957
It Happened at the World's Fair	M.G.M.	1962
It Happened in Brooklyn	M.G.M.	1947
It's a Date	Universal	1940
It's a Great Feeling	Warner Brothers	1949
It's a Great Life	M.G.M.	1929
It's Great to be Young	Associated British	1956
It's in the Air	A.B.F.D.	1938

It's Love Again	Gaumont British	1936
It's Magic	Warner Brothers	1948
It's Trad Dad	Columbia	1961
Italian Job, The	Paramount	1969
Jack Ahoy	Gaumont British	1934
Jack's the Boy	Gainsborough	1932
Jailhouse Rock	M.G.M.	1957
Jam Session	Columbia	1944
Jamboree	Warner Brothers	1957
James Dean Story	Warner Brothers	1957
Jaws	Universal	1975
Jazz Dance	Contemporary	1954
Jazz on a Summers Days	Galaxy	1959
Jazz Singer, The	Warner Brothers	1927
	Warner Brothers	1953
Jesus Christ, Superstar	Universal	1973
Joe Louis Story, The	United Artists	1953
John and Julie	British Lion	1955
Johnny Doughboy	Republic	1942
Johnny Guitar	Republic	1954
Joker is Wild, The	Paramount	1957
Jolson Sings Again	Columbia	1950
Jolson Story, The	Columbia	1947
Juke Girl, The	Warner Brothers	1942
Jumbo	M.G.M.	1962
Jungle Princess, The	Paramount	1936
Just For Fun	Columbia	1963
Just For You	Paramount	1952
Kansas City Kitty	Columbia	1944
Keep Your Seats Please	A.B.F.D.	1936
Kid From Spain, The	United Artists	1932
Kid Millions	United Artists	1934
King and I, The	20th Century Fox	1956
King Creole	Paramount	1958
King in New York, A	Attica	1957
King of Burlesque, The	20th Century Fox	1935
King of Jazz, The	Universal	1930
King of the Cowboys, The	Republic	1943
King Soloman's Mines	Gaumont British	1937
King Steps Out, The	Columbia	1936
King's Rhapsody	British Lion	1955
Kismet	M.G.M.	1955
Kiss Me Kate	M.G.M.	1953
Kiss the Boys Goodbye	Paramount	1941
Kiss Them For Me	20th Century Fox	1957
Kissin' Cousins	M.G.M.	1964
Kissing Bandit, The	M.G.M.	1948
Knickerbocker Holiday	United Artists	1944
Ladies Man, The	Paramount	1947
Lady be Good	M.G.M.	1941
Lady in the Dark, The	Paramount	1944
Lady on a Train, The	Universal	1945
Lady Sings the Blues	Paramount	1972

Las Vegas Nights (see Gay City, The)		
Las Vegas Story	R.K.O.	1952
Laughing Irish Eyes	Republic	1936
Laura	20th Century Fox	1944
Legions Last Patrol, The	Rank	1962
Let's Fall in Love	Columbia	1934
Let's Get Married	Eros	1959
Let's Make Love	20th Century Fox	1960
Let's Make Music	R.K.O.	1941
Let's Make Up (see Lilacs in the Spring)		
Let's Sing Again	R.K.O.	1936
Licence to Kill	U.I.P.	1989
Lied Einer Nacht (see Tell Me Tonight)		
Life of the Party, The	R.K.O.	1937
Lilacs in the Spring	Wilcox	1954
Lili	M.G.M.	1953
Lilian Russell	20th Century Fox	1940
Limelight	General	1936
	United Artists	1953
Lisbon	Republic	1956
Lisbon Story, The	Anglo-american	1946
Listen Darling	M.G.M.	1938
Little Boy Lost, The	Paramount	1953
Little Johnny Jones	First National	1929
Little Nellie Kelly	M.G.M.	1940
Live and Let Die	United Artists	1973
Living Daylights, The	United Artists	1987
Living it Up	Paramount	1954
London Town	Eagle-lion	1946
Looking For Love	M.G.M.	1964
Looking For the Silver Lining	Warner Brothers	1949
Lord Byron of Broadway	M.G.M.	1930
Lost Flight	Universal	1971
Louisiana Hayride	Columbia	1944
Louisiana Purchase	Paramount	1941
Love Affair	R.K.O.	1939
Love and Other Strangers	Cinerama	1970
Love Finds Andy Handy	M.G.M.	1938
Love Happy	United Artists	1950
Love, Honour and Behave	Warner Brothers	1938
Love in Bloom	Paramount	1935
Love in the Afternoon	Allied Artists	1957
Love in the Rough	M.G.M.	1930
Love is a Many Splendored Thing	20th Century Fox	1955
Love Letters	Paramount	1945
Love, Life and Laughter	A.B.F.D.	1934
Love Me or Leave Me	M.G.M.	1955
Love Me Tender	20th Century Fox	1956
Love Me Tonight	Paramount	1932
Love Parade, The	Paramount	1929
Love Story	Gainsborough	1958
	Paramount	1971
Love Thy Neighbour	Paramount	1940

Lovely to Look At	M.G.M.	1952
Lover Come Back	Universal	1946
Loving You	Paramount	1957
Lucky Boy	Tiffany-stahl	1929
Lucky Me	Warner Brothers	1954
Lullaby of Broadway	Warner Brothers	1951
M.A.S.H.	20th Century Fox	1972
Mad About Music	Universal	1938
Mad Dogs and Englishmen	M.G.M.	1970
Magic Christian, The	Commonwealth-United	1969
Magic Night, A (see Goodnight Vienna)		
Mahogany	Paramount	1975
Main Attraction, The	M.G.M.	1962
Make Believe Ballroom, The	Columbia	1949
Make Mine Music	R.K.O.	1946
Mammy	Warner Brothers	1930
Man Called Sullivan, A	United Artists	1945
Man Could Get Killed, A	Universal	1966
Man From Hong Kong, The	Golden Harvest	1975
Man From Laramie, The	Columbia	1955
Man From Music Mountain, The	Republic	1943
Man From Oklahoma, The	Republic	1945
Man From the Folies Bergere, The	20th Century Fox	1935
Man I Love, The	Warner Brothers	1947
Man In the White Suit, The	Universal	1952
Man on Fire	M.G.M.	1957
Man of La Mancha	United Artists	1972
Man Who Knew too Much, The	Paramount	1956
Man with the Golden Arm, The	United Artists	1955
Manhattan Merry-go-round (see Manhattan Music Box)		
Manhattan Music Box	Republic	1937
Margie	20th Century Fox	1946
Marianne	M.G.M.	1929
Marjorie Morningstar	Warner Brothers	1958
Mary Poppins	Disney	1964
Masquerade in Mexico	Paramount	1946
Maytime	M.G.M.	1937
Me and Marlborough	Gaumont British	1935
Me and My Girl	M.G.M.	1939
Meet Danny Wilson	Universal	1952
Meet Me in Las Vegas	M.G.M.	1956
Meet Me in St. Louis	M.G.M.	1944
Meet Miss Bobby Socks	Columbia	1944
Meet Mister Callaghan	Pinnacle	1954
Meet the People	M.G.M.	1944
Melba	United Artists	1953
Melody For Two	Warner Brothers	1937
Melody Lane	Universal	1929
Melody Time	Disney	1945
Memory For Two	Columbia	1945
Merry Widow, The	M.G.M.	1934
	M.G.M.	1952

Mexicali Rose	Republic	1939
Mexican Hayride	Universal	1948
Million Dollar Baby, A	Monogram	1935
Mississippi	Paramount	1935
Mister Bug Goes to Town (see Hoppity Goes to Town)		
Mister Dodd Takes to the Air	First National	1937
Mondo Cane	Times	1963
Monkey Business	Paramount	1931
Montana Moon	M.G.M.	1930
Monte Carlo	Paramount	1930
Moon Over Las Vegas	Universal	1944
Moon Over Miami	20th Century Fox	1941
Moonlight and Cactus	Universal	1944
Mother Wore Tights	20th Century Fox	1947
Moulin Rouge	United Artists	1934
	United Artists	1953
Move Over Darling	20th Century Fox	1963
Mule Train	Columbia	1950
Murder at the Vanities	Paramount	1934
Murder in the Music Hall	Republic	1946
Music Goes Round, The	Columbia	1936
Music in My Heart	Columbia	1939
Music in the Air	Fox	1934
Music Man, The	Warner Brothers	1962
My Blue Heaven	20th Century Fox	1950
My Dream is Yours	Warner Brothers	1949
My Fair Lady	Warner Brothers	1964
My Foolish Heart	R.K.O.	1950
My Gal Sal	20th Century Fox	1942
My Heart Goes Crazy (see London Town)		
My Man	Warner Brothers	1929
My Song Goes Around the World	Wardour	1934
Nancy Goes to Rio	M.G.M.	1940
Naughty Marietta	M.G.M.	1935
Naughty Nineties, The	Universal	1945
Near Rainbow's End	Tiffany-stahl	1930
Neptune's Daughter	M.G.M.	1949
Never Let Go	Rank	1960
Never on Sunday	United Artists	1960
Never Say Goodbye	Warner Brothers	1946
Never Too Young to Rock	G.T.O.	1975
New Faces	20th Century Fox	1954
New Faces of 1937	R.K.O.	1937
New Moon, The	M.G.M.	1930
	M.G.M.	1940
New York Town	Paramount	1941
New York, New York	United Artists	1977
Niagra	20th Century Fox	1953
Nice Girl	Universal	1941
Night and Day	Warner Brothers	1946
Night at the Opera, A	M.G.M.	1935
Night in Casablanca, A	United Artists	1946
Night is Young, The	M.G.M.	1935

Night Without Stars, A	R.K.O.	1953
No No Nanette	First National	1930
	R.K.O.	1940
No Trees in the Street	Warner-Pathe	1959
North to Alaska	20th Century Fox	1960
Nothing But the Truth	Paramount	1929
Now Voyager	Warner Brothers	1942
Off the Beaten Track	Universal	1942
Officer and a Gentleman, An	Paramount	1982
Oh You Beautiful Doll	20th Century Fox	1949
Oklahoma	20th Century Fox	1956
Old Barn Dance	Republic	1938
Oliver	Columbia	1968
On a Clear Day You Can See Forever	Paramount	1970
On an Island With You	M.G.M.	1948
On Moonlight Bay	Warner Brothers	1951
On Stage Everybody	Universal	1945
On the Avenue	20th Century Fox	1937
On the Riviera	20th Century Fox	1951
On the Town	M.G.M.	1949
On Wings of Song	Columbia	1935
On With the Show	Warner Brothers	1929
On Your Toes	First National	1939
One Hundred Men and a Girl	Universal	1937
One Minute to Zero	R.K.O.	1952
One Night of Love	Columbia	1934
One Sunday Afternoon	Warner Brothers	1949
One Touch of Venus	Universal	1950
Orchestra Wives	20th Century Fox	1942
Out of this World	Paramount	1945
Pagan, The	M.G.M.	1929
Pagan Love Song	M.G.M.	1929
Paint Your Wagon	Paramount	1969
Painting the Clouds With Sunshine	Warner Brothers	1951
Pajama Game, The	Warner Brothers	1957
Pal Joey	Columbia	1957
Paleface, The	Paramount	1948
Palooka (see Great Schnozzle, The)		
Pan-American	R.K.O.	1945
Panama Hattie	M.G.M.	1942
Pandora and the Flying Dutchman	M.G.M.	1952
Papa's Delicate Condition	Paramount	1963
Paramount on Parade	Paramount	1930
Parasites	First National	1929
Pardon My Rhythm	Universal	1944
Pardon My Sarong	Universal	1942
Parent Trap, The	Disney	1961
Paris	First National	1930
Paris Holiday	United Artists	1958
Paris Honeymoon	Paramount	1939
Paris Love Song	Paramount	1935
Passage to Marseilles	Warner Brothers	1944
Pat Garrett and Billy the Kid	M.G.M.	1973

Peg O' My Heart	M.G.M.	1933
Pennies From Heaven	Columbia	1936
Pepe	Columbia	1960
Perils of Pauline, The	Paramount	1947
Pete Kelly's Blues	Warner Brothers	1955
Peter Pan	R.K.O.	1953
Picnic	Columbia	1956
Picture of Dorian Gray, The	M.G.M.	1945
Pinocchio	R.K.O.	1940
Pirate, The	M.G.M.	1948
Play It Cool	Anglo-Amalgamated	1962
Playboy of Paris, The	Paramount	1930
Playmates	R.K.O.	1941
Poor Little Rich Girl	20th Century Fox	1936
Porgy and Bess	Columbia	1959
Postman Always Rings Twice, The	M.G.M.	1946
Powers Girl, The (see Hello Beautiful)		
Presenting Lily Mars	M.G.M.	1943
Priorities on Parade	Paramount	1942
Private Buckaroo	Universal	1942
Privilege	Universal	1967
Prize of Gold, The	Warwick	1954
Public Nuisance Number One	General	1936
Putting on the Ritz	United Artists	1930
Quadrophenia	Brent Walker	1979
Radio City Revels, The	R.K.O.	1938
Rain or Shine	Columbia	1930
Rainbow 'Round My Shoulder	Columbia	1952
Rainbow Man, The	Paramount	1929
Rainbow on the River	R.K.O.	1936
Rat Race, The	Paramount	1959
Razor's Edge, The	20th Century Fox	1947
Ready Willing and Able	Warner Brothers	1937
Rebecca of Sunnybrook Farm	20th Century Fox	1938
Red Headed Woman	M.G.M.	1932
Red Hot and Blue	Paramount	1949
Reveille With Beverly	Columbia	1943
Rhapsody in Blue	Warner Brothers	1945
Rhythm in the Clouds	Republic	1937
Rhythm on the Range	Paramount	1936
Rhythm on the River	Paramount	1940
Rhythm Parade	Monogram	1942
Rhythm Serenade	Columbia	1943
Rich, Young and Pretty	M.G.M.	1951
Ride 'Em Cowboy	Universal	1942
Ride Tenderfoot Ride	Republic	1940
Riders in the Sky	Columbia	1949
Riders of the Whistling Pines	Columbia	1949
Ridin' on a Rainbow	Republic	1941
Riding High	Paramount	1950
RIng of Fire	M.G.M.	1961
Ringside Maisie	M.G.M.	1941
Rio Rita	R.K.O.	1929

River of no Return, The	20th Century Fox	1954
Road House	20th Century Fox	1948
Road to Morocco, The	Paramount	1942
Road to Rio, The	Paramount	1947
Road to Singapore, The	Paramount	1940
Road to Utopia, The	Paramount	1946
Road to Zanzibar, The	Paramount	1941
Roberta	R.K.O.	1935
Rock a Bye Baby	Paramount	1958
Rock and Roll High School	New World	1979
Rock Around the Clock	Columbia	1956
Rock Rock Rock	Vanguard	1956
Rocky III	M.G.M./U.A.	1982
Rogue Song, The	M.G.M.	1930
Rolling in Money	Fox	1934
Roman Scandals	United Artists	1933
Romance and Rhythm	Warner Brothers	1938
Romance in the Dark	Paramount	1938
Romance on the High Seas (see It's Magic)		
Ronde, La	Curzon	1950
Rookies (see Buck Privates)		
Rosalie	M.G.M.	1937
Rose Marie	M.G.M.	1936
	M.G.M.	1954
Rose of Washington Square	20th Centruy Fox	1900
Royal Wedding (see Wedding Bells)		
Ruby Gentry	20th Century Fox	1952
Running Wild	Universal	1955
Sadie Mckee	M.g.m.	1934
Safety in Numbers	Paramount	1930
Sailors Three	A.B.F.D.	1940
Saint Louis Blues	Sack	1928
	Paramount	1958
Sally	First National	1929
Sally in Our Alley	Associated British Pathe	1931
Saludos Amigos	R.K.O.	1943
Samson and Delilah	Paramount	1951
San Antonio	Warner Brothers	1945
San Antonio Rose	Universal	1941
San Fernando Valley	Republic	1944
San Francisco	M.G.M.	1936
Sanders of the River	British Lion	1935
Sandpiper, The	M.G.M.	1965
Santa Fe Trail, The	First National	1940
Satchmo the Great	United Artists	1957
Saturday Night Fever	Paramount	1977
Say it With Music	British & Dominion	1932
Say it With Songs	Warner Brothers	1929
Sea Wife	20th Century Fox	1957
Second Chorus	Paramount	1941
Second Fiddle	20th Century Fox	1939
See Here Private Hargrove	M.G.M.	1944
Serenade	Warner Brothers	1956

Serious Charge	Eros	1958
Seven Brides For Seven Brothers	M.G.M.	1954
Seven Days Leave	R.K.O.	1942
Seven Hills of Rome, The	M.G.M.	1958
Seventh Heaven	20th Century Fox	1937
Shaft	M.G.M.	1971
Shall We Dance	R.K.O.	1937
Shane	Paramount	1953
She Loves Me Not	Paramount	1934
She Shall Have Music	Twickenham	1936
Shine on Harvest Moon	Warner Brothers	1944
Shipyard Sally	20th Century Fox	1939
Shiralee	M.G.M.	1957
Shocking Miss Pilgrim, The	20th Century Fox	1947
Shoot the Works	Paramount	1934
Shopworn Angel, The	Paramount	1929
Show Boat	Universal	1929
	Universal	1936
	M.G.M.	1951
Show Business	R.K.O.	1944
Show of Shows, The	Warner Brothers	1929
Sierra Sue	Republic	1941
Silk Stockings	M.G.M.	1957
Silver Dream Racer	Rank	1980
Silver Spurs	Republic	1943
Since You Went Away	United Artists	1944
Sincerely Yours	Warner Brothers	1955
Sing a Jingle	Universal	1944
Sing as We Go	A.B.F.D.	1934
Sing Baby Sing	20th Century Fox	1936
Sing Me a Love Song	First National	1936
Sing You Sinners	Paramount	1938
Sing Your Way Home	R.K.O.	1945
Singin' in the Rain	M.G.M.	1952
Singing Fool, The	Warner Brothers	1928
Singing Guns	Republic	1950
Singing Hill, The	Republic	1941
Sioux City Sue	Republic	1946
Sitting Pretty	Paramount	1933
Six Lessons From Madam La Zonga	Universal	1941
Six-Five Special	Anglo-Amalgamated	1958
Sky's the Limit, The	R.K.O.	1943
Slaughter Trail, The	R.K.O.	1951
Sleepy Lagoon	Republic	1943
Sleepy Time Gal	Republic	1942
Smart Girls Don't Talk	Warner Brothers	1948
Smiling Through	M.G.M	1941
Snow White and the Seven Dwarfs	R.K.O.	1938
So Dear to My Heart	R.K.O.	1948
So Long Letty	Warner Brothers	1929
Soldier Blue	Avco-Embassy	1970
Some Like it Hot	Paramount	1939
	United Artists	1959

Somebody Loves Me	Paramount	1952
Something in the Wind	Universal	1947
Something to Shout About	Columbia	1943
Song in My Heart	Fox	1930
Song is Born, A	R.K.O.	1948
Song of My Heart	Symphony	1947
Song of Norway, The	Cinerama	1970
Song of the Islands	20th Century Fox	1942
Song of the South	R.K.O.	1946
Sound of Music, The	20th Century Fox	1965
South of Dixie	Universal	1944
South Pacific	20th Century Fox	1958
Spetember Affair	Paramount	1951
Spring in Park Lane	British Lion	1949
Spring is Here	First National	1930
Spring Parade	Universal	1940
Springtime in the Rockies	20th Century Fox	1942
Spy Who Loved Me, The	United Artists	1977
Stage Door Canteen	United Artists	1943
Star	20th Century Fox	1968
Star is Born, A	Warner Brothers	1954
	Warner Brothers	1976
Star Maker, The	Paramount	1939
Star Spangled Rhythm	Paramount	1943
Star Wars	20th Century Fox	1977
Stardust on the Sage	Republic	1942
Starlift	Warner Brothers	1951
Stars on Broadway	Warner Brothers	1935
Stars on Parade	Columbia	1944
State Fair	20th Century Fox	1962
	20th Century Fox	1945
Step Lively	R.K.O.	1944
Stepping High	Film Booking Release	1928
Stooge, The	Paramount	1952
Stop the World - I Want to Get Off	Warner Brothers	1966
Stormy Weather	20th Century Fox	1943
Story of G.I. Joe, The	United Artists	1945
Story of Vernon & Irene Castle, The	R.K.O.	1939
Stowaway	20th Century Fox	1936
Strada, La	Curzon	1953
Strange Lady in Town	Warner Brothers	1955
Strange Laws	First National	1937
Strawberry Blonde, The	Warner Brothers	1941
Street Angel, The	Fox	1928
Streets of Laredo, The	Paramount	1949
Strictly Dishonourable	M.G.M.	1951
Strictly in the Groove	Universal	1942
Strike Up the Band	M.G.M.	1940
Strip, The	M.G.M.	1951
Stud, The	Brent Walker	1978
Student Prince, The	M.G.M.	1927
	M.G.M.	1954

Summer Holiday	M.G.M.	1948
	Warner-Pathé	1962
Summer Madness	London Films	1955
Summer of '42, The	Columbia-Warner	1971
Summer Place, A	Warner Brothers	1959
Summer Stock (see If You Feel Like Singing)		
Sun Also Rises, The	20th Century Fox	1957
Sun Valley Serenade	20th Century Fox	1941
Sunbonnet Sue	Monogram	1945
Sunburn	Hemdale	1979
Sunny	First National	1930
	R.K.O.	1941
Sunny Side of the Street, The	Columbia	1951
Sunny Side Up	Fox	1929
Sunset Boulevard	Paramount	1950
Sunshine Susie	Gainsborough	1932
Susan Slept Here	R.K.O.	1954
Suzy	M.G.M.	1936
Swanee River	20th Century Fox	1939
Sweater Girl, The	Paramount	1942
Sweden - Heaven and Hell	Embassy	1968
Sweet Adeline	Warner Brothers	1935
Sweet and Lowdown	20th Century Fox	1944
Sweet Charity	Universal	1969
Sweet Music	Warner Brothers	1935
Sweet Rosie O'Grady	20th Century Fox	1943
Sweetheart of Sigma Chi, The	Monogram	1946
Sweethearts	M.G.M.	1938
Sweethearts on Parade	Columbia	1930
Swing High, Swing Low	Paramount	1937
Swing in the Saddle	Columbia	1944
Swing Parade of 1946, The	Monogram	1946
Swing Teacher Swing	Paramount	1938
Swing Time	R.K.O.	1936
Swingtime Johnny	Universal	1944
Syncopation	Paramount	1929
	R.K.O.	1942
Take a Chance	Paramount	1933
Take Me Back to Oklahoma	Monogram	1940
Take Me Out to the Ball Game (see Everybody's Cheering)		
Tammy and the Bachelor	Universal	1957
Task Force	Warner Brothers	1949
Tea For Two	Warner Brothers	1950
Tell Me Tonight	Cine-Allianz	1932
Ten Cents a Dance	Columbia	1945
Ten Thousand Bedrooms	M.G.M.	1957
Tender Trap, The	M.G.M.	1955
Thank Your Lucky Stars	Warner Brothers	1943
Thanks a Million	20th Century Fox	1935
Thanks For the Memory	Paramount	1938
That Certain Age	Universal	1938
That Certain Feeling	Paramount	1956
That Dangerous Age	British Lion	1949

That Midnight Kiss	M.G.M.	1949
That Night in Rio	20th Century Fox	1941
That Summer	Columbia-Warner	1979
That Wonderful Urge	20th Century Fox	1949
That's a Good Girl	United Artists	1934
That's Right, You're Wrong	R.K.O.	1939
That's the Spirit	Universal	1945
There's No Business Like Show Business	20th Century Fox	1954
Things are Looking Up	Gaumont British	1934
Third Man, The	London Films	1949
Thirty Seconds Over Tokyo	M.G.M.	1945
This Could be the Night	M.G.M.	1957
This is the Army	Warner Brothers	1943
This is the Life	Universal	1944
This Time For Keeps	M.G.M.	1947
This Week of Grace	R.K.O.	1933
This'll Make You Whistle	Wilcox	1939
Thomas Crown Affair, The	United Artists	1968
Thoroughly Modern Millie	Universal	1967
Those Red Heads From Seattle	Paramount	1953
Thousands Cheer	M.G.M.	1944
Three Caballeros, The	R.K.O.	1944
Three Coins in a Fountain	20th Century Fox	1954
Three For the Show	Columbia	1955
Three Litle Pigs, The	Disney	1933
Three Little Girls in Blue	20th Century Fox	1946
Three Little Words	M.G.M.	1950
Three Smart Girls Grow Up	Universal	1939
Thrill of a Romance, The	M.G.M.	1945
Till the Clouds Roll By	M.G.M.	1946
Till the End of Time	R.K.O.	1946
Time, the Place and the Girl, The	Warner Brothers	1929
	Warner Brothers	1946
Times Square	Columbia-E.M.I.-Warner	1980
Times Square Lady, The	M.G.M.	1935
Tin Pan Alley	20th Century Fox	1940
To Have and Have Not	Warner Brothers	1945
To Mary With Love	20th Century Fox	1936
To The Victor	Warner Brothers	1948
Toast of New Orleans, The	M.G.M.	1950
Toast of New York, The	R.K.O.	1937
Tommy - a Rock Opera	Hemdale	1975
Tommy Steele Story, The	Anglo-Amalgamated	1957
Tommy the Toreador	Fanfare	1959
Too Many Girls	R.K.O.	1940
Too Much Harmony	Paramount	1933
Too Young to Know	Warner Brothers	1945
Top Gun	United Artists	1986
Top Hat	R.K.O.	1935
Top of the Town	Universal	1937
Torch Song, The	M.G.M.	1953
Trail of the Lonesome Pine, The	Paramount	1936
Transatlantic Merry-Go-Round	M.G.M.	1934

Trespasser, The	United Artists	1929
Trocadero	Republic	1944
Trouble in Store	Two Cities	1953
True to Life	Paramount	1943
Tumbling Tumbleweeds	Republic	1935
Twenty Million Sweethearts	Warner Brothers	1934
Two For Tonight	Paramount	1935
Two Girls and a Sailor	M.G.M.	1944
Two Guys From Milwaukee	Warner Brothers	1946
Two Hearts in Waltz Time	Associated Cinemas	1930
Two Latins From Manhattan	Columbia	1941
Two Little Bears	20th Century Fox	1961
Two Tickets to Broadway	R.K.O.	1951
Two Weeks with Love	M.G.M.	1950
Unchained	Warner Brothers	1955
Under the Clock	M.G.M.	1945
Under Water	R.K.O.	1955
Uninvited, The	Paramount	1944
Up in Arms	R.K.O.	1944
Up in Central Park	Universal	1948
Uptight	Paramount	1968
Vagabond King, The	Paramount	1930
	Paramount	1956
Vagabond Lover, The	R.K.O.	1929
Variety Jubilee	Butcher	1943
Varsity Show, The	Warner Brothers	1937
Vienese Nights	Warner Brothers	1930
View to a Kill, A	United Artists	1985
Vogues of 1938	United Artists	1937
Wabash Avenue	20th Century Fox	1950
Waikiki Wedding	Paramount	1937
Wait Till the Sun Shines Nellie	20th Century Fox	1952
Wake Up and Dream	20th Century Fox	1946
Wake Up and Live	20th Century Fox	1937
Wall, The		1979
Wallflower	Warner Brothers	1948
Watership Down	C.I.C.	1978
Way Out West	M.G.M.	1937
Way to the Stars, The	Two Cities	1945
Way We Were, The	Columbia-Warner	1973
We're Going to be Rich	20th Century Fox	1938
We're Not Dressing	Paramount	1934
Weary River	First National	1929
Wedding Bells	M.G.M.	1951
Weekend in Havana, A	20th Century Fox	1941
Weekend Pass	Universal	1944
Welcome Stranger	Paramount	1947
West of Zanzibar	Universal	1954
West Point Story, The (see Fine and Dandy)		
West Side Story	United Artists	1961
Wet Blanket Policy, The	United Artists	1948
Wharf Angel, The	Paramount	1934
What a Whopper	Viscount	1961

What Did You do in the War Daddy	United Artists	1966
What Lola Wants	Warner Brothers	1958
What's Cooking	Universal	1942
What's New Pussycat	United Artists	1965
When Johnny Comes Marching Home	Universal	1943
When My Baby Smiles at Me	20th Century Fox	1948
When Willie Comes Marching Home	20th Century Fox	1950
When You're in Love	Columbia	1937
Where the Boys Are	M.G.M.	1960
Where's Charley	Warner Brothers	1952
While I Live	20th Century Fox	1947
White Christmas	Paramount	1954
Who Done It	Universal	1942
Whoopee	United Artists	1930
Wicked Lady, The	Universal	1946
Wild Blue Yonder, The	Republic	1951
Wild in the Country	20th Century Fox	1961
Winged Victory	20th Century Fox	1944
Wings of the Navy, The	Warner Brothers	1939
With a Song in My Heart	20th Century Fox	1952
Wizard of Oz, The	M.G.M.	1939
Woman Commands, A	M.G.M.	1932
Woman in Love		1984
Wonder Bar	Warner Brothers	1934
Wonderful Life, A	Warner-Pathé	1964
Woodstock	Warner Brothers	1970
Words and Music	M.G.M.	1948
World is Full of Married Men, The	New Realm	1979
Written on the Wind	Universal	1957
Xanadu	Universal	1980
Yankee Doddle Dandy	Warner Brothers	1943
Yankee in King Arthur's Court, A	Paramount	1949
Yellow Submarine	United Artists	1968
Yes Giorgio	M.G.M.	1982
Yes Mister Brown	Gaumont British	1932
Yokel Boy, The	Republic	1942
You Are What You Eat	Commonwealth-United	1968
You Belong to My Heart	M.G.M.	1951
You Came Along	Paramount	1945
You Can't Have Everything	20th Century Fox	1937
You Light Up My Life	Columbia	1977
You Only Live Twice	United Artists	1967
You Were Meant For Me	20th Century Fox	1948
You Were Never Lovlier	Columbia	1942
You'll Find Out	R.K.O.	1940
You're a Sweetheart	Universal	1937
You're My Everything	20th Century Fox	1949
You're Never too Young	Paramount	1955
Young at Heart	Warner Brothers	1955
Young Eagles	Paramount	1030
Young Man of Music, A	Warner Brothers	1950
Young Ones, The	Warner-Pathé	1961
Youth on Parade	Republic	1942

CHRONOLOGICAL SECTION

This section lists all the songs by year. Starting with 1813, each year shows all the songs which first became popular during that year, in alphabetical order.

1813
Last Rose Of Summer

1856
Darling Nellie Gray

1861
Alice Where Art Thou?

1862
Killarny

1866
When You And I Were Young, Maggie

1868
Come Back To Erin

1869
Sweet Genevieve

1873
Eileen Alanna

1874
Silver Threads Among The Gold

1876
Grandfather's Clock

1877
In The Gloaming
Lost Chord, The

1880
Stephanie Gavotte, The

1881
Old Brigade, The

1884
Her Golden Hair Was Hanging Down Her Back
Love's Old Sweet Song

1889
Ask A Policeman
Little Annie Rooney
Oh Promise Me

1890
Comrades
Passing By
Where Did You Get That Hat

1891
Maggie Murphy's Home
Miner's Dream Of Home, The
Narcissus

Old Rustic Bridge By The Mill
Wot Cher

1892
Bowery, The
Daddy Wouldn't Buy Me A Bow-wow
Future Mrs 'awkins, The
Holy City, The
Man Who Broke The Bank At Monte Carlo, The
My Sweetheart's The Man In The Moon
Ta-ra-ra-boom-der-e

1893
After The Ball
Daisy Bell
Down The Road (Away Went Polly)
My Old Dutch
Oh Mr Porter
Say 'au Revoir' But Not 'goodbye'
Volunteer Organist, The

1894
At Trinity Church
I Don't Want To Play In Your Yard
If It Wasn't For The 'ouses In Between
Molly O!
Sidewalks Of New York, The
Two Little Girls In Blue

1895
Algy The Piccadilly Johnny
Band Played On, The
It's A Great Big Shame
She Was One Of The Early Birds
Soldiers Of The Queen
When The Summer Comes Again (Three Pots A Shilling)

1896
Amorous Goldfish, The
Beer, Beer, Glorious Beer
Chin Chin Chinaman
Chon Kina
El Capitan March
Sweet Rosie O'Grady
There'll Be A Hot Time In The Old Town Tonight
To A Wild Rose

1897
Asleep In The Deep
At A Georgia Camp Meeting
Beautiful Isle Of Somewhere, The
Break The News To Mother
Little Dolly Daydream
Our Lodger's Such A Nice Young Man
Sons Of The Sea
Stars And Stripes Forever, The

1898
For Old Times' Sake
Gipsy Love Song, The

Lily Of Laguna
Little Bit Off The Top, A
Romany Life
Rosary, The
She Is The Belle Of New York
Soldiers In The Park, The
Teach Me How To Kiss
They All Follow Me
When You Were Sweet Sixteen
Why Did I Leave My Little Back Room
Wine, Woman and Song

1899
Bird In a Gilded Cage, A
Hands Across The Sea
Hearts And Flowers
Hello Ma Baby
I'll Be Your Sweetheart
Maple Leaf Rag
My Wild Irish Rose
On The Banks of The Wabash
What Ho She Bumps
Whistling Rufus

1900
Goodbye Dolly Gray
I Want To Be A Military Man
Nirvana
Shade Of The Palm, The
Tell Me Pretty Maiden

1901
Blaze Away
Honeysuckle And The Bee, The
I Know Of Two Bright Eyes
Just A-wearyin' For You
Liza Johnson
Mighty Lak' A Rose
My Castle On The Nile
O Dry Those Tears

1902
Because
English Rose
Following In Father's Footsteps
I Live In Trafalgar Square
I May Be Crazy
In The Good Old Summertime
Just Like The Ivy
Land Of Hope And Glory
Melisands In The Wood
Try Again Johnnie
Under The Bamboo Tree
Under The Deodar
Where The Sunset Turns The Ocean's Blue To Gold
Won't You Come Home Bill Bailey
Yeoman Of England, The

1903
Down At The Old Bull And Bush (Under The Anheuser Bush)
I Know A Lovely Garden

Little Yellow Bird
March Of The Toys, The
Mother O' Mine
On A Sunday Afternoon
Picture No Artist Can Paint, A
Sweet Adeline
Thou Art My Rose
Toyland
Wine Of France

1904

Bluebell
Cigarette
Czardas
Garden Of Love, The
Give My Regards To Broadway
Gold And Silver Waltz, The
It's All Right In The Summertime
Kashmiri Love Song (from The Four
Indian Love Lyrics)
Mattinata ('Tis The Day)
Meet Me In St. Louis
My Ain Folk
My Dear Little Cingalee
Pearl Of Sweet Ceylon, The
Stop Your Tickling Jock
Swing Song
Teasing
Trumpeter, The
We All Walked Into The Shop
Yankee Doodle Boy

1905

Glorious Devon
I Don't Care
I Love A Lassie
I Wouldn't Leave My Little Wooden Hut
For You
If Those Lips Could Only Speak
In My Merry Oldsmobile
In The Shade Of The Old Apple Tree
Mary's A Grand Old Name
My Irish Molly-o
Nellie Dean
Sea Weed
She Is Ma Daisy
So Long Mary
Thora
Valeta
Wait Till The Sun Shines Nellie
Weymouth Chimes, The
Where The River Shannon Flows
Whistler And His Dog, The

1906

At Dawning
Billy Muggins
By The Side Of The Zuyder Zee
Don't Go In The Lions' Cage Tonight
Galloping Major, The
He's A Cousin Of Mine
I Just Can't Make My Eyes Behave
I Love You Truly
I Mean To Marry A Man
I Want What I Want When I Want It
Kiss Me Again

Little Bird On Nellie's Hat, The
Love Me And The World Is Mine
My Gal Sal
Poor John
Somewhere The Sun Is Shining
Waiting At The Church
Waltz Me Round Again Willie
We Parted On The Shore
What A Mouth
What's The Use Of Dreaming
When There Isn't A Girl About
Will You Love Me In December (As You
Do In May)

1907

Anchors Aweigh
Flying Dutchman, The
Glow Worm, The (Glühwünchen)
Golliwog's Cake Walk
Harrigan
High Society
Hobnailed Boots That Farver Wore, The
I Love You So (The Merry Widow Waltz)
I'm Afraid To Come Home In The Dark
Jolly Good Luck To The Girl Who Loves
A Soldier
Lighterman Tom
Maxim's
May Morning, A
Meet Me Jenny When The Sun Goes
Down
My Little Dietcher Girl
On The Road To Mandalay
Preacher And The Bear
Put Me Among The Girls
Red Wing
Rose In The Bud
School Days
She's A Lassie From Lancashire
Sussex By The Sea
Teddy Bear's Picnic, The
Vilia

1908

Boston Two Step
Call Round Any Old Time
Chip Off The Old Block
Down In Jungle Town
I Hear You Calling Me
I Wish I Had A Girl
In The Garden Of My Heart
In The Twi-twi-twilight
My Girl's A Yorkshire Girl
My Hero
Now I Have To Call Him Father
Oh Oh Antonio
She Sells Sea Shells
Shine On Harvest Moon
Sunbonnet Sue
Take Me Out To The Ball Game
Waltz Dream, The
Wedding O' Sandy McNab
Yama Yama Man, The
Yip I Addy Ay

1909

Arcady Is Ever Young
Archibald, Certainly Not
Beautiful Garden Of Roses, A
Boiled Beef And Carrots
By The Light Of The Silvery Moon
Cuddle Up A Little Closer
Dollar Princesses
For You Alone
Has Anybody Here Seen Kelly
I Do Like To Be Beside The Seaside
I Used To Sigh For The Silvery Moon
I Wonder Who's Kissing Her Now
If I Should Plant A Tiny Seed Of Love
La Golondrina (The Swallow)
Let's All Go Down The Strand
Letter Song, The
Little Shirt My Mother Made For Me
Meet Me Tonight In Dreamland
Molly O'Morgan
Moonstruck
My Dream Of Love
Nora Malone (Call Me By Phone)
Oh! I Must Go Home Tonight
Pipes Of Pan, The
Put On Your Old Gray Bonnet
Ship Ahoy
Sink Red Sun
Temptation Rag
When Father Papered The Parlour
Where My Caravan Has Rested
Yiddle On Your Fiddle
You Taught Me How To Love

1910

Ah Sweet Mystery Of Life
Caprice Viennois
Captain Gingah
Chinatown My Chinatown
Ciribiribin
Come Josephine In My Flying Machine
Come To The Ball
Don't Go Down The Mine Dad
Down By The Old Mill Stream
Every Little Movement
Fall In And Follow Me
Flanagan
Ginger You're Barmy
I Want To Sing In Opera
I'd Love To Live In Loveland With A Girl
Like You
I'm Falling In Love With Someone
I'm Henery The Eighth
I'm Shy, Mary Ellen I'm Shy
In The Shadows
Italian Street Song
Josh-u-ah
Let Me Call You Sweetheart
Mifanwy
Mother Machree
Mountains Of Mourne
'neath The Southern Moon
On Mobile Bay
Perfect Day, A
Play That Barbershop Chord
Put On Your Tat-ta Little Girlie
Put Your Arms Around Me Honey

Silver Bell
Some Of These Days
Steamboat Bill
Tony From America
Tramp, Tramp, Tramp Along The Highway
When I Take My Morning Promenade

1911

Alexander's Ragtime Band
All Alone
Any Old Iron
Black And White Rag
Do You Remember The Last Waltz
Down Home Rag
Everybody's Doing It
Floral Dance, The
Gaby Glide, The
Gipsy Maiden
I'm Twenty-One Today
I've Got Rings On My Fingers
In Summertime On Bredon
Just A Wee Deoch An' Doris
Little Grey Home In The West
Love And Wine
Macushla
My Message
Oh You Beautiful Doll
Photo Of The Girl I Left Behind, The
Pierette & Pierrot
Policeman's Holiday, The
Roamin' In The Gloamin'
Rose Of My Heart
Say Not Love Is A Dream
Somewhere A Voice Is Calling
Spaniard That Blighted My Life, The
Stein Song, The
Temple Bell, The
That Mysterious Rag
Till The Sands Of The Desert Grow Cold
To The Land Of My Own Romance
Until
We All Go The Same Way Home

1912

Are We To Part Like This
At Santa Barbara
Be My Comrade True
Casey Jones
Chicken Reel, The
Come Down Ma Evening Star
Danny Boy
Giannina Mia
Hail Caledonia
Here's To Love
Hitchy-Koo
I Love The Moon
I Want To Be In Dixie
I'm The Lonesomest Gal In Town
It's A Bit Of A Ruin That Cromwell Knocked About A Bit
It's A Long Way To Tipperary
Kitty The Telephone Girl
Little Love, A Little Kiss, A (Un Peu D'amour)
Moonlight Bay
My Beautiful Lady

My Melancholy Baby
Nights Of Gladness
Phil The Fluter's Ball
Polly Perkins Of Paddington Green
Ragtime Cowboy Joe
Rose Of Tralee, The
Row, Row, Row
Sweetheart Of Sigma Chi
They All Walk The Wibbly Wobbly Walk
Wedding Glide, The
When I Lost You
When Irish Eyes Are Smiling
When It's Apple Blossom Time In Normandy
When The Midnight Choo-Choo Leaves For Alabam'
When You Are In Love
Whispering Hope
Who Were You With Last Night
You're My Baby

1913

Ballin' The Jack
Blind Ploughman, The
Destiny Waltz
Fat Li'l' Feller Wid His Mammy's Eyes
Friend O' Mine
Get Out And Get Under
Goodbye Summer, So Long Fall, Hello Wintertime
Hold Your Hand Out Naughty Boy
I Love The Name Of Mary
If I Had My Way
International Rag
It's Nice To Get Up In The Morning
Memphis Blues
Peg O' My Heart
Sailing Down Chesapeake Bay
Shipmates O' Mine
Snooky Ookums
Sunshine Of Your Smile, The
There's A Long Long Trail
Trail Of The Lonesome Pine
Venus Waltz
Waiting For The Robert E. Lee
When A Man Comes Knocking At Your Heart
When You're All Dressed Up And No Place To Go
You Made Me Love You

1914

Aba Daba Honeymoon
All Aboard For Dixieland
All Pals Together
Are We Downhearted? No!
Army of Today's Alright, The
By Heck
By The Beautiful Sea
Can't You Hear Me Calling Caroline
Curse of An Aching Heart
End of My Old Cigar, The
Gilbert The Filbert
He's A Rag Picker
Hello, Hello, Who's Your Lady Friend
Here We Are, Here We Are, Here We Are Again
I Want To Go Back To Michigan

I Was A Good Little Girl Till I Met You
I Wonder If Love Is A Dream
I'll Make A Man Of You
I'll Take You Home Again Kathleen
In An Old Fashioned Town
Love's Garden Of Roses
Mate O' Mine
My Croony Melody
O Flower Divine
On The Five-Fifteen
Saint Louis Blues
Sing Joyous Bird
Sister Susie's Sewing Shirts For Soldiers
Sweethearts
Sylvia
There's A Girl In The Heart Of Maryland
They Didn't Believe Me
Too-ra-loo-ra-loo-ral
When It's Night Time In Dixieland
When The Angelus Is Ringing
When We've Wound Up The Watch On The Rhine
When You're A Long Long Way From Home
When You're Away
Wonderful Eyes
You Can't Get Many Pimples On A Pound Of Pickled Pork
You're Here And I'm Here
Your King And Country Want You

1915

Alabama Jubilee
All For You
Araby
Are You From Dixie
At The Foxtrot Ball
Back Home In Tennessee
Broken Doll
Burlington Bertie From Bow
Can It Be Love
Canadian Capers
Down Among The Sheltering Palms
Everybody's Crazy On The Foxtrot
Goodbye Virginia
Hello Frisco Hello
Hello Hawaii, How Are You
Hors D'oeuvres
Keep The Home Fires Burning
Little Bit Of Heaven, A
Little Of What You Fancy, A
Love Here Is My Heart (Mon Coeur Est Pour Toi)
M-O-T-H-E-R
Memories
Nola
Pack Up Your Troubles In Your Old Kit Bag
Paper Doll
Play A Simple Melody
Thank God For A Garden
Toy Town
Underneath The Stars
Violin Song, The
We'll Have A Jubilee In My Old Kentucky Home
When I Leave The World Behind

1916

Another Little Drink Wouldn't Do Us Any Harm
Any Time's Kissing Time
Arizona
Auf Wiederseh'n
Blue Eyes
Bohemia
Cobbler's Song, The
Cumparsita, La
Every Little While
Girl On The Magazine Cover, The
Good Morning Brother Sunshine
I Can't Do My Bally Bottom Button Up
I Love A Piano
If You Were The Only Girl In The World
Ireland Must Be Heaven For My Mother Came From There
It Is Only A Tiny Garden
Oh How She Could Yacki Hacki Wicki Wacki Woo
Poor Butterfly
Pretty Baby
Robber's Chorus
Roses Of Picardy
Something Seems Tingle-Ingle-Ing
Take Me Back To Dear Old Blighty
There's A Little Bit Of Bad In Every Good Little Girl
They're Wearing 'em Higher In Hawaii
Wait
What Do You Want To Make Those Eyes At Me For
When You Wore A Tulip
Where Did Robinson Crusoe Go With Friday On Saturday Night

1917

All The World Will Be Jealous Of Me
Allah's Holiday
Bachelor Gay, A
Beale Street Blues
Bells Of St. Mary's, The
Come To The Fair
Darktown Strutters Ball, The
Delilah
For Me And My Gal
Give Me The Moonlight
Good Bye-ee
Hawaiian Butterfly
Hello My Dearie
Homing
Indiana
Let The Great Big World Keep Turning
Little Miss Melody
Livery Stable Blues
Love Will Find A Way
McNamara's Band
Melody Of Love
M.I.S.S.I.S.S.I.P.P.I.
Oh It's A Lovely War
Oh! Johnny Oh!
On The Good Ship Yacki Hicki Doo La
Original Dixieland One-step
Paddy McGinty's Goat
Paradise For Two, A
Sympathy

There Are Fairies At The Bottom Of Our Garden
Thine Alone
Tickle Toe, The
Until We Meet Again
When You Look In The Heart Of A Rose
Where The Black Eyed Susans Grow
Where The Morning Glories Grow
Whisper To Me
Why Am I Always The Bridesmaid
Wild, Wild Women Are Making A Wild Man Out Of Me, The
Will You Remember (Sweetheart)
Yacka Hula Hickey Dula

1918

After You've Gone
Beautiful Ohio
Dear Old Pal Of Mine
First Love, Last Love, Best Love
Give Me A Little Cosy Corner
Going Up
Good Man Is Hard To Find, A
Heart Of A Rose
Hindustan
I Don't Want To Get Well
I Want A Girl Just Like The Girl That Married Dear Old Dad
I'm Sorry I Made You Cry
If You Could Care For Me
In A Monastery Garden
K-k-k-katy
Lilac Domino, The
Ma Blushin' Rosie
Madelon (Quand Madelon)
Mammy's Little Coal Black Rose
Missouri Waltz, The
Oh How I Hate To Get Up In The Morning
On The Level You're A Little Devil
Over There
Rock-a-bye Your Baby With A Dixie Melody
Russian Rag
Shim-Me-Sha-Wabble
Smiles
Smilin' Through
Some Sunday Morning
Somewhere In France With You
Sunrise And You
They Go Wild Simply Wild Over Me
They Were All Out Of Step But Jim
Till We Meet Again

1919

'N' Everything
And He'd Say "Oo-La-La Wee-wee"
At The Jazz Band Ball
Baby Won't You Please Come Home
Be My Little Baby Bumble Bee
Blues My Naughty Sweetie Gave To Me, The
By The Campfire
By The Waters Of Minnetonka
Country Gardens
Dardanella
Don't Dilly Dally On The Way
Everything Is Peaches Down In Georgia

How Ya Gonna Keep 'em Down On The Farm
I Ain't Gonna Give Nobody None O'This Jelly Roll
I'll Say She Does
I'm Always Chasing Rainbows
I'm Forever Blowing Bubbles
I've Got The Sweetest Girl In Maryland
In The Land Of Beginning Again
Indianola
Ja-da
Just Like A Gipsy
Let The Rest Of The World Go By
Love Sends A Little Gift Of Roses
Mademoiselle From Armentieres
Mammy O'Mine
Mandy (Berlin)
Maxina
My Isle Of Golden Dreams
Oh By Jingo, Oh By Gee
Oh How I Laugh When I Think How I Cried About You
Omaha
On The Beach At Waikiki
Philomel
Pretty Girl Is Like A Melody, A
Rose Room
Royal Garden Blues
Sanctuary
Sand Dunes
Someone Else May Be There When I'm Gone
Swanee
Tell Me
That Old Fashioned Mother Of Mine
Tiger Rag
Till The Clouds Roll By
Your Eyes Have Told Me So

1920

Abie My Boy
Alabama Moon
Alice Blue Gown
Avalon
Chong (He Come From Hong Kong)
El Relicario
I Belong To Glasgow
I Know Where The Flies Go In Wintertime
I'll Be With You In Apple Blossom Time
I've Got My Captain Working For Me Now
If You're Irish Come Into The Parlour
Indian Summer
Irene
Japanese Sandman
Left All Alone Again Blues
Mary
Mystery
Nobody Knows
Oh What A Pal Was Mary
Oh!
On Miami Shore
Pale Moon
Rose Of Washington Square
So Long, Oo-long (How Long You Gonna Be Gone)
Some Day Sweetheart

Sweet And Low
Tell Me Little Gipsy
That Naughty Waltz
Trees
Vamp, The
Venetian Moon
When The Harvest Moon Is Shining
Whispering
Wyoming
Wyoming Lullaby
You Ain't Heard Nothing Yet
You'd Be Surprised

1921

After You Get What You Want, You Don't Want It
Ain't We Got Fun
All By Myself
Amazon (River Of Dreams)
And Her Mother Came Too
Anytime, Anyday, Anywhere
Bright Eyes (Smith, Motzan, Jerome)
Broadway Rose
Cherie
Chili Bean
Chinaman's Song, The
Coal Black Mammy
Crooning
Dancing Time
Dapper Dan
Dear Love My Love
Do You Ever Think Of Me
Down Yonder
Feather Your Nest
Fishermen Of England, The
Goodnight (I'm Only A Strolling Vagabond)
Humming
I Might Be Your Once In A While
I Never Knew (I Could Love Anybody)
I Pitch My Lonely Caravan At Night
I Used To Love You (But It's All Over Now)
I'd Love To Fall Asleep And Wake Up In My Mammy's Arms
I'll See You In C-u-b-a
I'm Nobody's Baby
Ilo - A Voice From Mummy Land
In A Persian Market
Jazz Me Blues
Look For The Silver Lining
Love Nest
Margie
Mazie
Mello Cello
Moonlight
My Mammy
My Man (Mon Homme)
My Sunny Tennessee
Ours Is A Nice 'Ouse Ours Is
Palesteena
Playthings
Rose
Rosie (Make It Rosy For Me)
Salome
San
Singin' The Blues (Till My Daddy Comes Home)

Twelfth Street Rag
Vamping Rose
Wang Wang Blues, The
When My Baby Smiles At Me
Whip-Poor-Will
Whose Baby Are You
Wild Rose
Young Man's Fancy

1922

Amour Toujours L'Amour, L' (Love Everlasting)
Angel Child
April Showers
Bandana Days
Bimini Bay
Blue
Breeze (Blow My Baby Back To Me)
Brown Bird Singing, A
Bullfrog Patrol, The
Careless Love
Chicago (That Toddlin' Town)
Dear Old Southland
Everybody Step
Georgette
Hiawatha's Melody Of Love
Hot Lips
I Want Some Money
I'm Just Wild About Harry
If Winter Comes
Just For A While (Nur Eine Nacht)
Kalua
Kitten On The Keys
Leave Me With A Smile
Limehouse Blues
Ma! He's Making Eyes At Me
My Honey's Lovin' Arms
My Word You Do Look Queer
Nobody Lied (When They Said That I Cried Over You)
Oh Star Of Eve
On The Alamo
Parade Of The Wooden Soldiers
Peggy O'Neil
Please Do It Again
Robinson Crusoe's Isle
Sally, You Brought The Sunshine To Our Alley
Say It With Music
Second Hand Rose
Sheik Of Araby, The
Shufflin' Along
Some Sunny Day
Song Of Love
Stumbling
Swanee River Moon
T'aint Nobody's Bizness If I Do
Three O'clock In The Morning
Under The Lilac Bough
Wabash Blues
Wana (When I Wana, You No Wana)
Weeping Willow Lane
When Buddha Smiles
When Shall We Meet Again
When The Sun Goes Down
Why Waste Your Tears
Wimmin (I Gotta Have 'em That's All)
World Is Waiting For The Sunrise, The

1923

Aggravatin' Papa
Aunt Hagar's Blues
Barney Google
Beside A Babbling Brook
By The Shalimar
Carolina In The Morning
Cat's Whiskers, The
China Boy
Cielito Lindo
Cut Yourself A Piece Of Cake (And Make Yourself At Home)
Dirty Hands, Dirty Face
Estrellita
Farewell Blues
Fate
Golden Song, The
Homesick
House Of David Blues, The
I Ain't Nobody's Darling
I Cried For You
I Love Me
I Wish I Could Shimmy Like My Sister Kate
I'll Build A Stairway To Paradise
I'm Tickled To Death I'm Single
Just A Girl That Men Forget
Just Like A Thief
Kiss In The Dark, A
Lady Of The Evening
Last Night On The Back Porch
Little Nellie Kelly I Love You
Love Me Now
Maggie! Yes Ma?
Marchéta
Mister Gallagher And Mister Shean
Moon Love
My Buddy
(My Sweet) Hortense
My Sweetie Went Away
Oh Boy, What Joy We Had In Barefoot Days
Red Moon
Rose Of The Rio Grande
Runnin' Wild
Saw Mill River Road, The
Say It While Dancing
Shores Of Minnetonka
Song Of India
Sweet Indiana Home
Swingin' Down The Lane
That Red Head Gal
Toot Toot Tootsie Goodbye
Underneath The Mellow Moon
Until My Luck Comes Rolling Along
Way Down Yonder In New Orleans
When Hearts Are Young
When June Comes Along With A Song
When The Leaves Come Tumbling Down
Who Cares
Who's Sorry Now
Wonderful One
Yes We Have No Bananas
You Remind Me Of My Mother
You've Got To See Mama Every Night

1924

(Home In) Pasadena
After The Storm
Any Way The Wind Blows
Bells Across The Meadow
Bugle Call Rag
California Here I Come
Charley My Boy
Chili Bom Bom
Christopher Robin At Buckingham Palace
Don't Bring Me Posies (When It's Shoesies That I Need)
Don't Mind The Rain
Down On The Farm
Driftwood
Felix Kept On Walking
Gigolette
Girl In The Crinoline Gown, The
Hard Hearted Hannah
Horsey Keep Your Tail Up
I Love You
I Wonder What's Become Of Sally
I'm Going South
It Ain't Gonna Rain No Mo'
It Had To Be You
Jealous
June Brought The Roses
June Night
Linger Awhile
Little Wooden Whistle Wouldn't Whistle, The
Mama Goes Where Papa Goes
Mama Loves Papa - Papa Loves Mama
Memory Lane
My Time Is Your Time
Nights In The Wood (Les Nuits Du Bois)
Nobody's Sweetheart
Oh Gee, Oh Gosh, Oh Golly, I'm In Love
One I Love Belongs To Somebody Else, The
Parisian Pierrot
Riviera Rose
Roamin' To Wyomin'
Romany Rose
Rosita, La
Sahara
Say It With A Ukulele
Shine
Sleep
Smile Will Go A Long, Long Way, A
Sobbin' Blues
Somebody Loves Me
Somebody Stole My Gal
Spain
There's Yes! Yes! In Your Eyes
Tomorrow (I'll Be In My Dixie Home Again)
Twelve O'clock At Night
What'll I Do
When It's Night Time In Italy, It's Wednesday Over Here
When You And I Were Dancing
Who'll Buy My Violets (La Violetera)
Why Did I Kiss That Girl
You're In Kentucky As Sure As You're Born

1925

Ah-ha
Alabamy Bound
All Alone
Always (Berlin)
Babette
Bouquet (i Shall Always Think Of You)
Cake Walking Babies From Home
Charleston
Cheatin' On Me
Chick Chick Chicken
Collegiate
Copenhagen
Dear One
Did Tosti Raise His Bowler Hat When He Said Goodbye
Don't Bring Lulu
Doo Wacka Doo
Everybody Loves My Baby
Everything Is Hotsy Totsy Now
Follow The Swallow
Golden West, The
Honey I'm In Love With You
How Come You Do Me Like You Do
I Miss My Swiss - My Swiss Miss Misses Me
I Want To Be Happy
I'll See You In My Dreams
I'm A Little Blackbird Looking For A Bluebird
I'm Gonna Charleston Back To Charleston
I'm Knee Deep In Daisies
If You Hadn't Gone Away
If You Knew Susie
In Shadowland
Indian Love Call
Keep Smiling At Trouble
Let It Rain Let It Pour
Mandy Make Up Your Mind
Manhattan
Mexicali Rose
Mounties, The
Nobody Knows What A Red-head Mama Can Do
Ogo-Pogo, The
Oh How I Miss You Tonight
Oh, Katharina
On Mother Kelly's Doorstep
Paddlin' Madelin' Home
Pal Of My Cradle Days
Poor Little Rich Girl
Prisoner's Song, The
Red Hot Mamma
Remember
Rhapsody In Blue
Rose Marie
Save Your Sorrow For Tomorrow
Seminola
Serenade Frasquita (Farewell My Love, Farewell)
Shanghai
Show Me The Way To Go Home
Sometime
Sonya (Yup Alay Yup)
Stepping In Society
Sunny Havana
Sweet And Lowdown

Sweet Georgia Brown
Tea For Two
Tie A String Around Your Finger
Toy Drum Major, The
Ukulele Lady
When My Sugar Walks Down The Street
When The Sergeant Major's On Parade
When You And I Were Seventeen
Where The Lazy Daisies Grow
Where's My Sweetie Hiding
Who Takes Care Of The Caretaker's Daughter
Yearning (Just For You)
Yes Sir, That's My Baby

1926

(What Can I Say) After I Say I'm Sorry
Am I Wasting My Time On You
Angry
At Peace With The World
Baby Face
'Bam 'Bam 'Bammy Shore
Barcelona
Bird Songs At Eventide
Black Bottom, The
Brown Eyes Why Are You Blue
Bye Bye Blackbird
Cecilia
Clap Hands, Here Comes Charley
Cup Of Coffee, A Sandwich And You, A
Deep Henderson
Deep In My Heart
Dicky Bird Hop, The
Dinah
Don't Have Any More Missus Moore
Drifting And Dreaming
Drinking Song, The
End Of The Road, The
Fascinating Rhythm
Five Foot Two, Eyes Of Blue
Gimme A Little Kiss, Will Ya, Huh
Golden Days
Hey Gipsy (Play Gipsy) (Komm Tzizany)
Hi Diddle Diddle
Horses
I Found A New Baby
I Know That You Know
I Love My Baby, My Baby Loves Me
I Never Knew (That Roses Grew)
I Never Knew How Wonderful You Were
I Never See Maggie Alone
I Wonder Where My Baby Is Tonight
I'd Climb The Highest Mountain (If I Knew I'd Find You)
I'm Sitting On Top of The World
I've Never Seen A Straight Banana
Just A Cottage Small (By A Waterfall)
Keep Your Skirts Down Mary Ann
Leanin'
Let's All Go To Mary's House
Let's Talk About My Sweetie
Lonesome And Sorry
Looking For A Boy
Me Too
Moonlight And Roses
Moonlight On The Ganges

More We Are Together, The
Muskrat Ramble
Oh Lady Be Good
Poor Papa (He's Got Nothing At All)
Rolling Round The World
Roses Remind Me Of You
Say It Again
Serenade (Romberg, Donnelly)
Sleepy Time Gal
So Am I
So Is Your Old Lady
Sunny
Sweet Child (I'm Wild About You)
Sweet Man
Thanks For The Buggy Ride
That Certain Feeling
That Certain Party
Then I'll Be Happy
Tonight's My Night With Baby
Trudy
Two Little Blue Birds
Valencia
When Autumn Leaves Are Falling
When The Red Red Robin (Comes Bob
Bob Bobbin' Along)
Where'd You Get Those Eyes
Who

1927
Abdul Abulbul Amir
Ain't She Sweet
Ain't That A Grand And Glorious Feeling
Among My Souvenirs
At Sundown
Ay, Ay, Ay
Barbara
Because I Love You
Birth Of The Blues, The
Bless This House
Blue Room, The
Blue Skies
Breezin' Along With The Breeze
C'est Vous (it's You)
Ca C'est Paris
Charmaine
Clap Yo' Hands
Crazy Words, Crazy Tune
Dancing Tambourine
'Deed I Do
Desert Song, The
Diane
Do Do Do
Doll Dance, The
Fifty Million Frenchmen Can't Be Wrong
Flapperette
Forgive Me
French Military Marching Song
Girl Friend, The
Give Me A Night In June
Hallelujah
Hello Bluebird
Here In My Arms
I Can't Believe That You're In Love With
Me
I Left My Sugar Standing In The Rain
I Wonder How I Look When I'm Asleep
I'm Coming Virginia

I'm Going Back To Himazas
I'm In Love Again
I'm Looking For A Girl Named Mary
I'm Looking Over A Four-Leaf Clover
I'm Telling The Birds, Telling The Bees,
How I Love You
In A Little Spanish Town
In A Shady Nook By A Babbling Brook
It All Depends On You
Jealousy
Just Another Day Wasted Away
Just Like A Butterfly
Kentucky Lullaby
Looking At The World Through Rose
Coloured Glasses
Lucky Day
Magnolia
Mary Lou
Maybe (Gershwin)
Me And Jane In A Plane
Me And My Shadow
Meadowlark
Mississippi Mud
Moonbeam Kiss Her For Me
Mountain Greenery
Muddy Water
My Blue Heaven
My Cuties Due At Two To Two Today
My Heart Stood Still
Oh! If I Only Had You
On A Street Of Chinese Lanterns
One Alone
One Summer Night
Only A Rose
Perhaps You'll Think Of Me
Riff Song, The
Roses For Remembrance
Russian Lullaby
Sam The Old Accordion Man
Shepherd Of The Hills
Side By Side
Silver Rose
Since I Found You
So Blue
So Will I
Some Day
Some Sweet Day
Someone To Watch Over Me
Sometimes I'm Happy
Song Of The Vagabonds, The
Song Of The Wanderer, The
Sunday
Sunny Disposish
That Night In Araby
There Ain't No Maybe In My Baby's
Eyes
Ting-a-Ling (The Waltz Of The Bells)
Tonight You Belong To Me
Tree In A Park, A
What Do I Care What Somebody Said
What Do We Do On A Dew-dew-dewy
Day
What Does It Matter
When You Played The Organ And I
Sang "The Rosary"
Where's That Rainbow
Whispering Pines of Nevada, The

1928
After My Laughter Came Tears
Angela Mia
Are You Lonesome Tonight
Back In Your Own Back Yard
Bandanna Babies
Best Things In Life Are Free, The
Bill
Broken Hearted
Can't Help Lovin' Dat Man
Can't You Hear Me Say I Love You
Cheerie Beerie Be
Chiquita
Chloe
Constantinople
Coquette
Crazy Rhythm
Dance Little Lady
Dizzy Fingers
Don't Do That To The Poor Puss Cat
Everywhere You Go
Forty-Seven Ginger Headed Sailors
Funny Face
Garden In The Rain, A
Get Out And Get Under The Moon
Girl Of My Dreams
Gonna Get A Girl
Good News
He's Tall And Dark And Handsome
I Ain't Got Nobody
I Can't Do Without You
I Can't Give You Anything But Love
I'm Going Back To Old Nebraska
Ice Cream
In The Woodshed She Said She Would
Is She My Girl Friend
Janette
Jeannine, I Dream Of Lilac Time
Just A Memory
Just Imagine
Just Like A Melody Out Of The Sky
Laugh Clown Laugh
Let A Smile Be Your Umbrella
Louisiana
Lucky In Love
Make Believe
Man I Love, The
Marigold
Me And The Man In The Moon
Miss Annabelle Lee
Mistakes
My Ohio Home
My One And Only
My Pet
My Yiddishe Momme
Nagasaki
Oh You Have No Idea
Ol' Man River
Persian Rosebud
Persian Rug
Rain
Ramona
Roll Away Clouds
Room With A View
S'wonderful
Shaking The Blues Away
She Don't Wanna

She's A Great Girl
Short'nin' Bread
So Tired
Song I Love, The
Song Is Ended, The
South
Stay Out Of The South
Struttin' With Some Barbecue
Sugar
Sunshine
Sweet Sue-Just You
That's My Weakness Now
There's Everything Nice About You
Together
Under The Moon
Varsity Drag
Was It A Dream
When Day Is Done
Why Do I Love You

1929

Ain't Misbehavin'
All By Yourself In The Moonlight
Am I Blue
Because My Baby Don't Mean Maybe Now
Big City Blues
Breakaway, The
Broadway Melody, The
Button Up Your Overcoat
Carolina Moon
Cuckoo Waltz, The
Dear Little Cafe
Deep Night
Diga Diga Doo
Do Something
Doin' The New Lowdown
Doin' The Raccoon
Ever So Goosey
Fancy Our Meeting
Following The Sun Around
For Old Times' Sake
Gay Caballero, A
Glad Rag Doll
Goodnight
Happy Days And Lonely Nights
High Up On A Hill Top
Honey
How About Me
How Long Has This Been Going On
I Faw Down An' Go Boom
I Kiss Your Hand Madame (Ich Kusse Ihr Hand Madame)
I Lift Up My Finger And I Say Tweet Tweet
I'll Always Be In Love With You
I'll Get By
I'll See You Again
I'm A Ding Dong Daddy (From Dumas)
I'm A One Man Girl
I'm Crazy Over You
I'm Just A Vagabond Lover
I've Got A Feeling I'm Falling
If I Had You
If You Want The Rainbow
It Goes Like This (That Funny Melody)
King For A Day
Lady Divine

Let's Do It (Let's Fall In Love)
Little Pal
Liza (All The Clouds'll Roll Away)
Louise
Love (Your Magic Spell Is Everywhere)
Love Me Or Leave Me
Lover Come Back To Me
Makin' Whoopee
March Of The Grenadiers
Marie
Maybe - Who Knows
Mean To Me
Mia Bella Rosa
Misery Farm
Miss You
Mucking About The Garden
My Blackbirds Are Bluebirds Now
My Kinda Love
My Mother's Eyes
My Sin
My Song Of The Nile
One Kiss
Orange Blossom Time
Pagan Love Song, The
Piccolo Pete
Precious Little Thing Called Love, A
Ready For The River
S'posin'
She's Funny That Way
Shinaniki Da
Singin' In The Rain
Sleepy Valley
Softly As In A Morning Sunrise
Sonny Boy
Spread A Little Happiness
Stout Hearted Men
Sweetheart Of All My Dreams
That's A Plenty
That's You Baby
There'll Be Some Changes Made
There's A Blue Ridge Round My Heart, Virginia
There's A Rainbow 'round My Shoulder
There's Something Spanish In Your Eyes
Thinking Of You
Thou Swell
To-kay
Under The Roofs of Paris (Sous Les Toits de Paris)
Underneath The Russian Moon
Up In The Clouds
Valentine
Walking With Susie
Wanting You
Weary River
Wedding Bells Are Breaking Up That Old Gang Of Mine
Wedding Of The Painted Doll, The
What Is This Thing Called Love
When My Dreams Come True
When You're Smiling
Where The Shy Little Violets Grow
Why Is The Bacon So Tough
Yellow Dog Blues
You Do Something To Me
You Took Advantage Of Me
You Were Meant For Me

You're The Cream In My Coffee
Zigeuner

1930

All Alone Monday
Amy, Wonderful Amy
Around The Corner And Under The Tree
Basin Street Blues
Beyond The Blue Horizon
Blue Pacific Moonlight
Body And Soul
Bye Bye Blues
Cottage For Sale
Crying For The Carolines
Dancing With Tears In My Eyes
Dream Lover
Dream Mother
Elizabeth
Exactly Like You
Falling In Love Again
Get Happy
Gipsy Melody
Give Yourself A Pat On The Back
Go Home And Tell Your Mother
Great Day
Happy Days Are Here Again
Happy Feet
Have A Little Faith In Me
Honeysuckle Rose
Hora Staccato
How Am I To Know
I May Be Wrong But I Think You're Wonderful
I'm A Dreamer, Aren't We All
I'm In The Market For You
I've Got A Crush On You
If I Had A Talking Picture Of You
If You're In Love You'll Waltz
It Happened In Monterey
It Must Be True
Jollity Farm
Just A Gigolo
Just You, Just Me
Keeping Myself For You
King's Horses, The
Kinkajou, The
Kiss Waltz, The
Let Me Sing And I'm Happy
'leven-Thirty Saturday Night
Little Kiss Each Morning, A
Little White Lies
Lonesome Road
Malaguena
Molly
More Than You Know
My Baby Just Cares For Me
My Fate Is In Your Hands
My Love Parade
Nobody's Using It Now
Oh Donna Clara
Oh Maiden My Maiden
Over The Garden Wall
Painting The Clouds With Sunshine
Paris Stay The Same
Puttin' On The Ritz
Rangers' Song, The

Rio Rita
Ro-Ro-Rollin' Along
She's Such A Comfort To Me
Ship Without A Sail, The
Should I
Sing Something Simple
Sing You Sinners
Singing A Vagabond Song
Singing In The Bathtub
So Beats My Heart For You
Some Day I'll Find You
Something To Remember You By
Song of The Dawn
Song of The Islands (Na Lei O Hawaii)
Soon
Stop And Shop At The Co-Op Shop
Sunny Side Up
Sweeping The Clouds Away
Sweetheart We Need Each Other
Tell Me I'm Forgiven
There's A Good Time Coming
There's Danger In Your Eyes Cherie
Tip-toe Through The Tulips
When I'm Looking At You
When It's Springtime In The Rockies
When The Organ Played At Twilight
White Dove, The
Why Was I Born
With A Song In My Heart
Without A Song
You Brought A New Kind Of Love To Me
You Die If You Worry
You've Got That Thing

1931

Adeline
Ali Baba's Camel
Barnacle Bill The Sailor
Bathing In The Sunshine
Bench In A Park, A
Betty Co-ed
Blue Again
By The River Saint Marie
By The Sleepy Lagoon
Call Me Darling
Can't We Be Friends
Cheerful Little Earful
Choo Choo
Cuban Love Song
Dancing On The Ceiling
Dream A Little Dream Of Me
Drink, Drink Brothers Drink (Trink, Trink Bruderlein Trink)
Fiesta
Fine And Dandy
For You
Goodbye
Goodnight Sweetheart
Got A Date With An Angel
Hang Out The Stars In Indiana
Heartaches
Ho Hum
Hour Of Parting, The
I Bring A Love Song
I Don't Know Why - I Just Do
I Found You
I Still Get A Thrill (Thinking Of You)

I Surrender Dear
I'll Be Good Because Of You
I'm Alone Because I Love You
I'm Confessin'
I'm Happy When I'm Hiking
I'm Yours
I've Got Five Dollars
In The Jailhouse Now
It's The Darndest Thing
Jolly Good Company
Just One More Chance
Lady Of Spain
Lady Play Your Mandolin
Life Is Just A Bowl Of Cherries
Little Girl
Love For Sale
Love Letters In The Sand
Make Yourself A Happiness Pie
Mama Inez
Many Happy Returns Of The Day
Me
Memories Of You
Moanin' Low
Moment I Saw You, The
Mood Indigo
Moon Is Low
Moonlight On The Colorado
Moonlight Saving Time
My Future Just Passed
My Ideal
My Song Of Love
Nevertheless
Ninety-Nine Out Of A Hundred
Nobody Knows You When You're Down And Out
Of Thee I Sing
On A Little Balcony In Spain
On The Sunny Side Of The Street
Out Of Nowhere
Pardon Me Pretty Baby
Patiently Smiling
Peanut Vendor, The (El Manisero)
Please Don't Talk About Me When I'm Gone
Prisoner Of Love
Queen Was In The Parlour, The
Reaching For The Moon
Red River Valley
Rhymes
Ring Dem Bells
River Stay 'way From My Door
Rockin' Chair
Rockin' In Rhythm
Runaway Train, The
Sally
Siboney
Sing A Little Jingle
Singin' The Blues
Sitting On A Five Barred Gate
Smile, Darn Ya Smile
Somewhere In Old Wyoming
Speak To Me Of Love (Parlez Moi D'amour)
Springtime Reminds Me Of You (Deine Mutter Bleibt Immer Bei Mir)
Stardust
Sunny Days
Sweet And Lovely

Sweet Jenny Lee
Sweet Violets
Ten Cents A Dance
That's Why Darkies Were Born
Them There Eyes
There's Always Tomorrow
Three Little Words
Time On My Hands
Today I Feel So Happy
Twentieth Century Blues
Two Hearts In Three Quarter Time
Under The Bridges of Paris (Sous Les Ponts De Paris)
Vienna, City Of My Dreams
Walkin' My Baby Back Home
Were You Sincere
When I Take My Sugar To Tea
When The Bloom Is On The Sage
When The Guards Are On Parade
When The Moon Comes Over The Mountain
When You're Hair Has Turned To Silver
When Your Lover Has Gone
Whistling In The Dark
White Horse Inn, The
Who Am I
Would You Like To Take A Walk
Wrap Your Troubles In Dreams
You Are My Heart's Delight
You Too
You Will Remember Vienna
You're Driving Me Crazy
Your Eyes

1932

Adios
Ain't It Grand To Be Bloomin' Well Dead
All Of Me
Alone Together
As Time Goes By
As You Desire Me
At Your Command
Auf Wiederseh'n My Dear
Back Again To Happy-go-lucky-days
Beautiful Love
Bedtime Story, A
Bidin' My Time
But Not For Me
By The Fireside
Can't We Talk It Over
Carry On
Changing Of The Guard, The
Chinese Laundry Blues
Clouds Will Soon Roll By, The
Crazy People
Creole Love Call
Dancing In The Dark
Don't Say Goodbye
Dreaming
Eadie Was A Lady
Eleven More Months And Ten More Days
Embraceable You
Faded Summer Love, A
Fascination
Flies Crawled Up The Window, The
Georgia On My Mind
Ghost of a Chance, A

Gipsy Moon
Goodbye Blues
Goodnight Vienna
Goofus
Granada
Granny's Old Arm-Chair
Guilty
Happy Go Lucky You, And Broken Hearted Me
He Played His Ukulele As The Ship Went Down
He's Dead But He Won't Lie Down
Home
I Apologise
I Found A Million Dollar Baby
I Give My Heart
I Got Rhythm
I Guess I'll Have To Change My Plan
I Lost My Heart In Heidelberg
I Travel The Road
I Wanna Be Loved By You
I'll Follow You
I'll Never Be The Same
I'm Crazy 'bout My Baby
I'm Through With Love
I've Got The World On A String
I've Told Every Little Star
Ich Liebe Dich, My Dear
If I Could Be With You (One Hour To-night)
In A Shanty In Old Shanty Town
It Don't Mean A Thing (If It Ain't Got That Swing)
Just Friends
Just Humming Along
Just Once For All Time
Kicking The Going Around
Let's Have Another Cup o'coffee
Lies
Life's Desire
Linger A Little Longer In The Twilight
Liszt, Chopin And Mendelssohn
Live, Laugh And Love
Louisianna Hayride
Love Is Sweeping The Country
Love Is The Sweetest Thing
Love You Funny Thing
Lullaby Of The Leaves
Ma Curly Headed Babby
Mad About The Boy
Mad Dogs And Englishmen
Marching Along Together
Marta
Masquerade
Minnie The Moocher
Mona Lisa
Moon
Moonlight On The River
My Silent Love
New Sun In The Sky, A
Night Was Made For Love, The
Now's The Time To Fall In Love
Oh Monah
Old Kitchen Kettle, The
On The Air
Ooh That Kiss
Pagan Moon
Rogue Song, The

'Round The Marble Arch
Round The Bend Of The Road
Sentimental Gentleman From Georgia, A
She Didn't Say "Yes"
Shine On Your Shoes, A
Silver Hair And Heart Of Gold
Smoke Rings
Snuggled On Your Shoulder
Soft Lights And Sweet Music
Somebody Loves You
Song Is You, The
Sun Has Got His Hat On, The
Tell Me Tonight
There's Something In Your Eyes
They Cut Down The Old Pine Tree
Three's A Crowd
Thrill Is Gone, The
Too Many Tears
Underneath The Arches
Underneath The Harlem Moon
Voice In The Old Village Choir, The
Was That The Human Thing To Do
We Just Couldn't Say Goodbye
When It's Sleepy Time Down South
When We're Alone (Penthouse Seren-ade)
When Yuba Plays The Rumba On The Tuba
Where The Blue Of The Night
While We Danced At The Mardi Gras
Who's Your Little Who-zis
You Call It Madness
You Forgot Your Gloves
You Just You
You Rascal You
You're Blasé
You're Dancing On My Heart
You're My Everything

1933
After You - Who
All Over Italy
Balloons (Who'll Buy My Nice Balloons)
Black Moonlight
Blue Moments (Without You Dear)
Blue Prelude
Brother Can You Spare A Dime
Bungalow, A Piccolo And You, A
Butterflies In The Rain
Carry Me Back To Green Pastures
Castles In The Sand
Chewing Gum
Da-dar Da-dar
Darkness On The Delta
Day You Came Along, The
Dinner At Eight
Don't Blame Me
Down The Old Ox Road
Everything I Have Is Yours
Experiment
Fit As A Fiddle
Forty-Second Street
Gendarmes Duet, The
Girl In The Little Green Hat, The
Happy Ending
Have You Ever Been Lonely
Her Name Is Mary

Here Lies Love
Hiawatha's Lullaby
Hold Me
Home On The Range
How Deep Is The Ocean
I Cover The Waterfront
I Gotta Right To Sing The Blues
I Like Mountain Music
I'm Getting Sentimental Over You
I'm Sure Of Everything But You
I've Got To Sing A Torch Song
I've Got You On My Mind
In A Little Secondhand Store
In The Dim Dim Dawning
In The Valley Of The Moon
Isn't It Romantic
It's The Talk Of The Town
Jolly Brothers, The (Lustige Bruder)
Just An Echo In The Valley
Lazybones
Learn To Croon
Let Bygones Be Bygones
Let's All Sing Like The Birdies Sing
Let's Put Out The Lights And Go To Sleep
Little Street Where Old Friends Meet, A
Lover
Man On The Flying Trapeze, The
Mary Rose
Mimi
Moon Song (That Wasn't Meant For Me)
Moonstruck
My Darling
My Hat's On The Side Of My Head
My Moonlight Madonna
My Song Goes Round The World
Night And Day
'Oi' Song, The
Old Father Thames
Old Man Of The Mountain, The
One Girl
Orchids In The Moonlight
Paradise
Pettin' In The Park
Physician, The
Pink Elephants
Play Fiddle Play
Please
Pu-leeze Mr. Hemingway
Reflections In The Water
Roll Along Kentucky Moon
Rosetta
Say It Isn't So
Seven Years With The Wrong Woman
Shadow Waltz, The
Shuffle Off To Buffalo
Skirts
Snowball
Solomon
Sophisticated Lady
Stay On The Right Side Of The Road
Stormy Weather
Street Of Dreams
Sweetheart Darling
Temptation
Thanks
There's A Cabin In The Pines

Trouble In Paradise
Try A Little Tenderness
Under A Blanket Of Blue
We All Went Up Up Up The Mountain
We're In The Money
Wedding Of Mr Mickey Mouse
What A Perfect Combination
What Did I Do To Be So Black And Blue
Wheezy Anna
When It's Lamp Lighting Time In The Valley
Who Walks In (When I Walk Out)
Who's Afraid Of The Big Bad Wolf
Willow Weep For Me
Yes Mister Brown
You're An Old Smoothie
You're Getting To Be A Habit With Me
You've Got Me Crying Again
Young And Healthy

1934

All I Do Is Dream Of You
Always (Smith, Dyrenforth)
Annie Doesn't Live Here Anymore
April In Paris
As Long As I Live
Beside My Caravan
Boulevard Of Broken Dreams
Breeze, The (That's Bringing My Honey Back To Me)
By A Waterfall
Cafe In Vienna
Cage In The Window, A
Carioca, The
Close Your Eyes
Cocktails For Two
Continental, The
Coom Pretty One
Crest Of A Wave, The
Did You Ever See A Dream Walking
Does Santa Claus Sleep With His Whiskers
Don't Let Your Love Go Wrong
Fair And Warmer
Flying Down To Rio
For All We Know
Grinzing (Ich Muss Wieder Einmal In Grinzing Sein)
Hands Across The Table
Heat Wave
Hold My Hand
House Is Haunted, The
Hundred Years From Today, A
I Bought Myself A Bottle Of Ink
I Like The Likes Of You
I Saw Stars
I Took My Harp To A Party
I Wish I Were Twins
I'll Follow My Secret Heart
I'll String Along With You
I'm Humming, I'm Whistling, I'm Singing
I'm On A See-saw
If
In My Little Bottom Drawer
Inka Dinka Doo
Isle Of Capri
It's Only A Paper Moon
It's Time To Say Goodnight

Keep Young And Beautiful
La-Di-Da-Di-Da
Last Roundup, The
Let's All Go To The Music Hall
Let's Fall In Love
Little Dutch Mill
Little Man You've Had A Busy Day
Little Rock Getaway
Little Valley In The Mountains
Lost In A Fog
Love In Bloom
Love Thy Neighbour
Love's Last Word Is Spoken (Le Chaland Qui Passe)
Mama Don't Want No Peas, An' Rice, An' Coconut Oil
May I
Miss Otis Regrets
Mister And Mrs Is The Name
Moonglow
My Old Flame
Nasty Man
Night On The Desert
Nobody Loves A Fairy When She's Forty
Object Of My Affection, The
Oh Muki Muki Oh
Ol' Faithful
On A Steamer Coming Over
One Morning In May
One Night Of Love
Other People's Babies
Out In The Cold Cold Snow
Over My Shoulder
Over On The Sunny Side
P.S. I Love You
Play To Me Gipsy
Remember Me
Ridin' Around In The Rain
Rolling Home
Santa Claus Is Coming To Town
Sing As We Go
Sitting On A Back-Yard Fence
Smoke Gets In Your Eyes
Someone Stole Gabriel's Horn
Stars Fell On Alabama
Stay As Sweet As You Are
Sundown In Little Green Hollow
Sweet Lorraine
Tina
Touch Of Your Hand, The
Two Cigarettes In The Dark
Unless
Very Thought Of You, The
Wagon Wheels
We'll All Go Riding On A Rainbow
We'll Make Hay While The Sun Shines
What A Difference A Day Made
What A Little Moonlight Can Do
What Can You Give A Nudist On His Birthday
When A Soldier's On Parade
When You've Got A Little Springtime In Your Heart
With Her Head Tucked Underneath Her Arm
With My Eyes Wide Open I'm Dreamin'
Wonder Bar

Yesterdays
You Ought To See Sally On Sunday

1935

All For A Shilling A Day
All Through The Night
Anything Goes
Argentina
Back To Those Happy Days
Be Still My Heart
Believe It Beloved
Bess You Is My Woman Now
Blow, Gabriel, Blow
Blue Moon
Boots And Saddle
Canoe Song, The
Carry Me Back To The Lone Prairie
Cheek To Cheek
Christopher Robin Is Saying His Prayers
Cucaracha, La
Dancing With My Shadow
Dinner For One Please James
Don't Ever Leave Me
Down The Oregon Trail
Earful Of Music, An
East Of The Sun
Easter Parade
Every Single Little Tingle Of My Heart
Everything Stops For Tea
Everythings In Rhythm With My Heart
Fanlight Fanny
Fare-Thee-Well Annabelle
Flirtation Walk
Fold Your Wings
Friends
From The Top of Your Head (To The Tip Of Your Toes)
General's Fast Asleep, The
Gentlemen, The King
Gertie The Girl With The Gong
Getting Around And About
Gipsy In Me, The
Girl With The Dreamy Eyes
Glamorous Night
Goodbye Hawaii
Here Comes Cookie
His Majesty The Baby
Home Again
Home James And Don't Spare The Horses
How's Chances
I Believe In Miracles
I Get A Kick Out Of You
I Got Plenty Of Nuttin'
I Loves You Porgy
I Only Have Eyes For You
I Won't Dance
I'll Never Say "Never Again" Again
I'm Gonna Sit Right Down And Write Myself A Letter
I'm Gonna Wash My Hands Of You
I'm In The Mood For Love
I'm Popeye The Sailor Man
I'm Sitting High On A Hilltop
I've Had My Moments
If I Had A Million Dollars
In A Little Gipsy Tearoom

In The Middle Of A Kiss
Isn't This A Lovely Day
It Ain't Necessarily So
It's Easy To Remember
It's My Mother's Birthday Today
June In January
Lady In Red, The
Let's Have A Jubilee
Life Is A Song
Little Girl Blue
Little White Gardenia, A
Love Is Just Around The Corner
Love Me Forever
Lovely To Look At
Lullaby Of Broadway
Lulu's Back In Town
Making The Best Of Each Day
March Winds And April Showers
Me And The Old Folks At Home
Misty Islands Of The Highlands
Moon Was Yellow, The
Moonlight On The Alster
Most Beautiful Girl In The World
Mrs Worthington
My Kid's A Crooner
My Monday Date
My Very Good Friend The Milkman
No! No! A Thousand Times No
Nobody's Darlin' But Mine
Okay Toots
Old Ship Of Mine
Old Spinning Wheel, The
Old Timer
Olga Pulloffski (The Beautiful Spy)
On The Good Ship Lollipop
On Treasure Island
Out In The Cold Again
Paris In The Spring
Piccolino, The
Pig Got Up And Slowly Walked Away,
The
Put On An Old Pair Of Shoes
Red Sails In The Sunset
Rhythm Is Our Business
Rhythm Of The Rain
Roll Along Covered Wagon
Roll Along Prairie Moon
Rose In Her Hair, The
Saint James' Infirmary
Sarawaki
She's A Latin From Manhattan
Shine Through My Dreams
Sidewalks Of Cuba
Sleep My Baby Sleep
Song Of The Trees, The
Soon - There'll Just Be Two Of Us
South American Joe
Suddenly
Sugar Blues
Sunbonnet Blue, A
Sweetest Music This Side Of Heaven,
The
Take A Number From One To Ten
There's A Lovely Lake In London
There's Something About A Soldier
Things Are Looking Up
Top Hat, White Tie And Tails
Truckin'

Turn 'erberts Face To The Wall Mother
Way Back Home
We've Got To Keep Up With The
Joneses
Wheel Of The Wagon Is Broken, The
When I Grow Too Old To Dream
When My Ship Comes In
When The Gypsy Played
Who's Been Polishing The Sun
Winter Wonderland
With Every Breath I Take
Without A Word Of Warning
Words Are In My Heart, The
World Is Mine Tonight, The
You And The Night And The Music
You Can't Do That There 'ere
You Oughta Be In Pictures
You're The Top
Zing Went The Strings Of My Heart

1936

About A Quarter To Nine
Afterglow
Alone (Freed, Brown)
And The Great Big Saw Came Nearer
Animal Crackers In My Soup
At The Balalaika
At The Cafe Continental
Au Revoir But Not Goodbye
Between The Devil And The Deep Blue
Sea
Bird On The Wing
Broadway Rhythm
Broken Record, The
Celebratin'
Come Back To Sorrento (Tourna A Sur-
riento)
Cuban Pete
Darling, Je Vous Aime Beaucoup
Did I Remember
Did Your Mother Come From Ireland
Dream Time
Easy To Love
Empty Saddles
Feather In Her Tyrolean Hat, The
Fine Romance, A
Fleet's In Port Again, The
Gloomy Sunday (Szomoru Vasarnap)
Glory Of Love, The (Hill)
Goody Goody
Has Anybody Seen Our Ship
Here's To Romance
I Can't Dance, I Got Ants In My Pants
I Can't Escape From You
I Can't Get Started
I Dream Too Much
I Feel A Song Coming On
I Feel Like A Feather In The Breeze
I Like Bananas Because They Have No
Bones
I Wished On The Moon
I'm An Old Cow-hand
I'm Goin' Shoppin' With You
I'm In A Dancing Mood
I'm Putting All My Eggs In One Basket
I'm Shooting High
I've Got A Feelin' You're Foolin'
I've Got My Fingers Crossed

In A Sentimental Mood
In Caliente
Is It True What They Say About Dixie
It's A Sin To Tell A Lie
It's Been So Long
It's Love Again
King's Navee, The
Knock, Knock, Who's There
Laughing Irish Eyes
Let Yourself Go
Let's Face The Music And Dance
Let's Have A Tiddley At The Milk Bar
Lights Out
Little Bit Independent, A
Lost
Love Is A Dancing Thing
Lovely Lady
Magic Is The Moonlight (Te Quiero Dij-
iste)
Me And My Dog
Me And The Moon
Melody From The Sky, A
Moonburn
Music Goes 'round And 'round, The
My First Thrill
No Greater Love
No Regrets (Tobias, Ingraham)
No Strings
On A Sunday Afternoon (Freed, Brown)
On The Beach At Bali Bali
One Rose (That's Left In My Heart)
Organ Grinders Swing
Pick Yourself Up
Play Orchestra Play
Please Believe Me
Rainbow On The River
Rise 'N' Shine
Robins And Roses
Saddle Your Blues To A Wild Mustang
San Francisco
Serenade In The Night
Shoe Shine Boy
Sleep My Little One
Solitude
South Sea Island Magic
Star Fell Out Of Heaven, A
Stompin' At The Savoy
Sunset Trail, The
Sweetheart, Let's Grow Old Together
There Isn't Any Limit To My Love
These Foolish Things
This'll Make You Whistle
Touch Of Your Lips
Two Of Us, The
Until The Real Thing Comes Along
Viper's Drag
Waltz In Swing Time
Way You Look Tonight, The
We Saw The Sea
When A Lady Meets A Gentleman
Down South
When I'm Cleaning Windows
When Somebody Thinks You're Won-
derful
When The Guardsman Started Croon-
ing On Parade
When The Lights Are Low
When The Poppies Bloom Again

Whistling Waltz, The
Why Did She Fall For The Leader Of The Band
With All My Heart
Would You
You
You Are My Lucky Star
You Better Go Now
You Hit The Spot
You Were There
You've Got The Wrong Rumba
Your Feet's Too Big
Your Heart And Mine

1937

Afraid To Dream
All God's Chillun Got Rhythm
Alone At A Table For Two
Angel Of The Great White Way
Beginner's Luck
Blue Hawaii
Blue Turning Grey Over You
Bob White
Boo Hoo
Broken Hearted Clown
By Myself
Can I Forget You
Caravan
Carelessly
Climbing Up
Coronation Waltz, The
Cowboy
Delyse
Fairy On The Christmas Tree, The
Feather In Her Tyrolean Hat, The
First Time I Saw You, The
Foggy Day, A
Gangway
Girl On The Police Gazette, The
Girls Were Made To Love And Kiss
Gone With The Wind
Goodbye
Goodnight My Love
Greatest Mistake Of My Life, The
Harbour Lights
Head Over Heels In Love
Hi Tiddley Hi Ti Island
Home Town
Hurdy Gurdy Man, The
I Once Had A Heart Margarita
I'll Sing You A Thousand Love Songs
I'm Feeling Like A Million
I've Got My Love To Keep Me Warm
I've Got You Under My Skin
Ida, Sweet As Apple Cider
In The Chapel In The Moonlight
It Looks Like Rain In Cherry Blossom Lane
It's Raining Sunbeams
It's The Natural Thing To Do
La De De, La De Da
Leaning On A Lamp Post
Let Us Be Sweethearts All Over Again
Let's Call The Whole Thing Off
Little Boy That Santa Claus Forgot
Little Co-Operation From You, A
Little Old Lady

Love Bug Will Bite You, The
Magnolias In The Moonlight
May I Have The Next Romance With You
Merry-Go-Round Broke Down, The
Moon At Sea
Moon Got In My Eyes, The
Moon Of Manakoora, The
Moonlight And Shadows
My Funny Valentine
My Little Buckaroo
Never In A Million Years
Nice Cup Of Tea, A
Night Is Young And You're So Beautiful, The
Oh They're Tough Mighty Tough In The West
On A Little Bamboo Bridge
On Your Toes
One, Two, Button Your Shoe
Pennies From Heaven
Say "Si Si" (Para Vigo Me Voy)
September In The Rain
Seventh Heaven
She's My Lovely
Sing Baby Sing (Pollack, Yellen)
Sing, Sing, Sing
Slaughter On Tenth Avenue
Slumming On Park Avenue
So Do I
So Rare
Somebody Else Is Taking My Place
Stars In My Eyes
Swamp Fire
Sweet Heartache
Sweet Leilani
Ten Pretty Girls
That Old Feeling
There's A Lull In My Life
There's A Small Hotel
There's Something In The Air
They All Laughed
They Can't Take That Away From Me
This Year's Kisses
Through The Years
To Mary With Love
Trust In Me
Twilight In Turkey
Twilight On The Trail
Vieni, Vieni
Wake Up And Live
Walter, Walter (Lead Me To The Alter)
Wanderers
Was It Rain
What Will I Tell My Heart
When Did You Leave Heaven
When I'm With You
When My Dreamboat Comes Home
Where Are You
Whiffenpoof Song, The
With My Shillelagh Under My Arm
With Plenty Of Money And You
You Can't Have Everything
You Turned The Tables On Me

1938

A-tisket A-tasket
Alligator Crawl

Bei Mir Bist Du Schon
Biggest Aspidistra In The World, The
Change Partners
Chestnut Tree, The
Cinderella Stay In My Arms
Cinderella Sweetheart
Cry, Baby, Cry
Day Dreaming
Dearest Love
Dipsy Doodle, The
Don't Be That Way
Don't Ever Change
Donkey Serenade, The
Down Where The Trade Winds Blow
Ebbtide
Flat Foot Floogie, The
Folks Who Live On The Hill, The
Gipsy In My Soul
Girl In The Alice Blue Gown, The
Goodnight Angel
Have You Got Any Castles Baby
Hear My Song Violetta (Hor Mein Lied Violetta)
Heigh-Ho
Horsey, Horsey
How'd Ya Like To Love Me
I Can Dream Can't I
I Double Dare You
I Hadn't Anyone Till You
I Let A Song Go Out Of My Heart
I Love To Whistle
I Used To Be Colour Blind
I Wish I Were In Love Again
I Won't Tell A Soul (That I Love You)
I'll Take Romance
I'm Gonna Lock My Heart And Throw Away The Key
I'm Wishing
In My Little Red Book
In My Little Snapshot Album
In The Still Of The Night
It's D'lovely
Joint Is Jumpin', The
Joseph, Joseph
Knees Up Mother Brown
Lady Of Madrid
Lambeth Walk, The
Laughing Policeman, The
Little Drummer Boy, The (Noel & Pelosi)
Little Lady Make Believe
Love Walked In
Lullaby In Rhythm
Mama I Wanna Make Rhythm
Me And My Girl
Merrily We Roll Along
Music Maestro Please
My Heart Is Taking Lessons
Nice People
Nice Work If You Can Get It
Night Is Filled With Music, The
Now It Can Be Told
Oh Mama (The Butcher Boy)
Old Man Mose
On The Bridge Of Sighs
On The Bumpy Road To Love
On The Sentimental Side
Once In A While
One Song

417

Peckin'
Please Be Kind
Rags, Bottles Or Bones
Remember Me
Ride, Tenderfoot, Ride
Rosalie
Rose Of England
Roses In December
Sail Along Silvery Moon
Says My Heart
Shadrack
Shy Serenade
Sixty Seconds Got Together
Slap That Bass
Small Fry
Snake Charmer, The
So Many Memories
Some Day My Prince Will Come
Somebody's Thinking Of You Tonight
Stately Homes Of England, The
Summertime
Sweetest Song In The World, The
Swing High, Swing Low
Thanks For The Memory
Ti-Pi-Tin
Too Marvellous For Words
Toy Trumpet
Tu-Li-Tulip Time
When Mother Nature Sings Her Lullaby
When The Organ Played "O Promise Me"
When The Sun Goes Down
While A Cigarette Was Burning
Whistle While You Work
With A Smile And A Song
Yam, The
You Can Depend On Me
You Can't Stop Me From Dreaming
You Go To My Head
You're A Sweetheart
You're Laughing At Me

1939

And The Angels Sing
Apple For The Teacher, An
Are You Having Any Fun
Army, The Navy And The Air Force, The
Bach Goes To Town
Beer Barrel Polka, The
Begin The Beguine
Blue Skies Are Round The Corner
Boogie Woogie
Boom
Boomps-a-daisy
Cherokee
Comes Love
Could Be
Darn That Dream
Day In, Day Out
Deep In A Dream
Deep Purple
East Side Of Heaven
Faithful Forever
Ferdinand The Bull
Fiacre, Le (The Cab)
Franklin D. Roosevelt Jones
Funny Old Hills, The

Get Out Of Town
Handsome Territorial, A
Heart And Soul
Heaven Can Wait
Hold Tight, Hold Tight
Hong Kong Blues
Hooray For Hollywood
I Can Give You The Starlight
I Get Along Without You Very Well
I Have Eyes
I Paid For That Lie I Told You
I Poured My Heart Into A Song
I Shall Always Remember You Smiling
I Ups To Her, And She Ups To Me
I'll Walk Beside You
I'm Sending A Letter To Santa Claus
I've Got A Pocketful Of Dreams
If I Didn't Care
In An Eighteenth Century Drawing Room
In Between
It's In The Air
J'attendrai
Jeepers Creepers
Just A Kid Named Joe
Kiss Me Goodnight Sergeant-major
Lady's In Love With You, The
Life Is Nothing Without Music
Little Sir Echo
Lords Of The Air
Lydia The Tattooed Lady
Man And His Dream, A
Man With The Mandolin, The
Masquerade Is Over, The
Moonlight Serenade
Most Gentlemen Don't Like Love
My Dearest Dear
My Heart Belongs To Daddy
My Life Belongs To You
My Own
My Prayer
New Moon And An Old Serenade, A
New Orleans (Carmichael)
Nursie
Oh Nicholas Don't Be So Ridiculous
On The Outside Looking In
One Day When We're Young
Only When You're In My Arms
Penny Serenade, The
Primrose
Rancho Grande, El
Romany (Vivere)
Run Rabbit Run
Sing A Song Of Sunbeams
Sing For Your Supper
South of The Border
Stairway To The Stars
Start The Day Right
Summer Evening In Santa Cruz, A
Sunrise Serenade
T'aint What You Do
Tears On My Pillow (Nesbitt)
Tell Me Marianne (A Media Luz)
There'll Always Be An England
There's A Gold Mine In The Sky
They Say
This Can't Be Love
Three Little Fishes

Transatlantic Lullaby
Two Sleepy People
Umbrella Man, The
Undecided
Waltz Of My Heart
Washing On The Siegfried Line
We'll Meet Again
Well All Right
What's New
Wings Over The Navy
Wish Me Luck As You Wave Me Goodbye
Wishing
Woodchopper's Ball
You Grow Sweeter As The Years Go By
You Must Have Been A Beautiful Baby
You're As Pretty As A Picture
You're The Only Star In My Blue Heaven

1940

Adios Mariquita Linda
Adios Muchachos
April Played The Fiddle
Beautiful Dreamer
Between 18th And 19th On Chestnut Street
Boys In The Back Room, The
Breeze And I, The
Can't Get Indiana Off My Mind
Careless
Ding Dong The Witch Is Dead
Don't Worry 'bout Me
Down By The O-Hi-O
Dreaming (Duerme)
Falling In Love With Love
Fools Rush In
Gaucho Serenade, The
Give A Little Whistle
Good Morning
Goodbye Sally
Goodnight Children, Everywhere
Hang Your Heart On A Hickory Limb
Have You Met Miss Jones
Hi-Diddle-Dee-Dee (An Actors Life For Me)
I Can't Love You Anymore
I Haven't Time To Be A Millionaire
I Shall Be Waiting
I'll Never Smile Again
I'll Pray For You
I'm Stepping Out With A Memory Tonight
I've Got My Eyes On You
I've Got No Strings
If I Only Had A Heart
If I Only Had Wings
If I Should Fall In Love Again
Imagination
In An Old Dutch Garden
In The Mood
In The Quartermaster's Stores
It Makes No Difference Now
It's A Blue World
It's A Hap-Hap-Happy Day
It's A Hundred To One I'm In Love
It's A Lovely Day Tomorrow
It's Funny To Everyone But Me

Johnny One Note
Johnson Rag
Lady Is A Tramp, The
Lamp Is Low
Let The Curtain Come Down
Let The People Sing
Let's Have Another One
Lilacs In The Rain
Little Curly Hair In A High Chair
Little Rain Must Fall, A
Love Is All
Meet The Sun Half Way
Memories Live Longer Than Dreams
Mister Meadowlark
Moon And The Willow Tree, The
Nearness Of You, The
Nightingale Sang In Berkeley Square, A
Oh Mamma Mia
Oh What A Surprise For The Duce (Evviva La Torre Di Pisa)
On A Little Street In Singapore
One Sweet Letter From You
Over The Rainbow
Pavanne
Pennsylvania Six-Five-Thousand
Pessimistic Character, The (With The Crab Apple Face)
Playmates
Ride Cossack, Ride
Sailor With The Navy Blue Eyes, The
Say It
Scatterbrain
Seventeen Candles
Shake Down The Stars
Singing Hills, The
Six Lessons From Madame La Zonga
So Deep Is The Night (Tristesse)
Somewhere In France With You
South Rampart Street Parade
Sweet Potato Piper
That Sly Old Gentleman (From Featherbed Lane)
There's A Boy Coming Home On Leave
They Can't Black-out The Moon
Tiggerty Boo
Till The Lights Of London Shine Again
Too Romantic
Tuxedo Junction
Wabash Cannon Ball
Walkin' Thru Mockin' Bird Lane
We're Off To See The Wizard
When The Swallows Come Back To Capistrano
When You Wish Upon A Star
Where Or When
Who's Taking You Home Tonight
With The Wind And The Rain In Your Hair
Woodpeckers Song (Reginella Campagnola)
You Made Me Care When I Wasn't In Love
You Tell Me Your Dream
You've Done Something To My Heart

1941
Ain't It A Shame About Mame

All Over The Place
All The Things You Are
All This And Heaven Too
Along The Santa Fe Trail
Amapola
At Long Last Love
Aurora
Badge From Your Coat, The
Beat Me Daddy, Eight To The Bar
Beneath The Lights Of Home
Bewitched, Bothered And Bewildered
Bless 'em All
Blueberry Hill
Boa Noite
Boogie Woogie Bugle Boy
Call Of The Canyon, The
Chica Chica Boom Chic
Concerto For Clarinet
Corn Silk
Daddy
Do I Love You, Do I
Do I Worry
Dolores
Don't Take Your Love From Me
Down Argentine Way
Down Forget-Me-Not Lane
Echo Of A Serenade, The (Te Quiero Dijiste)
Falling Leaves
Ferry Boat Serenade (La Piccinina)
First Lullaby, The
Five O'clock Whistle, The
Flamingo
Frenesi
Goodnight And Bless You
Green Eyes (Aquellos Ojos Verdes)
Hawaiian War Chant, The
Hey Little Hen
Hut Sut Song
I Came, I Saw, I Conga'd
I Concentrate On You
I Didn't Know What Time It Was
I Don't Want To Set The World On Fire
I Guess I'll Have To Dream The Rest
I Hear A Rhapsody
I Understand
I Yi Yi Yi Yi I Like You Very Much
I'll Never Let A Day Pass By
I've Got Sixpence (As I Go Rolling Home)
Intermezzo (Souvenir De Vienne)
It Never Entered My Mind
It's A Great Day For The Irish
It's Always You
It's Foolish But It's Fun
Java Jive
Johnny Pedler
Just One Of Those Things
Kiss The Boys Goodbye
Last Time I Saw Paris, The
Lazy River
Let There Be Love
Let's Be Buddies
London I Love, The
London Pride
Mama Yo Quiero (I Want My Mama)
Maria Elena
Maybe (Madden, Flynn)

Minnie From Trinidad
Misirlou
Music Makers, The
My Romance
My Sister And I
On The Isle Of May
One O'clock Jump
Only Forever
Our Love Affair
Pair Of Silver Wings, A
Perfidia
Polka Dots And Moonbeams
Rhythm On The River
Ridin' High
Room Five Hundred And Four
Russian Rose
Saint Mary's In The Twilight
Sam You Made The Pants Too Long
San Antonio Rose
Sand In My Shoes
Scrub Me Mama With A Boogie Beat
Sleepy Serenade
South American Way
Starlight Serenade
That's For Me
Things I Love, The
This Is No Laughing Matter
Time Was (Duerme)
Tonight We Love
Trade Winds
Tumbling Tumbleweeds
Waltzing In The Clouds
We Three (My Echo, My Shadow And Me)
When April Sings
When I See An Elephant Fly
When That Man Is Dead And Gone
When The Moon Comes Over Madison Square
When The Sun Comes Out
When They Sound The Last All Clear
Whispering Grass
Why Don't We Do This More Often
Yes My Darling Daughter
You Don't Have To Tell Me, I Know
You Say The Sweetest Things Baby
You Started Something
You Stepped Out Of A Dream
You've Got Me This Way
Yours (Quierme Mucho)

1942
Always In My Heart
Anniversary Waltz, The
Arthur Murray Taught Me Dancing In A Hurry
At Last
Babalu
Baby Mine
Bambi
Be Careful It's My Heart
Blue Shadows And White Gardenias
Blues In The Night
Buckle Down Winsocki
By Candlelight
Cabin In The Sky
Caissons Go Rolling Along, The
Chattanooga Choo Choo

Conchita, Marquita, Lolita, Pepita, Rosita, Juanita Lopez
Day Dreaming
Deep In The Heart Of Texas
Do You Care
Don't Sit Under The Apple Tree
Elmer's Tune
Fleet's In, The
Friendship
Happiness Is A Thing Called Joe
Happy Holiday
How About You
How Green Was My Valley
Humpty Dumpty Heart
I Could Write A Book
I Don't Want To Walk Without You
I Got It Bad, And That Ain't Good
I Know Why
I Met Her On Monday
I Remember You
I Take To You
I Threw A Kiss In The Ocean
I'll Capture Your Heart
I'm Going To See You Today
I've Got A Gal In Kalamazoo
I've Heard That Song Before
Idaho
It Costs So Little
It Happened In Sun Valley
Jersey Bounce
Jim
Jingle, Jangle, Jingle
Just A-Sittin' And A-Rockin'
Katy Did, Katy Didn't
Keep An Eye On Your Heart
Lamplighter's Serenade, The
Let's Get Away From It All
Let's Start The New Year Right
Little April Shower
Love Is A Song
Lover Man (Oh Where Can You Be)
Ma, I Miss Your Apple Pie
Moonlight Becomes You
Moonlight Cocktail
My Paradise
My Ship
One Dozen Roses
One Love Forever
One More Kiss
Road To Morocco, The
Rolleo Rolling Along
Rose O'Day
Serenade In Blue
Shrine of St. Cecilia, The (Min Soldat)
Silver Wings In The Moonlight
Sing, Everybody Sing
Sinner Kissed An Angel, A
Skylark
Soft Shoe Shuffle, The
Some Sunny Day
Someone's Rocking My Dreamboat
Stage Coach
Story Of A Starry Night, The
String Of Pearls, A
Taboo
Taking A Chance On Love
Tangerine
That Lovely Weekend

That's The Moon My Son
There's A Land Of Begin Again
Thing-Ummy-Bob, The
This Is Worth Fighting For
This Time The Dream's On Me
Three Little Sisters
Tropical Magic
Waiter And The Porter And The Upstairs Maid, The
Warsaw Concerto, The
Watch The Birdie
What More Can I Say
When I Love, I Love
When The Lights Go On Again
Where In The World
Where The Waters Are Blue
Whistler's Mother-in-law, The
White Christmas
White Cliffs Of Dover, The
Wrap Yourself In Cotton Wool
You Are My Sunshine
You Walk By
Zoot Suit, A

1943

Ain't Got A Dime To My Name
All Or Nothing At All
All Our Tomorrows
American Patrol
Army Air Corps Song, The
At The Crossroads
Be Honest With Me
Better Not Roll Those Blue Blue Eyes
Brazil
Break Of Day
Can't Get Out Of This Mood
Close To You
Coming In On A Wing And A Prayer
Constantly
Daybreak
Dearly Beloved
Don't Ask Me Why
Don't Get Around Much Anymore
Easy Street
Every Night About This Time
Everything I've Got
Fuhrer's Face, Der
G'bye Now
He's My Guy
Hit The Road To Dreamland
Homecoming Waltz, The
I Came Here To Talk For Joe
I Get The Neck Of The Chicken
I Had The Craziest Dream
I Left My Heart At The Stage Door Canteen
I Lost My Sugar In Salt Lake City
I Love To Sing
I'll Be Around
I'm Getting Tired So I Can Sleep
I'm Gonna Get Lit Up
I'm Old Fashioned
I'm Thinking Tonight Of My Blue Eyes
If You Please
In My Arms
In The Blue Of Evening
It Can't Be Wrong

Jenny
Johnny Doughboy Found A Rose In Ireland
Johnny Zero
Lady Who Didn't Believe In Love, The
Let's Get Lost
Mister Five By Five
"Murder" He Says
My British Buddy
My Devotion
My Heart And I
My Shining Hour
Never Say Goodbye
Nightingale
Not Mine
Number Something Far Away Lane
Oh The Pity Of It All
Old Music Master, The
Pedro The Fisherman
Pennsylvania Polka
People Like You And Me
Perdido
Pistol Packin' Mama
Praise The Lord And Pass The Ammunition
Question And Answer (Demande Et Response)
Run Little Raindrop Run
Sing Me A Song Of The Islands
Smiths And The Joneses, The
Star Eyes
Sunday, Monday Or Always
That Old Black Magic
There Are Angels Outside Heaven
There Are Such Things
There Will Never Be Another You
There's A Harbour Of Dreamboats
There's No Two Ways About Love
This Is The Army Mister Jones
Thoughtless
Tico Tico
Time's A Wastin'
Touch Of Texas
Wait For Me Mary
Walking The Floor Over You
We Musn't Say Goodbye
Weep No More My Lady
What's The Good Word Mister Bluebird
When You Know You're Not Forgotten
Who Wouldn't Love You
Why Don't You Do Right
Why Don't You Fall In Love With Me
Yes Indeed
You Rhyme With Everything That's Beautiful
You Were Never Lovelier
You'd Be So Nice To Come Home To
You'll Never Know

1944

Amor
And Then You Kissed Me
Besame Mucho (Kiss Me)
Big Noise From Winnetka
Boy Next Door, The
By The River Of The Roses
Canteen Bounce, The
Cornish Rhapsody

Cow Cow Boogie
Dance With A Dolly
Day After Forever, The
Do Nothing Till You Hear From Me
Don't Sweetheart Me
Down In The Valley
Dreamer, The
For The First Time I've Fallen In Love
G.I. Jive, The
Going My Way
Goodnight Wherever You Are
Harlem Nocturne
Have Yourself A Merry Little Christmas
Hello Mom
His Rocking Horse Ran Away
Hold Back The Dawn
Holiday For Strings
Hour Never Passes, An
How Blue The Night
How Many Hearts Have You Broken
How Sweet You Are
I Couldn't Sleep A Wink Last Night
I Didn't Know About You
I Heard You Cried Last Night
I Like To Recognize The Tune
I Never Mention Your Name, Oh No
I'll Be Seeing You
I'll Remember April
I'll Walk Alone
I'm Gonna Move To The Outskirts Of Town
I'm Making Believe
I'm Riding For A Fall
If You Ever Go To Ireland
In The Spirit Of The Moment
Is My Baby Blue Tonight
Is You Is, Or Is You Ain't My Baby
It Could Happen To You
It Must Be Jelly, 'cause Jam Don't Shake Like That
It's Love, Love, Love
Journey To A Star, A
Let Me Love You Tonight (No Te Importe Saber)
Let's Take The Long Way Home
Life's Full Of Consequences
Lili Marlene
Long Ago And Far Away
Lovely Way To Spend An Evening, A
Mairzy Doats And Dozy Doats
Milkman Keep Those Bottles Quiet
Music Stopped, The
My Heart Tells Me
No Love, No Nothing
Now I Know
Poinciana
Roll Me Over
Sailor Who Are You Dreaming Of Tonight
San Fernando Valley
Say A Prayer For The Boys Over There
Shine On Victory Moon
Shoo Shoo Baby
Some Day I'll Meet You Again
Some Day Soon
Spring Will Be A Little Late This Year
Swinging On A Star
Take It Easy

Take The 'A' Train
Tenement Symphony, The
They're Either Too Young Or Too Old
Thinking About The Wabash
Till Stars Forget To Shine
Time Waits For No One
To Keep My Love Alive
Trolley Song, The
Victory Polka
When They Ask About You
You Belong To My Heart
You've Got Me Where You Want Me
Your Socks Don't Match

1945
Ac-cent-tchu-ate The Positive
After A While
And Her Tears Flowed Like Wine
Baia
Bell Bottom Trousers
Can't Help Singing
Can't You Read Between The Lines
Candy
Carolina
Chewing A Piece Of Straw
Cokey Cokey, The
Come Out, Come Out, Wherever You Are
Come With Me My Honey
Coming Home
Don't Fence Me In
Dream
Ev'ry Time We Say Goodbye
Friend Of Yours, A
Gipsy, The
Gonna Build A Big Fence Around Texas
How Little We Know
I Begged Her
I Hope To Die If I Told A Lie
I Love You
I Promise You
I Should Care
I Wanna Get Married
I Wish I Knew
I'd Rather Be Me
I'll Always Be With You
I'm Beginning To See The Light
I'm Gonna Love That Guy
I'm In Love With Two Sweethearts
In A Moment Of Madness
In Chi-chi Castenango
Into Each Life Some Rain Must Fall
Irresistible You
It's Been A Long Long Time
Juke Box Saturday Night
June Comes Around Every Year
Just A Little Fond Affection
Just A Prayer Away
Kiss In The Night, A (Anoche Te Bese)
Laura
Let Him Go, Let Him Tarry
Little On The Lonely Side, A
Lonely Footsteps
Love Is My Reason
Matelot
More And More
More I See You, The

My Dreams Are Getting Better All The Time
My Guy's Come Back
My Heart Sings
Nina
One Meat Ball
Opus Number One
Out Of The Night
Out Of This World
Pablo The Dreamer
Pretty Kitty Blue Eyes
Rum And Coca-cola
Sarie Marais
Saturday Night Is The Loneliest Night Of The Week
Sentimental Journey
She Broke My Heart In Three Places
Stella By Starlight
Straighten Up And Fly Right
Suddenly It's Spring
Sweet Dreams Sweetheart
Symphony
There Goes That Song Again
There I've Said It Again
There's No You
Three Caballeros, The (Ay Jalisco No Te Rajes)
We'll Gather Lilacs
What Makes The Sunset
Who Dat Up Dere
You, Fascinating You

1946
All Through The Day
Along The Navajo Trail
Amado Mio
Ampstead Way, The
Aren't You Glad You're You
As If I Didn't Have Enough On My Mind
Ashby De La Zouch (Castle Abbey)
Bless You
Caldonia
Cement Mixer
Charm Of You, The
Chickery Chick
Chiquita Banana
Close As Pages In A Book
Coax Me A Little Bit
Come Closer To Me (Acercate Mas)
Come Rain Or Come Shine
Come To Baby Do
Cruising Down The River
Cynthia's In Love
Day By Day
Dear Old Donegal
Did You Ever Get That Feeling In The Moonlight
Do You Love Me
Door Will Open, A
Enlloro (Voodoo Moon)
Everybody Knew But Me
Full Moon And Empty Arms
Getting Nowhere
Good, Good, Good
Gotta Be This Or That
Green Cockatoo, The
Her Bathing Suit Never Got Wet
Here Comes Heaven Again

Hey-Ba-Ba-Re-Bop
Homesick, That's All
I Can't Begin To Tell You
I Don't Know Enough About You
I Dream Of You
I Fall In Love Too Easily
I Fall In Love With You Every Day
I'll Buy That Dream
I'll Close My Eyes
I'm So All Alone
If You Are But A Dream
Isn't It Kinda Fun
It Might As Well Be Spring
It's A Grand Night For Singing
It's A Pity To Say Goodnight
Johnny Fedora
Kentucky
Laughing On The Outside
Let It Be Soon
Let It Snow
Let's Keep It That Way
Linger In My Arms A Little Longer Baby
Love Letters
Love Steals Your Heart
Make Mine Music
Mister Moon You've Got A Million Swee-
thearts
Money Is The Root Of All Evil
My Heart Goes Crazy
My Heart Isn't In It
Nancy (With The Laughing Face)
No Can Do
Oh What It Seemed To Be
Old Lamplighter, The
On The Atchison, Topeka And The
Santa Fe
Parrot On The Fortune Teller's Hat, The
Pompton Turnpike
Primrose Hill
Put It There Pal
Put The Blame On Mame
September Song
Shoo Fly Pie And Apple Pan Dowdy
Sioux City Sue
Skyliner
So Would I
Some Sunday Morning
Someday You'll Want Me To Want You
Soon It Will Be Sunday
Stars Will Remember, The
Strange Music
Surrender
Sweetheart, We'll Never Grow Old
Tampico
That's For Me
There's No One But You
This Heart Of Mine
Till The End Of Time
Till Then
To Each His Own
Too Many Irons In The Fire
Twilight Time
Two Silhouettes
Wait And See
Waiting For The Train To Come In
Welcome To My Dream
Without You (Tres Palabras)
Yah-Ta-Ta, Yah-Ta-Ta

You Always Hurt The One You Love
You Are Too Beautiful
You Can't Keep A Good Dreamer Down
You Keep Coming Back Like A Song
You Sang My Love Song To Somebody
Else
You Won't Be Satisfied
You're Nobody 'till Somebody Loves
You

1947

Accordion
Across The Alley From The Alamo
Ain't Nobody Hear But Us Chickens
Anniversary Song, The
Another Night Like This
Anything You Can Do
Apple Blossom Wedding, An
As Long As I'm Dreaming
Bloop Bleep
Chi-Baba Chi-Baba
Choo Choo Ch'boogie
Christmas Dreaming
Coffee Song, The
Country Style
Danger Ahead
Darktown Poker Club, The
Doin' What Comes Naturally
Don't Fall In Love
Down The Old Spanish Trail
Dream, Dream, Dream
Fellow Needs A Girl, A
Feudin' And Fightin'
Five Minutes More
For Sentimental Reasons
For You, For Me, For Everyone
Gal In Calico, A
Girl That I Marry
Golden Earrings
Hi-Jig-a-Jig (Follow The Band)
House Of Blue Lights, The
How Are Things In Glocca Morra
How Lucky You Are
Huggin' And Chalkin'
I Cain't Say No
I Get Up Every Morning (What Do I Do,
What Do I Do, What Do I Do)
I Got Lost In His Arms
I Got The Sun In The Morning
I Guess I'll Get The Papers And Go
Home
I Keep Forgetting To Remember
I Was Never Kissed Before
I Wish I Didn't Love You So
I'll Make Up For Everything
I'm Afraid To Love You
If I'm Lucky
If This Isn't Love
Is It A Sin
It's A Good Day
It's All Over Now (Skylar / Marcotte)
It's Dreamtime
It's The Same Old Dream
Linda
Little Old Mill
Love
Ma Belle Marguerita
Mam'selle

Managua Nicaragua
Maybe You'll Be There
Mer, La
My Adobe Hacienda
My Defenses Are Down
My First Love, My Last Love For Always
Near You
Now Is The Hour (Hearere Ra)
Oh But I Do
Oh What A Beautiful Morning
Oklahoma
Ol' Buttermilk Sky
Open The Door Richard
Out Of My Dreams
Patience And Fortitude
People Will Say We're In Love
Pretending
Rainy Night In Rio, A
Rickerty Rickshaw Man, The
Route Sixty-Six
Rumours Are Flying
Sewing Machine, The
Smile Right Back At The Sun
Sooner Or Later
South America, Take It Away
Sunday Kind Of Love, A
Surrey With The Fringe On Top, The
That's The Beginning Of The End
That's What I Like About The South
There's No Business Like Show Busi-
ness
They Say It's Wonderful
Things We Did Last Summer, The
This Is Always
This Is My Lovely Day
Time After Time
Toor-ie On His Bonnet, The
Turntable Song, The
We Could Make Such Beautiful Music
Together
Whole World Is Singing My Song
Woodman, Woodman Spare That Tree
You Can't Get A Man With A Gun
You Make Me Feel So Young
You Went Away And Left Me
Zip-a-Dee-Doo-Dah

1948

Ah But It Happens
All Dressed Up With A Broken Heart
And Mimi
Anything I Dream Is Possible
Ask Anyone Who Knows
At The Candlelight Cafe
Ballerina
Be A Clown
Bread And Butter Woman, A
Bumble Boogie
But Beautiful
Buttons And Bows
Civilization
Cool Water
Count Your Blessing
Cuanto Le Gusta
Down Sweetheart Avenue
Dream Of Owlen, The
Fella With An Umbrella, A

Fiddle Faddle
Fine Brown Frame
For Every Man There's A Woman
Galway Bay
Gentleman Is A Dope, The
Hair Of Gold, Eyes Of Blue
Heart Breaker
Hooray For Love
Hot Canary, The
I'll Dance At Your Wedding
I'm My Own Grandpa
I'm So Right Tonight
In Old Lisbon (Lisboa Antigua)
It Only Happens When I Dance With You
It's A Most Unusual Day
Jamaican Rumba
Laroo Laroo Lilli Bolero
Lazy Countryside
Life Get's Tedious, Don't It
Love Is Where You Find It
Love Somebody
Manana - Is Soon Enough For Me
Matinee
My Happiness
Nature Boy
Nice To Know You Care
No Orchids For My Lady
October Twilight
On A Slow Boat To China
Once Upon A Wintertime
Papa Won't You Dance With Me
Portrait Of A Flirt
Rambling Rose
Reflections On The Water
Sabre Dance
Serenade Of The Bells
Shoemaker's Serenade, The
Smoke, Smoke, Smoke (That Cigarette)
So Tired
Take Me To Your Heart Again (La Vie En Rose)
Tenderly
Teresa
That's My Desire
This Is My Mother's Day
Three Bells, The (Les Trois Cloches)
Time May Change
Too Fat Polka
Toolie Oolie Doolie
Tree In The Meadow, A
Tubby The Tuba
We'll Be Together Again
When You're In Love
Woody Woodpecker
You Call Everybody Darling
You Can't Be True Dear (Du Lannst Nicht Treu Sein)
You Don't Have To Know The Language
You've Changed

1949

'A' You're Adorable
Again
Almost Like Being In Love
Baby It's Cold Outside

Beautiful Eyes
Best Of All
Big Rock Candy Mountain, The
Blue Ribbon Gal
Bouquet Of Roses, A
Brush Those Tears From Your Eyes
Busy Doing Nothing
Candy Kisses
Careless Hands
Cigareets, Whusky And Wild Wild Women
Circus
Clancy Lowered The Boom
Clopin Clopant
Confidentially
Couple Of Swells, A
Crystal Gazer, The
December
Don't Cry Joe (Let Her Go, Let Her Go, Let Her Go)
Down By The Station
Down In The Glen
Dreamer With A Penny
Dreamer's Holiday, A
Dry Bones
Echo Told Me A Lie, The
Far Away Places
Forever And Ever
Four Winds And The Seven Seas
Ghost Riders In The Sky
Hang On The Bell Nellie
Harry Lime Theme, The
He's A Real Gone Guy
Heather On The Hill, The
Helene
Hop Scotch Polka
How Can You Buy Killarney
How High The Moon
How It Lies, How It Lies, How It Lies
Hurry On Down
I Don't See Me In Your Eyes Anymore
I'll Keep The Lovelight Burning
I've Got A Lovely Bunch Of Coconuts
If You Stub Your Toe On The Moon
In My Dreams
It All Comes Back To Me Now
It Happened In Adano
It's A Cruel Cruel World
It's Magic
It's You Or No-one
Jealous Heart
Jumping Bean
Kiss In Your Eyes
Kiss Me Sweet
Last Mile Home, The
Lavender Blue
Legend Of The Glass Mountain, The
Leicester Square Rag
Little Bird Told Me, A
Maharajah Of Magador, The
Maybe It's Because
Monkey And The Organ Grinder, The
Mule Train
My Darling, My Darling
My Dream Is Yours
My Golden Baby
My One And Only Highland Fling
My Two Front Teeth

New York, New York (Comden, Green, Bernstein)
No Moon At All
Now That I Need You
On The Five Forty-five
Once In Love With Amy
Our Love Story
Perhaps, Perhaps, Perhaps (Quizas, Quizas, Quizas)
Pigalle
Powder Your Face With Sunshine
Put 'em In A Box
Put Your Shoes On Lucy
Red Roses For A Blue Lady
Room Full Of Roses,a
Rose In A Garden Of Weeds, A
Rosewood Spinet, A
Seine, La
She's A Home Girl
Shoes With Wings On
Similau
Slipping Around
Snowy White Snow And Jingle Bells
Some Day My Heart Will Awake
Someone Like You
Song of Capri, The
Song of The Mountains, The (La Montanara)
Stanley Steamer, The
Stepping Out With My Baby
Strawberry Moon In A Blueberry Sky, A
Streets Of Laredo, The
Take Your Girl
That Lucky Old Sun
That Old Gang Of Mine
There's Nothing Rougher Than Love
Till All Our Dreams Come True
Twenty-Four Hours Of Sunshine
We'll Keep A Welcome
Wedding Of Lilli Marlene, The
Wedding Samba, The
While The Angelus Was Ringing
You're Breaking My Heart

1950

Ashes Of Roses
Ask Me No Questions
Autumn Leaves
Beloved Be Faithful
Bibbidi-Bobbidi-Boo
Bonaparte's Retreat
Busy Line
C'est Si Bon
Can Anyone Explain
Candy And Cake
Carousel Waltz, The
Chattanoogie Shoeshine Boy
Cherry Stones
Choo'n' Gum
Copper Canyon
Count Every Star
Cry Of The Wild Goose, The
Daddy's Little Girl
Dear Hearts And Gentle People
Dearie
Dream Is A Wish Your Heart Makes, A
Enjoy Yourself
Ferry Boat Inn, The

French Can Can Polka
Girls Were Made To Take Care Of Boys
Gone Fishin'
Goodnight Irene
Gordon For Me, A
Happy Times
Have I Told You Lately That I Love You
Hey Neighbour
Home Cooking
Hoop Dee-Doo
I Don't Care If The Sun Don't Shine
I Leave My Heart In An English Garden
I Remember The Cornfields
I Said My Pyjamas (And Put On My Prayers)
I Want You To Want Me To Want You
I'd've Baked A Cake
If I Had My Life To Live Over
If I Loved You
If I Were A Blackbird
It's So Nice To Have A Man Around The House
June Is Busting Out All Over
Just Say I Love Her
Let's Do It Again
Load Of Hay, A
Mambo Jambo
Me And My Imagination
M-I-S-S-I-S-S-I-P-P-I
Mister Snow
Mona Lisa
Moonlight In Vermont
Music, Music, Music
My Foolish Heart
My Thanks To You
Night The Floor Fell In, The
No Other Love
Oh You Sweet One
Old Master Painter, The
Old Piano Roll Blues, The
Orange Coloured Sky
Out Of A Clear Blue Sky
Petite Waltz, The
Quicksilver
Rag Mop
Rainy Day Refrain, A (Schnürlregen)
Rose I Bring You, The
Rudolph The Red Nosed Reindeer
Sam's Song
Scarlet Ribbons
Scottish Samba, The
Senora
Sentimental Me
She's A Lady
Silver Dollar
Six Times A Week And Twice On Sundays
Sleigh Ride
Speak Low
Sunshine Cake
Take Her To Jamaica (Where The Rum Comes From)
Tzena, Tzena, Tzena
Victory Test Match, The
We All Have A Song In Our Hearts
Wilhelmina
You'll Never Walk Alone
Your Heart And My Heart

1951
All My Love (Contet, Durand, Parish)
Allentown Jail
Always True To You In My Fashion
And So To Sleep Again
As We Are Today
At The End Of The Day
Bali Ha'i
Be My Love
Beautiful Brown Eyes
Because Of You
Beggar In Love, A
Belle, Belle, My Liberty Belle
Buffalo Billy
By Strauss
Can I Canoe You Up The River
Castle Rock
Castles In The Sand
Christopher Columbus
Cock-eyed Optimist, A
Cold Cold Heart
Come On A My House
Domino
From This Moment On
Frosty The Snowman
Get Out Those Old Records
Give Me The Simple Life
Good Luck, Good Health, God Bless You
Good Morning Mr Echo
Happy Talk
Hey Good Looking
Honey Bun
House Of Singing Bamboo, The
How Could You Believe Me, When I Said I Love You, When You Know I've Been A Liar All My Life
I Hate Men
I Love The Sunshine Of Your Smile
I Love The Way You Say 'Goodnight'
I Taut I Taw A Puddy Tat
I Wish I Wuz
I'll Always Love You
I'm Gonnna Wash That Man Right Out Of My Hair
I'm In Love With A Wonderful Guy
If I Can Help Somebody
In The Cool, Cool, Cool Of The Evening
Ivory Rag
Jezebel
Kentuckly Waltz, The
Kiss To Build A Dream On, A
Kisses Sweeter Than Wine
Little White Duck
London By Night
Loveliest Night Of The Year
Lovesick Blues
Lucky Lucky Lucky Me
Mademoiselle De Paris
Mariandl-andl-andl
May The Good Lord Bless And Keep You
Mocking Bird Hill
My Heart Cries For You
My Love And Devotion
My Resistance Is Low
My Truly Truly Fair
On Top Of Old Smokey

Our Very Own
Penny A Kiss, A Penny A Hug, A
Pink Champagne
Pretty Eyed Baby
Ronde De L'amour, La
Rose Rose I Love You (May Kway O May Kway)
Roving Kind, The
Shanghai
Shot Gun Boogie
Shrimp Boats
So In Love
So Long, It's Been Good To Know You
Some Enchanted Evening
Song Of Delilah, The
Sparrow In The Treetop
Tennessee Waltz, The
There Is Nothing Like A Dame
There's Always Room At Our House
There's No Tomorrow
Thing, The
This Nearly Was Mine
Too Darn Hot
Too Late Now
Too Young
Tulips And Heather
Unforgettable
Walking And Whistling Blues
Waltzing Cat, The
White Suit Samba, The
Why Can't You Behave
With These Hands
Would I Love You
Wunderbar
You Are My Destiny (Baynes/Ralton)
Younger Than Springtime

1952
'A' Round The Corner
Any Time
Anywhere I Wonder
At Last, At Last
Auf Wiederseh'n Sweetheart
Baby Doll
Be Anything - But Be Mine
Be My Life's Companion
Because Of Rain
Because You're Mine
Bella Musica
Belle Of The Ball
Blacksmith Blues, The
Blue Bell Polka
Blue Tango
Botch-a-Me
Brittania Rag
Congratulations
Cry
Dance Me Loose
Day Of Jubilo, The
Delicado
Didja Ever
Don't Laugh At Me
Down The Trail Of Aching Hearts
Ecstasy
El Cumbanchero
Faith Can Move Mountains
Feet Up

Flirtation Waltz, The
From The Time You Say Goodbye
Gandy Dancers Ball, The
Got You On My Mind
Guy Is A Guy, A
Half As Much
Here In My Heart
High Noon
Homing Waltz, The
I Thought Of You Last Night
I Wanna Say Hello
I Went To Your Wedding
I'm Glad There Is You
I'm Gonna Live Till I Die
I'm Yours (Mellin)
If You Go (Si Tu Partais)
Isle Of Innisfree
It's A Lovely Day Today
It's All In The Game
Jambalaya (On The Bayou)
Kiss Of Fire, The
Little White Cloud That Cried, The
Lullaby Of Birdland
Marching Strings
Marrying For Love
Meet Mister Callaghan
Moses
Never (Daniels, Newman)
No Two People
Oh Look At Me Now
Old Soft Shoe, The
Only Fools
Our Love Is Here To Stay
Padam, Padam
Please Mister Sun
Plink, Plank, Plunk
Rock Of Gibraltar
Saturday Rag
Sin
Slow Coach
Somewhere Along The Way
Star Of Hope
Sugar Bush
Take My Heart
Tell Me Why
That's Why
There's A Pawnshop On The Corner
To Be Worthy Of You
Turn Back The Hands Of Time
Under Paris Skies (Sous Le Ciel De Paris)
Walkin' To Missouri
We Won't Live In A Castle
Wheel Of Fortune, The
When I Fall In Love
When The World Was Young
When You're In Love
Where Did My Snowman Go
Why Worry
Wimoweh (Arr. Campbell)
Wonderful Copenhagen
You Belong To Me
You're Just In Love
Zing A Little Zong

1953

Adelaide's Lament

All The Time And Everywhere
Anna
Answer Me
April In Portugal (Coimbra)
Big Head
Big Mamou
Bridge Of Sighs, The
Broken Wings (Jerome, Grun)
Bushel And A Peck, A
Bye Bye Baby
Call Of The Faraway Hills, The
Can't I
Celebration Rag
Chick A Boom
Cloud Lucky Seven
Comes A-long A-love
Coronation Rag
Dancin' With Someone
Diamonds Are A Girl's Best Friend
Don't Let The Stars Get In Your Eyes
Donkey Song, The
Downhearted
Dragnet (Theme Of The Dragnet TV Programme)
Dummy Song, The
Ebb Tide
Eternally (Terry's Theme)
From Here To Eternity
Getting To Know You
Golden Tango, The
Have You Heard
Hello Young Lovers
Hey Joe (Bryant)
Hi lilli Hi-lo
Hold Me, Thrill Me, Kiss Me
Hot Toddy
I Believe
I Saw Mommy Kissing Santa Claus
I Talk To The Trees
I Whistle A Happy Tune
I'd Love To Fall Asleep
I'm Gonna Ring The Bell Tonight
I'm Praying To Saint Christopher
I'm Walking Behind You
I've Never Been In Love Before
If I Had A Golden Umbrella
If I Were A Bell
If You Love Me (Hyme A L'Amour)
In A Golden Coach
Is It Any Wonder
Istanbul (Not Constantinople)
Johnny Is The Boy For Me
Kiss
Let's Walk That-a-Way
Limelight
Little Red Monkey
Look At That Girl
Love Of My Life
Luck Be A Lady Tonight
Melba Waltz, The
Mister Tap-Toe
Mother Nature And Father Time
My Heart Belongs To You
My Love, My Life, My Happiness
My One And Only Love
Non Dimenticar (T'ho Voluto Bene)
Now
O Mein Papa

Oh Happy Day (Koplow, Reed)
Oo! What You Do To Me
Outside Of Heaven
Penny Whistle Song, The
Poppa Piccolono (Papaveri E Papere)
Pretend
Pretty Little Black Eyed Susie
Rachel
Rags To Riches
Ruby
Say You're Mine Again
Second Star To The Right, The
Settin' The Woods On Fire
Seven Lonely Days
Shall We Dance
She Wears Red Feathers
Sippin' Soda
Sit Down You're Rocking The Boat
Swedish Rhapsody
Takes Two To Tango
Tell Me A Story
Tell Me You're Mine (Per Un Bacio D'amor)
Tennessee Wig-walk, The
That Doggie In The Window
That's Amore
That's Entertainment
That's What Makes Paris Paree
They Call The Wind Maria
Till I Waltz Again With You
Till They've All Gone Home
Triplets
Ugly Duckling, The
Vaya Con Dios
We Kiss In The Shadow
Where Is Your Heart (Moulin Rouge Theme)
Where The Wind Blows
Why Don't You Believe Me
Wild Horses
Windsor Waltz, The
Wish You Were Here
You're A Pink Toothbrush
You, You, You
Your Cheating Heart
Your Mother And Mine

1954

Aleez Vous-En, Go Away
Autumn In New York
Bandit, The (O'Cangaceiro)
Bell Bottom Blues
Bimbo
Black Hills Of Dakota, The
Blowing Wild
Blue Bells Of Broadway, The
Book, The
C'est Magnifique
Can This Be Love
Cara Mia
Carnavalito
Changing Partners
Creep, The
Cross Over The Bridge
Crying In The Chapel
Cuff Of My Shirt, The
Deadwood Stage, The

Dime And A Dollar, A
Don't Leave Me Now
Eh Cumpari
Ev'ry Street's A Boulevard
Friends And Neighbours
From The Vine Came The Grape
Gang That Sang "Heart Of My Heart", The
Gilly-Gilly Ossenfeffer Katzen Ellen Bogen By The Sea
Give Me Your Word
Hajji Baba
Happy Wanderer, The
Heartless
Here's That Rainy Day
High And The Mighty, The
Hold My Hand
I Can't Tell A Waltz From A Tango
I Could Be Happy With You
I Get So Lonely
I Love Paris
I Need You Now
I See The Moon
I Still Believe
Idle Gossip
If I Gave My Heart To You
It's All Right With Me
It's Never Too Late To Fall In Love
Jilted
Johnny Guitar
Jones Boy, The
Kid's Last Fight, The
Little Shoemaker, The (Le Petit Cordonnier)
Little Things Mean A Lot
Lonely Ballerina
Luxembourg Polka
Make Love To Me
Mama Doll Song, The
Man (Uh-Huh)
Monotonous
My Friend
My Own True Love
My Son, My Son
Never Never Land
No One But You
Now And Forever (Oh Heideroslein)
Papa Loves Mambo
Pavements Of Paris, The (Sur Le Pavé
Rain, Rain, Rain
Ricochet
River Of No Return, The
Rock-a-Beatin' Boogie
Santo Natale
Secret Love
Sh-Boom
Shake, Rattle And Roll
Skin Deep
Skokiaan
Sky Blue Shirt And A Rainbow Tie, A
Smile
Sobbin' Women
Some Day You'll Be Sorry
Somebody
Somebody Bad Stole De Wedding Bell
Someone Else's Roses
Spring Is Here
Story Of Tina, The (Dio Prasina Matia)

Such A Night
Sway (Quien Sera)
Tara's Theme
That's What A Rainy Day Is For
There Must Be A Reason
This Ole House
Three Coins In The Fountain
Two Step, Side Step
Veni-Vidi-Vici
Wait For Me Darling
Wanted
West Of Zanzibar (Jambo)
Woman (Uh-Huh)
Young At Heart

1955
Adelaide
Ain't That A Shame
Alright, Okay, You Win
And This Is My Beloved
Anyone Can Be A Millionaire
Banjo's Back In Town, The
Baubles, Bangles And Beads
Beat Out Dat Rhythm On A Drum
Beyond The Stars
Bless Yore Beautiful Hide
Blossom Fell, A
Blue Star (The Medic Theme)
Boomerang
Bring Your Smile Along
Chee Chee-oo-chee
Cherry Pink And Apple Blossom White
Christmas Alphabet
Close The Door (They're Coming In The Window)
Crazy Otto Rag
Dam Busters March, The
Dance With Me Henry (Wallflower)
Danger, Heartbreak Ahead
Dat's Love
Day The Circus Left Town, The
Domani
Don't Worry
Dream Boat
Earth Angel
Evermore
Every Day Of My Life
Everywhere
Finger Of Suspicion, The
Give Me The Right
Go On By
Goin' Co'tin'
Guess Who I Saw Today
Hawkeye
Heartbeat
Hernando's Hideaway
Hey Mister Banjo
Hey There
How Important Can It Be
I See Your Face Before Me
I Wonder
I'll Be There
I'll Come When You Call
I'll Never Stop Loving You
I'm In Favour Of Friendship
If Anyone Finds This, I Love You
If You Believe

In Love For The Very First Time
John And Julie
Learning The Blues
Let Me Go Lover
Longing For You
Love Is A Many Splendoured Thing
Make Yourself Comfortable
Mama
Mambo Italiano
Man From Laramie, The
Man That Got Away, The
Meet Me On The Corner
Mister Sandman
Mobile
Moments To Remember
Most Beautiful Girl In The World, The
Naughty Lady Of Shady Lane, The
Night We Called It A Day, The
Once A Year Day
Open Up Your Heart
Paper Kisses
Portuguese Washerwomen, The (Les Lavandieres Du Portugal)
Prize Of Gold
Ready, Willing And Able
Relax-Ay-Voo
Rock Around The ClocK
Seventeen
Shifting, Whispering Sands
Sincerely
Softly, Softly
Song Of The Dreamer
Spring, Spring, Spring
Stars Shine In Your Eyes
Steam Heat
Stowaway
Strange Lady In Town
Stranger In Paradise
Suddenly (Cochran / Heuberger)
Suddenly There's A Valley
Summertime In Venice
Sweet And Gentle (Me Lo Dijo Adela)
Teach Me Tonight
That's How A Love Song Was Born
Three Galleons, The (Las Tres Carabelas)
Tomorrow (Hart, Geraldson)
Tweedle Dee
Twenty Tiny Fingers
Unchained Melody
Unsuspecting Heart
Wedding Bells (Hochzeitsglocken)
When You Lose The One You Love
Where Will The Dimple Be
Wonderful Wonderful Day
Yellow Rose Of Texas, The
You My Love

1956
Allegheny Moon
Arrivederci Darling (Arrivederci Roma)
Autumn Concerto
Bad Penny Blues
Ballad Of Davy Crockett, The
Band Of Gold, The
Be-Bop-A-Lula
Believe In Me (Sur Ma Vie)

Birds And The Bees, The
Bloodnoks Rock 'n' Roll
Blue Suede Shoes
Born To Be With You
Bring A Little Water Sylvie
By The Fountains Of Rome
Chain Gang
Christmas And You
Cindy, Oh Cindy
Come Home To My Arms
Come Next Spring
Cry Me A River
Detour Ahead
Don't Be Cruel
Don't Ring-a Da Bell
Dreams Can Tell A Lie
First Row Balcony
Georgian Rumba
Giddy-Up-a-Ding-Dong
Give Her My Love
Glendora
Great Pretender, The
Green Door, The
Guaglione (The Man Who Plays The
Mandolino)
Happiness Street
Happy Whistler, The
Heartbreak Hotel
Hot Diggity
Hound Dog
I louse With Love In It, A
I Hear Music
I Hear You Knocking
I Want You, I Need You, I Love You
I'll Be Home
It's Almost Tomorrow
Italian Theme, The (Mambo Caliente)
Ivory Tower
Jimmy Unknown
Just Walking In The Rain
Lay Down Your Arms
Left Bank, The (C'est A Hambourg)
Let's Take An Old Fashioned Walk
Letter To A Soldier
Long Tall Sally
Lost John
Love And Marriage
Love Me As Though There Were No
Tomorrow
Love Me Tender
Mack The Knife
Magic Touch
Majorca
Man With The Golden Arm
March Hare, The
Memories Are Made Of This
Miracle Of Love, The
Mister Cuckoo (Cuculino)
More (Alstone, Glazer)
My September Love
My Unfinished Symphony
Nellie The Elephant
Never Do A Tango With An Eskimo
No Other Love
Occasional Man, An
Old Pi-anna Rag, The
Only You (Ram, Rand)
Out Of Town

Pickin' A Chicken
Poor People Of Paris, The
Que Sera, Sera
Rip It Up (Blackwell / Marascalco)
Robin Hood
Rock And Roll Waltz
Rock Island Line
Rockin' Through The Rye
Rose Tattoo, The
Sadie's Shawl
Saint Therese Of The Roses
Saints Rock And Roll
Serenade (Cahn / Brodszky)
Singing The Blues
Sixteen Tons
Souvenir D'italie
Sweet Old Fashioned Girl
Tear Fell, A
Tender Trap, The
That Dear Old Gentleman
Too Young To Go Steady
True Love
Two Different Worlds
Walk Hand In Hand
Wayward Wind, The
Well, Did You Evah?
Westminster Waltz
When Mexico Gave Up The Rumba
Who Are We
Who Wants To Be A Millionaire
Why Do Fools Fall In Love
Willie Can
With Your Love (Mes Mains)
Woman In Love, A
You Are My First Love
You Can't Be True To Two
Young And Foolish
Zambesi

1957
Adoration Waltz, The
Affair To Remember, An
All
All Of You
All Shook Up
All The Way
Alone (Craft)
April Love
Armen's Theme
Around The World
Baby Baby
Be My Girl
Bernadine
Butterfingers
Butterfly
By You, By You, By You
Bye Bye Love
Ca C'est L'amour
Chances Are
Chantez Chantez
Chapel Of The Roses, The
Christmas Island
Cumberland Gap, The
Dark Moon
Day-O (Banana Boat Song)
Diana
Don't Forbid Me

Don't Knock The Rock
Don't You Rock Me Daddy-O
Elizabethan Serenade
Fabulous
Fire Down Below
Forgotten Dreams
Freight Train
Friendly Persuasion
Garden Of Eden, The
Girl Can't Help It, The
Gonna Find Me A Bluebird
Gonna Get Along Without You Now
Good Companions, The
Gotta Have Sometihng In The Bank,
Frank
Handful Of Songs, A
He's Got The Whole World In His Hands
Heart
Here I Am In Love Again
I Dreamed
I Love You Baby
I'd Give The World (Liebeslied)
I'll Find You
In The Middle Of A Dark Dark Night
In The Middle Of An Island
Island In The Sun
Just An Old-fashioned Girl
Just In Time
Knee Deep In The Blues
La Pansé (Mandy)
Last Train To San Fernando, The
Let Me Be Loved
Little Darlin'
Long Before I Knew You
Look Homeward Angel
Love Is A Golden Ring
Loving You
Man On Fire
Mandolin Serenade
Mangos
Marianne
Mary's Boy Child
Melodie D'amour (Maladie D'amour)
Mister Wonderful
Moonlight Gambler, The
My Dixie Darling
My House Is Your House (Mi Casa, Su
Casa)
My Special Angel
New Fangled Tango, A
Ninety-Nine Ways
Paralysed
Party
Party's Over, The
Passing Strangers
Peggy Sue
Puttin' On The Style
Rainbow
Razzle Dazzle
Remember You're Mine
Rock With The Cavemen
Rock-a-Billy
Round And Round
Santa Bring My Baby Back To Me
Shiralee
Shish Kebab
Something's Gotta Give
Start Movin'

Swedish Polka, The
Tammy
Teddy Bear
That'll Be The Day
Till
Too Close For Comfort
Too Much (Weinman)
Tutti Frutti
Wake Up Little Susie
Wandering Eyes
We Will Make Love
Wedding Ring
Whatever Lola Wants
White Silver Sands
White Sport Coat, A (And A Pink Carnation)
Whole Lotta Shakin' Goin' On
Wisdom Of A Fool, The
With All My Heart
Wonderful Wonderful
Worried Man Blues
Yes Tonight Josephine
You Don't Owe Me A Thing
You Me And Us
Young Love

1958

All I Have To Do Is Dream
Are You Sincere
Army Game, The
At The Hop
Baby Lover
Beep Beep
Big Man
Book Of Love
Born Too Late
Breathless
Catch A Falling Star
Certain Smile, A
Come On Lets Go
Come Prima (More Than Ever)
Dance, Everyone, Dance
Devotion
Dis Donc, Dis Donc
Do I Love You Because You're Beautiful
Don't
Dormi, Dormi, Dormi
Endless Sleep
Ev'ry Hour, Ev'ry Day Of My Life
Everybody Loves A Love
Fever
Fibbin'
Get Me To The Church On Time
Got A Match?
Grand Coolie Dam
Great Balls Of Fire
Hard Headed Woman
High Class Baby
House Of Bamboo, The
Hula Hoop Song, The
I Could Have Danced All Night
I Enjoy Being A Girl
I May Never Pass This Way Again
I'll Buy You A Star
I've Grown Accustomed To Her Face
If Dreams Came True
It's A Boy

It's Too Soon Too Know
Jailhouse Rock
Jingle Bell Rock
Kewpie Doll
Kiss Me, Honey Honey, Kiss Me
La Dee Dah
Left Right Out Of My Heart
Lights Of Lisbon, The
Little Serenade (Piccolissima Serenata)
Lollipop
Love Makes The World Go Round
Love Me Forever
Mad Passionate Love
Magic Moments
Mandolins In The Moonlight
Maybe Baby
My Heart Is An Open Book
My True Love
Nairobi
Oh Boy
Oh Oh I'm Falling In Love Again
On The Street Where You Live
Only Man On The Island, The
Our Language Of Love
Patricia
Poor Little Fool
Purple People Eater, The
Put A Light In The Window
Raunchy
Rave On
Reet Petite
Return To Me (Ritorna Ame)
River Kwai March
Secret Of Happiness, The
Splish Splash
Stairway Of Love
Story Of My Life, The
Stupid Cupid
Sugar Moon
Sugartime
Summer Is A-Comin' In
Swinging Shepherd Blues
Tequila
There's Never Been A Night
To Be Loved
Tom Hark
Torero
Trudie
Tulips From Amsterdam
Very Precious Love, A
Volare (Nel Blu Dipinto Di Blu)
Wear My Ring (Around Your Neck)
When
When The Boys Talk About The Girls
Whole Lotta Woman, A
Why Don't They Understand
Witch Doctor
Witchcraft
With A Little Bit Of Luck
Wonderful Time Up There
Wouldn't It Be Luverly
Yakity Yak
You Are My Destiny
You Need Hands

1959

Alvin's Harmonica

As I Love You
Ballad Of Bethnal Green, The
Battle Of New Orleans, The
Big Hunk Of Love, A
Bird Dog
Broken Hearted Melody
Bye Bye Baby, Goodbye
C'mon Everybody
Chantilly Lace
Charlie Brown
Chick
China Tea
Ciao Ciao Bambina (Piove)
Come Softly To Me
Day The Rains Came, The
Does Your Chewing Gum Lose It's Flavour
Donna
Dream Lover
Fool Such As I, A
Fort Worth Jail
Forty Miles Of Bad Road
Gal With The Yaller Shoes, The
Gigi
Goodbye Jimmy Goodbye
Guitar Boogie Shuffle
Happy Anniversary
Hawaiian Wedding Song
Heart Of A Man
Here Comes Summer
High Hopes
High School Confidential
Hold Back Tomorrow
Hoots Mon
I Feel Pretty
I Go Ape
I Got Stung
I've Waited So Long
If Only I Could Live My Life Again
It Doesn't Matter Anymore
It's A Wonderful World
It's Just A Matter Of Time
It's Late
It's Only Make Believe
Just A Little Too Much
Just As Much As Ever
King Creole
Lipstick On Your Collar
Little Donkey
Little Drummer Boy, The (Simeone, Onorati & Davis)
Little White Bull
Living Doll
Lonely Boy
Lonesome (Si Tu Vois Ma Mere)
Makin' Love
Maria
Mary Lou
May You Always
Maybe This Year
Milord
Mister Blue
Never Be Anyone Else But You
Never Mind
Oh Carol
Old Shep
One More Sunrise (Morgen)
One Night

Only Sixteen
Peggy Sue Got Married
Personality
Peter Gunn
Petite Fleur
Plenty Good Lovin'
Poison Ivy
Poor Jenny
Problems
Pub With No Beer, The
Put Your Head On My Shoulder
Rawhide
Red River Rock
Roulette
Sea Of Love
Seven Little Girls Sitting In The Back Seat
Side Saddle
Sing Little Birdie
Singing Piano, The
Sleep Walk
Snow Coach
So Many Ways
Someone
Somethin' Else
Something's Coming
Stagger Lee
Strollin'
Teen Beat
Teenager In Love, A
Thank Heaven For Little Girls
There Must Be A Way
This Old Man (Knick Knack Paddy Whack)
Three Stars
'Til I Kissed You
To Know Him Is To Love Him
Tom Dooley
Tomboy
Travellin' Light
Treble Chance
Twixt Twelve And Twenty
Venus (Marshall)
Village Of Saint Bernadette, The
Wait For Me (Ti Diro)
Waterloo
What Do You Want
What'd I Say
Willingly (Melodie Perdue)
Windows Of Paris
Wonder Of You, The
Wonderful Secret Of Love, The
World Outside, The

1960

Alley-Oop
Along Came Caroline
Angela Jones
Angela Mia
Apache
As Long As He Needs Me
Bad Boy
Be Mine
Beatnik Fly, The
Because They're Young
Beyond The Sea
Bonnie Came Back

Cathy's Clown
Chain Gang
Clementine
Colette
Consider Yourself
Cradle Of Love
Deck Of Cards
Delaware
Do You Mind
Dreamin'
El Paso
Everybody's Somebody's Fool
Fall In Love With You
Fings Ain't Wot They Used T'be
Footsteps
Four Little Heels
Girl Of My Best Friend, The
Good Timin'
Goodness Gracious Me
Green Fields
Gurney Slade Theme, The
Handy Man
He'll Have To Go
Heart Of A Teenage Girl
Heartaches By The Number
Hit And Miss
How About That
I Love You
I Wanna Go Home
I'd Do Anything
I'm Sorry
If She Should Come To You (la Montana)
Image Of A Girl
It's Now Or Never
Itsy Bitsy Teenie Weenie Yellow Polka Dot Bikini
Let It Be Me (Je T'appartiens)
Let's Think About Living
Lively
Lonely Pup (in A Christmas Shop)
Look For A Star
Looking High, High, High
Lorelei
Love Is Like A Violin (Mon Coeur Est Un Violin)
Lucille
Lucky Five
Made You
Mais Qui
Man Of Mystery
Mess Of Blues, A
Misty
Mustafa
My Heart Has A Mind Of It's Own
My Little Corner Of The World
My Love For You
My Old Man's A Dustman
Never On Sunday
Nine Times Out Of Ten
Oh So Wunderbar
Ol' Macdonald
Only The Lonely
Paper Roses
Passing Breeze
Please Don't Tease
Please Help Me I'm Falling
Poetry In Motion

Point Of No Return, The
Poor Me
Pretty Blue Eyes
Puppy Love
Robot Man
Rocking Goose
Romantica
Royal Event
Running Bear
Save The Last Dance For Me
Shakin' All Over
Shazam
Sixteen Reasons
So Sad
Someone Else's Baby
Staccato's Theme
Standing On The Corner
Starry Eyed
Stranger, The
Strawberry Fair
Stuck On You (Schroeder, Macfarland)
Summer Place, A
Summer Set
Sweet Nuthins
Tease Me
Tell Laura I Love Her
That's You
Theme From The Apartment, The
Three Step To Heaven
Tie Me Kangaroo Down Sport
Togetherness
Tom Pillibi
Voice In The Wilderness, A
Walk Don't Run
What In The World's Come Over You
When Johnny Comes Marching Home
When Will I Be Loved
Who Could Be Bluer
Why
Wild One
You Are Beautiful
You Got What It Takes

1961

African Waltz
Ain't Gonna Wash For A Week
And The Heavens Cried
Are You Sure
Baby I Don't Care
Baby Sittin' Boogie
Big Bad John
Bless You
Blue Angel
Breaking In A Brand New Broken Heart
Buona Sera
But I Do
Calendar Girl
Climb Ev'ry Mountain
Counting Teardrops
Crying
Cupid
Do-Re-Mi
Doll House
Don't Treat Me Like A Child
Don't You Know It
Easy Going Me
Ebony Eyes

Edelweiss
Exodus Theme, The
F.B.I.
Frightened City, The
Gee Whiz, It's You
Get Lost
Girl Like You, A
Gonna Build A Mountain
Halfway To Paradise
Hats Off To Larry
Have A Drink On Me
Hello Mary Lou, Goodbye Heart
Hey Look Me Over
His Latest Flame
Hit The Road Jack
How Many Tears
How Wonderful To Know (Aneme E Core)
Hundred Pounds Of Clay
I Love You Samantha
I Still Love You All
Johnny Remember Me
Kon-Tiki
Let It Rock
Let's Get Together
Let's Jump The Broomstick
Like Strangers
Little Boy Sad
Little Devil
Lot Of Living To Do, A
Maigret Theme, The
Make Someone Happy
Many Years Ago
Marry Me
Michael Row The Boat Ashore
Midnight In Moscow (Moscow Nights)
Moody River
Moon River
More Than I Can Say
Muskrat
My Boomerang Won't Come Back
My Favourite Things
My Friend The Sea
My Kind Of Girl
Mystery Girl
New Orleans (Guida, Royster)
No Regrets (Non Je Ne Regrette Rien)
North To Alaska
On The Rebound
Pepe
Pop Goes The Weasel
Portrait Of My Love, A
Put On A Happy Face
Quarter To Three
Reach For The Stars (Woner Ich Auch Komm, Wohin Ich Auch Geh)
Ring Of Fire
Romeo
Rubber Ball
Runaround Sue
Runaway
Running Scared
Sailor (Seeman Deine Heimat Ist Das Meer)
Savage, The
Second Time Around
Seventy-Six Trombones
So Long Baby

Sound Of Music, The
Stand By Me
Stay
Sucu Sucu
Surrender
Take Five
Take Good Care Of My Baby
That's My Home
Theme For A Dream
Theme From Dixie
Thousand Stars, A
Till There Was You
Time
Time Has Come, The
Tonight (Bernstein, Sondheim)
Tower Of Strength (Bacharach, Hilliard)
Toy Balloons
Trouble
Walk Right Back
Walking Back To Happiness
Warpaint
Weekend
Well I Ask Ya
What Kind Of Fool Am I
Wheels
When The Girl In Your Arms
Where Have All The Flowers Gone
Where The Boys Are
Who Am I
Wild In The Country
Wild Wind
Will You Love Me Tomorrow
Wooden Heart
You Don't Know
You'll Answer To Me
You're Sixteen
You're The Only Good Thing That's Happened To Me

1962
Ain't That Funny
As You Like It
Ballad Of The Paladin, The
Because Of Love
Bobby's Girl
Breaking Up Is Hard To Do
Call Me Irresponsible
Can't Help Falling In Love
Comancheros, The
Come Outside
Crying In The Rain
Dancin' Party
Desafinado
Devil Woman
Doctor Kildare Theme
Don't Ever Change
Don't Stop - Twist
Don't That Beat All
Dream Baby
English Country Garden
Eso Beso (That Kiss)
Everybody's Twisting
Follow That Dream
Forever Kind Of Love, A
Forget Me Not (Vandyke)
Ginny Come Lately
Good Luck Charm

Goodbye Cruel World
Green Leaves Of Summer, The
Guitar Man
Guitar Tango (Flamenco Guitar)
Happy Birthday Sweet Sixteen
Here Comes That Feeling
Hey Baby
Hey Little Girl
Hole In The Ground
How Can I Meet Her
I Can't Stop Loving You
I Love How You Love Me
I'd Never Find Another You
I'm Just A Baby
I'm Looking Out Of The Window
In San Francisco
It Might As Well Rain Until September
It Started All Over Again
It'll Be Me
James Bond Theme, The
Jeannie
Johnny Will
Keep Your Hands Off My Baby
Language Of Love, The
Last Night Was Made For Love
Let There Be Drums
Let's Dance
Let's Talk About Love
Let's Twist Again
Letter Full Of Tears
Lion Sleeps Tonight, The
Little Bitty Tear, A
Little Miss Lonely
Loco - Motion, The
Lonely
Lonely City
Lonesome
Love Me Do
Main Attraction, The
March Of The Siamese Children, The
Multiplication
Must Be Madison
Never Goodbye
Nicola
No One Can Make My Sunshine Smile
Norman
Nut Rocker
Oh Lonesome Me
Once Upon A Dream
Orange Blossom Special
Our Favourite Melodies
Pick A Bale Of Cotton
Picture Of You, A
Quando, Quando, Quando
Rambling Rose
Reminiscing
Return To Sender
Right Said Fred
Rock-a-Hula Baby
Rockin' Around The Christmas Tree
Roses Are Red
Run To Him
Sealed With A Kiss
Send Me The Pillow That You Dream On
Sharing You
She's Not You
Shelia

Sherry
So Do I (Bet Ami)
Softly As I Leave You (Piano)
Some Kinda Fun
Son, This Is She
Spanish Harlem
Speak To Me Pretty
Speedy Gonzales
Stranger On The Shore
Stripper, The
Sun Arise
Swiss Maid
Tell Me What He Said
Telstar
Things
Three Stars Will Shine Tonight
Twist, The
Twistin' The Night Away
Unsquare Dance, The
Vacation
Venus In Blue Jeans
Wanderer, The
What Now My Love (Et Maintenant)
When My Little Girl Is Smiling
Will I What
Wimoweh (Arr. Denver)
Wonderful Land
Wonderful World Of The Young, The
Ya Ya Twist
You Don't Know Me
Young Ones, The
Z Cars Theme

1963

Ain't Gonna Kiss Ya
All Alone Am I
All My Loving
Another Saturday Night
Applejack
Atlantis
Bachelor Boy
Bad To Me
Be My Baby
Big Girls Don't Cry
Blowing In The Wind
Blue Bayou
Bo Diddley
Bossa Nova Baby
Brown Eyed Handsome Man
Can't Get Used To Losing You
Comin' Home Baby
Cruel Sea, The
Cupboard Love
Da Doo Ron Ron
Dance On
Days Of Wine And Roses
Diamonds
Do You Love Me
Do You Want To Know A Secret
Dominique
Don't Talk To Him
Don't You Think It's Time
End Of The World, The
Everybody
Everything's Coming Up Roses
Falling
First Time, The

Flash Bang Wallop
Folk Singer, The
Foot Tapper
Forget Him
From A Jack To A King
From Me To You
From Russia With Love
Geronimo
Globetrotter
Go Away Little Girl
Harvest Of Love
Hava Nagila
He's A Rebel
He's So Fine
Hello Little Girl
Hello Muddah, Hello Fadduh
Hey Paula
How Do You Do It
I (Who Have Nothing) (Uno Dei Tanti)
I Like It
I Want To Stay Here
I Wonder
I'll Keep You Satisfied
I'll Never Get Over You
I'm Telling You Now
Ice Cream Man
If I Had A Hammer
If I Ruled The World
If You Gotta Make A Fool Of Somebody
In Dreams
In Summer
Island Of Dreams
It Only Took A Minute
It's My Party
Just Like Eddie
Legion's Last Patrol, The
Let's Turkey Trot
Like I Do
Like I've Never Been Gone
Little Girl
Little Town Flirt
Loop De Loop
Losing You (Un Ange Est Renn)
Lucky Lips
Memphis Tennessee
Money (That's What I Want)
More (Olivero, Ortolani, Newell)
My Colouring Book
Next Time
Night Has A Thousand Eyes, The
One Broken Heart For Sale
One Note Samba (Samba De Uma Nota So)
Our Day Will Come
Pipeline
Please Please Me
Puff The Magic Dragon
Rhythm Of The Rain
Robot
Say I Won't Be There
Say Wonderful Things
Scarlett O'Hara
Searchin'
She Loves You
Shindig
Still
Sugar And Spice
Sukiyaki (Ueo Muite Aruku)

Summer Holiday
Sweets For My Sweet
Take These Chains From Heart
Taste Of Honey, A
Tell Him
That's What Love Will Do
Then He Kissed Me
Twist And Shout
Two Kinds Of Teardrops
Up On The Roof
Walk Like A Man
Walk Right In
Welcome To My World
When Will You Say I Love You
Wipe Out
Wishing
You Can Never Stop Me Loving You
You Don't Have To Be A Baby To Cry
You Were Made For Me
You're The Devil In Disguise
Young Lovers

1964

All Day And All Of The Night
Always Something There To Remind Me
Anyone Who Had A Heart
As Tears Go By
As Usual
Baby I Love You
Baby Love
Bits And Pieces
Boys Cry
Can't Buy Me Love
Can't You See That She's Mine
Candy Man
Constantly (L'edera)
Crying Game, The
Do Wah Diddy Diddy
Do You Really Love Me Too (Fools Errand)
Don't Bring Me Down
Don't Let The Sun Catch You Crying
Don't Throw Your Love Away
Don't Turn Around
Down Town
Everybody Loves Somebody
Everything's Alright
Five-Four-Three-Two-One
From A Window
Girl From Ipanema, The
Glad All Over
Goggle Eye
Goldfinger
Good Golly Miss Molly
Hard Day's Night, A
Have I The Right
He's In Town
Hello Dolly
Here I Go Again (Shuman, Westlake)
Hippy Hippy Shake, The
House Of The Rising Sun, The
How Soon
How To Handle A Woman
I Feel Fine
I Get Around
I Just Don't Know What To Do With Myself

I Love You Because
I Only Want To Be With You
I Think Of You
I Understand
I Wanna Be Your Man
I Want To Hold Your Hand
I Will
I Won't Forget You
I Wouldn't Trade You For The World
I'm Crying
I'm Gonna Be Strong
I'm Into Something Good
I'm The Lonely One
I'm The One
If Ever I Would Leave You
In Other Words (Fly Me To The Moon)
It's All Over Now
It's An Open Secret
It's For You
It's Over
Juliet
Just One Look
Kiss Me Quick
Kissin' Cousins
Little Boxes
Little Children
Little Lovin', A
Little Red Rooster
Look At That Face
Losing You
March Of The Mods
Message To Martha
Move Over Darling
My Boy Lollipop
My Guy
Needles And Pins
No Particular Place To Go
Nobody I Know
Not Fade Away
Oh Pretty Woman
On The Beach
One Way Love
Over You
Pretty Paper
Quiet Nights Of Quiet Stars (Corcovado)
Rag Doll
Remember (Walking In The Sand)
Rise And Fall Of Flingle Bunt
Sha La La
She Loves Me
She's Not There
Shout (Isley)
Some Day We're Gonna Love Again
Someone, Someone
Stay Awhile
Sweetest Sounds, The
Tell Me When
That Girl Belongs To Yesterday
Theme For Young Lovers
There's A Heartache Following Me
This Is My Prayer (Non Ho L'eta Per Amarti)
Tobacco Road
Tokyo Melody
Twelfth Of Never
Twenty-Four Hours From Tulsa
Um Um Um Um Um

Walk Away (Warum Nur Warum)
Walk On By (Bacharach / David)
Walk On By (Hayes)
We Are In Love
We're Through
Wedding, The (La Novia)
When You Walk In The Room
Where Did Our Love Go
Who Can I Turn To
Wishin' And Hopin'
Wonderful Day Like Today, A
World Without Love, A
You Really Got Me
You're My World (Il Mio Mondo)
You're No Good

1965

All I Really Want To Do
All Over The World (Dans Le Monde Entier)
Almost There
Anyway, Anyhow, Anywhere
Baby Don't Go
Baby Please Don't Go
Bring It On Home To Me
Carnival Is Over, The
Cast Your Fate To The Wind
Catch The Wind
Catch Us If You Can
Chim Chim Cheree
Clapping Song, The
Colours
Come And Stay With Me
Come Tomorrow
Concrete And Clay
Day Tripper
Don't Bring Me Your Heartaches
Don't Let Me Be Misunderstood
Don't Make My Baby Blue
Don't Rain On My Parade
Eve Of Destruction, The
Everyone's Gone To The Moon
Evil Hearted You
Ferry 'cross The Mersey
For Your Love
Funny How Love Can Be
Game Of Love, The
Genie With The Light Brown Lamp
Get Off Of My Cloud
Girl Don't Come
Go Now
Goodbye My Love
Goodnight
Hang On Sloopy
He's Got No Love
Heart Full Of Soul
Help
Here Comes The Night
Here It Comes Again
How Can You Tell
I Can't Explain
I Can't Help Myself
I Could Easily Fall
I Got You Babe
I Know A Place
I Must Be Seeing Things
I Want Candy

I'll Be There
I'll Be True To You, Yes I Will
I'll Never Find Another You
I'll Stop At Nothing
I'm Alive
If You Gotta Go, Go Now
Iko Iko
In The Middle Of Nowhere
In The Midnight Hour
In Thoughts Of You
It Hurts So Much To See You Go
It's Good News Week
It's My Life
It's Not Unusual
It's The Same Old Song
Just A Little Bit Better
Keep Searchin' (We'll Follow The Sun)
King Of The Road
Last Time, The
Laugh At Me
Leader Of The Pack, The
Leave A Little Love
Let's Hang On
Like A Rolling Stone
Little Things
Long Live Love
Look Through Any Window
Looking Through The Eyes Of Love
Love Is Strange
Lovers Concerto
Make It Easy On Yourself
Mary Anne
Message Understood
Minute You're Gone, The
Mister Tambourine Man
Mrs. Brown You've Got A Lovely Daughter
My Generation
No Arms Can Ever Hold You
Not Until The Next Time
Oh No Not My Baby
On My Word
One Two Three
Poor Man's Son
Positively Fourth Street
Price Of Love, The
Princess In Rags
Reelin' And Rockin'
Satisfaction
See My Friend
Set Me Free
Silenzio, Il
Silhouettes
Some Of Your Lovin'
Somewhere
Special Years, The
Spoonful Of Sugar, A
Still I'm Sad
Stingray
Stop In The Name Of Love
Subterranean Homesick Blues
Summer Nights
Supercalifragilisticexpialidocious
Tears
Tell Me Why
Terry
That's The Way
There But For Fortune

This Little Bird
Ticket To Ride
Times They Are A-changin', The
Tired Of Waiting For You
To Know You Is To Love You
To Whom It Concerns
Too Many Rivers
Tossing And Turning
Trains And Boats And Planes
True Love Ways
Universal Soldier
Walk In The Black Forest (Eine Schwarzwaldfahrt)
Walk Tall
We Can Work It Out
We've Gotta Get Out Of This Place
What Have They Done To The Rain
What'cha Gonna Do About It
What's New Pussycat
Where Are You Now My Love
Wind Me Up (Let Me Go)
Windmill In Old Amsterdam, A
Wonderful World
Wooly Bully
World Of Our Own, A
Yeh Yeh
Yesterday
Yesterday Man
You've Got To Hide Your Love Away
You've Got Your Troubles
You've Lost That Lovin' Feelin'
You've Never Been In Love Like This Before
Zorba's Dance

1966

Alfie
All I See Is You
All Or Nothing
Back Stage
Bang Bang (My Baby Shot Me Down)
Barbara Ann
Bend It
Black Is Black
Blue Turns To Grey
Born Free
Bus Stop
California Dreamin'
Daydream
Dead End Street
Dedicated Follower Of Fashion, A
Distant Drums
Don't Answer Me (Ti Vedo Uscuiri)
Don't Bring Me Down
Eleanor Rigby
Elusive Butterfly, The
England Swings
Fool Am I, A (Dimmelo Parlami)
Friday On My Mind
Get Away
Gimme Some Loving
Girl
Girl Talk
God Only Knows
Goin' Back
Good Vibrations
Got To Get You Into My Life

Groovy Kind Of Love, A
Guantanamera
Have You Seen Your Mother, Baby, Standing In The Shadow
Help Me Girl
Hev Yew Gotta Loight Boy
Hey Girl
Hideaway
High Time
Hold Tight
Holy Cow
Homeward Bound
I Can't Control Myself
I Can't Let Go
I Couldn't Live Without Your Love
I Put A Spell On You
I Saw Her Again Last Night
I Want You
I'm A Boy
If Everyday Was Like Christmas
If I Were A Carpenter
In The Arms Of Love
Just Like A Woman
Just One Smile
Keep On Running
Lady Godiva
Lightin' Strikes
Like A Baby
Little By Little
Little Man
Love Like Yours, A
Love Me With All Of Your Heart (Caundo Caliente El Sol)
Love's Just A Broken Heart
Lovers Of The World Unite
Make The World Go Away
Mama
Man Without Love, A
May Each Day
Michelle
Mirror Mirror
Monday Monday
More Than Love
Must To Avoid, A
My Girl
My Love
My Mind's Eye
My Ship Is Coming In
Nineteenth Nervous Breakdown
No Milk Today
Nobody Needs Your Love
Nothing Comes Easy
On A Clear Day You Can See Forever
Out Of Time
Over Under Sideways Down
Paint It Black
Paperback Writer
People
Pied Piper, The
Pretty Flamingo
Promises
Rain
Rainy Day Woman Nos. 12 & 35
Reach Out I'll Be There
Rescue Me
River Deep, Mountain High
River, The (Le Colline Sono In Fiore)
Semi-Detached Suburban Mr James

Sha La La La Lee
Shadow Of Your Smile
Shapes Of Things
Shotgun Wedding
Sloop John B, The
Somebody Help Me
Someday One Day
Somewhere My Love (Lara's Theme)
Sorrow
Sound Of Silence, The
Spanish Flea
Stop Stop Stop
Strangers In The Night
Substitute
Summer In The City
Sun Ain't Gonna Shine Anymore, The
Sunny
Sunny Afternoon
Sweet Talkin' Guy
There Wont Be Many Coming Home
These Boots Are Made For Walking
They're Coming To Take Me Away Ha-haaa!
This Door Swings Both Ways
Till The End Of The Day
Time Drags By
Tomorrow (Andrews)
Too Soon To Know
Visions
Walk With Me
What Becomes Of The Brokenhearted
What Would I Be
When A Man Loves A Woman
Wild Thing
Winchester Cathedral
With A Girl Like You
Working In The Coalmine
Yellow Submarine
You Can't Hurry Love
You Don't Have To Say You Love Me (Lo Che Non Vivo)
You Keep Me Hangin' On
You Were On My Mind

1967

007 (Shanty Town)
All You Need Is Love
Alternate Title
Anyway That You Want Me
Autumn Almanac
Baby Now That I've Found You
Bernadette
Big Spender
Black Velvet Band, The
Boat That I Row, The
Call Her Your Sweetheart
Carrie Anne
Creeque Alley
Day I Met Marie, The
Death Of A Clown, The
Dedicated To The One I Love
Detroit City
Don't Sleep In The Subway
Even The Bad Times Are Good
Everybody Knows (I Still Love You)
Excerpt From A Teenage Opera (Grocer Jack)
Finchley Central

First Cut Is The Deepest
Flowers In The Rain
From The Underworld
Funny Familiar Forgotten Feelings
Georgy Girl
Green Green Grass Of Home, The
Groovin'
Ha Ha Said The Clown
Happening, The
Happy Jack
Here Comes My Baby
Heroes And Villains
Hey Joe (Roberts)
Hi-ho Silver Lining
Hole In My Shoe, A
Homburg
House That Jack Built, The
I Can Hear The Grass Grow
I Can See For Miles
I Was Kaiser Bill's Batman
I Was Made To Love Her
I Won't Come In While He's There
I'll Never Fall In Love Again (Bacharach / David)
I'm A Believer
I'm A Man
I'm Gonna Get Me A Gun
I've Been A Bad Bad Boy
If I Were A Rich Man
If My Friends Could See Me Now
In The Country
It Must Be Him (Seul Sur Son Etoile)
It Takes Two
It's All Over
Itchycoo Park
Just Loving You
Knock On Wood
Last Waltz, The
Let Me Cry On Your Shoulder
Let's Go To San Francisco
Let's Spend The Night Together
Letter, The
Little Bit Of Me, A Little Bit You, A
Look Of Love
Love Is All Around
Massachussetts
Matchmaker, Matchmaker
Matthew And Son
Mellow Yellow
Morningtown Ride
Music To Watch Girls By
New York Mining Disaster 1941, The
Night Of Fear
Nights In White Satin
Ode To Billy Joe
Okay
On A Carousel
Pamela Pamela
Paper Sun
Peek A Boo
Penny Lane
Pictures Of Lily
Puppet On A String
Purple Haze
Reflections
Release Me
Respect
Rhythm Of Life

Ruby Tuesday
San Franciscan Nights
San Francisco
Save Me
See Emily Play
Seven Drunken Nights
Seven Rooms Of Gloom
She'd Rather Be With Me
Silence Is Golden
Simon Smith And His Amazing Dancing Bear
Single Girl
Sitting In The Park
Snoopy Versus The Red Baron
Somethin' Stupid
Something's Gotten Hold Of My Heart
Standing In The Shadows Of Love
Strawberry Fields Forever
Sugar Town
Sunrise Sunset
Sunshine Superman
Sweet Soul Music
Talk To The Animals
Then I Kissed Her
There Goes My Everything
There Is A Mountain
There's A Kind Of Hush
This Is My Song
Thoroughly Modern Millie
Up Up And Away
Waterloo Sunset
We Love You
When I'm Sixty-four
When Will The Good Apples Fall
Whiter Shade Of Pale, A
Wind Cries Mary, The
With A Little Help From My Friends
You Only Live Twice
You've Not Changed
Zabadak

1968
Ain't Got No
Ain't Nothing But A Houseparty
All Along The Watchtower
All My Love (Arduini, Callander)
Am I That Easy To Forget
Aquarius
Baby Come Back
Ballad Of Bonnie And Clyde, The
Bend Me Shape Me
Bicyclettes De Belsize
Blue Eyes
Breaking Down The Walls Of Heartache
Cabaret
Can't Take My Eyes Off You
Captain Of Your Ship
Cinderella Rockafella
Classical Gas
Congratulations
Dance To The Music
Darlin'
Day Without Love, A
Daydream Believer
Days
Delilah
Do It Again

Do You Know The Way To San Jose
Dock Of The Bay, The
Don't Stop The Carnival
Elenore
Eloise
Everlasting Love
Everything I Am
Fire
Fire Brigade
Gimme Little Sign
Good Morning Starshine
Good, The Bad And The Ugly, The
Green Tambourine
Hard To Handle
Harper Valley P.T.A.
Hello Goodbye
Hello I Love You
Help Yourself (Gli Occhi Miei)
Here Comes The Judge
Here We Go Round The Mulberry Bush
Hey Jude
High In The Sky
Hold Me Tight
Honey
Hurdy Gurdy Man, The
Hush Not A Word To Mary
I Can Take Or Leave Your Loving
I Can't Let Maggie Go
I Close My Eyes And Count To Ten
I Don't Want Our Loving To Die
I Got Life
I Gotta Get A Message To You
I Pretend
I Say A Little Prayer
I Second That Emotion
I'm A Tiger
I'm Coming Home
Ice In The Sun
If I Knew Then (What I Know Now)
If I Only Had Time (Je N'aurai Pas Le Temps)
If The Whole World Stopped Loving
Importance Of Your Love, The (Important C'est La Rose)
Impossible Dream, The
In And Out Of Love
Jennifer Eccles
Jennifer Juniper
Joanna
Judy In Disguise
Jumping Jack Flash
Keep On
Kites
Lady Madonna
Lady Willpower
Last Night In Soho
Lazy Sunday
Legend Of Xanadu, The
Let The Heartaches Begin
Let The Sunshine In
Light My Fire
Listen To Me
LIttle Arrows
Little Green Apples
Love Is Blue (L'amour Est Bleu)
Lovin' Things
MacArthur Park

Man Without Love, A (Quando M'inna-moro)
May I Have The Next Dream With You
Me The Peaceful Heart
Mexico
Mighty Quinn
Money Song, The
Mony Mony
Mrs. Robinson
My Little Lady (Non Illuderti Mai)
My Name Is Jack
My Rainbow Valley
On The Road Again (Wilson, Jones)
One More Dance
One-Two-Three O'Leary
Only One Woman
Other Man's Grass, The
Pictures Of Matchstick Men
Race With The Devil
Red Balloon
Rosie
She Wears My Ring
Simon Says
Something Here In My Heart
Son Of Hickory Holler's Tramp, The
Step Inside Love
Suddenly You Love Me (Uno Tranquil-lo)
Sunshine Girl
Sunshine Of Your Love, The
Thank U Very Much
This Guy's In Love With You
This Old Heart Of Mine
This Wheel's On Fire
Those Were The Days
Tin Soldier
Universal
Walk Away Renee
What A Wonderful World
When Jesamine Goes
White Horses
Words
World
Wreck Of The Antoinette, The
Yesterday Has Gone
Young Girl
Yummy Yummy Yummy

1969

Ain't Got No - I Got Life (Medley)
Albatross
Aquarius - Let The Sun Shine In (med-ley)
Baby Make It Soon
Bad Moon Rising
Ballad Of John And Yoko, The
Behind A Painted Smile
Big Ship
Blackberry Way
Boom Bang-a-Bang
Boxer, The
Boy Named Sue, A
Break Away
Bringing On Back The Good Times
Build Me Up Buttercup
(Call Me) Number One
Chitty Chitty Bang Bang
Cloud Nine

Cold Turkey
Come Back And Shake Me
Come Together
Conversations
Curly
Dancing In The Street
Delta Lady
Dick-a-Dum Dum (Kings Road)
Dizzy
Do What You Gotta Do
Don't Forget To Remember
Early In The Morning
First Of May, The
For Once In My Life
Fox On The Run
Frozen Orange Juice
Galveston
Games People Play
Gentle On My Mind
Get Back
Get Ready
Gimme Good Lovin'
Give Peace A Chance
Goo Goo Babarabajagal (Love Is Hot)
Good Times (Better Times)
Goodbye
Goodnight Midnight
Half As Nice
Happy Heart
Harlem Shuffle
He Ain't Heavy, He's My Brother
Hello Susie
Higher & Higher
Honky Tonk Women
I Can Hear Music
I Can Sing A Rainbow
I Don't Know Why
I Guess I'll Always Love You
I Heard It Through The Grapevine
I'd Rather Go Blind
I'll Never Fall In Love Again
I'll Pick A Rose For My Rose
(I'm A) Road Runner
I'm Gonna Make You Love Me
I'm Gonna Make You Mine
I'm The Urban Spaceman
If I Can Dream
In The Bad Bad Old Days
In The Ghetto
In The Year 2525
Israelites, The
It Mek
It's Getting Better
Je T'aime, Moi Non Plus
Lay Lady Lay
Lights Of Cincinnati, The
Lily The Pink
Liquidator, The
Living In The Past
Love Child
Love Is All
Love Me Tonight (Alla Fine Della Stra-da)
Love's Been Good To Me
Make Me An Island
Man Of The World, A
Minute Of Your Time, A
Monsieur Dupont

My Cherie Amour
My Sentimental Friend
My Way
Natural Born Bugie
Nobody's Child
Ob-La-Di Ob-La-Da
Oh Happy Day (Hawkins)
Oh Well
On Days Like These
One Road
Onion Song, The
Pinball Wizard
Please Don't Go
Private Number
Proud Mary
Ragamuffin Man
Return Of Django, The
Ruby (Don't Take Your Love To Town)
Sabre Dance, The
Saved By The Bell
Something
Something In The Air
Something's Happening (Luglio)
Son Of Preacher Man
Sorry Suzanne
Space Oddity
Stop Her On Sight
Sugar Sugar
Surround Yourself With Sorrow
Sweet Dream
That's The Way God Planned It
Throw Down A Line
Time Is Tight
To Love Somebody
Too Busy Thinking About My Baby
Tracks Of My Tears, The
Viva Bobby Joe
Way It Used To Be, The
Way Of Life, The
What Does It Take (To Win Your Love)
Where Do You Go To My Lovely
Wichita Lineman
Windmills Of Your Mind
Winter World Of Love
With The Eyes Of A Child
Wonderful World, Beautiful People
Yester-me Yester-you Yesterday
You Got Soul

1970

A.B.C.
Abraham, Martin & John
Ain't No Mountain High Enough
All Kinds Of Everything
All Right Now
Back Home
Ball Of Confusion
Band Of Gold
Big Yellow Taxi
Black Night
Black Pearl
Both Sides Now
Bridge Over Troubled Water
Brontosaurus
But You Love Me Daddy
Close To You
Come And Get It

Cotton Fields
Daughter Of Darkness
Don't Cry Daddy
Don't Play That Song (You Lied)
Don't You Know
Down The Dustpipe
Durham Town (The Leaving)
Everything Is Beautiful
Farewell Is A Lonely Sound
Friends
Gasoline Alley Bred
Gimme Dat Ding
Give Me Just A Little More Time
Good Morning Freedom
Good Old Rock 'n' Roll
Goodbye Sam, Hello Samantha
Green Manalishi, The
Groovin' With Mr. Bloe
Hitchin' A Ride
Home Lovin' Man
Honey Come Back
I Can't Get Next To You
I Can't Tell The Bottom From The Top
I Don't Believe In If Any More
I Want You Back
I Will Survive
I'll Say Forever My Love
I've Got You On My Mind
I've Lost You
In The Summertime
Indian Reservation
Instant Karma
It's So Easy
It's Wonderful
Julie Do Ya Love Me
Knock Knock Who's There
Lady Barbara
Lady D'arbanville
Leavin' On A Jet Plane
Let It Be
Let's Get Together
Let's Work Together
Lola
Love Grows
Love Is Life
Love Like A Man
Love Of The Common People
Love You Save, The
Make It With You
Mama Told Me Not To Come
Melting Pot
Montego Bay
My Baby Loves Lovin'
Na Na Hey Hey Kiss Him Goodbye
Natural Sinner
Neanderthal Man
Never Had A Dream Come True
New World In The Morning, A
Our World
Paranoid
Patches
Question
Rag Mama Rag
Rainbow
Raindrops Keep Falling On My Head
Reflections Of My Life

San Bernadino
Signed, Sealed, Delivered, I'm Yours
Some Day We'll Be Together
Something's Burning
Spirit In The Sky
Still Water
Strange Band
Suspicious Minds
Sweet Inspiration
Tears Of A Clown, The
Temma Harbour
That Same Old Feeling
Tip Of My Finger, The
To Be Young Gifted And Black
Tracy
Travellin' Band
Twenty Five Or Six To Four
Two Little Boys
United We Stand
Up Around The Bend
Up The Ladder To The Roof
Venus
Voodoo Chile
Wanderin' Star
War
Wedding Bell Blues
What Are You Doing The Rest Of Your Life
When Julie Comes Around
Which Way You Goin' Billy?
Who Do You Love
Whole Lotta Love
Wild World
Witch, The
Witches Promise
Without Love (There Is Nothing)
Woodstock
Years May Come, Years May Go
Yellow River
You Can Get It If You Really Want It
You're Such A Good Looking Woman
You've Got Me Dangling On A String

1971

Amazing Grace
Another Day
Another Time Another Place
Apeman
Baby Jump
Back Street Luv
Banc, Un Arbre, Une Rue, Un
Bangla Desh
Banks Of The Ohio, The
Banner Man, The
Black And White
Black Skin Blue Eyed Boy
Blame It On The Pony Express
Brandy
Bridget The Midget
Broken Hearted (Cuore Cuore)
Brown Sugar
Butterfly
Candida
Chirpy Chirpy Cheep Cheep
Co-Co
(Come Round Here) I'm The One You Need

Cousin Norman
Coz I Luv You
Cracklin' Rosie
Daddy Don't You Walk So Fast
Devils' Answer, The
Did You Ever
Don't Let It Die
Double Barrel
Ernie (The Fastest Milkman In The West)
Everything's Tuesday
Fireball
For All We Know
Freedom Come Freedom Go
Funny Funny
Get It On
Grandad
Gypsys Tramps And Thieves
He's Gonna Step On You Again
Heaven Must Have Sent You
Hey Girl Don't Bother Me
Hot Love
I Am...I Said
I Believe (In Love)
I Did What I Did For Maria
I Don't Blame You At All
I Think Of You (Il Faut Trouver Le Temp D'aimer)
I Will Drink The Wine
I Will Return
I'll Be There
I'm Gonna Run Away From You
I'm Still Waiting
If Not For You
In My Own Time
Indiana Wants Me
Is This The Way To Amarillo
It Don't Come Easy
It's Impossible (Somos Novios)
It's Too Late
Jack In A Box
Jeepster
Jig A Jig
Johnny Reggae
Just My Imagination
Keep On Dancing
Knock Three Times
Lady Rose
Leap Up And Down
Let Your Yeah Be Yeah
Let's See Action
Life Is A Long Song
Look Around (And You'll Find Me There)
Maggie May
Malt And Barley Blues
Me And You And A Dog Named Boo
Monkey Spanner
Move On Up
Mozart 40
My Brother Jake
My Sweet Lord
Nathan Jones
Never Ending Song Of Love
Night They Drove Old Dixie Down, The
No Matter What
Nothing Rhymed
Oh You Pretty Thing
Power To The People

Pushbike Song, The
Rain
Remember Me
Ressurrection Shuffle, The
Ride A White Swan
Rose Garden
Rosetta
Run Baby Run
Rupert
Shaft (Theme From)
She's A Lady
Simple Game
Sing A Song Of Freedom
Soldier Blue
Something Old, Something New
Something Tells Me
Stoned Love
Strange Kind Of Woman, A
Sultana
Sunny Honey Girl
Surrender
Sweet Caroline
Tap Turns On The Water
Tired Of Being Alone
Tokoloshe Man
Tom-Tom Turnaround
Tomorrow Night
Tonight (Wood)
Tweedle Dee Tweedle Dum
Walkin'
We Will
What Are You Doing Sunday
When I'm Dead And Gone
When You Are A King
Where Do I Begin
Who Put The Lights Out
Witch Queen Of New Orleans
Won't Get Fooled Again
You're Ready Now
You've Got A Friend (King)
Your Song

1972

Ain't No Sunshine
All I Ever Need Is You
All The Young Dudes
Alone Again (Naturally)
American Pie
Angel
At The Club
Automatically Sunshine
Baby I'm... A Want You
Back Off Boogaloo
Beg Steal Or Borrow
Ben
Betcha By Golly Wow
Big Six
Blue Is The Colour
Borsalino
Brand New Key, A
Burlesque
Burning Love
California Man
Children Of The Revoloution, The
Circles
Clair
Come On Over To My Place

Come What May (Apres Toi)
Could It Be Forever
Crazy Horses
Crocodile Rock
Crying Laughing Loving Lying
Day After Day
Day By Day
Debora
Desiderata (You Are A Child Of The Universe)
Diamonds Are Forever
Donna
Elected
First Time Ever I Saw Your Face, The
Floy Joy
Goodbye To Love
Got To Be There
Gudbuy T'Jane
Guitar Man
Hallelujah Freedom
Happy Christmas (War Is Over)
Have You Seen Her
Heart Of Gold
Hold Your Head Up
Horse With No Name, A
How Can I Be Sure
I Can See Clearly Now
I Didn't Know I Loved You (Till I Saw You Rock 'n' Roll)
I Don't Know How To Love Him
I Get The Sweetest Feeling
I Just Can't Help Believing
I Won't Last A Day Without You
I'd Like To Teach The World To Sing
I'm Stone In Love With You
In A Broken Dream
Isn't Life Strange
It Must Be Love
It's Four In The Morning
It's One Of Those Nights
John I'm Only Dancing
Join Together
Lady Eleanor
Lay Down
Layla
Leeds United
Let's Stay Together
Little Bit Of Love, A
Little Willy
Living In Harmony
Look Wot Yu Dun
Looking Through The Windows
Loop Di Love
Mad About You
Mama Weer All Crazee Now
Mary Had A Little Lamb
Meet Me On The Corner
Metal Guru
Morning
Morning Has Broken
Mother And Child Reunion
Mother Of Mine
Mouldy Old Dough
My Ding a Ling
My World
No Matter How I Try
Oh Babe What Would You Say
Onedin Line, The

Ooh-Wakka-Doo-Wakka-Day
Popcorn
Poppa Joe
Radancer
Rock And Roll Part 1 & 2
Rocket Man
Rockin' Robin
Run Run Run
Run To Me
Saturday Night At The Movies
Schools Out
Seaside Shuffle
Silver Machine
Sister Jane
Sleepy Shores
Softly Whispering I Love You
Soley Soley
Son Of My Father
Song Sung Blue
Standing In The Road
Starman
Stay With Me
Stir It Up
Storm In A Teacup
Sugar Me
Superstar
Suzanne Beware Of The Devil
Sylvia's Mother
Take A Look Around
Take Me Back 'ome
Telegram Sam
Ten Thousand Five Hundred And Thirty Eight Overture
There Are More Questions Than Answers
Thing Called Love, A
Too Beautiful To Last
Tumbling Dice
Until It's Time For You To Go
Vincent
Virginia Plain
Walk In The Night
Walkin' In The Rain With The One I Love
What Is Life
Wig-Wam Bam
Without You
You Wear It Well
You're A Lady
Young New Mexican Pupeteer

1973

All Because Of You
All The Way From Memphis
Alright, Alright, Alright
Also Sprach Zarathustra
Always On My Mind
Amanda
Amoureuse
And I Love You So
Angel Fingers
Angie
Armed And Extremely Dangerous
Bad Bad Boy
Ball Park Incident
Ballroom Blitz
Big Eight
Big Seven

Blockbuster
Broken Down Angel
Brother Louie
Can The Can
Can You Do It
Can't Keep It In
Caroline
Cindy Incidentally
Could It Be I'm Falling In Love
Crazy
Cum On Feel The Noize
Dancing On A Saturday Night
Daniel
Daydreamer
Daytona Demon
Dean And I, The
Desperate Dan
Do You Wanna Dance
Do You Wanna Touch Me
Doctor My Eyes
Drive-In Saturday
Dynamite
Eye Level
Feel The Need In Me
Five Fifteen
Fool
For The Good Times
Fortyeight Crash
Gaye
Get Down
Ghetto Child
Give Me Love (Give Me Peace On Earth)
Giving It All Away
Going Home
Gonna Make You An Offer You Can't Refuse
Good Grief Christina
Goodbye Yellow Brick Road
Groover
Hard Rain's Gonna Fall, A
Heart Of Stone
Helen Wheels
Hell Raiser
Hello Hello I'm Back Again
Hello Hurray
Help Me Make It Through The Night
Hi Hi Hi
Honaloochie Boogie
I Am A Clown
I Wish It Could Be Christmas Everyday
I'm Doing Fine Now
I'm Free
I'm The Leader Of The Gang (I Am)
I've Been Hurt
If You Don't Know Me By Now
In The Rain
Jean Genie, The
Joybringer
Killing Me Softly With His Song
Knockin' On Heaven's Door
Laughing Gnome, The
Let Me In
Life On Mars
Like Sister And Brother
Live And Let Die
Long Haired Lover From Liverpool
Love Train

Me And Mrs Jones
Merry Xmas Everybody
Monster Mash
My Coo-Ca-Choo
My Friend Stan
My Love
Never, Never, Never (Grande, Grande, Grande)
Nice One Cyril
No More Mister Nice Guy
Nutbush City Limits
Old Fashioned Way, The (Les Plaisirs Demodes)
One And One Is One
Papa Was A Rolling Stone
Paper Plane
Part Of The Union
Photograph
Pick Up The Pieces
Pillow Talk
Power To All Our Friends
Pyjamarama
Randy
Rising Sun, The
Rock On
Rock-a-Doodle Doo
Roll Away The Stone
Roll Over Beethoven
Rubber Bullets
Saturday Night's Alright For Fighting
Say, Has Anyone Seen My Sweet Gypsy Rose
See My Baby Jive
Showdown
Skweeze Me Pleeze Me
Smarty Pants
Solid Gold Easy Action
Spanish Eyes (Moon Over Naples)
Step By Step
Stuck In The Middle With You
Summer (The First Time)
Superstition
Sweet Illusion
Sylvia
Take Me Girl I'm Ready
Take Me Home Country Road
Take Me To The Mardi Gras
This Flight Tonight
Tie A Yellow Ribbon
Top Of The World
Touch Me In The Morning
Truck On (Tyke)
Twentieth Century Boy
Walk On The Wild Side
Welcome Home (Vivre)
Whisky In The Jar
Why Can't We Live Together
Why Oh Why Oh Why
Wishing Well
Won't Somebody Dance With Me
Wonderful Dream (Tu Te Reconnaitras)
Yesterday Once More
Ying Tong Song, The
You Are The Sunshine Of My Life
You Can Do Magic
You Want It You Got It
You're So Vain

1974

Air That I Breathe, The
All I Want Is You
All Of Me Loves All Of You
All Of My Life
Always Yours
Amateur Hour
Angel Face
Annie's Song
Banana Rock
Band On The Run
Bangin' Man
Beach Baby
Billy Don't Be A Hero
Black-eyed Boys, The
Born With A Smile On My Face
Break The Rules
Can't Get Enough Of Your Love Babe
Candle In The Wind, A
Cat Crept In, The
Dance With The Devil
Devil Gate Drive
Doctor's Orders
Don't Let The Sun Go Down On Me
Don't Stay Away Too Long (Herzen Haben Keine Fenster)
Down On The Beach Tonight
Emma
Everyday
Everything I Own
Far Far Away
Farewell
Forever
Gee Baby
Get Dancing
Go (Before You Break My Heart)
Gonna Make You A Star
Guilty
Hang On In There Baby
Hanging On
Happy Anniversary
Having My Baby
He's Misstra Know It All
Hello Summertime
Hey Rock And Roll
Homely Girl
Honey Honey
How Come
I Can't Leave You Alone
I Can't Stop
I Get A Little Sentimental Over You
I Love You Love Me Love
I See A Star
I Shot The Sheriff
I'd Love You To Want Me
I'm Gonna Knock On Your Door
I'm Leaving It Up To You
If You Go Away (Ne Me Quitte Pas)
In Betweenies, The
In Crowd, The
Ire Feelings (Skanga)
It's Only Rock And Roll
It's You
Jarrow Song, The
Jealous Mind
Jet
Judy Teen

Juke Box Jive
Just For You
Killer Queen
Kissin' In The Back Row Of The Movies
Kung Fu Fighting
Lamplight
Let's Get Together Again
Let's Put It All Together
Liverpool Lou
Living For The City
Lonely Girl (Non Seitu)
Lonely This Christmas
Long Legged Woman Dressed In Black
Long Live Love
Long Tall Glasses
Love Me For A Reason
Love On A Mountain Top
Love's Theme
Lucy In The Sky With Diamonds
Magic
Man Who Sold The World, The
Mister Soft
Most Beautiful Girl, The
My Boy
Na Na Na
Never Turn Your Back On Mother Earth
Night Chicago Died, The
No Honestly
Oh Yes You're Beautiful
One Man Band
Pepper Box
Pool Hall Richard
Queen Of Clubs, The
Radar Love
Rebel Rebel
Red Dress
Reggae Tune
Remember (Sha-La-La)
Remember Me This Way
Remember You're A Womble
Rock And Roll Winter
Rock Me Gently
Rock The Boat (Holmes)
Rock Your Baby
Rock 'n' Roll Lady
Rocket
Rockin' Roll Baby
Roll Away The Stone
Sad Sweet Dreamer
School Love
Seasons In The Sun (Le Moribond)
Seven Seas Of Rhye, The
Shang-a-Lang
She
She's A Winner
Show Must Go On, The
Six Teens, The
Solitaire
Spiders And Snakes
Streak, The
Street Life
Sugar Baby Love
Summer Love Sensation
Teenage Rampage
Tell Me Why
There's A Ghost In My House
This Town Ain't Big Enough For The Both Of Us

Tiger Feet
Tonight (Bickerton, Waddington)
Too Good To Be Forgotten
Touch Too Much, A
Walkin' Miracle, A
Wall Street Shuffle
Waterloo
When Will I See You Again
Wild One, The
Wombling Merry Christmas
Wombling Song, The
Y Viva Espana
Year Of Decision
You Ain't Seen Nothing Yet
You Are Everything
You Little Trustmaker
You Make Me Feel Brand New
You Send Me
You Won't Find Another Fool Like Me
You You You
You're The First, The Last, My Everything

1975

All Around My Hat
Angie Baby
Are You Ready To Rock
Autobahn
Baby I Love You, O.K.
Barbados
Best Thing That Ever Happened To Me, The
Big Ten
Bimbo, El
Black Superman (Muhammed Ali)
Blanket On The Ground
Blue Guitar
Boogie On Reggae Woman
Bump, The
Bye Bye Baby (Baby Goodbye)
Can't Give You Anything (But My love)
Child's Prayer, A
Crying Over You
D.I.V.O.R.C.E.
Ding-a-Dong (Ding Dinge Dong)
Disco Queen
Disco Stomp
Doing Alright With The Boys
Dolly My Love
Don't Do It Baby
Don't Play Your Rock And Roll To Me
Down Down
Dreamer
Eighteen With A Bullet
Fancy Pants
Fattie Bum Bum
Feelings
Footsee
Fox On The Run
Funky Gibbon, The
Funky Moped, The
Girls
Give A Little Love
Good Love Can Never Die
Goodbye My Love
Heartbeat
Hold Back The Night

Hold Me Close
Hold On To Love
Honey
Hurt So Good
Hustle, The
I Ain't Lyin'
I Believe In Father Christmas
I Can Do It
I Can Help
I Wanna Dance Wit Choo (Do Dat Dance)
I Write The Songs
I'm Not In Love
I'm On Fire
If
If You Think You Know How To Love Me
Imagine
In For A Penny
Island Girl
It May Be Winter Outside (But In My Heart It's Spring)
It's Been So Long
It's Gonna Be A Cold Cold Christmas
It's In His Kiss
It's Time For Love
January
Jive Talkin'
Julie-ann
L-L-Lucy
Lady Marmalade (Voulez-vous Coucher Avec Moi Ce Soir)
Last Farewell, The
Let Me Be The One
Let Me Try Again (Laisse Moi Le Temps)
Life Is A Minestrone
Like A Butterfly
Listen To What The Man Said
Little Love And Understanding, A (Un Peu D'amour Et D'amitie)
Love Hurts
Love In The Sun
Love Is The Drug
Love Like You And Me, A
Love Me Love My Dog
Loving You
Make Me Smile (Come Up And See Me)
Mandy
Mister Raffles (Man It Was Mean)
Money Honey
Moonlighting
Moonshine Sally
Morningside Of The Mountain, The
Motor Biking
Ms Grace
My Eyes Adored You
My White Bicycle
Na Na Is The Saddest Word
Never Can Say Goodbye
New York City
New York Groove
Night, The
Now I'm Here
Oh What A Shame
Once Bitten Twice Shy
Only Yesterday
Only You Can
Pandora's Box

Philadelphia Freedom
Pick Up The Pieces
Play Me Like You Play Your Guitar
Please Mr. Postman
Please Tell Him That I Said Hello
Promised Land, The
Proud One, The
Purely By Coincidence
Rhinestone Cowboy, The
Ride A Wild Horse
Right Back Where We Started From
Roll Over Lay Down
Rolling Stone
S.O.S.
Sailing
Scotch On The Rocks
Secrets That You Keep, The
Send In The Clowns
Shame Shame Shame
Show Me You're A Woman
Sing Baby Sing
Skiing In The Snow
Sky High
Stand By Your Man
Star On A TV Show
Streets Of London, The
Sugar Candy Kisses
Summer Knows, The
Summertime City
Sweet Music
Swing Your Daddy
Take Good Care Of Yourself
Tears I Cried, The
Tears On My Pillow (Smith)
Thanks For The Memory (Wham Bam Thank You Mam)
That's The Way (I Like It)
There Goes My First Love
There's A Whole Lot Of Loving
Una Paloma Blanca
Under My Thumb
Way We Were, The
What Am I Gonna Do With You
Who Loves You
Why Did You Do It
You Can Make Me Dance Sing Or Anything
You Sexy Thing
Your Kiss Is Sweet

1976

All By Myself (Carmen)
Aria
Arms Of Mary, The
Art For Art's Sake
Baby We Better Try To Get It Together
Beautiful Noise
Blinded By The Light
Bohemian Rhapsody
Boston Tea Party, The
Boys Are Back In Town, The
Can I Take You Home Little Girl
Combine Harvester
Convoy
Convoy G.B.
Couldn't Get It Right
Dance Little Lady, Dance

Dancing Queen
Dancing With The Captain
Dat
December '63
Devil Woman
Disco Connection, The
Disco Duck
(Do The) Spanish Hustle
Do You Know Where You're Going To
Doctor Kiss Kiss
Doina De Jale
Don't Go Breaking My Heart
Don't Stop It Now
Don't Take Away The Music
Evil Woman
Falling Apart At The Seams
Fernando
Fool To Cry, A
Forever And Ever
Funky Weekend
Get Up And Boogie
Girls, Girls, Girls
Glass Of Champagne, A
Golden Years
Happy To Be On An Island In The Sun
Harvest For The World
Heart On My Sleeve
Heaven Must Be Missing An Angel
Hello Happiness
Here Comes The Sun
Here I Go Again (McDonald)
Howzat
Hurt
I Am A Cider Drinker
I Can't Ask For Anything More Than You
I Can't Get By Without You
I Love Music
I Love To Boogie
I Love To Love (But My Baby Just Loves To Dance)
I Wanna Stay With You
I'll Meet You At Midnight
I'm Mandy, Fly Me
I'm Your Puppet
If Not You
If You Leave Me Now
In Dulce Jubilo
In Zaire
It Only Takes A Minute
It Should Have Been Me
Jaws
Jeans On
Jolene
Jungle Rock
Killing Of Georgie, The
King Of The Cops
Kiss And Say Goodbye
Lean On Me (Withers)
Let 'em In
Let The Music Play
Let Your Love Flow
Let's Stick Together
Life Is Too Short Girl
Little Bit More, A
Little Brown Jug
Livin' Thing
Lost In France
Love And Affection

Love Hangover
Love Machine
Love Me
Love Me Like I Love You
Love Really Hurts Without You
Love To Love You Baby
Loving And Free
Low Rider
Mama Mia
Man To Man
Midnight Rider
Midnight Train To Georgia
Miss You Nights
Mississippi
Misty Blue
Money Money Money
More More More
Music
Mystery Song, The
No Charge
No Regrets (Rush)
Now Is The Time
People Like You And People Like Me
Play That Funky Music
Rain
Rock 'N' Me
Rodrigo's Concerto (Aranjuez Mon Amour)
Rubber Band Man, The
S-s-s-single Bed
Save Your Kisses For Me
Show Me The Way
Silly Love Songs
Silver Star
Sixteen Bars
Somebody To Love
Squeeze Box
Stop Me (If You've Heard It All Before)
Summer Of My Life, The
Take It To The Limit
This Is It
Tonight's The Night
Under The Moon Of Love
Walk Away From Love
We Do It
What I've Got In Mind
When A Child Is Born (Soleado)
When Forever Has Gone
Wide Eyed And Legless
You Are My Love
You Don't Have To Go
You Just Might See Me Cry
You Make Me Feel Like Dancing
You See The Trouble With Me
You Should Be Dancing
You To Me Are Everything
You'll Never Find Another Love Like Mine
You're My Best Friend
Young Hearts Run Free

1977

Ain't Gonna Bump No More
All Around The World
Angelo
Another Suitcase In Another Hall
Baby Don't Change Your Mind

Jack And Jill
Jamming
Jilted John
Just One More Night
Kiss You All Over
Let's All Chant
Let's Have A Quiet Night In
Like Clockwork
Little Bit Of Soap
Love Don't Live Here Anymore
Love Is In The Air
Love Is Like Oxygen
Lovely Day
Loves Unkind
Lucky Stars
Making Up Again
Man With The Child In His Eyes
Matchstalk Men And Matchstalk Cats And Dogs
Mind Blowing Decisions
Miss You
Mister Blue Sky
More Like The Movies
More Than A Woman
Mull Of Kintyre
My Best Friend's Girl
Native New Yorker
Never Let Her Slip Away
Night Fever
No-One Is Innocent
Northern Lights
Now That We've Found Love
Oh Carol
Oh What A Circus
Ole Ola
Only Women Bleed
Part Time Love
Picture This
Pretty Little Angel Eyes
Public Image
Rasputin
Rat Trap
Rivers Of Babylon, The
Rose Has To Die, A
Run For Home
Sandy
She's So Modern
Smurf Song, The
Sometimes When We Touch
Sorry I'm A Lady
Stayin' Alive
Substitute
Summer Night City
Summer Nights
Supernature
Sweet Talkin' Woman
Take A Chance On Me
Talking In Your Sleep
Three Times A Lady
Too Much Too Little Too Late
Up Town Top Ranking
Use Ta Be My Girl
Walk In Love
What A Waste
Who Pays The Ferryman
Wild West Hero
Wishing On A Star
With A Little Luck

Wuthering Heights
You Make Me Feel (Mighty Real)
You're The One That I Want

1979
After The Love Has Gone
Ain't Love A Bitch
Ain't No Stoppin' Us Now
Angel Eyes
Are 'Friends' Electric
Babylon's Burning
Banana Splits
Bang Bang
Beat The Clock
Boogie Wonderland
Born To Be Alive
Boys Keep Swingin'
Breakfast In America
Bright Eyes (Batt)
Can You Feel The Force
Can't Stand Losing You
Car 67
Cars
Chiquitita
Chosen Few, The
Complex
Confusion
Contact
Cool For Cats
Cool Meditation
Crazy Little Thing Called Love
Cruel To Be Kind
Dance Away
Deer Hunter Theme, The (Cavatina) (He Was Beautiful)
Devil Went Down To Georgia, The
Diary Of Horace Wimp, The
Does Your Mother Know
Don't Bring Me Down
Don't Stop Me Now
Don't Stop Till You Get Enough
Dreaming
Duke Of Earl
Eton Rifles
Every Day Hurts
Gangsters
Get Down
Get It
Gimme Gimme Gimme
Girls Talk
Go West
Good Times
Goodnight Tonight
Gotta Go Home
H.A.P.P.Y. Radio
Hallelujah
He's The Greatest Dancer
Heart Of Glass, A
Hello This Is Joannie
Hersham Boys
Hit Me With Your Rhythm Stick
Hold The Line
Hooray, Hooray, It's A Holi Holiday
Hot Stuff
I Don't Like Mondays
I Don't Wanna Lose You
I Want Your Love

I Was Made For Dancin'
I Will Survive
I'll Put You Together Again
I'm Every Woman
If I Said You Have A Beautiful Body
In The Navy
Into The Valley
Is She Really Going Out With Him
Jimmy Jimmy
Just The Way You Are
Just What I Needed
Just When I Needed You Most
Keep On Dancin'
King Rocker
Knocked It Off
Ladies Night
Lady Lynda
Lay Your Love On Me
Le Freak
Little More Love, A
Living On An Island
Living On The Front Line
Logical Song, The
Lone Ranger, The
Love's Gotta Hold On Me
Lucky Number
Making Plans For Nigel
Masquerade
Maybe
Message In A Bottle
Milk And Alcohol
Money In My Pocket
My Life
My Simple Heart
Night Owl
No More Tears (Enough Is Enough)
Number One Song In Heaven, The
Nunc Dimittis
O.K. Fred
Off The Wall
Oliver's Army
On My Radio
One Day At A Time
One Nation Under A Groove
One Step Beyond
One Way Ticket
Ooh What A Life
Painter Man
Parisienne Walkways
Pop Muzik
Que Sera Mi Vida (If You Should Go)
Queen Of Hearts
Rapper's Delight
Reasons To Be Cheerful
Reggae For It Now
Reunited
Ring My Bell
Roxanne
Rudy - A Message To You
Runner, The
Sail On
September
Shake Your Body (Down To The Ground)
She's In Love With You
Shine A Little Love
Shooting Star
Silly Games

Silly Thing
Since You've Been Gone
Some Girls
Song For Guy
Sound Of The Suburbs
Sparrow, The
Still
Street Life
Strut Your Funky Stuff
Sultans Of Swing
Sunday Girl
Take On The World
Too Much Heaven
Tragedy
Turn The Music Up
Tusk
Union City Blues
Up The Junction
Video Killed The Radio Star
Voulez-vous
Waiting For An Alibi
Walking On The Moon
Wanted
We Are Family
We Don't Talk Anymore
Whatever You Want
When You're In Love With A Beautiful Woman
Who Were You With In The Moonlight
Woman In Love, A
Wonderful Christmas Time
Wow
Y.M.C.A.
You Don't Bring Me Flowers

1980

All Night Long (Blackmore, Glover)
All Out Of Love
All Over The World
Amigo
And The Beat Goes On
And The Birds Were Singing (Et Les Oiseaux Chantaient)
Another Brick In The Wall
Another One Bites The Dust
Ashes To Ashes
Atomic
Babe
Babooshka
Back Together Again
Baggy Trousers
Banana Republic
Bank Robber
Behind The Groove
Better Love Next Time
Brass In Pocket
Call Me
Can't Stop The Music (La Musique N'a Pas De Fin)
Captain Beaky
Carrie
Casanova
Celebration
Check Out The Groove
Coming Up
Could You Be Loved
Coward Of The County
Cuba

D.I.S.C.O.
Dance Yourself Dizzy
Day Trip To Bangor
Do That To Me One More Time
Do You Feel My Love
Dog Eat Dog
Don't Make Waves
Don't Push It - Don't Force It
Don't Stand So Close To Me
Dreamin'
Earth Dies Screaming, The
Echo Beach
Eighth Day
Embarrassment
Emotional Rescue
Enola Gay
Everybody's Got To Learn Sometime
Fashion
Feels Like I'm In Love
Fool For Your Lovin'
Funkin' For Jamaica
Funky Town
Games Without Frontiers
Geno
Give Me The Night
Going Underground
Gotta Pull Myself Together
Green Onions
Groove, The
Hands Off - She's Mine
Hold On To My Love
I Can't Stand Up For Falling Down
I Could Be So Good For You
I Die, You Die
I Have A Dream
I Hear You Now
I Shoulda Loved Ya
I'm Coming Out
I'm In The Mood For Dancing
If You're Lookin' For A Way Out
Is It Love Your After
It's Different For Girls
It's Only Love
It's Still Rock And Roll To Me
January February
John I'm Only Dancing (Again)
Jump To The Beat
(Just Like) Starting Over
Killer On The Loose
King
Let's Get Serious
Let's Go Round Again
Living After Midnight
London Calling
Love Times Love (Love X Love)
Love Will Tear Us Apart
Masterblaster (Jammin')
Midnight Dynamos
Mirror In The Bathroom
Modern Girl
My Girl
My Old Piano
My Perfect Cousin
My Way Of Thinking
My World
Never Knew Love Like This Before
Nine To Five (Palmer)

No Doubt About It
Oh Yeah
On The Road Again
One Day I'll Fly Away
Oops Up Side Your Head
Over You
Play The Game
Please Don't Go
Rat Race
Rock With You
Seven Four Seven (Strangers In The Night)
Seventeen
Sexy Eyes
She's Out Of My Life
Silver Dream Machine
Simon Templer
So Good To Be Back Home
So Lonely
Someone's Looking At You
Spacer
Special Brew
Start
Stereotype
Stomp
Stop The Cavalry
Substitute
Suicide Is Painless
Super Trouper
Take That Look Off Your Face
Talk Of The Town
There There My Dear
There's No One Quite Like Grandma
Tide Is High, The
To Be Or Not To Be
To Cut A Long Story Short
Toccata
Together We Are Beautiful
Too Much Too Young
Turn It On Again
Turning Japanese
Two Pints Of Lager And A Packet Of Crisps Please
Upside Down
Use It Up And Wear It Out
Waterfalls
We Are Glass
What You're Proposing
What's Another Year
When You Ask About Love
Winner Takes It All
With You I'm Born Again
Woman In Love
Working My Way Back To You
Xanadu
You Gave Me Love

1981

Abacab
Absolute Beginners
All Stood Still
All The Love In The World
All Those Years Ago
And The Bands Played On
Ant Rap
Antmusic
Attention To Me

Ay Ay Ay Ay Moosey
Bed Sitter
Being With You
Bette Davis Eyes
Birdie Song, The (Tchip Tchip)
Body Talk
Cambodia
Can Can
Can You Feel It
Capstick Comes Home
Chant Number One
Chariots Of Fire
Chequered Love
Chi Mai
D-Days
Daddy's Home
Dancing On The Floor
Dancing Tight
De Do Do Do, De Da Da Da
Dead Ringer For Love
Do Nothing
Don't Stop The Music
Don't You Want Me
Einstein A Go-Go
Endless Love
Every Little Thing She Does Is Magic
Fade To Grey
Favourite Shirt
Flash
Flashback
For Your Eyes Only
Funeral Pyre
Ghost Town
Girls On Film
Going Back To My Roots
Good Thing Going, A
Good Year For The Roses
Grey Day
Hands Up (Give Me Your Heart)
Happy Birthday
Hold Me
Hold On Tight
How 'bout Us
Hucklebuck, The
I Ain't Gonna Stand For It
I Am The Beat
I Go To Sleep
I Surrender
I Want To Be Free
In The Air Tonight
Intuition
Invisible Sun
It's A Love Thing
It's Raining
Japanese Boy
Jealous Guy
Joan Of Arc
Just Can't Get Enough
Keep On Loving You
Kids In America
Kings Of The Wild Frontier
Labelled With Love
Lady
Lately
Lay All Your Love On Me
Let's Groove
Lies

Little In Love, A
Love Action (I Believe In Love)
Love On The Rocks
Making Your Mind Up
Memory
More Than In Love
Muscle Bound
My Own Way
New Life
Night Games
Nine To Five
No Woman No Cry
O Superman
Oldest Swinger In Town, The
Once In A Lifetime
One Day In Your Life
One In Ten
One Of Us
Open Your Heart
Ossie's Dream (The Way To Wembley)
Physical
Prince Charming
Rabbit
Rapture
Return Of The Los Palmas Seven, The
Reward
Rock This Town
Rock 'n' Roll
Romeo And Juliet
Runaway Boys
Shaddup You Face
She's Got Claws
Shut Up
Slow Hand
So This Is Romance
Something 'bout You Baby I Like
Southern Freeez
Souvenir
Spirits In The Material World
Stand And Deliver
Start Me Up
Steppin' Out)
Stray Cat Strut
Swords Of A Thousand Men
Tainted Love
Teddy Bear
Thunder In The Mountains
Tonight I'm Yours
Too Nice To Talk To
Under Pressure
Under Your Thumb
Vienna
Walk Right Now
Walkin' In The Sunshine
We'll Bring The House Down
When He Shines
When She Was My Girl
Will You
Wired For Sound
Woman
Wordy Rappinghood
You Better You Bet
You Drive Me Crazy
You Might Need Somebody
You'll Never Know
Young Parisians

1982

Abracadabra
Ain't No Pleasing You
All Of My Heart
Annie, I'm Not Your Daddy
Arthur's Theme
Beat Surrender
Being Boiled
Bitterest Pill, The
Blue Eyes
Centerfold
Classic
Come On Eileen
Computer Love
Da Da Da
Dear John
Do I Do
Do You Really Want To Hurt Me
Don't Go
Driving My Car
Drowning In Berlin
Ebony And Ivory
Eye Of The Tiger, The
Fame
Fantastic Day
Fantasy Island
Forget Me Nots
Friend Or Foe
Get Down On It
Ghosts
Girl Crazy
Girl Is Mine, The
Give Me Back My Heart
Go Wild In The Country
Golden Brown
Goody Two Shoes
Hard To Say I'm Sorry
Harry's Game
Have You Ever Been In Love
He Was Really Saying Something
Heartbreaker
Hi-fidelity
House Of Fun
Hungry Like The Wolf
Hymn
I Can Make You Feel Good
I Can't Go For That (No Can Do)
I Could Be Happy
I Don't Wanna Dance
I Eat Cannibals
I Love Rock 'n' Roll
I Wanna Do It With You
I Won't Let You Down
I'll Be Satisfied
I'll Find My Way Home
I'm A Wonderful Thing (Baby)
I've Never Been To Me
Inside Out
Instinction
It Started With A Kiss
Jackie Wilson Said
Just An Illusion
Just What I Always Wanted
Just Who Is The Five O'Clock Hero
Land Of Make Believe
Let's Go Dancing
Lifeline

Little Peace, A (Ein Bisschen Frieden)
Living On The Ceiling
Look Of Love, The
Love Come Down
Love Plus One
Mad World
Maid Of Orleans, The
Mama Used To Say
Maneater
Message, The
Mickey
Mirror Man
Mirror Mirror (Mon Amour)
Model, The
More Than This
Music And Lights
My Camera Never Lies
My Girl Lollipop
Night Birds
Night To Remember, A
Nobody's Fool
Now Those Days Are Gone
Oh Julie
One Step Further
Only Way Out, The
Only You (Clarke)
Other Side Of Love, The
Our House
Out Here On My Own
Papa's Got A Brand New Pigbag
Pass The Dutchie
Poison Arrow
Private Investigations
Promised You A Miracle
Rio
Run To The Hills
Saddle Up
Save A Prayer
Save Your Love
Say Hello, Wave Goodbye
See You
Senses Working Overtime
Seven Tears
(Sexual) Healing
Shirley
Shy Boy
Starmaker
Stool Pigeon
Strange Little Girl
There It Is
This Time (We'll Get It Right)
Time (Clock Of The Heart)
Torch
Town Called Malice, A
Truly
Waiting For A Girl Like You
Walking On Sunshine
We Have A Dream
We Take Mystery To Bed
Wedding Bells
What
Why
Wishing (If I Had A Photograph Of You)
Work That Body
Young Guns (Go For It)
Zoom

1983

Africa
All Night Long
Baby Come To Me
Baby Jane
Bad Boys
Beat It
Best Years of Our Lives
Big Apple
Billie Jean
Blind Vision
Blue Monday
Boxerbeat
Breakaway
Buffalo Gals
Buffalo Soldier
Calling Your Name
Can't Get Used To Losing You
Candy Girl
Chance
China Girl
Church Of The Poison Mind
Club Tropicana
Come Back And Stay
Come Live With Me
Communication
Crown, The
Cruel Summer
Cry Just A Little Bit
Cutter, The
Dead Giveaway
Dear Prudence
Dolce Vita
Don't Talk To Me About Love
Double Dutch
Down Under
Electric Avenue
European Female
Every Breath You Take
Everything Counts
Fields Of Fire
Flashdance - What A Feeling
Friday Night
Give It Up
Gloria
Gold
Heartache Avenue
Hey You The Rocksteady Crew
High Life
Hold Me Now
House That Jack Built
I Guess That's Why They Call It The
Blues
I'm Still Standing
I.O.U.
If You Can't Stand The Heat
In Your Eyes
Is There Something I Should Know
Islands In The Stream
It's Over
Just Got Lucky
Karma Chameleon
(Keep Feeling) Fascination
Lady Love Me (One More Time)
Last Night A D.J. Saved My Life
Let's Dance

Long Hot Summer
Love Cats, The
Love Is A Stranger
Love On Your Side
Love Town
Mama
Modern Love
Moonlight Shadow
My Oh My
Never Gonna Give You Up
Never Never
New Song
New Years Day
Nobody's Diary
Oh Diane
Old Rag Blues
Ooh To Be Ah
Orville's Song
Our Lips Are Sealed
Pale Shelter
Please Don't Fall In Love
Please Don't Make Me Cry
Puss 'n' Boots
Red Red Wine
Right By Your Side
Right Now
Rip It Up
Rockit
Rosana
Safety Dance
Say Say Say
She Means Nothing To Me
Sign Of The Times
Speak Like A Child
Steppin' Out
Story Of The Blues
Sun And The Rain, The
Sun Goes Down, The
Superman
Sweet Dreams (Are Made Of This)
Tahiti
Temptation
That's All
They Don't Know
This Is Not A Love Song
Thriller
Tomorrow's Just Another Day
Tonight I Celebrate My Love
Too Shy
Total Eclipse Of The Heart
True
Tunnel Of Love, The
Twisting By The Pool
Two Thousand Miles
Union Of The Snake
Up Where We Belong
Uptown Girl
Victims
Waiting For A Train
Walking In The Rain
Wanna Be Startin' Something
War Baby
Watching You, Watching Me
We Are Detective
Wham Rap (Enjoy What You Do)
What Am I Gonna Do

What Kinda Boy You Lookin' For Girl
When We Were Young
Wherever I Lay My Hat (That's My Home)
Whistle Down The Wind
Who's That Girl
Wings Of A Dove
Winter's Tale, A
Words
Wrapped Around Your Finger

1984

Agadoo
Against All Odds (Take A Look At Me Now)
Ain't Nobody
All Cried Out
An Innocent Man
Apollo 9
Automatic
Big In Japan
Bird Of Paradise
Blue Jean
Break My Stride
Breakdance Party
Breakin'... There's No Stopping Us
Careless Whisper
Caribbean Queen
Closest Thing To Heaven
Dancing Girls
Dancing With Tears In My Eyes
Do The Conga
Do They Know It's Christmas
Doctor Beat
Doctor! Doctor!
Don't Tell Me
Down On The Street
Drive
Everybody's Laughing
Farewell My Summer Love
(Feels Like) Heaven
Footloose
Freedom
Fresh
Ghostbusters
Gimme All Your Lovin'
Girls Just Want To Have Fun
Glad It's All Over
Groovin'
Hard Habit To Break
Heaven Knows I'm Miserable Know
Hello
Here Comes The Rain Again
Hide And Seek
High Energy
Hole In My Shoe
Holiday
I Am The Starlight
I Feel For You
I Feel Like Buddy Holly
I Just Called To Say I Love You
I Should Have Known Better
I Want To Break Free
I Won't Let The Sun Go Down On Me
I Won't Run Away
I'll Fly For You
I'm Falling

I'm Gonna Tear Your Playhouse Down
I'm So Excited
I've Been Losing You
If It Happens Again
In The Heart
It's A Hard Life
It's A Miracle
It's Raining Men
Joanna
Jump
Jump (For My Love)
Just Be Good To Me
Killing Moon, The
King Of Pain
Lay Your Hands On Me
Let The Music Play
Let's Hear It For The Boy
Letter To You
Like A Virgin
Like To Get To Know You Well
Locomotion
Lost In Music
Love Kills
Love Resurrection
Love Worth Waiting For, A
Love's Great Adventure
Madam Butterfly (Un Bel Di Verdremo)
Many Rivers To Cross
Marguerita Time
Master And Servant
Michael Caine
Missing You
My Ever Changing Moods
Nelson Mandela
Never Ending Story
New Moon On Monday
Ninety-nine Red Balloons
No More Lonely Nights
Nobody Told Me
On The Wings Of Love
One Love
One Night In Bankok
Only When You Leave
Passengers
Pearl In The Shell
People Are People
Pipes Of Peace, The
Power Of Love, The
Pride (In The Name Of Love)
Purple Rain
Radio Ga Ga
Reflex, The
Relax
Riddle, The
Robert De Niro's Waiting
Rockin' Good Way, A
Round And Round
Run Run Away
Running With The Night
Sad Songs (Say So Much)
Searchin'
Self Control
Sex Crime (Nineteen Eighty Four)
Shout To The Top
Small Town Boy
Some Guys Have All The Luck
Somebody Else's Guy

Somebody's Watching Me
Straight Ahead
Street Dance
Stuck On You
Talking Loud And Clear
Teardrops
Tell Her About It
That's Living Alright
Thinking Of You
Thorn Birds (Love Theme)
Time After Time
Together In Electric Dreams
Too Late For Goodbyes
Two Tribes
Wake Me Up Before You Go Go
Wanderer, The
War Song, The
We All Stand Together
What Difference Does It Make
What Do I Do
What Is Love
What's Love Got To Do With It
Whatever I Do (Wherever I Go)
When Doves Cry
When You're Young And In Love
White Lines (Don't Don't Do It)
Why
Wild Boys, The
Wishful Thinking
Wonderland
Wood Beez
Wouldn't It Be Good
You Take Me Up
Young At Heart
Your Love Is King

1985

Alive And Kicking
Alone Without You
Angel
Atmosphere
Axel F
Body And Soul
Body Rock
Born In The USA
Call Me
Cherish
Close (To The Edit)
Clouds Across The Moon
Could It Be I'm Falling In Love
Dancing In The Dark
Dancing In The Street
Do What You Do
Don Quixote
Don't Break My Heart
Don't Look Down
Don't You Forget About Me
Don't You Know It
Dress You Up
Easy Lover
Election Day
Every Time You Go Away
Everybody Wants To Rule The World
Everything Must Change
Everything She Wants
Feel So Real

Frankie
Friends
Gambler
Good Heart
Hanging On A String (Contemplating)
Head Over Heels
Heat Is On, The
History
Holding Out For A Hero
Howard's Way Theme
I Can Dream About You
I Know Him So Well
I Want To Know What Love Is
I Was Born To Love You
I Wonder If I Take You Home
I'm On Fire
I'm Your Man
If I Was
In Between Days
In Your Car
Into The Groove
Johnny Come Home
Kayleigh
Kiss Me
Last Christmas
Last Kiss
Lavender
Lean On Me
Let's Go Crazy
Lipstick, Powder And Paint
Little Red Corvette
Live Is Life
Living On Video
Look Mama
Love And Pride
Love Don't Live Here Anymore
Loverboy
Material Girl
Merry Christmas Everyone
Miami Vice
Money For Nothing
Move Closer
My Toot Toot
New England
Nightshift
Nikita
Nineteen
Obsession
One More Night
One Vision
Out In The Fields
Part Time Lover
Pie Jesu
Power Of Love, The
Rebel Yell
Rhythm Of The Night
Road To Nowhere
Round And Round
Run To You
Running Up That Hill
Saving All My Love For You
Say I'm Your Number One
Say You, Say Me
See The Day
Seperate Lives
She Sells Sanctuary
She's So Beautiful

Shout
Show, The
Since Yesterday
Sisters Are Doing It For Themselves
Slave to Love, A
Slave to The Rhythm
Solid
Something About You
Spend The Night
Spies Like Us
St. Elmo's Fire (Man In Motion)
Stairway To Heaven
Step Off
Suddenly
Sussudio
Take On Me
Tarzan Boy
Taste Of Your Tears
That Old Devil Called Love
That's What Friends Are For
There Must Be An Angel Playing With
My Heart
Things Can Only Get Better
Thinking Of You
Trapped
Unforgettable Fire, The
View To A Kill
Walking In The Air
Walking On Sunshine
Walls Come Tumbling Down
We All Follow Man. United
We Are The World
We Built This City
We Close Our Eyes
We Don't Need Another Hero
Welcome To The Pleasure Dome
White Wedding
Wide Boy
Word Girl, The
You Spin Me 'round (Like A Record)

1986

Absolute Beginners
Addicted To Love
Ain't Nothin' Goin' On But The Rent
Alice, I Want You Just For Me
All I Ask Of You
All The Things She Said
Always There
Amityville (The House On The Hill)
And She Was
Anyone Can Fall In Love
Bad Boy
Bang Zoom (Let's Go Go)
Borderline
Breakout
Broken Wings
Brother Louis
Burning Hearts
Calling All The Heroes
Camouflage
Can't Wait Another Minute
Captain Of Her Heart
Chain Reaction
Chicken Song, The
Dancing On The Ceiling

Died In Your Arms
Different Corner
Digging Your Scene
Do Ya Do Ya (Wanna Please Me)
Don't Get Me Wrong
Don't Give Up
Don't Leave Me This Way
Don't Waste My Time
Each Time You Break My Heart
Edge Of Heaven
Every Beat Of My Heart
Every Loser Wins
Final Countdown
Find The Time
Finest, The
For America
Forever Live And Die
French Kissin' In The Usa
Friends Will Be Friends
Girlie Girlie
Glory Of Love, The
Greatest Love Of All
Happy Hour
Hi Ho Silver
Hit That Perfect Beat
Holding Back The Years
How Will I Know
Human
Hunting High And Low
I Can Prove It
I Can't Wait
I Didn't Mean To Turn You On
I Want To Wake Up With You
In Too Deep
Invisible Touch
It's Alright (Baby's Coming Back)
Just Buggin'
Just Say No
Kind Of Magic, A
Kiss
Kyrie
Lady In Red
Land Of Confusion
Lessons In Love
Let's Go All The Way
Live To Tell
Living In America
Living On A Prayer
Look Away
Love Can't Turn Around
Love Missile F1-11
Manic Monday
Midas Touch, The
Move Away
My Favourite Waste Of Time
New Beginning
New York, New York
Notorious
On My Own
Only Love
Opportunities
Overjoyed
Panic
Papa Don't Preach
Phantom Of The Opera, The
Pull Up To The Bumper

Rage Hard
Rain Or Shine
Rise
Rock Me Amadeus
Rollin' Home
Roses
Sanctify Yourself
Saturday
Secret Lovers
Set Me Free
Shake You Down
Showing Out
Sing Our Own Song
Skye Boat Song, The
Sledgehammer
Smile
Snooker Loopy
So Cold The Night
So Macho
Sometimes
Spirit In The Sky
Starting Together
Stuck With You
Suburbia
Sun Always Shines On T.V., The
Sweet Freedom
System Addict
Take My Breath Away
Thorn In My Side
Through The Barricades
Touch Me (I Want Your Body)
Train Of Thought
True Blue
True Colours
Venus
Vienna Calling
Walk Like An Egyptian
Walk Of Life
Walk This Way
We Don't Have To Take Our Clothes Off
West End Girls
What Have You Done For Me Lately
What's The Colour Of Money
When I Think Of You
When The Going Gets Tough, The
Tough Get Going
Why Can't This Be Love
Word Up
You And Me Tonight
You Can Call Me Al
You Little Thief
You're In The Army Now

1987
Almaz
Alone
Always
Animal
Another Step Closer To You
Back And Forth
Bad
Barcelona
Big Love
Boy From Nowhere
Bridge To Your Heart
C'est La Vie

Can't Be With You Tonight
Caravan Of Love
Casanova
Causing A Commotion
China In Your Hand
Circus
Come Into My Life
Coming Around Again
Crazy Crazy Nights
Criticize
Crockett's Theme
Crush On You
Cry Wolf
Down To Earth
Ever Fallen In Love
Everything I Own
F.L.M.
Fairytale Of New York
Faith
Full Metal Jacket
Funky Town
Goodbye Stranger
Got My Mind Set On You
Heartache
Here I Go Again
Hey Matthew
Hold Me Now
House Nation
Hymn To Her
I Don't Want To Be A Hero
I Found Lovin'
I Heard A Rumour
I Just Can't Stop Loving You
I Knew You Were Waiting (For Me)
I Love My Radio
I Need Love
I Still Haven't Found What I'm Looking
For
I Think We're Alone Now
I Wanna Dance With Somebody (Who
Loves Me)
I Want Your Sex
If You Let Me Stay
Incommunicado
Irish Rover, The
Is This Love
It Didn't Matter
It Doesn't Have To Be
It Doesn't Have To Be This Way
It's A Sin
It's Over
Jack That House Built, The
Jack Your Body
Jive Talkin'
Just Don't Want To Be Lonely
La Bamba
La Isla Bonita
Labour Of Love
Let's Dance
Let's Wait Awhile
Letter From America
Lil' Devil
Little Boogie Woogie
Little Lies
Live It Up
Living Daylights, The

Living In A Box
Look Of Love
Love In The First Degree
Male Stripper
Misfit
Moonlighting
Music Of The Night
My Pretty One
Never Can Say Goodbye
Never Gonna Give You Up
No More The Fool
Nothing's Gonna Stop Me Now
Oh Carol
Once Upon A Long Ago
Open Your Heart
Pump Up The Volume
Rain
Real Thing, The
Real Wild Child
Rent
Respect Yourself
Respectable
Right Thing, The
Rock The Boat
Running In The Family
Serious
Shattered Dreams
She's On It
Sheila Take A Bow
Sign O' The Times
Slightest Touch
So Emotional
So Strong
Some People
Somewhere Out There
Star Trekkin'
Stay Out Of My Life
Surrender
Sweet Little Mystery
Sweetest Smile
This Corrosion
Time Of My Life
To Be With You Again
Toy Boy
True Faith
Turn Back The Clock
U Got The Look
Under The Boardwalk
Victim Of Love
Walk The Dinosaur
Wanted Dead Or Alive
Way You Make Me Feel, The
Weak In The Presence Of Beauty
What Have I Done To Deserve This
When Smokey Sings
Whenever You Need Somebody
Where The Streets Have No Name
Who Found Who
Who's That Girl
Wishing I Was Lucky
Wishing Well
With Or Without You
Wonderful Life
You Sexy Thing
You Win Again
You're The Voice

1988

All Day And All Of The Night
Alphabet Street
Anfield Rap, The
Angel Eyes (Home And Away)
Anything For You
Beat Dis
Big Fun
Blue Monday 1988
Boys (Summertime Love)
Breakfast In Bed
Burn It Up
Can I Play With Madness
Can You Party
Cat Among The Pigeons
Chains Of Love
Check This Out
Circles In The Sand
Clairvoyant, The
Could've Been
Crash
Cross My Broken Heart
Desire
Dirty Diana
Divine Emotions
Doctorin' The House
Doctorin' The Tardis
Domino Dancing
Don't Make Me Wait
Don't Turn Around
Don't Worry - Be Happy
Drop The Boy
Easy
Everywhere
Evil That Men Do
Fast Car
Find My Love
First Time, The
Foolish Beat
G.T.O.
Get Out Of My Dreams, Get Into My Car
Gimme Hope Jo'anna
Girl You Know It's True
Girlfriend
Good Tradition
Got To Be Certain
Groovy Kind Of Love, A
Hands To Heaven
Harder I Try, The
He Ain't No Competition
Heart
Heart And Soul
Heatseeker
Heaven Is A Place On Earth
Hot In The City
House Arrest
Hustle To The Music
I Don't Want To Talk About It
I Found Someone
I Get Weak
I Need You
I Owe You Nothing
I Quit
I Saw Him Standing There
I Should Be So Lucky
I Want You Back

I Want Your Love
I'm Gonna Be
I'm Not Scared
Ideal World
Je Ne Sais Pas, Pourquoi
Jingo
Joe Le Taxi
King Of Rock 'n' Roll, The
Left To My Own Devices
Let's All Chant
Little Respect
Love Bites
Love Changes Everything
Love Is Contagious
Love Will Save The Day
Lovely Day
Martha's Harbour
Mary's Prayer
Megablast
Missing You
Mistletoe And Wine
Monkey
My Love
My One Temptation
Nathan Jones
Need You Tonight
Never
Never Trust A Stranger
Nothing Can Divide Us
Nothing's Gonna Change My Love For You
O' L'amour
One Moment In Time
One More Try
One Two Three
Only Way Is Up, The
Orinoco Flow
Perfect
Pink Cadillac
Prove Your Love
Push It
Race, The
Real Gone Kid
Riding On A Train
Rise To The Occasion
Rok Da House
Roses Are Red
Rush Hour
Say A Little Prayer
Say It Again
Shake Your Love
She Makes My Day
She Wants To Dance With Me
She's Leaving Home
Ship Of Fools
Sign Your Name
Smooth Criminal
Somewhere In My Heart
Stand Up For Your Love Rights
Stay On These Roads
Stutter Rap
Suddenly
Suedhead
Superfly Guy
Take Me To Your Heart
Teardrops
Tell It To My Heart

That's The Way It Is
Theme From S-Express
Together Forever
Tower Of Strength
Tribute (Right On)
Two Hearts
Valentine
Voyage Voyage
Wap-Bam-boogie
We Call It Acieed
Wee Rule
When Will I Be Famous
Where Do Broken Hearts Go
Who's Leaving Who
Wild World
You Came

1989

Ain't Nobody Better
All Around The World
Americanos
Angel Of Harlem
Another Day In Paradise
Baby I Don't Care
Baby I Love Your Way
Back To Life
Batdance
Beds Are Burning
Belfast Child
Best Of Me, The
Best, The
Blame It On The Boogie
Blow The House Down
Buffalo Stance
Burning Bridges
C'mon And Get My Love
Can't Shake The Feeling
Can't Stay Away From You
Cherish
Cuddly Toy
Days
Don't Know Much
Don't Wanna Lose You
Drama
Especially For You
Eternal Flame
Eve Of The War
Every Day I Love You More
Every Little Step
Every Rose Has It's Thorn
Everyday Is Like Sunday
Express Yourself
Fine Time
Four Letter Word, A
French Kiss
Girl I'm Gonna Miss You
Good Life
Good Thing
Hand On Your Heart
Hey Music Lover
Hold Me In Your Arms
Homely Girl
I Beg Your Pardon
I Don't Wanna Get Hurt
I Don't Wanna Lose You
I Don't Want A Lover

I Drove All Night
I Feel The Earth Move
I Just Don't Have The Heart
I Need Your Lovin'
I Want It All
I Want That Man
I'd Rather Jack
If I Could Turn Back Time
If Only I Could
In Private
International Rescue
It Is Time To Get Funky
It's All Right
Just Keep Rockin'
Keep On Movin'
Keeping The Dream Alive
Lambada
Leave A Light On
Leave Me Alone
Licence To Kill
Like A Prayer
Living Years
Loco In Acapulco
London Nights
Look, The
Love Train
Manchild
Miss You Like Crazy
My Prerogative
Never Too Late
Nothing Has Been Proved
Numero Uno
On Our Own
On The Inside
One
Pacific
Paradise City
People Hold On
Poison
Pump Up The Jam
Requiem
Ride On Time
Right Back Where We Started From
Right Here Waiting
Road To Hell, The
Room In Your Heart
She Drives Me Crazy
Song For Whoever
Sowing The Seeds Of Love
Stop
Straight Up
Street Tuff
Superwoman
Sweet Child O' Mine
Sweet Surrender
That's The Way Love Is
This Time I Know It's For Real
Time Warp, The
Too Many Broken Hearts In The World
Too Much
Toy Soldiers
Wait
Waiting For A Star To Fall
We Didn't Start The Fire

Who's In The House
Wind Beneath My Wings
Wouldn't Change A Thing
You Are The One
You Got It
You Got It (The Right Stuff)
You Keep It All In
You'll Never Stop Me Loving You
You're History

1990

All I Wanna Do Is Make Love To You
All Together Now
Better The Devil You Know
Birdhouse In Your Soul
Black Velvet
Blue Savannah
Blue Velvet
Close To You
Could Have Told You So
Cover Girl
Dear Jessie
Dirty Cash
Doin' The Do
Don't Stop The Partyline
Don't Worry
Downtown Train
Dream's A Dream, A
Dub Be Good To Me
Enjoy The Silence
Falling
Fantasy
Fascinating Rhythm
Fog On The Tyne
From A Distance
Get A Life
Get Up (Before The Night Is Over)
Ghetto Heaven
Going Back To My Roots
Got To Get
Got To Have Your Love
Groove Is In The Heart
Groovy Train
Hang On To Your Love
Hangin' Tough
Hanky Panky
Happenin' All Over Again
Hardcore Uproar
Hear The Drummer Get Wicked
Hold On
How Am I Supposed To Live Without You
How Can We Be Lovers
I Can't Stand It
I Don't Know Anybody Else
I Wish It Would Rain Down
I'll Be Loving You (Forever)
I'll Be Your Baby Tonight
I'm Free
I'm Your Baby Tonight
I've Been Thinking About You
Ice Ice Baby
Infinity

It Must Have Been Love
It Takes Two
It's A Shame (My Sister)
It's My Life
Joker, The
Just Like Jesse James
Justify My Love
Killer
Kingston Town
Kinky Afro
Kinky Boots
Lily Was Here
Listen To Your Heart
Little Time, A
Love Shack
Mamma Gave Birth To The Soul Children
Megamix
Mona
Naked In The Rain
Natural Thing
Nessun Dorma
Nothing Compares 2 U
Nothing Ever Happens
One Love
Only One I Know, The
Only Rhyme That Bites, The
Opposites Attract
Power, The
Praying For Time
Put Your Hands Together
Rockin' Over The Beat
Sacrifice
Same Thing, The
Show Me Heaven
Silhouettes
Space Jungle, The
Star
Step Back In Time
Step On
Take Your Time
Tears On My Pillow
There She Goes
Thinking Of You
This Is How It Feels
To Love Somebody
Tom's Diner
Tonight
Touch Me
Turtle Power
U Can't Touch This
Unbelievable
Venus
Vision Of Love
Vogue
Wash Your Face In My Sink
What Time Is Love
When You Come Back To Me
Where Are You Baby
Won't Talk About It
Working Man
World In Motion
You Make Me Feel (Mighty Real)
You've Got A Friend

ACADEMY AWARD NOMINATIONS AND WINNING SONGS

The winning song in respect of each year is shown in *italics*.

1934
Continental, The
Carioca
Love in Bloom

1935
Lullaby of Broadway
Cheek to Cheek
Lovely to Look At

1936
Way You Look Tonight, The
Did I Remember
I've Got You Under My Skin
A Melody From the Sky
Pennies From Heaven
When Did You Leave Heaven?

1937
Sweet Leilani
Remember Me
That Old Feeling
They Can't Take That Away From Me
Whispers in the Dark

1938
Thanks For the Memory
Always and Always
Change Partners
Cowboy and the Lady, The
Dust
Jeepers Creepers
Merrily We Live
A Mist Over the Moon
My Own
Now it Can Be Told

1939
Over the Rainbow
Faithful Forever
I Poured My Heart into a Song
Wishing

1940
When You Wish Upon a Star
Down Argentine Way
I'd Know You Anywhere
It's a Blue World
Love of My Life
Only Forever
Our Love Affair
Waltzing in the Clouds
Who am I?

1941
Last Time I Saw Paris, The
Baby Mine
Be Honest With Me
Blues in the Night
Boogie Woogie Bugle Boy
Chattanooga Choo Choo
Dolores
Out of the Silence
Since I Kissed My Baby Goodbye

1942
White Christmas
Always in My Heart
Dearly Beloved
How About You
It Seems I Heard That Song Before
I've Got a Gal in Kalamazoo
Love is a Song
Pennies for Peppino
Pig Foot Pete
There's a Breeze on Lake Louise

1943
You'll Never Know
That Old Black Magic
Change of Heart
Happiness is a Thing Called Joe
My Shining Hour
Saludos Amigos
Say A Prayer For the Boys Over There
They're Either Too Young or Too Old
We Mustn't Say Goodbye
You'd Be So Nice to Come Home to

1944
Swinging on a Star
I Couldn't Sleep a Wink Last Night
I'll Walk Alone
I'm Making Believe
Long Ago and Far Away
Now I Know
Remember Me to Carolina
Rio de Janeiro
Silver Shadows and Golden Dreams
Sweet Dreams Sweetheart
Too Much in Love
Trolley Song, The

1945
It Might as Well Be Spring
Accentuate the Positive
Anywhere
Aren't You Glad You're You
Cat and the Canary, The

Endlessly
I Fall in Love Too Easily
I'll Buy That Dream
Linda
Love Letters
More and More
Sleighride in July
So in Love
Some Sunday Morning

1946
On The Atchison, Topeka and the Santa Fe
All Through the Day
I Can't Begin to Tell You
Ole Buttermilk Sky
You Keep Coming Back Like a Song

1947
Zip-a-dee-doo-dah
Gal in Calico, A
I Wish I Didn't Love You So
Pass That Peace Pipe
You Do

1948
Buttons and Bows
For Every Man There's a Woman
It's Magic
This is the Moment
Woody Woodpecker Song, The

1949
Baby It's Cold Outside
It's a Great Feeling
Lavender Blue
My Foolish Heart
Through a Long and Sleepless Night

1950
Mona Lisa
Be My Love
Bibbidi-bobbidi-boo
Mule Train
Wilhelma

1951
In the Cool, Cool, Cool of the Evening
Kiss to Build a Dream On, A
Never
Too Late Now
Wonder Why

1952
High Noon
Am I in Love
Because You're Mine
Thumbalina

Zing a Little Zong

1953
Secret Love
Moon is Blue, The
My Flaming Heart
Blue Pacific Blues
That's Amore

1954
Three Coins in the Fountain
Count Your Blessings Instead of Sheep
High and the Mighty, The
Hold My Hand
Man That Got Away, The

1955
Love is a Many Splendoured Thing
I'll Never Stop Loving You
Something's Gotta Give
Tender Trap, The
Unchained Melody

1956
Que Sera, Sera (Whatever Will Be, Will Be)
Friendly Persuasion
Julie
True Love
Written on the Wind

1957
All the Way
Affair to Remember, An
April Love
Tammy
Wild is the Wind

1958
Gigi
Almost in Your Arms
Certain Smile, A
To Love and Be Loved
Very Precious Love, A

1959
High Hopes
Best of Everything, The
Five Pennies, The
Hanging Tree, The
Strange Are the Ways of Love

1960
Never on a Sunday
Facts of Life, The
Faraway Part of Town
Green Leaves of Summer, The
Second Time Around, The

1961

Moon River
Bachelor in Paradise
Falcon and the Dove, The
Pocketful of Miracles
Town Without Pity

1962

Days of Wine and Roses
Follow Me
Second Chance
Tender is the Night
Walk on the Wild Side

1963

Call Me Irresponsible
Charade
It's A Mad, Mad, Mad, Mad World
More
So Little Time

1964

Chim Chim Cher-ee
Dear Heart
Hush Hush Sweet Caroline
My Kind of Town
Where Love Has Gone

1965

Shadow of Your Smile, The
Ballad of Cat Ballou
I Will Wait For You
Sweetheart Tree, The
What's New Pussycat?

1966

Born Free
Alfie
Georgy Girl
My Wishing Doll
Time For Love, A

1967

Talk to the Animals
Bare Necessities, The
Eyes of Love, The
Look of Love, The
Thoroughly Modern Millie

1968

Windmills of Your Mind
Chitty Chitty Bang Bang
For Love of Ivy
Funny Girl
Star

1969

Raindrops Keep Falling On My Head

Come Saturday Morning
Jean
True Grit
What Are You Doing the Rest of Your Life?

1970

For All We Know
Pieces of Dreams
Thank You Very Much
Till Love Touches Your Life
Whistling Away the Dark

1971

Shaft
Age of Not Believing
All His Children
Bless the Beasts and Children
Life is What You Make It

1972

Morning After, The
Ben
Come Follow, Follow Me
Marmalade, Molasses and Honey
Strange are the Ways of Love

1973

Way We Were, The
All That Love Went to Waste
Live and Let Die
Love
Nice to Be Around

1974

We May Never Love Like This Again
I Feel Love
Blazing Saddles
Little Prince
Wherever Love Takes Me

1975

I'm Easy
How Lucky Can You Get
Now That We're in Love
Richard's Window
Do You Know Where You're Going To?

1976

Evergreen
Ave Satani
Come To Me
Gonna Fly Now
World That Never Was, A

1977

You Light Up My Life
Candle on the Water
Nobody Does it Better

He Danced With Me
Someone's Waiting For You

1978
Last Dance, The
Hopelessly Devoted To You
Last Time I Felt Like This, The
Ready to Take a Chance Again
When You're Loved

1979
It Goes Like This
Rainbow Connection, The
It's Easy to Say
Through the Eyes of Love
I'll Never Say Goodbye

1980
Fame
Nine to Five
On the Road Again
Out Here On My Own
People Alone

1981
Arthur's Theme
Endless Love
First Time it Happens, The
For Your Eyes Only
One More Hour

1982
Up Where We Belong
Eye of the Tiger, The
How Do You Keep the Music Playing
If We Were in Love
It Might Be You

1983
Flashdance - What A Feeling
Manic
Over You
Papa Can You Hear Me?
Way He Makes Me Feel, The

1984
I Just Called To Say I Love You

Against All Odds (Take a Look at Me Now)
Footloose
Ghostbusters
Let's Hear It For the Boy

1985
Say You, Say Me
Miss Celie's Blues
Power of Love, The
Separate Lives
Surprise, Surprise

1986
Take My Breath Away
Glory of Love
Life in a Looking Glass
Mean Green Mother From Outer Space
Somewhere Out There

1987
(I've Had) The Time of My Life
Cry Freedom
Nothing's Gonna Stop Us Now
Shakedown
Storybook Love

1988
Let the River Run
Calling You
Two Hearts

1989
Under the Sea
After All
Girl Who Used to Be Me, The
I Love to See You Smile
Kiss the Girl

1990
Sooner or Later
Blaze of Glory
I'm Checking Out
Promise Me You'll Remember
Somewhere in My Memory

IVOR NOVELLO AWARDS AND NOMINATIONS

The winning song or songs in respect of each year are shown in *italics.*

1955
A Blossom Fell
Big City Blues
Dam Busters March, The
Everywhere
Fanfare Boogie
Got'n Idea
In Love For the Very First Time
Income Tax Collector, The
John and Julie
Man in a Raincoat

1956
By the Fountains of Rome
Experiments With Mice
Itinerary of an Orchestra
Lift Boy
March Hare, The
My September Love
My Unfinished Symphony
Nellie the Elephant
Out of Town
Toyshop Ballet
Westminster Waltz, The
You Are My First Love

1957
A Handful of Songs
Elizabethan Serenade
I'll Find You
Overdrive
Skiffling Strings
Streets of Sorrento, The
Three Brothers
Water, Water
We Will Make Love
Your Love is My Love

1958
Army Game, The
Colonel's Tune, The
I'm So Ashamed
Lingering Lovers
Melody From the Sea
Rock Bottom
There Goes My Lover
Trudie
Wind Cannot Read, The
You Need Hands

1959
Ballad of Bethnal Green, The
Beaulieu Festival Suite
Jazzboat
Little White Bull
Living Doll
Maybe This Year
Ring Ding
Side Saddle
Village of St. Bernadette, The
Windows of Paris

1960
Apache
As Long As He Needs Me
Belle of Barking Creek, The
Goodness Gracious Me
Gurney Slade Theme, The
Hit and Miss
Portrait of My Love
Seashore
What Do You Want if You Don't Want Money
Willow Waltz, The

1961
African Waltz
Are You Sure?
Avengers Theme, The
Duddly Dell
Maigret Theme, The
My Kind of Girl
No Greater Love
Portrait of My Girl
Secret of The Seine, The
Stranger on the Shore
Walking Back to Happiness
What Kind of Fool Am I?

1962
Bachelor Boy
Jeannie
My Love and Devotion
Nicola
Outbreak of Murder
Revival
Stranger on the Shore
Telstar
Turkish Coffee

Wonderful Land

1963
All My Loving
Carlos' Theme
Dance On
Flash, Bang Wallop
Harvest of Love
I Want to Hold Your Hand
If I Ruled the World
Scarlett O'Hara
She Loves You
Sweet September
What the Dickens
Bombay Duckling

1964
Can't Buy Me Love
Downtown
Hard Day's Night
I Feel Fine
Losing You

1965
A Windmill in Old Amsterdam
Catch the Wind
Help
I'll Never Find Another You
It's Not Unusual
Kiss, The
Look Through Any Window
March of the Mods
Mrs. Brown You've Got a Lovely Daughter
We Can Work it Out
Where Are You Now? (My Love)
Yesterday

1966
Born Free
Call Me
Dedicated Follower of Fashion
Have You Gotta Loight Boy?
Khartoum
Michelle
Power Game, The
Time Drags By
What Would I Be
Winchester Cathedral
Yellow Submarine

1967

A Whiter Shade of Pale
Ballad of Bonnie and Clyde, The
Don't Sleep in the Subway
Grocer Jack
Hello Goodbye
Last Waltz, The
Love in the Open Air
Puppet on a String
She's Leaving Home
This is My Song
To Sir With Love

1968

633 Squadron
Build Me Up Buttercup
Congratulations
Delilah
Hey Jude
I Close My Eyes and Count to Ten
I'm the Urban Spaceman
Jesamine
Ring of Kerry
Rosie

1969

Boom Bang-a-Bang
Get Back
Give Peace a Chance
Honky Tonk Women
Lights on Cincinnati
Love is All
Melting Pot
Ob-la-di Ob-la-da
Where Do You Go to My Lovely?

1970

17th March, The
Gimme Dat Ding
Grandad
Home Lovin' Man
In the Summertime
Knock, Knock, Who's There?
Let it Be
Light Flight
Love Grows
March From the Colour Suite
Something
Songs For My Father
United We Stand
We're Gonna Change the World
When I'm Dead And Gone

Who Do You Think You Are Kidding Mr. Hitler?
Yellow River
Your Song

1971

Don't Let it Die
Ernie
Freedom Come, Freedom Go
Hot Love
I Don't Know How to Love Him
My Sweet Lord
No Matter How I Try
Rosetta
Simple Game
Sleepy Shores
Superstar
When You Are a King
Why

1972

Alone Again (Naturally)
Beg Steal or Borrow
Clair
Colditz
Country Matters
Diamonds Are Forever
First Time Ever I Saw Your Face, The
Long Cool Woman in a Black Dress
Meet Me on the Corner
Mouldy Old Dough
Oh Babe What Would You Say
Our Jackie's Getting Married
People Tree, The
Solid Gold Easy Action
Without You

1973

Angie
Blockbuster
Children of Rome
Crocodile Rock
Daniel
Galloping Home
Get Down
I Love You Love Me Love
Like Sister and Brother
Merry Xmas Everybody
My Love
Nice One Cyril
Power to All Our Friends

Rubber Bullets
Won't Somebody Dance With Me
You Wont Find Another Fool Like Me

1974

Air That I Breathe
Billy Don't Be a Hero
Killer Queen
Kung Fu Fighting
Night Chicago Died, The
No Honestly
Sad Sweet Dreamer
Streets of London
Tiger Feet
Wombling Song

1975

Bohemian Rhapsody
Doctor's Orders
Good Word, The
Harry
I'm Not in Love
Island Girl
Last Farewell, The
Magic
Sailing
Sky High
Upstairs Downstairs (theme)

1976

Bouquet of Barbed Wire
Don't Cry For Me Argentina
Don't Go Breaking My Heart
Heart on My Sleeve
Miss You Nights
Music
Sam
Save Your Kisses For Me
Sweeny, The
We Do It
You Should Be Dancing

1977

Angelo
Boogie Nights
Cavatina
Don't Cry For Me Argentina
Don't Give Up on Us
Duellists, The
Heaven on the Seventh Floor
How Deep is Your Love?

I Don't Want to Put a Hold On You
Love For Lydia
Love Transformation
Matchstalk Men and Matchstalk Cats and Dogs
Mull of Kintyre
Poldark
Sam
Scarlet Buccaneer
Snow Goose, The
Wings

1978
39 Steps, The
Baker Street
Bright Eyes
Can't Smile Without You
Dr Who
Dreadlock Holiday
Fawlty Towers
Floral Dance, The
Grease
Heartsong
Hong Kong Beat
It's a Heartache
Lillie
Man With the Child in His Eyes, The
Matchstalk Men and Matchstalk Cats and Dogs
Mull of Kintyre
Night Fever
Railway Hotel
Rat Trap
Silent Witness, The
Song For Guy
Stayin' Alive
Watership Down
Wuthering Heights

1979
African Sanctus
Another Brick in the Wall
Bright Eyes
Caravans
Cavatina
He Was Beautiful
I Don't Like Mondays
Logical Song, The
Music Machine
Nunc Dimittis
Off the Wall

Secret Army
Shoestring
Too Much Heaven
Valley of Swords, The
Video Killed the Radio Star
War of the Worlds
We Don't Talk Anymore
Yanks

1980
Another Brick in the Wall
Another One Bites the Dust
Babooshka
Don't Stand So Close to Me
Flash
Fox
I Could Be So Good For You
I'm in the Mood For Dancing
January, February
Juliet Bravo
Silver Dream Machine
Stop the Cavalry
Take That Look Off Your Face
There's No One Quite Like Grandma
Together We Are Beautiful
What You're Proposing
Woman in Love
Xanadu
Your Ears Should Be Burning Now

1981
Don't You Want Me
Every Little Thing She Does is Magic
For Your Eyes Only
In the Air Tonight
Memory
Stand and Deliver
Vienna
When He Shines
Wired For Sound
Woman
You Drive Me Crazy

1982
Come on Eileen
Do You Really Want to Hurt Me?
Do You Want Me
Ebony and Ivory
Golden Brown
Harry's Game

Have You Ever Been in Love?
Heartbreaker
I Don't Wanna Dance
Land of Make Believe
Love Plus One
Now Those Days Are Gone
Oh Julie
Our House
Private Investigations

1983
Do You Really Want to Hurt Me?
Every Breath You Take
Karma Chameleon
Let's Dance
Moonlight Shadow
Only You
Pipes of Peace
Sweet Dreams
That's Living Alright
True
Walking in the Air

1984
Against All Odds
Careless Whisper
Caribbean Queen
Do They Know it's Christmas?
I Should Have Known Better
I Won't Let the Sun Go Down on Me
Reflex, The
Relax
Two Tribes
Wake Me Up Before You Go Go

1985
Easy Lover
Everybody Wants to Rule The World
Hit That Perfect Beat
I Know Him So Well
I Want to Know What Love Is
Money For Nothing
Nikita
Nineteen
Running Up That Hill
Shout
View to a Kill, A
We Don't Need Another Hero

1986
All I Ask of You

Chain Reaction
Don't Give Up
Edge of Heaven, The
Every Loser Wins
In Too Deep
It's Alright (Baby's Coming Back)
Kind of Magic, A
Living Doll
Nikita
Sledgehammer
Sweet Freedom
West End Girls

1987
China in Your Hand
I Knew You Were Waiting (For Me)
It's a Sin
Living Daylights, The
Living in a Box
Never Gonna Give You Up
Respectable

So Strong
What Have I Done to Deserve This?
You Win Again

1988
Especially For You
Faith
Get Out of My Dreams, Get Into My Car
I Should Be So Lucky
Little Respect, A
Love Changes Everything
Mary's Prayer
Mistletoe and Wine
Perfect
Two Hearts

1989
All Around the World
Another Day in Paradise
Back to Life
Buffalo Stance

Living Years, The
Nothing Has Been Proved
Room in Your Heart
She Drives Me Crazy
Something's Gotten Hold of My Heart
This Time I Know it's For Real
Too Many Broken Hearts

1990
All I Want to Do is Make Love to You
Blue Savannah
Don't Worry
Killer
Lily Was Here
Nothing Ever Happens
Sacrifice
Unbelievable
World in Motion

EUROVISION SONG CONTEST WINNERS

YEAR	SONG	COUNTRY
1956	Refrains	Switzerland
1957	Net Als Toen	Holland
1958	Dors Mon Amour	France
1959	Een Beetie	Holland
1960	Tom Pillibi	France
1961	Nous les Amoureux	Luxembourg
1962	Un Premier Amour	France
1963	Dansevise	Denmark
1964	Non Ho L'eta (This Is My Prayer)	Italy
1965	Poupee de Cire, Poupee de Son	Luxembourg
1966	Mercie Cherie	Austria
1967	Puppet on a String	United Kingdom
1968	La, La, La	Spain
1969 *	Viva Cantando	Spain
	Boom Bang A Bang	United Kingdom
	De Troubadour	Holland
	Un Jour un Enfant	France
1970	All Kinds of Everything	Ireland
1971	Un Banc, un Arbre, une Rue	Monaco
1972	Apres Toi (Come What May)	Luxembourg
1973	Tu Te Reconnaitras (Wonderful Dream)	Luxembourg
1974	Waterloo	Sweden
1975	Ding Dinge Dong	Holland
1976	Save Your Kisses For Me	United Kingdom
1977	L'oiseau et L'enfant	France
1978	A-ba-ni-bi	Israel
1979	Hallelujah	Israel
1980	What's Another Year?	Ireland
1981	Making Your Mind Up	United Kingdom
1982	Ein Bisschen Friden	Germany
1983	Si la Vie est Cadeau	Luxembourg
1984	Diggi-loo Diggi Ley	Sweden
1985	La de Swinge	Norway
1986	Jaime la Vie	Belgium
1987	Hold Me Now	Ireland
1988	Ne Partez Pas Sans Moi	Switzerland
1989	Rock Me	Yugoslavia
1990	Insieme 1992	Italy

* The 1969 contest was a four-way tie.

EUROVISON SONG CONTEST - UK ENTRIES

YEAR	SONG	FINAL PLACING
1956	No Entry	-
1957	All	Sixth
1958	No Entry	-
1959	Sing Little Birdie	Second
1960	Looking High, High, High	Second
1961	Are You Sure?	Second
1962	Ring-a-Ding Girl	Fourth
1963	Say Wonderful Things	Fourth
1964	I Love the Little Things	Second
1965	I Belong	Second
1966	A Man Without Love	Seventh
1967	Puppet on a String	*First*
1968	Congratulations	Second
1969	Boom Bang a Bang	*Joint First*
1970	Knock Knock	Second
1971	Jack in the Box	Fourth
1972	Beg, Steal or Borrow	Second
1973	Power to All Our Friends	Third
1974	Long Live Love	Fourth
1975	Let Me Be the One	Second
1976	Save Your Kisses For Me	*First*
1977	Rock Bottom	Second
1978	The Bad Old Days	Eleventh
1979	Mary Ann	Seventh
1980	Love Enough For Two	Third
1981	Making Your Mind Up	*First*
1982	One Step Further	Seventh
1983	I'm Never Giving Up	Sixth
1984	Love Games	Seventh
1985	Love Is	Fourth
1986	Runner in the Night	Seventh
1987	Only the Light	Thirteenth
1988	Go	Second
1989	Why Do I Always Get it Wrong	Second
1990	Give a Little Love Back to the World	Sixth

THEME SONGS AND SIGNATURE TUNES

An alphabetical list of artists and the songs they made their own.

ARTIST	TUNE
Ambrose	When Day is Done
Andrews Sisters, The	Bei Mir Bist Du Schon
Armstrong, Louis	When it's Sleepy Time Down South
Austin, Gene	My Blue Heaven
Barnet, Charlie	Skyliner
Basie, Count	One O'Clock Jump
Bayes, Nora	Shine on Harvest Moon
Bennett, Tony	Because of You
Benny, Jack	Love in Bloom
Black, Stanley	That Old Black Magic
Boyer, Lucienne	Speak to Me of Love
Brice, Fanny	Rose of Washington Square
Brisson, Carl	Cocktails for Two
Brown, Les	Sentimental Journey
Butterfield, Billy	What's New
Calloway, Cab	Minnie the Moocher
Calvert, Eddie	O Mein Papa
Cantor, Eddie	Makin' Whoopee
Carle, Frankie	Sunrise Serenade
Chevalier, Maurice	Louise
Clooney, Rosemary	Tenderly
Cohen, George M.	Give My Regards to Broadway
Cole, Nat 'King'	Straighten Up and Fly
Columbo, Russ	Sweet and Lovely
Como, Perry	Dream Along With Me
Cotton, Billy	Somebody Stole My Gal
Coward, Noel	I'll See You Again
Craig, Francis	Near You
Crosby, Bing	Where the Blue of the Night
Daniels, Billy	That Old Black Magic
Darewski, Herman	Back To Those Happy Days
Dixon, Reginald	I Do Like to be Beside the Seaside
Dorsey, Jimmy	So Rare (Closing Theme)
Dorsey, Tommy	I'm Getting Sentimental Over You
Durante, Jimmy	Inka Dinka Doo
Ellington, Duke	Take the 'A' Train
Elliott, G.H. (The Chocolate Coloured Coon)	I Used to Sigh for the Silvery Moon
Elrick, George	When You're Smiling
Fields, Gracie	Sally
Formby, George Jnr	Leaning on a Lamp Post
Fox, Roy	Whispering
Garland, Judy	Over the Rainbow
Gibbons, Carroll	On the Air
Goodman, Benny	Goodbye (Closing Theme)
Gray, Glen	Smoke Rings
Harris, Phil	That's What I Like About the South
Hartley, Fred	Life is Nothing Without Music
Hildegarde	Darling, Je Vous Aime Beaucoup
Hope, Bob	Thanks for the Memory
Horne, Lena	Stormy Weather
Hutchinson, Leslie (Hutch)	Begin the Beguine
Ink Spots, The	If I Didn't Care
James, Harry	Ciribiribin
Jolson, Al	My Mammy
Kunz, Charlie	Clap Hands Here Comes Charlie

REVIVALS

The following list is of those songs which have been a hit on more than one occasion. The year in which the song first became popular is in the middle column and the right-hand column details the years in which it subsequently became a hit, or "revived".

Song	First	Revived
After You've Gone	1918	1933
Ain't Misbehavin'	1929	May 1956 / Jul 1960
Ain't Nobody	Apr 1984	Jul 1989
Ain't That a Shame	Nov 1955	Feb 1957
Albatross	Feb 1969	Jul 1973
All By Myself	1921	1947
All Day and All of the Night	Nov 1964	Jan 1988
All I Have to Do is Dream	Jul 1958	Jan 1970
All of Me	1932	1947
All Pals Together	1914	1940
All Right Now	Aug 1970	Aug 1973
Am I Wasting My Time on You	1926	Nov 1958
Amazing Grace	Feb 1971	Jun 1972
Among My Souvenirs	1927	1947 / Dec 1959
Annie's Song	Oct 1974	Jul 1978
Anniversary Waltz, The	1942	Mar 1968
Another Saturday Night	Jun 1963	Sep 1974
Answer Me	Dec 1953	Feb 1976
Any Old Iron	1911	Sep 1957
Anything Goes	1935	Nov 1967
April Showers	1922	1947
Are You Lonesome Tonight?	1928	Feb 1961
As Time Goes By	1932	1943
Baby Face	1926	Nov 1949 / Jan 1959
Baby I Love You	Feb 1964	Mar 1973 / Mar 1980
Baby Love	Nov 1964	Sep 1974
Ballin' the Jack	1915	Aug 1948
Band Played on, The	1900	1941
Because	1902	1940
Because You're Mine	Nov 1952	Feb 1953
Begin the Beguine	1939	Dec 1981
Bells of St. Mary's, The	Apr 1917	1946
Ben	Dec 1972	Jul 1985
Bewitched, Bothered And Bewildered	1941	Jul 1950
Birth of the Blues	1927	1942
Black and White Rag	1913	Dec 1951
Black is Black	Aug 1966	Nov 1977
Blue Monday	Apr 1983	Oct 1983
Blue Moon	1935	May 1961
Blueberry Hill	1941	Oct 1956
Born to Be With You	Sep 1956	Jul 1973
Breaking Up is Hard to Do	Sep 1962	Aug 1972
Breeze and I, The	1940	Aug 1955
Bring it on Home to Me	May 1965	Oct 1974
Broken Hearted	1928	Mar 1952
C'est Si Bon	May 1950	Mar 1954
C'mon Everybody	Apr 1959	Jul 1979
Can't Help Falling Love	Apr 1962	May 1970 / May 1976
Can't Take My Eyes Off You	May 1968	Aug 1982
Candle in the Wind	Apr 1974	Feb 1988
Careless Hands	Jun 1949	Feb 1968
Charmaine	1927	Aug 1951 / Feb 1963
Cherry Pink & Apple Blossom White	Apr 1955	Sep 1982
Chicago	May 1922	Dec 1957
Chloe	1928	1946
Ciribiribin	1910	1935 / 1944

Clapping Song, The	Jun 1965	Aug 1982
Cocktails For Two	1934	1948
Come Back to Sorrento	Jun 1936	1947
Come Softly to Me	May 1959	Jan 1973
Concrete and Clay	Apr 1965	Apr 1976
Cool Water	Nov 1948	Oct 1955
Crying	Oct 1961	Jul 1980
Crying in the Chapel	Jan 1954	Jul 1965
Crying in the Rain	Feb 1962	Nov 1990
Cuckoo Waltz, The	1929	Dec 1948
Cuddle Up a Little Closer	1909	1943
Cupid	Sep 1961	May 1969, Aug 1980
Da Doo Ron Ron	Aug 1963	Nov 1974
Dance On	Jan 1963	Sep 1963
Dancin' Party	Sep 1962	Nov 1977
Darlin'	Feb 1968	Nov 1975
Deck of Cards	Jan 1960	Apr 1963 / Jun 1963 / Nov 1973
Deep Purple	1939	Dec 1957 / Jan 1964 / Feb 1976
Delilah	May 1968	Aug 1975
Diane	1927	Mar 1964
D.I.V.O.R.C.E.	Jul 1975	Nov 1975
Do They Know it's Christmas?	Dec 1984	Dec 1985 / Dec 1989
Do What You Gotta Do	Jan 1969	Oct 1969
Doctor Kildare Theme	Apr 1962	July 1962
Don't Blame Me	1933	Sep 1948 / Feb 1964
Don't Bring Lulu	1925	Dec 1961
Don't Cry For Me Argentina	Feb 1977	Feb 1979
Don't Go Breaking My Heart	Aug 1976	Nov 1988
Don't Leave Me This Way	Feb 1977	Sep 1986
Down By the O-hi-o	1921	1940
Down Yonder	1921	Feb 1952 / Jun 1960
Downtown	Dec 1964	Jan 1989
Dream a Little Dream of Me	1931	Sep 1968
Drive	Nov 1984	Sep 1985
Easy	Aug 1977	Sep 1988
Edelweiss	Jul 1961	May 1967
Embraceable You	1932	1945
Estrelita	Sep 1904	1945
Ev'ry Time We Say Goodbye	1945	Dec 1987
Everybody Wants to Rule the World	Apr 1985	Jun 1986
Everything I Have is Yours	1933	Mar 1953
Everything I Own	Nov 1974	Mar 1987
Everywhere You Go	1928	Aug 1949
Fanlight Fanny	1935	Apr 1962
Feel the Need in Me	Mar 1973	Jul 1977
Ferry 'Cross the Mersey	Jan 1965	Jun 1989
Flamingo	1941	Feb 1953
Floral Dance, The	1911	Dec 1977
Fool (If You Think it's Over)	Nov 1978	Feb 1982
Fools Rush In	1940	Nov 1963
For Me and My Gal	1918	1943
For You	1931	Apr 1949
Funky Town	Jan 1980	Sep 1987
Garden in the Rain, A	1928	1947
Get Back	Jun 1969	Dec 1976
Ghost Riders in the Sky	Jun 1949	Apr 1961 / Mar 1980
Ghostbusters	Oct 1984	Jan 1985
Girl of My Best Friend, The	Jul 1960	Oct 1976
Girl of My Dreams	1928	Apr 1958

Give Me the Moonlight	1918	Apr 1955
Glow Worm, The	1907	Nov 1952
Going Back to My Roots	1981	Jan 1990
Gonna Get Along Without You Now	Jan 1957	Nov 1979
Good Morning Starshine	Dec 1968	Oct 1969
Granada	1932	Apr 1954 / Sep 1961
Great Pretender	Feb 1956	Mar 1987
Green Door	Nov 1956	Aug 1981
Guilty	1932	1947
Happy Days and Lonely Nights	1929	Feb 1955
Happy Talk	Nov 1951	Jul 1982
Harbour Lights	1937	Mar 1960
Hard Day's Night, A	Sep 1964	Jan 1966
Hard Hearted Hannah	1924	Oct 1961
Harvest For the World	Aug 1976	Nov 1988
Have I the Right	May 1964	May 1977
Have You Ever Been Lonely	1933	Nov 1955
Have You Seen Her	Feb 1972	Jul 1975 / Oct 1990
Hawaiian Wedding Song	Jan 1959	Apr 1965 / Apr 1977
He Ain't Heavy, He's My Brother	Nov 1969	Oct 1988
He Was Beautiful	Jun 1979	Nov 1979
Heartaches	1931	1947 / May 1966
Heartbreak Hotel	Apr 1956	Aug 1971
Hello Dolly	Jul 1964	Feb 1966
Help	Aug 1965	Mar 1989
Help Me Make it Through the Night	Jan 1973	Jan 1975
Hey Gipsy	1926	1939
Hey Jude	Oct 1968	Feb 1969 / Apr 1976
Hi-Ho Silver Lining	May 1967	Dec 1972
Hi-Lilli Hi-lo	Jan 1953	Sep 1966
Hold Me	1933	Jul 1964
Hole in My Shoe	Oct 1967	Aug 1984
Holiday	Feb 1984	Aug 1985
Hora Staccato	1930	Mar 1948
Hors D'Oevres	May 1915	Nov 1949
House of the Rising Sun, The	Feb 1964	May 1970 / Oct 1982
How High the Moon	Dec 1949	May 1951
I Apologise	1932	Jun 1951, Apr 1965
I Belleve	May 1953	Apr 1964
I Can Dream, Can't I	1938	Dec 1949
I Can't Believe that You're in Love With Me	Apr 1927	May 1954
I Can't Help Myself	Aug 1965	Apr 1970 / Mar 1972
I Cried For You	1923	1939 / 1945 / Sep 1958 / Dec 1961
I Don't Know Why - I Just Do	1931	1946 / Jun 1962
I Get a Kick Out of You	1935	Nov 1974
I Get the Sweetest Feeling	Sep 1972	Mar 1987
I Got You Babe	Aug 1965	Sep 1985
I Hear You Knocking	Feb 1956	Jan 1971
I Heard it Through the Grapevine	Apr 1969	May 1986
I Love How You Love Me	Jan 1962	Aug 1966
I Love You Truly	1916	1934
I Never See Maggie Alone	1926	Dec 1949
I Only Have Eyes For You	1935	1946 / Oct 1975
I Only Wanna Be With You	Jan 1964	Oct 1976 / Dec 1979 / Feb 1989
I Remember You	1942	Aug 1962
I Sooond That Emotion	Oct 1969	Aug 1982
I Still Haven't Found What I'm Looking For	Jan 1987	Jun 1990
I Want to Hold Your Hand	Jan 1964	Feb 1980

I Will	May 1964	Dec 1977
I Wonder Who's Kissing Her Now	1909	1947
I'd Love to Live in Loveland With a Girl Like You	1910	1938
I'll Be With You in Apple Blossom Time	1920	1941
I'll Get By	1929	1944 / Dec 1961
I'll See You in My Dreams	1925	1962
I'll String Along With You	1934	Oct 1949 / Jan 1950
I'll Take You Home Again Kathleen	1914	May 1957
I'm a Man	Mar 1967	Feb 1970
I'm Always Chasing Rainbows	1919	1946
I'm Confessin'	1931	1946 / Jul 1963
I'm Every Woman	Jan 1979	May 1989
I'm Getting Sentimental Over You	1933	1938
I'm Gonna Sit Right Down and Write Myself a Letter	1935	Aug 1957
I'm Looking Over a Four Leaf Clover	1927	1948
I'm Nobody's Baby	1921	1941
I'm Sitting on Top of the World	1926	1953
I'm Stone in Love With You	Nov 1972	Mar 1976
I've Got You Under My Skin	1937	Nov 1966
I've Told Every Little Star	1932	Jun 1961
If	1934	Dec 1950
If I Didn't Care	1939	Jun 1974
If I Had My Way	1913	1940
If I Were a Carpenter	Dec 1966	Apr 1968
If You Don't Know Me By Now	Feb 1973	Apr 1989
Iko Iko	Jan 1965	Jul 1982
Imagine	Nov 1975	Jan 1981
In a Shady Nook By a Babbling Brook	1927	1944
In San Francisco	Dec 1962	Jul 1965
In the Air Tonight	Feb 1981	Jul 1988
In the Chapel in the Moonlight	1937	Nov 1965
In the Land of Beginning Again	1919	1946
In the Mood	1940	Feb 1976
Indian Love Call	Apr 1925	Apr 1952
Indian Summer	1920	1940
Instant Replay	Dec 1978	Feb 1990
Is it True What They Say About Dixie	1936	Feb 1950 / May 1950
Israelites, The	May 1969	Jun 1975
It Had to Be You	1924	1945
It Must Be Love	Jan 1972	Jan 1982
It Takes Two	Mar 1967	Dec 1990
It's a Sin to Tell a Lie	1936	May 1971
It's All in the Game	Feb 1952	Dec 1958 / Sep 1963 / Jul 1970
It's Almost Tomorrow	Feb 1956	Dec 1963
It's Late	May 1959	Aug 1983
It's My Party	Jul 1963	Oct 1981
It's Only Make Believe	Jan 1959	Aug 1964 / Dec 1970 / Sep 1978
It's the Same Old Song	Oct 1965	Feb 1971
Itchycoo Park	Sep 1967	Feb 1976
Its Bitsy Teeny Weeny Yellow Polka Dot Bikini	Aug 1960	Sep 1990
Ja-Da	1919	Mar 1961
Jambalaya	Oct 1952	Apr 1974
Je T'aime, Moi Non Plus	Oct 1969	Jul 1975
Jealousy	1927	1942 / Oct 1961
Johnson Rag	1940	Dec 1949
Just A-Wearyin' For You	1901	1938
Kiss	Mar 1986	Nov 1988
Kiss Me Again	1906	1945
Kisses Sweeter Than Wine	Sep 1951	Sep 1958

Knock on Wood	April 1967	Oct 1974 / May 1979 / Sep 1985
Last Christmas	Jan 1985	Jan 1986
Layla	Sep 1972	Apr 1982
Lazy River	1941	Apr 1961
Leader of the Pack, The	Feb 1965	Nov 1972 / Jul 1976
Lean On Me	Dec 1976	Apr 1987
Let Bygones Be Bygones	1933	1946
Let it Be	Apr 1970	Apr 1987
Let Me Go Lover	Feb 1955	Apr 1964
Let The Rest of the World Go By	1920	1945
Let There Be Love	1941	Aug 1962
Let's Dance	Nov 1962	Nov 1972
Let's Hang On	Nov 1965	Nov 1981
Let's Stay Together	Feb 1972	Jan 1984
Let's Twist Again	Apr 1962	Jan 1976
Lion Sleeps Tonight, The	Jan 1962	Mar 1982
Little Donkey	Dec 1959	Dec 1960
Little Drummer Boy, The	Mar 1959	Dec 1972 / Dec 1982
Little Girl	1931	Jan 1961
Little Love, a Little Kiss, A	1912	Jun 1962
Little White Lies	1930	Nov 1948
Living Doll	Aug 1959	Apr 1986
Loco-Motion, The	Oct 1962	Sep 1972 / Aug 1988
Look of Love	May 1967	Apr 1973
Looking Through the Eyes of Love	Jul 1965	Mar 1973
Love Here Is My Heart	1915	1945
Love Letters	1946	May 1962 / Aug 1966 / Dec 1987
Love Letters in the Sand	1931	Jul 1957
Love Me Do	Nov 1962	Nov 1982
Love Me or Leave Me	1929	Oct 1955
Love Me Tender	Dec 1956	Nov 1962
Love of the Common People	Aug 1970	Dec 1983
Lovely Day	Feb 1978	Oct 1988
Lover	1933	Aug 1949
Lovesick Blues	May 1951	Nov 1962
Ma He's Making Eyes at Me	1922	Nov 1957 / Mar 1974
Macarthur Park	Jul 1968	Nov 1978
Mack the Knife	Jun 1956	Oct 1959 / Nov 1959
Mademoiselle de Paris	May 1951	May 1965
Malaguena	1930	Nov 1955
Mama	Jul 1955	Jun 1960
Man With the Golden Arm	Sep 1956	Sep 1962
Marcheta	1923	Jul 1961
Maria	Jun 1959	Dec 1965
Maria Elena	1941	Dec 1963
Marie	1929	Jun 1965
Mary's a Grand Old Name	1905	1943
Mary's Boy Child	Nov 1957	Dec 1958 / Dec 1959 / Dec 1978
McNamara's Band	1917	1944
Me and My Shadow	1927	Jun 1950
Meet Me in St. Louis	1904	1945
Melody of Love	1917	May 1955
Memories Are Made of This	Feb 1956	Apr 1967
Merry Christmas Everybody	Dec 1973	Dec 1983
Mexicali Rose	1925	1939
Mexicali Rose	1925	1939 / Nov 1961
Miss You	1929	1942, Nov 1963
Mistakes	1928	Apr 1952
Misty	Jan 1960	Jul 1975

Mocking Bird Hill	May 1951	May 1964
Mona Lisa	July 1950	Sep 1959
Money (That's What I Want)	Dec 1963	Sep 1979
Montego Bay	Oct 1970	Oct 1986
Mony Mony	Aug 1968	Nov 1987
Moon River	Nov 1961	Feb 1972
Moonlight Serenade	1939	Feb 1976
More I See You, The	1945	Sep 1966
More Than I Can Say	Jun 1961	Aug 1980
More Than You Know	1930	1947
Mountain Greenery	1927	Aug 1956
Move Over Darling	Apr 1964	Dec 1983
My Baby Just Cares For Me	1930	Nov 1987
My Gal Sal	1906	1943
My Guy	Jun 1964	Aug 1972
My Happiness	Jun 1948	Mar 1959
My Heart Sings	1945	Feb 1959
My Love and Devotion	Nov 1951	Dec 1952
My Prayer	1939	Nov 1956 / Apr 1957 / Dec 1970
My Resistance is Low	May 1951	Jun 1976
My Way	Jun 1969	Nov 1970 / Mar 1971 / Jan 1978 / Aug 1978
Na Na Hey Hey Kiss Him Goodbye	Mar 1970	May 1983
Nathan Jones	Oct 1971	Dec 1988
Needles and Pins	Feb 1964	Nov 1977
Nellie The Elephant	Oct 1956	Dec 1984
Nevertheless	1931	Mar 1967
New Orleans	Feb 1961	Apr 1981
Nights in White Satin	Jan 1967	Dec 1972 / Dec 1979
No Greater Love	1936	1947
No Regrets	Feb 1976	Jul 1982
No Regrets (Non Je Ne Regrette Rien)	Mar 1961	Jun 1965
Nobody's Darlin' But Mine	1935	May 1963
Oh Boy	Feb 1958	May 1975
Oh How I Hate to Get Up in The Morning	1918	1943
Oh Johnny Oh	1918	1940
Oh No Not My Baby	May 1965	Sep 1973
On a Little Street in Singapore	1940	Jun 1978
On a Slow Boat to China	Dec 1948	Feb 1960
On the Banks of the Wabash	1899	1943
On the Sunny Side of the Street	1931	1945
Only You	May 1982	Dec 1983
Out of Nowhere	1931	1945
Papa Was a Rolling Stone	Feb 1973	Jun 1990
Paper Doll	1915	1944
Paper Roses	Sep 1960	Dec 1973
Paradise	1933	1946
Paranoid	Oct 1970	Sep 1980
Party's Over, The	Dec 1957	May 1962
Pasadena	May 1924	Jul 1961
Passing Strangers	Nov 1957	May 1969
Peanut Vendor, The (el Manisero)	1931	Jan 1949
Perfidia	1941	Jan 1961
Peter Gunn	Jul 1959	Apr 1986
Pied Piper, The	May 1966	Jul 1971
Pinball Wizard	May 1969	Mar 1973 / Apr 1976
Pistol Packin' Mama	1944	Jun 1960
Play a Simple Melody	1915	Dec 1950
Please Please Me	Mar 1963	Aug 1974

Poison Ivy	Oct 1959	Apr 1980
Power of Love, The (Lewis)	Sep 1985	Mar 1986
Preacher and the Bear	1907	1947
Pretend	Sep 1953	Oct 1981
Pretty Girl is Like a Melody, A	1919	1936
Prisoner's Song, The	1925	1937
Puppy Love	Apr 1960	Aug 1972
Put Your Arms Around Me Honey	1916	1944
Rags to Riches	Dec 1953	Jun 1971
Ragtime Cowboy Joe	1912	1943 / Aug 1959
Ramona	1928	Jul 1964
Reach Out I'll Be There	Nov 1966	Apr 1975 / Aug 1988
Red Roses For a Blue Lady	Jun 1949	Jul 1965
Reelin' and Rockin'	Apr 1965	Feb 1973
Reet Petite	Jan 1958	Jan 1987
Relax	Jun 1984	Jul 1984
Right Back Where We Started From	1935	Jun 1989
River Deep, Mountain High	Jul 1966	Aug 1971
River Stay 'Way From My Door	1931	Aug 1960
Rock Around the Clock	Dec 1955	Apr 1974
Rock the Boat	Aug 1974	Mar 1983
Rockin' Around the Christmas Tree	Dec 1962	Dec 1987
Rolling Round the World	May 1926	Jul 1949
Rose Marie	1925	Aug 1955
Roses of Picardy	1916	Jul 1967
Ruby Tuesday	Feb 1967	Nov 1970
Runaround Sue	Dec 1961	Dec 1980
Russian Lullaby	1927	1012
Sailing	Sep 1975	Oct 1976
Saint Louis Blues	1914	1929
Sally	1931	Jul 1970
Santa Claus is Comin' to Town	1934	Dec 1985
Sealed With a Kiss	Sep 1962	Aug 1975 / Jun 1989
Second Hand Rose	1922	Mar 1966
Secret Love	Feb 1954	Dec 1963
She's Not There	Sep 1964	Dec 1977
Sherry	Nov 1062	Aug 1975
Shine	1924	1941
Shine on Harvest Moon	1908	1945
Short'nin Bread	1928	1937
Shotgun Wedding	Jun 1966	Dec 1972
Shout	Jun 1964	Aug 1986
Side By Side	1927	Mar 1953
Singin' in the Rain	1929	May 1978
Singin' in the Rain	1929	1978
Smoke Gets in Your Eyes	1934	Mar 1959 / Sep 1974
Snoopy Versus the Red Baron	Feb 1967	Jul 1973
So Tired	Jun 1948	Dec 1967
Some Day You'll Want Me to Want You	1946	Dec 1958
Some Guys Have All the Luck	Sep 1984	Dec 1987
Somebody Stole My Gal	1924	May 1953
Someone to Watch Over Me	1927	1947
Somethin' Else	Nov 1959	Apr 1979
Something	Nov 1969	Aug 1970
Something to Remember You By	1930	1944
Something's Gotten Hold of My Heart	Dec 1967	Feb 1989
Sometime	1925	Nov 1950
Somewhere My Love (Lara's Theme)	Sep 1966	Aug 1967
Song of India	1923	1937

Sorrow	Jul 1966	Nov 1973
Space Oddity	Nov 1969	Nov 1975
Spanish Harlem	Aug 1962	Oct 1971
Spread a Little Happiness	1929	Sep 1982
Stand By Me	Aug 1961	Mar 1987
Stardust	1931	Jan 1975
Stay	Jan 1961	Jan 1964 / Aug 1978
Stein Song	1911	1930
Still Haven't Found What I'm Looking For	Apr 1987	Jun 1990
Strawberry Fields Forever	Apr 1967	1990
Substitute	May 1966	Nov 1976
Such a Night	Apr 1954	Sep 1964
Sugar Sugar	Dec 1969	May 1971
Suki Yaki	Feb 1963	Aug 1963
Summertime	1938	Aug 1982
Sunny	Nov 1966	Apr 1977
Sunshine of Your Smile, The	1914	Sep 1980
Suspicious Minds	Jan 1970	Feb 1986
Sway (Quien Sera)	May 1954	Jan 1961
Sweet Talkin' Guy	Jun 1966	Apr 1972
Sweet Violets	1931	Sep 1951
Sweetheart of All My Dreams	1929	1945
Swinging on a Star	1944	Jan 1964
Sympathy	1917	1937
T'aint What You Do	1939	Mar 1982
Take Me to Your Heart Again	Sep 1948	Feb 1966
Take My Breath Away	Dec 1986	Nov 1990
Tea For Two	1925	Jan 1959
Tears of a Clown, The	Oct 1970	Jan 1980
Teddy Bear's Picnic, The	1907	1933
Tell Him	Mar 1963	Dec 1974
Temptation	1933	1946 / Jul 1961
Tenderly	Jul 1948	May 1954
That Old Black Magic	1943	Jul 1952
Theme For a Dream	Mar 1961	Jul 1961
There Goes My Everything	Aug 1967	Apr 1971
There Must Be a Way	Apr 1959	Nov 1967
There'll Be Some Changes Made	1929	1941
This Old Heart of Mine	Dec 1968	Dec 1975
This Ole House	Oct 1954	Apr 1981
Three Bells, The	Nov 1948	Oct 1959
Three Steps to Heaven	Jun 1960	Jun 1975
Till	Oct 1957	Dec 1971
Together	1928	1945 / Oct 1961 / Oct 1964
Tom Hark	Apr 1958	Sep 1980
Tonight You Belong to Me	1927	Nov 1956
Too Busy Thinking About My Baby	Sep 1969	Sep 1972
Too Good to Be Forgotten	Dec 1974	Jul 1986
Too Young	Aug 1951	Oct 1972
Too-ra-loo-ra-loo-ral	1914	1944
Toot Toot Tootsie Goodbye	1923	Aug 1948
Trail of the Lonesome Pine, The	1913	Dec 1975
True Love Ways	May 1965	May 1983
Trust in Me	1937	May 1952
Try a Little Tenderness	1933	1947
Tuxedo Junction	1940	Mar 1976
Tweedle Dee	Apr 1955	May 1973
Twelfth of Never	Oct 1964	Apr 1973
Twelfth Street Rag	1921	Jan 1949

Twilight Time	1946	Jun 1958
Twist and Shout	Aug 1963	Dec 1988
Twist, The	Jan 1962	Jul 1988
Ugly Duckling, The	Apr 1953	Jun 1975
Unchained Melody	Jun 1955	Nov 1990
Under the Bridges of Paris	1931	May 1955
Unless	1934	Aug 1951
Vaya Con Dios	Sep 1953	Dec 1973
Virginia Plain	Sep 1972	Nov 1977
Walk Hand in Hand	May 1956	Dec 1965
Walk on By	May 1964	Feb 1990
Walkin' My Baby Back Home	1931	Jun 1952
Wanderer, The	Mar 1962	Nov 1984
Way Down Yonder in New Orleans	1923	Feb 1960
Wayward Wind, The	Jul 1956	Mar 1963
What a Difference a Day Made	1934	Nov 1975
What a Mouth	1906	Jul 1960
What Becomes of the Broken Hearted	Dec 1966	Sep 1974 / Apr 1981
What Do You Want to Make Those Eyes at Me For	1916	Nov 1959 / Dec 1987
What is This Thing Called Love	1929	1943
What Now My Love (et Maintenant)	Oct 1962	Mar 1966
What You Want to Make Those	1917	Dec 1987
What'd I Say	Jul 1959	Jun 1961
Wheels	Mar 1961	July 1961
When	Jul 1958	Apr 1977
When a Man Loves a Woman	Jul 1966	Mar 1987
When I Fall in Love	Oct 1952	May 1957 / Dec 1973 / Dec 1987
When You and I Were Young, Maggie	1866	Mar 1000
When You Ask About Love	Jan 1960	Nov 1980
When You Were Sweet Sixteen	1898	1941 / Jun 1948 / Nov 1981
Where Did Our Love Go	Oct 1964	Feb 1972
Whiffenpoof Song, The	1937	Aug 1948
Whipersing Grass	1941	Jul 1975
Whispering	1920	Sep 1963
White Christmas	1942	Dec 1952 / Dec 1977
Whiter Shade of Pale, A	Aug 1967	Jun 1972
Who's Sorry Now?	1923	Mar 1956 / Apr 1958
Why	Feb 1960	Dec 1972
Why Do Fools Fall in Love	Jul 1956	Dec 1981
Wild World	Sep 1970	Jun 1988
Will You Remember	1917	1937
Wimoweh	Mar 1952	Mar 1962
Wipe Out	Aug 1963	Sep 1987
With a Little Help From My Friends	Jul 1967	Nov 1968 / Jun 1988
With These Hands	Jul 1951	Aug 1965
Wonder of You, The	Aug 1959	Sep 1970
Wonderful World	May 1965	Apr 1986
Woodman, Woodman Spare That Tree	1913	1947
World is Waiting For the Sunrise, The	1920	Nov 1951
Yankee Doodle Boy, A	1905	1942
Yes My Darling Daughter	1941	Jul 1962
Yesterday	Nov 1965	Apr 1976
You Always Hurt the One You Love	1946	1958
You Always Hurt the One You Love	1946	Dec 1958 / Aug 1961
You Can't Hurry Love	Oct 1966	Jan 1983
You Don't Have To Say You Love Me (Lo Che Non Viro)	Jun 1966	Feb 1971 / Mar 1976
You Go to My Head	1938	1946
You Got What it Takes	Mar 1960	Sep 1977
You Keep Me Hangin' On	Dec 1966	Sep 1967 / Nov 1986

You Make Me Feel (Mighty Real)	Oct 1978	Jan 1990
You Must Have Been a Beautiful Baby	1939	Nov 1961
You to Me Are Everything	Jul 1976	Apr 1986
You'll Never Know	1943	Aug 1961
You'll Never Walk Alone	Jul 1950	Nov 1963 / Jun 1985
You're Breaking My Heart	Oct 1949	Apr 1965
You're Driving Me Crazy	1931	May 1961
You're Sixteen	Feb 1961	Mar 1974
You've Lost That Loving Feeling	Feb 1965	Mar 1969
Young Girl	Mar 1968	Aug 1974
Young Love	Feb 1957	Sep 1973
Your Cheating Heart	Mar 1953	Jan 1963
Your Cheating Heart	Mar 1953	1964
Yours	1941	Apr 1982
Zambezi	Jan 1956	Nov 1982

COMPOSERS

A list of composers and the songs they wrote, or co-wrote, in alphabetical order. Where a song was written by more than one composer, it will be listed under each of their names.

Adair, Tom
In the Blue of Evening
Let's Get Away From it All
Night We Called it a Day, The
There's No You

Adams, Stanley
In the Dim Dim Dawning
Little Old Lady
There are Such Things
What a Difference a Day Made

Adamson, Harold
Affair to Remember, An
Around the World
Aurora
Coming In on a Wing and a Prayer
Daybreak
Did I Remember
Everything I Have Is Yours
Ferry Boat Serenade (La Piccinina)
Here Comes Heaven Again
I Couldn't Sleep a Wink Last Night
I Love to Whistle
It's a Most Unusual Day
It's a Wonderful World
It's Been So Long
Love Me as Though There Were No Tomorrow
Lovely Way to Spend an Evening, A
Music Stopped, The
My Own
My Resistance is Low
There's Something in the Air
Time on My Hands
Too Young to Go Steady
Where Are You
Woodpeckers Song (Reginella Campagnola)
You
You're a Sweetheart
You're as Pretty as a Picture

Adamson, Stuart
Chance
In the Navy
Into the Valley
Look Away
Masquerade

Adler, Richard
Everybody Loves a Lover
Heart
Hernando's Hideaway
Hey There
Once a Year Day
Rags to Riches
Steam Heat
Whatever Lola Wants

Ager, Milton
Ain't She Sweet
Ain't That a Grand and Glorious Feeling
Auf Wiederseh'n My Dear
Bench in a Park, A
Crazy Words, Crazy Tune
Everything Is Peaches Down in Georgia
Forgive Me
Glad Rag Doll
Happy Days Are Here Again
Happy Feet
I Wonder What's Become of Sally
I'm Nobody's Baby
Is She My Girl Friend
Mama Goes Where Papa Goes
My Pet
She Don't Wanna
Song of the Dawn

Trouble in Paradise
Trust in Me
Who Cares
Young Man's Fancy

Ahlert, Fred
I Don't Know Why - I Just Do
I'd Love to Fall Asleep and Wake Up in My Mammy's Arms
I'll Follow You
I'll Get By
I'm Gonna Sit Right Down and Write Myself a Letter
In Shadowland
Life is a Song
Love You Funny Thing
Mean to Me
Moon Was Yellow, The
Walkin' My Baby Back Home
Where the Blue of the Night

Aitken, Matt
Better the Devil You Know
Can't Shake the Feeling
Cross My Broken Heart
Especially For You
Every Day I Love You More
F.L.M.
G.T.O.
Got to Be Certain
Hand on Your Heart
Hang on to Your Love
Happenin' All Over Again
Harder I Try, The
He Ain't No Competition
I Don't Wanna Get Hurt
I Heard a Rumour
I Just Don't Have the Heart
I Should Be So Lucky
I Want You Back
I'd Rather Jack
Je Ne Sais Pas, Pourquoi
Let's all Chant
Love In the First Degree
Never Gonna Give You Up
Never Too Late
Nothing Can Divide Us
Nothing's Gonna Stop Me Now
Respectable
Say I'm Your Number One
Showing Out
Step Back in Time
Take Me to Your Heart
That's the Way it is
This Time I Know It's For Real
Together Forever
Too Many Broken Hearts in the World
Toy Boy
Whatever I Do (Wherever I Go)
When You Come Back to Me
Whenever You Need Somebody
Who's Leaving Who
Wouldn't Change a Thing
You'll Never Stop Me Loving You
You've Got a Friend

Akst, Harry
Am I Blue
Baby Face
Dinah
Guilty
Smile Will Go a Long, Long Way, A
Stepping in Society
What a Perfect Combination

Allen, Robert
Chances Are

Everybody Loves a Lover
If Dreams Came True
Moments to Remember

Alstone, Alex
Dancin' With Someone
More
Symphony
Till They've All Gone Home

Alter, Louis
Circus
Dolores
Melody From the Sky, A
My Kinda Love
Rainbow on the River
Twilight on the Trail
You Turned the Tables on Me

Altman, Arthur
All Alone Am I
All or Nothing at All
Play Fiddle Play
There's a Harbour of Dreamboats

Anderson, Ian
Life is a Long Song
Living in the Past
Sweet Dream
Witches Promise

Anderson, Leroy
Belle of the Ball
Blue Tango
Fiddle Faddle
Forgotten Dreams
Penny Whistle Song, The
Plink, Plank, Plunk
Sleigh Ride
Waltzing Cat, The

Anderson, Stig
Dancing Queen
Fernando
Honey Honey
Knowing Me, Knowing You
Mama Mia
S.O.S.
Waterloo

Andersson, Benny
Angel Eyes
Chiquitita
Dancing Queen
Does Your Mother Know
Fernando
Gimme Gimme Gimme
Honey Honey
I Have a Dream
I Know Him So Well
Knowing Me, Knowing You
Lay All Your Love on Me
Mama Mia
Money Money Money
Name of the Game
One Night in Bang kok
One of Us
S.O.S.
Summer Night City
Super Trouper
Take a Chance on Me
Voulez-Vous
Waterloo
Winner Takes it All

Andrews, Chris
First Time, The
Girl Don't Come
How Can You Tell

I'll Stop at Nothing
Long Live Love
Message Understood
Nothing Comes Easy
To Whom it Concerns
Tomorrow
We Are in Love
Yesterday Man
You've Not Changed

Anka, Paul
Diana
Having My Baby
I Love You Baby
It Doesn't Matter Anymore
Let Me Try Again (Laisse Moi Le Temps)
Lonely Boy
My Way
Puppy Love
Put Your Head on My Shoulder
She's a Lady
You Are My Destiny

Ant, Adam
Ant Rap
Antmusic
Apollo 9
Dog Eat Dog
Friend or Foe
Goody Two Shoes
Kings of the Wild Frontier
Prince Charming
Puss 'n' Boots
Stand and Deliver
Young Parisians

Arden, Rodd
Celebration Rag
Hold Your Head Up
Me and the Old Folks at Home
Old Ship of Mine
She's Not There
When You Lose the One You Love

Arlen, Harold
Ac-cent-tchu-ate the Positive
As Long as I Live
Between the Devil and the Deep Blue Sea
Blues in the Night
Come Rain Or Come Shine
Ding Dong the Witch is Dead
For Every Man There's a Woman
Get Happy
Happiness is a Thing Called Joe
Hit the Road to Dreamland
Hooray For Love
How Blue the Night
I Gotta Right to Sing the Blues
I Promise You
I've Got the World on a String
If I Only Had a Heart
It's Only a Paper Moon
June Comes Around Every Year
Kicking the Going Around
Let's Fall in Love
Let's Take the Long Way Home
Life's Full Of Consequences
Lydia the Tattooed Lady
Man That Got Away, The
My Shining Hour
Now I Know
Out of This World
Over the Rainbow
Stormy Weather
That Old Black Magic
This Time the Dream's on Me
We're Off to See the Wizard
When the Sun Comes Out

Ashford, Nicholas
Ain't No Mountain High Enough

I'm Every Woman
Onion Song, The
Remember Me
Solid
Surrender

Austin, Gene
How Come You Do Me Like You Do
Lonesome Road
Ridin' Around In the Rain
When My Sugar Walks Down the Street

Ayer, Nat. D.
Another Little Drink Wouldn't Do Us Any Harm
At the Foxtrot Ball
First Love, Last Love, Best Love
If You Were the Only Girl In the World
Let the Great Big World Keep Turning
Oh You Beautiful Doll
Shufflin' Along
You're My Baby

Bacharach, Burt
Alfie
Always Something There to Remind Me
Anyone Who Had a Heart
Arthur's Theme
Close to You
Do You Know the Way to San Jose
I Just Don't Know What to Do With Myself
I Say a Little Prayer
I'll Never Fall In Love Again
Look of Love
Magic Moments
Make It Easy on Yourself
Message to Martha
On My Own
Raindrops Keep Falling on My Head
Story of My Life, The
That's What Friends Are For
This Guy's In Love With You
Tower Of Strength
Trains and Boats and Planes
Twenty-Four Hours From Tulsa
Walk on By
What's New Pussycat
Wishin' and Hopin'

Baer, Abel
Chapel of the Roses, The
High Up on a Hill Top
I Miss My Swiss - My Swiss Miss Misses Me
June Night
Mama Loves Papa - Papa Loves Mama
My Mother's Eyes
There Are Such Things

Bagdasarian, Ross
Alvin's Harmonica
Armen's Theme
Come on a My House
Witch Doctor

Bailey, Tom
Doctor! Doctor!
Hold Me Now
I Want That Man
Lay Your Hands on Me
Love on Your Side
We Are Detective
You Take Me Up

Ball, Ernest
All the World Will Be Jealous of Me
In the Garden of My Heart
Let the Rest of the World Go By
Little Bit Of Heaven, A
Love Me and the World Is Mine
Mother Machree

'Till the Sands of the Desert Grow Cold
When Irish Eyes Are Smiling
Will You Love Me In December (as You Do In May)

Ballard, Clint
Ev'ry Hour, Ev'ry Day of My Life
Game of Love, The
I'm Alive
You're No Good

Ballard, Russ
I Surrender
New York Groove
No More the Fool
Since You've Been Gone
So You Win Again

Banks, Anthony
Abacab
Follow You Follow Me
In Too Deep
Invisible Touch
Land of Confusion
Mama
That's All
Turn It on Again

Barnes, Howard
Accordion
Blossom Fell, A
Butterfly
Chewing a Piece of Straw
Dreams Can Tell a Lie
Echo Told Me a Lie, The
Load of Hay, A
Lonely Footsteps
Number Something Far Away Lane

Barris, Harry
At Your Command
I Surrender Dear
It Must Be True
Lies
Little Dutch Mill
Mississippi Mud
Wrap Your Troubles in Dreams

Barry, Jeff
Baby I Love You
Be My Baby
Da Doo Ron Ron
Do Wah Diddy Diddy
I Can Hear Music
Leader of the Pack, The
Montego Bay
River Deep, Mountain High
Sugar Sugar
Tell Laura I Love Her
Tell Me What He Said
Then He Kissed Me
Then I Kissed Her

Barry, John
Born Free
Diamonds Are Forever
Down Deep Inside
Goldfinger
Hit and Miss
Living Daylights, The
Made You
View to a Kill
You Only Live Twice

Barson, Michael
Baggy Trousers
Driving in My Car
Embarrassment
Grey Day
House of Fun
My Girl

Return Of the Los Palmas Seven, The
Sun and the Rain, The
Tomorrow's Just Another Day

Bart, Lionel
As Long as He Needs Me
Butterfingers
Consider Yourself
Do You Mind
Easy Going Me
Fings Ain't Wot They Used T'be
From Russia With Love
Handful of Songs, A
I'd Do Anything
Little White Bull
Living Doll
Rock With the Cavemen
Tokyo Melody

Batt, Mike
Banana Rock
Bright Eyes
I Feel Like Buddy Holly
Please Don't Fall in Love
Remember You're a Womble
Summertime City
Winter's Tale, A
Wombling Merry Christmas
Wombling Song, The

Bayer Sager, Carole
Arthur's Theme
Don't Cry Out Loud
Groovy Kind of Love, A
Nobody Does It Better
On My Own
Starmaker
When I Need You
You're Moving Out Today

Becaud, Gilbert
Day the Rains Came, The
If Only I Could Live My Life Again
Importance of Your Love, The (Import
ant C'est La Rose)
It Must Be Him (Seul Sur Son Etoile)
Let It Be Me (Je T'appartiens)
Little Love and Understanding, A (Un
Peu D'amour Et D'amitie)
Love on the Rocks
What Now My Love (Et Maintenant)
With Your Love (Mes Mains)

Bell, Andrew
Blue Savannah
Chains Of Love
Circus
Drama
It Doesn't Have to Be
Little Respect
O' L'amour
Ship Of Fools
Sometimes
Star
Victim Of Love

Bell, Ronald
Celebration
Cherish
Get Down on It
In the Heart
Steppin' Out

Bell, Thomas
Betcha By Golly Wow
Ghetto Child
I'm Stone In Love With You
Rockin' Roll Baby
Rubber Band Man, The
You Are Everything
You Make Me Feel Brand New

Bellotte, Pete
From Here to Eternity
Givin' Up Givin' In
Good Grief Christina
Hot Stuff
I Feel Love
I Remember Yesterday
Love to Love You Baby
Loves Unkind
Son of My Father

Belolo, Henri
Can't Stop the Music (La Musique N'a
Pas De Fin)
Go West
Street Dance
Y.M.C.A.

Benatzky, Ralph
Goodbye
Grinzing (Ich Muss Wieder Einmal In
Grinzing Sein)
My Song of Love
White Horse Inn, The
You Too
Your Eyes

Benjamin, Bennie
Can Anyone Explain?
Cross Over the Bridge
Dancin' With Someone
Don't Let Me Be Misunderstood
How Important Can it Be
I Don't See Me in Your Eyes Anymore
I Don't Want to Set the World on Fire
I'll Keep the Lovelight Burning
Oh What It Seemed to Be
Rumours Are Flying
Surrender
Wheel Of Fortune, The
When the Lights Go on Again

Bennett, Brian
Genie With the Light Brown Lamp
I Could Easily Fall
In the Country
Rise and Fall of Flingle Bunt
Summer Holiday
Time Drags By

Bennett, Roy C.
Naughty Lady Of Shady Lane, The
Stairway of Love
Travellin' Light
Twenty Tiny Fingers
Wonderful World Of the Young, The
Young Ones, The

Bergman, Alan
Guaglione (The Man Who Plays the
Mandolino)
Way We Were, The
What Are You Doing the Rest of Your
Life?
Windmills Of Your Mind

Berlin, Irving
After You Get What You Want, You
Don't Want It
Alexander's Ragtime Band
All Alone
All By Myself
Always
Anything You Can Do
Araby
At Peace With the World
Be Careful It's My Heart
Because I Love You
Blue Skies
Change Partners
Cheek to Cheek
Couple Of Swells, A

Doin' What Comes Naturally
Easter Parade
Everybody Knew But Me
Everybody Step
Everybody's Doing It
Fella With An Umbrella, A
Getting Nowhere
Girl on the Magazine Cover, The
Girl on the Police Gazette, The
Girl That I Marry
Happy Holiday
He's a Rag Picker
Heat Wave
Homesick
How About Me
How Deep is the Ocean
How's Chances
I Can't Do Without You
I Got Lost in His Arms
I Got the Sun in the Morning
I Left My Heart at the Stage Door Can-
teen
I Love a Piano
I Poured My Heart Into a Song
I Threw a Kiss in the Ocean
I Used to Be Colour Blind
I Want to Be in Dixie
I Want to Go Back to Michigan
I'll Capture Your Heart
I'll See You In C-U-B-A
I'm Getting Tired So I Can Sleep
I'm Putting All My Eggs in One Basket
I've Got My Captain Working For Me Now
I've Got My Love to Keep Me Warm
If You Believe
International Rag
Isn't This a Lovely Day
It Only Happens When I Dance With
You
It's a Lovely Day Today
It's a Lovely Day Tomorrow
Lady of the Evening
Let Me Sing and I'm Happy
Let Yourself Go
Let's Face the Music and Dance
Let's Have Another Cup O'Coffee
Let's Start the New Year Right
Let's Take An Old Fashioned Walk
Mandy
Marie
Marrying For Love
Me
My British Buddy
My Defences Are Down
Night Is Filled With Music, The
No Strings
Nobody Knows
Now It Can Be Told
Oh How I Hate to Get Up In the Morning
Piccolino, The
Play a Simple Melody
Pretty Girl Is Like a Melody, A
Puttin' on the Ritz
Reaching For the Moon
Remember
Russian Lullaby
Say It Isn't So
Say It With Music
Shaking the Blues Away
Slumming on Park Avenue
Snooky Ookums
Soft Lights and Sweet Music
Some Sunny Day
Someone Else May Be There When I'm
Gone
Song Is Ended, The
Stepping Out With My Baby
Sunshine
Tell Me Little Gipsy

That Mysterious Rag
There's No Business Like Show Business
They Say It's Wonderful
They Were All Out Of Step But Jim
This Is the Army Mister Jones
This Year's Kisses
Top Hat, White Tie and Tails
We Saw the Sea
What Does It Matter
What'll I Do
When I Leave the World Behind
When I Lost You
When It's Night Time in Dixieland
When My Dreams Come True
When That Man is Dead and Gone
When the Midnight Choo-Choo Leaves
For Alabam'
White Christmas
Woodman, Woodman Spare That Tree
Yam, The
Yiddle on Your Fiddle
You Can't Get a Man With a Gun
You Keep Coming Back Like a Song
You'd Be Surprised
You're Just In Love
You're Laughing At Me

Bernstein, Leonard
I Feel Pretty
Maria
New York, New York
Something's Coming
Somewhere
Tonight

Berry, Chuck
Brown Eyed Handsome Man
Let It Rock
Memphis Tennessee
My Ding-a-Ling
No Particular Place to Go
Promised Land, The
Reelin' and Rockin'
Roll Over Beethoven
Tulane

Bettis, John
Body Rock
Goodbye to Love
One Moment In Time
Only Yesterday
Slow Hand
Top Of the World
Yesterday Once More

Bickerton, Wayne
Don't Do it Baby
I Can Do it
Juke Box Jive
Like a Butterfly
Sugar Baby Love
Sugar Candy Kisses
Tonight
We Can Do it

Black, Don
Always There
Anyone Can Fall in Love
Ben
Born Free
Diamonds Are Forever
I'll Put You Together Again
Sam
Take That Look Off Your Face
Walk Away (Warum Nur Warum)

Blackwell, Otis
All Shook Up
Breathless
Don't Be Cruel

Great Balls of Fire
Handy Man
Nine Times Out of Ten
One Broken Heart For Sale
Paralysed
Return to Sender
Space Jungle, The

Blaikley, Alan
Bend It
(Call Me) Number One
Hideaway
I've Lost You
My Little Lady (Non Illuderti Mai)
Save Me
Me and My Life

Blaikley, Howard
From the Underworld
Have I the Right?
I Don't Want Our Loving to Die
Last Night In Soho
Legend of Xanadu, The
Okay
That's the Way
Wreck of the Antoinette, The
Zabadak

Blane, Ralph
Boy Next Door, The
Buckle Down Winsocki
Girl Next Door, The
Girls Were Made to Take Care of Boys
Have Yourself a Merry Little Christmas
Love
My Dream Is Yours
Occasional Man, An
Someone Like You
Stanley Steamer, The
Trolley Song, The

Block, Martin
I Guess I'll Have to Dream the Rest
New Moon and An Old Serenade, A
This Is No Laughing Matter
Waiting For the Train to Come In

Bloom, Rube
Day In, Day Out
Don't Worry 'Bout Me
Everybody's Twisting
Fools Rush In
Give Me the Simple Life
Maybe You'll Be There
Out In the Cold Again
Stay on the Right Side of the Road
Truckin'
Your Heart and Mine

Blossom, Henry
All For You
I Want What I Want When I Want It
Kiss Me Again
Thine Alone
When You're Away

Blue, Barry
Dancing on a Saturday Night
Do You Wanna Dance
I Eat Cannibals
School Love

Bock, Jerry
If I Were a Rich Man
Matchmaker, Matchmaker
Mister Wonderful
She Loves Me
Sunrise Sunset
Too Close For Comfort

Bolan, Marc
Children Of the Revolution, The

Debora
Get It on
Groover
Hot Love
I Love to Boogie
Jeepster
Metal Guru
New York City
Ride a White Swan
Solid Gold Easy Action
Telegram Sam
Truck On (Tyke)
Twentieth Century Boy

Bono, Sonny
Baby Don't Go
Bang Bang (My Baby Shot Me Down)
I Got You Babe
Laugh At Me
Little Man
Needles and Pins

Bowie, David
Absolute Beginners
All the Young Dudes
Ashes to Ashes
Blue Jean
Boys Keep Swingin'
China Girl
Drive-in Saturday
Fashion
Golden Years
Jean Genie, The
John I'm Only Dancing
Laughing Gnome, The
Life on Mars
Man Who Sold the World, The
Modern Love
Oh You Pretty Thing
Rebel Rebel
Sound and Vision
Space Oddity
Starman
Under Pressure

Box, Elton
Angel Of the Great White Way
Horsey, Horsey
I'm In Love With Two Sweethearts
I've Got Sixpence (As I Go Rolling Home)
In the Quartermaster's Stores
Just a Little Fond Affection
We All Went Up Up Up the Mountain
When You Know You're Not Forgotten

Bray, Steve
Angel
Causing a Commotion
Each Time You Break My Heart
Express Yourself
Into the Groove
True Blue

Bricusse, Leslie
Goldfinger
Gonna Build a Mountain
If I Ruled the World
Look At That Face
My Kind of Girl
Out of Town
Summer Is a-Comin' In
Talk to the Animals
What Kind of Fool Am I
Who Can I Turn to
Wonderful Day Like Today, A
You Only Live Twice

Bristol, Johnny
Hang on in There Baby
Love Me For a Reason
Some Day We'll Be Together

Take Me Girl I'm Ready
Walk In the Night
What Does It Take (to Win Your Love)

Britten, Terry
Bang Bang
Carrie
Devil Woman
Knocked It Off
To Be Or Not to Be
We Don't Need Another Hero
What's Love Got to Do With It

Brodszky, Nicholas
Be My Love
Because You're Mine
Gal With the Yaller Shoes, The
I'll Never Stop Loving You
No One But You
Serenade

Brooks, Jack
It's Dreamtime
Ol' Buttermilk Sky
Rose Tattoo, The
That's Amore

Brown, Errol
Brother Louie
Child's Prayer, A
Disco Queen
Don't Stop It Now
Emma
Everyone's a Winner
I Believe (In Love)
Lady Barbara
Love Is Life
Man to Man
Put Your Love In Me
What Kinda Boy You Lookin' For Girl
You Sexy Thing

Brown, George
Celebration
Clouds Will Soon Roll By, The
Have You Ever Been Lonely
Ladies Night
Old Man Of the Mountain, The
They Cut Down the Old Pine Tree
Toor-ie on His Bonnet, The

Brown, Lew
Beer Barrel Polka, The
Best Things In Life Are Free, The
Birth Of the Blues, The
Black Bottom, The
Broken Hearted
Button Up Your Overcoat
Chili Bean
Collegiate
Comes Love
Dapper Dan
Don't Bring Lulu
Don't Sit Under the Apple Tree
Dummy Song, The
For Old Times' Sake
Georgette
Give Me the Moonlight
Good News
I Came Here to Talk For Joe
I Used to Love You (But It's All Over Now)
I Wonder How I Look When I'm Asleep
I'd Climb the Highest Mountain (If I Knew I'd Find You)
I'm a Dreamer, Aren't We All
I'm Telling the Birds, Telling the Bees, How I Love You
I'm the Lonesomest Gal in Town
If I Had a Talking Picture of You
If You Hadn't Gone Away
It All Depends on You

Johnny Pedler
Just a Memory
Just Imagine
Last Night on the Back Porch
Life Is Just a Bowl of Cherries
Little Pal
Lucky Day
Lucky In Love
Magnolia
My Sin
Oh By Jingo, Oh By Gee
Oh Mama (The Butcher Boy)
One Sweet Letter From You
Red Moon
Shine
So Blue
So Will I
Song I Love, The
Sonny Boy
Sunny Side Up
That Old Feeling
That's Why Darkies Were Born
Then I'll Be Happy
Thrill Is Gone, The
Together
Varsity Drag
When It's Night Time In Italy, It's Wednesday Over Here
Where the Lazy Daisies Grow
Why Did I Kiss That Girl
You're the Cream In My Coffee

Brown, Nacio Herb
All I Do is Dream Of You
Alone
Broadway Melody, The
Broadway Rhythm
Doll Dance, The
Eadie Was a Lady
Good Morning
I'm Feeling Like a Million
I've Got a Feelin' You're Foolin'
Love Is Where You Find It
Moon Is Low
On a Sunday Afternoon
Pagan Love Song, The
Paradise
Should I
Singin' In the Rain
Temptation
We'll Make Hay While the Sun Shines
Wedding of the Painted Doll, The
When Buddha Smiles
Would You
You Are My Lucky Star
You Stepped Out of a Dream
You Were Meant For Me
You're An Old Smoothie

Bryan, Alfred
Brown Eyes Why Are You Blue
Come Josephine In My Flying Machine
Hiawatha's Melody of Love
I Want You to Want Me to Want You
My Song of the Nile
Peg O' My Heart
There's a Blue Ridge Round My Heart, Virginia
There's Everything Nice About You
You Taught Me How to Love

Bryant, Boudleaux
All I Have to Do Is Dream
Bird Dog
Bye Bye Love
Hawkeye
Hey Joe
Let's Think About Living
Like Strangers
Love Hurts

Poor Jenny
Problems
She Wears My Ring
Wake Up Little Susie
Willie Can

Bryant, Felice
Bye Bye Love
Poor Jenny
Problems
She Wears My Ring
Wake Up Little Susie
Willie Can

Bugatti, Dominic
Dancing With the Captain
Grandma's Party
Modern Girl
My Simple Heart
When He Shines
Woman in Love, A

Burke, Joe
By the River of the Roses
Carolina Moon
Dancing With Tears in My Eyes
Dear One
Dream Mother
For You
I Never Knew How Wonderful You Were
In a Little Gipsy Tearoom
In the Valley of the Moon
It Looks Like Rain in Cherry Blossom Lane
Kiss Waltz, The
Little Bit Independent, A
Many Happy Returns of the Day
My Very Good Friend the Milkman
Oh How I Miss You Tonight
On Treasure Island
Pagan Moon
Painting the Clouds With Sunshine
Rambling Rose
Robins and Roses
Roses Remind Me of You
So Is Your Old Lady
Tip-Toe Through the Tulips
Yearning (Just For You)

Burke, Johnny
Ain't Got a Dime to My Name
Ain't it a Shame About Mame
Annie Doesn't Live Here Anymore
Apple For the Teacher, An
April Played the Fiddle
Aren't You Glad You're You
As Long as I'm Dreaming
Busy Doing Nothing
But Beautiful
Constantly
Country Style
Day After Forever, The
East Side of Heaven
Friend of Yours, A
Going My Way
Hang Your Heart on a Hickory Limb
Here's That Rainy Day
His Rocking Horse Ran Away
Humpty Dumpty Heart
I've Got a Pocketful of Dreams
If You Please
If You Stub Your Toe on the Moon
Imagination
It Could Happen to You
It's Always You
It's the Natural Thing to Do
Kiss In Your Eyes
Man and His Dream, A
Meet the Sun Half Way
Misty
Moon and the Willow Tree, The

Moon Got in My Eyes, The
Moonlight Becomes You
My Heart Goes Crazy
My Heart is Taking Lessons
On the Sentimental Side
One, Two, Button Your Shoe
Only Forever
Pennies From Heaven
Pessimistic Character, The (With the Crab Apple Face)
Polka Dots and Moonbeams
Put it There Pal
Rhythm on the River
Road to Morocco, The
Scatterbrain
Sing a Song of Sunbeams
Smile Right Back at the Sun
So Do I
So Would I
Suddenly It's Spring
Sunday, Monday or Always
Sunshine Cake
Sweet Potato Piper
Swinging on a Star
That Sly Old Gentleman (From Featherbed Lane)
That's For Me
Too Romantic
Welcome to My Dream
What's New
When the Moon Comes Over Madison Square
Yah-ta-ta, Yah-ta-ta
You Can't Keep a Good Dreamer Down
You Don't Have to Know the Language

Bush, Kate
Babooshka
Man With the Child in His Eyes
Running Up That Hill
Wow
Wuthering Heights

Butler, Ralph
All Over Italy
Ever So Goosey
Give Yourself a Pat on the Back
Hey Little Hen
Horsey, Horsey
I'm Happy When I'm Hiking
Let's All Go to the Music Hall
Nellie the Elephant
Never Never Land
Ogo-Pogo, The
'Round the Marble Arch
Run Rabbit Run
Sun Has Got His Hat on, The
There's a Good Time Coming
There's a Lovely Lake in London

Caesar, Irving
Animal Crackers in My Soup
Crazy Rhythm
Hold My Hand
I Want to Be Happy
Is it True What They Say About Dixie
It Goes Like This (That Funny Melody)
Just a Gigolo
Lady Play Your Mandolin
My Blackbirds Are Bluebirds Now
Nasty Man
Sometimes I'm Happy
South American Joe
Swanee
Tea For Two
There's Something Spanish in Your Eyes
Tonight's My Night With Baby
Under the Roofs of Paris (Sous Les Toits De Paris)

Cahn, Sammy
All the Way
And Then You Kissed Me
Be My Love
Because You're Mine
Bei Mir Bist Du Schon
Call Me Irresponsible
Can't You Read Between the Lines
Charm of You, The
Come Out, Come Out, Wherever You Are
Day By Day
Dormi, Dormi, Dormi
Five Minutes More
Gal With the Yaller Shoes, The
High Hopes
Hurdy Gurdy Man, The
I Begged Her
I Fall in Love Too Easily
I Should Care
I'll Never Stop Loving You
I'll Walk Alone
I'm Gonna Ring the Bell Tonight
I've Heard That Song Before
It's Been a Long Long Time
It's the Same Old Dream
It's You or No-One
Joseph, Joseph
Let it Snow
Let Me Try Again (Laisse Moi Le Temps)
Love and Marriage
Papa Won't You Dance With Me
Please Be Kind
Put 'Em in a Box
Relax-ay-Voo
Rhythm Is Our Business
Saturday Night is the Loneliest Night Of the Week
Second Star to the Right, The
Second Time Around
Serenade
Shoe Shine Boy
Teach Me Tonight
Tender Trap, The
That's What Makes Paris Paree
There Goes That Song Again
There's Nothing Rougher Than Love
Things We Did Last Summer, The
Thinking About the Wabash
Thoroughly Modern Millie
Three Coins in the Fountain
Time After Time
Until the Real Thing Comes Along
Victory Polka
What Makes the Sunset
Your Mother and Mine

Caldwell, Anne
Bullfrog Patrol, The
I Know That You Know
Kalua
Left All Alone Again Blues
Whose Baby Are You

Callander, Peter
All My Love
Ballad Of Bonnie and Clyde, The
Billy Don't Be a Hero
Black-Eyed Boys, The
Daddy Don't You Walk So Fast
Don't Answer Me (Ti Vedo Uscuiri)
Even the Bad Times Are Good
Fool Am I, A (Dimmelo Parlami)
Goodbye Sam, Hello Samantha
Hitchin' a Ride
Hush Not a Word to Mary
I Did What I Did For Maria
Monsieur Dupont
Night Chicago Died, The
Ragamuffin Man
Suddenly You Love Me (Uno Tranquillo)

Campbell, James
By the Fireside
Goodnight Sweetheart
I Found You
I'm Happy When I'm Hiking
If I Had You
Just An Echo in the Valley
Linger a Little Longer in the Twilight
Old Kitchen Kettle, The
On a Street of Chinese Lanterns
Try a Little Tenderness
Two of Us, The

Campbell-Hunter, Roma
Boom
Fairy on the Christmas Tree, The
Oh Mamma Mia
Romany (vivere)

Cann, Warren
All Stood Still
Dancing With Tears in My Eyes
Hymn
Love's Great Adventure
Vienna

Carlton, Harry
Constantinople
Mademoiselle From Armentieres
'Oi' Song, The
Shinaniki Da

Carmichael, Hoagy
Can't Get Indiana off My Mind
Georgia on My Mind
Heart and Soul
Hong Kong Blues
How Little We Know
I Get Along Without You Very Well
In the Cool, Cool, Cool of the Evening
Katy Did, Katy Didn't
Lamplighter's Serenade, The
Lazy River
Lazybones
Little Old Lady
Moonburn
My Resistance is Low
Nearness of You, The
New Orleans
Ol' Buttermilk Sky
Old Music Master, The
One Morning in May
Rockin' Chair
Skylark
Small Fry
Snowball
Stardust
Two Sleepy People

Carpenter, Richard
Goodbye to Love
Only Yesterday
Top of the World
Yesterday Once More

Carr, Leon
Bell Bottom Blues
There's No Tomorrow
Young New Mexican Pupeteer
Your Socks Don't Match

Carr, Michael
Cinderella Stay In My Arms
Cowboy
Did Your Mother Come From Ireland
Dinner For One Please James
First Lullaby, The
General's Fast Asleep, The
Getting Around and About
Girl With the Dreamy Eyes
Handsome Territorial, A

Home Town
I Love to Sing
Kon-Tiki
Little Boy That Santa Claus Forgot
Lonely Ballerina
Man Of Mystery
Merrily We Roll Along
Misty Islands of the Highlands
Ol' Faithful
Old Timer
On the Outside Looking In
One-Two-Three O'Leary
Pair of Silver Wings, A
Somewhere In France With You
South Of the Border
Sunset Trail, The
Washing on the Siegfried Line
Wheel Of the Wagon Is Broken, The
White Horses
Why Did She Fall For the Leader of the
Band

Carroll, Harry
By the Beautiful Sea
I'm Always Chasing Rainbows
There's a Girl In the Heart Of Maryland
Trail Of the Lonesome Pine

Carson, Milton
My Love and Devotion
My Love, My Life, My Happiness
My Unfinished Symphony
Someone Else's Roses
Tulips and Heather

Carter, Desmond
I Took My Harp to a Party
I'm on a See-saw
La-di-da-di-da
Mona Lisa
Today I Feel So Happy
You Just You

Carter, John
Beach Baby
Funny How Love Can Be
Knock Knock Who's There?
Let's Go to San Francisco
My Sentimental Friend
Peek a Boo
Semi-Detached Suburban Mr James
Sunshine Girl
Tossing and Turning

Caryll, Ivan
Moonstruck
My Beautiful Lady
Soldiers In the Park, The
Thou Art My Rose
Venus Waltz, The

Casey, H.W.
Gimme Some
I Ain't Lyin'
I Can't Leave You Alone
It's Been So Long
Queen Of Clubs, The
Rock Your Baby
That's the Way (I Like It)

Castling, Harry
Are We to Part Like This?
Don't Have Any More Missus Moore
Just Like the Ivy
Let's All Go Down the Strand
Meet Me Jenny When the Sun Goes
Down
Oh Nicholas Don't Be So Ridiculous
We All Go the Same Way Home
We All Walked Into the Shop
What Ho She Bumps
When There Isn't a Girl About

Cavanaugh, James
Buffalo Billy
Did You Ever Get That Feeling in the
Moonlight
Gaucho Serenade, The
I Came, I Saw, I Conga'd
I Like Mountain Music
Little on the Lonely Side, A
Man With the Mandolin, The
Mississippi Mud
Umbrella Man, The
You're Nobody 'till Somebody Loves You

Chaplin, Charles
Eternally (Terry's Theme)
Limelight
Mandolin Serenade
Smile
This is My Song

Chaplin, Saul
Anniversary Song, The
Bei Mir Bist Du Schon
Hurdy Gurdy Man, The
Joseph, Joseph
Please Be Kind
Shoe Shine Boy
Until the Real Thing Comes Along

Chapman, Mike
Ballroom Blitz
Best, The
Blockbuster
Can the Can
Cat Crept In, The
Co-Co
Crazy
Daytona Demon
Devil Gate Drive
Doctorin' the Tardis
Don't Play Your Rock and Roll to Me
Dynamite
Forty-Eight Crash
Funny Funny
Hell Raiser
I'll Meet You at Midnight
If You Can't Give Me Love
If You Think You Know How to Love Me
It's Your Life
Kiss You All Over
Lay Back in the Arms of Someone
Lay Your Love on Me
Little Willy
Living Next Door to Alice
Lonely This Christmas
Mickey
Moonshine Sally
Oh Carol
Poppa Joe
Rocket
Secrets That You Keep, The
She's In Love With You
Sister Jane
Six Teens, The
Some Girls
Teenage Rampage
Tiger Feet
Tom-Tom Turnaround
Touch Too Much, A
Wig-Wam Bam
Wild One, The

Charig, Phil
Fancy Our Meeting
I Wanna Get Married
Sunny Disposish
There's Always Tomorrow

Charles, Hugh
Blue Skies Are Round the Corner
By Candlelight

I Shall Always Remember You Smiling
I Shall Be Waiting
I Won't Tell a Soul (That I Love You)
Russian Rose
Silver Wings In the Moonlight
There'll Always Be an England
There's a Land of Begin Again
Till Stars Forget to Shine
We'll Meet Again
Where the Waters Are Blue

Child, Desmond
How Can We Be Lovers
Just Like Jesse James
Living on a Prayer
Poison

Chinn, Nicky
Ballroom Blitz
Blockbuster
Can the Can
Cat Crept In, The
Co-Co
Crazy
Daytona Demon
Devil Gate Drive
Doctorin' the Tardis
Don't Play Your Rock and Roll to Me
Dynamite
Fortyeight Crash
Funny Funny
Hell Raiser
I'll Meet You At Midnight
If You Can't Give Me Love
If You Think You Know How to Love Me
It's Your Life
Kiss You All Over
Lay Back In the Arms Of Someone
Lay Your Love on Me
Little Willy
Living Next Door to Alice
Lonely This Christmas
Mickey
Moonshine Sally
Oh Carol
Poppa Joe
Rocket
Secrets That You Keep, The
She's In Love With You
Sister Jane
Six Teens, The
Some Girls
Teenage Rampage
Tiger Feet
Tom-Tom Turnaround
Touch Too Much, A
Use Ta Be My Girl
Who Found Who
Wig-Wam Bam
Wild One, The

Churchill, Frank
Baby Mine
Bambi
Heigh-Ho
I'm Wishing
Little April Shower
Love Is a Song
One Song
Some Day My Prince Will Come
Whistle While You Work
Who's Afraid of the Big Bad Wolf
With a Smile and a Song

Ciccone, Madonna
Angel
Causing a Commotion
Cherish
Dear Jessie
Each Time You Break My Heart

Express Yourself
Gambler
Hanky Panky
Into the Groove
Justify My Love
La Isla Bonita
Like a Prayer
Live to Tell
Look of Love
Open Your Heart
Papa Don't Preach
True Blue
Vogue
Who's That Girl?

Clare, Sidney
Ah-Ha
I'd Climb the Highest Mountain (if I Knew I'd Find You)
Keeping Myself For You
Ma! He's Making Eyes At Me
Making the Best of Each Day
Miss Annabelle Lee
On the Good Ship Lollipop
One Sweet Letter From You
Please Don't Talk About Me When I'm Gone
Since I Found You
Then I'll Be Happy
What Do I Care What Somebody Said

Clark, Dave
Bits and Pieces
Can't You See That She's Mine
Catch Us if You Can
Everybody Knows (I Still Love You)
Glad All Over

Clarke, Allan
Carrie Anne
Jennifer Eccles
On a Carousel
Stop Stop Stop

Clarke, Grant
Am I Blue
Blue
Dirty Hands, Dirty Face
Everything Is Peaches Down in Georgia
Get Out and Get Under
Goodbye Virginia
(Home in) Pasadena
I'm a Little Blackbird Looking For a Blue-bird
In the Land of Beginning Again
Mandy Make Up Your Mind
Ragtime Cowboy Joe
Rosie (Make It Rosy For Me)
Second Hand Rose
There's a Little Bit of Bad In Every Good Little Girl
Weary River

Clarke, Vincent
Blue Savannah
Chains of Love
Circus
Don't Go
Drama
It Doesn't Have to Be
Just Can't Get Enough
Little Respect
Never Never
New Life
O' L'amour
Only You
Other Side Of Love, The
Ship of Fools
Sometimes
Star
Victim of Love

Cliff, Jimmy
Let Your Yeah Be Yeah
Many Rivers to Cross
Wonderful World, Beautiful People
You Can Get It If You Really Want It

Clifford, Gordon
I Surrender Dear
It Must Be True
Paradise
Who Am I?

Coates, Eric
Bird Songs At Eventide
By the Sleepy Lagoon
Dam Busters March, The
I Pitch My Lonely Caravan At Night

Cobb, Will
Are You From Dixie
Goodbye Dolly Gray
I Just Can't Make My Eyes Behave
School Days
Sunbonnet Sue
Waltz Me Round Again Willie
Yip I Addy Ay

Coben, Cy
Nobody's Child
Old Piano Roll Blues, The
She's a Lady
Sweet Violets

Cohan, George M.
Give My Regards to Broadway
Harrigan
Little Nellie Kelly I Love You
Over There
So Long Mary
Until My Luck Comes Rolling Along
When June Comes Along With a Song
Yankee Doodle Boy
You Remind Me of My Mother

Coleman, Cy
Big Spender
Hey Look Me Over
If My Friends Could See Me Now
Rhythm of Life
Witchcraft

Coleman, Larry
Changing Partners
Just as Much as Ever
Ricochet
Tennessee Wig-Walk, The

Collins, Charles
Any Old Iron
Are We to Part Like This
Boiled Beef and Carrots
Don't Dilly Dally on the Way
I Wouldn't Leave My Little Wooden Hut For You
Now I Have to Call Him Father
When There Isn't a Girl About
Why Am I Always the Bridesmaid

Collins, Phil
Abacab
Against All Odds (Take a Look At Me Now)
Another Day In Paradise
Easy Lover
Follow You Follow Me
I Wish It Would Rain Down
In the Air Tonight
In Too Deep
Invisible Touch
Land Of Confusion
Loco In Acapulco
Mama
One More Night

Sussudio
That's All
Turn It on Again
Two Hearts

Comden, Betty
Just In Time
Long Before I Knew You
Make Someone Happy
Moses
Party's Over, The

Connelly, Reginald
By the Fireside
Dreaming
Falling in Love Again
Goodnight Sweetheart
Homecoming Waltz, The
I Found You
I'm Happy When I'm Hiking
If I Had You
Just An Echo In the Valley
Linger a Little Longer In the Twilight
Old Kitchen Kettle, The
On a Street Of Chinese Lanterns
Sunny Days
Try a Little Tenderness
Two of Us, The
When the Organ Played at Twilight

Connor, Tommie
Biggest Aspidistra In the World, The
Chestnut Tree, The
Down In the Glen
Give Her My Love
Hang on the Bell Nellie
Homing Waltz, The
I Love to Sing
I Once Had a Heart Margarita
I Saw Mommy Kissing Santa Claus
It's My Mother's Birthday Today
Lili Marlene
Little Boy That Santa Claus Forgot
Never Do a Tango With an Eskimo
Rose I Bring You, The
Scottish Samba, The
Till the Lights Of London Shine Again
Wedding of Lilli Marlene, The
When the Guardsman Started Crooning on Parade
Who's Taking You Home Tonight?

Conrad, Con
Barney Google
Big City Blues
Breakaway, The
Continental, The
Goodnight
Here's to Romance
Honey I'm In Love With You
Let's All Go to Mary's House
Lonesome and Sorry
Ma! He's Making Eyes at Me
Margie
Memory Lane
Moonlight
Only When You're In My Arms
Palesteena
Prisoner Of Love
Singin' the Blues (Till My Daddy Comes Home)
That's You Baby
Walking With Susie
You Call It Madness
You've Got to See Mama Every Night

Cook, Paul
Holidays In the Sun
No-One Is Innocent
Pretty Vacant
Silly Thing

Cook, Roger
Banner Man, The
Blame It on the Pony Express
Conversations
Doctor's Orders
Freedom Come Freedom Go
Gasoline Alley Bred
Good Times (Better Times)
Hello Summertime
Home Lovin' Man
I Was Kaiser Bill's Batman
I'd Like to Teach the World to Sing
I've Got You on My Mind
Like Sister and Brother
Lovers Of the World Unite
Melting Pot
My Baby Loves Lovin'
Randy
Softly Whispering I Love You
Something Old, Something New
Something Tells Me
Something's Gotten Hold of My Heart
Sunny Honey Girl
Talking In Your Sleep
Way It Used to Be, The
Way of Life, The
You've Got Your Troubles

Cooke, Sam
Another Saturday Night
Bring It on Home to Me
Chain Gang
Cupid
Sweet Soul Music
Twistin' the Night Away
You Send Me

Cooper, Alice
Elected
No More Mister Nice Guy
Only Women Bleed
Poison
School's Out

Coots, J. Fred
Doin' the Raccoon
Dream Time
For All We Know
I Still Get a Thrill (Thinking Of You)
Love Letters in the Sand
Precious Little Thing Called Love, A
Santa Claus is Coming to Town
You Go to My Head

Cosby, Henry
I Was Made to Love Her
My Cherie Amour
Never Had a Dream Come True
Tears of a Clown, The

Coslow, Sam
Black Moonlight
Cocktails For Two
Day You Came Along, The
Down the Old Ox Road
I'd Rather Be Me
In the Middle of a Kiss
It's Love Again
It's Raining Sunbeams
Just One More Chance
Learn to Croon
Little White Gardenia, A
Moon Song (That Wasn't Meant For Me)
Moonstruck
My Old Flame
New Moon and an Old Serenade, A
One Summer Night
Sing You Sinners
Sweeping the Clouds Away
Thanks

Was It a Dream
When Autumn Leaves Are Falling

Coulter, Phil
All of Me Loves All of You
Baby I Love You, O.K.
Back Home
Bump, The
Congratulations
Fancy Pants
Forever and Ever
Heart Of Stone
Julie-Ann
My Boy
Puppet on a String
Remember (Sha-la-la)
Shang-a-Lang
Summer Love Sensation
Surround Yourself With Sorrow

Courtney, David
Giving It All Away
Long Tall Glasses
One Man Band
Shooting Star
Who Were You With in the Moonlight

Coward, Noel
Dance Little Lady
Dear Little Cafe
Dearest Love
Has Anybody Seen Our Ship
I'll Follow My Secret Heart
I'll See You Again
London Pride
Mad About the Boy
Mad Dogs and Englishmen
Matelot
Mrs Worthington
Nina
Parisian Pierrot
Play Orchestra Play
Poor Little Rich Girl
Room With a View
Some Day I'll Find You
Stately Homes of England, The
To-Kay
Twentieth Century Blues
You Were There
Zigeuner

Cox, Desmond
Angel of the Great White Way
Horsey, Horsey
I'm In Love With Two Sweethearts
I've Got Sixpence (As I Go Rolling Home)
In the Quartermaster's Stores
Just a Little Fond Affection
We All Went Up Up Up the Mountain
Wheel Of the Wagon Is Broken, The
When You Know You're Not Forgotten

Craig, Michael
Church Of The Poison Mind
Do You Really Want to Hurt Me
It's a Miracle
Karma Chameleon
Move Away
Victims

Crane, Jimmy
Every Day Of My Life
Hurt
I Need You Now
If I Gave My Heart to You

Creamer, Henry
After You've Gone
Any Way the Wind Blows
Dear Old Southland
If I Could Be With You (One Hour Tonight)

Way Down Yonder In New Orleans

Creatore, Luigi
Can't Give You Anything (But My Love)
Can't Help Falling In Love
Funky Weekend
Let's Put It All Together
Na Na Is the Saddest Word
Sing Baby Sing
Sixteen Bars
Star on a TV Show
Walkin' Miracle, A
Wild In the Country

Creed, Linda
Betcha By Golly Wow
Ghetto Child
Greatest Love of All
I'm Stone In Love With You
Rockin' Roll Baby
Rubber Band Man, The
You Are Everything
You Make Me Feel Brand New

Creme, Lol
Dean and I, The
Donna
I'm Mandy, Fly Me
Life is a Minestrone
Rubber Bullets
Under Your Thumb
Wedding Bells

Crewe, Bob
Big Girls Don't Cry
Bye Bye Baby (Baby Goodbye)
Can't Take My Eyes Off You
Daddy Cool - the Girl Can't Help It
Get Dancing
I Wanna Dance Wit Choo (Do Dat Dance)
La Dee Dah
Lady Marmalade (Voulez-Vous Coucher Avec Moi Ce Soir)
Let's Hang on
My Eyes Adored You
Proud One, The
Rag Doll
Silence Is Golden
Silhouettes
Sun Ain't Gonna Shine Anymore, The
Walk Like a Man
You're Ready Now

Cropper, Steve
Dock Of the Bay, The
Green Onions
In the Midnight Hour
Knock on Wood

Cross, Christopher
All Stood Still
Arthur's Theme
Dancing With Tears In My Eyes
Vienna

Cunningham, Tom
Angel Eyes (Home and Away)
Sweet Little Mystery
Sweet Surrender
Wishing I Was Lucky

Currie, Alannah
Doctor! Doctor!
Hold Me Now
I Want That Man
Lay Your Hands on Me
Love on Your Side
We Are Detective
You Take Me Up

Currie, William
All Stood Still

Dancing With Tears In My Eyes
Fade to Grey
Hymn
Vienna

Curtis, Mann
Choo'n' Gum
Didja Ever
I'm Gonna Live Till I Die
Jones Boy, The
Let It Be Me (Je T'appartiens)
Mais Qui
My Dreams Are Getting Better All the Time
Pretty Kitty Blue Eyes
Story Of a Starry Night, The
That's What a Rainy Day Is For
Whole World Is Singing My Song

Curtis, Sonny
Little Girl
More Than I Can Say
Reminiscing
Walk Right Back
When You Ask About Love

Dallin, Sarah
I Heard a Rumour
I Want You Back
Love In the First Degree
Robert De Niro's Waiting
Young at Heart

Damerell, Stanley
Argentina
Butterflies In the Rain
Da-dar Da-dar
Friends
I Bought Myself a Bottle Of Ink
If
Lady of Madrid
Lady of Spain
Let's All Sing Like the Birdies Sing
Life's Desire
Sailor Who Are You Dreaming of Tonight
Sitting on a Five Barred Gate
Song of the Trees, The
There's a Lovely Lake in London
Unless
You Die if You Worry

Dammers, Jerry
Do Nothing
Gangsters
Ghost Town
Nelson Mandela
Stereotype
Too Much Too Young

Darewski, Herman
Army, The Navy and the Air Force, The
I Used to Sigh For the Silvery Moon
If You Could Care For Me
In the Twi-Twi-Twilight
Sister Susie's Sewing Shirts For Soldiers
When We've Wound Up the Watch on the Rhine

Darin, Bobby
Dream Lover
I'll Be There
Multiplication
Splish Splash
Things

David, Hal
Alfie
Always Something There to Remind Me
Anyone Who Had a Heart
Bell Bottom Blues
Broken Hearted Melody

Close to You
Do You Know the Way to San Jose?
Four Winds and the Seven Seas
I Just Don't Know What to Do With Myself
I Say a Little Prayer
I'll Never Fall In Love Again
It Only Took a Minute
Look of Love
Magic Moments
Make It Easy on Yourself
Message to Martha
No Regrets (Non Je Ne Regrette Rien)
Raindrops Keep Falling on My Head
Story of My Life, The
That's What Friends Are For
This Guy's in Love With You
Trains and Boats and Planes
Twenty-Four Hours From Tulsa
Walk on By
What's New Pussycat?
Wishin' and Hopin'
You'll Answer to Me

David, Mack
At the Candlelight Cafe
Bibbidi-Bobbidi-Boo
Birds and the Bees, The
Call of the Faraway Hills, The
Cherry Pink and Apple Blossom White
Chi-Baba Chi-Baba
Come With Me My Honey
Dream is a Wish Your Heart Makes, A
Falling Leaves
I Don't Care if the Sun Don't Shine
It Must Be Him (Seul Sur Son Etoile)
It's Love, Love, Love
Johnny Zero
Just a Kid Named Joe
My Own True Love
On the Isle Of May
Singing Hills, The
Sinner Kissed An Angel, A
Sixty Seconds Got Together
Thoughtless

David, Worton
Are We Downhearted? No!
Heart of a Rose
Hello, Hello, Who's Your Lady Friend?
Hold Your Hand Out Naughty Boy
I Want to Sing in Opera
Omaha
Playthings
That Old Fashioned Mother of Mine

Davies, Ray
All Day and All of the Night
Apeman
Autumn Almanac
Days
Dead End Street
Death of a Clown, The
Dedicated Follower of Fashion, A
I Go to Sleep
Lola
See My Friend
Set Me Free
Sunny Afternoon
Till the End of the Day
Tired of Waiting For You
You Really Got Me
Waterloo Sunset

Davies, Raymond
Death of a Clown, The
Lola
Waterloo Sunset

Davis, Benny
Angel Child

Baby Face
Bring Your Smile Along
Carolina Moon
Dream Time
Driftwood
How Green Was My Valley
I Still Get a Thrill (Thinking Of You)
I'm Nobody's Baby
It's a Cruel Cruel World
Lonesome and Sorry
Margie
Oh How I Miss You Tonight
Roses Remind Me Of You
Say It While Dancing
She's a Home Girl
Smile Will Go a Long, Long Way, A
There Must Be a Reason
With These Hands
Yearning (Just For You)

Davis, Jimmy
It Makes No Difference Now
Lover Man (Oh Where Can You Be)
Nobody's Darlin' But Mine
You Are My Sunshine

De Lange, Eddie
All This and Heaven Too
Along the Navajo Trail
Darn That Dream
Deep in a Dream
Heaven Can Wait
If I'm Lucky
Solitude
String of Pearls, A
This is Worth Fighting For

De Lugg, Milton
Be My Life's Companion
Hoop Dee-Doo
Orange Coloured Sky
Shanghai

De Paul, Gene
Bless Yore Beautiful Hide
Cow Cow Boogie
Goin' Co'tin'
He's My Guy
I'll Remember April
Irresistible You
Milkman Keep Those Bottles Quiet
Mister Five By Five
Sobbin' Women
Spring, Spring, Spring
Star Eyes
Teach Me Tonight
Watch the Birdie
Wonderful Wonderful Day

De Paul, Lynsey
Dancing on a Saturday Night
No Honestly
School Love
Sugar Me
Won't Somebody Dance With Me

De Rose, Peter
Buona Sera
Cloud Lucky Seven
Deep Purple
Down the Oregon Trail
Have You Ever Been Lonely
La De De, La De Da
Lamp is Low
Lilacs in the Rain
Muddy Water
Oh Muki Muki Oh
On a Little Street In Singapore
Rolling Home
Somebody Loves You
Twenty-Four Hours Of Sunshine

Wagon Wheels
When You're Hair Has Turned to Silver

De Shannon, Jackie
Bette Davis Eyes
Breakaway
Come and Stay With Me
When You Walk In the Room

De Sylva, Buddy
Alabamy Bound
April Showers
Avalon
Best Things In Life Are Free, The
Birth Of the Blues, The
Black Bottom, The
Broken Hearted
Button Up Your Overcoat
California Here I Come
Eadie Was a Lady
For Old Times' Sake
Good News
I Wonder How I Look When I'm Asleep
I'll Build a Stairway to Paradise
I'll Say She Does
I'm a Dreamer, Aren't We All
If I Had a Talking Picture Of You
If You Knew Susie
It All Depends on You
Just a Cottage Small (By a Waterfall)
Just a Memory
Just Imagine
Keep Smiling At Trouble
Kiss in the Dark, A
Little Pal
Look For the Silver Lining
Lucky Day
Lucky in Love
Magnolia
Memory Lane
My Sin
'N' Everything
Please Do It Again
Rise 'n' Shine
Save Your Sorrow For Tomorrow
So Blue
Somebody Loves Me
Song I Love, The
Sonny Boy
Sunny Side Up
Together
Varsity Drag
When Day Is Done
Whip-Poor-Will
Wishing
You Ain't Heard Nothing Yet
You're An Old Smoothie
You're the Cream in My Coffee

Deacon, John
Another One Bites the Dust
Friends Will Be Friends
I Want to Break Free
You're My Best Friend

Dean, James
Farewell is a Lonely Sound
I'll Say Forever My Love
It's Wonderful
What Becomes of the Brokenhearted
You Don't Have to Be a Star

Dee, Sylvia
Chickery Chick
End of the World, The
House With Love in it, A
If Anyone Finds This, I Love You
Laroo Laroo Lilli Bolero
Robot Man
Too Young

Dees, Bill
Goodnight
It's Over
Oh Pretty Woman
There Won't Be Many Coming Home

Dehr, Rich
Green Fields
Love Is a Golden Ring
Marianne
Memories Are Made of This
Mister Tap-Toe

Del Riego, Teresa
Homing
O Dry Those Tears
Sink Red Sun
Thank God For a Garden

Delanoe, Pierre
Day the Rains Came, The
If Only I Could Live My Life Again
Let It Be Me (Je T'Appartiens)
What Now My Love (Et Maintenant)
With Your Love (Mes Mains)

Diamond, Neil
Beautiful Noise
Boat That I Row, The
Cracklin' Rosie
I Am...I Said
I'm a Believer
Little Bit of Me, A Little Bit You, A
Love on the Rocks
Red Red Wine
Song Sung Blue
Sweet Caroline
You Don't Bring Me Flowers

Dietz, Howard
Alone Together
By Myself
Dancing in the Dark
I Guess I'll Have to Change My Plan
I See Your Face Before Me
Louisianna Hayride
Love is a Dancing Thing
Moanin' Low
Moment I Saw You, The
New Sun in the Sky, A
Shine on Your Shoes, A
Something to Remember You By
That's Entertainment
Triplets

Dillon, William
All Alone
End of the Road, The
I Want a Girl Just Like the Girl That
Married Dear Old Dad

Dixon, Mort
'Bam 'Bam 'Bammy Shore
Bye Bye Blackbird
Fare-Thee-Well Annabelle
Flirtation Walk
Follow the Swallow
I Found a Million Dollar Baby
I'm Looking Over a Four-Leaf Clover
If You Want the Rainbow
In Caliente
Just Like a Butterfly
Lady In Red, The
Mister and Mrs is the Name
Moonbeam Kiss Her For Me
Nagasaki
Ooh That Kiss
Pink Elephants
River Stay 'Way From My Door
Sing a Little Jingle
Stay Out of the South
That Old Gang Of Mine

Would You Like to Take a Walk
You're My Everything

Donaldson, Walter
At Sundown
Back Home In Tennessee
Because My Baby Don't Mean Maybe
Now
Beside a Babbling Brook
Carolina In the Morning
Chili Bom Bom
Could Be
Did I Remember
Earful Of Music, An
Hiawatha's Lullaby
How Ya Gonna Keep 'Em Down on the
Farm
I Wonder Where My Baby is Tonight
I've Got the Sweetest Girl in Maryland
I've Had My Moments
It's Been So Long
Just Like a Melody Out of the Sky
Let It Rain Let it Pour
Let's Talk About My Sweetie
Little White Lies
Love Me or Leave Me
Makin' Whoopee
Mister Meadowlark
My Baby Just Cares For Me
My Blue Heaven
My Buddy
My Mammy
My Ohio Home
(My Sweet) Hortense
Okay Toots
Roamin' to Wyomin'
Sam the Old Accordion Man
Sweet Indiana Home
Sweet Jenny Lee
That Certain Party
There Ain't No Maybe in My Baby's Eyes
We'll Have a Jubilee in My Old Kentucky
Home
(What Can I Say) After I Say I'm Sorry
When My Ship Comes in
Where'd You Get Those Eyes
Yes Sir, That's My Baby
You
You're Driving Me Crazy

Donnelly, Dorothy
Deep in My Heart
Drinking Song, The
Golden Days
Serenade
Song of Love

Dorset, Ray
Baby Jump
Feels Like I'm in Love
In the Summertime
Lady Rose
Long Legged Woman Dressed in Black

Dozier, Lamont
Baby Love
Bernadette
(Come Round Here) I'm the One You
Need
Going Back to My Roots
Happening, The
Heaven Must Have Sent You
I Can't Help Myself
I Guess I'll Always Love You
(I'm a) Road Runner
In and Out of Love
It's the Same Old Song
Loco in Acapulco
Love Like Yours, A
Reach Out I'll Be There
Reflections

Seven Rooms of Gloom
Standing in the Shadows of Love
Stop in the Name of Love
There's a Ghost in My House
This Old Heart of Mine
Two Hearts
Where Did Our Love Go
You Can't Hurry Love
You Keep Me Hangin' on

Drake, Ervin
Beloved Be Faithful
Castle Rock
I Believe
My Friend
Perdido
Rickerty Rickshaw Man, The
Tico Tico

Drake, Milton
Ashby De La Zouch (Castle Abbey)
Java Jive
Kiss Me Sweet
Mairzy Doats and Dozy Doats
Pu-leeze Mr. Hemingway
She Broke My Heart In Three Places

Dreyer, Dave
Back in Your Own Back Yard
Cecilia
In a Little Secondhand Store
Inka Dinka Doo
Me and My Shadow
There's a Rainbow 'Round My Shoulder

Dubin, Al
About a Quarter to Nine
All the World Will Be Jealous of Me
Along the Santa Fe Trail
Anniversary Waltz, The
Boulevard Of Broken Dreams
Crooning
Cup Of Coffee, A Sandwich and You, A
Dancing With Tears in My Eyes
Fair and Warmer
Feudin' and Fightin'
For You
Forty-Second Street
I Only Have Eyes For You
I'll Sing You a Thousand Love Songs
I'll String Along With You
I'm Goin' Shoppin' With You
I've Got to Sing a Torch Song
Indian Summer
Just a Girl That Men Forget
Keep Young and Beautiful
Kiss Waltz, The
Lullaby of Broadway
Lulu's Back In Town
Many Happy Returns of the Day
Nobody Knows What a Red-head Mama Can Do
Pagan Moon
Painting the Clouds With Sunshine
Pettin' In the Park
Remember Me
Rose in Her Hair, The
September in the Rain
Shadow Waltz, The
She's a Latin From Manhattan
Shuffle Off to Buffalo
So Is Your Old Lady
South American Way
Three's a Crowd
Tip-toe Through the Tulips
Too Many Tears
We're in the Money
With Plenty of Money and You
Wonder Bar
Words Are in My Heart, The

You're Getting to Be a Habit With Me
Young and Healthy

Duke, Vernon
April in Paris
Autumn in New York
Cabin in the Sky
I Can't Get Started
I Like the Likes of You
I'm Gonna Ring the Bell Tonight
Suddenly
Taking a Chance on Love
That's What Makes Paris Paree

Dunbar, Ronald
Band of Gold
Everything's Tuesday
Give Me Just a Little More Time
Patches
You've Got Me Dangling on a String

Dylan, Bob
All Along the Watchtower
All I Really Want to Do
Baby Stop Crying
Blowing in the Wind
Hard Rain's Gonna Fall, A
I Want You
I'll Be Your Baby Tonight
If Not For You
If You Gotta Go, Go Now
Just Like a Woman
Knockin' on Heaven's Door
Lay Lady Lay
Like a Rolling Stone
Mighty Quinn
Mister Tambourine Man
Positively Fourth Street
Rainy Day Woman (Nos. 12 & 35)
Subterranean Homesick Blues
This Wheel's on Fire
Times They Are a-Changin', The

Eaton, Jimmy
Cry, Baby, Cry
Dance With a Dolly
I Double Dare You
I'm Gonna Lock My Heart and Throw Away the Key
Turn Back the Hands of Time

Ebb, Fred
Cabaret
Close the Door (They're Coming In the Window)
Money Song, The
My Colouring Book
New York, New York

Eddy, Duane
Bonnie Came Back
Forty Miles Of Bad Road
Guitar Man
Ring Of Fire
Shazam

Edens, Roger
In Between
It's a Great Day For the Irish
Minnie From Trinidad
Moses
Our Love Affair

Edwards, Bernard
Dance, Dance, Dance
Everybody Dance
Good Times
He's the Greatest Dancer
I Want Your Love
I'm Coming Out
Le Freak
Lost In Music

My Old Piano
Rapper's Delight
Spacer
Thinking Of You
Upside Down
We Are Family
Why

Edwards, Gus
By the Light Of the Silvery Moon
I Just Can't Make My Eyes Behave
In My Merry Oldsmobile
Orange Blossom Time
School Days
Sunbonnet Sue

Edwards, Sherman
Broken Hearted Melody
First Row Balcony
Wonderful Wonderful
You'll Answer to Me

Egan, Ray
Japanese Sandman
Mammy's Little Coal Black Rose
Sleepy Time Gal
Some Sunday Morning
There Ain't No Maybe In My Baby's Eyes

Egan, Raymond
Ain't We Got Fun
Bimini Bay
I Never Knew (I Could Love Anybody)
When Shall We Meet Again
Where the Morning Glories Grow

Eliscu, Edward
Carioca, The
Flying Down to Rio
Great Day
Orchids In the Moonlight
They Cut Down the Old Pine Tree
Without a Song
You Forgot Your Gloves

Ellington, Duke
Caravan
Creole Love Call
Do Nothing Till You Hear From Me
Don't Get Around Much Anymore
I Didn't Know About You
I Got It Bad, and That Ain't Good
I Let a Song Go Out of My Heart
I'm Beginning to See the Light
In a Sentimental Mood
It Don't Mean a Thing (If It Ain't Got That Swing)
Just a-Sittin' and a-Rockin'
Mood Indigo
Ring Dem Bells
Rockin' in Rhythm
Solitude
Sophisticated Lady
Time's a-Wastin'

Elliot, Jack
Do You Care
It's So Nice to Have a Man Around the House
Ivory Rag
La Pansé (Mandy)
Our Very Own
Sam's Song

Ellis, Vivian
Flies Crawled Up the Window, The
I Was Never Kissed Before
I'm on a See-saw
Ma Belle Marguerita
Me and My Dog
Other People's Babies

She's My Lovely
Spread a Little Happiness
There's Always Tomorrow
This Is My Lovely Day

English, Scott
Bend Me Shape Me
Brandy
Help Me Girl
Hi-ho Silver Lining
Mandy

Essex, David
Gonna Make You a Star
Hold Me Close
Lamplight
Rock on
Rolling Stone
Silver Dream Machine
Tahiti

Estefan, Gloria
Anything For You
Can't Stay Away From You
Don't Wanna Lose You
One Two Three

Evans, Paul
Hello This Is Joannie
Johnny Will
Roses Are Red
When

Evans, Ray
As I Love You
Buttons and Bows
Copper Canyon
Dime and a Dollar, A
G'bye Now
Golden Earrings
Home Cooking
I'll Always Love You
In the Arms of Love
Let Me Be Loved
Mona Lisa
Que Sera, Sera
Song of Delilah, The
Streets of Laredo, The
Tammy
To Each His Own

Evans, Tolchard
Argentina
Barcelona
Da-dar Da-dar
Everywhere
Friends
I Bought Myself a Bottle of Ink
I'll Find You
If
Lady of Madrid
Lady of Spain
Let's All Sing Like the Birdies Sing
Life's Desire
My September Love
Sailor Who Are You Dreaming of Tonight
Singing Piano, The
Song of the Trees, The
There's a Lovely Lake In London
Unless

Everly, Don
Cathy's Clown
It's All Over
Price of Love, The
So Sad

Eyton, Frank
All Over the Place
Body and Soul
Don't Do That to the Poor Puss Cat
Gipsy Moon

Let the People Sing
Take Me to Your Heart Again (La Vie en Rose)
Tell Me Tonight
Today I Feel So Happy
You've Done Something to My Heart

Fahey, Siobhan
I Heard a Rumour
I Want You Back
Love In the first Degree
Robert De Niro's Waiting
You're History
Young At Heart

Fain, Sammy
April Love
Are You Having Any Fun
Black Hills Of Dakota, The
Blue Bells Of Broadway, The
By a Waterfall
Certain Smile, A
Deadwood Stage, The
Dear Hearts and Gentle People
I Can Dream Can't I
I Left My Sugar Standing In the Rain
I'll Be Seeing You
Let a Smile Be Your Umbrella
Love Is a Many Splendoured Thing
Man on Fire
Nobody Knows What a Red-head Mama Can Do
Second Star to the Right, The
Secret Love
Sitting on a Back-yard Fence
Sunbonnet Blue, A
That Old Feeling
Very Precious Love, A
Was That the Human Thing to Do
Wedding Bells Are Breaking Up That Old Gang Of Mine
When I Take My Sugar to Tea
You Brought a New Kind of Love to Me
Your Mother and Mine

Fall, Leo
Be My Comrade True
Dollar Princesses
Love Me Now
My Dream of Love

Farian, Frank
Daddy Cool
Girl I'm Gonna Miss You
Gotta Go Home
Hooray, Hooray, It's a Holi Holiday
Ma Baker
Rasputin
Rivers of Babylon, The

Farrar, John
Hopelessly Devoted to You
Little More Love, A
Sam
You're the One That I Want

Farrell, Wes
Could It Be Forever
Hang on Sloopy
I Can't Stop
Our Favourite Melodies

Ferry, Bryan
All I Want is You
Angel Eyes
Dance Away
Love is the Drug
Oh Yeah
Over You
Pyjamarama
Street Life
This is Tomorrow

Virginia Plain

Fields, Dorothy
Bandanna Babies
Big Spender
Blue Again
Close as Pages in a Book
Cuban Love Song
Diga Diga Doo
Dinner at Eight
Doin' the New Lowdown
Don't Blame Me
Fine Romance, A
Go Home and Tell Your Mother
Goodbye Blues
I Can't Give You Anything But Love
I Dream Too Much
I Feel a Song Coming on
I Won't Dance
I'll Buy You a Star
If My Friends Could See Me Now
It's the Darndest Thing
Lost in a Fog
Lovely to Look At
On the Sunny Side of the Street
Rhythm of Life
Singin' the Blues
Stars in My Eyes
Waltz in Swing Time
Way You Look Tonight, The

Finch, Richard
Gimme Some
I Ain't Lyin'
I Can't Leave You Alone
It's Been So Long
Please Don't Go
Rock Your Baby

Finck, Herman
Gilbert the Filbert
I'll Make a Man of You
In the Shadows
Toy Town
Whisper to Me

Findon, Ben
Atmosphere
Attention to Me
Chosen Few, The
Don't Make Waves
Gotta Pull Myself Together
I'm In the Mood For Dancing
Love of My Life
Love Really Hurts Without You
Red Light Spells Danger
Rose Has to Die, A
Stop Me (If You've Heard It All Before)
Think I'm Gonna Fall In Love With You
Wanted

Fiorito, Ted
Alone at a Table For Two
Charley My Boy
I Never Knew (That Roses Grew)
Laugh Clown Laugh
Meadowlark
Roll Along Prairie Moon
Sometime

Fischer, Carl
Bring Your Smile Along
We'll Be Together Again
When You're in Love
Who Wouldn't Love You
You've Changed

Fisher, Doris
Amado Mio
Good, Good, Good
Into Each Life Some Rain Must Fall

Put the Blame on Mame
Tampico
That Old Devil Called Love
Whispering Grass
You Always Hurt the One You Love
You Sang My Love Song to Somebody
Else

Fisher, Fred
Chicago (That Toddlin' Town)
Come Josephine In My Flying Machine
Dardanella
Fifty Million Frenchmen Can't Be Wrong
Happy Days and Lonely Nights
I Want You to Want Me to Want You
Ireland Must Be Heaven For My Mother
Came From There
Peg O' My Heart
They Go Wild Simply Wild Over Me
Whispering Grass
Wimmin (I Gotta Have 'Em That's All)

Fisher, Mark
Dear One
Everywhere You Go
Oh How I Miss You Tonight
Wap-Bam-Boogie
When You're Smiling

Fishman, Jack
Arrivederci Darling (Arrivederci Roma)
Half as Nice
Help Yourself (Gli Occhi Miei)
If I Only Had Time (Je N'aurai Pas Le
Temps)
My Friend the Sea
Something's Happening (Luglio)
West Of Zanzibar (Jambo)
Why Don't They Understand
Years May Come, Years May Go

Fletcher, Guy
I Can't Tell the Bottom From the Top
Power to All Our Friends
Sing a Song of Freedom
With the Eyes of a Child

Flett, Doug
I Can't Tell the Bottom From the Top
Power to All Our Friends
Sing a Song of Freedom
With the Eyes of a Child

Flowers, Herbie
Banner Man, The
Grandad
Oh What a Shame
Our World
Randy

Fogerty, John
Bad Moon Rising
Proud Mary
Rockin' All Over the World
Travellin' Band
Up Around the Bend

Forrest, George
And This Is My Beloved
Baubles, Bangles and Beads
Pink Champagne
Ride Cossack, Ride
Strange Music
Stranger In Paradise

Forsey, Keith
Don't You Forget About Me
Flashdance - What a Feeling
Heat is on, The
Never Ending Story

Foster, David
Best Of Me, The

Glory Of Love, The
Hard to Say I'm Sorry
St. Elmo's Fire (Man In Motion)

Franklin, Dave
Anniversary Waltz, The
Merry-go-round Broke Down, The
When My Dreamboat Comes Home
You Can't Stop Me From Dreaming

Freed, Arthur
All I Do Is Dream Of You
Alone
Broadway Melody, The
Broadway Rhythm
Fit As a Fiddle
Good Morning
House Of Singing Bamboo, The
I Cried For You
I'm Feeling Like a Million
I've Got a Feelin' You're Foolin'
Little Dutch Mill
Moon Is Low
On a Sunday Afternoon
Our Love Affair
Pagan Love Song, The
Should I
Singin' In the Rain
Temptation
This Heart Of Mine
We'll Make Hay While the Sun Shines
Wedding Of the Painted Doll, The
When Buddha Smiles
Would You
You Are My Lucky Star
You Were Meant For Me

Freed, Ralph
Hawaiian War Chant, The
How About You
I Thought Of You Last Night
In a Moment Of Madness
Swing High, Swing Low
Who Walks In (When I Walk Out)

Friend, Cliff
Broken Record, The
Chili Bom Bom
Don't Sweetheart Me
Give Me a Night In June
Gonna Build a Big Fence Around Texas
Hello Bluebird
I'm Telling the Birds, Telling the Bees,
How I Love You
It Goes Like This (That Funny Melody)
June Night
Let It Rain Let It Pour
Lovesick Blues
Mama Loves Papa - Papa Loves Mama
Merry-go-round Broke Down, The
My Blackbirds Are Bluebirds Now
Oh! If I Only Had You
So Will I
South American Joe
Sweetest Music This Side Of Heaven,
The
Then I'll Be Happy
There's Something Spanish In Your Eyes
There's Yes! Yes! in Your Eyes
Time Waits For No One
Trade Winds
Wana (When I Wana, You No Wana)
When My Dreamboat Comes Home
Where the Lazy Daisies Grow
You Can't Stop Me From Dreaming

Frimi, Rudolf
Allah's Holiday
L'amour Toujours L'amour, (Love Ever-
lasting)
Dear Love My Love

Donkey Serenade, The
Giannina Mia
Indian Love Call
Mounties, The
Only a Rose
Rose Marie
Some Day
Something Seems Tingle-ingle-ing
Song Of the Vagabonds, The
Sympathy
When a Man Comes Knocking At Your
Heart

Furber, Douglas
Bells Of St. Mary's, The
Fancy Our Meeting
Flies Crawled Up the Window, The
Lambeth Walk, The
Me and My Girl
She's Such a Comfort to Me
Yes Mister Brown

Furholmen, Magne
Cry Wolf
Living Daylights, The
Take on Me
You Are the One

Gabriel, Pascal
Don't Make Me Wait
Megablast
Superfly Guy
Theme From S-Express

Gabriel, Peter
Don't Give Up
Games Without Frontiers
Sledgehammer
Solsbury Hill

Gallop, Sammy
Count Every Star
Elmer's Tune
Maybe You'll Be There
Outside of Heaven
Shoo Fly Pie and Apple Pan Dowdy
Somewhere Along the Way
That's the Moon My Son
That's You
There Must Be a Way

Gamble, Kenny
Don't Leave Me This Way
I Love Music
I'm Gonna Make You Love Me
If You Don't Know Me By Now
Love Train
Me and Mrs Jones
Now That We've Found Love
She's a Winner
Show You the Way to Go
Step Off
Take Good Care of Yourself
Use Ta Be My Girl
When Will I See You Again
Year of Decision
You'll Never Find Another Love Like
Mine

Gannon, Kim
Always In My Heart
Dreamer's Holiday, A
Five O'Clock Whistle, The
I Understand
It Can't Be Wrong
Lady Who Didn't Believe in Love, The
Moonlight Cocktail

Garson, Mort
Gotta Have Sometihng In the Bank,
Frank
It Only Took a Minute

Left Right Out Of My Heart
Our Day Will Come
Starry Eyed
Theme For a Dream

Gaskill, Clarence
Doo Wacka Doo
I Can't Believe That You're In Love With Me
Minnie the Moocher
Prisoner of Love

Gates, David
Baby I'm... a Want You
Everything I Own
Guitar Man
If
Make it With You

Gaudio, Bob
Big Girls Don't Cry
Bye Bye Baby (Baby Goodbye)
Can't Take My Eyes Off You
December '63
Let's Hang on
Night, The
Proud One, The
Rag Doll
Silence is Golden
Silver Star
Sun Ain't Gonna Shine Anymore, The
Walk Like a Man
Who Loves You
You're Ready Now

Gay, Byron
Fate
Horses
Oh!
Sand Dunes
Vamp, The

Gay, Noel
Ali Baba's Camel
All For a Shilling a Day
All Over the Place
Fleet's In Port Again, The
Hey Little Hen
I Took My Harp to a Party
King's Horses, The
La-di-da-di-da
Lambeth Walk, The
Leaning on a Lamp Post
Let the People Sing
Let's Have a Tiddley at the Milk Bar
Me and My Girl
My Thanks to You
'Round the Marble Arch
Run Rabbit Run
Sun Has Got His Hat on, The
There's Something About a Soldier
Things Are Looking Up
Toor-ie on His Bonnet, The
Who's Been Polishing the Sun
You've Done Something to My Heart

Gaye, Marvin
Dancing In the Street
Got to Give It Up
(Sexual) Healing
Wherever I Lay My Hat (That's My Home)

Geldof, Bob
Banana Republic
Do They Know It's Christmas
I Don't Like Mondays
Like Clockwork
Looking After Number One
Mary Of the Fourth Form
Rat Trap
She's So Modern
Someone's Looking at You

George, Don
Door Will Open, A
I Never Mention Your Name, Oh No
I'm Beginning to See the Light
Yellow Rose of Texas, The

Gershwin, George
Beginner's Luck
Bess You Is My Woman Now
Bidin' My Time
But Not For Me
By Strauss
Clap Yo' Hands
Do Do Do
Embraceable You
Fascinating Rhythm
Foggy Day, A
For You, For Me, For Everyone
Funny Face
How Long Has This Been Going on
I Got Plenty of Nuttin'
I Got Rhythm
I Loves You Porgy
I'll Build a Stairway to Paradise
I've Got a Crush on You
It Ain't Necessarily So
Let's Call the Whole Thing Off
Liza (All the Clouds'll Roll Away)
Looking For a Boy
Love is Sweeping the Country
Love Walked in
Man I Love, The
Maybe
My One and Only
Nice Work If You Can Get It
Of Thee I Sing
Oh Lady Be Good
Our Love is Here to Stay
Please Do it Again
Rhapsody In Blue
S'wonderful
Slap That Bass
So Am I
Somebody Loves Me
Someone to Watch Over Me
Soon
Summertime
Swanee
Sweet and Lowdown
That Certain Feeling
They All Laughed
They Can't Take That Away From Me

Gershwin, Ira
Beginner's Luck
Bess You Is My Woman Now
Bidin' My Time
Blow, Gabriel, Blow
But Not For Me
By Strauss
Cheerful Little Earful
Clap Yo' Hands
Do Do Do
Embraceable You
Fascinating Rhythm
Foggy Day, A
For You, For Me, For Everyone
Funny Face
How Long Has This Been Going on
I Can't Get Started
I Got Plenty Of Nuttin'
I Got Rhythm
I Loves You Porgy
I've Got a Crush on You
It Ain't Necessarily So
Jenny
Let's Call the Whole Thing Off
Liza (All the Clouds'll Roll Away)
Long Ago and Far Away

Looking For a Boy
Love is Sweeping the Country
Love Walked In
Man I Love, The
Man That Got Away, The
Maybe
My One and Only
My One and Only Highland Fling
My Ship
Nice Work if You Can Get It
Of Thee I Sing
Oh Lady Be Good
Our Love is Here to Stay
S'wonderful
Shoes With Wings on
Slap That Bass
So Am I
Someone to Watch Over Me
Soon
Summertime
Sunny Disposish
Sweet and Lowdown
That Certain Feeling
They All Laughed
They Can't Take That Away From Me

Gibb, Barry
All the Love In the World
An Everlasting Love
Chain Reaction
Don't Forget to Remember
Emotions
First Of May, The
Grease
Heartbreaker
How Deep Is Your Love
I Gotta Get a Message to You
If I Can't Have You
Islands In the Stream
Jive Talkin'
Love Me
Massachussetts
More Than a Woman
My World
New York Mining Disaster 1941, The
Night Fever
Nights on Broadway
Only One Woman
Run to Me
Stayin' Alive
To Love Somebody
Too Much Heaven
Tragedy
Woman in Love
Words
World
You Should Be Dancing
You Win Again

Gibb, Maurice
All the Love In the World
Chain Reaction
Don't Forget to Remember
First of May, The
Heartbreaker
How Deep Is Your Love
I Gotta Get a Message to You
If I Can't Have You
Islands in the Stream
Jive Talkin'
Massachussetts
More Than a Woman
New York Mining Disaster 1941, The
Night Fever
Nights on Broadway
Only One Woman
Run to Me
Stayin' Alive
Too Much Heaven

Tragedy
Words
World
You Should Be Dancing
You Win Again

Gibb, Robin
All the Love in the World
Chain Reaction
Emotions
First of May, The
Heartbreaker
Hold on to My Love
How Deep Is Your Love
I Gotta Get a Message to You
If I Can't Have You
Islands In the Stream
Jive Talkin'
Love Me
Massachusetts
More Than a Woman
My World
New York Mining Disaster 1941, The
Night Fever
Nights on Broadway
Only One Woman
Run to Me
Saved By the Bell
Stayin' Alive
To Love Somebody
Too Much Heaven
Tragedy
Woman In Love
Words
World
You Should Be Dancing
You Win Again

Gideon, Melville
Arizona
Girl In the Crinoline Gown, The
I'm Tickled to Death I'm Single
If Winter Comes
One Girl
When the Sun Goes Down

Gifford, Harry
Fanlight Fanny
Kitty the Telephone Girl
She Sells Sea Shells
When I'm Cleaning Windows
When It's Apple Blossom Time In Normandy

Gilbert, Joe
Amy, Wonderful Amy
Bathing In the Sunshine
Me and Jane in a Plane
Silver Hair and Heart Of Gold

Gilbert, Joseph
Adeline
Au Revoir But Not Goodbye
Delyse
I'm So All Alone
Let Bygones Be Bygones
Let Us Be Sweethearts All Over Again
Shine on Victory Moon
When You Played the Organ and I Sang
The Rosary

Gilbert, L. Wolfe
By Heck
Chiquita
Down Yonder
Green Eyes (Aquellos Ojos Verdes)
Hitchy-Koo
I Miss My Swiss - My Swiss Miss Misses
Me
Jeannine, I Dream of Lilac Time
Mama Don't Want No Peas, an' Rice,
an' Coconut Oil

Mama Inez
Marta
My Mother's Eyes
Oh, Katharina
Peanut Vendor, The (El Manisero)
Ramona
Waiting For the Robert E. Lee

Gilbert, Ray
Adios Mariquita Linda
Baia
Cuanto le Gusta
Hot Canary, The
Johnny Fedora
Muskrat Ramble
Sooner or Later
That's a Plenty
Three Caballeros, The (Ay Jalisco No
Te Rajes)
Two Silhouettes
Without You (Tres Palabras)
You Belong to My Heart
Zip-a-dee-doo-dah

Gilkyson, Terry
Christopher Columbus
Cry of the Wild Goose, The
Day of Jubilo, The
Green Fields
Love is a Golden Ring
Marianne
Memories Are Made Of This
Mister Tap-Toe
Rock of Gibraltar
Tell Me a Story
Where the Wind Blows

Gill, Peter
Power Of Love, The
Rage Hard
Relax
Two Tribes
Welcome to the Pleasure Dome

Gillespie, Haven
Beautiful Love
Breezin' Along With the Breeze
Drifting and Dreaming
Honey
Kiss
Old Master Painter, The
Santa Claus Is Coming to Town
That Lucky Old Sun
You Go to My Head
You're In Kentucky As Sure As You're
Born

Gimbel, Norman
Killing Me Softly With His Song
Ricochet
Sway (Quien Sera)
Tennessee Wig-Walk, The

Glazer, Tom
Give Me the Right
Melody Of Love
More
Skokiaan

Glitter, Gary
Always Yours
Do You Wanna Touch Me
Doctorin' the Tardis
Doing Alright With the Boys
Hello Hello I'm Back Again
I Didn't Know I Loved You (Till I Saw You
Rock 'n' Roll)
I Love You Love Me Love
I'm the Leader Of the Gang (I Am)
Little Boogie Woogie
Love Like You and Me, A
Oh Yes You're Beautiful

Remember Me This Way
Rock and Roll Part 1 & 2

Goddard, Geoffrey
Don't You Think It's Time
Johnny Remember Me
Just Like Eddie
Lonely City
Son, This Is She
Wild Wind

Godfrey, Fred
Blue Eyes
Meet Me Jenny When the Sun Goes
Down
Molly O'Morgan
Now I Have to Call Him Father
Take Me Back to Dear Old Blighty
Who Were You With Last Night

Godley, Kevin
Dean and I, The
Donna
Neanderthal Man
Rubber Bullets
Under Your Thumb
Wedding Bells

Goell, Kermit
Clopin Clopant
How Wonderful to Know (Aneme E
Core)
Huggin' and Chalkin'
Near You

Goetz, E. Ray
Don't Go In the Lions' Cage Tonight
For Me and My Gal
In the Shadows
My Croony Melody
We'll Have a Jubilee In My Old Kentucky
Home
Who'll Buy My Violets (La Violetera)
Yacka Hula Hickey Dula

Goffin, Gerry
At the Club
Do You Know Where You're Going to?
Don't Bring Me Down
Don't Ever Change
Forever Kind of Love, A
Go Away Little Girl
Goin' Back
Halfway to Paradise
He's in Town
How Can I Meet Her
How Many Tears
I Want to Stay Here
I'd Never Find Another You
I'll Be True to You, Yes I Will
I'm Into Something Good
It Might as Well Rain Until September
It Started All Over Again
Keep Your Hands Off My Baby
Let's Turkey Trot
Loco - Motion, The
Miss You Like Crazy
No One Can Make My Sunshine Smile
Nothing's Gonna Change My Love For
You
Oh No Not My Baby
Run to Him
Saving All My Love For You
Sharing You
Some Of Your Lovin'
Take Good Care of My Baby
Up on the Roof
When My Little Girl is Smiling
Will You Love Me Tomorrow

Gold, Wally
Because They're Young

Good Luck Charm
It's My Party
It's Now or Never
Look Homeward Angel

Goldstein, Jerry
I Can't Stop
I Want Candy
Low Rider
Sorrow

Goodhart, Al
Auf Wiederseh'n My Dear
Better Not Roll Those Blue Blue Eyes
Everything Stops For Tea
Everythings in Rhythm With My Heart
Fit As a Fiddle
Gangway
Happy Go Lucky You, and Broken Hearted Me
I Apologise
I Saw Stars
I Ups to Her, and She Ups to Me
I'm In a Dancing Mood
In the Dim Dim Dawning
Johnny Doughboy Found a Rose in Ireland
Little Co-operation From You, A
My First Thrill
Serenade Of the Bells
Smiths and the Joneses, The
There Isn't Any Limit to My Love
This'll Make You Whistle
Who Walks in (When I Walk Out)
You've Got the Wrong Rumba

Goodwin, Joe
Breeze (Blow My Baby Back to Me)
Everywhere You Go
I'm Knee Deep In Daisies
My Croony Melody
On a Steamer Coming Over
Orange Blossom Time
They're Wearing 'em Higher In Hawaii
When You're Smiling

Gordon, Irving
Allentown Jail
Be Anything - But Be Mine
Christmas Dreaming
Delaware
Unforgettable
Wonderful Secret of Love, The

Gordon, Mack
Afraid to Dream
At Last
Blue Shadows and White Gardenias
Boa Noite
Chattanooga Choo Choo
Chica Chica Boom Chic
Did You Ever See a Dream Walking
Down Argentine Way
From the Top Of Your Head (to the Tip of Your Toes)
Goodnight My Love
Head Over Heels in Love
Here Comes Cookie
I Can't Begin to Tell You
I Feel Like a Feather in the Breeze
I Had the Craziest Dream
I Know Why
I Take to You
I Wish I Knew
I Yi Yi Yi I Like You Very Much
I'm Humming, I'm Whistling, I'm Singing
I'm Making Believe
I've Got a Gal in Kalamazoo
In an Old Dutch Garden
It Happened in Sun Valley
Love Thy Neighbour

Mam'selle
May I
May I Have the Next Romance With You
More I See You, The
My Heart Tells Me
Never in a Million Years
Paris in the Spring
People Like You and Me
Run Little Raindrop Run
Serenade in Blue
Sing Me a Song of the Islands
Star Fell Out of Heaven, A
Stay As Sweet as You Are
Take a Number From One to Ten
There Will Never Be Another You
There's a Lull in My Life
This is Always
Time on My Hands
To Mary With Love
Tropical Magic
Underneath the Harlem Moon
Wake Up and Live
When I Love, I Love
When I'm With You
Wilhelmina
With My Eyes Wide Open I'm Dreamin'
Without a Word Of Warning
You Can't Have Everything
You Hit the Spot
You Make Me Feel So Young
You My Love
You Say the Sweetest Things Baby
You'll Never Know

Gordy Jnr, Berry
Do You Love Me?
I'll Be Satisfied
I'll Be There
Money (That's What I Want)
Reet Petite
To Be Loved
You Got What It Takes

Gore, Martin
Enjoy the Silence
Everything Counts
Master and Servant
People Are People
See You

Gould, Rowland
Lessons in Love
Running in the Family
Something About You
To Be With You Again

Gouldman, Graham
Art For Art's Sake
Bridge to Your Heart
Bus Stop
Dreadlock Holiday
Evil Hearted You
For Your Love
Good Morning Judge
Heart Full of Soul
I'm Mandy, Fly Me
I'm Not in Love
Look Through Any Window
No Milk Today
Pamela Pamela
Rubber Bullets
Things We Do For Love, The
Wall Street Shuffle

Graham, Harry
Goodbye
King's Horses, The
Love Me Now
Love Will Find a Way
My Song of Love
Patiently Smiling

Robinson Crusoe's Isle
White Horse Inn, The
You Are My Heart's Delight
You Too
Your Eyes

Grant, Eddy
Do You Feel My Love
Electric Avenue
Gimme Hope Jo'anna
I Don't Wanna Dance
Living on the Front Line
Walking on Sunshine

Grant, Ian
Let the People Sing
Let There Be Love
So Do I (Bet Ami)
You've Done Something to My Heart

Green, Adolph
Just In Time
Long Before I Knew You
Make Someone Happy
Moses
New York, New York
Party's Over, The

Green, Bud
Alabamy Bound
Castles in the Sand
Do Something
Flat Foot Floogie, The
I Love My Baby, My Baby Loves Me
I'll Always Be in Love With You
Moonlight on the River
Once in a While
Sentimental Journey
That's My Weakness Now

Green, Johnny
Body and Soul
Coquette
I Cover the Waterfront
I'm Yours
Out Of Nowhere
Turntable Song, The

Green, Peter
Albatross
Green Manalishi, The
Man of the World, A
Oh Well

Green, Philip
John and Julie
March Hare, The
Say Wonderful Things
That's How a Love Song Was Born

Greenaway, Roger
Banner Man, The
Blame It on the Pony Express
Can I Take You Home Little Girl
Conversations
Doctor's Orders
Down on the Beach Tonight
Freedom Come Freedom Go
Gasoline Alley Bred
Good Times (Better Times)
Hello Happiness
Hello Summertime
Home Lovin' Man
I Was Kaiser Bill's Batman
I'd Like to Teach the World to Sing
I've Got You on My Mind
It's Gonna Be a Cold Cold Christmas
Jeans on
Kissin' In the Back Row of the Movies
Like Sister and Brother
Lovers of the World Unite
Melting Pot

My Baby Loves Lovin'
Randy
Softly Whispering I Love You
Something Old, Something New
Something Tells Me
Something's Gotten Hold of My Heart
Sunny Honey Girl
There Goes My First Love
Way It Used to Be, The
Way of Life, The
You Just Might See Me Cry
You're More Than a Number in My Little Red Book
You've Got Your Troubles

Greenbank, Percy
Chin Chin Chinaman
Chon Kina
Come to the Ball
Garden of Love, The
Little Miss Melody
Pearl of Sweet Ceylon, The
Swing Song
Violin Song, The
When You Are In Love
Wonderful Eyes

Greenfield, Howard
Breaking in a Brand New Broken Heart
Breaking Up is Hard to Do
Calendar Girl
Counting Teardrops
Crying In the Rain
Everybody's Somebody's Fool
Happy Birthday Sweet Sixteen
I Go Ape
Is This the Way to Amarillo
Little Devil
My Heart Has a Mind of It's Own
Oh Carol
Stupid Cupid
Venus in Blue Jeans
Warpaint
Where the Boys Are

Greenwich, Ellie
Baby I Love You
Be My Baby
Da Doo Ron Ron
Do Wah Diddy Diddy
I Can Hear Music
Leader of the Pack, The
River Deep, Mountain High
Sunshine After the Rain
Then He Kissed Me

Grever, Maria
Echo Of a Serenade, The (Te Quieo Dijiste)
Magic Is the Moonlight (Te Quiero Dijiste)
Ti-pi-tin
Tu-li-tulip Time
What a Difference a Day Made

Grey, Clifford
All For a Shilling a Day
Another Little Drink Wouldn't Do Us Any Harm
Dream Lover
First Love, Last Love, Best Love
Got a Date With An Angel
Hey Gipsy (Play Gipsy) (Komm Tzizany)
I'm a One Man Girl
If Winter Comes
If You Were the Only Girl In the World
Let the Great Big World Keep Turning
March Of the Grenadiers
My Love Parade
Nobody's Using It Now
Paris Stay the Same
Rogue Song, The

Sometimes I'm Happy
Valencia
When I'm Looking At You
White Dove, The
Wild Rose

Grosz, Will
Along the Santa Fe Trail
At the Cafe Continental
Bird on the Wing
In An Old Dutch Garden
Isle of Capri
Ten Pretty Girls
Tina

Haines, Will
Biggest Aspidistra in the World, The
He's Dead But He Won't Lie Down
In My Little Bottom Drawer
Sally

Hammerstein II, Oscar
All the Things You Are
All Through the Day
Bali Hi
Beat Out Dat Rhythm on a Drum
Bill
Can I Forget You
Can't Help Lovin' Dat Man
Climb Ev'ry Mountain
Cock-Eyed Optimist, A
Dat's Love
Desert Song, The
Do I Love You Because You're Beautiful
Do-Re-Mi
Don't Ever Leave Me
Edelweiss
Fellow Needs a Girl, A
Folks Who Live on the Hill, The
French Military Marching Song
Gentleman is a Dope, The
Getting to Know You
Happy Talk
Hello Young Lovers
Honey Bun
I Bring a Love Song
I Cain't Say No
I Enjoy Being a Girl
I Whistle a Happy Tune
I Won't Dance
I'll Take Romance
I'm Gonnna Wash That Man Right Out of My Hair
I'm in Love With a Wonderful Guy
I've Told Every Little Star
If I Loved You
Indian Love Call
Isn't It Kinda Fun
It Might As Well Be Spring
It's a Grand Night For Singing
June is Bustin' Out All Over
Kiss to Build a Dream on, A
Last Time I Saw Paris, The
Lover Come Back to Me
Make Believe
Mister Snow
Mounties, The
My Favourite Things
No Other Love
Oh What a Beautiful Morning
Oklahoma
Ol' Man River
One Alone
One Day When We're Young
One Kiss
Out of My Dreams
People Will Say We're In Love
Riff Song, The
Rose Marie
Shall We Dance?

Softly As in a Morning Sunrise
Some Enchanted Evening
Song is You, The
Sound Of Music, The
Stout Hearted Men
Sunny
Surrey With the Fringe on Top, The
That's For Me
There is Nothing Like a Dame
This Nearly Was Mine
Two Little Blue Birds
Wanting You
We Kiss in the Shadow
When I Grow Too Old to Dream
Who
Why Do I Love You?
Why Was I Born?
You Are Beautiful
You Will Remember Vienna
You'll Never Walk Alone
Younger Than Springtime

Hammond, Albert
Air That I Breathe, The
Blow the House Down
Don't Turn Around
Freedom Come Freedom Go
Gimme Dat Ding
Good Morning Freedom
I Don't Wanna Lose You
Little Arrows
Make Me An Island
Nothing's Gonna Stop Us Now
One Moment in Time
Room In Your Heart
When I Need You
You're Such a Good Looking Woman

Handman, Lou
Are You Lonesome Tonight?
Blue
Don't Ever Change
I'm Gonna Charleston Back to Charleston
Is My Baby Blue Tonight
Me and the Moon
My Sweetie Went Away
On a Steamer Coming Over
Was it Rain?

Handy, William C.
Aunt Hagar's Blues
Beale Street Blues
Careless Love
Memphis Blues
Saint Louis Blues
Yellow Dog Blues

Hanley, James
Any Way the Wind Blows
Breeze (Blow My Baby Back to Me)
I'm In the Market For You
Indiana
Just a Cottage Small (By a Waterfall)
Rose Of Washington Square
Second Hand Rose
Sleepy Valley
Zing Went the Strings Of My Heart

Harbach, Otto
Allah's Holiday
Cuddle Up a Little Closer
Desert Song, The
Every Little Movement
French Military Marching Song
Giannina Mia
Going Up
I Want to Be Happy
I Won't Dance
Indian Love Call
Love Nest
Mounties, The

Night Was Made For Love, The
One Alone
Riff Song, The
Rose Marie
She Didn't Say "Yes"
Smoke Gets in Your Eyes
Something Seems Tingle-ingle-ing
Sunny
Sympathy
Tea For Two
Tickle Toe, The
Touch of Your Hand, The
Two Little Blue Birds
When a Man Comes Knocking at Your Heart
Who
Yesterdays

Harburg, E.Y.
April In Paris
Brother Can You Spare a Dime
Can't Help Singing
Ding Dong the Witch Is Dead
Happiness is a Thing Called Joe
How Are Things in Glocca Morra?
I Like the Likes of You
I'm Yours
If I Only Had a Heart
If This Isn't Love
It's Only a Paper Moon
Life's Full of Consequences
Lydia the Tattooed Lady
More and More
Over the Rainbow
Suddenly
We're Off to See the Wizard

Hargreaves, Robert
Butterflies In the Rain
Da-dar Da-dar
If
Lady of Madrid
Lady of Spain
Let's All Sing Like the Birdies Sing
Life's Desire
Song of the Trees, The
Unless
You Die If You Worry

Harley, Steve
Judy Teen
Make Me Smile (Come Up and See Me)
Mister Raffles (Man It Was Mean)
Mister Soft

Harline, Leigh
Give a Little Whistle
Hi-diddle-dee-dee (an Actors Life For Me)
I've Got No Strings
When You Wish Upon a Star

Harnick, Sheldon
If I Were a Rich Man
Matchmaker, Matchmaker
She Loves Me
Sunrise Sunset

Harper, Jimmy
Biggest Aspidistra In the World, The
Celebration Rag
In My Little Bottom Drawer
In My Little Snapshot Album
When You Lose the One You Love

Harris, Clifford
Bachelor Gay, A
Give Me a Little Cosy Corner
I Was a Good Little Girl Till I Met You
Paradise For Two, A

Harris, James
Dub Be Good to Me

Human
I Didn't Mean to Turn You on
Just Be Good to Me
Let's Wait Awhile
Saturday
When I Think of You

Harrison, George
All Those Years Ago
Bangla Desh
Give Me Love (Give Me Peace on Earth)
Here Comes the Sun
My Sweet Lord
Photograph
Something
What Is Life

Harry, Deborah
Atomic
Call Me
Dreaming
Heart of Glass, A
Picture This
Rapture
Union City Blues

Hart, Lorenz
Bewitched, Bothered and Bewildered
Blue Moon
Blue Room, The
Dancing on the Ceiling
Everything I've Got
Falling In Love With Love
Girl Friend, The
Have You Met Miss Jones
Here In My Arms
I Could Write a Book
I Didn't Know What Time is Was
I Like to Recognize the Tune
I Wish I Were In Love Again
It's Easy to Remember
I've Got Five Dollars
Isn't It Romantic
It Never Entered My Mind
Johnny One Note
Lady Is a Tramp, The
Little Girl Blue
Lover
Manhattan
Mimi
Most Beautiful Girl in the World, The
Mountain Greenery
My Funny Valentine
My Heart Stood Still
My Romance
On Your Toes
Ship Without a Sail, The
Sing For Your Supper
Soon - There'll Just Be Two Of Us
Spring Is Here
Ten Cents a Dance
There's a Small Hotel
This Can't Be Love
Thou Swell
To Keep My Love Alive
Tree In a Park, A
Where or When
Where's That Rainbow
With a Song in My Heart
You Are Too Beautiful
You Took Advantage of Me

Hart, Peter
Meet Me on the Corner
Nellie the Elephant
Soon It Will Be Sunday
Tomorrow

Hartman, Dan
I Can Dream About You

Instant Replay
Living In America
Ride on Time

Hassall, Christopher
Fold Your Wings
Glamorous Night
I Can Give You the Starlight
I Leave My Heart in an English Garden
My Dearest Dear
My Life Belongs to You
Primrose
Rose of England
Shine Through My Dreams
Story of Tina, The (Dio Prasina Matia)
Take Your Girl
Waltz of My Heart
When the Gypsy Played

Hatch, Tony
Don't Sleep In the Subway
Down Town
I Couldn't Live Without Your Love
I Know a Place
Joanna
My Love
Other Man's Grass, The
Where Are You Now My Love?

Hawker, Mike
Don't Treat Me Like a Child
I Only Want to Be With You
Little Miss Lonely
Stay Awhile
Walking Back to Happiness
You Don't Know

Hay, Roy
Church Of the Poison Mind
Do You Really Want to Hurt Me?
It's a Miracle
Karma Chameleon
Move Away
Victims

Hazlewood, Lee
Bonnie Came Back
Guitar Man
Shazam
Sugar Town
These Boots Are Made For Walking

Hazlewood, Mike
Air That I Breathe, The
Freedom Come Freedom Go
Gimme Dat Ding
Good Morning Freedom
Little Arrows
Make Me an Island
You're Such a Good Looking Woman

Hazzard, Tony
Fox on the Run
Ha Ha Said the Clown
Listen to Me
Me the Peaceful Heart

Heaton, Paul
Happy Hour
Little Time, A
Song For Whoever
You Keep it All In

Henderson, Joe
Chick
Somebody
Treble Chance
Trudie
Why Don't They Understand

Henderson, Ray
Alabamy Bound
Animal Crackers In My Soup

'Bam 'Bam 'Bammy Shore
Best Things in Life Are Free, The
Birth of the Blues, The
Black Bottom, The
Broken Hearted
Button Up Your Overcoat
Bye Bye Blackbird
Don't Bring Lulu
Dummy Song, The
Five Foot Two, Eyes of Blue
Follow the Swallow
For Old Times' Sake
Georgette
Good News
Hold My Hand
Humming
I Wonder How I Look When I'm Asleep
I'm a Dreamer, Aren't We All
I'm Sitting on Top of the World
If I Had a Talking Picture of You
If You Hadn't Gone Away
It All Depends on You
Just a Memory
Just Imagine
Keep Your Skirts Down Mary Ann
Life Is Just a Bowl of Cherries
Little Pal
Lucky Day
Lucky in Love
Magnolia
My Sin
Nasty Man
So Blue
Song I Love, The
Sonny Boy
Sunny Side Up
That Old Gang of Mine
That's Why Darkies Were Born
Thrill is Gone, The
Together
Varsity Drag
Why Did I Kiss That Girl?
You're the Cream in My Coffee

Hendrix, Jimi
Angel
Purple Haze
Voodoo Chile
Wind Cries Mary, The

Heneker, David
Dis Donc, Dis Donc
Flash Bang Wallop
Only Fools
Our Language of Love
Thing-ummy-Bob, The

Herbert, A.P.
Girls Were Made to Love and Kiss
Ma Belle Marguerita
Nice Cup of Tea, A
Other People's Babies

Herbert, Victor
Ah Sweet Mystery Of Life
All For You
Gipsy Love Song, The
I Might Be Your Once in a While
I Want What I Want When I Want It
I'm Falling in Love With Someone
Indian Summer
Italian Street Song
Kiss in the Dark, A
Kiss Me Again
March of the Toys, The
'Neath the Southern Moon
Romany Life
Sweethearts
Thine Alone
To the Land of My Own Romance

Toyland
Tramp, Tramp, Tramp Along the Highway
When You're Away

Heyman, Edward
Blue Star (The Medic Theme)
Body and Soul
Boo Hoo
Ho Hum
I Cover the Waterfront
Love Letters
Moonburn
My Darling
Out of Nowhere
They Say
Through the Years
When I Fall In Love
You Oughta Be In Pictures

Heyward, Nick
Fantastic Day
Favourite Shirt
Love Plus One
Nobody's Fool
Whistle Down the Wind

Hill, Andy
Have You Ever Been in Love?
If You Can't Stand the Heat
Land of Make Believe
Making Your Mind Up
My Camera Never Lies
Now Those Days Are Gone

Hill, Billy
Alone at a Table For Two
Call Of the Canyon, The
Down the Oregon Trail
Empty Saddles
Glory of Love, The
In the Chapel in the Moonlight
Last Roundup, The
Lights Out
Night on the Desert
Oh Muki Muki Oh
Old Spinning Wheel, The
On a Little Street in Singapore
Put on an Old Pair of Shoes
Rolling Home
There's a Cabin in the Pines
Wagon Wheels

Hiller, Tony
Angelo
Figaro
Save Your Kisses For Me
Sunny Honey Girl
United We Stand

Hilliard, Bob
Be My Life's Companion
Bouquet of Roses, A
Careless Hands
Castles in the Sand
Civilization
Coffee Song, The
Dear Hearts and Gentle People
Dearie
Downhearted
Ev'ry Street's a Boulevard
Gotta Have Something in the Bank, Frank
I'm in Favour of Friendship
Moonlight Gambler, The
My Little Corner of the World
Only Man on the Island, The
Our Day Will Come
Seven Little Girls Sitting In the Back Seat
Shanghai
Somebody Bad Stole de Wedding Bell
Strawberry Moon in a Blueberry Sky, A

Till They've All Gone Home
Tower of Strength
Zambesi

Hirsch, Louis
Don't Ever Change
Gaby Glide, The
Going Up
Hello Frisco Hello
Love Nest
Tickle Toe, The
Wedding Glide, The

Hirsch, Walter
'Deed I Do
Horsey Keep Your Tail Up
Lullaby in Rhythm
Me and the Moon
Who's Your Little Who-Zis

Hodges, Charles
Ain't No Pleasing You
Ossie's Dream (The Way to Wembley)
Rabbit
Snooker Loopy

Hoffman, Al
Allegheny Moon
Ashby De La Zouch (Castle Abbey)
Auf Wiederseh'n My Dear
Bibbidi-Bobbidi-Boo
Chi-baba Chi-baba
Close to You
Dream Is a Wish Your Heart Makes, A
Everything Stops For Tea
Everythings in Rhythm With My Heart
Fit as a Fiddle
Gangway
Gilly-Gilly Ossenfeffer Katzen Ellen Bogen By the Sea
Goodnight Wherever You Are
Happy Go Lucky You, and Broken Hearted Me
Hawaiian Wedding Song
Heartaches
Hot Diggity
I Apologise
I Can't Tell a Waltz From a Tango
I Paid For That Lie I Told You
I Saw Stars
I Ups to Her, and She Ups to Me
I'd've Baked a Cake
I'm Gonna Live Till I Die
I'm In a Dancing Mood
In the Dim Dim Dawning
Little Co-operation From You, A
Little Man You've Had a Busy Day
Mairzy Doats and Dozy Doats
Me and My Imagination
My First Thrill
My House Is Your House (Mi Casa, Su Casa)
Oh Oh I'm Falling In Love Again
On the Bumpy Road to Love
Papa Loves Mambo
Sailor With the Navy Blue Eyes, The
Santo Natale
She Broke My Heart In Three Places
Story of a Starry Night, The
Takes Two to Tango
There Isn't Any Limit to My Love
There's No Tomorrow
This'll Make You Whistle
Torero
What's the Good Word Mister Bluebird
Where Will the Dimple Be?
Who Walks In (When I Walk Out)
You Can't Be True to Two
You've Got the Wrong Rumba

Hoffman, Jack
Dream Boat
I Love the Sunshine of Your Smile
I Wanna Say Hello
Teresa

Holder, Neville
Bangin' Man
Coz I Luv You
Cum on Feel the Noize
Everyday
Far Far Away
Gudbuy T'Jane
In For a Penny
Look Wot Yu Dun
Mama Weer All Crazee Now
Merry Xmas Everybody
My Friend Stan
My Oh My
Run Run Away
Skweeze Me Pleeze Me
Take Me Back 'Ome
Thanks For the Memory (Wham Bam Thank You Mam)
We'll Bring the House Down

Holland, Brian
Baby Love
Bernadette
(Come Round Here) I'm the One You Need
Happening, The
Heaven Must Have Sent You
I Can't Help Myself
I Guess I'll Always Love You
(I'm a) Road Runner
In and Out of Love
It's the Same Old Song
Love Like Yours, A
Please Mr. Postman
Reach Out I'll Be There
Reflections
Seven Rooms of Gloom
Standing in the Shadows of Love
Stop in the Name of Love
There's a Ghost In My House
This Old Heart of Mine
Where Did Our Love Go?
You Can't Hurry Love
You Keep Me Hangin' on

Holland, Eddie
Baby Love
Bernadette
(Come Round Here) I'm the One You Need
Happening, The
He Was Really Saying Something
Heaven Must Have Sent You
I Can't Help Myself
I Guess I'll Always Love You
(I'm a) Road Runner
In and Out of Love
It's the Same Old Song
Love Like Yours, A
Reach Out I'll Be There
Reflections
Seven Rooms of Gloom
Standing on the Shadows of Love
Stop in the Name of Love
There's a Ghost in My House
This Old Heart of Mine
Where Did Our Love Go?
You Can't Hurry Love
You Keep Me Hangin' on

Hollander, Frederick
Boys in the Back Room, The
Falling in Love Again
It's Raining Sunbeams
Moonlight and Shadows

Holly, Buddy
Maybe Baby
Peggy Sue
Peggy Sue Got Married
That'll Be the Day
True Love Ways
Wishing

Hooker, Brian
Dear Love My Love
Only a Rose
Some Day
Song of the Vagabonds, The

Horn, Trevor
Close (To the Edit)
Double Dutch
Give Me Back My Heart
Mirror Mirror (Mon Amour)
Slave to the Rhythm
Video Killed the Radio Star

Howard, Ken
Bend It
Hideaway
Hold Tight
Save Me

Huff, Leon
Don't Leave Me This Way
I Love Music
If You Don't Know Me By Now
Love Train
Me and Mrs Jones
Now That We've Found Love
Put Your Hands Together
She's a Winner
Show You the Way to Go
Step Off
Take Good Care of Yourself
When Will I See You Again?
Year of Decision
You'll Never Find Another Love Like Mine

Hughes, Alex
Big Eight
Big Seven
Big Six
Big Ten

Hunter, Ian
All the Way From Memphis
Honaloochie Boogie
Once Bitten Twice Shy
Roll Away the Stone

Hupfeld, Herman
As Time Goes By
Let's Put Out the Lights and Go to Sleep
Sing Something Simple
When Yuba Plays the Rumba on the Tuba

Hynde, Chrissie
Brass in Pocket
Don't Get Me Wrong
Talk of the Town
Two Thousand Miles

Idol, Billy
Hot in the City
King Rocker
Rebel Yell
White Wedding

Ilda, Lewis
Getting Around and About
I'm In Love With Two Sweethearts
Just a Little Fond Affection
Little Old Mill
Old Timer

Jackson, Michael
Bad

Beat It
Billie Jean
Can You Feel It
Dirty Diana
Don't Stop Till You Get Enough
Girl Is Mine, The
I Just Can't Stop Loving You
Leave Me Alone
Say Say Say
Shake Your Body (Down to the Ground)
Smooth Criminal
Walk Right Now
Wanna Be Startin' Something
Way You Make Me Feel, The
We Are the World

Jacobs, Al
Every Day of My Life
Hurt
I Need You Now
If I Gave My Heart to You
Please Believe Me

Jaffe, Moe
Bell Bottom Trousers
Collegiate
Gipsy in My Soul
I'm My Own Grandpa
If I Had My Life to Live Over
If You Are But a Dream
Oh You Sweet One

Jagger, Mick
Angie
As Tears Go By
Blue Turns to Grey
Brown Sugar
Emotional Rescue
Fool to Cry, A
Get Off of My Cloud
Have You Seen Your Mother, Baby, Standing in the Shadow?
Honky Tonk Women
I'm Free
It's Only Rock and Roll
Jumping Jack Flash
Last Time, The
Let's Spend the Night Together
Miss You
Nineteenth Nervous Breakdown
Out of Time
Paint it Black
Ruby Tuesday
Satisfaction
Start Me Up
That Girl Belongs to Yesterday
Tumbling Dice
Under My Thumb
We Love You

James, Harry
As If I Didn't Have Enough on My Mind
I'm Beginning to See the Light
Music Makers, The
One O'Clock Jump
Peckin'

James, Mark
Always on My Mind
It's Only Love
Moody Blue
Suspicious Minds

Jay, Fred
Gotta Go Home
Hooray, Hooray, It's a Holi Holiday
Ma Baker
Rasputin
Wedding, The (La Novia)
When a Child Is Born (Soleado)

Jaymes, David
Ay Ay Ay Ay Moosey
Best Years of Our Lives
High Life
Walking in the Rain

Jenkins, Gordon
Blue Prelude
Goodbye
Homesick, That's All
P.S. I Love You
San Fernando Valley

Jerome, John
Broken Wings
Cherry Stones
Paper Kisses
Saturday Rag
You Me and Us

Jerome, M.K.
Bright Eyes
My Little Buckaroo
Some Sunday Morning
Sweet Dreams Sweetheart

Jerome, William
Back Home In Tennessee
Chinatown My Chinatown
Get Out and Get Under the Moon
My Irish Molly-O
Row, Row, Row

Jessel, George
And He'd Say "Oo-la-la Wee-Wee"
Oh How I Laugh When I Think How I
Cried About You
Roses in December

Jobim, Antonio Carlos
Desafinado
Girl From Ipanema, The
One Note Samba (Samba De Uma Nota So)
Quiet Nights Of Quiet Stars (Corcovado)

Joel, Billy
It's Still Rock and Roll to Me
Just the Way You Are
My Life
Tell Her About It
Uptown Girl
We Didn't Start the Fire

John, Dominic
Blossom Fell, A
Dreams Can Tell a Lie
Echo Told Me a Lie, The
When You're In Love

John, Elton
Blue Eyes
Candle In the Wind, A
Crocodile Rock
Daniel
Don't Let the Sun Go Down on Me
Goodbye Yellow Brick Road
I Guess That's Why They Call It the
Blues
I'm Still Standing
Island Girl
Nikita
Part Time Love
Passengers
Philadelphia Freedom
Rocket Man
Sacrifice
Sad Songs (Say So Much)
Saturday Night's Alright For Fighting
Song For Guy
Your Song

Johnson, Holly
Americanos

Love Train
Power of Love, The
Rage Hard
Relax
Two Tribes
Welcome to the Pleasure Dome

Johnson, Howard
Am I Wasting My Time on You?
Feather Your Nest
I Don't Want to Get Well
Ice Cream
In the Woodshed She Said She Would
Ireland Must Be Heaven For My Mother
Came From There
M-O-T-H-E-R
Mystery
What Do We Do on a Dew-Dew-Dewy
Day
What Do You Want to Make Those Eyes
at Me For?
When the Moon Comes Over the Moun-
tain

Johnson, James P.
Charleston
If I Could Be With You (One Hour Tonight)
Joint is Jumpin', the
There's No Two Ways About Love

Johnston, Arthur
Black Moonlight
Cocktails For Two
Day You Came Along, The
Down the Old Ox Road
I'm a Little Blackbird Looking For a Blue-
bird
I'm Sitting High on a Hilltop
It's the Natural Thing to Do
Just One More Chance
Learn to Croon
Moon Got In My Eyes, The
Moon Song (That Wasn't Meant For Me)
Moonstruck
My Old Flame
One, Two, Button Your Shoe
Pennies From Heaven
So Do I
Thanks

Jolly, Steve
All Cried Out
Body Talk
Cruel Summer
Flashback
Just An Illusion
Love Resurrection
Music and Lights
Robert De Niro's Waiting
Shy Boy

Jolson, Al
Anniversary Song, The
Avalon
Back in Your Own Back Yard
California Here I Come
Dirty Hands, Dirty Face
I'll Say She Does
Keep Smiling at Trouble
Little Pal
Me and My Shadow
'N' Everything
Sonny Boy
There's a Rainbow 'Round My Shoulder
You Ain't Heard Nothing Yet

Jones, Alan
Hard to Handle
I Can't Stand Up For Falling Down
Over You
Standing In the Road

Jones, Howard
Hide and Seek
Like to Get to Know You Well
Look Mama
New Song
Pearl In the Shell
Things Can Only Get Better

Jones, Isham
I'll See You in My Dreams
It Had to Be You
No Greater Love
on the Alamo
One I Love Belongs to Somebody Else,
The
Spain
Swingin' Down the Lane
You've Got Me Crying Again

Jones, Steve
Holidays In the Sun
No-one is Innocent
Pretty Vacant
Silly Thing

Jurgens, Dick
Careless
Elmer's Tune
It's a Hundred to One I'm in Love
One Dozen Roses

Jurmann, Walter
All God's Chillun Got Rhythm
Beneath the Lights of Home
In the Spirit Of the Moment
San Francisco
Springtime Reminds Me of You (Deine
Mutter Bleibt Immer Bei Mir)

Kahal, Irving
By a Waterfall
Corn Silk
I Can Dream Can't I
I Left My Sugar Standing in the Rain
I'll Be Seeing You
Let a Smile Be Your Umbrella
Moonlight Saving Time
Night Is Young and You're So Beautiful,
The
Sitting on a Back-Yard Fence
Sunbonnet Blue, A
Three's a Crowd
Wedding Bells Are Breaking Up That
Old Gang of Mine
When I Take My Sugar to Tea
You Brought a New Kind Of Love to Me

Kahn, Gus
Ain't We Got Fun
All God's Chillun Got Rhythm
Around the Corner and Under the Tree
Beside a Babbling Brook
Bimini Bay
Carioca, The
Carolina in the Morning
Charley My Boy
Chloe
Coquette
Day Dreaming
Dream a Little Dream of Me
Earful of Music, An
Flying Down to Rio
Goofus
Guilty
Hour of Parting, The
I Never Knew (That Roses Grew)
I Wish I Had a Girl
I Wonder Where My Baby Is Tonight
I'll Never Be the Same
I'll Say She Does
I'll See You in My Dreams
I'm Sitting High on a Hilltop

I'm Through With Love
I've Had My Moments
It Had to Be You
It's Foolish But It's Fun
Let's Talk About My Sweetie
Little Street Where Old Friends Meet, A
Love Me Forever
Love Me or Leave Me
Makin' Whoopee
Memories
My Baby Just Cares For Me
My Buddy
My Isle Of Golden Dreams
My Ohio Home
Nobody's Sweetheart
Oh! If I Only Had You
Okay Toots
One I Love Belongs to Somebody Else,
The
One Night of Love
Orchids in the Moonlight
Persian Rug
Pretty Baby
Ready For the River
Roses For Remembrance
San Francisco
Some Sunday Morning
Spain
Sweetheart Darling
Swingin' Down the Lane
Sympathy
That Certain Party
There Ain't No Maybe In My Baby's
Eyes
Toot Toot Tootsie Goodbye
Ukulele Lady
Voice in the Old Village Choir, The
Waltzing in the Clouds
When April Sings
When My Ship Comes In
When You and I Were Seventeen
Where the Morning Glories Grow
Where the Shy Little Violets Grow
With All My Heart
Yes Sir, That's My Baby
You Ain't Heard Nothing Yet
You Stepped Out of a Dream
You Toll Mo Your Dream
Your Eyes Have Told Me So

Kalmar, Bert
All Alone Monday
Hello Hawaii, How Are You
I Wanna Be Loved By You
Kiss to Build a Dream on, A
My Sunny Tennessee
Nevertheless
Oh What a Pal Was Mary
Only When You're in My Arms
So Long, Oo-long (How Long You
Gonna Be Gone)
Thinking of You
Three Little Words
Up in the Clouds
What a Perfect Combination
Who's Sorry Now

Kamosi, Manuela
Get Up (Before the Night Is Over)
Megamix
Pump Up the Jam
Rockin' Over the Beat

Kander, John
Cabaret
Money Song, The
My Colouring Book
New York, New York

Kassel, Art
Around the Corner and Under the Tree

Chewing Gum
Sobbin' Blues
That's the Moon My Son

Kaye, Buddy
'A' You're Adorable
Boys Cry
Christmas Alphabet
Full Moon and Empty Arms
In the Middle of Nowhere
Italian Theme, The (Mambo Caliente)
Little By Little
Next Time
Oh So Wunderbar
Penny a Kiss, A Penny a Hug, A
Speedy Gonzales
This Is My Prayer (Non Ho L'eta Per
Amarti)
'Till the End of Time
Time

Keller, Jack
Breaking In a Brand New Broken Heart
Everybody's Somebody's Fool
Forever Kind of Love, A
How Can I Meet Her
It Started All Over Again
My Heart Has a Mind of It's Own
No One Can Make My Sunshine Smile
One Way Ticket
Run to Him
Venus in Blue Jeans

Kelly, Tom
Alone
Eternal Flame
I Drove All Night
Like a Virgin
So Emotional
True Colours

Kemp, Gary
Chant Number One
Communication
Gold
I'll Fly For You
Instinction
Lifeline
Muscle Bound
Only When You Leave
Round and Round
Through the Barricades
To Cut a Long Story Short
True

Kendis, James
Feather Your Nest
If I Had My Way
Underneath the Russian Moon
When It's Night Time In Italy, It's Wed-
nesday Over Here

Kennedy, Jimmy
All Our Tomorrows
And Mimi
Apple Blossom Wedding, An
April in Portugal (Coimbra)
At the Cafe Continental
Beside My Caravan
Bird on the Wing
Cafe In Vienna
Chestnut Tree, The
Cinderella Stay In My Arms
Coronation Waltz, The
Did Your Mother Come From Ireland?
Down the Old Spanish Trail
Down the Trail of Aching Hearts
French Can Can Polka
General's Fast Asleep, The
Handsome Territorial, A
Harbour Lights

Home Town
Hour Never Passes, An
Isle Of Capri
Istanbul (Not Constantinople)
Little Valley In the Mountains
Love Is Like a Violin (Mon Coeur Est Un
Violin)
Misty Islands of the Highlands
My Prayer
My Song Goes Round the World
Never Goodbye
Oh Donna Clara
Oh Nicholas Don't Be So Ridiculous
Ol' Faithful
Pigalle
Play to Me Gipsy
Red Sails in the Sunset
Roll Along Covered Wagon
Romeo
Saint Mary's in the Twilight
Serenade in the Night
South of the Border
Sunset Trail, The
Teddy Bear's Picnic, The
Ten Pretty Girls
There's a Boy Coming Home on Leave
Washing on the Siegfried Line
Why Did She Fall For the Leader of the
Band?

Kenny, Charles
After a While
Gone Fishin'
Love Letters In the Sand
There's a Gold Mine In the Sky
While a Cigarette Was Burning

Kenny, Nick
After a While
Carelessly
Gone Fishin'
Love Letters In the Sand
There's a Gold Mine In the Sky
While a Cigarette Was Burning

Kent, Walter
Ah But It Happens
I Never Mention Your Name, Oh No
I'm Gonna Live Till I Die
Last Mile Home, The
Mama I Wanna Make Rhythm
Pu-leeze Mr. Hemingway
White Cliffs of Dover, The
Who Dat Up Dere

Kern, Jerome
All the Things You Are
All Through the Day
Bill
Bullfrog Patrol, The
Can I Forget You
Can't Help Lovin' Dat Man
Can't Help Singing
Dancing Time
Day Dreaming
Dearly Beloved
Don't Ever Leave Me
Fine Romance, A
Folks Who Live on the Hill, The
I Dream Too Much
I Won't Dance
I'm Old Fashioned
I've Told Every Little Star
Kalua
Last Time I Saw Paris, The
Left All Alone Again Blues
Long Ago and Far Away
Look For the Silver Lining
Lovely to Look At
Make Believe
Moon Love

More and More
Night Was Made For Love, The
Ol' Man River
Pick Yourself Up
She Didn't Say "Yes"
Smoke Gets in Your Eyes
Song Is You, The
Sunny
They Didn't Believe Me
Till the Clouds Roll By
Touch of Your Hand, The
Two Little Blue Birds
Waltz in Swing Time
Way You Look Tonight, The
Whip-Poor-Will
Who
Whose Baby Are You?
Why Do I Love You?
Why Was I Born?
Wild Rose
Yesterdays
You Were Never Lovelier
You're Here and I'm Here

Kershaw, Nik
Dancing Girls
Don Quixote
I Won't Let the Sun Go Down on Me
Riddle, The
Wide Boy
Wouldn't it Be Good

King, Carole
At the Club
Crying in the Rain
Don't Bring Me Down
Don't Ever Change
Go Away Little Girl
Goin' Back
Halfway to Paradise
He's In Town
How Many Tears
I Feel the Earth Move
I Want to Stay Here
I'd Never Find Another You
I'm Into Something Good
It Might as Well Rain Until September
It's Too Late
Keep Your Hands Off My Baby
Let's Turkey Trot
Loco - Motion, The
Oh No Not My Baby
Sharing You
Some of Your Lovin'
Take Good Care of My Baby
Up on the Roof
When My Little Girl Is Smiling
Will You Love Me Tomorrow
You've Got a Friend

King, Mark
It's Over
Lessons in Love
Running in the Family
Something About You
Sun Goes Down, The
To Be With You Again

King, Robert
I Ain't Nobody's Darling
Ice Cream
Keep Your Skirts Down Mary Ann
Moonlight on the Colorado
Seminola
Why Did I Kiss That Girl

Klages, Ray
Doin' the Raccoon
Just You, Just Me
Pardon Me Pretty Baby
to Be Worthy of You

Klenner, John
Heartaches
Just Friends
Round the Bend of the Road
Walk In Love

Kluger, Jean
Cuba
D.I.S.C.O.
Hands Up (Give Me Your Heart)
Que Sera Mi Vida (If You Should Go)

Knopfler, Mark
Money For Nothing
Private Investigations
Romeo and Juliet
Sultans of Swing
Twisting By the Pool
Walk of Life

Koehler, Ted
Animal Crackers in My Soup
As Long as I Live
Between the Devil and the Deep Blue Sea
By the Shalimar
Don't Worry 'Bout Me
Every Night About This Time
Everybody's Twisting
Get Happy
I Gotta Right to Sing the Blues
I'm Shooting High
I've Got My Fingers Crossed
I've Got the World on a String
Kicking the Going Around
Let's Fall In Love
Lovely Lady
Mia Bella Rosa
Now I Know
Out In the Cold Again
Some Sunday Morning
Stay on the Right Side of the Road
Stormy Weather
Sweet Dreams Sweetheart
There's No Two Ways About Love
Truckin'
When the Sun Comes Out
Wrap Your Troubles In Dreams

Kongos, John
Kinky Afro
Step on
Tokoloshe Man

Kramer, Alex
Ain't Nobody Hear But Us Chickens
Candy
Come With Me My Honey
Far Away Places
It All Comes Back to Me Now
It's Love, Love, Love
Money Is the Root of All Evil
My Sister and I
That's the Beginning of the End
Weep No More My Lady

Lane, Burton
Everything I Have is Yours
Feudin' and Fightin'
How About You
How Are Things In Glocca Morra
How'd Ya Like to Love Me
I Hear Music
If This Isn't Love
Lady's in Love With You, The
On a Clear Day You Can See Forever
Says My Heart
Swing High, Swing Low

Lane, Ronnie
How Come
Itchycoo Park

My Mind's Eye
Tin Soldier
Universal

Lauder, Harry
End of the Road, The
I Love a Lassie
It's Nice to Get Up in the Morning
Just a Wee Deoch An' Doris
Roamin' In the Gloamin'
She is Ma Daisy
Stop Your Tickling Jock
We Parted on the Shore
Wedding O' Sandy McNab

Lawrence, Jack
All or Nothing At All
Beyond the Sea
Hold My Hand
If I Didn't Care
In An Eighteenth Century Drawing Room
It's Funny to Everyone But Me
Johnson Rag
Linda
My Heart Isn't in it
No One But You
Play Fiddle Play
Poor People of Paris, The
Sunrise Serenade
Symphony
Tenderly
Tu-li-Tulip Time
What Will I Tell My Heart
With the Wind and the Rain in Your Hair
Yes My Darling Daughter

Le Bon, Simon
Election Day
Notorious
Reflex, The
Wild Boys, The

Le Brunn, George
If It Wasn't For the 'Ouses In Between
It's a Great Big Shame
Liza Johnson
Oh Mr Porter

Le Clerq, Arthur
He Played His Ukulele As the Ship Went Down
I Bought Myself a Bottle Of Ink
Nobody Loves a Fairy When She's Forty
What Can You Give a Nudist on His Birthday

Lea, James
Gudbuy T'Jane
In For a Penny
Look Wot Yu Dun
Mama Weer All Crazee Now
My Oh My
Take Me Back 'ome

Lea, Jimmy
Bangin' Man
Coz I Luv You
Cum on Feel the Noize
Everyday
Far Far Away
Merry Xmas Everybody
My Friend Stan
Skweeze Me Pleeze Me
Thanks For the Memory (Wham Bam Thank You Mam)

Leander, Mike
Always Yours
Another Time Another Place
Boy From Nowhere
Do You Wanna Touch Me
Doing Alright With the Boys

Early In the Morning
Hello Hello I'm Back Again
High Time
I Didn't Know I Loved You ('Till I Saw You Rock 'n' Roll)
I Love You Love Me Love
I'm the Leader of the Gang (I Am)
I've Been a Bad Bad Boy
Lady Godiva
Little Boogie Woogie
Love Like You and Me, A
Oh Yes You're Beautiful
Remember Me This Way
Rock and Roll Part 1 & 2

Lecuona, Ernesto
Always In My Heart
Another Night Like This
As We Are Today
Say "Si Si" (Para Vigo Me Voy)
Siboney

Lee, Bert
And the Great Big Saw Came Nearer
Good Bye-ee
Hello, Hello, Who's Your Lady Friend
Josh-u-ah
Knees Up Mother Brown
My Little Dietcher Girl
My Word You Do Look Queer
Olga Pulloffski (The Beautiful Spy)
Paddy McGinty's Goat
Stop and Shop At the Co-Op Shop
With Her Head Tucked Underneath Her Arm

Lee, Lester
Bread and Butter Woman, A
Christmas Dreaming
Dreamer With a Penny
Fire Down Below
Man From Laramie, The
Pennsylvania Polka
Prize Of Gold
Sabre Dance

Lee, Peggy
I Don't Know Enough About You
It's a Good Day
Johnny Guitar
Manana - Is Soon Enough For Me

Leeway, Joe
Doctor! Doctor!
Hold Me Now
Lay Your Hands on Me
Love on Your Side
We Are Detective
You Take Me Up

Lehar, Franz
Gigolette
Gipsy Maiden
Girls Were Made to Love and Kiss
Gold and Silver Waltz, The
I Love You So (The Merry Widow Waltz)
Love and Wine
Maxim's
Oh Maiden My Maiden
Patiently Smiling
Pierette & Pierrot
Say Not Love Is a Dream
Serenade Frasquita (Farewell My Love, Farewell)
Vilia
White Dove, The
You Are My Heart's Delight

Leiber, Jerry
Baby I Don't Care
Bossa Nova Baby
Charlie Brown

Hound Dog
I (Who Have Nothing) (Uno Del Tanti)
Jailhouse Rock
King Creole
Lorelei
Loving You
Lucky Lips
Pearl's a Singer
Searchin'
She's Not You
Spanish Harlem
Stand By Me
Yakity Yak

Leigh, Carolyn
Day the Circus Left Town, The
Hey Look Me Over
Stowaway
Witchcraft
Young At Heart

Leigh, Fred W.
Army of Today's Alright, The
Captain Gingah
Don't Dilly Dally on the Way
Galloping Major, The
Jolly Good Luck to the Girl Who Loves a Soldier
Little Bit Off the Top, A
Little of What You Fancy, A
Poor John
Put on Your Tat-ta Little Girlie
Waiting At the Church
Why Am I Always the Bridesmaid

Leigh, Rowland
Elizabeth
I Give My Heart
Just Once For All Time
Live, Laugh and Love
Tell Me I'm Forgiven

Leitch, Donovan
Goo Goo Babarabajagal (Love Is Hot)
Hurdy Gurdy Man, The
Jennifer Juniper
Mellow Yellow
Sunshine Superman
There Is a Mountain
Walkin'

Lennon, John
All My Loving
All You Need Is Love
Bad to Me
Ballad of John and Yoko, The
Can't Buy Me Love
Cold Turkey
Come Together
Day Tripper
Dear Prudence
Do You Want to Know a Secret
Eleanor Rigby
From a Window
From Me to You
Get Back
Girl
Give Peace a Chance
Goodbye
Got to Get You Into My Life
Happy Christmas (War Is Over)
Hard Day's Night, A
Hello Goodbye
Hello Little Girl
Help
Hey Jude
I Feel Fine
I Saw Him Standing There
I Wanna Be Your Man
I Want to Hold Your Hand
I'll Keep You Satisfied

Imagine
Instant Karma
It's For You
Jealous Guy
(Just Like) Starting Over
Lady Madonna
Let It Be
Love Me Do
Lucy In the Sky With Diamonds
Michelle
Nobody I Know
Nobody Told Me
Ob-la-di Ob-la-da
Paperback Writer
Penny Lane
Please Please Me
Power to the People
Rain
She Loves You
She's Leaving Home
Step Inside Love
Strawberry Fields Forever
Ticket to Ride
We Can Work It Out
When I'm Sixty-Four
With a Little Help From My Friends
Woman
World Without Love, A
Yellow Submarine
Yesterday
You've Got to Hide Your Love Away

Lennox, Annie
Here Comes the Rain Again
It's Alright (Baby's Coming Back)
Love Is a Stranger
Right By Your Side
Sex Crime (Nineteen Eighty Four)
Sisters Are Doing It For Themselves
Sweet Dreams (Are Made of This)
There Must Be An Angel Playing With My Heart
Thorn In My Side
Who's That Girl

Leon, Harry
Bedtime Story, A
Goodbye Hawaii
In a Golden Coach
Liszt, Chopin and Mendelssohn
Me and the Old Folks At Home
Sally

Leonard, Patrick
Cherish
Dear Jessie
Hanky Panky
Like a Prayer
Live to Tell
Look Of Love
Who's That Girl

Lerner, Alan Jay
Almost Like Being In Love
Get Me to the Church on Time
Gigi
Heather on the Hill, The
How Could You Believe Me When I Said I Love You, When You Know I've Been a Liar All My Life
How to Handle a Woman
I Could Have Danced All Night
I Talk to the Trees
I've Grown Accustomed to Her Face
If Ever I Would Leave You
Night They Invented Champagne, The
On a Clear Day You Can See Forever
On the Street Where You Live
Thank Heaven For Little Girls
They Call the Wind Maria
Too Late Now

Wanderin' Star
With a Little Bit of Luck
Wouldn't It Be Luverly

Leslie, Edgar
Among My Souvenirs
Blue
By the River Saint Marie
Crazy People
Dirty Hands, Dirty Face
For Me and My Gal
Get Out and Get Under
Hello Hawaii, How Are You
(Home In) Pasadena
I Wish I Were Twins
In a Little Gipsy Tearoom
It Looks Like Rain in Cherry Blossom
Lane
Little Bit Independent, A
Me and Jane in a Plane
Me and the Man In the Moon
Mistakes
Moon Was Yellow, The
Oh What a Pal Was Mary
On Treasure Island
Perhaps You'll Think of Me
Robins and Roses
Rose of the Rio Grande
Shepherd of the Hills
When You Played the Organ and I Sang
The Rosary

Letters, William
Check Out the Groove
Flanagan
Has Anybody Here Seen Kelly
Molly O'Morgan

Levine, Irwin
Black Pearl
Candida
I Must Be Seeing Things
Knock Three Times
Say, Has Anyone Seen My Sweet
Gypsy Rose
Tie a Yellow Ribbon
What Are You Doing Sunday

Lewis, Al
Adoration Waltz, The
Blueberry Hill
Breeze, The (That's Bringing My Honey
Back to Me)
Bungalow, a Piccolo and You, A
Dream Mother
Finger Of Suspicion, The
Gonna Get a Girl
I'm Crazy Over You
Ninety-Nine Out of a Hundred
No! No! A Thousand Times No
Now's the Time to Fall In Love
On the Bumpy Road to Love
Rose O'Day
Start the Day Right
Sweet Child (I'm Wild About You)
Way Back Home
Why Don't You Fall In Love With Me?

Lewis, Bunny
Beyond the Stars
Let's Talk About Love
Milord
Voice in the Wilderness, A

Lewis, Sam M.
Cheerie Beerie Be
Crying For the Carolines
Dinah
Five Foot Two, Eyes of Blue
For All We Know
Gloomy Sunday (Szomoru Vasarnap)
Have a Little Faith In Me

How Ya Gonna Keep 'Em Down on the
Farm
I Believe In Miracles
I Kiss Your Hand Madame (Ich Kusse
Ihr Hand Madame)
I Wonder
I'd Love to Fall Asleep and Wake Up In
My Mammy's Arms
I'm Sitting on Top of the World
In a Little Spanish Town
In Shadowland
Just Friends
King For a Day
La De De, La De Da
Laugh Clown Laugh
My Mammy
(My Sweet) Hortense
Rock-a-bye Your Baby With a Dixie
Melody
Round the Bend of the Road
Sam You Made the Pants Too Long
Street of Dreams
When You're a Long Long Way From
Home
Where Did Robinson Crusoe Go With
Friday on Saturday Night

Lewis, Terry
Finest, The
Human
I Didn't Mean to Turn You on
Just Be Good to Me
Let's Wait Awhile
Saturday
What Have You Done For Me Lately
When I Think of You

Linzer, Sandy
Breaking Down the Walls of Heartache
If You're Lookin' For a Way Out
Let's Hang on
Lovers Concerto
Native New Yorker
Skiing in the Snow
Use it Up and Wear it Out
Working My Way Back to You
You Can Do Magic

Lippman, Sidney
'A' You're Adorable
Chickery Chick
House With Love in it, A
If Anyone Finds This, I Love You
Laroo Laroo Lilli Bolero
Too Young

Lipton, Dan
My Girl's a Yorkshire Girl
Oh Oh Antonio
Put Me Among the Girls
She's a Lassie From Lancashire

Lisbona, Eddie
Don't Fall In Love
Don't Leave Me Now
I Get Up Every Morning (What Do I Do,
What Do I Do, What Do I Do)
I Keep Forgetting to Remember
I Once Had a Heart Margarita
It's My Mother's Birthday Today
Out of the Night
Shoemaker's Serenade, The
When the Guardsman Started Crooning
on Parade

Little, Jack
Hold Me
I Hope to Die If I Told a Lie
In a Shanty In Old Shanty Town
Jealous
Little Rain Must Fall, A
Ting-a-ling (The Waltz of the Bells)

Where's My Sweetie Hiding

Livingston, Jay
As I Love You
Buttons and Bows
Copper Canyon
Dime and a Dollar, A
Golden Earrings
Home Cooking
I'll Always Love You
In the Arms of Love
Let Me Be Loved
Mona Lisa
Que Sera, Sera
Streets of Laredo, The
Tammy
To Each His Own

Livingston, Jerry
Ashby De La Zouch (Castle Abbey)
Bibbidi-Bobbidi-Boo
Chi-baba Chi-baba
Close to You
Darkness on the Delta
Dream is a Wish Your Heart Makes, A
It's the Talk of the Town
Just a Kid Named Joe
Mairzy Doats and Dozy Doats
She Broke My Heart in Three Places
Sixty Seconds Got Together
Song of Delilah, The
Story of a Starry Night, The
Stowaway
Thoughtless
Twelfth of Never
Under a Blanket of Blue
Veni-Vidi-Vici
What's the Good Word Mister Bluebird
Who Are We

Lloyd Webber, Andrew
All I Ask of You
Another Suitcase in Another Hall
Don't Cry For Me Argentina
I Am the Starlight
I Don't Know How to Love Him
Memory
Music of the Night
Oh What a Circus
Phantom of the Opera, The
Pie Jesu
Superstar
Take That Look Off Your Face

Loeb, John Jacob
Boo Hoo
Get Out Those Old Records
Ma, I Miss Your Apple Pie
Masquerade
Reflections in the Water

Loesser, Frank
Adelaide
Adelaide's Lament
Anywhere I Wonder
Baby It's Cold Outside
Bloop Bleep
Boys In the Back Room, The
Bushel and a Peck, A
Can't Get Out of This Mood
Dolores
Dreamer, The
Hello Mom
Hoop Dee-doo
How Sweet You Are
How'd Ya Like to Love Me
I Don't Want to Walk Without You
I Get the Neck of the Chicken
I Hear Music
I Wish I Didn't Love You So
I Wish I Were Twins

I'll Never Let a Day Pass By
I'm Riding For a Fall
I've Never Been In Love Before
If I Were a Bell
In My Arms
Jingle, Jangle, Jingle
Katy Did, Katy Didn't
Kiss the Boys Goodbye
Lady's In Love With You, The
Let's Get Lost
Luck Be a Lady Tonight
Moon Of Manakoora, The
My Darling, My Darling
"Murder" He Says
No Two People
Now That I Need You
On a Slow Boat to China
Once In Love With Amy
Praise the Lord and Pass the Ammunition
Sand In My Shoes
Say It
Says My Heart
Sewing Machine, The
Sit Down You're Rocking the Boat
Small Fry
Spring Will Be a Little Late This Year
Standing on the Corner
They're Either Too Young or Too Old
Touch of Texas
Two Sleepy People
Ugly Duckling, The
Woman In Love, A
Wonderful Copenhagen

Loewe, Frederick
Almost Like Being In Love
Get Me to the Church on Time
Gigi
Heather on the Hill, The
How to Handle a Woman
I Could Have Danced All Night
I Talk to the Trees
I've Grown Accustomed to Her Face
If Ever I Would Leave You
Night They Invented Champagne, The
On the Street Where You Live
Thank Heaven For Little Girls
They Call the Wind Maria
Wanderin' Star
With a Little Bit of Luck
Wouldn't It Be Luverly

Lombardo, Carmen
Boo Hoo
Coquette
Get Out Those Old Records
Ma, I Miss Your Apple Pie
Powder Your Face With Sunshine
Return to Me (Ritorna Ame)
Ridin' Around in the Rain
Snuggled on Your Shoulder
Sweetest Music This Side of Heaven, The

Lordan, Jerry
Apache
Atlantis
Conversations
Diamonds
Girl Like You, A
Good Times (Better Times)
I'm Just a Baby
I've Waited So Long
Mary Anne
Scarlett O'Hara
Who Could Be Bluer
Wonderful Land

Loudermilk, John D.
Angela Jones
Ebony Eyes

Goggle Eye
Indian Reservation
Language of Love, The
Norman
This Little Bird
Tobacco Road
Waterloo

Lowe, Bernie
Remember You're Mine
Teddy Bear
Wandering Eyes
Wild One

Lowe, Chris
Domino Dancing
Heart
I'm Not Scared
In Private
It's a Sin
Left to My Own Devices
Nothing Has Been Proved
Opportunities
Rent
Suburbia
West End Girls
What Have I Done to Deserve This

Lubin, Joe
Don't Fall In Love
I Get Up Every Morning (What Do I Do, What Do I Do, What Do I Do)
I Keep Forgetting to Remember
Move Over Darling
Shoemaker's Serenade, The
'Till Stars Forget to Shine
Tutti Frutti

Lyle, Graham
Heart on My Sleeve
I Don't Wanna Lose You
I Should Have Known Better
I Wanna Stay With You
Malt and Barley Blues
We Don't Need Another Hero
What's Love Got to Do With It
When I'm Dead and Gone

Lyle, Kenneth
Army Of Today's Alright, The
Here We Are, Here We Are, Here We Are Again
Jolly Good Luck to the Girl Who Loves a Soldier

Lyman, Abe
Driftwood
I Cried For You
Mary Lou
(What Can I Say) After I Say I'm Sorry

Lynne, Jeff
10538 Overture
All Over the World
Confusion
Diary of Horace Wimp, The
Don't Bring Me Down
Evil Woman
Hold on Tight
Livin' Thing
Mister Blue Sky
Rockaria
Shine a Little Love
Showdown
Sweet Talkin' Woman
Telephone Line
Wild West Hero
Xanadu
You Got It

Lynot, Phil
Boys Are Back In Town, The

Dancin' In the Moonlight
Don't Believe a Word
Killer on the Loose
Parisienne Walkways
Waiting For An Alibi

MacAulay, Tony
Baby Make It Soon
Baby Now That I've Found You
Blame It on the Pony Express
Build Me Up Buttercup
Don't Give Up on Us
Down on the Beach Tonight
Falling Apart At the Seams
Gasoline Alley Bred
Going In With My Eyes Open
Home Lovin' Man
I Get a Little Sentimental Over You
In the Bad Bad Old Days
It Sure Brings Out the Love In Your Eyes
Kissin' In the Back Row Of the Movies
Let the Heartaches Begin
Let's Have a Quiet Night In
Lights Of Cincinnati, The
Love Grows
Mexico
Play Me Like You Play Your Guitar
Silver Lady
Something Here In My Heart
Something Old, Something New
Sorry Suzanne
That Same Old Feeling
You Won't Find Another Fool Like Me
You're More Than a Number In My Little Red Book

MacDermot, Galt
African Waltz
Ain't Got No
Aquarius
Good Morning Starshine
I Got Life
Let the Sunshine in

MacDonald, Ballard
Beautiful Ohio
Breeze (Blow My Baby Back to Me)
Clap Hands, Here Comes Charley
If I Should Plant a Tiny Seed of Love
Parade of the Wooden Soldiers
Play That Barbershop Chord
Rose of Washington Square
There's a Girl In the Heart of Maryland
Trail of the Lonesome Pine

Mack, Cecil
Charleston
He's a Cousin of Mine
Shine
Teasing

MacLeod, John
Baby Now That I've Found You
Let the Heartaches Begin
Mexico
Something Here In My Heart
That Same Old Feeling

Madonna (See Ciccone, Madonna)

Madden, Edward
Bluebell
By the Light of the Silvery Moon
Down In Jungle Town
Goodbye Summer, So Long Fall, Hello Wintertime
Moonlight Bay
Silver Bell
Two Little Boys

Mael, Ron
Amateur Hour
Beat the Clock
Never Turn Your Back on Mother Earth
Number One Song In Heaven, The
This Town Ain't Big Enough For the
Both of Us

Magidson, Herb
Conchita, Marquita, Lolita, Pepita, Ro-
sita, Juanita Lopez
Continental, The
Enjoy Yourself
Gone With the Wind
Goodnight Angel
Here's to Romance
I Can't Love You Anymore
I'll Buy That Dream
I'll Dance At Your Wedding
I'm Stepping Out With a Memory Tonight
Linger in My Arms a Little Longer Baby
Masquerade is Over, The
Music Maestro Please
Roses in December
Say a Prayer For the Boys Over There

Magine, Frank
Balloons (Who'll Buy My Nice Balloons)
By the Shalimar
Mia Bella Rosa
Rose
Venetian Moon

Mancini, Henry
Days of Wine and Roses
How Soon
In the Arms of Love
Moon River
Peter Gunn
Thorn Birds (Love Theme)

Mann, Barry
Bless You
Come on Over to My Place
Counting Teardrops
Don't Know Much
Don't Make My Baby Blue
Footsteps
How Much Love
I Just Can't Help Believing
I Love How You Love Me
I'm Gonna Be Strong
In the Rain
It's Getting Better
Looking Through the Eyes of Love
Saturday Night at the Movies
Sometimes When We Touch
Somewhere Out There
Warpaint
We've Gotta Get Out of This Place
You've Lost That Lovin' Feelin'

Mann, Dave
Castles In the Sand
Dearie
Downhearted
I'm In Favour of Friendship
No Moon at All
Only Man on the Island, The
Somebody Bad Stole De Wedding Bell
There I've Said It Again

Mann, Kal
Dancin' Party
Let's Twist Again
Remember You're Mine
Teddy Bear
Wandering Eyes
Wild One

Manning, Dick
Allegheny Moon

Fascination
Gilly-Gilly Ossenfeffer Katzen Ellen
Bogen By the Sea
Hawaiian Wedding Song
Hot Diggity
I Can't Tell a Waltz From a Tango
Jilted
Like I Do
Morningside of the Mountain, The
My House Is Your House (Mi Casa, Su
Casa)
Oh Oh I'm Falling In Love Again
Papa Loves Mambo
Santo Natale
Takes Two to Tango
Torero
While the Angelus Was Ringing
You Can't Be True to Two

Marcus, Sol
Ask Anyone Who Knows
Don't Let Me Be Misunderstood
I Don't Want to Set the World on Fire
Till Then
When the Lights Go on Again

Marley, Bob
Buffalo Soldier
Could You Be Loved
Exodus
I Shot the Sheriff
Is This Love
Jamming
One Love
Stir It Up

Marr, John
Heaven Knows I'm Miserable Now
Panic
Sheila Take a Bow
What Difference Does It Make

Marriott, Steve
All or Nothing
Hey Girl
Itchycoo Park
Lazy Sunday
My Mind's Eye
Natural Born Bugie
Tin Soldier
Universal

Martin, Bill
All of Me Loves All of You
Baby I Love You, O.K.
Back Home
Bump, The
Congratulations
Fancy Pants
Forever and Ever
Heart of Stone
Julie-Ann
My Boy
Puppet on a String
Remember (Sha-la-la)
Shang-a-lang
Summer Love Sensation
Surround Yourself With Sorrow

Martin, Hugh
Boy Next Door, The
Buckle Down Winsocki
Have Yourself a Merry Little Christmas
Love
Occasional Man, An
Trolley Song, The

Marvin, Hank B.
Day I Met Marie, The
Foot Tapper
Gee Whiz, It's You
Genie With the Light Brown Lamp

Geronimo
I Could Easily Fall
In the Country
On the Beach
Rise and Fall of Flingle Bunt
Shindig
Throw Down a Line
Time Drags By

Maschwitz, Eric
At the Balalaika
Climbing Up
Goodnight Vienna
Mademoiselle De Paris
Mariandl-Andl-Andl
Nightingale Sang In Berkeley Square, A
Pair of Silver Wings, A
Rainy Day Refrain, A (Schnürlregen)
Room Five Hundred and Four

Mason, Barry
Bicyclettes De Belsize
Can I Take You Home Little Girl
Delilah
Don't Turn Around
Good Love Can Never Die
Here It Comes Again
I Pretend
I'm Coming Home
Last Waltz, The
Love Grows
Love Is All
Love Me Tonight (Alla Fine Della Strada)
Man Without Love, A (Quando M'innamo-
ro)
One-Two-Three O'Leary
There Goes My First Love
When Forever Has Gone
Winter World of Love
You Just Might See Me Cry

Masser, Michael
Do You Know Where You're Going to
Greatest Love of All
In Your Eyes
Miss You Like Crazy
Nothing's Gonna Change My Love For You
Saving All My Love For You
Tonight I Celebrate My Love
Touch Me in the Morning

May, Hans
Break of Day
Love of My Life
Love Steals Your Heart
My Song Goes Round the World
Starlight Serenade
Windsor Waltz, The

May, Simon
Always There (Howard's Way Theme)
Anyone Can Fall In Love
Born With a Smile on My Face
Every Loser Wins
More Than in Love
Summer of My Life, The

McCarthy, Joseph
Alice Blue Gown
Following the Sun Around
I'm Always Chasing Rainbows
I'm In the Market For You
If You're In Love You'll Waltz
Ireland Must Be Heaven For My Mother
Came From There
Irene
Kinkajou, The
Rambling Rose
Rio Rita
Saw Mill River Road, The
Sweetheart We Need Each Other

They Go Wild Simply Wild Over Me
What Do You Want to Make Those Eyes
At Me For
You Made Me Love You

McCartney, Paul
All My Loving
All You Need Is Love
Another Day
Bad to Me
Ballad of John and Yoko, The
Band on the Run
Can't Buy Me Love
Come and Get It
Come Together
Coming Up
Day Tripper
Dear Prudence
Do You Want to Know a Secret
Ebony and Ivory
Eleanor Rigby
From a Window
From Me to You
Get Back
Girl
Give Peace a Chance
Goodbye
Goodnight Tonight
Got to Get You Into My Life
Hard Day's Night, A
Helen Wheels
Hello Goodbye
Hello Little Girl
Help
Hey Jude
Hi Hi Hi
I Feel Fine
I Saw Her Standing There
I Wanna Be Your Man
I Want to Hold Your Hand
I'll Keep You Satisfied
It's For You
Jet
Lady Madonna
Let 'Em In
Let It Be
Listen to What the Man Said
Live and Let Die
Love Me Do
Lucy In the Sky With Diamonds
Mary Had a Little Lamb
Michelle
Mull of Kintyre
My Love
No More Lonely Nights
Nobody I Know
Ob-la-di Ob-la-da
Once Upon a Long Ago
Paperback Writer
Penny Lane
Pipes Of Peace, The
Please Please Me
Rain
Say Say Say
She Loves You
She's Leaving Home
Silly Love Songs
Spies Like Us
Step Inside Love
Strawberry Fields Forever
Ticket to Ride
Waterfalls
We All Stand Together
We Can Work It Out
When I'm Sixty-Four
With a Little Help From My Friends
With a Little Luck
Wonderful Christmas Time
World Without Love, A

Yellow Submarine
Yesterday
You've Got to Hide Your Love Away

McCoy, Van
Baby Don't Change Your Mind
Come Back and Finish What You
Started
Hustle, The
I Get the Sweetest Feeling
Shuffle, The
This Is It
When You're Young and In Love

McGlennon, Felix
Comrades
Her Golden Hair Was Hanging Down
Her Back
Sons of the Sea

McHugh, Jimmy
Bandanna Babies
Blue Again
Can't Get Out of This Mood
Coming In on a Wing and a Prayer
Cuban Love Song
Diga Diga Doo
Dinner at Eight
Doin' the New Lowdown
Don't Blame Me
Everything is Hotsy Totsy Now
Go Home and Tell Your Mother
Goodbye Blues
Here Comes Heaven Again
How Blue the Night
I Can't Believe That You're In Love With
Me
I Can't Give You Anything But Love
I Couldn't Sleep a Wink Last Night
I Feel a Song Coming on
I Get the Neck of the Chicken
I Love to Whistle
I Won't Dance
I'm In the Mood For Love
I'm Shooting High
I've Got My Fingers Crossed
In a Moment of Madness
It's a Most Unusual Day
It's the Darndest Thing
Let's Get Lost
Lost In a Fog
Love Me As Though There Were No
Tomorrow
Lovely Lady
Lovely to Look At
Lovely Way to Spend An Evening, A
"Murder" He Says
Music Stopped, The
My Own
On the Sunny Side of the Street
Say a Prayer For the Boys Over There
Say It
Singin' the Blues
South American Way
There's Something In the Air
Too Young to Go Steady
Touch of Texas
When My Sugar Walks Down the Street
Where Are You
With All My Heart
You're a Sweetheart
You're as Pretty as a Picture
You've Got Me This Way

McKuen, Rod
I Think of You (Il Faut Trouver Le Temp
D'Aimer)
If You Go Away (Ne Me Quitte Pas)
Love's Been Good to Me
Seasons In the Sun (Le Moribond)

Meek, Joe
Don't You Think It's Time
Globetrotter
Ice Cream Man
Robot
Telstar

Mellin, Robert
I'm Yours
My One and Only Love
Stranger on the Shore
Wedding Bells (Hochzeitsglocken)
You, You, You

Mellor, Tom
I Wouldn't Leave My Little Wooden Hut
For You
Kitty the Telephone Girl
When It's Apple Blossom Time in Nor-
mandy

Melson, Joe
Blue Angel
Blue Bayou
Crying
Only the Lonley
Run Baby Run
Running Scared

Mercer, Johnny
Ac-cent-tchu-ate the Positive
And the Angels Sing
Arthur Murray Taught Me Dancing In a
Hurry
Autumn Leaves
Baby Doll
Bernadine
Bless Yore Beautiful Hide
Blues in the Night
Bob White
Come Rain or Come Shine
Could Be
Day Dreaming
Day In, Day Out
Days of Wine and Roses
Dearly Beloved
Dream
Fleet's in, The
Fools Rush in
G.I. Jivo, Tho
Goin' Co'tin'
Goody Goody
Have You Got Any Castles Baby
Hit the Road to Dreamland
Hooray For Hollywood
How Little We Know
I Promise You
I Remember You
I'm an Old Cow-Hand
I'm Old Fashioned
If I Had a Million Dollars
In the Cool, Cool, Cool of the Evening
Jeepers Creepers
June Comes Around Every Year
Laura
Lazybones
Let's Take the Long Way Home
Lost
Mister Meadowlark
Moon River
My Shining Hour
Not Mine
Old Music Master, The
On the Atchison, Topeka and the Santa
Fe
Out Of This World
P.S. I Love You
Ride, Tenderfoot, Ride
Skylark
Sobbin' Women
Something's Gotta Give

Spring, Spring, Spring
Tangerine
That Old Black Magic
This Time the Dream's on Me
Too Marvellous For Words
Wait and See
Waiter and the Porter and the Upstairs Maid, The
When the World Was Young
While We Danced At the Mardi Gras
Wings Over the Navy
Wonderful Wonderful Day
You Grow Sweeter as the Years Go By
You Must Have Been a Beautiful Baby
You Were Never Lovelier
You've Got Me This Way
You've Got Me Where You Want Me
Your Heart and Mine

Mercury, Freddie
Barcelona
Bicycle Race
Bohemian Rhapsody
Crazy Little Thing Called Love
Don't Stop Me Now
Friends Will Be Friends
I Was Born to Love You
It's a Hard Life
Killer Queen
Love Kills
Play the Game
Seven Seas of Rhye, The
Somebody to Love
We Are the Champions

Merrill, Bob
All the Time and Everywhere
Beggar in Love, A
Belle, Belle, My Liberty Belle
Candy and Cake
Chick a Boom
Christopher Columbus
Cuff of My Shirt, The
Don't Rain on My Parade
Feet Up
I'd've Baked a Cake
If I Had a Golden Umbrella
In the Middle of a Dark Dark Night
Kid's Last Fight, The
Look at That Girl
Make Yourself Comfortable
Mambo Italiano
Me and My Imagination
Miracle of Love, The
Mustafa
My Truly Truly Fair
Nairobi
People
She Wears Red Feathers
Sparrow in the Treetop
Sweet Old Fashioned Girl
That Doggie in the Window
That's Why
There's a Pawnshop on the Corner
There's Always Room At Our House
Walkin' to Missouri
We Won't Live in a Castle
When the Boys Talk About the Girls
Where Will the Dimple Be
You Don't Have to Be a Baby to Cry

Meskill, Jack
On the Beach At Bali Bali
Pardon Me Pretty Baby
Rhythm of the Rain
Smile, Darn Ya Smile
There's Danger in Your Eyes Cherie
Were You Sincere
When the Organ Played O Promise Me

Meyer, George W.
Brown Eyes Why Are You Blue?
Everything Is Peaches Down in Georgia
For Me and My Gal
Hiawatha's Melody of Love
I Believe In Miracles
I'm a Little Blackbird Looking For a Bluebird
I'm Sure of Everything But You
In the Land of Beginning Again
Mandy Make Up Your Mind
My Song of the Nile
Silver Rose
There Are Such Things
When You're a Long Long Way From Home
Where Did Robinson Crusoe Go With Friday on Saturday Night?
You Taught Me How to Love
You're Dancing on My Heart

Meyer, Joseph
California Here I Come
Clap Hands, Here Comes Charley
Crazy Rhythm
Cup Of Coffee, a Sandwich and You, A
Fancy Our Meeting
I Wish I Were Twins
I Wonder
Idle Gossip
If You Knew Susie
My Honey's Lovin' Arms
Tonight's My Night With Baby

Michael, George
Bad Boys
Careless Whisper
Club Tropicana
Different Corner
Edge of Heaven
Everything She Wants
Faith
Freedom
I Want Your Sex
I'm Your Man
Last Christmas
Monkey
One More Try
Praying For Time
Wake Me Up Before You Go Go
Wham Rap (Enjoy What You Do)
Young Guns (Go For It)

Miller, Frank
Green Fields
If You're Irish Come Into the Parlour
Love is a Golden Ring
Marianne
Memories Are Made of This
Mister Tap-Toe

Miller, Ned
Dark Moon
Don't Mind the Rain
From a Jack to a King
Sunday

Miller, Roger
England Swings
King of the Cops
King of the Road
Swiss Maid

Miller, Ron
For Once in My Life
I've Never Been to Me
Touch Me in the Morning
Yester-Me Yester-You Yesterday

Miller, Sonny
By Candlelight
Don't Ring-a Da Bell

Got a Date With An Angel
I'd Love to Fall Asleep
I'll Come to You
Pavements of Paris, The (Sur Le Pavé)
Remember Me
Russian Rose
Seventeen Candles
Silver Wings in the Moonlight
Starlight Serenade
They Can't BlackOut the Moon
'Till Stars Forget to Shine
Vieni, Vieni
Where the Waters Are Blue

Mills, A.J.
By the Side of the Zuyder Zee
Do You Remember the Last Waltz
Everybody's Crazy on the Foxtrot
Fall in and Follow Me
Just Like the Ivy
Ship Ahoy
Take Me Back to Dear Old Blighty
We All Walked Into the Shop
What Ho She Bumps
When I Take My Morning Promenade
Why Did I Leave My Little Back Room

Mills, Irving
Caravan
Everything Is Hotsy Totsy Now
House of David Blues, The
I Let a Song Go Out of My Heart
In a Sentimental Mood
It Don't Mean a Thing (If i t Ain't Got That Swing)
Let's Have a Jubilee
Lovesick Blues
Minnie the Moocher
Mood Indigo
Moonglow
Nobody Knows What a Red-Head Mama Can Do
Organ Grinders Swing
Ring Dem Bells
Rockin' in Rhythm
Sidewalks of Cuba
Solitude
Someone Stole Gabriel's Horn
Sophisticated Lady
Straighten Up and Fly Right
There's No Two Ways About Love
When My Sugar Walks Down the Street

Mills, Kerry
At a Georgia Camp Meeting
Meet Me in St. Louis
Red Wing
Whistling Rufus

Mitchell, Joni
Big Yellow Taxi
Both Sides Now
This Flight Tonight
Woodstock

Mitchell, Neil
Angel Eyes (Home and Away)
Sweet Little Mystery
Sweet Surrender
Wishing I Was Lucky

Mitchell, Sidney
Ashes of Roses
Big City Blues
Breakaway, The
Laughing Irish Eyes
Melody From the Sky, A
Seventh Heaven
Sugar
That's You Baby

Toy Trumpet
Twilight on the Trail
Walking With Susie
You Turned the Tables on Me

Mizzy, Vic
Choo'n' Gum
Didja Ever
Jones Boy, The
My Dreams Are Getting Better All the Time
Pretty Kitty Blue Eyes
Sailor With the Navy Blue Eyes, The
Take it Easy
That's What a Rainy Day is For
Three Little Sisters
Whole World is Singing My Song

Moll, Billy
Hang Out the Stars in Indiana
Ice Cream
Moonlight on the Colorado
Ro-ro-Rollin' Along
Wrap Your Troubles in Dreams

Monaco, Jimmy
Ah-Ha
Ain't it a Shame About Mame
Apple For the Teacher, An
April Played the Fiddle
Crazy People
Dirty Hands, Dirty Face
East Side of Heaven
Every Night About This Time
Hang Your Heart on a Hickory Limb
I Can't Begin to Tell You
I Haven't Time to Be a Millionaire
I'm Making Believe
I've Got a Pocketful of Dreams
Man and His Dream, A
Me and the Man In the Moon
Meet the Sun Half Way
My Heart Is Taking Lessons
On the Sentimental Side
Only Forever
Pessimistic Character, The (With the Crab Apple Face)
Rhythm on the River
Row, Row, Row
Sing a Song of Sunbeams
Six Lessons From Madame La Zonga
Sweet Potato Piper
That Sly Old Gentleman (From Featherbed Lane)
That's For Me
Too Romantic
We Musn't Say Goodbye
What Do You Want to Make Those Eyes At Me For?
When the Moon Comes Over Madison Square
You Made Me Love You

Monckton, Lionel
Arcady Is Ever Young
Come to the Ball
Little Miss Melody
Moonstruck
My Dear Little Cingalee
Pearl of Sweet Ceylon, The
Pipes of Pan, The
Soldiers In the Park, The
Temple Bell, The
Tony From America
Toy Town
Try Again Johnnie
Under the Deodar
When You Are in Love
Whisper to Me

Monnot, Marguerite
Dis Donc, Dis Donc
If You Love Me (Hyme a L'amour)
Left Bank, The (C'est a Hambourg)
Milord
Our Language of Love
Poor People of Paris, The

Montgomery, Bob
Heartbeat
Honey
Misty Blue
Wind Me Up (Let Me Go)
Wishing

Morali, Jacques
Can't Stop the Music (La Musique N'a Pas De Fin)
Go West
Street Dance
Y.M.C.A.

Moret, Neil
Chloe
Mello Cello
Moonlight and Roses
Persian Rug
Ready For the River
She's Funny That Way
Song of the Wanderer, The

Morey, Larry
Bambi
Ferdinand the Bull
Heigh-Ho
I'm Wishing
Lavender Blue
Little April Shower
Love Is a Song
One Song
Some Day My Prince Will Come
Whistle While You Work
With a Smile and a Song

Moroder, Giorgio
Call Me
Flashdance - What a Feeling
From Here to Eternity
Givin' Up Givin' In
Good Grief Christina
I Feel Love
I Remember Yesterday
Love Kills
Love to Love You Baby
Love's Unkind
Never Ending Story
Runner, The
Son of My Father
Take My Breath Away
Together in Electric Dreams

Morris, Ken
Heartless
Hong Kong Garden
Mister Moon You've Got a Million Sweethearts
Primrose Hill

Morrisey, Steven
Everyday is Like Sunday
Heaven Knows I'm Miserable Now
Panic
Sheila Take a Bow
What Difference Does It Make

Morse, Theodore F.
Bluebell
Down in Jungle Town
I'm Sorry I Made You Cry
M-O-T-H-E-R
Two Little Boys

Morton, Hugh
She Is the Belle of New York
Teach Me How to Kiss
They All Follow Me
Wine, Woman and Song

Moss, Jonathan
Church of the Poison Mind
Do You Really Want to Hurt Me
Time (Clock of the Heart)
Victims

Moy, Sylvia
I Was Made to Love Her
It Takes Two
My Cherie Amour
Never Had a Dream Come True

Moyet, Alison
All Cried Out
Is This Love
Love Resurrection
Nobody's Diary
Other Side of Love, The

Muir, Lewis
Hitchy-Koo
Play That Barbershop Chord
Ragtime Cowboy Joe
Waiting For the Robert E. Lee

Murphy, C.w.
Flanagan
Has Anybody Here Seen Kelly?
Hold Your Hand Out Naughty Boy
I Live in Trafalgar Square
Let's All Go Down the Strand
Little Yellow Bird
My Girl's a Yorkshire Girl
Oh Oh Antonio
Put Me Among the Girls
She's a Lassie From Lancashire
We All Go the Same Way Home

Murphy, Stanley
Be My Little Baby Bumble Bee
Oh How She Could Yacki Hacki Wicki Wacki Woo
On the Five-fifteen
Put on Your Old Gray Bonnet

Murray, Fred
Boiled Beef and Carrots
Ginger You're Barmy
I'm Henery the Eighth
It's All Right in the Summertime
Little Bit Off the Top, A
Our Lodger's Such a Nice Young Man

Murray, Mitch
Ballad of Bonnie and Clyde, The
Billy Don't Be a Hero
Black-Eyed Boys, The
Even the Bad Times Are Good
Goodbye Sam, Hello Samantha
Hitchin' a Ride
How Do You Do It
Hush Not a Word to Mary
I Did What I Did For Maria
I Like It
I'm Telling You Now
Night Chicago Died, The
Ragamuffin Man
You Were Made For Me

Musel, Bob
Band of Gold, The
Homecoming Waltz, The
Out of the Night
Poppa Piccolono (Papaveri E Papere)
Tell Me Marianne (A Media Luz)

Musker, Frank
Dancing With the Captain
Grandma's Party
Modern Girl
My Simple Heart
Woman in Love, A

Myers, Mike
Attention to Me
Don't Make Waves
Gotta Pull Myself Together
I'm in the Mood For Dancing
Love of My Life
New Beginning
Think I'm Gonna Fall in Love With You
Wanted

Myers, Sherman
Butterflies in the Rain
Just Humming Along
Moonlight on the Ganges
Queen Was in the Parlour, The

Myrow, Joseph
Five O'Clock Whistle, The
If I'm Lucky
Wilhelmina
You Make Me Feel So Young

Nash, Graham
Carrie Anne
Jennifer Eccles
On a Carousel
Stop Stop Stop

Neiburg, Al
Darkness on the Delta
I'm Confessin'
It's a Hap-Hap-Happy Day
It's the Talk of the Town
Under a Blanket of Blue

Newell, Norman
By the Fountains of Rome
Come What May (Apres Toi)
Go (Before You Break My Heart) (Si)
Importance of Your Love, The (Important C'est La Rose)
Jeannie
Melba Waltz, The
More
More Than Love
My Thanks to You
Never, Never, Never (Grande, Grande, Grande)
Nice to Know You Care
Portrait of My Love, A
Promises
Say Wonderful Things
Song of Capri, The
That's How a Love Song Was Born

Newley, Anthony
Goldfinger
Gonna Build a Mountain
Look At That Face
What Kind of Fool Am I?
Who Can I Turn to?
Wonderful Day Like Today, A

Newman, Lionel
Again
As if I Didn't Have Enough on My Mind
I Met Her on Monday
Kiss
Never
River of No Return, The

Newman, Randy
Just One Smile
Mama Told Me Not to Come
My Way of Thinking
Nobody Needs Your Love

Simon Smith and His Amazing Dancing Bear

Nicholls, Horatio
Adeline
Among My Souvenirs
Amy, Wonderful Amy
Babette
Back to Those Happy Days
Badge From Your Coat, The
Bathing in the Sunshine
Bedtime Story, A
Blue Eyes
Bouquet (I Shall Always Think of You)
Delilah
Delyse
Down Forget-Me-Not Lane
Gipsy Melody
Golden West, The
Heart of a Rose
It Costs So Little
Janette
Just Like a Thief
Let's All Go to the Music Hall
Liszt, Chopin and Mendelssohn
Mistakes
Omaha
Persian Rosebud
Playthings
Riviera Rose
Romany Rose
Sahara
Shanghai
Shepherd of the Hills
Sunny Havana
That Old Fashioned Mother of Mine
Toy Drum Major, The
When the Guards Are on Parade
Whispering Pines of Nevada, The

Noble, Ray
By the Fireside
Cherokee
Goodnight Sweetheart
I Found You
I Hadn't Anyone 'Till You
I'll Be Good Because of You
Love is the Sweetest Thing
Touch of Your Lips
Very Thought of You, The

Noel, Art
Broken Hearted Clown
If You Ever Go to Ireland
Kiss Me Goodnight Sergeant-Major
Little Drummer Boy, The
Nursie
What More Can I Say
You Don't Have to Tell Me, I Know

Nolan, Kenny
Get Dancing
Lady Marmalade (Voulez-Vous Coucher Avec Moi Ce Soir)
My Eyes Adored You
Ride a Wild Horse
Swing Your Daddy

Novello, Ivor
And Her Mother Came Too
Fold Your Wings
Glamorous Night
I Can Give You the Starlight
Keep the Home Fires Burning
Love is My Reason
My Dearest Dear
My Life Belongs to You
Primrose
Rose of England
Shine Through My Dreams
Some Day My Heart Will Awake

Take Your Girl
Waltz of My Heart
We'll Gather Lilacs
When the Gypsy Played

Numan, Gary
Are 'Friends' Electric
Cars
Complex
I Die, You Die
She's Got Claws
We Are Glass
We Take Mystery to Bed

O'Connor, Desmond
How Lucky You Are
Let's Do it Again
Let's Keep it That Way
Roll Me Over
'Till All Our Dreams Come True
When You're in Love

O'Dowd, George
Church of the Poison Mind
Do You Really Want to Hurt Me?
It's a Miracle
Karma Chameleon
Move Away
Time (Clock of the Heart)
Victims

O'Sullivan, Gilbert
Alone Again (Naturally)
Clair
Get Down
No Matter How I Try
Nothing Rhymed
Ooh-Wakka-Doo-Wakka-Day
We Will
Why Oh Why Oh Why

O'Toole, Mark
Power of Love, The
Rage Hard
Relax
Two Tribes
Welcome to the Pleasure Dome

Oakey, Philip
Being Boiled
Don't You Want Me
(Keep Feeling) Fascination
Love Action (I Believe in Love)
Mirror Man
Open Your Heart
Together In Electric Dreams

Oakland, Ben
I'll Dance at Your Wedding
I'll Take Romance
Java Jive
Roses In December
Sidewalks of Cuba

Ocean, Billy
Caribbean Queen
Get Out of My Dreams, Get Into My Car
Suddenly
When the Going Gets Tough, The Tough Get Going

Olman, Abe
Down Among the Sheltering Palms
Down By the O-Hi-O
Oh! Johnny Oh!
Some Sweet Day

Orbison, Roy
Blue Angel
Blue Bayou
Crying
Falling
Goodnight

In Dreams
It's Over
Oh Pretty Woman
Only the Lonely
Running Scared
There Won't Be Many Coming Home
You Got It

Orzabal, Roland
Chance
Everybody Wants to Rule the World
Head Over Heels
Mad World
Pale Shelter
Shout
Sowing the Seeds of Love

Osborne, Gary
Amoureuse
Blue Eyes
Forever Autumn
Part Time Love

Owens, Harry
Blue Shadows and White Gardenias
Down Where the Trade Winds Blow
Linger Awhile
Sing Me a Song of the Islands
Sweet Leilani

Pace, Daniele
Do It, Do It Again (A Far L'amore Comincia Tu)
Go (Before You Break My Heart) (Si)
Love Me Tonight (Alla Fine Della Strada)
My Little Lady (Non Illuderti Mai)
Suddenly You Love Me (Uno Tranquillo)

Padilla, Jose
Ca C'est Paris
Relicairo, El
Valencia
Who'll Buy My Violets (La Violetera)

Paich, David
Africa
Hold the Line
Lady Love Me (One More Time)
Lido Shuffle

Panzeri, Mario
Come Prima (More Than Ever)
Go (Before You Break My Heart) (Si)
Love Me Tonight (Alla Fine Della Strada)
My Little Lady (Non Illuderti Mai)
Poppa Piccolono (Papaveri E Papere)
Suddenly You Love Me (Uno Tranquillo)
This is My Prayer (Non Ho L'Eta Per Amarti)

Paramor, Norrie
Frightened City, The
Let's Talk About Love
Lonely
Once Upon a Dream
Savage, The
Voice in the Wilderness, A

Parfitt, Richard
Again and Again
Living on An Island
Mystery Song, The
Roll Over Lay Down
Whatever You Want

Parish, Mitchell
All My Love
Ciao Ciao Bambina (Piove)
Deep Purple
Don't Be That Way
Hands Across the Table

Lamp Is Low
Let Me Love You Tonight (No Te Importe Saber)
Lilacs in the Rain
Moonlight Serenade
One Morning in May
Ruby
Sentimental Gentleman From Georgia, A
Sidewalks of Cuba
Sleigh Ride
Sophisticated Lady
Stairway to the Stars
Stardust
Stars Fell on Alabama
Sweet Lorraine
Tzena, Tzena, Tzena
Volare (Nel Blu Dipinto Di Blu)

Parker, Ross
Blue Ribbon Gal
Blue Skies Are Round the Corner
Girl in the Alice Blue Gown, The
Hang on the Bell Nellie
Hey Neighbour
I Shall Always Remember You Smiling
I Shall Be Waiting
I Won't Tell a Soul (That I Love You)
I'll Make Up For Everything
Memories Live Longer Than Dreams
There'll Always Be An England
There's a Land of Begin Again
We'll Meet Again
Your Heart and My Heart

Parr-Davies, Harry
Fairy on the Christmas Tree, The
Happy Ending
I Leave My Heart in An English Garden
In My Little Snapshot Album
It's in the Air
Mary Rose
My Paradise
Never Say Goodbye
Pedro the Fisherman
Sing As We Go
Sweetest Song In the World, The
Wish Me Luck As You Wave Me Goodbye

Parsons, Geoffrey
Autumn Concerto
Believe In Me (Sur Ma Vie)
Bella Musica
Chee Chee-oo-Chee
Eternally (Terry's Theme)
Good Companions, The
If You Go (Si Tu Partais)
If You Love Me (Hyme a L'amour)
Little Serenade (Piccolissima Serenata)
Little Shoemaker, The (Le Petit Cordonnier)
Mama
Mandolin Serenade
Mister Cuckoo (Cuculino)
O Mein Papa
Seine, La
Smile
Stars Shine In Your Eyes
With Your Love (Mes Mains)

Peacock, Trevor
Mrs. Brown You've Got a Lovely Daughter
Mystery Girl
That's What Love Will Do

Pease, Harry
I Don't Want to Get Well
In a Little Secondhand Store
In a Shady Nook By a Babbling Brook
Moon at Sea

Peggy O'Neil

Pellow, Marti
Angel Eyes (Home and Away)
Sweet Little Mystery
Sweet Surrender
Wishing I Was Lucky

Pelosi, Don
Angel of the Great White Way
Broken Hearted Clown
Ferry Boat Inn, The
It Happened in Adano
Kiss Me Goodnight Sergeant-Major
Little Drummer Boy, The
Little Old Mill
Nursie
Old Ship of Mine
Stars Will Remember, The
When the Poppies Bloom Again
When You Lose the One You Love
You Don't Have to Tell Me, I Know

Pepper, Harry S.
Carry Me Back to Green Pastures
Drink, Drink Brothers Drink (Trink, Trink Bruderlein Trink)
Hear My Song Violetta (Hor Mein Lied Violetta)
I Lost My Heart in Heidelberg
Oh Maiden My Maiden
Rags, Bottles or Bones

Peretti, Hugo
Can't Give You Anything (But My Love)
Can't Help Falling in Love
Funky Weekend
Let's Put it All Together
Na Na Is the Saddest Word
Sing Baby Sing
Sixteen Bars
Star on a TV Show
Walkin' Miracle, A
Wild in the Country

Perren, Freddie
Don't Take Away the Music
Heaven Must Be Missing An Angel
I Will Survive
Reunited
Whodunit

Petrie, Henry W.
Asleep In the Deep
I Don't Want to Play in Your Yard
Where the Sunset Turns the Ocean's Blue to Gold

Petty, Norman
Heartbeat
Maybe Baby
Not Fade Away
Oh Boy
Peggy Sue
Rave on
That'll Be the Day
True Love Ways
Wheels

Phillips, John
California Dreamin'
Creeque Alley
I Saw Her Again Last Night
Monday Monday
San Francisco

Pilat, Lorenzo
Go (Before You Break My Heart) (Si)
Love Me Tonight (Alla Fine Della Strada)
My Little Lady (Non Illuderti Mai)
Suddenly You Love Me (Uno Tranquillo)

Pinkard, Maceo
Gimme a Little Kiss, Will Ya, Huh
Mammy O'Mine
Sugar
Sweet Georgia Brown
Sweet Man
Them There Eyes

Pirroni, Marco
Antmusic
Apollo 9
Dog Eat Dog
Friend or Foe
Goody Two Shoes
Kings of the Wild Frontier
Prince Charming
Puss 'n' Boots
Stand and Deliver

Pitchford, Dean
Fame
Footloose
Holding Out For a Hero
Let's Hear It For the Boy

Pockriss, Lee
Catch a Falling Star
Four Little Heels
Itsy Bitsy Teenie Weenie Yellow Polka
Dot Bikini
Kites
My Heart is An Open Book
My Little Corner of the World
Seven Little Girls Sitting in the Back
Seat
Tracy
When Julie Comes Around

Pola, Eddie
Girl With the Dreamy Eyes
I Love the Way You Say 'Goodnight'
I Said My Pyjamas (And Put on My
Prayers)
I'm Gonna Wash My Hands of You
Marching Along Together
Quicksilver
Sleep My Baby Sleep
'Till the Lights of London Shine Again
Wedding of Mr Mickey Mouse

Pollack, Lew
Angela Mia
Charmaine
Cheatin' on Me
Diane
Miss Annabelle Lee
My Yiddishe Momme
Seventh Heaven
Sing Baby Sing
That's a Plenty
Toy Trumpet

Pomus, Doc
Can't Get Used to Losing You
His Latest Flame
Kiss Me Quick
Mess of Blues, A
Save the Last Dance For Me
She's Not You
Surrender
Suspicion
Sweets For My Sweet
Teenager in Love, A

Popp, Andre
Love Is Blue (L'amour Est Bleu)
Portuguese Washerwomen, The (Les
Lavandieres Du Portugal)
Tom Pillibi
Years May Come, Years May Go

Porter, Cole
After You - Who
Aleez Vous-en, Go Away
All of You
All Through the Night
Always True to You In My Fashion
Anything Goes
At Long Last Love
Be a Clown
Begin the Beguine
Blow, Gabriel, Blow
C'est Magnifique
Ca C'est L'amour
Do I Love You, Do I
Don't Fence Me In
Easy to Love
Ev'ry Time We Say Goodbye
Experiment
Friendship
From This Moment on
Get Out of Town
Gipsy In Me, The
I Concentrate on You
I Get a Kick Out of You
I Hate Men
I Love Paris
I Love You
I Love You Samantha
I'm in Love Again
I've Got My Eyes on You
I've Got You on My Mind
I've Got You Under My Skin
In the Still of the Night
It's All Right With Me
It's D'Lovely
Just One of Those Things
Let's Be Buddies
Let's Do It (let's Fall In Love)
Love For Sale
Miss Otis Regrets
Most Gentlemen Don't Like Love
My Heart Belongs to Daddy
Night and Day
Physician, The
Ridin' High
Rosalie
So in Love
Solomon
Too Darn Hot
True Love
Well, Did You Evah?
What is This Thing Called Love
Who Wants to Be a Millionaire
Why Can't You Behave
Wunderbar
You Do Something to Me
You'd Be So Nice to Come Home to
You're the Top
You've Got That Thing

Posford, George
At the Balalaika
Goodnight Vienna
London I Love, The
Room Five Hundred and Four
World is Mine Tonight, The

Powell, Teddy
Boots and Saddle
March Winds and April Showers
Snake Charmer, The
Somebody's Thinking of You Tonight

Presley, Elvis
All Shook Up
Don't Be Cruel
Heartbreak Hotel
Love Me Tender
Space Jungle, The

Prince, Hughie
Beat Me Daddy, Eight to the Bar
Boogie Woogie Bugle Boy
I Guess I'll Get the Papers and Go Home
Let's Have Another One

Puzey, Robert
Attention to Me
Don't Make Waves
Gotta Pull Myself Together
I'm In the Mood For Dancing
Wanted

Rado, James
Ain't Got No
Aquarius
Good Morning Starshine
Let the Sunshine In

Ragni, Gerome
Ain't Got No
Aquarius
Good Morning Starshine
Let the Sunshine In

Rainger, Ralph
Blue Hawaii
Ebbtide
Faithful Forever
Funny Old Hills, The
Here Lies Love
I Have Eyes
I Wished on the Moon
June in January
Love in Bloom
Moanin' Low
Oh the Pity of it All
Please
Thanks For the Memory
With Every Breath I Take
You Started Something

Raleigh, Ben
Do You Really Love Me Too (Fools
Errand)
Donkey Song, The
Faith Can Move Mountains
First Row Balcony
Laughing on the Outside
Tell Laura I Love Her
Wonderful Wonderful
You Walk By

Ram, Buck
Afterglow
Great Pretender, The
Magic Touch
Only You
Twilight Time

Randell, Denny
Breaking Down the Walls of Heartache
I Wanna Dance Wit Choo (Do Dat
Dance)
Let's Hang on
Lovers Concerto
Native New Yorker
Skiing In the Snow
Working My Way Back to You

Raye, Don
Beat Me Daddy, Eight to the Bar
Boogie Woogie Bugle Boy
Cow Cow Boogie
Domino
He's My Guy
House of Blue Lights, The
I Still Love You All
I'll Remember April
Irresistible You
Let's Have Another One
Milkman Keep Those Bottles Quiet

Mister Five By Five
Music Makers, The
Scrub Me Mama With a Boogie Beat
Star Eyes
Struttin' With Some Barbecue
Watch the Birdie
Well All Right

Razaf, Andy
Ain't Misbehavin'
Blue Turning Grey Over You
Honeysuckle Rose
I'm Gonna Move to the Outskirts of Town
In the Mood
Joint is Jumpin', the
Louisiana
Memories of You
My Fate is in Your Hands
S'posin'
Stompin' at the Savoy
That's What I Like About the South
What Did I Do to Be So Black and Blue

Record, Eugene
Have You Seen Her
Homely Girl
It's Time For Love
Too Good to Be Forgotten
You Don't Have to Go

Redding, Otis
Dock of the Bay, The
Hard to Handle
Respect
Sweet Soul Music

Redmond, John
Buffalo Billy
Dream, Dream, Dream
Gaucho Serenade, The
I Came, I Saw, I Conga'd
Man With the Mandolin, The
Sky Blue Shirt and a Rainbow Tie, A

Reed, Les
Bicyclettes De Belsize
Daughter of Darkness
Delilah
Don't Bring Me Your Heartaches
Hello Happiness
Here it Comes Again
I Pretend
I'm Coming Home
It's Not Unusual
Last Waltz, The
Leave a Little Love
Leeds United
Love is All
Please Don't Go
Tell Me When
There's a Kind of Hush
Winter World of Love

Reid, Billy
Anything I Dream Is Possible
Bridge of Sighs, The
Coming Home
Danger Ahead
Gipsy, The
I Still Believe
I'll Close My Eyes
I'm Walking Behind You
It's a Pity to Say Goodnight
My First Love, My Last Love For Always
Reflections on the Water
Snowy White Snow and Jingle Bells
This is My Mother's Day
Tree in the Meadow, A

Reid, L.A.
Every Little Step

Girlfriend
I'm Your Baby Tonight
On Our Own
Roses Are Red
Superwoman

Reine, Michael
Give Her My Love
Homing Waltz, The
Love of My Life
Rose I Bring You, The
Wedding of Lilli Marlene, The
Windsor Waltz, The

Rene, Leon
I Lost My Sugar In Salt Lake City
Someone's Rocking My Dreamboat
When It's Sleepy Time Down South
When the Swallows Come Back to Capistrano

Revel, Harry
Afraid to Dream
Did You Ever See a Dream Walking
From the Top of Your Head (To the Tip of Your Toes)
Goodnight My Love
Head Over Heels In Love
Here Comes Cookie
I Feel Like a Feather In the Breeze
I'm Going Back to Old Nebraska
I'm Humming, I'm Whistling, I'm Singing
Love Thy Neighbour
May I
May I Have the Next Romance With You
Never In a Million Years
Paris in the Spring
Star Fell Out of Heaven, A
Stay As Sweet As You Are
Take a Number From One to Ten
There's a Lull in My Life
To Mary With Love
Underneath the Harlem Moon
Wake Up and Live
When I'm With You
With My Eyes Wide Open I'm Dreamin'
Without a Word of Warning
You Can't Have Everything
You Hit the Spot

Reyam, George
Daddy Cool
Ma Baker
Rasputin
Rivers of Babylon, The

Rhodes, Nick
Election Day
Notorious
Reflex, The
Wild Boys, The

Rice, Tim
Another Suitcase in Another Hall
Don't Cry For Me Argentina
I Don't Know How to Love Him
I Know Him So Well
Oh What a Circus
One Night in Bankok
Superstar
Winter's Tale, A

Richard(s), Keith
Angie
As Tears Go By
Blue Turns to Grey
Brown Sugar
Emotional Rescue
Fool to Cry, A
Get Off of My Cloud
Have You Seen Your Mother, Baby, Standing in the Shadow

Honky Tonk Women
I'm Free
It's Only Rock and Roll
Jumping Jack Flash
Last Time, The
Let's Spend the Night Together
Nineteenth Nervous Breakdown
Out of Time
Paint it Black
Ruby Tuesday
Satisfaction
Start Me Up
That Girl Belongs to Yesterday
Tumbling Dice
Under My Thumb
We Love You

Richie, Lionel
All Night Long
Dancing on the Ceiling
Easy
Endless Love
Hello
Lady
Running With the Night
Sail on
Say You, Say Me
Still
Stuck on You
Three Times a Lady
Truly
We Are the World

Richman, Harry
C'est Vous (It's You)
Miss Annabelle Lee
Moonlight Saving Time
Ro-ro-Rollin' Along
Say it Again
Singing a Vagabond Song
There's Danger in Your Eyes Cherie
Walkin' My Baby Back Home

Robbins, Marty
Devil Woman
El Paso
White Sport Coat, A (And a Pink Carnation)
You Don't Owe Me a Thing

Roberts, Allan
Amado Mio
Bread and Butter Woman, A
Dreamer With a Penny
Every Single Little Tingle of My Heart
Good, Good, Good
Into Each Life Some Rain Must Fall
Put the Blame on Mame
Sabre Dance
Tampico
That Old Devil Called Love
What's the Good Word Mister Bluebird
You Always Hurt the One You Love
You Sang My Love Song to Somebody Else

Roberts, Paddy
Angel of the Great White Way
Ballad of Bethnal Green, The
Book, The
Evermore
Good Companions, The
Heart of a Man
Horsey, Horsey
In Love For the Very First Time
It's a Boy
Johnny is the Boy For Me
Lay Down Your Arms
Meet Me on the Corner
Pickin' a Chicken
Softly, Softly

That Dear Old Gentleman
Three Galleons, The (Las Tres Carabelas)
You Are My First Love

Robertson, B.A.
Bang Bang
Carrie
Hold Me
Knocked It Off
Living Years
To Be or Not to Be
We Have a Dream
Wired For Sound

Robin, Leo
All Through the Day
Beyond the Blue Horizon
Blue Hawaii
Bye Bye Baby
Diamonds Are a Girl's Best Friend
Ebbtide
Faithful Forever
For Every Man There's a Woman
Funny Old Hills, The
Gal In Calico, A
Hallelujah
Here Lies Love
Hooray For Love
I Can't Escape From You
I Have Eyes
I'm a One Man Girl
Journey to a Star, A
June In January
Louise
Love In Bloom
Love Is Just Around the Corner
Moonlight and Shadows
My Cuties Due At Two to Two Today
My Ideal
No Love, No Nothing
Oh But I Do
Oh the Pity of It All
Please
Prisoner of Love
Rainy Night In Rio, A
Thanks For the Memory
Turntable Song, The
With Every Breath I Take
You Started Something
Zing a Little Zong

Robin, Sid
Congratulations
My Monday Date
That's My Home
Undecided

Robinson, J. Russel
Margie
Mary Lou
Palesteena
Singin' the Blues ('Till My Daddy Comes Home)
Tomorrow (I'll Be In My Dixie Home Again)

Robinson, Sylvia
Message, The
Pillow Talk
Shame Shame Shame
White Lines (Don't Don't Do It)

Robinson, William
Automatically Sunshine
Floy Joy
I Don't Blame You At All
My Girl
My Guy
Still Water
Tears of a Clown, The

Robison, Carson
Barnacle Bill the Sailor
Carry Me Back to the Lone Prairie
Life Get's Tedious, Don't It
Runaway Train, The

Rodgers, Nile
Dance, Dance, Dance
Everybody Dance
Good Times
He's the Greatest Dancer
I Want Your Love
I'm Coming Out
Le Freak
Lost In Music
My Old Piano
Rapper's Delight
Thinking of You
Upside Down
We Are Family
Why

Rodgers, Richard
Bali Ha'i
Bewitched, Bothered and Bewildered
Blue Moon
Blue Room, The
Carousel Waltz, The
Climb Ev'ry Mountain
Cock-Eyed Optimist, A
Dancing on the Ceiling
Do I Love You Because You're Beautiful
Do-Re-Mi
Edelweiss
Everything I've Got
Falling in Love With Love
Fellow Needs a Girl, A
Gentleman Is a Dope, The
Getting to Know You
Girl Friend, The
Happy Talk
Have You Met Miss Jones
Hello Young Lovers
Here in My Arms
Honey Bun
I Cain't Say No
I Could Write a Book
I Didn't Know What Time is Was
I Enjoy Being a Girl
I Like to Recognize the Tune
I Whistle a Happy Tune
I Wish I Were in Love Again
I'm Gonna Wash That Man Right Out of My Hair
I'm in Love With a Wonderful Guy
I've Got Five Dollars
If I Loved You
Isn't it Kinda Fun
Isn't it Romantic
It Might As Well Be Spring
It Never Entered My Mind
It's a Grand Night For Singing
It's Easy to Remember
Johnny One Note
June Is Busting Out All Over
Lady Is a Tramp, The
Little Girl Blue
Lover
Manhattan
March of the Siamese Children, The
Mimi
Mister Snow
Most Beautiful Girl in the World
Mountain Greenery
My Favourite Things
My Funny Valentine
My Heart Stood Still
My Romance
No Other Love
Oh What a Beautiful Morning

Oklahoma
On Your Toes
Out of My Dreams
People Will Say We're in Love
Shall We Dance
Ship Without a Sail, The
Sing For Your Supper
Slaughter on Tenth Avenue
Some Enchanted Evening
Soon - There'll Just Be Two of Us
Sound of Music, The
Spring is Here
Surrey With the Fringe on Top, The
Sweetest Sounds, The
Ten Cents a Dance
That's For Me
There is Nothing Like a Dame
There's a Small Hotel
This Can't Be Love
This Nearly Was Mine
Thou Swell
To Keep My Love Alive
Tree in a Park, A
We Kiss in the Shadow
Where or When
Where's That Rainbow
With a Song in My Heart
You Are Beautiful
You Are Too Beautiful
You Took Advantage of Me
You'll Never Walk Alone
Younger Than Springtime

Roker, Ron
Dance Little Lady, Dance
Do You Wanna Dance
Rupert
Storm in a Teacup

Romberg, Sigmund
Auf Wiederseh'n
Close As Pages in a Book
Deep In My Heart
Desert Song, The
Drinking Song, The
French Military Marching Song
Golden Days
I Bring a Love Song
Lover Come Back to Me
One Alone
One Kiss
Riff Song, The
Serenade
Softly As in a Morning Sunrise
Song of Love
Stout Hearted Men
Wanting You
When Hearts Are Young
When I Grow Too Old to Dream
Will You Remember (Sweetheart)
You Will Remember Vienna

Rome, Harold
Franklin D. Roosevelt Jones
My Heart Sings
South America, Take it Away
Wish You Were Here

Romeo, Beresford
Back to Life
Dream's a Dream, A
Get a Life
Keep on Movin'

Romeo, Tony
I Am a Clown
I'm Gonna Make You Mine
It's One Of Those Nights
Oh Boy (The Mood I'm in)

Rose, Billy
Back in Your Own Back Yard
Barbara
Barney Google
Cheerful Little Earful
Clap Hands, Here Comes Charley
Cup Of Coffee, a Sandwich and You, A
Does Your Chewing Gum Lose it's Flavour?
Don't Bring Lulu
Dummy Song, The
Fifty Million Frenchmen Can't Be Wrong
Follow the Swallow
Great Day
Happy Days and Lonely Nights
House is Haunted, The
I Found a Million Dollar Baby
I've Got a Feeling I'm Falling
If You Hadn't Gone Away
If You Want the Rainbow
It Happened in Monterey
It's Only a Paper Moon
Me and My Shadow
More Than You Know
Night Is Young and You're So Beautiful, The
Poor Papa (He's Got Nothing At All)
Suddenly
That Night in Araby
That Old Gang of Mine
There's a Rainbow 'Round My Shoulder
Tonight You Belong to Me
Twelve O'Clock At Night
Without a Song
Would You Like to Take a Walk
You've Got to See Mamma Every Night

Rose, Fred
Be Honest With Me
'Deed I Do
Deep Henderson
Don't Bring Me Posies (When It's Shoesies That I Need)
Red Hot Mamma
Settin' the Woods on Fire
Take These Chains From My Heart

Rose, Vincent
Avalon
Blueberry Hill
Linger Awhile
Moon at Sea
Pardon Me Pretty Baby
Umbrella Man, The
Were You Sincere
Whispering

Ross, Adrian
Bohemia
Come to the Ball
Gipsy Maiden
Golden Song, The
Goodnight (I'm Only a Strolling Vagabond)
Little Love, a Little Kiss, A (un Peu D'amour)
Little Miss Melody
Love and Wine
Love Here Is My Heart (Mon Coeur Est Pour Toi)
Pearl Of Sweet Ceylon, The
Philomel
Say Not Love Is a Dream
Try Again Johnnie
Under the Deodar
Under the Lilac Bough
Waltz Dream, The
Whisper to Me

Ross, Adrian
Can It Be Love
Dollar Princesses

I Love You So (The Merry Widow Waltz)
Maxim's
My Dear Little Cingalee
My Dream Of Love
Vilia

Ross, Jerry
Heart
Hernando's Hideaway
Hey There
I'm Gonna Make You Love Me
Once a Year Day
Rags to Riches
Steam Heat
Whatever Lola Wants

Rossi, Francis
Break the Rules
Burning Bridges
Caroline
Down Down
Lies
Marguerita Time
Paper Plane
Pictures Of Matchstick Men
Rock 'n' Roll
Roll Over Lay Down
What You're Proposing

Rostill, John
Genie With the Light Brown Lamp
I Could Easily Fall
In the Country
Rise and Fall of Flingle Bunt
Time Drags By

Rubens, Paul
Bohemia
Can it Be Love
Flying Dutchman, The
Here's to Love
I Love the Moon
Little Pink Petty From Peter
Violin Song, The
Wonderful Eyes
Your King and Country Want You

Ruby, Harry
All Alone Monday
And He'd Say "Oo-la-la Wee-Wee"
Another Night Like This
Do You Love Me?
Give Me the Simple Life
I Wanna Be Loved By You
I'll Always Be In Love With You
Kiss to Build a Dream on, A
Maybe It's Because
My Sunny Tennessee
Nevertheless
So Long, Oo-Long (How Long You Gonna Be Gone)
Thinking of You
Three Little Words
Up In the Clouds
What a Perfect Combination
Who's Sorry Now?

Ruby, Herman
Cecilia
My Honey's Lovin' Arms
My Sunny Tennessee
Only When You're in My Arms
Twelve O'Clock at Night

Russell, Bert
Hang on Sloopy
Little Bit of Soap
One Way Love
Tell Him
Twist and Shout

Russell, Bob
At the Crossroads
Babalu
Ballerina
Brazil
Circus
Do Nothing Till You Hear From Me
Don't Get Around Much Anymore
Frenesi
He Ain't Heavy, He's My Brother
Honey
I Didn't Know About You
Little Green Apples
Matinee
No Other Love
Taboo
Time Was (Duerme)
Who Dat Up Dere?
Would I Love You

Rutherford, Mike
Follow You Follow Me
In Too Deep
Invisible Touch
Land of Confusion
Living Years
Mama
That's All
Turn It on Again

Saint-Marie, Buffy
Soldier Blue
Universal Soldier
Until It's Time For You to Go
Up Where We Belong

Samwell, Ian
Fall In Love With You
Gee Whiz, It's You
High Class Baby
Never Mind
You Can Never Stop Me Loving You

Sarony, Leslie
Ain't It Grand to Be Bloomin' Well Dead
Coom Pretty One
Dicky Bird Hop, The
Don't Do That to the Poor Puss Cat
Flirtation Waltz, The
Forty-seven Ginger Headed Sailors
I Lift Up My Finger and I Say Tweet Tweet
Jollity Farm
Mucking About the Garden
Over the Garden Wall
Rhymes
Wheezy Anna
When a Soldier's on Parade
When the Guards Are on Parade

Sayer, Leo
Dreamin'
Giving It All Away
How Much Love
Long Tall Glasses
Moonlighting
One Man Band
Show Must Go on, The
You Make Me Feel Like Dancing

Schertzinger, Victor
Arthur Murray Taught Me Dancing In a Hurry
Dream Lover
Fleet's in, The
I Remember You
I'll Never Let a Day Pass By
Kiss the Boys Goodbye
Love Me Forever
Magnolias in the Moonlight
March of the Grenadiers

Marchéta
Moon and the Willow Tree, The
My Love Parade
Nobody's Using It Now
Not Mine
One Night of Love
Paris Stay the Same
Sand in My Shoes
Tangerine

Schoebel, Elmer
Bugle Call Rag
Farewell Blues
House of David Blues, The
Nobody's Sweetheart

Schroeder, Aaron
Because They're Young
Big Hunk of Love, A
Good Luck Charm
I Got Stung
I'm Gonna Knock on Your Door
It's Now or Never
Love's Theme
Mandolins in the Moonlight
Rubber Ball
Santa Bring My Baby Back to Me
Stuck on You
Twixt Twelve and Twenty

Schroeder, John
Don't Treat Me Like a Child
Little Miss Lonely
Walking Back to Happiness
You Don't Know

Schuster, Ira
Did You Ever Get That Feeling in the Moonlight
Hold Me
Somebody's Thinking of You Tonight
There's a Blue Ridge Round My Heart, Virginia
Vamping Rose

Schwartz, Arthur
Alone Together
By Myself
Dancing in the Dark
Dreamer, A
Gal in Calico, A
How Sweet You Are
I Guess I'll Have to Change My Plan
I See Your Face Before Me
I'll Buy You a Star
I'm Riding For a Fall
Louisianna Hayride
Moment I Saw You, The
New Sun in the Sky, A
Oh But I Do
Rainy Night In Rio, A
Relax-ay-voo
She's Such a Comfort to Me
Shine on Your Shoes, A
Something to Remember You By
That's Entertainment
Triplets
You and the Night and the Music

Schwartz, Jean
Chinatown My Chinatown
Goodbye Virginia
Hello Hawaii, How Are You
My Irish Molly-O
On the Level You're a Little Devil
Rock-a-Bye Your Baby With a Dixie Melody
Trouble In Paradise
Trust In Me

Scott, Bennett
By the Side of the Zuyder Zee

Do You Remember the Last Waltz
Everybody's Crazy on the Foxtrot
Fall in and Follow Me
Ship Ahoy
Take Me Back to Dear Old Blighty
When I Take My Morning Promenade

Scott, Ronnie
I'm a Tiger
Ice in the Sun
It's a Heartache
Lost in France

Sedaka, Neil
Breaking Up Is Hard to Do
Calendar Girl
Happy Birthday Sweet Sixteen
I Go Ape
Is This the Way to Amarillo
Little Devil
Oh Carol
Solitaire
Stupid Cupid
Where the Boys Are

Seiler, Eddie
Ask Anyone Who Knows
I Don't Want to Set the World on Fire
'Till Then
When the Lights Go on Again

Shand, Terry
Cry, Baby, Cry
Dance With a Dolly
I Double Dare You
I'm Gonna Lock My Heart and Throw Away the Key
I'm So Right Tonight
You Don't Have to Be a Baby to Cry

Shannon, Del
Hats Off to Larry
Hey Little Girl
Keep Searchin' (We'll Follow the Sun)
Little Town Flirt
Runaway
So Long Baby
Two Kinds of Teardrops

Shay, Larry
Everywhere You Go
Get Out and Get Under the Moon
I'm Knee Deep In Daisies
When You're Smiling
You're In Kentucky as Sure as You're Born

Shelley, Peter
Ever Fallen In Love
Gee Baby
Good Love Can Never Die
Jealous Mind
Love Me Love My Dog
My Coo-ca-choo
Red Dress
Tell Me Why
You You You

Shephard, Gerry
Angel Face
Goodbye My Love
Just For You
Let's Get Together Again
Love In the Sun
People Like You and People Like Me
Tears I Cried, The

Sherman, Al
Bungalow, a Piccolo and You, A
Comes A-long A-love
Dream Mother
He's Tall and Dark and Handsome
I Paid For That Lie I Told You

I'm Crazy Over You
Me Too
Ninety-nine Out of a Hundred
No! No! A Thousand Times No
Nows the Time to Fall In Love
On a Little Bamboo Bridge
On the Beach at Bali Bali
Pretending
Roses Remind Me of You
Save Your Sorrow For Tomorrow
There's a Harbour of Dreamboats
Trudy
What Do We Do on a Dew-Dew-Dewy Day
When the Organ Played O Promise Me

Sherman, Richard M.
Chim Chim Cheree
Chitty Chitty Bang Bang
Let's Get Together
Spoonful of Sugar, A
Supercalifragilisticexpialidocious

Sherman, Robert B.
Chim Chim Cheree
Chitty Chitty Bang Bang
Let's Get Together
Spoonful of Sugar, A
Supercalifragilisticexpialidocious

Shilkret, Nat
First Time I Saw You, The
Jeannine, I Dream of Lilac Time
Lady Divine
Lonesome Road

Shipley, Ellen
Circle In the Sand
Heaven Is a Place on Earth
Leave a Light on
Same Thing, The

Shirl, Jimmy
Beloved Be Faithful
Castle Rock
I Believe
My Friend

Shuman, Earl
Left Right Out of My Heart
Seven Lonely Days
Starry Eyed
Theme For a Dream

Shuman, Mort
Can't Get Used to Losing You
Here I Go Again
His Latest Flame
Kiss Me Quick
Love's Just a Broken Heart
Mess of Blues, A
Save the Last Dance For Me
Sha La La La Lee
Surrender
Suspicion
Sweets For My Sweet
Teenager in Love, A

Sievier, Bruce
Her Name Is Mary
J'Attendrai
Love's Last Word is Spoken (Le Cha-land Qui Passe)
Speak to Me of Love (Parlez Moi D'amour)
Under the Roofs of Paris (Sous Les Toits De Paris)
You're Blasé

Sigler, Maurice
Everything Stops For Tea
Everything's in Rhythm With My Heart
I Saw Stars

I'm in a Dancing Mood
Little Man You've Had a Busy Day
My First Thrill
There Isn't Any Limit to My Love
This'll Make You Whistle
You've Got the Wrong Rumba

Sigman, Carl
Answer Me
Arrivederci Darling (Arrivederci Roma)
Ballerina
Buona Sera
Careless Hands
Civilization
Creep, The
Day the Rains Came, The
Ebb Tide
Enjoy Yourself
Fool
Hop Scotch Polka
It's All in the Game
Losing You (Un Ange Est Renn)
Matinee
My Heart Cries For You
Pennsylvania Six-Five-Thousand
Right Now
Robin Hood
Souvenir D'Italie
Summertime In Venice
Till
Twenty-Four Hours of Sunshine
What Now My Love (Et Maintenant)
Where Do I Begin
Willingly (Melodie Perdue)
World Outside, The
You're My World (Il Mio Mondo)

Silver, Abner
After a While
Angel Child
Barbara
C'est Vous (it's You)
How Green Was My Valley
I'm Going South
It's a Cruel Cruel World
My Love For You
New Moon and An Old Serenade, A
No! No! A Thousand Times No
On the Beach At Bali Bali
Pu-leeze Mr. Hemingway
Say It Again
Say It While Dancing
She's a Home Girl
When Autumn Leaves Are Falling
When the Organ Played O Promise Me
Wisdom of a Fool, The
With These Hands

Simon, Nat
And Mimi
Apple Blossom Wedding, An
Coax Me a Little Bit
Down the Trail of Aching Hearts
Every Single Little Tingle of My Heart
Gaucho Serenade, The
Her Bathing Suit Never Got Wet
In My Little Red Book
Istanbul (Not Constantinople)
Little Curly Hair In a High Chair
Little Lady Make Believe
Mama Doll Song, The
No Can Do
Old Lamplighter, The
Poinciana
Rosewood Spinet, A
Wait For Me Mary

Simon, Paul
Boxer, The
Bridge Over Troubled Water

Homeward Bound
Mother and Child Reunion
Mrs. Robinson
Someday One Day
Sound of Silence, The
Take Me to the Mardi Gras
You Can Call Me Al

Simpson, Valerie
Ain't No Mountain High Enough
I'm Every Woman
Onion Song, The
Remember Me
Solid
Surrender

Sinfield, Peter
Have You Ever Been In Love
I Believe In Father Christmas
Land of Make Believe
Rain or Shine

Singleton, Charles
Don't Forbid Me
Just as Much as Ever
Spanish Eyes (Moon Over Naples)
Strangers in the Night

Skylar, Sunny
Amor
And So to Sleep Again
Besame Mucho (Kiss Me)
Gotta Be This or That
Hair Of Gold, Eyes of Blue
It Must Be Jelly, 'Cause Jam Don't Shake Like That
It's All Over Now
Waiting For the Train to Come in
You're Breaking My Heart

Smith, Harry B.
Bright Eyes
Romany Life
Sheik of Araby, The
To the Land of My Own Romance
You're Here and I'm Here

Smith, Robert
Good Old Rock 'n' Roll
I Might Be Your Once in a While
In Between Days
Lilac Domino, The
Love Cats, The
Sweethearts

Snyder, Ted
I Want to Be in Dixie
Sheik of Araby, The
That Mysterious Rag
That Night in Araby
Under the Moon
Who's Sorry Now

Sondheim, Stephen
Everything's Coming Up Roses
I Feel Pretty
Maria
Send in the Clowns
Something's Coming
Somewhere
Tonight

Sonin, Ray
Best of All
Gertie the Girl With the Gong
Homecoming Waltz, The
Madelon (Quand Madelon)

Spector, Phil
Baby I Love You
Be My Baby
Black Pearl
Da Doo Ron Ron

I Can Hear Music
In the Rain
River Deep, Mountain High
Spanish Harlem
Then He Kissed Me
Then I Kissed Her
To Know Him Is to Love Him
You've Lost That Lovin' Feelin'

Spina, Harold
Annie Doesn't Live Here Anymore
I'd Give the World (Liebeslied)
It's So Nice to Have a Man Around the House
Long Live Love
My Very Good Friend the Milkman
Nice One Cyril
Would I Love You

Spoliansky, Mischa
Canoe Song, The
Climbing Up
Hour of Parting, The
Melba Waltz, The
Song of Capri, The
Tell Me Tonight

Springfield, Tom
Carnival Is Over, The
Georgy Girl
I'll Never Find Another You
Island of Dreams
Just Loving You
Losing You
Promises
Say I Won't Be There
Walk With Me
World of Our Own, A

Springsteen, Bruce
Because the Night
Blinded By the Light
Born in the USA
Dancing In the Dark
I'm on Fire
Pink Cadillac

Stanford, Trevor
China Tea
Jeannie
Lucky Five
Passing Breeze
Roulette
Royal Event
Side Saddle
Snow Coach

Starr, Maurice
Candy Girl
Cover Girl
Hangin' Tough
I'll Be Loving You (Forever)
Tonight
You Got It (The Right Stuff)

Steele, David
Good Thing
Hands Off - She's Mine
It's a Shame (My Sister)
Johnny Come Home
Mirror In the Bathroom
She Drives Me Crazy

Steele, Tommy
Butterfingers
Handful of Songs, A
Rock With the Cavemen
Shiralee

Steinberg, William
Alone
I Drove All Night

Like a Virgin
So Emotional

Steiner, Max
Come Next Spring
It Can't Be Wrong
My Own True Love
Some Day I'll Meet You Again
Summer Place, A
Tara's Theme

Stellman, Marcel
Be Mine
Johnny is the Boy For Me
Little Love and Understanding, A (Un
Peu D'amour Et D'amitie)
Maybe This Year
Melodie D'amour (Maladie D'amour)
Tom Pillibi

Stept, Sammy
Comes Love
Do Something
Don't Sit Under the Apple Tree
I Came Here to Talk For Joe
I Fall in Love With You Every Day
I'll Always Be in Love With You
I'm Looking For a Girl Named Mary
Laughing Irish Eyes
Please Don't Talk About Me When I'm
Gone
Sweet Heartache
That's My Weakness Now
When They Ask About You

Sterling, Andrew
Down at the Old Bull and Bush (Under
the Anheuser Bush)
Keep Your Skirts Down Mary Ann
Meet Me in St. Louis
Sleepy Valley
When My Baby Smiles At Me
Wait 'Till the Sun Shines Nellie

Stevens, Cat
Can't Keep It In
First Cut Is the Deepest
Here Comes My Baby
I Don't Want to Talk About It
I'm Gonna Get Me a Gun
Lady D'Arbanville
Matthew and Son
Wild World

Stevens, Geoff
Crying Game, The
Daddy Don't You Walk So Fast
Daughter of Darkness
Doctor's Orders
Finchley Central
Goodbye Sam, Hello Samantha
I Get a Little Sentimental Over You
I'll Put You Together Again
It Sure Brings Out the Love in Your Eyes
It's Gonna Be a Cold Cold Christmas
Knock Knock Who's There
Leeds United
Lights of Cincinnati, The
Like Sister and Brother
Peek a Boo
Semi-Detached Suburban Mr James
Sorry Suzanne
Sunshine Girl
Tell Me When
There's a Kind of Hush
Winchester Cathedral
You Won't Find Another Fool Like Me

Stevenson, William
Dancing in the Street
He Was Really Saying Something
It Should Have Been Me

It Takes Two

Stewart, Dave
Here Comes the Rain Again
Is This Love
It's Alright (Baby's Coming Back)
Love is a Stranger
Right By Your Side
Sex Crime (Nineteen Eighty Four)
Sisters Are Doing it For Themselves
Sweet Dreams (Are Made of This)
There Must Be An Angel Playing With
My Heart
Thorn in My Side
Who's That Girl?

Stewart, Eric
Art For Art's Sake
Dreadlock Holiday
Good Morning Judge
I'm Mandy, Fly Me
I'm Not in Love
Life is a Minestrone
Neanderthal Man
Things We Do For Love, The

Stewart, Rod
Ain't Love a Bitch
Baby Jane
Cindy Incidentally
Da' Ya Think I'm Sexy
Every Beat of My Heart
Farewell
Hot Legs
Killing of Georgie, The
Maggie May
Ole Ola
Pool Hall Richard
Stay With Me
Tonight I'm Yours
Tonight's the Night
What Am I Gonna Do
You Belong to Me
You Can Make Me Dance, Sing or Any-
thing
You Wear It Well
You're In My Heart

Stilgoe, Richard
All I Ask of You
I Am the Starlight
Music of the Night
Phantom of the Opera, The

Stillman, Al
Afterglow
Breeze and I, The
Chances Are
Happy Anniversary
How Soon
I Believe
If Dreams Came True
In My Little Red Book
Juke Box Saturday Night
Mama Yo Quiero (I Want My Mama)
Moments to Remember
Say "Si Si" (Para Vigo Me Voy)

Stock, Larry
Adoration Waltz, The
Blueberry Hill
Did You Ever Get That Feeling in the
Moonlight
Moon At Sea
Morningside of the Mountain, The
Umbrella Man, The
You Won't Be Satisfied
You're Nobody 'Till Somebody Loves You

Stock, Mike
Better the Devil You Know
Can't Shake the Feeling

Cross My Broken Heart
Especially For You
Every Day I Love You More
F.L.M.
G.T.O.
Got to Be Certain
Hand on Your Heart
Hang on to Your Love
Happenin' All Over Again
Harder I Try, The
He Ain't No Competition
I Don't Wanna Get Hurt
I Heard a Rumour
I Just Don't Have the Heart
I Should Be So Lucky
I Want You Back
I'd Rather Jack
Je Ne Sais Pas, Pourquoi
Let's All Chant
Love in the First Degree
Never Gonna Give You Up
Never Too Late
Nothing Can Divide Us
Nothing's Gonna Stop Me Now
Respectable
Say I'm Your Number One
Showing Out
Step Back in Time
Take Me to Your Heart
That's the Way It Is
This Time I Know It's For Real
Together Forever
Too Many Broken Hearts in the World
Toy Boy
Whatever I Do (Wherever I Go)
When You Come Back to Me
Whenever You Need Somebody
Who's Leaving Who
Wouldn't Change a Thing
You'll Never Stop Me Loving You
You've Got a Friend

Stoller, Mike
Baby I Don't Care
Bossa Nova Baby
Charlie Brown
Don't
Hound Dog
I (Who Have Nothing) (Uno Dei Tanti)
Jailhouse Rock
King Creole
Lorelei
Loving You
Lucky Lips
Pearl's a Singer
Poison Ivy
Searchin'
She's Not You
Stand By Me
Yakity Yak

Stolz, Robert
Don't Ask Me Why
Don't Say Goodbye
Goodbye
It's Foolish But It's Fun
My Song of Love
Robinson Crusoe's Isle
Romeo
Salome
Two Hearts in Three Quarter Time
Waltzing in the Clouds
When April Sings
White Horse Inn, The
You Just You
You Too
Your Eyes

Stothart, Herbert
Cuban Love Song

Donkey Serenade, The
I Wanna Be Loved By You
Ride Cossack, Ride
Rogue Song, The
Sweetheart Darling
When I'm Looking At You

Stranks, Alan
All
Break Of Day
Love Steals Your Heart
No Orchids For My Lady

Straus, Oscar
Letter Song, The
My Hero
Ronde De L'amour, La
Waltz Dream, The

Strauss, Art
Cinderella Sweetheart
Saint Therese of the Roses
Seventeen Candles
They Can't Black-Out the Moon

Strong, Barrett
Ball of Confusion
Cloud Nine
I Can't Get Next to You
I Heard It Through the Grapevine
Just My Imagination
Papa Was a Rolling Stone
Take a Look Around
War

Stuart, Leslie
I May Be Crazy
I Want to Be a Military Man
Lily of Laguna
Little Dolly Daydream
Shade of the Palm, The
Soldiers of the Queen
Tell Me Pretty Maiden

Styne, Jule
And Then You Kissed Me
Bye Bye Baby
Can't You Read Between the Lines
Charm of You, The
Come Out, Come Out, Wherever You Are
Conchita, Marquita, Lolita, Pepita, Rosita, Juanita Lopez
Diamonds Are a Girl's Best Friend
Don't Rain on My Parade
Ev'ry Street's a Boulevard
Everything's Coming Up Roses
Five Minutes More
I Begged Her
I Don't Want to Walk Without You
I Fall in Love Too Easily
I'll Walk Alone
I've Heard That Song Before
It's Been a Long Long Time
It's Magic
It's the Same Old Dream
It's You or No-one
Just in Time
Lady Who Didn't Believe in Love, The
Let it Snow
Long Before I Knew You
Make Someone Happy
Party's Over, The
People
Put 'Em in a Box
Saturday Night is the Loneliest Night of the Week
There Goes That Song Again
There's Nothing Rougher Than Love
Things We Did Last Summer, The
Thinking About the Wabash
Three Coins in the Fountain

Time After Time
Victory Polka
What Makes the Sunset

Suesse, Dana
Ho Hum
My Silent Love
Night is Young and You're So Beautiful, The
Whistling in the Dark
You Oughta Be in Pictures

Summer, Donna
Down Deep Inside
I Feel Love
I Remember Yesterday
Love to Love You Baby
Loves Unkind
This Time I Know it's For Real

Swain, Tony
All Cried Out
Body Talk
Cruel Summer
Flashback
Just An Illusion
Love Resurrection
Music and Lights
Robert De Niro's Waiting
Shy Boy

Symes, Marty
By the River of the Roses
Darkness on the Delta
How Many Hearts Have You Broken
It's the Talk of the Town
No Greater Love
Pretending
Somebody's Thinking of You Tonight
Under a Blanket of Blue

Tarney, Alan
Dreamin'
January February
Last Kiss
Little in Love, A
Living in Harmony
My Pretty One
Some People
We Don't Talk Anymore
Wired For Sound

Tate, James W.
Bachelor Gay, A
Broken Doll
Every Little While
Give Me a Little Cosy Corner
I Was a Good Little Girl 'Till I Met You
If I Should Plant a Tiny Seed of Love
Paradise For Two, A
Somewhere In France With You

Taupin, Bernie
Candle in the Wind, A
Crocodile Rock
Daniel
Don't Let the Sun Go Down on Me
Goodbye Yellow Brick Road
I Guess That's Why They Call it the Blues
I'm Still Standing
Island Girl
Nikita
Passengers
Philadelphia Freedom
Rocket Man
Sacrifice
Saturday Night's Alright For Fighting
We Built This City
Your Song

Taylor, Chip
Anyway That You Want Me

I Can't Let Go
On My Word
Wild Thing

Taylor, Irving
Everybody Loves Somebody
Give Me Your Word
Knees Up Mother Brown
Quicksilver
Sailor With the Navy Blue Eyes, The
Take It Easy
Three Little Sisters

Taylor, James
Cherish
Fresh
Get Down on it
In the Heart
Joanna
Straight Ahead

Taylor, John
Notorious
Reflex, The
Wild Boys, The

Taylor, Roger
Election Day
Reflex, The
Wild Boys, The

Temperton, Rodney
Always and Forever
Baby Come to Me
Boogie Nights
Give Me the Night
Groove Line, The
Love Times Love (Love X Love)
Off the Wall
Rock With You
Stomp
Sweet Freedom
Thriller
Too Hot to Handle

Tennant, Neil
Domino Dancing
Heart
I'm Not Scared
In Private
It's a Sin
Nothing Has Been Proved
Opportunities
Rent
Suburbia
West End Girls
What Have I Done to Deserve This

Tepper, Sid
Kewpie Doll
Naughty Lady of Shady Lane, The
Red Roses For a Blue Lady
Stairway of Love
Travellin' Light
Twenty Tiny Fingers
When the Girl in Your Arms
Wonderful World of the Young, The
Young Ones, The

Terriss, Dorothy
I Never Knew How Wonderful You Were
Three O'Clock in the Morning
Wonderful One

Teschemacher, Edward
Because
I Know a Lovely Garden
I Wonder if Love is a Dream
Mattinata ('Tis the Day)
O Flower Divine
Until
Where My Caravan Has Rested

Tierney, Harry
Alice Blue Gown
Following the Sun Around
If You're in Love You'll Waltz
Irene
Kinkajou, The
M.I.S.S.I.S.S.I.P.P.I.
Rangers' Song, The
Rio Rita
Saw Mill River Road, The
Sweetheart We Need Each Other

Tiomkin, Dimitri
Blowing Wild
Friendly Persuasion
Green Leaves of Summer, The
Hajji Baba
High and the Mighty, The
High Noon
Rawhide
Strange Lady in Town

Tobias, Charles
After My Laughter Came Tears
As We Are Today
Broken Record, The
Cloud Lucky Seven
Coax Me a Little Bit
Comes Love
Don't Sit Under the Apple Tree
Don't Sweetheart Me
For the First Time I've Fallen in Love
Get Out and Get Under the Moon
He's Tall and Dark and Handsome
Her Bathing Suit Never Got Wet
I Came Here to Talk For Joe
If I Knew Then (What I Know Now)
In the Valley of the Moon
Just a Prayer Away
Just Another Day Wasted Away
Little Curly Hair In a High Chair
Little Lady Make Believe
Making the Best of Each Day
Mama Doll Song, The
May I Have the Next Dream With You
Me Too
Miss You
No Can Do
Old Lamplighter, The
Rose O'Day
Rosewood Spinet, A
Somebody Loves You
Start the Day Right
Time Waits For No One
Trade Winds
Trudy
Wait For Me Mary
What Do We Do on a Dew-Dew-Dewy Day
When You're Hair Has Turned to Silver

Tobias, Fred
Born Too Late
Good Timin'
Hello This is Joannie
Johnny Will

Tobias, Harry
Ashes of Roses
At Your Command
If I Knew Then (What I Know Now)
Love Is All
May I Have the Next Dream With You
Miss You
No Regrets
Rolleo Rolling Along
Sail Along Silvery Moon
Star of Hope
Sweet and Lovely
Wait For Me Mary

Tobias, Henry
If I Had My Life to Live Over
If I Knew Then (What I Know Now)
May I Have the Next Dream With You
Rolleo Rolling Along

Towers, Leo
Bedtime Story, A
Liszt, Chopin and Mendelssohn
Little Old Mill
Me and the Old Folks At Home
Sally
Silver Wings in the Moonlight
Stars Will Remember, The
When the Poppies Bloom Again

Townshend, Peter
Anyway, Anyhow, Anywhere
Five Fifteen
Happy Jack
I Can See For Miles
I Can't Explain
I'm a Boy
I'm Free
Join Together
Let's See Action
My Generation
Pictures Of Lily
Pinball Wizard
Squeeze Box
Substitute
Won't Get Fooled Again
You Better You Bet

Tracey, William
Is My Baby Blue Tonight
Mammy O'Mine
Play That Barbershop Chord
Them There Eyes

Trenet, Charles
At Last, At Last
Beyond the Sea
Boom
La Mer

Trent, Jackie
Don't Sleep in the Subway
I Couldn't Live Without Your Love
Joanna
Other Man's Grass, The
What Would I Be
Where Are You Now My Love

Troup, Bobby
Daddy
Girl Can't Help It, The
Girl Talk
Route Sixty-Six

Turk, Roy
After My Laughter Came Tears
Aggravatin' Papa
Are You Lonesome Tonight
Gimme a Little Kiss, Will Ya, Huh
I Don't Know Why - I Just Do
I'll Follow You
I'll Get By
I'm a Little Blackbird Looking For a Blue-bird
I'm Gonna Charleston Back to Charleston
Just Another Day Wasted Away
Love You Funny Thing
Mandy Make Up Your Mind
Mean to Me
My Sweetie Went Away
Oh How I Laugh When I Think How I Cried About You
Sweet Man
Tomorrow (I'll Be in My Dixie Home Again)
Walkin' My Baby Back Home

Where the Blue of the Night

Turner, John
Auf Wiederseh'n Sweetheart
Autumn Concerto
Bandit, The (O'Cangaceiro)
Believe In Me (Sur Ma Vie)
Chee Chee-oo-Chee
Eternally (Terry's Theme)
Little Shoemaker, The (Le Petit Cordon-nier)
Mama
Mandolin Serenade
Mister Cuckoo (Cuculino)
O Mein Papa
Smile
Stars Shine in Your Eyes
Walkin' Thru Mockin' Bird Lane
With Your Love (Mes Mains)

Twomey, Kay
Better Not Roll Those Blue Blue Eyes
Johnny Doughboy Found a Rose in Ire-land
Let's Walk That-a-way
Mother Nature and Father Time
Oo! What You Do to Me
Pretty Little Black Eyed Susie
Serenade of the Bells
Smiths and the Joneses, The
Wooden Heart

Ulvaeus, Bjorn
Angel Eyes
Chiquitita
Dancing Queen
Does Your Mother Know
Gimme Gimme Gimme
Honey Honey
I Have a Dream
Knowing Me, Knowing You
Lay All Your Love on Me
Money Money Money
Name of the Game
One Night In Bangkok
One of Us
S.O.S.
Summer Night City
Super Trouper
Take a Chance on Me
Voulez-Vous
Waterloo
Winner Takes it All

Ure, Midge
All Stood Still
Do They Know it's Christmas?
Fade to Grey
If I Was
Vienna

Vallee, Rudy
Betty Co-Ed
Deep Night
I'm Just a Vagabond Lover
Oh Mama (The Butcher Boy)

Van Alstyne, Egbert
Beautiful Love
Drifting and Dreaming
I'm Afraid to Come Home in the Dark
In the Shade of the Old Apple Tree
Memories
Pretty Baby
Your Eyes Have Told Me So

Van Heusen, Jimmy
Ain't Got a Dime to My Name
All the Way
All This and Heaven Too
Ampstead Way, The
Aren't You Glad You're You

As Long As I'm Dreaming
Busy Doing Nothing
But Beautiful
Call Me Irresponsible
Constantly
Country Style
Darn That Dream
Day After Forever, The
Deep in a Dream
Friend of Yours, A
Going My Way
Heaven Can Wait
Here's That Rainy Day
High Hopes
His Rocking Horse Ran Away
Humpty Dumpty Heart
If You Please
If You Stub Your Toe on the Moon
Imagination
It Could Happen to You
It's Always You
Love and Marriage
Moonlight Becomes You
My Heart Goes Crazy
Nancy (With the Laughing Face)
Polka Dots and Moonbeams
Put it There Pal
Road to Morocco, The
Second Time Around
Shake Down the Stars
Smile Right Back at the Sun
So Would I
Suddenly it's Spring
Sunday, Monday or Always
Sunshine Cake
Swinging on a Star
Tender Trap, The
Thoroughly Modern Millie
Welcome to My Dream
Yah-ta-ta, Yah-ta-ta
You Can't Keep a Good Dreamer Down
You Don't Have to Know the Language
You My Love

Vance, Paul
Catch a Falling Star
Four Little Heels
Itsy Bitsy Teenie Weenie Yellow Polka Dot Bikini
Tracy
When Julie Comes Around

Vandyke, Les
Ain't That Funny
Applejack
As You Like It
Cupboard Love
Don't That Beat All
Don't You Know It
Forget Me Not
Get Lost
How About That
Poor Me
Someone Else's Baby
Time Has Come, The
Well I Ask Ya
What Do You Want
Who Am I

Vangarde, Daniel
Cuba
D.I.S.C.O.
Hands Up (Give Me Your Heart)
Ooh What a Life
Que Sera Mi Vida (If You Should Go)

Verdi, Beatrice
Behind a Painted Smile
I Can't Get You Outa My Mind
In the Middle Of Nowhere

Little By Little

Von Tilzer, Albert
Chili Bean
Dapper Dan
Give Me the Moonlight
I Used to Love You (But It's All Over Now)
I'll Be With You In Apple Blossom Time
I'm Praying to Saint Christopher
I'm the Lonesomest Gal in Town
My Cuties Due At Two to Two Today
Nora Malone (Call Me By Phone)
Oh By Jingo, Oh By Gee
Oh How She Could Yacki Hacki Wicki Wacki Woo
Put Your Arms Around Me Honey
Roll Along Prairie Moon
Take Me Out to the Ball Game
Teasing

Von Tilzer, Harry
All Alone
Bird in a Gilded Cage, A
Down At the Old Bull and Bush (Under the Anheuser Bush)
I Want a Girl Just Like the Girl That Married Dear Old Dad
Little Wooden Whistle Wouldn't Whistle, The
On a Sunday Afternoon
Wait 'Till the Sun Shines Nellie

Waaktaar, Pal
Cry Wolf
Hunting High and Low
I've Been Losing You
Living Daylights, The
Stay on These Roads
Sun Always Shines on T.V., the
Take on Me
Train of Thought
You Are the One

Waddington, Tony
Don't Do It Baby
I Can Do It
Juke Box Jive
Like a Butterfly
Sugar Baby Love
Sugar Candy Kisses
Tonight
We Can Do It

Walden, Narada Michael
Divine Emotions
How Will I Know
I Shoulda Loved Ya
Jump to the Beat
Licence to Kill
We Don't Have to Take Our Clothes Off

Wallace, Oliver
Baby Mine
Fuhrer's Face, Der
Hindustan
When I See An Elephant Fly

Wallace, Raymond
Back Again to Happy-Go-Lucky-Days
Ever So Goosey
Give Yourself a Pat on the Back
I'm Happy When I'm Hiking
Jolly Good Company
Merrily We Roll Along
Old Father Thames
There's a Good Time Coming
When the Organ Played At Twilight
With My Shillelagh Under My Arm
You Can't Do That There 'Ere

Waller, Thomas
Ain't Misbehavin'

Alligator Crawl
Blue Turning Grey Over You
Honeysuckle Rose
I'm Crazy 'Bout My Baby
I've Got a Feeling I'm Falling
Joint is Jumpin', the
My Fate is in Your Hands
Viper's Drag
What Did I Do to Be So Black and Blue

Warren, Diane
Don't Turn Around
How Can We Be Lovers
I Get Weak
If I Could Turn Back Time
Just Like Jesse James
Nothing's Gonna Stop Us Now
Rhythm of the Night

Warren, Harry
About a Quarter to Nine
Affair to Remember, An
At Last
Baby Doll
Birds and the Bees, The
Boa Noite
Boulevard of Broken Dreams
By the River Saint Marie
Chattanooga Choo Choo
Cheerful Little Earful
Chica Chica Boom Chic
Crying For the Carolines
Day Dreaming
Dormi, Dormi, Dormi
Down Argentine Way
Fair and Warmer
Forty-Second Street
Have a Little Faith in Me
(Home In) Pasadena
House of Singing Bamboo, The
I Found a Million Dollar Baby
I Had the Craziest Dream
I Know Why
I Love My Baby, My Baby Loves Me
I Only Have Eyes For You
I Take to You
I Wish I Knew
I Yi Yi Yi Yi I Like You Very Much
I'll Sing You a Thousand Love Songs
I'll String Along With You
I'm Goin' Shoppin' With You
I've Got a Gal In Kalamazoo
I've Got to Sing a Torch Song
It Happened in Sun Valley
Jeepers Creepers
Journey to a Star, A
Keep Young and Beautiful
Lullaby of Broadway
Lulu's Back in Town
More I See You, The
My Dream is Yours
My Heart Tells Me
My One and Only Highland Fling
Nagasaki
No Love, No Nothing
On the Atchison, Topeka and the Santa Fe
One Sweet Letter From You
Ooh That Kiss
People Like You and Me
Pettin' in the Park
Remember Me
Rose in Her Hair, The
Rose of the Rio Grande
Rose Tattoo, The
Run Little Raindrop Run
Seminola
September in the Rain
Serenade in Blue
Shadow Waltz, The

Please Don't Tease
Shindig
Summer Holiday
Theme For Young Lovers
Time Drags By

Weldon, Frank
Buffalo Billy
Goodnight Wherever You Are
I Came, I Saw, I Conga'd
I Like Mountain Music
Little on the Lonely Side, A
Man With the Mandolin, The

Weller, Paul
Absolute Beginners
All Around the World
Beat Surrender
Bitterest Pill, The
Eton Rifles
Going Underground
Groovin'
It Didn't Matter
Just Who is the Five O'Clock Hero
Long Hot Summer
My Ever Changing Moods
Shout to the Top
Speak Like a Child
Start
Town Called Malice, A
Walls Come Tumbling Down

Wendling, Pete
I Believe in Miracles
I Wonder
I'm Sure of Everything But You
Oh What a Pal Was Mary
There's Danger in Your Eyes Cherie
There's Everything Nice About You
Yacka Hula Hickey Dula

Wenrich, Percy
By the Campfire
Goodbye Summer, So Long Fall, Hello
Wintertime
Moonlight Bay
Put on Your Old Gray Bonnet
Sail Along Silvery Moon
Shores of Minnetonka
Silver Bell
When You Wore a Tulip

Westlake, Clive
All I See is You
Here I Go Again
How Come
I Close My Eyes and Count to Ten
Losing You
Minute of Your Time, A

Weston, Paul
Congratulations
Day By Day
Gandy Dancers Ball, The
I Should Care
No Other Love
Shrimp Boats

Weston, R.P.
And the Great Big Saw Came Nearer
End of My Old Cigar, The
Good Bye-ee
Hobnailed Boots That Farver Wore, The
I'm Henery the Eighth
I've Got Rings on My Fingers
My Word You Do Look Queer
Olga Pulloffski (The Beautiful Spy)
Paddy McGinty's Goat
Sister Susie's Sewing Shirts For Soldiers
Stop and Shop at the Co-Op Shop
What a Mouth
When Father Papered the Parlour

With Her Head Tucked Underneath Her
Arm

Whitcup, Leonard
Boots and Saddle
Fiesta
From the Vine Came the Grape
March Winds and April Showers
Snake Charmer, The

White, Barry
Baby We Better Try to Get it Together
Can't Get Enough of Your Love Babe
It May Be Winter Outside (But in My
Heart it's Spring)
Let the Music Play
Love's Theme
Walkin' in the Rain With the One I Love
What Am I Gonna Do With You
You See the Trouble With Me
You're the First, The Last, My Every-
thing

White, Maurice
Best of My Love, The
Boogie Wonderland
Fantasy
Let's Groove
September

Whitfield, Norman
Ball Of Confusion
Car Wash
Cloud Nine
He Was Really Saying Something
I Can't Get Next to You
I Heard It Through the Grapevine
It Should Have Been Me
Just My Imagination
Papa Was a Rolling Stone
Take a Look Around
Too Busy Thinking About My Baby
War
Wherever I Lay My Hat (That's My Home)

Whiting, George
Believe It Beloved
Don't Let Your Love Go Wrong
High Up on a Hill Top
My Blue Heaven
Saddle Your Blues to a Wild Mustang

Whiting, Richard A.
Beyond the Blue Horizon
Bimini Bay
Breezin' Along With the Breeze
Eadie Was a Lady
Guilty
Have You Got Any Castles Baby
Honey
Hooray For Hollywood
Horses
I Can't Escape From You
Japanese Sandman
Louise
Mammy's Little Coal Black Rose
My Future Just Passed
My Ideal
On the Good Ship Lollipop
Ride, Tenderfoot, Ride
She's Funny That Way
Sleepy Time Gal
Some Sunday Morning
Sundown in Little Green Hollow
Sweet Child (I'm Wild About You)
'Till We Meet Again
Too Marvellous For Words
Ukulele Lady
When Did You Leave Heaven
When Shall We Meet Again
Where the Black Eyed Susans Grow

Where the Morning Glories Grow
You're An Old Smoothie

Whitney, Joan
Ain't Nobody Hear But Us Chickens
Candy
Come With Me My Honey
Far Away Places
It All Comes Back to Me Now
It's Love, Love, Love
Love Somebody
Money is the Root of All Evil
My Sister and I
That's the Beginning of the End
Weep No More My Lady

Whittaker, Roger
Durham Town (The Leaving)
I Don't Believe in if Any More
Last Farewell, The
New World in the Morning, A

Wilde, Marty
Bad Boy
Cambodia
Chequered Love
Four Letter Word, A
I'm a Tiger
Ice in the Sun
Kids in America
Love Me Love My Dog

Wilde, Ricky
Cambodia
Chequered Love
Four Letter Word, A
Kids in America
Never Trust a Stranger

Williams, Clarence
Baby Won't You Please Come Home
Cake Walking Babies From Home
I Ain't Gonna Give Nobody None O'This
Jelly Roll
I Can't Dance, I Got Ants In My Pants
Royal Garden Blues
Sugar Blues
T'Aint Nobody's Bizness If I Do

Williams, Hank
Cold Cold Heart
Hey Good Looking
Jambalaya (On the Bayou)
Your Cheating Heart

Williams, Harry
I'm Afraid to Come Home In the Dark
In the Shade Of the Old Apple Tree
It's a Long Way to Tipperary
Mello Cello
Rose Room

Williams, Spencer
Basin Street Blues
Careless Love
Everybody Loves My Baby
I Ain't Gonna Give Nobody None O'This
Jelly Roll
I Ain't Got Nobody
I Found a New Baby
I'm Sending a Letter to Santa Claus
Royal Garden Blues
Shim-Me-Sha-Wabble
Soft Shoe Shuffle, The
When the Lights Are Low

Wilson, Brian
Break Away
Darlin'
Do It Again
God Only Knows
Good Vibrations
Heroes and Villains

I Get Around
Sloop John B, The

Wilson, Frank
Love Child
Still Water
Stoned Love
Up the Ladder to the Roof

Wilson, Meredith
I See the Moon
May the Good Lord Bless and Keep You
Seventy-Six Trombones
Till There Was You
Trouble

Wilson, Tony
Brother Louie
Disco Queen
Emma
I Believe (In Love)
Lady Barbara
Love is Life
You Sexy Thing

Wimperis, Arthur
Arcady is Ever Young
Canoe Song, The
Gilbert the Filbert
Here's to Love
I'll Make a Man of You
If You Could Care For Me
Pipes of Pan, The
Temple Bell, The
Tony From America

Wine, Toni
Black Pearl
Candida
Groovy Kind of Love, A
What Are You Doing Sunday?

Winwood, Steve
Gimme Some Loving
Here We Go Round the Mulberry Bush
I'm a Man
Paper Sun

Wise, Fred
'A' You're Adorable
Follow That Dream
Kissin' Cousins
Let's Walk That-a-Way
Mother Nature and Father Time
Nightingale
Oo! What You Do to Me
Pretty Little Black Eyed Susie
Rock-a-Hula Baby
Wooden Heart

Wiseman, Ben
Follow That Dream
Let's Walk That-a-Way
Mother Nature and Father Time
Rock-a-Hula Baby
Wooden Heart

Witherspoon, William
Farewell Is a Lonely Sound
I'll Pick a Rose For My Rose
I'll Say Forever My Love
It's Wonderful
What Becomes of the Brokenhearted

Wonder, Stevie
Boogie on Reggae Woman
Crown, The
Do I Do
Happy Birthday
He's Misstra Know It All
I Ain't Gonna Stand For It
I Don't Know Why
I Just Called to Say I Love You

I Was Made to Love Her
I Wish
Isn't She Lovely?
Lately
Let's Get Serious
Living For the City
Masterblaster (Jammin')
My Cherie Amour
My Love
Never Had a Dream Come True
Overjoyed
Part Time Lover
Signed, Sealed, Delivered, I'm Yours
Sir Duke
Superstition
Tears of a Clown, The
You Are the Sunshine of My Life
Your Kiss is Sweet

Wood, Guy
Donkey Song, The
Faith Can Move Mountains
My One and Only Love
October Twilight
Till Then

Wood, Haydn
Brown Bird Singing, A
It is Only a Tiny Garden
Love's Garden of Roses
O Flower Divine
Roses of Picardy

Wood, Ron
Cindy Incidentally
Pool Hall Richard
Stay With Me
You Can Make Me Dance Sing or Anything

Wood, Roy
Angel Fingers
Are You Ready to Rock?
Ball Park Incident
Blackberry Way
Brontosaurus
California Man
Curly
Fire Brigade
Flowers in the Rain
Forever
Hello Susie
I Can Hear the Grass Grow
I Wish It Could Be Christmas Everyday
Night Of Fear
Rock and Roll Winter
See My Baby Jive
Tonight

Woods, Harry
Celebratin'
Clouds Will Soon Roll By, The
Dancing With My Shadow
Goodnight
Hang Out the Stars In Indiana
I'll Never Say "Never Again" Again
I'm Going South
I'm Looking Over a Four-Leaf Clover
Just An Echo In the Valley
Just Like a Butterfly
Let's All Go to Mary's House
Linger a Little Longer In the Twilight
Little Kiss Each Morning, A
Little Street Where Old Friends Meet, A
Me Too
Moonbeam Kiss Her For Me
My Hat's on the Side of My Head
Old Kitchen Kettle, The
Over My Shoulder
Paddlin' Madelin' Home
Pink Elephants

Poor Papa (He's Got Nothing At All)
River Stay 'Way From My Door
She's a Great Girl
Side By Side
Since I Found You
So Many Memories
Stay Out of the South
Try a Little Tenderness
Voice In the Old Village Choir, The
We Just Couldn't Say Goodbye
We'll All Go Riding on a Rainbow
What a Little Moonlight Can Do
What Do I Care What Somebody Said?
When Somebody Thinks You're Wonderful
When the Moon Comes Over the Mountain
When the Red Red Robin (Comes Bob Bob Bobbin' Along)
When You've Got a Little Springtime In Your Heart
Whistling Waltz, The
You Ought to See Sally on Sunday

Wright, Robert
And This Is My Beloved
Baubles, Bangles and Beads
Donkey Serenade, The
It's a Blue World
Jersey Bounce
Pink Champagne
Ride Cossack, Ride
Strange Music
Stranger in Paradise

Wrubel, Allie
As You Desire Me
Fare-Thee-Well Annabelle
First Time I Saw You, The
Flirtation Walk
Gone With the Wind
Goodnight Angel
I Can't Love You Anymore
I Met Her on Monday
I'll Buy That Dream
I'm Stepping Out With a Memory Tonight
In Caliente
Johnny Fedora
Lady In Red, The
Masquerade Is Over, The
Music Maestro Please
Why Don't We Do This More Often
Zip-a-Dee-Doo-Dah

Wyle, George
Give Me Your Word
I Love the Way You Say 'Goodnight'
I Said My Pyjamas (And Put on My Prayers)
May Each Day
Quicksilver

Yellen, Jack
Ain't She Sweet?
Ain't That a Grand and Glorious Feeling
Alabama Jubilee
All Aboard For Dixieland
Are You From Dixie?
Are You Having Any Fun
Bench In a Park, A
Cheatin' on Me
Crazy Words, Crazy Tune
Down By the O-hi-o
Forgive Me
Glad Rag Doll
Happy Days Are Here Again
Happy Feet
Hard Hearted Hannah
Hold My Hand
I Wonder What's Become of Sally
Is She My Girl Friend

Mama Goes Where Papa Goes
My Pet
My Yiddishe Momme
Nasty Man
She Don't Wanna
Sing Baby Sing
Song of the Dawn
Who Cares
Young Man's Fancy

Youmans, Vincent
Carioca, The
Flying Down to Rio
Great Day
Hallelujah
I Know That You Know
I Want to Be Happy
Keeping Myself For You
More Than You Know
One Girl
Orchids In the Moonlight
Rise 'n' Shine
Sometimes I'm Happy
Tea For Two
Through the Years
Tie a String Around Your Finger
Time on My Hands
Without a Song

Young, Joe
Annie Doesn't Live Here Anymore
Cheerie Beerie Be
Crying For the Carolines
Dinah
Don't Ask Me Why
Five Foot Two, Eyes Of Blue
Have a Little Faith In Me
Hiawatha's Lullaby
How Ya Gonna Keep 'Em Down on the Farm
I Kiss Your Hand Madame (Ich Kusse Ihr Hand Madame)
I'd Love to Fall Asleep and Wake Up In My Mammy's Arms

I'm Alone Because I Love You
I'm Gonna Sit Right Down and Write Myself a Letter
I'm Sitting on Top of the World
In a Little Spanish Town
In a Shanty in Old Shanty Town
In Shadowland
King For a Day
Laugh Clown Laugh
Life Is a Song
Long Haired Lover From Liverpool
Lullaby of the Leaves
My Mammy
My Mammy's Arms
(My Sweet) Hortense
On the Level You're a Little Devil
Ooh That Kiss
Rock-a-Bye Your Baby With a Dixie Melody
Snuggled on Your Shoulder
Two Hearts In Three Quarter Time
Was That the Human Thing to Do?
When the Angelus is Ringing
Where Did Robinson Crusoe Go With Friday on Saturday Night?
Yacka Hula Hickey Dula
You're My Everything

Young, Kenny
Captain of Your Ship
Come Back and Shake Me
Doin' the Do
Goodnight Midnight
Just a Little Bit Better
Just One More Night
Only You Can
S-s-s-Single Bed
Under the Boardwalk
When Will the Good Apples Fall

Young, Rida Johnson
Ah Sweet Mystery Of Life
I'm Falling in Love With Someone

Italian Street Song
Mother Machree
'Neath the Southern Moon
Tramp, Tramp, Tramp Along the High-way
Will You Remember (Sweetheart)?

Young, Robert
Break the Rules
Caroline
Down Down
Living on an Island
Mystery Song, The
Paper Plane
Roll Over Lay Down

Young, Victor
Around the World
Beautiful Love
Blue Star (The Medic Theme)
Call of the Faraway Hills, The
Can't We Talk It Over
Ghost of a Chance, A
Golden Earrings
Hundred Years From Today, A
Johnny Guitar
Love Letters
My Foolish Heart
Our Very Own
Sam You Made the Pants Too Long
Song of Delilah, The
Stella By Starlight
Street of Dreams
Sweet Sue-Just You
When I Fall In Love

Zaret, Hy
It All Comes Back to Me Now
My Sister and I
One Meat Ball
Unchained Melody

SONGS BY SUBJECT CLASSIFICATION

A list, by subject matter, giving songs which are about that subject or have the subject matter in the title of the song. If the subject is the first word in the title, the song will not be included in this index as it can be easily located in the alphabetical section. Some of the classifications are musical genres, such as **Big Band Hits.**

Age

All The Young Dudes
Arcady Is Ever Young
Because They're Young
Call Round Any Old Time
Dear Old Pal Of Mine
Down By The Old Mill Stream
Down The Old Ox Road
Excerpt From A Teenage Opera (Grocer Jack)
For Old Times' Sake
Granny's Old Arm-Chair
Happy Birthday Sweet Sixteen
Heart Of A Teenage Girl
Hello Young Lovers
I Want A Girl Just Like The Girl That Married Dear Old Dad
I'm An Old Cow-Hand
I'm Old Fashioned
I'm Twenty-One Today
In Old Lisbon (Lisboa Antigua)
In The Good Old Summertime
It's The Same Old Dream
Keep Young And Beautiful
Little Old Lady
Little Old Mill
Love's Old Sweet Song
Me And The Old Folks At Home
My Old Dutch
My Old Flame
New Moon And An Old Serenade, A
Nineteen
Nobody Loves A Fairy When She's Forty
One Day When We're Young
Only Sixteen
Our Lodger's Such A Nice Young Man
Put On An Old Pair Of Shoes
Seventeen
So Is Your Old Lady
Something Old, Something New
Sweetheart, Let's Grow Old Together
That Dear Old Gentleman
That Old Black Magic
That Old Fashioned Mother Of Mine
That Old Feeling
That Old Gang Of Mine
That Same Old Feeling
That Sly Old Gentleman (From Featherbed Lane)
Theme For Young Lovers
There'll Be A Hot Time In The Old Town Tonight
They're Either Too Young Or Too Old
To Be Young Gifted And Black
Too Much Too Young
Too Young To Go Steady
Voice In The Old Village Choir, The
When I Grow Too Old To Dream
When I'm Sixty-four
When The World Was Young
When We Were Young
When You And I Were Seventeen
When You And I Were Young, Maggie
When You Were Sweet Sixteen
Wonderful World Of The Young, The
You Make Me Feel So Young
You're An Old Smoothie
You're Sixteen
Young Girl
Young Lovers
Young Ones, The

Air

In The Air Tonight
It's In The Air
Lords Of The Air
Love Is In The Air
On The Air
Something In The Air
There's Something In The Air
Walking In The Air

American States

Alabama Jubilee
Alabama Moon
Alabamy Bound
Arizona
At A Georgia Camp Meeting
Back Home In Tennessee
Black Hills Of Dakota, The
California Here I Come
California Man
Can't Get Indiana Off My Mind
Carolina
Carolina In The Morning
Carolina Moon
Deep In The Heart Of Texas
Devil Went Down To Georgia, The
Down The Oregon Trail
Everything Is Peaches Down In Georgia
From New York To L.A.
Georgia On My Mind
Gonna Build A Big Fence Around Texas
Goodbye Hawaii
Goodbye Virginia
Hang Out The Stars In Indiana
Hawaiian Butterfly
Hello Hawaii, How Are You
Hotel California
I Want To Go Back To Michigan
I'm Coming Virginia
I'm Going Back To Old Nebraska
I've Got The Sweetest Girl In Maryland
Idaho
Indiana
Indiana Wants Me
Kentucky
Kentucky Lullaby
Kentucky Waltz, The
Louisiana
Louisiana Hayride
Massachusetts
Memphis Tennessee
Miami Vice
Missouri Waltz, The
My Ohio Home
My Sunny Tennessee
North To Alaska
Oklahoma
Omaha
Pennsylvania Polka
Roamin' To Wyomin'
Roll Along Kentucky Moon
Sentimental Gentleman From Georgia, A
Somewhere In Old Wyoming
Stars Fell On Alabama
Sweet Indiana Home
Tennessee Waltz, The
Tennessee Wig-Walk, The
There's A Blue Ridge Round My Heart, Virginia
There's A Girl In The Heart Of Maryland
They're Wearing 'Em Higher In Hawaii
Touch Of Texas
Walkin' To Missouri
We'll Have A Jubilee In My Old Kentucky Home
When The Midnight Choo-Choo Leaves For Alabam'
Whispering Pines Of Nevada, The
Wyoming
Yellow Rose Of Texas, The
You're In Kentucky As Sure As You're Born

Anatomy

Angel Eyes
Angel Face
Arms Of Mary, The
Baby Face
Beautiful Brown Eyes
Beautiful Eyes
Bette Davis Eyes
Better Not Roll Those Blue Blue Eyes
Big Head
Black Bottom, The
Black Skin Blue Eyed Boy
Black-eyed Boys, The
Blue Eyes
Body And Soul
Born With A Smile On My Face
Bright Eyes
Brown Eyed Handsome Man
Brown Eyes Why Are You Blue
Brush Those Tears From Your Eyes
Butterfingers
Can't Take My Eyes Off You
Careless Hands
Cheek To Cheek
Cheerful Little Earful
China In Your Hand
Clap Hands, Here Comes Charley
Clap Yo' Hands
Close Your Eyes
Cock-Eyed Optimist, A
Come Home To My Arms
Dancing With Tears In My Eyes
Died In Your Arms
Dirty Hands, Dirty Face
Dizzy Fingers
Doctor My Eyes
Don't It Make My Brown Eyes Blue
Don't Let The Stars Get In Your Eyes
Dry Bones
Earful Of Music, An
Ebony Eyes
Eye Level
Eye Of The Tiger, The
Feet Up
Finger Of Suspicion, The
First Time Ever I Saw Your Face, The
Five Foot Two, Eyes Of Blue
Flat Foot Floogie, The
Foot Tapper
Footloose
For Your Eyes Only
Forty-seven Ginger Headed Sailors
Four Little Heels
From The Top Of Your Head (To The Tip Of Your Toes)
Fuhrer's Face, Der
Full Moon And Empty Arms
Funny Face
Girl With The Dreamy Eyes
Give Yourself A Pat On The Back

Goggle Eye
Going In With My Eyes Open
Goldfinger
Green Eyes (Aquellos Ojos Verdes)
Hair Of Gold, Eyes Of Blue
Hands Across The Table
Hands Off - She's Mine
Happy Feet
Hard Headed Woman
Hawkeye
He's Got The Whole World In His Hands
Head Over Heels
Head Over Heels In Love
Here In My Arms
Hold Me In Your Arms
Hold My Hand
Hold Your Hand Out Naughty Boy
Hold Your Head Up
Hot Legs
Hot Lips
I Close My Eyes And Count To Ten
I Don't See Me In Your Eyes Anymore
I Have Eyes
I Just Can't Make My Eyes Behave
I Know Of Two Bright Eyes
I Lift Up My Finger And I Say Tweet Tweet
I Only Have Eyes For You
I See Your Face Before Me
I Want To Hold Your Hand
I'd Love To Fall Asleep And Wake Up In My Mammy's Arms
I'll Close My Eyes
I'm Gonna Wash My Hands Of You
I'm Gonna Wash That Man Right Out Of My Hair
I'm Knee Deep In Daisies
I'm Thinking Tonight Of My Blue Eyes
I've Got My Eyes On You
I've Got My Fingers Crossed
I've Got Rings On My Fingers
I've Got You Under My Skin
I've Grown Accustomed To Her Face
If Those Lips Could Only Speak
If You Stub Your Toe On The Moon
In My Arms
In The Arms Of Love
In Your Eyes
It Sure Brings Out The Love In Your Eyes
Keep An Eye On Your Heart
Keep Your Hands Off My Baby
Kiss In Your Eyes
Knee Deep In The Blues
Knees Up Mother Brown
Laughing Irish Eyes
Lay Back In The Arms Of Someone
Lay Your Hands On Me
Let Me Cry On Your Shoulder
Linger In My Arms A Little Longer Baby
Long Haired Lover From Liverpool
Long Legged Woman Dressed In Black
Look At That Face
Looking Through The Eyes Of Love
Lucky Lips
Ma! He's Making Eyes At Me
Man With The Child In His Eyes
Man With The Golden Arm
Moon Got In My Eyes, The
My Eyes Adored You
My Fate Is In Your Hands
My Hat's On The Side Of My Head
My Honey's Lovin' Arms
My Mind's Eye
My Mother's Eyes
My Two Front Teeth
Night Has A Thousand Eyes, The
No Arms Can Ever Hold You
On Your Toes
Only When You're In My Arms

Oops Up Side Your Head
Our Lips Are Sealed
Over My Shoulder
Powder Your Face With Sunshine
Pretty Eyed Baby
Pretty Kitty Blue Eyes
Pretty Little Angel Eyes
Pretty Little Black Eyed Susie
Put On A Happy Face
Put Your Arms Around Me Honey
Put Your Hands Together
Put Your Head On My Shoulder
Put Your Shoes On Lucy
Raindrops Keep Falling On My Head
Rose In Her Hair, The
Rudolph The Red Nosed Reindeer
Sailor With The Navy Blue Eyes, The
Sexy Eyes
Shaddup You Face
Shake Your Body (Down To The Ground)
Silver Hair And Heart Of Gold
Slow Hand
Smoke Gets In Your Eyes
Snuggled On Your Shoulder
Spanish Eyes (Moon Over Naples)
Star Eyes
Starry Eyed
Stars In My Eyes
Stars Shine In Your Eyes
Take That Look Off Your Face
That Red Head Gal
Them There Eyes
There's A Rainbow 'Round My Shoulder
There's Danger In Your Eyes Cherie
There's Something In Your Eyes
There's Something Spanish In Your Eyes
There's Yes! Yes! In Your Eyes
Tickle Toe, The
Tie A String Around Your Finger
Tiger Feet
Time On My Hands
Tip Of My Finger, The
Touch Of Your Hand, The
Touch Of Your Lips
Twenty Tiny Fingers
Under Your Thumb
Walk Hand In Hand
Wandering Eyes
Wash Your Face In My Sink
We Close Our Eyes
What A Mouth
What Do You Want To Make Those Eyes At Me For
When The Girl In Your Arms
When You're Hair Has Turned To Silver
Where The Black Eyed Susans Grow
Where Will The Dimple Be
Where'd You Get Those Eyes
Wide Eyed And Legless
With Her Head Tucked Underneath Her Arm
With My Eyes Wide Open I'm Dreamin'
With The Eyes Of A Child
With The Wind And The Rain In Your Hair
With These Hands
Wonderful Eyes
Work That Body
Wrapped Around Your Finger
You Go To My Head
You Need Hands
Your Eyes
Your Feet's Too Big

Angel

And The Angels Sing
Blue Angel
Broken Down Angel
Earth Angel

Goodnight Angel
Got A Date With An Angel
Heaven Must Be Missing An Angel
Look Homeward Angel
My Special Angel
Pretty Little Angel Eyes
Sinner Kissed An Angel, A
There Are Angels Outside Heaven
There Must Be An Angel Playing With My Heart

Animals

Ali Baba's Camel
Bird Dog
Blame It On The Pony Express
Brontosaurus
Buffalo Billy
Buffalo Gals
Buffalo Soldier
Buffalo Stance
Bullfrog Patrol, The
Cat Among The Pigeons
Cat Crept In, The
Cat's Whiskers, The
Chick Chick Chicken
Chicken Reel, The
Chicken Song, The
Cool For Cats
Count Your Blessings Instead Of Sheep
Crazy Horses
Crocodile Rock
Cry Wolf
Daddy Wouldn't Buy Me A Bow-wow
Deer Hunter Theme, The
Dog Eat Dog
Don't Do That To The Poor Puss Cat
Don't Go In The Lions' Cage Tonight
Donkey Serenade, The
Donkey Song, The
Down On The Farm
Eye Of The Tiger, The
Felix Kept On Walking
Ferdinand The Bull
Fox On The Run
Funky Gibbon, The
Hi Ho Silver
Holy Cow
Home James And Don't Spare The Horses
Horse With No Name, A
Horses
Horsey Keep Your Tail Up
Horsey, Horsey
Hound Dog
Hungry Like The Wolf
I Go Ape
I Taut I Taw A Puddy Tat
I'm A Tiger
Jollity Farm
Karma Chameleon
King's Horses, The
Kitten On The Keys
Little Donkey
Little Red Monkey
Little White Bull
Livery Stable Blues
Lonely Pup (In A Christmas Shop)
Love Cats, The
Love Me Love My Dog
Mad Dogs And Englishmen
March Hare, The
Mary Had A Little Lamb
Matchstalk Men And Matchstalk Cats And Dogs
Me And My Dog
Me And You And A Dog Named Boo
Misery Farm
Monkey
Monkey And The Organ Grinder, The

Monkey Spanner
Mule Train
Muskrat
Muskrat Ramble
Nellie The Elephant
Old Shep
Paddy McGinty's Goat
Pig Got Up And Slowly Walked Away, The
Pink Elephants
Pop Goes The Weasel
Puff The Magic Dragon
Puss 'N' Boots
Rat Race
Rat Trap
Ride A Wild Horse
Rudolph The Red Nosed Reindeer
Run Rabbit Run
Running Bear
Saddle Your Blues To A Wild Mustang
Simon Smith And His Amazing Dancing Bear
Stray Cat Strut
Talk To The Animals
That Doggie In The Window
They Shoot Horses Don't They
Tie Me Kangaroo Down Sport
Tiger Feet
Tiger Rag
Turtle Power
Walk The Dinosaur
Waltzing Cat, The
What's New Pussycat
When I See An Elephant Fly
Whistler And His Dog, The
White Horse Inn, The
White Horses
Who's Afraid Of The Big Bad Wolf
Wild Horses
Yellow Dog Blues

Answers (see Questions)

Apparel

Alice Blue Gown
All Around My Hat
Baggy Trousers
Bell Bottom Blues
Bell Bottom Trousers
Blue Suede Shoes
Boots And Saddle
Button Up Your Overcoat
Buttons And Bows
Chantilly Lace
Cuff Of My Shirt, The
Did Tosti Raise His Bowler Hat When He Said Goodbye
Dress You Up
Fancy Pants
Favourite Shirt
Feather In Her Tyrolean Hat, The
Full Metal Jacket
Gal In Calico, A
Gal With The Yaller Shoes, The
Girl In The Alice Blue Gown, The
Girl In The Crinoline Gown, The
Girl In The Little Green Hat, The
Goody Two Shoes
Hats Off To Larry
Her Bathing Suit Never Got Wet
Hobnailed Boots That Farver Wore, The
Hole In My Shoe
Homburg
I Can't Dance, I Got Ants In My Pants
I Can't Do My Bally Bottom Button Up
I Said My Pyjamas (And Put On My Prayers)

Itsy Bitsy Teenie Weenie Yellow Polka Dot Bikini
Jeans On
Johnny Fedora
Keep Your Skirts Down Mary Ann
Kinky Boots
Lady In Red
Lipstick On Your Collar
Little Bird On Nellie's Hat, The
Little Shirt My Mother Made For Me
My Hat's On The Side Of My Head
Old Soft Shoe, The
One, Two, Button Your Shoe
Parrot On The Fortune Teller's Hat, The
Princess In Rags
Puss 'N' Boots
Put On An Old Pair Of Shoes
Put On Your Old Gray Bonnet
Put On Your Tat-Ta Little Girlie
Rags To Riches
Red Dress
Sadie's Shawl
Sand In My Shoes
Scarlet Ribbons
She Wears Red Feathers
Shine On Your Shoes, A
Shoe Shine Boy
Shoes With Wings On
Sister Susie's Sewing Shirts For Soldiers
Skirts
Sky Blue Shirt And A Rainbow Tie, A
Smarty Pants
Soft Shoe Shuffle, The
Sun Has Got His Hat On, The
Sunbonnet Blue, A
Sunbonnet Sue
These Boots Are Made For Walking
They're Wearing 'em Higher In Hawaii
Tie A Yellow Ribbon
Toor-le On His Bonnet, The
Top Hat, White Tie And Tails
Venus In Blue Jeans
We Don't Have To Take Our Clothes Off
When You're All Dressed Up And No Place To Go
Where Did You Get That Hat
Wherever I Lay My Hat (That's My Home)
White Sport Coat, A (And A Pink Carnation)
White Suit Samba, The
You Forgot Your Gloves
Zoot Suit, A

Armed Forces

Army Air Corps Song, The
Army Game, The
Army Of Today's Alright, The
Badge From Your Coat, The
Be My Comrade True
Bell Bottom Blues
By The Side Of The Zuyder Zee
Caissons Go Rolling Along, The
Captain Gingah
Changing Of The Guard, The
Comrades
Don't Stop The Music
Fleet's In Port Again, The
Fleet's In, The
Forty-seven Ginger Headed Sailors
French Military Marching Song
Handsome Territorial, A
I Want To Be A Military Man
I've Got My Captain Working For Me Now
In The Navy
In The Quartermaster's Stores
Jolly Good Luck To The Girl Who Loves A Soldier
King's Navee, The
Kiss Me Goodnight Sergeant-Major

Letter To A Soldier
Lords Of The Air
March Of The Grenadiers
Sailor (Seeman Deine Heimat Ist Das Meer)
Sailor Who Are You Dreaming Of Tonight
Sailor With The Navy Blue Eyes, The
Sister Susie's Sewing Shirts For Soldiers
Soldier Blue
Soldiers In The Park, The
Stop The Cavalry
There's A Boy Coming Home On Leave
There's Something About A Soldier
This Is The Army Mister Jones
Universal Soldier
When A Soldier's On Parade
When The Guards Are On Parade
When The Guardsman Started Crooning On Parade
When The Sergeant Major's On Parade
Wings Over The Navy
Yeoman Of England, The
You're In The Army Now

Baby

Angie Baby
Bandanna Babies
Be My Baby
Beach Baby
Because My Baby Don't Mean Maybe Now
Bossa Nova Baby
Bye Bye Baby
Bye Bye Baby (Baby Goodbye)
Bye Bye Baby, Goodbye
Come To Baby Do
Comin' Home Baby
Don't Do It Baby
Don't Make My Baby Blue
Dream Baby
Everybody Loves My Baby
Gee Baby
Hang On In There Baby
Having My Baby
Hello Ma Baby
Here Comes My Baby
Hey Baby
High Class Baby
His Majesty The Baby
I Found A Million Dollar Baby
I Found A New Baby
I Got You Babe
I Love My Baby, My Baby Loves Me
I Love You Baby
I Wonder Where My Baby Is Tonight
I'll Be Your Baby Tonight
I'm Crazy 'Bout My Baby
I'm Just A Baby
I'm Nobody's Baby
I'm Your Baby Tonight
It's All Over Baby Blue
Keep Your Hands Off My Baby
Like A Baby
Linger In My Arms A Little Longer Baby
Love To Love You Baby
Ma Curly Headed Babby
Maybe Baby
My Baby Just Cares For Me
My Baby Loves Lovin'
My Golden Baby
My Melancholy Baby
Oh No Not My Baby
Other People's Babies
Pardon Me Pretty Baby
Pretty Baby
Pretty Eyed Baby
Rock Your Baby
Rock-A-Bye Your Baby With A Dixie Melody

Rock-a-hula Baby
Rockin' Roll Baby
Run Baby Run
See My Baby Jive
Sleep My Baby Sleep
So Long Baby
Someone Else's Baby
Something 'Bout You Baby I Like
Stepping Out With My Baby
Sugar Baby Love
Take Good Care Of My Baby
That's You Baby
There Ain't No Maybe In My Baby's Eyes
Tonight's My Night With Baby
Too Busy Thinking About My Baby
Walkin' My Baby Back Home
War Baby
When My Baby Smiles At Me
Whose Baby Are You
Yes Sir, That's My Baby
You Don't Have To Be A Baby To Cry
You Must Have Been A Beautiful Baby
You Say The Sweetest Things Baby
You're My Baby

Bad

Big Bad John
Even The Bad Times Are Good
Good, The Bad And The Ugly, The
I've Been A Bad Bad Boy
There's A Little Bit Of Bad In Every Good
Little Girl

Beautiful

Bless Yore Beautiful Hide
But Beautiful
By The Beautiful Sea
Do I Love You Because You're Beautiful
Keep Young And Beautiful
Most Beautiful Girl In The World
Most Beautiful Girl, The
My Beautiful Lady
Night Is Young And You're So Beautiful,
The
Oh What A Beautiful Morning
Oh Yes You're Beautiful
Oh You Beautiful Doll
She's So Beautiful
Together We Are Beautiful
Too Beautiful To Last
We Could Make Such Beautiful Music
Together
Weak In The Presence Of Beauty
When You're In Love With A Beautiful
Woman
You Are Beautiful
You Must Have Been A Beautiful Baby

Believe

Daydream Believer
Don't Believe A Word
How Could You Believe Me, When I Said
I Love You, When You Know I've Been A
Liar All My Life
I Believe
I Believe In Father Christmas
I Believe In Miracles
I Can't Believe That You're In Love With
Me
I Don't Believe In If Any More
I Just Can't Help Believing
I Still Believe
I'm A Believer
I'm Making Believe
If You Believe
It's Only Make Believe
Lady Who Didn't Believe In Love, The
Land Of Make Believe

Little Lady Make Believe
Make Believe
Please Believe Me
They Didn't Believe Me
Why Don't You Believe Me

Bell

Blue Bell Polka
Blue Bells Of Broadway, The
Don't Ring-a Da Bell
Hang On The Bell Nellie
I'm Gonna Ring The Bell Tonight
If I Were A Bell
Jingle Bell Rock
Ring Dem Bells
Ring My Bell
Saved By The Bell
Serenade Of The Bells
Snowy White Snow And Jingle Bells
Somebody Bad Stole De Wedding Bell
Three Bells, The (Les Trois Cloches)
Ting-a-ling (The Waltz Of The Bells)
Wedding Bell Blues
Wedding Bells
Wedding Bells Are Breaking Up That Old
Gang Of Mine
While The Angelus Was Ringing

Big Band Hits

Adios Mariquita Linda
Amapola
American Patrol
And Her Tears Flowed Like Wine
And The Angels Sing
At Last
Begin The Beguine
Big Noise From Winnetka
Breeze And I, The
Bumble Boogie
Caldonia
Chattanooga Choo Choo
Cherokee
Concerto For Clarinet
Dipsy Doodle, The
Do Nothing Till You Hear From Me
Don't Get Around Much Anymore
Elmer's Tune
Frenesi
Green Eyes (Aquellos Ojos Verdes)
Hawaiian War Chant, The
I Can't Get Started
I Got It Bad, And That Ain't Good
I Remember You
I'm Beginning To See The Light
I'm Getting Sentimental Over You
I've Got A Gal In Kalamazoo
In The Mood
It Don't Mean A Thing (If It Ain't Got That
Swing)
It Happened In Sun Valley
Jersey Bounce
Johnson Rag
Juke Box Saturday Night
Just A-Sittin' And A-Rockin'
Maria Elena
Mood Indigo
Moonlight Cocktail
Moonlight Serenade
Music Makers, The
My Guy's Come Back
On The Sunny Side Of The Street
One O'Clock Jump
Opus Number One
Peanut Vendor, The (El Manisero)
Pennsylvania Six-Five-Thousand
Perdido
Perfidia
Polka Dots And Moonbeams

Pompton Turnpike
Rockin' In Rhythm
Serenade In Blue
Skyliner
So Rare
Solitude
Sophisticated Lady
South Rampart Street Parade
Stage Coach
Star Eyes
Stompin' At The Savoy
Story Of A Starry Night, The
String Of Pearls, A
Sunrise Serenade
Take The 'A' Train
Tangerine
Time's A Wastin'
Tuxedo Junction
Woodchopper's Ball
Yes Indeed

Birds

Albatross
And The Birds Were Singing (Et Les
Oiseaux Chantaient)
Bye Bye Blackbird
Cat Among The Pigeons
Cold Turkey
Cry Of The Wild Goose, The
Cuckoo Waltz, The
Dicky Bird Hop, The
Disco Duck
Follow The Swallow
Gonna Find Me A Bluebird
Green Cockatoo, The
Hello Bluebird
Hey Little Hen
Hot Canary, The
I'm A Little Blackbird Looking For A Blue-
bird
I'm Telling The Birds, Telling The Bees,
How I Love You
If I Were A Blackbird
In The Chapel In The Moonlight
La Golondrina (The Swallow)
Let's All Sing Like The Birdies Sing
Let's Turkey Trot
Little Bird On Nellie's Hat, The
Little Bird Told Me, A
Little Red Rooster
Little White Duck
Little Yellow Bird
Meadowlark
Mister Cuckoo (Cuculino)
Mister Meadowlark
Mocking Bird Hill
My Blackbirds Are Bluebirds Now
Night Birds
Night Owl
Nightingale
Nightingale Sang In Berkeley Square, A
Parrot On The Fortune Teller's Hat, The
Philomel
Pickin' A Chicken
Pretty Flamingo
Red Wing
Ride A White Swan
Robins And Roses
Rockin' Robin
Rocking Goose
She Was One Of The Early Birds
Sing Joyous Bird
Sing Little Birdie
Skylark
Sparrow, The
This Little Bird
Two Little Blue Birds
Ugly Duckling, The
Walkin' Thru Mockin' Bird Lane

Watch The Birdie
What's The Good Word Mister Bluebird
When Doves Cry
When The Red Red Robin (Comes Bob Bob Bobbin' Along)
When The Swallows Come Back To Capistrano
White Dove, The
Wings Of A Dove
Woodpeckers Song (Reginella Campagnola)
Woody Woodpecker

Birthday

Happy Birthday
Happy Birthday Sweet Sixteen
I'm Twenty-One Today
It's My Mother's Birthday Today
What Can You Give A Nudist On His Birthday

Blues

Aunt Hagar's Blues
Bad Penny Blues
Basin Street Blues
Beale Street Blues
Bell Bottom Blues
Big City Blues
Birth Of The Blues, The
Blacksmith Blues, The
Bye Bye Blues
Chinese Laundry Blues
Farewell Blues
Goodbye Blues
Hong Kong Blues
House Of David Blues, The
I Gotta Right To Sing The Blues
I Guess That's Why They Call It The Blues
Jazz Me Blues
Knee Deep In The Blues
Learning The Blues
Left All Alone Again Blues
Limehouse Blues
Livery Stable Blues
Lovesick Blues
Malt And Barley Blues
Memphis Blues
Mess Of Blues, A
Old Piano Roll Blues, The
Old Rag Blues
Royal Garden Blues
Saddle Your Blues To A Wild Mustang
Saint James' Infirmary
Saint Louis Blues
Shaking The Blues Away
Singin' The Blues
Singin' The Blues (Till My Daddy Comes Home)
Singing The Blues
Sobbin' Blues
Story Of The Blues
Subterranean Homesick Blues
Swinging Shepherd Blues
Twentieth Century Blues
Wabash Blues
Wang Wang Blues, The
Wedding Bell Blues
Worried Man Blues
Yellow Dog Blues

Boats / Ships

Anchors Aweigh
Big Ship
Boat That I Row, The
Canoe Song, The
Captain Of Your Ship
Day-O (Banana Boat Song)

Dream Boat
Ferry Boat Inn, The
Ferry Boat Serenade (La Piccinina)
Fleet's In, The
Has Anybody Seen Our Ship
He Played His Ukulele As The Ship Went Down
Michael Row The Boat Ashore
My Ship
My Ship Is Coming In
Old Ship Of Mine
On A Slow Boat To China
On A Steamer Coming Over
On The Good Ship Lollipop
On The Good Ship Yacki Hicki Doo La
Onedin Line, The
Red Sails In The Sunset
Rock The Boat
Row, Row, Row
Sail On
Sailing
Sailing Down Chesapeake Bay
Shrimp Boats
Sit Down You're Rocking The Boat
Skye Boat Song, The
Sloop John B, The
Someone's Rocking My Dreamboat
Steamboat Bill
Stowaway
There's A Harbour Of Dreamboats
Three Galleons, The (Las Tres Carabelas)
Trains And Boats And Planes
Waiting For The Robert E. Lee
When My Ship Comes In
Wreck Of The Antoinette, The

Boogie

Baby Sittin' Boogie
Blame It On The Boogie
Bumble Boogie
Get Up And Boogie
Guitar Boogie Shuffle
Honaloochie Boogie
I Love To Boogie
Little Boogie Woogie
Rock-A-Beatin' Boogie
Scrub Me Mama With A Boogie Beat
Shot Gun Boogie
Wap-Bam-Boogie
Yes Sir I Can Boogie

Boy

Bachelor Boy
Bad Bad Boy
Bad Boy
Bad Boys
Black Skin Blue Eyed Boy
Black-Eyed Boys, The
Boy From Nowhere
Chattanoogie Shoeshine Boy
China Boy
Doing Alright With The Boys
Drop The Boy
Girls Were Made To Take Care Of Boys
Hersham Boys
Hev Yew Gotta Loight Boy
Hold Your Hand Out Naughty Boy
I'm A Boy
I've Been A Bad Bad Boy
It's A Boy
Japanese Boy
Jones Boy, The
Kiss The Boys Goodbye
Let's Hear It For The Boy
Little Boy Sad
Little Boy That Santa Claus Forgot
Little Curly Hair In A High Chair

Little Drummer Boy, The
Lonely Boy
Looking For A Boy
Mad About The Boy
Mary's Boy Child
My Boy
My Boy Lollipop
Nature Boy
Oh Boy
Oh Boy (The Mood I'm In)
Pretty Blue Eyes
Runaway Boys
Shy Boy
Small Town Boy
Sorry Boy
Tarzan Boy
Toy Boy
Twentieth Century Boy
Two Little Boys
What Kinda Boy You Lookin' For Girl
When The Boys Talk About The Girls
Where The Boys Are
Wide Boy
Wild Boys, The
Yankee Doodle Boy

Buildings

At Trinity Church
Bells Of St. Mary's, The
Bless This House
Blow The House Down
Bungalow, A Piccolo And You, A
Cafe In Vienna
Castles In The Sand
Chapel Of The Roses, The
Christopher Robin At Buckingham Palace
Come On A My House
Cottage For Sale
Doll House
Ferry Boat Inn, The
Have You Got Any Castles Baby
Heartbreak Hotel
Hotel California
House Is Haunted, The
House Of Bamboo, The
House Of David Blues, The
House Of Singing Bamboo, The
House Of The Rising Sun, The
House That Jack Built
House That Jack Built, The
House With Love In It, A
If It Wasn't For The 'Ouses In Between
In A Little Secondhand Store
In A Monastery Garden
In A Shanty In Old Shanty Town
In The Chapel In The Moonlight
In The Middle Of The House
It's So Nice To Have A Man Around The House
Jack That House Built, The
Just A Cottage Small (By A Waterfall)
Let's All Go To Mary's House
Let's All Go To The Music Hall
Little Dutch Mill
My Castle On The Nile
My House Is Your House (Mi Casa, Su Casa)
Our House
Ours Is A Nice 'Ouse Ours Is
Saint James' Infirmary
Stately Homes Of England, The
Tara's Theme
Temple Bell, The
Tenement Symphony, The
There's A Cabin In The Pines
There's A Ghost In My House
There's A Pawnshop On The Corner
There's A Small Hotel

There's Always Room At Our House
This Ole House
Up On The Roof
We Won't Live In A Castle
White Horse Inn, The
Who's In The House
Winchester Cathedral
Windmill In Old Amsterdam, A
Windmills Of Your Mind

Child / Children

All God's Chillun Got Rhythm
Belfast Child
Don't Have Any More Missus Moore
Don't Treat Me Like A Child
Ghetto Child
Goodnight Children, Everywhere
If The Kids Are United
Little Children
Little Curly Hair In A High Chair
Love Child
Mamma Gave Birth To The Soul Children
Man With The Child In His Eyes
Mary's Boy Child
Mother And Child Reunion
Nobody's Child
Real Wild Child
Small Fry
Speak Like A Child
Sweet Child O' Mine
Voodoo Chile
When A Child Is Born (Soleado)
With The Eyes Of A Child

Christmas

Do They Know It's Christmas
Does Santa Claus Sleep With His Whis-
kers
Fairy On The Christmas Tree, The
Happy Christmas (War Is Over)
Have Yourself A Merry Little Christmas
I Believe In Father Christmas
I Saw Mommy Kissing Santa Claus
I Wish It Could Be Christmas Everyday
I'm Sending A Letter To Santa Claus
If Everyday Was Like Christmas
It's Gonna Be A Cold Cold Christmas
Last Christmas
Little Boy That Santa Claus Forgot
Little Donkey
Lonely Pup (In A Christmas Shop)
Lonely This Christmas
Merry Christmas Everyone
Merry Xmas Everybody
Rockin' Around The Christmas Tree
Santa Bring My Baby Back To Me
Santa Claus Is Coming To Town
Santo Natale
Snowy White Snow And Jingle Bells
White Christmas
Wombling Merry Christmas
Wonderful Christmas Time

Circus/Clown

Be A Clown
Broken Hearted Clown
Cathy's Clown
Day The Circus Left Town, The
Death Of A Clown, The
Ha Ha Said The Clown
I Am A Clown
Laugh Clown Laugh
Merry-go-round Broke Down, The
Oh What A Circus
On A Carousel
Send In The Clowns
Tears Of A Clown, The

Colours

Alice Blue Gown
Am I Blue
Beautiful Brown Eyes
Better Not Roll Those Blue Blue Eyes
Beyond The Blue Horizon
Big Yellow Taxi
Bob White
Carry Me Back To Green Pastures
Coal Black Mammy
Deep Purple
Don't It Make My Brown Eyes Blue
Evergreen
Fade To Grey
Fine Brown Frame
Five Foot Two, Eyes Of Blue
Genie With The Light Brown Lamp
Girl In The Alice Blue Gown, The
Girl In The Little Green Hat, The
Goodbye Yellow Brick Road
Hair Of Gold, Eyes Of Blue
How Blue The Night
How Green Was My Valley
I Used To Be Colour Blind
I'm Thinking Tonight Of My Blue Eyes
In My Little Red Book
It's A Blue World
It's All Over Baby Blue
Lady In Red
Lily The Pink
Little Brown Jug
Little Girl Blue
Little Green Apples
Little Grey Home In The West
Little Red Monkey
Little Red Rooster
Little White Bull
Little White Cloud That Cried, The
Little White Duck
Little White Gardenia, A
Little White Lies
Little Yellow Bird
Looking At The World Through Rose Col-
oured Glasses
Love Is Blue (L'Amour Est Bleu)
Mammy's Little Coal Black Rose
Mellow Yellow
Mister Blue
Misty Blue
Mood Indigo
Moody Blue
Moon Was Yellow, The
My Blackbirds Are Bluebirds Now
My Blue Heaven
My Colouring Book
Nights In White Satin
Ninety-Nine Red Balloons
Out Of A Clear Blue Sky
Paint It Black
Pretty Blue Eyes
Pretty Kitty Blue Eyes
Pretty Little Black Eyed Susie
Put On Your Old Gray Bonnet
Rhapsody In Blue
Ride A White Swan
Roses Are Red
Rudolph The Red Nosed Reindeer
Sailor With The Navy Blue Eyes, The
Serenade In Blue
Sink Red Sun
Sky Blue Shirt And A Rainbow Tie, A
Soldier Blue
Song Sung Blue
Sundown In Little Green Hollow
That Old Black Magic
That Red Head Gal
There's A Blue Ridge Round My Heart,
Virginia

Tie A Yellow Ribbon
True Blue
Two Little Blue Birds
Two Little Girls In Blue
Under A Blanket Of Blue
Under The Lilac Bough
What Did I Do To Be So Black And Blue
When The Red Red Robin (Comes Bob
Bob Bobbin' Along)
Where The Black Eyed Susans Grow
Where The Blue Of The Night
Where The Waters Are Blue
Who Could Be Bluer
You're A Pink Toothbrush
You're More Than A Number In My Little
Red Book
You're The Only Star In My Blue Heaven

Communication

Busy Line
Hanging On The Telephone
Hold The Line
I Gotta Get A Message To You
I Heard It Through The Grapevine
I Just Called To Say I Love You
Kitty The Telephone Girl
Message In A Bottle
Message Understood
Message, The
My Message
Pennsylvania Six-five-thousand
Private Number
Telegram Sam
Telephone Line
Telephone Man

Confectionery

Big Rock Candy Mountain, The
Candy And Cake
Candy Girl
Candy Kisses
Candy Man
Chewing Gum
Choo'n' Gum
Cut Yourself A Piece Of Cake (And Make
Yourself At Home)
Does Your Chewing Gum Lose It's Fla-
vour
I Ain't Gonna Give Nobody None O'This
Jelly Roll
I Want Candy
I'd've Baked A Cake
Ice Cream
Ice Cream Man
Lollipop
My Boy Lollipop
On The Good Ship Lollipop
Popcorn
Sugar And Spice
Sugar Candy Kisses
Sunshine Cake
Sweets For My Sweet

Correspondence / Letter

I'm Gonna Sit Right Down And Write
Myself A Letter
I'm Sending A Letter To Santa Claus
If Anyone Finds This, I Love You
Love Letters
Love Letters In The Sand
One Sweet Letter From You
Please Mr. Postman
Return To Sender

Counties

Dear Old Donegal
Glorious Devon
How Can You Buy Killarney

It's A Long Way To Tipperary
Mountains Of Mourne
My Girl's A Yorkshire Girl
Rose Of Tralee, The
She's A Lassie From Lancashire

Countries

All Over Italy
April In Portugal (Coimbra)
Big In Japan
Born In The Usa
Breakfast In America
Don't Cry For Me Argentina
Down Argentine Way
Fishermen Of England, The
For America
French Kissin' In The USA
From Russia With Love
Hindustan
I'll See You In C-U-B-A
If You Ever Go To Ireland
In A Persian Market
In Zaire
Hail Caledonia
Johnny Doughboy Found A Rose In Ireland
Kids In America
Lady Of Spain
Letter From America
Living In America
Lost In France
Managua Nicaragua
On A Little Balcony In Spain
On A Slow Boat To China
Pearl Of Sweet Ceylon, The
Road To Morocco, The
Rock Of Gibraltar
Rose Of England
Sidewalks Of Cuba
Somewhere In France With You
Song Of India
Stately Homes Of England, The
Sunny Havana
There'll Always Be An England
Tony From America
Viva Espana, Y
When It's Night Time In Italy, It's Wednesday Over Here
When Mexico Gave Up The Rumba
Wine Of France
Young And Foolish

Crying

All Cried Out
And Her Tears Flowed Like Wine
And The Heavens Cried
Baby Stop Crying
Big Girls Don't Cry
Boo Hoo
Boys Cry
Don't Cry Daddy
Don't Cry For Me Argentina
Don't Cry Joe (Let Her Go, Let Her Go, Let Her Go)
Don't Cry Out Loud
Don't Let The Sun Catch You Crying
Fool To Cry, A
I'm Crying
I'm Sorry I Made You Cry
Let Me Cry On Your Shoulder
Little White Cloud That Cried, The
My Heart Cries For You
No Woman No Cry
Oh How I Laugh When I Think How I Cried About You
Sobbin' Blues
Sobbin' Women
Tears I Cried, The

Weep No More My Lady
When Doves Cry
Willow Weep For Me
You Don't Have To Be A Baby To Cry
You Just Might See Me Cry
You've Got Me Crying Again

Dance

Adoration Waltz, The
African Waltz
After The Ball
Anniversary Waltz, The
Arthur Murray Taught Me Dancing In A Hurry
At The Foxtrot Ball
At The Hop
At The Jazz Band Ball
Ballerina
Batdance
Beer Barrel Polka, The
Begin The Beguine
Belle Of The Ball
Blue Bell Polka
Blue Monday
Blue Tango
Bossa Nova Baby
Boston Two Step
Calendar Girl
Can Can
Canteen Bounce, The
Carioca, The
Carousel Waltz, The
Charleston
Chicken Reel, The
Cokey Cokey, The
Come To The Ball
Continental, The
Coronation Waltz, The
Creep, The
Cuckoo Waltz, The
Darktown Strutters Ball, The
Destiny Waltz
Do The Conga
Do You Remember The Last Waltz
Do You Wanna Dance
Doin' The New Lowdown
Doin' The Raccoon
Doll Dance, The
Domino Dancing
Don't Stop - Twist
Everybody's Crazy On The Foxtrot
Everybody's Twisting
Flirtation Waltz, The
Floral Dance, The
French Can Can Polka
Friday Night
G.I. Jive, The
Gaby Glide, The
Gandy Dancers Ball, The
Georgian Rumba
Get Dancing
Gold And Silver Waltz, The
Golden Tango, The
Guitar Boogie Shuffle
Guitar Tango
Harlem Shuffle
He's The Greatest Dancer
Hippy Hippy Shake, The
Homecoming Waltz, The
Homing Waltz, The
Hop Scotch Polka
I Came, I Saw, I Conga'd
I Can't Dance, I Got Ants In My Pants
I Can't Tell A Waltz From A Tango
I Could Have Danced All Night
I Don't Wanna Dance
I Wanna Dance Wit Choo (Do Dat Dance)

I Wanna Dance With Somebody (Who Loves Me)
I Was Made For Dancin'
I Wish I Could Shimmy Like My Sister Kate
I Won't Dance
I'll Dance At Your Wedding
I'm Gonna Charleston Back To Charleston
I'm In A Dancing Mood
If You're In Love You'll Waltz
It Only Happens When I Dance With You
Jamaican Rumba
Java Jive
Jersey Bounce
John I'm Only Dancing
Keep On Dancin'
Kentucky Waltz, The
Kiss Waltz, The
Lambada
Last Waltz, The
Let Yourself Go
Let's Dance
Let's Go Dancing
Let's Turkey Trot
Let's Twist Again
Lido Shuffle
Loco - Motion, The
Love Is A Dancing Thing
Luxembourg Polka
Mambo Italiano
Mambo Jambo
Melba Waltz, The
Must Be Madison
Never Do A Tango With An Eskimo
New Fangled Tango, A
Old Soft Shoe, The
One More Dance
One Note Samba (Samba De Uma Nota So)
Original Dixieland One-step
Papa Loves Mambo
Papa Won't You Dance With Me
Pennsylvania Polka
Petite Waltz, The
Rock And Roll Waltz
Sabre Dance
Sabre Dance, The
Safety Dance
Save The Last Dance For Me
Say It While Dancing
Scottish Samba, The
Shadow Waltz, The
Shall We Dance
Shuffle, The
Simon Smith And His Amazing Dancing Bear
Six Lessons From Madame La Zonga
Soft Shoe Shuffle, The
Stephanie Gavotte, The
Stompin' At The Savoy
Street Dance
Swedish Polka, The
Takes Two To Tango
Ten Cents A Dance
Tennessee Waltz, The
That Naughty Waltz
Tickle Toe, The
Till I Waltz Again With You
Too Fat Polka
Twist, The
Twistin' The Night Away
Two Hearts In Three Quarter Time
Unsquare Dance, The
Valeta
Venus Waltz, The
Wedding Glide, The
Wedding Samba, The
Westminster Waltz

When Mexico Gave Up The Rumba
When You And I Were Dancing
When Yuba Plays The Rumba On The Tuba
While We Danced At The Mardi Gras
Whistling Waltz, The
White Suit Samba, The
Windsor Waltz, The
Won't Somebody Dance With Me
Yam, The
You Can Make Me Dance Sing Or Anything
You Make Me Feel Like Dancing
You Should Be Dancing
You're Dancing On My Heart
You've Got The Wrong Rumba
Zorba's Dance

Day

All Alone Monday
All Day And All Of The Night
All For A Shilling A Day
All Through The Day
Another Day
Another Day In Paradise
Another Saturday Night
As We Are Today
At The End Of The Day
Back Again To Happy-Go-Lucky-Days
Back To Those Happy Days
Bad Old Days, The
Blue Monday
Break Of Day
D-days
Dancing On A Saturday Night
Dippety Day
Drive-in Saturday
Eighth Day
Election Day
Eleven More Months And Ten More Days
Ev'ry Hour, Ev'ry Day Of My Life
Every Day Hurts
Every Day Of My Life
Everybody Dance
Everyday
Everyday Is Like Sunday
Everything's Tuesday
Fantastic Day
Foggy Day, A
Friday On My Mind
Golden Days
Great Day
Happy Days And Lonely Nights
Happy Days Are Here Again
Hard Day's Night, A
I Don't Like Mondays
I Fall In Love With You Every Day
I Met Her On Monday
I'll Never Let A Day Pass By
If Everyday Was Like Christmas
In Between Days
In The Bad Bad Old Days
Isn't This A Lovely Day
It's A Good Day
It's A Great Day For The Irish
It's A Hap-Hap-Happy Day
It's A Lovely Day Today
It's A Most Unusual Day
It's My Mother's Birthday Today
Juke Box Saturday Night
Just Another Day Wasted Away
King For A Day
Lazy Sunday
Little Man You've Had A Busy Day
Love Will Save The Day
Lovely Day
Lucky Day
Making The Best Of Each Day

Manic Monday
Many Happy Returns Of The Day
May Each Day
Monday Monday
My Monday Date
Never On Sunday
New Moon On Monday
New Years Day
Night And Day
Night We Called It A Day, The
Now Those Days Are Gone
Oh Boy, What Joy We Had In Barefoot Days
Oh Happy Day
On A Clear Day You Can See Forever
On A Sunday Afternoon
On Days Like These
Once A Year Day
One Day At A Time
One Day When We're Young
Only Yesterday
Our Day Will Come
Perfect Day, A
Rainy Day Refrain, A (Schnürlregen)
Ruby Tuesday
Saturday
Saturday Night At The Movies
Saturday Night Is The Loneliest Night Of The Week
Saturday Night's Alright For Fighting
School Days
See The Day

She Makes My Day
Six Times A Week And Twice On Sundays
Some Day
Some Day I'll Find You
Some Day I'll Meet You Again
Some Day My Prince Will Come
Some Day Sweetheart
Some Day We'll Be Together
Some Day We're Gonna Love Again
Some Day You'll Be Sorry
Some Sunday Morning
Some Sunny Day
Some Sweet Day
Someday One Day
Soon It Will Be Sunday
Start The Day Right
Sunday
Sunday Girl
Sunday Kind Of Love, A
Sunday, Monday Or Always
Sunny Days
That Girl Belongs To Yesterday
That'll Be The Day
That's What A Rainy Day Is For
This Is My Lovely Day
This Is My Mother's Day
Those Were The Days
Till The End Of The Day
Tomorrow's Just Another Day
What A Difference A Day Made
What Are You Doing Sunday
When Day Is Done
When It's Night Time In Italy, It's Wednesday Over Here
Where Did Robinson Crusoe Go With Friday On Saturday Night
Wonderful Day Like Today, A
Wonderful Wonderful Day
Yester-Me Yester-You Yesterday
Yesterday
Yesterday Man
Yesterdays
You Ought To See Sally On Sunday

Devil

Dance With The Devil
Lil' Devil
Little Devil
On The Level You're A Little Devil
Race With The Devil
Suzanne Beware Of The Devil
That Old Devil Called Love
You're The Devil In Disguise

Dixieland

Original Dixieland One-step

Doctor

Physician, The
Witch Doctor

Dream

Afraid To Dream
All I Do Is Dream Of You
All I Have To Do Is Dream
Amazon (River Of Dreams)
Anything I Dream Is Possible
Beautiful Dreamer
Boulevard Of Broken Dreams
Darn That Dream
Day Dreaming
Daydream
Daydream Believer
Daydreamer
Deep In A Dream
Did You Ever See A Dream Walking
Drifting And Dreaming
Follow That Dream
Forgotten Dreams
Get Out Of My Dreams, Get Into My Car
Girl Of My Dreams
Girl With The Dreamy Eyes
Hit The Road To Dreamland
I Can Dream About You
I Can Dream Can't I
I Dream Of You
I Dream Too Much
I Dreamed
I Guess I'll Have To Dream The Rest
I Had The Craziest Dream
I Have A Dream
I Wonder If Love Is A Dream
I'll Buy That Dream
I'll See You In My Dreams
I'm A Dreamer, Aren't We All
I've Got A Pocketful Of Dreams
If Dreams Came True
If I Can Dream
If You Are But A Dream
Impossible Dream, The
In Dreams
In My Dreams
Island Of Dreams
It's Dreamtime
It's The Same Old Dream
Jeannine, I Dream Of Lilac Time
Keeping The Dream Alive
Kiss To Build A Dream On, A
Little Dolly Daydream
Man And His Dream, A
May I Have The Next Dream With You
Meet Me Tonight In Dreamland
Miner's Dream Of Home, The
My Dream Is Yours
My Dream Of Love
My Dreams Are Getting Better All The Time
My Isle Of Golden Dreams
Never Had A Dream Come True
Once Upon A Dream
Ossie's Dream (The Way To Wembley)

Out Of My Dreams
Pablo The Dreamer
Sad Sweet Dreamer
Sailor Who Are You Dreaming Of Tonight
Say Not Love Is A Dream
Send Me The Pillow That You Dream On
Shattered Dreams
Shine Through My Dreams
Silver Dream Machine
Someone's Rocking My Dreamboat
Song Of The Dreamer
Street Of Dreams
Sweet Dream
Sweet Dreams (Are Made Of This)
Sweet Dreams Sweetheart
Sweetheart Of All My Dreams
Theme For A Dream
There's A Harbour Of Dreamboats
This Time The Dream's On Me
Till All Our Dreams Come True
Together In Electric Dreams
Vienna, City Of My Dreams
Waltz Dream, The
Was It A Dream
We Have A Dream
What's The Use Of Dreaming
When I Grow Too Old To Dream
When My Dreams Come True
With My Eyes Wide Open I'm Dreamin'
Wonderful Dream (Tu Te Reconnaitras)
Wrap Your Troubles In Dreams
You Can't Keep A Good Dreamer Down
You Can't Stop Me From Dreaming
You Stepped Out Of A Dream
You Tell Me Your Dream

Drink

And Her Tears Flowed Like Wine
Another Little Drink Wouldn't Do Us Any Harm
Applejack
Beer Barrel Polka, The
Beer, Beer, Glorious Beer
Boston Tea Party, The
Brandy
China Tea
Cigaroote, Whusky And Wild Wild Women
Cocktails For Two
Cup Of Coffee, A Sandwich And You, A
Days Of Wine And Roses
Down At The Old Bull And Bush (Under The Anheuser Bush)
Everything Stops For Tea
Frozen Orange Juice
Glass Of Champagne, A
Have A Drink On Me
Hot Toddy
I Am A Cider Drinker
I Will Drink The Wine
Ida, Sweet As Apple Cider
Kisses Sweeter Than Wine
Let's Have A Tiddley At The Milk Bar
Let's Have Another Cup O' Coffee
Let's Have Another One
Love And Wine
Marguerita Time
Milk And Alcohol
Mistletoe And Wine
Moonlight Cocktail
Nice Cup Of Tea, A
No Milk Today
Pink Champagne
Pub With No Beer, The
Red Red Wine
Rum And Coca-Cola
Scotch On The Rocks
Seven Drunken Nights
Sippin' Soda

Stein Song, The
Tea For Two
Tequila
Two Pints Of Lager And A Packet Of Crisps Please
When I Take My Sugar To Tea
Whisky In The Jar
Wine Of France
Wine, Woman And Song

Father / Dad

But You Love Me Daddy
Don't Go Down The Mine Dad
Following In Father's Footsteps
Hello Muddah, Hello Fadduh
Hobnailed Boots That Farver Wore, The
I Want A Girl Just Like The Girl That Married Dear Old Dad
I'm A Ding Dong Daddy (From Dumas)
Mama Goes Where Papa Goes
Mama Loves Papa - Papa Loves Mama
Mother Nature And Father Time
Now I Have To Call Him Father
O Mein Papa
Papa Loves Mambo
Papa Won't You Dance With Me
Poor Papa (He's Got Nothing At All)
Son Of My Father
When Father Papered The Parlour

Film

Girls On Film
If I Had A Talking Picture Of You
In My Little Snapshot Album
Kissin' In The Back Row Of The Movies
More Like The Movies
My Camera Never Lies
Only You
Photo Of The Girl I Left Behind, The
Watch The Birdie
You Oughta Be In Pictures

Fire

Beds Are Burning
Blaze Away
Burn It Up
Burning Bridges
Burning Hearts
By The Fireside
Chariots Of Fire
Eternal Flame
Funeral Pyre
Great Balls Of Fire
I Don't Want To Set The World On Fire
I'm On Fire
Keep The Home Fires Burning
Kiss Of Fire, The
Light My Fire
Man On Fire
My Old Flame
Ring Of Fire
Settin' The Woods On Fire
Something's Burning
St. Elmo's Fire (Man In Motion)
Swamp Fire
Unforgettable Fire, The
We Didn't Start The Fire

Flower

Apple Blossom Wedding, An
Ashes Of Roses
Beautiful Garden Of Roses, A
Blossom Fell, A
Blue Shadows And White Gardenias
Bouquet Of Roses, A
Broadway Rose
Build Me Up Buttercup

By The River Of The Roses
Chapel Of The Roses, The
Cherry Pink And Apple Blossom White
Days Of Wine And Roses
Don't Bring Me Posies (When It's Shoesies That I Need)
English Rose
Every Rose Has It's Thorn
Everything's Coming Up Roses
Floral Dance, The
Good Year For The Roses
Heart Of A Rose
Hearts And Flowers
I Never Knew (That Roses Grew)
I'll Be With You In Apple Blossom Time
I'll Pick A Rose For My Rose
I'm Knee Deep In Daisies
Jeannine, I Dream Of Lilac Time
Johnny Doughboy Found A Rose In Ireland
June Brought The Roses
Last Rose Of Summer
Little White Gardenia, A
Love Sends A Little Gift Of Roses
Love's Garden Of Roses
Mammy's Little Coal Black Rose
Mexicali Rose
Mighty Lak' A Rose
Moonlight And Roses
My Wild Irish Rose
No Orchids For My Lady
O Flower Divine
One Dozen Roses
One Rose (That's Left In My Heart)
Only A Rose
Pansé, La (Mandy)
Paper Roses
Persian Rosebud
Red Roses For A Blue Lady
Relicairo, El
Riviera Rose
Robins And Roses
Romany Rose
Room Full Of Roses, A
Russian Rose
Saint Therese Of The Roses
San Antonio Rose
Silver Rose
Someone Else's Roses
Thou Art My Rose
Tip-Toe Through The Tulips
To A Wild Rose
Tu-Li-Tulip Time
Under The Lilac Bough
Vamping Rose
We'll Gather Lilacs
When The Bloom Is On The Sage
When The Poppies Bloom Again
When You Look In The Heart Of A Rose
When You Wore A Tulip
Where Have All The Flowers Gone
Where The Lazy Daisies Grow
Where The Shy Little Violets Grow
Who'll Buy My Violets (La Violetera)
Yellow Rose Of Texas, The
You Don't Bring Me Flowers

Flying

Airport
Amy, Wonderful Amy
Apollo 9
Army Air Corps Song, The
Broken Wings
Calling Occupants Of Interplanetary Craft
Come Josephine In My Flying Machine
Coming In On A Wing And A Prayer
Fold Your Wings
I Lost My Heart To A Starship Trooper

I'll Fly For You
I'm Mandy, Fly Me
If I Only Had Wings
Leavin' On A Jet Plane
Lords Of The Air
Man On The Flying Trapeze, The
Me And Jane In A Plane
One Day I'll Fly Away
Pair Of Silver Wings, A
Paper Plane
Rumours Are Flying
Shoes With Wings On
Silver Wings In The Moonlight
Skyliner
Straighten Up And Fly Right
Trains And Boats And Planes
When I See An Elephant Fly
Wind Beneath My Wings
Wings Over The Navy

Food

American Pie
Boiled Beef And Carrots
Candy And Cake
Cup Of Coffee, A Sandwich And You, A
Dinner At Eight
Dinner For One Please James
Home Cooking
Hors D'Oeuvres
I'd've Baked A Cake
I'm Putting All My Eggs In One Basket
Life Is A Minestrone
Ma, I Miss Your Apple Pie
Make Yourself A Happiness Pie
One Meat Ball
Shish Kebab
Shoo Fly Pie And Apple Pan Dowdy
Short'nin' Bread
Shrimp Boats
Sing For Your Supper
Stop And Shop At The Co-op Shop
Sunshine Cake
Taste Of Honey, A
Why Is The Bacon So Tough
You Can't Get Many Pimples On A Pound Of Pickled Pork

Fool

Everybody's Somebody's Fool
I've Got A Feelin' You're Foolin'
If You Gotta Make A Fool Of Somebody
It's Foolish But It's Fun
My Foolish Heart
No More The Fool
Nobody's Fool
Only Fools
Poor Little Fool
Ship Of Fools
These Foolish Things
What Kind Of Fool Am I
Why Do Fools Fall In Love
Wisdom Of A Fool, The
Won't Get Fooled Again
You Won't Find Another Fool Like Me

Friend

All Pals Together
Amigo
Are 'Friends' Electric
Can't We Be Friends
Dear Old Pal Of Mine
Diamonds Are A Girl's Best Friend
Girl Friend, The
Girl Of My Best Friend, The
Hello, Hello, Who's Your Lady Friend
I'm In Favour Of Friendship
If My Friends Could See Me Now
Is She My Girl Friend

Just Friends
Let's Be Buddies
Little Pal
Little Street Where Old Friends Meet, A
Mate O' Mine
My Best Friend's Girl
My Buddy
My Friend
My Friend Stan
My Friend The Sea
My Sentimental Friend
My Very Good Friend The Milkman
Oh What A Pal Was Mary
Pal Of My Cradle Days
Power To All Our Friends
Put It There Pal
See My Friend
That's What Friends Are For
With A Little Help From My Friends
You've Got A Friend

Fruit

Big Apple
Day-o (Banana Boat Song)
Don't Sit Under The Apple Tree
Everything Is Peaches Down In Georgia
From The Vine Came The Grape
Here We Go Round The Mulberry Bush
I Like Bananas Because They Have No Bones
I'll Be With You In Apple Blossom Time
I've Got A Lovely Bunch Of Coconuts
I've Never Seen A Straight Banana
In The Shade Of The Old Apple Tree
Life Is Just A Bowl Of Cherries
Little Green Apples
When It's Apple Blossom Time In Normandy
When Will The Good Apples Fall
Yes We Have No Bananas

Fun

Big Fun
Isn't It Kinda Fun
It's Foolish But It's Fun
Some Kinda Fun

Games

Darktown Poker Club, The
Deck Of Cards
Domino Dancing
Gambler
Harry's Game
Hide And Seek
I Don't Want To Play In Your Yard
I'm Forever Blowing Bubbles
I'm On A See-Saw
It's All In The Game
Kites
Name Of The Game
Night Games
Pinball Wizard
Play The Game
Pool Hall Richard
Roulette
Silly Games
Snooker Loopy
Solitaire
Take Me Out To The Ball Game
Tumbling Dice
Winner Takes It All

Garden

Beautiful Garden Of Roses, A
Country Gardens
English Country Garden
Hong Kong Garden

I Know A Lovely Garden
I Leave My Heart In An English Garden
In A Monastery Garden
In An Old Dutch Garden
In The Garden Of My Heart
In The Woodshed She Said She Would
It Is Only A Tiny Garden
Love's Garden Of Roses
Mucking About The Garden
Over The Garden Wall
Rose Garden
Rose In A Garden Of Weeds, A
Royal Garden Blues
Thank God For A Garden
There Are Fairies At The Bottom Of Our Garden

Gentleman

Most Gentlemen Don't Like Love
Sentimental Gentleman From Georgia, A
That Dear Old Gentleman
That Sly Old Gentleman (From Featherbed Lane)
When A Lady Meets A Gentleman Down South

Geography

Ain't No Mountain High Enough
Bells Across The Meadow
Big Rock Candy Mountain, The
Black Hills Of Dakota, The
Blue Bayou
Blueberry Hill
By A Waterfall
Call Of The Canyon, The
Call Of The Faraway Hills, The
Carry Me Back To Green Pastures
Carry Me Back To The Lone Prairie
Climb Ev'ry Mountain
Copper Canyon
Cotton Fields
Darkness On The Delta
Delta Lady
Down In The Glen
Down In The Valley
Faith Can Move Mountains
Fields Of Fire
Funny Old Hills, The
Gonna Build A Mountain
Green Fields
Heather On The Hill, The
High Up On A Hill Top
Home On The Range
How Green Was My Valley
I Like Mountain Music
I Remember The Cornfields
I'd Climb The Highest Mountain (If I Knew I'd Find You)
I'm Sitting High On A Hilltop
In The Valley Of The Moon
It Happened In Sun Valley
Itchycoo Park
Just An Echo In The Valley
Kings Of The Wild Frontier
Legend Of The Glass Mountain, The
Little Valley In The Mountains
Love On A Mountain Top
Macarthur Park
Misty Islands Of The Highlands
Morningside Of The Mountain, The
My One And Only Highland Fling
My Rainbow Valley
Night On The Desert
Old Man Of The Mountain, The
Out In The Fields
Pettin' In The Park
Primrose Hill
River Deep, Mountain High

Sahara
San Fernando Valley
Singing Hills, The
Sitting In The Park
Soldiers In The Park, The
Solsbury Hill
Song Of The Mountains, The (La Montanara)
Strawberry Fields Forever
Suddenly There's A Valley
There Is A Mountain
Thunder In The Mountains
Voice In The Wilderness, A
Walk In The Black Forest (Eine Schwarzwaldfahrt)
Waterfalls
We All Went Up Up Up The Mountain
When It's Lamp Lighting Time In The Valley
When The Moon Comes Over The Mountain
White Cliffs Of Dover, The
Wonderful Land

Ghost

House Is Haunted, The
With Her Head Tucked Underneath Her Arm

Gipsy

Hey Gipsy (Play Gipsy) (Komm Tzizany)
I'm Just A Vagabond Lover
In A Little Gipsy Tearoom
Just Like A Gipsy
Play To Me Gipsy
Romany (vivere)
Romany Life
Romany Rose
Say, Has Anyone Seen My Sweet Gypsy Rose
Singing A Vagabond Song
Song Of The Vagabonds, The
Tell Me Little Gipsy
When The Gypsy Played

Girl

Be My Girl
Big Girls Don't Cry
Bobby's Girl
Brown Girl In The Ring
Can I Take You Home Little Girl
Candy Girl
China Girl
Daddy's Little Girl
Dancing Girls
Diamonds Are A Girl's Best Friend
Georgy Girl
Go Away Little Girl
Gonna Get A Girl
Heart Of A Teenage Girl
Hello Little Girl
Help Me Girl
Hey Girl
Hey Girl Don't Bother Me
Hey Little Girl
Homely Girl
I Enjoy Being A Girl
I Love A Lassie
I Want A Girl Just Like The Girl That Married Dear Old Dad
I'd Love To Live In Loveland With A Girl Like You
I'm A One Man Girl
I'm Looking For A Girl Named Mary
I'm The Lonesomest Gal In Town
I've Got The Sweetest Girl In Maryland
If You Were The Only Girl In The World
Image Of A Girl
Is She My Girl Friend

Island Girl
It's Different For Girls
Jolly Good Luck To The Girl Who Loves A Soldier
Just A Girl That Men Forget
Just An Old-Fashioned Girl
Life Is Too Short Girl
Little Girl
Little Girl Blue
Lonely Girl (Non Seitu)
Look At That Girl
Material Girl
Me And My Girl
Modern Girl
Most Beautiful Girl In The World
Most Beautiful Girl, The
Music To Watch Girls By
My Best Friend's Girl
My Girl
My Girl Lollipop
My Girl's A Yorkshire Girl
My Kind Of Girl
My Little Dietcher Girl
Mystery Girl
One Girl
Photo Of The Girl I Left Behind, The
Poor Little Rich Girl
Pretty Girl Is Like A Melody, A
Put Me Among The Girls
Seven Little Girls Sitting In The Back Seat
She's A Home Girl
She's A Lassie From Lancashire
Single Girl
Sleepy Time Gal
Somebody Stole My Gal
Strange Little Girl
Sunday Girl
Sunny Honey Girl
Sunshine Girl
Sweet Old Fashioned Girl
Take Me Girl I'm Ready
Take Your Girl
Tell Me Pretty Maiden
Ten Pretty Girls
Thank Heaven For Little Girls
That Girl Belongs To Yesterday
There's A Girl In The Heart Of Maryland
There's A Little Bit Of Bad In Every Good Little Girl
Two Little Girls In Blue
Uptown Girl
Use Ta Be My Girl
Waiting For A Girl Like You
Waltz Me Round Again Willie
West End Girls
When My Little Girl Is Smiling
When She Was My Girl
When The Boys Talk About The Girls
When The Girl In Your Arms
When There Isn't A Girl About
Who's That Girl
Why Did I Kiss That Girl
With A Girl Like You
Word Girl, The
Young Girl

Go

Allez Vous-en, Go Away
And The Beat Goes On
Anything Goes
As Tears Go By
Baby Please Don't Go
Bach Goes To Town
Bang Zoom (Let's Go Go)
Don't Go
Don't Go In The Lions' Cage Tonight
Every Time You Go Away
Everywhere You Go

He'll Have To Go
Here I Go Again
I Can't Go For That (No Can Do)
I Can't Let Go
I Can't Let Maggie Go
I Go To Sleep
I Wanna Go Home
I'd Rather Go Blind
If You Go (Si Tu Partais)
If You Go Away (Ne Me Quitte Pas)
If You Gotta Go, Go Now
It Hurts So Much To See You Go
Let Him Go, Let Him Tarry
Let Me Go Lover
Let Yourself Go
Let's Go All The Way
Let's Go Crazy
Let's Go Dancing
Let's Go Round Again
Let's Go To San Francisco
Make The World Go Away
No Particular Place To Go
Please Don't Go
Show You The Way To Go
Sing As We Go
There Goes That Song Again
Wake Me Up Before You Go Go
We All Go The Same Way Home
When You're All Dressed Up And No Place To Go
Where Did Robinson Crusoe Go With Friday On Saturday Night
Where Do Broken Hearts Go
Where Do You Go To My Lovely
You Better Go Now
You Don't Have To Go
You Grow Sweeter As The Years Go By

Gold

Band Of Gold
Hair Of Gold, Eyes Of Blue
Heart Of Gold
If I Had A Golden Umbrella
In A Golden Coach
Love Is A Golden Ring
Man With The Golden Arm
My Golden Baby
My Isle Of Golden Dreams
Prize Of Gold
Silence Is Golden
Silver Hair And Heart Of Gold
Silver Threads Among The Gold
Solid Gold Easy Action
There's A Gold Mine In The Sky

Good

Bringing On Back The Good Times
Even The Bad Times Are Good
For The Good Times
Gimme Good Lovin'
Hey Good Looking
I Can Make You Feel Good
I Could Be So Good For You
I Was A Good Little Girl Till I Met You
I'll Be Good Because Of You
I'm Into Something Good
It's A Good Day
It's Good News Week
Jolly Good Company
Love's Been Good To Me
May The Good Lord Bless And Keep You
Take Good Care Of Yourself
There's A Good Time Coming
There's A Little Bit Of Bad In Every Good Little Girl
When Will The Good Apples Fall
Wouldn't It Be Good
You're No Good

You're Such A Good Looking Woman
You're The Only Good Thing That's Happened To Me

Goodbye

Adios
Adios Mariquita Linda
Adios Muchachos
Bye Bye Baby, Goodbye
Did Tosti Raise His Bowler Hat When He Said Goodbye
Don't Say Goodbye
Ev'ry Time We Say Goodbye
Fare-Thee-Well Annabelle
Farewell Blues
From The Time You Say Goodbye
G'bye Now
Hello Goodbye
Kiss And Say Goodbye
Kiss The Boys Goodbye
Last Farewell, The
Na Na Hey Hey Kiss Him Goodbye
Never Can Say Goodbye
Never Goodbye
Never Say Goodbye
Say Hello, Wave Goodbye
So Long, It's Been Good To Know You
So Long, Oo-long (How Long You Gonna Be Gone)
Too Late For Goodbyes
Toot Toot Tootsie Goodbye
We Just Couldn't Say Goodbye
We Musn't Say Goodbye
Wish Me Luck As You Wave Me Goodbye

Goodnight

Boa Noite
I Love The Way You Say 'Goodnight'
It's Time To Say Goodnight

Greetings

Give My Regards To Broadway
Good Morning Brother Sunshine
Happy Birthday
Please Tell Him That I Said Hello

Happy

Back Again To Happy-Go-Lucky-Days
Back To Those Happy Days
Don't Worry - Be Happy
Enjoy Yourself
Get Happy
Hello Happiness
Holidays In The Sun
I Could Be Happy
I Could Be Happy With You
I Want To Be Happy
I Whistle A Happy Tune
I'm Happy When I'm Hiking
It's A Hap-Hap-Happy Day
Let Me Sing And I'm Happy
Make Someone Happy
Make Yourself A Happiness Pie
Many Happy Returns Of The Day
My Love, My Life, My Happiness
Oh Happy Day
Put On A Happy Face
Secret Of Happiness, The
Sometimes I'm Happy
Spread A Little Happiness
Then I'll Be Happy
Today I Feel So Happy
Walking Back To Happiness

Heart

All Dressed Up With A Broken Heart
All Of My Heart
Always In My Heart
Anyone Who Had A Heart
Be Careful It's My Heart
Be Still My Heart
Breaking Down The Walls Of Heartache
Broken Hearted
Broken Hearted (Cuore Cuore)
Broken Hearted Clown
Broken Hearted Melody
Captain Of Her Heart
Cold Cold Heart
Cross My Broken Heart
Curse Of An Aching Heart
Danger, Heartbreak Ahead
Dear Hearts And Gentle People
Deep In My Heart
Don't Break My Heart
Don't Bring Me Your Heartaches
Don't Go Breaking My Heart
Every Beat Of My Heart
Every Single Little Tingle Of My Heart
Everythings In Rhythm With My Heart

Gang That Sang "Heart Of My Heart", The
Give Me Back My Heart
Good Heart
Hand On Your Heart
Hang Your Heart On A Hickory Limb
Happy Go Lucky You, And Broken Hearted Me
Happy Heart
Hello Mary Lou, Goodbye Heart
Here In My Heart
Humpty Dumpty Heart
I Give My Heart
I Just Don't Have The Heart
I Leave My Heart In An English Garden
I Let A Song Go Out Of My Heart
I Lost My Heart In Heidelberg
I Once Had A Heart Margarita
I Poured My Heart Into A Song
I'll Capture Your Heart
I'll Follow My Secret Heart
I'm Gonna Lock My Heart And Throw Away The Key
If I Gave My Heart To You
If I Only Had A Heart
In The Garden Of My Heart
In The Heart
It's A Heartache
Jealous Heart
Keep An Eye On Your Heart
Left Right Out Of My Heart
Let The Heartaches Begin
Love Here Is My Heart (Mon Coeur Est Pour Toi)
Love Me With All Of Your Heart (Caundo Caliente El Sol)
Love Steals Your Heart
Love's Just A Broken Heart
Me The Peaceful Heart
My Foolish Heart
My Heart Belongs To Daddy
My Heart Belongs To You
My Heart Cries For You
My Heart Goes Crazy
My Heart Has A Mind Of It's Own
My Heart Is An Open Book
My Heart Is Taking Lessons
My Heart Isn't In It
My Heart Sings
My Heart Stood Still
My Simple Heart
One Broken Heart For Sale
Open Up Your Heart
Open Your Heart
Peg O' My Heart

Room In Your Heart
Rose Of My Heart
Says My Heart
Silver Hair And Heart Of Gold
So Beats My Heart For You
Some Day My Heart Will Awake
Something Here In My Heart
Something's Gotten Hold Of My Heart
Stout Hearted Men
Sweet Heartache
Take Me To Your Heart Again (La Vie En Rose)
Take My Heart
Take These Chains From Heart
There Must Be An Angel Playing With My Heart
There's A Blue Ridge Round My Heart, Virginia
There's A Heartache Following Me
This Old Heart Of Mine
Too Many Broken Hearts In The World
Total Eclipse Of The Heart
Two Hearts
Two Hearts In Three Quarter Time
Unsuspecting Heart
Waltz Of My Heart
We All Have A Song In Our Hearts
What Becomes Of The Brokenhearted
When Hearts Are Young
When You Look In The Heart Of A Rose
When You've Got A Little Springtime In Your Heart
Where Do Broken Hearts Go
Where Is Your Heart (Moulin Rouge Theme)
With A Song In My Heart
With All My Heart
Wooden Heart
Words Are In My Heart, The
You Are My Heart's Delight
You Belong To My Heart
You're Breaking My Heart
You're Dancing On My Heart
You're In My Heart
You're My Best Friend
You've Done Something To My Heart
Young At Heart
Your Cheating Heart
Your Heart And Mine
Your Heart And My Heart
Zing Went The Strings Of My Heart

Heaven

All This And Heaven Too
And The Heavens Cried
Closet Thing To Heaven
East Side Of Heaven
Edge Of Heaven
Ghetto Heaven
Hands To Heaven
Here Comes Heaven Again
Ireland Must Be Heaven For My Mother Came From There
Knockin' On Heaven's Door
Little Bit Of Heaven, A
Number One Song In Heaven, The
Outside Of Heaven
Pennies From Heaven
Seventh Heaven
Show Me Heaven
Stairway To Heaven
Star Fell Out Of Heaven, A
Sweetest Music This Side Of Heaven, The
Thank Heaven For Little Girls
There Are Angels Outside Heaven
Three Step To Heaven
Too Much Heaven
When Did You Leave Heaven

You're The Only Star In My Blue Heaven   I've Been Hurt

Holiday

Allah's Holiday
Dreadlock Holiday
Dreamer's Holiday, A
Happy Holiday
Hooray, Hooray, It's A Holi Holiday
Policeman's Holiday, The
Summer Holiday
Vacation

Home

Baby Won't You Please Come Home
Back Home
Back Home In Tennessee
Beneath The Lights Of Home
Bring It On Home To Me
Butterflies In The Rain
Can I Take You Home Little Girl
Capstick Comes Home
Comin' Home Baby
Coming Home
Cucaracha, La
Daddy's Home
Down Home Rag
Go Home And Tell Your Mother
Going Home
Gotta Go Home
Green Green Grass Of Home, The
I Wanna Go Home
I Wonder If I Take You Home
I'll Be Home
I'll Find My Way Home
I'm Afraid To Come Home In The Dark
I'm Coming Home
It's So Nice To Have A Man Around The House
Johnny Come Home
Keep The Home Fires Burning
Last Mile Home, The
Let's Take The Long Way Home
Little Grey Home In The West
Look Homeward Angel
Maggie Murphy's Home
Miner's Dream Of Home, The
My Ohio Home
Oh! I Must Go Home Tonight
Paddlin' Madelin' Home
Rollin' Home
Rolling Home
Run For Home
She's A Home Girl
She's Leaving Home
Show Me The Way To Go Home
So Good To Be Back Home
Subterranean Homesick Blues
Sweet Indiana Home
Take Me Back 'ome
Take Me Home Country Road
That's My Home
There Wont Be Many Coming Home
Till They've All Gone Home
Walkin' My Baby Back Home
Way Back Home
We All Go The Same Way Home
Welcome Home (Vivre)
When Johnny Comes Marching Home
When You're A Long Long Way From Home
Who's Taking You Home Tonight
Won't You Come Home Bill Bailey
You'd Be So Nice To Come Home To

Hurt

Do You Really Want To Hurt Me
Every Day Hurts
I Don't Wanna Get Hurt

Insects

Beatnik Fly, The
Birds And The Bees, The
Butterfly
Elusive Butterfly, The
Flies Crawled Up The Window, The
Hawaiian Butterfly
Honeysuckle And The Bee, The
I Can't Dance, I Got Ants In My Pants
I'm Telling The Birds, Telling The Bees, How I Love You
Just Like A Butterfly
Like A Butterfly
Magic Fly
Poor Butterfly
Spanish Flea
Spiders And Snakes

Islands

Barbados
Beautiful Isle Of Somewhere, The
Blue Hawaii
Carribean Queen
Christmas Island
Crying For The Carolines
Cuba
Fantasy Island
Funkin' For Jamaica
Goodbye Hawaii
Happy To Be On An Island In The Sun
Hi Tiddley Hi Ti Island
Hong Kong Blues
I'll See You In C-U-B-A
In The Middle Of An Island
Living On An Island
Majorca
Make Me An Island
Minnie From Trinidad
Misty Islands Of The Highlands
My Isle Of Golden Dreams
On A Little Street In Singapore
On The Beach At Bali Bali
On The Isle Of May
On Treasure Island
Only Man On The Island, The
Robinson Crusoe's Isle
Sidewalks Of Cuba
Sing Me A Song Of The Islands
Skye Boat Song, The
Song Of Capri, The
Song Of The Islands (Na Lei O Hawaii)
South Sea Island Magic
Tahiti
Take Her To Jamaica (Where The Rum Comes From)
West Of Zanzibar (Jambo)

Jazz

Angry
At The Jazz Band Ball
Avalon
Ballin' The Jack
Black Bottom, The
Bugle Call Rag
Cake Walking Babies From Home
Charleston
China Boy
Chinatown My Chinatown
Collegiate
Dardanella
Darktown Strutters Ball, The
Doo Wacka Doo
Everybody Loves My Baby
Farewell Blues
I Ain't Gonna Give Nobody None O'this Jelly Roll

I Want A Girl Just Like The Girl That Married Dear Old Dad
I Wish I Could Shimmy Like My Sister Kate
I'm Gonna Charleston Back To Charleston
Indiana
Ja-Da
Maple Leaf Rag
Memphis Blues
Muskrat Ramble
Nobody's Sweetheart
Palesteena
Red Wing
Rose Of The Rio Grande
Royal Garden Blues
Runnin' Wild
Sheik Of Araby, The
Shim-Me-Sha-Wabble
Shine
Sobbin' Blues
Spain
That Red Head Gal
There'll Be A Hot Time In The Old Town Tonight
Tiger Rag
Under The Bamboo Tree
Way Down Yonder In New Orleans
Who's Sorry Now
Won't You Come Home Bill Bailey

Jewellery

Baubles, Bangles And Beads
Black Pearl
Lucy In The Sky With Diamonds
String Of Pearls, A
Wear My Ring (Around Your Neck)

Kiss

Ain't Gonna Kiss Ya
And Then You Kissed Me
Any Time's Kissing Time
Botch-A-Me (Baciami)
Candy Kisses
Doctor Kiss Kiss
Eso Beso (That Kiss)
French Kiss
French Kissin' In The Usa
Gimme A Little Kiss, Will Ya, Huh
Girls Were Made To Love And Kiss
Hold Me, Thrill Me, Kiss Me
I Kiss Your Hand Madame (Ich Kusse Ihr Hand Madame)
I Saw Mommy Kissing Santa Claus
I Threw A Kiss In The Ocean
I Was Never Kissed Before
I Wonder Who's Kissing Her Now
In The Middle Of A Kiss
It Started With A Kiss
It's In His Kiss
Last Kiss
Little Kiss Each Morning, A
Little Love, A Little Kiss, A (Un Peu D'amour)
Moonbeam Kiss Her For Me
Na Na Hey Hey Kiss Him Goodbye
One Kiss
One More Kiss
Ooh That Kiss
Paper Kisses
Penny A Kiss, A Penny A Hug, A
Save Your Kisses For Me
Sealed With A Kiss
Sinner Kissed An Angel, A
Sugar Candy Kisses
Teach Me How To Kiss
Then He Kissed Me
Then I Kissed Her
'Til I Kissed You

We Kiss In The Shadow
Why Did I Kiss That Girl
Your Kiss Is Sweet

Lady

Dance Little Lady, Dance
Delta Lady
Eadie Was A Lady
If You Knew Susie
Little Lady Make Believe
Little Old Lady
Lovely Lady
Lydia The Tattooed Lady
My Beautiful Lady
My Little Lady (Non Illuderti Mai)
No Orchids For My Lady
Red Roses For A Blue Lady
Rock 'n' Roll Lady
She's A Lady
Silver Lady
Sophisticated Lady
Sorry I'm A Lady
Strange Lady In Town
Three Times A Lady
When A Lady Meets A Gentleman Down South
You're A Lady

Latin

Adios
Adios Mariquita Linda
Adios Muchachos
Amapola
Amor
Another Night Like This
At The Crossroads
Aurora
Babalu
Baia
Bandit, The (O'Cangaceiro)
Brazil
Breeze And I, The
Carnavalito
Cielito Lindo
Come Closer To Me (Acercate Mas)
Cuanto Le Gusta
Cucaracha, La
Cumparsita, La
Delicado
Desafinado
Echo Of A Serenade, The (Te Quieo Dijiste)
Estrellita
Frenesi
Girl From Ipanema, The
Granada
Green Eyes (Aquellos Ojos Verdes)
It's Impossible (Somos Novios)
La Golondrina (The Swallow)
Let Me Love You Tonight (No Te Importe Saber)
Love Me With All Of Your Heart (Caundo Caliente El Sol)
Loveliest Night Of The Year
Malaguena
Mama Inez
Mama Yo Quiero (I Want My Mama)
Mambo Jambo
Maria Elena
Marta
One Note Samba (Samba De Uma Nota So)
Pablo The Dreamer
Parrot On The Fortune Teller's Hat, The
Peanut Vendor, The (El Manisero)
Perfidia
Perhaps, Perhaps, Perhaps (Quizas, Quizas, Quizas)
Poinciana

Quiet Nights Of Quiet Stars (Corcovado)
Rancho Grande, El
Say "Si Si" (Para Vigo Me Voy)
Siboney
Sucu Sucu
Sway (Quien Sera)
Sweet And Gentle (Me Lo Dijo Adela)
Taboo
Three Caballeros, The (Ay Jalisco No Te Rajes)
Ti-Pi-Tin
Tico Tico
Time Was (Duerme)
Wedding, The (La Novia)
What A Difference A Day Made
Without You (Tres Palabras)
You Belong To My Heart
Yours (Quierme Mucho)

Laugh

After My Laughter Came Tears
Don't Laugh At Me
Everybody's Laughing
Oh How I Laugh When I Think How I Cried About You
This Is No Laughing Matter
You're Laughing At Me

Law / Police

Ask A Policeman
Gendarmes Duet, The
Girl On The Police Gazette, The
Good Morning Judge
King Of The Cops
Laughing Policeman, The
Miami Vice
Mounties, The
Watching The Detectives

Letter (see Correspondence)

Lie

Dreams Can Tell A Lie
Echo Told Me A Lie, The
Fibbin'
How It Lies, How It Lies, How It Lies
I Ain't Lyin'
I Hope To Die If I Told A Lie
I Paid For That Lie I Told You
It's A Sin To Tell A Lie
Little Lies
My Camera Never Lies
Nobody Lied (When They Said That I Cried Over You)

Life / Live

Ah Sweet Mystery Of Life
All Of My Life
Annie Doesn't Live Here Anymore
As Long As I Live
Back To Life
Be My Life's Companion
Best Things In Life Are Free, The
Best Years Of Our Lives
C'est La Vie
Come Into My Life
Ev'ry Hour, Ev'ry Day Of My Life
Folks Who Live On The Hill, The
For Once In My Life
Get A Life
Give Me The Simple Life
Good Life
Got To Get You Into My Life
Greatest Mistake Of My Life, The
High Life
How Am I Supposed To Live Without You

How Could You Believe Me, When I Said I Love You, When You Know I've Been A Liar All My Life
I Got Life
I'd Love To Live In Loveland With A Girl Like You
I'm Gonna Live Till I Die
If I Had My Life To Live Over
If Only I Could Live My Life Again
Into Each Life Some Rain Must Fall
Isn't Life Strange
It's A Hard Life
It's My Life
It's Your Life
Last Night A D.J. Saved My Life
Let's Think About Living
Long Live Love
Lot Of Living To Do, A
Love Don't Live Here Anymore
Love Is Life
Love Of My Life
Me And My Life
Memories Live Longer Than Dreams
My Kinda Life
My Life
My Life Belongs To You
My Love, My Life, My Happiness
New Life
On The Street Where You Live
Once In A Lifetime
One Day In Your Life
Ooh What A Life
Reflections Of My Life
Seperate Lives
She's Out Of My Life
Spaniard That Blighted My Life, The
Stay Out Of My Life
Story Of My Life, The
Street Life
Summer Of My Life, The
That's Living Alright
There's A Lull In My Life
Time Of My Life
Walk Of Life
Way Of Life, The
What Are You Doing The Rest Of Your Life
What Is Life
Why Can't We Live Together
Wild Side Of Life, The
Wonderful Life
You Are The Sunshine Of My Life
You Light Up My Life

Lonely

All Alone Am I
Are You Lonesome Tonight
Farewell Is A Lonely Sound
Have You Ever Been Lonely
I Get So Lonely
I Live In Trafalgar Square
I'm The Lonely One
I'm The Lonesomest Gal In Town
Just Don't Want To Be Lonely
Little Miss Lonely
Little On The Lonely Side, A
No More Lonely Nights
Oh Lonesome Me
Only The Lonely
Saturday Night Is The Loneliest Night Of The Week
So Lonely

Look

Hey Look Me Over
I Wonder How I Look When I'm Asleep
I'll Be Seeing You
I'm Looking For A Girl Named Mary

I'm Looking Out Of The Window
I'm Looking Over A Four-Leaf Clover
If You're Lookin' For A Way Out
Just One Look
Lovely To Look At
Oh Look At Me Now
On The Outside Looking In
Searchin'
Someone's Looking At You
Sound And Vision
Take A Look Around
Take That Look Off Your Face
Things Are Looking Up
U Got The Look
Way You Look Tonight, The
What Kinda Boy You Lookin' For Girl
When I'm Looking At You
When You Look In The Heart Of A Rose
You're Such A Good Looking Woman

Love

Addicted To Love
All My Love
All My Loving
All Of Me Loves All Of You
All You Need Is Love
Almost Like Being In Love
Amor
And I Love You So
Anyone Can Fall In Love
April Love
Baby Love
Back Street Luv
Be My Love
Beautiful Love
Because Of Love
Beggar In Love, A
Big Hunk Of Love, A
Book Of Love
Breaking In A Brand New Broken Heart
Burning Love
Bye Bye Love
C'mon And Get My Love
Can It Be Love
Can This Be Love
Can't Buy Me Love
Can't Get Enough Of Your Love Babe
Can't Help Falling In Love
Can't You Hear Me Say I Love You
Careless Love
Chanson D'amour
Chequered Love
Comes Love
Could It Be I'm Falling In Love
Cradle Of Love
Creole Love Call
Crying Laughing Loving Lying
Cupboard Love
Cynthia's In Love
Dat's Love
Day Without Love, A
Dead Ringer For Love
Dear Love My Love
Dedicated To The One I Love
Do You Love Me
Do You Really Love Me Too (Fools Errand)
Doctor Love
Dolly My Love
Don't Let Your Love Go Wrong
Don't Take Your Love From Me
Don't Talk To Me About Love
Don't Throw Your Love Away
Dream Lover
Endless Love
Everlasting Love
Everybody Loves A Love
Everybody Loves Somebody

Faded Summer Love, A
Fall In Love With You
Falling In Love Again
Falling In Love With Love
Farewell My Summer Love
First Love, Last Love, Best Love
For Your Love
Forever Kind Of Love, A
From Russia With Love
Funny How Love Can Be
Game Of Love, The
Garden Of Love, The
Gimme Some Loving
Give Her My Love
Glory Of Love, The
Goodbye My Love
Goodbye To Love
Goodnight My Love
Greatest Love Of All
Groovy Kind Of Love, A
Harvest Of Love
Have I Told You Lately That I Love You
He's Got No Love
Hello I Love You
Hello Young Lovers
Here I Am In Love Again
Here Lies Love
Here's To Love
Hiawatha's Melody Of Love
Hold On To Love
Honey I'm In Love With You
Hooray For Love
Hot Love
How Could You Believe Me, When I Said
I Love You, When You Know I've Been A
Liar All My Life
How Deep Is Your Love
How Much Love
How'd Ya Like To Love Me
I Bring A Love Song
I Can Take Or Leave Your Loving
I Can't Believe That You're In Love With
Me
I Can't Give You Anything But Love
I Can't Love You Anymore
I Can't Stop Loving You
I Couldn't Live Without Your Love
I Didn't Know I Loved You (Till I Saw You
Rock 'n' Roll)
I Don't Know How To Love Him
I Don't Want Our Loving To Die
I Fall In Love Too Easily
I Fall In Love With You Every Day
I Guess I'll Always Love You
I Just Called To Say I Love You
I Left My Heart At The Stage Door Canteen
I Love How You Love Me
I Love My Baby, My Baby Loves Me
I Love Paris
I Love To Love (But My Baby Just Loves
To Dance)
I Love You
I Love You Because
I Love You Love Me Love
I Love You Samantha
I Love You Truly
I Still Love You All
I Used To Love You (But It's All Over
Now)
I Wanna Be Loved By You
I Want To Know What Love Is
I Was Born To Love You
I Was Made To Love Her
I Wish I Didn't Love You So
I Wish I Were In Love Again
I Wonder If Love Is A Dream
I'll Always Be In Love With You
I'll Never Fall In Love Again
I'm Afraid To Love You

I'm Alone Because I Love You
I'm Falling In Love With Someone
I'm Gonna Make You Love Me
I'm In Love Again
I'm In Love With A Wonderful Guy
I'm In Love With Two Sweethearts
I'm In The Mood For Love
I'm Not In Love
I'm Stone In Love With You
I'm Telling The Birds, Telling The Bees,
How I Love You
I'm Through With Love
I've Got My Love To Keep Me Warm
I've Never Been In Love Before
If I Should Fall In Love Again
If I Should Plant A Tiny Seed Of Love
If This Isn't Love
If You Love Me (Hyme A L'amour)
If You're In Love You'll Waltz
Importance Of Your Love, The (Important
C'est La Rose)
In And Out Of Love
In Love For The Very First Time
In The Arms Of Love
Indian Love Call
It Must Be Love
It Sure Brings Out The Love In Your Eyes
It's A Love Thing
It's Love Again
It's Love, Love, Love
It's Time For Love
Julie Do Ya Love Me
Just Loving You
Just Say I Love Her
Kashmiri Love Song (From The Four Indian Love Lyrics)
Labelled With Love
Labour Of Love
Lady Who Didn't Believe In Love, The
Lady's In Love With You, The
Language Of Love, The
Last Night Was Made For Love
Lay All Your Love On Me
Leave A Little Love
Lessons In Love
Let Me Be Loved
Let Me Go Lover
Let Me Love You Tonight (No Te Importe
Saber)
Let There Be Love
Let Your Love Flow
Let's Fall In Love
Let's Talk About Love
Little Bit Of Love, A
Little In Love, A
Little Love And Understanding, A (Un
Peu D'amour Et D'amitie)
Little Love, A Little Kiss, A (Un Peu
D'amour)
Little Lovin', A
Little Nellie Kelly I Love You
Live, Laugh And Love
Long Haired Lover From Liverpool
Long Live Love
Look Of Love
Looking Through The Eyes Of Love
Lucky In Love
Make Love To Me
Makin' Love
Man I Love, The
Man Without Love, A
Man Without Love, A (Quando M'innamoro)
Marrying For Love
Melodie D'amour (Maladie D'amour)
Melody Of Love
Miracle Of Love, The
Modern Love
Moon Love
More Than In Love

More Than Love
Most Gentlemen Don't Like Love
My Baby Loves Lovin'
My Dream Of Love
My First Love, My Last Love For Always
My Heart And I
My Heart Tells Me
My Kinda Love
My Love
My Love And Devotion
My Love For You
My Love Parade
My Love, My Life, My Happiness
My One And Only Love
My Own True Love
My September Love
My Silent Love
My Song Of Love
Never Ending Song Of Love
Night Was Made For Love, The
No Greater Love
No Love, No Nothing
No Other Love
No Other Love
Nobody Needs Your Love
Nothing's Gonna Change My Love For You
Nows The Time To Fall In Love
Oh Gee, Oh Gosh, Oh Golly, I'm In Love
On The Bumpy Road To Love
Once In Love With Amy
One Love Forever
One Night Of Love
One Way Love
Our Language Of Love
Our Love Affair
Our Love Is Here To Stay
Our Love Story
P.S. I Love You
Pagan Love Song, The
Part Time Lover
People Will Say We're In Love
Portrait Of My Love, A
Power Of Love, The
Precious Little Thing Called Love, A
Price Of Love, The
Prisoner Of Love
Puppy Love
Radar Love
Rose Rose I Love You (May Kway O May Kway)
Say Not Love Is A Dream
Sea Of Love
Secret Love
She Loves Me
So In Love
Softly Whispering I Love You
Some Day We're Gonna Love Again
Somebody Loves Me
Somebody Loves You
Somewhere My Love (Lara's Theme)
Speak To Me Of Love (Parlez Moi D'Amour)
Stairway Of Love
Step Inside Love
Stoned Love
Stop In The Name Of Love
Suddenly You Love Me (Uno Tranquillo)
Sugar Baby Love
Taking A Chance On Love
Teenager In Love, A
Tell Laura I Love Her
That Lucky Old Sun
That Old Devil Called Love
That's Amore
That's How A Love Song Was Born
That's What Love Will Do
Theme For Young Lovers
There Goes My First Love

There Isn't Any Limit To My Love
There's No Two Ways About Love
There's Nothing Rougher Than Love
Thing Called Love, A
Things I Love, The
Things We Do For Love, The
This Can't Be Love
This Is Not A Love Song
To Keep My Love Alive
To Know Him Is To Love Him
To Know You Is To Love You
To Love Somebody
Torn Between Two Lovers
True Love
True Love Ways
Very Precious Love, A
Walkin' In The Rain With The One I Love
We Are In Love
We Will Make Love
What Is This Thing Called Love
What Now My Love (Et Maintenant)
When A Man Loves A Woman
When I Fall In Love
When Will I Be Loved
When Will You Say I Love You
When You Are In Love
When You Ask About Love
When You Lose The One You Love
When You're In Love
Where Are You Now My Love
Who Do You Love
Who Wouldn't Love You
Whole Lotta Love
Why Do Fools Fall In Love
Why Do I Love You
Why Don't You Do Right
Will You Love Me In December (As You Do In May)
Will You Love Me Tomorrow
Winter World Of Love
With Your Love (Mes Mains)
Without Love (There Is Nothing)
Woman In Love, A
World Without Love, A
You Are My First Love
You Brought A New Kind Of Love To Me
You Can Never Stop Me Loving You
You Can't Hurry Love
You Don't Have To Say You Love Me (Lo Che Non Vivo)
You Made Me Care When I Wasn't In Love
You Made Me Love You
You Taught Me How To Love
You're Just In Love
You've Got To Hide Your Love Away
You've Lost That Lovin' Feelin'
You've Never Been In Love Like This Before
Young Love
Young Lovers

Luck

Beginner's Luck
Cloud Lucky Seven
Good Luck Charm
Good Luck, Good Health, God Bless You
Happy Go Lucky You, And Broken Hearted Me
I Should Be So Lucky
If I'm Lucky
It's Never Too Late To Fall In Love
Jolly Good Luck To The Girl Who Loves A Soldier
Just Got Lucky
Some Guys Have All The Luck
There But For Fortune
Until My Luck Comes Rolling Along
Wheel Of Fortune, The

Wish Me Luck As You Wave Me Good-bye
Wishing I Was Lucky
With A Little Bit Of Luck
With A Little Luck

Lullaby

Kentucky Lullaby

Magic

Every Little Thing She Does Is Magic
I Put A Spell On You
It's Magic
Kind Of Magic, A
Puff The Magic Dragon
Tropical Magic
You Can Do Magic

Man

An Innocent Man
Big Man
Brown Eyed Handsome Man
California Man
Can't Help Lovin' Dat Man
Candy Man
Evil That Men Do
For Every Man There's A Woman
Good Man Is Hard To Find, A
Guitar Man
Handy Man
Heart Of A Man
Home Lovin' Man
I Hate Men
I Mean To Marry A Man
I Wanna Be Your Man
I Want That Man
I'll Make A Man Of You
I'm A Man
I'm A One Man Girl
I'm Gonnna Wash That Man Right Out Of My Hair
Ice Cream Man
If I Were A Rich Man
It's Raining Men
Listen To What The Man Said
Little Man
Little Man You've Had A Busy Day
Love Like A Man
Lover Man (Oh Where Can You Be)
Me And The Man In The Moon
Mirror Man
Mister Tambourine Man
My Man (Mon Homme)
Nasty Man
Neanderthal Man
Occasional Man, An
Old Man Mose
Old Man Of The Mountain, The
Only Man On The Island, The
Our Lodger's Such A Nice Young Man
Poor Man's Son
Ragamuffin Man
Robot Man
Rocket Man
Stand By Your Man
Starman
Stout Hearted Men
Superman (Gioca Jouer)
Sweet Man
Telephone Man
This Old Man (Knick Knack Paddy Whack)
Tokoloshe Man
Umbrella Man, The
Walk Like A Man
When A Man Loves A Woman
Wild, Wild Women Are Making A Wild Man Out Of Me, The

Worried Man Blues
Yesterday Man
You Can't Get A Man With A Gun

March

Anchors Aweigh
Blaze Away
Dam Busters March, The
El Capitan March
French Military Marching Song
River Kwai March
Stars And Stripes Forever, The
Tramp, Tramp, Tramp Along The Highway
When Johnny Comes Marching Home

Marriage / Wedding

Aba Daba Honeymoon
Apple Blossom Wedding, An
Band Of Gold
Band Of Gold, The
D.I.V.O.R.C.E.
Get Me To The Church On Time
Hawaiian Wedding Song
I Mean To Marry A Man
I Wanna Get Married
I Want A Girl Just Like The Girl That Married Dear Old Dad
I Went To Your Wedding
I'll Dance At Your Wedding
Jilted John
Love And Marriage
Peggy Sue Got Married
Shotgun Wedding
Somebody Bad Stole De Wedding Bell
Wear My Ring (Around Your Neck)
White Wedding
Why Am I Always The Bridesmaid

Me

All Of Me
All The World Will Be Jealous Of Me
Answer Me
As You Desire Me
Blues My Naughty Sweetie Gave To Me, The
But Not For Me
Call Me
Can't You Hear Me Calling Caroline
Do You Ever Think Of Me
Do You Love Me
Don't Ask Me Why
Don't Blame Me
Don't Bring Me Down
Don't Ever Leave Me
Don't Take Your Love From Me
Easy Going Me
Every Little Movement
For Me And My Gal
From Me To You
Gipsy In Me, The
Give Me A Little Cosy Corner
Give Me The Moonlight
Have A Little Faith In Me
Hey Look Me Over
Hold Me, Thrill Me, Kiss Me
How About Me
I Hear You Calling Me
I Love Me
I Love My Baby, My Baby Loves Me
I Miss My Swiss - My Swiss Miss Misses Me
I Ups To Her, And She Ups To Me
I Want You To Want Me To Want You
I'd Rather Be Me
I've Got My Captain Working For Me Now
If You Could Care For Me
Just You, Just Me

Kiss Me Again
Knowing Me, Knowing You
Leave Me With A Smile
Let Me Call You Sweetheart
Love Me And The World Is Mine
Love Me Forever
Love Me Now
Lover Come Back To Me
Ma! He's Making Eyes At Me
Mean To Me
Meet Me In St. Louis
Meet Me Jenny When The Sun Goes Down
Meet Me Tonight In Dreamland
Perhaps You'll Think Of Me
Put Your Arms Around Me Honey
Sentimental Me
She Loves Me
Show Me The Way To Go Home
Somebody Loves Me
Someone To Watch Over Me
Take Me Back To Dear Old Blighty
Take Me Out To The Ball Game
Tell Me Little Gipsy
Tell Me Tonight
Tell Me What He Said
Tell Me When
They All Follow Me
They Can't Take That Away From Me
They Didn't Believe Me
They Go Wild Simply Wild Over Me
Tonight You Belong To Me
Waltz Me Round Again Willie
What Do You Want To Make Those Eyes At Me For
When My Baby Smiles At Me
Wild, Wild Women Are Making A Wild Man Out Of Me, The
Will You Love Me In December (As You Do In May)
You Do Something To Me
You Remind Me Of My Mother
You Taught Me How To Love
You Took Advantage Of Me
You Were Meant For Me
You're Getting To Be A Habit With Me
You've Got Me Where You Want Me

Memory / Remember

Affair To Remember, An
Do You Remember The Last Waltz
Don't Forget To Remember
I Remeber Elvis Presley
I Remember You
I Shall Always Remember You Smiling
I'll Remember April
I'm Stepping Out With A Memory Tonight
It's Easy To Remember
Just A Memory
Moments To Remember
Night To Remember, A
Roses For Remembrance
So Many Memories
Something To Remember You By
Stars Will Remember, The
Thanks For The Memory
Will You Remember (Sweetheart)
You Will Remember Vienna

Metal

Copper Canyon
Quicksilver

Mind

Always On My Mind
As If I Didn't Have Enough On My Mind
Can't Get Indiana Off My Mind
Church Of The Poison Mind

Got My Mind Set On You
I Can't Get You Outa My Mind
I've Got You On My Mind
It Never Entered My Mind

Money

Ain't Got A Dime To My Name
All For A Shilling A Day
Anyone Can Be A Millionaire
Bad Penny Blues
Big Spender
Brass In Pocket
Brother Can You Spare A Dime
Dime And A Dollar, A
Dirty Cash
Dollar Princesses
Dreamer With A Penny
I Found A Million Dollar Baby
I Haven't Time To Be A Millionaire
I Want Some Money
I.O.U.
If I Had A Million Dollars
If I Were A Rich Man
In For A Penny
Man Who Broke The Bank At Monte Carlo, The
Pennies From Heaven
Penny A Kiss, A Penny A Hug, A
Penny Serenade, The
Silver Dollar
Ten Cents A Dance
Three Coins In The Fountain
We're In The Money
What's The Colour Of Money
Who Pays The Ferryman
Who Wants To Be A Millionaire

Month

Calendar Girl
Eleven More Months And Ten More Days
First Of May, The
Give Me A Night In June
I'll Remember April
It Might As Well Rain Until September
My September Love
One Morning In May
Roses In December
When April Sings
When June Comes Along With A Song

Mood

Can't Get Out Of This Mood
I'm In A Dancing Mood
I'm In The Mood For Dancing
In A Sentimental Mood
My Ever Changing Moods

Moon

Alabama Moon
All By Yourself In The Moonlight
Allegheny Moon
Bad Moon Rising
Blue Pacific Moonlight
By The Light Of The Silvery Moon
Carolina Moon
Clouds Across The Moon
Dancin' In The Moonlight
Dark Moon
Did You Ever Get That Feeling In The Moonlight
Enlloro (Voodoo Moon)
Everyone's Gone To The Moon
Full Moon And Empty Arms
Get Out And Get Under The Moon
Gipsy Moon
Give Me The Moonlight
How High The Moon

I Love The Moon
I See The Moon
I Used To Sigh For The Silvery Moon
If You Stub Your Toe On The Moon
In Other Words (Fly Me To The Moon)
In The Chapel In The Moonlight
In The Valley Of The Moon
It's Only A Paper Moon
Killing Moon, The
Magic Is The Moonlight (Te Quiero Dij-iste)
Magnolias In The Moonlight
Me And The Man In The Moon
Me And The Moon
Mister Moon You've Got A Million Swee-thearts
My Moonlight Madonna
My Sweetheart's The Man In The Moon
'Neath The Southern Moon
New Moon And An Old Serenade, A
New Moon On Monday
No Moon At All
Orchids In The Moonlight
Pagan Moon
Pale Moon
Penny Whistle Song, The
Polka Dots And Moonbeams
Reaching For The Moon
Roll Along Kentucky Moon
Sail Along Silvery Moon
Shine On Harvest Moon
Shine On Victory Moon
Silver Wings In The Moonlight
Strawberry Moon In A Blueberry Sky, A
Sugar Moon
Swanee River Moon
That's The Moon My Son
They Can't Black-Out The Moon
Under The Moon
Under The Moon Of Love
Underneath The Harlem Moon
Underneath The Mellow Moon
Underneath The Russian Moon
Venetian Moon
Walking On The Moon
What A Little Moonlight Can Do
When The Harvest Moon Is Shining
When The Moon Comes Over Madison Square
When The Moon Comes Over The Mountain
Who Were You With In The Moonlight

Mother

And Her Mother Came Too
Break The News To Mother
Coal Black Mammy
Does Your Mother Know
Dream Mother
Fat Li'l' Feller Wid His Mammy's Eyes
Go Home And Tell Your Mother
Have You Seen Your Mother, Baby, Standing In The Shadow
Hello Mom
I Saw Mommy Kissing Santa Claus
I'd Love To Fall Asleep And Wake Up In My Mammy's Arms
Ireland Must Be Heaven For My Mother Came From There
It's My Mother's Birthday Today
Little Shirt My Mother Made For Me
Ma! He's Making Eyes At Me
Maggie! Yes Ma?
My Mammy
My Mother's Eyes
My Yiddishe Momme
On Mother Kelly's Doorstep
Sylvia's Mother
That Old Fashioned Mother Of Mine

This Is My Mother's Day
Turn 'Erberts Face To The Wall Mother
When Mother Nature Sings Her Lullaby
Will You Love Me In December (As You Do In May)
You Remind Me Of My Mother
Your Mother And Mine

Music

All God's Chillun Got Rhythm
Alvin's Harmonica
And The Bands Played On
Antmusic
Aria
Armen's Theme
Autumn Concerto
Ballad Of Bethnal Green, The
Ballad Of Davy Crockett, The
Ballad Of John And Yoko, The
Banjo's Back In Town, The
Beat Me   Daddy, Eight To The Bar
Beat Out Dat Rhythm On A Drum
Blue Prelude
Bohemian Rhapsody
Broken Hearted Melody
Can't Stop The Music (La Musique N'a Pas De Fin)
Concerto For Clarinet
Cornish Rhapsody
Crazy Rhythm
Dance To The Music
Do-Re-Mi
Don't Take Away The Music
Donkey Serenade, The
Earful Of Music, An
Echo Of A Serenade, The (Te Quieo Dijiste)
Elizabethan Serenade
Everythings In Rhythm With My Heart
Fanfare For The Common Man
Fascinating Rhythm
First Lullaby, The
Gaucho Serenade, The
Guitar Boogie Shuffle
Harlem Nocturne
Hey Music Lover
Hiawatha's Lullaby
Hiawatha's Melody Of Love
I Can Hear Music
I Got Rhythm
I Hear A Rhapsody
I Hear Music
I Like Mountain Music
I Love Music
It Goes Like This (That Funny Melody)
Johnny Guitar
Just Like A Melody Out Of The Sky
Lamplighter's Serenade, The
Let The Music Play
Let Yourself Go
Let's All Go To The Music Hall
Life Is Nothing Without Music
Little Miss Melody
Little Serenade (Piccolissima Serenata)
Living In Harmony
Lovers Concerto
Lullaby In Rhythm
Lullaby Of Birdland
Lullaby Of Broadway
Make Mine Music
Mama I Wanna Make Rhythm
Mandolin Serenade
Mcnamara's Band
Melodie D'amour (Maladie D'amour)
Melody From The Sky, A
Melody Of Love
Moonlight Serenade
My Croony Melody
My Kid's A Crooner

My Unfinished Symphony
New Moon And An Old Serenade, A
Night Is Filled With Music, The
Old Music Master, The
One Note Samba (Samba De Uma Nota So)
Our Favourite Melodies
Pavanne
Penny Serenade, The
Play A Simple Melody
Play That Barbershop Chord
Play That Funky Music
Pop Muzik
Rainy Day Refrain, A (Schnürlregen)
Rhapsody In Blue
Rhythm Is Our Business
Rhythm Of Life
Rhythm Of The Night
Rhythm Of The Rain
Rhythm On The River
Rock-A-Bye Your Baby With A Dixie Melody
Rockin' In Rhythm
Say It With Music
Serenade In Blue
Serenade In The Night
Serenade Of The Bells
Shy Serenade
Slave To The Rhythm
Sleepy Serenade
Soft Lights And Sweet Music
Sound Of Music, The
Starlight Serenade
Strange Music
Sunrise Serenade
Swedish Rhapsody
Sweet Music
Sweet Potato Piper
Sweet Soul Music
Sweetest Music This Side Of Heaven, The
Symphony
Tenement Symphony, The
Tokyo Melody
Transatlantic Lullaby
Travellin' Band
Turn The Music Up
Unchained Melody
Warsaw Concerto, The
We Could Make Such Beautiful Music Together
When Mother Nature Sings Her Lullaby
You And The Night And The Music

Musical Instruments

April Played The Fiddle
At The Balalaika
Beat Out Dat Rhythm On A Drum
Blue Guitar
Boogie Woogie Bugle Boy
Bugle Call Rag
Bungalow, A Piccolo And You, A
Concerto For Clarinet
Dancing Tambourine
Distant Drums
Fiddle Faddle
Fit As A Fiddle
Gertie The Girl With The Gong
Green Tambourine
Guaglione (The Man Who Plays The Mandolino)
He Played His Ukulele As The Ship Went Down
Hey Mister Banjo
I Love A Piano
I Took My Harp To A Party
Kicking The Going Around
Kitten On The Keys
Lady Play Your Mandolin

Let There Be Drums
Little Wooden Whistle Wouldn't Whistle, The
Love Is Like A Violin (Mon Coeur Est Un Violin)
Man With The Mandolin, The
Mello Cello
Mister Tambourine Man
Monkey And The Organ Grinder, The
My Old Piano
Old Pi-Anna Rag, The
Old Piano Roll Blues, The
Phil The Fluter's Ball
Play Fiddle Play
Play Me Like You Play Your Guitar
Play Orchestra Play
Sam The Old Accordion Man
Say It With A Ukulele
Seventy-six Trombones
Singing Piano, The
Slap That Bass
Someone Stole Gabriel's Horn
Squeeze Box
Toy Drum Major, The
Toy Trumpet
Tubby The Tuba
Weymouth Chimes, The
When The Organ Played "O Promise Me"
When The Organ Played At Twilight
When You Played The Organ And I Sang "The Rosary"
When Yuba Plays The Rumba On The Tuba
Yiddle On Your Fiddle

Names (Male)

Ballad Of Bonnie And Clyde, The
Ballad Of Davy Crockett, The
Ballad Of John And Yoko, The
Ballin' The Jack
Barnacle Bill The Sailor
Big Bad John
Brother Louie
Brother Louis
Buffalo Billy
Burlington Bertie From Bow
Clap Hands, Here Comes Charley
Cousin Norman
Crazy Otto Rag
Dance With Me Henry (Wallflower)
Dapper Dan
Dear John
Desperate Dan
Diary Of Horace Wimp, The
Dinner For One Please James
Don Quixote
Don't Cry Joe (Let Her Go, Let Her Go, Let Her Go)
Goodbye Jimmy Goodbye
Goodbye Sam, Hello Samantha
Gotta Have Somethng In The Bank, Frank
Gurney Slade Theme, The
Happiness Is A Thing Called Joe
Happy Jack
Has Anybody Here Seen Kelly
Hats Off To Larry
Hey Joe
Hey Matthew
Hit The Road Jack
Home James And Don't Spare The Horses
House Of David Blues, The
House That Jack Built
Hurry Up Harry
I Came Here To Talk For Joe
I Feel Like Buddy Holly
I Loves You Porgy
I Remeber Elvis Presley

I'm Henery The Eighth
I'm Just Wild About Harry
Jilted John
Jumping Jack Flash
Just A Kid Named Joe
Just Like Eddie
Lighterman Tom
Little Pink Petty From Peter
Little Willy
Lost John
Making Plans For Nigel
My Brother Jake
My Friend Stan
My Name Is Jack
Nice One Cyril
O.K. Fred
Ode To Billy Joe
Oh! Johnny Oh!
Oh Nicholas Don't Be So Ridiculous
Oh Oh Antonio
Old Man Mose
Open The Door Richard
Piccolo Pete
Pool Hall Richard
Poor John
Poppa Joe
Pu-Leeze Mr. Hemingway
Ragtime Cowboy Joe
Right Said Fred
Rock Me Amadeus
Rockin' Robin
Song For Guy
South American Joe
Steamboat Bill
Telegram Sam
They Were All Out Of Step But Jim
Try Again Johnnie
Turn 'Erberts Face To The Wall Mother
Waiting For The Robert E. Lee
Wedding O' Sandy McNab
When Johnny Comes Marching Home
When Yuba Plays The Rumba On The Tuba
Where Did Robinson Crusoe Go With Friday On Saturday Night
Which Way You Goin' Billy?
Whistling Rufus
Won't You Come Home Bill Bailey
Yes Mister Brown
You Can Call Me Al

Names (Female)

Adios Mariquita Linda
Ain't It A Shame About Mame
Along Came Caroline
And Mimi
Arms Of Mary, The
Baby Jane
Ballad Of Bonnie And Clyde, The
Ballad Of John And Yoko, The
Boy Named Sue, A
Can't You Hear Me Calling Caroline
Come Josephine In My Flying Machine
Come On Eileen
Cracklin' Rosie
Darling Nellie Gray
Day I Met Marie, The
Dear Jessie
Dear Prudence
Dirty Diana
Don't Bring Lulu
Dream Of Olwen, The
Fanlight Fanny
Fare-Thee-Well Annabelle
Gimme Hope Jo'anna
Good Golly Miss Molly
Good Grief Christina
Goodbye Dolly Gray

Goodbye Sally
Goodbye Sam, Hello Samantha
Goodbye Virginia
Goodnight Irene
Gudbuy T'jane
Hang On The Bell Nellie
Hard Hearted Hannah
Hear My Song Violetta (Hor Mein Lied Violetta)
Hello Dolly
Hello Mary Lou, Goodbye Heart
Hello Susie
Hello This Is Joannie
Her Name Is Mary
Hey Paula
Hush Not A Word To Mary
I Can't Let Maggie Go
I Did What I Did For Maria
I Love The Name Of Mary
I Love You Samantha
I Never See Maggie Alone
I Once Had A Heart Margarita
I Want Candy
I Wish I Could Shimmy Like My Sister Kate
I Wonder What's Become Of Sally
I'll Pick A Rose For My Rose
I'll Take You Home Again Kathleen
I'm Looking For A Girl Named Mary
I'm Mandy, Fly Me
I'm Shy, Mary Ellen I'm Shy
If You Knew Susie
Keep Your Skirts Down Mary Ann
Knees Up Mother Brown
Lady Barbara
Lady Eleanor
Lady Lynda
Lady Madonna
Lady Rose
Let's All Go To Mary's House
Little Bird On Nellie's Hat, The
Little Dolly Daydream
Little Nellie Kelly I Love You
Liverpool Lou
Living Next Door To Alice
Long Tall Sally
Ma Belle Marguerita
Ma Blushin' Rosie
Me And Jane In A Plane
Meet Me Jenny When The Sun Goes Down
Message To Martha
Mia Bella Rosa
Miss Annabelle Lee
Miss Otis Regrets
Moonshine Sally
Mrs Worthington
My Irish Molly-O
Oh Carol
Oh Diane
Oh Donna Clara
Oh Julie
Oh Monah
Oh What A Pal Was Mary
Oh, Katharina
Once In Love With Amy
Paddlin' Madelin' Home
Pansé, La (Mandy)
Pictures Of Lily
Poison Ivy
Poor Jenny
Poor Little Angeline
Pretty Kitty Blue Eyes
Pretty Little Black Eyed Susie
Proud Mary
Put The Blame On Mame
Put Your Shoes On Lucy
Romany Rose
Runaround Sue

Say, Has Anyone Seen My Sweet Gypsy Rose
Second Hand Rose
See Emily Play
She Is Ma Daisy
Sierra Sue
Sioux City Sue
Sister Jane
Sister Susie's Sewing Shirts For Soldiers
So Long Mary
Song Of Delilah, The
Sorry Suzanne
Story Of Tina, The (Dio Prasina Matia)
Sunbonnet Sue
Sweet Adeline
Sweet Caroline
Sweet Genevieve
Sweet Georgia Brown
Sweet Jenny Lee
Sweet Leilani
Sweet Lorraine
Sweet Sue - Just You
Tell Laura I Love Her
Tell Me Marianne (A Media Luz)
They Call The Wind Maria
Thoroughly Modern Millie
Thou Art My Rose
Wait For Me Mary
Wake Up Little Susie
Walk Away Renee
Walking With Susie
Wedding Of Lilli Marlene, The
Whatever Lola Wants
Wheezy Anna
When Jesamine Goes
When Julie Comes Around
When You And I Were Young, Maggie
Wilhelmina
Wind Cries Mary, The
Yes Tonight Josephine
You Ought To See Sally On Sunday

Nationality

Chin Chin Chinaman
(Do The) Spanish Hustle
Double Dutch
Down The Old Spanish Trail
Fifty Million Frenchmen Can't Be Wrong
Flying Dutchman, The
I Leave My Heart In An English Garden
I Miss My Swiss - My Swiss Miss Misses Me
If You're Irish Come Into The Parlour
In A Little Spanish Town
In An Old Dutch Garden
It's A Great Day For The Irish
Laughing Irish Eyes
Little Dutch Mill
Mad Dogs And Englishmen
Mambo Italiano
March Of The Siamese Children, The
My Dear Little Cingalee
My Irish Molly-o
On A Street Of Chinese Lanterns
There's Something Spanish In Your Eyes
Turning Japanese
Underneath The Russian Moon
Walk Like An Egyptian
When Irish Eyes Are Smiling
Who's Taking You Home Tonight
Yankee Doodle Boy
You And The Night And The Music
Young New Mexican Pupeteer

Night / Tonight

All Day And All Of The Night
All Night Long
All Through The Night
Another Night Like This
Another Saturday Night
Are You Lonesome Tonight
Because The Night
Black Night
Blues In The Night
Boogie Nights
Crazy Crazy Nights
Dancing On A Saturday Night
Deep Night
Down On The Beach Tonight
Every Night About This Time
Friday Night
Give Me The Night
Glamorous Night
Goodnight Midnight
Goodnight Tonight
Hard Day's Night, A
Help Me Make It Through The Night
Here Comes The Night
Hold Back The Night
How Blue The Night
I Could Have Danced All Night
I Couldn't Sleep A Wink Last Night
I Drove All Night
I Pitch My Lonely Caravan At Night
I Saw Her Again Last Night
I Thought Of You Last Night
I Wonder Where My Baby Is Tonight
I'll Be Your Baby Tonight
I'm Gonna Ring The Bell Tonight
I'm Stepping Out With A Memory Tonight
I'm Your Baby Tonight
If I Could Be With You (One Hour Tonight)
In The Air Tonight
In The Middle Of A Dark Dark Night
In The Midnight Hour
In The Still Of The Night
It's One Of Those Nights
Juke Box Saturday Night
June Night
Just One More Night
Ladies Night
Last Night A D.J. Saved My Life
Last Night In Soho
Last Night On The Back Porch
Last Night Was Made For Love
Let Me Love You Tonight (No Te Importe Saber)
Let's Have A Quiet Night In
Let's Spend The Night Together
London By Night
London Nights
Love Me Tonight (Alla Fine Della Strada)
Luck Be A Lady Tonight
Meet Me Tonight In Dreamland
Midnight In Moscow (Moscow Nights)
Miss You Nights
Music Of The Night
Need You Tonight
No More Lonely Nights
Oh How I Miss You Tonight
Oh! I Must Go Home Tonight
One More Night
One Night
One Night In Bankok
One Night Of Love
Out Of The Night
Quiet Nights Of Quiet Stars (Corcovado)
Rainy Night In Rio, A
Rhythm Of The Night
Rock The Boat (Tempest)
Running With The Night
Sailor Who Are You Dreaming Of Tonight
San Franciscan Nights
Saturday Night At The Movies
Saturday Night Is The Loneliest Night Of The Week
Saturday Night's Alright For Fighting
Serenade In The Night
So Cold The Night
So Deep Is The Night (Tristesse)
Somebody's Thinking Of You Tonight
Spend The Night
Story Of A Starry Night, The
Strangers In The Night
Such A Night
Summer Night City
Summer Nights
Teach Me Tonight
Tell Me Tonight
That Night In Araby
There'll Be A Hot Time In The Old Town Tonight
There's Never Been A Night
This Flight Tonight
Tomorrow Night
Twistin' The Night Away
Walk In The Night
Way You Look Tonight, The
When It's Night Time In Italy, It's Wednesday Over Here
Where The Blue Of The Night
Who Were You With Last Night
Yes Tonight Josephine
You And Me Tonight
You've Got To See Mama Every Night

Numbers

007 (Shanty Town)
Between 18th And 19th On Chestnut Street
Big Eight
Big Seven
Big Six
(Call Me) Number One
Chant Number One
Cloud Nine
Cocktails For Two
Counting Teardrops
Dinner At Eight
Heartaches By The Number
Hundred Years From Today, A
I Close My Eyes And Count To Ten
I Found A Million Dollar Baby
I'm Feeling Like A Million
I've Got Five Dollars
In The Year 2525
It Takes Two
It's A Hundred To One I'm In Love
Knock Three Times
Looking After Number One
Lucky Five
Lucky Number
Mister Moon You've Got A Million Sweethearts
Multiplication
Never In A Million Years
Night Has A Thousand Eyes, The
No! No! A Thousand Times No
Number One Song In Heaven, The
Numero Uno
Opus Number One
Pennsylvania Six-Five-Thousand
Rainy Day Woman Nos. 12 & 35
Room Five Hundred And Four
Say I'm Your Number One
Take A Number From One To Ten
Twixt Twelve And Twenty
You Only Live Twice
You're More Than A Number In My Little Red Book

Occupations

Apple For The Teacher, An
Ask A Policeman

Ballerina
Blacksmith Blues, The
Boxer, The
Candy Man
Chattanoogie Shoeshine Boy
Cobbler's Song, The
Cowboy
Crystal Gazer, The
Deer Hunter Theme, The
Fishermen Of England, The
Folk Singer, The
Gambler
Guitar Man
Hurdy Gurdy Man, The
I Was Kaiser Bill's Batman
I'm An Old Cow-Hand
If I Were A Carpenter
Lamplighter's Serenade, The
Lighterman Tom
Little Drummer Boy, The
Little Shoemaker, The (Le Petit Cordonnier)
Lonely Ballerina
Male Stripper
Man With The Mandolin, The
Matchmaker, Matchmaker
Milkman Keep Those Bottles Quiet
Miner's Dream Of Home, The
Mister Tambourine Man
Monkey And The Organ Grinder, The
My Very Good Friend The Milkman
Nursie
Old Lamplighter, The
Old Master Painter, The
Painter Man
Paperback Writer
Peanut Vendor, The (El Manisero)
Pearl's A Singer
Pedro The Fisherman
Picture No Artist Can Paint, A
Pied Piper, The
Please Mr. Postman
Policeman's Holiday, The
Portuguese Washerwomen, The (Les Lavandieres Du Portugal)
Rags, Bottles Or Bones
Rickerty Rickshaw Man, The
Sam The Old Accordion Man
Shepherd Of The Hills
Shoe Shine Boy
Shoemaker's Serenade, The
Snake Charmer, The
Stripper, The
Sweet Potato Piper
Swinging Shepherd Blues
Three Caballeros, The (Ay Jalisco No Te Rajes)
Umbrella Man, The
Waiter And The Porter And The Upstairs Maid, The
When I'm Cleaning Windows
Who Pays The Ferryman
Who Takes Care Of The Caretaker's Daughter
Wichita Lineman
Woodchopper's Ball
Working In The Coalmine
Young New Mexican Pupeteer

Party

Ain't Nothing But A Houseparty
Breakdance Party
Can You Party
It's My Party

People

Crazy People
Dear Hearts And Gentle People

Games People Play
Let The People Sing
Love Of The Common People
Nice People
No Two People
Other People's Babies
Poor People Of Paris, The
Power To The People
Some People
Two Sleepy People
Wonderful World, Beautiful People

Periodicals

Close As Pages In A Book
Girl On The Magazine Cover, The
Girl On The Police Gazette, The
I Could Write A Book
In My Little Red Book
My Colouring Book
My Heart Is An Open Book

Plants

From The Vine Came The Grape
Green Green Grass Of Home, The
Here We Go Round The Mulberry Bush
House Of Bamboo, The
House Of Singing Bamboo, The
I Can Hear The Grass Grow
I Remember The Cornfields
I'm Looking Over A Four-Leaf Clover
Just Like The Ivy
Load Of Hay, A
Lullaby Of The Leaves
Malt And Barley Blues
Other Man's Grass, The
Pick A Bale Of Cotton
Rockin' Through The Rye
Tumbling Tumbleweeds
When The Bloom Is On The Sage
Whispering Grass

Questions & Answers

Ask Me No Questions
Devils' Answer, The
Don't Answer Me (Ti Vedo Uscuiri)
There Are More Questions Than Answers
You'll Answer To Me

Radio / Television

I Love My Radio
On My Radio
On The Air
Sun Always Shines On T.V., The
Video Killed The Radio Star

Rag

Alexander's Ragtime Band
Black And White Rag
Brittania Rag
Bugle Call Rag
Celebration Rag
Coronation Rag
Crazy Otto Rag
Down Home Rag
He's A Rag Picker
International Rag
Ivory Rag
Johnson Rag
Leicester Square Rag
Maple Leaf Rag
Old Pi-Anna Rag, The
Old Rag Blues
Russian Rag
Saturday Rag
Temptation Rag
That Mysterious Rag

Tiger Rag
Twelfth Street Rag

Relatives

Good Morning Brother Sunshine
He Ain't Heavy, He's My Brother
I Wish I Could Shimmy Like My Sister Kate
I Wish I Were Twins
I'm My Own Grandpa
Jolly Brothers, The (Lustige Bruder)
Kissin' Cousins
Like Sister And Brother
Matthew And Son
Me And The Old Folks At Home
Mister And Mrs Is The Name
Mrs. Brown You've Got A Lovely Daughter
My Ain Folk
My Brother Jake
My Old Dutch
My Perfect Cousin
My Sister And I
My Son, My Son
Poor Man's Son
Running In The Family
That's The Moon My Son
There's No One Quite Like Grandma
Three Little Sisters
Triplets
We Are Family
Whistler's Mother-In-Law, The
Who Takes Care Of The Caretaker's Daughter
Yes My Darling Daughter

Religion

At Trinity Church
Bless This House
Blow, Gabriel, Blow
Child's Prayer, A
Christopher Robin Is Saying His Prayers
Church Of The Poison Mind
Get Me To The Church On Time
God Only Knows
Holy City, The
Hymn
Hymn To Her
I Say A Little Prayer
I'll Pray For You
I'm Praying To Saint Christopher
Living On A Prayer
May The Good Lord Bless And Keep You
My Sweet Lord
Oh Lord
Praying For Time
Save A Prayer
Say A Little Prayer
Someone Stole Gabriel's Horn
Son Of A Preacher Man
Temple Bell, The
That's The Way God Planned It
This Is My Prayer (Non Ho L'eta Per Amarti)
To Know Him Is To Love Him
Waiting At The Church
Winchester Cathedral

Residence

Beside My Caravan
Caravan
Caravan Of Love
Have You Got Any Castles Baby
I Wouldn't Leave My Little Wooden Hut For You
It's So Nice To Have A Man Around The House
Just A Cottage Small (By A Waterfall)

Ours Is A Nice 'Ouse Ours Is
Tara's Theme
This Ole House
Why Did I Leave My Little Back Room

Rivers

Banks Of The Ohio, The
By The River Of The Roses
By The River Saint Marie
Can I Canoe You Up The River
Cruising Down The River
Cry Me A River
Down By The O-Hi-O
Down By The Old Mill Stream
Ferry 'Cross The Mersey
Fog On The Tyne
In A Shady Nook By A Babbling Brook
Lazy River
Many Rivers To Cross
Moody River
Moon River
Moonlight On The Colorado
Moonlight On The Ganges
Moonlight On The River
My Castle On The Nile
My Song Of The Nile
Ol' Man River
Old Father Thames
On The Alamo
On The Banks Of The Wabash
Rainbow On The River
Ready For The River
Rhythm On The River
Rose Of The Rio Grande
Saw Mill River Road, The
Shores Of Minnetonka
Too Many Rivers
Weary River
When We've Wound Up The Watch On
The Rhine
Where The River Shannon Flows

Rock

Are You Ready To Rock
Banana Rock
Bloodnoks Rock 'n' Roll
Castle Rock
Crocodile Rock
Don't Knock The Rock
Don't Play Your Rock And Roll To Me
Don't You Rock Me Daddy-O
Good Old Rock 'n' Roll
Hey Rock And Roll
I Didn't Know I Loved You (Till I Saw You
Rock 'n' Roll)
I Love Rock 'n' Roll
It's Only Rock And Roll
It's Still Rock And Roll To Me
Jailhouse Rock
Jingle Bell Rock
Jungle Rock
Just A-Sittin' And A-rockin'
Just Keep Rockin'
King Of Rock 'n' Roll, The
King Rocker
Let It Rock
Little Rock Getaway
Nut Rocker
Red River Rock
Reelin' And Rockin'
Saints Rock And Roll

Royalty

Carribean Queen
Coronation Rag
Coronation Waltz, The
Crown, The
Dollar Princesses

Gentlemen, The King
His Majesty The Baby
Soldiers Of The Queen
Some Day My Prince Will Come
When You Are A King
Your King And Country Want You

Sea

Asleep In The Deep
'Bam 'Bam 'Bammy Shore
Barnacle Bill The Sailor
Beach Baby
Beyond The Sea
Blue Pacific Moonlight
By The Beautiful Sea
Circles In The Sand
Crest Of A Wave, The
Cruel Sea, The
Dock Of The Bay, The
Don't Make Waves
Down On The Beach Tonight
Driftwood
Ebb Tide
Ebbtide
Echo Beach
Four Winds And The Seven Seas
Gilly-Gilly Ossenfeffer Katzen Ellen
Bogen By The Sea
Hands Across The Sea
Harbour Lights
Her Bathing Suit Never Got Wet
How Deep Is The Ocean
I Cover The Waterfront
I Do Like To Be Beside The Seaside
I Threw A Kiss In The Ocean
Martha's Harbour
Mer, La
Montego Bay
Moon At Sea
Moonlight Bay
My Friend The Sea
On Miami Shore
On The Beach
On The Beach At Bali Bali
On The Beach At Waikiki
Sailing Down Chesapeake Bay
Sand Dunes
Seven Seas Of Rhye, The
She Sells Sea Shells
Shifting, Whispering Sands
Sleepy Shores
Sons Of The Sea
South Sea Island Magic
Stranger On The Shore
Sussex By The Sea
Temma Harbour
There's A Harbour Of Dreamboats
Tide Is High, The
We Parted On The Shore
We Saw The Sea
White Silver Sands

Seasons

Come Next Spring
Cruel Summer
Faded Summer Love, A
Farewell My Summer Love
Forever Autumn
Goodbye Summer, So Long Fall, Hello
Wintertime
Green Leaves Of Summer, The
Hello Summertime
Here Comes Summer
If Winter Comes
In Summer
In Summertime On Bredon
In The Good Old Summertime
In The Summertime

Indian Summer
It May Be Winter Outside (But In My
Heart It's Spring)
It's All Right In The Summertime
Last Rose Of Summer
Long Hot Summer
Once Upon A Wintertime
One Summer Night
Paris In The Spring
Seasons In The Sun (Le Moribond)
Silver Dream Machine
Sing A Song Of Sunbeams
Suddenly It's Spring
When Autumn Leaves Are Falling
When It's Springtime In The Rockies
When The Summer Comes Again (Three
Pots A Shilling)
When You've Got A Little Springtime In
Your Heart
Where Did My Snowman Go
Younger Than Springtime

Silver

By The Light Of The Silvery Moon
Gold And Silver Waltz, The
Hi Ho Silver
Hi-Ho Silver Lining
I Used To Sigh For The Silvery Moon
Pair Of Silver Wings, A
When You're Hair Has Turned To Silver
White Silver Sands

Sing / Song

And The Angels Sing
And The Birds Were Singing (Et Les
Oiseaux Chantaient)
Annie's Song
Birdie Song, The (Tchip Tchip)
Brown Bird Singing, A
Can't Help Singing
Canoe Song, The
Chanson D'amour
Chantez Chantez
Chicken Song, The
Clapping Song, The
Cobbler's Song, The
Crooning
Day-O (Banana Boat Song)
Don't Play That Song (You Lied)
Donkey Song, The
Gang That Sang "Heart Of My Heart",
The
Handful Of Songs, A
Hawaiian Wedding Song
Hear My Song Violetta (Hor Mein Lied
Violetta)
House Of Singing Bamboo, The
Hula Hoop Song, The
Humming
Hut Sut Song
I Bring A Love Song
I Can Sing A Rainbow
I Feel A Song Coming On
I Let A Song Go Out Of My Heart
I Love To Sing
I Poured My Heart Into A Song
I Write The Songs
I'd Like To Teach The World To Sing
I'll Sing You A Thousand Love Songs
I'm Humming, I'm Whistling, I'm Singing
I've Got To Sing A Torch Song
I've Heard That Song Before
It's The Same Old Song
Killing Me Softly With His Song
Learn To Croon
Let The People Sing
Let's All Sing Like The Birdies Sing
Life Is A Long Song
Life Is A Song

Logical Song, The
Love Is A Song
Love's Old Sweet Song
Mama Doll Song, The
Moon Song (That Wasn't Meant For Me)
My Croony Melody
My Heart Sings
My Kid's A Crooner
Mystery Song, The
Never Ending Song Of Love
New Song
Number One Song In Heaven, The
Of Thee I Sing
One Song
Onion Song, The
Orville's Song
Pagan Love Song, The
Pearl's A Singer
Penny Whistle Song, The
Pushbike Song, The
Sad Songs (Say So Much)
Sam's Song
September Song
Skye Boat Song, The
Smurf Song, The
Sweetest Song In The World, The
Swing Song
That's How A Love Song Was Born
There Goes That Song Again
This Is My Song
This Is Not A Love Song
Trolley Song, The
Violin Song, The
War Song, The
We All Have A Song In Our Hearts
When April Sings
When Mother Nature Sings Her Lullaby
When Smokey Sings
Whole World Is Singing My Song
Wine, Woman And Song
With A Smile And A Song
Wombling Song, The
Woodpeckers Song (Reginella Campagnola)
You Can Make Me Dance Sing Or Anything
Your Song
Zing A Little Zong

Sky

Blue Skies
Blue Skies Are Round The Corner
Cabin In The Sky
Ghost Riders In The Sky
High In The Sky
Just Like A Melody Out Of The Sky
Lucy In The Sky With Diamonds
Melody From The Sky, A
Mister Blue Sky
New Sun In The Sky, A
Orange Coloured Sky
Spirit In The Sky
There's A Gold Mine In The Sky
Under Paris Skies (Sous Le Ciel De Paris)

Sleep

And So To Sleep Again
Asleep In The Deep
By The Sleepy Lagoon
Does Santa Claus Sleep With His Whiskers
Don't Sleep In The Subway
Endless Sleep
General's Fast Asleep, The
I Couldn't Sleep A Wink Last Night
I Go To Sleep
I Wonder How I Look When I'm Asleep

I'd Love To Fall Asleep
I'd Love To Fall Asleep And Wake Up In My Mammy's Arms
I'm Getting Tired So I Can Sleep
Japanese Sandman
Let's Put Out The Lights And Go To Sleep
Mister Sandman
So Tired
Talking In Your Sleep
Two Sleepy People
When It's Sleepy Time Down South

Smile

Born With A Smile On My Face
Bring Your Smile Along
Certain Smile, A
I Shall Always Remember You Smiling
I'll Never Smile Again
Just One Smile
Keep Smiling At Trouble
Leave Me With A Smile
Let A Smile Be Your Umbrella
Make Me Smile (Come Up And See Me)
No One Can Make My Sunshine Smile
Patiently Smiling
Shadow Of Your Smile
Sunshine Of Your Smile, The
Sweetest Smile
When Buddha Smiles
When Irish Eyes Are Smiling
When My Baby Smiles At Me
When My Little Girl Is Smiling
When You're Smiling
With A Smile And A Song

Space

Apollo 9
I Lost My Heart To A Starship Trooper
I'm The Urban Spaceman
Rocket Man

Speak / Talk

Body Rock
Can't We Talk It Over
Conversations
Don't Talk To Him
Don't Talk To Me About Love
Girls Talk
Happy Talk
I Came Here To Talk For Joe
I Don't Want To Talk About It
I Talk To The Trees
Idle Gossip
If I Had A Talking Picture Of You
If Those Lips Could Only Speak
It's The Talk Of The Town
Jive Talkin'
Let's Talk About Love
Let's Talk About My Sweetie
Love's Last Word Is Spoken (Le Chaland Qui Passe)
Pillow Talk
Please Don't Talk About Me When I'm Gone
Rabbit
Sweet Talkin' Guy
Sweet Talkin' Woman
Too Nice To Talk To
We Don't Talk Anymore
Won't Talk About It
Yakity Yak

Sport

Alley's Tartan Army
Anfield Rap, The
Bicycle Race
Boxer, The

Gone Fishin'
Leeds United
Ossie's Dream (The Way To Wembley)
Runner, The
Victory Test Match, The
We All Follow Man. United
We Can Do It

Star

Beyond The Stars
Blue Star (The Medic Theme)
Catch A Falling Star
Come Down Ma Evening Star
Count Every Star
Don't Let The Stars Get In Your Eyes
Estrellita
Gonna Make You A Star
Good Morning Starshine
Hang Out The Stars In Indiana
I Am The Starlight
I Can Give You The Starlight
I Saw Stars
I See A Star
I'll Buy You A Star
I've Told Every Little Star
Look For A Star
Lucky Stars
Oh Star Of Eve
Quiet Nights Of Quiet Stars (Corcovado)
Reach For The Stars (Woner Ich Auch Komm, Wohin Ich Auch Geh)
Second Star To The Right, The
Shake Down The Stars
Shooting Star
Silver Star
Stairway To The Stars
Stella By Starlight
Story Of A Starry Night, The
Swinging On A Star
Telstar
Thousand Stars, A
Three Stars
Till Stars Forgot To Shine
Underneath The Stars
Waiting For A Star To Fall
Wanderin' Star
When You Wish Upon A Star
Wishing On A Star
You Are My Lucky Star
You Don't Have To Be A Star
You're The Only Star In My Blue Heaven

Stop

Breakin'... There's No Stopping Us
Don't Stop It Now
Don't Stop Me Now
Don't Stop The Carnival
Don't Stop The Music
Don't Stop Till You Get Enough
Everything Stops For Tea
I Can't Stop
I Can't Stop Loving You
I Just Can't Stop Loving You
I'll Stop At Nothing
Nothing's Gonna Stop Me Now
Nothing's Gonna Stop Us Now
You Can't Stop Me From Dreaming
You'll Never Stop Me Loving You

Sun

Ain't No Sunshine
At Sundown
Automatically Sunshine
Bathing In The Sunshine
Don't Let The Sun Catch You Crying
Don't Let The Sun Go Down On Me
East Of The Sun
Following The Sun Around

Good Morning Brother Sunshine
Happy To Be On An Island In The Sun
Here Comes The Sun
Holidays In The Sun
House Of The Rising Sun, The
I Don't Care If The Sun Don't Shine
I Got The Sun In The Morning
I Love The Sunshine Of Your Smile
I Won't Let The Sun Go Down On Me
Ice In The Sun
Invisible Sun
Island In The Sun
It Happened In Sun Valley
It's Raining Sunbeams
Keep Searchin' (We'll Follow The Sun)
Let The Sunshine In
Love In The Sun
Meet Me Jenny When The Sun Goes Down
Meet The Sun Half Way
My Sunny Tennessee
New Sun In The Sky, A
No One Can Make My Sunshine Smile
On The Sunny Side Of The Street
One More Sunrise (Morgen)
Over On The Sunny Side
Painting The Clouds With Sunshine
Paper Sun
Please Mister Sun
Powder Your Face With Sunshine
Rising Sun, The
Sally, You Brought The Sunshine To Our Alley
Seasons In The Sun (Le Moribond)
Sing A Song Of Sunbeams
Sink Red Sun
Smile Right Back At The Sun
Softly As In A Morning Sunrise
Some Sunny Day
Somewhere The Sun Is Shining
That Lucky Old Sun
Twenty-Four Hours Of Sunshine
Walkin' In The Sunshine
Walking On Sunshine
Waterloo Sunset
We'll Make Hay While The Sun Shines
What Makes The Sunset
When The Sun Comes Out
When The Sun Goes Down
Who's Been Polishing The Sun
World Is Waiting For The Sunrise, The
You Are My Sunshine
You Are The Sunshine Of My Life

Sweetheart

Auf Wiederseh'n Sweetheart
Call Her Your Sweetheart
Down Sweetheart Avenue
Goodnight Sweetheart
I'll Be Your Sweetheart
I'm In Love With Two Sweethearts
Let Me Call You Sweetheart
Let Us Be Sweethearts All Over Again
Mister Moon You've Got A Million Sweethearts
My Sweetheart's The Man In The Moon
Nobody's Sweetheart
Some Day Sweetheart
Sweet Dreams Sweetheart
You're A Sweetheart

Tears

After My Laughter Came Tears
As Tears Go By
Brush Those Tears From Your Eyes
Counting Teardrops
Dancing With Tears In My Eyes
How Many Tears

Letter Full Of Tears
Little Bitty Tear, A
Many Years Ago
No More Tears (Enough Is Enough)
O Dry Those Tears
Seven Tears
Taste Of Your Tears
Too Many Tears
Tracks Of My Tears, The
Two Kinds Of Teardrops
Why Waste Your Tears

Temperature

Fair And Warmer
Frozen Orange Juice
I've Got My Love To Keep Me Warm
If You Can't Stand The Heat
In The Cool, Cool, Cool Of The Evening
It's Gonna Be A Cold Cold Christmas
Long Hot Summer
Out In The Cold Again
Out In The Cold Cold Snow
Red Hot Mamma
Southern Freeez
Steam Heat
There'll Be A Hot Time In The Old Town Tonight
Till The Sands Of The Desert Grow Cold
Too Darn Hot
Too Hot To Handle

Thoroughfares

Algy The Piccadilly Johnny
Along The Navajo Trail
Along The Santa Fe Trail
Angel Of The Great White Way
At The Crossroads
Autobahn
Back Street Luv
Baker Street
Basin Street Blues
Between 18th And 19th On Chestnut Street
Blackberry Way
Blue Bells Of Broadway, The
Boulevard Of Broken Dreams
Bowery, The
Broadway Melody, The
Broadway Rose
Cross Over The Bridge
Dancing In The Street
Davy's On The Road Again
Dead End Street
Detour Ahead
Down Forget-Me-Not Lane
Down On The Street
Down Sweetheart Avenue
Down The Old Ox Road
Down The Old Spanish Trail
Down The Oregon Trail
Easy Street
Electric Avenue
End Of The Road, The
Ev'ry Street's A Boulevard
Forty Miles Of Bad Road
Forty-Second Street
Give My Regards To Broadway
Goodbye Yellow Brick Road
Happiness Street
Heartache Avenue
Hit The Road Jack
Hit The Road To Dreamland
I Live In Trafalgar Square
I Travel The Road
It Looks Like Rain In Cherry Blossom Lane
Italian Street Song
King Of The Road

Lambeth Walk, The
Leicester Square Rag
Let's All Go Down The Strand
Little Street Where Old Friends Meet, A
Lonesome Road
Lullaby Of Broadway
Meet Me On The Corner
Naughty Lady Of Shady Lane, The
Nightingale Sang In Berkeley Square, A
Nights On Broadway
Number Something Far Away Lane
On A Little Street In Singapore
On A Street Of Chinese Lanterns
On The Road Again
On The Road To Mandalay
On The Street Where You Live
On The Sunny Side Of The Street
One Road
Pavements Of Paris, The (Sur Le Pavé)
Penny Lane
Polly Perkins Of Paddington Green
Pompton Turnpike
Positively Fourth Street
Relicairo, El
Round The Bend Of The Road
'Round The Marble Arch
Route Sixty-Six
Sally, You Brought The Sunshine To Our Alley
Saw Mill River Road, The
Sidewalks Of Cuba
Sidewalks Of New York, The
Slaughter On Tenth Avenue
Slumming On Park Avenue
South Rampart Street Parade
Standing In The Road
Stay On The Right Side Of The Road
Stay On These Roads
Sunset Trail, The
Swingin' Down The Lane
Take Me Home Country Road
There's A Long Long Trail
Tobacco Road
Trail Of The Lonesome Pine
Tramp, Tramp, Tramp Along The Highway
Twelfth Street Rag
Two Four Six Eight Motorway
Walkin' Thru Mockin' Bird Lane
Wall Street Shuffle
Weeping Willow Lane
When My Sugar Walks Down The Street
When The Moon Comes Over Madison Square
Where The Streets Have No Name

Time

About A Quarter To Nine
All The Time And Everywhere
Am I Wasting My Time On You
Another Time Another Place
As Time Goes By
At Dawning
Beat The Clock
Bidin' My Time
Bird Songs At Eventide
Bringing On Back The Good Times
Call Round Any Old Time
Can't Wait Another Minute
Carolina In The Morning
Come Down Ma Evening Star
Dinner At Eight
Don't Waste My Time
Don't You Think It's Time
Early In The Morning
Every Night About This Time
Every Time You Go Away
Find The Time
Fine Time

First Time Ever I Saw Your Face, The
First Time I Saw You, The
First Time, The
Five O'Clock Whistle, The
For Old Times' Sake
For The Good Times
Give Me Just A Little More Time
Good Times
Good Times (Better Times)
Good Timin'
Happy Hour
Happy Times
High Noon
High Time
Hour Of Parting, The
I Didn't Know What Time It Was
I Haven't Time To Be A Millionaire
I'll Meet You At Midnight
If I Could Turn Back Time
If I Only Had Time (Je N'aurai Pas Le Temps)
In Love For The Very First Time
In My Own Time
In The Good Old Summertime
In The Midnight Hour
In The Twi-Twi-Twilight
It Only Takes A Minute
It Only Took A Minute
It's Been A Long Long Time
It's Four In The Morning
It's Just A Matter Of Time
It's Nice To Get Up In The Morning
It's Time To Say Goodnight
Just In Time
Just Once For All Time
Just Who Is The Five O'Clock Hero
Lady Of The Evening
Last Time, The
Little Time, A
Living After Midnight
May Morning, A
Midnight In Moscow (Moscow Nights)
Minute Of Your Time, A
Moonlight Saving Time
Mother Nature And Father Time
My Cuties Due At Two To Two Today
My Dreams Are Getting Better All The Time
My Favourite Waste Of Time
My Time Is Your Time
New World In The Morning, A
Next Time
Nine Times Out Of Ten
Nine To Five
Not Until The Next Time
Now Is The Hour (Hearere Ra)
Now Is The Time
Oh How I Hate To Get Up In The Morning
On The Five Forty-Five
One Moment In Time
One O'Clock Jump
Out Of Time
Part Time Love
Part Time Lover
Quarter To Three
Ride On Time
Rock Around The Clock
Rush Hour
Second Time Around
Sign Of The Times
Six Times A Week And Twice On Sundays
Sixty Seconds Got Together
Some Sunday Morning
Song Of The Dawn
Step Back In Time
Take Five
Take Your Time
There's A Good Time Coming

This Time I Know It's For Real
This Time The Dream's On Me
Three O'Clock In The Morning
Three Times A Lady
Tu-Li-Tulip Time
Turn Back The Clock
Turn Back The Hands Of Time
Twelve O'Clock At Night
Twenty-Four Hours From Tulsa
Twenty-Four Hours Of Sunshine
Until It's Time For You To Go
What Time Is Love
When It's Lamp Lighting Time In The Valley
When It's Night Time In Dixieland
When It's Sleepy Time Down South
When The Midnight Choo-Choo Leaves For Alabam'
Wonderful Time Up There

Tomorrow

All Our Tomorrows
Come Tomorrow
Hold Back Tomorrow
It's A Lovely Day Tomorrow
It's Almost Tomorrow
Love Me As Though There Were No Tomorrow
Save Your Sorrow For Tomorrow
There's Always Tomorrow
There's No Tomorrow
This Is Tomorrow
Will You Love Me Tomorrow

Town / City

All The Way From Memphis
Along The Santa Fe Trail
April In Paris
At Santa Barbara
Autumn In New York
Battle Of New Orleans, The
Big Noise From Winnetka
Boy From New York City
By The Fountains Of Rome
Ca C'est Paris
Cafe In Vienna
Day The Circus Left Town, The
Day Trip To Bangor
Do You Know The Way To San Jose
Down Town
Drowning In Berlin
Fairytale Of New York
Flying Down To Rio
From New York To L.A.
Get Out Of Town
Girl From Ipanema, The
Goodnight Vienna
He's In Town
Hello Frisco Hello
Home Town
Hooray For Hollywood
I Belong To Glasgow
I Lost My Heart In Heidelberg
I Lost My Sugar In Salt Lake City
I Love Paris
I'm Gonna Charleston Back To Charleston
I'm In Love With Vienna
I've Got A Gal In Kalamazoo
In Chi-Chi Castenango
In Old Lisbon (Lisboa Antigua)
In San Francisco
Is This The Way To Amarillo
It Happened In Adano
It Happened In Monterey
It's The Talk Of The Town
Lady Of Madrid
Last Time I Saw Paris, The

Last Train To San Fernando, The
Let's Go To San Francisco
Lights Of Cincinnati, The
Lights Of Lisbon, The
Little Town Flirt
Loco In Acapulco
Long Haired Lover From Liverpool
Mademoiselle De Paris
Mademoiselle From Armentieres
Maid Of Orleans, The
Man From Laramie, The
Man Who Broke The Bank At Monte Carlo, The
Managua Nicaragua
Maybe It's Because I'm A Londoner
Meet Me In St. Louis
Midnight In Moscow (Moscow Nights)
Midnight Train To Georgia
Native New Yorker
Night Chicago Died, The
On A Little Street In Singapore
On Miami Shore
On Mobile Bay
On The Road To Mandalay
One Night In Bankok
Out Of Town
Pavements Of Paris, The (Sur Le Pavé)
Poor People Of Paris, The
Rainy Night In Rio, A
Return Of The Los Palmas Seven, The
Rio
Rivers Of Babylon, The
She Is The Belle Of New York
Shuffle Off To Buffalo
Sidewalks Of New York, The
Streets Of Laredo, The
Streets Of London, The
Summer Evening In Santa Cruz, A
Summertime In Venice
Sweetheart Of Sigma Chi
That's What Makes Paris Paree
There's A Lovely Lake In London
Till The Lights Of London Shine Again
Tulips From Amsterdam
Twenty-four Hours From Tulsa
Under Paris Skies (Sous Le Ciel De Paris)
Under The Bridges Of Paris (Sous Les Ponts De Paris)
Under The Roofs Of Paris (Sous Les Toits De Paris)
Way Down Yonder In New Orleans
When The Swallows Come Back To Capistrano
White Cliffs Of Dover, The
Windmill In Old Amsterdam, A
Windows Of Paris
Witch Queen Of New Orleans
You Will Remember Vienna

Toys

Balloons (who'll Buy My Nice Balloons)
Broken Doll
Cuddly Toy
Doll Dance, The
Golliwog's Cake Walk
His Rocking Horse Ran Away
Kewpie Doll
Little Wooden Whistle Wouldn't Whistle, The
March Of The Toys, The
Paper Doll
Parade Of The Wooden Soldiers
Playthings
Rag Doll
Teddy Bear
Teddy Bear's Picnic, The
Wedding Of The Painted Doll, The

Transport

Bicyclettes De Belsize
Big Yellow Taxi
Chattanooga Choo Choo
Chitty Chitty Bang Bang
Come Josephine In My Flying Machine
Convoy
Deadwood Stage, The
Driving My Car
Fast Car
Ferry 'Cross The Mersey
Fiacre, Le (The Cab)
Finchley Central
Freight Train
Get Out Of My Dreams, Get Into My Car
Groovy Train
I Pitch My Lonely Caravan At Night
In A Golden Coach
In My Merry Oldsmobile
In Your Car
Last Train To San Fernando, The
Leavin' On A Jet Plane
Little Red Corvette
Love Train
Me And Jane In A Plane
Midnight Train To Georgia
Motor Biking
Mule Train
My White Bicycle
On The Atchison, Topeka And The Santa Fe
On The Five Forty-Five
On The Five-fifteen
Orange Blossom Special
Pink Cadillac
Pushbike Song, The
Riding On A Train
Rock Island Line
Roll Along Covered Wagon
Runaway Train, The
Seven Little Girls Sitting In The Back Seat
Sleigh Ride
Slow Coach
Snow Coach
Stage Coach
Stanley Steamer, The
Surrey With The Fringe On Top, The
Take The 'A' Train
Thanks For The Buggy Ride
Ticket To Ride
Tuxedo Junction
Wagon Wheels
Waiting For A Train
Waiting For The Train To Come In
Wheel Of The Wagon Is Broken, The
When The Midnight Choo-Choo Leaves For Alabam'
Where My Caravan Has Rested
Yellow Submarine

Travel

Bus Stop
Calling Occupants Of Interplanetary Craft
Cruising Down The River
Day Tripper
Drive
Finchley Central
Hitchin' A Ride
I Drove All Night
I Travel The Road
Leavin' On A Jet Plane
Oh Mr Porter
Passengers
Riding On A Train
Ro-Ro-Rollin' Along
Roamin' In The Gloamin'

Sentimental Journey
Sleigh Ride
Thanks For The Buggy Ride
Trains And Boats And Planes
Travellin' Light
Trolley Song, The
Up Up And Away
Voyage Voyage
We'll All Go Riding On A Rainbow

Trees

Around The Corner And Under The Tree
Autumn Leaves
Don't Sit Under The Apple Tree
Down Among The Sheltering Palms
Fairy On The Christmas Tree, The
Falling Leaves
Hang Your Heart On A Hickory Limb
I Talk To The Trees
In The Shade Of The Old Apple Tree
Moon And The Willow Tree, The
Nights In The Wood (Les Nuits Du Bois)
Shade Of The Palm, The
Song Of The Trees, The
There's A Cabin In The Pines
They Cut Down The Old Pine Tree
Trail Of The Lonesome Pine
Under The Bamboo Tree
Under The Deodar
Under The Lilac Bough
When The Leaves Come Tumbling Down
Whispering Pines Of Nevada, The

TV Themes

Always There
Army Game, The
Ballad Of The Paladin, The
Chi Mai
Doctor Kildare Theme
Doina De Jale
Eye Level
Gurney Slade Theme, The
Harry's Game
Heat Is On, The
Hit And Miss
How Soon
Howard's Way Theme
I Could Be So Good For You
Maigret Theme, The
Miami Vice
Moonlighting
No Honestly
Nunc Dimittis
On The Inside
Onedin Line, The
Only Love
Peter Gunn
Rawhide
She
Sleepy Shores
Staccato's Theme
Stranger On The Shore
Thorn Birds (Love Theme)
Tom Hark
Walking In The Air
Who Pays The Ferryman
Wombling Song, The
Z Cars Theme

Twist

Don't Stop - Twist
Everybody's Twisting
Let's Twist Again
Ya Ya Twist

Vegetables

Boiled Beef And Carrots

Green Onions
Jumping Bean
Mama Don't Want No Peas, An' Rice, An' Coconut Oil
Sweet Potato Piper

Walk

Break My Stride
Cake Walking Babies From Home
Daddy Don't You Walk So Fast
Did You Ever See A Dream Walking
Felix Kept On Walking
Flirtation Walk
Footsteps
I Don't Want To Walk Without You
I'll Walk Beside You
I'm Happy When I'm Hiking
I'm Walking Behind You
Let's Take An Old Fashioned Walk
Let's Walk That-A-Way
Love Walked In
Pig Got Up And Slowly Walked Away, The
Shufflin' Along
Sleep Walk
Strollin'
Stumbling
These Boots Are Made For Walking
They All Walk The Wibbly Wobbly Walk
We All Walked Into The Shop
When I Take My Morning Promenade
When My Sugar Walks Down The Street
When You Walk In The Room
Who Walks In (When I Walk Out)
Would You Like To Take A Walk
You Walk By
You'll Never Walk Alone

War / Wartime Songs

Army Air Corps Song, The
Army Of Today's Alright, The
Army, The Navy And The Air Force, The
Badge From Your Coat, The
Bless 'Em All
Caissons Go Rolling Along, The
Canteen Bounce, The
Dam Busters March, The
Don't Sit Under The Apple Tree
Eve Of The War
Fuhrer's Face, Der
G.I. Jive, The
Goodbye Sally
Hello Mom
Hey Little Hen
I Came Here To Talk For Joe
I Left My Heart At The Stage Door Canteen
I'll Pray For You
I'm Gonna Get Lit Up
I've Got Sixpence (As I Go Rolling Home)
If I Only Had Wings
In The Quartermaster's Stores
It's A Long Way To Tipperary
Johnny Doughboy Found A Rose In Ireland
Johnny Zero
Let The People Sing
Let's Be Buddies
Lili Marlene
Lords Of The Air
Ma, I Miss Your Apple Pie
Milkman Keep Those Bottles Quiet
My British Buddy
No Love, No Nothing
Oh It's A Lovely War
Oh What A Surprise For The Duce (Evviva La Torre Di Pisa)
Over There

Pack Up Your Troubles In Your Old Kit Bag
Praise The Lord And Pass The Ammunition
River Kwai March
Run Rabbit Run
Shine On Victory Moon
Somewhere In France With You
Star Wars Theme
Take Me Back To Dear Old Blighty
There'll Always Be An England
There's A Boy Coming Home On Leave
They Can't Black-out The Moon
They're Either Too Young Or Too Old
Thing-Ummy-Bob, The
This Is The Army Mister Jones
This Is Worth Fighting For
Till The Lights Of London Shine Again
Washing On The Siegfried Line
When That Man Is Dead And Gone
When The Lights Go On Again
When They Sound The Last All Clear
When We've Wound Up The Watch On The Rhine
White Cliffs Of Dover, The
Wings Over The Navy

Water

Ain't Gonna Wash For A Week
Bridge Over Troubled Water
By A Waterfall
By The Waters Of Minnetonka
Cool Water
Her Bathing Suit Never Got Wet
Muddy Water
Reflections In The Water
Singing In The Bathtub
Splish Splash
Still Water
Tap Turns On The Water
Three Coins In The Fountain
Twisting By The Pool
Where The Waters Are Blue

Weather

After The Storm
Any Way The Wind Blows
April Showers
Baby It's Cold Outside
Because Of Rain
Blowing In The Wind
Blowing Wild
Breeze (Blow My Baby Back To Me)
Breeze And I, The
Breeze, The (That's Bringing My Honey Back To Me)
Breezin' Along With The Breeze
Butterflies In The Rain
Candle In The Wind, A
Cast Your Fate To The Wind
Catch The Wind
Cloud Nine
Clouds Across The Moon
Clouds Will Soon Roll By, The
Come Rain Or Come Shine
Crying In The Rain
Day The Rains Came, The
Don't Mind The Rain
Don't Rain On My Parade
Down Where The Trade Winds Blow
Fair And Warmer
Flowers In The Rain
Fog On The Tyne
Foggy Day, A
Four Winds And The Seven Seas
Frosty The Snowman
Garden In The Rain, A
Get Off Of My Cloud

Gone With The Wind
Hard Rain's Gonna Fall, A
Here Comes The Rain Again
I Can Sing A Rainbow
I Can't Stand The Rain
I Feel Like A Feather In The Breeze
I Left My Sugar Standing In The Rain
I Wish It Would Rain Down
I'm Always Chasing Rainbows
Ice In The Sun
If You Want The Rainbow In The Rain
Into Each Life Some Rain Must Fall
It Ain't Gonna Rain No Mo'
It Looks Like Rain In Cherry Blossom Lane
It Might As Well Rain Until September
It's Raining
It's Raining Men
It's Raining Sunbeams
Just Walking In The Rain
Let It Rain Let It Pour
Let It Snow
Lightin' Strikes
Lilacs In The Rain
Little April Shower
Little Rain Must Fall, A
Little White Cloud That Cried, The
Lost In A Fog
March Winds And April Showers
Mister Snow
My Rainbow Valley
Naked In The Rain
Ol' Buttermilk Sky
Out In The Cold Cold Snow
Out Of A Clear Blue Sky
Over The Rainbow
Painting The Clouds With Sunshine
Passing Breeze
Purple Rain
Rhythm Of The Rain
Ridin' Around In The Rain
Roll Away Clouds
Run Little Raindrop Run
September In The Rain
Singin' In The Rain
Skiing In The Snow
Sweeping The Clouds Away
That's What A Rainy Day Is For
There's A Rainbow 'Round My Shoulder
They Call The Wind Maria
Thunder In The Mountains
Till The Clouds Roll By
Trade Winds
Up In The Clouds
Walkin' In The Rain With The One I Love
Walking In The Rain
Waltzing In The Clouds
Wayward Wind, The
We'll All Go Riding On A Rainbow
What Do We Do On A Dew-Dew-Dewy Day
What Have They Done To The Rain
Where The Wind Blows
Where's That Rainbow
Whistle Down The Wind
Wild Wind
Wind Beneath My Wings
Wind Cries Mary, The
With The Wind And The Rain In Your Hair

Whistle

Five O'Clock Whistle, The
Give A Little Whistle
Happy Whistler, The
I Love To Whistle
I Whistle A Happy Tune
I'm Humming, I'm Whistling, I'm Singing

Penny Whistle Song, The
This'll Make You Whistle
Walking And Whistling Blues
Whistle While You Work
Whistler And His Dog, The
Whistler's Mother-in-law, The
Whistling In The Dark
Whistling Rufus
Whistling Waltz, The

Wish

I Wish
I Wish I Didn't Love You So
I Wish I Knew
I Wish I Were In Love Again
I Wish I Were Twins
I Wished On The Moon
I'm Wishing
When You Wish Upon A Star
Wish Me Luck As You Wave Me Goodbye
Wish You Were Here
Wishful Thinking
Wishing
Wishing On A Star
Wishing Well

Woman

Bess You Is My Woman Now
Cigareets, Whusky And Wild Wild Women
Devil Woman
Evil Woman
For Every Man There's A Woman
Hard Headed Woman
How To Handle A Woman
I'm Every Woman
Just Like A Woman
Long Legged Woman Dressed In Black
More Than A Woman
No Woman No Cry
Oh Pretty Woman
Only One Woman
Only Women Bleed
Rainy Day Woman Nos. 12 & 35
Senora
Show Me You're A Woman
Sobbin' Women
Strange Kind Of Woman, A
Superwoman
Sweet Talkin' Woman
When A Man Loves A Woman
When You're In Love With A Beautiful Woman
Whole Lotta Woman, A
Wild World
Wild, Wild Women Are Making A Wild Man Out Of Me, The
Wimmin (I Gotta Have 'em That's All)
Wine, Woman And Song
Winter World Of Love
You're Such A Good Looking Woman

World

All Around The World
All Over The World (Dans Le Monde Entier)
All The Love In The World
All The World Will Be Jealous Of Me
Around The World
At Peace With The World
End Of The World, The
Everybody Wants To Rule The World
Globetrotter
Goodbye Cruel World
Harvest For The World
He's Got The Whole World In His Hands
I Don't Want To Set The World On Fire

I Wouldn't Trade You For The World
I'd Give The World (Liebeslied)
I'd Like To Teach The World To Sing
I'm Sitting On Top Of The World
I've Got The World On A String
Ideal World
If The Whole World Stopped Loving
If You Were The Only Girl In The World
It's A Blue World
It's A Cruel Cruel World
It's A Wonderful World
Let The Great Big World Keep Turning
Looking At The World Through Rose Coloured Glasses
Love Makes The World Go Round
Love Me And The World Is Mine
Lovers Of The World Unite
Mad World
Make The World Go Away
Man Of The World, A
Man Who Sold The World, The
Most Beautiful Girl In The World
My Little Corner Of The World
My Song Goes Round The World
My World
Never Turn Your Back On Mother Earth
New World In The Morning, A
Our World
Out Of This World
Rockin' All Over The World
Rolling Round The World
Spirits In The Material World
Top Of The World
Two Different Worlds
We Are The World
Welcome To My World
What A Wonderful World
What In The World's Come Over You
When I Leave The World Behind
When The World Was Young
Where In The World
Whole World Is Singing My Song
Wild World
Wonderful World
Wonderful World Of The Young, The
Wonderful World, Beautiful People
You're My World (Il Mio Mondo)

Year

All Those Years Ago
Best Years Of Our Lives
Calendar Girl
Golden Years
Good Year For The Roses
Holding Back The Years
Hundred Years From Today, A
In The Year 2525
June Comes Around Every Year
Let's Start The New Year Right
Living Years
Loveliest Night Of The Year
Maybe This Year
Never In A Million Years
New Years Day
Once A Year Day
Seven Years With The Wrong Woman
Special Years, The
Spring Will Be A Little Late This Year

What's Another Year
You Grow Sweeter As The Years Go By

You

After You - Who
All For You
All I Do Is Dream Of You
Am I Wasting My Time On You
Brown Eyes Why Are You Blue
Can I Forget You
Close To You
Come Out, Come Out, Wherever You Are
Cup Of Coffee, A Sandwich And You, A
Do You Care
Do You Love Me
Do You Remember The Last Waltz
Don't You Know It
Embraceable You
Exactly Like You
First Time I Saw You, The
For You
From Me To You
Gee Whiz, It's You
Getting To Know You
Gimme A Little Kiss, Will Ya, Huh
Hello Hawaii, How Are You
Honey I'm In Love With You
How Come You Do Me Like You Do
How Sweet You Are
I Ain't Nobody's Darling
I Can't Begin To Tell You
I Can't Do Without You
I Can't Escape From You
I Didn't Know About You
I Double Dare You
I Found You
I Get A Kick Out Of You
I Get Along Without You Very Well
I Hadn't Anyone Till You
I Like The Likes Of You
I Love You
I Love You Truly
I Never Knew How Wonderful You Were
I Only Have Eyes For You
I Only Want To Be With You
I Take To You
I Think Of You
I Wanna Be Loved By You
I Want You To Want Me To Want You
I Want You, I Need You, I Love You
I Wouldn't Leave My Little Wooden Hut For You
I'd Never Find Another You
I'll Be Good Because Of You
I'll Be Seeing You
I'll Be With You In Apple Blossom Time
I'll Follow You
I'll Make A Man Of You
I'll Never Get Over You
I'll See You Again
I'll See You In My Dreams
I'll String Along With You
I'm Getting Sentimental Over You
I'm Goin' Shoppin' With You
I'm Going To See You Today
I'm In The Market For You
I'm Sure Of Everything But You
I'm Telling You Now

I've Got A Crush On You
If Ever I Would Leave You
If I Could Be With You (One Hour Tonight)
If I Had You
If You Could Care For Me
If You Hadn't Gone Away
If You Were The Only Girl In The World
Irresistible You
It Could Happen To You
It Had To Be You
It's For You
Just A-Wearyin' For You
Just You, Just Me
Keeping Myself For You
Knowing Me, Knowing You
Little Co-operation From You, A
Little Of What You Fancy, A
Longing For You
Losing You
Losing You (Un Ange Est Renn)
Love Bug Will Bite You, The
Love You Funny Thing
Memories Of You
Miss You
Moment I Saw You, The
More I See You, The
My Life Belongs To You
My Love For You
My Word You Do Look Queer
Oh How I Laugh When I Think How I Cried About You
Oh! If I Only Had You
Oh You Have No Idea
Over You
Picture Of You, A
Roses Remind Me Of You
Sharing You
Since I Found You
Sing You Sinners
Softly As I Leave You (Piano)
Somebody Loves You
Someone Like You
Somewhere In France With You
Song Is You, The
Sunrise And You
T'aint What You Do
That's You Baby
There's Everything Nice About You
There's No You
Thinking Of You
Till There Was You
To Know You Is To Love You
Tonight You Belong To Me
Wanting You
Were You Sincere
When They Ask About You
When You And I Were Dancing
When You And I Were Seventeen
When You Are In Love
When You Were Sweet Sixteen
When You Wore A Tulip
Where'd You Get Those Eyes
Who Were You With Last Night
Whose Baby Are You
Why Do I Love You
Will You Remember (Sweetheart)
Without You (Tres Palabras)
Would You

FOREIGN LANGUAGE SONGS

Argentina
Adios Muchachos
Carnavalito
Cumparsita, La
Kiss of Fire, The
Pablo The Dreamer
Sucu Sucu
Tell Me Marianne (A Media Luz)
Wedding, The (La Novia)

Australia
All Out of Love
Carry On
Dear John
Funky Town
Heatseeker
Howzat
Live is Life
Love is in The Air
Need You Tonight
On the Inside
Pub With No Beer, The
Real Wild Child
Shaddup You Face
Suddenly
Sun Arise
Tie Me Kangaroo Down Sport

Austria
Caprice Veinnois
Cigolette
Gipsy Maiden
Girls Were Made to Love and Kiss
Gold and Silver Waltz, The
Golden Song, The
Hear My Song Violetta (Hor Mein Lied Violetta)
Hey Gipsy (Play Gipsy)
Hot Canary, The
I Give My Heart
I Love You So (The Merry Widow Waltz)
Just a Gigolo
Love and Wine
Maxim's
Oh Donna Clara
Oh Katharina
Oh Maiden My Maiden
Patiently Smiling
Pierette & Pierrot
Sailor (Seeman Deine Heimat Ist Das Meer)
Say Not Love is a Dream
Serenade Frasquita (Farewell My Love, Farewell)
Vienna, City of My Dreams
Vilia
Waltz Dream, The
When Day is Done
White Dove, The
You Are My Heart's Delight

Belgium
Birdie Song, The (Tchip Tchip)
Ca Plane Pour Moi
Dominique
Don't Stop the Partyline
Get Up (Before the Night is Over)
Megamix
Petite Waltz, The
Pump Up the Jam
Rockin' Over the Beat
Una Paloma Blanca
Y Viva Espana

Brazil
Aurora
Baia
Bandit, The (O'Cangaceiro)
Brazil
Delicado
Desafinado
Feelings
Girl From Ipanema, The
Mama Yo Quiero (I Want My Mama)
One Note Samba (Samba de Uma Nota So)
Parrot on the Fortune Teller's Hat, The
Quiet Nights of Quiet Stars (Corcovado)
Tico Tico

Canada
Black Velvet
British Hustle, The
Echo Beach
Living on Video
Run to You
Safety Dance
Wash Your Face in My Sink
Which Way You Goin' Billy?
Working Man

Cuba
Another Night Like This
At the Crossroads
Babalu
Breeze and I, The
Green Eyes (Aquellos Ojos Verdes)
Let Me Love You Tonight (No Te Importe Saber)
Malaguena
Mama Inez
Marta
Peanut Vendor, The (El Manisero)
Poinciana
Say "Si Si" (Para Vigo Me Voy)
Siboney
Sweet and Gentle (Me Lo Dijo Adela)
Taboo
Yours (Quierme Mucho)

Czechoslovakia

Beer Barrel Polka, The
Little Valley in the Mountains

Denmark

Jealousy

France

Accordion
Agadoo
All Over the World (Dans le Monde Entier)
Alright, Alright, Alright
Amoureuse
And the Birds Were Singing (Et les Oiseaux Chantaient)
At Last, At Last
Autumn Leaves
Believe in Me (Sur Ma Vie)
Bella Musica
Beyond the Sea
Bimbo, El
Boom
Born to Be Alive
Borsalino
Butterfly
C'est Si Bon
Ca C'est Paris
Can't Stop the Music (La Musique N'a Pas De Fin)
Cherry Pink and Apple Blossom White
Clopin Clopant
Cuba
D.I.S.C.O.
Day the Rains Came, The
Dis Donc, Dis Donc
Domino
Fascination
Fiacre, Le (The Cab)
French Can Can Polka
From New York To L.a.
Garden of Love, The
Gendarmes Duet, The
Go West
Golliwog's Cake Walk
Guitar Tango (Flamenco Guitar)
Hands Up (Give Me Your Heart)
I Love to Love (But My Baby Just Loves To Dance)
I Love to Sing
I Still Love You All
I Think of You (Il Faut Trouver le Temp D'aimer)
I'm So All Alone
If I Only Had Time (Je N'aurai Pas le Temps)
If Only I Could Live My Life Again
If You Go (Si Tu Partais)
If You Go Away (Ne Me Quitte Pas)
If You Love Me (Hyme A L'amour)
Importance of Your Love, The (Important C'est la Rose) It Must Be Him (Seul Sur Son Etoile)
It's Over

J'attendrai
Je T'aime, Moi Non Plus
Joe Le Taxi
Left Bank, The (C'est A Hambourg)
Let it Be Me (Je T'appartiens)
Let Me Try Again (Laisse Moi le Temps)
Little Love and Understanding, A (Un Peu D'amour Et D'amitie)
Little Love, a Little Kiss, A (Un Peu D'amour)
Little Shoemaker, The (Le Petit Cordonnier)
Losing You (Un Ange Est Renn)
Love Here is My Heart (Mon Coeur Est Pour Toi)
Love is Blue (L'amour Est Bleu)
Love is Like a Violin (Mon Coeur Est Un Violin)
Love on the Rocks
Love's Last Word is Spoken (Le Chaland Qui Passe)
Madelon (Quand Madelon)
Mademoiselle de Paris
Magic Fly
Melodie D'Amour (Maladie D'Amour)
Mer, La
Milord
Mustafa
My Heart Sings
My Man (Mon Homme)
My Message
My Prayer
My Way
Nights in the Wood (Les Nuits Du Bois)
No Regrets (Non Je Ne Regrette Rien)
Old Fashioned Way, The (Les Plaisirs Demodes)
Only Love
Ooh What a Life
Our Language of Love
Oxygene
Padam, Padam
Pavements of Paris, The (Sur le Pavé)
Pepper Box
Petite Fleur
Philomel
Pigalle
Poor People of Paris, The
Portuguese Washerwomen, The (Les Lavandieres du Portugal)
Que Sera Mi Vida (If You Should Go)
Ronde de L'amour, La
Saddle Up
Seasons in the Sun (Le Moribond)
Seine, La
Shanghai
She
Speak to Me of Love (Parlez Moi D'amour)
Sultana
Supernature
Swing Song
Symphony
Take Me to Your Heart Again (La Vie En Rose)

Three Bells, The (Les Trois Cloches)
Tom Pillibi
Under Paris Skies (Sous Le Ciel De Paris)
Under the Bridges of Paris (Sous les Ponts de Paris)
Under the Roofs of Paris (Sous les Toits de Paris)
Valencia
Valentine
Vieni, Vieni
Voyage Voyage
Waiting For a Girl Like You
Welcome Home (Vivre)
What Now My Love (Et Maintenant)
When Forever Has Gone
When the World Was Young
Where is Your Heart (Moulin Rouge Theme)
While the Angelus Was Ringing
Willingly (Melodie Perdue)
With Your Love (Mes Mains)
Wonderful Dream (Tu Te Reconnaitras)
Words
Y.M.C.A.
Years May Come, Years May Go

Germany
Also Sprach Zarathustra
Answer Me
Auf Wiederseh'n Sweetheart
Autobahn
Automatic Lover
Axel F
Be Mine
Be My Comrade True
Belfast
Big in Japan
Blame it on The Boogie
Brother Louis
Brown Girl in the Ring
Call Me Darling
Da Da Da
Daddy Cool
Don't Ask Me Why
Don't Say Goodbye
Don't Stay Away Too Long (Herzen Haben Keine Fenster)
Drink, Drink Brothers Drink (Trink, Trink Bruderlein Trink)
Elizabeth
Falling in Love Again
Fool
Forever and Ever
Get Up and Boogie
Girl I'm Gonna Miss You
Girls, Girls, Girls
Glass of Champagne, A
Glow Worm, The (Glühwünchen)
Goodbye
Goodnight (I'm Only a Strolling Vagabond)
Gotta Go Home
Grinzing (Ich Muss Wieder Einmal in Grinzing Sein)

Happy Heart
Happy Wanderer, The
Hooray, Hooray, it's a Holi Holiday
I Kiss Your Hand Madame (Ich Kusse Ihr Hand Madame)
I Lost My Heart in Heidelberg
I Once Had a Heart Margarita
I'd Give the World (liebeslied)
If Only I Could
Jolly Brothers, The (Lustige Bruder)
Just For a While (Nur Eine Nacht)
Just Once For All Time
Keeping the Dream Alive
Letter Song, The
Lights of Lisbon, The
Lilac Domino, The
Lili Marlene
Little Peace, A (Ein Bisschen Frieden)
Live, Laugh and Love
London Nights
Love Me Now
Luxembourg Polka
Ma Baker
Mack the Knife
Mariandl Andl Andl
Mississippi
Mister Cuckoo (Cuculino)
Model, The
Monsieur Dupont
Moonlight on the Alster
My Golden Baby
My Hero
My Song Goes Round The World
My Song of Love
Ninety-Nine Red Balloons
Now and Forever (Oh Heideroslein)
Oh So Wunderbar
One More Sunrise (Morgen)
Parade of the Wooden Soldiers
Pepe
Power of Love, The
Power, The
Race, The
Rainy Day Refrain, A (Schnürlregen)
Rasputin
Reach For the Stars (Woner Ich Auch Komm, Wohin Ich Auch Geh)
Requiem
Rivers of Babylon, The
Robinson Crusoe's Isle
Romeo
Salome
Serenade
Seven Tears
So Do I (Bet Ami)
Sorry I'm a Lady
Springtime Reminds Me of You (Deine Mutter Bleibt Immer Bei Mir)

Tell Me I'm Forgiven
There's Something in Your Eyes
Today I Feel So Happy
Tokyo Melody
Tulips From Amsterdam
Two Hearts in Three Quarter Time
Walk Away (Warum Nur Warum)
Walk in the Black Forest (Eine Schwarzwaldfahrt)
Wedding Bells (Hochzeitsglocken)
White Horse Inn, The
Witch, The
Yes Mister Brown
Yes Sir I Can Boogie
You Can't Be True Dear (du Lannst Nicht Treu Sein) You
Just You
You Too
Your Eyes

Greece
All Alone Am I
Helene
Misirlou
Never on Sunday
Story of Tina, The (Dio Prasina Matia)

Hawaii
Hawaiian Wedding Song
On the Beach At Waikiki
One Rose (That's Left in My Heart)

Holland
Body and Soul
Computer Love
Ding-a-Dong (Ding Dinge Dong)
Dippety Day
Fantasy Island
Final Countdown
History
I Can't Stand It
I Don't Want to Be a Hero
I Remember Elvis Presley
I See a Star
Radar Love
Rock Me Amadeus
Rock the Boat
Shattered Dreams
Smurf Song, The
Sylvia
Venus
Vienna Calling
You're in the Army Now
Gipsy Moon
Gloomy Sunday

Ireland
All Kinds of Everything
Tarzan Boy

What's Another Year?

Israel
A Ba Ni Bi
Hallelujah
Tzena, Tzena, Tzena

Italy
All My Love
Anna
Aria
Arrivederci Darling (Arrivederci Roma)
Autumn Concerto
Boys (Summertime Love)
Broken Hearted (Cuore Cuore)
Call Me
Chee Chee-oo-Chee
Chi Mai
Chirpy Chirpy Cheep Cheep
Ciao Ciao Bambina (Piove)
Ciribiribin
Come Back to Sorrento (Tourna A Surriento)
Come Prima (More Than Ever)
Constantly (M'edera)
Do it, Do it Again (A Far L'amore Comincia Tu)
Dolce Vita
Don't Answer Me (Ti Vedo Uscuiri)
Donkey Song, The
Ferry Boat Serenade (La Piccinina)
Fool Am I, A (dimmelo Parlami)
Go (Before You Break My Heart) (si)
Guaglione (The Man Who Plays the Mandolino)
Half As Nice
Help Yourself (Gli Occhi Miei)
How Wonderful to Know (Aneme E Core)
I (Who Have Nothing) (Uno Dei Tanti)
I Don't Know Anybody Else
I Love My Radio
Italian Theme, The (Mambo Caliente)
Lady Barbara
Legion's Last Patrol, The
Little Serenade (Piccolissima Serenata)
Lonely Girl (Non Seitu)
Love Me Tonight (Alla Fine Della Strada)
Mah Na Mah Na
Mais Qui
Majorca
Mama
Man Without Love, A (Quando M'innamoro)
Mattinata (Tis The Day)
May Morning, A
More
My Little Lady (Non Illuderti Mai)
Nessun Dorma
Never, Never, Never (Grande, Grande, Grande)
Non Dimenticar (T'ho Voluto Bene)

Numero Uno
Oh Mama (The Butcher Boy)
Oh What a Surprise For the Duce (Evviva La Torre Di Pisa)
Pansé, La (Mandy)
Poppa Piccolono (Papaveri E Papere)
Quando, Quando, Quando
Ride on Time
River, The (Le Colline Sono In Fiore)
Romantica
Romany (Vivere)
Self Control
Serenade in the Night
Silenzio, Il
Softly As I Leave You (Piano)
Something's Happening
Song of The Mountains, The (La Montanara)
Souvenir D'italie
Stars Shine in Your Eyes
Suddenly You Love Me (Uno Tranquillo)
Summertime in Venice
Superman (Gioca Jouer)
Tell Me You're Mine (Per Un Bacio D'amor)
This is My Prayer (Non Ho L'eta Per Amarti)
Torero
Touch Me
Tweedle Dee Tweedle Dum
Volare (Nel Blu Dipinto Di Blu)
Wait For Me (Ti Diro)
Way it Used to Be, The
When a Child is Born (Soleado)
Woodpecker's Song (Reginella Campagnola)
You Don't Have to Say You Love Me (Lo Che Non Vivo)
You, Fascinating You
You're My World (Il Mio Mondo)

Jamaica
Cool Meditation
Double Barrel
Israelites, The
Liquidator, The
Return of Django, The
Up Town Top Ranking

Japan
Sukiyaki (Ueo Muite Aruku)

Luxembourg
Come What May (Apres Toi)

Mexico
Adios Mariquita Linda
Amapola
Amor
Besame Mucho (Kiss Me)
Cielito Lindo
Come Closer to Me (Acercate Mas)
Cuanto le Gusta
Cucaracha, La

Cumbanchero, El
Echo of a Serenade, The
Estrellita
Frenesi
Granada
It's Impossible (Somos Novios)
La Golondrina (The Swallow)
Love Me With All of Your Heart (Caundo Caliente El Sol)
Loveliest Night of the Year
Magic is The Moonlight
Mambo Jambo
Maria Elena
Perfidia
Perhaps, Perhaps, Perhaps (Quizas, Quizas, Quizas)
Rancho Grande, El
Sway (Quien Sera)
Three Caballeros, The (Ay Jalisco No Te Rajes)
Ti-pi-tin
Time Was (Duerme)
Tu-li-Tulip Time
What a Difference a Day Made
Without You (Tres Palabras)
You Belong to My Heart

Monaco
Banc, Un Arbre, Une Rue, Un

New Zealand
Now is the Hour (Hearere Ra)

Portugal
April in Portugal (Coimbra)
In Old Lisbon (Lisboa Antigua)

Romania
Doina de Jale
Hora Staccato

Russia
Onedin Line, The
Sabre Dance, The
Song of India

South Africa
'A' Round the Corner
Pickin' a Chicken
Sadie's Shawl
Sarie Marais
Skokiaan
Sugar Bush
Tom Hark
Zambesi

Spain
Ay, Ay, Ay
El Relicario
If She Should Come to You (La Montana)

Kiss in the Night, A (Anoche Te Bese)
Relicairo, El
Rodrigo's Concerto (Aranjuez Mon Amour)
Three Galleons, The (Las Tres Carabelas)
Who'll Buy My Violets (La Violetera)

Sweden
Angel Eyes
Chiquitita
Cuckoo Waltz, The
Dancing Queen
Does Your Mother Know
Fernando
Gimme Gimme Gimme
Got to Get
Honey Honey
I Have a Dream
Intermezzo (Souvenir de Vienne)
It Must Have Been Love
Knowing Me, Knowing You

Lay All Your Love on Me
Lay Down Your Arms
Listen to Your Heart
Look, The
Mama Mia
Money Money Money
Name of the Game
One of Us
S.O.S.
Shrine of St. Cecilia, The (Min Soldat)
Summer Night City
Super Trouper
Swedish Polka, The
Swedish Rhapsody
Take a Chance on Me
Voulez-Vous
Waterloo
Winner Takes it All
O Mein Papa
Toolie Oolie Doolie

NOTES

NOTES

NOTES

MUSIC MASTER

other titles available in this series:-

CD Catalogue

Tracks Catlaogue

Country Music Catalogue

Price Guide for Record Collectors

Films and Shows Catalogue

Video Catalogue

Albums Catalogue

Jazz Catalogue

Master Catalogue (The Big Red Book)

To order any of the above titles, please use the order form on the facing page.

ORDER BY TELEPHONE 081 953 5433

MUSIC MASTER
SUBSCRIPTIONS & CATALOGUES ORDER FORM

SUBSCRIPTIONS

TITLE	CODE	PRICE (£)	QUANTITY	SUB-TOTAL
1992 MUSIC MASTER SUBSCRIPTION (Master Catalogue '92 (Available July '92), all supplements from July '92 to June '93 and 1992 Tracks Catalogue (4th edition))	C92	209.50		

CATALOGUES

TITLE	CODE	PRICE	QUANTITY	SUB-TOTAL
CD Catalogue 12th Edition	CD12	10.95		
Jazz Catalogue	J1	10.95		
Price Guide for Record Collectors	G1	9.95		
Albums Catalogue	P18	14.95		
Tracks Catalogue	T3	16.95		
Music on Video Catalogue (2nd Edition)	V2	9.95		
Films and Shows Catalogue	E1	7.95		
Country Music Catalogue	K1	9.95		
NEW FOR 1992				
Directory of Popular Music (available May '92)	PM1	14.95		
Spoken Word Catalogue (available June '92)	SW1	14.95		
Master Catalogue '92 (available July '92)	H92	134.00		
TOTAL				
POSTAGE & PACKING				
GRAND TOTAL				

POSTAGE & PACKING
SUBSCRIPTIONS   UK: no extra charge   EUROPE: add £25.00   REST OF WORLD: add £90.00
CATALOGUES   UK: add £1.50 per book (max order £5.00)   EUROPE: add £2.50 per book
(Master Catalogue £8.50)   REST OF WORLD: add £7.00 per book (Master Catalogue £35.00)

☐ I enclose a cheque for the above amount made payable to MUSIC MASTER
☐ Please debit my credit card   ☐ Access/Mastercard   ☐ Visa/Eurocard   ☐ American Express

Credit Card Holder's Name ·
Address ·
Card No · · · · · · · · · · · · Expiry Date · · · · · · · · · ·

Mr/Mrs/Miss/Ms ·
Company Name ·
Address ·
Country · · · · · · · · · Post Code/Zip Code · · · · · · · · ·
Telephone Number · · · · · · Fax Number · · · · · · Date · · · · · ·

MUSIC MASTER, UNIT 4, DURHAM RD, BOREHAM WOOD, HERTS, WD6 1LW
TELEPHONE: 081 953 5433 FAX: 081 207 5814

☐ I would prefer not to receive literature about related products (Tick box as appropriate)